W9-AVC-564

The Gender and Science Reader brings together key writings by leading scholars to provide a comprehensive feminist analysis of the nature and practice of science. Challenging the self-proclaimed objectivity of scientific practice, the contributors uncover the gender, class and racial prejudices of modern science. The Reader draws from a range of media, including feminist criticism, scientific literature, writings about scientific education, and the popular press. Articles are grouped into six thematic sections which address:

- Women in Science – women's access to study and employment in science, combining both analytical evidence and personal testimonies
- Creating Androcentric Science – exploring the gendered origins of science at the time of the Enlightenment
- Analyzing Gendered Science – feminist methodologies and epistemology for the study of science
- Gendered Praxis – examples of how gender bias can affect and distort scientific work
- Science and Identity – how science reinforces gender and racial stereotypes
- Feminist Restructuring of Science – what is the future of feminist science studies?

In addition to a general introduction by the editors to the volume, and introductions to each of the thematic sections, the Reader also includes a comprehensive bibliography of feminist science studies, making it an indispensable resource for anyone involved in the teaching, research or study of science.

Contributors: Sharon Begley, Lynda Birke, Susan Bordo, Suzanne G. Brainard, Linda Carlin, Margaret A. Eisenhart, Anne Fausto-Sterling, Elizabeth Finkel, Donna Haraway, Sandra Harding, Ruth Hubbard, Evelyn Fox Keller, Gisela Kaplan, E. Anne Kerr, Muriel Lederman, Helen E. Longino, John Lukacs, Curtis L. Meinert, Carolyn Merchant, Lesley J. Rogers, Hilary Rose, Sue V. Rosser, Londa Schiebinger, Vandana Shiva, Bonnie Jean Shulman, Edward R. Silverman, Bonnie Spanier, Lisa Weasel, Christine Wenneras, Liz Whitelegg, Agnes Wold, Helen Zweifel.

Editors: Muriel Lederman is an Associate Professor of Biology and affiliated with the Women's Studies Program at Virginia Polytechnic Institute. **Ingrid Bartsch** is an Assistant Professor of Women's Studies at the University of South Florida and is a practising ecologist.

Edited by

Muriel Lederman and Ingrid Bartsch

London and New York

First published 2001 by Routledge
11 New Fetter Lane, London EC4P 4EE

Simultaneously published in the USA and Canada
by Routledge
29 West 35th Street, New York, NY 10001

Routledge is an imprint of the Taylor and Francis Group

Typeset in Perpetua and Bell Gothic by Keystroke, Jacaranda Lodge, Wolverhampton
Printed and bound in Great Britain by TJ International Ltd, Padstow, Cornwall

British Library Cataloging in Publication Data
A catalogue record for this book is available from the British Library

Library of Congress Cataloging in Publication Data
A catalogue record for this book has been requested.

ISBN 0–415–21357–6 (hbk)
ISBN 0–415–21358–4 (pbk)

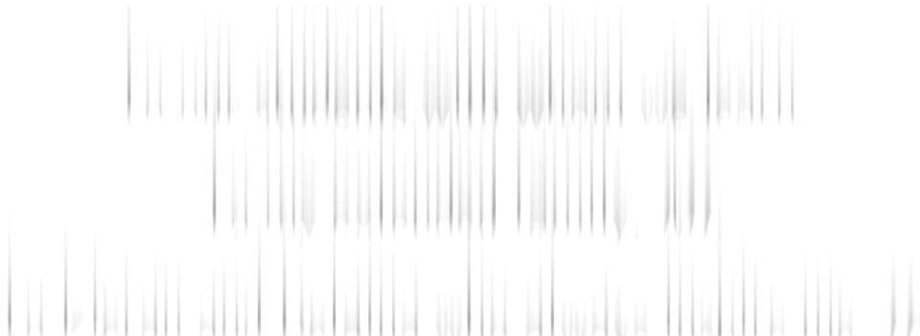

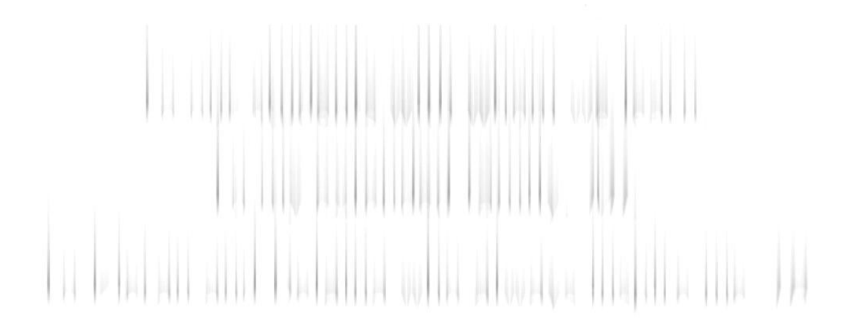

Acknowledgements xi

Introduction 1

SECTION ONE
Women in Science 9

1 Margaret A. Eisenhart and Elizabeth Finkel
WOMEN (STILL) NEED NOT APPLY 13

2 Suzanne G. Brainard and Linda Carlin
A SIX-YEAR LONGITUDINAL STUDY OF UNDERGRADUATE WOMEN IN ENGINEERING AND SCIENCE 24

3 Edward R. Silverman
NSF EMPLOYMENT STUDY CONFIRMS ISSUES FACING WOMEN, MINORITIES 38

4 Christine Wenneras and Agnes Wold
NEPOTISM AND SEXISM IN PEER-REVIEW 42

5 Ruth Hubbard
SCIENCE AND SCIENCE CRITICISM 49

6 Bonnie Spanier
HOW I CAME TO THIS STUDY 52

7 Evelyn Fox Keller
FROM WORKING SCIENTIST TO FEMINIST CRITIC 59

SECTION TWO 63
Creating Androcentric Science

8 Carolyn Merchant
DOMINION OVER NATURE 68

9 Susan Bordo
SELECTIONS FROM *THE FLIGHT TO OBJECTIVITY* 82

10 Evelyn Fox Keller
SECRETS OF GOD, NATURE, AND LIFE 98

11 National Academy of Sciences
METHODS AND VALUES 111

12 Sharon Begley
THE SCIENCE WARS 114

SECTION THREE 119
Analyzing Gendered Science

13 Sue V. Rosser
ARE THERE FEMINIST METHODOLOGIES APPROPRIATE FOR THE NATURAL SCIENCES AND DO THEY MAKE A DIFFERENCE? 123

14 Sandra Harding
FEMINIST STANDPOINT EPISTEMOLOGY 145

15 Donna Haraway
SITUATED KNOWLEDGES: THE SCIENCE QUESTION IN FEMINISM AND THE PRIVILEGE OF PARTIAL PERSPECTIVE 169

16 Sandra Harding
IS SCIENCE MULTICULTURAL? CHALLENGES, RESOURCES, OPPORTUNITIES, UNCERTAINTIES 189

17 Helen E. Longino
SUBJECTS, POWER, AND KNOWLEDGE: DESCRIPTION AND PRESCRIPTION IN FEMINIST PHILOSOPHIES OF SCIENCE 213

18 **John Lukacs**
HEISENBERG'S RECOGNITIONS: THE END OF THE SCIENTIFIC WORLD VIEW 225

[illegible]

THE BIOPOLITICS OF A MULTICULTURAL FIELD 252

21 **Bonnie Spanier**
FOUNDATIONS FOR A "NEW BIOLOGY," PROPOSED IN *MOLECULAR CELL BIOLOGY* 272

22 **Helen Zweifel**
THE GENDERED NATURE OF BIODIVERSITY CONSERVATION 289

23 **Curtis L. Meinert**
THE INCLUSION OF WOMEN IN CLINICAL TRIALS 303

SECTION FIVE
Science and Identity 307

24 **Lynda Birke**
IN PURSUIT OF DIFFERENCE: SCIENTIFIC STUDIES OF WOMEN AND MEN 309

25 **Gisela Kaplan and Lesley J. Rogers**
RACE AND GENDER FALLACIES: THE PAUCITY OF BIOLOGICAL DETERMINIST EXPLANATIONS OF DIFFERENCE 323

26 **Anne Fausto-Sterling**
GENDER, RACE, AND NATION: THE COMPARATIVE ANATOMY OF "HOTTENTOT" WOMEN IN EUROPE, 1815-1817 343

27 **Bonnie Spanier**
FROM MOLECULES TO BRAINS, NORMAL SCIENCE SUPPORTS SEXIST BELIEFS ABOUT DIFFEENCES 367

28 Liz Whitelegg
GIRLS IN SCIENCE EDUCATION: OF RICE AND FRUIT TREES 373

SECTION SIX
Feminist Restructuring of Science 383

29 E. Anne Kerr
TOWARD A FEMINIST NATURAL SCIENCE: LINKING THEORY AND PRACTICE 386

30 Bonnie Jean Shulman
IMPLICATIONS OF FEMINIST CRITIQUES OF SCIENCE FOR THE TEACHING OF MATHEMATICS AND SCIENCE 407

31 Lisa Weasel
THE CELL IN RELATION: AN ECOFEMINIST REVISION OF CELL AND MOLECULAR BIOLOGY 423

32 Muriel Lederman
STRUCTURING FEMINIST SCIENCE 437

33 Vandana Shiva
DEMOCRATIZING BIOLOGY: REINVENTING BIOLOGY FROM A FEMINIST, ECOLOGICAL, AND THIRD WORLD PERSPECTIVE 447

34 Londa Schiebinger
CREATING SUSTAINABLE SCIENCE 466

35 Hilary Rose
EPILOGUE: WOMEN'S WORK IS NEVER DONE 483

Afterword 491
Bibliography 495
Index 503

Permission given by the following publishers and authors is gratefully acknowledged:

Chapter 1 Margaret A. Eisenhart and Elizabeth Finkel. "Women (Still) Need Not Apply," in *Women's Science: Learning and Succeeding from the Margins* (Chicago and London: University of Chicago Press, 1988), pp. 17–27. Courtesy of The University of Chicago Press.

Chapter 2 Suzanne G. Brainard and Linda Carlin. "A Six-Year Longitudinal Study of Undergraduate Women in Engineering and Science," in *Journal of Engineering Education*, October 1998, pp. 369–375. Courtesy of the *Journal of Engineering Education* and the American Society for Engineering Education.

Chapter 3 Edward R. Silverman. "NSF Employment Study Confirms Issues Facing Women, Minorities," in *The Scientist* (April 14, 1997) © *The Scientist*. Reproduced by permission.

Chapter 4 Christine Wenneras and Agnes Wold. "Nepotism and Sexism in Peer-Review." Reprinted by permission from *Nature*, Vol. 387, pp. 341–343. Copyright © 1997 Macmillan Magazines Ltd.

Chapter 5 Ruth Hubbard. *The Politics of Women's Biology*. Copyright © 1990 by Rutgers, The State University. Reprinted by permission of Rutgers University Press.

Chapter 6 Bonnie Spanier. "How I Came to This Study," in *Im/Partial Science*. (Bloomington and Indianapolis: Indiana University Press, 1995), pp. xi–xv. Courtesy of Indiana University Press.

Chapter 7 Evelyn Fox Keller. "From Working Scientist to Feminist Critic," in *Secrets of Life, Secrets of Death* (New York and London: Routledge,

1992), pp. 21–25, 56–72. Reproduced by permission of Taylor and Francis/ Routledge Inc.

Chapter 8 Carolyn Merchant. "Dominion Over Nature," chapter 7 (adapted) from *The Death of Nature: Women, Ecology and The Scientific Revolution.* Copyright © 1980 by Carolyn Merchant. Reprinted by permission of HarperCollins Publishers, Inc.

Chapter 9 Susan Bordo. "Selections from *The Flight to Objectivity,*" in *Feminist Interpretations of René Descartes* (Pennsylvania State University Press, 1999), pp. 48–69. Copyright © 1999 The Pennsylvania State University. Reproduced by permission of The Pennsylvania State University Press.

Chapter 10 Evelyn Fox Keller. "Secrets of God, Nature, and Life," in *Secrets of Life, Secrets of Death* (New York and London: Routledge, 1992), pp. 21–25, 56–72. Reproduced by permission of Taylor and Francis/ Routledge Inc.

Chapter 11 National Academy of Sciences. "Methods and Values." Reprinted from *On Being a Scientist.* Copyright © 1989 by the National Academy of Sciences. Courtesy of the National Academy Press.

Chapter 12 Sharon Begley. "The Science Wars," from *Newsweek* (April 21, 1997) © (1997) Newsweek, Inc. All rights reserved. Reprinted by permission.

Chapter 13 Sue V. Rosser. "Are There Feminist Methodologies Appropriate for the Natural Sciences and Do They Make a Difference?" 1988. Reprinted from *Women's Studies International Forum,* Vol. 15, No. 5/6, pp. 535–550, with permission from Elsevier Science.

Chapter 14 Sandra Harding. "Feminist Standpoint Epistemology," in *Whose Science? Whose Knowledge? Thinking from Women's Lives* (Ithaca, Cornell University Press, 1991) pp. 119–163 (abridged). Used by permission of the Publisher, Cornell University Press.

Chapter 15 Donna Haraway. "Situated Knowledges: The Science Question in Feminism and the Privilege of Partial Perspective," in *Feminist Studies,* Vol. 14, No. 3 (Fall 1988), pp. 575–599, by permission of the publisher, *Feminist Studies,* Inc.

Chapter 16 Sandra Harding. "Is Science Multicultural? Challenges, Resources, Opportunities, Uncertainties," in *Configurations,* Vol. 2, 1994, pp. 301–330. Copyright © 1994. The Johns Hopkins University Press and Society for Literature and Science.

Chapter 17 Helen E. Longino. "Subjects, Power, and Knowledge: Description and Prescription in Feminist Philosophies of Science." Copyright © 1992. From *Feminist Epistemologies,* ed. Linda Alcoff and Elizabeth Potter. Reproduced by permission of Taylor and Francis/Routledge Inc.

Chapter 18 John Lukacs. "Heisenberg's Recognitions: The End of the Scientific World View," from *Historical Consciousness,* ed. John G. Burke. Copyright © 1994 by Transaction Publishers. All rights reserved.

Chapter 19 Anne Fausto-Sterling. "Life in the XY Corral," 1989. Reprinted from *Women's Studies International Forum,* Vol. 12, No. 3, pp. 319–331, with permission from Elsevier Science.

Chapter 20 Donna Haraway. "The Biopolitics of a Multicultural Field." Copyright © 1989. From *Primate Visions* by Donna Haraway, pp. 244–278. Reproduced by permission of Taylor and Francis/Routledge, Inc.

Chapter 21 Bonnier Spanier. From *Im/Partial Science* (Bloomington and [illegible]

Chapter 24 Lynda Birke. "In Pursuit of Difference: Scientific Studies of Women and Men," in *Inventing Women*, ed. Gill Kirkup and Laurie Smith, 1992. Copyright © 1992 by Blackwell Publishers, by permission of the publishers.

Chapter 25 Gisela Kaplan and Lesley J. Rogers. "Race and Gender Fallacies: The Paucity of Biological Determinist Explanations of Difference," in *Challenging Racism and Sexism: Alternatives to Genetic Explanations of Difference*, ed. Ethel Tobach and Betty Rosoff (New York: The Feminist Press at The City University of New York, 1994). Copyright © 1994 by Gisela Kaplan and Lesley J. Rogers. Reprinted by permission of the authors and The Feminist Press at The City University of New York.

Chapter 26 Anne Fausto-Sterling. "Gender Race, and Nation: The Comparative Anatomy of 'Hottentot' Women in Europe, 1815–1817," in *Deviant Bodies*, ed. Jennifer Terry and Jacqueline Urla (Bloomington and Indianapolis: Indiana University Press, 1996), pp. 19–48. Courtesy of Indiana University Press.

Chapter 27 Bonnier Spanier. "From Molecules to Brains, Normal Science Supports Sexist Beliefs About Differences," in *Im/Partial Science* (Bloomington and Indianapolis: Indiana University Press, 1995), pp. 72–77. Courtesy of Indiana University Press.

Chapter 28 Liz Whitelegg. "Girls in Science Education: Of Rice and Fruit Trees," in *Inventing Women*, ed. Gill Kirkup and Laurie Smith, 1992, pp. 178–187. Copyright © 1992 by Blackwell Publishers, by permission of the publishers.

Chapter 29 E. Anne Kerr. "Toward a Feminist Natural Science: Linking Theory and Practice." Reprinted from *Women's Studies International Forum*, Vol. 21, pp. 95–109, 1998, with permission of Elsevier Science.

Chapter 30 Bonnie Jean Shulman. "Implications of Feminist Critiques of Science for the Teaching of Mathematics and Science," from *The Journal of Women and Minorities in Science and Engineering*, 1, pp. 1–28, 1994. Reprinted by permission of Begell House, Inc.

Chapter 31 Lisa Weasel. "The Cell in Relation: An Ecofeminist Revision of Cell and Molecular Biology." Reprinted from *Women's Studies International*

Forum, Vol. 20, No. 1, pp. 49–59, 1996, with permission from Elsevier Science.

Chapter 32 Muriel Lederman. "Structuring Feminist Science." Reprinted from *Women's Studies International Forum*, Vol. 16, 1993, with permission from Elsevier Science.

Chapter 33 Vandana Shiva. "Democratizing Biology: Reinventing Biology from a Feminist, Ecological, and Third World Perspective," in *Reinventing Biology*, ed. Lynda Birke and Ruth Hubbard (Bloomington and Indianapolis: Indiana University Press, 1995). Courtesy of Indiana University Press.

Chapter 34 Londa Schiebinger. "Creating Sustainable Science," in *Osiris* 12 (1997), pp. 201–16. Courtesy of University of Chicago Press.

Chapter 35 Hilary Rose. "Epilogue: Women's Work is Never Done," in *Love, Power and Knowledge* (Bloomington and Indianapolis: Indiana University Press, 1994), pp. 230–238. Courtesy of University of Chicago Press. Reprinted by permission of Indiana University Press and Blackwell Publishers.

The editors wish to thank Doreene Valentine for her encouragement at the beginning of this venture and Rebecca Barden, our editor at Routledge, for her quick, sensible answers to a multitude of questions and for her patience.

I (M.L.) would like to thank Robin Andrews for (inadvertently) starting me down the trail that led to this book; Carol Burger, Ann LaBerge, Duncan Porter, Bruce Turner, and Doris Zallen for walking with me for twenty years; the members of the Women's Studies community at Virginia Tech, who helped me learn how to walk the walk; the EO/AA Office at Virginia Tech, which supported me financially so I could develop the "Gender and Science" course; the Center for Excellence in Teaching at Virginia Tech for their support; the Head of the Department of Biology, Joe Cowles, who validates my walking two paths at once; the MJ group, for keeping me sane, and especially David Bleich. There is a New Yorker cartoon in which ski tracks approach a tree, go around it, and then run parallel again. I see our lives each as one of those tracks. Thank you for skiing with me, even though neither of us skis in the real world. Last but not least - Brian, Esther, Hannah, and my parents, who would have been tickled pink to hold this book.

I (I.B.) am very grateful to Janice Snook and David Stamps, who made it possible for a plant ecologist to secure a tenure line in Women's Studies. And I am thankful for many friendships, particularly those with Carolyn DiPalma, Linda Whiteford, and Peg Ostrenko who have guided me patiently through many issues, both personal and professional.

The publication of this book was supported by a grant from the University of South Florida Publication Council.

MODERN SCIENCE, AS DEFINED AND PRACTICED in post-industrial, technologically driven nations, is currently being scrutinized at a number of levels. One outcome of this probing has been devaluation of basic research, and funding patterns that are increasingly mission-driven, with programs defined more by legislators than by investigators. At another level, there are intensive local and national efforts to reconstruct and revitalize science education. Ultimately, because science plays a powerful role in Western societies, its practitioners are being held accountable for producing information that is incomprehensible to most citizens and, from their perspective, presents conflicting results about dietary supplements or medical advisories from one study to the next. Diminished scientific literacy, coupled with growing diversity within the population, inevitably results in tensions between science and a society asked to support it. A broader awareness of how science is shaped, that is, of the culture of science, would reduce the tensions and open the way for a dialogue among and between scientists and all people. Dr. Mae Jemison, science literacy advocate, points out that our goal should not simply be to inspire more students to become scientists, but to give people the interest in asking and answering questions about the world around them (Jemison, 1998). Making science more accessible, creating the "civic science" proposed by the former United States National Science Foundation (NSF) director Neal Lane (1996), can only improve the public image of science and serve to attract and stimulate those with the most creative minds, irrespective of their gender, race, and class.

Most Western practitioners of science are white males. A variety of books and articles raise the question of why women are under-represented at all levels of scientific endeavors, addressing the "leaky pipeline," the issue of "women in science." Some of the data that demonstrate this phenomenon were generated by NSF and were sufficiently compelling to prompt that agency to create programs to bring more girls and women into the sciences. These programs resulted in modest increases in the number of women receiving advanced degrees or becoming employed in scientific occupations. Disturbingly, the most recent findings indicate that some of the original gains are now being reversed as women trained as scientists choose other paths (Smaglik, 1998). In effect, the education and mentoring programs that provided same sex role models, reduced gender stereotypes, increased leadership opportunities, and access to the full curriculum were insufficient for retaining women scientists.

Why does this matter? No social endeavor can continue to be successful if half of humanity is un-represented in its practice. Why is this happening? We believe that the lack of women per se is merely a symptom of a more basic problem with science. This volume is entitled *The Gender and Science Reader* to indicate that the emphasis of its contents is on *gender* in several senses – the socially defined, gender role of women in society that impacts their access to a life in science, the socially defined role of women in science, and the gendered norms within the culture of science. To us, gender and science (in contrast to women in science) refers to the culture of science and the social situatedness of women, through which girls and women receive incompatible cultural messages. On the one hand, society has normalized women's role as females, with the nurturing and cooperative behaviors that this entails. On the other hand, scientists are expected to be rational, unemotional and, driven by funding and recognition, highly competitive.

The associations between gender, science and women are complex, but their examination is crucial, particularly for scientists. Most scientists have not recognized that unmasking the relationships between these categories (race can be added to the mix) has had, and will continue to have, a profound impact upon their life's work. It is they who may ultimately benefit from a better understanding of both the culture of science and of how their unexamined assumptions about science impact how they train future scientists, from kindergartners to post-doctoral researchers.

Although of greatest benefit to scientists themselves, unveiling the nature and practice of science is a product of other disciplines including sociology of science, new history, philosophy of science, the feminist critique of science, and post-modernism. The first three areas come together under the rubric of "science and technology studies" (STS), a new, synergistic melding in which each field informs the others. The feminist critiques of science, which began with (usually) women scientists becoming dissatisfied with various aspects of practice, now inform STS and vice versa. Within these fields, there is the nearly universal assumption that the problems identified with science have cultural bases – derived from both the mores of science and the societies in which it functions.

Scientists, in general, believe that their work is beyond cultural or social influence – that they are discovering, rather than inventing, Nature. This perception has permeated the general population such that it is difficult to convince people that science is not objective truth. Moreover, it is the self-proclaimed "objectivity" of science, along with its elitist, gendered and racist stances (whether overt, covert, or unintentional) that create friction with social studies of science. Scientists should become aware of analyses of their disciplines based on class and race. Feminist analyses unveil the achievements and struggles of women scientists and offer suggestions for a science that is more inclusive. Feminist analyses also claim that the institutions, language, methods, and interpretations of science comfortably follow a masculine model (Bleier, 1984, Fee, 1982, Haraway, 1978, Hubbard, 1990, Keller, 1982, Maynard, 1997, Merchant, 1996, Rose, 1994). What has become "normal" in science is, in [illegible]

A second strain was the women's health movement, through which women recaptured control of their bodies from the medical industry by teaching themselves about themselves. A third strain was the recognition of humanity's effect on Earth – that we were putting ourselves at risk by not living in harmony with the environment, of which we are but one component.

These strains were braided through the academic discipline now called the social studies of science – an analysis of science based in its history and in epistemology – how we know that which we know. Other studies of the history of science (beginning with Thomas Kuhn's *The Structure of Scientific Revolutions*) demonstrated that science is an activity with rules and regulations established by its practitioners. Stephen Shapin describes the characteristics of the Scientific Revolution in ways that show the origins of the contemporary structure of science and how it operates. These are:

> First, the mechanization of nature: the increasing use of mechanical metaphors to construe natural knowledge processes and phenomena; second, the depersonalization of natural knowledge; the growing separation between human subjects and the natural objects of their knowledge . . . ; third, the attempted mechanization of knowledge making, that is the proposed deployment of explicitly formulated rules of method that aims at disciplining the production of knowledge by managing or eliminating the effects of human passions and interest; and fourth; the aspiration to use the resulting reformed natural knowledge to achieve moral, social, and political ends.
>
> (Shapin, 1996, 13)

Each of these characteristics is addressed in some way in the feminist analyses of science. What makes these analyses distinctively feminist is that they take as their basis the social situation of women and, in some cases, women's biology. The feminist point of view offers a lens on science that is not available from the perspective of its majority practitioners.

The mechanization of nature results in dissecting its processes to finer and finer levels of organization – reducing one field of science to the next higher or lower in the hierarchy of rigor. Biological phenomena are explained by their chemistry, chemistry is explained by physics, physics by mathematics. The systems investigated in this way take on a life of their own and seldom is the attempt made to re-integrate information gained by these methods. If this effort were made, those who generate scientific knowledge might be more respectful of the objects of their investigation. Nature should not just be a force to be tamed for the benefit of humanity; humanity is an integral part of the Nature it defines and an equilibrium between the two should be a goal.

Science education itself has been presented as a contributor to declining participation in the sciences for both women and minorities and curriculum transformation has been at the heart of some feminist analyses (Barr and Birke, 1998, Rosser, 1995, 1997, Seymour and Hewitt, 1994). How to follow the rules of science is instilled from a child's earliest experience. They are told that there is a strict set of rules about what constitutes natural phenomena, what are the appropriate questions to ask about natural phenomena, and what are the appropriate ways to ask those questions and interpret the answers. What they are not told is that these rules are not absolute but keep shifting and evolving, changed by scientists' requirements for defensible knowledge claims. Science defends itself from non-conforming views by claiming objectivity. It states that there are constants not subject to alternative description or explanation from a viewpoint other than the one currently adopted. Of course, this is an unassailable tautology.

Shapin's third point about the Scientific Revolution is "eliminating the effects of human passions and interest." Inventing Nature takes into account creative human activity. It suggests that there are natural phenomena, but the explanation of these phenomena is influenced by the life experiences (including the social setting) of the interpreter. It may be only from such a situated perspective, whether the perspective is that of being female, being non-white, being non-Western and bearing in mind that these categories are mutually informing, that the methods and results of science can be critiqued effectively. The feminist unveiling of "bad science," questioning why women were not included in medical studies of heart disease, why drugs are tested only on male rats, are examples of countering this gendered view. Unfortunately, it is only through political intervention that equity was achieved.

Many scientists distance themselves from the political nature of science, claiming that research is undertaken solely for the sake of discovery. Science is political in the sense that it supports outcomes defined as advantageous by the Western, capitalist society that, ironically, has evolved in parallel to modern science (Harding, 1998). Mathematics and physics, both basic and applied are, and historically have been, in the service of the military. Much of basic biology is justified by medical applications. Feminist analyses of how science is politicized have raised numerous issues about the implications of, for example, genetic research. Science has also been pressed into the service of supporting the social status quo. To do so, it has been used by those with power to insure the continued marginalization of those who could be threats, who might demand and succeed in grabbing a share of that power, thereafter possibly using it in more judicious ways. Thus emerge "scientific" studies that "demonstrate" the inherent inability of girls to do mathematics, or the genetic deficiency in native intelligence among non-white races.

Why did we want to create this anthology that we hope will bring the feminist analyses of science to the attention of many? Its genesis is a thoroughly modern event;

the editors found each other through the Internet. As subscribers to WISENET (the Women in Science and Engineering Network), we had both received a message soliciting collaborators for an anthology centered in "Women in Science." One of us (M.L.), after much deliberation about the consequences of receiving a positive response, [illegible]

help "spread the word." We envision this book addressing the need for a source book in upper-division undergraduate and graduate level courses that address issues related to women, gender, and the sciences. At the practical level, we both teach courses at the undergraduate level. Both of us have had problems delivering readings to students. We have required students to purchase several available books, but supplements still were required. Alternatively, we have created duplicated packets of readings that were still very pricey. We believe strongly that social and political perspectives on science must be part of any general education, for prospective scientists as well as for prospective poets.

Even before the material included here gets to the students, it will have to become more familiar to instructors. This book will be a resource for faculty members in Women's Studies and natural science programs, increasing their familiarity with the feminist analysis of science. This analysis is not often presented in "Introduction to Women's Studies" courses, since most of the instructors for these courses are trained in the humanities or social sciences and are not sufficiently conversant with science to integrate this field into their research and pedagogy. Even though social analyses of science are foreign to scientists, they are the bread and butter of science and technology studies, a field under attack by science. The philosophers, historians, and sociologists of science working in science and technology studies may not be familiar with the feminist analysis because of its gendered base, not traditionally a mainstream component of programs in their fields. We hope this book will heighten the awareness of teachers and scholars across disciplines with regard to the feminist analysis of science, as well as provide them with useful materials so that they will feel more comfortable including this analysis in their courses. Even more fervently, we hope that practitioners of science will be impacted by this volume and elect to add social and feminist analyses to their science courses. Most scientists are not self-reflexive with respect to their work; becoming familiar with these fields may begin to change attitudes and practice to the advantage not only of women scientists but of all scientists.

This volume is meant to include multiple perspectives rather than be simply comprehensive, which explains the wide variety of readings and size of the book. We hope, first, that instructors will find the selection sufficient to minimize the need for supplemental readings. We have included some "classics" (Haraway's "Situated Knowledges" and Harding's *Whose Science? Whose Knowledge?* for example) as well as some more recent material and even some articles from outside academic journals. The book is meant to provide brief accounts of women's participation in the sciences as well as feminist visions for a new approach to science. We realize fully that the selections have a leaning toward the life sciences. This reflects what is available in the literature rather than our own inclination to favor this field. Historically, it has been women trained as biologists – Ruth Hubbard, Donna Haraway, Sue Rosser, Anne Fausto-Sterling – who have led the way. Moreover, concepts presented in the life sciences can often be interpreted by mirroring (androcentric) society. The materials that present a feminist analysis of the physical sciences are more situated in education in part because, as in the classroom, it is easier to begin with the obvious. Physics, chemistry and mathematics have presented a greater challenge to feminists because they are perceived to be more "exact" and grounded in truth. Recent works, by Karen Barad for example (Barad, 1998), are beginning to etch away this rigid coating.

The contents cover our "take" on the term "gender and science". The pieces selected are arranged in six sections and are a blend of the way both our courses are organized. The first section is "Women in Science." This topic begins the book because I.B. finds that it allows even reluctant people to recognize the absence of women in the sciences on their own, creating less resistance to the theory that follows. Scientists also might be more willing to accept the notion that science has been historically and culturally constructed if they see the unnatural absence of women early on. The next section, "Creating Androcentric Science," grounds all further readings in the historical and philosophical basis of why Western science is the way it is. This is followed by a group of papers that cover the essence of the feminist analysis of science. In M.L.'s course, these last two sections begin the course. Students feel that this order helps them to grasp the specifics of gendered practice (Section Four). Linked to these essays is a section on how science reinforces traditional definitions of gender/race and gender/race roles. The book ends with a group of papers devoted to alternatives to "the way it is," both in terms of education and theory. The idea of a "successor science" can be problematic; taking the position that women do science differently can result in "feminine" rather than "feminist" science. Experience tells us that "feminine" science will be rendered invisible; a science that accounts for the problems raised by the feminist analysis will be potent.

Finally, we fully acknowledge our privilege as white, middle-class, North American women. M.L.'s parents were immigrants from Poland. Her becoming a scientist with a Ph.D. was the ultimate in success. I.B. had no mentors or guidance that would help explain her "success" as a scientist but would probably not have gotten to where she is without this privilege. That we are now in a position to focus a portion of our efforts on the feminist critique of science may be the ultimate recognition of our good fortune.

References

Barad, Karen (1998) "Agential Realism: Feminist Interventions in Understanding Scientific Practices." In Biagioli, Mario, *The Science Studies Reader*. New York: Routledge.

Barr, Jean and Birke, Lynda (1998) *Common Science? Women, Science and Knowledge*. Bloomington and Indianapolis: Indiana University Press.

Bleier, Ruth (1984) *Science and Gender: A Critique of Biology and its Theories on Women*. Oxford: Pergamon Press.

[illegible]

Jemison, Mae, as reported in the Newsletter of the Ecological Society of America, June, 1998.

Keller, Evelyn Fox (1982) "Feminism and Science." *Signs: Journal of Women in Culture and Society* 7: 589–602.

Lane, Neal (1996) as reported in *Science* 271: 904.

Maynard, Mary (1997) "Revolutionizing the Subject: Women's Studies and the Sciences." In Maynard, Mary (ed.) *Science and the Construction of Women*. London: UCL Press.

Merchant, Carolyn (1996) *Earthcare: Women and the Environment*. London and New York: Routledge.

Rose, Hilary (1994) *Love, Power, and Knowledge: Towards a Feminist Transformation of the Sciences*. Bloomington and Indianapolis: Indiana University Press.

Rosser, Sue V. (ed.) (1995) *Teaching the Majority: Breaking the Gender Barrier in Science, Mathematics, and Engineering*. New York and London: Teachers College Press.

Rosser, Sue V. (1997) *Re-Engineering Female Friendly Science*. New York and London: Teachers College Press.

Seymour, Elaine and Hewitt, Nancy M. (1994) *Talking About Leaving*. Boulder, CO: University of Colorado Press.

Shapin, Stephen (1996) *The Scientific Revolution*. Chicago and London: University of Chicago Press.

Smaglik, Paul (1998) "Exodus of Women from Science is Jeopardizing Recent Gains." *The Scientist*, April 13.

WOMEN ARE UNDER-REPRESENTED in the natural sciences at all levels. In North America, this condition for women means fewer girls and women in science in high school and college programs, lower rates of employment, lower salaries and slower advancement, and concentration in places and positions of low prestige – in effect, all indicators of lesser "success" based on what counts in Western culture. Because women have been actively recruited into the sciences over the last two decades, many attribute these gender issues to women themselves – that is, that women are "choosing" not to pursue these fields or high-status positions in them. In reality, girls and women report that the climate of science is hostile in a multitude of ways and illustrates that recruitment in the absence of retention is ineffective in changing conditions for women in the sciences.

The absence of women in the sciences is symptomatic of a much deeper issue associated with the norms and expectations of science. Because the normal image of scientists has been, and continues to be, white, middle/upper-class, solitary, laboratory-oriented man, it is necessary to modify "scientist" when we try to include other types of people. Thus, we have created special categories for people who are field biologists or women scientists, placing the difference-generating modifier even before the discipline. Practicing women scientists face such a wide variety of issues (from reduced access and visibility to lower rates of promotion and funding) that they never question why they have been given this label. The fact that our culture does not make it possible for us to assume that scientists can be women means that women scientists *are* an anomaly, that they are categorized as exceptions that deserve a special title. Even when we claim to acknowledge the accomplishments of women in the sciences, we maintain the notion of rarity, sprinkling science textbooks and "who's whos" with the well-worn names of a few women. Although naming existing women scientists, survivors in a sense, provides visibility and positive role models for young women, it does nothing to change the culture of science or the conditions for girls and women pursuing scientific activities.

People (especially scientists) who are introduced to the concept of "woman scientist" typically come to the conclusion that feminists are promoting the idea that women "do" science differently. This conclusion has two rather unproductive outcomes. First, assuming that all that women want is to acknowledge the importance of a female style to science meets with intense objection from practicing women scientists, who do not want their work perceived as "other." Second, if we accept that women do science differently then we can rationalize that science will "change" if we add more women. Twenty-five years of recruitment initiatives by the National Science Foundation show us that this is not the case. Adding more women changes nothing if the norms and expectations of the culture of science remain unaltered. Furthermore, new information suggests that the inroads that women have made are in jeopardy as women choose to pursue lives that are incompatible with the expectations of scientists (Smaglik, 1998).

What of the survivors, the women and other under-represented groups whom we can identify and count as practicing scientists? A number of studies have documented the condition of women in the sciences from historical, disciplinary and even cross-cultural perspectives (Rossiter, 1982, 1995; NSF, 1992, 1996; Vetter, 1992). In short, these data show the same trends – lower numbers and lesser success – that were initially identified in more qualitative terms. In this section, the contributions by Eisenhart and Finkel, Brainard and Carlin, Silverman, and Wenneras and Wold offer statistical information about the training, employment, and productivity of women in the sciences. These articles underscore the need for improving programs for women and the subtle ways that women's work in the sciences is undervalued either in terms of where and how women are conducting research or how that research comes to be recognized by the scientific community. Rather than offering a bleak picture, these selections offer quantitative evidence of the imbalance in participation and opportunities for women in science. Often, it is this evidence that is most convincing and surprising for those who believe that women who are scientists are seen only as scientists and that being a woman has no influence.

Another way to understand women in science is to listen to the experiences of women scientists. Stories by women scientists raise familiar themes which are well presented in several recently published books (Eisenhart and Finkel, 1998; Morse, 1995; Pattatucci, 1998). These narratives tell of the surprise and confusion of double standards related to personal choices like marriage and parenthood; they tell of frustration in publishing and attaining grants; they speak to the lack of role models and mentors. Women perceive these issues as barriers to success in science. The remaining pieces in this section are short, personal accounts by three women trained as natural scientists, all of whom have become prominent analysts of the culture of science. Ruth Hubbard, Bonnie Spanier and Evelyn Fox Keller share a love for science but also an awareness of the need to reconceptualize how we see the natural world. They speak of the paths that led them to this understanding and of the events that made it clear that they could not separate their scientific and political roles.

References

Eisenhart, Margaret A. and Finkel, Elizabeth (1998) *Women's Science: Learning and Succeeding From the Margins*. Chicago and London: University of Chicago

London: Sage.

Rossiter, M.W. (1982) *Women Scientists in America: Struggles and Strategies to 1940*. Baltimore: Johns Hopkins University Press.

Rossiter, M.W. (1995) *Women Scientists in America: Before Affirmative Action 1940–1972*. Baltimore: Johns Hopkins University Press.

Smaglik, Paul (1998) "Exodus of Women from Science is Jeopardizing Recent Gains." *The Scientist*, April 13.

Vetter, B.M. (1992) "Women in Science: Ferment, Yes; Progress, Maybe; Change, Slow." *Mosaic* 23: 34–41.

Additional Resources

AAAS (1992) "Women in Science: First Annual Survey." *Science* 255: 1365–1388.

AAAS (1993) "Gender and the Culture of Science." *Science* 260: 383–430.

AAAS (1994) "Comparisons Across Cultures." *Science* 261: 1467–1496.

Abir-Am, P. and D. Outram (1987) *Uneasy Careers and Intimate Lives: Women in Science 1789–1979*. New Brunswick, NJ: Rutgers University Press.

Association for Women in Science (1995) *A Hand Up: Women Mentoring Women in Science*. Washington, DC: AWIS.

Bertsch-McGrayne, S. (1993) *Nobel Prize Women in Science: Their Lives, Struggles, and Momentous Discoveries*. New York: Birch Lane Press.

Brush, S.G. (1991) "Women in Science and Engineering." *American Scientist* 79: 404–419.

Etzkowitz, H. *et al.* (1994) "The Paradox of a Critical Mass for Women in Science." *Science* 266: 51–54.

Evetts, Julia (1996) *Gender and Career in Science and Engineering*. London: Taylor & Francis.

Grinstein, L.S., R.K. Rose, and M.H. Rafailovich (eds) (1993) *Women in Chemistry and Physics: A Biobibliographic Sourcebook*. Westport, CT: Greenwood Publishing.

Hanson, Sandra L. (1996) *Lost Talent: Women in the Sciences*. Philadelphia: Temple University Press.

Holloway, M. (1993) "A Lab of Her Own." *Scientific American*, November, 94–103.

Jones, M.G. and J. Wheatley (1988) "Factors Influencing the Entry of Women into Science and Related Fields." *Science Education* 72: 127–142.

Kahle, J.B. (1988) "Recruitment and Retention of Women in College Science Majors." *Journal of College Science Teaching* 17: 382–384.

Kass-Simon, G. and P. Farnes (eds) (1990) *Women of Science: Righting the Record.* Bloomington and Indianapolis: Indiana University Press.

Kelly, A. (1982) *Why Young Women Don't Do Science."* New Scientist 94: 497–500.

National Research Council (1991) *Women in Science and Engineering: Increasing Their Numbers in the 1990s.* Washington, DC: National Academy Press.

National Research Council (1992) *Science and Engineering Programs: On Target for Women?* Washington, DC: National Academy Press.

Rosser, S.V. (1994) *Educating Women for Success in Science and Mathematics: A University of South Carolina Model.* USC Columbia: University Publications.

Seymour, E. and N. Hewitt (1994) *Talking About Leaving.* Boulder: Greenhaven Press.

Shepherd, L.J. (1993) *Lifting the Veil: The Feminine Face of Science.* Boston: Shambhala.

University of Wisconsin Women's Studies Librarian's Office (1994) *History of Women and Science, Health, and Technology: A Bibliographic Guide to the Professions and the Disciplines.* Madison: University of Wisconsin.

Ware, N.C., N.A. Steckler, and J. Leserman (1985) "Undergraduate Women: Who Chooses a Science Major?" *Journal of Higher Education* 56: 73–84.

Zuckerman, H. *et al.* (1991) *The Outer Circle: Women in the Scientific Community.* New York: W.W. Norton.

Chapter 1

[S]tarting in 1968 and essentially complete by 1972, there was a legal revolution in women's education and employment rights. It promised, even seemed to guarantee, broad ramifications for women's careers in science and engineering, but its full implementation would require many battles in the years ahead. One era had ended and a new, more equitable one was beginning.

(Rossiter 1995, 382)

[Women's] career attainments continue, on average [as of 1991], to be more modest than those of men in all sectors – in academia, industry, and government – and the gap in attainments grows as men and women age. Moreover, while some distinguished women scientists and engineers have become insiders and members of the scientific establishment, those who have often feel themselves to be outsiders and on the margin. It is not clear at this juncture whether parity will be achieved in the careers of men and women scientists and engineers and, if so, when.

(Zuckerman 1991, 56)

Patterns in the participation of women in science and engineering

Despite the hope for the equal participation of women in science and engineering noted by Margaret Rossiter above, women have been and continue to be found in the lower-status activities and workplaces of science and engineering practice. Although many believe that women in the 1990s are well on their way to achieving parity with men in science and engineering, there is evidence to the contrary. The gap between men's and women's success, especially in elite science and engineering, remains significant.

This chapter begins with an examination of women's involvement in science or engineering in the United States today. We investigate the distribution of women in science and engineering degree programs and workplaces and summarize changes in their participation over the past four decades. We then examine and critique current proposals for educational reform developed with the goal of addressing the absence of women and their inequitable treatment in science and engineering activities in school and at work.

Before proceeding, we want to note that our search for information about where the women are in science and engineering was not easy. Although considerable data are available on the numbers and types of degrees earned by female and male scientists and engineers, there are many fewer sources of information on the employment of men and women in science and engineering. We found, as did Rossiter (1995), that "the statistical picture is badly incomplete . . . [has] many gaps, and fail[s] to probe very deeply or meaningfully into . . . aspects of the women's situation" (95).

Particularly significant in our opinion were the limited trend data on the employment of scientists who do not have doctoral degrees (not available during the period 1970–1995) and the lack of information on employment of scientists in nonprofit organizations (with the exception of government). Given Rossiter's finding that (as of 1966), of people employed as scientists, 38.1 percent of the women (26.5 percent of the men) held master's degrees (1995, 105), and our own finding of large proportions of female scientists in environmental and other nonprofit organizations, the absence of detailed information in these two areas was especially notable.

A brief history of women in science and engineering

Rossiter's description, quoted above, of the optimism about women's increased opportunities in science and engineering produced by the passage of equal rights legislation in the late 1960s and early 1970s initially appeared to be well founded. The number of science and engineering doctorates awarded to women rose from a mere 7 percent in 1970 to 24 percent in 1985 (Zuckerman 1991, 29), and in engineering alone the number of bachelor's degrees awarded to women rose from only 385 in 1975 (less than 1 percent of all undergraduate degrees awarded in engineering) to more than 11,000 in 1985 (approximately 16 percent of the total) (National Science Board (NSB) 1993, 79). Similarly, the percentages of white females with doctoral degrees in science or engineering employed as academic faculty increased from 12.1 percent in 1979 to 18.1 percent in 1989 (NSB 1993, 409–11). At the same time, the numbers of men in these fields also increased, thus making women's achievements all the more impressive (NSB 1993, 409–10).

Unfortunately, by the mid-1980s the picture seemed to be changing, and the late 1980s brought sobering news. Analyzing the enrollment of men and women in college-degree programs, Jerry Jacobs (1995) found that the rate of improvement in what he refers to as the "integration," or balance, of women and men in twenty-four degree programs slowed substantially in the late 1980s after increasing markedly from the late 1960s through the early 1980s. Among those receiving bachelor's degrees in computer science, life sciences, mathematics, and engineering, increases in the proportion of women during the period of 1980–85 slowed during the period 1985–90, and, except in the life sciences, women's percentages remained considerably below men's (Jacobs 1995, 88). In the physical sciences, small increases occurred over the entire period 1980–90, but women's enrollment had reached only about 30 percent in 1990. Jacobs concludes his report with this ominous note:

> [illegible]

[illegible] currently as rosy as that predicted in the 1960s, nor even as rosy as that described by people examining trends in enrollment, hiring, and employment between the late 1960s and the mid-1980s. In fact, current figures on women's participation in science and engineering, as well as the details of women's increased participation in scientific and engineering fields between 1960 and 1985, reveal that although there are currently more opportunities for women to become scientists and engineers than in the past, the opportunities are still limited.

Figures on the percentages of women receiving master's and doctoral degrees in natural science or engineering show a pattern similar to that reported by Jacobs (National Science Foundation (NSF) 1996). Although the percentages of women in these fields have increased dramatically since 1971, their percentages continue to be considerably lower than those of men, as tables 1.1 and 1.2 reveal. Thus, despite substantial gains, women continue to be underrepresented in science and engineering degree programs.

Even women who do succeed in academic science or engineering have more trouble than men do in finding satisfying and rewarding employment. Rates of unemployment and underemployment among scientists and engineers (those looking for work) are consistently higher for women than men (Vetter 1992; Zuckerman 1991, 32). Harriet Zuckerman's (1991) study of the careers of male and female scientists and engineers reveals that even when men and women are similarly qualified and get jobs, their career trajectories tend to be different, to women's disadvantage.

Beginning with their initial qualifications, Zuckerman traces scientists' careers between 1970 and 1980. She includes indicators such as the timing of tenure and

Table 1.1 Percentages of women receiving master's degrees, 1971 and 1991

Field	*1971*	*1991*
Engineering	1.1%	14.0%
Natural sciences	22.2%	35.6%

Source: National Science Foundation, Division of Research, Evaluation, and Communication, Directorate for Education and Human Resources, *Indicators of Science and Mathematics Education, 1995,* ed. Larry E. Suter (Arlington, VA: National Science Foundation [NSF 96–52], 1996), 186.

Table 1.2 Percentages of women receiving doctoral degrees, 1971 and 1991

Field	*1971*	*1991*
Engineering	0.5%	8.7%
Natural sciences	9.7%	26.0%

Source: National Science Foundation, Division of Research, Evaluation, and Communication, Directorate for Education and Human Resources, *Indicators of Science and Mathematics Education*, 1995, ed. Larry E. Suter (Arlington, VA: National Science Foundation [NSF 96–52], 1996), 187.

promotion; salary; research impact; honors; and reputation. She reports that the intellectual caliber of men and women entering science or engineering with doctoral degrees is the same (as measured by either standardized test scores or by prior academic performance) and that men and women now earn their doctoral degrees at much the same age (34). These similarities, as well as the fact that approximately equal numbers of women and men are awarded and accept postdoctoral positions (an expected step in the trajectory toward high-status academic positions in most science fields), suggest that men and women begin their careers as scientists equally well prepared for success (34–35). However, female scientists in academe are considerably more likely to hold their first professional position as instructors, lecturers, and other "off-ladder" academic positions, whereas men are more likely to work first in tenure-track positions (36).

The initial tendency for female scientists to fill lower-status positions continues into the later stages of their careers. While data on women's positions in educational institutions, industry, and government are less than thorough,

> they are relentlessly consistent . . . women, on average, started out in lower ranks than men, and the disparity in their ranks continues. . . . [For] example, Ashern and Scott . . . report that among matched men and women who received Ph.D.s in the 1940s and 1950s, 86 percent of men had become full professors by 1979 as against 64 percent of women (a ratio of 1.3:1). In the cohort that got Ph.D.s in the 1960s, a smaller proportion of both men (52 percent) and women (30 percent) had become full professors by 1979, but men proportionately outnumbered women by a ratio of 1.7: 1. . . . And finally, among those who had gotten Ph.D.s between 1970 and 1974, just 6 percent of men and 3 percent of women had become full professors [by 1979].
>
> (Zuckerman 1991, 37)

Salary figures for male and female scientists and engineers reported in 1991 reveal another disparity between men and women. Despite the calls for more women to be employed in science or engineering, median annual salaries for full-time employed civilian scientists and engineers are less for women at every level of experience, beginning with scientists and engineers employed less than five years. For people employed less than five years, the median salary for men is $48,000, and that for women is $42,000 (NSF 1994, 374). The disparity remains even after more experience, with women consistently earning between 87.5 percent and 83.6 percent of men's salaries.

The statistics cited above from Zuckerman's review reflect a picture of women in science that is particularly grim: in general, while women and men seem to be completing doctorates with similar credentials and experience, the positions and rewards they find are not comparable. While many of the reports Zuckerman summarizes were produced in the late 1980s and based upon studies conducted [illegible] as assistant professors in four-year colleges and universities were women (NSF 1994, 376–77). As Smith and Tang comment,

> Surprisingly, this pattern remains the same even in fields where women have relatively high representation in doctoral training. In 1989, less than half of all female doctoral scientists and engineers held full professorships in psychology or the social sciences, compared to two-thirds among males. Experience apparently only explains a portion of the gender disparity in academic rank.
>
> (117)

According to the National Science Board (NSB 1993), "no profession exhibits a greater disparity in the employment of men and women than engineering" (79). As of 1991, women made up 3.4 percent of the US engineering workforce. Due in large part to the scarcity of qualified female engineers, starting salaries for women in engineering are higher than those for men and higher than those offered to women in any other field (Vandervoort 1985, 140). However, a salary gap begins to appear after several years. According to Vandervoort, "women engineers who have worked fifteen years have salaries only 84.9 percent of men" (140). And we find that "men's salaries continue to increase with years of experience, but women's reach a plateau. The chief explanation for this widening gap is that significantly more men are promoted to managerial positions than women" (NSB 1993, 79).

According to a study by Judith McIlwee and Gregg Robinson (1992), many female engineers graduate from college and find well-paid jobs, receiving starting salaries at or above those of their male counterparts. However, within ten years, women occupy lower-status positions than men. According to the authors, "men who had been out of school longest and with their current employer longest held the highest ranked jobs. In contrast, there was no similar association for women" (84). Furthermore, "a significant number of women who started their careers in high-status design jobs actually experienced downward mobility over time" (84).

Thus, despite increases in women's involvement in science and engineering degree programs after the passage of equal rights legislation in the late 1960s and early 1970s, women's participation in the work of science and engineering remains unequal to that of men, and is less well rewarded. Women tend to be concentrated in fields of low prestige and in jobs and positions with less status and less salary, than those enjoyed by men. This distribution of people in the disciplines and places of scientific and engineering practice suggests why, when we went looking for women practicing science, we found them where we did: in lower-status workplaces, and in lower-status activities of science and engineering.[1]

This continued disparity has not escaped the notice of educators and policy makers, who have proposed a series of educational reforms designed to rectify some of the inequities that still exist for women interested in pursuing careers in science and engineering. Although these reforms do not directly address women's concentration in lower-status and lower-paying science positions, they seek improvements in science education that will raise the number of well-trained women prepared to enter science or engineering fields.[2]

The effort to improve opportunities for female scientists and engineers through education[3]

For many people, the key to solving the problem of women's underrepresentation in science and engineering lies in increasing the numbers and improving the academic preparation of girls and young women in science and mathematics. If schools did a better job of teaching science and mathematics, more people, especially women, might pursue degrees and jobs in science or engineering and be more successful in them. Concerns such as these have led to the recent development of three national level proposals for science education reform, including the American Association for the Advancement of Science's (AAAS) Project 2061 (AAAS 1989, 1993; Rutherford and Ahlgren 1990); the National Science Teachers Association's (NSTA) project, *Scope, Sequence, and Coordination of Secondary School Science* (Aldridge 1992; NSTA 1992, 1995); and the National Research Council's (NRC) *National Science Education Standards* (1994, 1996). In one way or another, all three reform proposals aim to improve science education for the benefit of girls (among other goals). For example, the NRC makes equity for all students the first principle of its reform agenda. Its first principle reads as follows:

> Science is for all students. This principle is one of equity and excellence. Science in our schools must be for all students: All students, regardless of age, sex, cultural or ethnic background, disabilities, aspirations, or interest and motivation in science, should have the opportunity to attain high levels of scientific literacy. The standards . . . emphatically reject any situation in science education where some people – for example, members of certain populations – are discouraged from pursuing science and excluded from opportunities to learn science.
>
> (NRC 1996, 20)

This goal is also addressed in both the NSTA and AAAS proposals, although to different degrees. NSTA's scope, sequence and coordination proposal (1992) includes a more general statement about equity, focusing on the need to develop "instructional strategies [that are] . . . appropriate for heterogeneous groups, with no tracking" (15), and aiming at what they describe as "an ambitious, but not unrealistic" final goal: "Science learning for all students that is interesting, relevant, challenging, and personally rewarding" (16). The authors of AAAS's *Science for All Americans* (1989) are more explicit:

> The recommendations in this report apply to all students. The set of recommendations constitutes a common core of learning . . . for all young people,
>
> [illegible]

[illegible] discouraged, barred, or chased from science.

The processes thought to contribute to the underrepresentation of girls and women in science are many and varied. They include the mass media's stereotyped portrayals of scientists as nerdy and male (e.g., Nelkin 1987); the "chilly climate" of science classrooms and degree programs (e.g., Hall and Sandler 1982; Sadker and Sadker 1994; Seymour and Hewitt 1994; Tobias 1990); the ways women and minorities are culturally defined as the type of "people who leave" science and engineering programs (Downey, Hegg, and Lucena 1993); the known manipulation of some scientific findings for corporate or political gain (e.g., Greider 1992; Nelkin 1987); and the systematic exclusion of non-Western, non-male interests and perspectives from science (e.g., Harding 1991; Keller 1985).

Yet the current reform proposals suggest that relatively minor changes in science content and classroom instruction can overcome these barriers. The following excerpt from *Science for All Americans* is illustrative:

> We are convinced that – given clear goals, the right resources, and good teaching throughout 13 years of school – essentially all students . . . will be able to reach all of the recommended learning goals by the time they graduate from high school.
>
> (Rutherford and Ahlgren 1990, x–xi)

In essence, the reform proposals suggest that better teaching, higher standards, and sensitivity to differences among students can overcome long-standing obstacles to participation. The proposals do not address feminist or minority critiques of science.

Over a decade ago, Evelyn Fox Keller (1982) argued that feminist and minority critiques of science could be arranged on a four-point continuum from liberal to radical. The liberal critique suggests that women and minorities are underrepresented in science because they have not been treated in the same encouraging way as have men. The liberal solution is to find ways for girls, women, and minorities to gain equal access to the range and depth of positive science experiences already available to boys and men.

This is the approach taken by AAAS, NSTA, and NRC. An excerpt from NRC's national standards provides an example. The second underlying principle of the national standards (after the principle of equity) states that "[a]ll students will learn all science in the content standards" (1–7). Later in the document, NRC explains what teachers should do to meet this principle:

> Teachers of science orchestrate their classes so that all have equal opportunities to participate in learning activities. Students with physical disabilities might require modified equipment; students with limited English ability might need to be encouraged to use their own language as well as English . . . students with learning disabilities might need more time to complete science activities.
> (1996, 11–13)

Yet in Keller's scheme, the liberal approach is the most conservative one.

A second, more radical, critique by Keller suggests that the predominance of men in the sciences has led to a bias in the choice and definition of the problems scientists have addressed. For example, in the health sciences, problems associated with conceiving a child have, until very recently, received little attention. The focus of work (generally by male researchers) has been on contraceptive techniques and devices to be used by women to prevent conception. From this perspective, science is likely to discourage women and minorities because it does not address many of the topics that concern them.

Other, more radical critiques advanced by Keller question the fundamental processes and foundations of science. A third critique suggests the possibility of bias in the design and interpretation of research. The study of primatology provides a good example (e.g., Haraway 1989). When white males were the only primate researchers, they viewed the primate troop, composed of a single adult male with several females and young, as a harem and interpreted their data from the assumption that the male was the troop leader. Years of field observation studies by female researchers (e.g., Jane Goodall and Dian Fossey) have shown that the social organization of some primate troops is better explained by matriarchy: males are used by females as a resource for sperm, protection, and friendship. The possibility of this type of bias suggests that science discourages women and minorities because its theoretical stances tend to privilege white male standpoints.

The most radical critique of science offered by Keller is a challenge to the truth and warrant of the conclusions of natural science on the grounds that they reflect the judgments of only one group of people: men. Keller writes, "It is not true [that] 'the conclusions of natural science are true and necessary, and the judgment of man has nothing to do with them'; it is the judgment of women that they [the conclusions of science] have nothing to do with" (1982, 590).

The means of lowering barriers for women and minorities suggested by AAAS, NSTA, and NRC address only the type of bias identified in Keller's first and most conservative critique. The changes are all "compensatory" strategies (e.g., Howe 1993) to provide access to science for previously underrepresented groups. Compensatory strategies treat disadvantaged persons according to their special needs, but only with the aim of enabling them to measure up to a standard already set by the advantaged group. The content and modes of inquiry in the science activities of the current reform projects in science education are not open to the kind of revisions that Keller's other three critiques suggest. In all three proposals, the nature of the science to be learned is specifically described in the content standards, and they describe, almost exclusively, the content and methods of conventional science.

The same criticisms can be made of college-level reform efforts. Programs such as those for "women in engineering" or those that encourage cooperative work groups and single-sex classes are usually compensatory in that they aim to raise women's performance to the level of men's (see Tonso 1997 for an extended discussion in the case of engineering).

If we are serious about increasing the numbers and kinds of people in science, new curriculum plans and outcome measures that focus on conventional science do not

Notes

1 We should also note that women in science or engineering are predominantly white. The numbers of nonwhite women in science and engineering are very small, although in comparison to their percentage in the population, their representation is not as dispiriting as for white women. In 1991, minority women, approximately 8 percent of the population as a whole, earned about 5 percent of all bachelor's degrees in the physical sciences and about 7 percent of all bachelor's degrees in the biological sciences (NSF 1994, 231–34). Numbers at the doctoral level are far lower, with black, non-Hispanic women (5 percent of the population) earning just 1.1 percent of all science and engineering doctorates in 1992, and American Indian/Alaskan Native women (0.5 percent of the population) earning 0.2 percent of those degrees (NSF 1994, 345–46). These figures suggest why, when we did find women working in science or engineering, most of them were white.

2 Some readers will no doubt think that the inequities facing women in the science and engineering workforce have more to do with discrimination against women or with women's decisions about family matters than with education. We take up these issues in chapter 2 [of *Women's Science: Learning and Succeeding from the Margins*]. Here we focus on the current, large-scale, national effort to improve women's opportunities through education.

3 Scott Marion contributed to this review of educational reforms. A longer critique of the reforms can be found in Eisenhart, Finkel, and Marion (1996).

References

Aldridge, B. 1992. Project on scope, sequence, and coordination: A new synthesis for improving science education. *Journal of Science Education* 1 (1):13–21.

American Association for the Advancement of Science (AAAS). 1989. *Science for all Americans: A Project 2061 report on literacy goals in science, mathematics, and technology.* Washington, DC: American Association for the Advancement of Science.

American Association for the Advancement of Science (AAAS). 1993. *Benchmarks for scientific literacy*. New York: Oxford University Press.

Downey, G., Hegg, S., and Lucena, J. 1993, November. Weeded out: Critical reflection in engineering education. Paper presented at the American Anthropological Association, Washington, DC.

Eisenhart, M., Finkel, E., and Marion, S. 1996. Creating the conditions for scientific literacy: A reexamination. *American Educational Research Journal* 33 (2): 261–95.

Greider, M. 1992. *Who will tell the people? The betrayal of American democracy*. New York: Simon and Schuster.

Hall, R. and Sandler, B. 1982. *The classroom climate: A chilly one for women?* Washington, DC: Association of American Colleges, Project on the Status and Education of Women.

Haraway, D. 1989. *Primate visions: Gender, race, and nature in the world of modern science*. New York: Routledge.

Harding, S. 1991. *Whose science? Whose knowledge? Thinking from women's lives*. Ithaca, NY: Cornell University Press.

Holland, D. and Eisenhart, M. 1990. *Educated in romance: Women, achievement, and college culture*. Chicago: University of Chicago Press.

Howe, K. 1993. Equality of educational opportunity and the criterion of equal educational worth. *Studies in Philosophy and Education* 11: 329–37.

Jacobs, J. 1995. Gender and academic specialties: Trends among recipients of college degrees in the 1980s. *Sociology of Education* 68: 81–98.

Keller, E. 1982. Feminism and science. *Signs: Journal of Women in Culture and Society* 7 (3): 589–902.

Keller, E. 1985. *Reflections on gender and science*. New Haven, CT: Yale University Press.

Lave, J. 1990. Views of the classroom: Implications for math and science learning research. In M. Gardner, J. Greeno, A. Reif, A. Schoenfeld, A. DiSessa, and E. Stage, eds., *Toward a scientific practice of science education*, pp. 203–17. Hillsdale, NJ: Erlbaum Associates.

McIlwee, J. and Robinson, G. 1992. *Women in engineering: Gender, power, and workplace culture*. Albany, NY: SUNY Press.

National Research Council. 1994, November. *National science education standards: Draft*. Washington, DC: National Academy Press.

National Research Council. 1996. *National science education standards*. Washington, DC: National Academy Press.

National Science Board, 1993. *Science and engineering indicators, 1993*. Washington, DC: U.S. Government Printing Office (NSB 93–1).

National Science Foundation. 1994. *Women, minorities, and persons with disabilities in science and engineering: 1994*. Washington, DC: National Science Foundation (NSF 94–333).

National Science Foundation. 1996. *Women, minorities, and persons with disabilities in science and engineering: 1996*. Washington, DC: National Science Foundation (NSF 96–311).

National Science Teachers Association. 1992. *Scope, sequence, and coordination of secondary school science*. Vol. 1. Arlington, VA: Author.

National Science Teachers Association. 1995. *Scope, sequence, and coordination of secondary school science*. Vol. 3. Arlington, VA: Author.

Nelkin, K. 1987. *Selling science: How the press covers science and technology*. New York: W.H. Freeman.

Rossiter, M. 1995. *Women scientists in America: Before affirmative action, 1940–1972*. Baltimore, MD: Johns Hopkins University Press.

Rutherford, J. and Ahlgren, A. 1990. *Science for all Americans*. New York: Oxford University Press.

Sadker, M. and Sadker, D. 1994. *Failing at fairness: How America's schools cheat girls*. New York: Scribner.

Seymour, E. and Hewitt, N. 1994. *Talking about leaving: Why undergraduates leave the sciences*. Boulder, CO: Westview Press.

Smith, E., and Tang, J. 1994. Trends in science and engineering doctorate production [illegible]

[illegible] Participation and recognition. In J. Kahle, ed., *Women in science: A report from the field*, pp. 124–47. Philadelphia, PA: Falmer Press.

Vetter, B. 1992. What's holding up the glass ceiling? Barriers to women in the science and engineering workplace. Occasional Paper 92–3, Commission on Professionals in Science and Technology.

Zuckerman, H. 1991. The careers of men and women scientists: A review of current research. In H. Zuckerman, J. Cole, and J. Bruer, eds., *The outer circle: Women in the science community*, pp. 28–56. New Haven, CT: Yale University Press.

Chapter 2

Suzanne G. Brainard and Linda Carlin

A SIX-YEAR LONGITUDINAL STUDY OF UNDERGRADUATE WOMEN IN ENGINEERING AND SCIENCE

Abstract

In 1991, the Women in Engineering (WIE) Initiative at the University of Washington was funded by the Alfred P. Sloan Foundation to conduct a longitudinal study of undergraduate women pursuing degrees in science or engineering. Cohorts of approximately 100 students have been added to the study each year, for a current total of 672 participants. The objectives are: (a) to determine an accurate measure of retention by tracking individual students through their science and engineering academic careers; (b) to examine factors affecting retention of women in science and engineering; and (c) to evaluate the effectiveness of WIE's programs targeted at increasing enrollment and retention of women in science and engineering. These programs include interventions primarily during the freshman and sophomore years, which are critical attrition points. The results of this study are reported annually to the Dean of Engineering and related departments for consideration in policy formulation. Annual results of the study have shown consistent patterns of persistence factors and barriers for these high-achieving women; most notably a significant drop in academic self-confidence during their freshman year in college. In addition, individual tracking of these women has shown a retention that is much higher than the estimated national average for engineering and science students.

I. Introduction

Undergraduate engineering enrollments in the United States reached an all-time high of 406,144 students in 1983. By 1996, this figure had decreased to only 317,772 students. However, this decline in engineering enrollment was disproportionate between females and males. The enrollment of males declined 25% from 1983 to 1996 (341,495 to 256,013), while the enrollment of females declined only 4% during the same period of time (64,649 to 61,759) and has actually increased almost every year since 1989. However, it still has not returned to the 1983 peak level.[†]

On the other hand, undergraduate engineering degrees granted in the US [illegible] actually happening.

Current national retention rate estimates for women, calculated as the ratio of students who complete an engineering program to the number of incoming freshmen four years earlier, are slightly below 60%.[2] Similarly calculated retention rates of female engineering students at the University of Washington in 1991, obtained from the Registrar's Office prior to the initiation of the present study, were about 55%. This aggregate retention calculation fails to account for students who transfer into engineering after the freshman year, resulting in an inflated retention rate. A more accurate retention rate can only be determined by tracking individual students from the beginning to completion of a program.

At the University of Washington, about 4000 freshmen (50% are female) are enrolled annually. During their freshman year, all students planning to pursue a degree in science or engineering are enrolled in the College of Arts and Sciences. Most students do not enter the College of Engineering or science departments until their junior year. It is only at the beginning of their junior year that students can be tracked individually by their college or department and more accurate persistence rates determined. Thus, there is no tracking of students who switch degree programs or who transfer to the University during their first two years.

The inadequacy and inconsistency of collection and maintenance of evaluation and retention data is a national problem and was identified in 1988 by the National Research Council (NRC) as a major hindrance to projecting future manpower needs as well as identifying problem areas in the pipeline. The NRC established a committee to investigate ways to improve this process both at the federal and institutional levels. Although mandates can be put in place for federal agencies, it is more difficult to do so for educational institutions. Collecting longitudinal data and maintaining tracking systems on all registered students is complicated and expensive. As a result, only a handful of institutions have implemented such systems, since most do not have an incentive to bear the cost.

The Women in Engineering Initiative (WIE) at the University of Washington was established in 1988 with the mission of increasing enrollment and retention of women pursuing degrees in engineering, primarily through a network of support programs for students. In 1991, supported by a grant from the Alfred P. Sloan Foundation, WIE began a longitudinal study of undergraduate women pursuing degrees in science or engineering. The study has three primary goals, the first of which is to obtain a more accurate measure of retention of females pursuing science and engineering (S&E) degrees by tracking individual students until they graduate.[3]

To date, WIE is able to report retention rates for women in S&E based on individual tracking of 672 women who have participated in the study over a span of six years. There are currently no comparison data available on retention rates for men in S&E, or women pursuing other degrees. To further investigate factors specifically related to the retention of women in S&E, the current study may eventually be expanded to include individual tracking of students in these groups.

The importance of determining accurate retention rates is related to the influx of women and other minority groups into the job market. Despite the growing proportion of these groups in the general workforce, they are underrepresented in the fields of science and engineering. For example, although women make up 46% of the total labor force, they comprise only 31% of the science professions (excluding social science) and only 8% of the engineering professions.[4] As the demographics of the workforce continue to change, a lack of technical education and experience in this growing portion of the workforce would prove detrimental to our increasingly technology-oriented society.[5]

A second goal of the study is to determine what factors influence the persistence of women in S&E degree programs. Early research investigating the underrepresentation of women in technical fields focused on ability. However, Seymour and Hewitt, in their benchmark 1994 study comparing students persisting in S&E undergraduate degree programs with those who chose to switch to another field of study, or drop out of college altogether, found that there were no real differences in the factors of high school preparation, ability, or effort expended in their coursework between students who remain and those who switch.[6] Although these results applied to both male and female undergraduates, they have been confirmed for women by other studies of female S&E undergraduates.[7,8]

Seymour and Hewitt identify two categories of students who switch out of S&E programs: students who become bored or disappointed with the S&E curriculum, and students who feel forced to leave due to a loss of academic self-confidence in a competitive environment.[9] Seymour and Hewitt's findings place many women and students of color in this second category.

These findings are supported by an earlier study of young women in high school who tended to suffer from a loss of perceived academic competence.[10] While only males of low competence dropped out of math and science courses, females of high competence were often also dropping out. These young women had experienced a loss of self-confidence prior to any exhibited loss of performance in their math and science classes. Therefore, it was not lack of academic ability that diverted these young women from continuing in math and science, but a lack of self-confidence.

The establishment and successful continuation of women in engineering programs at several universities[11] is an acknowledgment of the theory that, given support and opportunity, women can not only survive, but thrive in a traditionally male-dominated field.

The third goal of the study is to evaluate the impact of WIE programs on retention rates of women pursuing S&E undergraduate degrees at the University of Washington.

In summary, in order to have a better picture of how well female S&E students are faring, the goals of WIE's retention program and longitudinal study are:

- to determine a more accurate measure of retention by tracking individual students through their science and engineering academic careers
- to examine the factors affecting retention of females in science and engineering
- to evaluate the effectiveness of WIE's programs targeted at increasing recruit-

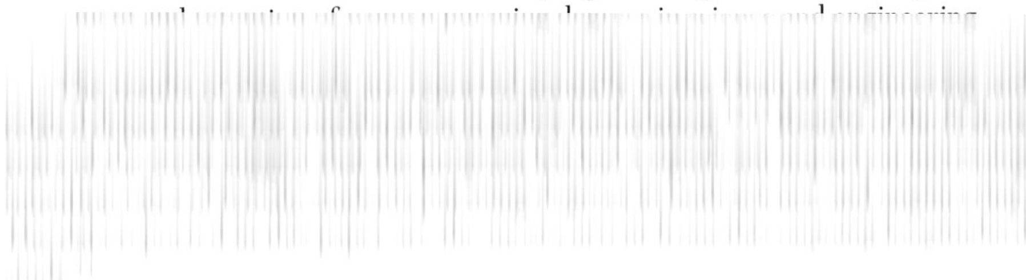

II. Method

A. Instrument design and data gathering

Six instruments have been designed to gather information: the Annual Freshman Interest Survey, Freshman Initial Interview Form, Freshman Follow-up Interview Form, Sophomore Follow-up Questionnaire, Junior Follow-up Questionnaire, and Senior Follow-up Questionnaire.

The Annual Freshman Interest Survey is mailed in August of each year to all incoming female freshmen at the University of Washington to determine how many are interested in pursuing degrees in science or engineering. Although early response rates in the first three years of the study were low, averaging 11%, the most recent three years' survey response rates have doubled to 22% of the approximately 2000 surveys sent out each year.

Of those responding to the survey, approximately 100 students interested in engineering and 25 students interested in science are selected to participate in the study.* Using a structured interview form, an initial, personal interview is conducted with each student at the WIE Study Center during the Autumn Quarter. A second, follow-up interview is conducted either in person or over the telephone during the Spring Quarter. Sophomores, juniors, and seniors are sent (via email) an annual follow-up questionnaire. Students not responding to the annual questionnaire are tracked by their registration status in the University Registrar's student database.

Reviewed and approved by the University of Washington Human Rights Committee, the structured interview forms are used to ensure that the students' rights of confidentiality and safety are honored and the same information is gathered on each student. The following information is gathered: demographic information; education

* At least 70% of the approximately 100–150 female students who enter engineering each year respond to the survey. It would appear that these students are representative of the population. We have found that students expressing an interest in both science and engineering are less likely to persist than those who are only interested in engineering. The reasons for this are unclear, but perhaps a student who initially declares an interest in both is less committed to a specific major, and therefore less likely to persist.

and professional background; academic interests; amount of family, peer and financial support; confidence level; and perceptions of campus climate and quality of teaching. Students participating in the study must sign a release form consenting to participate.

B. Tracking system

The WIE tracking system provides a mechanism for measuring retention rates, monitoring student participation in activities, and analyzing data each year. Utilizing the SPSS statistical package, data from the tracking system are analyzed:

- to determine retention rates
- to identify individual problems potentially leading to changing majors or dropping out of science and engineering
- to analyze trends and patterns of barriers that tend to influence the retention of entering female freshmen
- to provide a mechanism for accountability in measuring the effectiveness of the WIE's efforts to increase the retention rates of female freshmen.

C. Interventions

A series of interventions (or contact points) are implemented by personal contact with each student throughout her academic career at the University of Washington, focusing primarily on the freshman and sophomore years, when students are not yet accepted into their respective departments and are at the greatest risk of switching out of science and engineering. These contact points involve academic and social support. Students are interviewed to discuss their academic goals, make plans for the future, and participate in activities with a community of peers. The contact points include personal interviews, an orientation session, peer tutoring, peer mentoring, and quarterly seminars and events. WIE also offers an engineering mentoring program that matches students with professionals working in their field of interest. This program, now in its seventh year, has had great success in providing students with "real-world" experience, as well as improving their self-confidence in their academic challenges.[15]

III. Analyses and results

A. Freshman Interest Survey

Since 1991, the Annual Freshman Interest Survey has been mailed to six consecutive cohorts of all incoming first-year female students at the beginning of Autumn Quarter. Table 2.1 summarizes the response rates of students to the survey and the number of students forming each cohort.

B. Persistence in engineering

The student responses to the interviews show that there are a number of common factors influencing a student's decision to persist in engineering or science, to switch

Table 2.1 Response rates to the Freshman Interest Survey

	Year	*Initial Interest Surveys response rate*	*Students interested*	*Students interviewed (initial cohort*	*1997*
Cohort 5	1995	22% (474/2118)	394	127	Sophomore
Cohort 6	1996	23% (485/2126)	427	118	Freshman

to another major, or to drop out of school altogether. Tables 2.2–2.5 summarize the factors that have shown, based on Chi-square analyses, a significant correlation (based on an exploratory study alpha level of $p< 0.1$) with persistence in engineering or science. These factors are then ranked according to their relative importance as a predictive factor of persistence, based on a stepwise logistic regression analysis model using persistence as the dependent variable. Persistence factors of 5th- and 6th-year students could not be calculated because persistence rates for both cohorts 1 and 2 in their 5th year were 100%, and only one of the two remaining 6th-year students from cohort 1 responded to the survey.

In the first two years of preparation for entering an engineering or science department, students at the University of Washington are required to take technical core courses, which include a series in math, physics and chemistry. The primary factors which seem to help these women decide to continue in S&E beyond their freshman year in college are interest in their math and science courses, being able to work independently, a positive influence of faculty, career opportunities, and the presence of WIE (table 2.2). Interestingly, many students who rated WIE as a persistence factor did not actually participate in any WIE programs, reflecting the support that the mere presence of a program like WIE appears to have for some students. Newly emerging persistence factors this year for freshman students were positive ratings of the quality of their math instruction, involvement in the Society of Women Engineers (SWE), and feeling supported by their mothers.

By the end of the sophomore year, the primary factor related to persistence continues to be the student's experience in math and science classes (table 2.3). In addition, committing to an engineering or science degree by registering as a pre-engineering or pre-science student (as indicated by their registration status), and gaining acceptance into a department become major factors in persistence. The positive influence of an advisor and working during the school year are also consistently related to persistence. Participation in SWE and internships and co-ops emerged as persistence

Table 2.2 Persistence factors in science and engineering at the end of the freshman year, cohorts 1–6*

Variables	χ^2	χ^2 *p-value*	*Logistic regression p-value*
Enjoy science classes	29.90	.000	.000
Enjoy math classes	27.11	.000	.010
Participation in WIE	11.92	.103	.053
Career opportunities	24.99	.002	.061
Society of Women Engineers	8.16	.086	.150
Positive influence of mother	17.01	.030	.210
Quality of math instruction	15.31	.009	.321
Positive influence of Faculty/TAs	15.07	.001	.685
No problem working independently	15.67	.074	.812

*N=466; due to refinements to the questionnaire, not all students responded to all questions

Table 2.3 Persistence factors in science and engineering at the sophomore year, cohorts 1–5*

Variables	χ^2	χ^2 *p-value*	*Logistic regression p-value*
Influence of math and science classes	36.13	.000	.050
Registration status	42.17	.000	.020
Acceptance into the department	8.10	.017	.057
Positive influence of internship/co-op	8.29	.141	.097
Working during the school year	7.56	.023	.145
Positive influence of an advisor	16.21	.013	.396
Society of Women Engineers			

**N=369; due to refinements to the questionnaire, not all students responded to all questions*

Table 2.4 Persistence factors in science and engineering at the junior year, cohorts 1–4*

Variables	χ^2	χ^2 *p-value*	*Logistic regression p-value*
Society of Women Engineers	9.72	.137	.264
Registration status	11.30	.010	.481
Positive influence of a mentor	7.19	.126	.535
Influence of math and science classes	17.74	.001	.694
Acceptance into the department	3.05	.081	.703
Participation in conferences and events	8.38	.079	.758

**N=284; due to refinements to the questionnaire, not all students responded to all questions*

Table 2.5 Persistence factors in science and engineering at the senior year, cohorts 1–3*

Variables	χ^2	χ^2 *p-value*	*Logistic regression p-value*
Seeing an academic advisor	3.17	.075	.031

preparing for their careers.

By the junior year, most students have been accepted into a department, reflected by registration status as a predictor of persistence (table 2.4). Other persistence factors include the positive influence of a mentor and math and science courses, and participation in conferences and events. A new factor for juniors this year, but consistent with the freshmen and sophomore findings, is participation in SWE.

Consistent with past years, persistence factors for seniors include a positive influence of science classes, seeing an academic advisor, and participation in conferences and events. New factors emerging this year are a positive influence of engineering classes and teaching quality.

C. Perceived barriers to persistence

For those women who do choose to remain in engineering and science, there are a number of barriers to persistence frequently perceived at each stage of their education. The most frequently reported barriers are summarized by year in school in table 2.6. Because of ongoing refinements to the annual interviews and questionnaires, not all questions were asked of all cohorts. Therefore, as shown in the column headings, the response rates represent only those students who responded to these questions, rather than the entire study population.

As in previous years, lack of self-confidence is consistently reported by at least one-fourth of the students in each year of school. A disturbing trend in this finding is that, rather than becoming more confident in their abilities as they make their way through college, the proportion of women reporting lack of self-confidence nearly doubles by the senior year. Because this trend is a key focus of this study, it will be discussed in more detail in the next section of this paper. Similarly disturbing trends are found for feeling isolated and losing interest. The proportion of students reporting feeling intimidated also increases to over 41% by the junior year, and then drops to about one-fourth of the students in the senior year.

Approximately 20% (a 5–10% decrease from last year) of the freshmen, sophomores and juniors report that they feel no barriers to persisting in their engineering or science education. Surprisingly, by the time they are 4th- and 5th-year seniors, almost all of the remaining women in our study, many of whom had earlier reported perceiving no barriers to their academic progress, report at least some barriers. In addition to the barriers reported in table 2.6, these 4th- and 5th-year seniors report feeling discouraged by low grades (45.0%), and complain about poor teaching (54.1%) and unapproachable faculty (37.9%). Financial problems continue to be a concern for about 20–30% of students throughout college.

D. *Level of confidence*

Levels of self-confidence in academic achievement in S&E are measured each year on the basis of responses to questions asking the students to rate themselves as math and science students compared with their peers on a 1–5 Likert-type scale. As in previous years, most of these women intending to major in engineering or science begin with a very high level of self-confidence in their abilities in math and science (mean scores: math=4.01; science=3.98). However, both of these levels of self-confidence drop significantly ($p < 0.001$) over the course of their first year (mean scores: math=3.37; science=3.52).

Students who do maintain a high level of self-confidence in the freshman year report enjoyment of math and science classes, a high rating of instruction in math and science classes, and participation in WIE.

By the end of the sophomore year, overall self-confidence levels begin to increase slightly from the general decline in the freshman year. High self-confidence scores at this point are significantly correlated with level of interest in choice of major, a high rating of instruction in math and science classes, a positive influence of math and science classes and faculty/TAs (teaching assistants), and persistence.

The continued increase in confidence at the end of the junior year reflects having been accepted into a department. In addition, self-confidence is significantly correlated with a positive influence of math and science classes and faculty/TAs, interest in coursework, and persistence.

High levels of self-confidence for 4th- and 5th-year seniors are significantly correlated to a high rating of instruction in math and science classes, a positive influence of math classes and an advisor, participation in student professional societies and WIE seminars, and feeling prepared for a career and that educational expectations were met. The students who maintain a high level of math and science self-confidence through graduation in S&E as a group had higher initial levels of self-confidence (initial math=4.47 compared to 4.01; initial science=4.24 compared to 3.98). It should be noted, however, that the overall levels of self-confidence, even for these exceptional students, never return to the original high level of entering freshman students.

E. *Retention*

One of the primary goals of this study is to calculate accurate retention rates of women in S&E. The retention rates reported in table 2.7 are the first accurate calculations based on tracking individual women throughout their college career. With no intervention in place, it would be expected that these rates would fall below the over-inflated estimated rate of 55% reported by the University Registrar. The results of this study indicate that the retention rates of women in engineering and science at the University of Washington have increased substantially, to more than 72% in most cases, since the inception of the WIE Undergraduate Retention Program.

An analysis of incremental retention rates reveals patterns of switching out of S&E. As shown in table 2.8, most women who leave S&E do so during their sophomore year. This switching coincides with the time when most students find out if they have been accepted into a department, as well as the point of lowest academic self-confidence that [illegible] For those women who remain in S&E beyond their sophomore [illegible] in the retention rate at the junior and senior years is expected, since

- these students have persevered through the hurdles of the lower-level prerequisite courses and acceptance in their department at the end of their sophomore year
- the cost of switching, in terms of lost time and effort, increases as time goes on.

The most frequent reasons given for switching are summarized in table 2.9. Responses from all cohorts over the six years of the study have been fairly consistent: loss of interest in engineering and science, other majors appear more interesting, and discouragement by conceptual difficulties and perception of low grades. This discouragement corresponds to the drop in self-confidence over the course of the freshman year. Note that the responses in table 2.9 do not reflect the entire 187 students who have switched or dropped out, but only the 142 students who responded to the survey at the point of switching or leaving the University of Washington.

A comparison of math and science self-confidence levels for women persisting in S&E or switching to another degree program shows that women who switch at the end

Table 2.6 Most frequently reported perceived barriers

Barrier	*Freshmen (n=561)*	*Sophomores (n=291)*	*Juniors (n=144)*	*Seniors (n=137)*	*5th Year (n=35)*	*Average*
Lack of self-confidence	23.0%	26.8%	26.4%	44.5%	48.6%	33.9%
Not being accepted into department	29.4%	33.2%	9.7%	N/A	N/A	32.8%
Feeling intimidated	22.6%	35.7%	41.7%	19.0%	25.7%	28.4%
Isolation	7.6%	13.4%	8.3%	51.8%	45.7%	25.4%
Financial problems	17.8%	23.6%	25.7%	30.7%	28.6%	25.3%
Lack of interest	12.6%	18.2%	17.4%	38.0%	31.4%	23.5%
None	22.8%	17.9%	22.2%	2.9%	8.6%	14.9%

Table 2.7 Retention rates of female students in science and engineering at the UW

Cohort	*Current status*	*Original N*	*Still in S&E*	*%*
1	Graduated	92	65	71%
2	End of 5th year or graduated	107	78	73%
3	End of senior year or graduated	103	61	59%
4	End of junior year	125	81	65%
5	End of sophomore year	127	93	73%
6	End of freshman year	118	107	91%

Table 2.8 Incremental retention by year in school

Cohort	*Freshman year*	*Sophomore*	*Junior*	*Senior*	*5th year*	*6th year*
1	97%	84%	97%	95%	100%	94%
2	93%	89%	94%	94%	100%	
3	87%	83%	83%	98%		
4	80%	87%	93%			
5	90%	82%				
6	91%					

Table 2.9 Most frequent reasons for not persisting in science and engineering

Reasons	*Freshman year (n=59)*	*Sophomores (n=58)*	*Juniors (n=17)*	*Seniors (n=8)*	*5th year (n=0)*
Other majors more interesting	37%	41%	41%	50%	N/A
Lost interest in S&E	56%	60%	59%	63%	N/A
Conceptual difficulties	37%	45%	44%	38%	N/A
Discouraged by low grades	41%	60%	47%	50%	N/A
Rewards not worth the effort	34%	18%	19%	38%	N/A
Poor teaching	27%	28%	81%	38%	N/A

Total N=142 students who responded to the annual questionnaire stating that they were switching out of science/engineering or dropping out of college altogether. Total does not include those 45 students who did not return the questionnaire when they left or changed majors.

of their freshman year feel significantly less confident in science ($p < 0.05$) than those who persist; however, there is no difference in levels of math confidence. Self-confidence scores are clearly divergent between persisters and switchers at the end of the sophomore year, with both scores significantly lower ($p < 0.05$) for switchers. By the junior and senior years, only science self-confidence is significantly lower for switchers ($p < 0.05$). Surprisingly, math self-confidence does not appear to be related to persistence for those women who switch in the later years of their education. It is more likely that women who switch in later years do so due to the alienating S&E educational climate.[16]

IV. Conclusion

In summary, there are several factors forming a general, consistent pattern describing the academic experiences influencing the decisions of women to persist in, or switch out of, degree programs in engineering and science.

program do so in the first or sophomore year. The primary reasons they give for switching are losing interest in science/engineering, being attracted by another field, or being discouraged by academic difficulties and perception of low grades.

- Not surprisingly, the reasons for leaving are also the most frequently reported concerns, or "barriers" reported by women students who persist: fear of losing interest, intimidation, lack of self-confidence, poor advising, and not being accepted in their department. Although 20% of first-year students, sophomores and juniors reported no barriers, nearly all seniors reported at least one barrier.
- Women who are most likely to persist through the freshman year chose to pursue their major primarily because they enjoyed their science and math classes in high school, continue to enjoy those classes in college, and work well independently. In addition, they consider WIE and faculty to have a positive influence on them during their first year in college. New persistence factors emerging in this year's results are positive ratings of the quality of math instruction, involvement in SWE, and feeling supported by their mothers.
- In the sophomore year, persistence factors focus primarily on a positive relationship with an advisor, the influence of math and science classes, working, and gaining acceptance into a department. Participating in SWE and internships and co-ops also emerged as persistence factors this year.
- In the junior year, after most students have been accepted into a department, persistence factors shift to positive influence of a mentor, math and science classes, participation in conferences and events, and, for the first time, SWE.
- For seniors, persistence factors are a positive influence of science classes, seeing an academic advisor, and participation in conferences and events. New factors emerging this year were a positive influence of engineering classes and quality of instruction.
- Only science self-confidence levels are consistently lower for switchers than persisters. Math self-confidence is only significantly lower for those women who switch in their sophomore year; for those who switch in the first, junior, or senior year, there is no difference in math self-confidence.
- Despite differences in self-confidence, comparison at the time of switching showed no difference in actual performance, measured by GPA, between women who persist in S&E and women who switch to a nonscience major.
- Students who maintain high levels of math and science self-confidence throughout

college were likely to have had higher initial self-confidence levels. Continued high self-confidence is correlated with a number of other factors which have been shown to be related to persistence in S&E, such as higher levels of interest in coursework, positive relationships with faculty/TAs, involvement in student societies, seminars, conferences and events, participating in internships, and generally better preparation for a career.

- Overall retention rates for women participating in this study are consistently significantly higher than the estimated national average.

These findings suggest that factors other than ability play a major part in women's decisions to persist or switch from an engineering or science degree program. Maintaining a feeling of interest and involvement with coursework, and a sense of doing well academically, and finally the commitment that comes with acceptance into a department appear to be major influences for these women. In response to the finding that many students lose interest and change majors during the first two years when they take only prerequisite courses, some departments in the College of Engineering have instituted policy changes making it possible for students to begin the engineering curriculum in the sophomore year rather than the junior year. This policy will more than likely positively influence retention rates. The impact on retention of this and other changes in the curriculum will be examined as an ongoing part of the present study.

Note

[†] Based on "A Longitudinal Study of Undergraduate Women in Engineering and Science" by Suzanne G. Brainard and Linda Carlin which appeared in the Proceedings of the 1997 Frontiers in Education Conference, Pittsburgh, PA, November 5–8, IEEE Catalog No. 97CH36099, pp. 134–143, @ 1997 IEEE.

References

1 *Engineering and Technology Degrees Granted*, Engineering Workforce Commission of the American Association of Engineering Societies, Inc., New York, 1997.

2 Babco, E., "Women in Engineering," *Comments*, vol. 32, no. 4, 1994, pp. 22–24.

3 Brainard, S., S. Laurich-McIntyre, and L. Carlin, "Retaining Female Undergraduate Students in Engineering and Science," *Journal of Women and Minorities in Science and Engineering*, vol. 2, no. 4, 1995, pp. 255–267.

4 Women, Minorities, and Persons with Disabilities in Science and Engineering, NSF 94–333, National Science Foundation (NSF), Arlington, VA, 1994.

5 Ref. 4.

6 Seymour, E., and N. Hewitt, Talking about Leaving – Factors Contributing to High Attrition Rates Among Science, Mathematics and Engineering Undergraduate Majors, Final Report to the Alfred P. Sloan Foundation, Ethnography and Assessment Research, Bureau of Sociological Research, University of Colorado, Boulder, CO, 1994.

7 Laurich-McIntyre, S., and S. Brainard, "Retaining Women Freshmen in Engineering and Science: A Success Story," Proceedings, Fifth Annual WEPAN Conference, Washington, DC, 1995, pp. 227–232.

8 Ginorio, A., Warming the Climate for Women in Academic Science, Association of American Colleges, Washington, DC, 1995.

[illegible]

13 Ref. 7.

14 Ref. 3.

15 Brainard, S., and L. Ailes-Sengers, "Mentoring Female Engineering Students: A Model Program at the University of Washington," *Journal of Women and Minorities in Science and Engineering*, vol. 1, no. 4, 1994, pp. 123–135.

16 Ref. 8.

Chapter 3

Edward R. Silverman

NSF EMPLOYMENT STUDY CONFIRMS ISSUES FACING WOMEN, MINORITIES

Women and underrepresented minorities – African Americans, Hispanics, and Native Americans – generally are paid lower salaries and occupy fewer supervisory positions than their white, male counterparts in industry, according to a recent study conducted by the National Science Foundation. The study also sheds light on the issues that women and minorities say often impede their chances of entering or advancing in the workplace. Women, for instance, report fears that their careers may be incompatible with raising a family. Minorities say it's hard to secure high-level jobs when they lack sufficient experience or education to compete.

The results, reported in "Women, Minorities and Persons with Disabilities in Science and Engineering: 1996" (National Science Foundation, NSF-96–311, 1996), revealed a host of discrepancies in education and salary among different groups. The nearly 300-page report compiled a wealth of 1993 employment data in an effort to address ongoing concerns about the lack of equal opportunity for women and minorities.

For example, the study found a notable difference in the average salaries of male and female researchers with Ph.D.s. The average salary for female doctorate holders was $50,200, compared with $63,600 for men. In other words, women made 79 percent of what their male counterparts earned. Discrepancies among racial and ethnic groups also were clear. Science and engineering Ph.D.s who are African American, Native American, Asian, and Hispanic made an average of $5,875 less than their white counterparts.

"The picture is still bleak," says Joan Buffelli, a senior science resource analyst in the Science Resource Studies division at NSF, who helped prepare the study. However, she adds, "things are improving faster for women than for minorities. The percentage of science and engineering degrees [awarded] to women, for instance, has increased at a faster rate than for men. But change is slow."

In 1993, for example, women made up 20 percent of the doctoral scientists and engineers in the United States labor force, up from 19 percent in 1991. Of the 470,500 estimated science Ph.D.s in the labor force in 1993, approximately 11 percent were Asians, 2 percent were blacks, 2 percent were Hispanics, and less than 1 percent were Native Americans.

[illegible]

sector. Yet the study found that only 21 percent of [illegible] in the private sector – compared with 33 percent of male Ph.D.s. And within industry, women were less likely than men to be in management positions.

Work-related employee characteristics – including additional degrees, enhanced job skills, and professional licenses – accounted for another 19 percent, or $2,500, of the salary gap. Field of degree contributed 11 percent, or $1,500. For example, the study found that women are disproportionately represented in psychology and social sciences, which traditionally pay less. Type of work performed – meaning occupation in general and whether the position was a management or a postdoctoral post – explained 15 percent, or $2,000, of the gap. Another factor was years since receipt of doctorate, which explained about 24 percent, or $3,200 of the salary difference. The study found that in 1993 the average female Ph.D. received her degree 10.4 years before the survey date, vs. 15.7 years among men. About 10 percent of the difference, or $1,400, was listed as "unexplained." According to the report, "some or all of the 'unexplained' gender salary gap may be attributable to 'unequal pay for equal work.' Indeed, the size of the unexplained gap may even be underestimated."

Perhaps the most controversial gender-related finding was the significance of "life choices," which accounted for about 10 percent, or $1,400, of the salary gap. It underscored the decisions some women make to juggle the responsibilities associated with nurturing both careers and families. The study noted that "employers are likely to find that they can offer relatively low salaries to fill positions with high non-salary rewards or low non-salary costs. Men and women may place different values on these non-salary aspects of jobs, and this may result in salary differentials. For example, if, on the average, women place a higher value on having a short work week than do men (i.e. because of greater responsibilities for child care), women may be more likely to choose positions with relatively low salaries and fewer hours per week."

In fact, the study explored the compatibility of marriage and science for women. It found that female Ph.D. scientists and engineers are less likely than men to be married – 66 percent of women are married compared with 83 percent of men. Women with Ph.D.s are twice as likely as men never to have married or to be divorced. The study also found that about 54 percent of women, compared with 35 percent of men, were married to another scientist or engineer.

"The climate in industry may be perceived as less favorable to women for a number of reasons, including recruitment and hiring practices, a corporate culture hostile to women, sexual harassment, lack of opportunities for career development and critical developmental assignments, failure to accommodate work–family issues, lack of mentoring and lack of access to informal networks of communication," the study concluded.

In the view of Catherine Didion, executive director of the Washington, DC-based Association for Women in Science, many women are not willing to acknowledge these impediments. "I think we still want to view everything through a filter that shows how good your research or hypothesis is, as opposed to chit-chatting with the right people. Often, women don't want to complain because it'll seem they can't get along and will be labeled a troublemaker."

Although there is little difference between the unemployment rates of female and male doctorates in life sciences – 1.8 percent compared with 1.4 percent – some female Ph.D. researchers are worried about their employment prospects or their ability to advance, given the concerns about discrimination or the difficulties in balancing work and family life. "Family status influences exit rates out of science and engineering employment," the study notes. "Married scientists and engineers and those with children are more likely to leave science and engineering employment than those who are not married and do not have children."

"When I got out of grad school, I didn't think these issues would be a problem. But after I got my doctorate and tried to get a faculty position, I saw it was a striking trend," reports Jong-on Hahm, a 37-year-old neuroscientist and postdoctoral fellow at Georgetown University, who is married with two children. She is about to begin a job search among biotechnology companies. "I doubt if someone will ask a guy if [his] personal life will affect the job, but from what I've heard from other women who are job-hunting, it comes up a lot," she notes.

Racial/ethnic gaps

Underrepresented minorities face similar problems when it comes to salaries and opportunities. The study found that African American Ph.D.s in science and engineering made an average of $7,100 less than their white counterparts. Native American and Hispanic doctorate holders also made less than whites – $6,500 and $5,700 on average, respectively. Asians, who aren't considered underrepresented, had a $4,100 salary gap.

As with women, two categories – years since receipt of doctorate and employer characteristics – accounted for a substantial portion of the respective gaps. For instance, the fact that African Americans earned their Ph.D.s later than whites was responsible for a $2,300 average salary differential, and employer characteristics accounted for another $2,500 in differences. However, Asians did not experience such difficulties, in part because they tend to be employed in higher-paying engineering jobs and, like whites, occupy jobs in industry to a greater extent than other minorities.

The findings don't surprise John Alderete, a professor of microbiology at the University of Texas Health Center in San Antonio and president of the Society for Advancement of Chicanos and Native Americans in Science. He attributes the differences to systemic problems heavily ingrained in society.

He cites soaring school drop-out rates, poverty, little or no health care, poor environmental conditions among urban poor and migrant farm workers, homelessness, teen pregnancies, and domestic violence as overwhelming social issues that, through neglect, have accounted for the lack of minorities in a position to pursue careers in science.

Alderete also criticizes universities for relying on standardized high school tests administered to ill-prepared minority populations and for not doing enough to recruit [illegible] recruitment drives, she says, "we're not overwhelmed with such candidates."

However, she adds, Synaptic employs a large number of women. Of four department directors, one is female. And one of nine Ph.D. researchers in the company's chemistry group is a woman. However Mullinix contends that she doesn't come across such representation at most other companies, which confirms some of the findings of the study. The observation only strengthens her belief that women will continue to find it difficult to secure high-ranking jobs. "Overall, the NSF data is very depressing when you look at the [number of] higher-level jobs out there."

Chapter 4

Christine Wenneras and Agnes Wold

NEPOTISM AND SEXISM IN PEER-REVIEW

In the first-ever analysis of peer-review scores for postdoctoral fellowship applications, the system is revealed as being riddled with prejudice. The policy of secrecy in evaluation must be abandoned.

Throughout the world, women leave their academic careers to a far greater extent than their male colleagues.[1] In Sweden, for example, women are awarded 44 per cent of biomedical PhDs but hold a mere 25 percent of the postdoctoral positions and only 7 percent of professorial positions. It used to be thought that once there were enough entry-level female scientists, the male domination of the upper echelons of academic research would automatically diminish. But this has not happened in the biomedical field, where disproportionate numbers of men still hold higher academic positions, despite the significant numbers of women who have entered this research field since the 1970s.

Reasons for lack of success

Why do women face these difficulties? One view is that women tend to be less motivated and career-oriented than men, and therefore are not as assiduous in applying for positions or grants. Another is that women are less productive than men, and consequently their work has less scientific merit. Yet another is that women suffer discrimination due to gender. We decided to investigate whether the peer-review system of the Swedish Medical Research Council (MRC), one of the main funding agencies for biomedical research in Sweden, evaluates women and men on an equal basis. Our investigation was prompted by the fact that the success rate of female scientists applying for postdoctoral fellowships at the MRC during the 1990s has been less than half that of male applicants.

Our study strongly suggests that peer reviewers cannot judge scientific merit independent of gender. The peer reviewers over-estimated male achievements and/or under-estimated female performance, as shown by multiple-regression analyses of the relation between defined parameters and scientific productivity and competence scores.

[illegible] yielding a final score that is the basis on which the applicants to each committee are ranked.

The MRC board, which includes the chairmen of the 11 committees, ultimately decides to whom the fellowships will be awarded. Usually each committee chooses between one and three of the top-ranked applicants. Of the 114 applicants for the 20 postdoctoral fellowships offered in 1995, there were 62 men and 52 women, with a mean age of 36 years, all of whom had received a PhD degree within the past five years. Most of the female applicants had basic degrees in science (62 percent), and the rest had medical (27 percent) or nursing (12 percent) degrees; the corresponding figures for the male applicants were 38, 59 and 3 percent.

Traditionally, peer-review scores are not made public, and indeed the MRC officials initially refused us access to the documents dealing with evaluation of the applicants. In Sweden, however, the Freedom of the Press Act grants individuals access to all documents held by state or municipal authorities. Only documents defined as secret by the Secrecy Act are exempt, for example those that may endanger the security of the state, foreign relations or citizens' personal integrity. Accordingly, we appealed against the refusal of the MRC to release the scores.

In 1995, the Administrative Court of Appeal judged the evaluation scores of the MRC to be official documents. Hence, to our knowledge, this is the first time that genuine peer-reviewer evaluation sheets concerning a large cohort of applicants have become available for scientific study.

We found that the MRC reviewers gave female applicants lower average scores than male applicants on all three evaluation parameters: 0.25 fewer points for scientific competence (2.21 versus 2.46 points); 0.17 fewer points for quality of the proposed methodology (2.37 versus 2.54); and 0.13 fewer points for relevance of the research proposal (2.49 versus 2.62). Because these scores are multiplied with each other, female applicants received substantially lower final scores compared with male applicants (13.8 versus 17.0 points on average). That year, 4 women and 16 men were awarded postdoctoral fellowships.

As shown by these figures, the peer reviewers deemed women applicants to be particularly deficient in scientific competence. As it is generally regarded that this parameter is related to the number or quality of scientific publications,[2,3,4,5] it seemed reasonable to assume that women earned lower scores on this parameter than men because they were less productive. We explored this hypothesis by determining the scientific productivity of all 114 applicants and then comparing the peer-reviewer ratings of groups of male and female applicants with similar scientific productivity.

Productivity variables

We measured the scientific productivity of each applicant in six different ways. First, we determined the applicant's total number of original scientific publications, and second, the number of publications on which the applicant was first author. Both figures were taken from the applicant's bibliography, which we double-checked in the Medline database. (We call these measures "total number of publications" and "total number of first-author publications.")

To take into account the fact that the prestige of biomedical journals varies widely, we constructed measures based on journals' impact factors. The impact factor of a scientific journal is listed in the independent Institute of Scientific Information's *Journal Citation Reports*, and describes the number of times an average paper published in a particular journal is cited during one year. Our third measure was to add together the impact factors of each of the journals in which the applicant's papers were published, generating the "total impact measure" of applicant's total number of publications.

Fourth, we generated the "first-author impact measure" by adding together the impact factors of the journals in which the applicant's first-author papers appeared. The unit of measure for both total impact and first-author impact is "impact points" with one impact point equalling one paper published in a journal with an impact factor of 1.

Fifth, using the science citation database, we identified the number of times the applicant's scientific papers were cited during 1994, which yielded the measure "total citations." And sixth, we repeated this procedure for papers on which the applicant was first author, giving the measure "first-author citations."

Did men and women with equal scientific productivity receive the same competence rating by the MRC reviewers? No! For the productivity variable "total impact," the peer reviewers gave female applicants lower scores than male applicants who displayed the same level of scientific productivity. In fact, the most productive group of female applicants, containing those with 100 total impact points or more, was the only group of women judged to be as competent as men, although only as competent as the least productive group of male applicants (the one whose members had fewer than 20 total impact points).

Why women score low

Although the difference in scoring of male and female applicants of equal scientific productivity suggested that there was indeed discrimination against women researchers, factors other than the applicant's gender could, in principle, have been responsible for the low scores awarded to women. If, for example, women were mainly to conduct research in areas given low priority by the MRC, come from less-renowned universities, or have less collaboration with academic decision-makers, their lower scores could depend on such factors, rather than on their gender *per se*.

To determine the cause of women's lower scores, we performed a multiple-regression analysis, which reveals the factors that exert a primary influence on a certain outcome (for example, competence scores) and the size of such an influence. Multiple regression permits the elimination of factors whose influence on a certain outcome merely reflects their dependence on other factors

accompanied the application; and whether the applicant was affiliated with any of the members of the evaluation committee. The last piece of information is noted on the MRC evaluation protocols, in which case the reviewer in question is not allowed to participate in the scoring of that applicant. It was as frequent for female (12 percent) as for male (13 percent) applicants to be associated with a committee member.

The outcome of the regression analysis is shown in Table 4.1. Three out of the six productivity variables generated statistically significant models capable of predicting the competence scores the applicants were awarded: total impact, first-author impact and first-author citations. The model that provided the highest explanatory power was the one based on total impact ($r^2 = 0.47$). In all three models, we found two factors as well as scientific productivity that had a significant influence on competence scores: the gender of the applicant and the affiliation of the applicant with a committee member.

Table 4.1 Factors that significantly influenced peer reviewers' ratings of scientific competence, according to three multiple regression models

	Scientific productivity			*Additional points given by the reviewers for the following factors*		
Multiple regression model based on:	r^2	*Intercept*	*Competence points per productivity unit*	*Male gender*	*Reviewer affiliation*	*Recommendation letter*
Total impact	0.47	2.09	0.0033 *<0.00005**	0.21 *<0.00005*	0.22 *0.0008*	0.10 *0.04*
First-author impact	0.44	2.13	0.0094 *<0.0001*	0.24 *<0.00005*	0.22 *0.005*	NS
First-author citations	0.41	2.17	0.0054 *0.0001*	0.23 *<0.00005*	0.23 0.001	NS

*Italicized numbers indicate *P*-values for the variable in question.
NS, not statistically significant, *P*-value >0.05.

According to the multiple-regression model based on total impact, female applicants started from a basic competence level of 2.09 competence points (the intercept of the multiple regression curve) and were given an extra 0.0033 competence points by the reviewers for every impact point they had accumulated. Independent of scientific productivity, however, male applicants received an extra 0.21 points for competence. So, for a female scientist to be awarded the same competence score as a male colleague, she needed to exceed his scientific productivity by 64 impact points (95 percent confidence interval: 35–93 impact points).

This represents approximately three extra papers in *Nature* or *Science* (impact factors 25 and 22, respectively), or 20 extra papers in a journal with an impact factor of around 3, which would be an excellent specialist journal such as *Atherosclerosis*, *Gut*, *Infection and Immunity*, *Neuroscience* or *Radiology*. Considering that the mean total impact of this cohort of applicants was 40 points, a female applicant had to be 2.5 times more productive than the average male applicant to receive the same competence score as he received (40+64)/40=2.6).

Friendship bonus

According to the same multiple-regression model, applicants who were affiliated with a committee member received competence scores 0.22 points higher than applicants of the same gender and scientific productivity who lacked such ties (Table 4.1). This "affiliation bonus" was worth 67 impact points (confidence interval: 29–105 impact points). Hence, an applicant lacking personal ties with the reviewers needed to have 67 more impact points than an applicant of the same sex who was associated with one of the reviewers, to be perceived as equally competent. So, although MRC policy does not allow "biased" reviewers to participate in the scoring of applicants they are associated with, this rule was insufficient, as the "neutral" committee members compensated by raising their scores when judging applicants affiliated with one of their peers.

Because the affiliation bonus was of the same magnitude as the "male gender" bonus, a woman applicant could make up for her gender (–0.21 competence points) by being affiliated with one of the reviewers (+0.22 competence points). On the other hand, a female (–0.21 competence points) lacking personal connections in the committee (–0.22 competence points) had to present an additional 131 impact points to the MRC reviewers to receive the same competence score as a male applicant affiliated with one of the reviewers.

Such a level of productivity was attained by only three of the 114 applicants, one male and two female. Hence, being of the female gender and lacking personal connections was a double handicap of such severity that it could hardly be compensated for by scientific productivity alone.

The two other regression models, based on first-author impact and first-author citations, yielded almost identical results to the first with regard to the effect of gender and affiliation (Table 4.1). This congruity was not a statistical artefact due to a high degree of interrelation between the three productivity variables, as the total impact and first-author impact of the applicants were only moderately correlated (r=0.63), as were total impact and first-author citations (r=0.62). We therefore believe that male gender and reviewer affiliation were real determinants of scientific competence in the eyes of the MRC reviewers.

The applicant's nationality, education, field of research or postdoctoral experience did not influence competence scores in any of the models. A letter of recommendation had a positive effect on the competence score in the model based on total impact, but [illegible]

Changing the system

The peer-review system, characterized as "the centrepiece of the modern scientific review process," has been criticized on many grounds, including poor inter-reviewer reliability[6] and because reviewers may favor projects confirming their own views.[7] Our study is the first analysis based on actual peer-reviewer scores and provides direct evidence that the peer-review system is subject to nepotism, as has already been suggested anecdotally.[8,9,10]

One might argue that young researchers affiliated with peer reviewers are part of a scientific elite that has received superior training and are therefore more competent than average applicants. Indeed, applicants with such ties had higher total impact levels on average than applicants without such connections (data not shown). Hence, applicants with personal alliances justly benefited from higher competence scores because of their higher scientific productivity. However, on top of that, they were given extra competence points not warranted by scientific productivity. We see no reason why an applicant who manages to produce research of high quality despite not being affiliated with a prestigious research group should not be similarly rewarded.

Several studies have shown that both women and men rate the quality of men's work higher than that of women when they are aware of the sex of the person to be evaluated, but not when the same person's gender is unknown.[11,12,13] It is somewhat surprising that the results of these studies have not discouraged the scientific community from relying on evaluation systems that are vulnerable to reviewer prejudice.

An interesting question that we could not address here is whether the harsher evaluation of female researchers was due to the paucity of women among the peer reviewers. The small number of women reviewers (5 out of 55) and their uneven distribution among the MRC's committees made a statistical analysis of their scoring behavior impossible. However, a few studies have indicated that female evaluators may be more objective in assessing the achievement of women than their male counterparts.[14] Nevertheless, we are not confident that a simple increase in the percentage of women reviewers would solve the problem of gender-based discrimination.

If gender discrimination of the magnitude we have observed is operative in the peer-review systems of other research councils and grant-awarding organizations, and in countries other than Sweden, this could entirely account for the lower success rate of female as compared with male researchers in attaining high academic rank. The United Nations has recently named Sweden as the leading country in the world with respect to equal opportunities for men and women, so it is not too far-fetched to assume that gender-based discrimination may occur elsewhere. It is therefore essential that more studies such as ours are conducted in different countries and in different areas of scientific research.

An in-depth analysis of other peer-review systems can be achieved only if the policy of secrecy is abandoned. We could perform our study only because of the Swedish Freedom of the Press Act. It is often claimed that secrecy in scoring will protect reviewers from improper influences. But our results cast doubt on these claims. It has also been suggested that the recruitment of peer reviewers of high quality would be impeded if reviewers were not granted anonymity. Such fears seem to be exaggerated because, although reviewer evaluation scores have been accessible to everyone in Sweden since the court ruling of 1995, there have been no large-scale defections of peer reviewers from the evaluation committees.

Most important, the credibility of the academic system will be undermined in the eyes of the public if it does not allow a scientific evaluation of its own scientific evaluation system. It is our firm belief that scientists are the most suited to evaluate research performance. One must recognize, however, that scientists are no less immune than other human beings to the effects of prejudice and comradeship. The development of peer-review systems with some built-in resistance to the weaknesses of human nature is therefore of high priority. If this is not done, a large pool of promising talent will be wasted.

Notes

1 Widnal, S.E. *Science* 241, 1740–1745 (1988).
2 Cole, S., Cole, J.R. and Simon, G.A. *Science* 214, 881–886 (1981).
3 Long, J.S. *Social Forces* 71, 159–178 (1992).
4 Sonnert, G. *Social Stud. Sci.* 25, 35–55 (1995).
5 Sonnert, G. and Holton, G. *Am. Sci.* 84, 63–71 (1996).
6. Glantz, S.A. and Bero, L.A. J. *Am. Med. Assoc.* 272, 114–116 (1994).
7 Ernst, E., Resch, K.L. and Uher, R.M. *Ann. Intern. Med.* 116, 958 (1992).
8 Forsdyke, D.R. *FASEB J.* 7, 619–621 (1993).
9 Calza, L. and Gerbisa, S. *Nature* 374, 492 (1995).
10 Perez-Enciso, M. *Nature* 378, 760 (1995).
11 Goldberg, P. *Trans-Action* 5, 28–30 (1968).
12 Nieva, V.F. and Gutek, B.A. *Acad. Manag. Rev.* 5, 267–276 (1980).
13 O'Leary, V.E. and Wallston, B.S. *Rev. Pers. Soc. Psychol.* 2, 9–13 (1982).
14 Frieze, I.H. in *Women and Achievement: Social and Motivational Analyses* (ed. Mednick, M.T., Tangri, S.S. and Hoffman, L.W.), 158–171 (Hemisphere, Washington, DC: 1975).

Chapter 5

Nature is part of history and culture, not the other way around. Sociologists and historians of science tend to know that. Most scientists do not. Because I was trained as a scientist, it has taken me many years to understand that "in science, just as in art and in life, only that which is true to culture is true to nature" (Fleck, [1935] 1979, p. 35).

From 1947 until the late 1960s I was a devout scientist. I did experiments and wrote papers and reviews in the accepted tradition and did not ask myself how what I was doing fit into the culture. Like many scientists, I assumed I was probing nature and that that was an unquestionable good and reason enough to go on doing it.

The Vietnam War and the women's movement led me to look closely at these assumptions. The war made me see that science and the universities help maintain differences in wealth and power between nations and between the ethnic, racial, and economc groups within them. The women's liberation movement sharpened and focused these issues and gave them special urgency, for in the mid-1970s, no doubt in response to the renewed activism for women's rights, biological theories began to be revived that threaten women's struggle for equality. Sociobiologists and other biological determinists breathed new life into old arguments that derived differences in the positions women and men occupy in the workplace, the home, and the political sphere from the differences in our procreative functions. They needed to be answered.

That I was able to turn my attention to these issues was due to the fact that in 1973, owing in large part to the political work of the women's movement, the tenuous position I had held at Harvard became stable. In an unusual step, the university promoted a few of us from the typical women's ghetto of "research associate and lecturer" to tenured professorships. This promotion carried with it increased freedom to decide what work I wanted to do and what I wanted to teach. I could pursue my changing interests and share my new questions and analyses with a growing group of interested and interesting students. I could develop a network of colleagues from a secure professional and economic base.

My 1990 book describes my journey from observing nature to observing science, from doing science to studying it. The book is divided into three parts: "How do we know?" "What do we know?" "How do we use it?" The first is concerned primarily with feminist issues in the sociology of science, the second with feminist criticisms of subject matter, the third with current applications of biological knowledge in procreative technologies. As might be expected, this arrangement is to some extent arbitrary and involves cross-currents and overlaps.

I want to stress at the outset that I think the subject of women's biology is profoundly political – hence the book's title [*The Politics of Women's Biology*]. The predominantly male scientists who have described our biology have done so at least in part to explain why it is "natural" for us to function as we do in society. To assert power over our lives women, of course, need the economic and political conditions that make it possible even to conceive of doing so. But we also need to recognize our biological capabilities in order to value them and use them to benefit us.

To go beyond defining ourselves as victims of male power and domination, we have to acquire the sense that our individual histories and needs, as well as our collective experiences and actions, are important. We need not only to accept but to appreciate our bodies and bodily functions, which is difficult to do in the face of the barrage of disabling information we encounter at home, in the media, and from health professionals.

Women's health activists have tried to reeducate us about our bodies. But to free ourselves from debilitating misrepresentations, we need to understand the ideological bases of the medical/scientific misinformation and disinformation we get about how genes, hormones, muscles – in a word, our bodies – function. To reconceptualize our biology and make it truly ours is important the same way it has been important for us to gain control of our language and interpret our own experiences. This book is intended to contribute to that process.

It seems contradictory that as our political awareness has increased, many of us scientists who are feminists have turned from doing scientific experiments to the social studies of science and science criticism. Feminist poets, novelists, and artists by and large have not needed to make such a change. They have been more able to incorporate their political consciousness into their work than we have.

I am not sure of all the reasons why this is so. One surely is that the way scientists define objectivity renders the various guises in which politics enter into scientific explanations invisible. For example, social class has never been a category in US health statistics, and recently the Thatcher government ceased to specify social class in British health statistics. The US statistics are usually expressed in the quasi-biological terms of race and sex, which obscure the economic and social differences between the different races and sexes. We will encounter other examples as we go along. The important point for now is that political and social realities can be incorporated in subtle ways so that they are hard to discern in what are presented as descriptions of biology or, in this instance, health.

Another reason is that doing science requires institutional support. In literature and the arts, the most original work is not produced in universities or subject to review by funding agencies. It may require a sponsor or a publisher, but in the arts it is possible to find someone who will take the risk to publish or exhibit innovative work or, if need be, to form alternative collectives that take that risk. Probably, also, the rigid training scientists undergo limits our own imaginations and constrains our originality more than happens to artists.

It is appropriate to raise these issues because in science, as in the arts, we create stories and images about nature, including people, and transmit them through language.

And, in both, the stories must be "true" in the sense that they must reflect other people's experiences. A writer who misrepresents people's life experiences is as "wrong" as a scientist who misrepresents or misinterprets cultural beliefs about nature.

At present, some social critics of science argue that, much like writers, all scientists [illegible] animals and plants into hierarchies, like the societies in which they have lived. They speak of the animal and plant "kingdoms," of "higher" and "lower" organisms. And, of course, they rank human beings at the top. Darwin's evolutionary theory is based on the idea that the history of organisms has unfolded in a world of scarce resources where individuals have to compete. In this world the individual is the most important unit, far more important than the group. Both assumptions reflect basic beliefs of Darwin's class and society. You will find other examples, worked out in detail, in the chapters that follow.

The question I want to ask here is, can feminists hope to improve science by bringing into consciousness the implicit assumptions that underlie standard scientific descriptions and interpretations? I believe we can, which is why I think of myself as a scientist, even though I no longer do laboratory science. I consider myself a scientist because I continue to be keenly curious about nature and want to understand how it works. I do not think science as currently practiced is the way to find out, among other reasons because it proceeds by breaking nature into smaller and smaller bits, and then usually ignores, loses, or misreads their connections. Scientists engage in this practice, called reductionism, in the hope that once they get to understand the ultimate bits, they will be able to put them together and understand nature. But, as with Humpty Dumpty, that is going at it the wrong way around. I remain a scientist because I think we can understand nature. But we must be respectful of the connections and relationships within it.

Like most poets and novelists, scientists do not want their work to be read only as self-revelation and societal text. Writers are probing the psyche, human relationships, our place in society and the cosmos. Similarly, most scientists wish to probe nature, including people. In the current debate within feminist science criticism, I stand with those who argue that the political insights feminism provides can lead us to more accurate, hence truer, accounts of nature than we now have. But we must rigorously analyze the assumptions scientists make and specify as best we can the political, economic, and social realities that inform these assumptions. Maybe then we will be able to interpret scientific accounts – which are the stories scientists tell – in ways that allow us to understand nature less imperiously and to misuse and abuse it less.

Reference

Fleck, Ludwick [1935] (1979). *The Dialectic of Sex*. New York: Morrow.

Chapter 6

Bonnie Spanier

HOW I CAME TO THIS STUDY

Scanning the science section in the University at Albany's bookstore a few years back, I pulled from the shelf an attractive new molecular biology textbook entitled *Molecular Cell Biology*. The three authors, James Darnell, Harvey Lodish, and David Baltimore, were familiar to me as leading figures in molecular biology and virology, my fields of graduate study. In fact, as a very green and eager graduate student at Harvard, I had the pleasure and challenge of working in the MIT lab of David Baltimore, who later received a Nobel Prize. Opening the six-pound textbook, costing $42.95, I was, in a way, coming home. But I had changed. I had removed old lenses, so that I saw what had been invisible to me and to many others: the distorting effects of cultural biases about gender.[1]

It was almost a decade since I had left laboratory research on the molecular biology of viral infections, had left the equally rewarding teaching of biology, biochemistry, molecular and cell biology, microbiology, and immunology to pursue three simple goals: increasing the public's access to science; answering the simple question of why a world-famous embryologist, my mentor, had spent her career at a small women's college; and following a complex desire to expand my skills, creative scope, and knowledge beyond the science to which I was trained and from which I had received ample rewards. A privileged daughter, I had a faculty appointment at the State University of New York at Albany, where I was the Women's Studies Program Director, equivalent to a department chair, but in a relatively young interdisciplinary field.[2] At the moment that I discovered the textbook, I was starting a year's leave, supported by an affirmative action program for untenured faculty, to advance my research on the impact of feminism in the natural sciences. My gender consciousness governed the perspective of my engagement with that textbook and, consequently, dramatically changed the focus of my research.

In that moment in the summer of 1987 and in the years following, I brought together three major factors that shape my view of the world: an education in classical biology and biochemistry, credentials and experience in molecular biology, and a feminist awareness of the significance of gender in society and the importance of placing knowledge into its historical and political contexts. This effort at synthesis, this lifting of the constructed barriers separating these three aspects of my being, has been an experience that I hope proves useful to others as well.

I fell in love with DNA and enzymes sometime before junior high school, when [illegible] of New York City, microbiologist Mary (Polly) Bunting was on the cover of *Time* or *Newsweek* as the new president of Radcliffe College. I remember being instantly impressed. She was a scientist, she had built her own home with her husband, and she was raising their children by herself after his death. This role model was all I needed, it seems in retrospect, for me to ignore the stereotyping of woman and scientist as contradictory terms. (Indeed, I later learned of Dr. Bunting's pronouncement: "I decided many years ago that I was far more interested in being a fact than in living anyone else's theory.")[3]

With the help of a National Merit Scholarship, I attended an elite, traditionally white women's college with strong science departments and a commitment to liberal arts education and the love of learning for its own sake (perhaps more typical of college experience in the '60s than can be imagined by students today). At Bryn Mawr College I found another inspiration, the brilliant embryologist and teacher Jane Oppenheimer, who mentored me in a number of ways, including teaching me both research skills and care and respect for animals used in experiments. She applied her very high expectations of students to herself, always pushing beyond current boundaries by combining perspectives from classical biology with insights from new experimental techniques and approaches to the study of life. She also made us aware of one implicit hierarchy: one of her specialties was to dethrone mammals, primates, and humans as the pinnacle of evolution in favor of birds.

Miss Oppenheimer (we called all the female professors of her generation "Miss" and all the younger, male professors "Doctor," even though all had doctorates) engaged in her history of science research "on the side," as she said, always claiming it was an avocation for her, while her colleagues recognized those writings as significant contributions to the history of biology. However, as she did not teach history of science courses at Bryn Mawr when I was there, I gained only a limited perspective on historical studies of science. During the period of my college years (1963–67), molecular biology was the rage, but the requirements for the biology major at Bryn Mawr continued to emphasize a classical approach to biology: intensive study of invertebrate as well as vertebrate physiology, classification of organisms, embryology, and traditional biochemistry. As a consequence, I developed an appreciation for the diversity of living beings as well as of macromolecules.

Although I was a white, middle-class, female graduate of a prestigious women's college, my access to graduate school in the late 1960s in biochemistry and, eventually, the molecular biology of viruses was made possible as much by the post-Sputnik push for the US to gain supremacy in science and technology as it was by the efforts for equal opportunity for women, which became visible in the second wave of the women's liberation movement beginning in the late 1960s.[4] I eagerly sought research jobs as an undergraduate and was mentored first by Jane Oppenheimer and later by biochemist W. Eugene Knox in Harvard University's Department of Biological Chemistry located at Harvard Medical School.

Eventually, in Michael A. Bratt's lab in Harvard's Department of Microbiology and Molecular Genetics, I found the perfect complement to elegant and abstract molecular biology with my growing concern for improving the quality of life for others. We attempted to understand the molecular workings of disease by studying interactions of viruses (specifically, different strains of the paramyxovirus Newcastle disease virus) with the cells they infect. Having persevered with the help of several mentors, I learned quickly what it means to be an insider in science, being asked to represent our lab at major animal virology conferences and then gaining access to opportunities for postdoctoral fellowships at prestigious research centers.

By 1975, doctorate in hand, I had a position in the Biology Department at Wheaton College in Massachusetts, a small women's college which felt comfortably like Bryn Mawr. As most young researcher/educators do, I applied for research grants. With the support of my thesis advisor and a gifted colleague and friend, Chuck Madansky, and after the usual first rejection, I was fortunate to obtain two coveted grants for young investigators, one from the National Institutes of Health and the other from the American Lung Association.

Just before this time, something had tugged at my sleeve. In my search for grants I had come across a new program at the Bunting Institute at Radcliffe College, renamed around that time for the same Dr. Polly Bunting who had inspired me; she had started the Radcliffe Institute in 1960 to allow women with children some free time and space to pursue their creative or educational dreams. The Bunting grant offered two years of postdoctoral-level support and research expenses for studies of women in American society. Never actually expecting to get the grant, I proposed to interview three women scientists about their work and to write about their science in their own words, making women scientists visible and making science interesting to a wider public. I also planned to take courses in the history of science, a specialty at Harvard. I was motivated by my respect for and curiosity about Jane Oppenheimer. Knowing that she had received her doctorate from Yale and had spent sabbaticals at Johns Hopkins, I wondered why she had stayed at Bryn Mawr, where the teaching load was much greater and the resources and prestige much less than that at research universities. The question suggests the degree of my ignorance about women's education and opportunities, particularly in the sciences. Such ignorance was not unusual, however, even for a graduate of a (white) women's college, since the women's colleges I knew were not hotbeds of feminist consciousness-raising in the early years of the women's movement. And it was not until 1982 that Margaret Rossiter published her eye-opening historical study of women in American science. Although important feminist scholarship had been published by 1977, I was not at all familiar with it, having spent the previous decade being trained as a scientist at some of the best institutions of higher learning in the United States.[5]

Unexpectedly, Radcliffe offered me the two-year grant at the same time that the National Institutes of Health and American Lung Association grants came through. The choice was difficult because I would be forced as an untenured faculty member to give up my tenure-track position.[6] I chose the Bunting grant, opting for time to develop a different part of me, to learn to see science differently, and to learn about my foremothers. At the Bunting Institute, I met women scholars and artists, nearly forty

and female.[7] Donna Haraway's more recent elaboration captures the extreme nature of sexual politics as "a polyvalent term covering a host of life-and-death issues and struggles for meanings."[8]

While I was working in quaint Cambridge, Massachusetts, a white, middle-class woman was raped and murdered in broad daylight in a park near the Bunting Institute. One of the gifted writers at the Institute flew across the country to testify at the trial of the man who had raped her and had walked her into the hills near the writers' colony to kill her, as he had done to other women. She had managed to escape, had lived to tell her story and help convict the rapist-murderer. Several black women, each walking late at night in Boston's Back Bay area where I was staying, were murdered and the killers never found. I learned nearly firsthand that the struggles around gender, race, and class for meanings in society have deadly consequences for many of us.

Meanwhile, I was auditing courses at Harvard in the history and social study of science, especially Everett Mendelsohn's legendary classes. I found Ruth Hubbard's Biology and Women's Issues, a course that had grown from a seminar's handful of students to the 100 students who filled the biology lecture hall.[9] Along with women's concerns in science, I discovered women's history, and with that, the absences, the gaping lacunae in my education. Thus I began an education that continues to this day, now within the legitimized and legitimizing academic territory of women's studies, an education that has moved me beyond the solipsisms of privilege to recognize the interconnections among the many struggles for freedom.[10]

It was with that background of classical biology and biochemistry, molecular biology, history and social study of science, and feminism that I opened *Molecular Cell Biology* and read:

> *E. coli* F (male) plasmid determines the difference between male and female strains, and encodes the proteins required for cell-to-cell contact during sexual mating. These plasmids are of great use to experimental molecular biologists – they are essential tools of recombinant *DNA technology* . . . [11]

Male and female bacteria? The male signifier as an essential tool of research. Here was the tip of the iceberg of gender ideology in molecular biology.

Notes

1 "Re-vision – the act of looking back, of seeing with fresh eyes, of entering an old text from a new critical direction – is for women more than a chapter in cultural history; it is an act of survival" (Adrienne Rich, "When We Dead Awaken: Writing as Re-vision," in *On Lies, Secrets, and Silence* (New York: Norton, 1979), 35).

2 Women's Studies is an interdisciplinary academic discipline that has celebrated an anniversary of two decades. The women's studies major was recently evaluated by the National Women's Studies Association as part of the Association of American Colleges' project to assess undergraduate liberal learning. The following statements from the report suggest the purpose and scope of women's studies as an academic field:

> [W]omen's studies both critiques existing theories and methodologies and formulates new paradigms and organizing concepts in all academic fields. It provides students with tools to uncover and analyze the ideological dynamics of their lives and become active participants in processes of social, political, and personal change. . . .
>
> The central organizing category of analysis in women's studies is the concept of gender, which we understand as a pervasive social construction reflecting and determining differentials of power and opportunity. From their inception, however, feminist scholarship and pedagogy also have emphasized the diversity of women's experiences and the importance of the differences among women as necessary correctives to the distortions inherent in androcentric views of human behavior, culture, and society. Women's studies therefore establishes the social construction of gender as a focal point of analysis in a complex matrix with class, race, age, ethnicity, nationality, and sexual identity as fundamental categories of social, cultural, and historical analysis. . . .
>
> From its position on the margin and by its willingness to identify its own ideologies, women's studies brings to light the ideological nature of all structures of knowledge – most particularly the masculine bias in curricula that once seemed complete and impartial. Perhaps the most important skill women's studies can pass on to students is the ability to recognize those biases where they seem most invisible.
>
> Johnnella Butler *et al.*, "Women's Studies Task Force Report," in *Reports from the Fields – Project on Liberal Learning, Study-in-Depth, and the Arts and Sciences Major*, vol. 2 (Washington, DC: Association of American Colleges, 1990), 208, 209, 211.

3 Jacquelyn A. Mattfield and Carol G. Van Aken, eds., *Women and the Scientific Professions* (Cambridge: MIT Press, 1965), 22. In contrast to the interest I developed in biology and chemistry, I remember high school physics, with its ballistics and pulleys, as irrelevant to me. I was one of two females in the advanced physics class, and the teacher made his dislike of girls, or at least me, clear when he consistently marked wrong just enough of my correct test answers to bring my grade just below A–. When I politely pointed this out, he simply mumbled and never changed my grades. I regret his influence on me and who knows how many others.

The invisible (in that I reached this awareness only later in life) role model was my mother, who raised three children and cared for a husband and also taught young children for many years. She had majored in mathematics and minored in physics at Hunter College, graduating with honors and Phi Beta Kappa. She shared with me her love of Rachel Carson's *The Sea Around Us* as we walked along the South Jersey shore, when I was still a child capable of wonder. Roselyn Solomon Spanier's love of math and ease with science and technology in everyday life (fixing toasters, [illegible] College, not one biology student that I knew was admitted to medical school, while most of the students who applied to graduate schools were accepted, including those rejected from medical school. Half of the students admitted on government fellowships with me to Harvard's Biological Chemistry Department were women. In contrast, most medical schools still had a tiny quota of women, certainly less than ten percent.

5 Margaret W. Rossiter, *Women Scientists in America: Struggles and Strategies to 1940* (Baltimore: Johns Hopkins University Press, 1982). Elite women's colleges were not hotbeds of radical feminism in the early years of the women's movement. Just one example from academic literature I could have known about: sociologist Jesse Bernard's *Academic Women* (University Park, Pa.: Pennsylvania State University Press, 1964; reprint, New American Library, 1974). More politically radical and less academic was Leslie Tanner's *Voices from Women's Liberation* (New York: Mentor Books, 1970), a book I did not meet until 1979. I now know the context in which to appreciate the brilliant women scientists who were able to make their careers at women's colleges. Miss Oppenheimer is a very private person, so I do not know the particular answer to my original motivating question.

6 A key player was the chair of the biology department at Wheaton, who told me that if he suspected I would turn to the women and science topic after doing the funded laboratory research required for tenure, he would not support me for a permanent position in biology. Also, he would not allow me a two-year leave from the biology position, saying that was too long to hold my position for me. Clearly, he did not see my development in the area of women and science or the history of science as a plus in his biology department. Although I disagreed with his attitude, I never questioned his right to make those decisions. I have since learned to be more disobedient.

7 Kate Millett, *Sexual Politics* (Garden City, NY: Doubleday, 1970). I wish to thank the feminists who inspired and educated me at the Bunting, including MaryAnn Amacher, Joyce Antler, Ann J. Lane, Linda Perkins, Temma Nason, Sue Standing, and Ines Talamantez.

8 Donna J. Haraway, "Investment Strategies for the Evolving Portfolio of Primate Females," in *Body/Politics: Women and the Discourse of Science*, ed. Mary Jacobus, Evelyn Fox Keller, and Sally Shuttleworth (New York: Routledge, 1990), 141.

9 The original seminar produced the first version of Ruth Hubbard, Mary Sue Henifin, and Barbara Fried's *Biological Woman – The Convenient Myth* under the title *Women Look at Biology Looking at Women: A Collection of Feminist Critiques* (Cambridge, Mass.: Schenkman, 1979).

10 In 1980 I was fortunate to be called back to Wheaton College to administer a FIPSE-funded project, Toward a Balanced Curriculum: Integrating the New Scholarship on Women into the Curriculum; coediting a sourcebook for curriculum transformation projects; and helping women's studies grow at Wheaton. See Bonnie Spanier, Alexander Bloom, and Darlene Boroviak, *Toward a Balanced Curriculum* (Cambridge, Mass.: Schenkman, 1984); and Bonnie Spanier, "Inside an Integration Project: A Case Study of the Relationship between Balancing the Curriculum and Women's Studies," *Women's Studies International Forum* 7, no. 3 (1984): 153–59. The new biology chair, John Kricher, gave me the great pleasure of offering a biology department course on "Women in Science: The Difference They Make," a transformational experience with wonderful students I shall never forget. In the eye-opening and challenging years spent with Wheaton's Balanced Curriculum Project, I chose women's studies as my discipline. Through a fortuitous opportunity, I was offered the women's studies program director position at Albany in 1984.

11 James Darnell, Harvey Lodish, and David Baltimore, *Molecular Cell Biology*, 1st ed. (New York: Scientific American Books, 1986), 137.

Chapter 7

I begin with three vignettes, all drawn from memory.

1965. In my first few years out of graduate school, I held quite conventional beliefs about science. I believed not only in the possibility of clear and certain knowledge of the world, but also in the uniquely privileged access to this knowledge provided by science in general, and by physics in particular. I believed in the accessibility of an underlying (and unifying) "truth" about the world we live in, and I believed that the laws of physics gave us the closest possible approximation of this truth. In short, I was well trained in both the traditional realist worldviews assumed by virtually all scientists and the conventional epistemological ordering of the sciences. I had, after all, been trained, first, by theoretical physicists, and later, by molecular biologists. This is not to say that I lived my life according to the teachings of physics (or molecular biology), only that when it came to questions about what "really is," I knew where, and how, to look. Although I had serious conflicts about my own ability to be part of this venture, I fully accepted science, and scientists, as arbiters of truth. Physics (and physicists) were, of course, the highest arbiters.

Somewhere around this time, I came across the proceedings of the first major conference held in the United States on "Women and the Scientific Professions" (Mattfield and Van Aiken 1965) – a subject of inevitable interest to me. I recall reading in those proceedings an argument for more women in science, made by both Erik Erikson and Bruno Bettelheim, based on the invaluable contributions a "specifically female genius" could make to science. Although earlier in their contributions both Erikson and Bettelheim had each made a number of eminently reasonable observations and recommendations, I flew to these concluding remarks as if waiting for them, indeed forgetting everything else they had said. From the vantage point I then occupied, my reaction was predictable: to put it quite bluntly, I laughed. Laws of nature are universal – how could they possibly depend on the sex of their discoverers? Obviously, I snickered, these psychoanalysts know little enough about science (and by implication, about truth).

1969. I was living in a suburban California house and found myself with time to think seriously about my own mounting conflicts (as well as those of virtually all my female cohorts) about being a scientist. I had taken a leave to accompany my husband on his sabbatical, remaining at home to care for our two small children. Weekly, I would talk to the colleague I had left back in New York and hear his growing enthusiasm as he reported the spectacular successes he was having in presenting our joint work. In between, I would try to understand why my own enthusiasm was not only not growing, but actually diminishing. How I went about seeking such an understanding is worth noting: what I did was to go to the library to gather data about the fate of women scientists in general – more truthfully, to document my own growing disenchantment (even in the face of manifest success) as part of a more general phenomenon reflecting an underlying misfit between women and science. And I wrote to Erik Erikson for further comment on the alarming (yet somehow satisfying) attrition data I was collecting. In short, only a few years after ridiculing his thoughts on the subject, I was ready to at least entertain if not embrace an argument about women in, or out of, science based on "women's nature." Not once during that entire year did it occur to me that at least part of my disenchantment might be related to the fact that I was in fact not sharing in the *kudos* my colleague was reaping for our joint work.

1974. I had not dropped out of science, but I had moved into interdisciplinary, undergraduate teaching. And I had just finished teaching my first women's studies course when I received an invitation to give a series of "Distinguished Lectures" on my work in mathematical biology at the University of Maryland. It was a great honor, and I wanted to do it, but I had a problem. In my women's studies course, I had yielded to the pressure of my students and colleagues to talk openly about what it had been like, as a woman, to become a scientist. In other words, I had been persuaded to publicly air the exceedingly painful story of the struggle that had actually been[1] – a story I had previously only talked about in private, if at all. The effect of doing this was that I actually came to see that story as public, that is, of political significance, rather than as simply private, of merely personal significance. As a result, the prospect of continuing to present myself as a disembodied scientist, of talking about my work as if it had been done in a vacuum, as if the fact of my being a woman was entirely irrelevant, had come to feel actually dishonest.

I resolved the conflict by deciding to present in my last lecture a demographic model of women in science – an excuse to devote the bulk of that lecture to a review of the many barriers that worked against the survival of women as scientists, and to a discussion of possible solutions. I concluded my review with the observation that perhaps the most important barrier to success for women in science derived from the pervasive belief in the intrinsic masculinity of scientific thought. Where, I asked, does such a belief come from? What is it doing in science, reputedly the most objective, neutral, and abstract endeavor we know? And what consequences does that belief have for the actual doing of science?

In 1974 "women in science" was not a proper subject for academic or scientific discussion; I was aware of violating professional protocol. Having given the lecture – having "carried it off" – I felt profoundly liberated. I had passed an essential milestone.

Although I did not know it then, and wouldn't recognize it for another two years, this lecture marked the beginning of my work as a feminist critic of science. In it I raised three of the central questions that were to mark my research and writing over the next decade. I can now see that, with the concluding remarks of that lecture, I had also completed the basic shift in mind-set that made it possible to begin such a venture. Even though my views about gender, science, knowledge, and truth were to evolve

depends), nor for the possibility that beliefs could affect science – a possibility that requires a distinction analagous to that between sex and gender, only now between nature and science. I was, of course, able to accommodate a distinction between belief and reality, but only in the sense of "false" beliefs, that is, mere illusion, or mere prejudice; "true" beliefs I took to be synonomous with the "real."

It seems to me that in that mind-set, beliefs *per se* were not seen as having any real force – neither the force to shape the development of men and women, nor the force to shape the development of science. Some people may "misperceive" nature, human or otherwise, but properly seen, men and women simply *are*, faithful reflections of male and female biology – just as science simply is, a faithful reflection of nature. Gravity has (or is) a force, DNA has force, but beliefs do not. In other words, as scientists, we are trained to see the locus of real force in the world as physical, not mental.

There is of course a sense in which they are right: beliefs *per se* cannot exert force on the world. But the people who carry such beliefs can. Furthermore, the language in which their beliefs are encoded has the force to shape what others – as men, as women, and as scientists – think, believe, and, in turn, actually do. It may have taken the lens of feminist theory to reveal the popular association of science, objectivity, and masculinity as a statement about the social rather than natural (or biological) world, referring not to the bodily and mental capacities of individual men and women, but to a collective consciousness; that is, as a set of beliefs given existence by language rather than by bodies, and by that language, granted the force to shape what individual men and women might (or might not) do. But to see how such culturally laden language could contribute to the shaping of science takes a different kind of lens. That requires, first and foremost, a recognition of the social character (and force) of the enterprise we call "science," a recognition quite separable from – and in fact, historically independent of the insights of contemporary feminism.

Note

1 This story was subsequently published in S. Ruddick and P. Daniels's *Working It Out* (1977) New York: Pantheon.

IF WE ARE GOING TO analyze science through a feminist lens, we must know how science operates and how these operations fit together within a coherent framework. In order to get a sense of the framework of science, we must go back to its origins, at the time of the so-called Scientific Revolution. A standard beginning for this period is 1542, when Copernicus proposed the heliocentric universe, and the end is 1687, when Newton published his "Mathematical Principles." Thus, this revolution dates from approximately 1500–1700. Those involved in developing a different perspective on Nature weren't "scientists" (as this term wasn't invented until the nineteenth century (Shapin, 1996, p. 6), but natural philosophers. The term "scientific revolution" was not applied to their strategies for understanding Nature until well after this time.

In short, a mechanistic worldview replaced two earlier streams of thought, the Aristotelian view and the Renaissance Hermetical tradition. The Greeks believed that Nature was composed of four "natures": earth, fire, water, and air. Each of the natures could move and their motion was vertical, either up or down. Each natural body had its own nature, Nature had an inherent purpose, and the universe was cyclical. Knowledge about Nature was gained by observation and reflection and the purpose of knowledge was contemplative. The Greeks were interested in final causes, asking "why" questions. They believed in reason and developed standards for rational argument, although mathematics was not a primary tool in their investigation of Nature.

During the "scientific revolution," changes were introduced in two spheres: the nature of Nature and the nature of knowledge. Nature was no longer a living organism and humans did not live in harmony with it. Nature no longer had an inherent purpose but was considered inert and available for exploitation by Man for his benefit. Valid knowledge about Nature was to be obtained by answering questions designed to elucidate mechanisms. The Greek "why" questions were replaced by "how" questions, answers to which were to be found through experiment. This mechanistic worldview still prevails today; its metaphor is the clock – in order to understand how the clock works, it must be taken apart. The mechanistic explanations obtained were held to hold throughout the universe. For the Greeks, motion was up or down; after the "scientific revolution," motion was not limited to two directions. Once started, it continued in the initial direction until changed by a force. This determinism could also apply to a broader sphere; instead of the rhythms of the universe being cyclical, they were now linear, with recurrence being replaced by the possibility of progress.

In this mechanistic worldview, God became the giver of the laws of nature, which were defined by mathematics. An inevitable consequence of both mechanization and the idealization of mathematics is the detachment of the investigator from that which is being studied, of the knower from the known. The combination of the universality of natural laws and the use of mathematics to explicate these laws solidified not only the separateness of nature but also the idea that there was only one correct method of investigating Nature. This is objectivity, the lack of personal bias or agenda in science.

The Renaissance Hermetical tradition, named after Hermes Trismegistus, a Greek whose works were rediscovered in the mid-fifteenth century, included magic and alchemy. It was both a precursor of and in conflict with the new worldview:

> the most important feature of the Hermetic writing lay in the notion that man was created by God with an intellect so that he could know and appreciate God's works and with a body so that he could use his spark of divine knowledge "to regulate all things . . . and take care of terrestrial things and govern them." Every man is potentially a magus (magician), capable of both recognizing and directing the forces inherent but sometimes hidden in nature, in order to fashion the world according to his designs.
>
> (Burke, 1987, p. 47)

This description points out that the Hermetical tradition contributed to the active program of the science that was to follow. The parts of the tradition that were in opposition to the new worldview were alchemy and magic. In the old tradition, magic was used for the benefit of the individual rather than for society. Alchemy was not solely the transmutation of elements, but a philosophy based in a hermaphroditic earth – clearly in conflict with a science that, as we will soon see, is characterized as masculine.

Stephen Shapin describes science after the "scientific revolution" thus:

> First, the mechanization of nature: the increasing use of mechanical metaphors to construe natural knowledge processes and phenomena; second, the depersonalization of natural knowledge; the growing separation between human subjects and the natural objects of their knowledge . . . ; third, the attempted mechanization of knowledge making, that is the proposed deployment of explicitly formulated rules of method that aims at disciplining the production of knowledge

> by managing or eliminating the effects of human passions and interest; and fourth, the aspiration to use the resulting reformed natural knowledge to achieve moral, social, and political ends.
>
> (Shapin, 1996, p. 13)

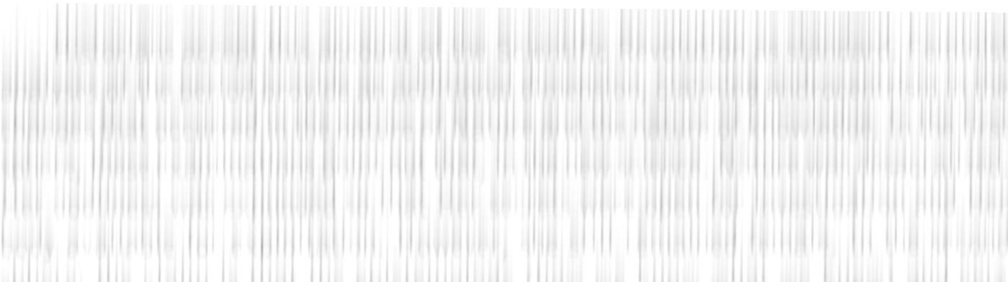

structure of science is masculine. It is masculine in three ways; almost all the individuals who developed the new methodology were men; it is self-identified as masculine by the use of phrases such as "The Masculine Birth of Time" and "virile mind"; and its characteristics map onto the traits society defines as masculine.

Feminist scholars apply tools such as historical and linguistic analysis, as well as psychological approaches, to the writings of philosophers such as Bacon and Descartes, who were the dominant forces driving these changes. Sir Francis Bacon, as described in the first selection in this section, "Dominion over Nature" from Carolyn Merchant's *The Death of Nature: Women, Ecology and the Scientific Revolution*, was a courtier to James I of England. Merchant concentrates especially on Bacon's description of how nature is to be dissected and used for human good. Bacon's language to describe Man's dominion over nature uses "bold sexual imagery"; his words reinforce the female not only as an object, but an object for exploitation. It is Man's proper role to investigate Nature, and, for Bacon, Man's mind is a virile agent for this task. Once Bacon's program was adopted by the newly formed Royal Society, it became institutionalized and codified. Merchant also notes social and economic changes that illustrate Shapin's statement on the use of the newly changed natural knowledge.

Descartes was a French philosopher (1596–1650) whose goal was to create a unified system of knowledge based in pure reason and mathematical principles. He is best known for the phrase "cogito, ergo sum," "I think, therefore I am." For the Greeks, humans were "in nature" and used intellect for their inner world and their senses for the outer world. Descartes was concerned that such use of the senses would be subjective and lead to distortions in perception. For him, it was an epistemological problem to relate the thinking self (*res cogitans*) with the external world (*res extensa*). In "Selections from *The Flight to Objectivity*," the second selection in this section, Susan Bordo asserts that the psychology of child development and oedipal interpretations can explain Cartesian philosophy. Just as the child doesn't believe that a thing exists unless it is directly in view, the world doesn't exist in a constant fashion for Descartes without God's attention. Just as a child must separate from its mother, humans must separate from nature. Man's reason is the tool to insure this separation, leading to the denial of mother/Nature and an unemotional, objective, measured (literally), masculine assessment of the universe. This is ultimately alienated knowing, "The otherness of Nature is now what allows it to be known."

The essay by Evelyn Fox Keller, "Secrets of God, Nature, and Life" from *Secrets of Life, Secrets of Death: Essays on Language, Gender and Science*, lays out very clearly the "schism . . . between God and Nature, God and woman but also between woman and man" that underpinned the new mechanistic science. Women's/Nature's residual power of procreation that cannot be eliminated is destroyed by the biological research program of reducing life to genes.

The third of Shapin's characteristics of the Scientific Revolution is the "mechanization of knowledge making . . . the proposed development of explicitly formulated rules of method that aims at disciplining the production of knowledge" (p. 13). Anyone who has studied science has been taught these rules, that still endure three centuries after their promulgation. Individuals trained in history, philosophy and sociology have, since the Second World War, analyzed the philosophical and social forces involved in knowledge production, reaching conclusions that have been distressing to some practicing scientists. In 1962, Thomas Kuhn, himself a physicist, published *The Structure of Scientific Revolutions*, which laid out, using the history of the physical sciences as a basis, an analysis of the "glue" that holds science together. His definition of a paradigm included a set of rules for science-making, including the appropriate questions to ask, the appropriate ways to ask these questions, the appropriate instruments to use, and how appropriate answers be understood. Any one who wants to be a participant in science has to follow the rules.

These methods are not foolproof, as related in the first section ("Methods and Their Limitations") of *On Being a Scientist*, a report from the Committee on the Conduct of Science of the National Academy of Sciences of the United States. If methods are defined by practitioners, science is not solitary fact-finding but a social endeavor. Since scientists are also imbedded in the larger culture, the values of the culture can influence science practice, as described in "Values in Science." The importance of recognizing these influences is underscored by the report's being published by the most influential and prestigious science organization in the United States.

If the structure of science is androcentric, as the pieces in this section assert, and women have been systematically excluded and their contributions to science devalued, as shown in Section Two, the feminist and other critiques of science may challenge theory and practice. "Scientific theories are always capable of being reexamined and if necessary replaced" (On Being a Scientist, p. 13). Recently, science has been challenged in just these ways. Predictably, scientists have disagreed vehemently, resulting in what has been called "The Science Wars." The last article in this section is a popular account of this tempest, with examples of research that has been influenced significantly by cultural factors. Broader discussions of feminist analysis of the epistemology of science and of gender influences on science practice are found in Sections Four and Five.

References

Burke, John G. (ed.) (1987) *Science and Culture in the Western Tradition.* Scottsdale, AZ: Gorsuch Scarisbruck.

National Academy of Science (1989) *On Being a Scientist*, Washington, DC: National Academy Press.

Shapin, Stephen (1996) *The Scientific Revolution*. Chicago and London: University of Chicago Press.

Keller, Evelyn Fox (1992) *Secrets of Life, Secrets of Death*. New York and London: Routledge.

Kuhn, Thomas S. (1970) *The Structure of Scientific Revolutions, Second Edition Enlarged*. Chicago and London: University of Chicago Press.

Latour, Bruno (1987) *Science in Action*. Milton Keynes: Open University Press.

Lloyd, Genevieve (1996) "Reason, Science and the Domination of Matter." In Evelyn Fox Keller and Helen Longino, eds. *Feminism and Science*. Oxford and New York: Oxford University Press.

Longino, Helen (1990) *Science as Social Knowledge: Values and Objectivity in Scientific Inquiry*. Princeton: Princeton University Press.

Macilwain, Colin (1997) "Campuses Ring to a Stormy Clash Over Truth and Reason." *Nature* 387: 331–333.

Merchant, Carolyn (1980) *The Death of Nature: Women, Biology and the Scientific Revolution*. San Francisco: Harper & Row.

Noble, David (1992) *A World Without Women: The Christian Clerical Culture of Western Science*. New York: Knopf.

Schiebinger, Londa (1989) *The Mind Has No Sex: Women in the Origins of Modern Science*. Cambridge and London: Harvard University Press.

Schiebinger, Londa (1993) *Nature's Body: Gender in the Making of Modern Science*. Boston: Beacon Press.

Toulmin, Stephen (1990) *Cosmopolis: The Hidden Agenda of Modernity*. New York: Free Press.

Chapter 8

Carolyn Merchant

DOMINION OVER NATURE

Disorderly, active nature was soon forced to submit to the questions and experimental techniques of the new science. Francis Bacon (1561–1626), a celebrated "father of modern science," transformed tendencies already extant in his own society into a total program advocating the control of nature for human benefit. Melding together a new philosophy based on natural magic as a technique for manipulating nature, the technologies of mining and metallurgy, the emerging concept of progress and a patriarchal structure of family and state, Bacon fashioned a new ethic sanctioning the exploitation of nature.

Bacon has been eulogized as the originator of the concept of the modern research institute, a philosopher of industrial science, the inspiration behind the Royal Society (1660), and as the founder of the inductive method by which all people can verify for themselves the truths of science by the reading of nature's book.[1] But from the perspective of nature, women, and the lower orders of society emerges a less favorable image of Bacon and a critique of his program as ultimately benefitting the middle-class male entrepreneur. Bacon, of course, was not responsible for subsequent uses of his philosophy. But, because he was in an extremely influential social position and in touch with the important developments of his time, his language, style, nuance, and metaphor become a mirror reflecting his class perspective.

Sensitive to the same social transformations that had already begun to reduce women to psychic and reproductive resources, Bacon developed the power of language as political instrument in reducing female nature to a resource for economic production. Female imagery became a tool in adapting scientific knowledge and method to a new form of human power over nature. The "controversy over women" and the inquisition of witches – both present in Bacon's social milieu – permeated his description of nature and his metaphorical style and were instrumental in his transformation of the earth as a nurturing mother and womb of life into a source of secrets to be extracted for economic advance.

Bacon's roots can be found in middle-class economic development and its progressive interests and values. His father was a middle-class employee of the queen, his mother a Calvinist whose Protestant values permeated his early home life. Bacon took steps to gain the favor of James I soon after the latter's ascent to the throne in 1603. He moved from "learned counsel" in 1603 to attorney general in 1613, privy councillor

year of his English reign, James I replaced the milder witch laws of Elizabeth I, which evoked the death penalty only for killing by witchcraft, with a law that condemned to death all practitioners.[3]

It was in the 1612 trials of the Lancashire witches of the Pendle Forest that the sexual aspects of witch trials first appeared in England. The source of the women's confessions of fornication with the devil was a Roman Catholic priest who had emigrated from the Continent and planted the story in the mouths of accused women who had recently rejected Catholicism.

These social events influenced Bacon's philosophy and literary style. Much of the imagery he used in delineating his new scientific objectives and methods derives from the courtroom, and, because it treats nature as a female to be tortured through mechanical inventions, strongly suggests the interrogations of the witch trials and the mechanical devices used to torture witches. In a relevant passage, Bacon stated that the method by which nature's secrets might be discovered consisted in investigating the secrets of witchcraft by inquisition, referring to the example of James I:

> *For you have but to follow and as it were hound nature in her wanderings, and you will be able when you like to lead and drive her afterward to the same place again.* Neither am I of opinion in this history of marvels that superstitious narratives of *sorceries, witchcrafts, charms*, dreams, divinations, and the like, where there is an assurance and clear evidence of the fact, should be altogether excluded . . . howsoever the use and practice of such arts is to be condemned, yet from the speculation and consideration of them . . . a useful light may be gained, not only for a true judgment of the offenses of persons charged with such practices, *but likewise for the further disclosing of the secrets of nature. Neither ought a man to make scruple of entering and penetrating into these holes and corners, when the inquisition of truth is his whole object – as your majesty has shown in your own example.*[4]
>
> (italics added)

The strong sexual implications of the last sentence can be interpreted in the light of the investigation of the supposed sexual crimes and practices of witches. In another example, he compared the interrogation of courtroom witnesses to the inquisition of nature: "I mean (according to the practice in civil causes) in this great plea or suit granted by the divine favor and providence (whereby the human race seeks to recover its right over nature) *to examine nature herself* and the arts upon interrogatories."[5] Bacon pressed the idea further with an analogy to the torture chamber: "For like as a man's disposition is never well known or proved till he be crossed, nor Proteus ever changed shapes till he was *straitened* and *held fast*, so nature exhibits herself more clearly under the *trials* and *vexations* of art [mechanical devices] than when left to herself."[6]

The new man of science must not think that the "inquisition of nature is in any part interdicted or forbidden." Nature must be "bound into service" and made a "slave," put "in constraint" and "molded" by the mechanical arts. The "searchers and spies of nature" are to discover her plots and secrets.[7]

This method, so readily applicable when nature is denoted by the female gender, degraded and made possible the exploitation of the natural environment. As woman's womb had symbolically yielded to the forceps, so nature's womb harbored secrets that through technology could be wrested from her grasp for use in the improvement of the human condition:

> There is therefore much ground for hoping that there are still laid up in the womb of nature many secrets of excellent use having no affinity or parallelism with anything that is now known . . . only by the method which we are now treating can they be speedily and suddenly and simultaneously presented and anticipated.[8]

Bacon transformed the magical tradition by calling on the need to dominate nature not for the sole benefit of the individual magician but for the good of the entire human race. Through vivid metaphor, he transformed the magus from nature's servant to its exploiter, and nature from a teacher to a slave. Bacon argued that it was the magician's error to consider art (technology) a mere "assistant to nature having the power to finish what nature has begun" and therefore to despair of ever "changing, transmuting, or fundamentally altering nature."[9]

The natural magician saw himself as operating within the organic order of nature – he was a manipulator of parts within that system, bringing down the heavenly powers to the earthly shrine. Agrippa, however, had begun to explore the possibility of ascending the hierarchy to the point of cohabiting with God. Bacon extended this idea to include the recovery of the power over nature lost when Adam and Eve were expelled from paradise.

Due to the Fall from the Garden of Eden (caused by the temptation of a woman), the human race lost its "dominion over creation." Before the Fall, there was no need for power or dominion, because Adam and Eve had been made sovereign over all other creatures. In this state of dominion, mankind was "like unto God." While some, accepting God's punishment, had obeyed the medieval strictures against searching too deeply into God's secrets, Bacon turned the constraints into sanctions. Only by "digging further and further into the mine of natural knowledge" could mankind recover that lost dominion. In this way, "the narrow limits of man's dominion over the universe" could be stretched "to their promised bounds."[10]

Although a female's inquisitiveness may have caused man's fall from his God-given dominion, the relentless interrogation of another female, nature, could be used to regain it. As he argued in *The Masculine Birth of Time*, "I am come in very truth leading to you nature with all her children to bind her to your service and make her your slave." "We have no right," he asserted, "to expect nature to come to us." Instead, "Nature must be taken by the forelock, being bald behind." Delay and subtle argument "permit one only to clutch at nature, never to lay hold of her and capture her."[11]

Nature existed in three states – at liberty, in error, or in bondage:

> She is either free and follows her ordinary course of development as in the [illegible]

[illegible] growing, self-actualizing being. The second state was necessary to explain the malfunctions and monstrosities that frequently appeared and that could not have been caused by God or another higher power acting on his instruction. Since monstrosities could not be explained by the action of form or spirit, they had to be the result of matter acting perversely. Matter in Plato's Timaeus was recalcitrant and had to be forcefully shaped by the demiurge. Bacon frequently described matter in female imagery, as a "common harlot." "Matter is not devoid of an appetite and inclination to dissolve the world and fall back into the old Chaos." It therefore must be "restrained and kept in order by the prevailing concord of things." "The vexations of art are certainly as the bonds and handcuffs of Proteus, which betray the ultimate struggles and efforts of matter."[13]

The third instance was the case of art (techné), man operating on nature to create something new and artificial. Here "nature takes orders from man and works under his authority." Miners and smiths should become the model for the new class of natural philosophers who would interrogate and alter nature. They had developed the two most important methods of wresting nature's secrets from her, "the one searching into the bowels of nature, the other shaping nature as on an anvil." "Why should we not divide natural philosophy into two parts, the mine and the furnace?" For "the truth of nature lies hid in certain deep mines and caves," within the earth's bosom. Bacon, like some of the practically minded alchemists, would "advise the studious to sell their books and build furnaces" and, "forsaking Minerva and the Muses as barren virgins, to rely upon Vulcan."[14]

The new method of interrogation was not through abstract notions, but through the instruction of the understanding "that it may in very truth dissect nature." The instruments of the mind supply suggestions, those of the hand give motion and aid the work. "By art and the hand of man," nature can then be "forced out of her natural state and squeezed and molded." In this way, "human knowledge and human power meet as one."[15]

Here, in bold sexual imagery, is the key feature of the modern experimental method – constraint of nature in the laboratory, dissection by hand and mind, and the penetration of hidden secrets – language still used today in praising a scientist's "hard facts," "penetrating mind," or the "thrust of his argument." The constraints against penetration in Natura's lament over her torn garments of modesty have been turned into sanctions in language that legitimates the exploitation and "rape" of nature for human good. The seventeenth-century experimenters of the Accademia del Cimento of Florence (i.e., the Academy of Experiment, 1657–1667) and the Royal Society of London who placed mice and plants in the artificial vacuum of the barometer or bell jar were vexing nature and forcing her out of her natural state in true Baconian fashion.[16]

Scientific method, combined with mechanical technology, would create a "new organon," a new system of investigation, that unified knowledge with material power. The technological discoveries of printing, gunpowder, and the magnet in the fields of learning, warfare, and navigation "help us to think about the secrets still locked in nature's bosom." "They do not, like the old, merely exert a gentle guidance over nature's course; they have the power to conquer and subdue her, to shake her to her foundations." Under the mechanical arts, "nature betrays her secrets more fully . . . than when in enjoyment of her natural liberty."[17]

Mechanics, which gave man power over nature, consisted in motion; that is, in "the uniting or disuniting of natural bodies." Most useful were the arts that altered the materials of things – "agriculture, cookery, chemistry, dying, the manufacture of glass, enamel, sugar, gunpowder, artificial fires, paper, and the like." But in performing these operations, one was constrained to operate within the chain of causal connections; nature could "not be commanded except by being obeyed." Only by the study, interpretation, and observation of nature could these possibilities be uncovered; only by acting as the interpreter of nature could knowledge be turned into power. Of the three grades of human ambition, the most wholesome and noble was "to endeavor to establish and extend the power and dominion of the human race itself over the universe." In this way "the human race [could] recover that right over nature which belongs to it by divine bequest."[18]

The interrogation of witches as symbol for the interrogation of nature, the courtroom as model for its inquisition, and torture through mechanical devices as a tool for the subjugation of disorder were fundamental to the scientific method as power. For Bacon, as for Harvey, sexual politics helped to structure the nature of the empirical method that would produce a new form of knowledge and a new ideology of objectivity seemingly devoid of cultural and political assumptions.

[. . .]

Capitalism and scientific progress

Bacon's utopian *New Atlantis*, written in 1624, shortly before his death, postulated a program of scientific study that would be a foundation for the progress and advancement of "the whole of mankind."

By the time Bacon wrote his *New Atlantis*, a significant cleavage existed in English society between wage laborers and merchants. The rift between middle-class society and the poorer sectors was developing in the textile industry, mining industry, and the crafts.[19]

In seventeenth-century England, the rural poor became servants for the families of gentleman landlords, husbanders, and yeoman farmers. The cottager's son or daughter who became a servant in husbandry left home around the age of ten and was cared for, fed, clothed, and housed by the surrogate family for the next ten to twenty years. After marriage, probably to another servant, the cottage-laborer might well face the rest of his or her short life in poverty, earning small sums for daily labor contracts.

Cottagers supplied much of the labor for the rural putting-out systems, which combined large numbers of households in the production of textiles under the direction of a clothier capitalist. When not employed in planting, plowing, and harvesting operations, farmers and their families engaged in the sorting, carding, and spinning of wool. The subsequent weaving, dying, and dressing of cloth was performed by [illegible] fulling mills and workshops where the cloth was stretched and pressed. In 1618, an English writer estimated that a clothier who made twenty broadcloths a week provided work for 500 persons, counting wool sorters, carders, spinners, weavers, burlers, fullers, cloth finishers, dyers, and loom and spinning wheel makers. In the West Country, the capital investments were larger and the number of operations directed by the clothier more extensive than in the Yorkshire country of the north.

The transition from craft production to preindustrial capitalism taking place throughout the century was more pronounced in the rural rather than the urban putting-out systems. A clothier in the rural putting-out system was freer than his urban counterpart from municipal taxes and regulations and from restrictions on the quality of his product, the number of his employees, and his methods of production. "The expansive years between 1460 and 1560 are particularly important because the balance of tradition and innovation shifted gradually but decisively. . . . But by 1560 the cleavage between capital and labor . . . was firmly and widely established in many parts of industrial Europe."[20] Rising prices widened the separation between wages and profits with a larger share of community wealth going to the capitalist.

A second industry that employed the poor as wage workers was mining.[21] Large-scale operations were rare, with only about 100 workers being employed in each of the larger mines. In England, the coal industries at Newcastle upon Tyne and Wear developed rapidly in the late sixteenth century, impelled by the increasing scarcity of timber.

In the British copper and brass industry that developed in the 1560s, large capital investments were necessary for opening and developing the mining shafts, smelting the ore, producing brass wire, and flattening ingots. Since neither the workers nor any single capitalist had the necessary funds, capital was supplied by English and German shareholders – members of the nobility, clergy, state officials, and merchants. Separation of worker and capitalist was thus a prerequisite for the start of this industry.[22] In the iron industry, foundry and forge were owned and products marketed by entrepreneurs. Free and independent miners and metal workers were a decreasing group.

A similar separation was taking place within the crafts, created by decreasing upward mobility for journeypeople. By hard and diligent work or by marrying the master's daughter, a journeyman might succeed.[23] But more and more masters tended to pass their craft to their sons, making the group hereditary. Masters became "small-scale industrial capitalists," and journeypeople became their paid workers, with less chance for independence. The journeyman weaver, for example, owned neither the material, as did the clothier, nor the looms, as did the master weaver.

Within the craft guilds, some masters accumulated money and extended the markets beyond their own towns. Lower craftspersons became more dependent on them. The same phenomenon of market extension and dependence also took place between one craft and another.

Francis Bacon's early interest in writing a "History of Trades" was a manifestation of his desire to discover those secrets of the craft workshops that could be applied to the practical needs and interests of middle-class society. Growth and progress could be achieved from the study of the mechanical arts, "for these . . . are continually thriving and growing."[24]

The concept of scientific progress that Bacon developed as a program sanctioned the gap between journeyman and master craftsman. Much has been made of the concept of progress in Western society, through which standards of living for "all mankind" are presumably improved. But did the "public good" really include the cottager, journeyperson, and peasant, or did it function so as to benefit the master craftsman, clothier, and merchant?

The idea of scientific progress has been associated with the rise of technology and "the requirements of early capitalistic economy" by scholars who have argued that the idea of cooperation and the sharing of knowledge for both the construction of theory and the public good stemmed from the intellectual attitudes of sixteenth-century master craftsmen, mechanical engineers, and a few academic scholars and humanists. "The absence of slavery, the existence of machinery, the capitalistic spirit of enterprise and economic rationality seem to be prerequisites without which the ideal of scientific progress cannot unfold."[25]

The sixteenth-century groups that evolved the concept of progress are the same groups that right up until the present have pressed for increased growth and development: entrepreneurs, military engineers, humanist academics, and scientists and technicians.

[. . .]

What had been merely prefaces and statements advocating a utilitarian concept of progress in these sixteenth-century treatises became a whole program and ideology in the utopian thought of Francis Bacon. In the *New Atlantis*, progress was placed in the hands of a group of scientists and technicians who studied nature altered by "the mechanical arts" and "the hand of man" that her secrets might be utilized to benefit society.

Mechanism and the *New Atlantis*

The scientific research institute designed to bring progress to Bensalem, the community of the *New Atlantis*, was called Salomon's House. The patriarchal character of this utopian society was reinforced by designating the scientists as the "Fathers of Salomon's House." In the *New Atlantis*, politics was replaced by scientific administration. No real political process existed in Bensalem. Decisions were made for the good of the whole by the scientists, whose judgment was to be trusted implicitly, for they alone possessed the secrets of nature.

Scientists decided which secrets were to be revealed to the state as a whole and which were to remain the private property of the institute rather than becoming public knowledge: "And this we do also, we have consultations, which of the inventions and experiences which we have discovered shall be published, and which not: and all take an oath of secrecy for the concealing of those which we think fit to keep secret, though

"robe of fine black cloth with wide sleeves and a cape," an "undergarment . . . of excellent white linen," and a girdle and a clerical scarf, also of linen. His gloves were set with stone, his shoes were of peach-colored velvet, and he wore a Spanish helmet.

The worship to be accorded to the scientist was further enhanced by his vehicle, a "rich chariot" of cedar and gilt carried like a litter between four richly velveted horses and two blue-velveted footmen. The chariot was decorated with gold, sapphires, a golden sun, and a small cherub of gold with wings outspread" and was followed by fifty richly dressed footmen. In front walked two bareheaded men carrying a pastoral staff and a bishop's crosier.

Bacon's scientist not only looked but behaved like a priest who had the power of absolving all human misery through science. He "had an aspect as if he pitied men"; "he held up his bare hand as he went, as blessing the people, but in silence." The street was lined with people who, it would seem, were happy, orderly, and completely passive: "The street was wonderfully well kept, so that there was never any army [which] had their men stand in better battle array than the people stood. The windows were not crowded, but everyone stood in them as if they had been placed."

Bacon's "man of science" would seem to be a harbinger of many modern research scientists. Critics of science today argue that scientists have become guardians of a body of scientific knowledge, shrouded in the mysteries of highly technical language that can be fully understood only by those who have had a dozen years of training. It is now possible for such scientists to reveal to the public only information they deem relevant. Depending on the scientist's ethics and political viewpoint, such information may or may not serve the public interest.

Salomon's House, long held to be the prototype of a modern research institute, was a forerunner of the mechanistic mode of scientific investigation. The mechanical method that evolved during the seventeenth century operated by breaking down a problem into its component parts, isolating it from its environment, and solving each portion independently. Bacon's research center maintained separate "laboratories" for the study of mining and metals, weather, fresh- and salt-water life, cultivated plants, insects, and so on.

The tasks of research were divided hierarchically among the various scientists, novices, and apprentices. Some abstracted patterns from other experiments, some did preliminary book research, some collected experiments from other arts and sciences; others tried out new experiments, or compiled results or looked for applications. The interpreters of nature raised the discoveries into greater observations, axioms, and aphorisms. This differentiation of labor followed the outlines of Bacon's inductive methodology.

In the laboratories of Salomon's House, one of the goals was to recreate the natural environment artificially through applied technology. Large, deep caves called the Lower Region were used for "the imitation of natural mines and the producing of new artificial metals by compositions and materials."[27] In another region were "a number of artificial wells and fountains, made in imitation of the natural sources and baths." Salt water could be made fresh, for "we have also pools, of which some do strain fresh water out of salt, and others by art do turn fresh water into salt."

Not only was the manipulation of the environment part of Bacon's program for the improvement of mankind, but the manipulation of organic life to create artificial species of plants and animals was specifically outlined. Bacon transformed the natural magician as "servant of nature" into a manipulator of nature and changed art from the aping of nature into techniques for forcing nature into new forms and controlling reproduction for the sake of production: "We make a number of kinds of serpents, worms, flies, fishes of putrefaction, where of some are advanced (in effect) to be perfect creatures like beasts or birds, and have sexes, and do propagate. Neither do we this by chance, but we know beforehand of what matter and commixture what kind of those creatures will arise."

These examples were taken directly from Delia Porta's *Natural Magic* (1558), the second book of which dealt specifically with putrefaction and the generation of the living organisms mentioned by Bacon – worms, serpents, and fishes. The chapter dealing with putrefaction had discussed the generation of canker worms from mud, so that "we may also learn how to procreate new creatures."[28] "Serpents," wrote Delia Porta, "may be generated of man's marrow, of the hairs of a menstrous woman, and of a horsetail, or mane," while "certain fishes," such as groundlings, carp, and shellfish, "are generated out of putrefaction." New beasts and birds could be generated through knowledge and carefully controlled coupling.

Delia Porta also set down instructions as to how to produce a new organism in a series of trials. Such creatures "must be of equal pitch; they must have the same reproductive cycle, and one must be equally "as lustful as the other." Furthermore "if any creatures want appetite . . . we may make them eager in lust."

The *New Atlantis* had parks and enclosures for beasts and birds where just such experiments were performed: "By art likewise we make them greater or taller than their kind is, and contrariwise dwarf them, and stay their growth; we make them more fruitful and bearing than their kind is, and contrariwise barren and not generative. Also we make them differ in color, shape, activity, many ways."[29]

The scientists of Salomon's House not only produced new forms of birds and beasts, but they also altered and created new species of herbs and plants: "We have also means to make divers plants rise by mixtures of earths without seeds, and likewise to make divers new plants differing from the vulgar, and to make one tree or plant turn into another."

Rather than respecting the beauty of existing organisms, Bacon's *New Atlantis* advocated the creation of new ones:

> We have also large and various orchards and gardens, wherein we do not so much respect beauty as variety of ground and soil, proper for diverse trees and herbs. . . . And we make (by art) in the same orchards and gardens, trees and flowers to come earlier or later than their seasons, and to come up and bear more speedily [illegible] they do. We make them by art greater much than their [illegible]

ultimately directed toward [illegible] and enclosures of all sorts of beasts and birds, which we use not only for view or rareness but likewise for dissections and trials, that thereby we may take light [i.e., enlightenment] what may be wrought upon the body of man. . . . We also try all poisons and other medicines upon them as well of chirurgery as physic."[31]

Much of Bacon's strategy in the *New Atlantis* was directed at removing ethical strictures against manipulative magic, of the sort found in Agrippa's *Vanity of Arts and Science* (1530), a polemic probably written for Agrippa's own self-protection, containing important arguments against transforming and altering nature. Just as Agricola had been obliged to refute Agrippa's views on mining in order to liberate that activity from the ethical constraints imposed by ancient writers, so Bacon was obliged to refute the constraints against the manipulation of nature. Agrippa had argued against tampering with nature and maiming living organisms:

> Those exercises appurtenant to agriculture . . . might in some measure deserve commendation, could it have retained itself within moderate bounds and not shown us so many devices to make strange plants, so many portentous graftings and metamorphoses of trees; how to make horses copulate with asses, wolves with dogs, and so to engender many wondrous monsters contrary to nature: and those creatures to whom nature has given leave to range the air, the seas and earth so freely, to captivate and confine in aviaries, cages, warrens, parks, and fish ponds, and to fat them in coops, having first put out their eyes, and maimed their limbs.[32]

Agrippa had further inveighed against the manipulators of nature who had tried to discover "how to prevent storms, make . . . seed fruitful, kill weeds, scare wild beasts, stop the flight of beasts and birds, the swimming of fishes, to charm away all manner of diseases; of all which those wise men before named have written very seriously and very cruelly."

Much of Bacon's program in the *New Atlantis* was meant to sanction just such manipulations, his whole objective being to recover man's right over nature, lost in the Fall. Agrippa had observed that after the Fall nature, once kind and beneficent, had become wild and uncontrollable: "For now the earth produces nothing without our labor and our sweat, but deadly and venomous . . . nor are the other elements less kind to us: many the seas destroy with raging tempests, and the horrid monsters devour the air making war against us with thunder, lightning and storms; and with a crowd of pestilential diseases, the heavens conspire our ruin."

In order to control the ravages of wild tempestuous nature, Bacon set as one of the objectives of Salomon's House the artificial control of the weather and its concomitant monsters and pestilences: "We have also great and spacious houses, where we imitate and demonstrate meteors, as snow, hail, rain, some artificial rains of bodies and not of water, thunder, lightnings, also generation of bodies in air, as frogs, flies, and diverse others." Tempests (like that produced by Shakespeare's magician, Prospero) could also be created for study by using "engines for multiplying and enforcing of winds."[33]

The Baconian program, so important to the rise of Western science, contained within it a set of attitudes about nature and the scientist that reinforced the tendencies toward growth and progress inherent in early capitalism. While Bacon himself had no intimation as to where his goals might ultimately lead, nor was he responsible for modern attitudes, he was very sensitive to the trends and directions of his own time and voiced them eloquently. The expansive tendencies of his period have continued, and the possibility of their reversal is highly problematical.

Bacon's mechanistic utopia was fully compatible with the mechanical philosophy of nature that developed during the seventeenth century. Mechanism divided nature into atomic particles, which, like the civil citizens of Bensalem, were passive and inert. Motion and change were externally caused: in nature, the ultimate source was God, the seventeenth century's divine father, clockmaker, and engineer; in Bensalem, it was the patriarchal scientific administration of Salomon's House. The atomic parts of the mechanistic universe were ordered in a causal nexus such that by contact the motion of one part caused the motion of the next. The linear hierarchy of apprentices, novices, and scientists who passed along the observations, experimental results, and generalizations made the scientific method as mechanical as the operation of the universe itself. Although machine technology was relatively unadvanced in Bensalem, the model of nature and society in this utopia was consistent with the possibilities for increased technological and administrative growth.

In the *New Atlantis* lay the intellectual origins of the modern planned environments initiated by the technocratic movement of the late 1920s and 1930s, which envisioned totally artificial environments created by and for humans. Too often these have been created by the mechanistic style of problem solving, which pays little regard to the whole ecosystem of which people are only one part. The antithesis of holistic thinking, mechanism neglects the environmental consequences of synthetic products and the human consequences of artificial environments. It would seem that the creation of artificial products was one result of the Baconian drive toward control and power over nature in which "The end of our foundation is the knowledge of causes and secret motions of things and the enlarging of the bounds of human empire, to the effecting of all things possible."[34] To this research program, modern genetic engineers have added new goals – the manipulation of genetic material to create human life in artificial wombs, the duplication of living organisms through cloning, and the breeding of new human beings adapted to highly technological environments.

[. . .]

Notes

1 Treatment of Francis Bacon's contributions to science include Paolo Rossi, *Francis Bacon: From Magic to Science* (London: Routledge & Kegan Paul, 1968); Lisa Jardine, *Francis Bacon and the Art of Discourse* (Cambridge, England: Cambridge University [illegible]

(London: Baker, 1967), p. 83.

4 Bacon, "De Dignitate et Augmentis Scientiarum" (written 1623), *Works*, ed. James Spedding, Robert Leslie Ellis, Douglas Devon Heath, 14 vols. (London: Longmans Green, 1870), vol. 4, p. 296. The ensuing discussion was stimulated by William Leiss's *The Domination of Nature* (New York: Braziller, 1972), Chap. 3, pp. 45–71.

5 Bacon, "Preparative Towards a Natural and Experimental History," *Works*, vol. 4, p. 263. Italics added.

6 Bacon, "De Dignitate," *Works*, vol. 4, p. 298. Italics added.

7 Bacon, "The Great Instauration" (written 1620), *Works*, vol. 4, p. 20; "The Masculine Birth of Time," ed. and trans. Benjamin Farrington, in *The Philosophy of Francis Bacon* (Liverpool, England: Liverpool University Press, 1964), p. 62; "De Dignitate," *Works*, vol. 4, pp. 287, 294.

8 Quoted in Moody E. Prior, "Bacon's Man of Science," in Leonard M. Marsak, ed., *The Rise of Modern Science in Relation to Society* (London: Collier-Macmillan, 1964), p. 45.

9 Rossi, p. 21; Leiss, p. 56; Bacon, *Works*, vol. 4, p. 294; Henry Cornelius Agrippa, *De Occulta Philosophia Libri Tres* (Antwerp, 1531): "No one has such powers but he who has cohabited with the elements, vanquished nature, mounted higher than the heavens, elevating himself above the angels to the archetype itself, with whom he then becomes cooperator and can do all things," as quoted in Frances A. Yates, *Giordano Bruno and the Hermetic Tradition* (New York: Vintage Books, 1964), p. 136.

10 Bacon, "Novum Organum," Part 2, in *Works*, vol. 4, p. 247; "Valerius Terminus," *Works*, vol. 3, pp. 217, 219; "The Masculine Birth of Time," trans. Farrington, p. 62.

11 Bacon, "The Masculine Birth of Time," and "The Refutation of Philosophies," trans. Farrington, pp. 62, 129, 130.

12 Bacon, "De Augmentis," *Works*, vol. 4, p. 294; see also Bacon, "Aphorisms," *Works*, vol. 4.

13 "De Augmentis," *Works*, vol. 4, pp. 320, 325; Plato, "The Timaeus," in *The Dialogues of Plato*, trans. B. Jowett (New York: Random House, 1937), vol. 2, p. 17; Bacon, "Parasceve," *Works*, vol. 4, p. 257.

14 Bacon, "De Augmentis," *Works*, vol. 4, pp. 287, 343, 393.

15 Bacon, "Novum Organum," *Works*, vol. 4, p. 246; "The Great Instauration," *Works*, vol. 4, p. 29; "Novum Organum," Part 2, *Works*, vol. 4, p. 247.

16 Alain of Lille, *De Planctu Naturae*, in T. Wright, ed., *The Anglo-Latin Satirical Poets and Epigrammatists* (Wiesbaden: Kraus Reprint, 1964) vol. 2, pp. 441, 467; Thomas

Kuhn, "Mathemetical vs. Experimental Traditions in the Development of Physical Science," *Journal of Interdisciplinary History* 7, no. 1 (Summer, 1976): 1–31, see p. 13. On the Accademia del Cimento's experiments see Martha Ornstein [Bronfenbenner], *The Role of Scientific Societies in the Seventeenth Century* (reprint ed., New York: Arno Press, 1975, p. 86.

17 Bacon, "Thoughts and Conclusions on the Interpretation of Nature or A Science of Productive Works," trans. Farrington, *The Philosophy of Francis Bacon*, pp. 93, 96, 99.

18 Bacon, "De Augmentis," *Works*, vol. 4, p. 294; "Parasceve," *Works*, vol. 4, p. 257; "Plan of the Work," vol. 4, p. 32; "Novum Organun," *Works*, vol. 4, pp. 114, 115.

19 The following discussion of the effects of early capitalist organization in the textile industry draws on Laslett, pp. 15–17; Eugene F. Rice, Jr., *The Foundations of Early Modern Europe, 1460–1559* (New York: Norton, 1970), pp. 52–53; E. Lipson, *The Economic History of England* (London: Black, 1943) vol. 2, pp. 9, 11–15, 17, 31; E. Lipson, *A Short History of Wool and Its Manufacture (Mainly in England)* (Cambridge, Mass.: Harvard University Press, 1953); Henry Kamen, *The Iron Century: Social Change in Europe, 1550–1660* (London: Wiedenfeld and Nicolson, 1971), p. 114. For late sixteenth-century laws regulating the textile industry, see R.H. Tawney and Eileen Power, *Tudor Economic Documents* (London: Longmans Green, 1924), vol. 1, pp. 169–228; see also Thomas Deloney, "The Pleasant History of John Winchcomb, in his Younger Years Called Jack of Newburie," in F.O. Mann, ed., *The Works of Thomas Deloney* (Oxford, 1912).

20 Rice, pp. 53–54.

21 The discussion of capitalist organization in the mining industry draws on Lipson, *Economic History*, vol. 2, pp. 114, 162; John U. Nef, "Coal Mining and Utilization," in Charles Singer and others, eds., *A History of Technology* (New York: Oxford University Press, 1957), vol. 3, p. 77; J.U. Nef, *The Rise of the British Coal Industry* (London: Routledge & Kegan Paul, 1932), vol. 1. On laws regulating the mining industry see Tawney and Power, pp. 229–92.

22 Henry Hamilton, *The English Brass and Copper Industries to 1880* (London: Cass, 1967; first published 1926), pp. 70, 17, 76.

23 For example, see Deloney. On declining upward mobility for journeymen see J.U. Nef, *Industry and Government in France and England, 1540–1640* (Philadelphia: American Philosophical Society, 1940), pp. 17–19; Christopher R. Friedrichs, "Capitalism, Mobility, and Class Formation in the Early Modern German City," *Past and Present*, no. 69 (Nov. 1975): 24–49; E.F. Rice, *Foundations of Early Modern Europe*, pp. 48–49; Natalie Z. Davis, *Society and Culture in Early Modern France* (Stanford, Cal.: Stanford University Press, 1975), pp. 4–15. See also Lipsom, *Economic History*, vol. 2, p. 35; Hamilton, p. 71.

24 Walter E. Houghton, Jr., "The History of Trades: Its Relation to Seventeenth Century Thought," in Philip P. Wiener and Aaron Noland, eds., *Roots of Scientific Thought* (New York: Basic Books, 1953), pp. 355–60. Bacon, *Works*, vol. 4, pp. 74–75.

25 Edgar Zilsel, "The Genesis of the Concept of Scientific Progress," in *Roots of Scientific Thought*, pp. 251–55, quotation on p. 275. A.C. Keller, "Zilsel, the Artisans, and the Idea of Progress in the Renaissance," in *Roots of Scientific Thought*, pp. 281–86. Paolo Rossi, *Philosophy, Technology and the Arts in the Early Modern Era* (New York: Harper & Row, 1970), Chap. 1, 2, pp. 1–99. J.B. Bury, *The Idea of Progress* (New York: Dover, 1955). For a criticism of the scholar-craftsman theory and its relation to technological progress, see A. Rupert Hall, "The Scholar and the Craftsman in the Scientific Revolution," in Marshall Clagett, ed., *Critical Problems in*

the History of Science (Madison: University of Wisconsin Press, 1959), pp. 3–23. As cited in Zilsel, Keller, and Rossi, sixteenth-century treatises advocating cooperative sharing of knowledge for human progress included: Master craftsmen: Kaspar Brunner, "Grundlicher Bericht des Buchsengiessens" (1547); *Archive fur die Geschichte der Naturwissenschaften und Technik* 7 (1916), p. 171; Robert Norman, *The*

Humanists and academics: Abraham Ortelius (1527–1598), *Theatrum Orbis Terrarum* (Antwerp, 1570); Francois Rebelais (1490–1553), *Gargantua and Pantagruel* (Paris, 1533), last chapter; Jean Bodin, *Methodus and Facilem Historiarum Cognitionem* (Paris, 1566), Chap. 7; Loys Leroy, *Les Politiques d'Aristotle* (Paris, 1568), argument to Book II. Political theorist J. Schaar has pointed out that the full humanization of life logically implies a human environment filled with humans at the expense of nature.

26 Bacon, "The New Atlantis," *Works*, vol. 3, subsequent quotations on pp. 165, 154, 155. On politics and science in "The New Atlantis," see Joseph Haberer, *Politics and the Community of Science* (New York: Van Nostrand Reinhold, 1969), pp. 46, 47; see M.E. Prior, "Bacon's Man of Science," in L.M. Marsak, ed., pp. 41–53; P. Rossi, *Francis Bacon*, Chap. 1. On critiques of technology, see John McDermott, "Technology: The Opiate of the Intellectuals," *New York Review of Books*, July 31, 1969; Theodore Roszak, *Where the Wasteland Ends* (Garden City, NY: Doubleday, 1963), Chap. 2.

27 Bacon, "The New Atlantis," *Works*, vol. 3, quotations on pp. 157, 158, 159.

28 G. Della Porta, *Natural Magic*, ed. D.J. Price (facsimile of 1658 ed., New York: Basic Books, 1957; first published 1558), pp. 27, 29, 31–40.

29 Bacon, *Works*, vol. 3, quotations on pp. 158, 159. Cf. Della Porta, pp. 59, 61, 62.

30 Bacon, *Works*, vol. 3, p. 158. Cf. Della Porta, pp. 61–62, 73, 74–75, 81, 95–99.

31 Bacon, *Works*, vol. 3, p. 159.

32 Henry Cornelius Agrippa, *The Vanity of Arts and Sciences* (London, 1694; first published 1530), pp. 252–53.

33 Bacon, *Works*, vol. 3, pp. 157, 158.

34 *Ibid.*, p. 156.

Chapter 9

Susan Bordo

SELECTIONS FROM *THE FLIGHT TO OBJECTIVITY*

Author's note

In selecting a piece of my own work for this collection, the simplest thing would have been to reprint "The Cartesian Masculinization of Thought," which originally appeared in *Signs* and has since been reprinted in a number of collections. "The Cartesian Masculinization of Thought" was drawn from *The Flight to Objectivity*, and does focus on the gender dimensions of Cartesianism. I have found, however, that this article – for a variety of reasons – is too frequently misinterpreted as an historical application of Nancy Chodorow's work. I admire Chodorow's work, but, as discussed in the Introduction to this volume, the point of my argument is different from that of Chodorow and other "gender difference" theorists. As I write in the Introduction to *Flight*, "My use of developmental theory focuses, not on gender difference, but on very general categories – individuation, separation anxiety, object permanence – in an attempt to explore their relevance to existential changes brought about by the dissolution of the organic, finite, maternal universe of the Middle Ages and Renaissance" (6–7). In order to avoid perpetuating further misunderstandings of my project, I have chosen to construct a new piece, culled from both the article and other sections of the book, but which puts greater emphasis on the argument that I believed myself to be making in the book. My apologies for any gaps or points that seem to be made too swiftly in the interests of an accurate "précis" of the argument.

On November 10, 1619, Descartes had a series of dreams – bizarre, richly imaginal sequences manifestly full of anxiety and dread. He interpreted these dreams – which most readers would surely regard as nightmares – as revealing to him that mathematics is the key to understanding the universe. Descartes's resolute and disconcertingly positive interpretation has become a standard textbook anecdote, a symbol of the seventeenth-century rationalist project. That project, in the official story told in most philosophy and history texts, describes seventeenth-century culture as Descartes described his dreams: in terms of intellectual beginnings, fresh confidence, and a new belief in the ability of science – armed with the discourses of mathematics and the "new philosophy" – to decipher the language of nature.

Recent scholarship, however, has detected a certain instability, a dark underside, [illegible] dizzying vacillations, the constant requestioning of the self, the determination, if only temporary, to stay within confusion and contradiction, to favor interior movement rather than clarity and resolve.

All that, of course, is ultimately left behind by Descartes, as firmly as his bad dreams (as he tells his correspondent, Elizabeth of Bohemia) were conquered by the vigilance of his reason. The model of knowledge that Descartes bequeathed to modern science, and of which he is often explicitly described as the father, is based on clarity, dispassion, and detachment. Yet the transformation from the imagery of nightmare (the *Meditations'* demons, dreamers, and madmen) to the imagery of objectivity remains unconvincing. The sense of experience conveyed by the first two Meditations – what Karl Stern calls the sense of "reality founded on uncertainty" (1965, 99) – is not quite overcome for the reader by the positivity of the later Meditations. Descartes's critics felt this in his own time. Over and over, the objection is raised: given the power of the first two Meditations, how can you really claim to have extricated yourself from the doubt and from the dream?

Drawing on the work of Margaret Mahler and Jean Piaget, I will undertake a cultural reexamination of Cartesian doubt and of Descartes's seeming triumph over the epistemological insecurity of the first two Meditations. I will suggest that in an important sense the separate self, conscious of itself and of its own distinctness from a world outside it, is born in the Cartesian era. This was a *psychocultural* birth – of "inwardness" of "subjectivity," of locatedness in time and space – generating new anxieties and, ultimately, new strategies for maintaining equilibrium in an utterly changed and alien world. In interpreting those anxieties and strategies, I propose, much can be learned from those theorists for whom the concepts of psychological birth, separation anxiety, and the defenses that may be employed against such anxiety, are central to a picture of human development. Such theories provide an illuminative framework for a fresh reading of the *Meditations*.

I will suggest that we view the "great Cartesian anxiety," although manifestly expressed in epistemological terms, as anxiety over separation from the organic female universe of the Middle Ages and the Renaissance. The Cartesian reconstruction, correspondingly, will be explored as a rebirthing of nature (as machine) and knowledge (as objectivity), a "masculine birth of time," as Francis Bacon called it, in which the more intuitive, empathic, and associational elements were exorcised from science and philosophy. The result was a "supermasculinized" model of knowledge in which detachment, clarity, and transcendence of the body are all key requirements.

Separation and individuation themes in the *Meditations*

The need for God's guarantee, in the *Meditations*, is a need for a principle of continuity and coherence for what is experienced by Descartes as a disastrously fragmented and discontinuous mental life. For Descartes, indeed, discontinuity is the central fact of human experience. Nothing – neither certainty, nor temporal existence itself – endures past the present moment without God. Time – both external and internal – is so fragmented that "in order to secure the continued existence of a thing, no less a cause is required than that needed to produce it at the first" (Haldane and Ross 1969, 1: 56 (hereafter referred to as HR)). This means not only that our continued existence is causally dependent on God (HR 1: 158–59), but that God is required to provide continuity and unity to our inner life as well. That inner life, without God, "is always of the present moment"; two and two may equal four right now, while we are attending to it, but we need God to assure us that two and two will always form four, whether we are attending to it or not. Even the most forcefully experienced insights – save the *cogito* – become open to doubt once the immediacy of the intuition passes:

> For although I am of such a nature that as long as I understand anything very clearly and distinctly, I am naturally impelled to believe it to be true, yet because I am also of such a nature that I cannot have my mind constantly fixed on the same object in order to perceive it clearly, and as I often recollect having formed a past judgement without at the same time properly recollecting the reasons that led me to make it, it may happen meanwhile that other reasons present themselves to me, which would easily cause me to change my opinion, if I were ignorant of the facts of the existence of God, and thus I should have no true and certain knowledge, but only vague and vacillating opinion.
>
> (HR 1: 183–84)

This strong sense of the fragility of human cognitive relations with the object world is closely connected to the new Cartesian sense (which Descartes shared with the culture around him) of what Stephen Toulmin has called "the inwardness of mental life" (1976): the sense of experience as occurring deeply within and bounded by a self. According to many scholars of the era, such a sense was not prominent in the medieval experience of the world:

> When we think causally, we think of consciousness as situated at some point in space . . . even those who achieve the intellectual contortionism of denying that there is such a thing as consciousness, feel that this denial comes from inside their own skins. . . . This was not the background picture before the scientific revolution. The background picture then was of man as a microcosm within the macrocosm. It is clear that he did not feel himself isolated by his skin from the world outside to quite the same extent that we do. He was integrated or mortised into it, each different part of him being united to a different part of it by some invisible thread. In his relation to his environment, the man of the middle ages was rather less like an island, rather more like an embryo.
>
> (Barfield 1965, 78)

During the Renaissance, as Claudio Guillen argues, European culture became "interiorized" (1971). It is in art and literature that the change is most dramatically expressed. For the medievals and the early Renaissance, there is no radical disjunction between the "inner" reality and outward appearance, but rather "a close relation between the movement of the body and movement of the soul" (Baxandall 1972, 60).

inward, I fix it there and keep it busy . . . I look inside myself; I continually observe myself, I take stock in myself, I taste myself . . . I roll about in myself" (1963, 273). "Myself" here is neither the public self, a social or familial identity, nor even the voice of personal conscience, belief, or commitment. It is an experiential "space," deeply interior, and at the same time capable of objectification and examination.

In philosophy, the interiorization of the self is marked by a change from the notion of "mind-as-reason" to the notion of "mind-as-consciousness" (Rorty 1979, 53). For Aristotle, there had been two modes of knowing, corresponding to the two ways that things may be known. On the one hand, there is *sensing*, which is the province of the body, and which is of the particular and material; on the other hand, there is *thought* (or reason), which is of the universal and immaterial. For Descartes, both these modes of knowing become subsumed under the category of *penser*, which embraces perceptions, images, ideas, pains, and volitions alike: "What is a thing which thinks? It is a thing which doubts, understands, [conceives], affirms, denies, wills, refuses, which also imagines and feels" (HR 1: 153). The characteristic that unites all these states is that they are all *conscious* states: "Thought is a word which covers everything that exists in us in such a way that we are immediately conscious of it. Thus all the operations of will, intellect, imagination, and of the senses are thoughts" (HR 2: 52).

"Consciousness" was a new categorical umbrella which was at once to suggest the appropriateness of new imagery and metaphors. Whereas "Reason," for the Greeks and medievals, was a human faculty, resisting metaphors of locatedness, neither "inside" nor "outside" the human being, "consciousness," for Descartes, was the quality of a certain sort of event – the sort of event distinguished from all other events precisely by being located in inner "space" rather than in the external world. The *Meditations*, in both form and content, remains one of the most thoroughgoing and compelling examples we have of exploration of that inner space. Augustine's *Confessions* embody a stream of consciousness, to be sure, but they very rarely confront that stream as an object of exploration. Descartes provides the first real phenomenology of the mind, and one of the central results of that phenomenology is the disclosure of the deep epistemological alienation that attends the sense of mental interiority: the enormous gulf that must separate what is conceived as occurring "in here" from that which, correspondingly, must lie "out there."

Consider, in this connection, the difference between the Greek and medieval view of the nature of error and the Cartesian view. The principal form that error takes, for

Descartes, is in the judgment that the ideas that are in me "are similar or conformable to the things which are outside me" (HR 1: 160). For the Greeks and medievals, such a formulation would have made no sense. Completely absent in their thought is the image of an unreliable, distorting inner faculty; rather, there are two worlds (for Aristotle, it might be more correct to say two aspects of the same world) and two human faculties – intellect and sense – appropriate to each. Error is the result of confusion *between* worlds – the sensible and the unchanging – not the result of inner misrepresentation of external reality. For Descartes, constrastingly, the central inquiry of Meditation 2, and the first formulation of what was to become *the* epistemological question for philosophers until Kant, is "whether any of the objects of which I have ideas *within* me exist *outside of me*" (HR 1: 161, emphasis added). Under such circumstances, *cogito ergo sum* is, indeed, the only emphatic reality, for to be assured of its truth, we require nothing but confrontation with the inner stream itself. Beyond the direct and indubitable "I am," the meditation on the self can lead to no other truths without God to bridge the gulf between the "inner" and the "outer."

The profound Cartesian experience of self as inwardness ("I think, therefore I am") and its corollary – the heightened sense of distance from the "not I" – inspires a deeper consideration of the popular imagery that describes the transition from the Middle Ages to the early modern period through metaphors of birth and infancy. "The world did in her Cradle take a fall," mourned Donne in the *Anatomy of the World* (1611), grieving for a lost world as well as for Elizabeth Drury. Ortega y Gasset describes the "human drama which began in 1400 and ends in 1650" as a "drama of parturition" (1958, 184). Arthur Koestler compares the finite universe to a nursery and, later, to a womb: "Homo sapiens had dwelt in a universe enveloped by divinity as by a womb; now he was being expelled from the womb" (1959, 218). Such imagery may be more appropriate than any of these authors intended. As individuals, according to Margaret Mahler, our true psychological birth comes when we begin to experience our separateness from the mother, when we begin to individuate from her. That process, whose stages are described in detail by Mahler, involves a slowly unfolding reciprocal delineation of self and world (1972). For Mahler (as for Piaget, in describing cognitive development), as subjectivity becomes ever more internally aware, so the object world (via its principal representative, the mother) becomes ever more external and autonomous. Thus, the normal adult experience of "being both fully 'in' and at the same time basically separate from the world out there" is developed from an original state of unity with the mother (Mahler 1972, 333).

This is not easy for the child, for every major step in the direction of individuation revives an "eternal longing" for the "ideal state of self" in which mother and child were one, and recognition of our ever increasing distance from it. "Side by side with the growth of his emotional life, there is a noticeable waning . . . of his [previous] relative obliviousness to the mother's presence. Increased separation anxiety can be observed . . . a seemingly constant concern with the mother's whereabouts" (Mahler 1972, 337). Although we become more or less reconciled to our separateness, the process of individuation and its anxieties "reverberates throughout the life cycle. It is never finished, it can always be reactivated" (33).

I offer these insights not in the service of a "developmental" science of Western history (such as that, for example, that Piaget has proposed). Theories of separation and individuation describe *individual* development on the level of *infant* object relations, and arguable within a particular cultural milieu and a particular form of family life. The categories and developmental schema presented by Mahler cannot simply be transposed into a grand narrative of historical change or evolutionary development. But they *do* offer a way of seeing the Cartesian era empathically, psychologically, and "personally." They enable us to ask whether separation anxiety might not "reverberate," too, on the [illegible] central motifs in the *Meditations*.

Recall, in this connection, Descartes's concern over the inability of the mind to be "constantly fixed on the same object in order to perceive it clearly" (and thus, without God's guarantee, to be assured only of "vague and vacillating opinion"; HR 1: 183–84). The original model of epistemological security (which Descartes knows cannot be fulfilled – thus the need for God) is a constant state of mental vigilance over the object; in the absence of that, nothing can be certain. To put this in more concrete terms: no previously reached conclusions, no past insights, no remembered information can be trusted. Unless the object is present and immediately in sight, it ceases to be available to the knower.

Consider this epistemological instability in connection with Piaget's famous experiments on the development of "permanent object concert" (or objectivity) in children (1954). That development is from an egocentric state, in which the self and world exist on an unbroken continuum and the child does not distinguish between events occurring in the self and events occurring in the world, to one in which the sense of a mutually juxtaposed self and world is distinct, firm, and stable. At first, the developing child does not perceive objects as having enduring stability, "firm in existence though they do not directly affect perception." Instead, the object world is characterized by "continuous annihilations and resurrections," depending upon whether or not the object is within the child's perceptual field. When an object leaves the child's sight, it (effectively) leaves the universe (103).

In a sense, this is Descartes's dilemma, too, and the reason he needs God. Neither the self nor objects are stable, and the lack of stability in the object world is, indeed, experienced as concern over the whereabouts of the world. This is not to say that Descartes saw the world as a child does. He, of course, had "permanent object concert." In speaking of perceiving objects, he is talking not about rudimentary perception but of the intellectual apprehension of the essences of things. The structural similarity between his "doubt by inattention" (as Robert Alexander calls it (1972, 121)) and the developing child's perceptual deficiencies is suggestive, however. At the very least, such similarities open up the imagination to a consideration of the thoroughly *historical* character of our modern structuring of the relation between self and world. They urge us to entertain the notion that the categories that we take for granted as experiential or theoretical "givens" – subjectivity, perspectivity, inwardness, locatedness, and objectivity (all "moments" of the subject/object distinction) – may not be universals, but specific to the history of dominant Western norms of consciousness, each with its own birth, life, and decline.

Without my making any unsupportable claims about how medievals "saw" the world, it seems clear that for the medieval aesthetic and philosophical imagination, the categories of self and world, inner and outer, human and natural were not as rigorously opposed as they came to be during the Cartesian era. The most striking evidence for this comes not only from the organic, holistic imagery of the cosmos and the animistic science that prevailed until the seventeenth century, but from medieval art as well. That art, which seems so distorted and spatially incoherent to a modern viewer, does so precisely because it does not represent the point of view of a detached, discretely located observer confronting a visual field of separate objects. The latter mode of representation – that of the perspective painting – had become the dominant artistic convention by the seventeenth century. In the medieval painting, by contrast, the fiction of the fixed beholder is entirely absent; instead, the spectator, as art historian Samuel Edgerton describes the process, is invited to become "absorbed within the visual world . . . to walk about, experiencing structures, almost tactilely, from many different sides, rather than from a single, overall vantage" (1975, 9). Often, sides of objects that could not possibly be seen at once (from one perceptual point of view) are represented as though the (imagined) movement of the subject in relating to the object – touching it, considering it from all angles – constitutes the object itself. The re-created experience is of the world and self as an unbroken continuum.

Owen Barfield suggests that the reason that perspective was not discovered before the Renaissance was because people did not need it: "Before the scientific revolution the world was more like a garment men wore about them than a stage on which they moved. In such a world the convention of perspective was unnecessary. . . . It was as if the observers were themselves in the picture. Compared with us, they felt themselves and the objects around them and the words that expressed those objects, immersed together in something like a clear lake of – what shall we say? – of 'meaning,' if you choose" (Barfield 1965, 94–95). By extreme contrast, consider Pascal's despair at what seems to him an arbitrary and impersonal "allotment" in the "infinite immensity of spaces of which I know nothing and which know nothing of me. . . . There is no reason for me to be here rather than there, now rather than then. Who put me here?" (Pascal 1966). Pascal's sense of homelessness and abandonment, his apprehension of an almost personal indifference on the part of the universe, is closely connected here to an acute anxiety at the experience of personal boundedness and locatedness, of "me-here-now" (and *only* "here-now"). A similar anxiety, as I have suggested, is at the heart of Descartes's need for a God to sustain both his existence and his inner life from moment to moment, to provide a reassurance of permanence and connection between self and world. Once, such connection had not been in question.

The Cartesian rebirth and reconstruction

> Descartes envisages himself a kind of rebirth. Intellectual salvation comes only to the twice-born.
>
> Harry Frankfurt, *Demons, Dreamers, and Madmen*

If the transition from Middle Ages to Renaissance can be looked on as a kind of protracted birth – from which the human being emerges as a decisively separate entity, no longer continuous with the universe with which it had once shared a soul – so the possibility of objectivity, strikingly, is conceived by Descartes as a kind of rebirth, on one's own terms, this time.

[illegible]

between subject and object. It is this feature of infancy that is responsible for all the "childhood prejudices" that later persist in the form of adult philosophical confusion between primary and secondary qualities, the "preconceptions of the senses," and the dictates of reason. As children, we judged subjectively, determining "that there was more or less reality in each body, according as the impressions made [on our own bodies] were more or less strong." So, we attributed much greater reality to rock than air, believed the stars were actually as small as "tiny lighted candles," and believed that heat and cold were properties of the objects themselves (HR 1: 250). These "prejudices" stay with us, "we quite forget we had accepted them without sufficient examination, admitting them as though they were of perfect truth and certainty"; thus, "it is almost impossible that our judgments should be as pure and solid as they would have been if we had had complete use of our reason since birth and had never been guided except by it" (HR I: 88).

It is crucial to note that it is the lack of differentiation between subject and object, between self and world, that is construed here as the epistemological threat. The medieval sense of relatedness to the world had not depended on such "objectivity" but on continuity between the human and physical realms, on the interpenetrations, through meanings and associations, of self and world. Now, a clear and distinct sense of the boundaries of the self has become the ideal; the lingering of infantile subjectivism has become the impediment to solid judgment.

The precise form of that subjectivism, as we have seen, is the inability to distinguish properly what is happening solely "inside" the subject from what has an external existence. "Swamped" inside the body, one simply didn't have a perspective from which to discriminate, to examine, to judge. In Meditation 1, Descartes re-creates that state of utter entrapment by luring the reader through the continuities between madness, then dreaming – that state each night when each of us loses our adult clarity and detachment – and finally to the possibility that the whole of our existence may be like a dream, a grand illusion so encompassing that there is no conceivable perspective from which to judge its correspondence with reality. This, in essence, is the Evil Demon hypothesis – a specter of complete enclosedness and entrapment within the self. The difference, of course, is that, in childhood, we assumed that what we felt was a measure of external reality; now, as mature Cartesian doubters we reverse that prejudice. We assume nothing. We refuse to let our bodies mystify us: "I shall close my eyes, I shall stop my ears, I shall call away all my senses" (HR 1: 157). We begin afresh.

For Descartes, then, the state of childhood can be revoked, through a deliberate and methodical reversal of all the prejudices acquired within it, and a beginning anew with reason as one's only parent. This is precisely what the *Meditations* attempts to do. The mind is emptied of all that it has been taught. The body of infancy, preoccupied with appetite and sense experience, is transcended. The clear and distinct ideas are released from their obscuring material prison. The end result is a philosophical reconstruction that secures all the boundaries that in childhood (and at the start of the *Meditations*) are so fragile between the "inner" and the "outer," between the subjective and the objective, between self and world.

The Cartesian reconstruction has two interrelated dimensions. On the one hand, the ontological blueprint of the order of *things* is refashioned. The spiritual and the corporeal are now two distinct substances that share no qualities (other than being created), permit of interaction but no merging, and are each defined precisely in opposition to the other. *Res cogitans* is "a thinking and unextended thing"; *res extensa* is "an extended and unthinking thing." This metaphysical reconstruction has important epistemological implications, too. For the mutual exclusion of *res cogitans* and *res extensa* makes possible the conceptualization of complete intellectual independence from the body, *res extensa* of the human being and chief impediment to human objectivity.

Descartes, of course, was not the first philosopher to view the body with disdain. Nor was Descartes the first to view human existence as bifurcated into the realms of the physical and the spiritual, with the physical cast in the role of the alien and impure. For Plato, the body is often described via the imagery of separateness from the self: it is "fastened and glued" to me, "nailed" and "riveted" to me (*Phaedo*, 66c). Images of the body as confinement from which the soul struggles to escape – "prison," "cage" – abound in Plato, as they do in Descartes. For Plato, as for Augustine later, the body is the locus of all that which threatens our attempts at control. It overtakes, it overwhelms, it erupts and disrupts. This situation becomes an incitement to battle the unruly forces of the body. Although less methodically than Descartes, Plato provides instruction on how to gain control over the body, how to achieve intellect, independence from the lure of its illusion, and become impervious to its distractions. A central theme of the *Phaedo*, in fact, is the philosopher's training in developing such independence from the body.

But while dualism runs deep in our traditions, it is only with Descartes that body and mind are *defined* in terms of mutual exclusivity. For Plato (and Aristotle), the living body is permeated with soul, which can only depart the body at death. For Descartes, on the other hand, soul and body become two distinct substances. The body is pure *res extensa* – unconscious, extended stuff, brute materiality. "Every kind of thought which exists in use," he says in the *Passions of the Soul*, "belongs to the soul" (HR 1: 33). The soul, on the other hand, is pure *res cogitans* – mental, incorporeal, without location, *bodyless*: "in its nature entirely independent of body, and not in any way derived from the power of matter" (HR 1: 118). Plato's and Aristotle's view that "soul" is a principle of life is one that Descartes takes great pains to refute in the *Passions of the Soul*. The "life" of the body, he insists, is a matter of purely mechanical functioning: "We may judge that the body of a living man differs from that of a dead man just as does a watch or other automation (i.e., a machine moves of itself), when it is wound up and contains in itself the corporeal principle of those movements for which it is designated along with all that is requisite for its action, from the same watch or other machine when it is broken and when the principle of its movement ceases to act" (HR 1: 333).

While the body is thus likened to a machine, the mind (having been conceptually purified of all material contamination) is defined by precisely and only those qualities that the human being shares with God: freedom, will, consciousness. For Descartes there is no ambiguity or complexity here. The body is excluded from all participation, all connection with God; the soul alone represents the godliness and the goodness

knowledge," Plato unequivocally declares in the *Phaedo* (Plato 1953, 121).

For the Greeks, then, there are definite limits to the human intellect. For Descartes, on the other hand, epistemological hubris knows few bounds. The dream of purity is realizable during one's lifetime. For given the right method, one can transcend the body. This is, of course, what Descartes believed himself to have accomplished in the *Meditations*. Addressing Gassendi as "O flesh!" he describes himself as "a mind so far withdrawn from corporeal things that it does not even know that anyone has existed before it" (HR 2: 214). Such a mind, being without body, would be unaffected by distracting disruption and "commotion" in the heart, blood, and animal spirits. It would see through the deceptiveness of the senses. And it would be above the idiosyncrasies and biases of individual perspective. For the body is the most ubiquitous reminder of how *located* and perspectival our experience and thought are, how bounded in time and space. The Cartesian knower, on the other hand, being without a body, not only has "no need of any place" (HR 1: 101) but actually *is* "no place." He therefore cannot "grasp" the universe – which would demand a place "outside" the whole. But, assured of his own transparency, he can relate with absolute neutrality to the objects he surveys, unfettered by the perspectival nature of embodied vision. He has become, quite literally, "objective."

In the new Cartesian scheme of things, neither bodily response (the sense or the emotional) nor associational thinking, exploring the various personal or spiritual meanings the object has for us, can tell us anything about the object "itself." *It* can only be grasped, as Gillispie puts it, "by measurement rather than sympathy" (1960, 42). It now became inappropriate to speak, as the medievals had done, in anthropocentric terms about nature, which for Descartes is "totally devoid of mind and thought." Also, the values and significances of things in relation to the human realm must be understood as purely a reflection of how we feel about them, having nothing to do with their "objective" qualities. "Thus," says Whitehead, in sardonic criticism of the characteristic scientific philosophy of the seventeenth century, "the poets are entirely mistaken. They should address their lyrics to themselves, and should turn them into odes of self-congratulation. . . . Nature is a dull affair, soundless, scentless, colorless; merely the hurrying of material, endlessly, meaninglessly" (1967b, 54). But this colorless impersonality, for the Cartesian model of knowledge, is the mark of truth. Resistant to human will, immune to every effort of the knower to make it what *he* would have it be rather than what it "is," purified of all "inessential" spiritual associations and connections with the rest of the universe, the clear and distinct idea is both compensation for and conqueror of the cold, new world.

The Cartesian "masculinization" of thought

> If a kind of Cartesian ideal were ever completely fulfilled, i.e., if the whole of nature were only what can be explained in terms of mathematical relationships – then we would look at the world with that fearful sense of alienation, with that utter loss of reality with which a future schizophrenic child looks at his mother. A machine cannot give birth.
>
> Karl Stern, *The Flight from Woman*

The Cartesian reconstruction may also be described in terms of separation from the *maternal* – the immanent realms of earth, nature, the authority of the body – and a compensatory turning toward the *paternal* for legitimization through external regulation, transcendent values, and the authority of law. For the medieval cosmos whose distinction gave birth to the modern sensibility was a *mother*-cosmos, and the soul which Descartes drained from the natural world was a *female* soul. Carolyn Merchant, whose groundbreaking interdisciplinary study, *The Death of Nature*, chronicles the changing imagery of nature in this period, describes the "organic cosmology" that mechanism overthrew: "Minerals and metals ripened in the uterus of the Earth Mother, mines were compared to her vagina, and metallurgy was the human hastening of the living metal in the artificial womb of the furnace. . . . Miners offered propitiation to the deities of the soil, performed ceremonial sacrifices . . . sexual abstinence, fasting, before violating the sacredness of the living earth by sinking a mine" (1980, 4).

The notion of the natural world as *mothered* has sources for the Western tradition in both Plato and Aristotle. In Plato's *Timeaus*, the formless "receptacle" or "nurse" provides the substratum of all determinate materiality. The "receptacle" is likened to a mother because of its receptivity to impression; the father is the "source or spring" – the eternal forms that "enter" and "stir and inform her." The child is the determinate nature that is formed through their union: the *body* of nature (1949, 4). In this account, the earth is not a mother, but is itself a child of the union of "nurse" and forms. The notion that the earth *itself* mothers things, for example, metals and minerals, required the inspiration of the Aristotelian theory of animal reproduction. In that theory, the female provides not only matter as "substratum," but matter as sensible "stuff": the *catamenia*, or menstrual material, which is "worked upon" and shaped by the "effective and active" element, the semen of the male (729a–b).

In the fifteenth and sixteenth centuries, the Aristotelian account of animal generation was "projected" onto the cosmos. A "stock description" of biological generation in nature was the marriage of heaven and earth and the impregnation of the (female) earth by the dew and rain created by the movements of the (masculine) celestial heavens (Merchant 1980, 16). The female element here is *natura naturata*, of course – passive rather than creative nature. But passivity here connotes *receptivity* rather than inertness; only a living, breathing earth can be impregnated. And indeed, for Plato most explicitly, the world *has* a soul – a female soul – which permeates the corporeal body of the universe. In the seventeenth century, as Merchant argues, that female world-soul died – or more precisely, was *murdered* – by the mechanist re-visioning of nature.

The re-visioning of the universe as a *machine* (most often, a clockwork) was not the work of philosophers alone. Astronomy and anatomy had already changed the dominant picture of the movements of the heavens and the processes of the body by

[illegible]

and that apparently played a large and respected role in Hermetic philosophy and, it might be argued, in the pre-scientific orientation toward the world in general. If the key terms in the Cartesian hierarchy of epistemological values are *clarity* and *distinctness* – qualities that mark each object off from the other and from the knower – the key term in this alternative scheme of values might be designated (following Gillispie's contrast here) as *sympathy*. Various writers have endeavored to articulate such a notion. Henri Bergson names it "intellectual sympathy" and argues that the deepest understanding of that which is to be known comes not from analysis of parts but from "placing oneself within" the full being of an object and allowing *it* to speak. "Sympathetic" understanding of the object, according to Karl Stern, is that which understands it through "union" with it (1965, 42), or, as James Hillman describes it, through "merging with" or "marrying" it. To merge with or marry that which is to be known means, for Hillman, to grant personal or intuitive response a positive epistemological value, even (perhaps especially) when such response is contradictory or fragmented (1972, 293).

For sympathetic thinking, the objective and subjective *merge*, participate in the creation of meaning. This does not necessarily mean a rejection, but rather a *re-visioning* of "objectivity." Sympathetic thinking, Marcuse suggests, is the only mode that *truly* respects the object, that is, that allows the variety of its meanings to unfold without coercion or too focused interrogation (Marcuse 1972, 74). More recently Evelyn Fox Keller has offered the conception of "dynamic objectivity":

> Dynamic objectivity is . . . a pursuit of knowledge that makes use of subjective experience . . . in the interests of a more effective objectivity. Premised on continuity, it recognizes difference between self and other as an opportunity for a deeper and more articulated kinship. The struggle to disentangle self from other is itself a source of insight – potentially into the nature of both self and other. It is a principal means for divining what Poincaré calls "hidden harmonies and relations." To this end, the scientist employs a form of attention to the natural world that is like one's ideal attention to the human world: it is a form of love.
>
> (1985, 117)

Various writers, including Keller, have argued that "sympathetic" thinking was a valued mode of knowledge in the pre-Renaissance world. Morris Berman finds such thinking in the "common denominators" of medieval consciousness (whether

Aristotelian or Hermetic) – the doctrines of *resemblance, sympathy, antipathy* – which connect all domains of the universe through a network of shared meanings. More specifically, the alchemical and marginal traditions – the "hermetic wisdom" – are "dedicated to the notion that real knowledge occurred only via the union of subject and object, in a psychic-emotional identification with images rather than a purely intellectual examination of concepts" (1981, 73). In contrast, Cartesian objectivity has as its ideal the rendering *impossible* of any such continuity between subject and object. The scientific mind must be cleansed of all its sympathies toward the objects it tries to understand. It must cultivate absolute *detachment*.

Recognizing the centrality of such ideals to modern science has led writers such as Sandra Harding to characterize modern science in terms of a "super-masculinization of rational thought." Similarly, Karl Stern has said that "[what] we encounter in Cartesian rationalism is the pure masculinization of thought" (1965, 104). The notion that modern science crystallizes masculinist modes of thinking is a theme, too, in the work of James Hillman: "The specific consciousness we call scientific, Western and modern," says Hillman, "is the long sharpened tool of the masculine mind that has discarded parts of its own substance, calling it "Eve," "female," and "inferior" (1972, 250). What these writers have in mind in describing modern science as masculine is *not* the fact that science has been male dominated, or that it has had problematic attitudes toward women. Science has, of course, a long history of discrimination against women, insisting that women cannot measure up to the rigor, persistence, or clarity that science requires. It also has its share of explicitly misogynist doctrine, as do its ancient forefathers, Aristotle and Galen. What Harding, Stern, and Hillman are criticizing, however, are not these features of science, but a dominant *intellectual* style required of men *and* women working in the sciences today. In the words of Evelyn Fox Keller: "The scientific mind is set apart from what is to be known, i.e., from nature, and its autonomy is guaranteed . . . by setting apart its modes of knowing from those in which the dichotomy is threatened. In this process, the characterization of both the scientific mind and its modes of access to knowledge as masculine is indeed significant. Masculine here connotes, as it so often does, autonomy, separation, and distance . . . a radical rejection of any commingling of subject and object" (1985, 79).

The remarkable and provocative notion that knowledge became masculinized at a certain point in our intellectual history suggests that it is misleading to view the history of philosophy as consistently and obsessively devoted to the exclusion or transcendence of those qualities identified as or associated with the feminine. Although men have been the cultural architects of our dominant scientific and philosophic traditions, the structures they have built are not "male" in the same way in all eras and cultures – for what it has meant to *be* male (or scientific) has historically and culturally varied dramatically. The images, language, and principles central to the Hermetic science that mechanism dethroned in the seventeenth century are precisely those traditionally associated with the feminine; moreover, they were attacked as such by the opposition. Medieval philosophy, too, for all its retreat from sexuality, did *not* disparage the body's role in knowledge, nor was it especially impressed with distance and detachment as paths to understanding. Rather, it is precisely because all that was changed by the scientific and intellectual revolutions of the seventeenth century that we can today find meaning in describing those revolutions as effecting some sort of masculinization of thought.

Such notions, moreover, are not unique to contemporary thought. According to Francis Bacon, the new scientific and philosophic culture of the seventeenth century inaugurated "a truly masculine birth of time." Similarly and strikingly, Henry Oldenberg, secretary of the Royal Society, asserted in 1664 that the business of that society was to raise "a masculine philosophy." Keller pays very serious attention to such historical [illegible] what emerges with clarity, despite any subtleties in the attitudes of individual thinkers, is that the notion of science as masculine is hardly a twentieth-century invention or feminist fantasy. The founders of modern science consciously and explicitly proclaimed the masculinity of science as inaugurating a new era. And they associated that masculinity with a clearer, purer, more objective, and more disciplined epistemological relation to the world.

Psychoanalytic theory urges us to examine that which we actively repudiate for the shadow of a loss we mourn. Freud, in *Beyond the Pleasure Principle*, tells the story of an eighteen-month-old boy – an obedient, orderly little boy, as Freud describes him – who, although "greatly attached to his mother," never cried when she left him for a few hours.

> This good little boy, however, had an occasional disturbing habit of taking any small objects he could get hold of and throwing them away from him into a corner, under the bed, and so on, so that hunting for his toys and picking them up was often quite a business. As he did this he gave vent to a loud, long-drawn-out "o-o-o-o" accompanied by an expression of interest and satisfaction. His mother and the writer of the present account were agreed in thinking that this was not a mere interjection but represented the German word "*fort*" ("gone"). I eventually realized that it was a game and that the only use he made of any of his toys was to play "gone" with them. . . . [T]he complete game [was] disappearance and return. . . . The interpretation . . . became obvious. It was related to the child's great cultural achievement, the instinctual renunciation (that is, the renunciation of instinctual satisfaction) which he had made in allowing his mother to go away without protesting. He compensated himself for this, as it were, by himself staging the disappearance and return of the objects within his reach. . . . Throwing away the object so that it was "gone" might satisfy an impulse of the child's, which was suppressed in his actual life, to revenge himself on his mother for going away from him. In that case it would have a defiant meaning: "All right, then, go away! I don't need you, I'm sending you away myself."
>
> (1959, 33–35)

The "fort-da" game and Freud's interpretation of it places the Cartesian facility for transforming anxiety into confidence, loss into mastery, in a striking new perspective.

The Cartesian reconstruction of the world can be seen as a "fort-da" game – a defiant gesture of independence from the female cosmos, a gesture that is at the same time compensation for a profound loss. The sundering of the organic ties between person and nature – originally experienced as epistemological estrangement, as the opening up of a chasm between self and world – is reenacted, *this* time with the human being as the engineer and architect of the separation. Through the Cartesian "rebirth," a new masculine theory of knowledge is delivered, in which detachment from nature acquires a positive epistemological value. A new *world* is reconstructed, too, one in which all generativity and creativity fall to God, the spiritual father, rather than to the female "flesh" of the world.

With the same masterful stroke – the mutual opposition of the spiritual and the corporeal – the formerly female earth becomes inert matter and the objectivity of science is insured. "She" becomes "it" – and "it" can be understood and controlled. Not through sympathy, of course, but by virtue of the very *object*-ivity of the "it." At the same time, the "wound" of separateness is healed through the *denial* that there "was" any union. For the mechanists, unlike Donne, the female world-soul did not die – rather the world is dead. There is nothing to mourn, nothing to lament. Indeed, the "new" epistemological anxiety is evoked, not over loss, but by the "memory" or suggestion of *union*; sympathetic, associational, or bodily response obscures objectivity, feeling for nature muddies the clear lake of the mind. The "otherness" of nature is now what allows it to be known.

References

Alexander, Robert, 1972. "The Problem of Metaphysical Doubt and Its Removal." In R.J. Butler, ed., *Cartesian Studies*, 106–22. New York: Barnes & Noble.

Aristotle. 1941. *Basic Works*. Edited by Richard McKoen. New York: Random House.

Barfield, Owen. 1965. *Saving the Appearances: A Study in Idolatry*. New York: Harcourt Brace Jovanovich.

Baxandall, Michael. 1972. *Painting and Experience in Fifteenth-Century Italy*. Oxford: Oxford University Press.

Berman, Morris. 1981. *The Re-enchantment of the World*. Ithaca: Cornell University Press.

Bernstein, Richard. 1980. "Philosophy in the Conversation of Mankind." *Review of Metaphysics* 33, no. 4: 745–75.

Descartes, René. 1969. *Philosophy Works*. Vols. 1 and 2. Edited by Elizabeth Haldane and G.R.T. Ross. Cambridge: Cambridge University Press.

—— 1976. *Conversations with Burman*. Translated by John Cottingham. Oxford: Clarendon Press.

Easlea, Brian. 1980. *Witch-hunting, Magic, and the New Philosophy*. Atlantic Highlands, NJ: Humanities Press.

Edgerton, Samuel, Jr. 1975. *The Renaissance Rediscovery of Linear Perspective*. New York: Harper and Row.

Farrington, Benjamin. 1951. *Temporis Partus Masculus: An Untranslated Writing of Francis Bacon*. N.p.: Centaurus I.

Frankfurt, Harry. 1970. *Demons, Dreamers, and Madmen*. New York: Bobbs-Merrill.

Freud, Sigmund. 1959. *Beyond the Pleasure Principle*. New York: Bantam.

Furth, Hans. 1969. *Piaget and Knowledge*. Englewood Cliffs, NJ: Prentice-Hall.

Gibson, James J. 1950. *The Perception of the Visual World*. Boston: Houghton Mifflin.
Gillispie, Charles. 1960. *The Edge of Objectivity*. Princeton: Princeton University Press.
Guillen, Claudio. 1971. "On the Concept and Metaphor of Perspective." In *Literature as System*. Princeton: Princeton University Press.
Harries, Karsten. 1973. "Descartes, Perspective, and the Angelic Eye." *Yale French Studies*, [illegible]

[illegible]

Merchant, Carolyn. 1980. *The Death of Nature*. San Francisco: Harper and Row.
Montaigne, Michel de. 1963. *Essays*. Translated and edited by Donald Frame. New York: St. Martin's Press.
Ortega y Gasset, Jose. 1958. *Man and Crisis*. New York: W.W. Norton.
Pascal, Blaise. 1966. *Pensées*. Translated by A.J. Krailsheimer. Hammondsworth, UK: Penguin.
Piaget, Jean. 1954. *The Construction of Reality in the Child*. New York: Random House.
Plato, 1949. *Timeaus*. Translated by Benjamin Jowett. Indianapolis: Bobbs-Merrill.
—— 1953. *Phaedo. The Dialogues of Plato*. Translated by Benjamin Jowett. 4th edition. Rev. Oxford: Clarendon Press.
—— 1957. *Theatetus and Sophist*. Translated by Francis Cornford. New York: Library of Liberal Arts.
Popkin, Richard. 1979. *History of Scepticism from Erasmus to Spinoza*. Berkeley and Los Angeles: University of California Press.
Rorty, Richard. 1979. *Philosophy and the Mirror of Nature*. Princeton: Princeton University Press.
Shakespeare, William. 1946. *Hamlet*. New York: Appleton-Century-Crofts.
Stern, Karl. 1965. *The Flight from Woman*. New York: Noonday.
Toulmin, Stephen. 1976. "The Inwardness of Mental Life." *Critical Inquiry* 6 (Autumn): 1–16.
Whitehead, Alfred North. (1933) 1967a. *Adventures of Ideas*. New York: Collier Macmillan.
—— (1925) 1967b. *Science and the Modern World*. Toronto: Collier Macmillan.

Chapter 10

Evelyn Fox Keller

SECRETS OF GOD, NATURE, AND LIFE

Introduction

One virtually infallible way to apprehend the thickness (or "viscosity") of language and culture is to take a key image employed by a culture in transition and attempt to track its shifting meanings, referents, and evocative force. This indeed was the task that Raymond Williams set himself in compiling his now famous *Keywords* (1983). Almost inevitably, one quickly finds (as Williams himself found) that an entire critical vocabulary is called forth, all of its terms shifting in concert. And as the individual meanings of these words shift and reorient themselves, their collective meaning, the worldview the vocabulary (or "lexicon") represents, is transformed. Tracking such a collection of keywords can thus yield a temporal and cognitive map of a cultural transformation in process.

Take, for instance, the image of "secrets" as it was evoked in sixteenth- and seventeenth-century English discourses of nature, attending in particular to how that image changed over the course of the scientific revolution – how it changed in its usage, in its denotative or connotative force; in its referentiality and its consequentiality. Of these changes, one aspect alone might be said to provide an almost perfect marker of the origins of modern science. I am thinking, of course, of the rhetorical shift in the locus of essential secrets from God to Nature. Over time, the metaphorical import of this shift was momentous; above all, it came to signal a granting of permission to enquiring minds – permission that was a psychologically necessary precursor for the coming Enlightenment. Indeed, Kant's own answer to the question "What is Enlightenment?" was simply this: "*sapere aude*" – to dare to know.

Arcana Dei signaled forbidden knowledge, the hidden affairs or workings of God, "the secret[s] which god hath set Ayein a man mai noght be let" (*OED*: 357) – "hyd to alle men," or at best revealed to only a chosen few. To be allowed to share in God's secrets meant to be enclosed by the same protective veil. The knowledge acquired by those privileged few who *had* gained such access remained similarly (and properly) shrouded in secrecy. Once known, secrets did not become open knowledge in our sense of the term; rather, knowledge itself remained secret. Indeed, knowledge and secrets were at times almost interchangeable terms (see, for example, Eamon 1984).

But between the sixteenth and early eighteenth centuries, the term "secrets"

one of disclosure rather than enclosure. If the idea of *Arcana Dei* invited privileged entrance into a veiled inner sanctum, the expression "secrets of nature" came to be heard as an invitation to dissolving, or to ripping open, the veil of secrecy.

However, in order for the passage of secrets from God to Nature to have such import for the pursuit (and with it, for the definition) of knowledge, many other terms had to shift in concert. Perhaps especially, the terms God and Nature had themselves to undergo subtle transformation as they came to mark a different – simultaneously more distant and more authoritarian – relation between God and the natural world. Once alive and intelligent, participating in (even having) soul, by the beginning of the eighteenth century, Nature had given way to nature: devoid of both intelligence and life. As Carlo Ginzburg has written, "the secrets of Nature are no longer secrets; the intellectual boldness of scientists will put Nature's gifts at our feet" (1976: 41). He might have said as well that Nature, relieved of God's presence, had itself become transformed – newly available to inquiry precisely because it was newly defined as an object.

But still, between availability and compulsion is quite a long way, and in order to understand why the move from God to Nature lent to "secrets" the sense not merely of accessibility, but in addition, of demanding penetration, something else is needed. In particular, it is necessary to add the terms "woman" and "life" to the shifting lexicon,[1] paying special note, as we do, to the rhetorical import of the role of gender in that discursive transformation.

Women, life and nature

Recent literature in feminist theory has called for a critical examination by historians and sociologists of science of the significance of the gender markings that have pervaded virtually all of the discourse of modern science, and that were especially prominent in early writings. In particular, a series of arguments has been put forth for the central role played by the metaphoric equation, first, between woman and nature, and collaterally, between man and mind, in the social construction of modern science, especially in the articulation of new criteria for certain knowledge, and in the demarcation of scientific from other forms of knowledge (see, especially, Merchant 1980; Keller 1985; Harding 1986). From this perspective, it would be tempting indeed to think of the passage of secrets from God to Nature in the sixteenth and seventeenth centuries as a simple re-tagging from male to female – as it were, a sex-change operation on the term "secrets." But such a view is itself a consequence of the reconfiguration that this passage signaled – a reconfiguration in which the meanings of male and female (as well as of God and Nature) were themselves both participants and products. In other words, along with the change of meaning for the terms God and Nature went a simultaneous change of meaning for the terms man and woman. The very construction, "secrets of nature," called forth a metaphoric convergence between women, life and nature that bound these terms together in a new way, and in so doing, contributed to changes in all their meanings. What was new was not the metonymic use of women to stand for life, or even, by extension, as representation of nature; rather, the newness lay in the naming of the conjunction between women, life, and nature as the locus (or refuge) of secrets that *did not belong to God*. It is in this move – in the wedge between Nature and God that was rhetorically inserted by such a shift in reference – that the language of secrets acquired its most radically new implication: not respect for the status of things as they are and must be, but first, permission, then, a challenge, and finally, a moral imperative for change.

Of course, it might be argued, since the affiliation between Woman, Nature, and Life had been established long before the period we are discussing, that it had always served to guarantee a latent antithesis between God and Nature, even before those terms had themselves become officially separate. Indeed, as Gillian Beer has observed, one effect of personifying nature as female is to promote just this separation, to distinguish nature from God (Beer, in Jordanova 1986: 233). But in fact, before naming nature as female could work to properly effect such a distinction, any residual trace of a divine image had itself to be more fully erased from the term "woman." The latent antithesis between God and Nature, or for that matter, between God and female, does not become fully manifest until a wedge has been inserted between both parts of the dyadic construct, woman/nature, and the divine. God cannot stand in antithetical relation to either nature or woman until He is first made to stand apart; antithesis can only work to drive deeper a wedge that is already in place. However, once in place, the tension between male and female then can (and inescapably does) come to work on behalf of a process that ends in radical schism – finally, not only between God and Nature, God and woman, but also between male and female.

It is just this complex process of interlocking separations growing into demarcations that, I am suggesting, is marked, and facilitated, by the naming (or renaming) of "secrets" as belonging to "Nature" rather than to "God." That renaming *could* come to signal the loss of His protection precisely because of the preexisting tension between the terms. Yet it is only with such a renaming that the language of secrets could now be heard as an invitation to exposure, as a call to arms. The net effect of the demarcations that emerged from the new configurations – demarcations between God and Nature, between God and woman, and between woman and man – was to transform the implication of Nature's obscure interiority for enquiring men from an intimation of exclusion to a certainty; banishing forever any possibility of participation; making of that interiority a secret that, once no longer forbidden, must be exposed precisely because it cannot be shared.

It might be said that the cultural function of secrets is always to articulate a boundary – an interior not visible to outsiders, the demarcation of a separate domain, a sphere of autonomous power. Belonging to God, that sphere was inviolable. And as long as the power associated with women, nature, and life was seen as belonging to, or at least blessed by, God, it too was inviolable. The critical move in the transformation of these relations came in the disassociation of these powers from God, and accordingly, in the dissolution of the sanctions an earlier association had guaranteed. Unless severely checked, the power that had been and continued to be associated with women, nature, and life, once disassociated from God, automatically took on an autonomy that seemed

The connections between Reformation theology in seventeenth-century England and the scientific revolution, and the particular notion of "positive sanctions," first argued by Robert Merton in 1938, have in the intervening fifty years become familiar territory to historians of science. Gary Deason (1986) reminds us of one such link that is surely pertinent here. Though more than one hundred and fifty years separated the architects of the scientific revolution from the beginnings of Protestantism, many of their arguments bear a striking resemblance to those of Luther and Calvin before them. For Calvin, as for Luther, to assure God's "radical sovereignty" it was necessary to retrieve the world of animate and inanimate objects from the Aristotelians and Thomists, relieving these objects of their intrinsic activity, and recast as His "instruments." To godly men, "These are . . . nothing but instruments to which God continually imparts as much effectiveness as he wills, and according to his own purpose bends and turns them to either one action or another" (Calvin, quoted in Deason 1986: 176–77). In almost identical language, Robert Boyle argued against the Aristotelian view of a personified nature on the grounds that it "seems to detract from the honour of the great author and governor of the world" (Boyle 1744, 4: 361). To grant activity to nature is to detract from "the profound reverence we owe the divine majesty, since it seems to make the Creator differ too little by far from a created (not to mention an imaginary) Being" (Boyle 1744, 4: 366; in Deason 1986: 180). Moses, Boyle reminds us,

> has not a word of nature: and whereas philosophers presume, that she, by her plastic power and skill, forms plants and animals out of the universal matter, the divine historian ascribes the formation of them to God's immediate fiat.
>
> (1744, 4: 368)

In much the same spirit, Newton may have been even more deeply committed to the belief that homage to God required that matter be seen as brute, passive, in a word, pure inertia – capable only of resistance to force, and not of generating (or causing) it. That even gravity, the force that by his own account derives from "the quantity of solid matter which [particles] contain,"

> should be innate, inherent and essential to Matter . . . is to me so great an Absurdity, that I believe no Man who has in philosophical Matters a competent Faculty of thinking, can ever fall into it.
>
> (in Deason 1986: 183)

For Newton, all motion and all life derived from without, from "active Principles" associated not with material nature, but with God.

> And if it were not for these Principles, the Bodies of the Earth, Planets, Comets, Sun, and all things in them would grow cold and freeze, and become inactive Masses; and all Putrefaction, Generation, Vegetation and Life would cease, and the Planets and Comets would not remain in their Orbs.
>
> (in Deason 1986: 184)

As Deason writes, "the radical sovereignty of God required the animation of nature to come from God alone and not from matter" (p. 183).

Deason's point is well taken. But still missing from his analysis is the work done on and by the marks of gender in the language of God and nature. There are not two terms in the transformation to which Boyle and Newton contribute so importantly, but in fact three, each of which is itself at least dual. Rather than a simple renegotiation between God and nature, seventeenth-century rhetoric aimed at a renegotiation of the relation between sets of cultural entities that could at the time still be treated as relatively coherent dyads: God and father; nature and mother; man and brother. (The last dyad, man and brother, is generally tacit in these texts, appearing only obliquely, if at all.) To see the actually workings of this rhetoric, it is necessary to reread the same texts for the marks of gender. I choose one essay in particular, Boyle's *A Free Inquiry into the Vulgarly Received Notion of Nature*, to illustrate how only a slightly more attentive reading permits us to see much of the complexity of the linguistic and cultural reorientation that Boyle, here as elsewhere, actively sought to effect. Boyle himself was of course only one actor among many in this transformation, and the rhetorical structures of his writing were effective precisely to the extent that they spoke to the readers of his time. My primary purpose in singling out this particular essay, however, is as much to exemplify a method of reading as it is to make an example of a particular method of writing.

Rereading Boyle

Boyle announces both his intention and his strategy in the title itself: one notion of nature, already devalued by the label "vulgar," is to be replaced by another, the result of "free inquiry." The term "free" is used by Boyle throughout his text interchangeably with "bold." His title thus announces the author as one who (anticipating Kant) "dares to know." The object of Boyle's inquiry is clear enough – it is "right ideas" of "nature herself." But before Boyle even identifies the "wrong" or "vulgar" ideas of nature from which he dissents (we learn only along the way that it is the picture of nature as active, potent, and intelligent), he sets out to examine the constraints that bond some men to "vulgar" notions – that is, those commonly (but mistakenly) held scruples that require a special freedom and daring to overcome.

Two such scruples are named in the very first section of his discourse. First, is the compunction of filial obligation, raised only to be cast in immediate a priori doubt:

> [I]t may seem an ingrateful and unfilial thing to dispute against nature, that is taken by mankind for the common parent of us all. But though it be an undutiful thing, to express a want of respect for an acknowledged parent, yet I know not, [illegible]
>
> I might add, that it not being half so evident to me, that what is called nature is my parent, as that all men are my brothers, by being the offspring of God . . . I may justly prefer the doing of them a service, by disabusing them, to the paying of her a ceremonial respect.

But even "setting allegories aside,"

> I have sometimes seriously doubted, whether the vulgar notion of nature has not been both injurious to the glory of God, and a great impediment to the solid and useful discovery of his works.
>
> (Boyle 1744, 4: 361)

Thus Boyle begins his opening argument for transferring veneration from nature to God with a tacit reversal, invoking not paternal but maternal uncertainty, inserting doubt where there had heretofore been none. As in Boyle's other writings, skepticism is employed here as a "rhetorical tool" – invoked to "challenge the authority of a particular discursive tradition" (Golinski 1987: 59).[2] Doubt is, after all, the very stuff of "free inquiry" – so long, that is, as it is not debarred by faith. Assurance that *this* question at least is not so debarred is given promptly: "I know not," he writes, "why it may not be allowable to question . . . whether she be so or no." In other words, Boyle's first task is to create the space for a question, and this he accomplishes by invoking the authority of "free inquiry." But from where does that authority derive? From the very first moment of his text, the authority of "free inquiry" is rooted in the tacit opposition between "free" and "vulgar" that Boyle has inserted in his opening title.

Having thus authorized himself – and his readers – to replace what had commonly been taken to be a certainty by a question, the field is now open for new (or newly invoked) kinds of certification. For this, Boyle looks with one eye to the evidence of his own senses, and, with the other, to biblical authority. Though philosophers may presume of nature "that she, by her plastic power and skill, forms plants and animals out of the universal matter," Boyle reminds us that the Bible tells us differently:

> *God said, let the earth bring forth the living creature after its kind. . . . And God* (without any mention of nature) *made the beast of the earth after his kind.*
>
> (Boyle 1744, 4: 368)

The particular difference Boyle wishes to note is underscored by both the subject of and the actual verb designating creation, and by the gender of the originary parent or model of living beings: From "she," with "her" plastic powers, the biblical quotation shifts, first, to "it," the earth, still retaining sufficient active power to enable it to "bring forth," and finally, to "Him," who "made" the beast of the earth (as it were) after "his" kind.

At the very least, the reader feels obliged to conclude that it is not "half so evident" that nature is not a true parent after all, and accordingly, that the scruple of filial respect does not apply. Instead, a counterscruple – wedding scientific doubt with religious certainty – ought to prevail. Together, the logical doubt that will be revealed by a free inquiry, and the theological certainty that is by definition not open to question, combine to argue for a reorientation of affiliation. Fraternal duty (propelled by free inquiry) and paternal gratitude (guaranteed by faith) are made one: true veneration belongs only to Him who "makes me a man," who, "setting allegories aside," binds all men in a brotherhood dedicated to "the solid and useful discovery of his works."

The second scruple that Boyle attributes to common belief is closely related to the first: it follows from the view of nature as an agent, or "viceregent" of God, and hence as sacrosanct. The identification of this second scruple, a "scruple of conscience," is in fact preceded by just the sort of rhetorical polarization Deason describes:

> I think it more consonant to the respect we owe to divine providence to conceive . . . God [as] a most free, as well as a most wise agent. . . . This, I say, I think to be a notion more respectful to divine providence, than to imagine, as we commonly do, that God has appointed an intelligent and powerful Being, called nature, to be as his viceregent, continually watchful for the good of the universe in general . . . I am the more tender of admitting such a lieutenant to divine providence, as nature is fancied to be, because I shall hereafter give you some instances, in which it seems, that, if there were such a thing, she must be said to act too blindly and impotently, to discharge well the part she is to be trusted with.
>
> (Boyle 1744, 4: 362–63)

Nature is demoted from her position as viceregent, first, in the name of "the respect we owe to divine providence," and second, in the name of a promised (empirical) demonstration. Having thus disparaged the role of nature, any lingering "scruple of conscience" concerning the "removal of [her] boundaries" is automatically undermined:

> To this I add, that the veneration, wherewith men are imbued for what they call nature, has been a discouraging impediment to the empire of man over the inferior creatures of God: for many have not only looked upon it, as an impossible thing to compass, but as something of impious to attempt, the removing of those boundaries, which nature seems to have put and settled among her productions;

> and whilst they look upon her as such a venerable thing, some make a kind of scruple of conscience to endeavor so to emulate any of her works, as to excel them.
>
> (Boyle 1744, 4: 363)

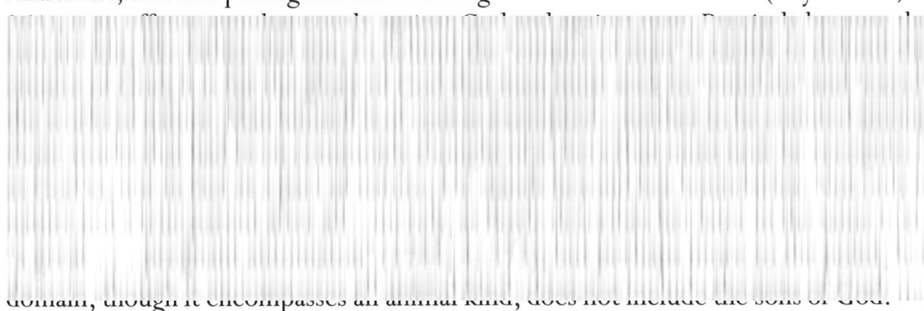

The offense committed in making "a Goddess" of nature, "as if it were a kind of Antichrist, that usurped a great share in the government of the world" (Boyle 1744, 4: [illegible] domain, though it encompasses all animal kind, does not include the sons of God.

> I shall here consider the world [that is, the "corporeal works of God"] but as the great system of things corporeal, as it once really was towards the close of the sixth day of the creation, when God had finished all his material works, but had not yet created man.
>
> (Boyle 1744, 4: 364)

Arriving only on the seventh day, man stands apart, and above – his proximity to God measured by his distance from nature, and proven by his ability to examine "the nature of the spring, that gets all [the parts of "the great automaton"] amoving" (Boyle 1744, 4: 358) – in short, by his capacity to "emulate" and "excel" the workings of her parts. The knowledge thus acquired provides not only proof of (at least some) men's proximity to God, but, as well, to each other. Its function is to cement the brotherhood of man under the fatherhood of God. So conceived, knowledge must be "freely and generously communicated" (Boyle 1655) – not secreted for either personal glory or personal gain.[3]

On the place of woman in this new cosmology, Boyle is virtually silent.[4] But though unspoken, she is doubly figured, and doubly dispossessed: once, explicitly, as the mother who is not, and again, implicitly, as the unnamed wife of the man who is. Truly a spokesman of his time, Boyle leaves her to oscillate ambiguously between deconstructed nature and reconstructed man. And indeed, there she will remain for almost the entire history of modern science, dislocated without a clearly viable relocation in view.

The problem of life

At least part of the reason for the enduring uncertainty in the status of "woman," oscillating between nature and man, can be identified quite readily: it lies in the problem of life, a problem that can be described simultaneously in terms of the science of life and in terms of the language of life – but perhaps especially, as a problem evident in the life of the language of science.

There is indeed a sense in which the workings of language can be said to have a life of their own, yet more complex than the above (already rather convoluted) reading suggests. Especially, it might be said that the metaphor of "secrets of nature" has had a life of its own, with its own built-in mortality. Notice, for example, how, with the reorientation between God and Nature just described, the conjunction between Woman, Nature, and life that was itself so useful a rhetorical resource in the secularization of nature is set on a course that ultimately works toward its own dissolution: once Nature's secrets are penetrated, nature no longer holds that which had marked it with the personalizing "N," that is, as alive; "Nature" can no longer serve as a trope (or prosopopeia) for the world of living creatures. If the metaphoric passage of "secrets" marked a wedge between Nature and God that in turn licensed an all-out crusade on Nature's secrets, the very success of that crusade guaranteed the emergence of a new kind of wedge, now between nature and life. It is this new wedge that leads Richard Westfall (1972) to write in hindsight of the revolution that "banished life from the universe," and that, even before much had happened, had led Henry More to complain to Descartes of "the sharp and cruel blade [with] which in one blow, so to speak, [you] dared to despoil of life and sense practically the whole race of animals, metamorphosing them into marble statues and machines" (Easlea 1983: 23). The life of Man was of course not so despoiled; for Boyle, as for Descartes, man is set apart by his "rational soul" (1744, 4: 364), arriving on the scene only on the seventh day of creation. Indeed, in certain respects, the deanimation of nature seemed merely to enhance man's own sense of animation, an animation now, however, marked more by difference from than by kinship with the rest of the natural world.

Were it the case that the same wedge that had "banished life from the universe" had placed Woman squarely on the side of Man, equally (or similarly) severed from nature, the history of science might have looked quite different. As it was, however, the metaphoric structure of the entire discourse precluded such a turn. That structure propelled the tropic course of scientific language in a rather different direction, a direction that, for the short run at least, left the identification of women with nature ambiguously intact. On the one hand, it was precisely the survival of the metaphoric link between woman and nature that facilitated the reflection of nature's deanimation, desanctification, and mechanization in the social domain; that is, that facilitated the parallel and contemporaneous taming (or "passification") of the image of Woman that has been noted by social historians.[5] On the other hand, it was precisely the survival of women's still mysterious relation to the production of life – especially, of the life that mattered most (that is, our own) – that sustained the identification of women with nature, and that simultaneously provided the irreducible ground of resistance to the final mechanization of nature. As long as the generation of life – human life/all life – remained beyond our grasp, both women and nature would retain some of their/its sense of residual potency.[6] Machines might be powerful, but they are not omnipotent; to imagine them capable of generation, as Descartes did, was to go beyond the bounds of credulity. Fontanelle (d. 1657) put it quite simply in his early retort to Descartes:

> Do you say that Beasts are Machines just as Watches are? Put a Dog Machine and a Bitch Machine side by side, and eventually a third little Machine will be the

> result, whereas two Watches will lie side by side all their lives without ever producing a third Watch.
>
> (from Jacob 1973: 63)

In other words, as long as mechanism failed to provide a plausible solution to the mysteries of genesis and generation, a trace of divine blessing survived; one pocket of secrecy remained sacrosanct.

For a brief while, a radically different solution to the problem of generation enjoyed [illegible] that here, in the twin problems of genesis and generation, where the domains of women, life, nature, and God could not be clearly demarcated, a limit to man's "dare to know" stood firm.

Conclusion

For all the rhetorical persuasiveness and scientific acumen of Bacon, Descartes, Boyle, and Newton; long after Henry Oldenburg's invitation to suitors with "boldness and importunity," who could "penetrate into Nature's antechamber to her inner closet" (from Easlea 1983: 26); long after Halley had sung his praises of Newton's prowess in "penetrating into the abstrusest secrets of Nature"; long even after Alexander Pope's dictum that, after Newton, "All was *Light*," the most vital of nature's laws lay, still, "hid in Night." A full two centuries would follow in which the most "penetrating genius" of human culture would reveal many of the "most mysterious recesses of nature," and yet, even so, it would still have to be granted that the secrets of greatest importance to men remained as they'd begun, as Davenant had written in 1630, "lock'd" in Nature's "cabinet" (*OED*: 357). In the early nineteenth century, Sir Humphry Davy complained that "The skirt only of the veil which conceals these mysterious and sublime processes has been lifted up" (quoted in Easlea 1983: 28). Across the channel, using almost identical language, François Magendie wrote: "Nature has not up to the present permitted man to raise the veil which hides from him the understanding of vital phenomena" (quoted in Mendelson 1965: 216). The same basic observation would be heard, again and again, in England, in France, and in Germany, until well into the second half of the nineteenth century.

As long as the problems of genesis and generation would remain recalcitrant, the ambiguity that continued to animate the metaphoric relation between women, nature, and life would also endure. Indeed, it could be said that it is these mysteries that constitute the very source of the ambiguity. In turn, however, that same ambiguity functioned as a force impinging on the status of "woman" in the larger cultural field, a force that was simultaneously generative and constraining. Above all, it permitted, and even required, an understanding of "woman" that could mediate, at one and the same time, between man and nature, and between animate and inanimate. One might say that it is just this ambiguity that is captured by the enduring trope "secrets of nature" – indeed, that maintains its entire metaphoric structure.

But there is also a dynamic at work within this language that is itself quintessentially dialectical. The survival of the ambiguous relation between women, life, and nature rests on the endurance of an inaccessible domain – on a domain of difference that maintains the life of the metaphor, "secrets of nature." At the same time, however, the tropic structure of this metaphor itself constitutes a relentless pressure aimed at its dissolution. Once resolved, once the secrets of genesis and generation are completely revealed, once nature has become truly lifeless, so too, in that moment, the metaphor of "secrets of nature" will also have died. And because the life of language is always *in* culture, it should come as no surprise that many of the social norms that had served all along to nourish and animate it will also have died.[8]

Perhaps the only surprise is how very long this process would take to work itself out. We might marvel at the longevity of the language that has continued to animate the scientific project even as both that project, and that language, worked to deanimate the sources that provided them with their vital energies.

In retrospect, we might say that those who had "dared to know" had lacked the means to know; that Davy's (or Magendie's) remarks reflected the inadequacy of the instruments (both conceptual and technological) available to seventeenth- and eighteenth-century mechanists for fully penetrating N/nature's ultimate secret, that the force of nature's resistance was too great. But in actuality, these remarks also reflected a human (or cultural) resistance that worked alongside natural resistance to keep this boldest of all crusades beyond the reach of Newton's gaze.

In the late eighteenth and early nineteenth centuries, this human resistance manifested itself in the demarcation of a separate domain of nature for living beings, and with it, a separate domain of science. And for a while at least, the demarcation of "life," and the parallel demarcation of "biology," served to provide living beings with something of a refuge from the incursions of seventeenth- and eighteenth-century mechanism. Eventually, of course, mechanism did prevail. But before this final conquest, indeed, before the "secret of life" could even be named as a fitting quest for natural science, life itself would first have to be relieved of the residual sense of sublimity that had, despite all the efforts of the mechanical philosophers, continued to attach to the nature of animal and plant forms. Secrets would have to make a final passage, from nature to life – a passage that both marked and facilitated the transformation of twentieth-century science and culture, much as the earlier passage, from God to nature, had marked and facilitated the transformations of that period; a passage that was necessary if the ordinary people that scientists are were to condone the rhetoric and the technology required for the dissolution of this last stronghold. When that happened, a new religion would be resurrected: a God neither of "man" nor "woman," but of atoms and molecules. For the one religious reference that Francis Crick is willing to embrace, he quotes Salvador Dali:

> And now the announcement of Watson and Crick about DNA. This is for me the real proof of the existence of God.
>
> (Crick 1966: 1)

I am indebted to the National Endowment for the Humanities for supporting the work for this essay during my stay at the Institute for Advanced Study in 1987–88.

Notes

1 It is T.S. Kuhn who has introduced the term "lexicon" into the history and philosophy of science to denote a "structured vocabulary" of scientific terms (see.

implicit in Boyle's arguments against "the retention of 'secrets and receipts' for commercial gain."

4 Elizabeth Potter makes an interesting argument showing that the absence of women in Boyle's discourse and cosmology is neither natural nor idle, but rather that it actively works to frame man as *the* scientific presence (see Potter 1989).

5 The significance of this transformation for shifting social norms of gender (that is, for actual men and women) is not an explicit subject of this paper, but it is an obviously related question of fundamental importance. A brief discussion, as well as some references to the literature on this subject, can be found in Keller (1985) (cf. especially chapter 3).

6 As well, it might be added, as sexual agency. Consider, for example, that it was only toward the end of the eighteenth century that "medical science and those who relied upon it cease[d] to regard the female orgasm as relevant to generation" (Laqueur 1986: 1).

7 Although, to my knowledge, Boyle himself was not an explicit advocate of such preformationist (or preexistence) theories, and even seems to have vacillated both on the question of preexistence and on the adequacy of purely mechanical accounts of generation (see, for example, Pyle 1987), I think it can be argued that his argument in "A Free Inquiry . . . " did help to set the stage for the preformationist arguments that followed. (For further discussion of seventeenth-century preformationism, see Bowler 1971; Roger 1971; Gasking 1967.)

8 The change in the language of science of the second half of the twentieth century, and the parallel changes in social norms that we witness around us, are of course a subject of their own. Some of the interactions between scientific language, technology and social norms characteristic of our own time will be elaborated in a later essay; here I wish only to call attention to the existence of such interactions.

References

Bowler, P. (1971) Preformation and Pre-Existence in the Seventeenth Century. *J. Hist. Biol.* 4: 221–244.

Boyle, Robert (1655) "An Invitation to a Free and Generous Communication of Secrets and Receipts in Physick." In ed. Samuel Sartlib, *Chymical, Medicinal and Chyrurgical Addresses: Made to Samuel Hartlib Esquire*. London, pp. 113–150.

Boyle, Robert (1744) *The Works of Robert Boyle*, ed. Thomas Birch. London: A. Millar.

Crick, Francis (1966) *Of Molecules and Men*. Seattle: University of Washington Press.

Deason, G. (1986) "Reformation Theology and the Mechanistic Conception of Nature." In ed. D. Lindberg and R. Numbers, *God and Nature*. Berkeley: University of California Press, pp. 167–191.

Eamon, W. (1984) Arcana Disclosed: The Advent of Printing, the Books of Secrets, Tradition and the Development of Experimental Science in the Sixteenth Century. *Hist. Sci*. xxii: 111–150.

Easlea, Brian (1983) *Fathering the Unthinkable: Masculinity, Scientists, and the Nuclear Arms Race*. London: Pluto Press.

Gasking, E. (1967) *Investigations into Generation: 1651–1828*. London: Hutchinson.

Ginzburg, C. (1976) High and Low: The Theme of Forbidden Knowledge in the Sixteenth and Seventeenth Centuries. *Past and Present* 73: 28–41.

Golinski, J.V. (1987) "Robert Boyle: Skepticism and Authority in Seventeenth-century Chemical Discourse." In ed. A.E. Benjamin, G.N. Cantor, J.R.R. Christie, *The Figural and the Literal: Problems of Language in the History of Science and Philosophy*. Manchester: Manchester University Press, pp. 58–82.

Harding, Sandra (1986) *The Science Question in Feminism*. Milton Keynes: Open University Press.

Jacob, François (1973) *The Logic of Life*. New York: Vintage.

Jordanova, L. ed. (1986) *Languages of Nature*. New Brunswick: Rutgers University Press.

Keller, Evelyn Fox (1985) *Reflections on Gender and Science*. New Haven: Yale University Press.

Kuhn, T.S. (1989) "Possible Worlds in the History of Science." In ed. A Sture, *Possible Worlds in Humanities, Arts, and Sciences*. Proceedings of Nobel Symposium 65. Berlin: Walter de Gruyter.

Laqueur, T. (1986) "Organism, Generation and the Politics of Reproductive Biology." In ed. C. Gallagher and T. Laqueur, *The Making of the Modern Body*. Berkeley: University of California Press, pp. 1–41.

Lloyd, G. (1984) *The Man of Reason*. Minneapolis: University of Minnesota Press.

Mendelson, E. (1965) Physical Models and Physiological Concepts. *Brit. J. for Hist. of Sci*. 2(7): 201–218.

Merchant, Carolyn (1980) *The Death of Nature: Women, Biology and the Scientific Revolution*. San Francisco: Harper & Row.

Potter, E. (1989) "Making the Gender Politics in Science." In ed. N. Tuana, *Feminism and Science*. Bloomington: Indiana University Press, pp. 132–146.

Pyle, A.J. (1987) Animal Generation and the Mechanical Philosophy. *Hist. Phil. Life Sci*. 9: 225–254.

Roger, J. (1971) *Les Sciences de la Vie dans la Pensée Française du XVII Siecle*. Paris: Armand Colin.

Westfall, R. (1972) "Newton and the Hermetic Tradition." In ed. A.G. Debus, *Science, Medicine and Man in the Renaissance*. New York: Science History Publications.

Williams, R. (1983) *Keywords*. Oxford: Oxford University Press.

Chapter 11

National Academy of Sciences

Values in science

Scientists bring more than just a toolbox of techniques to their work. Scientists must also make complex decisions about the interpretation of data, about which problems to pursue, and about when to conclude an experiment. They have to decide the best ways to work with others and exchange information. Taken together, these matters of judgment contribute greatly to the craft of science, and the character of a person's individual decisions helps determine that person's scientific style (as well as, on occasion, the impact of that person's work).

Much of the knowledge and skill needed to make good decisions in science is learned through personal experience and interactions with other scientists. But some of this ability is hard to teach or even describe. Many of the intangible influences on scientific discovery – curiosity, intuition, creativity – largely defy rational analysis, yet they are among the tools that scientists bring to their work.

When judgment is recognized as a scientific tool, it is easier to see how science can be influenced by values. Consider, for example, the way people judge between competing hypotheses. In a given area of science, several different explanations may account for the available facts equally well, with each suggesting an alternate route for further research. How do researchers pick among them?

Scientists and philosophers have proposed several criteria by which promising scientific hypotheses can be distinguished from less fruitful ones. Hypotheses should be internally consistent so that they do not generate contradictory conclusions. Their ability to provide accurate experimental predictions, sometimes in areas far removed from the original domain of the hypothesis, is viewed with great favor. With disciplines in which experimentation is less straightforward, such as geology, astronomy, or many of the social sciences, good hypotheses should be able to unify disparate observations. Also highly prized are simplicity and its more refined cousin, elegance.

Other kinds of values also come into play in science. Historians, sociologists, and other students of science have shown that social and personal beliefs – including philosophical, thematic, religious, cultural, political, and economic beliefs – can shape scientific judgment in fundamental ways. For example, Einstein's rejection of quantum mechanics as an irreducible description of nature – summarized in his insistence that "God does not play dice" – seems to have been based largely on an aesthetic conviction that the physical universe could not contain such an inherent component of randomness. The nineteenth-century geologist Charles Lyell, who championed the idea that geological change occurs incrementally rather than catastrophically, may have been influenced as much by his religious views as by his geological observations. He favored the notion of a God who is an unmoved mover and does not intervene in His creation. Such a God, thought Lyell, would produce a world in which the same causes and effects keep cycling eternally, producing a uniform geological history.

Does holding such values harm a person's science? In some cases the answer has to be "yes." The history of science offers a number of episodes in which social or personal beliefs distorted the work of researchers. The field of eugenics used the techniques of science to try to demonstrate the inferiority of certain races. The ideological rejection of Mendelian genetics in the Soviet Union beginning in the 1930s crippled Soviet biology for decades.

Despite such cautionary episodes, it is clear that values cannot – and should not – be separated from science. The desire to do good work is a human value. So is the conviction that standards of honesty and objectivity need to be maintained. The belief that the universe is simple and coherent has led to great advances in science. If researchers did not believe that the world can be described in terms of a relatively small number of fundamental principles, science would amount to no more than organized observation. Religious convictions about the nature of the universe have also led to important scientific insights, as in the case of Lyell discussed above.

The empirical link between scientific knowledge and the physical, biological, and social world constrains the influence of values in science. Researchers are continually testing their theories about the world against observations. If hypotheses do not accord with observations, they will eventually fall from favor (though scientists may hold on to hypotheses even in the face of some conflicting evidence since sometimes it is the evidence rather than the hypothesis that is mistaken).

The social mechanisms of science also help eliminate distorting effects that personal values might have. They subject scientific claims to the process of collective validation, applying different perspectives to the same body of observations and hypotheses.

The challenge for individual scientists is to acknowledge and try to understand the suppositions and beliefs that lie behind their own work so that they can use that self-knowledge to advance their work. Such self-examination can be informed by study in many areas outside of science, including history, philosophy, sociology, literature, art, religion, and ethics. If narrow specialization and a single-minded focus on a single activity keep a researcher from developing the perspective and fine sense of discrimination needed to apply values in science, that person's work can suffer.

Conflicts of interest

Sometimes values conflict. For example, a particular circumstance might compromise – or appear to compromise – professional judgments. Maybe a researcher has a financial interest in a particular company, which might create a bias in scientific decisions affecting the future of that company (as might be the case if a researcher with stock in a company were paid to determine the usefulness of a new device produced by the company). Or a scientist might receive a manuscript or proposal to review that discusses

[illegible]

of parents and students in universities), and public confidence in the integrity of research.

Disclosure of conflicts of interest subjects these concerns to the same social mechanisms that are so effective elsewhere in society. In some cases it may only be necessary for the researcher to inform a journal editor of a potential conflict of interest, leaving it for the editor to decide what action is necessary. In other cases careful monitoring of research activities can allow important research with a potential conflict of interest to go forward while protecting the integrity of the institution and of science. In any of these cases the intent is to involve outside monitors or otherwise create checks to reduce the possibility that bias will enter into science.

Chapter 12

Sharon Begley

THE SCIENCE WARS

Scientists worship at the shrine of objectivity, but even the pious occasionally lapse. A century ago archeologists who discovered the great stone ruins of Zimbabwe went through all sorts of contortions to prove that the magnificent oval palace and other structures were built by the Phoenicians of King Solomon's time – or by anyone other than the ancestors of the Bantus. In the 1960s biologists studying conception described the "whiplashlike motion and strong lurches" of sperm "delivering" genes required to "activate the developmental program of the egg," which "drifted" along passively. The model portrayed sperm as macho adventurers, eggs as coy damsels. And throughout the 1970s and later, ornithologists gathered sheaves of data proving that, in birds, a female's success laying eggs and rearing hatchlings was always enhanced by the presence of a male.

These acolytes of scientific objectivity were spectacularly wrong. The Bantus' ancestors did build the great stone complex. The human egg does play an active role in conception. And in some bird species, particularly the eastern bluebird, the father's presence makes little or no difference to the survival of hatchlings. But why did scientists get it wrong in all three cases, and many others? That question lies at the heart of the "science wars." The combatants are, on the one side, bench scientists who study the biological and physical world and, on the other, sociologists and others who study scientists as if they were exotic Borneo tribesmen. Their battlegrounds are scholarly journals and books where the two sides attack each other. And the issue they're fighting over goes to the heart of the scientific enterprise: is science an objective pursuit?

The critics of science say that the practice of science – the questions it asks, the way it interprets observations, even what counts as data – is subject to the political, cultural and social influences of the times. If society considers females passive, say the critics, then scientists will tend to see the same characteristics in the egg. And if social values mean that an intact nuclear family is best for kids, then most scientists look for, find or give more credence to examples of birds or other species where that holds true. It is not that evil scientists intentionally set out to enshrine the prejudices of the day in their research conclusions. But as mere mortals, they cannot escape their influence. Science, say its critics, is therefore a "social construct," and its discoveries and conclusions have no special claim on truth.

To many scientists, those are fighting words. But they have been slow to react. The early criticism came from academic fields like women's studies and literary criticism that few scientists pay attention to, so they didn't even realize they were under attack in the 1980s. When they finally woke up to the bombardment, they found the criticism [illegible] constructivists' ideas. Now some of the more extreme science-bashers have modified their views: the feminist critic who called Isaac Newton's *Principia* "a rape manual" now regrets her choice of words. Of more than 20 science critics interviewed for this article, every one offered a version of the disclaimer "Science is still the best game in town when it comes to producing knowledge," as philosopher Ann Cudd of the University of Kansas put it.

But a much more important change is also underway. As the extremists on both sides are frozen out, more thoughtful criticisms of science are winning over even some physicists, astronomers and biologists. One of the world's leading journals of science, *Nature*, editorialized recently that scholars who describe science as a social construction should "not be dismissed," since "fashionable ideas" do affect what "becomes accepted as scientific truth." At Princeton University, an informal group of lab scientists and the scholars who study them is meeting once a month to talk about how science can be skewed by ideology and how to make it more objective. They call themselves Reality Check. And last month at a conference on "Science and Its Critics" at the University of Kansas, working scientists presented compelling examples of how science got wrong answers when social and political values influenced the work. Says physicist Kurt Gottfried of Cornell University, who co-authored a paper on the science wars in the current issue of *Nature*, "Cultural and other extraneous factors are more important in the creation of science than most people realize."

Most often, such factors are brought to bear on emotionally or ideologically charged subjects, like sex or race. Countless studies have "proved" the intellectual inferiority of women, blacks or immigrants. But values have also skewed other sciences.

Hubble trouble

What could be more removed from politics than the expansion of the universe? But even this subject, as astrophysicist Keith Ashman of the University of Kansas recounted at the science-wars conference, was distorted by subjective factors, in particular loyalty and careerism. Throughout the 1970s and 1980s, two groups of researchers, one in

Texas and one in California, consistently found wildly different values for the rate at which the universe is expanding, which is called the Hubble constant. Texas got 100, California got 50 (don't worry what the numbers mean). Each group became set in its view of how to measure distances to galaxies and stars, and how to measure the speed of a receding galaxy. (There is no simple or agreed-on formula for either measurement.) Both are used to calculate the Hubble constant. "These were highly technical issues that outsiders had a hard time judging," says Ashman. "So for 20 years the community was far too influenced by the reputation of these people, and that hindered attempts to find a consensus figure for the Hubble constant." Depending on who a cosmologist's friends were and on whom she or he studied under, the scientist aligned with one camp or the other. The few lone voices suggesting that the correct value might lie between 50 and 100 were ignored. The right value, as determined by the orbiting Hubble Space Telescope, is indeed around 75. With more objectivity, astronomers might have learned that sooner, says Ashman.

A monkey's uncle

About 40 years ago, primatologists began studying savanna baboons in the hope that they might shed light on how human ancestors lived. Baboons form some of the most male-dominated troops of any primate. They also form shifting alliances with other males to get better access to females. The males' behavior was seen as the social glue that held the troop together; the females were widely interpreted as being superfluous to the troop's cohesion. Even though another researcher, as early as the 1930s, had studied gibbons and other primates where the males were less aggressive, it was the baboon studies that "became an instant paradigm of how to understand primate behavior as well as a model for human society," says primatologist Hrdy. "It fit people's conceptions of male and female behavior. The baboons were supposedly telling us what our hunter-gatherer ancestors were like," and therefore how modern humans were naturally inclined to behave.

But then the social winds shifted. Primatologists, influenced by feminism, realized that they have to study every individual in a troop – not just the biggest, strongest or most conspicuous – to understand primate society. They began amassing examples of apes where females rather than males select mates, females as well as males maintain social cohesion, and cooperation rather than aggression characterizes the life of the troop. The behavior of animals other than the alpha males was suddenly deemed worthy of study, and researchers corrected their one-sided view of how primate societies work. How had they misstepped in the first place? "In nature, things do not come with labels saying 'This is data'," says Kansas's Cudd. "In deciding what is data – whether it's the baboon pounding his chest or also the female grooming her mother – scientists impose their values. That's what we mean by the social construction of theories."

Scrambled eggs

For decades biologists described sperm as the more active participant in conception. The egg merely drifted and waited; the sperm had "velocity" and "penetrated." But in the mid-1980s biologists measured the force a sperm exerts while swimming. It turned out that sperm are ineffectual swimmers: they flounder around, meander sideways and expend 10 times more power on turning the head of the cell side to side than on moving forward. The sperm was as likely to scoot away from the egg as to reach it. Biologists had hardly considered the possibility that the egg actively grabbed the sperm, but it does. It's not that researchers had no clue that the egg contributes to conception – in 1964 they knew that genetic material in the egg guides the fertilized cell during the hours right after conception. But research indicating an active role for the egg “just got [illegible]

generations and measured how reliably males inherit their father's ornamentation. Their consensus: ornamentation has a “heritability” of 37 percent. (A value of 100 percent means a trait is always inherited, as eye color is; a value of 0 means it never is.) But after 1988, the heritabilities published in science journals suddenly shot up, to an average of 67 percent, finds Rauno Alatalo of the University of Jyvaskyla. What happened? The birds hadn't changed. Fancy tails and other decorations didn't suddenly become more heritable. What did change, says Alatalo, is that a new theory of why females choose the fanciest birds as mates suddenly became fashionable. The new theory holds that ornaments are signs of a male's strength and fitness, qualities he would pass on to his offspring. If this theory is right, the heritability of ornaments would be high. The popularity of the new theory, says Alatalo, skewed the data. He suspects that biologists, enamored of the new theory, were more likely to believe, and publish, findings of high heritabilities.

At one level, the science wars might seem to be an intellectual brawl holding no interest for anyone outside the precious environs of academia. But society is driven by science. The conclusions of researchers answer questions as important to ordinary people as the heritability of alcoholism and the merits of using IQ scores to assign 5-year-olds to “gifted” school programs. Science, in short, matters. It matters if its conclusions are no sturdier than the latest intellectual fashion. If they are not – if the truths of science depend on who's doing the research – then “science forfeits its credibility,” warns archeologist Bruce Trigger of McGill University.

That is already a danger, as shown in the ways lawyers and policymakers use and abuse science. If a senator wants a scientist to testify that lead poses little threat to children's intelligence, he can find one. If a lawyer wants an expert to testify that an endangered species isn't, she can find one. Even worse are cases where the actual science that is done – not what laymen do with the science – is pummeled by politics. That happened to epidemiologist Janet Daling of the Fred Hutchinson Cancer Research Center in Seattle. She was struck by findings that early pregnancy releases hormones that might increase the risk of breast cancer, and late pregnancy changes the breasts in ways that may protect against cancer. Might abortion, then, increase the risk of breast cancer? In 1994 Daling published, in the *Journal of the National Cancer Institute*, a study of 1,806 women indicating that it did. *JNCI* was evidently uncomfortable with this conclusion: it ran an editorial pointing out several ways the study might have erred. In contrast, a study published this January in *The New England Journal of Medicine* found no additional risk of breast cancer after abortion. The editorial about it implied that the question had been resolved forever: "A woman need not worry about the risk of breast cancer" rising after an abortion. It did not point out that this study, no less than Daling's, might have flaws. "I'm not saying I'm sure our studies are right," says Daling. "But let's be objective and not let emotional issues into it."

In some cases, then, values rather than facts inflect research. Nevertheless, science differs from, say, literary criticism, in a crucial way. First, it has built-in mechanisms to catch and correct the results of human foibles. After all, researchers did finally recognize that molecules in the egg actively participate in conception, and that baboons are probably not the only model for the behavior of human ancestors. "So yes, scientists are influenced by factors we shouldn't be," says Kansas astrophysicist Ashman. "But despite all this, we are still measuring something real, something that is not a social construct, and with better data the scientific method allowed us to converge on the right answer." Or, as McGill's Trigger puts it, "the constraints of the data are what make the difference between writing a novel about the past and doing archeology." The real trick, for scientists and for those who base public policy on their work, is to tell when the research is still being skewed by social and political values, and when those biases have been recognized and neutralized by the scientific method. That's a war worth fighting.

SECTION THREE

Analyzing Gendered Science

IN SECTION TWO, WE PRESENTED essays that compared the relationship between humans and Nature before and after the Scientific Revolution. In this comparison, feminist scholars show how both the perception of Nature and the new methods for investigating it came to be gendered during this change in worldview. Since the science established at the time of the Scientific Revolution has been carried on and functions essentially unchanged today, feminists analyze the epistemology of current science – how the way we claim to know the natural world through science can be explicated and justified.

Some of science's androcentric hallmarks are objectivity, alienated knowing, experimentation, and the resulting gendered practice, examples of which are given in Section Four. Feminists have many objections to this masculinist method for investigating Nature; developing an alternative has been a central concern for at least two decades. The materials in this section question the central claim of Western science, that it is an objective, value-free methodology for finding "truth" about the natural world.

Sue Rosser's "Are There Feminist Methodologies Appropriate for the Natural Sciences and Do They Make a Difference?" gives a clear and concise summary of the positions held by the main schools of feminist criticism of scientific epistemology. It is clear that, like most other human endeavors, feminist epistemology is not monolithic. Some schools (liberal and psychoanalytic feminism) would assimilate women (and men) into a "gender-free" science. Such a methodology is appealing to many. It would obviate the problems of masculine science without replacing it with a "feminine" science. "Feminine" science is an anathema to some women, who love science and have struggled to overcome social barriers and be successful at its practice. They fear that such a science would be derided, they would automatically be associated with it based on their sex, and their work completely denied.

The essentialist school uses women's biology as a foundation for developing feminist methodologies for the sciences. Many object to this basis since women's bodies have for so long been degraded (Section Five). The Marxist strain brought social location into the analysis by raising the question "Who controls the means of production?" of science. Rosser concludes that "As long as oppression of women and patriarchy continue, it is unlikely that the effects of feminist methodologies derived from the feminist theories that present some challenge to the status quo will be felt."

In Western society, Nature, women and the female remain subjugated, devalued objects identified as Other. One of the threads of the feminist epistemology is to revalue this otherness, literally to resurrect it and give it meaning as a vantage point from which to look at science. The claim is made that looking at Nature from the standpoint of woman can give a unique perspective, an enhanced vision, a different viewpoint; these words are found constantly in feminist arguments.

In the excerpt from *Whose Science, Whose Knowledge: Thinking from Women's Lives*, Sandra Harding characterizes a feminist standpoint by identifying those areas of women's lives that characterize "otherness," and shows how these can be a resource instead of a disadvantage. She then critiques objectivity (objectivism) from this standpoint and suggests the implementation of "strong objectivity," "extending the notion of scientific research to include systematic examination of . . . background beliefs," including those that devalue contributions to science from groups other than those privileged to have practiced it for centuries.

One of the difficulties with a standpoint is how to justify one particular view in contrast to others. Leaving aside the notion that gendered science is itself an unacknowledged standpoint, feminist scholars are extremely sensitive to this point, as they take into account not only gender but race and class in their analyses. Is there a unique feminist standpoint or are there multiple standpoints that count as feminist? If an alternative *feminist* story about Nature has credence, does that mean that *all* alternative stories about nature have equal value? Persons of good will who are receptive to feminist critiques of science, balk at the notion of relativism, validating all stories about nature, and feel, as an abstract principle, that allowing feminist standpoints starts down the slippery slope of authenticating what Longino calls "crackpot" science (p. 223).

Donna Haraway's "Situated Knowledges: The Science Question in Feminism and the Privilege of Partial Perspective" addresses these questions. Haraway, together with the other authors whose work is included in this section, is one of the foremost American writers in feminist science studies. This rich selection is one of the earliest in which her distinctive vision and especially her unique "voice" appear. The content echoes the title – there is more than one perspective by which to interpret her theses. Several themes are present: a means to a faithful account of the natural world that is socially egalitarian; the rejection of disembodied views of Nature and of relativism, since both exclude responsibility for the consequences of those views (the god trick); the embodiment of vision, but an embodiment that recognizes multiple bodies and multiple perspectives, that must recognize, relate, and revalue each other to transform science.

The second selection by Harding ("Is Science Multicultural? Challenges, Resources, Opportunities, Uncertainties") suggests that even though science today is primarily white and Western, post-colonial science studies reveal that other cultures have made significant contributions to its development, even if these contributions are unrecognized (and unrecognizable under the current paradigm). By recognizing that "what counts as an 'aspect of nature's regularities' in daily life is itself shaped by . . . cultures and subcultures located in different environments" (Harding, 1997, p. 191), the feminist objectivity debate can be broadened to include the concerns of more than white, Western women. It is not only gender or race or social location, but physical situation and local culture, that defines how Nature is interpreted. [illegible] and Harding and suggests a practical way to eliminate the inherent power disparity between the predominant practitioners of science and the marginal others. She suggests developing communities that recognize the value of partial perspectives, that acknowledge that science is modeling the natural world and that models come from various locations, any of which can provide insights into Nature's workings. This community would develop standards for epistemic adequacy that represent all interested parties.

In some respects, the arguments about objectivity may be moot. Lukacs proposes ten ways, derived from the work of physicist Werner Heisenberg, by which the bases of Western science (objectivity, the universality of mechanistic laws) may be an untenable position. Heisenberg is a Nobel laureate who discovered the "uncertainty principle," that it is impossible to know simultaneously the position and momentum of an electron. If certainty is lacking at the level of subatomic particles in the field that claims to offer the most certainty in describing the natural world, then gendered claims to certainty in all aspects of science must be seriously questioned.

References

Harding, Sandra (1997) "Women's Standpoints on Nature: What Makes Them Possible?" *Osiris* 12: 186–200.

Suggested readings

Cartwright, Nancy (1983) *How the Laws of Physics Lie*. Oxford: Clarendon Press.

Cartwright, Nancy (1989) *Nature's Capacities and their Measurement*. Oxford: Clarendon Press.

Gilligan, Carol (1982) *In a Different Voice*. Cambridge and London: Harvard University Press.

Goldberger, Nancy, Tarule, Jill, Clinchy, Blythe, and Belenky, Mary (1996) *Knowedge, Difference, and Power: Essays Inspired by Women's Ways of Knowing*. New York: Basic Books.

Hacking, Ian (1983) *Representing and Intervening*. Cambridge: Cambridge University Press.

Harding, Sandra (1986) *The Science Question in Feminism*. Milton Keynes: Open University Press.

Harding, Sandra (1991) *Whose Science? Whose Knowledge?* Ithaca: Cornell University Press.

Harding, Sandra and Hintikka, Merrill (eds) (1983) Discovering *Reality: Feminist Perspectives on Epistemology, Metaphysics, Methodology, and Philosophy of Science*. Dordrecht: Reidel.

Heckman, Susan (1997) "Truth and Method: Feminist Standpoint Theory Revisited." *Signs: Journal of Women in Culture and Society* 22: 341–365.

Henrion, Claudia (1997) *Women in Mathematics: The Addition of Difference*. Bloomington and Indianapolis: Indiana University Press.

Hesse, Mary (1996) *Models and Analogies in Science*. Notre Dame, IN: Notre Dame Press.

Keller, Evelyn Fox (1983) *A Feeling for the Organism: The Life and Work of Barbara McClintock*. San Francisco: W.H. Freeman.

McCaughey, Martha (1993) "Redirecting Feminist Critiques of Science." *Hypatia* 8: 72–84.

Needham, Joseph (1969) *The Grand Titration: Science and Society in East and West*. Toronto: University of Toronto Press.

Rose, Hilary (1983) "Hand, Brain and Heart: Towards a Feminist epistemology for the Natural Sciences." *Signs: Journal of Women in Culture and Society* 9: 73–96.

Chapter 13

Sue V. Rosser

MAKE A DIFFERENCE?

Synopsis

Examination of the questions raised about feminist methodologies for the natural sciences reveals that answers are complex and dependent upon the feminist theory from which the methodology springs. The jumble of descriptors for feminist methodology – rejects dualisms, is based on women's experience, shortens the distance between observer and object of study, rejects unicausal, hierarchical approaches, unites application with problem – seems contradictory when portrayed as feminist methodology. They become much more understandable when viewed as a lumping together of possible methodological implications for science resulting from different feminist theories. Radical feminism, and particularly lesbian separatism, suggest strong reasons why we are not able to see the results of a feminist methodology. As long as oppression of women and patriarchy continue, it is unlikely that the effects of feminist methodologies derived from the feminist theories that challenge the status quo will be felt.

The debates surrounding feminist methodology (Alcoff, 1989; Christ, 1987; Harding, 1987; MacKinnon, 1987) constitute a major focus for discussion in many of the disciplines, such as anthropology, literature, history, and psychology, in which the feminist critique has had a profound impact upon the knowledge base and theoretical framework of the field. In Women's Studies the debates serve as yet another issue that crosses disciplinary lines and demonstrates the strengths and uniqueness of this interdisciplinary field.

These debates raise basic and fundamental questions for all disciplines: is there a feminist methodology or methodologies? If there are, what are they and how do they differ from other non-mainstream or non-positivist methodologies? What kinds of new and different questions might be explored using feminist methodologies that haven't been explored with previous methodologies? How would results of research done with feminist methodologies look compared to results obtained using more traditional methodologies?

For the sciences, the debates reveal the significant diversity among the disciplines and the values and status accorded by most of Western society to results from the traditional methodologies. Researchers in the social sciences have been the individuals most actively challenging the traditional methods by feminist critiques and development of feminist methodologies. In the early 1970s women social scientists began to recognize that women were often excluded as subjects and that androcentric experimental designs sought to uncover data to answer questions of importance to men based on male experience. Sociologists (Bart, 1971; Oakley, 1981; Roberts, 1981), psychologists (Chodorow, 1974; Wallston, 1981; Weisstein, 1971), and anthropologists (Collier and Rosaldo, 1981; Leacock, 1981; Linton, 1974; Ortner, 1974) began to evolve methodologies that centered on women's experience and that might answer questions of interest to women.

In the physical sciences, virtually no attempts have been made to explore feminist methodologies. In fact, very few feminist critiques of the traditional methodologies exist; the two or three existing critiques take a historical approach. Griffin (1978) and Merchant (1979) explore the historical roots of twentieth-century mechanistic science, which becomes the rational, objective approach to problem solving that men use to dominate both women and nature. Keller (1985), in her work on Bacon, also examines the extent to which the scientific method becomes an androcentric approach to the world which might be used not only to dominate women but to exclude women and women's experience. To my knowledge Keller (1985) is the only one who has begun to extend the critique to an examination of the influence on the methodologies in physics in her essay "Cognitive Repression in Contemporary Physics."

That virtually no further explorations of feminist methodologies in the physical sciences exist is not surprising given the dearth of women physical scientists – in the United States 14.9% employed in 1988 (National Science Foundation, 1990) and 16.8% receiving Ph.D.s. The status of the physical sciences and the scientific method as a paradigm of the objective approach to problem solving in our current society provide other barriers to the evolution of feminist methodologies in the physical sciences.

The natural sciences, and biology in particular, represent a field in which women form a growing segment of the scientists – in the United States 36.56% of the Ph.D.s in 1988 and 29.79% of employed biologists in 1988 (National Science Foundation, 1990). Despite their lower wages, documented discrimination that prevents advancement (National Science Foundation, 1990), and the overwhelming pressure they face to adopt mainstream theories, approaches, and practices in order to achieve success, a considerable volume of feminist critique has been produced by courageous feminist biologists (Birke, 1986; Bleier, 1984; Fausto-Sterling, 1985; Hubbard, 1990; Rosser, 1990) and philosophers of science (Fee, 1982; Haraway, 1990; Harding, 1986). Building upon these critiques, some feminists in science (Birke, 1986; Keller, 1985; Rosser, 1990) and philosophy (Haraway, 1990; Harding, 1987) have begun to raise the interesting parameters that the question of feminist methodologies in biology might reveal: are the critiques raised by feminists simply examples of bad science? Is good science gender-free? Would feminist methodologies lead to better practice of the scientific method or do they imply that the scientific method as we know it is inadequate or unacceptable? What are these feminist methodologies? If they exist, would these feminist methodologies result in major differences in the types of problems that might be solved or just minor variations in the types of problems currently explored in science? Could men develop and use feminist methodologies? What might be the practical results or applications of feminist methodologies?

method is really a methodology to read a more lengthy, complex discussion of each term. The brief definitions I will give here are based on the work of Harding (1987). An *epistemology* is a theory of knowledge which considers what kinds of things can be known, who can be a knower, and how (through what tests) beliefs are legitimated as knowledge. The epistemology associated with traditional biology suggests that the physiological, chemical, and anatomical characteristics of living beings can be known by observers trained as scientists who test their observations by validation through the scientific method. Feminist critiques of the epistemology of biology (Fee, 1981, 1982, 1983; Harding, 1986; Keller, 1985, 1987) have suggested that its theory of knowledge constitutes a masculine view of the world. To be trained to be a scientist is to be trained to observe the characteristics of living beings of interest to men in an objective, distant, autonomous fashion that resonates with an androcentric perspective on the world.

Methods are techniques for gathering evidence or data. Most biological methods fall under the broad category of observation, including observation of animals, plants, and chemical behavior either directly or indirectly on the organic, structural, and microscopic level. Some biological methods involve examining historical traces and records, particularly in the study of paleontology and evolution. Although feminists use these same methods, what they choose to observe and examine may differ quite markedly from the choices of a traditional scientist with a masculine world view. For example, female primatologists (Fedigan, 1982; Hrdy, 1979, 1981, 1986; Lancaster, 1975; Small, 1984) discovered many new insights regarding primate social behavior simply by observing female–female primate interaction. Because of their masculine world view, male primatologists had virtually ignored female–female lower primate interactions. Presumably this oversight came from the fact that as human males they had experienced male–male and male–female interactions. Since their own identity as a male precluded their *experiencing* female–female interactions, their masculine world view led them to fail to *observe* female–female interaction in other primate species.

Methodology constitutes a theory and analysis of how research proceeds or should proceed; it examines how "the general structure of theory finds its application in particular scientific disciplines" (Caws, 1967, p. 339). The discussion of the scientific method, using the example of the number of legs an insect has for illustration, given in most introductory biology texts, provides an example of methodology. Application of the scientific method to explore problems such as the length of exposure to video display terminals (VDTs) that cause possible cluster miscarriages or birth defects are examples that shift the focus from problems traditionally explored to women's experience and concerns.

Epistemology, methods, and methodology are related concepts and are usually connected during the process of research. As Harding states: "Epistemological issues certainly have crucial implications for how general theoretical structures can and should be applied in particular disciplines and for the choice of methods of research" (1987, p. 3). However, in talking about feminist methodology in biology I will attempt to describe how research does or should proceed when feminist theory and analysis are applied to the discipline of biology.

Feminist theories

Individuals unfamiliar with feminism or Women's Studies often assume that feminist theory provides a singular and unified framework for analysis. In one sense this is correct; all feminist theory posits gender as a significant characteristic that interacts with other characteristics, such as race and class, to structure relationships between individuals, within groups, and within society as a whole. However, using the lens of gender to view the world results in diverse images or theories: liberal feminism, Marxist feminism, socialist feminism, African-American feminism, lesbian separatist feminism, conservative or essentialist feminism, existential feminism, psychoanalytic feminism, and radical feminism. The variety and complexity of these various feminist theories provide a framework through which to explore interesting methodology issues raised in biology.

Liberal feminism

Beginning in the eighteenth century, political scientists, philosophers, and feminists (Wollstonecraft, 1975; Mill (John Stuart), 1970; Mill (Harriet Taylor), 1970; Friedan, 1974; Jaggar, 1983) have described the parameters of liberal feminism. The differences between nineteenth-century and twentieth-century liberal feminists have varied from libertarian to egalitarian, and numerous complexities exist among definitions of liberal feminists today. However, a general definition of liberal feminism is the belief that women are suppressed in contemporary society because they suffer unjust discrimination (Jaggar, 1983). Liberal feminists seek no special privileges for women and simply demand that everyone receive equal consideration without discrimination on the basis of sex.

Most scientists would assume that the implications of liberal feminism for biology and other disciplines within the sciences are that scientists should work to remove the documented overt and covert barriers (National Science Foundation, 1990; Rosser, 1990; Rossiter, 1984; Vetter, 1988) that have prevented women from entering and succeeding in science. Although they might hold individual opinions as to whether or not women deserve equal pay for equal work, access to research resources, and equal opportunities for advancement, most scientists, even those who are brave enough to call themselves feminists, assume that the implications of liberal feminism extend only to employment, access, and discrimination issues.

In fact, the implications of liberal feminism extend beyond this. Liberal feminism shares two fundamental assumptions with the foundations of the traditional method for scientific discovery: (1) Both assume that human beings are highly individualistic and obtain knowledge in a rational manner that may be separated from their social conditions; and (2) Both accept positivism as the theory of knowledge. Positivism [illegible] interests, and emotions. Objectivity is thus contingent upon value neutrality or freedom from values, interests, and emotions associated with a particular class, race, or sex.

Although each scientist strives to be as objective and value-free as possible, most scientists, feminists, and philosophers of science recognize that no individual can be neutral or value-free. Instead, "objectivity is defined to mean independence from the value judgments of any particular individual" (Jaggar, 1983, p. 357).

In the past two decades feminist historians and philosophers of science (Fee, 1982; Haraway, 1990; Harding, 1986) and feminist scientists (Birke, 1986; Bleier, 1984, 1986; Fausto-Sterling, 1985; Keller, 1983, 1985; Rosser, 1988; Spanier, 1982) have pointed out a source of bias and absence of value neutrality in science, particularly biology. By excluding females as experimental subjects, focusing on problems of primary interest to males, faulty experimental designs, and interpretations of data based in language or ideas constricted by patriarchal parameters, experimental results in several areas in biology have been demonstrated to be biased or flawed. Feminist critiques (Keller, 1985; Harding, 1986) suggest that these flaws and biases were permitted to become part of the mainstream of scientific thought and were perpetuated in the scientific literature for decades, in some cases (Sayers, 1982) for more than a century, because virtually all of the individuals who were scientists were men. Since most or all scientists were male, values held by most males were not distinguishable as biasing; they became synonymous with the "objective" view of the world.

Three examples from within three different areas in biology illustrate the flawed research resulting from male bias in the discipline:

Animal behavior

Some researchers have observed behavior in lower animals in a search for "universal" behavior patterns that occur in males of all species or in all males of a particular order or class, such as primates or mammals. This behavior is than extrapolated to humans in an attempt to demonstrate a biological or innate basis for the behavior. Sociobiologists such as Barash (1977), Dawkins (1976), and Wilson (1975) have based their new discipline on biological determinism in stating that behavior is genetically determined and that differences between males and females in role, status, and performance are biologically based.

Feminist critiques of sociobiology have centered around criticisms of the assumption that behaviors such as aggression, homosexuality, promiscuity, selfishness, and altruism are biologically determined. Critiques also underline problems involved with anthropomorphosis in animal behavior studies. The anthropomorphosis occurs in at least two forms: (a) the use of human language and frameworks to describe animal behavior which is then used to "prove" that certain human behaviors are innate since they are also found in animals; and (b) the selective choice of species for study that mirror human society. The data from those selected species is then assumed to be the universal behavior of all species. Some scientists have suggested that these feminist critiques are obvious. However, the most renowned sociobiologists (Dawkins, 1976; Trivers, 1972; Wilson, 1978) have continued to assume that genes do determine behavior and that the behaviors described as aggression, homosexuality, rape, selfishness, and altruism in animals are equivalent to those behaviors in humans, even though more than one decade of criticism by feminists (Birke, 1986; Bleier, 1976; Fausto-Sterling, 1985; Hubbard and Lowe, 1979; Lowe, 1978) has been leveled against the "obvious" flaws in the sociobiological theories and assumptions.

Primatology

Similarly, although it was clear in the early primatology work (Yerkes, 1943) that particular primate species, such as the baboon and chimpanzee, were chosen for study primarily because their social organization was seen by the observers as closely resembling that of human primates, subsequent researchers forgot the "obvious" limitations imposed by such selection of species and proceeded to generalize the data to universal behavior patterns for all primates. It was not until a significant number of women entered primatology that concepts of the universality and male leadership of dominance hierarchies among primates (Lancaster, 1975; Leavitt, 1975; Leibowitz, 1975; Rowell, 1974) were questioned and shown to be inaccurate for many primate species. The "evident" problems discussed by feminist critics (Bleier, 1984) of studying non-human primates in an attempt to discover what the true nature of humans would be without the overlay of culture have also been largely ignored by many of the sociobiologists and scientists studying animal behavior.

Neurosciences

In the neurosciences, a substantial amount of work has been done relating to sex differences in the brains of men and women. The studies on brain lateralization, genes, brain structure, and effects of prenatal and postpubertal androgens and estrogens on the nervous system have been carried out in an attempt to discern biological bases for differences between males and females in behavioral or performance characteristics, such as aggression, or verbal, visuospatial, and mathematical ability. Excellent critiques have been made by feminists of the faulty experimental designs and unfounded extrapolations beyond the data of the work in brain lateralization (Star, 1979), hormones (Bleier, 1984), genes (Fennema and Sherman, 1977), and brain structure (Bleier, 1986). Although most scientists accept the validity of the critiques, reputable scientific journals (see Bleier, 1988, for an account of her encounters with *Science* over this matter), textbooks, and the popular press continue to publish studies biased by similar methodological inconsistencies, extrapolations in data from one species to another and over-generalizations of data.

These examples of flawed research and other examples resulting from the critiques of feminists have raised fundamental questions regarding gender and good science: do these examples simply represent "bad science"? Is good science really gender-free or [illegible]

1 It does not question the integrity of the scientific method itself or of its supporting corollaries of objectivity and value neutrality. Liberal feminism reaffirms the idea that it is possible to find a perspective from which to observe that is truly impartial, rational, and detached. Lack of objectivity and presence of bias occur because of human failure to properly follow the scientific method and avoid bias due to situation or condition. Liberal feminists argue that it was through attempts to become more value-neutral that the possible androcentrism in previous scientific research has been revealed.
2 Liberal feminism also implies that good scientific research is not conducted differently by men and women and that in principle men can be just as good feminists as women. Now that feminist critiques have revealed flaws in research due to gender bias, both men and women will use this revelation to design experiments, gather and interpret data, and draw conclusions and theories that are more objective and free from bias, including gender bias (Biology and Gender Study Group, 1989).

In contrast to liberal feminism, all other feminist theories call into question the fundamental assumptions underlying the scientific method, its corollaries of objectivity and value neutrality, or its implications. They reject individualism for a social construction of knowledge and question positivism and the possibility of objectivity obtained by value neutrality. Many also imply that men and women may conduct scientific research differently, although each theory posits a different cause for the gender distinction. Just as examination of liberal feminism uncovered interesting information about methodology in biology, exploration of other feminist theories reveals fruitful points.

Marxist-feminism

Marxist-feminism serves as the clearest example of a feminist theory that contrasts with liberal feminism in its rejection of individualism and positivism as approaches to knowledge. Marxist critiques of science, the historical precursors and foundation for Marxist-feminist critiques, view all knowledge as socially constructed and emerging from practical human involvement in production that takes a definite historic form. According to Marxism, knowledge, including scientific knowledge, cannot be solely individualistic. Since knowledge is a productive activity of human beings, it cannot be objective and value-free because the basic categories of knowledge are shaped by human purposes and values. Marxism proposes that the form of knowledge is determined by the prevailing mode of production. In the twentieth-century United States, according to Marxism, scientific knowledge would be determined by capitalism and reflect the interests of the dominant class. In strict Marxist-feminism, where class is emphasized over gender, only bourgeois (liberal) feminism or proletarian feminism can exist. A bourgeois woman scientist would be expected to produce scientific knowledge that would be the same as that produced by a bourgeois man scientist but which would be different from that produced by a proletarian woman scientist.

Although feminists have critiqued Marxism for decades (Flax, 1981; Foreman, 1977; Goldman, 1931; Vogel, 1983) about its shortcomings on the woman question, the Marxist critique of science opened the door for three insights shared by feminist theories and methodologies:

1 It proposed that scientific knowledge was socially constructed and could not be dichotomized from other human values the scientist holds. Beginning with the work of Thomas Kuhn (1970) and his followers, historians and philosophers of science have pointed out that scientific theories and practice may not be dichotomized from other human values held by the scientist. The scientific paradigms that are acceptable to the mainstream of the practicing scientists are convincing precisely because they reinforce or support the historical, economic, and social, racial, political, and gender policies of the majority of scientists at that particular time. Rose and Rose (1980) underline the fact that the reason Darwin's theory of natural selection was acceptable to ninteenth-century England, was that it was laden with the values of the upper classes of that Victorian period:

> Its central metaphors drawn from society and in their turn interacting with society were of the competition of species, the struggle for existence, the ecological niche, and the survival of the fittest.
>
> (Rose and Rose, 1980, p. 28)

These metaphors reflected Victorian society and were acceptable to it because they, and the social Darwinism quickly derived from it, seemed to ground its norm solidly in a biological foundation. The use of craniometry provides a ninteenth-century example of the acceptance of incorrect biological measurements and false conclusions drawn from accurate measurements because the biological "facts" permitted a justification for the inferior social position of colonials (especially Blacks) and women (Gould, 1981).

Feminist critics today (Bleier, 1984, 1986; Fee, 1982; Haraway, 1978; Hein, 1981; Hubbard, 1979) have discussed the extent to which the emphasis upon sex differences research (when in fact for most traits there are no differences or only very small mean differences characterized by a large range of overlap between the sexes) in the neurosciences and endocrinology, and upon the search for genetic bases to justify sex role specialization and the division of labor, comes from the desire to find a biological basis for the social inequality between the sexes. The measurement of hormone levels in homosexuals compared to heterosexuals and the search for a "gene" for homosexuality provide other examples of an attempt to separate biological from environmental determinants and to seek biological bases for the discriminatory treatment against homosexuals (Birke, 1986). One can imagine that a society free from inequality between the sexes and lacking homophobia would not view sex differences and sexual

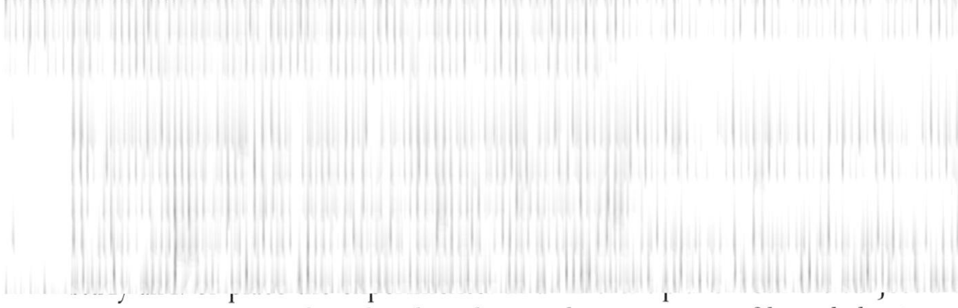

seen as more scientific only when the social construction of knowledge is not recognized.

African-American critique

African-American or Black feminism also rejects individualism and positivism for social construction as an approach to knowledge. It is based on the African-American critique of a Eurocentric approach to knowledge. In addition to the rejection of objectivity and value-neutrality associated with the positivist approach accepted by liberal feminism, the African-American approach critiques dichotomization of knowledge or at least the identification of science with the first half and African-American with the latter half of the following dichotomies: culture/nature; rational/feeling; objective/subjective; quantitative/qualitative; active/passive; focused/diffuse; independent/dependent; mind/body; self/others; knowing/being. Like Marxism, African-American critiques question methods that distance the observer from the object of study, thereby denying a facet of the social construction of knowledge.

Whereas Marxism posits class as the organizing principle around which the struggle for power exists, African-American critiques maintain that race is the primary oppression. Neo-Marxists view the entire scientific enterprise as a function of context and class-specific interests with scientific methodology itself constituted by these interests. African-Americans critical of the scientific enterprise may view it as a function of white Eurocentric interests with the methodology a reflection of those interests. Just as Marxists view class oppression as primary and superseding gender oppression, African-American critiques place race above gender as an oppression. A strict, traditional interpretation of African-American critiques would suggest that scientific knowledge produced by African-American women would more closely resemble scientific knowledge produced by African-American men than that produced by white women.

Many feminists were attracted by certain tenets – particularly the ideas of the social construction of knowledge, rejection of objectivity and other dualisms, and locating the observer in the same plane as the object of study – of both Marxist and African-American critiques. However, as feminists, they had experienced and recognized the oppression of gender and found it unacceptable to have it ignored or subsumed as a secondary oppression under class or race. Both socialist feminism and African-American feminism have examined the respective intersection of class and gender or race and gender in an attempt to provide a more complex and comprehensive view of reality.

Socialist feminism and African-American feminism

The addition of Socialist feminism and African-American feminism to classical Marxist and African-American critiques is the assertion that the special position of women within (or as) a class or race gives them a special standpoint that provides them with a particular world view. This world view from the standpoint of women is supposed to be more reliable and less distorted than that of men from the same class or race. Implicit in the acceptance of the social construction of knowledge is the rejection of the standpoint of the neutral, disinterested observer of liberal feminism; Marxist and African-American critiques posit differing standpoints. They suggest that the prevailing knowledge and science reflect the interests and values of the dominant race and class. Because the dominant race and class have an interest in concealing, and may not in fact recognize the way they dominate, the science and picture of reality they present will be distorted. Classical Marxist and African-American critiques suggest that individuals oppressed by class (Marxist) and/or race (African-American) have an advantageous and more comprehensive view of reality. Because of their oppression, they have an interest in perceiving problems with the status quo and the science and knowledge produced by the dominant class and race. Simultaneously, their position requires them to understand the science and condition of the dominant group in order to survive. Thus, the standpoint of the oppressed comprehends and includes that of the dominant group, so it is superior.

Socialist-feminist (Hartmann, 1981; Jaggar, 1983; Mitchell, 1971, 1974; Young, 1980, 1981) and African-American feminist critiques (Giddings, 1984; Hooks, 1981, 1983, 1990; Lorde, 1984) assert that in contemporary society, women suffer oppression due to their gender. Women oppressed by both class and gender (socialist-feminist) or both race and gender (African-American feminists) have a more comprehensive, inclusive standpoint than that of the working-class men or Black men. Socialist-feminist and African-American feminist theory implies that women scientists, through a collective process of political and scientific struggle (Jaggar, 1983) might produce a science and knowledge different from that produced by men of any race or class.

Other feminist theories also maintain that women, because they are women, possess a different perspective or standpoint than men. Common to these other feminist theories is the assumption that diversity among women due to race, class, religion, ethnic background, sexual orientation, age, and other factors exists. However, gender is a predominant factor which provides women with a sufficiently unique and unified perspective that their knowledge, science, and view of reality are likely to differ from that of men. The primary difference among these other feminist theories is their position on the source of gender differences between men and women. Because the theories differ on the source of gender differences, some variation exists among them about its effects upon methodology.

Essentialist feminism

Essentialist feminist theory posits that women are different from men because of their biology, specifically their secondary sex characteristics and their reproductive systems. Frequently, essentialist feminism may extend to include gender differences in visuospatial and verbal ability, aggression and other behavior, and other physical and mental traits based on prenatal or pubertal hormone exposure. Nineteenth-century essentialist feminists (Blackwell (1875), 1976; Calkins, 1896; Tanner, 1896) often [illegible]

In the earlier phases of the current wave of feminism, most feminist scientists (Bleier, 1979; Fausto-Sterling, 1985; Hubbard, 1979; Rosser, 1982) fought against some sociobiological research such as that by Wilson (1975), Trivers (1972), and Dawkins (1976) and some hormone and brain lateralization research (Buffery and Gray, 1972; Gorski, Harlan, Jacobson, Shryne, and Southam, 1980; Goy and Phoenix, 1971; Sperry, 1974) which seemed to provide biological evidence for differences in mental and behavioral characteristics between males and females. Essentialism was seen as a tool for conservatives who wished to keep women in the home and out of the work place. More recently, feminists have re-examined essentialism from perspectives ranging from conservative to radical (Corea, 1985; Dworkin, 1983; MacKinnon, 1982, 1987; O'Brien, 1981; Rich, 1976) with a recognition that biologically based differences between the sexes might imply superiority and power for women in some arenas.

Essentialist feminism would imply that because of their biology, differential hormonal effects on the brain, the physical experiences of menstrual cycles, pregnancy, childbirth, lactation, and menopause, and/or other differing anatomical or physiological characteristics, women scientists would produce a different science from that of men. It seems logical and understandable that due to their biological experiences women might be interested in different problems than men. However, essentialism would imply that these differences would lead them to different methods in approaching these problems, that is, experiencing menstruation might lead women to different methods than those used by men for studying menstruation.

A contradiction within essentialist feminism would seem to be that although it rejects the positivist "neutral observer" standpoint of liberal feminism, its relationship with the social construction of knowledge seems somewhat different from that of other feminist theories. Liberal feminism is usually equated not only with the positivist neutral observer but also with non-essentialism or at least the assumption of equality between the sexes. Essentialism is based on biological differences between men and women rather than the social construction of gender posited by other feminist theories, including liberal feminism. Yet, essentialist feminism, in its suggestion that male and female scientists might approach problems differently because of their gender, implies a social construction of knowledge and science.

Existentialist feminism

Existentialist feminism, first described by Simone de Beauvoir (1974), suggests that women's "otherness" and the social construction of gender rest on society's interpretation of biological differences:

> The enslavement of the female to the species and the limitations of her various powers are extremely important facts; the body of woman is one of the essential elements in her situation in the world. But that body is not enough to define her as woman; there is no true living reality except as manifested by the conscious individual through activities and in the bosom of a society. Biology is not enough to give an answer to the question that is before us; why is woman the Other?
>
> (de Beauvoir, 1974, p. 51)

In other words, it is the value that society assigns to biological differences between males and females which has led woman to play the role of the Other (Tong, 1989); it is not the biological differences themselves. It is possible to imagine a society without gender differences.

The methodological implications which flow from existentialist feminism are that a society which emphasized gender differences would produce a science which emphasized sex differences. In such a society, men and women might be expected to create very different sciences because of the social construction of both gender and science. The possibility of a gender-free or gender-neutral (positivist) science evolving in such a society is virtually nil. Elizabeth Fee (1982) summed up the situation very well: she states that a sexist society should be expected to develop a sexist science. Conceptualizing a feminist science from within our society is "like asking a medieval peasant to imagine the theory of genetics or the production of a space capsule" (Fee, 1982, p. 31).

Psychoanalytic feminism

In many ways, psychoanalytic feminism takes a stance similar to that of existentialist feminism. Derived from Freudian theory, psychoanalysis posits that girls and boys develop contrasting gender roles because they experience their sexuality differently and deal differently with the stages of psychosexual development. Based on the Freudian prejudice that anatomy is destiny, psychoanalytic theory assumes that biological sex will lead to different ways for boys and girls to resolve the Oedipus and castration complexes which arise during the phallic stage of normal sexual development. As was the situation with existentialism, psychoanalysis recognizes that gender construction is not biologically essential; in "normal" gender construction the biological sex of the child–caretaker interaction differs depending on the sex of the child (and possibly that of the primary caretaker). However, psychoanalytic theory is not strictly biologically deterministic since cases of "abnormal" sexuality may result when gender construction is opposite or not congruent with biological sex.

Simone de Beauvoir admired Freud for advancing the idea that sexuality is the ultimate explanation for the form of civilization and gender relations (Tong, 1989). However, she rejected Freud's interpretation as overly simplistic. She particularly rejected his theory of women's castration complex as a psychological explanation for their inferior social status. De Beauvoir suggested that the reason women may suffer from so-called penis envy is that they desire the material and psychological privileges permitted men in our society rather than the anatomical organ itself.

Numerous feminists (Firestone, 1970; Friedan, 1974; Millett, 1970) in the 1960s and 1970s attacked Freud and the successor psychoanalytic theories because of their negative view of women and the considerable damage that application of those theories

why the construction of gender and sexuality in this stage usually results in male dominance. They conclude that the gender differences resulting in male dominance can be traced to the fact that, in our society, women are the primary caretakers for most infants and children.

Accepting most Freudian ideas about the Oedipus complex, Chodorow and Dinnerstein conclude that boys are pushed to be independent, distant, and autonomous from their female caretakers while girls are permitted to be more dependent, intimate, and less individuated from their mothers or female caretakers. Building upon the work of Chodorow and Dinnerstein, feminists (Keller, 1982; Harding, 1986; Hein, 1981) have explored how the gender identity proposed by object relations theory with women as caretakers might lead to more men choosing careers in science. Keller (1982, 1985) in particular applied the work of Chodorow and Dinnerstein to suggest how science has become a masculine province which excludes women and causes women to exclude themselves from it. Science is a masculine province not only in the fact that it is populated mostly by men but also in the choice of experimental topics, use of male subjects for experimentation, interpretation and theorizing from data, as well as the practice and applications of science undertaken by the scientists. Keller suggests (1982, 1985) that since the scientific method stresses objectivity, rationality, distance, and autonomy of the observer from the object of study (i.e., the positivist neutral observer), individuals who feel comfortable with independence, autonomy, and distance will be most likely to become scientists. Because most caretakers during the Oedipal phase are female, most individuals in our culture who will be comfortable as scientists will be male. The type of science they create will also be reflective of those same characteristics of independence, distance, and autonomy. It is upon this basis that feminists have suggested that the objectivity and rationality of science are synonymous with a male approach to the physical, natural world.

According to psychoanalytic feminism, women scientists might be more likely to use approaches that shorten the distance between them as observer and their object of study, might develop a relationship with their object of study, and might appear to be less objective. The biography of Barbara McClintock, *A Feeling For the Organism*, written by Evelyn Fox Keller (1983), demonstrates this. McClintock's statement on receiving the Nobel Prize was that "it might seem unfair to reward a person for having so much pleasure over the years, asking the maize plant to solve specific problems and then watching its responses" (Keller, 1984, p. 44). Works by Goodfield (1981) and Hynes (1989) have also discussed this more "feminine" approach taken by women scientists.

Psychoanalytic feminism does not necessarily imply that biological males will take a masculine approach and that biological females will take a feminine approach. In most cases, due to the resolution of the Oedipal complex with a female caretaker, this will be the case. Proponents of psychoanalytic feminism (Keller, 1985) suggest that this is why so many more males than females are attracted to science. However, many of the biological females who are currently scientists probably take a more masculine approach, due not only to resolution of psychosexual development phases but also to training by male scientists. Psychoanalytic feminism also suggests that biological males could take a "feminine" approach.

Psychoanalytic feminism also opens the door for "gender-neutral" or "gender-free" (Keller, 1984) science. Chodorow (1978) and Dinnerstein (1977) find the solution to gender differences which result in male dominance to be the father's or other male's having a much more active role in caretaking the child. They suggest that the active involvement of both women and men in caretaking will lead children to recognize that both men and women have strengths and weaknesses. It would also presumably result in less polarization in gender roles and the possibility of a gender-free science. Although the gender-free potential of psychoanalytic feminism seems similar to the neutral, detached observer of liberal feminism, psychoanalytic feminism is premised on a type of social construction of knowledge – knowledge of sexuality and gender.

Radical feminism

Radical feminism, in contrast to psychoanalytic feminism and liberal feminism, rejects the possibility of a gender-free science or a science developed from a neutral, objective perspective. Radical feminism maintains that women's oppression is the first, most widespread, and deepest oppression (Jaggar and Rothenberg, 1984). Since men dominate and control most institutions, politics, and knowledge in our society, they reflect a male perspective and are effective in oppressing women. Scientific institutions, practice, and knowledge are particularly male-dominated and have been documented by many feminists (Bleier, 1984; Fee, 1982; Griffin, 1978; Haraway, 1978, 1990; Hubbard, 1990; Keller, 1985; Merchant, 1979; Rosser, 1990) to be especially effective patriarchal tools to control and harm women. Radical feminism rejects most scientific theories, data, and experiments precisely because they not only exclude women but also because they are not women-centered.

The theory that radical feminism proposes is evolving (Tong, 1989) and is not as well developed as some of the other feminist theories discussed above. The reasons that its theory is less developed spring fairly directly from the nature of radical feminism itself. First, it is radical. That means that it rejects most of currently accepted ideas about scientific epistemology – what kinds of things can be known, who can be a knower, and how beliefs are legitimated as knowledge – and methodology – the general structure of how theory finds its application in particular scientific disciplines. Second, unlike the feminisms previously discussed, radical feminism does not have its basis in a theory such as Marxism, positivism, psychoanalysis, or existentialism, already developed for decades by men. Since radical feminism is based in women's experience, it rejects feminisms rooted in theories developed by men based on their experience and world view. Third, the theory of radical feminism must be developed by women and based in women's experience (MacKinnon, 1987). Because radical feminism maintains that the oppression of women is the deepest, most widespread, and historically first oppression, women have had few opportunities to come together, understand [illegible] knowers. Because women have been oppressed, they know more than men. They must see the world from the male perspective in order to survive, but their double vision from their experience as an oppressed group allows them to see more than men. In this respect radical feminism parallels Marxist-feminist and African-American feminist critiques of who has the most accurate view of reality.

However, radical feminism deviates considerably from other feminisms in its view of how beliefs are legitimated as knowledge. A successful strategy that women use to obtain reliable knowledge and correct distortions of patriarchal ideology is the consciousness-raising group (Jaggar, 1983). Using their personal experiences as a basis, women meet together in communal, non-hierarchical groups to examine their experiences to determine what counts as knowledge (MacKinnon, 1987).

Because of the belief of radical feminists in connection and a conception of the world as an organic whole, they reject dualistic and hierarchical approaches. Dichotomies such as rational/feeling, objective/subjective, mind/body, culture/nature, and theory/practice are viewed as patriarchal conceptions which fragment the organic whole of reality. Linear conceptions of time and what is considered to be "logical" thinking in the Western traditions are frequently rejected by radical feminists. Cyclicity as a conception of time and thinking as an upward spiral seem more appropriate approaches to studying a world in which everything is connected in a process of constant change (Daly, 1978, 1984).

Radical feminists view all human beings and, most particularly, themselves as connected to the living and non-living world. Consequently, radical feminists view themselves as "participators" (Jaggar, 1983) connected in the same plane with rather than distanced from their object of study. Many radical feminists also believe that because of this connection, women can know things by relying on intuition and/or spiritual powers. Radical feminists vary in their belief as to whether the special ways of knowing of women are due to their biology (Daly, 1978; Griffin, 1978) or to their common social experiences as an oppressed group (Belenky, Clinchy, Goldberger, and Tarule, 1986) or both.

Lesbian separatism

By its very nature, radical feminism emphasizes connection among the diverse beliefs held by women about ways to obtain knowledge, and rejects the examination of a constantly changing, complex whole by looking at one of its parts. However, lesbian separatism, usually viewed as a subgroup theory within radical feminism, has some interesting implications for feminist methodology in science. To the tenets of radical feminist theory and their methodological implications for a feminist science, lesbian separatism provides one major addition. Lesbian separatists suggest that daily interaction with the patriarchal world and compulsory heterosexuality (Rich, 1976) make it impossible for women to completely understand their oppression and its distortion of their experience of reality. Therefore, in order to connect with other women and nature to understand reality, women must separate themselves from men. Only when freed from male oppression and patriarchy for a considerable period of time will women be able to understand their experiences and ways of knowing. Although based on separation from one part of reality – men – presumably lesbian separatists seek separation in order to enhance connection with the rest of reality. Radical feminism in general, and lesbian separatism in particular, suggest that their methods, arising from an extremely different view of reality, would result in a very different science and scientific method. Given the current oppression of women and male dominated scientific hierarchy which controls the scientific problems considered worthy of funding for study, and the acceptable approaches that might be used to study those problems, the results of a radical feminist science and especially of lesbian separatism are unimaginable.

Conclusion

A re-examination of the questions raised about feminist methodologies in the introduction to this paper reveals that answers are complex and dependent upon the feminist theory from which the methodology springs. There is certainly not just one feminist methodology, just as there is not one feminist theory. The jumble of descriptors for feminist methodology – rejects dualisms, is based on women's experience, shortens the distance between observer and object of study, rejects unicausal, hierarchical approaches, unites application with problem – seems contradictory when portrayed as feminist methodology. They become much more understandable when viewed as a lumping together of possible methodological implications for science resulting from different feminist theories. This lumping together explains why some feminist theories (liberal and psychoanalytic) posit that feminist methodologies would lead to gender-free or gender-neutral science that could be carried out by male or female scientists. Meanwhile, other feminist theories (essentialist and radical) suggest that only women could develop feminist methodologies. Most feminist theories, with the exception of liberal feminism, reject the neutral objective observer for a social construction of scientific knowledge based upon the standpoint of the observer, which is influenced by gender, as well as other factors such as race or class. Radical feminism, and particularly lesbian separatism, suggest strong reasons for why we are not able to see the results of a feminist methodology. As long as oppression of women and patriarchy continue, it is unlikely that the effects of feminist methodologies derived from the feminist theories that present some challenge to the status quo will be felt. Certainly, the biology and its accompanying feminist methodologies that would evolve under radical feminism are impossible to imagine under current circumstances.

References

Mattuck. (1986). *Women's ways of knowing*. New York: Basic Books.

Biology and Gender Study Group. (1989). The importance of feminist critique for contemporary cell biology. In Nancy Tuana (Ed.), *Feminism and science* (pp. 172–187). Bloomington, IN: Indiana University Press.

Birke, Lynda. (1986). *Women, feminism, and biology: The feminist challenge*. New York: Methuen.

Blackwell, Antoinette. [1875] (1976). *The sexes throughout nature*. New York: G.P. Putnam's Sons; reprinted, Westport, CT: Hyperion Press, Inc.

Bleier, Ruth. (1976). Myths of the biological inferiority of women: An exploration of the sociology of biological research. *University of Michigan Papers in Women's Studies, 2*, 39–63.

Bleier, Ruth. (1979). Social and political bias in science: An examination of animal studies and their generalizations to human behavior and evolution. In Ruth Hubbard and Marian Lowe (Eds.), *Genes and gender II: Pitfalls in research on sex and gender* (pp. 49–70). New York: Gordian Press.

Bleier, Ruth. (1984). *Science and gender: A critique of biology and its theories on women*. Tarrytown, NY: Pergamon Press.

Bleier, Ruth. (1986). Sex differences research: Science or belief? In Ruth Bleier (Ed.), *Feminist approaches to science* (pp. 147–164). Tarrytown, NY: Pergamon Press.

Bleier, Ruth. (1988). Science and the construction of meanings in the neurosciences. In Sue V. Rosser (Ed.), *Feminism within the science and health care professions: Overcoming resistance*. Tarrytown, NY: Pergamon Press.

Buffery, William, and Gray, J. (1972). Sex differences in the development of spatial and linguistic skills. In C. Ounsted and D.C. Taylor (Eds.), *Gender differences: Their ontogeny and significance*. Edinburgh: Churchill Livingstone.

Calkins, Mary. (1896). Community ideas of men and women. *Psychological Review, 3*(4): 426–430.

Capra, Fritzof. (1973). *The Tao of physics*. New York: Bantam Books.

Caws, Peter. (1967). Scientific method. In Pat Edwards (Ed.), *The encyclopedia of philosophy*. New York: Macmillan.

Chodorow, Nancy. (1974). Family structure and feminine personality. In Michelle Z. Rosaldo and Louise Lamphere (Eds.), *Women, culture, and society* (pp. 43–66). Stanford, CA: Stanford University Press.

Chodorow, Nancy. (1978). *The reproduction of mothering: Psychoanalysis and the sociology of gender*. Berkeley and Los Angeles: University of California Press.

Christ, Carol P. (1987). Toward a paradigm shift in the academy and in religious studies. In Christie Farnham (Ed.), *The impact of feminist research in the academy* (pp. 53–76). Bloomington, IN: Indiana University Press.

Collier, Jane, and Rosaldo, Michell Z. (1981). Politics and gender in simple societies. In Sherry Ortner and Harriet Whitehead (Eds.), *Sexual meanings* (pp. 275–329). New York: Cambridge University Press.

Corea, Gena. (1985). *The mother machine: Reproductive technologies from artificial insemination to artificial wombs*. New York: Harper & Row.

Daly, Mary. (1978). *Gyn-Ecology: The metaethics of radical feminism*. Boston: Beacon Press.

Daly, Mary. (1984). *Pure lust: Elemental feminist philosophy*. Boston: Beacon Press

Dawkins, Richard. (1976). *The selfish gene*. New York: Oxford University Press.

Dinnerstein, Dorothy. (1977). *The mermaid and the minotaur: Sexual arrangements and human malaise*. New York: Harper Colophon Books.

Dubois, Ellen, Kelly, Gail P., Kennedy, Elizabeth, Korsmeyer, Carolyn, and Robinson, Lillian S. (1985). *Feminist scholarship: Kindling in the groves of academe*. Urbana, IL: University of Illinois Press.

Dworkin, Andrea. (1983). *Right-wing women*. New York: Coward-McCann.

Fausto-Sterling, Anne. (1985). *Myths of gender*. New York: Basic Books.

Fedigan, Linda Marie. (1982). *Primate paradigms: Sex roles and social bonds*. Montreal: Eden Press.

Fee, Elizabeth. (1981). Is feminism a threat to scientific objectivity? *International Journal of Women's Studies 4*(4), 213–233.

Fee, Elizabeth. (1982). A feminist critique of scientific objectivity. *Science for the People*, 14(4), 8.

Fee, Elizabeth. (1983). Women's nature and scientific objectivity. In Marian Lowe and Ruth Hubbard (Eds.), *Women's nature: Rationalization of inequality*. Tarrytown, NY: Pergamon Press.

Fennema, Elizabeth, and Sherman, Julie. (1977). Sex related differences in mathematics achievement, spatial visualization and affective factors. *American Educational Research Journal, 14*, 51–71.

Firestone, Shulamith. (1970). *The dialectic of sex*. New York: Bantam Books.

Flax, Jane. (1981). Do feminists need Marxism? *Building feminist theory: Essays from "Quest," A Feminist Quarterly* (pp. 174–185). New York: Longman.

Foreman, Ann. (1977). *Femininity as alienation: Women and the family in Marxism and psychoanalysis.* London: Pluto Press.

Friedan, Betty. (1974). *The feminine mystique*. New York: Dell.

Friedan, Betty. (1981). *The second stage*. New York: Summit Books.

Giddings, Paula. (1984). *When and where we enter: The impact of Black women on race and sex in America*. New York: Morrow.

Goldman, Emma. (1931). *Living my life* (Vol. 2). New York: Alfred A. Knopf. Reprinted, New York: Dover Publications, 1970.

Goodfield, June. (1981). *An imagined world*. New York: Penguin Books.

Gorski, Robert, Harlan, R.E., Jacobson, C.D., Shryne, J.E., and Southam, A.M. (1980). Evidence for the existence of a sexually dimorphic nucleus in the preoptic area of the rat. *Journal of Comparative Neurology, 193*, 529–539.

Gould, Stephen Jay. (1981). *The mismeasure of man*. New York: W.W. Norton.

Goy, Robert, and Phoenix, Charles H. (1971). The effects of testosterone propionate administered before birth on the development of behavior in genetic female rhesus monkeys. In Charles H. Sawyer and Robert A. Gorski (Eds.), *Steroid hormones and brain function*. Berkeley: University of California Press.

Griffin, Susan. (1978). *Women and nature: The roaring inside her*. New York: Harper & Row.

Haraway, Donna. (1978). Animal sociology and a natural economy of the body politic, Part I: A political physiology of dominance; Animal sociology and a natural economy of the body politic, Part II: The past is the contested zone: Human nature and theories of production and reproduction in primate behavior studies. *Signs:* [illegible]

Hartmann, Heidi. (1981). The unhappy marriage of Marxism and feminism: Towards a more progressive union. In Lydia Sargent (Ed.), *Women and revolution: A discussion of the unhappy marriage of Marxism and feminism* (pp. 1–41). Boston: South End Press.

Hein, Hilde. (1981). Women and science: Fitting men to think about nature. *International Journal of Women's Studies, 4*, 369–377.

Hollingsworth, Leta S. (1914). Variability as related to sex differences in achievement. *American Journal of Sociology, 19*(4), 510–530.

hooks, bell. (1981). *Talking back: Thinking feminist, thinking Black*. Boston: South End Press.

hooks, bell. (1983). *Feminist theory from margin to center*. Boston: South End Press.

hooks, bell. (1990). *Yearning: Race, gender, and cultural politics*. Boston: South End Press.

Hrdy, Sarah B. (1979). Infanticide among animals: A review, classification and examination of the implications for the reproductive strategies of females. *Ethology and Sociobiology, 1*, 3–40.

Hrdy, Sarah B. (1981). *The woman that never evolved*. Cambridge, MA: Harvard University Press.

Hrdy, Sarah B. (1986). Empathy, polyandry, and the myth of the coy female. In Ruth Bleier (Ed.), *Feminist approaches to science* (pp. 119–146) Tarrytown, NY: Pergamon Press.

Hubbard, Ruth. (1979). Have only men evolved? In Ruth Hubbard, Mary S. Henifin and Barbara Fried (Eds.), *Women look at biology looking at women* (pp. 7–35). Cambridge, MA: Schenkman.

Hubbard, Ruth. (1990). *Politics of women's biology*. New Brunswick, NJ: Rutgers University Press.

Hubbard, Ruth, and Lowe, Marian. (1979). Introduction. In Ruth Hubbard and Marian Lowe (Eds.), *Genes and gender II: Pitfalls in research on sex and gender* (pp. 9–34). New York: Gordian Press.

Hynes, H. Patricia. (1989). *The recurring silent spring*. Tarrytown, NY: Pergamon Press

Jaggar, Alison M. (1983). *Feminist politics and human nature*. Totowa, NJ: Rowman & Allanheld.

Jaggar, Alison, and Rothenberg, Paula. (Eds.) (1984). *Feminist frameworks*. New York: McGraw-Hill

Keller, Evelyn Fox. (1982). Feminism and science. *Signs* 7(3), 589–602.

Keller, Evelyn Fox. (1983). *A feeling for the organism: The life and work of Barbara McClintock*. New York: W.H. Freeman.

Keller, Evelyn Fox. (1984, November/December). Women and basic research: Respecting the unexpected. *Technology Review*, 44–47.

Keller, Evelyn Fox. (1985). *Reflections on gender and science*. New Haven, CT: Yale University Press.

Keller, Evelyn Fox. (1987). Women, scientists and feminist critics of science. *Daedalus*, 77–91.

Kuhn, Thomas S. (1970). *The structure of scientific revolutions* (2nd ed.). Chicago: University of Chicago Press.

Lancaster, Jane. (1975). *Primate behavior and the emergence of human culture*. New York: Holt, Rinehart & Winston.

Leacock, Eleanor. (1981). *Myths of male dominance*. New York: Monthly Review Press.

Leavitt, Ruth R. (1975). *Peaceable primates and gentle people: Anthropological approaches to women's studies*. New York: Harper & Row.

Leibowitz, Lila. (1975). Perspectives in the evolution of sex differences. In Rayna Reiter (Ed.), *Toward an anthropology of women* (pp. 20–35). New York: Monthly Review Press.

Linton, Sally. (1974). Woman the gatherer. In Rayna Reiter (Ed.), *Toward an anthropology of women* (pp. 36–50). New York: Monthly Review Press.

Lorde, Audre. (1984). *Sister outsider*. Trumansburg, NY: Crossing Press.

Lowe, Marian. (1978). Sociobiology and sex differences. *Signs: Journal of Women in Culture and Society, 4*(1), 118–125.

MacKinnon, Catherine. (1982). Feminism, Marxism, method and the state: An agenda for theory. *Signs: Journal of Women in Culture and Society, 7*(3), 515–544.

MacKinnon, Catherine A. (1987). *Feminism unmodified: Discourses on life and law*. Cambridge, MA and London: Harvard University Press.

Merchant, Carolyn. (1979). *The death of nature: Women, ecology and the scientific revolution*. New York: Harper & Row.

Mill, Harriet Taylor. (1970). Enfranchisement of women. In Alice S. Rossi (Ed.), *Essays on sex equality* (pp. 89–122). Chicago: University of Chicago Press.

Mill, John Stuart. (1970). The subjection of women. In John Stuart Mill and Harriet Taylor Mill (Eds.), *Essays on sex equality* (pp. 123–242). Alice A. Rossi (Ed.). Chicago: University of Chicago Press.

Millett, Kate. (1970). *Sexual politics*. Garden City, NY: Doubleday.

Mitchell, Juliet. (1971). *Woman's estate*. New York: Pantheon Books.

Mitchell, Juliet. (1974). *Psychoanalysis and feminism*. New York: Vintage Books.

National Science Foundation. (1990). *Women and minorities in science and engineering*. (NSF 90–301). Washington, DC: Author.

Oakley, Ann. (1981). Interviewing women: A contradiction in terms. In Helen Roberts (Ed.), *Doing feminist research* (pp. 30–61). London and Boston: Routledge & Kegan Paul.

O'Brien, Mary. (1981). *The politics of reproduction*. Boston: Routledge & Kegan Paul.

Ortner, Sherry. (1974). Is female to male as nature to culture? In Michelle Rosaldo and Louise Lamphero (Eds.), *Woman, culture, and society* (pp. 67–87). Stanford, CA: Stanford University Press.

Rich, Adrienne. (1976). *Of woman born: Motherhood as experience*. New York: W.W. Norton.

Roberts, Helen. (1981). *Doing feminist research*. London and Boston: Routledge & Kegan Paul.

Rose, Hilary, and Rose, Steven. (1980). The myth of the neutrality of science. *Science and liberation* (pp. 17–32). Boston: South End Press.

Rosser, Sue V. (1982). Androgyny and sociobiology. *International Journal of Women's Studies, 5*(5), 435–444.

Rosser, Sue V. (1988). Women in science and health care: A gender at risk. In Sue V. Rosser (Ed.), *Feminism within the science and health care professions: Overcoming resistance* (pp. 3–15). Tarrytown, NY: Pergamon Press.

Rosser, Sue V. (1990). *Female-friendly science*. Tarrytown, NY: Pergamon Press.

[illegible]

Spanier, Bonnie. (1982). Toward a balanced curriculum: The study of women at Wheaton College. *Change, 14* (April), 31–34.

Sperry, Robert W. (1974). Lateral specialization in the surgically separated hemispheres. In Francis O. Schmitt and Frederic G. Wardon (Eds.), *The neurosciences: Third study program*. Cambridge, MA: MIT Press.

Star, Susan Leigh. (1979). Sex differences and the dichotomization of the brain: Methods, limits and problems in research on consciousness. In Ruth Hubbard and Marian Lowe (Eds.), *Genes and gender II: Pitfalls in research on sex and gender* (pp. 113–130). New York: Gordian Press.

Tanner, Ann. (1896). The community of ideas of men and women. *Psychological Review, 3*(5), 548–550.

Tong, Rosemarie. (1989). *Feminist thought: A comprehensive introduction*. Boulder, CO: Westview Press.

Trivers, Robert L. (1972). Parental investment and sexual selection. In B. Campbell (Ed.), *Sexual selection and the descent of man* (pp. 136–179). Chicago, IL: Aldine.

Vetter, Betty. (1988). Where are the women in the physical sciences? In Sue V. Rosser (Ed.), *Feminism within the science and health care professions: Overcoming resistance* (pp. 19–32). Tarrytown, NY: Pergamon Press.

Vogel, Lise. (1983). *Marxism and the oppression of women: Towards a unitary theory*. New Brunswick, NJ: Rutgers University Press.

Wallston, Barbara S. (1981). What are the questions in the psychology of women? A feminist approach to research. *Psychology of Women Quarterly, 5*, 597–617.

Weisstein, Maomi. (1971). Psychology constructs in the female, or the fantasy life of the male psychologist. In Michelle H. Garskof (Ed.), *Roles women play: Readings toward women's liberation* (pp. 68–83). Belmont, CA: Brooks/Cole Publishing Co.

Wilson, Edward O. (1975). *Sociobiology: The new synthesis*. Cambridge, MA: Harvard University Press.

Wilson, Edward O. (1978). *On human nature*. Cambridge, MA: Harvard University Press.

Wollstonecraft, Mary. (1975). *A vindication of the rights of woman*. Carol H. Poston (Ed.). New York: W.W. Norton.

Yerkes, R.M. (1943). *Chimpanzees*. New Haven: Yale University Press.

Young, Iris. (1980). Socialist feminism and the limits of dual systems theory. *Socialist Review 10*(2–3), 174.

Young, Iris. (1981). Beyond the unhappy marriage: A critique of the dual systems theory. In Lydia Sargent (Ed.), *Women and revolution: A discussion of the unhappy marriage of Marxism and feminism* (pp. 43–69). Boston: South End Press.

Chapter 14

Sandra Harding

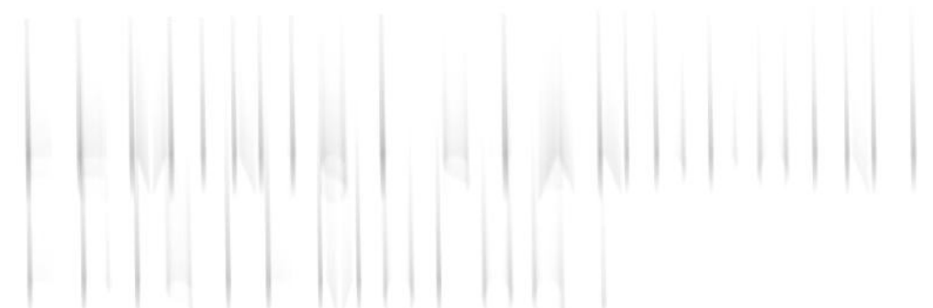

Description

Another response to the question about how to justify the results of feminist research is provided by the feminist standpoint theorists. They argue that not just opinions but also a culture's best beliefs – what it calls knowledge – are socially situated. The distinctive features of women's situation in a gender-stratified society are being used as resources in the new feminist research. It is these distinctive resources, which are not used by conventional researchers, that enable feminism to produce empirically more accurate descriptions and theoretically richer explanations than does conventional research. Thus, the standpoint theorists offer an explanation different from that of feminist empiricists of how research directed by social values and political agendas can nevertheless produce empirically and theoretically preferable results.

Just who are these "standpoint theorists"? Three in particular have made important contributions: Dorothy Smith, Nancy Hartsock, and Hilary Rose.[1] In addition, Jane Flax's early work developed standpoint themes; Alison Jaggar used standpoint arguments in her *Feminist Politics and Human Nature*, and I developed briefly one version of this theory and later discussed the emergence of a number of them in *The Science Question in Feminism*.[2] Standpoint arguments are also implicit and, increasingly, explicit in the work of many other feminist thinkers.[3]

[. . .]

The feminist standpoint theories focus on gender differences, on differences between women's and men's situations which give a scientific advantage to those who can make use of the differences. But what are these differences? On what grounds should we believe that conventional research captures only "the vision available to the rulers"? Even if one is willing to admit that any particular collection of research results provides only a partial vision of nature and social relations, isn't it going too far to say that it is also perverse or distorted?[4] What is it about the social situation of conventional researchers that is thought to make their vision partial and distorted? Why is the standpoint of women – or of feminism – less partial and distorted than the picture of nature and social relations that emerges from conventional research?

We can identify many differences in the situations of men and women that have been claimed to provide valuable resources for feminist research. These can be thought of as the "grounds" for the feminist claims.[5]

(1) Women's different lives have been erroneously devalued and neglected as starting points for scientific research and as the generators of evidence for or against knowledge claims. Knowledge of the empirical world is supposed to be grounded in that world (in complex ways). Human lives are part of the empirical world that scientists study. But human lives are not homogeneous in any gender-stratified society. Women and men are assigned different kinds of activities in such societies; consequently, they lead lives that have significantly different contours and patterns. Using women's lives as grounds to criticize the dominant knowledge claims, which have been based primarily in the lives of men in the dominant races, classes, and cultures, can decrease the partialities and distortions in the picture of nature and social life provided by the natural and social sciences.[6]

Sometimes this argument is put in terms of personality structures. Jane Flax and other writers who draw on object relations theory point to the less defensive structure of femininity than of masculinity. Different infantile experiences, reinforced throughout life, lead men to perceive their masculinity as a fragile phenomenon that they must continually struggle to defend and maintain. In contrast, women perceive femininity as a much sturdier part of the "self." Stereotypically, "real women" appear as if provided by nature; "real men" appear as a fragile social construct. Of course, "typical" feminine and masculine personality structures are different in different classes, races, and cultures. But insofar as they are different from each other, it deteriorates objectivity to devalue or ignore what can be learned by starting research from the perspective provided by women's personality structures.[7]

Sometimes this argument is put in terms of the different modes of reasoning that are developed to deal with distinctive kinds of human activity. Sara Ruddick draws our attention to the "maternal thinking" that is characteristic of people (male or female) who have primary responsibility for the care of small children. Carol Gilligan identifies those forms of moral reasoning typically found in women's thought but not found in the dominant Western "rights orientation" of ethics. And Mary Belenky and her colleagues argue that women's ways of knowing exhibit more generally the concern for context that Gilligan sees in moral knowing.[8]

One could argue also that the particular forms of any emotion that women experience as an oppressed, exploited, and dominated gender have a distinctive content that is missing from all those parallel forms in their brothers' emotional life. Consider suffering, for example. A woman suffers not only as a parent of a dying child, as a child of sick parents, as a poor person, or as a victim of racism. Women suffer in ways peculiar to *mothers* of dying children, to *daughters* of sick parents, to poor *women*, and in the special ways that racist policies and practices affect *women's* lives. Mother, daughter, poor woman, and racially oppressed woman are "nodes" of historically specific social practices and social meanings that mediate when and how suffering occurs for such socially constructed persons. Women's pleasures, angers, and other emotions too are in part distinctive to their social activities and identities as historically determinate women, and these provide a missing portion of the human lives that human knowledge is supposed to be both grounded in and about.

Whatever the kind of difference identified, the point of these arguments is that women's "difference" is only difference, not a sign of inferiority. The goal of maximizing the objectivity of research should require overcoming excessive reliance on distinctively masculine lives and making use also of women's lives as origins for scientific problematics, sources of scientific evidence, and checks against the validity of knowledge claims.

[illegible]

marriage. Women had experienced these assaults not as something that could be called rape but only as part of the range of heterosexual sex that wives should expect.

Moreover, women (feminists included) say all kinds of things – misogynist remarks and illogical arguments; misleading statements about an only partially understood situation; racist, class-biased, and heterosexist claims – that are scientifically inadequate. (Women, and feminists, are not worse in this respect than anyone else; we too are humans.) Furthermore, there are many feminisms, and these can be understood to have started their analyses from the lives of different historical groups of women: liberal feminism from the lives of women in eighteenth- and nineteenth-century European and American educated classes; Marxist feminism from the lives of working-class women in nineteenth- and twentieth-century industrializing societies; Third World feminism from late twentieth-century Third World women's lives. Moreover, we all change our minds about all kinds of issues. So while both "women's experiences" and "what women say" certainly are good places to begin generating research projects in biology and social science, they would not seem to be reliable grounds for deciding just which claims to knowledge are preferable.

For a position to count as a standpoint, rather than as a claim – equally valuable but for different reasons – for the importance of listening to women tell us about their lives and experiences, we must insist on an objective location – women's lives – as the place from which feminist research should begin. We would not know to value that location so highly if women had not insisted on the importance of their experiences and voices. (Each woman can say, "I would not know to value my own experience and voice or those of other women if women had not so insisted on the value of women's experiences and voices.") But it is not the experiences or the speech that provide the grounds for feminist claims; it is rather the subsequently articulated observations of and theory about the rest of nature and social relations – observations and theory that start out from, that look at the world from the perspective of, women's lives. And who is to do this "starting out"? With this question it becomes clear that knowledge-seeking requires democratic, participatory politics. Otherwise, only the gender, race, sexuality, and class elites who now predominate in institutions of knowledge-seeking will have the chance to decide how to start asking their research questions, and we are entitled to suspicion about the historic location from which those questions will in fact be asked. It is important both to value women's experiences and speech and also to be able to specify carefully their exact role in the production of feminist knowledges.

(2) Women are valuable "strangers" to the social order. Another basis claimed for feminist research by standpoint thinkers is women's exclusion from the design and direction of both the social order and the production of knowledge. This claim is supported by the sociological and anthropological notion of the stranger or outsider. Sociologist Patricia Hill Collins summarizes the advantages of outsider status as identified by sociological theorists. The stranger brings to her research just the combination of nearness and remoteness, concern and indifference, that are central to maximizing objectivity. Moreover, the "natives" tend to tell a stranger some kinds of things they would never tell each other; further, the stranger can see patterns of belief or behavior that are hard for those immersed in the culture to detect.[9] Women are just such outsiders to the dominant institutions in our society, including the natural and social sciences. Men in the dominant groups are the "natives" whose life patterns and ways of thinking fit all too closely the dominant institutions and conceptual schemes.

In the positivist tendencies in the philosophy of the social sciences, these differences between the stranger and the natives are said to measure their relative abilities to provide causal explanations of the natives' beliefs and behaviors. Only understanding, not explanation, can result from the natives' own accounts of their beliefs and behaviors, or from the accounts of anthropologists or sociologists who "go native" and identify too closely with the natives. Because women are treated as strangers, as aliens – some more so than others – by the dominant social institutions and conceptual schemes, their exclusion alone provides an edge, an advantage, for the generation of causal explanations of our social order from the perspective of their lives. Additionally, however, feminism teaches women (and men) how to see the social order from the perspective of an outsider. Women have been told to adjust to the expectations of them provided by the dominant institutions and conceptual schemes. Feminism teaches women (and men) to see male supremacy and the dominant forms of gender expectations and social relations as the bizarre beliefs and practices of a social order that is "other" to us. *It* is "crazy"; we are not.

This claim about the grounds for feminist research also captures the observation of so many sociologists and psychologists that the social order is dysfunctional for women. There is a closer fit for men in the dominant groups between their life needs and desires and the arrangement of the social order than there is for any women. But this kind of claim has to be carefully stated to reflect the extremely dysfunctional character of the US social order for men who are *not* members of dominant groups – for example, African Americans and Hispanics. It is clearly more dysfunctional for unemployed African American and Hispanic men than it is for economically privileged white women. Nevertheless, with extremely important exceptions, this insight illuminates the comparison of the situation of women and men in many of the same classes, races, and cultures. It also captures the observation that within the same culture there is in general a greater gap for women than for men between what they say or how they behave, on the one hand, and what they think, on the other hand. Women feel obliged to speak and act in ways that inaccurately reflect what they would say and do if they did not so constantly meet with negative cultural sanctions. The socially induced need for women always to consider "what men (or 'others') will think" leads to a larger gap between their observable behavior and speech and their thoughts and judgments.

(3) Women's oppression gives them fewer interests in ignorance. The claim has been made that women's oppression, exploitation, and domination are grounds for transvaluing women's differences because members of oppressed groups have fewer interests in ignorance about the social order and fewer reasons to invest in maintaining or justifying the status quo than do dominant groups. They have less to lose by distancing themselves from the social order; thus, the perspective from their

example, the perception that women believe they are firmly saying no to certain sexual situations in which men consistently perceive them to have said yes or "asked for it" (rape, battering) becomes explainable if one believes that there can never be objectively consensual relations between members of oppressor and oppressed groups. It is from the perspective of women's interests that certain situations can be seen as rape or battering which from the perspective of the interests of men and the dominant institutions were claimed to be simply normal and desirable social relations between the sexes.

(4) Women's perspective is from the other side of the "battle of the sexes" that women and men engage in on a daily basis. "The winner tells the tale," as historians point out, and so trying to construct the story from the perspective of the lives of those who resist oppression generates less partial and distorted accounts of nature and social relations.

Far from being inert "tablets" – blank or not – human knowers are active agents in their learning. Knowledge emerges for the oppressed through the struggles they wage against their oppressors. It is because women have struggled against male supremacy that research starting from their lives can be made to yield up clearer and more nearly complete visions of social reality than are available only from the perspective of men's side of these struggles. "His resistance is the measure of your oppression" said the early 1970s slogan that attempted to explain why it was that men resisted so strenuously the housework, child care, and other "women's work" that they insisted was so easy and required so few talents and so little knowledge.

As I put the point earlier, knowledge is produced through "craft" procedures, much as a sculptor comes to understand the real nature of the block of marble only as she begins to work on it. The strengths and weaknesses of the marble – its unsuspected cracks or surprising interior quality – are not visible until the sculptor tries to give it a shape she has in mind. Similarly, we can come to understand hidden aspects of social relations between the genders and the institutions that support these relations only through struggles to change them. Consider an example from the history of science: it is only because of the fierce struggles waged in the nineteenth and early twentieth centuries to gain formal equality for women in the world of science that we can come to understand that formal equality is not enough. As Margaret Rossiter points out, all the formal barriers to women's equity in education, credentialing, lab appointments, research grants, and teaching positions have been eliminated, yet there are still relatively few women to be found as directors and designers of research enterprises in the natural sciences.[10] The struggles to end discrimination against women in the sciences enabled people to see that formal discrimination was only the front line of defense against women's equity in scientific fields.

Hence, feminist politics is not just a tolerable companion of feminist research but a necessary condition for generating less partial and perverse descriptions and explanations. In a socially stratified society the objectivity of the results of research is increased by political activitism by and on behalf of oppressed, exploited, and dominated groups. Only through such struggles can we begin to see beneath the appearances created by an unjust social order to the reality of how this social order is in fact constructed and maintained. This need for struggle emphasizes the fact that a feminist standpoint is not something that anyone can have simply by claiming it. It is an achievement. A standpoint differs in this respect from a perspective, which anyone can have simply by "opening one's eyes." Of course, not all men take the "men's position" in these struggles; there have always been men who joined women in working to improve women's conditions, just as there have always been women who – whatever their struggles with men in their private lives – have not thought it in their interest to join the collective and institutional struggles against male supremacy. Some men have been feminists, and some women have not.

(5) Women's perspective is from everyday life. A fifth basis for the superiority of starting research from the lives of women rather than men in the dominant groups has been pointed out in one form or another since the early 1970s. The perspective from women's everyday activity is scientifically preferable to the perspective available only from the "ruling" activities of men in the dominant groups. Dorothy Smith has developed this argument most comprehensively: women have been assigned the kinds of work that men in the ruling groups do not want to do, and "women's work" relieves these men of the need to take care of their bodies or of the local places where they exist, freeing them to immerse themselves in the world of abstract concepts. The labor of women "articulates" and shapes these men's concepts of the world into those appropriate for administrative work.[11] Moreover, the more successfully women perform "women's work," the more invisible it becomes to men. Men who are relieved of the need to maintain their own bodies and the local places where they exist come to see as real only what corresponds to their abstracted mental world. This is why men see "women's work" not as real human activity – self-chosen and consciously willed (even within the constraints of a male-dominated social order) – but only as natural activity, a kind of instinctual labor such as bees and ants perform. Women are thus excluded from men's conceptions of culture and history.

[. . .]

(6) Women's perspective comes from mediating ideological dualisms: nature versus culture. Other standpoint theorists have stressed the ways in which women's activities mediate the divisions and separations in contemporary Western cultures between nature and culture and such manifestations of this polarity as intellectual work, on the one hand, and manual or emotional work, on the other hand. For example, as Nancy Hartsock has noted,

women's labor, like that of the male worker, is contact with material necessity. Their contribution to subsistence, like that of the male worker, involves them in a world in which the relation to nature and to concrete human requirements is central, both in the form of interaction with natural substances whose quality, rather than quantity, is important to the production of meals, clothing, etc., and in the form of close attention to the natural changes in these substances. Women's labor both for wages and even more in household production involves a unification of mind and body for the purpose of trans- [illegible]

into cultural ones – from men's typical kinds of labor: "The female experience of bearing and rearing children involves a unity of mind and body more profound than is possible in the worker's instrumental activity." Women's work processes children, food, all bodies, balky machines, and social relations. It makes possible men's retreat to and appropriation of "abstract masculinity."[13]

Starting our research from women's activities in these gender divisions of labor enables us to understand how and why social and cultural phenomena have taken the forms in which they appear to us. Women's transformation of natural objects into cultural ones remains invisible, as a social activity, to men. More objective research requires restoring to our vision as necessary human social activity these "lost" processes and their relation to the activities centered in men's discourses.

(7) Women, and especially women researchers, are "outsiders within." Sociologist Patricia Hill Collins has developed feminist standpoint theory to explain the important contributions that African American feminist scholars can make to sociology – and, I would add, to our understanding of nature and social life more generally: "As outsiders within, Black feminist scholars may be one of many distinct groups of marginal intellectuals whose standpoints promise to enrich sociological discourse. Bringing this group, as well as those who share an outsider within status *vis-à-vis* sociology, into the center of analysis may reveal views of reality obscured by more orthodox approaches."[14] It is not enough to be only on the "outside" – to be immersed only in "women's work" or in "black women's work" – because the relations between this work and "ruling work" are not visible from only one side of this division of human activity. Instead, it is when one works on both sides that there emerges the possibility of seeing the relation between dominant activities and beliefs and those that arise on the "outside." bell hooks captures this point in the title of her book *Feminist Theory: From Margin to Center*.[15] The strangers and outsiders discussed in the older anthropological and sociological writings were, consciously or not, assumed to be members of the dominant or "center" culture who were observing the residents in the dominated or marginalized cultures. No one expected the "natives" to write books about the anthropologists or sociologists (let alone be expected to sit on their tenure and promotion committees). Yet "studying up" and "studying oneself" as an "outsider within" offer resources for decreasing the

partiality and distortion of research additional to those available to researchers who restrict their work to "studying down."

Dorothy Smith develops this ground when she points out in a geological metaphor that for women sociologists (may I add "women researchers" more generally?) a "line of fault" opens up between their experiences of their lives and the dominant conceptual schemes, and that it is this disjuncture along which much of the major work in the women's movement has focused, especially centering on issues about women's bodies and violence against women. So objectivity is increased by thinking out of the gap between the lives of "outsiders" and the lives of "insiders" and their favored conceptual schemes.

(8) This is the right time in history. A final reason for the greater adequacy of research that begins with women's lives is suggested by parallels between feminist standpoint theories and Marxist discussions of the "standpoint of the proletariat."[16] It was not possible to see the class system of bourgeoisie and proletariat until the mid-nineteenth century, Engels argued. Utopian socialists such as Charles Fourier and Robert Owens could see the unnecessary misery and excessive wealth created at opposite ends of this emerging class system at the turn of the nineteenth century, but they could not identify in capitalism the mechanism that was producing these two classes from the peasants, artisans, merchants, and aristocrats that preceded them. The problem was not that the utopians were lacking in intellectual brilliance or that they were victims of false social myths; the reason they could not produce an adequate causal account was that the class system had not yet appeared in forms that made such explanations possible: "The great thinkers of the Eighteenth Century could, no more than their predecessors, go beyond the limits imposed upon them by their epoch," observed Engels. Only with the emergence of a "conflict between productive forces and modes of production" – a conflict that "exists, in fact, objectively, outside us, independently of the will and actions even of the men that have brought it on" – could the class structure of earlier societies be detected for the first time. "Modern socialism is nothing but the reflex, in thought, of this conflict in fact; its ideal reflection in the minds, first, of the class directly suffering under it, the working class."[17]

Similarly, the sex/gender system appeared as a possible object of knowledge only with various recent changes in the situation of women and men – changes created by shifts in the economy, by the so-called sexual revolution, by the increased entrance of women into higher education, by the civil rights struggles of the 1960s, and by other identifiable economic, political, and social phenomena. The cumulative result is that the social order generates conflicting demands on and expectations for women in each and every class. Looking at nature and social relations from the perspective of these conflicts in the sex/gender system – in our lives and in other women's lives – has enabled feminist researchers to provide empirically and theoretically better accounts than can be generated from the perspective of the dominant ideology, which cannot see these conflicts and contradictions as clues to the possibility of better explanations of nature and social life.[18]

Comments

Several comments are in order before I proceed to evaluate standpoint epistemology as I did feminist empiricism. First, note that none of the foregoing claims suggests that the biological differences between women and men provide the resources for feminist analyses. Nor do these accounts appeal to women's intuition.

Second, the eight claims should be understood not as competing but as complementary ways to describe these resources. Nor should they be thought to constitute a

as the perspective from the lives of men in the dominant group to assumptions that the world is "out there," ready for reflecting in our mirrorlike minds, or whether it is not more easily apparent that language is never a transparent medium and that the world-as-object-of-knowledge is and will always remain socially constructed.

[. . .]

Third, I must stress that these standpoint approaches enable one to appropriate and redefine objectivity. In a hierarchically organized society, objectivity cannot be defined as requiring (or even desiring) value neutrality.

Virtues

Standpoint epistemologies are most convincing to thinkers who are used to investigating the relationship between patterns of thought and the historical conditions that make such patterns reasonable. Consequently, many historians, political theorists, and sociologists of knowledge can find these explanations of why feminist research can generate improved research results more plausible than feminist empiricism.

The diversity of the resources that in other forms are familiar in the social sciences, and that feminists can call on in defending the greater objectivity attainable by starting research from women's lives, is another great advantage. It is hard to imagine how to defeat this entire collection of arguments – and the others to be found in feminist research – since they are grounded in a variety of relatively conventional understandings in the social sciences.

Moreover, the standpoint theories, like feminist empiricism, can claim historical precedents. Many (though not necessarily all) of the grounds identified above are used by the new histories of science to explain the emergence of modern science.[19] Scientific method itself was created by a "new kind of person" in the early modern era. Feudalism's economic order separated hand and head labor so severely that neither serfs nor aristocrats could get the necessary combination of a trained intellect and willingness to get one's hands dirty that are necessary for experimental method. One can also point to pre-Newtonian science's involvement in political struggles against the aristocracy.

Or one can focus on the "fit" of Ptolemaic astronomy's conceptual scheme with the hierarchical social structure of the Catholic Church and feudal society while, in contrast, the Copernican astronomy mirrored the more democratic social order that was emerging. Or one can note the way the problematics of the new physics were "for" the rise of the new merchant classes: it was not that Newton set out to "conspire" with these classes; rather, his new physics solved problems that had to be solved if transportation, mining, and warfare were to be more efficient.[20] So the feminist empiricists' appeals to historical precedent can be made in a different way by the standpoint theorists.

[. . .]

Strong objectivity and socially situated knowledge

In the preceding section I argued that a feminist standpoint theory can direct the production of less partial and less distorted beliefs. This kind of scientific process will not merely acknowledge the social-situatedness – the historicity – of the very best beliefs any culture has arrived at or could in principle "discover" but will use this fact as a resource for generating those beliefs.[21] Nevertheless, it still might be thought that this association of objectivity with socially situated knowledge is an impossible combination. Has feminist standpoint theory really abandoned objectivity and embraced relativism? Or, alternatively, has it remained too firmly entrenched in a destructive objectivism that increasingly is criticized from many quarters?

The declining status of "objectivism"

Scientists and science theorists working in many different disciplinary and policy projects have objected to the conventional notion of a value-free, impartial, dispassionate objectivity that is supposed to guide scientific research and without which, according to conventional thought, one cannot separate justified belief from mere opinion, or real knowledge from mere claims to knowledge. From the perspective of this conventional notion of objectivity – sometimes referred to as "objectivism" – it has appeared that if one gives up this concept, the only alternative is not just a cultural relativism (the sociological assertion that what is thought to be a reasonable claim in one society or subculture is not thought to be so in another) but, worse, a judgmental or epistemological relativism that denies the possibility of any reasonable standards for adjudicating between competing claims. Some fear that to give up the possibility of one universally and eternally valid standard of judgment is perhaps even to be left with no way to argue rationally against the possibility that *each person's* judgment about the regularities of nature and their underlying causal tendencies must be regarded as equally valid. The reduction of the critic's position to such an absurdity provides a powerful incentive to question no further the conventional idea that objectivity requires value-neutrality. From the perspective of objectivism, judgmental relativism appears to be the only alternative.

[. . .]

My concern is to state as clearly as possible how issues of objectivity and relativism appear from the perspective of a feminist standpoint theory.

Feminist critics of science and the standpoint theorists especially have been interpreted as supporting either an excessive commitment to value-free objectivity or, alternatively, the abandonment of objectivity in favor of relativism. Because there are clear commitments within feminism to tell less partial and distorted stories about women, men, nature, and social relations, some critics have assumed that feminism must be committed to value-neutral objectivity. Like other feminists, however, the standpoint theorists have also criticized conventional sciences for their arrogance in [illegible] and social sciences to claims that feminist images or representations of the world hold any special epistemological or scientific status. Such policing of thought is exactly what they have objected to in criticizing the authority of their disciplinary canons on the grounds that such authority has had the effect of stifling the voices of marginalized groups. In ignoring these views, feminist epistemologists who are concerned with natural or social science agendas appear to support an epistemological divide between the sciences and humanities, a divide that feminism has elsewhere criticized.

The arguments of this book move away from the fruitless and depressing choice between value-neutral objectivity and judgmental relativism. The last chapter stressed the greater objectivity that can be and has been claimed to result from grounding research in women's lives. This chapter draws on some assumptions underlying the analyses of earlier chapters in order to argue that the conventional notion of objectivity against which feminist criticisms have been raised should be regarded as excessively weak. A feminist standpoint epistemology requires strengthened standards of objectivity. The standpoint epistemologies call for recognition of a historical or sociological or cultural relativism – but not for a judgmental or epistemological relativism. They call for the acknowledgment that all human beliefs – including our best scientific beliefs–are socially situated, but they also require a critical evaluation to determine which social situations tend to generate the most objective knowledge claims. They require, as judgmental relativism does not, a scientific account of the relationships between historically located belief and maximally objective belief. So they demand what I shall call *strong objectivity* in contrast to the weak objectivity of objectivism and its mirror-linked twin, judgmental relativism. This may appear to be circular reasoning – to call for scientifically examining the social location of scientific claims – but if so, it is at least not viciously circular.[22]

This chapter also considers two possible objections to the argument presented, one that may arise from scientists and philosophers of science, and another that may arise among feminists themselves.

Objectivism's weak conception of objectivity

The term "objectivism" is useful for the purposes of my argument because its echoes of "scientism" draw attention to ways in which the research prescriptions called for by a value-free objectivity only mimic the purported style of the most successful scientific practices without managing to produce their effects. Objectivism results only in semi-science when it turns away from the task of critically identifying all those broad, historical social desires, interests, and values that have shaped the agendas, contents, and results of the sciences much as they shape the rest of human affairs. Objectivism encourages only a partial and distorted explanation of why the great moments in the history of the natural and social sciences have occurred.

Let me be more precise in identifying the weaknesses of this notion. It has been conceptualized both too narrowly and too broadly to be able to accomplish the goals that its defenders claim it is intended to satisfy. Taken at face value it is ineffectively conceptualized, but this is what makes the sciences that adopt weak standards of objectivity so effective socially: objectivist justifications of science are useful to dominant groups that, consciously or not, do not really intend to "play fair" anyway. Its internally contradictory character gives it a kind of flexibility and adaptability that would be unavailable to a coherently characterized notion.

Consider, first, how objectivism operationalizes too narrowly the notion of maximizing objectivity. The conception of value-free, impartial, dispassionate research is supposed to direct the identification of all social values and their elimination from the results of research, yet it has been operationalized to identify and eliminate only those social values and interests that differ among the researchers and critics who are regarded by the scientific community as competent to make such judgments. If the community of "qualified" researchers and critics systematically excludes, for example, all African Americans and women of all races, and if the larger culture is stratified by race and gender and lacks powerful critiques of this stratification, it is not plausible to imagine that racist and sexist interests and values would be identified within a community of scientists composed entirely of people who benefit – intentionally or not – from institutional racism and sexism.

This kind of blindness is advanced by the conventional belief that the truly scientific part of knowledge-seeking – the part controlled by methods of research – is only in the context of justification. The context of discovery, where problems are identified as appropriate for scientific investigation, hypotheses are formulated, key concepts are defined – this part of the scientific process is thought to be unexaminable within science by rational methods. Thus "real science" is restricted to those processes controllable by methodological rules. The methods of science – or, rather, of the special sciences – are restricted to procedures for the testing of already formulated hypotheses. Untouched by these careful methods are those values and interests entrenched in the very statement of what problem is to be researched and in the concepts favored in the hypotheses that are to be tested. Recent histories of science are full of cases in which broad social assumptions stood little chance of identification or elimination through the very best research procedures of the day.[23] Thus objectivism operationalizes the notion of objectivity in much too narrow a way to permit the achievement of the value-free research that is supposed to be its outcome.

But objectivism also conceptualizes the desired value-neutrality of objectivity too broadly. Objectivists claim that objectivity requires the elimination of all social values and interests from the research process and the results of research. It is clear, however, that not all social values and interests have the same bad effects upon the results of research. Some have systematically generated less partial and distorted beliefs than others – or than purportedly value-free research – as earlier chapters have argued.

Nor is this so outlandish an understanding of the history of science as objectivists frequently intimate. Setting the scene for his study of nineteenth-century biological determinism, Stephen Jay Gould says:

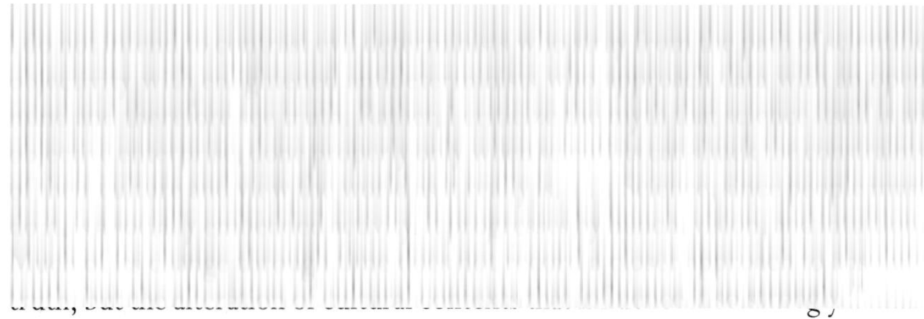

Other historians agree with Gould.[25] Modern science has again and again been reconstructed by a set of interests and values – distinctively Western, bourgeois, and patriarchal – which were originally formulated by a new social group that intentionally used the new sciences in their struggles against the Catholic Church and feudal state. These interests and values had both positive and negative consequences for the development of the sciences.[26] Political and social interests are not "add-ons" to an otherwise transcendental science that is inherently indifferent to human society; scientific beliefs, practices, institutions, histories, and problematics are constituted in and through contemporary political and social projects, and always have been. It would be far more startling to discover a kind of human knowledge-seeking whose products could – alone among all human products – defy historical "gravity" and fly off the earth, escaping entirely their historical location. Such a cultural phenomenon would be cause for scientific alarm; it would appear to defy principles of "material" causality upon which the possibility of scientific activity itself is based.[27]

Of course, people in different societies arrive at many of the same empirical claims. Farmers, toolmakers, and child tenders in every culture must arrive at similar "facts" about nature and social relations if their work is to succeed. Many of the observations collected by medieval European astronomers are preserved in the data used by astronomers today. But what "facts" these data refer to, what further research they point to, what theoretical statements they support and how such theories are to be applied, what such data signify in terms of human social relations and relations to nature – all these parts of the sciences can differ wildly, as the contrast between medieval and contemporary astronomy illustrates.

[. . .]

The best as well as the worst of the history of the natural sciences has been shaped by – or, more accurately, constructed through and within – political desires, interests, and values. Consequently, there appear to be no grounds left from which to defend the claim that the objectivity of research is advanced by the elimination of all political values and interests from the research process. Instead, the sciences need to legitimate *within scientific research*, as part of practicing science, critical examination of historical values and interests that may be so shared within the scientific community, so invested in by the very constitution of this or that field of study, that they will not show up as a cultural bias between experimenters or between research communities. What objectivism cannot conceptualize is the need for critical examination of the "intentionality of nature" – meaning not that nature is no different from humans (in having intentions, desires, interests, and values or in constructing its own meaningful "way of life," and so on) but that nature-as-the-object-of-human-knowledge never comes to us "naked"; it comes only as already constituted in social thought.[28] Nature-as-object-of-study simulates in this respect an intentional being. This idea helps counter the intuitively seductive idea that scientific claims are and should be an epiphenomenon of nature. It is the development of strategies to generate just such critical examination that the notion of strong objectivity calls for.

Not everyone will welcome such a project; even those who share these criticisms of objectivism may think the call for strong objectivity too idealistic, too utopian, not realistic enough. But is it more unrealistic than trying to explain the regularities of nature and their underlying causal tendencies scientifically but refusing to examine *all* their causes? And even if the ideal of identifying all the causes of human beliefs is rarely if ever achievable, why not hold it as a desirable standard? Anti-litter laws improve social life even if they are not always obeyed.[29]

Weak objectivity, then, is a contradictory notion, and its contradictory character is largely responsible for its usefulness and its widespread appeal to dominant groups. It offers hope that scientists and science institutions, themselves admittedly historically located, can produce claims that will be regarded as objectively valid without their having to examine critically their own historical commitments, from which – intentionally or not – they actively construct their scientific research. It permits scientists and science institutions to be unconcerned with the origins or consequences of their problematics and practices, or with the social values and interests that these problematics and practices support. It offers the possibility of enacting what Francis Bacon promised: "The course I propose for the discovery of sciences is such as leaves but little to the acuteness and strength of wits, but places all wits and understandings nearly on a level." His "way of discovering sciences goes far to level men's wits, and leaves but little to individual excellence; because it performs everything by surest rules and demonstrations."[30]

For those powerful forces in society that want to appropriate science and knowledge for their own purposes, it is extremely valuable to be able to support the idea that ignoring the constitution of science within political desires, values, and interests will somehow increase the reliability of accounts of nature and social life. The ideal of the disinterested rational scientist advances the self-interest of both social elites and, ironically, scientists who seek status and power. Reporting on various field studies of scientific work, Steve Fuller points out that Machiavellian judgments

> simulate those of the fabled "rational" scientist, since in order for the Machiavellian to maximize his advantage he must be ready to switch research programs when he detects a change in the balance of credibility – which is, after all, what philosophers of science would typically have the rational scientist do. To put the point more strikingly, it would seem that as the scientist's motivation approximates total *self-interestedness* (such that he is always able to distance his own

> interests from those of any social group which supports what may turn out to be a research program with diminishing credibility), his behavior approximates total *disinterestedness*. And so we can imagine the ultimate Machiavellian scientist pursuing a line of research frowned upon by most groups in the society – perhaps determining the racial component in intelligence is an example – simply because he knows of its potential for influencing the course of future research and hence for enhancing his credibility as a scientist.[31]

[illegible]

values silence and destroy the most likely sources of evidence against [illegible] That is what makes them rational for elites.

Strong objectivity: a competency concept

At this point, what I mean by a concept of strong objectivity should be clear. In an important sense, our cultures have agendas and make assumptions that we as individuals cannot easily detect. Theoretically unmediated experience, that aspect of a group's or an individual's experience in which cultural influences cannot be detected, functions as part of the evidence for scientific claims. Cultural agendas and assumptions are part of the background assumptions and auxiliary hypotheses that philosophers have identified. If the goal is to make available for critical scrutiny all the evidence marshaled for or against a scientific hypothesis, then this evidence too requires critical examination *within* scientific research processes. In other words, we can think of strong objectivity as extending the notion of scientific research to include systematic examination of such powerful background beliefs. It must do so in order to be competent at maximizing objectivity.

The strong objectivity that standpoint theory requires is like the "strong programme" in the sociology of knowledge in that it directs us to provide *symmetrical* accounts of both "good" and "bad" belief formation and legitimation.[32] We must be able to identify the social causes of good beliefs, not just of the bad ones to which the conventional "sociology of error" and objectivism restrict causal accounts. However, in contrast to the "strong programme," standpoint theory requires causal analyses not just of the micro processes in the laboratory but also of the macro tendencies in the social order, which shape scientific practices. Moreover, a concern with macro tendencies permits a more robust notion of reflexivity than is currently available in the sociology of knowledge or the philosophy of science. In trying to identify the social causes of good beliefs, we will be led also to examine critically the kinds of bad beliefs that shape our own thought and behaviors, not just the thought and behavior of others. [. . .]

It is important to remember that in a certain sense there are no "women" or "men" in the world – there is no "gender" – but only women, men, and gender constructed through particular historical struggles over just which races, classes, sexualities, cultures, religious groups, and so forth, will have access to resources and power. Moreover, standpoint theories of knowledge, whether or not they are articulated as such, have been advanced by thinkers concerned not only with gender and class hierarchy (recollect that standpoint theory originated in class analyses) but also with other "Others."[33] To make sense of any actual woman's life or the gender relations in any culture, analyses must begin in real, historic women's lives, and these will be women of particular races, classes, cultures, and sexualities. The historical particularity of women's lives is a problem for narcissistic or arrogant accounts that attempt, consciously or not, to conduct a cultural monologue. But it is a resource for those who think that our understandings and explanations are improved by what we could call an intellectual participatory democracy.

The notion of strong objectivity welds together the strengths of weak objectivity and those of the "weak subjectivity" that is its correlate, but excludes the features that make them only weak. To enact or operationalize the directive of strong objectivity is to value the Other's perspective and to pass over in thought into the social condition that creates it – not in order to stay there, to "go native" or merge the self with the Other, but in order to look back at the self in all its cultural particularity from a more distant, critical, objectifying location. One can think of the subjectivism that objectivism conceptualizes as its sole alternative as only a "premodern" alternative to objectivism; it provides only a premodern solution to the problem we have here and now at the moment of postmodern criticisms of modernity's objectivism. Strong objectivity rejects attempts to resuscitate those organic, occult, "participating consciousness" relationships between self and Other which are characteristic of the premodern world.[34] Strong objectivity requires that we investigate the relation between subject and object rather than deny the existence of, or seek unilateral control over, this relation.

Historical relativism versus judgmental relativism

It is not that historical relativism is in itself a bad thing. A respect for historical (or sociological or cultural) relativism is always useful in starting one's thinking. Different social groups tend to have different patterns of practice and belief and different standards for judging them; these practices, beliefs, and standards can be explained by different historical interests, values, and agendas. Appreciation of these empirical regularities is especially important at this moment of unusually deep and extensive social change, when even preconceived schemes used in liberatory projects are likely to exclude less-well-positioned voices and to distort emerging ways of thinking that do not fit easily into older schemes. Listening carefully to different voices and attending thoughtfully to others' values and interests can enlarge our vision and begin to correct for inevitable ethnocentrisms. (The dominant values, interests, and voices are not among these "different" ones; they are the powerful tide against which "difference" must swim.)

To acknowledge this historical or sociological fact, as I have already argued, does not commit one to the further epistemological claim that there are therefore no rational or scientific grounds for making judgments between various patterns of belief and their originating social practices, values, and consequences. Many thinkers have pointed out that judgmental relativism is internally related to objectivism. For example, science historian Donna Haraway argues that judgmental relativism is the other side of the very same coin from "the God trick" required by what I have called weak objectivity. To insist that no judgments at all of cognitive adequacy can legitimately be made amounts to the same thing as to insist that knowledge can be produced only from "no place at all": that is, by someone who can be every place at once.[35]

[. . .]

Responding to objections

Two possible objections to the recommendation of a stronger standard for objectivity must be considered here. First, some scientists and philosophers of science may protest that I am attempting to specify standards of objectivity for all the sciences. What could it mean to attempt to specify *general* standards for increasing the objectivity of research? Shouldn't the task of determining what counts as adequate research be settled within each science by its own practitioners? Why should practicing scientists revise their research practices because of what is thought by a philosopher or anyone else who is not an expert in a particular science?

But the issue of this chapter is an epistemological issue – a metascientific one – rather than an issue within any single science. It is more like a directive to operationalize theoretical concepts than like a directive to operationalize in a certain way some particular theoretical notion within physics or biology. The recommended combination of strong objectivity with the acknowledgment of historical relativism would, if adopted, create a culture-wide shift in the kind of epistemology regarded as desirable. Certainly, strategies for enacting commitments to strong objectivity and the acknowledgment of historical relativism would have to be developed within each particular research program; plenty of examples already exist in biology and the social sciences. My position is that the natural sciences are backward in this respect; they are not immune from the reasonableness of these directives, as conventionalists have assumed.

The notion of strong objectivity developed here represents insights that have been emerging from thinkers in a number of disciplines for some decades – not just "wishful thinking" based on no empirical sciences at all. Criticisms of the dominant thought of the West from both inside and outside the West argue that its partiality and distortions are the consequence in large part of starting that thought only from the lives of the dominant groups in the West. Less partiality and less distortion result when thought starts from peasant life, not just aristocratic life; from slaves' lives, not just slaveowners' lives; from the lives of factory workers, not just those of their bosses and managers; from the lives of people who work for wages and have also been assigned responsibility for husband and child care, not just those of persons who are expected to have little such responsibility. This directive leaves open to be determined within each discipline or research area what a researcher must do to start thought from women's lives or the lives of people in other marginalized groups, and it will be easier – though still difficult – to provide reasonable responses to such a request in history or sociology than in physics or chemistry. But the difficulty of providing an analysis in physics or chemistry does not signify that the question is an absurd one for knowledge-seeking in general, or that there are no reasonable answers for those sciences too.

The second objection may come from feminists themselves. Many would say that the notion of objectivity is so hopelessly tainted by its historical complicity in justifying the service of science to the dominant groups that trying to make it function effectively and progressively in alternative agendas only confuses the matter. If feminists want to breathe new life into such a bedraggled notion as objectivity, why not at least invent an alternative term that does not call up the offenses associated with the idea of value-neutrality, that is not intimately tied to a faulty theory of representation, to a faulty psychic construction of the ideal agent of knowledge, and to regressive political tendencies.

Let us reorganize some points made earlier in order to get the full force of this objection. The goal of producing results of research that are value-free is part of the notion of the ideal mind as a mirror that can reflect a world that is "out there," ready-made. In this view, value-free objectivity can locate an Archimedean perspective from which the events and processes of the natural world appear in their proper places. Only false beliefs have social causes – human values and interests that blind us to the real regularities and underlying causal tendencies in the world, generating biased results of research. True beliefs have only natural causes: those regularities and underlying causal tendencies that are *there*, plus the power of the eyes to see them and of the mind to reason about them. This theory of representation is a historically situated one: it is characteristic only of certain groups in the modern West. Can the notion of objectivity really be separated from this implausible theory of representation?

Value-free objectivity requires also a faulty theory of the ideal agent – the subject – of science, knowledge, and history. It requires a notion of the self as a fortress that must be defended against polluting influences from its social surroundings. The self whose mind would perfectly reflect the world must create and constantly police the borders of a gulf, a no-man's-land, between himself as the subject and the object of his research, knowledge, or action. Feminists have been among the most pointed critics of this self-versus-Other construct,[36] referring to it as "abstract masculinity."[37] Moreover, its implication in Western constructions of the racial Other against which the "white" West would define its admirable projects is also obvious.[38] Can the notion of objectivity be useful in efforts to oppose such sexism and racism?

Equally important, the notion of value-free objectivity is morally and politically regressive for reasons additional to those already mentioned. It justifies the construction of science institutions and individual scientists as "fast guns for hire." It has been used to legitimate and hold up as the highest ideal institutions and individuals that are, insofar as they are scientific, to be studiously unconcerned with the origins or consequences of their activities or with the values and interests that these activities advance. This nonaccidental, determined, energetic lack of concern is supported by science education that excludes training in critical thought and that treats all expressions of social and political concern – the concerns of the torturer and the concerns of the tortured – as being on the same low level of scientific "rationality." Scandalous examples of the institutional impotence of the sciences as sciences to speak to the moral and political issues that shape their problematics, consequences, values, and interests have been identified for decades. The construction of a border between scientific method and violations of human and, increasingly, animal rights must be conducted "outside" that method, by government statements about what constitutes acceptable methods of research on human and animal subjects, what constitutes consent to experimentation, [illegible] regard to morals and politics, yet still apply rational standards to sorting less from more partial and distorted belief. Indeed, my argument is that these standards are more rational and more effective at producing maximally objective results than the ones associated with what I have called weak objectivity.

As I have been arguing, objectivity is one of a complex of inextricably linked notions. Science and rationality are two other terms in this network. But it is not necessary to accept the idea that there is only one correct or reasonable way to think about these terms, let alone that the correct way is the one used by dominant groups in the modern West. Not all reason is white, masculinist, modern, heterosexual, Western reason. Not all modes of rigorous empirical knowledge-seeking are what the dominant groups think of as science – to understate the point. The procedures institutionalized in conventional science for distinguishing between how we want the world to be and how it is are not the only or best ways to go about maximizing objectivity. It is important to work and think outside the dominant modes, as the minority movements have done. But it is important, also, to bring the insights developed there into the heart of conventional institutions, to disrupt the dominant practices from within by appropriating notions such as objectivity, reason, and science in ways that stand a chance of compelling reasoned assent while simultaneously shifting and displacing the meanings and referents of the discussion in ways that improve it. It is by thinking and acting as "outsiders within" that feminists and others can transform science and its social relations for those who remain only insiders or outsiders.

Reflexivity revisited

The notion of "strong objectivity" conceptualizes the value of putting the subject or agent of knowledge in the same critical, causal plane as the object of her or his inquiry. It permits us to see the scientific as well as the moral and political advantages of this way of trying to achieve a reciprocal relationship between the agent and object of knowledge. The contrast developed here between weak and strong notions of objectivity permits the parallel construction of weak versus strong notions of reflexivity.

Reflexivity has tended to be seen as a problem in the social sciences – and only there. Observation cannot be as separated from its social consequences as the directives of "weak objectivity," originating in the natural sciences, have assumed. In social inquiry, observation changes the field observed. Having recognized his complicity in the lives of his objects of study, the researcher is then supposed to devise various strategies to try to democratize the situation, to inform the "natives" of their options, to make them participants in the account of their activities, and so forth.[39]

Less commonly, reflexivity has been seen as a problem because if the researcher is under the obligation to identify the social causes of the "best" as well as the "worst" beliefs and behaviors of those he studies, then he must also analyze his own beliefs and behaviors in conducting his research project – which have been shaped by the same kinds of social relations that he is interested to identify as causes of the beliefs and behaviors of others. (Here, reflexivity can begin to be conceptualized as a "problem" for the natural sciences, too.) Sociologists of knowledge in the recent "strong programme" school and related tendencies, who emphasize the importance of identifying the social causes of "best belief," have been aware of this problem from the very beginning but have devised no plausible way of resolving it – primarily because their conception of the social causes of belief in the natural sciences (the subject matter of their analyses) is artificially restricted to the micro processes of the laboratory and research community, explicitly excluding race, gender, and class relations. This restricted notion of what constitutes appropriate subject matter for analyses of the social relations of the sciences is carried into their understanding of their own work. It generates ethnographies of their own and the natural science communities which are complicitous with positivist tendencies in insisting on the isolation of research communities from the larger social, economic, and political currents in their societies. (These accounts are also flawed by their positivist conceptions of the object of natural science study.)[40]

These "weak" notions of reflexivity are disabled by their lack of any mechanism for identifying the cultural values and interests of the researchers, which form part of the evidence for the results of research in both the natural and social sciences. Anthropologists, sociologists, and the like, who work within social communities, frequently appear to desire such a mechanism or standard; but the methodological assumptions of their disciplines, which direct them to embrace either weak objectivity or judgmental relativism, have not permitted them to develop one. That is, individuals express "heartfelt desire" not to harm the subjects they observe, to become aware of their own cultural biases, and so on, but such reflexive goals remain at the level of desire rather than competent enactment. In short, such weak reflexivity has no possible operationalization, or no competency standard, for success.

A notion of strong reflexivity would require that the objects of inquiry be conceptualized as gazing back in all their cultural particularity and that the researcher, through theory and methods, stand behind them, gazing back at his own socially situated research project in all its cultural particularity and its relationships to other projects of his culture – many of which (policy development in international relations, for example, or industrial expansion) can be seen only from locations far away from the scientist's actual daily work. "Strong reflexivity" requires the development of oppositional theory from the perspective of the lives of those Others ("nature" as already socially constructed, as well as other peoples), since intuitive experience, for reasons discussed earlier, is frequently not a reliable guide to the regularities of nature and social life and their underlying causal tendencies.

Standpoint theory opens the way to stronger standards of both objectivity and reflexivity. These standards require that research projects use their historical location as a resource for obtaining greater objectivity.

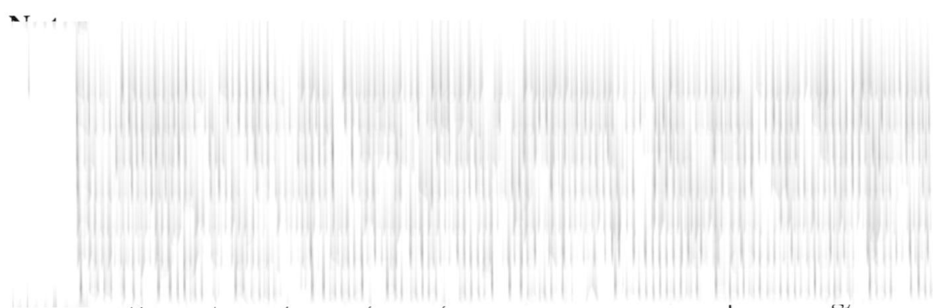

Natural Sciences," *Signs* 9: 1 (1983).

2 Jane Flax, "Political Philosophy and the Patriarchal Unconscious: A Psychoanalytic Perspective on Epistemology and Metaphysics," in Harding and Hintikka, *Discovering Reality*; Alison Jaggar, *Feminist Politics and Human Nature* (Totowa, NJ; Rowman & Allenheld, 1983), esp. chap. 11; Sandra Harding, "Why Has the Sex-Gender System Become Visible Only Now?" in Harding and Hintikka, *Discovering Reality*; Sandra Harding, *The Science Question in Feminism* (Ithaca: Cornell University Press, 1986), chap. 6.

3 Standpoint theory arguments have been made in the context of other liberatory social movements as well (a point to which I return later): see, e.g., Samir Amin, *Eurocentrism* (New York: Monthly Review Press, 1989); Bettina Aptheker, *Tapestries of Life: Women's Work, Women's Consciousness, and the Meaning of Daily Life* (Amherst: University of Massachusetts Press, 1989); Patricia Hill Collins, "Learning from the Outsider Within: The Sociological Significance of Black Feminist Thought," *Social Problems* 33 (1986); Walter Rodney, *How Europe Underdeveloped Africa* (Washington, DC: Howard University Press, 1982); Edward Said, *Orientalism* (New York: Pantheon Books, 1978); Edward Said, Foreword to *Selected Subaltern Studies*, ed. Ranajit Guha and Gayatri Chakravorty Spivak (New York: Oxford University Press, 1988), viii.

4 I have substituted "distorted" for "perverse," since one person's "perversities" may be another's most highly valued pleasures. "Distorted" appears less amenable to this kind of transvaluation.

5 In *The Science Question in Feminism*, I discussed differences between the grounds proposed by four standpoint theorists: Rose, Hartsock, Flax, and Smith. Here I consider additional grounds proposed to justify feminist research.

6 Standpoint theories need not commit essentialism. *The Science Question in Feminism* contributed to such a misreading of their "logic"; in this book I contest an essentialist reading.

7 Flax, "Political Philosophy." See also Nancy Hirschmann's use of object relations theory to ground a standpoint epistemology in her "Freedom, Recognition, and Obligation: A Feminist Approach to Political Theory," *American Political Science Review* 83: 4 (1989).

8 Sara Ruddick, *Maternal Thinking: Towards a Politics of Peace* (Boston: Beacon Press); Carol Gilligan, *In a Different Voice: Psychological Theory and Women's Development* (Cambridge, Mass.: Harvard University Press, 1982); Mary Belenky *et al.*, *Women's Ways of Knowing: The Development of Self, Voice and Mind* (New York: Basic Books, 1986). I said above that Ruddick, Gilligan, and Belenky – among others – do not develop their criticisms of the generalization from stereotypically masculine to paradigmatically human reason into a standpoint epistemology. My point here is that their arguments can be used to do so.

9 Collins, "Learning from the Outsider Within," S14.

10 Margaret W. Rossiter, *Women Scientists in America: Struggles and Strategies to 1940* (Baltimore: Johns Hopkins University Press, 1982).

11 Smith, *Everyday World*. See Hartsock's similar argument in "The Feminist Standpoint."

12 Hartsock, "The Feminist Standpoint," 291–92.

13 Ibid., 293, 294, 296.

14 Collins, "Learning from the Outsider Within," S14.

15 Bell Hooks, *Feminist Theory: From Margin to Center* (Boston: South End Press, 1983).

16 I examined this parallel in "Why Has the Sex/Gender System Become Visible Only Now?"

17 Friedrich Engels, "Socialism: Utopian and Scientific," in *The Marx and Engels Reader*, ed. Richard Tucker (New York: Norton, 1972), 606, 624.

18 For one illuminating analysis of such contradictions, see Natalie Sokoloff, "Motherwork and Working Mothers," in *Feminist Frameworks*, ed. Alison M. Jaggar and Paula S. Rothenberg (New York: McGraw-Hill, 1978).

19 A good overview for modern science is Wolfgang Van den Daele, "The Social Construction of Science," in *The Social Production of Scientific Knowledge*, ed. Everett Mendelsohn, Peter Weingart, and Richard Whitley (Dordrecht: Reidel, 1977).

20 See, e.g., Boris Hessen, *The Economic Roots of Newton's Principia* (New York: Howard Fertig, 1971); Edgar Zilsel, "The Sociological Roots of Science," *American Journal of Sociology* 47 (1942). A historical precedent of a different sort is claimed by Marxist theorist Fredric Jameson, who argues that although it was the Hungarian Marxist Georg Lukács who was responsible for the original development of standpoint theory, it is not Lukács's defenders today or other contemporary Marxists but feminist standpoint theorists who now exhibit "the most authentic descendency of Lukács' thinking." See Jameson, "*History and Class Consciousness* as an 'Unfinished Project,'" in *Rethinking Marxism* I: I (1988), 49–72; Lukács, *History and Class Consciousness* (Cambridge, Mass.: MIT Press, 1971), claimed that there is a feminist epistemology which holds that women's experiences ground feminist knowledge claims. Some critics think that this is what feminist standpoint theory holds. Sometimes this purported epistemology is referred to as gynocentric epistemology or "female-centered" epistemology. The articulation of women's experiences does play an important role in feminist epistemologies; as I argue in Chapters 6 and 11, articulating women's experiences does make possible less partial and distorted knowledge, but it does not provide knowledge with firm foundations – it does not ground it.

21 See Donna Haraway, "Situated Knowledges: *The Science Question in Feminism* and the Privilege of Partial Perspective," *Feminist Studies* 14: 3 (1988).

22 Additional writings informing this chapter include esp. Haraway, "Situated Knowledges"; Donna Haraway, *Primate Visions: Gender, Race, and Nature in the World of Modern Science* (New York: Routledge, 1989); Jane Flax, *Thinking Fragments: Psychoanalysis,*

Feminism, and Postmodernism in the Contemporary West (Berkeley: University of California Press, 1990); and the writings of standpoint theorists themselves, esp. Nancy Hartsock, "The Feminist Standpoint,"; Dorothy Smith, *The EverydayWorld as Problematic*; Hilary Rose, "Hand, Brain, and Heart,"; Patricia Hill Collins, "Learning from the OutsiderWithin," though each of these theorists would no doubt disagree with various aspects of my argument.

23 This is the theme of many feminist, left, and antiracist analyses of biology and social sciences. See, e.g., Anne Fausto-Sterling, *Myths of Gender: Biological Theories about*

[illegible]

Mass.: Harvard University Press, 1989).

24 Gould, *Mismeasure of Man*, 21–22.

25 E.g.,William Leiss, *The Domination of Nature* (Boston: Beacon Press, 1972); Carolyn Merchant, *The Death of Nature: Women, Ecology, and the Scientific Revolution* (NewYork: Harper & Row, 1980); Wolfgang Van den Daele, "The Social Construction of Science."

26 The usefulness of such political movements to the growth of knowledge in the sciences is discussed in Chapter 3.

27 See Chapter 4. Joseph Rouse, *Knowledge and Power: Towards a Political Philosophy of Science* (Ithaca: Cornell University Press, 1987), provides a good analysis of the implications for science of Foucauldian notions of politics and power.

28 See Haraway, *Primate Visions*, esp, chap. 10, for analysis of differences between the Anglo-American, Japanese, and Indian constructions of "nature" which shape the objects of study in primatology.

29 Steve Fuller uses the anti-litter law example in another context in *Social Epistemology* (Bloomington: Indiana University Press, 1991).

30 Quoted in Van den Daele, "Social Construction of Science," 34.

31 Fuller, *Social Epistemology*, 267.

32 I use "good" and "bad" here to stand for "true" and "false," "better confirmed" and "less well confirmed," "plausible" and "implausible," and so on.

33 See, e.g., Samir Amin, *Eurocentrism*; Bettina Aptheker, *Tapestries of Life*; Collins, "Learning from the Outsider Within"; Walter Rodney, *How Europe Underdeveloped Africa*; Edward Said, *Orientalism*; Edward Said, Foreword to *Selected Subaltern Studies*, viii.

34 See Morris Berman, *The Reenchantment of theWorld* (Ithaca: Cornell University Press, 1981), for an analysis of the world that modernity lost, and lost for good. Some feminists have tried to dismantle modernist projects with premodernist tools.

35 Haraway, "Situated Knowledges," makes these points and uses the phrase "the God trick."

36 See, e.g., Nancy Chodorow, *The Reproduction of Mothering* (Berkeley: University of California Press, 1978); Dorothy Dinnerstein, *The Mermaid and the Minotaur: Sexual Arrangements and Human Malaise* (NewYork: Harper & Row, 1976); Carol Gilligan, *In a Different Voice: Psychological Theory and Women's Development* (Cambridge, Mass.:

Harvard University Press, 1982); Evelyn Fox Keller, *Reflections on Gender and Science* (New Haven, Conn.: Yale University Press, 1984).

37 Hartsock, "The Feminist Standpoint."

38 See, e.g., Sander Gilman, *Difference and Pathology: Stereotypes of Sexuality, Race, and Madness* (Ithaca: Cornell University Press, 1985); V.Y. Mudimbe, *The Invention of Africa: Gnosis, Philosophy and the Order of Knowledge* (Bloomington: Indiana University Press, 1988); Said, *Orientalism*, and Foreword to *Subaltern Studies*.

39 A fine account of the travails of such a project reports Robert Blauner and David Wellman's dawning recognition that nothing they did could eliminate the colonial relationship between themselves and their black informants in the community surrounding Berkeley; see their "Toward the Decolonization of Social Research," in Ladner, *The Death of White Sociology*. Economist Vernon Dixon argues that from the perspective of an African or African American world view, the idea that observation would not change the thing observed appears ridiculous; see his "World Views and Research Methodology," in *African Philosophy: Assumptions and Paradigms for Research on Black Persons*, ed. L.M. King, Vernon Dixon, and W. W. Nobles (Los Angeles: Fanon Center, Charles R. Drew postgraduate Medical School, 1976), and my discussion of the congruence between African and feminine world views in *The Science Question in Feminism*, chap. 7.

40 See, e.g., David Bloor, *Knowledge and Social Imagery* (London: Routledge & Kegan Paul, 1976); and Steve Woolgar's nevertheless interesting paper, "Reflexivity is the Ethnographer of the Text," as well as other (somewhat bizarre) discussions of reflexivity in Woolgar, *Knowledge and Reflexivity: New Frontiers in the Sociology of Knowledge* (London and Beverly Hills: Sage, 1988).

Chapter 15

Donna Haraway

Academic and activist feminist enquiry has repeatedly tried to come to terms with the question of what we might mean by the curious and inescapable term 'objectivity'. We have used a lot of toxic ink and trees processed into paper decrying what *they* have meant and how it hurts *us*. The imagined 'they' constitute a kind of invisible conspiracy of masculinist scientists and philosophers replete with grants and laboratories; and the imagined 'we' are the embodied others, who are not allowed *not* to have a body, a finite point of view, and so an inevitably disqualifying and polluting bias in any discussion of consequence outside our own little circles, where a 'mass'-subscription journal might reach a few thousand readers composed mostly of science-haters. At least, I confess to these paranoid fantasies and academic resentments lurking underneath some convoluted reflections in print under my name in the feminist literature in the history and philosophy of science. We, the feminists in the debates about science and technology, are the Reagan era's 'special interest groups' in the rarefied realm of epistemology, where traditionally what can count as knowledge is policed by philosophers codifying cognitive canon law. Of course, a special interest group is, by Reaganoid definition, any collective historical subject which dares to resist the stripped-down atomism of Star Wars, hypermarket, postmodern, media-simulated citizenship. Max Headroom doesn't have a body; therefore, he alone sees everything in the great communicator's empire of the Global Network. No wonder Max gets to have a naïve sense of humour and a kind of happily regressive, pre-oedipal sexuality, a sexuality which we ambivalently – and dangerously incorrectly – had imagined was reserved for lifelong inmates of female and colonized bodies, and maybe also white male computer hackers in solitary electronic confinement.

It has seemed to me that feminists have both selectively and flexibly used and been trapped by two poles of a tempting dichotomy on the question of objectivity. Certainly I speak for myself here, and I offer the speculation that there is a collective discourse on these matters. On the one hand, recent social studies of science and technology have made available a very strong social constructionist argument for *all* forms of knowledge claims, most certainly and especially scientific ones.[2] In these tempting views, no insider's perspective is privileged, because all drawings of inside–outside boundaries in knowledge are theorized as power moves, not moves towards truth. So, from the strong social constructionist perspective, why should we be cowed by scientists' descriptions of their activity and accomplishments; they and their patrons have stakes in throwing sand in our eyes. They tell parables about objectivity and scientific method to students in the first years of their initiation, but no practitioner of the high scientific arts would be caught dead acting on the textbook versions. Social constructionists make clear that official ideologies about objectivity and scientific method are particularly bad guides to how scientific knowledge is actually *made*. Just as for the rest of us, what scientists believe or say they do and what they really do have a very loose fit.

The only people who end up actually *believing* and, goddess forbid, acting on the ideological doctrines of disembodied scientific objectivity enshrined in elementary textbooks and technoscience booster literature are nonscientists, including a few very trusting philosophers. Of course, my designation of this last group is probably just a reflection of residual disciplinary chauvinism from identifying with historians of science and too much time spent with a microscope in early adulthood in a kind of disciplinary pre-oedipal and modernist poetic moment when cells seemed to be cells and organisms, organisms. *Pace*, Gertrude Stein. But then came the law of the father and its resolution of the problem of objectivity, solved by always already absent referents, deferred signifieds, split subjects, and the endless play of signifiers. Who wouldn't grow up warped? Gender, race, the world itself – all seem just effects of warp speeds in the play of signifiers in a cosmic force field. All truths become warp speed effects in a hyper-real space of simulations. But we cannot afford these particular plays on words – the projects of crafting reliable knowledge about the 'natural' world cannot be given over to the genre of paranoid or cynical science fiction. For political people, social constructionism cannot be allowed to decay into the radiant emanations of cynicism.

In any case, social constructionists could maintain that the ideological doctrine of scientific method and all the philosophical verbiage about epistemology were cooked up to distract our attention from getting to know the world *effectively* by practicing the sciences. From this point of view, science – the real game in town, the one we must play – is rhetoric, the persuasion of the relevant social actors that one's manufactured knowledge is a route to a desired form of very objective power. Such persuasions must take account of the structure of facts and artefacts, as well as of language mediated actors in the knowledge game. Here, artefacts and facts are parts of the powerful art of rhetoric. Practice is persuasion, and the focus is very much on practice. All knowledge is a condensed node in an agonistic power field. The strong programme in the sociology of knowledge joins with the lovely and nasty tools of semiology and deconstruction to insist on the rhetorical nature of truth, including scientific truth. History is a story Western culture buffs tell each other; science is a contestable text and a power field; the content is the form.[3] Period. The form in science is the artefactual-social rhetoric of crafting the world into effective objects. This is a practice of world-changing persuasions that take the shape of amazing new objects – like microbes, quarks, and genes.

But whether or not they have the structure and properties of rhetorical objects, late twentieth-century scientific entities – infective vectors (microbes), elementary particles (quarks), and biomolecular codes (genes) – are not Romantic or modernist objects with internal laws of coherence.[4] They are momentary traces focused by force fields, or they are information vectors in a barely embodied and highly mutable semiosis ordered by acts of recognition and misrecognition. Human nature, encoded in its genome and its other writing practices, is a vast library worthy of Umberto Eco's

So, the further I get with the description of the radical social constructionist programme and a particular version of postmodernism, coupled to the acid tools of critical discourse in the human sciences, the more nervous I get. Like all neuroses, mine is rooted in the problem of metaphor, that is, the problem of the relation of bodies and language. For example, the force field imagery of moves in the fully textualized and coded world is the matrix for many arguments about socially negotiated reality for the postmodern subject. This world-as-code is, just for starters, a high-tech military field, a kind of automated academic battlefield, where blips of light called players disintegrate (what a metaphor!) each other in order to stay in the knowledge and power game. Technoscience and science fiction collapse into the sun of their radiant (ir)reality – war.[5] It shouldn't take decades of feminist theory to sense the enemy here. Nancy Hartsock (1983b) got all this crystal clear in her concept of abstract masculinity.

I, and others, started out wanting a strong tool for deconstructing the truth claims of hostile science by showing the radical historical specificity, and so contestability, of *every* layer of the onion of scientific and technological constructions, and we end up with a kind of epistemological electro-shock therapy, which far from ushering us into the high stakes tables of the game of contesting public truths, lays us out on the table with self-induced multiple personality disorder. We wanted a way to go beyond showing bias in science (that proved too easy anyhow), and beyond separating the good scientific sheep from the bad goats of bias and misuse. It seemed promising to do this by the strongest possible constructionist argument that left no cracks for reducing the issues to bias versus objectivity, use versus misuse, science versus pseudo-science. We unmasked the doctrines of objectivity because they threatened our budding sense of collective historical subjectivity and agency and our 'embodied' accounts of the truth, and we ended up with one more excuse for not learning any post-Newtonian physics and one more reason to drop the old feminist self-help practices of repairing our own cars. They're just texts anyway, so let the boys have them back. Besides these textualized postmodern worlds are scary, and we prefer our science fiction to be a bit more utopic, maybe like *Woman on the Edge of Time* or even *Wanderground*.

Some of us tried to stay sane in these disassembled and dissembling times by holding out for a feminist version of objectivity. Here, motivated by many of the same political desires, is the other seductive end of the duplicitous objectivity problem. Humanistic Marxism was polluted at the source by its structuring ontological theory of the domination of nature in the self-construction of man and by its closely related impotence to historicize anything women did that didn't qualify for a wage. But Marxism was still a promising resource in the form of epistemological feminist mental hygiene that sought our own doctrines of objective vision. Marxist starting points offered tools to get to our versions of standpoint theories, insistent embodiment, a rich tradition of critiques of hegemony without disempowering positivisms and relativisms, and nuanced theories of mediation. Some versions of psychoanalysis aided this approach immensely, especially anglophone object relations theory, which maybe did more for US socialist-feminism for a time than anything from the pen of Marx or Engels, much less Althusser or any of the late pretenders to sonship treating the subject of ideology and science.[6]

Another approach, 'feminist empiricism', also converges with feminist uses of Marxian resources to get a theory of science which continues to insist on legitimate meanings of objectivity and which remains leery of a radical constructivism conjugated with semiology and narratology (Harding, 1986, pp. 24–6, 161–2). Feminists have to insist on a better account of the world; it is not enough to show radical historical contingency and modes of construction for everything. Here, we, as feminists, find ourselves perversely conjoined with the discourse of many practising scientists, who, when all is said and done, mostly believe they are describing and discovering things *by means of* all their constructing and arguing. Evelyn Keller has been particularly insistent on this fundamental matter, and Harding calls the goal of these approaches a 'successor science'. Feminists have stakes in a successor science project that offers a more adequate, richer, better account of a world, in order to live in it well and in critical, reflexive relation to our own as well as others' practices of domination and the unequal parts of privilege and oppression that make up all positions. In traditional philosophical categories, the issue is ethics and politics perhaps more than epistemology.

So, I think my problem and 'our' problem is how to have *simultaneously* an account of radical historical contingency for all knowledge claims and knowing subjects, a critical practice for recognizing our own 'semiotic technologies' for making meanings, *and* a no-nonsense commitment to faithful accounts of a 'real' world, one that can be partially shared and friendly to earth-wide projects of finite freedom, adequate material abundance, modest meaning in suffering, and limited happiness. Harding calls this necessary multiple desire a need for a successor science project and a postmodern insistence on irreducible difference and radical multiplicity of local knowledges. *All* components of the desire are paradoxical and dangerous, and their combination is both contradictory and necessary. Feminists don't need a doctrine of objectivity that promises transcendence, a story that loses track of its mediations just where someone might be held responsible for something, and unlimited instrumental power. We don't want a theory of innocent powers to represent the world, where language and bodies both fall into the bliss of organic symbiosis. We also don't want to theorize the world, much less act within it, in terms of Global Systems, but we do need an earth-wide network of connections, including the ability partially to translate knowledges among very different – and power-differentiated – communities. We need the power of modern critical theories of how meanings and bodies get made, not in order to deny meaning and bodies, but in order to live in meanings and bodies that have a chance for a future.

Natural, social, and human sciences have always been implicated in hopes like these. Science has been about a search for translation, convertibility, mobility of meanings, and universality – which I call reductionism, when one language (guess whose) must be enforced as the standard for all the translations and conversions. What money does in the exchange orders of capitalism, reductionism does in the powerful mental orders of global sciences: there is finally only one equation. That is the deadly fantasy that feminists and others have identified in some versions of objectivity doctrines [illegible] tivity, I and most other feminists in the objectivity debates have alternatively, or even simultaneously, held on to both ends of the dichotomy, which Harding describes in terms of successor science projects versus postmodernist accounts of difference and I have sketched in this chapter as radical constructivism versus feminist critical empiricism. It is, of course, hard to climb when you are holding on to both ends of a pole, simultaneously or alternately. It is, therefore, time to switch metaphors.

The persistence of vision[7]

I would like to proceed by placing metaphorical reliance on a much maligned sensory system in feminist discourse: vision. Vision can be good for avoiding binary oppositions. I would like to insist on the embodied nature of all vision, and so reclaim the sensory system that has been used to signify a leap out of the marked body and into a conquering gaze from nowhere. This is the gaze that mythically inscribes all the marked bodies, that makes the unmarked category claim the power to see and not be seen, to represent while escaping representation. This gaze signifies the unmarked positions of Man and White, one of the many nasty tones of the word *objectivity* to feminist ears in scientific and technological, late industrial, militarized, racist and male dominant societies, that is, here, in the belly of the monster, in the United States in the late 1980s. I would like a doctrine of embodied objectivity that accommodates paradoxical and critical feminist science projects: feminist objectivity means quite simply *situated knowledges*.

The eyes have been used to signify a perverse capacity – honed to perfection in the history of science tied to militarism, capitalism, colonialism, and male supremacy – to distance the knowing subject from everybody and everything in the interests of unfettered power. The instruments of visualization in multinationalist, postmodernist culture have compounded these meanings of dis-embodiment. The visualizing technologies are without apparent limit; the eye of any ordinary primate like us can be endlessly enhanced by sonography systems, magnetic resonance imaging, artificial intelligence-linked graphic manipulation systems, scanning electron microscopes, computer-aided tomography scanners, colour enhancement techniques, satellite surveillance systems, home and office VDTs, cameras for every purpose from filming the mucous membrane lining the gut cavity of a marine worm living in the vent gases on a fault between continental plates to mapping a planetary hemisphere elsewhere in the solar system. Vision in this technological feast becomes unregulated gluttony; all perspective gives way to infinitely mobile vision, which no longer seems just mythically about the god-trick of seeing everything from nowhere, but to have put the myth into ordinary practice. And like the god-trick, this eye fucks the world to make techno-monsters. Zoe Sofoulis (1988) calls this the cannibal-eye of masculinist extra-terrestrial projects for excremental second birthing.

A tribute to this ideology of direct, devouring, generative, and unrestricted vision, whose technological mediations are simultaneously celebrated and presented as utterly transparent, the volume celebrating the 100th anniversary of the National Geographic Society closes its survey of the magazine's quest literature, effected through its amazing photography, with two juxtaposed chapters. The first is on 'Space', introduced by the epigraph, 'The choice is the universe – or nothing' (Bryan, 1987, p. 352). Indeed. This chapter recounts the exploits of the space race and displays the colour enhanced 'snapshots' of the outer planets reassembled from digitalized signals transmitted across vast space to let the viewer 'experience' the moment of discovery in immediate vision of the 'object'.[8] These fabulous objects come to us simultaneously as indubitable recordings of what is simply there and as heroic feats of techno-scientific production. The next chapter is the twin of outer space: 'Inner Space', introduced by the epigraph, 'The stuff of stars has come alive' (Bryan, 1987, p. 454). Here, the reader is brought into the realm of the infinitesimal, objectified by means of radiation outside the wave lengths that 'normally' are perceived by hominid primates, i.e., the beams of lasers and scanning electron microscopes, whose signals are processed into the wonderful full-colour snapshots of defending T cells and invading viruses.

But of course that view of infinite vision is an illusion, a god-trick. I would like to suggest how our insisting metaphorically on the particularity and embodiment of all vision (though not necessarily organic embodiment and including technological mediation), and not giving in to the tempting myths of vision as a route to disembodiment and second-birthing, allows us to construct a usable, but not an innocent, doctrine of objectivity. I want a feminist writing of the body that metaphorically emphasizes vision again, because we need to reclaim that sense to find our way through all the visualizing tricks and powers of modern sciences and technologies that have transformed the objectivity debates. We need to learn in our bodies, endowed with primate color and stereoscopic vision, how to attach the objective to our theoretical and political scanners in order to name where we are and are not, in dimensions of mental and physical space we hardly know how to name. So, not so perversely, objectivity turns out to be about particular and specific embodiment, and definitely not about the false vision promising transcendence of all limits and responsibility. The moral is simple: only partial perspective promises objective vision. This is an objective vision that initiates, rather than closes off, the problem of responsibility for the generativity of all visual practices. Partial perspective can be held accountable for both its promising and its destructive monsters. All Western cultural narratives about objectivity are allegories of the ideologies of the relations of what we call mind and body, of distance and responsibility, embedded in the science question in feminism. Feminist objectivity is about limited location and situated knowledge, not about transcendence and splitting of subject and object. In this way we might become answerable for what we learn how to see.

These are lessons which I learned in part walking with my dogs and wondering how the world looks without a fovea and very few retinal cells for colour vision, but with a huge neural processing and sensory area for smells. It is a lesson available from photographs of how the world looks to the compound eyes of an insect, or even from the camera eye of a spy satellite or the digitally transmitted signals of space probe-perceived differences 'near' Jupiter that have been transformed into coffee table [illegible] loving care people might take to learn how to see faithfully from another's point of view, even when the other is our own machine. That's not alienating distance; that's a *possible* allegory for feminist versions of objectivity. Understanding how these visual systems work, technically, socially, and psychically ought to be a way of embodying feminist objectivity.

Many currents in feminism attempt to theorize grounds for trusting especially the vantage points of the subjugated; there is good reason to believe vision is better from below the brilliant space platforms of the powerful (Hartsock, 1983a; Sandoval, n.d.; Harding, 1986; Anzaldúa, 1987). Linked to this suspicion, this chapter is an argument for situated and embodied knowledges and against various forms of unlocatable, and so irresponsible, knowledge claims. Irresponsible means unable to be called into account. There is a premium on establishing the capacity to see from the peripheries and the depths. But here lies a serious danger of romanticizing and/or appropriating the vision of the less powerful while claiming to see from their positions. To see from below is neither easily learned nor unproblematic, even if 'we' 'naturally' inhabit the great underground terrain of subjugated knowledges. The positionings of the subjugated are not exempt from critical re-examination, decoding, deconstruction, and interpretation; that is, from both semiological and hermeneutic modes of critical enquiry. The standpoints of the subjugated are not 'innocent' positions. On the contrary, they are preferred because in principle they are least likely to allow denial of the critical and interpretative core of all knowledge. They are savvy to modes of denial through repression, forgetting, and disappearing acts – ways of being nowhere while claiming to see comprehensively. The subjugated have a decent chance to be on to the god-trick and all its dazzling – and, therefore, blinding – illuminations. 'Subjugated' standpoints are preferred because they seem to promise more adequate, sustained, objective, transforming accounts of the world. But *how* to see from below is a problem requiring at least as much skill with bodies and language, with the mediations of vision, as the 'highest' techno-scientific visualizations.

Such preferred positioning is as hostile to various forms of relativism as to the most explicitly totalizing versions of claims to scientific authority. But the alternative to relativism is not totalization and single vision, which is always finally the unmarked category whose power depends on systematic narrowing and obscuring. The alternative to relativism is partial, locatable, critical knowledges sustaining the possibility of webs of connections called solidarity in politics and shared conversations in epistemology. Relativism is a way of being nowhere while claiming to be everywhere equally. The 'equality' of positioning is a denial of responsibility and critical enquiry. Relativism is the perfect mirror twin of totalization in the ideologies of objectivity; both deny the stakes in location, embodiment, and partial perspective; both make it impossible to see well. Relativism and totalization are both 'god-tricks' promising vision from everywhere and nowhere equally and fully, common myths in rhetorics surrounding Science. But it is precisely in the politics and epistemology of partial perspectives that the possibility of sustained, rational, objective enquiry rests.

So, with many other feminists, I want to argue for a doctrine and practice of objectivity that privileges contestation, deconstruction, passionate construction, webbed connections, and hope for transformation of systems of knowledge and ways of seeing. But not just any partial perspective will do; we must be hostile to easy relativisms and holisms built out of summing and subsuming parts. 'Passionate detachment' (Kuhn, 1982) requires more than acknowledged and self-critical partiality. We are also bound to seek perspective from those points of view, which can never be known in advance, which promise something quite extraordinary, that is, knowledge potent for constructing worlds less organized by axes of domination. In such a viewpoint, the unmarked category would *really* disappear – quite a difference from simply repeating a disappearing act. The imaginary and the rational – the visionary and objective vision – hover close together. I think Harding's plea for a successor science and for postmodern sensibilities must be read to argue that this close touch of the fantastic element of hope for transformative knowledge and the severe check and stimulus of sustained critical enquiry are jointly the ground of any believable claim to objectivity or rationality not riddled with breathtaking denials and repressions. It is even possible to read the record of scientific revolutions in terms of this feminist doctrine of rationality and objectivity. Science has been utopian and visionary from the start; that is one reason 'we' need it.

A commitment to mobile positioning and to passionate detachment is dependent on the impossibility of innocent 'identity' politics and epistemologies as strategies for seeing from the standpoints of the subjugated in order to see well. One cannot 'be' either a cell or molecule – or a woman, colonized person, labourer, and so on – if one intends to see and see from these positions critically. 'Being' is much more problematic and contingent. Also, one cannot relocate in any possible vantage point without being accountable for that movement. Vision is *always* a question of the power to see – and perhaps of the violence implicit in our visualizing practices. With whose blood were my eyes crafted? These points also apply to testimony from the position of 'oneself'. We are not immediately present to ourselves. Self-knowledge requires a semiotic-material technology linking meanings and bodies. Self-identity is a bad visual system. Fusion is a bad strategy of positioning. The boys in the human sciences have called this doubt about self-presence the 'death of the subject', that single ordering point of will and consciousness. That judgement seems bizarre to me. I prefer to call this generative doubt the opening of non-isomorphic subjects, agents, and territories of stories unimaginable from the vantage point of the cyclopian, self-satiated eye of the master subject. The Western eye has fundamentally been a wandering eye, a travelling lens.

These peregrinations have often been violent and insistent on mirrors for a conquering self – but not always. Western feminists also *inherit* some skill in learning to participate in revisualizing worlds turned upside down in earth-transforming challenges to the views of the masters. All is not to be done from scratch.

The split and contradictory self is the one who can interrogate positionings and be accountable, the one who can construct and join rational conversations and fantastic imaginings that change history.[9] Splitting, not being, is the privileged image for feminist epistemologies of scientific knowledge. 'Splitting' in this context

taneously in all, or wholly in any, of the privileged (subjugated) positions structured by gender, race, nation, and class. And that is a short list of critical positions. The search for such a 'full' and total position is the search for the fetishized perfect subject of oppositional history, sometimes appearing in feminist theory as the essentialized Third World Woman (Mohanty, 1984). Subjugation is not grounds for an ontology; it might be a visual clue. Vision requires instruments of vision; an optics is a politics of positioning. Instruments of vision mediate standpoints; there is no immediate vision from the standpoints of the subjugated. Identity, including self-identity, does not produce science; critical positioning does, that is, objectivity. Only those occupying the positions of the dominators are self-identical, unmarked, disembodied, unmediated, transcendent, born again. It is unfortunately possible for the subjugated to lust for and even scramble into that subject position – and then disappear from view. Knowledge from the point of view of the unmarked is truly fantastic, distorted, and so irrational. The only position from which objectivity could not possibly be practised and honoured is the standpoint of the master, the Man, the One God, whose Eye produces, appropriates, and orders all difference. No one ever accused the God of monotheism of objectivity, only of indifference. The god-trick is self-identical, and we have mistaken that for creativity and knowledge, omniscience even.

Positioning is, therefore, the key practice grounding knowledge organized around the imagery of vision, as so much Western scientific and philosophic discourse is organized. Positioning implies responsibility for our enabling practices. It follows that politics and ethics ground struggles for the contests over what may count as rational knowledge. That is, admitted or not, politics and ethics ground struggles over knowledge projects in the exact, natural, social, and human sciences. Otherwise, rationality is simply impossible, an optical illusion projected from nowhere comprehensively. Histories of science may be powerfully told as histories of the technologies. These technologies are ways of life, social orders, practices of visualization. Technologies are skilled practices. How to see? Where to see from? What limits to vision? What to see for? Whom to see with? Who gets to have more than one point of view? Who gets blinkered? Who wears blinkers? Who interprets the visual field? What other sensory powers do we wish to cultivate besides vision? Moral and political discourse should be the paradigm of rational discourse in the imagery and technologies of vision. Sandra Harding's claim, or observation, that movements of social revolution have most contributed to improvements in science might be read as a claim about the knowledge consequences of new technologies of positioning. But I wish Harding had spent more time remembering that social and scientific revolutions have not always been liberatory, even if they have always been visionary. Perhaps this point could be captured in another phrase: the science question in the military. Struggles over what will count as rational accounts of the world are struggles over *how* to see. The terms of vision: the science question in colonialism; the science question in exterminism (Sofoulis, 1988); the science question in feminism.

The issue in politically engaged attacks on various empiricisms, reductionisms, or other versions of scientific authority should not be relativism, but location. A dichotomous chart expressing this point might look like this:

universal rationality	ethnophilosophies
common language	heteroglossia
new organon	deconstruction
unified field theory	oppositional positioning
world system	local knowledges
master theory	webbed accounts

But a dichotomous chart misrepresents in a critical way the positions of embodied objectivity which I am trying to sketch. The primary distortion is the illusion of symmetry in the chart's dichotomy, making any position appear, first, simply alternative and, second, mutually exclusive. A map of tensions and resonances between the fixed ends of a charged dichotomy better represents the potent politics and epistemologies of embodied, therefore accountable, objectivity. For example, local knowledges have also to be in tension with the productive structurings that force unequal translations and exchanges – material and semiotic – within the webs of knowledge and power. Webs *can* have the property of systematicity, even of centrally structured global systems with deep filaments and tenacious tendrils into time, space and consciousness, the dimensions of world history. Feminist accountability requires a knowledge tuned to resonance, not to dichotomy. Gender is a field of structured and structuring difference where the tones of extreme localization, of the intimately personal and individualized body, vibrate in the same field with global high tension emissions. Feminist embodiment, then, is not about fixed location in a reified body, female or otherwise, but about nodes in fields, inflections in orientations, and responsibility for difference in material-semiotic fields of meaning. Embodiment is significant prosthesis; objectivity cannot be about fixed vision when what counts as an object is precisely what world history turns out to be about.

How should one be positioned in order to see in this situation of tensions, resonances, transformations, resistances, and complicities? Here, primate vision is not immediately a very powerful metaphor or technology for feminist political-epistemological clarification, since it seems to present to consciousness already processed and objectified fields; things seem already fixed and distanced. But the visual metaphor allows one to go beyond fixed appearances, which are only the end products. The metaphor invites us to investigate the varied apparatuses of visual production, including the prosthetic technologies interfaced with our biological eyes and brains. And here we find highly particular machineries for processing regions of the electromagnetic spectrum into our pictures of the world. It is in the intricacies of these visualization technologies in which we are embedded that we will find metaphors and means for understanding and intervening in the patterns of objectification in the world, that is, the patterns of reality for which we must be accountable. In these metaphors, we find means for appreciating simultaneously *both* the concrete, 'real' aspect and the aspect of semiosis and production in what we call scientific knowledge.

translation, stuttering, and the partly understood. Feminism is about the sciences of the multiple subject with (at least) double vision. Feminism is about a critical vision consequent upon a critical positioning in homogeneous gendered social space.[10] Translation is always interpretative, critical, and partial. Here is a ground for conversation, rationality, and objectivity – which is power-sensitive, not pluralist, 'conversation'. It is not even the mythic cartoons of physics and mathematics – incorrectly caricatured in anti-science ideology as exact, hyper-simple knowledges – that have come to represent the hostile other to feminist paradigmatic models of scientific knowledge, but the dreams of the perfectly known in high technology, permanently militarized scientific productions and positionings, the god-trick of a Star Wars paradigm of rational knowledge. So location is about vulnerability; location resists the politics of closure, finality, or, to borrow from Althusser, feminist objectivity resists 'simplification in the last instance'. That is because feminist embodiment resists fixation and is insatiably curious about the webs of differential positioning. There is no single feminist standpoint because our maps require too many dimensions for that metaphor to ground our visions. But the feminist standpoint theorists' goal of an epistemology and politics of engaged, accountable positioning remains eminently potent. The goal is better accounts of the world, that is, 'science'.

Above all, rational knowledge does not pretend to disengagement: to be from everywhere and so nowhere, to be free from interpretation, from being represented, to be fully self-contained or fully formalizable. Rational knowledge is a process of ongoing critical interpretation among 'fields' of interpreters and decoders. Rational knowledge is power-sensitive conversation (King, 1987a):

> knowledge: community: : knowledge: power
> hermeneutics: semiology: : critical interpretation: codes.

Decoding and transposing plus translation and criticism; all are necessary. So science becomes the paradigmatic model not of closure, but of that which is contestable and contested. Science becomes the myth not of what escapes human agency and responsibility in a realm above the fray, but rather of accountability and responsibility for translations and solidarities linking the cacophonous visions and visionary voices that characterize the knowledges of the subjugated. A splitting of senses, a confusion of voice and sight, rather than clear and distinct ideas, becomes the metaphor for the ground of the rational. We seek not the knowledges ruled by phallogocentrism (nostalgia for the presence of the one true Word) and disembodied vision, but those ruled by partial sight and limited voice. We do not seek partiality for its own sake, but for the sake of the connections and unexpected openings situated knowledges make possible. The only way to find a larger vision is to be somewhere in particular. The science question in feminism is about objectivity as positioned rationality. Its images are not the products of escape and transcendence of limits, i.e., the view from above, but the joining of partial views and halting voices into a collective subject position that promises a vision of the means of ongoing finite embodiment, of living within limits and contradictions, i.e., of views from somewhere.

Objects as actors: the apparatus of bodily production

Throughout this reflection on 'objectivity', I have refused to resolve the ambiguities built into referring to science without differentiating its extraordinary range of contexts. Through the insistent ambiguity, I have foregrounded a field of commonalities binding exact, physical, natural, social, political, biological, and human sciences; and I have tied this whole heterogeneous field of academically (and industrially, for example, in publishing, the weapons trade, and pharmaceuticals) institutionalized knowledge production to a meaning of science that insists on its potency in ideological struggles. But, partly in order to give play to both the specificities and the highly permeable boundaries of meanings in discourse on science, I would like to suggest a resolution to one ambiguity. Throughout the field of meanings constituting science, one of the commonalities concerns the status of any object of knowledge and of related claims about the faithfulness of our accounts to a 'real world', no matter how mediated for us and no matter how complex and contradictory these worlds may be. Feminists, and others who have been most active as critics of the sciences and their claims or associated ideologies, have shied away from doctrines of scientific objectivity in part because of the suspicion that an 'object' of knowledge is a passive and inert thing. Accounts of such objects can seem to be either appropriations of a fixed and determined world reduced to resource for the instrumentalist projects of destructive Western societies, or they can be seen as masks for interests, usually dominating interests.

For example, 'sex' as an object of biological knowledge appears regularly in the guise of biological determinism, threatening the fragile space for social constructionism and critical theory, with their attendant possibilities for active and transformative intervention, called into being by feminist concepts of gender as socially, historically, and semiotically positioned difference. And yet, to lose authoritative biological accounts of sex, which set up productive tensions with its binary pair, gender, seems to be to lose too much; it seems to be to lose not just analytic power within a particular Western tradition, but the body itself as anything but a blank page for social inscriptions, including those of biological discourse. The same problem of loss attends a radical 'reduction' of the objects of physics or of any other sciences to the ephemera of discursive production and social construction.[11]

But the difficulty and loss are not necessary. They derive partly from the analytical tradition, deeply indebted to Aristotle and to the transformative history of 'White Capitalist Patriarchy' (how may we name this scandalous Thing?) that turns everything into a resource for appropriation, in which an object of knowledge is finally itself only matter for the seminal power, the act, of the knower. Here, the object both guarantees and refreshes the power of the knower, but any status as *agent* in the productions of knowledge must be denied the object. It – the world – must, in short, be objectified as thing, not as an agent; it must be matter for the self-formation of the only social

sex/gender distinction in the recent history of feminist theory. Sex is 'resourced' for its re-presentation as gender, which 'we' can control. It has seemed all but impossible to avoid the trap of an appropriationist logic of domination built into the nature/culture binarism and its generative lineage, including the sex/gender distinction.

It seems clear that feminist accounts of objectivity and embodiment – that is, of a world – of the kind sketched in this chapter require a deceptively simple manoeuvre within inherited Western analytical traditions, a manoeuvre begun in dialectics, but stopping short of the needed revisions. Situated knowledges require that the object of knowledge be pictured as an actor and agent, not a screen or a ground or a resource, never finally as slave to the master that closes off the dialectic in his unique agency and authorship of 'objective' knowledge. The point is paradigmatically clear in critical approaches to the social and human sciences, where the agency of people studied itself transforms the entire project of producing social theory. Indeed, coming to terms with the agency of the 'objects' studied is the only way to avoid gross error and false knowledge of many kinds in these sciences. But the same point must apply to the other knowledge projects called sciences. A corollary of the insistence that ethics and politics covertly or overtly provide the bases for objectivity in the sciences as a heterogeneous whole, and not just in the social sciences, is granting the status of agent/actor to the 'objects' of the world. Actors come in many and wonderful forms. Accounts of a 'real' world do not, then, depend on a logic of 'discovery', but on a power-charged social relation of 'conversation'. The world neither speaks itself nor disappears in favour of a master decoder. The codes of the world are not still, waiting only to be read. The world is not raw material for humanization; the thorough attacks on humanism, another branch of 'death of the subject' discourse, have made this point quite clear. In some critical sense that is crudely hinted at by the clumsy category of the social or of agency, the world encountered in knowledge projects is an active entity. In so far as a scientific account has been able to engage this dimension of the world as object of knowledge, faithful knowledge can be imagined and can make claims on us. But no particular doctrine of representation or decoding or discovery guarantees anything. The approach I am recommending is not a version of 'realism', which has proved a rather poor way of engaging with the world's active agency.

My simple, perhaps simple-minded, manoeuvre is obviously not new in Western philosophy, but it has a special feminist edge to it in relation to the science question in feminism and to the linked questions of gender as situated difference and of female embodiment. Ecofeminists have perhaps been most insistent on some version of the world as active subject, not as resource to be mapped and appropriated in bourgeois, Marxist, or masculinist projects. Acknowledging the agency of the world in knowledge makes room for some unsettling possibilities, including a sense of the world's independent sense of humour. Such a sense of humour is not comfortable for humanists and others committed to the world as resource. Richly evocative figures exist for feminist visualizations of the world as witty agent. We need not lapse into an appeal to a primal mother resisting becoming resource. The Coyote or Trickster, embodied in American Southwest Indian accounts, suggests our situation when we give up mastery but keep searching for fidelity, knowing all the while we will be hoodwinked. I think these are useful myths for scientists who might be our allies. Feminist objectivity makes room for surprises and ironies at the heart of all knowledge production; we are not in charge of the world. We just live here and try to strike up non-innocent conversations by means of our prosthetic devices, including our visualization technologies. No wonder science fiction has been such a rich writing practice in recent feminist theory. I like to see feminist theory as a reinvented coyote discourse obligated to its enabling sources in many kinds of heterogeneous accounts of the world.

Another rich feminist practice in science in the last couple of decades illustrates particularly well the 'activation' of the previously passive categories of objects of knowledge. The activation permanently problematizes binary distinctions like sex and gender, without however eliminating their strategic utility. I refer to the reconstructions in primatology, especially but not only women's practice as primatologists, evolutionary biologists, and behavioural ecologists, of what may count as sex, especially as female sex, in scientific accounts (Haraway, 1989). The *body*, the object of biological discourse, itself becomes a most engaging being. Claims of biological determinism can never be the same again. When female 'sex' has been so thoroughly re-theorized and revisualized that it emerges as practically indistinguishable from 'mind', something basic has happened to the categories of biology. The biological female peopling current biological behavioural accounts has almost no passive properties left. She is structuring and active in every respect; the 'body' is an agent, not a resource. Difference is theorized *biologically* as situational, not intrinsic, at every level from gene to foraging pattern, thereby fundamentally changing the biological politics of the body. The relations between sex and gender have to be categorically reworked within these frames of knowledge. I would like to suggest this trend in explanatory strategies in biology as an allegory for interventions faithful to projects of feminist objectivity. The point is not that these new pictures of the biological female are simply true or not open to contestation and conversation. Quite the opposite. But these pictures foreground knowledge as situated conversation at every level of its articulation. The boundary between animal and human is one of the stakes in this allegory, as well as that between machine and organism.

So I will close with a final category useful to a feminist theory of situated knowledges: the apparatus of bodily production. In her analysis of the production of the poem as an object of literary value, Katie King offers tools that clarify matters in the objectivity debates among feminists. King suggests the term 'apparatus of literary production' to highlight the emergence of what is embodied as literature at the intersection of art, business, and technology. The apparatus of literary production is a matrix from which 'literature' is born. Focusing on the potent object of value called the 'poem', King applies her analytic frame to the relation of women and writing technologies (King, 1987b). I would like to adapt her work to understanding the generation – the actual production and reproduction – of bodies and other objects of value in scientific knowledge projects. At first glance, there is a limitation to using King's scheme inherent in the 'facticity' of biological discourse that is absent from literary discourse and its knowledge claims. Are biological bodies 'produced' or [illegible] of such objects or, what is the same thing, their final or unique determination of what can count as objective knowledge at a particular historical juncture. Like King's objects called 'poems', which are sites of literary production where language also is an actor independent of intentions and authors, bodies as objects of knowledge are material-semiotic generative nodes. Their *boundaries* materialize in social interaction. Boundaries are drawn by mapping practices; 'objects' do not pre-exist as such. Objects are boundary projects. But boundaries shift from within; boundaries are very tricky. What boundaries provisionally contain remains generative, productive of meanings and bodies. Siting (sighting) boundaries is a risky practice.

Objectivity is not about dis-engagement, but about mutual *and* usually unequal structuring, about taking risks in a world where 'we' are permanently mortal, that is, not in 'final' control. We have, finally, no clear and distinct ideas. The various contending biological bodies emerge at the intersection of biological research and writing, medical and other business practices, and technology, such as the visualization technologies enlisted as metaphors in this chapter. But also invited into that node of intersection is the analogue to the lively languages that actively intertwine in the production of literary value: the coyote and protean embodiments of a world as witty agent and actor. Perhaps the world resists being reduced to mere resource because it is – not mother/matter/mutter – but coyote, a figure for the always problematic, always potent tie of meaning and bodies. Feminist embodiment, feminist hopes for partiality, objectivity and situated knowledges, turn on conversations and codes at this potent node in fields of possible bodies and meanings. Here is where science, science fantasy, and science fiction converge in the objectivity question in feminism. Perhaps our hopes for accountability, for politics, for ecofeminism, turn on revisioning the world as coding trickster with whom we must learn to converse.

Notes

1 This chapter originated as a commentary on Harding (1986), at the Western Division meetings of the American Philosophical Association, San Francisco, March

1987. Support during the writing of this paper was generously provided by the Alpha Fund of the Institute for Advanced Study, Princeton, New Jersey. Thanks especially to Joan Scott, Rayna Rapp, Judy Newton, Judy Butler, Lila Abu-Lughod, and Dorinne Kondo.

2 For example, see Knorr-Cetina and Mulkay (1983); Bijker *et al.* (1987); and especially Latour (1984, 1988). Borrowing from Michel Tournier's *Vendredi* (1967), Latour's brilliant and maddening aphoristic polemic against all forms of reductionism makes the essential point for feminists: 'Méfiez-vous de la pureté; c'est le vitriol de l'ame' (Latour, 1984, p. 171). Latour is not otherwise a notable feminist theorist, but he might be made into one by readings as perverse as those he makes of the laboratory, that great machine for making significant mistakes faster than anyone else can, and so gaining world changing power. The laboratory for Latour is the railroad industry of epistemology, where facts can only be made to run on the tracks laid down from the laboratory out. Those who control the railroads control the surrounding territory. How could we have forgotten? But now it's not so much the bankrupt railroads we need as the satellite network. Facts run on lightbeams these days.

3 For an elegant and very helpful elucidation of a non-cartoon version of this argument, see White (1987). I still want more; and unfulfilled desire can be a powerful seed for changing the stories.

4 In her analysis exploring the fault line between modernism and postmodernism in ethnography and anthropology – in which the high stakes are the authorization or prohibition to craft *comparative* knowledge across 'cultures', from some epistemologically grounded vantage point *either* inside, outside, or in dialogical relation with any unit of analysis – Marilyn Strathern (1987) made the crucial observation that it is not the written ethnography that is parallel to the work of art as object-of-knowledge, but the *culture*. The Romantic and modernist natural-technical objects of knowledge, in science and in other cultural practice, stand on one side of this divide. The postmodernist formation stands on the other side, with its 'anti-aesthetic' of permanently split, problematized, always receding and deferred 'objects' of knowledge and practice, including signs, organisms, systems, selves, and cultures. 'Objectivity' in a postmodern frame cannot be about unproblematic objects; it must be about specific prosthesis and translation. Objectivity, which at root has been about crafting *comparative* knowledge (how to name things to be stable and to be like each other), becomes a question of the politics of redrawing of boundaries in order to have non-innocent conversations and connections. What is at stake in the debates about modernism and postmodernism is the pattern of relationships between and within bodies and language.

5 Zoe Sofoulis (1988) has produced a dazzlingly (she will forgive me the metaphor) theoretical treatment of technoscience, the psychoanalysis of science fiction culture, and the metaphorics of extra-terrestrialism, including a wonderful focus on the ideologies and philosophies of light, illumination, and discovery in Western mythics of science and technology. My essay was revised in dialogue with Sofoulis's arguments and metaphors in her PhD dissertation.

6 Crucial to this discussion are Harding (1986), Keller (1985), Hartsock (1983a, 1983b), Flax (1983, 1987), Keller and Grontkowski (1983), Rose (1986), Haraway (1985), and Petchesky (1987).

7 John Varley's science fiction short story called 'The Persistence of Vision' is part of the inspiration for this section. In the story, Varley constructs a utopian community

designed and built by the deaf-blind. He then explores these people's technologies and other mediations of communication and their relations to sighted children and visitors (Varley, 1978). In 'Blue Champagne', Varley (1986) transmutes the theme to interrogate the politics of intimacy and technology for a paraplegic young woman whose prosthetic device, the golden gypsy, allows her full mobility. But since the infinitely costly device is owned by an intergalactic communications and entertainment empire for which she works as a media star making 'feelies', she may keep her technological, intimate, enabling, other self only in exchange for her complicity in [illegible] communication.

8 I owe my understanding of the experience of these photographs to Jim Clifford, University of California at Santa Cruz, who identified their 'land ho!' effect on the reader.

9 Joan Scott reminded me that Teresa deLaurentis (1986, pp. 14–15) put it like this:

> Differences among women may be better understood as differences within women. . . . But once understood in their constitutive power – once it is understood, that is, that these differences not only constitute each woman's consciousness and subjective limits but all together define the *female subject of feminism* in its very specificity, its inherent and at least for now irreconcilable contradiction – these differences, then, cannot be again collapsed into a fixed identity, a sameness of all women as Woman, or a representation of Feminism as a coherent and available image.

10 Harding (1986, p. 18) suggested that gender has three dimensions, each historically specific: gender symbolism, the social-sexual division of labour, and processes of constructing individual gendered identity. I would enlarge her point to note that there is no reason to expect the three dimensions to co-vary or co-determine each other, at least not directly. That is, extremely steep gradients between contrasting terms in gender symbolism may very well not correlate with sharp social-sexual divisions of labour or social power, but may be closely related to sharp racial stratification or something else. Similarly, the processes of gendered subject formation may not be directly illuminated by knowledge of the sexual division of labour or the gender symbolism in the particular historical situation under examination. On the other hand, we should expect mediated relations among the dimensions. The mediations might move through quite different social axes of organization of both symbols, practice, and identity, such as race. And vice versa. I would suggest also that science, as well as gender or race, might usefully be broken up into such a multi-part scheme of symbolism, social practice, and subject position. More than three dimensions suggest themselves when the parallels are drawn. The different dimensions of, for example, gender, race, and science might mediate relations

among dimensions on a parallel chart. That is, racial divisions of labour might mediate the patterns of connection between symbolic connections and formation of individual subject positions on the science or gender chart. Or formations of gendered or racial subjectivity might mediate the relations between scientific social division of labour and scientific symbolic patterns.

The chart below begins an analysis by parallel dissections. In the chart (and in reality?), both gender and science are analytically asymmetrical; i.e., each term contains and obscures a structuring hierarchicalized binarism, sex/gender and nature/science. Each binarism orders the silent term by a logic of appropriation, as resource to product, nature to culture, potential to actual. Both poles of the binarism are constructed and structure each other dialectically. Within each voiced or explicit term, further asymmetrical splittings can be excavated, as from gender, masculine to feminine, and from science, hard sciences to soft sciences. This is a point about remembering how a particular analytical tool works, willy nilly, intended or not. The chart reflects common ideological aspects of discourse on science and gender and may help as an analytical tool to crack open mystified units like Science or Woman.

Gender	Science
symbolic system	symbolic system
social division of labour (by sex, by race, etc.)	social division of labour (by craft, industrial, or post-industrial logics)
individual identity/subject position (desiring/desired; autonomous/relational)	individual identity/subject position (knower/known; scientist/other)
material culture (gender paraphernalia and daily gender technologies: the narrow tracks on which sexual difference runs)	material culture (laboratories: the narrow tracks on which facts run)
dialectic of construction and discovery	dialectic of construction and discovery

11 Evelyn Keller (1987) insists on the important possibilities opened up by the construction of the intersection of the distinction between sex and gender, on the one hand, and nature and science, on the other. She also insists on the need to hold to some non-discursive grounding in 'sex' and 'nature', perhaps what I am calling the 'body' and 'world'.

References

Anzaldúa, Gloria (1987) *Borderlands/LaFrontera*. San Francisco: Spinsters/Aunt Lute.

Bryan, C.D.B. (1987) *The National Geographic Society: 100 Years of Adventure and Discovery*. New York: Abrams.

Bijker, Wiebe E., Hughes, Thomas P. and Pinch, Trevor. eds. (1987) *The Social Construction of Technological Systems*. Cambridge, MA: MIT Press.

deLaurentis, Teresa (1986) 'Feminist Studies/Critical Studies.' In ed. Teresa deLaurentis, *Feminist Studies/Critical Studies*. Bloomington: Indiana University Press.

Eco, Umberto (1983) *The Name of the Rose*, trans. William Weaver. New York: Harcourt Brace Jovanovich.

Flax, Jane (1983) 'Political Philosophy and the Patriarchal Unconscious: A Psychoanalytical Perspective on Epistemology and Metaphysics.' In Harding and Hintikka (1983) pp. 245–282.

Flax, Jane (1987) Postmodernism and Gender Relations in Feminist Theory. *Signs* 12: 621–643.

Haraway, Donna (1985) Manifesto for Cyborgs: Science, Technology and Social Feminism [illegible]

[illegible] Specifically Feminist Historical Materialism.' In Harding and Hintikka (1983).

Hartsock, Nancy (1983b) *Money, Sex, and Power*. New York: Longman; Boston: Northeastern University Press.

Keller, Evelyn Fox (1985) *Reflections on Gender and Science*. New Haven: Yale University Press.

Keller, Evelyn Fox (1987) The Gender/Science System: Or is Sex to Gender as Nature is to Science? *Hypatia* 2: 37–49.

Keller, Evelyn Fox and Grontkowski, Christine (1983) 'The Mind's Eye.' In Harding and Hintikka (1983).

King, Katie (1987a) 'Canons without Innocence', University of California at Santa Cruz, PhD thesis.

King, Katie (1987b) *The Passing Dreams of Choice . . . Once Before and After: Audre Lord and the Apparatus of Literary Production*, book prospectus, University of Maryland at College Park.

Knorr-Cetina, Karin and Mulkay, Michael. eds. (1983) *Science Observed: Perspectives on the Social Study of Science*. Beverly Hills: Sage.

Kuhn, Annette (1982) *Women's Pictures: Feminism and Cinema*. London: Routledge & Kegan Paul.

Latour, Bruno (1984) *Les Microbes, guerre et paix, suivi des irreductions*. Paris: Metailie.

Latour, Bruno (1988) *The Pasteurization of France, Followed by Irreductions: A Politico-Scientific Essay*. Cambridge, MA: Harvard University Press.

Mohanty, Chandra Talpade (1984) Under Western Eyes: Feminist Scholarship and Colonial Discourse. *Boundary* 2: 333–358.

Petchesky, Rosalind Pollack (1987) Fetal Images: The Power of Visual Culture in the Politics of Reproduction. *Feminist Studies* 13: 263–292.

Rose, Hilary (1986) 'Women's Work, Women's Knowledge.' In ed. Juliet Mitchell and Ann Oakley, *What is Feminism: A Re-examination*. New York: Pantheon, pp. 161–183.

Sandoval, Chela (n.d.) *Yours in Struggle: Women Respond to Racism, a Report on the National Women's Studies Association*. Oakland, CA: Center for Third World Organizing.

Sofoulis, Zoe (1988) 'Through the Lumen: Frankenstein and the Optics of Re-origination', University of California at Santa Cruz, PhD thesis.

Strathern, Marilyn (1987) Out of Context: the Persuasive Fictions of Anthropology. *Anthropology* 28: 251–281.

Tournier, Michel (1967) *Vendredi*. Paris: Gallimard.
Varley, John (1978) 'The Persistence of Vision.' In *The Persistence of Vision*. New York: Dell, pp. 265–316.
Varley, John (1986) 'Blue Champagne.' In *Blue Champagne*. New York: Berkeley, pp. 17–79.
White, Hayden (1987) *The Content of Form: Narrative Discourse and Historical Representation*. Baltimore: Johns Hopkins University Press.

Chapter 16

Sandra Harding

Challenges and resources

Are the natural sciences multicultural? Could they and should they be? Such questions initially may seem ignorant, or at least odd, since it is exactly the lack of cultural fingerprints that conventionally is held responsible for the great successes of the sciences. The sciences "work," they are universally valid, it is said, because they transcend culture. They can tell us how nature really functions rather than merely how the British, Native Americans, or Chinese fear or want it to work.

There are good reasons to wonder whether one should regard this "universal science" claim as ending the matter, however. Multicultural perspectives are providing more-comprehensive and less distorted understandings of history, literature, the arts, and the social sciences. They are beginning to reshape public consciousness as they are disseminated through television specials, new elementary and high-school history and literature textbooks, and, indeed, daily news reports of perspectives on the West (or should one say the "North"?) that conflict with the conventional beliefs that many Westerners now understand to be Eurocentric. Do the challenges raised by multicultural perspectives in other fields have no consequences for the natural sciences?

We can identify three central questions for anyone who wishes to explore this issue. First, to what extent does modern science have origins in non-European cultures? Second, have there been and could there be other sciences, culturally distinctive ones, that also "work" and thus are universal in this sense? Third, in what ways is modern science culturally European or European-American? Fortunately, pursuit of these questions has been made easier by the appearance in English recently of a small but rich set of writings on such topics. These "postcolonial science studies," as I shall refer to them, are authored by scientists and engineers, a few anthropologists, and historians of science, who are of both European and Third World descent (the latter live in the Third *and* First Worlds).

The proceedings of two recent conferences give a sense of the increasing international interest in these topics. *Science and Empires: Historical Studies about Scientific Development and European Expansion* contains about one-third of the 120 papers presented at a UNESCO sponsored conference in Paris in 1986. The conference was organized by the French government's National Center for Scientific Research, and these proceedings are published by one of the most prestigious and largest science studies publishers in the world. *The Revenge of Athena: Science, Exploitation and the Third World* contains twenty of the thirty-five or so papers presented at a 1986 conference in Penang, Malaysia, where Asian scientists, engineers, and science policy analysts were joined by several historians of science of European descent. The final version of the conference's policy statement, the Third World Network's *Modern Science in Crisis: A Third World Response*, has been published separately.[1]

Now is none too soon to note that the terms of this discussion are and must be controversial, for whoever gets to name natural and social realities gets to control how they will be organized. Moreover, it is not just language that is at issue, but also a "discourse" – a conceptual framework with its logic linking my words in ways already familiar to readers – that is adequate to the project of this essay.[2] For example, for conventional science theorists it is controversial to use the term "science" to refer to the sciences' social institutions, technologies and applications, metaphors, language, and social meanings: they insist on restricting the term's reference to sciences' abstract cognitive core – the laws of nature and/or the legendary scientific method, thereby excluding the other parts of sciences' practices and culture, which many contemporary science theorists insist are also fundamental constituents of the sciences.[3]

Moreover, the terms of multicultural discourse are and must be controversial. Do my references to "Western" replicate the dualistic, orientalist thinking that has been so widely criticized? Is it not precisely from the borderlands between "Western" and "non-Western" that this paper and the thought of its cited authors arise?[4] How "Western" is Western science anyway (a topic to be pursued below)? And which of the diverse peoples currently living in Europe and North America get to count as Western? Is Japan "non-Western" and "Third World"? Additionally, Third World cultures are immensely diverse, and they are internally heterogeneous by class, gender, ethnicity, religion, politics, and other features. Does ignoring or marginalizing these differences not disseminate characteristic Eurocentric tendencies to homogenize, and to refuse to think carefully about, peoples that Westerners have constructed as their Others? Furthermore, does "neocolonial" not designate better than "postcolonial" the present relations between the West and its former colonies? And are African and Indigenous Americans appropriately thought of as "colonized"? What are the politics of continuing to refer to the First and Third Worlds, when this contrast is the product of the Eurocentric Cold War? Finally, should the knowledge traditions of non-Western cultures be referred to as "sciences" rather than only as "ethnosciences" (a topic I take up below)?

We cannot easily settle such questions. In some cases, it is the familiar languages that are at issue in the questions raised in this essay. In other cases, less controversial terms have not yet been found or have not yet reached general circulation. Moreover, changing language sometimes advances the growth of knowledge – but in other cases it simply substitutes an acceptable veneer under which ignorance and exploitative politics can continue to flourish. Discourses, conceptual schemes, paradigms, and epistemes are at issue, not just words. I hope readers can penetrate beyond these inadequate languages to the issues that can help us develop less-problematic thinking, speech, and actions. I shall primarily use the terms that the postcolonial authors use, though their own usages are diverse and sometimes conflicting.

One term worth clarifying, however, is "Eurocentrism." Here I refer to a cluster of assumptions, central among which are that peoples of European descent, their institutions, practices, and conceptual schemes, express the unique heights of human [illegible] – who are concerned to rethink critically those social relations past and present and the role of the sciences in them, and who wish to bring about more-effective links between scientific projects and those of advancing democratic social relations.

The universal science view – that modern sciences are uniquely successful exactly because they have eliminated cultural fingerprints from their results of research – incorporates some assumptions that are probably false, or that at least have not been supported by evidence. For example, it assumes that no other sciences could generate the laws of gravity, or antibiotics; that modern science does not also "work" for producing human and natural disasters; that what has worked best to advance the West will and should work best to advance other societies; that modern sciences are the best ones for discovering all of the laws of nature; and that the kinds of projects for which modern sciences have worked best in the past are the ones at which any possible sciences – past, present, and future – should want to succeed.[6] Yet in spite of these problematic assumptions, the conventional view contains important insights. Such insights are more reasonably explained, however, in ways that give up these problematic assumptions and locate modern sciences on the more accurate historical and geographical maps produced by the postcolonial accounts.[7]

Let us turn to the three questions that will help to determine the degree to which science may be multicultural.

Question 1: Does modern science have non-Western origins?

The least controversial response is to acknowledge that modern sciences have borrowed from other cultures. Most people are aware of at least a couple of such examples. However, the borrowings have been far more extensive and important than the conventional histories reveal. Modern sciences have been enriched by contributions not only from the so-called complex cultures of China, India, and other east Asian and Islamic societies, but also from the so-called simpler ones of Africa, the pre-Columbian Americas, and others that interacted with the expansion of European cultures.

To list just a few examples: Egyptian mystical philosophies and premodern European alchemical traditions were far more useful to the development of sciences in Europe than is suggested by the conventional view that these are only irrational and marginally valuable elements of immature Western sciences.[8] The Greek legacy of scientific and mathematical thought was not only fortuitously preserved but also developed in Islamic culture, to be claimed by the sciences of the European Renaissance.[9] Furthermore, the identification of Greek culture as European is questionable on several counts. For one thing, the idea of Europe and the social relations that such an idea made possible only came into existence centuries later: some would date the emergence of "Europe" to Charlemagne's achievements; others, to fifteenth-century events. Another point here is that through the spread of Islam, diverse cultures of Africa and Asia can also claim Greek culture as their legacy.[10]

Some knowledge traditions that were appropriated and fully integrated into modern sciences are not acknowledged at all. Thus the principles of pre-Columbian agriculture, which provided potatoes for almost every European ecological niche and thereby had a powerful effect on the nutrition and subsequent history of Europe, were subsumed into European science.[11] Mathematical achievements from India and Arabic cultures provide other examples. The magnetic needle, the rudder, gunpowder, and many other technologies useful to Europeans and the advance of their sciences (were these not part of scientific instrumentation?) were borrowed from China. Knowledge of local geographies, geologies, animals, plants, classification schemes, medicines, pharmacologies, agriculture, navigational techniques, and local cultures that formed significant parts of European sciences' picture of nature were provided in part by the knowledge traditions of non-Europeans. ("We took on board a native of the region, and dropped him off six weeks further up the coast," reputedly report voyagers' accounts.) Summarizing the consequences for modern sciences of British imperialism in India, one recent account points out that in effect "India was added as a laboratory to the edifice of modern science."[12] We could say the same for all of the lands to which the "voyages of discovery" and later colonization projects took the Europeans.[13]

Thus modern science already is multicultural, at least in the sense that elements of the knowledge traditions of many different non-European cultures have been incorporated into it. There is nothing unusual about such scientific borrowing: it is evident in the ordinary, everyday borrowing that occurs when scientists revive models, metaphors, procedures, technologies, or other ideas from older European scientific traditions, or when they borrow such elements from the culture outside their laboratories and field stations, or from other contemporary sciences.[14] After all, a major point of professional conferences and international exchange programs, not to mention "keeping up with the literature," is to permit everyone to borrow everyone else's achievements. As we shall shortly see, without such possibilities, sciences wither and lose their creativity. What is at issue here is only the Eurocentric failure to acknowledge the origins and importance to "real science" of these borrowings from non-European cultures, thereby trivializing the achievements of other scientific traditions.

To give up this piece of Eurocentrism does not challenge the obvious accomplishments of modern sciences. Every thinking person should be able to accept the claim that modern science is multicultural in this sense. Of course, it is one thing to accept a claim that conflicts with one's own, and quite another to use it to transform one's own thinking. To do the latter would require historians of science and the rest of us to locate our accounts on a global civilizational map, rather than only on the Eurocentric map of Europe that we all learned.

There are implications here also for philosophies and social studies of science. For example, the standard contrast of the objectivity, rationality, and progressiveness of modern scientific thought vs. the only-locally-valid, irrational, and backward or primitive thought of other cultures begins to seem less explanatorily useful and, indeed, less accurate after the postcolonial accounts. Whether overtly stated or only discreetly assumed, such contrasts damage our ability not only to appreciate the strengths of other scientific traditions, but also to grasp what are the real strengths and limitations of modern sciences[illegible]

[illegible]

Do any other knowledge traditions deserve to be called sciences? The conventional view is that only modern sciences are entitled to this designation. In such an account, science is treated as a cultural emergent in early modern Europe. While a shift in social conditions may have made it possible in the first place, what emerged was a form of knowledge-seeking that is fundamentally self-generating; its "internal logic" is responsible for its great successes. This "logic of scientific research" has been characterized in various ways – as inductivism, crucial experiments, the hypothetico-deductive method, or a cycle of normal science–revolution–normal science. Whatever the logic attributed to scientific research, it is conceptualized as "inside" science, and not "outside" it "in society." Though Chinese or African astronomers may have made discoveries before Europeans, this is not sufficient to indicate that the former were really doing what is reasonably regarded as "science."[15] Thus while science is said to need a supportive social climate in order to flourish, the particular form of that climate is claimed to leave no distinctive cultural fingerprints on science's results of research.

Is this a reasonable position? Is the content of the successes of modern sciences due entirely to the sciences' "internal" features? For one thing, not all of the successes attributed to Western science are unique to it. In many cases, "what has been ascribed to the European tradition has been shown on closer examination to have been done elsewhere by others earlier. (Thus Harvey was not the first to discover the circulation of blood, but an Arabic scientist was; Paracelsus did not introduce the fourth element 'salt' and start the march towards modern chemistry, but a twelfth-century alchemist from Kerala did so teaching in Saudi Arabia.)"[16] Many other cultures made sophisticated astronomical observations repeated only centuries later in Europe. For example, many of the observations that Galileo's telescope made possible were known to the Dogon peoples of West Africa more than 1500 years earlier: either they had invented some sort of telescope, or they had extraordinary eyesight.[17] Many mathematical achievements of Indians and other Asian peoples were adopted or invented in Europe much later. Indeed, it is as revealing to examine the ideas that European sciences *did not* borrow from the knowledge traditions they encountered as it is to examine what they did borrow. Among the notions "unborrowed" are the ability to deal with very large numbers (such as 10^{53}), the zero as a separate number with its own arithmetical logic, and irrational and negative numbers.[18]

Joseph Needham points out that "between the first century B.C. and fifteenth century A.D. Chinese civilization was much more efficient than the occidental in applying human natural knowledge to practical human needs . . . in many ways this was much more congruent with modern science than was the world outlook of Christendom."[19] Thus other knowledge traditions "worked" at projects that Western sciences could accomplish only much later. If the achievements of modern science should be attributed to its "internal logic," then evidently this logic is not unique to it.

This brings us to a second point: nobody has discovered an eleventh commandment handed down from the heavens specifying what may and may not be counted as a science. Obviously the project of drawing a line between science and nonscience is undertaken because it emphasizes a contrast thought to be important. Belief in the reality of this demarcation, as in the reality of the science vs. pseudo-science duality, is necessary in order to preserve the mystique of the uniqueness and purity of the West's knowledge-seeking. Thus the sciences, as well as the philosophies that are focused on describing and explaining the kind of rationality so highly valued in the modern West, have been partners with anthropology in maintaining a whole series of Eurocentric contrasts whether or not individual scientists, philosophers, or anthropologists so intended. The self-image of the West depends on contrasts, not only between the rational and irrational, but also between civilization and the savage or primitive, the advanced or progressive and the backward, dynamic and static societies, developed and undeveloped, the historical and the natural, the rational and the irrational. Through these and other contrasts the European Self has constructed its Other, and has thereby justified its exploitative treatment of various peoples.[20] My point here is that even though there clearly are obvious and large differences between modern sciences and the traditions of seeking systematic knowledge of the natural world to be found in other cultures, it is useful to think of them all as sciences in order to gain a more objective understanding of the causes of Western successes, the achievements of other sciences, and possible directions for future local and global sciences.[21]

One cannot avoid noticing, moreover, that European scholars disagree on exactly which distinctive features are responsible for the success of European sciences. It is instructive to look at four accounts of Western scientific uniqueness made by distinguished and otherwise progressive Western analysts – ones whose work has in important ways challenged conventional Eurocentric assumptions. Anthropologist Robin Horton, who has shown how African traditional thought is surprisingly similar to Western scientific thought, attributes the residual crucial differences to the fact that modern scientific thought takes a critical stance toward tradition and is aided in this project by its rejection of magical relations between language and the world; it holds that we can manipulate language without thereby changing the world.[22] However, as philosopher J.E. Wiredu points out, Horton undervalues the extent to which noncritical and dogmatic assumptions prevail in modern Western scientific thought. After all, "classical" British empiricism is "traditional thought" for Western scientific communities and those who value scientific rationality: the once-radical claims of Locke and Hume have become uncontroversial assumptions for us – and yet an anthropologist from another culture might refer to them as our "folk beliefs." So how accurate is it to claim that a critical approach to tradition is responsible for the successes of modern sciences? Moreover, if science is modern in its rejection of magical relations between language and the world, scientists surely are not, Wiredu continues, since many also hold religious beliefs that invest in just such magical relations.[23] Many commentators have noted the sacred – dare one say "magical" – faith in the accuracy and progressiveness of modern science that is characteristic of many scientists and of the "educated classes" more generally.

Historian Thomas Kuhn would agree with Wiredu's assessment that Western sciences are in significant respects uncritical of conventional assumptions; indeed, he [illegible]

four centuries. No other place and time has supported the very special communities from which scientific productivity comes."[24] Though one might think that a social community is not "internal" to the logic of science, Kuhn insists that in an important sense it is; the "very special" scientific communities are ones trained to follow modern science's success-producing internal logic of paradigm creation, puzzle solving with anomaly tolerance, paradigm breakdown, and then, eventually, another paradigm shift. Kuhn directed attention to the importance of the distinctive social organization of modern scientific communities. However, one can also see that his problematic here, his concern to identify a different, distinctive cause of modern science's successes, is inseparable in his thought from the widespread Eurocentric assumptions he articulates about the origins and virtues of European civilization.

Historian Joseph Needham – who does refer to Chinese knowledge traditions as sciences when comparing them to those of the modern West, and who would contest Kuhn's characterization of non-European sciences as primitive and the West's as uniquely descended from the Greek – proposes yet another kind of cause of the success of modern European sciences:

> When we say that modern science developed only in Western Europe at the time of Galileo in the late Renaissance, we mean surely that there and then alone there developed the fundamental bases of the structure of the natural sciences as we have them today, namely the application of mathematical hypotheses to Nature, the full understanding and use of the experimental method, the distinction between primary and secondary qualities, the geometrisation of space, and the acceptance of the mechanical model of reality. Hypotheses of primitive or medieval type distinguish themselves quite clearly from those of modern type.[25]

For Needham, success came, not from the attitudes on which Horton focuses, nor from the organization of scientific communities that appears so important to Kuhn, but from a specific set of assumptions about the nature of reality and appropriate methods of research.

Finally, sociologist Edgar Zilsel, asking why modern science developed only in Renaissance Europe rather than in China or some other "high culture," claims it was the emergence of a new social class that, in contrast to the classes of aristocratic or slave societies, was permitted to combine a trained intellect with willingness to do manual labor, that allowed the invention of experimental method. Only in early modern Europe, where there was an absence of slavery and where aristocracy was being challenged, was there a progressive culture, he implies, that gave individuals reasons to want to obtain both intellectual and manual training.[26]

No doubt one could find additional features of the cultures and practices of modern sciences to which other historians would attribute their successes. These different purported causes are probably not entirely independent of each other, and each would win its supporters. However, my point is only that there is no general agreement, even among the most distinguished and progressive Western science theorists, about the distinctive causes of modern science, and that the search for such an explanation and the kinds of accounts on which such scholars settle usually remain tied to Eurocentric dualisms.

A third source of skepticism about conventional claims for the unique efficacy of Western sciences arises from an often-repeated argument in the postcolonial accounts: European sciences advanced because they focused on describing and explaining those aspects of nature's regularities that permitted the upper classes of Europeans to multiply and thrive, especially through the prospering of their military, imperial, and otherwise expansionist projects. Interestingly, evidence for this claim can now easily be gathered from many of the museum exhibits and scholarly publications associated with the 1992 quincentennial of the Columbian encounter, which drew attention, intentionally or not, to the numerous ways European expansion in the Americas advanced European sciences. A detailed account of how British colonialism in India advanced European sciences is provided by R.K. Kochhar. The British needed better navigation, so they built observatories, funded astronomers, and kept systematic records of their voyages. The first European sciences to be established in India were, not surprisingly, geography and botany.[27] Nor is the intimate relation between scientific advance in the West and expansionist efforts a matter only of the distant past (or only of expansion into foreign lands, as noted earlier): by the end of World War II, the development of US physics had been virtually entirely handed over to the direction of US militarism and nationalism, as historian Paul Forman has shown in detail.[28]

Thus European expansionism has changed the "topography" of global scientific knowledge, causing the advance of European sciences and the decline or under-development of scientific traditions of other cultures: "The topography of the world of knowledge before the last few centuries could be delineated as several hills of knowledge roughly corresponding to the regional civilizations of, say, West Asia, South Asia, East Asia and Europe. The last few centuries have seen the levelling of the other hills and from their debris the erection of a single one with its base in Europe."[29]

These arguments begin to challenge the idea that the causes of modern science's achievements are to be located entirely in their purported inherently transcultural character. It turns out that what makes them "work" (and appear uniquely to do so) is at least partly their focus on kinds of projects that European expansion could both advance and benefit from while simultaneously clearing the field of potentially rival scientific traditions. This is not to deny that Western sciences can claim many great and, so far, unique scientific achievements. Instead, it is to argue, contrary to conventional views, that scientific "truths," no less than false beliefs, are caused by social relations as well as by nature's regularities and the operations of reason.[30]

But could there be other, culturally distinctive sciences that also "work"? The postcolonial accounts have shown how rich and sophisticated were the scientific traditions of Asia, Islam, and "simpler" societies of the past. But what about the future? We return to this issue shortly.

[illegible] in the very "laws of nature" that form their cognitive/technical core. Here I can identify only five of the distinctively "Western" features persistently noted in the postcolonial literature.

First, as indicated above, the particular aspects of nature that modern sciences describe and explain, and the ways in which they are described and explained, have been selected in part by the conscious purposes and unconscious interests of European expansion. Of course these are not the only factors shaping these sciences – androcentric, religious, local bourgeois, and other purposes and interests have also had powerful effects, as many recent accounts have shown – but they are significant. The "problems" that have gotten to count as scientific are those for which expansionist Europe needed solutions; the aspects of nature about which the beneficiaries of expansionism have not needed or wanted to know have remained uncharted. Thus culturally distinctive patterns of both systematic knowledge and systematic ignorance in modern sciences' picture of nature's regularities and their underlying causal tendencies can be detected from the perspective of cultures with different preoccupations. For example, modern sciences answered questions about how to improve European land and sea travel, to mine ores, to identify the economically useful minerals, plants, and animals of other parts of the world, to manufacture and farm for the benefit of Europeans living in Europe, the Americas, Africa, and India, to improve their health (and occasionally that of the workers who produced profit for them), to protect settlers in the colonies from settlers of other nationalities, to gain access to the labor of the indigenous residents, and to do all this to benefit only local European citizens – the Spanish vs. the Portuguese, French, or British. These sciences have not been concerned to explain how the consequences of interventions in nature for the benefit of Europeans of the advantaged gender, classes, and ethnicities would change the natural resources available to the majority of the world's peoples, or what the economic, social, political, and ecological costs to less-advantaged groups in and outside Europe would be of the interventions in nature and social relations that science's experimental methods "foresaw" and to which it directed policy-makers. Sciences with other purposes – explaining how to shift from unrenewable to renewable natural resources, to maintain a healthy but less environmentally destructive standard of living in the overdeveloped societies, to clean up toxic wastes, to benefit women in every culture, and so on – could generate other, perhaps sometimes conflicting, descriptions and explanations of nature's regularities and underlying causal tendencies.

Second, early modern sciences' conception of nature is distinctively Western, or at least alien to many other cultures. For the resident of medieval Europe, nature was enchanted; the "disenchantment of nature" was a crucial element in the shift from the medieval to the modern mentality, from feudalism to capitalism, from Ptolemaic to Galilean astronomy, and from Aristotelian to Newtonian physics.[32] Modern science related to a worldly power in nature, not to power that lay outside the material universe. To gain power over nature would, for modern man, violate no moral or religious principles.

Moreover, the Western conception of laws of nature drew on both Judeo-Christian religious beliefs and the increasing familiarity in early modern Europe with centralized royal authority, with royal absolutism. Needham points out that this Western idea that the universe was a "great empire, ruled by a divine Logos"[33] was never comprehensible at any time in the long history of Chinese science because a common thread in the diverse Chinese traditions was that nature was self-governed, a web of relationships without a weaver, with which humans interfered at their own peril: "Universal harmony comes about not by the celestial fiat of some King of Kings, but by the spontaneous co-operation of all beings in the universe brought about by their following the internal necessities of their own natures. . . . [A]ll entities at all levels behave in accordance with their position in the greater patterns (organisms) of which they are parts."[34] Compared to Renaissance science, the Chinese conception of nature was problematic, blocking their interest in discovering "precisely formulated abstract laws ordained from the beginning by a celestial lawgiver for non-human nature": "There was no confidence that the code of Nature's laws could be unveiled and read, because there was no assurance that a divine being, even more rational than ourselves, had ever formulated such a code capable of being read."[35]

Of course, such notions of "command and duty in the 'Laws' of Nature" have disappeared from modern science, replaced by the notion of statistical regularities that describe rather than prescribe nature's order – in a sense, a return, Needham comments, to the Taoist perspective. And yet other residues of the earlier conception remain. Evelyn Fox Keller has pointed to the positive political implications of conceptualizing nature simply as ordered rather than as law-governed."[36] My point here is only that Western conceptions of nature have been intimately linked to historically shifting Western religious and political ideals.

Third, the European, Christian conception of the laws of nature was just one kind of regional resource used to develop European sciences – elements of medieval scientific and classical Greek thought, and other religious, national, class, and gender metaphors, models, and assumptions also were available. The adoption of these cultural resources is familiar from the writings of conventional historians of Western sciences. In the context of the postcolonial literatures, these now appear as distinctively European cultural elements, ones that make modern sciences foreign to peoples in many other cultures.

Another kind of regional resource available only "in Europe" was created through the intermingling and integration of non-European elements with each other and with resources already available in Europe to make more useful elements for modern science. That is, the non-European elements indicated above were not only borrowed, but also frequently transformed through processes possible only for a culture at the center of global exchanges. Thus the map and route of European expansion could be traced in the expansion of the content of European sciences. Prior to European expansion, African, Asian, and indigenous American cultures had long traded scientific and technological ideas among themselves as they exchanged other products, but this possibility was reduced or eliminated for them and transferred to Europe during the [illegible]

racial and ethnic minorities and women located at the periphery of local and global economic and political networks.[38]

The causes of this distribution are not mysterious or unforeseen. For one thing, it is not "man" whom sciences enable to make better use of nature's resources, but only those already positioned in social hierarchies. As Khor Kok Peng puts the point, the latter already own and control both nature, in the form of land with its forests, water, plants, animals, and minerals, and the tools to extract and process such resources. These people are the ones who are in a position to decide "what to produce, how to produce it, what resources to use up to produce, and what technology to use":

> We thus have this spectacle, on the one hand, of the powerful development of technological capacity, so that the basic and human needs of every human being could be met if there were an appropriate arrangement of social and production systems; and, on the other hand, of more than half the world's population (and something like two-thirds the Third World's people) living in conditions where their basic and human needs are not met.[39]

Not only are the benefits and costs of modern science distributed in ways that disproportionately benefit elites in the West and elsewhere, but science's accounting practices are distorted to make this distribution invisible to those who gain the benefits. All consequences of sciences and technologies that are not planned or intended are externalized as "not science."[40] The critics argue that such an "internalization of profits and externalization of costs is the normal consequence when nature is treated as if its individual components were isolated and unrelated."[41]

Fifth, and finally, even if modern sciences bore none of the above cultural fingerprints, their value-neutrality would itself mark them as culturally distinctive. Of course, this is a contradiction ("If it's value-free, then it's not value-free"), or at least highly paradoxical. The point is that maximizing cultural neutrality, not to mention claiming it, is itself a culturally specific value; both the reality and the claim are at issue here. Most cultures do not value neutrality, so one that does is easily identifiable. Moreover, the claim to neutrality is itself characteristic of the administrators of modern, Western cultures organized by principles of scientific rationality.[42] Surprisingly, it turns out that abstractness and formality express distinctive cultural features, not the absence of any culture at all. Thus when modern science is introduced into many other societies, it is experienced as a rude and brutal cultural intrusion precisely because of this feature, too. Modern sciences' "neutrality" devalues not only local scientific traditions, but also the culturally defining values and interests that make a tradition Confucian rather than Protestant or Islamic. Claims for modern sciences' universality and objectivity are "a politics of disvaluing local concerns and knowledge and legitimating 'outside experts.'"[43]

Interesting issues emerge from the discovery of the cultural specificity of modern sciences. For example, the conventional understanding of the universality of modern science is contested in two ways. First, these accounts argue that universality is established as an empirical consequence of European expansion, not as an epistemological cause of valid claims, to be located "inside science" – for example, in its method. As one author puts it, "The epistemological claim of the 'universality of science' . . . covers what is an empirical fact, the material and intellectual construction of this 'universal science' and its 'international character.' The 'universality of science' does not appear to be the cause but the effect of a process that we cannot explain or understand merely by concentrating our attention on epistemological claims."[44]

Second, a wedge has been driven between the universality of a science and its cultural neutrality. While the laws of nature "discovered" by modern sciences that explain, for instance, how gravity and antibiotics work, will have their effects on us regardless of our cultural location, they are not the only possible such universal laws of nature; there could be many universally valid but culturally distinctive sciences.

> [I]f we were to picture physical reality as a large blackboard, and the branches and shoots of the knowledge tree as markings in white chalk on this blackboard, it becomes clear that the yet unmarked and unexplored parts occupy a considerably greater space than that covered by the chalk tracks. The socially structured knowledge tree has thus explored only certain partial aspects of physical reality, explorations that correspond to the particular historical unfoldings of the civilization within which the knowledge tree emerged.
>
> Thus entirely different knowledge systems corresponding to different historical unfoldings in different civilizational settings become possible. This raises the possibility that in different historical situations and contexts sciences very different from the European tradition could emerge. Thus an entirely new set of "universal" but socially determined natural science laws are possible.[45]

These accounts thus provide additional evidence for the claim that fully modern sciences could be constructed within other cultures – the argument I left incomplete in the last section. Significant cultural features of modern sciences have not blocked their development as fully modern, according to the postcolonial accounts; indeed, they are responsible for just these successes.[46] Moreover, one can now ask, which of the original cultural purposes of modern science that continue today to shape its conceptual framework are still desirable? Should we want to continue to develop sciences that, intentionally or not, succeed by extinguishing or obscuring all other scientific traditions, directing limitless consumption of scarce and unrenewable resources, distributing their benefits internally and their costs externally, and so forth? Furthermore, these arguments show that if culture shapes science, then changes in local and global cultures can shape different sciences "here" as well as "there."

Future sciences: opportunities and uncertainties

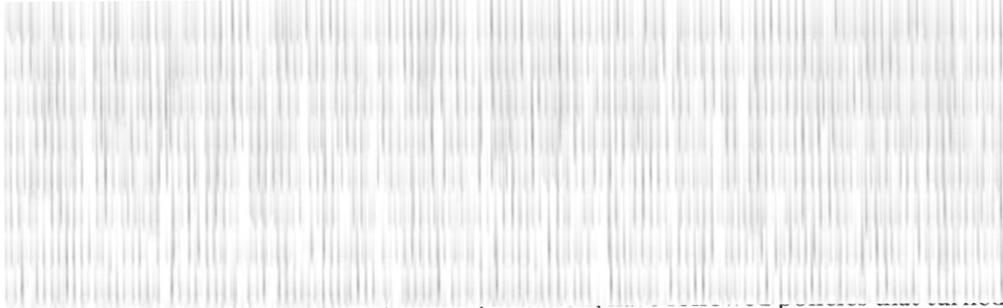

out not to be wise, and have suffered from natural and social processes that they could not escape. The point, instead, is that the balance sheet for both modern sciences and those of other knowledge traditions looks different from the perspective of the lives of the majority of the world's peoples than it does from that of the lives of advantaged groups in the West and elsewhere, and there are good reasons to think that in some respects the perspective of the elites is not less objective."[47] We should also recollect that sciences of European or other civilizational histories have different effects on the lives of women and men, and of peoples in different classes and ethnicities.[48] This important issue cannot be pursued further here, but it has to be kept in mind when thinking about the very general options that I now turn to review.

Projects starting in the Third World

One's location in local and global social relations gives urgency to partially different projects, and also gives one access to different resources. In the balance of this essay I wish to consider some of these different priorities and resources, although, of course, those who value the advancing of democracy and, especially, the bringing of modern sciences under more democratic social controls will share a great deal. One's social location both enables and limits what one can see and do. Here I wish to focus on the resources of certain kinds of social locations. (As stressed earlier, both the "Third World" and the "West" are socially diverse.) Of course, no one would deny that there are aspects of modern sciences, their cultures and practices, that can and should be used to benefit all peoples living in every society. What is at issue here is not that claim, but a host of others having to do with who will decide which aspects these are, how they should be used in different cultures, and how the benefits and costs of their production and use are to be distributed.

To begin with, we must note that for the small middle-classes in most Third World societies, modern sciences represent desirable resources for the ways that these groups participate in industry, agriculture, medicine, and the state organization of social life, and for the higher status and increased power that are awarded there as well as here to most things of European origin. Moreover, it is modern scientific practices that are demanded as a condition of economic aid by such international organizations as the World Bank and the International Monetary Fund. Thus, many people of Third World descent whose voices reach Western ears are no more critical of modern sciences than are many Westerners. However, great social changes often have been stimulated by the far-sighted projects of a few visionaries. (Think, for example, of the effects of the work of people recently regarded as "kooks" such as Rachel Carson, critics of "passive smoking," and vitamin advocates.) Many features of the postcolonial critical analyses express perspectives that appear in virtually every Third World culture, and that are rapidly gathering support in the West. What is needed is more extensive respectful public discussion of the issues raised in and by these writings.

What are the alternatives envisioned in Third World postcolonial science analyses to the continued suppression of indigenous scientific goals, practices, and culture by Western ones? One proposal is to integrate endangered Third World sciences into modern sciences. The continued expansion of European social relations and their modernization pressures are rapidly causing the extinction of many non-Western cultures, thus possibly losing for humanity the unique and valuable kinds of knowledge that they have achieved:

> just as forest peoples possess much knowledge of plants and animals that is valid and useful, regional civilizations possess stores of elaborate knowledge on a wide variety of topics. These stores, the results of millennia of human enquiry, were lost from view because of the consequences of the European "discovery." But now it appears they will be increasingly opened up, foraged for valid uses and what is worthy opportunistically used. The operative word should be "opportunistically," to guard against a mere romantic and reactionary return to assumed past golden ages of these civilizations.[49]

Just as modernization pressures are reducing the diversity of plant, animal, and even human genetic pools, so, too, they are reducing the diversity of cultures and the valuable human ideas developed in them. These scientific legacies are interesting and valuable to preserve for their own sake – but they also can make even greater contributions to modern sciences.

This proposal raises many questions. If this were the only strategy for using other scientific legacies, would it not be a self-fulfilling one, offering no resistance to the eventual extinction of all "freestanding" non-Western scientific traditions? Is it presumed that only those non-Western elements that *could* be incorporated without dissonance into modern sciences would be, and that other kinds of valuable knowledge would be abandoned because they conflicted with modern scientific paradigms, thus leaving one global science that is distinctively the product of the European civilizational tradition? Is it inevitable that modern science/culture end up the global one? How should Westerners feel about extracting for the benefit of their cultural legacy the resources that become available from cultures that are dying as a consequence of the policies of overadvantaged groups? (But how much should it matter what Westerners feel about such things?)

A second proposal is to integrate in the other direction – thus, indigenous scientific traditions around the world would be strengthened through adopting those parts of modern sciences that could be integrated into *them*. This kind of process has already occurred in many places. For example, one report describes how modern sciences were integrated into local knowledge systems in China.[50] Indian anthropologist Ashis Nandy argues for a comprehensive program of this sort. He points out that India

> is truly bicultural. It has had six hundred years of exposure to the west and at least two hundred years of experience in incorporating and internalizing not merely the west but specifically western systems of knowledge. It need not necessarily exercise the option that it has of defensively rejecting modern

In this scenario, there would be many culturally distinctive scientific traditions that shared some common elements with modern Western sciences. Here there could again be "many hills" of scientific knowledge. Both forms of multiculturalism would be advanced: culturally diverse sciences around the globe, and diverse cultural origins within each local science. Is this proposal possible? Few of the marginalized cultures are strong enough to resist the continued expansion of Western-originated modernization, but some may be able to do so. And Western societies are not static; they may find their own reasons to want a more democratic balance of their own and other cultures' projects.

A third proposal argues that Third World scientific projects should be "delinked" from Western ones.[52] This is thought to be necessary if Third World societies are to construct fully modern sciences within their indigenous scientific traditions. Otherwise, capitalism inevitably succeeds in turning Third World cultures into markets that can increase profits for elites in the West (just as it continually extends into more and more aspects of daily life in the West). The Third World Network puts the issue this way:

> Only when science and technology evolve from the ethos and cultural milieu of Third World societies will it become meaningful for our needs and requirements, and express our true creativity and genius. Third World science and technology can only evolve through a reliance on indigenous categories, idioms and traditions in all spheres of thought and action. A major plank of any such strategy should be the delinking of the Third World from the secular dynamic which institutionalizes the hegemony of the west.[53]

This strategy makes sense when one recognizes that there are many more "universal laws of nature" that such delinked sciences could discover if they were permitted to develop out of civilizational settings different from those that have been directed by European projects. Such a delinking program could make a world of different, but interrelated, culturally diverse sciences.

How delinked can the cultures that make up our shrinking world become? Like the earlier proposals, this one, too, raises knotty issues. However, even if a complete social, political, and economic delinking proves impossible, does not attempting to delink as much as possible – even just daring to think about it! – enable more creative strategizing? Let us begin to try to imagine what scientific culture and practices in the West would/should look like if the Third World no longer provided so much of the raw materials, "laboratories," or markets (voluntary or involuntary) for modern sciences and the kinds of "development" they have advanced.

A fourth proposal goes even further in revaluing non-Western scientific traditions: it argues that Third World sciences and their cultures can provide useful models for global sciences of the future. Many elements of the distinctively modern scientific ethic are unsuitable, not only for disadvantaged peoples in the Third World and elsewhere, but also for any future human or nonhuman cultures at all. For example, modern sciences' commitments to a utilitarian approach to nature, to externalizing the costs and internalizing the benefits of scientific advances, and to an ethic of increasing consumption ("development") are not ones that can support future life on earth: "[M]odern science has become the major source of active violence against human beings and all other living organisms in our times. Third World and other citizens have come to know that there is a fundamental irreconcilability between modern science and the stability and maintenance of all living systems, between modern science and democracy."[54]

Thus non-Western scientific traditions that do not share such problematic commitments can provide models for the kinds of global sciences that our species must have, in order for it and the rest of nature to survive. As two biologists put the point, Western sciences should realistically be assessed as a transitional stage in scientific development.[55] The point here is not that non-Western cultures and their scientific traditions are all good and Western ones all bad, but that all of us can learn and benefit from the achievements of non-European civilizations' traditions also.

For example, some Third World societies have learned to negotiate with a powerful West. The forms of multiculturalism that they have chosen and/or been forced to adopt give them valuable knowledge about how to live in a world where they, unlike Western elites, cannot afford the illusion that they are dependent on no other culture, that they can take what they wish from nature and other peoples, that they are the one model of the uniquely and admirably human, and that their ideas are uniquely and universally valid. Third World scientific traditions can offer valuable models for global sciences here, too.

In this scenario, presumably Western groups would integrate into their sciences and culture precisely those Third World cultural elements that would transform modern sciences. In contrast to the first proposal, it would be some of the elements of Third World cultures most incompatible with modern sciences that would be valued: the Third World forms of democratic, pacific, life-maintaining, and communal tendencies so at odds with the imperialistic, violent, consuming, and possessively individualistic ones that critics find in Western sciences and culture. (Obviously the former are not always well practiced in Third World cultures prior to the expansion into them of European culture, nor are they absent from First World cultures, as the postcolonial critics are perfectly aware and as they always caution.) The result would be many, culturally different sciences, each with culturally diverse origins – but central among the elements most valued in each case would be those that advance cooperation, democracy, the richness of indigenous achievements, and sustainable development.

Is this a real possibility? Will people of European descent be able to accept the idea that their democratic traditions are not the only viable ones? It is time to turn to examine what those living in the West can contribute to the development of sciences that have greater validity and are less imperial.

[illegible]

[illegible] thinkers put the point) retrieving and developing the best in European cultural traditions for sciences suitable for the emerging postcolonial world. Obviously, adding to our local environments – our classrooms, faculties, conferences, syllabi, footnotes, policy circles, television interviews, and the like – the voices and presence of peoples whose groups have less benefited from modern sciences will immeasurably enable the rest of us. But there are also important steps we can take beyond "add postcolonials and stir" (to borrow a phrase from feminist writings). I mention here just three contributions that appear fairly obvious (though not uncontroversial); we should make it a project to identify more of them.

First, we can relocate the projects of sciences and science studies that originate in the West on the more accurate historical map created by the new postcolonial studies, instead of on the familiar one charted by Eurocentric accounts of mainly European and US history. This will require rethinking what it is that sciences and science studies should be describing and explaining and how they do so – for example, in "rational reconstructions" of scientific progress, and historical, sociological, and ethnographic accounts of sciences, their cultures and practices. In what ways have the existing projects in physics, chemistry, engineering, biology, geology, and the history, sociology, anthropology, and philosophies of the sciences been excessively contained by Eurocentric assumptions and goals? Moreover, we can disseminate these accounts outside of university circles – for example, in the new diversity-focused US and global history texts currently being produced for elementary and high-school students in the US, in media accounts that reach the general public, and in journals, conferences, and other forms of communication that reach scientists.

Second, to this kind of new "science education" about the history of scientific traditions we can add a new education *in* the sciences both for schoolrooms and for public discussion in journals, newspapers, television, and other resources through which a citizenry educates itself. Obviously, one important assistance in this project will be to achieve more culturally diverse science communities, including especially their directors and funders; in terms of what happens in the laboratory as well as later, "science communities" are far more extensive than only those who work in laboratories. However, other equally important transformations are necessary here. "Science criticism" that draws on the postcolonial analyses needs to be introduced into all science education programs – both inside and outside classroom contexts, in media accounts and in museum exhibits.

Existing science programs are supposed to instill in students a commitment to the most rigorous criticism of traditional assumptions, but the postcolonial accounts show that Eurocentric assumptions have blocked a crucial range of such criticisms. Scientists and humanists have usually spoken as if intellectual life should be divided up between their two kinds of projects, as if the sciences and humanities are parallel projects.[56] But they are not: the sciences are parallel to the arts, and the humanities to the social studies of science, which are not considered part of science at all. Persons well educated in the humanities are expected to have a good training in literary, art, drama and other forms of humanist *criticism* – in the "history, theory, and sociology" *about* the arts – but we do not expect them to be accomplished poets, sculptors, or playwrights. And this humanist critical education is not considered to be a lesser field than the performance of the arts. It is not an introductory project of explaining "arts for nonmajors," it is an equal and different project with its own principles and goals – one in which poets, sculptors, and playwrights can gain greater resources through exposure to the achievements and limitations of past efforts in their fields. It is a kind of parallel program for the sciences that I suggest is needed.

There are many reasonable answers to the question of why no such field of "science criticism" exists already within science departments: "the history of physics is not physics"; "the methods of history and sociology are not really scientific"; "there is not enough time in the curriculum"; "where are the faculty to teach such courses?" – and so on. (And some may reasonably object to my drawing this parallel between the arts and the sciences at all, because artists, in contrast to scientists, are not primarily trained in universities.) My point here is that these answers are *not reasonable enough*. Failing to locate any significant critical studies of the sciences in universities, and especially in science departments, indicates to students that no one thinks these studies important for learning to do science or for making reasoned decisions about scientific issues in public life. This is unfortunate, since, as the postcolonial accounts show, philosophical, sociological, and historical assumptions form part of scientific understanding *about nature*. Scientists unknowingly use distorting cultural assumptions as part of the *evidence* for their research results if they are taught that social studies of science are irrelevant to doing science, and that they should assiduously "avoid politics" rather than learning how to identify cultural features in their scientific assumptions, and how to sort the distorting and knowledge-limiting from the knowledge-enlarging cultural values and interests.

Of course, the kinds of philosophy and social studies of science needed for this project are not widely practiced. These fields have enthusiastically adopted the goal of serving as "handmaids to the sciences," as John Locke put it, and lack the empirical and theoretical adequacy required to come to terms with postcolonial histories and critiques. Nevertheless, more accurate and critical studies of sciences in their historical context should form an important part of science education as well as of general education.

Imagine if every science department contained the same proportion of "science critics" to scientists that English departments do of literary critics to creative writers anywhere in the world. Imagine having scientists, science policy makers, and the rest of us educated in "The Role of Biology, Chemistry, and Physics in the Modern European Empire – and Vice Versa"; "Chinese (Islamic, South Asian, African, Indigenous American, etc.) Sciences: Past, Present, and Future"; "The Sexual Meanings of the Scientific Revolution in the European Expansion"; "From Craft to Factory Production of Twentieth-Century Science: Benefits and Losses"; "Objectivity as Ideal and Ideology"; "The Science and Political Economy of the Human Genome Project"; "Science and Democracy: Enemies or Friends?"; and, especially, a course on the meanings and effects [illegible]

critically use their indigenous cultural legacies, rather than – as they point out – only European ones. Those of us who value features of the European tradition can similarly strengthen notions of objectivity, rationality and scientific method, notions central not only to our scientific tradition, but also to such other Western institutions as the law and public policy."[58] Paradoxically, these postcolonial analyses, which can appear to come from outside modern science, are also very much inside its historical processes, as I have been arguing throughout. They are exactly what is called for by its conventional goal of increasing the growth of knowledge through a critical examination of cultural superstitions and unwarranted assumptions.

To conclude: asking questions about the hidden but real multiculturalism of global sciences can lead to far more accurate and valuable understandings, not only of other cultures' scientific legacies, but also of rich possibilities in the legacy of European culture and practice.

Notes

1 Patrick Petitjean *et al.*, *Science and Empires: Historical Studies about Scientific Development and European Expansion* (Dordrecht: Kluwer, 1992); Z. Sardar, ed., *The Revenge of Athena: Science, Exploitation and the Third World* (London: Mansell, 1988); Third World Network, *Modern Science in Crisis: A Third World Response* (Penang, Malaysia: Third World Network, 1988). Many of the works cited below are useful far beyond the particular claim I cite. Additional writings that I have also found especially useful in thinking about the possible multiculturalism of science include Michael Adas, *Machines as the Measure of Man* (Ithaca, NY: Cornell University Press, 1989); Donna Haraway, *Primate Visions: Gender, Race, and Nature in the World of Modern Science* (New York: Routledge, 1989); Charles Moraze, ed., *Science and the Factors of Inequality* (Paris: UNESCO, 1979); Vandana Shiva, *Staying Alive: Women, Ecology and Development* (London: Zed Press, 1989); Sharon Traweek, *Beamtimes and Lifetimes* (Cambridge, Mass.: Harvard University Press, 1988). See also Sandra Harding, *The Science Question in Feminism* (Ithaca, NY: Cornell University Press, 1986) and "After Eurocentrism: Challenges for the Philosophy of Science," in *Philosophy of Science*

Association 1992 Proceedings, vol. 2., ed. David Hull, Micky Forbes, and Kathleen Okruhlik (East Lansing: Philosophy of Science Association, 1993), in addition to other works cited below.

2 Laurel Graham pointed this out.

3 For examples of the latter, see Andrew Pickering, ed., *Science as Practice and Culture* (Chicago: University of Chicago Press, 1992).

4 The term "borderlands" is from Gloria Anzaldúa's *Borderlands/La Frontera: The New Mestiza* (San Francisco: Spinsters/Aunt Lute Book Company, 1987). The notion appears in the writing of many other "borderlands" thinkers.

5 See, e.g., Samir Amin, *Eurocentrism* (New York: Monthly Review Press, 1989).

6 Scientists usually claim that all they mean by the statement that "science works" is that it makes accurate predictions. However, in the next breath they usually defend the extraordinarily high US investment in scientific establishments on what I take to be the only grounds that anyone could find reasonable in a society professing a commitment to democratic social relations – namely, that the results of science improve social life. Thus "science works" in this enlarged sense, which is conflated with the more technical sense of the phrase. As we shall see below, the success of sciences' empirical predictions depends in part on social relations; there are good historical reasons for the conflation.

7 I am tempted to keep inserting "Western" into "modern science" – modern *Western* science – to avoid the standard Eurocentric assumption that non-Western traditions, including their scientific practices and cultures, are static; that only Western sciences are dynamic and thus only they have developed since the fifteenth century. However, that locution has other problems: it emphasizes the dualistic "West vs. the rest" framework, it ignores the non-Western components of modern science, etc.

8 See Frances Yates, *Giordano Bruno and the Hermetic Tradition* (New York: Vintage, 1969).

9 Donald E. Lach, *Asia in the Making of Europe, vol. 2* (Chicago: University of Chicago Press, 1977); Seyyed Hossein Nasr, "Islamic Science, Western Science: Common Heritage, Diverse Destinies," in Sardar, *Revenge of Athena* (above, n. 1), pp. 239–248.

10 See Martin Bernal, *Black Athena: The Afroasiatic Roots of Classical Civilization, vol. I* (New Brunswick, NJ: Rutgers University Press, 1987); Cheikh Anta Diop, *The African Origin of Civilization: Myth or Reality?* trans. M. Cook (Westport, Conn.: L. Hill, 1974); Lacinay Keita, "African Philosophical Systems: A Rational Reconstruction," *Philosophical Forum* 9: 2–3 (1977–78): 169–189; Lach, *Asia* (above, n. 9); I.A. Sabra, "The Scientific Enterprise," in *The World of Islam*, ed. B. Lewis (London: Thames and Hudson, 1976); E. Frances White, "Civilization Denied: Questions on *Black Athena*," *Radical America* 21: 5 (1987): 38–40.

11 Jack Weatherford, *Indian Givers: What the Native Americans Gave to the World* (New York: Crown, 1988).

12 R.K. Kochhar, "Science in British India," parts I and II, *Current Science* (India) 63: 11 (1992): 694. Cf. also ibid. 64: 1 (1993): pp. 55–62.

13 And, as V.Y. Mudimbe pointed out to me, of Europe itself, for European sciences also constituted European lands, cities, and peoples as their laboratories. Consider, for example, the way women, the poor, children, the sick, the mad, rural and urban populations, and workers have been continuously studied by natural and social sciences.

14 Susantha Goonatilake makes this point in "The Voyages of Discovery and the Loss

and Re-Discovery of 'Other's' Knowledge," *Impact of Science on Society* 167 (1993): 241–264.

15 For one thing, Westerners note that Chinese or African astronomy is done within culturally local projects of a sort devalued by scientific rationality, such as (in some cases) astrology, or culturally local meanings of the heavens or other natural phenomena. So, whatever their accuracy, such astronomical discoveries could not be admitted as "real science" without permitting the possibility of assigning such a status also to astrology or Confucian religious beliefs. Alternatively, one could say

19 Joseph Needham, *The Grand Titration: Science and Society in East and West* (Toronto: University of Toronto Press, 1969), pp. 55–56.

20 See, e.g., Susan Bordo, *The Flight to Objectivity* (Albany: State University of New York Press, 1987); Genevieve Lloyd, *The Man of Reason* (Minneapolis: University of Minnesota Press, 1984); Tzvetan Todorov, *The Conquest of America: The Question of the Other*, trans. Richard Howard (New York: Harper & Row, 1984).

21 See Needham's discussion of seven conceptual errors in standard Western thought about "universal science" that lead to erroneous devaluations of the scientific achievements of non-European sciences, in *Grand Titration* (above, n. 19).

22 Robert Horton, "African Traditional Thought and Western Science," parts 1 and 2, *Africa*, 37 (1967): 50–71; 155–187.

23 J.E. Wiredu, "How Not to Compare African Thought with Western Thought," in *African Philosophy*, ed. Richard Wright, 3rd ed. (Lanham, Md.: University Press of America, 1984), pp. 149–162.

24 Thomas S. Kuhn, *The Structure of Scientific Revolutions*, 2nd ed. (Chicago: University of Chicago Press, 1970), p. 167.

25 Needham, *Grand Titration* (above, n. 19), pp. 14–15.

26 Edgar Zilsel, "The Sociological Roots of Science," *American Journal of Sociology* 47 (1941–42): 544–562.

27 Kochhar, "Science in British India" (above, n. 12); Alfred Crosby, *Ecological Imperialism: The Biological Expansion of Europe* (Cambridge: Cambridge University Press, 1987); V.V. Krishna, "The Colonial 'Model' and the Emergence of National Science in India: 1876–1920," in Petitjean *et al.* (above, n. 1), pp. 57–72; Deepak Kumar, "Problems in Science Administration: A Study of the Scientific Surveys in British India 1757–1900," in ibid., pp. 269–280.

28 Paul Forman, "Behind Quantum Electronics: National Security as Basis for Physical Research in the U.S., 1940–1960," *Historical Studies in Physical and Biological Sciences* 18 (1987): pp. 149–229.

29 Susantha Goonatilake, "A Project for Our Times," in Sardar, *Revenge of Athena* (above, n. 1), pp. 235–236. (Should not African and indigenous American civilizations also count as regional ones containing scientific traditions?)

30 The "Strong Programme" in the sociology of knowledge has developed this analysis.

See, e.g., David Bloor, *Knowledge and Social Imagery* (London: Routledge and Kegan Paul, 1977).

31 This section reviews the arguments of Sandra Harding, "Is Western Science an Ethnoscience?" (forthcoming).

32 See, e.g., Morris Berman, *The Reenchantment of the World* (Ithaca, NY: Cornell University Press, 1981); Bordo, *Flight to Objectivity* (above, n. 20); Carolyn Merchant, *The Death of Nature. Women, Ecology, and the Scientific Revolution* (New York: Harper & Row, 1980); Nasr, "Islamic Science" (above, n. 9).

33 Needham, *Grand Titration* (above, n. 19), p. 302.

34 Ibid., p. 323.

35 Ibid., p. 327.

36 "[L]aws of nature, like laws of the state, are historically imposed from above and obeyed from below"; in contrast, "the concept of order, wider than law and free from its coercive, hierarchical, and centralizing implications has the potential to expand our conception of science. Order is a category comprising patterns of organization that can be spontaneous, self-generated, or externally imposed" (Evelyn Fox Keller, *Reflections on Gender and Science* (New Haven: Yale University Press, 1984), pp. 131, 132). See also the interesting discussion of Needham's argument in Jatinder K. Bajaj, "Francis Bacon, the First Philosopher of Modern Science: A Non-Western View," in *Science, Hegemony and Violence: A Requiem for Modernity*, ed. Ashis Nandy (Delhi: Oxford University Press, 1990).

37 See Bruno Latour's discussion of the importance to science of "centres of calculation," in chap. 6 of his *Science in Action* (Cambridge, Mass.: Harvard University Press, 1987).

38 The complexity of these sentences arises from the fact that elites in Third World cultures also enjoy luxurious access to the benefits of modern sciences, and the majority of citizens in most First World cultures – that is, the poor and other disadvantaged groups – do not.

39 Khor Kok Peng, "Science and Development Underdeveloping the Third World," in Sardar, *Revenge of Athena* (above, n. 1), pp. 207–208.

40 Claude Alvares, "Science, Colonialism and Violence: A Luddite View," in Nandy, *Science, Hegemony and Violence* (above, n. 36), p. 108.

41 J. Bandyopadhyay and V. Shiva, "Science and Control: Natural Resources and Their Exploitation," in Sardar, *Revenge of Athena* (above, n. 1), p. 63.

42 Dorothy Smith is especially eloquent on this point: see *The Conceptual Practices of Power* (Boston: Northeastern University Press, 1990) and *The Everyday World as Problematic: A Feminist Sociology* (Boston: Northeastern University Press, 1987). However, abstractness is not unique to such cultures. As Vaola Rachetta pointed out (by letter), certain forms of ancient Hinduism are based on philosophical abstractions.

43 Bandyopadhyay and Shiva, "Science and Control" (above, n. 41), p. 60.

44 Xavier Polanco, "World-Science: How is the History of World-Science to be Written?" in Petijean *et al.*, *Science and Empires* (above, n. 1), p. 225.

45 Susantha Goonatilake, *Aborted Discovery: Science and Creativity in the Third World* (London: Zed Press, 1984), pp. 229–230.

46 This kind of critique enables one to see that sleeping in the feminist science analyses lies a direct challenge to conventional assumptions about the necessity of value-neutrality to the universality of science. A form of this challenge has been to question the necessity of value-neutrality to the maximal objectivity of science;

see Sandra Harding, "After the Neutrality Ideal: Science, Politics and 'Strong Objectivity,"' *Social Research* 59: 3 (1992): pp. 568–587, reprinted in *The Politics of Western Science, 1640–1990*, ed. Margaret Jacob (Atlantic Highlands, NJ: Humanities Press, forthcoming).

47 Some readers may be troubled by my retention of notions that seem so central to modern science and its mentality, such as "objectivity," "less distorted," "valid," and the like. I cannot take the space here to discuss the reasons why I, like many other science critics, find these to be important terms to appropriate, "reoccupy," and

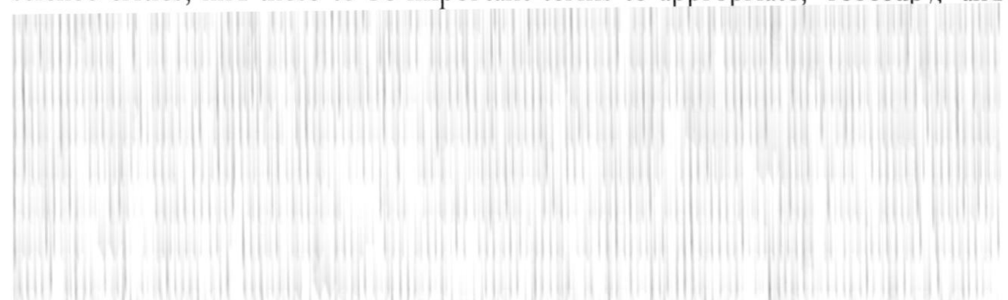

Knowledge? Thinking from Women's Lives (Ithaca, NY: Cornell University Press, 1991), and "After the Neutrality Ideal" (above, n. 46).

48 One particularly good discussion of this is in Bina Agarwal, "The Gender and Environment Debate: Lessons from India," *Feminist Studies* 18: 1 (1992): pp. 119–158.

49 Goonatilake, "Voyages of Discovery" (above, n. 14), p. 25. This approach is by no means unique to Third World theorists; it has been appearing even in Western popular accounts of "endangered societies." (Notice the extension to non-Western peoples of language initially used to describe animals.) For example, *Time* magazine ran a cover story in 1992 reporting on the "endangered knowledge" that Western culture should gather from cultures disappearing under modernization and development pressures. ("Modernization" and "development" for whom?)

50 Elizabeth Hsu, "The Reception of Western Medicine in China: Examples from Yunnan," in Petitjean *et al.*, *Science* and *Empires* (above, n. 1), p. 89.

51 Ashis Nandy, Introduction to *Science, Hegemony and Violence* (above, n. 36), p. 11.

52 This language has been developed by Samir Amin; see, e.g., *Eurocentrism* (above, n. 5).

53 Third World Network, *Modern Science in Crisis* (above, n. 1), reprinted in *The "Racial" Economy of Science: Toward a Democratic Future*, ed. Sandra Harding (Bloomington: Indiana University Press, 1993), p. 333.

54 Ibid., p. 31.

55 Richard Levins and Richard Lewontin, "Applied Biology in the Third World," in *The Dialectical Biologist* (Cambridge, Mass.: Harvard University Press, 1988); reprinted in Harding, *"Racial" Economy of Science* (above, n. 53), pp. 315–325.

56 See, e.g., C.P. Snow, *The Two Cultures, and A Second Look* (Cambridge: Cambridge University Press, 1964). The following argument draws from Sandra Harding, "Women and Science in Historical Context," *National Women's Studies Association Journal* 5: 1 (1993): 49–55.

57 I refer here to the discussion of the meanings and other effects that authors never intended their works to have that is indicated by the phrase "the 'death' of the author."

58 The last two decades of feminist and antiracist critiques in philosophy, science studies,

political theory, and the social sciences will provide especially useful resources here since they have focused on just such projects of transforming standards of objectivity, rationality, and method into ones more effective at preventing distorting cultural assumptions and conceptual frameworks from shaping the results of research and public policy.

Chapter 17

Helen E. Longino

Prologue

Feminists, faced with traditions in philosophy and in science that are deeply hostile to women, have had practically to invest new and more appropriate ways of knowing the world. These new ways have been less invention out of whole cloth than the revival or re-evaluation of alternative or suppressed traditions. They range from the celebration of insight into nature through identification with it to specific strategies of survey research in the social sciences. Natural scientists and lay persons anxious to see the sciences change have celebrated Barbara McClintock's loving identification with various aspects of the plants she studied, whether whole organism or its chromosomal structure revealed under the microscope. Social scientists from Dorothy Smith to Karen Sacks have stressed designing research *for* rather than merely about women, a goal that requires attending to the specificities of women's lives and consulting research subjects themselves about the process of gathering information about them. Such new ways of approaching natural and social phenomena can be seen as methods of discovery, ways of getting information about the natural and social worlds not available via more traditional experimental or investigative methods.

Feminists have rightly pointed out the blinders imposed by the philosophical distinction between discovery and justification; a theory of scientific inquiry that focuses solely on the logic of justification neglects the selection processes occurring in the context of discovery that limit what we get to know about.

[. . .]

Nevertheless, ignoring the context of justification for the context of discovery is equally problematic. I wish in this essay to explore some of the tensions between descriptivism and normativism (or prescriptivism) in the theory of knowledge, arguing that although many of the most familiar feminist accounts of science have helped us to redescribe the process of knowledge (or belief) acquisition, they stop short of an adequate normative theory. However, these accounts do require a new approach in normative epistemology because of their redescription.

Feminists have also been struck by the interlocking character of several aspects of knowledge and power in the sciences. Women have been excluded from the practice of science, even as scientific inquiry gets described both as a masculine activity and as demonstrating women's unsuitability to engage in it, whether because of our allegedly deficient mathematical abilities or our insufficient independence. Some of us notice the location of women in the production of the artifacts made possible by new knowledge: swift and nimble fingers on the microelectronics assembly line. Others notice the neglect of women's distinctive health issues by the biomedical sciences, even as new techniques for preserving the fetuses they carry are introduced into hospital delivery rooms. The sciences become even more suspect as analysis of their metaphors (for example, in cell biology and in microbiology) reveals an acceptance (and hence reinforcement) of the cultural identification of the male with activity and of the female with passivity. Finally, feminists have drawn a connection between the identification of nature as female and the scientific mind as male and the persistent privileging of explanatory models constructed around relations of unidirectional control over models constructed around relations of interdependence. Reflection on this connection has prompted feminist critics to question the very idea of a scientific method capable of adjudicating the truth or probability of theories in a value-neutral way.

Although the sciences have increased human power over natural processes, they have, according to this analysis, done so in a lopsided way, systematically perpetuating women's cognitive and political disempowerment (as well as that of other groups marginalized in relation to the Euro-American drama). One obvious question, then, is whether this appropriation of power is an intrinsic feature of science or whether it is an incidental feature of the sciences as practised in the modern period, a feature deriving from the social structures within which the sciences have developed. A second question is whether it is possible to seek and possess empowering knowledge without expropriating the power of others. Is seeking knowledge inevitably an attempt at domination? And are there criteria of knowledge other than the ability to control the phenomena about which one seeks knowledge? Feminists have answered these questions in a number of ways. I will review some of these before outlining my own answer.

Feminist epistemological strategies 1: Changing the subject

Most traditional philosophy of science (with the problematic exception of Descartes's) has adopted some form of empiricism. Empiricism's silent partner has been a theory of the subject, that is, of the knower.[1] The paradigmatic knower in Western epistemology is an individual – an individual who, in several classic instances, has struggled to free himself from the distortions in understanding and perception that result from attachment. Plato, for example, maintained that knowledge of the good is possible only for those whose reason is capable of controlling their appetites and passions, some of which have their source in bodily needs and pleasures and others of which have their source in our relations with others. The struggle for epistemic autonomy is even starker for Descartes, who suspends belief in all but his own existence in order to recreate a body of knowledge cleansed of faults, impurities, and uncertainties. For Descartes, only those grounds available to a single, unattached, disembodied mind are acceptable principles for the construction of a system of beliefs. Most subsequent epistemology has granted Descartes's conditions and disputed what those grounds are and whether any proposed grounds are sufficient grounds for knowledge. Descartes's creation of the radically and in principle isolated individual as the ideal epistemic agent has for the most part gone unremarked.[2] Locke, for example, adopts the Cartesian identification of the thinking subject with the disembodied soul without even remarking upon the individualism of the conception he inherits and then struggles with the problem of

[illegible]

and so are more descriptively adequate than the theories they challenge, they fall short of normative adequacy. The strategies identify the problems of contemporary science as resulting from male or masculinist bias. Each strategy understands both the bias and its remedy differently. One holds out the original ideal of uncontaminated or unconditioned subjectivity. A second identifies bias as a function of social location. A third identifies bias in the emotive substructure produced by the psychodynamics of individuation.

Feminist empiricism has by now taken a number of forms. That form discussed and criticized by Sandra Harding is most concerned with those fields of scientific research that have misdescribed or misanalysed women's lives and bodies.

[. . .]

From this perspective, certain areas of science having to do with sex and gender are deformed by gender ideology, but the methods of science are not themselves masculinist and can be used to correct the errors produced by ideology. The ideal knower is still the purified mind, and epistemic or cognitive authority inheres in this purity. This strategy, as Harding has observed, is not effective against those research programmes that feminists find troublesome but that cannot be faulted by reference to the standard methodological precepts of scientific inquiry. I have argued, for example, that a critique of research on the influence of prenatal gonadal hormones on behavioural sex differences that is limited to methodological critique of the data fails to bring out the role of the explanatory model that both generates the research and gives evidential relevance to that data.[3]

Another approach is, therefore, the standpoint approach. There is no one position from which value-free knowledge can be developed, but some positions are better than others.

By valorizing the perspectives uniquely available to those who are socially disadvantaged, standpoint theorists turn the table on traditional epistemology; the ideal epistemic agent is not an unconditioned subject but the subject conditioned by the social experiences of oppression. The powerless are those with epistemic legitimacy, even if they lack the power that could turn that legitimacy into authority. One of the difficulties of the standpoint approach comes into high relief, however, when it is a women's or a feminist standpoint that is in question. Women occupy many social locations in a racially and economically stratified society. If genuine or better knowledge depends on the correct or a more correct standpoint, social theory is needed to ascertain which of these locations is the epistemologically privileged one. But in a standpoint epistemology, a standpoint is needed to justify such a theory. What is that standpoint and how do we identify *it*? If no single standpoint is privileged, then either the standpoint theorist must embrace multiple and incompatible knowledge positions or offer some means of transforming or integrating multiple perspectives into one. Both of these moves require either the abandonment or the supplementation of standpoint as an epistemic criterion.

Standpoint theory faces another problem as well. It is by now commonplace to note that standpoint theory was developed by and for social scientists. It has been difficult to see what its implications for the natural sciences might be. But another strategy has seemed more promising. Most standpoint theorists locate the epistemic advantage in the productive/reproductive experience of the oppressed whose perspective they champion. A different change of subject is proposed by those identifying the problems with science as a function of the psychodynamics of individuation. Evelyn Fox Keller has been asking, among other things, why the scientific community privileges one kind of explanation or theory over others. In particular she has asked why, when both linear reductionist and interactionist perspectives are available, the scientific community has preferred the linear or 'master molecule' theory that understands a natural process as controlled by a single dominant factor. This question was made vivid by her discussion of her own research on slime mould aggregation and the fate of Barbara McClintock's work on genetic transposition.[4]

Keller's original response, spelled out in *Reflections on Gender and Science*, involved an analysis of the traditional ideal of scientific objectivity, which she understood as the ideal of the scientist's detachment from the object of study.[5]

[. . .]

She, therefore, proposed an alternative conceptualization of autonomy, contrasting static autonomy with what she called dynamic autonomy, an ability to move in and out of intimate connection with the world. Dynamic autonomy provides the emotional substructure for an alternative conception of objectivity: dynamic objectivity. The knower characterized by dynamic objectivity, in contrast to the knower characterized by static objectivity, does not seek power over phenomena but acknowledges instead the ways in which knower and phenomena are in relationship as well as the ways in which phenomena themselves are complexly interdependent.

[. . .]

Both standpoint theory and the psychodynamic perspective suggest the inadequacy of an ideal of a pure transparent subjectivity that registers the world as it is in itself (or, for Kantians, as structured by universal conditions of apperception or categories of understanding). I find it most useful to read them as articulating special instances of more general descriptive claims that subjectivity is conditioned by social and historical location and that our cognitive efforts have an ineluctably affective dimension. Classical standpoint theory identifies relation to production/reproduction as the key, but there are multiple, potentially oppositional relations to production/reproduction in a complex society, and there are other kinds of social relation and location that condition subjectivity. For example, one of the structural features of a male-dominant society is asymmetry of sexual access. Men occupy a position of entitlement to women's bodies, whereas women, correspondingly, occupy the position of that to which men are entitled. Complications of the asymmetry arise in class- and race-stratified societies. There may be other structural features as well, such as those related to the institutions of heterosexuality, that condition subjectivity. Because each individual occupies a location in a multidimensional grid marked by numerous interacting structures of power asymmetry, the analytical task is not to determine which is epistemically most adequate. Rather, the task is to understand how these

Although either transferring or diffusing power, the strategies discussed so far have in common a focus on the individual epistemic agent, on the autonomous subject. (The subject in the second and third approaches comes to be in a social context and as a consequence of social interactions, but its knowledge is still a matter of some relation between it and the subject matter.) The standpoint and psychodynamically based theories recommend certain new positions and orientations as superior to others but fail to explain how we are to decide or to justify decisions between what seem to be conflicting claims about the character of some set of natural processes. On what grounds can one social location or affective orientation be judged epistemically superior to another?

Feminist science critics have provided analyses of the context of discovery that enable us to see how social values, including gender ideology in various guises, could be introduced into science. Some theories that have done so go on to recommend an alternate subject position as epistemically superior. But arguments are missing – and it's not clear that any particular subject position could be adequate to generate knowledge. Can a particular subject position be supported by an a priori argument? It can, but only by an argument that claims a particular structure for the world and then identifies a particular subjectivity as uniquely capable of knowing that structure. The problem with such arguments is that they beg the question. The one subject position that could be advanced as epistemically superior to others without presupposing something about the structure of the world is the unconditioned position, the position of no position that provides a view from nowhere. Attractive as this ideal might seem, arguments in the philosophy of science suggest that this is a chimera. Let me turn to them.

Feminist epistemological strategies 2: Multiplying subjects

The ideal of the unconditioned (or universally conditioned) subject is the traditional proposal for escaping the particularity of subjectivity. Granting the truth of the claim that individual subjectivities are conditioned, unconditioned subjectivity is treated as an achievement rather than a natural endowment. The methods of the natural sciences constitute means to that achievement. . . . The difficulty just outlined for the feminist epistemological strategy of changing the subject, however, has a parallel in developments in the philosophy of science. Both dilemmas suggest the individual knower is an inappropriate focus for the purpose of understanding (and changing) science.

In the traditional view, the natural sciences are characterized by a methodology that purifies scientific knowledge of distortions produced by scientists' social and personal allegiances. The essential features of this methodology – explored in great detail by positivist philosophers of science – are observation and logic. Much philosophy of science in the last twenty-five years has been preoccupied with two potential challenges to this picture of scientific methodology – the claim of Kuhn, Feyerabend, and Hanson that observation is theory laden and the claim of Pierre Duhem that theories are underdetermined by data. One claim challenges the stability of observations themselves, the other the stability of evidential relations. Both accounts have seemed (at least to their critics and to some of their proponents) to permit the unrestrained expression of scientists' subjective preferences in the content of science. If observation is theory laden, then observation cannot serve as an independent constraint on theories, thus permitting subjective elements to constrain theory choice. Similarly, if observations acquire evidential relevance only in the context of a set of assumptions, a relevance that changes with a suitable change in assumptions, then it's not clear what protects theory choice from subjective elements hidden in background assumptions. Although empirical adequacy serves as a constraint on theory acceptance, it is not sufficient to pick out one theory from all contenders as the true theory about a domain of the natural world. These analyses of the relation between observation, data, and theory are often thought to constitute arguments against empiricism, but, like the feminist epistemological strategies, they are more effective as arguments against empiricism's silent partner, the theory of the unconditioned subject. The conclusion to be drawn from them is that what has been labelled scientific method does not succeed as a means to the attainment of unconditioned subjectivity on the part of individual knowers. And as long as the scientific knower is conceived of as an individual, knowing best when freed from external influences and attachment (that is, when detached or free from her/his context), the puzzles introduced by the theory-laden nature of observation and the dependence of evidential relations on background assumptions will remain unsolved.

It need not follow from these considerations, however, that scientific knowledge is impossible of attainment. Applying what I take to be a feminist insight – that we are all in relations of interdependence – I have suggested that scientific knowledge is constructed not by individuals applying a method to the material to be known but by individuals in interaction with one another in ways that modify their observations, theories and hypotheses, and patterns of reasoning. Thus scientific method includes more than just the complex of activities that constitutes hypothesis testing through comparison of hypothesis statements with (reports of) experiential data, in principle an activity of individuals. Hypothesis testing itself consists of more than the comparison of statements but involves equally centrally the subjection of putative data, of hypotheses, and of the background assumptions in light of which they seem to be supported by those data to varieties of conceptual and evidential scrutiny and criticism.[6] Conceptual criticism can include investigation into the internal and external consistency of a hypothesis and investigation of the factual, moral, and social implications of background assumptions; evidential criticism includes not only investigation of the quality of the data but of its organization, structuring, and so on. Because background assumptions can be and most frequently are invisible to the members of the scientific community for which they are background, and because unreflective acceptance of such assumptions can come to define what it is to be a member of such a community (thus making criticism impossible), effective criticism of background, assumptions requires the [illegible] practice of inquiry is productive of knowledge to the extent that it facilitates transformative criticism. The constitution of the scientific community is crucial to this end as are the interrelations among its members. Community level criteria can, therefore, be invoked to discriminate among the products of scientific communities, even though context-independent standards of justification are not attainable. At least four criteria can be identified as necessary to achieve the transformative dimension of critical discourse:

1. There must be publicly recognized forums for the criticism of evidence, of methods, and of assumptions and reasoning.
2. The community must not merely tolerate dissent, but its beliefs and theories must change over time in response to the critical discourse taking place within it.
3. There must be publicly recognized standards by reference to which theories, hypotheses, and observational practices are evaluated and by appeal to which criticism is made relevant to the goals of the inquiring community. With the possible exception of empirical adequacy, there needn't be (and probably isn't) a set of standards common to all communities. The general family of standards from which those locally adopted might be drawn would include such cognitive virtues as accuracy, coherence, and breadth of scope, and such social virtues as fulfilling technical or material needs or facilitating certain kinds of interactions between a society and its material environment or among the society's members.
4. Finally, communities must be characterized by equality of intellectual authority. What consensus exists must not be the result of the exercise of political or economic power or of the exclusion of dissenting perspectives; it must be the result of critical dialogue in which all relevant perspectives are represented.

Although requiring diversity in the community, this is not a relativist position. True relativism, as I understand it, holds that there are no legitimate constraints on what counts as reasonable to believe apart from the individual's own beliefs. Equality of intellectual authority does not mean that anything goes but that everyone is regarded as equally capable of providing arguments germane to the construction of scientific knowledge. The position outlined here holds that both nature and logic impose constraints. It fails, however, to narrow reasonable belief to a single one among all contenders, in part because it does not constrain belief in a wholly unmediated way. Nevertheless, communities are constrained by the standards operating within them, and individual members of communities are further constrained by the requirement of critical interaction relative to those standards. To say that there may be irreconcilable but coherent and empirically adequate systems for accounting for some portion of the world is not to endorse relativism but to acknowledge that cognitive needs can vary and that this variation generates cognitive diversity.

Dilemmas of pluralism

This sort of account is subject to the following dilemma.[7] What gets produced as knowledge depends on the consensus reached in the scientific community. For knowledge to count as genuine, the community must be adequately diverse. But the development of a theoretical idea or hypothesis into something elaborate enough to be called knowledge requires a consensus. The questions must stop somewhere, at some point, so that a given theory can be developed sufficiently to be applied to concrete problems. How is scientific knowledge possible while pursuing socially constituted objectivity? That is, if objectivity requires pluralism in the community, then scientific knowledge becomes elusive, but if consensus is pursued, it will be at the cost of quieting critical oppositional positions.

My strategy for avoiding this dilemma is to detach scientific knowledge from consensus, if consensus means agreement of the entire scientific community regarding the truth or acceptability of a given theory. This strategy also means detaching knowledge from an ideal of absolute and unitary truth. I suggest that we look at the aims of inquiry (at least some) as satisfied by embracing multiple and, in some cases, incompatible theories that satisfy local standards. This detachment of knowledge from universal consensus and absolute truth can be made more palatable than it might first appear by two moves. One of these is implicit in treating science as a practice or set of practices; the other involves taking up some version of a semantic or model-theoretic theory of theories.

Beginning with the second of these, let me sketch what I take to be the relevant aspects of implications of the semantic view.[8] This view is proposed as an alternative to the view of theories as sets of propositions (whether axiomatized or not). If we take the semantic view, we understand a theory as a specification of a set of relations among objects or processes characterized in a fairly abstract way. Another characterization would be that on the semantic view, a theory is the specification of a structure. The structure as specified is neither true nor false; it is just a structure. The theoretical claim is that the structure is realized in some actual system. As Mary Hesse has shown, models are proposed as models of some real world system on the basis of an analogy between the model and the system, that is, the supposition that the model and the system share some significant features in common.[9] Models often have their start as metaphors. Examples of such metaphoric models are typical philosophers' examples like the billiard ball model of particle interactions or the solar system model of the atom. What many feminists have pointed out (or can be understood as having pointed out) is the use of elements of gender ideology and social relations as metaphors for natural processes and relations. Varieties of heterosexual marriage have served as the metaphoric basis for models of the relation between nucleus and cytoplasm in the cell, for example.[10] The master molecule approach to gene action, characterized by unidirectional control exerted on organismal processes by the gene, reflects relations of authority in the patriarchal household. Evelyn Fox Keller has recently been investigating the basis of models in molecular biology in androcentric metaphors of sexuality and procreation.[11] [illegible] are put.

The adequacy of a theory conceived as a model is determined by our being able to map some subset of the relations/structures posited in the model onto some portion of the experienced world. (How the portions of the world stand in many relations to many other portions.) Any given model or schema will necessarily select among those relations. So its adequacy is not just a function of isomorphism of one of the interpretations of the theory with a portion of the world but of the fact that the relations it picks out are ones in which we are interested. A model guides our interactions with the interventions in the world. We want models that guide the interactions and interventions we seek. Given that different subcommunities within the larger scientific community may be interested in different relations or that they may be interested in objects under different descriptions, different models (that if taken as claims about an underlying reality would be incompatible) may well be equally adequate and provide knowledge, in the sense of an ability to direct our interactions and interventions, even in the absence of a general consensus as to what's important. Knowledge is not detached from knowers in a set of propositions but consists in our ability to understand the structural features of a model and to apply it to some particular portion of the world; it is knowledge of that portion of the world through its structuring by the model we use. The notion of theories as sets of propositions requires that we view the adequacy of a theory as a matter of correspondence of the objects, processes, and relations described in the propositions of the theory with the objects, processes, and relations in the domain of the natural world that the theory purports to explain; that is, it requires that adequacy be conceptualized as truth. The model-theoretic approach allows us to evaluate theories in relation to our aims as well as in relation to the model's isomorphism with elements of the modelled domain and permits the adequacy of different and incompatible models serving different and incompatible aims. Knowledge is not contemplative but active.

The second move to escape the dilemma develops some consequences of treating science as practice. There are two worth mentioning. If we understand science as practice, then we understand inquiry as ongoing, that is, we give up the idea that there is a terminus of inquiry that just is the set of truths about the world. (What LaPlace's demon knew, for example.) Scientific knowledge from this perspective is not the static end point of inquiry but a cognitive or intellectual expression of an ongoing interaction with our natural and social environments. Indeed, when we attempt to identify the goals of inquiry that organize scientific cognitive practices, it becomes clear that there are several, not all of which can be simultaneously pursued.[13] Scientific knowledge, then, is a body of diverse theories and their articulations onto the world that changes over time in response to the changing cognitive needs of those who develop and use the theories, in response to the new questions and anomalous empirical data revealed by applying theories, and in response to changes in associated theories. Both linear-reductionist and interactionist models reveal aspects of natural processes, some common to both and some uniquely describable with the terms proper to one but not both sorts of model. If we recognize the partiality of theories, as we can when we treat them as models, we can recognize pluralism in the community as one of the conditions for the continued development of scientific knowledge in this sense.

In particular, the models developed by feminists and others dissatisfied with the valuative and affective dimensions of models in use must at the very least (given that they meet the test of empirical adequacy) be recognized as both revealing the partiality of those models in use and as revealing some aspects of natural phenomena and processes that the latter conceal. These alternative models may have a variety of forms and a variety of motivations, and they need not repudiate the aim of control. We engage in scientific inquiry to direct our interactions with the interventions in the world. . . . If we aim for effective action in the natural world, something is to be controlled. The issue should be not whether but what and how. Rather than repudiate it, we can set the aim of control within the larger context of overall purposes and develop a more refined sense of the varieties of control made possible through scientific inquiry.

A second consequence for feminist and other oppositional scientists of adopting both the social knowledge thesis and a model-theoretic analysis of theories is that the constructive task does not consist in finding the one best or correct feminist model. Rather, the many models that can be generated from the different subject positions ought to be articulated and elaborated. Very few will be exclusively feminist if that means exclusively gender-based or developed only by feminists. Some will be more appropriate for some domains, others for others, and some for none. We can't know this unless models get sufficiently elaborated to be used as guides for interactions. Thus, this joint perspective implies the advocacy of subcommunities characterized by local standards. To the extent that they address a common domain and to the extent that they share some standards in common, these subcommunities must be in critical dialogue with each other as well as with those subcommunities identified with more mainstream science. The point of dialogue from this point of view is not to produce a general and universal consensus but to make possible the refinement, correction, rejection, and sharing of models. Alliances, mergers, and revisions of standards as well as of models are all possible consequences of this dialogic interaction.

Conclusions

Understanding scientific knowledge in this way supports at least two further reflections on knowledge and power. First of all, the need for models within which we can situate ourselves and the interactions we desire with the natural world will militate against the inclusiveness required for an adequate critical practice, if only because the elaboration of any model requires a substantial commitment of material and intellectual resources on the part of a community.[14] This means that, in a power-stratified society, the inclusion of the less powerful and hence of models that could serve as a resource for criticism of the received wisdom in the community of science will always be a matter of conflict. At the same time, the demand for inclusiveness should not be taken to mean that every [illegible] grain of some of the institutionalized aspects of science in the industrialized nations, but as long as they do satisfy some of the central standards of those communities, then the perspectives they embody must be included in the critical knowledge-constructive dialogue. Although there is always a danger that the politically marginal will be conflated with the crackpot, one function of public and common standards is to remind us of that distinction and to help us draw it in particular cases. I do not know of any simple or formulaic solution to this problem.

Second . . . the structures of cognitive authority themselves must change. No segment of the community, whether powerful or powerless, can claim epistemic privilege. If we can see our way to the dissolution of those structures, then we need not understand the appropriation of power in the form of cognitive authority as intrinsic to science. Nevertheless, the creation of cognitive democracy, of democratic science, is as much a matter of conflict and hope as is the creation of political democracy.

Notes

1 Empiricist philosophers have found themselves in great difficulty when confronting the necessity to make their theory of the knower explicit, a difficulty most eloquently expressed in David Hume's Appendix to *A Treatise of Human Nature*, ed. L.A. Selby-Bigge (Oxford: Clarendon Press, 1960).

2 The later philosophy of Wittgenstein does challenge the individualist ideal. Until recently few commentators have developed the anti-individualist implications of his work. See Naomi Scheman, 'Individualism and the Objects of Psychology', in Sandra Harding and Merrill Hintikka (eds.), *Discovering Reality* (Boston: Reidel, 1983), 225–44.

3 Cf. Longino, 'Can There Be A Feminist Science?', in *Hypatia* 2/3 (Autumn 1987); and ch. 7 of Longino, *Science as Social Knowledge* (Princeton: Princeton University Press, 1990).

4 Cf. Evelyn F. Keller, 'The Force of the Pacemaker Concept in Theories of Slime Mold Aggregation', in *Perspectives in Biology and Medicine*, 26 (1983), 515–21; and *A Feeling for the Organism* (San Francisco: W.H. Freeman, 1983).

5 Evelyn F. Keller, *Reflections on Gender and Science* (New Haven: Yale University Press, 1984).

6 For argument for and exposition of these points, see Longino, *Science as Social Knowledge*, esp. ch. 4.

7 Thanks to Sandra Mitchell for this formulation.

8 My understanding of the semantic view is shaped by its presentations in Bas van Fraassen, *The Scientific Image* (New York: Oxford University Press, 1980); and Ronald Giere, *Explaining Science* (Chicago: University of Chicago Press, 1988).

9 Mary Hesse, *Models and Analogies in Science* (Notre Dame, Ind.: Notre Dame University Press, 1966).

10 The Gender and Biology Study Group, 'The Importance of Feminist Critique for Contemporary Cell Biology', in *Hypatia*, 3/1 (1988).

11 Evelyn Fox Keller, 'Making Gender Visible in the Pursuit of Nature's Secrets', in Teresa de Lauretis (ed.), *Feminist Studies/Critical Studies* (Bloomington: Indiana University Press, 1986), 67–77; and 'Gender and Science', in *The Great Ideas Today* (Chicago: Encyclopedia Britannica, 1990).

12 Donna Haraway, 'The Biological Enterprise: Sex, Mind, and Profit from Human Engineering to Sociobiology', in *Radical History Review*, 20 (1979): 206–37.

13 This point is developed further in *Science as Social Knowledge*, ch. 2.

14 For a somewhat different approach to a similar question, see Philip Kitcher, 'The Division of Cognitive Labour', in *Journal of Philosophy*, 87/1 (Jan. 1990), 5–23.

Chapter 18

John Lukacs

John Lukacs is an historian of twentieth-century European culture who brings a strongly religious perspective to his discussion of the intellectual implications of quantum mechanics. Like many theologians, he views the indeterminacy principle as a warrant for a renewed emphasis on free will, and like many humanistically inclined students of history, he welcomes the new challenge to traditional notions of objectivity.

Let me . . . insist that what follows is not the breathless attempt of an enthusiastic historian to hitch his wagon to Heisenberg's star, or to jump on Heisenberg's bandwagon. . . . Rather, the contrary: my wagon is self-propelled, and a Heisenberg bandwagon does not exist (at least in the United States, among one hundred people who know the name of Einstein, not more than one may know of Heisenberg). It is the philosophical, rather than the experimental, part of Heisenberg's physics that I am qualified to discuss; my principal interest . . . springs from the condition that among the physicists of this century who have made excursions into philosophy I have found Heisenberg's philosophical exposition especially clear, meaningful and relevant . . . and I have drawn upon some of his writings . . . because I want to present some of his courageous epistemological recognitions in a form which every English-speaking historian may read and understand easily. I have arranged these matters in order to sum them up in the form of ten propositions, the phrasing, the selection, and the organization of which is entirely my own: it is but their illustrations which come from the sphere of physics, described . . . by Heisenberg. . . . They are illustrations in the literal sense: they are intended to illustrate, to illuminate new recognitions, certain truths, in the assertion of which this writer, as indeed any historian in the twentieth century, is no longer alone.

First: there is no scientific certitude. Atomic physics found that the behavior of particles is considerably unpredictable: but, what is more important, this uncertainty is not "the outcome of defects in precision or measurement but a principle that could be demonstrated by experiment." Physicists have now found that while they can reasonably predict the average reactions of great numbers of electrons in an experiment, they cannot predict what a single electron will do, and not even when it will do it. The implications of this are, of course, the limitations of measurement; of accuracy; of scientific predictability – all fundamental shortcomings of "classical," or Newtonian physics – they suggest the collapse of absolute determinism even in the world of matter.

Second: the illusory nature of the ideal of objectivity. In quantum mechanics the very act of observing alters the nature of the object, "especially when its quantum numbers are small." Quantum physics, Heisenberg says, "do not allow a completely objective description of nature." "As it really happened" (or "as it is really happening") is, therefore, an incomplete statement in the world of matter, too. . . . "In our century," Heisenberg wrote . . . "it has become clear that the desired objective reality of the elementary particle is too crude an oversimplification of what really happens. . . ." "We can no longer speak of the behaviour of the particle independently of the process of observation. As a final consequence, the natural laws formulated mathematically in quantum theory no longer deal with the elementary particles themselves but with our knowledge of them."

[. . .]

In biology, too, "it may be important for a complete understanding that the questions are asked by the species man which itself belongs to the genus of living organisms, in other words, that we already know what life is even before we have defined it scientifically." The recognition of personal participation is inescapable.

Third: the illusory nature of definitions. It seems that the minds of most physicists during the present interregnum still clung to the old, "logical" order of things: they were always giving names to newly discovered atomic particles, to such elements of the atomic kernel that did not "fit." Yet the introduction of the name "wavicle" does preciously little to solve the problem of whether light consists of waves or of particles; and it may be that the continuing nominalistic habit of proposing new terms (sometimes rather silly-sounding ones, such as "neutrino") suggests that illusion of the modern mind which tends to substitute vocabulary for thought, tending to believe that once we name or define something we've "got it." Sometimes things may get darker through definitions, Dr. Johnson said; and Heisenberg seems to confirm the limited value of definitions even in the world of matter:

> Any concepts or words which have been formed in the past through the interplay between the world and ourselves are not really sharply defined with respect to their meaning; that is to say, we do not know exactly how far they will help us in finding our way in the world. We often know that they can be applied to a wide range of inner or outer experience but we practically never know precisely the limits of their applicability. This is true even of the simplest and most general concepts like "existence" and "space" and "time." . . . The words "position" and "velocity" of an electron, for instance, seemed perfectly well defined as to both their meaning and their possible connections, and in fact they were clearly defined concepts within the mathematical framework of Newtonian mechanics. But actually they were not well defined, as is seen from the relations of uncertainty. One may say that regarding their position in Newtonian mechanics they were well defined, but in their relation to nature they were not.

Fourth: the illusory nature of the absolute truthfulness of mathematics. The absoluteness of mathematical "truth" was disproven by Gödel's famous theorem in 1931, but even before that, in the 1920s, physicists were beginning to ask themselves this uneasy question; as Heisenberg put it:

> Is it true that only such experimental situations can arise in nature as can be expressed in the mathematical formalism? The assumption that this was actually [illegible]

scale there can be no action smaller than the quantum of action; and under certain physical conditions two by two do not always amount to four). Quantum theory found, too, that certain mathematical statements depend on the time element: Heisenberg realized that p times q is not always the equivalent of q times p in physics (when, for example, p means momentum and q position). What this suggests is that certain basic mathematical operations are not independent of human concepts of time and perhaps not even of purpose. That certain quantities do not always obey arithmetical rules was suggested already in the 1830s by the Irish mathematical genius Hamilton; and the Englishman Dirac, still to some extent influenced by nominalism, tried in the 1920s to solve this problem by asserting the necessity to deal with a set of so-called "Q numbers" which do not always respond to the rules of multiplication. But perhaps the "problem" may be stated more simply: the order in which certain mathematical (and physical) operations are performed affects their results.

Fifth: the illusory nature of "factual" truth. Change is an essential component of all nature: this ancient principle reappears within quantum physics. We have seen that the physicist must reconcile himself to the condition that he cannot exactly determine both the position and the speed of the atomic particle. He must reconcile himself, too, to the consequent condition that in the static, or factual, sense a basic unit of matter does not exist. It is not measurable; it is not even ascertainable; it is, in a way, a less substantial concept than such "idealistic" concepts as "beauty" or "mind." We can never expect to see a static atom or electron, since they do not exist as "immutable facts"; at best, we may see the trace of their motions. Einstein's relativity theory stated that matter is transmutable, and that it is affected by time; but the full implications of this condition were not immediately recognized, since they mean, among other things, that the earlier watertight distinctions between "organic" and "inorganic" substances no longer hold. "A sharp distinction between animate and inanimate matter," writes Heisenberg, "cannot be made." "There is only one kind of matter, but it can exist in different discrete stationary conditions." Heisenberg doubts "whether physics and chemistry will, together with the concept of evolution, some day offer a complete description of the living organism."

Sixth: the breakdown of the mechanical concept of causality. We have seen how, for the historian, *causa* must be more than the *causa efficiens* (Aristotle's efficient cause), and that the necessarily narrow logic of mechanical causality led to deterministic systems that have harmed our understanding of history, since in reality, through life and in history this kind of causation almost always "leaks." But now not even in physics is this kind of causation universally applicable: it is inadequate, and moreover, "fundamentally and intrinsically undemonstrable." There is simply no satisfactory way of picturing the fundamental atomic processes of nature in categories of space and time and causality. The multiplicity and the complexity of causes reappear in the world of physical relationships, in the world of matter.

Seventh: the principal importance of potentialities and tendencies. Quantum physics brought the concept of potentiality back into physical science – a rediscovery, springing from new evidence, of some of the earliest Greek physical and philosophical theories. Heraclitus was the first to emphasize this in the reality of the world: his motto, "Everything Moves," "imperishable change that renovates the world"; he did not, in the Cartesian and Newtonian manner, distinguish between being and becoming; to him fire was *both* matter and force. Modern quantum theory comes close to this when it describes energy, according to Heisenberg, anything that moves: "it may be called the primary cause of all change, and energy can be transformed into matter or heat or light." To Aristotle, too, matter was not by itself a reality but a *potentia* (potentiality), which existed by means of form: through the processes of nature the Aristotelian "essence" passed from mere possibility through form into actuality. When we speak of the temperature of the atom, says Heisenberg, we can only mean an expectation, "an objective tendency or possibility, a *potentia* in the sense of Aristotelian philosophy." An accurate description of the elementary particle is impossible: "the only thing which can be written down as description is a probability function"; the particle "exists" only as a possibility, "a possibility for being or a tendency for being." But this probability is not merely the addition of the element of "chance," and it is something quite different from mathematical formulas of probabilities.

[. . .]

We have already met Heisenberg's question: "What happens 'really' in an atomic event?" The mechanism of the results of the observation can always be stated in the terms of the Newtonian concepts: "but what one deduces from an observation is a probability function . . . [which] does not itself represent a course of events in the course of time. It represents a tendency for events and our knowledge of events."

Eighth: not the essence of "factors" but their relationship counts. Modern physics now admits, as we have seen, that important factors may not have clear definitions: but, on the other hand, these factors may be clearly defined, as Heisenberg puts it, "with regard to their connections." These relationships are of primary importance: just as no "fact" can stand alone, apart from its associations with other "facts" and other matters, modern physics now tends to divide its world not into "different groups of objects but into different groups of connections." In the concepts of modern mathematics, too, it is being increasingly recognized how the functions of dynamic connections may be more important than the static definitions of "factors." Euclid had said that a point is something which has no parts and which occupies no space. At the height of positivism, around 1890, it was generally believed that an even more perfect statement would consist in exact definitions of "parts" and of "space." But certain mathematicians have since learned that this tinkering with definitions tends to degenerate into the useless nominalism of semantics, and consequently they do not bother with definitions of "points" or "lines" or "connection"; their interest is directed, instead, to the axiom that two points can be always connected by a line, to the relationships of lines and points and connections.

Ninth: the principles of "classical" logic are no longer unconditional: new concepts of truths are recognized. "Men fail to imagine any relation between two opposing truths and so they assume that to state one is to deny the other," Pascal wrote. Three centuries later

[illegible]

In quantum theory this law . . . is to be modified. . . . Weizaecker points out that one may distinguish various levels of language. . . . In order to cope with [certain quantum situations] Weizaecker introduced the concept "degree of truth". . . . [By this] the term "not decided" is by no means equivalent to the term "not known." . . . There is still complete equivalence between the two levels of language with respect to the correctness of a statement, but not with respect to the incorrectness.

[. . .]

Knowledge means not certainty, and a halftruth is not 50 percent truth; everyday language cannot be eliminated from any meaningful human statement of truth, including propositions dealing with matter; after all is said, logic is human logic, our own creation.

Tenth: at the end of the Modern Age the Cartesian partition falls away. Descartes's framework, his partition of the world into objects and subjects, no longer holds:

> The mechanics of Newton [Heisenberg writes] and all the other parts of classical physics constructed after its model started out from the assumption that one can describe the world without speaking about God or ourselves. This possibility seemed almost a necessary condition for natural science in general.
>
> But at this point the situation changed to some extent through quantum theory . . . we cannot disregard the fact [I would say: the condition] that science is formed by men. Natural science does not simply describe and explain nature; it is a part of the interplay between nature and ourselves; it describes nature as exposed to our method of questioning. This was a possibility of which Descartes could not have thought [?] but it makes the sharp separation between the world and the I impossible.
>
> . . . The Cartesian partition . . . has penetrated deeply into the human mind during the three centuries following Descartes and it will take a long time for it to be replaced by a really different attitude toward the problem of reality

We cannot avoid the condition of our participation. . . . The recognition of this marks the beginning of a revolution not only in physical and philosophical but also in biological (and, ultimately, medical) concepts, springing from the empirical realization that there is a closer connection between mind and matter than what we have been taught to believe. Still, because of our interregnum, decades and disasters may have to pass until this revolution will bring its widely recognizable results. Yet we may at least look back at what we have already begun to leave behind.

After three hundred years the principal tendency in our century is still to believe that life is a scientific proposition, and to demonstrate how all of our concepts are but the products of complex mechanical causes that may be ultimately determinable through scientific methods. Thus Science, in Heisenberg's words, produced "its own, inherently uncritical" – and, let me add, inherently unhistorical – philosophy. But now "the scientific method of analysing, [defining] and classifying has become conscious" – though, let me add, far from sufficiently conscious – "of its limitations, which rise out of the [condition] that by its intervention science alters and refashions the object of investigation. In other words, methods and object can no longer be separated. *The scientific world-view has ceased to be a scientific view in the true sense of the word*."

These are Heisenberg's italics. They correspond with the arguments . . . in which I have tried to propose the historicity of reality as something which is prior to its mathematicability. They represent a reversal of thinking after three hundred years: but, in any event, such recognitions involve not merely philosophical problems or problems of human perception but the entirety of human involvement in nature, a condition from which we, carriers of life in its highest complexity, cannot separate ourselves. The condition of this participation is the recognition of our limitations which is . . . our gateway to knowledge. "There is no use in discussing," Heisenberg writes, "what could be done if we were other beings than what we are." We must even keep in mind that the introduction of the "Cartesian" instruments such as telescopes and microscopes, which were first developed in the seventeenth century, do not, in spite of their many practical applications, bring us *always and necessarily* closer to reality – since they are interpositions, *our* interpositions, between our senses and the "object." We may even ask ourselves whether *our* task is still to "see" more rather than to see better, since not only does our internal deepening of human understanding now lag behind our accumulation of external information, but too, this external information is becoming increasingly abstract and unreal. Hence the increasing breakdown of internal communications: for, in order to see better, we must understand our own limitations better and also trust ourselves better. At the very moment of history when enormous governments are getting ready to shoot selected men hermetically encased in plastic bubbles out of the earth onto the moon, the importance of certain aspects of the "expanding universe" has begun to decline, and not only for humanitarian reasons alone; we are, again, in the center of the universe – inescapably as well as hopefully so.

Our problems – all of our problems – concern primarily human nature. The human factor is the basic factor. These are humanistic platitudes. But they have now gained added meaning, through the unexpected support from physics. It is thus that the recognitions of the human condition of science, and of the historicity of science – let me repeat that Heisenberg's approach is also historical – may mark the way toward the next phase in the evolution of human consciousness, in the Western world at least.

SECTION FOUR

THE PREVIOUS TWO SECTIONS have focused on analyses of scientific epistemology – how and why scientists see and understand the world the way they do. Does this perspective affect the questions that scientists ask, the focus of their research, and which theories are accepted and promoted within the scientific community? In this section, we consider the model we have for scientific inquiry, the perception that science is an autonomous and objective enterprise, and the gap that exists between the evidence we have and the stories we choose to construct with this evidence.

Science, as we recognize it today, came about as a result of the development and rigorous application of the experimental approach when simple observation was deemed insufficient to explain cause and effect relationships. The scientific method, so uniformly and unquestioningly recited by students as objective, essentially reduces both questions and answers by narrowing the inquiry to find *an* answer to a question. It requires that complex natural systems be reduced to their parts, ignoring the interactions that take place among the components of the system(s). The reductionism required by the scientific (experimental) method means that the findings of research are often difficult to re-integrate into an understanding of more complex phenomena. Ultimately, we find that we actually understand very little.

One fundamental assumption in the traditional method of scientific discovery is that human beings are individualistic and obtain knowledge in a rational manner that can be separated from their social condition. This ignores the fact that who is asking the question affects what questions get asked and how the answers to the questions are constructed. In effect, we can only find what we are looking for and, if only one type of person (usually white, Western, and male) is seeking answers, only some answers will be sought. And, because reason, fact, and object represent rational discourse and scientific knowledge and are, not surprisingly, qualities synonymous with masculinity, only some answers will be validated.

Although we have numerous examples of how gender-based patterns of exclusion, structured by power relations, have affected the norms and methods of scientific practice and inquiry, science is still presumed to be neutral, lacking any societal agenda or possibility for bias among its practitioners. "Science-as-usual" prevails because scientists are taught to be passive recipients of knowledge and not encouraged to think about the epistemology of science. Scientists are trained to believe that, through logical inquiry and detachment from the objects of inquiry, it is possible to derive an understanding of the natural world. This approach fails to recognize that there are multiple ways to interpret data, particularly when the empirical evidence represents a small piece of a more complex picture. In "Life in the XY Corral," Anne Fausto-Sterling argues that assumptions about gender, race, and sexuality shape scientific theorizing as well as the interpretation of what we claim to observe. She asserts that developmental biologists, who emphasize male factors in sex determination research while leaving female factors uninvestigated, are simply reflecting the societal norm that recognizes males as powerful and females as invisible. In the struggle for scientific authority, theories that support existing presumptions about gender, race, and sexuality are given priority over those that challenge societal assumptions.

The authority of science has been used to marginalize and discriminate among and between women and to misrepresent women's nature. The search for "difference," whether sexual or racial, has dominated scientific research on humans and other animals and has been used to reaffirm societal attitudes toward gender and race. The chapters by Donna Haraway, Bonnie Spanier, and Helen Zweifel are examples of how these organizing principles are used in the fields of primatology, molecular biology, and conservation biology to create and reinforce gendered and racial hierarchies. Similar evidence for bias exists in subdisciplines such as botany and evolutionary biology (Gates and Shteir 1997, Hager 1997, Schiebinger 1993). These writings provide clear examples of how societal bias becomes part of the explanation provided for "natural" phenomena and how standard methods (developed from a particular perspective) used in various disciplines are justified as objective and value-neutral. Are these examples of "bad science" as a result of failing to follow the scientific method properly, or do they reveal androcentrism in research? Given this type of evidence, most could see that bias exists in research, particularly when it involves humans and other primates. However, in "The Inclusion of Women in Clinical Trials," Curtis Meinert argues that although large, heterogeneous samples are desirable in clinical trials involving human health, we should trust scientists to know how to be selective about who is suitable for the research. He rationalizes the use of selectivity to reduce variance because understanding the main effects of treatments is more important than understanding how the effects might vary among different subgroups. As always, reductionism makes it difficult to re-integrate partial information into an understanding of more complex phenomena.

References and additional resources

Birke, Lynda and Ruth Hubbard (1995) *Reinventing Biology: Respect for Life and the Creation of Knowledge*. Bloomington and Indianapolis: Indiana University Press.

Gates, Barbara T. and Ann B. Shteir (1997) *Natural Eloquence: Women Reinscribe Science*. Madison: University of Wisconsin Press.

Signs 24: 171–200.

Schiebinger, Londa (1987) "The History and Philosophy of Women in Science: A Review Essay." *Signs* 12: 305–332.

Schiebinger, Londa (1993) *Nature's Body. Gender in the Making of Modern Science*. Boston: Beacon Press.

Van Den Wijngaard, Marianne (1997) *Reinventing the Sexes: The Biomedical Construction of Femininity and Masculinity*. Bloomington and Indianapolis: Indiana University Press.

Chapter 19

Anne Fausto-Sterling

LIFE IN THE XY CORRAL

Synopsis

This essay outlines some of the ways in which contemporary developmental biology has been shaped by the exigencies of particular social movements and ideologies. The work is divided into three parts. Part One explores how the removal of the developing organism from its environmental context and the placement of the nucleus rather than the integrated cell at the head of a developmental control hierarchy has powerfully advanced our abilities to create chimeric organisms, to use genetic engineering for better and for worse and even to create mammalian clones. Part Two outlines a relationship between a central tenet of developmental and evolutionary theory, the continuity of the germ line, and the eugenics movement active during the first quarter of the twentieth century. Part Three discusses how assumptions about gender which are deeply embedded in our language have affected theories of male and female development.

> The Hip Young Gunslingers of modern developmental biology shoot fast, hard and often inaccurately.
>
> (Jackson, 1986, p. 193)

Introduction

Origin myths have a venerable place in the history of human cultures. Such tales lurk even in the groves of academe, finding their way into the disciplinary lore of the sciences and social sciences (Haraway, 1984–85; Tanner, 1981). A recent example from the pages of a new journal, *Trends in Genetics (TIG)*, illustrates the point. In an article entitled "A molecular season for descriptive embryology," Alfonso Martinez-Arias (1986) tells an origin story about contemporary developmental biology, the research field which in an earlier era biologists called embryology. He starts with Thomas Hunt Morgan, the stern American father of Mendelian genetics B.C. (Before the Code). According to Martinez-Arias, Morgan was interested in embryology until "he got distracted . . . and set up the foundations of modern genetics." While Morgan's genetic baby "grew into molecular genetics with all its flair and charisma," embryology stagnated. But finally, the charismatic molecular geneticists have turned their attention to Morgan's first love. [illegible]

[illegible]

experiments in developmental biology, but rather the review's ritual format. The author first appeals to an originator, a father, who abandoned his child for many long years (during which time the child languished, unable to develop). Now finally the father's heirs, the "hip, young gunslingers of modern developmental biology," have returned to rescue the stunted offspring and help it, with the heavenly blessing of the Father, to grow to manhood. In writing this piece Martinez-Arias clearly had no intention of offering an accurate historical account of twentieth century genetics and developmental biology. Instead, his article asserts that developmental biology and its precursor field, embryology, is a subdiscipline of genetics, one with no independent body of thought, experiment, method, problematic, or theory. That the article appeared in a new journal entitled *Trends in Genetics (TIG)* and subtitled "DNA, Differentiation and Development," is entirely appropriate to its task. Sapp (1987, p. 223) describes the process as follows:

> . . . scientists are engaged in a struggle for scientific authority. What is at stake in this struggle is the power to impose a definition of field: what questions are important, what phenomena are interesting, what techniques are suitable, and what theories are acceptable.

Two of the "weapons" used in this struggle, as Sapp has so nicely shown, are the rewriting of the history of a field and the establishment of new scientific journals. As a brand new journal *TIG* sets out to consolidate information and experimentation from the past twenty years and to provide a new forum for writing about certain important developmental questions.[1] Such a move is both reasonable and given the explosion of journal articles which no one has time to read laudable. But even well-deserved praise need not prevent us from examining the significance of the journal's intellectual construction. This particular new journal places development and differentiation into a sub-division of genetics. Although the editor recognizes that there are legitimate nongenetic approaches to the study of development, he sees these as stop-gap. In accounting for placing development in a subtitle underneath genetics, the editor writes (Prentis, 1985, p. 1):

> By using the subtitle "DNA, Differentiation and Development" the journal has been given the opportunity to focus on issues in developmental biology *which at present* may have no well-defined genetic component.
>
> (emphasis added)

The fact is that the fields of embryology and genetics have been locked in a power struggle for much of the twentieth century (Allen, 1974, 1985). Traditionally historians of science have looked at such struggles by closely examining the sequence of experimentation and debate found in the scientific literature (Churchill, 1974). In this essay I argue that such an approach is necessary but insufficient for understanding how scientific beliefs become established and how once established, they can once again change. In the sections which follow, I will discuss the development of two central concepts in developmental biology, differential gene expression and the continuity of the germ line; I argue that social and political factors combined with particular experimental results to shape the ideas which have come now, in the last half of the 1980s, to be accepted into the biological canon. Specifically, I contend that the social relations of race, gender, and class have left their imprints on the field of developmental biology. In providing such arguments I offer an origin story which differs markedly from that presented by Martinez-Arias.

During the past dozen years a new field of scholarship broadly referred to as the social studies of science has appeared on the scene. The basic assumption of scholars in this area is that scientific research forms an integral part of our cultural, social, and political systems. Rejected is the notion of the scientist as a fully independent and objective agent able to seek out an unfettered truth. Placed in the context of the social studies of science the claim that the imprints of racial, gender, and class ideology may be found in developmental biology is not really a very strange one, although to working scientists it seems odd indeed. But geneticists and embryologists focus centrally on sexual reproduction, the origin of species types, and the transmission from one generation to the next of both similarity and difference. That the explanatory systems which have emerged in these fields reflect in some way our beliefs and our political struggles around these issues should not surprise us. In pointing to such reflections, I am *not* claiming a one-to-one correlation between the biases and prejudices of individual scientists and the work they produce. Nor am I arguing that the presence of such imprinting necessarily renders the theories under discussion wrong or incoherent. Indeed much of the power of contemporary molecular biology lies in its comprehensive and cohering explanatory capabilities. Rather, my purpose in pursuing such a line of inquiry is to "work out in what sense and to what degree we can speak coherently of (scientific) knowledge as being rooted in social life" (Knorr-Cetina and Mulkay, 1983, p. 6).

The essay is divided into three parts. In part One I discuss how both the organism and the egg cell have become literally and conceptually decontextualized as their study has been placed into a sub-category of molecular genetics. In part Two I discuss the establishment of the idea of a separate and sequestered germ line and suggest a relationship between its acceptance during the first quarter of the twentieth century and a contemporary enthusiasm for eugenics, a social program which combined particular class, gender, and race interests. In part Three I discuss the ways in which unconscious beliefs and modes of speaking about gender have affected current discussions about sex determination in mammals. In all three segments I argue that the direction, subject matter, and scope of the field have been affected in particular ways and that scientists operating in other cultures under other belief systems might well have constructed other equally valid accounts of development.

Decontextualization and the quest for control

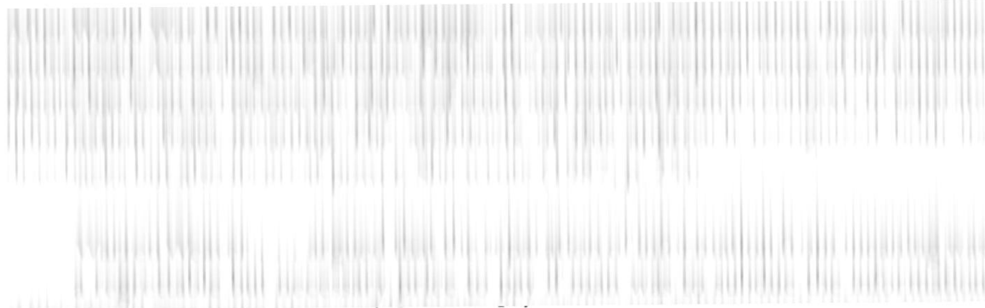

channel he likened to a discreet "office girl" who processes all that comes to her desk without regard for its meaning.

The application of systems theory to the embryo has involved two sorts of decontextualization, that of the egg cell and that of the organism. The account of animal development represented in *Trends in Genetics* and other new journals such as *Genes and Development* and *Developmental Genetics* gives primary importance to the gene. In modern terminology the gene is understood to represent specific base sequences in a DNA molecule, which is in higher organisms organized into complex arrangements of protein and nucleic acid called chromosomes. Chromosomes reside in the cell nucleus, and all cells in all tissues of an organism are believed to have the same DNA/information content.[2] Despite their identical DNA/information content the cells of different organs and tissues within the body differ from one another both structurally, chemically, and functionally. Developmental biologists explain this apparent paradox by invoking something they call *Differential Gene Expression*. According to this account of development, the fertilized egg begins to divide and a multicellular organism develops as different genes in different cells express their potential. Thus the hemoglobin genes, which reside in all cells of the body, only express their hemoglobin potential in the red blood cell; the myosin and acting genes become especially active in muscle cells, etc. In this view, the problem of embryonic development reduces to a problem of understanding how genes important for development are organized within the chromosomes and what controls their differential readout. The genetic code, that linear sequence of bases in the DNA molecule, *becomes* the organism.[3] To quote François Jacob, who shared the Nobel prize for his work on the control of gene expression in bacteria (1982, p. 2):

> In the chromosomes received from its parents, each egg . . . contains its entire future: the stages of its development, the shape and the properties of the living being which will emerge. The organism thus *becomes* the realization of a programme prescribed by its heredity.
>
> (emphasis added)

One important implication of the idea that the mature organism exists preformed in the DNA code of the zygote is that the context in which it develops, be it the ocean, a fresh-water pond or a woman's uterus, becomes irrelevant. If the code *is* the organism then it should be possible to gain power over the developmental process by removing it from its original context and placing it in the laboratory. This sort of power has already become part of our existence. With test tube babies, for example, the disembodied embryo has many parents. Thus we are now regularly treated on television to the sight of physicians involved in *in vitro* fertilizations (IVF) presenting themselves as proud and powerful parents. In addition to the IVF doctor, children may also have biological parents, surrogate parents and adoptive parents. The legal and ethical implications of separating the human egg from its uterine context have been dramatically brought to light by the Baby M case. As Katherine Hayles (1987, p. 26) describes it: "Never before in human history had the cultural context itself been constituted through a technology that makes it possible to fragment, manipulate and reconstitute informational texts at will."

The language of fragmentation in the biological literature and the cubist images evoked is quite striking. Biochemist W. Szybalski, in the founding editorial of a journal called *Gene* (1976, pp. 1–2), writes the following:

> The journal *Gene* is intended to serve . . . as the main repository for articles on the elements of physically controlled recombination processes, including chemical or enzymatic disassembly and *in vitro* assembly of genomes, specialized recombination processes, and the properties of reconstructed genes and genomes.

A recent example of such fragmentation involves the cloning of domestic livestock by fusing individual cells obtained from fragmented embryos with oocyte fragments (Marx, 1988). The potential pay-off for the livestock industry, of being able to obtain genetically identical animals, is great. The potential applications to humans cannot be that far off.

Decontextualization of the egg cell

For much of the twentieth century biologists have debated about the relative roles of the cell nucleus and cytoplasm in heredity. Embryologists in the first quarter of the century provided a great deal of experimental evidence pointing to the importance of the egg cytoplasm in the control of embryonic form and character. In contrast American Mendelian geneticists, with Thomas Hunt Morgan leading the way, down-played the importance of the cytoplasm, emphasizing instead the presence in the nucleus of genetic factors which alone served to determine the characteristics of the adult organism.

While acknowledging that Mendelian genes controlled superficial characteristics such as eye color, many embryologists could not fathom the idea that these hypothetical constructs accounted for the varied and complex behaviors of the egg and early embryo. Furthermore, the problem of genetic constancy in different cell types proved a conceptual stumbling block for many. The nucleus may contain genes, but if all cells contain the same set of genes, how indeed could different cell types arise during embryonic development? The answer, for which considerable experimental evidence existed, was to be found in a highly complex and differentiated egg cytoplasm. That this answer emphasized the special importance of the female parent is evident in the following quote from embryologist E.G. Conklin (in Sapp, 1987, p. 170):

> We are vertebrates because our mothers were vertebrates and produced eggs of the vertebrate pattern; but the color of our skin and hair and eyes, our sex, stature and mental peculiarities were determined by the sperm as well as by the egg [illegible]

[illegible] network which attempted to discredit scientist Ruth Sager's ground-breaking work on cytoplasmic inheritance, carried out under difficult circumstances because she was a woman and working on a stigmatized subject, by referring to it as "Ruth's defense of the egg" (Sapp, 1987, p. 206). While embryologists today would continue to agree that the egg is, embryologically speaking, the more important germ cell (an egg can develop a new organism without a sperm, but the reverse is not possible), a vision of development which focuses on the dominant role of the nucleus in cell processes will quite reasonably emphasize the equal nuclear contributions of egg and sperm. A more diffuse notion of inheritance, which looks both at cytoplasmic as well as nuclear genes and which emphasizes the complex structure of the egg places greater influence at the feet of the female parent.

The intellectual move of the 1970s which consolidated the central role of the nucleus in developmental theory was made by none other than James Watson. His book *The Molecular Biology of the Gene* (1976) is perhaps the clearest statement of the hopes and accomplishments of molecular biology in the 1970s. Incorporating embryology into the fold involved a major reshaping of the traditional subject matter of development. One chapter sub-heading states the matter clearly: "The heart of embryology is the problem of cell differentiation" (Watson, 1976, p. 500). Framing the problem in this fashion accomplishes two tasks. First, it awards priority to the nucleus redefining *the* problem of development as one of the control of gene activity. Second, it removes from the field those problems less well suited to the methods and concepts of molecular genetics, problems such as embryonic regulation, cleavage, gastrulation morphogenesis, cellular determination, regeneration, and multicellular pattern formation, in other words, most of what traditionally trained embryologists would consider to be their subject matter.

The 1980s application of molecular biology to development may be found in a far more sophisticated and major new text, *Molecular Cell Biology* (Darnell, Lodish, and Baltimore, 1986), a book written expressly to consolidate the knowledge gained by researchers in the past decade and to shape the field for the coming one. The chapter on animal development discusses many topics omitted by James Watson and updates the reader on the attention focused on early embryonic development by researchers working with several key organisms.[4] In general the authors' treatment of embryology is both more humble and more thorough than Watson's, but the focus remains nucleocentric. The conceptual blinders imposed by such a focus can be seen clearly in their discussion of the classical nuclear transplantation experiments.

Since earlier in this century when Hans Spemann constricted a developing egg with a fine baby's hair in order to see if the nucleus of different embryonic cells changed during development (Spemann, 1928), scientists have performed large numbers of ingenious experiments all aimed at asking the same question: can the nucleus of a fully differentiated cell, if placed in an undivided egg cell, direct the development of a complete and well-formed new organism, or as they say in the trade, do nuclei from differentiated cells remain totipotent? The theoretical framework of differential gene expression rests on the "right" answer to this question, for if development is merely the controlled reading out of the genetic code, all nuclei in all cells ought to be equivalent. If, on the other hand, there is no nuclear equivalence, something other than or in addition to the expression of the DNA code must be part of the secret of embryonic development. Since the 1950s studies of nuclear potency have involved the physical transfer of nuclei from differentiated cells into fertilized, enucleated egg cells. The results of hundreds of experiments and a great deal of wrangling can be briefly summarized: the more differentiated the cell from which the donor nucleus is taken, the less capable the nucleus is of supporting full development. Since the DNA content of these nuclei is thought to be identical, the inability of just any old nucleus to support full development is puzzling.

The authors of *Molecular Cell Biology* (Darnell *et al.*, 1986) spend three paragraphs wrestling with the puzzle, but are unable to solve it. The source of this inability, I argue, lies not in a lack of knowledge of the differentiated nucleus so much as it does in a conception of the nucleus as something which has meaning and control outside of its cellular context. The nuclear transplantation literature provides abundant evidence that nuclear activities can only be understood when studied and interpreted in their cellular context. For example, the nucleus of a brain cell which has been actively involved in synthesizing specialized proteins of the brain, changes its activities when placed in a nonbrain cytoplasmic context. The question to ask is not how does a cell nucleus change during differentiation, but how does the dynamic nuclear-cytoplasmic interaction alter? The body of work on nuclear transplantations is inconclusive because it is at a conceptual impasse which cannot be overcome as long as the code remains separate from the context which gives it meaning.

Eugenics and the acceptance of the germ-line theory

In addition to the concept of differential gene expression, the concept of a *Continuous Germ Line* provides a cornerstone to contemporary theories of development. Although the egg cell itself has the capacity to develop all of the different cell types found in the adult, as the egg divides, its daughter cells lose this ability. If differentiated cells lose their ability to form new organisms, however, then how do we explain the appearance of new reproductively competent cells, eggs and sperm, in each generation? The German biologist August Weismann proposed in the late nineteenth century that in the early embryo a special cell lineage, the germ line, is sequestered from participation in larval or adult development and it is from this special cell line, and this line alone, that the gametes arise in the sexually mature organism. None of the other cells, the so-called somatic cells, play a role in the making of future generations. Weismann argued that the germ line was immortal, that each generation of germ cells gave rise to the next, while at the same time throwing off a somatic line, which died out with each animal generation. Evolutionary change could only occur if a germ-line nucleus is changed; characteristics acquired by the soma would not be passed on to the next [illegible]

combination of the ideas of differential gene expression, the inheritance of a blueprint for development in the DNA code, and the transmission of that code (including an occasional mutation or code change) through the sequestered germ line of multicellular animals has provided a coherent and powerful joining point for the fields of development and heredity (Browder, 1984). Why shouldn't the story end here?

When August Weismann first proposed his viewpoint it was rejected by many embryologists (Maienschein, 1987). Yet, by 1915 it had become a central part of embryological theory. Historian Jane Maienschein suggests that the rapid change in the viewpoints of US biologists resulted from two factors: the experimental evidence accumulated to support the idea of a sequestered and continuous germ line, and what she calls "a pragmatic desire for progress" (Maienschein, 1987, p. 88). I believe, however, that such an explanation is incomplete. While the ultimate success of Weismann's germ-line theory depended in part on the experimental evidence which supported it, it also resulted from the profound implications of this theory for contemporary architects of social change, especially those enamored of eugenics. Some of the evidence to support this claim and a sketch of the implications for contemporary theories of development and evolution follow. Theoretically, I am working with a model of scientific theory-making very similar to that elaborated by Elizabeth Potter in her account of Robert Boyle's adoption of a corpuscular theory of matter (Potter, 1988). Agreeing with mainstream philosophers of science that theory choice is over-determined, she shows how the political and social compatibilities of a particular vision of nature can swing the balance of choice in one direction or another. The point is not that political philosophies cause bad theory choice, but that there are often several fairly good accounts of existing data available. Which theory finally predominates depends on much more than just how well the data and the facts fit together.

Historian John Burnham argues that the Anglo-American response to Weismannism had everything to do with theories of social change. "A large number of the most influential English and American intellectuals," he writes, "had posited general social theories upon assumptions concerning the permanent (inherited) influence that environmental changes have upon the race" (Burnham, 1972, p. 323). Weismann argued directly against the inheritance of acquired characteristics suggesting instead that only genetic changes in the human population could lead to racial betterment. A letter to *Nature* written in 1888 by P. Chalmers Mitchell spells out how the problem was conceptualized. He writes that Weismann's view, "Obviously . . . excludes the inheritance of acquired, characters. . . . " In humans:

> Instincts are elaborated, not by the accumulation of transmitted individual experience, but by continual selection of mental variations in the required direction. . . . Talent and even genius often run through several generations; and certainly mental powers can be much increased in individual lives. But the exhibition of talent and genius depends on a combination of many physical and mental conditions in which constitutional variation is ever present, and these variations are undoubtedly inheritable.
>
> (Mitchell, 1888, pp. 156–157)

Historian Ruth Schwartz Cowan points out that the founder of modern eugenics, Sir Francis Galton, came up with the idea of the continuity of the germ plasm a decade before Weismann. While Galton was not that interested in the idea from the standpoint of a biologist, he did insist upon it as part of his political program of eugenics (Cowan, 1968). The application of the germ plasm theory to social problems did not escape US embryologists and geneticists during the first quarter of the twentieth century. To the contrary, many of them wrote extensively on the topic and integrated their concerns into basic textbooks (Castle, 1920; Jennings, 1930; Osborn, 1920). A consideration of some of the writings of E.G. Conklin, a key figure in US embryology, will serve to illustrate the point. In the preface to his 1915 edition of *Heredity and Environment in the Development of Men*, Conklin, a professor of biology at Princeton, wrote, "Within recent years the experimental study of heredity and development has led to a new epoch in our knowledge . . . and it does not seem unreasonable to suppose that in time it will produce a better breed of men" (Conklin, 1915, p. v). He continues in the following vein:

> If human heredity, development and evolution may be controlled to even a slight extent, we may expect that sooner or later the human race will be changed for the better. At least *no other form of social betterment* and race improvement can compare . . . with that which attempts to change the natures of men and to establish in the blood, the qualities which are desired.
>
> (emphasis added)

In Chapter IV of *Heredity and Environment* (1915), Conklin follows his account of Weismann's disproof of the inheritance of acquired characteristics, with a discussion of euthenics, the bettering of the race through environmental changes. While acknowledging the importance of good education and opportunity, he concludes "if society is really to advance . . . the natures of men must improve as well as their environment" (Conklin, 1915, p. 363). Over a period of three decades Conklin wrote extensively about the application of embryology and genetics to human affairs (Conklin, 1921, 1930, 1935, 1943). The continuity of the germ plasm as postulated by Weismann and modified by experimental observation played a key role in his visions. This essay is not the place to spell out in detail Conklin's feelings about the "race question," bolshevism and democracy, or the education of women, all of which he considers as he connects the lessons taught by development to his social concerns; I simply contend that the acceptance of the idea of a continuous germ line cannot be separated from the social implications read into it by biologists of this period.

A fully embraced theory of the continuous germ line profoundly influenced the shape of contemporary developmental biology. Darnell *et al.* (1986, p. 1001), for example, make the following statement: "The initial determination of cells as primordial germ cells occurs very early in *all* animals" (emphasis added). This generalization is striking because it is inaccurate. It was known to be so in 1900 and its inaccuracies are

animals), Buss (1987) points out that the first three kingdoms completely violate Weismann's doctrine, that is, that fungi, plants, and protists do not have a sequestered, continuous germ line; neither do all taxonomic groups represented by the animal kingdom. In fact no fewer than 9 of 18 animal phyla contain at least some species which violate Weismann's doctrine. Looked at this way, one can see that the theory of development which emerged early in the twentieth century and which continues to hold center stage today is accurately applicable to only a small part of the biotic world. There are multiple explanations for this state of affairs, but the ready applicability of Weismann's writings to political struggles over issues in race, class, and gender (all of which are profoundly intermixed in the eugenics movement) must certainly be counted among them. Social ideologies have indeed affected the content of contemporary developmental biology. Nor would it be difficult to envision a different canon, developing in a different culture which would be equally "correct" from a scientific view-point, but which would choose paradigm organisms whose biology exemplified social interaction and cooperative change. Perhaps in such a culture the results obtained from in-depth studies of colonial animals and plants (which do not have sequestered germ lines) would provide the building blocks for a theory of development while the embryology of higher metazoans would be seen as discomfort-producing "exceptions." Such a theory would allow for the incorporation of somatic change into future generations and would be philosophically compatible with no biological theories of social change[5] (Mulkay and Gilbert, 1982).

Development and the language of gender

A number of scholars have written about the importance of language and metaphor choice in the development of scientific theory (The Biology and Gender Study Group, 1988; Bleier, 1984; Haraway, 1976; Keller, 1985; Stepan, 1986). This essay concludes with an analysis of the role of language choice in the production of theories about male and female development. I argue that unconscious assumptions about gender, hidden within the language we use to write about it, have worked to create implausible theories of sexual development. The issues have been most recently highlighted by a great deal of publicity about the discovery of what some have called a sex determining gene on the human Y chromosome.

In December 1987, we were treated to a memorable media blast. Scientists at MIT, we learned, had discovered the secret of sex determination; the secret, they said, consisted of a master gene on the Y chromosome. In the TV and newspaper interviews, Dr. David Page, the researcher in question, suggested that his discovery had fundamental and new importance for all of developmental biology. Had Page, who calls his laboratory at MIT's Whitehead Institute the XY Corral (Roberts, 1988), really uncovered the secrets of sex?

In analyzing the work of Page and others on mammalian sex determination three intersecting issues arise.[6] The first is the use of the universal language of man; in much of the literature discoveries billed as the key to sex determination are in fact only keys to male development. The second concerns the representation of male as presence and female as absence. This representation has been widely written about in psychoanalytic and linguistic feminist analyses, but it also extends into the heart of biological theories about male and female. The third is the treatment of "sex" as something clearcut and unambiguous. Feminist theorists have critically examined the categories of sex and gender (Flax, 1987), but despite the "data" at their fingertips, biologists continue to write about sex as if it were an uncomplicated dualism. In the pages which follow I will show how each of these issues plays out in the current work on sex determination. Some of the territory I cover has also been traversed by the Swarthmore Biology and Gender Study Group, and also with both prescience and good humor by Ruth Herschberger (The Biology and Gender Study Group, 1988; Herschberger, 1948).

Scientists usually divide the process of sex determination into two phases. Primary sex determination refers to the initial decision of a bipotential embryonic gonad to develop as either a testis or an ovary, while secondary sex determination refers to the decisions of a bipotential embryo to develop either male or female accessory organs (fallopian tubes, epididymal structures, etc.) and either male or female external genitalia. I have analyzed accounts of secondary sex determination elsewhere (Fausto-Sterling, 1987), and will here consider only very recent work on primary sex determination.

Sex determination = male determination

In the summary of the article by Page *et al.* (1987), published in the prestigious journal *Cell*, he and his co-authors (there are eight, of whom at least five are women) write, "We report the cloning of a 230 kilo-base segment of the human Y chromosome that contains some or all of the testis-determining factor gene (TDF), the master sex determining locus" (Page *et al.*, 1987, p. 1091). The language in this sentence collapses the phrases "sex determination" and "testis-determination" into one another; "ovary determination" remains invisible and unmentionable. Geneticists Eva Eicher and Linda L. Washburn, in a paper critical of the sex determination literature (a publication to which Page and co-authors do not refer), write the following (Eicher and Washburn, 1986, pp. 328–329):

Some investigators have overemphasized the hypothesis that the Y chromosome is involved in testis determination by presenting the induction of testicular tissue as an active (gene-directed, dominant) event while presenting the induction of ovarian tissue as a passive (automatic) event. Certainly the induction of ovarian tissue is as much an active, genetically directed developmental process as is the induction of testicular tissue, or for that matter, the induction of any cellular differentiation process. Almost nothing has been written about genes involved in the induction of ovarian tissue from the undifferentiated gonad.

[illegible]

Presence and absence

In the opening sentence of the *Cell* article, Page *et al.* write: "The presence or absence of the Y chromosome determines whether a mammalian embryo develops as male or female." In the introduction, they restate the theme: "The mammalian Y chromosome, by its presence or absence, constitutes a binary switch upon which hinge all sexually dimorphic characteristics" (Page *et al.*, 1987, p. 1091). And again in the conclusion they open with "Our studies suggest that the sex of an individual is determined by the presence or absence of a very small portion of the human Y chromosome . . . female WHT1013 carries 99.8% of the Y chromosome; she lacks only the 160 kb that comprise intervals 1A2 and 1B – yet she is a female" (Page *et al.*, 1987, p. 1099). Usually, development of specific tissue types is understood to involve the activation of specific genes or gene sequences. Yet, the generally accepted theory of sex determination claims that female differentiation is determined by the *absence* of something, that a female develops when something is lacking. I suggest that the pervasiveness of our cultural construction of female as absence, seen in everything from Freudian theory to the non-equivalence of the words male and female in our language (the opposite of male is not female, but non-male), has also insinuated itself into biological theories about male and female development. The process by which this has happened is completely unconscious, and it has gone unnoticed until feminists, by focusing an alternate prism on the subject, became able to "see" what had previously appeared invisible.

Eicher and Washburn (1986) constructed a model of sex determination which includes both male and female. They propose the presence of parallel genetic pathways for gonadal determination, one involved in testis formation and the other in ovarian formation. Using the word induction to describe the activation of each pathway, they suggest that the crucial task for the indifferent embryo is "to guarantee that only one of the gonadal-determination pathways is normally realized in any one individual" (Eicher and Washburn, 1986, p. 341). In their model the critical difference in male and female development is timing. If the testis pathway is induced, the first gene to act in that pathway (which may well be the gene identified by Page and co-workers) could produce a chemical which represses the activation of the ovarian pathway. The question of why gonadal pathway activation occurs earlier in XY mammals than in XX ones remains unanswered, but Eicher and Washburn's model opens up a research program in which both ovarian and testis determining genes are sought after. In fact they propose a number of strategies for looking for information about the control of ovarian development.

The complications of sex

David Page investigated sex determination using the following tactic. He obtained DNA samples from unusual clinical cases in which individuals with two X chromosomes had been designated as males (XX males) and ones with an XYchromosomal constitution had been designated as females (XY females). He and his co-workers reasoned that if there is a male-determining gene on the Y chromosome, then what must be going on in these unusual cases is that the gene, that is, a small stretch of DNA not visible under the microscope, had been translocated from the Y chromosome to some other chromosome. If this were the case then even though an XX male had no microscopically detectable Y chromosome, he must have the key piece of DNA responsible for maleness present on one of his other chromosomes. Similarly, even though the XY females appeared to have a normal Y chromosome, they must have lost a key submicroscopic portion of the Y, the so-called testis determining factor. By collecting DNA samples from a number of different XX males and XY females, and by examining them with the most modern of molecular techniques, Page *et al.* (1987) confirmed that a small stretch of Y chromosome DNA was indeed present in the genome of XX males and missing from that of XY females.

But then came the puzzling result. This same stretch of DNA, or at least one very similar to it in base sequence, is also present on the X chromosomes of normal females. If this Y-chromosome DNA sequence is the "master sex-determining locus" and if its presence means male and its absence means female, then what is it doing on both X and Y chromosomes? Page and co-authors offer several hypotheses. The first, and least satisfactory, is that although the gene is on the X chromosome, it does nothing when there, i.e., it is passive in a female but active in a male. The other models, while somewhat more plausible, fall short because these researchers understand the word "sex" in too simple a fashion. In fact the subjects from whom they obtained DNA samples present a more complex story.

In the *Cell* paper Page *et al.* (1987) give no hint that the XX males and XY females from whom they obtained DNA samples were anything other than fully normal representatives of their sex. But this is not the case. (If it were they would probably have never been discovered, since it was clinical symptoms which brought them to attention in the first place.) For example, the four XX males whom they studied[7] were all sterile (no sperm production), had small testes which totally lacked germ cells, that is, the precursor cells for sperms, high follicle stimulating hormone levels and low testosterone levels. Presumably they were classified as males because of their external genitalia and the presence of testes. But clearly their development had not been fully normal (Guellaen *et al.*, 1984). Similarly, the development of the XY females was abnormal. Although both of these patients' external genitalia were normal, their ovaries lacked germ cells. In both XX males and XY females, then, what does the notion of a sex-determining gene mean? Is maleness decided on the basis of external genital structure? Often not, since sometimes physicians decide that an individual with female genitalia is really a male and surgically correct the external structures so that they match the chromosomal and hormonal sex. Is it the presence of an ovary or testis that decides the matter? If so, oughtn't the gonad to have germ cells in it to "count"? Or is it enough to be in the right place and have the right superficial histological structure? There are no good answers to these questions because EVEN biologically speaking sex is not such an either/or construct. Page and co-workers chose to leave [illegible]

Although considerable scholarship now backs up the claim that the social relations marked by race, class, and gender have affected the development of contemporary science, the idea remains puzzling to many. In this essay I have outlined some of the ways in which contemporary theories of developmental biology have been shaped by the exigencies of particular social movements and ideologies. This sculpting may be seen at several different levels.

In the first part of this essay I discussed the ways in which the removal of the developing organism from its environmental context and the placement of the nucleus rather than the integrated cell at the head of a developmental control hierarchy has powerfully advanced our abilities to create chimeric organisms, to use genetic engineering for better and for worse, and even to arrive at that moment in science fiction when we can create mammalian clones. These technological successes should not obscure the fact that the vision behind the research program comes from very specific cultural and historical places. It is not the task of this essay to locate the development of information theory in its appropriate context, one of weaponry development, the scientific management of labor, and the development of psychological and sexual norms to be imposed upon diverse North Atlantic populations. A number of others have explicated this claim in some detail (Haraway, 1979, 1983; Hayles, 1987). In this essay I have merely pointed to a few of the ways that the language of information theory has become an integral and therefore often unnoticed part of theories of development. That there might have been other themes which generated other research programs seems also to be a plausible claim.

From this most general argument about the structure of theories of development I then moved to a more specific account of one of the central tenets of embryological theory: the notion of a sequestered and immortal germ line. When first suggested in the late 1800s, the idea fit well with an emerging movement for social betterment, the eugenics movement. Although mostly discredited, but certainly not dead today, in its own time this movement claimed among its adherents large numbers of intellectuals in the sciences and social sciences. The Anglo-American version of eugenics concerned itself with the influx of non-Nordic peoples into England and the United States (Fisher, 1958; MacKenzie, 1981; Stepan, 1982), and wove together in intricate fashion the social relations of race, class, and gender. American embryologists were involved in this movement and were quick to argue the relevance of the germ-line theory to theories of social change through selective breeding.

The germ-line theory had experimental support from a large number of different organisms. Thus a combination of scientific experiments and social utility helped it to become a cornerstone of contemporary embryology. It did and does not, however, provide an all-inclusive account of development. Rather it accurately applies to selected animal phyla while remaining inappropriate for major sectors of the biotic world. Organisms which belong to these sectors are simply not used as objects appropriate for embryological investigations. Once again, the argument is not that contemporary development theories are wrong, or biased or unscientific, but rather that they are more limited than they claim to be, and that the shape of the field of study in 1988, which organisms are taken as prototypes for investigation, and which theories provide the framework for experiments deemed worthy of financial support and scholarly recognition, is not determined or driven solely by the logic of the science.

In the final section of this essay I discussed how assumptions about gender which are embedded deeply in our language have affected theories of male and female development. Specifically, I show how the use of the male as universal leads to a slippage in which ideas presented as accounts of sexual development only account for male development. In such cases female development remains invisible and uninvestigated. Furthermore biologists' inability to break away from a strict binary account of male and female has led them to ignore data, which are better accounted for in approaches which accept the existence of intermediate states of sexuality.

We can return finally to the task which framed this essay, that of working out "in what sense and to what degree we can speak coherently of knowledge as being rooted in social life" (Knorr-Cetina and Mulkay, 1983, p. 6). What we can see from an examination of developmental biology is that the social relations of power represented by race, class, and gender, have influenced field definition and theory choice, and in one case, that of the study of the control of male and female development, have prevented the articulation of a coherent theory. It will require a variety of specific case studies in different fields of science to assess the generality of these answers.

Notes

1 This opening editorial lists the following questions "What controls early development? How is sex determined? Which genetic processes are involved in evolution? What defects underlie genetic diseases? How do differentiated cells maintain their correct functional, spatial, and temporal relationships?
2 This is not literally true, but the exceptions can be fitted into the overall scheme.
3 This is a predominant but by no means monolithic vision of embryonic development. It is, however, the one represented most strongly in the new journals mentioned in this article, and it represents the most powerful vision in terms of research funding and the interests of new graduate students.
4 The three paradigmatic organisms of contemporary developmental biology are a tiny roundworm, *CAENORHABDITIS ELEGANS*, the fruitfly, *DROSOPHILA MELANOGASTER*, and the laboratory mouse, *MUS MUSCULUS*. All three organisms have a germ line which separates out from the somatic cell line early in development,

and two of the three (the fly and the roundworm) follow very rigid developmental plans. One would be hard-put to posit that these particular organisms are generally representative of the biotic world; thus, it is argued in the next section of this paper, one must ask why these three have become so important.

5 Some readers will be tempted to read this as covert support for Lysenkoism. I consider Lysenkoism to be an example of "bad science." However, since Lysenko and his followers applied political ideology to biology even when the experimental evidence didn't fit. My intent here is to point out that in a society with very different

[illegible]

analysis.

7 It is virtually impossible to correlate their numbered DNA samples with the clinical histories, which makes reading the paper very difficult; but it is no accident that Page *et al.* do not find the clinical accounts worthy of discussion when building their theories of sex determination.

References

Allen, Gar. (1974). Opposition to the Mendelian-chromosome theory: The physiological and developmental genetics of Richard Goldschmidt. *Journal of the History of Biology*, 7, 49–92.

Allen, Gar. (1985). T.H. Morgan and the split between embryology and genetics, 1910–1935. In T.H. Jorder, J.A. Witkowski, and C.C. Wylie (Eds.), *A history of embryology* (pp. 113–147). Cambridge: Cambridge University Press.

The Biology and Gender Study Group. (1988). The importance of feminist critique for contemporary cell biology. *Hypatia*, 3, 61–76.

Bleier, Ruth. (1984). *Science and gender*. Elmsford, NY: Pergamon Press.

Browder, Leon W. (1984). *Developmental biology*. Philadelphia: Saunders.

Burnham, John C. (1972). Instinct theory and the German reaction to Weismannism. *Journal of the History of Biology*, 5, 321–326.

Buss, Leo. (1987). *The evolution of individuality*. Princeton, NJ: Princeton University Press.

Castle, W.E. (1920). *Genetics and eugenics*. Cambridge: Harvard University Press.

Churchill, Frederick B. (1974). William Johannsen and the genotype concept. *Journal of the History of Biology*, 7, 530.

Conklin, Edwin Grant. (1915). *Heredity and environment in the development of men*. Princeton, NJ: Princeton University Press.

Conklin, Edwin Grant. (1921). *The direction of human evolution*. New York: Charles Scribner's.

Conklin, Edwin Grant. (1930). *Science and the future of man*. Providence, RI: Brown University Papers IX.

Conklin, Edwin Grant. (1935). *Freedom and responsibility: A biological view of some problems of democracy*. Boston: Houghton Mifflin.

Conklin, Edwin Grant. (1943). *Man, real and ideal: Observations and reflections on man's nature, development and destiny*. New York: Charles Scribner's.
Cowan, Ruth Schwartz. (1968). Sir Francis Galton and the continuity of germ plasm: A biological idea with political roots. Proc. X11 Congress International D'Histoire Des Sciences, Paris.
Darnell, James, Lodish, Harvey, and Baltimore, David. (1986). *Molecular cell biology*. New York: Freeman.
Eicher, Eva M., and Washburn, Linda L. (1986). Genetic control of primary sex determination in mice. *Annual Review of Genetics*, 20, 327–360.
Fausto-Sterling, Anne. (1987). Society writes biology/biology constructs gender. *Daedalus*, 116, 61–76.
Flax, Jane. (1987). Postmodernism and gender relations in feminist theory. *Signs*, 12, 621–643.
Fisher, Ronald A. (1958). *The genetical theory of natural selection*. New York: Dover.
Gilbert, Scott F. (1988). *Developmental biology* (2nd ed.), Sunderland, MA: Siftauer Assoc.
Guellaen, Georges, Casanove, Myriam, Bishop, Colin, Geldwerth, Danielle, Andre, Gabriel, Fellous, Marc, and Weissenbach, Jean. (1984). Human XX males with Y single-copy DNA fragments. *Nature*, 307, 172–173.
Haraway, Donna. (1976). *Crystals, fabrics, and fields. Metaphors of organicism in 20th century developmental biology*. New Haven, CT: Yale University Press.
Haraway, Donna. (1979). The biological enterprise: Sex, mind and profit from human engineering to sociobiology. *Radical History Review*, Spring/Summer, 206–237.
Haraway, Donna. (1981–82). The high cost of information in post World War II evolutionary biology: Ergonomics, semiotics and the sociobiology of communication systems. *Philosophical Forum*, XIII, 244–278.
Haraway, Donna. (1983). Signs of dominance: From a physiology to a cybernetics of primate society, C.R. Carpenter, 1930–1970. *Studies in the History of Biology*, 6, 129–278.
Haraway, Donna. (1984–85). Teddy bear patriarchy: Taxidermy in the Garden of Eden, New York City, 1908–1936. *Social Text*, 20–64.
Hayles, N. Katherine. (1987). Text out of context: Situating post modernism within an information society. *Discourse*, 9, 24–36.
Herschberger, Ruth. (1948). *Adam's rib*. New York: Pelligrini and Cudahy.
Jackson, Ian. (1986). A solid foundation for developmental biology. *Trends in Genetics*, 2, 193.
Jacob, François. (1982). *The logic of life: A history of heredity* (p. 2). New York: Pantheon edition. (Original pub. date, 1976.)
Jennings, H.S. (1930). *The biological basis of human nature*. New York: W.W. Norton.
Keller, Evelyn Fox. (1985). *Reflections on gender and science*. New Haven, CT: Yale University Press.
Knorr-Cetina, Karen D., and Mulkay, Michael. (1983). Introduction: Emerging principles in social-studies of science. In *Science observed: Perspectives on the social study of science* (p. 6). London: Sage.
MacKenzie, Donald A. (1981). *Statistics in Britain 1865–1930*. Edinburgh: Edinburgh University Press.
Maienschein, Jane. (1987). Heredity/development in the United States, circa 1900. *History and Philosophy of the Life Sciences*, 9, 79–93.
Martinez-Arias, Alfonso. (1986). A molecular season for descriptive embryology. *Trends in Genetics*, 146.

Marx, Jean L. (1988). Cloning sheep and cattle embryos. *Science*, 239, 463–464.

Mitchell, P. Chalmers. (1888). Weismann on heredity. *Nature*, 38: 156–157.

Mulkay, Michael, and Gilbert, G. Nigel. (1982). Accounting for error: How scientists construct their social world when they account for correct and incorrect belief. *Sociology*, 2, 153–183.

Osborn, Henry Fairfield. (1920). Preface. In Madison Grant, *The passing of the great race*. New York: Scribner's.

Page, David C., Mosher, Rebecca, Simpson, Elizabeth M., Fisher, Elizabeth M.C. [illegible]

Spemann, Hans. (1928). Die Entwicklung seitlicher und dorsoventraler Keimhhalften bei verzogerter Kernversorgung. *Zeitschrift fur Wissenschaftliche Zoologie*. 132, 105–134.

Stepan, Nancy. (1982). *The idea of race in science: Great Britain 1800–1960*. Hamden, CT: Archon Books.

Stepan, Nancy Leys. (1986). Race and gender: The role of analogy in science. *ISIS*, 77, 261–277.

Szybalski, W. (1976). Founding editorial. Gene, 1, 1–2.

Tanner, Nancy. (1981). *On becoming human*. Cambridge: Cambridge University Press.

Watson, James D. (1976). *Molecular biology of the gene* (3rd ed.). Menlo Park, CA: W.A. Benjamin.

Wilson, J.D., George, F.W., and Griffin, J.E. (1981). The hormonal control of sexual development. *Science*, 211, 1278–1284.

Chapter 20

Donna Haraway

THE BIOPOLITICS OF A MULTICULTURAL FIELD

The mirror and the mask: the drama of Japanese primates

Japanese field study of an indigenous monkey inaugurated post-World War II naturalistic studies of nonhuman primates. The origin of the post-war primate story is within non-Western narrative fields. In the beginning, Japanese primatology was both autonomous and autochthonous – but not innocent, not without history. Human and animal, the actors and authors appeared on an island stage that was not set by the story of Paradise Lost. The Japanese monkeys became part of a complex cultural story of a domestic science and a native scientific identity for an industrial power in the "E/east."

Japanese primate studies originated in 1948 among a group of animal ecologists, including Imanishi Kinji, who had earned a doctor of science degree from Kyoto University in 1940. In the first generation of Japanese to pursue studies of animals in their natural environments, Imanishi led expeditions to several areas outside Japan. The Japanese primatologists were well aware of the Western work, and they cited Yerkes, Carpenter, and others with appreciation and critical evaluation. But the Japanese forged an independent primatology, whose characteristics were part of cultural narratives just as they have been in the West. As tropical primates have been mirrors for Western humans, domestic Japanese monkeys have been mirrors for their skilled indigenous observers.

Before turning to primates, Imanishi studied Japanese wild horses. In 1950 Imanishi and Miyade Denzaburo formed the Primates Research Group. Provisioning began in 1952, about the time of the establishment of the Kyoto University Anthropology Research Group. In Tokyo a medically oriented Experimental Animal Research Committee started up, and in 1956 the Kyoto and Tokyo groups established the Japan Monkey Center, followed in 1967 by the national Primate Research Institute of Kyoto University. By 1961, more than twenty Japanese macaque groups had been provisioned and brought into systematic operation.[1] In 1961 the Japanese began langur monkey studies, with the cooperation of Indian scientists in India, and launched the Kyoto University African Primatological Expedition. In 1965 they initiated a long-term chimpanzee project in Tanzania's Mahale Mountains.[2] In 1972, Japanese workers started groundwork for their study of pygmy chimpanzees in Zaire.[3]

Westerners were unaware of the Japanese work until after 1956. About 1957, Yale medical primatologist Gertrude van Wagenen found a book with a picture of monkeys in a bookstore in Japan. She wrote Stuart Altmann at the National Institutes [illegible] international language politics. From about 1959–60, Japanese and Western workers have been in regular contact, despite on-going difficulties of linguistic, cultural, and scientific communication.

National primates

It is ideologically and technically relevant that the Japanese studies were initiated on a species, *Macaca fuscata*, native to Japan. Although Japan had been a colonial power since the late nineteenth century, Japanese founding frameworks for watching monkeys and apes did not depend on the structure of colonial discourse – that complex search for primitive, authentic, and lost self, sought in the baroque dialectic between the wildly free and subordinated other. Rather, Japanese monkeys have been a part of the construction of a specifically Japanese scientific cultural identity. Constructing that identity has been a major theme in recent Japanese social, cultural, and intellectual history.[6]

Japanese monkeys might be viewed as actors in a Kabuki drama or a Noh performance. Their stylized social gestures and intricate rule-ordered lives are like dramatic masks that necessarily both conceal and reveal complex cultural meanings about what it means to be simultaneously social, indigenous, and individual for Japanese observers. Seeking the truth of nature underneath the thin, often obscuring layer of culture, the Westerner tends to see in our primate kin a deeper shared animal nature. In contrast, perhaps, Japanese primate observers have seen simian masks expressing the essential double-sidedness of the relations of individual and society and of knower and known.[7] It is not a "truer" nature behind the mask that is sought within the Japanese cultural frame; nature is not the bare face behind the mask of culture. Instead, the figure of the Japanese dramatic mask alludes to a powerful abstract stylization of the specific social intricacies and profoundly individual qualities that pattern primate life. The dramatic mask in Japan is a figure of the co-determining relations of inside and outside and of the subtle reversals of position that change inside into outside. Masks cannot be stripped away to reveal the truth; rather the mask is a figure of the two-sidedness of the structure of life, person, and society. I am suggesting that Japanese primatologists constructed simians as masks in these culturally specific senses. Japanese monkeys were crafted as objects of knowledge showing the structure of an interactionist, relational, contextual self in a highly differentiated social world like that inhabited by their skilled observers (R. Smith 1983: 68–105). "Nature" was made into an object of study in Japanese primatology, but it was nature as a social object, as itself composed of conventional social processes and specifically positioned actors, that intrigued early Japanese monkey watchers.

Let us follow some of the issues raised by this highly modern, richly traditional, indigenous science. Through a gesture appropriate to the Western structures of appropriation of the "other" that this book [*Primate Visions. Gender, Race and Nature in the World of Modern Science*] has not escaped, Japanese primatology can be mined for resources to illuminate questions about gender, feminism, and orientalism. The early ethnographies of Japanese monkeys can be useful distorting mirrors for Euro-American feminists tangled in a culturally given story about nature and organic unity.

The search for the untouched heart of nature seems not to be a dream shared by the Japanese with Western observers. In a dissertation and other writing on different forms of anthropomorphism in Japanese and Western primatology, Pamela Asquith investigates the historical and philosophical roots of Japan's extensive studies of the social lives of nonhuman primates.[8] She argues that the particular related boundaries between human and animal and between mind and body, so crucial to Western Greek and Judeo-Christian mythology and to derivative ideologies of scientific objectivity, are not part of Buddhist or Confucian Japanese cultural heritage. While concern with status, personality, social change and stability, and leadership pervades Japanese primate studies, the split between observer and observed, so crucial to the Western quest for a healing touch across the breach, is missing.

When the human–animal boundary is not culturally crucial, two things change which matter immensely to the themes of this book. First, "nature" cannot be constructed as a health spa for the ills of industrial society; i.e., the tortured negotiation of touch with the representatives of a region from which "man" is banned does not dominate popular consciousness and covertly inform positivist science. A corollary of this first point is that "woman" will not be symbolically and socially required to cross taboo lines in scientific primate studies, in order to allow the field to include certain kinds of practices and theories coded as empathic or intuitive in the West, and so suspect for scientific men. The crucial question of identification with the "object' of study will not have the same gender load. It is hard to know what effect large numbers of Japanese women might have had on Japanese primate studies, which have been more male-dominated than in the United States.[9] The *particular* scientific-gender coding characterizing Western analysis or the relations of women and science are not meaningful in the Japanese context. The second point is that the reliability of scientific knowledge does not depend on enforcing the boundary against the forbidden desire of touch with nature. The dialectic of touch and transcendence in "Teddy Bear Patriarchy" is not a Japanese story. The eros, the politics, and the epistemology of primate science are culturally and historically specific.

Instead, as Asquith (1981) argues in her interpretations of the publications of Japanese primatologists Imanishi Kinji and Kawai Masao, strong Japanese cultural sources posit a "unity" of human beings and animals.[10] But it is hardly a unity that would be comfortable to those who seek in mystifications of the "Oriental" a solution to the norms of alienation built into Western scientific and social practice; it is not a unity innocent of cruelty and power. For example, Kawai explains why children's throwing stones at and bullying animals is not considered unacceptable in Japanese culture. Relations between species are like relations between older and younger siblings or parents and children. What Westerners might consider violence might be seen as acceptable "family" behavior. Kawai argues that the Western (apparently) moral stance [illegible] body as punishment for past imperfections (Asquith 1981: 353). Buddhist approaches can easily insist on the polluting aspects of animals, women, and the body. The ease of interchange among beings can be a source of considerable danger and anxiety. Similarly, within Confucian cultural resources in their Japanese form, the idea of a continuum between animals and humans is not inconsistent with a hierarchy within the unity. What is excluded is the idea of "special creation" or Christian stewardship that has been critical in the Western history of natural history, evolutionary biology, and conservation (Asquith 1981: 352). Buddhist ideals of compassion can ground relationships to animals, women, or other suffering beings in ways similar to masculinist human stewardship in Christian cultures, and certainly Japanese relations with human and nonhuman entities do not exclude, but insist on dominance and subordination within a social and ontological unity.

Stressing the troubling or contradictory dimensions for Westerners of Japanese cultural tendencies in human–animal relations is not to claim that the Japanese are cruel to animals or to categories of humans, but is rather a caution against the cannibalistic Western logic that readily constructs other cultural possibilities as resources for Western needs and action. It is important not to make Japanese primatology "other" in that sense, so that important differences can be appreciated, rather than mystified. In addition to the relevance for primate studies of Japanese reinventions of Buddhism and Confucianism, those early importations from Japan's first "West" (i.e., China and Korea), there is also another relevant "traditional" stand in Japanese cultural reinventions: Shinto and its emphasis on matrilineality and the importance and power of mothers in social life. But it is not simply the obviously "religious" or "cultural" stories that frame the drama of Japanese monkeys' lives. The narratives of modern sciences themselves are equally "traditional" and equally "reinvented" from the point of view of the post-World War II constructions of primate studies.

Asquith emphasizes that Japanese primatology, as it was developed by Imanishi and his co-workers, was neither traditional nor especially congenial to other mid-century Japanese scientists. To make nature an *object* of study is precisely not a Japanese move, and all of Japanese modern science has been in tension with groups crudely lumped as "traditionalists." Neither was Imanishi's science, with its emphasis on identification with the animals and on a disciplined subjectivity, congenial to "Westernizers" or "modernists," who regarded Japanese cultural sources as unproductive for the development of modern science. Imanishi's Japanese scientific contemporaries initially rejected his primatology as excessively subjective or anthropomorphic (Asquith 1981: 350–51).

Asquith argues that Imanishi's approach was an original, "individualistic" synthesis of Western and Japanese strands. Such "individualistic" groups arose in several areas of natural science with the lifting of severe regulations on research (accepting Western technology but rejecting Western philosophies of nature and science) at the end of Meiji Japan in the early twentieth century. And after World War II, the Japanese forged a nationally specific organization of research and cognitive style in science. Imanishi's and Kawai's version of the synthesis has been part of the framework for a productive, collective Japanese branch of life science in primatology involving several institutions, international study sites, state support, and the training of graduate students in numbers rivaling the largest Western institutions.

What have been the special characteristics of Japanese studies of primates? First, several commentators have remarked on the early introduction of "provisionization" (Imanishi 1963: 70) of the free-ranging animals with food, thereby systematically increasing the observability of the highly mobile animals and altering the relation of observer and observed that compromises the "wild" or "natural" status of the animals from Western points of view. The "wild" status of the primates for the Japanese referred more to their running away from observers than to an essential character that would offer epistemological and symbolic guarantees. In the Japanese view, provisionization expressed an exchange or relationship that *already* existed (Asquith 1981: chap. 6).

A contemporary Western tourist in Japan is impressed by the *visibly* constructed nature which is loved and cultivated. The cultivation of domestication is not only found in the Japanese gardens, which have become such a popular commodity in Western architecture and landscaping. An ancient gnarled tree will be duly marked with a plaque as a national treasure. A famous natural scene, the changing seasons, trees in blossom: all these are deep in literary and other aesthetic practices. Nature is not just beyond the frontier, just beneath the crust of culture, the animal as opposed to the human. Nature is not presented as valuable because it is wild in Teddy Roosevelt's sense.[11] Nature is an aesthetic value and understood to require careful tending, arrangement, and rearrangement. Nature in Japan is a *work* of art. A provisionized monkey troop was seen to be in the process of domestication (Imanishi 1963: 70); that process in no way violated its natural status, which rested not on non-interference but on the particular quality of relationship.

Western observers have experimentally fed animals in the field, prominently in Carpenter's and all following work on Cayo Santiago and in Goodall's chimpanzee studies, but overwhelmingly, Westerners try to maintain – or apologize for violating – a "neutral" relation to the animals, which is believed to minimize the "interference" of the observer with the natural character of the object of knowledge that will be so important to the epistemological status of the resulting report. Deliberate experiment is one thing; "uncontrolled" interaction with the animals quite another. The repeated allegories of violation of this rule in Western primate studies are the stuff of informal culture, popular presentation, admonitory stories of polluted science, or personal idiosyncracy that should never be allowed to interfere with real science. Studies of provisionized animals do not have quite the same status for Western observers as observations of a previously undescribed species in an area far from human activity. To study monkeys on Cayo Santiago is surely valuable, and much cheaper in a period of declining funding for primate studies, but nothing like the pleasures of the Kibale forest in Uganda or Amboseli National Park in Kenya. The fully controlled laboratory and the fully "natural" field situation ground the most reliable science for Westerners. The intermediate zones have been areas of great nervousness. Pollution of a study is easy if the boundary between human and animal is incautiously crossed (Douglas 1966). [illegible] allow no greater identification than their male peers, repeatedly report having to guard against incautious admission or cultivation of their feelings, in order to be respected scientifically or to avoid being labeled "naturally" intuitive.

The second marked characteristic of Japanese primatology has been Japanese workers' renown for their individual identifications of large numbers of animals. It has not been atypical for all the Japanese associated with a macaque study site to recognize by face at a glance more than 200 individuals, most of whom are named (and numbered). Western observers also pride themselves on recognizing animals, and many Western scientists name their study animals rather than number them, but the comprehensive, detailed catalogue of the lives of *every* animal in a group is a Japanese trademark. It is instructive to compare the North American Stuart Altmann's tattooing of each rhesus monkey on Cayo Santiago in 1956 and his subsequent system of data collection with the field system of the Japanese. Both recorded detailed information on individual animals, and both pursued long-term research at stable sites. But Altmann's report was severely "objective," while Japanese writing of that period was highly "ethnographic," a kind of interpretation of primate cultures.[12] Altmann's report was at least as laden with cultural values as the Japanese accounts, and in particular I read both literatures of that period to fit comfortably with culturally specific, scientifically coded masculinist concepts and practices.[13]

The skill of recognizing the unmarked animals is associated with a strong sense of the individual animals' "personalities." Practiced Western observers are also renowned for recognition feats, for example, Iain Douglas-Hamilton with elephants and Linda Fedigan with Japanese macaques transplanted to Texas. But the story surrounding Douglas-Hamilton emphasizes the photographs of each elephant and patient memorizing of each nick in the ear or another discrete, tattoo-like natural marker, not the complex "personality" of a physiognomy (I. and O. Douglas-Hamilton 1975). The "technology" of identification is narratively emphasized despite the book's overwhelming story of the hero scientist's and his photographer wife's personal touch with a nature dangerous to ordinary people. The issue of recognition, like each of the "special" characters of Japanese primatology, also is differentiated by gender for Western observers – in a way that puts Western women and Japanese (mostly male) observers in a common symbolic location.

For example, Linda Marie Fedigan notes her "misgivings about female empathy" partly as a response to an annoying experience that warned her about the difficulty of women's being credited with their hard-won scientific accomplishments. After "having put many hours of effort into learning to identify the individual female monkeys of a large group, my ability was dismissed as being inherent in my sex, by a respected and senior male colleague" (Fedigan 1984: 308). Conversely, Irven DeVore reported disappointment that *his* naming and recognition of many animals other than the dominant males went unremarked in the partly gender-determined narrative of his responsibility for masculinist theories of male dominance supposedly based in his failure to see most individuals.[14] The point is not that Western women, Western men, and Japanese scientists have different, mysterious ways of learning the identities of particular animals; all the ways involve quite ordinary hard work and concentration. But the feats or failures of identification carry different cultural meanings according to the powerful markers of national and gender identities. From a structurally Western point of view, to be Japanese is more than a "nationality"; it is to be a representative of the "Orient." White women and the Japanese live in the "East," where Man is not alienated. The *narrative* is more revealing than the method. Similarly, the narrative that leads historians of primatology, including this one, to construct allegories of identification or alienation in discussing the neutral subject of "scientific methods" is as important as any technical protocol.

The dialectical relationship of the specific personal character of each animal with the whole social system of relationships has been the basis of a special concept (*specia*), introduced by Imanishi into the primate literature, but never taken very seriously by puzzled Western primate scientists. Asquith related the Japanese arguments that their technique or personal recognition was bound up with a different approach to evolutionary theory and the concept of adaptation. The theory of natural selection was not understood as the center of Darwinism in Western countries until well into the twentieth century, and different national understandings of Darwin and evolution have received considerable attention from historians of biology.

Evolutionary theory in Japan was worked into culturally specific patterns too. The founding Japanese primatologists had no difficulty with the fact of evolution, but their questions and resulting explanatory systems were directed to sociology and social anthropology, and not to questions of fitness and strategies of adaptation. Most Japanese primate writing stressed what Western observers were more likely to see as "proximate" explanation, i.e., the social interactions themselves, their patterns of change and specificity, while neglecting "theory" or the "ultimate" explanation of adaptive strategies and reproductive fitness maximization.

Imanishi explained the concept of *specia* to "denote the aggregation of all individuals belonging to the same species which occupies a definite area on the globe." In addition, he proposed the term *oikia* to refer to the organization of higher vertebrates into particular aggregations denoted usually by terms like family or troop, i.e., by terms stressing social organization.[15] Both terms were constructed within a "culture and personality" framework for studying primates. Japanese workers in this period used definitions of culture suggested by the Boasian culture and personality theorists, and they explicitly compared their observations to issues raised by Margaret Mead.[16] Asquith points out how difficult, or more, superfluous, the concepts of *specia* and *oikia* have seemed to Western primatologists. But Imanishi's suggestions are a window onto

Japanese constructions of nature. The social conventions of the monkeys were precisely the natural-technical object of knowledge constructed by the Japanese observers. The gap between natural and conventional is not the crucial issue; but the subtle social surface, the mask, is the essence of the *specia*. The *specia*, specific to an area of the globe, and the *oikia*, specific to a particular troop or monkey kin-organized group, are concepts grounding Japanese concern with the rootedness, i.e., with the native status, of a social entity. Nature as "wild" does not concern the Japanese in the way it does Euro- [illegible]

monkeys for ten years and beyond. This orientation persisted in their expansion of primate observations to species outside Japan. While long-term, collective sites have come to characterize Western primate studies as well, initially a person who wanted to make a mark on the field sought an "untouched" species in an "undisturbed" environment. Western stories about the origins of the long-term sites tend to de-emphasize the presence of many people and to stress the role of an individual founder. The popular stories of Jane Goodall and Dian Fossey are perhaps the most extreme version of this common narrative. The tensions among generations of Western workers between those who founded sites, and in some sense see those sites as their personal achievement in making a section of "nature" into an object of knowledge, as well as a personal spiritual resource, and later workers, described by founders as seeking only data and not really caring about the animals, surfaced in my interviews. The quality of Western scientific primatology as travel and quest literature, wherein the individual hero brings back a prize valuable for the whole community, is a covert but important dimension that seems foreign to the social and symbolic organization of Japanese primate studies. Similarly, the story of the isolated Western observer who stays too long and loses his Western rationality – or his life – in a bodily touch with nature which went too far does not seem present in Japan's narratives of natural history.[18]

The final aspect of Japanese method is a philosophic synthesis of the meaning of the practices of provisionization, individual identification, and long-term collective work. Asquith presented in English for the first time Kawai's *Nihonzaru no seitai* (*Life of Japanese Monkeys*, 1969), in which he proposes the concept of *kyokan* ("feel-one") to designate the particular method and attitude resulting from feelings of mutual relations, personal attachment, and shared life with the animals *as the foundation of reliable scientific knowledge*. *Kyokan* means "becoming fused with the monkeys' lives where, through an intuitive channel, feelings are mutually exchanged" (Asquith 1981: 343). The "sympathetic method," not to be confused with a Western romanticized organicism that excludes power and violence, is crucial to the question of "objectivity." "It is our view, however, that by positively entering the group, by making contact at some level, objectivity can be established. It is on this basis that the experimental method can be introduced into natural behaviour study and which makes scientific analysis possible.

It is probably permissible to describe the method of the Primates Research Group as 'the new subjectivity'" (Kawai, in Asquith 1981: 346).

In her interviews with over forty Japanese primatologists, Asquith found that no one but Kawai used the term *kyokan*. The other workers attributed the word to Kawai's eccentricity, and Kawai noted his uniqueness on the point. But perhaps only the word, and not the underlying positions on the subtlety of the connections of subjectivity and objectivity, is at issue. Asquith reported that Itani, professor of the Laboratory of Human Evolution, preferred to call their method "anthropomorphic," stressing their assumption that since monkeys have "minds" of some sort, some kind of empathetic method would be reasonable and likely required to understand simian societies.[19]

Females: a site of discourse on social order

Both the *kyokan* methodological attitude and the possible cultural tones from Shinto sources sounded in several of the early discoveries of the Japanese primatologists raise interesting questions for a history concerned with the relations of feminism, women, females, and life sciences. Western primatology's "early" notorious focus on males to the exclusion of females and consequent masculinist interpretations of primate life have been noted in many historical accounts of the field. Many of these historical claims are part of a reassurance that the problem is well in hand now, with both women and men properly chastened by the lesson of the bad old days. Heroes who led the way out of biased science differ in the various accounts. Feminist-inclined women tend to emphasize the entry of their conspecifics (congenerics?) into the field in the context of a political women's movement,[20] and others look to ordinary progress in the self-cleansing scientific history of ideas.[21]

The early influential presence of Western women in primatology makes the case complex. It is impossible to separate cleanly their stories from those of their male peers in the same explanatory traditions and moments of primatology. For example, Sherwood Washburn's first two students of primate social life, Irven DeVore and Phyllis Jay, both theorized about male dominance hierarchies as organizers of social cooperation, although differences that could be considered gender related were also prominent. The two principals do not have the same retrospective opinion about their own and each other's work on these issues, and my reading of their early papers adds a third and dissimilar interpretation from either of theirs. Also, current sociobiological male and female theorists emphasize female biology and behavior for excellent reasons, which are *now* seen to be built in neo-Darwinian selection theory. Why now? Is it women who matter? or feminism? or neither? or both? and matter to what?

In the 1950s the Japanese were reporting that the basic structure of Japanese macaque society was "matrilineal," i.e., organized around descent groups of hierarchically related groups of females and their offspring (Kawai 1958). The rank of a male depended more on his mother's rank than on his individual exploits, and the rank of a daughter was stably predicted from her birth order and matrilineage.[22] Upsets could occur, but it did not make sense to see troop structure as the function of dominant males, who nonetheless filled a leadership role-function. Imanishi emphasized that for a male to be accepted into the core group of an *oikia*, so as to be part of the cluster of dominant males and females with their young, he had first to be accepted by the dominant females (Imanishi 1963: 79). He speculated that a psychological process of identification with high-status males was available for the male young of a high-status female. Those males would have the proper confident attitude that would lead to acceptance and high rank later. Males without the crucial maternal history would be permanently peripheralized and possibly leave the troop. Kawamura Syunzo (1958) also reported on a female-led troop, the since famous Minoo-B group, referred to as having a "matriarchal social order." Itani reported on frequent "paternal care" of young by males, especially those of unstable rank who appeared to perform this role [illegible] The other youngsters and females got the idea from her in a pattern that flowed through the female-lineage hierarchies. Sub-adult males got the important dental-care idea last because they were most peripheralized from the core group of females and young. However, if a top central male did get a new idea, his practice would spread even more quickly through the society. But social and technical innovation emerged from the practices of youngsters and their mothers.[23] The reports were not about the question of sex in cultural innovation, but about the processes of "tradition" or "protocultural behavior" in a nonhuman species. Read retrospectively in relation to Western debates about gender and science, the description of females stands out in comparison to the early male-authored Western accounts.

That all of these events in the history of a monkey species entered popular and technical literatures in several languages itself speaks to complex interest in the question of female "power." The matrilineal troop structure data were particularly damaging for the male dominance hierarchy explanations of macaques, and these data were cited by some Western (male and female) primatologists as early as they were published in English (Losos 1985). Both Japanese and Western men were interested in reporting what females and youngsters did, and these observers were capable of relating what they saw to explanations of how primate societies worked. Japanese men, not members of a culture famous for its congeniality to women, at least in the last millennium or so, made these points in their original reports in the 1950s. What else must be said about these narratives?

First, they *are* narratives – culturally important stories with plots, heroes, obstacles, and achievements.[24] The presence of females, even powerful females, hardly makes a narrative women-centered, much less "feminist." And to be *Woman*-centered and *women*-centered are quite different things. In Japanese (and Western) primatology the bulk of discussion about female-centered organization was directed toward understanding *male* life patterns and to explaining social conservation.

However, there is a strong Japanese cultural preoccupation with mothering and with mother–son relations that has different tones from Western versions. Japanese historians stress the importance of Shinto tradition, with its female shamans and major female deities, especially the sun goddess, Amaterasu. The absence of a monotheistic, patriarchal father god challenges men's imagination about women and females. Contemporary Japanese culture is replete with fiction, films, varieties of pornography, and social commentary on the ideology of mother-determined Japanese men's lives (Buruma 1985: 1–63). In complex interplay with Japanese histories of gender domination and conflict, these stories affect how both women and men conceive the social and natural worlds. Neither the stories nor the social and natural worlds split in the same way as in the West.

In addition, Japanese women are traditionally regarded as the source of the most crucial innovation for a modern people concerned about its native roots: Japanese women, from the period of Lady Murasaki's *Tale of Gerlji* in Heian Japan, originated Japanese written literature, while the men were writing in Chinese. Japanese women, as mothers at the node of kin groups, but also as literary figures, are at the sources of Japanese historical accounts of what it means to be Japanese, to be native, to have one's own language.[25] For the Japanese, the issue, echoing in primate studies as in other cultural practices, seems to be less the origin of language, the boundary between animal and human, than the *uniqueness* of one's own language, the boundary between native and stranger, the subtle play between conservation and change. Females and women seem socially and imaginatively to be located at dense intersections of meaning for these issues in Japan. I am not arguing that there was a direct determination between these broad cultural patterns and what Kawai or Kawamura saw Japanese monkeys doing in the 1950s. But the narrative field – the story-laden quality of observation, description, and explanation general to the life sciences, and especially primatology – for any particular Japanese account was structured by different axes of meaning and possibility. The period since Japan's defeat in World War II has been a critical one for Japanese cultural reinvention of identities in extraordinarily complex patterns of "scientific" and "traditional," native and foreign, revolutionary and conservative. In that context, the primatology of a native species may be read for its stories about gender, innovation, and conservation.

For Westerners, it is not remarkable that social stability has reported to rest on female-offspring networks. Nineteenth-century doctrines of the organization of the female around the uterus required that and more. Scientific attention to females has not been lacking. Indeed, the reproductive and nurturing female body has been constructed as a core scientific object of knowledge co-extensive with the history of biology as a discourse on systems of production and reproduction.[26] Women and females appear as scientists and as objects of scientific attention in the wake of twentieth-century global women's political movements; but the kinds of stories, the kinds of narrative fields of meanings, in which those beings appear were profoundly restructured. Feminism, as well as primatology, is a story-telling practice.

The percentage of women among Japanese observers is among the lowest in the world. The 1980 membership lists of the International Primatological Society indicate that about 9 percent of the Japanese members were women. Japanese women primatologists have not had the visibility of their Western counterparts. But from very early there were women; for example, Mori Umeyo's mother was also a primate scientist, resulting in probably the first mother–daughter lineage of primate watchers.[27] Mori Umeyo was a participant in Shirley Strum's 1976 Wenner-Gren baboon conference. Senior Japanese male scientists have commented in publications on the relevance of women observers to the content and accuracy of research.

For example, Pamela Asquith quotes Kawai Masao on his frustration at not being able to remember well enough the identities of females in troops he was observing. Kawai admitted:

> We had always found it more difficult to distinguish among females as we could not see any particular differences among them. However a female researcher who joined our study could recognize individual females easily and understood [illegible]

[illegible] Would the unique "female researcher" have seen her results as the fruit of natural affinity, or would she with Fedigan have remembered hours of work, perhaps invisible to the men because most of her life was invisible? Was the barrier between Kawai and the female monkeys a lack of natural affinity or the social history of patriarchy?

Kawai went further, and Asquith, a Western woman writing a history of primatology, noted his usage in a masterpiece of understatement in a modest footnote. Like Yerkes before him, in a different culture which still somehow fostered male researchers' feelings of annoyance at female animals seen to take advantage of their sexual politics to curry undeserved favor, Kawai described an incident in which females chased off a high-ranking male, relying on the implicit support of a still higher ranking male. Kawai perceived the females as "swaggering" and "taking advantage of" their relation to the ascendant male.[29] In *Adam's Rib*, written between 1941 and 1946, and so the first feminist commentary on the history of primatology, Ruth Herschberger (1970 [1948]: 5–15) had the chimpanzee Josie comment on Yerkes's similar perceptions in the 1930s. Herschberger, prescient about the dilemma of male observers isolated from women in the field, titled her first chapter ironically, "How to Tell a Woman from a Man." Between seeing no differences among females and perceiving their actions in terms of his own solidarity with the offended male, Kawai's description of matrilineal rank structure, supposedly crucial to deposing male dominance hierarchy theory as the explanation of the organization of macaque primate society, makes this reader remember that matrilineal organization is eminently compatible with male power and masculinist standpoints in social theory. *The River Ki*, a contemporary popular Japanese fiction written by a major Japanese woman author, makes the same point (Ariyoshi 1980).

My concluding moral is simple: holism, appreciation of intuitive method, presence of "matriarchal" myth systems and histories of women's cultural innovation, cultivation of emotional and cognitive connection between humans and animal absence of dualist splits in objects of knowledge, qualitative method subtly integrated with rigorous and long-term quantification, extensive attention to the female social organization as the infrastructure grounding more visible male activities, and lack of culturally reinforced fear of loss of personal boundaries in loving scientific attention to the world are all perfectly compatible with masculinism in epistemology and male dominance in politics.

The lessons of Japanese primatology for current analyses in Western feminist philosophical and social studies of science are clear on these points. Western science suggests the same message, but perhaps it is more obvious in the context of sharp cultural difference, the sharpest, in fact – that between the mythic world historical structures called "West" and "East."

Both nineteenth- and twentieth-century Western feminist theorists have argued that the self-contained, autonomous, Western masculinist self, and the knowledge of the world he produces, is somehow truly opposed by women's putatively less rigid selves, issuing messages in another voice. The knowledge of the world imagined to come from this point of view, called women's, is variously described as more holist, less hostile to the body and to nature, promising a healing touch for alienation in industrial societies, and able to circumvent condemnation to the endless chain of substitutions for elusive true knowledge of nature, sometimes called a fully human knowledge. Psychoanalytic theory, history of science, and cognitive psychology are some of the disciplinary tools feminists have used to make these arguments.[30]

In complex sympathy with these claims, the feminist philosopher of science Sandra Harding (1986) noted that contemporary criticism of "Western" science by Afro-American theorist Vernon Dixon aligns him neatly with organicist ideologies of contemporary white women. Elizabeth Fee (1986) systematically showed how oppositional movements in science in the last twenty years have echoed each other's rhetoric and ideologies about science, while each movement claimed to ground its insights in an historically unique, sufficient, and necessary experience of domination, mediated by "dualist" science. In these arguments, there is little or no analysis of the historical and textual forms of power and violence built into "holist," "non-Western" frameworks. It has become clear to critics of anthropology how the observed and described peoples are turned into resources for the solution of other people's dilemmas (Fabian 1983). Those studied are regularly found to have just those properties that the writer's culture lacks and needs or fears and rejects. It is this structure that defines the logical move that constructs what will count as "primitive," "natural," "other."

Feminist theory has repeatedly replicated this "naturalizing" structure of discourse in its own oppositional constructions. It is at least odd that the *kyokan* method described in Japanese primatology (Kawai 1969), a description of the moment of transcendence of gender in a Western white woman's relation to cells she was observing (Keller 1983), a male activist's description of Native Americans' relation to nature before white violation (Means 1980), and an Afro-American man's discussion of organicism (Dixon 1976) – not to mention the sordid history of organicism and rejection of "dualism" in explicitly racist, fascist twentieth-century movements – make similar ideological and analytical moves (Fee 1986). That each of these constructions could be seen as eccentric or exceptional, e.g., not representative of most Japanese workers' views of their method or of women geneticists' approaches to sub-cellular structure, does not weaken their power as privileged allegory about oppositional practice.

What is the generative structure of oppositional discourse that insists on privileging "unity" at the expense of painful self-critical analyses of power and violence in one's own politics? There is at least a century-long tradition of Japanese writing about the difference of its philosophy of science compared to the procedures of Western science, which have played such a crucial role in modern Japanese history. This tradition is an important kind of oppositional literature produced within a culture that both maintained its national independence and adapted the modern sciences to its traditions and institutions, so as to challenge Western scientific hegemony very successfully in critical fields, including particle physics and micro-electronics. But Japan's complex oppositional-assimilationist approach to the sciences has not found a natural unity innocent of power and domination.

Japanese monkeys and those who watch them are inserted in the oppositional-assimilationist discourse on science, in a story-telling practice about themselves as [illegible] a dominant scientific ideology and practice, perceived as Western in the one case and as masculinist in the other. And both posit a "new subjectivity" in response to the cultural domination of "objectivity."[31] Both are discourses about a "native" or original unity. Both also have much to say about the charged symbolic and social status of mothers. Both are laced with structurally suppressed internal complexities about power. Perhaps the chief lesson of Japanese primates for feminist theories of science is that living in the "East" – no matter whether that place is found inside a cell, in the right half of the brain, in the Sacred Hills of Dakota, in mothering before or beyond patriarchy, or on Koshima Island in a matrilineal *Macaca fuscata* colony – is no solution for living in the "West."

Notes

1 Asquith (1981: 211); Itani (1954, 1975). I have followed the Japanese convention of placing the family name first and personal name second.
2 Nishida (1968, 1979); Hiraiwa-Hasegawa *et al.* (1983).
3 Kuroda (1980); Kano (1979, 1982); Kano and Mulavwa (1984); Nishida (1972).
4 S.A. Altmann interview, 1 April 1982.
5 Frisch (1959); Kitahara-Frisch resides in Japan. Altmann (1965).
6 See Traweek (1988) for cultural similarities and differences among United States, European, and Japanese high-energy physicists. She traces the threads of elite international scientific cultures, particular national variants, and gender-specific scientific practices and imaginations woven into the fabric of field theories and built into the hardware of test devices.
7 Doi (1986: 23–33, 76–86).
8 Asquith (1981, 1983, 1984, 1986a, 1986b).
9 Nakane (1982) provides one Japanese woman's account of becoming an anthropologist. I have not found a comparable account by a woman anthropologist studying primates.
10 Just as the Christian ideal of stewardship is complex, historically dynamic, and able to accommodate mutually contradictory forms of social relationship with nature, so too Japanese cultural reworkings of Buddhism, Confucianism, and Western

science are multifaceted and historically mobile. For some sense of how modern cultural reinvention works in Japanese popular culture, see Buruma (1985). However, Buruma's "Orientalist" treatment reinscribes for an American audience stereotyped Japanese exoticisms (Kondo 1984). In a structuralist analysis, Ohnuki-Tierney (1987) examines Japanese concepts of self and other by inquiring into the meanings of monkeys and the "special status" people who produce the popular monkey performances. In Japan monkeys have been mediators between deities and people, scapegoats, and clowns linked to social criticism. On "cultural reinvention" and ethnographic narratives of the self, see Clifford (1988).

11 Hern's (1971, orig. 1899) retelling of Japanese ghost stories evokes the regions outside the world of ordinary humans, a kind of naturalistic and demon-filled wilderness, but not one closely resembling the modern Western idea of wilderness (where the deer and the antelope play, etc.). From its origin, this Western wilderness is permeated with nostalgia and a sense of the impending disappearance of nature. That is, this concept of wilderness is implicit in European and Euro-American culture only after the "penetration" and "discovery" of colonized others, including the landscape with its plants and animals, were underway. However, one should not assume that Japanese constructions of nature are necessarily more compatible with conservation or broadly non-exploitative practices necessary for species and habitat survival, nationally or globally, compared to Western constructions. Both inside and outside Japan, the Japanese are enmeshed in terrible environmental problems. My point is that the different ways of loving, knowing, and otherwise constructing "nature" have different strengths or hazards for building non-exploitative conservation and survival practices.

12 Altmann (1962); Itani (1963); Imanishi (1960); Kawamura (1958).

13 Haraway (1981–82); Keller (1985).

14 DeVore (1962, 1963, 1965), interview, 18 March 1982; Smuts interview, 18 March 1982.

15 Imanishi (1963: 69); Asquith (1981, 1984).

16 Kawamura (1963); Itani (1963).

17 Japan has been a colonial power, and I do not intend to romanticize Japanese treatment of its colonial "others," for example, the Koreans. But Japan's indigenous species have not been enlisted in its cultural symbology marking insider–outsider.

18 Tournier (1972); Akeley (1923); Fossey (1983); Mowat (1987).

19 Asquith, personal communication, 28 August 1985.

20 Hrdy (1986); Hrdy and Williams (1983); Haraway (1978a, 1978b, 1983); Rowell (1984); M. Small (1984).

21 Altmann (1967); Losos (1985); Clutton-Brock (1983).

22 A U.C. Berkeley student, Donald Sade, reported this same structure among the rhesus monkeys of Cayo Santiago (Sade 1965, 1967). Sade discounted influence from the women's movement in primatology, and he was not comfortably part of the Washburn network (Losos 1985: 16–19). Losos's citation analysis showed that members of the Washburn network who continued to emphasize the male dominance hierarchy as the organizing axis of society did not often cite Sade on matrilineal rhesus social organization. Losos argued that male dominance hierarchy explanations, never hegemonic, were undermined by socioecology through the late 1960s and early 1970s independently of feminism.

23 For a film stressing that "the young revolutionize the culture" (soundtrack), see National Geographic's *Monkeys, Apes, and Man* (1971). The remark comes right after

the filmic narration of Gray and Eileen Eaton's research with a *Macaca fuscata* colony at Oregon Regional Primate Research Center. The soundtrack calls the Oregon Japanese monkeys "ambassadors from some foreign nation – the animal kingdom." The rich ambiguities implicit in the words ambassador, colony, and nation resonate with the move from human nation to animal species. The next filmic scene is the monkey's "home" – Japan. The first stop, in a snowstorm, shows the adaptation of the monkey citizens in the extreme northern part of their distribution. The viewer learns that this simian is not a tropical creature. The point silently joins the reso- [illegible] The codes of race and colonization in the drama of "civilization" in the animal kingdom could hardly be more explicit. Here, the codes override the usual placement of monkeys and apes, in which the apes are ascribed the greater social and behavioral complexity and form the link between animal and human. The film moves out of the rain forest into the open, where progress and civilization can begin, here represented in Adriaan Kortlandt's studies of chimpanzees' understanding of death and of their use of clubs to beat up a threatening stuffed leopard.

24 Landau (1981, 1984).

25 The *Kinjiki* and the *Nihongi*, the earliest written historical chronicles, from about 720 CE, were written in Chinese. They are full of accounts of important roles of women and female deities in Japan as a nation, e.g, the story of the Empress Suiko (692–628 BCE). Her title was posthumously bestowed because the writing of history was considered to be an important innovation of her reign. The close association of women with writing at the origin of Japan as a national and linguistic community contrasts markedly with the symbolic function of Eve's eating from the tree of knowledge of good and evil for the Western and Islamic peoples of the Book.

26 Haraway (1979, 1985).

27 S.A. Altmann, speech to the American Society of Primatologists, 3 June 1980.

28 Kawai (1969: 293), in Asquith (1981: 344).

29 Kawai (1965); Asquith (1981: 344n).

30 Chodorow (1978); Irigaray (1985); Gilligan (1982); Keller (1983, 1985); Merchant (1980).

31 *IPPL Newsletter* 14 (2), July 1987: 10.

Bibliography

Akeley, Carl E. 1923. *In Brightest Africa*. New York: Doubleday, Page & Co.

Akeley, Carl E. and Mary Jobe Akeley. 1922. *Lions, Gorillas, and their Neighbors*. New York: Dodd & Mead.

Altmann, Stuart A. 1962. A field study of the sociobiology of rhesus monkeys, *Macaca mulatta*. *Annals of the New York Academy of Sciences* 102(2): 338–435.

Altmann, Stuart A., ed. 1965. *Japanese Monkeys: A Collection of Translations*. Selected by Kinji Imanishi. Atlanta: Yerkes Primate Research Center.

Altmann, Stuart A., ed. 1967. *Social Communication among Primates*. Chicago: University of Chicago Press.

Ariyoshi, Sawako. 1980. *The River Ki*. Translated by Mildred Tahata. Tokyo and New York: Kodansha Ltd.

Asquith, Pamela. 1981. Some aspects of anthropomorphism in the terminology and philosophy underlying Western and Japanese studies of the social behaviour of non-human primates. Ph.D. thesis, Oxford University.

Asquith, Pamela. 1983. The Monkey Memorial Service of Japanese primatologists. *RAIN*, no. 54 (February): 3–4.

Asquith, Pamela. 1984. Bases for difference in Japanese and Western primatology. Paper delivered at the 12th Meeting of CAPA/AAPC, University of Alberta, November 15–18.

Asquith, Pamela. 1986a. Imanishi's impact in Japan. *Nature* 323: 675–76.

Asquith, Pamela. 1986b. Anthropomorphism and the Japanese and Western traditions in primatology. In J. Else and P. Lee, eds. *Primate Ontogeny, Cognition and Behavior: Developments in Field and Laboratory Research*. New York: Academic Press, pp. 61–71.

Bermant, Gordon and Donald Lindberg, eds. 1975. *Primate Utilization and Conservation*. New York: Wiley-Interscience.

Bleier, Ruth, ed. 1986. *Feminist Approaches to Science*. New York: Pergamon.

Buruma, Ian. 1985. *Behind the Mask: On Sexual Demons, Sacred Mothers, Transvestites, Gangsters, Drifters and Other Japanese Cultural Heroes*. New York: Pantheon.

Chodorow, Nancy. 1978. *The Reproduction of Mothering*. Los Angeles: University of California Press.

Clifford, James. 1988. *The Predicament of Culture*. Cambridge, Mass.: Harvard University Press.

Clutton-Brock, Timothy H. 1983. Behavioural ecology and the female. *Nature* 306: 716.

DeVore, Irven. 1962. The social behavior and organization of baboon troops. Ph.D. thesis, University of Chicago.

DeVore, Irven. 1963. Mother–infant relations in free ranging baboons. In Harriet L. Rheingold, ed., *Maternal Behavior in Mammals*. New York: John Wiley & Sons, pp. 305–35.

DeVore, Irven, ed. 1965. *Primate Behavior: Field Studies of Monkeys and Apes*. New York: Holt, Rinehart & Winston.

Dixon, Vernon. 1976. World views and research methodology. In L.M. King, V. Dixon, and W.W. Nobles, eds. *African Philosophy: Assumptions and Paradigms for Research on Black Persons*. Los Angeles: Fanon Center, Charles R. Drew, graduate school.

Doi, Iakeo. 1986. *The Anatomy of Self*. Translated by Mark Harbison. Tokyo: Kodansha International Ltd.

Douglas, Mary. 1966. *Purity and Danger: An Analysis of the Concepts of Pollution and Taboo*. London: Routledge & Kegan Paul.

Douglas-Hamilton, Iain, and Oria Douglas-Hamilton. 1975. *Life among the Elephants*. New York: Viking.

Fabian, Johannes. 1983. *Time and the Other: How Anthropology Makes Its Object*. New York: Columbia University Press.

Fedigan, Linda Marie. 1984. Sex ratios and sex differences in primatology. *American Journal of Primatology* 7: 305–8.

Fee, Elizabeth. 1986. Critiques of modern science: The relationship of feminism to other radical epistemologies. In Bleier 1986: 42–56.

Fossey, Dian. 1983. *Gorillas in the Mist*. Boston: Houghton Mifflin.

Frisch, Jean (Kitahara). 1959. Research on primate behavior in Japan. *American Anthropologist* 61: 584–96.

Gilligan, Carol. 1982. *In a Different Voice*. Cambridge, Mass.: Harvard University Press.

Hamburg, David A., and Elizabeth McCown, eds. 1979. *The Great Apes*. Menlo Park, Calif.: Benjamin/Cummings.

[illegible]

[illegible] systems. *Philosophical Forum* XIII (2–3): 244–78.

Haraway, Donna J. 1983. The contest for primate nature: Daughters of man the hunter in the field, 1960–80. In Mark Kann, ed. *The Future of American Democracy: Views from the Left*. Philadelphia: Temple University Press, pp. 175–207.

Haraway, Donna J. 1985. A manifesto for cyborgs: Science, technology, and socialist feminism in the 1980s. *Socialist Review* 15(2): 65–108.

Harding, Sandra. 1986. *The Science Question in Feminism*. Ithaca: Cornell University Press.

Hern, Lafcadio. 1971 [1899]. *In Ghostly Japan*. Rutland, Vt., and Tokyo: Charles E. Tuttle & Co.

Herschberger, Ruth. 1970 [1948]. *Adam's Rib*. New York: Harper & Row.

Hiraiwa-Hasegawa, Mariko, Hasegawa Toshisada, and Nishida Toshisada. 1983. Demographic study of a large-sized unit group of chimpanzees in the Mahale Mountains, Tanzania. Mahale Mountains Chimpanzee Research Project, Ecological Report, no. 30.

Hrdy, Sarah Blaffer. 1986. Empathy, polyandry, and the myth of the coy female. In Bleier 1986: 119–46.

Hrdy, Sarah Blaffer, and George C. Williams. 1983. Behavioral biology and the double standard. In Wasser 1983b: 3–17.

Imanishi, Kinji. 1960. Social organization of subhuman primates in their natural habitat. *Current Anthropology* 1(5–6): 390–405.

Imanishi, Kinji. 1961. The origin of the human family – a primatological approach. *Japanese Journal of Ethnology* 25: 119–30.

Imanishi, Kinji. 1963. Social behavior in Japanese monkeys, *Macaca fuscata*. In Southwick 1963: 68–81.

Irigaray, Luce. 1985. Is the subject of science sexed? *Cultural Critique* 1: 73–88.

Itani, Junichiro. 1954. Japanese monkeys at Takasakiyama. In Imanishi Kinji, ed. *Social Life of Animals in Japan* (in Japanese). Tokyo: Kobunsya.

Itani, Junichiro. 1958. On the acquisition and propagation of new food habits in the troop of Japanese monkeys at Takasakiyama. *Primates* 1: 84–98.

Itani, Junichiro. 1963. Paternal care in the wild Japanese monkey, *Macaca fuscata*. In Southwick 1963: 91–97.

Itani, Junichiro. 1975. Twenty years with the Mount Takasaki monkeys. In Bermant and Lindberg 1975: 197–249.

Kano, Takayoshi. 1979. A pilot study on the ecology of pygmy chimpanzees *Pan paniscus*. In Hamburg and McCown 1979: 123–35.

Kano, Takayoshi. 1982. The social group of pygmy chimpanzees (*Pan paniscus*) of Wamba. *Primates* 23: 171–88.

Kano, Takayoshi, and Mbangi Mulavwa. 1984. Feeding ecology of the pygmy chimpanzees (*Pan paniscus*) of Wamba. In Sussman 1984: 233–74.

Kawai, Masao. 1958. On the rank system in a natural group of Japanese monkeys, I and II. *Primates* 1 (2) 48, in Japanese with English summary.

Kawai, Masao. 1965. Newly acquired precultural behaviour of the natural troop of Japanese monkeys on Koshima Islet. *Primates* 6: 1–30.

Kawai, Masao. 1969. Nihonzam no seitai (*Life of Japanese Monkeys*). Tokyo.

Kawamura, Syunzo. 1958. Matriarchal social ranks in the Muloo-B troop: A study of the rank system of Japanese monkeys. *Primates* 1 (2): 149–56 (in Japanese).

Kawamura, Syunzo. 1963. The progress of sub-culture propagation among Japanese monkeys. In Southwick 1963: 82–90.

Keller, Evelyn Fox. 1983. *A Feeling for the Organism*. New York: Freeman.

Keller, Evelyn Fox. 1985. *Reflections on Gender and Science*. New Haven: Yale University Press.

Kondo, Dorinne. 1984. If you want to know who they are . . . *The New York Times Book Review* (September 16): 13–14.

Kuroda, Suehisa. 1980. Social behavior of the pygmy chimpanzees. *Primates* 21(2): 181–97.

Landau, Misia. 1981. The anthropogenic: Paleoanthropological writing as a genre of literature. Ph.D. thesis, Yale University.

Landau, Misia. 1984. Human evolution as narrative. *American Scientist* 72: 362–68.

Losos, Elizabeth. 1985. Monkey see, monkey do: Primatologists' conceptions of primate societies. Senior thesis, Harvard University.

Means, Russell. 1980. Fighting words on the future of the earth. *Mother Jones*, December, pp. 22–38.

Merchant, Carolyn. 1980. *The Death of Nature: Women, Ecology, and the Scientific Revolution*. New York: Harper & Row.

Mowat, Farley. 1987. *Woman in the Mists: The Story of Dian Fossey and the Mountain Gorillas of Africa*. New York: Warner Books.

Nakane, Chie. 1982. Becoming an anthropologist. In Derek Richter, ed. *Women Scientists: The Road to Liberation*. London: Macmillan, pp. 45–60.

Nishida, Toshisada. 1968. The social group of wild chimpanzees in the Mahale Mountains. *Primates* 9: 167–224.

Nishida, Toshisada. 1972. Preliminary information on the pygmy chimpanzees (Pan paniscus) of the Congo Basin. *Primates* 13: 415–25.

Nishida, Toshisada. 1979. The social structure of chimpanzees in the Mahale Mountains. In Hamburg and McCown 1979: 73–121.

Ohnuki-Tierney, Emiko. 1987. *The Monkey as Mirror: Symbolic Transformations in Japanese History and Ritual*. Princeton: Princeton: University Press.

Rowell, Thelma. 1984. Introduction. In Small 1984: 13–16.

Sade, Donald S. 1965. Some aspects of parent–offspring and sibling relations in a group of rhesus monkeys, with a discussion of grooming. *American Journal of Physical Anthropology* 23(1) 1–17.

Sade, Donald S. 1967. Determinants of dominance in a group of free-ranging rhesus monkeys. In S.A. Altmann 1967: 99–114.

Small, Meredith, ed. 1984. *Female Primates: Studies by Women Primatologists*. New York: Allan Liss.

Smith, Robert J. 1983. *Japanese Society: Tradition, Self, and the Social Order*. Cambridge: Cambridge University Press.

Southwick, Charles, ed. 1963. *Primate Social Behavior*. Princeton: Van Nostrand.

Sussman, Randall L., ed. 1984. *The Pygmy Chimpanzee: Evolutionary Biology and Behavior*

Chapter 21

Bonnie Spanier

FOUNDATIONS FOR A "NEW BIOLOGY," PROPOSED IN *MOLECULAR CELL BIOLOGY*

James Darnell, Harvey Lodish, and David Baltimore claim that a set of techniques called recombinant DNA technologies, rather than a concept, should function to unify all of experimental biology. This explicit proposal of a unifying principle for all of molecular biology has significant ramifications for all biology's subfields. In the first edition of *Molecular Cell Biology*, the authors announced the foundation of a "new biology"[1] in which three previously distinct fields were to be reorganized and subsumed under the new molecular cell biology. The 1990 edition repeats and emphasizes this point that what is "required" is "a reformulation of a body of related information formerly classified under the separate headings of genetics, biochemistry, and cell biology." This reformulation of these three disciplines does not occur around a unifying concept or theory but from a "group of techniques collectively referred to as molecular genetics." The reasons for giving molecular genetics this central role in reorganizing biology are the "powerful analytic force" of the techniques and their ability "to unify all experimental biology in language and concerns." The second reason is actually circular; by placing the techniques at the center of biology, the language and concerns of molecular genetics become the filter through which nature will be studied and conceptualized. Indeed, the authors state, "With the tools of molecular genetics, genes for all types of proteins – enzymes, structural proteins, regulatory proteins – can be purified, sequenced, changed at will, reintroduced into individual cells of all kinds (even into germ lines of organisms) and expressed there as proteins." And, in circular justification, they again assert that "[m]ost of experimental biology now relies heavily on molecular genetics."[2]

What is particularly significant about their declaration is that, while the rationale for reformulating those areas of biology appears to be the new information obtained in the past decade (particularly that about eukaryotic cells) with recombinant DNA techniques,[3] it soon becomes clear that the analytical power of recombinant DNA techniques, not the new information, is *itself* seen as sufficient reason for the proposed reorganization of biological knowledge into a new hierarchy. Circular reasoning starts with the power of this particular technique to provide certain kinds of information and ends up using the set of techniques for organizing knowledge systems at the cellular and molecular levels.[4]

In case there was any doubt about the new dominance of recombinant DNA techniques, the authors open the preface to the second edition with the following point:

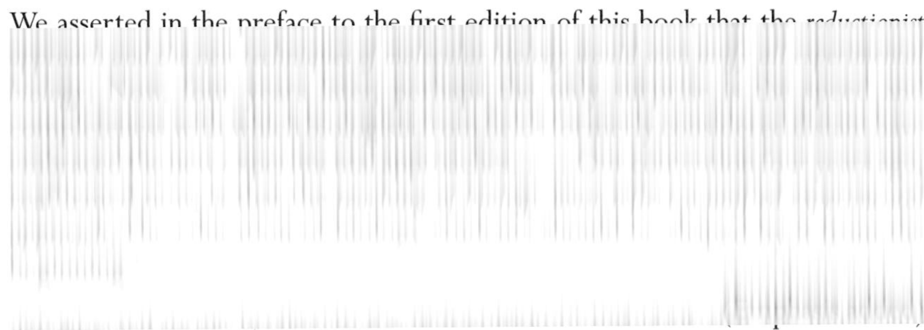

In *Molecular Cell Biology*, the authors have articulated and formalized what has been taking place within the field since the 1970s. While other textbooks may not be as explicit in calling for a reorganization of knowledge in biology, most of them proceed from the same underlying assumptions about the power and significance of recombinant DNA technology.[6]

Molecular genetics techniques are not the only ones credited with great advances in molecular biology, but they are the only ones elevated to the status of a central technology for reorganizing the study of life. The paragraph following the declaration points to "comparable advances" in culturing cells and in "sophisticated instrumentation," such as electron microscopy and computers. The chapter devoted to the "tools of molecular cell biology," molecular technology," or, in the second edition, "manipulating macromolecules"[7] makes the following statement about the importance of radioactive tracers: "Almost all experimental biology depends on the use of radioactive compounds."[8] Yet only one set of techniques is singled out as an organizing principle for the field of biology, in part due to the view that "many deep biological secrets were locked up in the sequence of the bases in DNA."

> Almost overnight, this group of techniques, often collectively called *molecular genetics*, became the dominant approach to the study of many basic biological questions, including how gene expression is regulated in eukaryotic cells and how protein or domains of proteins function. The power and success of the new technology have raised high hopes that the practical rise of our ever-increasing, biological knowledge will bring many benefits to mankind.[9]

Why is it so important to claim *one* dominant approach? Although each subfield of biology declares a central place for itself relative to the other subfields, these authors want molecular genetics to be the *sole* unifying principle for studying life. Within this framework of the preeminence and power of recombinant DNA techniques, reference to "older procedures still widely used in molecular experiments today" sounds almost patronizing.

There is little doubt that each historical epoch in the development of this science has advanced, in part, through the new opportunities brought about by major new techniques such as enzyme assays, spectroscopy, radioactive tracers, scintillation counting, and nucleic acid hybridization. Recalling the importance of specific techniques in the descriptions of various subfields,[10] what justifies singling out the techniques of recombinant DNA as the only ones worthy of the label *technology*? Such categorization clearly implies the elevated importance of those techniques over other equally necessary and effective ones. I suggest that raising recombinant DNA technology to the status of an organizing principle for a new molecular biology and then a new biology (no, *the* new biology) closes down other ways of approaching the study of life at the cellular and molecular levels. While that would not have to be the case, my analysis below suggests that a *singular* approach is being promoted at this time. Furthermore, the oddity of using a technique, rather than a concept, as an explicit unifying principle raises fundamental problems about the epistemology of this stance (is there only one way of knowing molecular biology?) and suggests hidden contradictions about the meaning of molecular biology that must be investigated.

Evelyn Fox Keller has argued provocatively that the genetic origins of molecular biology came from scientists (mainly physicists) committed to a reductionist view of life intertwined with the desire to control life by solving its mysteries ("deep biological secrets were locked up in the sequence of the bases in DNA"). Life's secret, cast as reproduction, is held by women; dominance relations in society compel Western male scientists to ferret out the last vestiges of female power. In this light, it is not surprising that the techniques of molecular genetics are the chosen organizing principle for the definition and study of "life."[11] Other views that emphasize the close relationship of science and capitalism would also place the new molecular biology into a context of social control.[12]

The pronouncement made by the authors of *Molecular Cell Biology* raises to a new level of concern several of the problems cited elsewhere in this book [*Im/Partial Science*]. These problems include presenting science as a nonpolitical and value-neutral endeavor based on objective methods as a means to accurate knowledge, with techniques in particular seen as value-neutral; privileging molecular genetics as the lens for understanding and explaining "life," with the attendant problems of biology as a rigid determinant of life's activities and behavior, along with a polarized view of nature in relation to nurture; and consequently narrowing the frame of reference for the meaning of "life."

Techniques are Seen as Value-Neutral. By defining molecular genetics as a set of techniques (that turn out to be primarily recombinant DNA technologies), rather than an explicit conceptual framework, the authors reinforce the traditional belief in scientific objectivity and the neutrality of science. Although advances in techniques have had a central impact on the development of all the fields in biology (the light microscope, for example), it seems odd that a whole field is explicitly organized around a set of techniques, rather than a concept. For example, advances in microscopy have contributed enormously to our understanding of cells and the organelles and substructures within them, but microscopy is not claimed as a unifying principle of cell biology. Instead, structure/function relationships of subcellular structures and a "cell theory" that holds that the cell is the basic structural unit of "life" are explicit principles of the field of cell biology.

What does the dominance of a technology mean with regard to hidden values and beliefs? Techniques seem to be value-neutral, but in fact they are big business in both economics and epistemology. Any technique or technology is designed to provide specific kinds of information and produces certain material consequences from its methodology. Corlann Bush proposes that tools and technologies have valences, "analogous to that of atoms that have lost or gained electrons through ionization. A particular technological system, even an individual tool, has a tendency to interact in similar situations in identifiable and predictable ways."[13]

[illegible]

By accepting this formulation without question, molecular biologists sidestep the political and social implications of the principle actually underpinning the new biology; since knowledge of "the gene" and its "expression" is knowledge of "life," and since the gene is the fundamental unit of life, then the major questions in the study of biology are to be organized around the gene. With studies of the functioning of proteins that "work together to make a living cell," conceived within a framework of proteins as "the ultimate gene products," research problems are cast primarily in terms of genes and their products. Less attention is given to the other "factors," such as the organism's environment or the organism's history, which in this view can only "affect" predetermined biological processes. Ultimately, the paradigm of molecular genetics as the basis of the study of biology forces us to view all of life, including behavior and social structures, as "gene products." When you study to be a molecular biologist, very little of your education is usually spent on the ecology and physiology of whole organisms.

Not only does recombinant DNA technology set the conceptual framework of "life," it also organizes scientific research. In the recent controversy about the Human Genome Project, Bernard D. Davis and colleagues from the Department of Microbiology and Molecular Genetics at Harvard Medical School argued that the Human Genome Project, rather than expanding the sources of funds for research, has instead cut small grants for untargeted research in the biomedical sciences. Although those small projects are considered to have the greatest potential for promising discoveries, funding has decreased dramatically in the past few years.[15] Tracing the history of the Human Genome Project, Davis asserts that the idea came from an administrator in the government who was "convinced that the powerful tools of molecular biology made it appropriate to introduce centrally administered 'big science' into biomedical research."[16] Considering the conceptual and psychological power of certain models of what is naturally "best," it may not be accidental that the power of recombinant DNA techniques seems valenced toward a hierarchical, centralized organization of scientific research.[17]

Using a set of techniques as an ostensibly value-neutral approach to the study of life masks deeply political and powerful commitments, some of which are clearly implicated in the highly charged struggles around the Human Genome Project, its scientific value, fund-raising strategies, and safety and ethical issues of recombinant DNA experiments and applications. Yet the debates about potential biohazards and applications of recombinant DNA technology (which have been at times highly acrimonious) are absent from Darnell, Lodish, and Baltimore's 1,000+ pages, making molecular biology look value-neutral and free of politics. Since overt political analysis is rarely included in science courses, this depoliticization is very effective in socializing scientists to ignore or dismiss the political content of scientific work.

As Molecular Genetics Becomes Molecular Biology, the Values and Ideology of Biological Determinism Become Entrenched, but Less Visible. The current formalizing step articulated by Darnell, Lodish, and Baltimore strongly supports my earlier argument that molecular genetics as a successful methodology has become molecular genetics as an encompassing worldview of biology. The powerful techniques of molecular genetics, now applicable to animal and plant cells, are being used *not just as techniques, but as organizing principles for all of biology*.

Much of the molecular biology represented in scientific journals supports the hegemonic influence of molecular genetics within biology. We see a prime example in a new journal, *The Plant Cell*, published by the American Society of Plant Physiologists. In the table of contents of the first issue, published in January 1989, thirteen of the fifteen research articles feature "genes" or "DNA" or "mutant" in the title. Clearly, this new journal is devoted to studying plant cells primarily through the lens of genes and genetic control.[18] That scientists treat the "new biology" as a *fait accompli* in some quarters is evident in a new textbook: *Biotechnology: The Science and the Business*, in which the first subheading under the major section, "Underlying Technologies and Economics," is: "The New Biology."[19]

With this worldview of "the new biology" come undetected ideologies embedded in molecular genetics, intertwined with gender beliefs. The focus on nuclear or chromosomal genes as the most important units of life follows from and, in turn, reinforces a reductionist and biological determinist belief that what is coded into the DNA sequence determines what is scientifically important about the cell's activities and, hence, life. Watson's reference to the human genome as the Book of Life is further clarified by his assertion that the objective of the Human Genome Project is "to find out what being human is."[20] This fundamentalist ideology embraces a rigidity in the meaning given to "biology," since the DNA sequence must be a conservative one, both for the cell to function properly (as a product of evolutionary adaptation to its environment) and for the next generation of cells and organisms to function similarly (heredity). The ideology is also hereditarian in the belief that what is fixed in our biology is inherited, passed on unchanged to subsequent generations. "Biology" is understood as fixed and unchanging, when it is actually elastic and variable. Despite such phenomena as jumping genes, mutations and other changes in base sequence, diverse modifications in chemical constituents that affect the functioning of DNA, and associations in complexes, the belief in a rigid biology applies in the realm of DNA and genes. Some of these molecular events are part of normal processes of development and aging, while others may lead to diseases such as cancers, but all are examples of changes that DNA and genes undergo during the lifetime of an organism.

The combination of reductionism, reification, and the elevation of the stripped-down gene to the top of a hierarchy of control obscures the valid perspective that mechanisms involved in heredity and control of protein synthesis are equally dependent on enzymes, other proteins, cofactors, water molecules, structural organization, and complex interactive processes among components of the cell and the surrounding environs. A reductionist fallacy first distinguishes complex processes (protein synthesis, information transfer, DNA replication, organizational assembly) from a single original cause (such as DNA sequence and gene expression) and then conflates the complex processes with the causal entity. Reification and reductionism substitute a piece of DNA for a complex process. As a consequence of the assumptions embedded in the new

Narrowing the Frame of Reference for the Meaning of "Life": Proposed Reorganization of Subfields of Biology. One could argue that every subfield has its focus and that the orientation of molecular biology, which places the gene in the center of the field, is just one of many approaches taken in the life sciences. That argument might be valid if students in biology and molecular biology were taught several subfields equally, valuing different approaches to understanding "life" at the level of macromolecules and in relation to other levels of organization of "life." But implicit in the call for a common language and a common set of concerns is a concomitant narrowing of perspectives.

Formal descriptions of different subfields of biology foreground certain characteristics and levels of organization, while setting others as secondary although necessary and supporting. For example, the field description for developmental biology in *Peterson's Guide* places genetics as a subdiscipline under development, while stressing the essential interrelationship of the two designated areas. What distinguishes Darnell, Lodish, and Baltimore's pronouncement is its explicit placement of molecular genetics over all other areas of biology to function as an organizing principle for conceptualizing biological life.

The authors make the aim of their textbook quite clear in the preface. After claiming that scientists have created a new biology in the last decade, the authors explain that the purpose of their book is not just to present this new information, but to reorganize the framework within which all of biology is to be comprehended fully.

> It was our purpose to teach a one-year course that integrates molecular biology with biochemistry, cell biology, and genetics, and that *applies this coherent insight to such fascinating problems* as development, immunology, and cancer. We hope that the availability of this material in a unified form will stimulate the teaching of molecular biology as an integral subject and that such integrated courses will be *offered to students as early as possible in their undergraduate education*. Only then will students be *truly able to grasp the findings of the new biology* and its relation to the *specialized areas* of cell biology, genetics, and biochemistry.[22]
>
> (Emphasis added)

The intention is to fit the lens of molecular genetics into the glasses of undergraduate science students at the start of their education in biology, whether teachers emphasize "the gene or the cell."[23]

The authors' goal is to be *comprehensive*, as well as to merge molecular biology with the three new *sub*disciplines ("specialized areas") of cell biology, genetics, and biochemistry. Such reorganization significantly narrows students' perspectives on the study of "life" to mean only reproduction and gene control. And among those students are not only undergraduates and graduate students in the life sciences, but also medical and dental students. Furthermore, this textbook has been used for faculty seminars on molecular biology and is certainly an important resource for science writers.[24]

The paradigm of the new molecular biology excludes other frameworks for visualizing the functioning of cells at the molecular level in relation to organismic functioning. This was brought home to me in a conversation with an audience member after a presentation on this work. Recently immersed in learning molecular biology so that she could teach science teachers the fundamentals, a teacher interested in feminist perspectives expressed her discomfort. Was I denying the truth about DNA, RNA, and protein when I challenged the Central Dogma? If so, she could not imagine an alternative view. What does it mean to have only one conceptualization of molecular and cellular life – and to be unable to place the roles of DNAs, RNAs, and proteins into a context that would allow shifts of foreground and background?[25] Those of us trained in traditional biochemistry and also in cell biology, developmental biology, ecology, and classical biology have a range of ways of conceptualizing life's activities at the level of molecules, organelles, cells, organisms, populations, and biosphere participants. How much are students training to be science teachers – or research molecular biologists – required to know about the extraordinary variety of species of life and the array of their physiological, metabolic, and developmental capabilities? As scientist-educators reorganize curricula around this new version of molecular biology, upcoming generations of students lose this diversity of perspectives.

Further, the concept of "information" promotes a reification of life processes into a universal causal code that is inadequate to account for the specificity and diversity found among molecules and organisms. While proteins are considered important in the work they do in the cell, and different kinds of RNAs play central roles in the translation of the linear sequence of nucleotides in DNA to protein structure and function, the sequence of DNA termed "the gene" holds the focus of the field of molecular biology and thus supposedly holds the answer to life's mysteries (disease, evolution, and development). And we are to reorganize all of experimental biology around that focus.

Understanding life as a consequence of the flow of energy from the sun or as the physicochemical reactions that maintain life or the complex interactions of organisms with their environments, including other organisms, has been displaced in the landscape of molecular biology and in biology in general, so that life is characterized primarily as the reproduction of genetic information, even at a time when global and local ecological issues threaten the very "life" of this planet. Recent developments in the field of molecular biology, therefore, tend to cut off alternative ways of conceptualizing life processes, reducing molecular genetics with a biological determinist ideology embedded with gender beliefs.

Molecular-biology-as-genetics is rarely questioned in *Science*, other than in debates among scientists about the significance and value of the Human Genome Project.[26] In a notable exception, on the thirtieth anniversary of the discovery of the double-helical structure of DNA, reporter Jeffrey Fox used the "rather traditional gathering of the most successful members of the molecular biology club" as an occasion to comment on the limitations of putting all our biology eggs in one molecular genetics basket. The article contrasted Watson, "still an enthusiastic lobbyist for molecular biology, particularly genetics," against Crick, who "by contrast, has left that subject behind and set his mind to studying the brain." DNA technology may not be "adequate to the [illegible] obscure the inscrutability of the information often thereby produced." Raising the specter of the contrast between true, all-seeing knowledge ("all there is to know") and insignificant manipulations, one noted scientist criticized molecular biology when he said, "Perhaps we're only 'genetics mechanics,' today."[28]

Another broadly critical perspective was expressed when Paul Doty, longtime Harvard physical biochemist, was quoted as saying: "Because experts are burdened with too much knowledge, they have done poorly at predicting the future in science."[29] The reporter offered an interpretation of this view as "a warning to those who have become too enthralled with the powerful tools now available to molecular biologists. Thus, even the best and the brightest of these scientists may be running the risk of stagnation by burdening themselves with too much of but one kind of data."[30]

The price of ideology: limited approaches to cancer research

What difference does it make to our understanding of "life" to be guided by the basic question: how do the genes control everything in the cell? And, remembering Watson's prescriptive and descriptive injunction that "[h]ardly any contemporary experiment on gene structure or function is done today without recourse to ever more powerful methods for cloning and sequencing genes,"[31] what difference does it make to have research programs based primarily on recombinant DNA technologies that involve sequencing pieces of DNA and proteins?

A striking example of the consequences of this definition of molecular biology is found in the Darnell, Lodish, and Baltimore chapter on cancer – with important changes in the second edition (1990), to which I will refer. In the first edition (1986), the chapter treats cancer as a subject of molecular genetics. However, the authors point to poorly understood areas of cancer research. Comprehension of cell-to-cell interactions, cell surface biology, the ability of tumor cells to escape the surveillance of the immune system, cellular factors that affect cell division in the whole organism, and other growth controls was "stymied by complexity." Their explicit preoccupation with what the tools of molecular genetics have revealed about cancer is justified in the following way: "Enormous progress has been made in the areas that allow for genetic analysis because of the extraordinary power that molecular genetics has developed in recent years."[32]

This is another case of a misleading conflation of a successful methodology with an explanatory stance. The methodology of molecular genetics has, indeed, provided much information about a genetic analysis of cancer. But it does not necessarily follow that a genetic analysis is "enormous progress" or that genetic research is the best approach for understanding what causes cancer or how to prevent it.

Only in the chapter summary do the authors note some limitations: "This composite picture [of how a cancer develops] is certainly simplistic – for one thing, *it does not include nongenetic influences* – but it represents *a framework for future research*, and, we hope, for the development of new methods of prevention and therapy for this dread disease" (emphasis added).[33] The considerable omission of "nongenetic influences" is quickly countered by repeating the assertion that the genetic framework offers the (implied best) hope against cancer.

Furthermore, although the authors also point to the "enormous progress . . . made toward understanding how some external agents initiate cancer," they are more concerned about "how the initiating events affect the mechanisms that regulate cell growth and why abnormal cells fail to obey the rules of normal tissue organization."[34] Messages are mixed. Some information is given about cancer as it exists as a disease, but the emphasis is clear in the rest of the chapter, which is predominantly occupied by the genetic basis of cancer as it is studied in cell culture.

The authors sound almost apologetic about including a chapter on cancer in a book on molecular biology: "In focusing on a medical problem, cancer, this chapter may seem to have departed from the subject matter of the rest of the book. Cancer represents such a fundamental problem in cellular behavior however, that many aspects of molecular biology are relevant to understanding the cancer cell."[35] That the authors justify a focus on cancer by casting it as "a fundamental problem in cellular behavior" suggests how tightly constraining are the boundaries separating molecular genetics and cell biology from the whole organism and from societal concerns at this time.

The provocative title of the last section of the chapter exacerbates the focus on genetics and cancer by asking: "Is Susceptibility to Cancer Inherited?" The answer provided: very rarely in humans. The authors' question as posed no doubt reflects widespread interest in the heritability of cancer. Yet the way the question was posed and highlighted tends to counteract the actual answer given. My question is: why aren't other equally widespread concerns included, such as occupational hazards and environmental carcinogens? Even diet and nutrition are only mentioned in passing.

Consider the difference between thinking that cancer is primarily a problem of an individual's unfortunate genetic makeup, rather than a problem influenced significantly by cancer-promoting chemicals and irradiation in our air, water, and food, produced in good measure or affected by industrial processes, and societal conditions and habits.[36] By viewing the problem of cancer through the abstract (but ideologically powerful) concern of heritability, readers are kept ignorant of the importance of factors we know contribute to cancer in various populations – and that we could change.

Several significant changes in the 1990 edition illustrate the problem of focusing on genetics in considering cancer, as well as how improvements can be made. The newer edition substitutes a section under "Human Cancer" entitled: "Rare Susceptibilities to

Cancer Point to Antioncogenes."[37] The first sentence, while convoluted, stresses the *minor* role that genetic inheritance is thought to play in human cancer: "A corollary to the belief that multiple interacting events in our environment are the major risk factors for cancer is the belief that genetic inheritance plays only a small role in carcinogenesis."[38] The evidence immediately given is that "people who migrate to a new environment take on the profile of cancers in their new environment within a generation. For instance, when Japanese citizens move to California, they rapidly [illegible]

Then too, the discourse subtly discourages pursuing possible risk factors in human cancer in other ways, by focusing on "clear-cut," "hard evidence" as the only kind that deserves attention. After acknowledging that cancer research aims at changing the course of human cancer, the authors stress the "slow and frustrating activity" of identifying "clear-cut" risk factors, especially because scientists believe that "natural cancers result from the interaction of multiple events over time."[41] With that criterion, the only "successful endeavor" is "the identification of cigarette smoking as a crucial risk factor in lung cancer. A risk factor of this potency gives a clear indication of how to act to avoid lung cancer: avoid cigarettes."[42]

The language the authors use strongly suggests that we should not waste our time being concerned about risk factors that have not yet been as conclusively proven as cigarette smoking: "Animal fat is thought to be a risk factor for colon and breast cancer, and many viruses and chemicals have been correlated with minor cancers; however, hard evidence that would help us avoid breast cancer, colon cancer, prostate cancer, leukemias, and others is generally lacking."[43]

Readers are not exhorted to take up great challenges, such as getting the "hard evidence." Nor is it clear just what "hard evidence" is, as compared to other forms of evidence. No suggestions are given about avenues to follow to address this central problem in cancer research. *Nothing* follows to suggest that, *because cancer is multicausal and multistep*, we need to actively change the monocausal thinking to which we are trained (and to which we continue to train our students) in order to be more creative – and, ultimately, more successful in our research. The authors provide little incentive to study complex interactions among different factors or economic priorities that influence our health, nothing more than a glimpse of epidemiological evidence that places the study of cancer into the context of society. Perhaps the best example of the consequences of this perspective is the refusal, until recently, of the National Institutes of Health to fund research on the effects of diet on breast cancer.[44]

Even with the second edition's changes, of the forty-two pages in the chapter on cancer, only the last two and a half focus on the "multicausal, multistep nature of carcinogenesis" and explicitly couple nongenetic influences with oncogene activity.[45] The changes made in the 1990 edition are significant (including more space on cell surfaces and other nongenetic components of the cell) and suggest increased awareness of the issues I raise, but they are not sufficient to construct a balanced view of cancer. Furthermore, the summary still ends by holding up the oncogene model as the hope for prevention and therapy against cancer.[46]

To say that "DNA alteration is at the heart of cancer induction"[47] is misleading both about the disease and what we can do to prevent or cure it, and confuses mechanism with cause. What actually causes one person to get cancer while another does not is not the *mechanism* of oncogenes but the *effects* on the oncogenes (or proto-oncogenes). A straightforward statement to that effect could suggest that, if we want to prevent cancer, we have to change many things in our world, not just produce vaccines.

Here, an opportunity is lost to *integrate* the genetic and nongenetic influences conceptually, and to prepare minds to generate "a framework for future research" that encompasses, rather than excludes, the complex interaction of such factors. Instead, the text reinforces an artificial and polarizing boundary between genetic and non-genetic, which current science actually shows to be specious. Not only does our scientific understanding of this disease suffer as a consequence, but this form of the nature/nurture fallacy privileges the promise of a gene therapy approach to curing cancer, while ignoring the data that a large majority of human cancers are influenced or promoted by environmental carcinogens in our workplaces, in air, water, and food, in such cultural habits as sunbathing and tobacco use, and in our social conditions, such as poverty and stress. Rather than thinking of cancer as a disease not only of whole human beings but of society, the future researcher is encouraged by example to ignore major economic, political, and social forces that contribute significantly to this disease.

What is lost in minimizing "nongenetic factors" is critical. Many diseases are as multicausal and multistep as cancer, and focusing on eliminating only one risk factor or causal agent is narrow and counterproductive.[48] The representation of molecular biology in textbooks and journal articles generally keeps science separate from society. Unless we challenge the current values and assumptions of molecular biology, our efforts to understand the workings of nature and the problems of disease will be partial, at best.

What must be changed is not only the paradigmatic polarization that occurs at all levels, constructing dichotomies such as genetic/nongenetic and nature/nurture, but also the sociopolitical values and assumptions that structure and define molecular biology. Having examined the effects of cultural beliefs in molecular biology, we can imagine correcting some of those biases by eliminating gender-associated language and by bringing a historical understanding of the social construction of purportedly biological categories of gender and race to scientific studies of sex and sexuality, as well as race and class. We can present the parts of the cell as equally important in "life" and in "regulation" and avoid fallacies inherent in a reductionist worldview by understanding qualitative differences among the levels of organization we consider "life." And we can teach the history and sociopolitical significance of genetics, molecular biology, molecular genetics, and related subfields as an integral part of the construction of knowledge. Reconstructing systems of knowledge is not a simple task, but it is possible to imagine a fairly easy application of the dictum that feminist awareness functions as a necessary experimental control to eliminate pervasive and often unconscious gender bias. Other issues, such as that raised about the use of equality and inequality in genetics or the definition of "life" based on the gene, require more radical reconceptualizing of whole areas of biology.

Alternatives: a beginning

An alternative understanding of genetics and the gene would balance many components [illegible] these counterexamples are brought forward to offset the predominant ideologies, they cannot serve as models for change.

Among the changes required to correct the imbalances I have delineated are explicit statements in textbook introductions, repeated throughout the books, that the molecular genetics approach is but one of several particular approaches that conceptualize "life." Scientists could point out that molecular genetics brings to the foreground the characteristics of growth and reproduction (the crystalline tradition), while other approaches (the fluid tradition) foreground maintenance of structures and functions amidst the flux of metabolism, energy, and physicochemical components – or the dynamic interactions of living beings with their environmental context.[49] Constant reminders should create more than a list of different views of life. Textbooks could interweave the differing perspectives at key points. Alternative epistemologies of "life" from other cultures could be compared to our culturally bound, Western scientific notions of "life."

Ruth Hubbard reminds us of Niels Bohr's use of "complementarity" in reconciling scientific characteristics of light as both particles and waves: "Classical physicists argued over which they really were. Bohr and the other quantum theorists asserted that they were both, and by complementarity Bohr meant that they were both at all times, not sometimes one, sometimes the other."[50] Countering a tendency to choose either one version or another, the notion of scientific complementarity will be particularly useful as a corrective to competing definitions of life. "Complementarity provides a fruitful model for integrating the different levels of organization we can use to describe living organisms. The phenomena we observe at the subatomic, atomic, molecular, cellular, organismic, or societal levels are all taking place simultaneously and constitute a single reality."[51] Both Bohr's notion of complementarity and feminist philosophy reject either/or polarities and hierarchies of differences.

Those of us concerned with refocusing molecular biology can work on such a transformation in many ways. These may include creatively exploring radical alternatives to language and concepts, developing new and more neutral language for balanced concepts, and looking for alternative language in existing scientific literature. I cite one example from a recent Nobel Prize address: Rita Levi-Montalcini received the Nobel Prize in Physiology of Medicine in 1986 (with Stanley Cohen) for her research, from the 1940s to the present, on a protein called nerve growth factor (NGF) that has many effects in a wide range of tissues. Her address describes the current understanding of nerve growth factor relative to its scientific history. In this case, the properties of the material itself – "a protein molecule from such diverse and unrelated sources as mouse sarcomas, snake venom, and mouse salivary glands [that] elicited such a potent and disrupting action of normal neurogenetic processes" – may have promoted a less reductionist and hereditarian view of the subject. In addition, it "did not fit into any conceptual preexisting schemes." Dr. Levi-Montalcini hints that she may also have resisted forcing NGF into the dominant framework derived from the study of bacterial viruses because her approach is more consonant with some traditions of animal physiology. She also suggests a view from the margin: "In spite of, or perhaps because of, its unusual and almost extravagant deeds in living organisms and in vitro systems, NGF did not at first find enthusiastic reception by the scientific community, as also indicated by the reluctance of other investigators to engage in this line of research."[52]

Levi-Montalcini's language suggests an alternative molecular biology, one that uses the latest techniques without having the results overpower and crowd out other components of interest.

[. . .]

Notes

1 James Darnell, Harvey Lodish, and David Baltimore, *Molecular Cell Biology*, 1st ed. (New York: Scientific American Books, 1986), viii; (2nd ed., xii). The context in which the authors use this key term is as follows:

> We hope that the availability of this material in a unified form will stimulate the teaching of molecular cell biology as an integral subject and that such integrated courses will be offered to students as early as possible in their undergraduate education. Only then will students be truly able to grasp the findings of the new biology and its relation to the specialized areas of biology, genetics, and biochemistry.

2 Ibid., 2nd ed., xi–xii.

3 This new information includes nonlinearity of genes, post-transcriptional processing of RNA, mobile genetic elements, and no identifiable function for "junk" DNA.

4 This is a good example of the way a technique's "valence" interacts with the context in which the technique is used and given meaning to produce a constraining framework.

5 Darnell, Lodish, and Baltimore, *Molecular Cell Biology*, 2nd ed., vii–viii. Here is an example of how a self-fulfilling prophecy contributes to an epistemology or system of knowledge.

6 I stand by that assertion, in spite of the following statement from the final pages of Watson *et al.*, *Molecular Biology of the Gene* (Menlo Park, Calif.: Benjamin/Cummings, 1987), highlighted by the subheading in bold:

Molecular Biology Is a Subdiscipline of Biology

The evolution of genes is necessarily complex because genes exist only within organisms, and organisms can interact with one another and with the environment in exceedingly subtle ways. Although molecular biology is concerned primarily with molecules, it must always be seen as a subdiscipline of biology. As the next two sections will illustrate, we simply cannot expect to understand the structure and function of genes unless we are prepared to understand the biology of the organisms in which those genes reside.

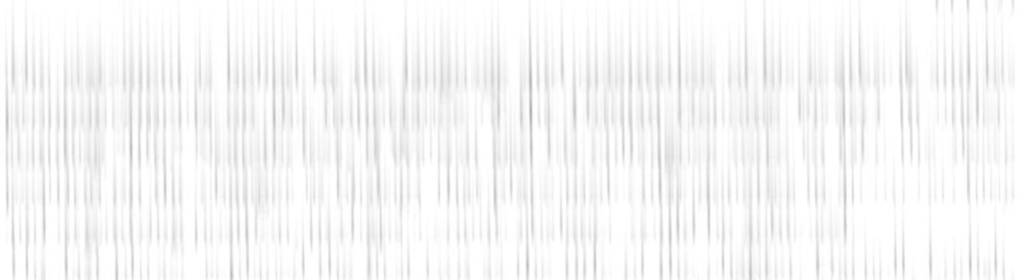

and Baltimore, *Molecular Cell Biology*, 1st ed., 221; 2nd ed., 189. Subsequent quotes from this chapter are from the newer edition, unless otherwise noted.

8 Darnell, Lodish, and Baltimore, *Molecular Cell Biology*, 190.

9 An avalanche of technical advances in the 1970s drastically changed this perspective. First, enzymes were discovered that cut the DNA from any organism at specific short nucleotide sequences, generating a reproducible set of pieces. The availability of these enzymes, called *restriction endonucleases*, greatly facilitated two important developments: DNA cloning and DNA sequencing.

Ibid., 189–190. A notable change in wording eliminated "The power and the success of the new technology *have given birth to* many hopes for . . ." (1st ed., 222).

10 See chapter 2 and Appendixes B and C.

11 Evelyn Fox Keller, "Physics and the Emergence of Molecular Biology," *Journal of History of Biology* 23 (1990): 389–409; and "From Secrets of Life to Secrets of Death," in Keller, *Secrets of Life, Secrets of Death: Essays on Language, Gender, and Science* (New York: Routledge, 1992), 39–55, esp. 51. My study provides support for extending to the present Keller's claims about the philosophical origins of molecular biology; see chapter 2.

12 For example, Hilary Rose and Steven Rose, "The Incorporation of Science," in *Ideology of/in the Natural Sciences*, ed. Hilary Rose and Steven Rose (Cambridge: Schenkman, 1979), 16–33; and Sal Restivo, "Modern Science as a Social Problem," *Social Problems* 35 (1988): 206–25.

13 For example, a gun is valenced toward violence, and television is valenced toward viewer passivity (Corlann Bush, "Women and the Assessment of Technology: to Think, to Be; to Unthink, to Free," in *Machina ex Dea: Feminist Perspectives on Technology*, ed. Joan Rothschild (New York: Pergamon, 1983), 154–55).

14 Bush specifies four types of contexts that must be taken into account in any feminist analysis of a technique or technology (which she defines as "the organized systems of interactions that utilize tools and involve techniques for the performance of tasks and the accomplishment of objectives"). These are: the design or developmental context, the user context, the environmental context, and the cultural

context of "norms, values, myths, aspirations, laws, and interactions of the society of which the tool or technique is a part" (Ibid., esp. 157–58).

15 Funding for new projects and competing renewals in NIH (Nationals Institutes of Health) study sections has been cut from 6,000 to 4,600 projects/renewals a year, while, among the total grants approved for funding by the study sections, the proportion actually funded has dropped from forty percent to twenty-five percent. Furthermore, all awarded grants had their individual budgets cut by ten to twenty percent (Bernard D. Davis *et al.*, "The Human Genome and Other Initiatives." *Science* 249 (July 27, 1990): 342–43).

16 Bernard D. Davis *et al.*, "The Human Genome." The cosigners, among them Harold Amos, Jonathan R. Beckwith, Alice S. Huang, Ruth Sager, and Priscilla Schaffer, reflect a very broad spectrum of political positions.

17 The concern expressed about continued support for new and ongoing peer-reviewed research was also used as a forum for a "deeper" concern of many scientists that stemmed

> from doubts about the scientific justification for the present status of the HGP. Many are not convinced that a crash program for analyzing the structure of genomes will advance either health or the life sciences, for many years to come as much as studies of specific physiological and biochemical functions and their abnormalities.
>
> (Bernard D. Davis *et al.*, "The Human Genome," 342)

Thus, these scientists criticized the proposed project to sequence all of the human genome for its own sake as an inefficient and skewed effort to understand human diseases and physiology.

18 Advertisement, *Science* 243 (January 20, 1989): 328. Another straightforward example of the reorganization of fields is found in another relatively new journal, *Trends in Genetics*, in which development and differentiation are places as subcategories under genetics, with guiding questions such as "What controls early development? How is sex determined? [W]hich genetic processes are involved in evolution? [W]hat defects underlie genetic diseases?" (Alfonso Martinez-Arias, "A Molecular Season for Descriptive Embryology," *Trends in Genetics* 2 (1986): 146, as quoted in Anne Fausto-Sterling, "Life in the XY Corral," *Women's Studies International Forum* 12 (1989): 319–33, esp. 319–20, 332).

19 Advertisement for Vivian Moses and Ronald E. Cape, eds., *Biotechnology, The Science and the Business* (Reading, UK: Harwood, 1991) in *Science* 251 (January 11, 1991).

20 Leslie Roberts, "Genome Project Under Way, at Last," *Science 243* (January 13, 1989): 167–68; quote, 167. James D. Watson was, until recently, the director of the Human Genome Project.

21 See Ruth Hubbard and Elijah Wald, *Exploding the Gene Myth* (Boston: Beacon, 1993), for a close analysis of some of the consequences for medical and health concerns.

22 Darnell, Lodish, and Baltimore, *Molecular Cell Biology*, 1st ed., viii; 2nd edn., xii.

23 Ibid.

24 For example, the Darnell, Lodish, and Baltimore textbook was used at the Massachusetts Institute of Technology for a faculty seminar. While science writers probably consult the current science textbooks, Natalie Angier, known increasingly for being enamored of a molecular genetics approach to biology, made specific

mention of reading this particular textbook. Natalie Angier, *Natural Obsessions: The Search for the Oncogene* (Boston: Houghton Mifflin, 1988), 173.

25 The view that, politics aside, DNA *is* a "master molecule" is not limited to science novices.

26 The predominant view in *Science*, whether reflected in the editorials, particularly those of Daniel Koshland, Jr., or the assumptions undergirding research and review articles, is that gene cloning and sequencing is the most promising and exciting approach to understanding molecular mechanisms of life. In my analysis in this and

> genuinely criticized.
>
> (Ibid., 30)

29 Ibid.

30 Ibid.

31 Watson *et al.*, *Gene*, v.

32 Darnell, Lodish, and Baltimore, *Molecular Cell Biology*, 1st ed., 1036.

33 Ibid., 1076. Note that this summary is nearly unchanged in the second edition (998).

34 Ibid., 1036.

35 Ibid., 1075.

36 That this arena is controversial should be no surprise, since so much is at stake in determining what causes cancer. Views on the risks of substances found to be mitogenic and carcinogenic in mice when given in very large doses have recently shifted away from an extremist position that everything causes cancer. Bruce Ames, for one, has changed his position on the kinds of evidence that are useful in ascertaining what promotes cancer, but the complex debate continues. Letters, *Science* 250 (December 21, 1990): 1644–46; and *Science* 251 (February 8, 1991): 606–08.

37 Oncogenes are genes involved in transforming or changing the growth characteristics of cells in tissue culture or in inducing cancer in animals. Antioncogenes are hypothetical genes presumed to be involved in countering the effects of oncogenes (Darnell, Lodish, and Baltimore, *Molecular Cell Biology*, 996).

38 Ibid.

39 Ibid.

40 Another example:

> Nongenetic mechanisms may play some role in cancer induction. For example, some chemicals, called promoters, can potentiate the activity of electrophilic carcinogens. The best-understood promoters are the phorbol esters, which cause nongenetic changes that often mimic transformation. These substances activate a cellular protein kinase. Long-term treatment with phorbol esters leads to permanent cellular alterations that may or may not be genetic. An

> apparently clear-cut case of a nongentic change that causes cancer is the epigenetic alteration leading to a teratocarcinoma. These tumor cells revert to normal when they are implanted into early embryos.
>
> (Ibid., 997)

41 Ibid., 995.

42 Ibid.

43 Ibid., 996.

44 National Women's Health Network communication, June 1993; and Ann Gibbons, "Women's Health Issues Take Center Sage at the IOM," *Science* 258 (October 30, 1992): 733.

45 Darnell, Lodish, and Baltimore, *Molecular Cell Biology*, 994–96.

46 Ibid., 998.

47 Ibid., 956.

48 Cast in leftist language, the central assertion is clear and, whether or not you agree with the political stance, quite accurately highlights the power of the framework or paradigm in shaping answers:

> But whether the cause of tuberculosis is said to be a bacillus or the capitalist exploitation of workers, whether the death rate from cancer is best reduced by studying oncogenes or by seizing control of factories – these questions can be decided objectively only within the framework of certain sociopolitical assumptions.
>
> Richard Levins and Richard Lewontin, *The Dialectical Biologist* (Cambridge: Harvard University Press, 1985), 5.

49 See chapter 2; and Scott Gilbert, "Intellectual Traditions in the Life Sciences: Molecular Biology and Biochemistry," *Perspectives in Biology and Medicine* 26 (1982): 151–52.

50 Hubbard, *Politics*, 116–17.

51 Ibid.

52 Rita Levi-Montalcini, "The Nerve Growth Factor 35 Years Later," *Science* 237 (September 4, 1987): 1154–62; quote, 1157. Dr. Levi-Montalcini is at the Institute of Cell Biology, NRC, Rome, Italy.

Chapter 22

Helen Zweifel

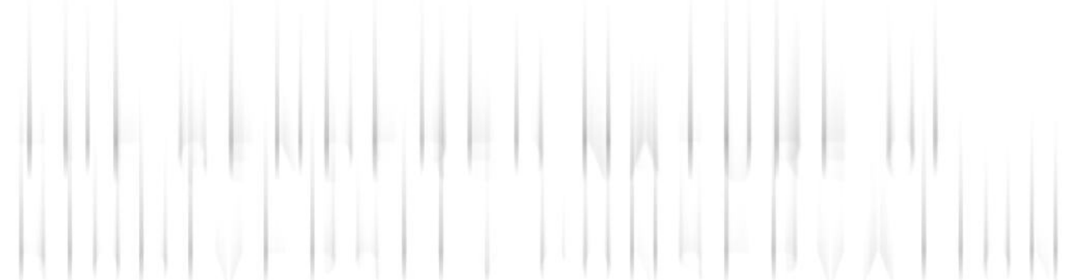

"I do not despair ever, for I guard one seed, a little life seed that I shall safeguard and plant again" (Shiva 1996, 129). This song, sung by Indian women farmers, reflects the important role of women as custodians of the seed and its significance for food security and autonomy. The central role of women in the conservation and sustainable use of natural resources has been overlooked in studies on biodiversity, most of which have been done from the perspective of natural science. In more recent debates on environmental and development issues, women have gradually become visible. The emerging importance of participatory approaches in the context of applied research and practice has led to a growing interest in "indigenous" or "local knowledge" in resource management. However, in development work and nature conservation at the practical level, gender issues, if mentioned at all, are often considered as "special issues" or "further aspects." One implication of this is that "half or more of indigenous ecological science has been obscured by the prevailing invisibility of women, their work, their interests and especially their knowledge" (Rocheleau 1991, 157). The United Nations Conference on Environment and Development in Rio de Janeiro in 1992 and the United Nations Women's Conference in Beijing in 1995 were important impulses that stimulated interest in the gendered nature of biodiversity management and conservation. The Convention on Biological Diversity, which was signed at the Rio Earth Summit in June 1992, explicitly recognizes in its preamble "the vital role that women play in the conservation and sustainable use of biological diversity" and affirms "the need for the full participation of women at all levels of policy-making and implementation for biological diversity conservation" (UNEP 1992, 2).

This article explores gendered roles, skills, and knowledge in the fields of conservation, development, and management of genetic resources in Africa, Asia, and Latin America. An actor-oriented approach will be adopted, which conceptualizes women and men as social actors who attempt to solve problems, learn how to intervene in the flow of social events around them, use their own strategies within an arena of limited opportunities, and participate in the societal process as decision makers and negotiators in resource management. After a brief survey of the discussion on women and environment in international gender studies and of the practice of development assistance, the following issues will be highlighted: gendered roles and responsibilities, and skills of local farmers in the conservation and sustainable use of biological diversity; gendered knowledge; and research on the issue of gender and biodiversity in the wider context of international politics. To sum up, this article will discuss the efforts that are required at all levels to develop and implement research and policies that empower women and at the same time contribute to the conservation and sustainable use of biodiversity.

Gender, environment, and development

Different approaches to women in the international context have emerged in social science research and in institutions concerned with foreign aid and development. In the seventies, researchers "discovered" women, and they were followed a few years later by development agencies. Women, who had been overlooked by mostly male experts, were now to be integrated into existing aid programs to make development work more efficient (Women in Development (WID). By the end of the eighties, this concept was partially replaced by the gender approach (Gender and Development (GAD)). Gender is defined as a socially constructed category and involves roles, expectations and responsibilities that are not biologically determined. In contrast to the integration approach, the gender approach highlights power relations between men and women and within society at large, and demands socioeconomic and political changes. This approach analyses the sexual division of labor in agriculture, the different relationships of men and women with the natural resource base, and the impact of male migration on women's work and responsibilities (gender analysis). Women are perceived not merely as passive recipients of aid but as agents of change (see Braidotti *et al.* 1994, 82–83). There are different viewpoints and evaluations of the relevance of the GAD approach. It has been argued that "a Gender and Development perspective leads to a fundamental re-examination of social structures and institutions, to rethinking of hierarchical gender relations and ultimately to the loss of power of entrenched elites, which will affect some women as well as men" (Rathgeber 1995, 206). Women from the South, however, have charged that both the WID and the GAD concept dilute feminist issues and that women are only added to existing structures without anyone questioning basic paradigms such as Western views of modernization or the economic growth model (Braidotti *et al.* 1994, 88). Approaches used by researchers and activists from the countries of Africa, Asia, and Latin America focus on "empowerment" or the "autonomy" of women.

The debate on gender, environment, and development is still at an early stage. Several authors recognize a clear connection between gender equity and environmental problems and the development process (Joekes *et al.* 1996; Abramovitz 1994; Agarwal 1992; Braidotti *et al.* 1994; Rocheleau 1995; Dankelmann and Davidson 1988; Douma *et al.* 1994; Harcourt 1995; Mies and Shiva 1993). The quality of the relationship between gender and environment, and the implications of this relationship for women and the diversity of life forms, still needs to be explored. The evolving perspectives on gender, development, and environment are quite heterogeneous. In theory and practice, six concepts can be identified.

1 *Women as victims of development and environmental degradation*. When women became an issue in environment and development debates, the first picture to emerge was that of women as victims of development and the environmental crisis. Typical images were groups of women walking long distances every day, carrying heavy [illegible]

[illegible] groups all over the world became actively engaged in grassroots movements defending the environment against destruction. In the Chipko movement in India and the Green Belt movement in Kenya, women emerged as fearless defenders of the environment and powerful actors in environmental protest (Harcourt 1995, 2). The other side of the coin is that women, though lacking political power, have been given a key role and responsibility for the survival of the planet. Women are called upon to save our planet, as mothers, caretakers of the family, of nature, and of the environment (Leach 1992, 14).

4 *Women in harmony with nature*. The ecofeminist perspective, particularly as represented in the work of Maria Mies and Vandana Shiva (1993), criticizes Western science and development practice and links women's subordination with the exploitation of the environment (Joekes *et al*. 1996, 30). Some Non-Governmental Organizations and development agencies perceive women's interests and environmental needs as identical to a certain degree: the need for environmental protection is portrayed as a (poor, Third World) women's preoccupation (Harcourt 1995, 2). Different strategies for environmental recovery are proposed. While some authors question the very basic parameters in the development model, others look for improvements within existing social and economic structures (Braidotti *et al*. 1994, 120).

5 *Women as managers of natural resources*. This approach recognizes the strength of women and the importance of their work in the management of natural resources such as forests, water, and soils. The amount of work women do – productive, reproductive, and environmental management work – has been recognized, along with their specific knowledge and their perspectives on resources. Women are seen as active participants, decision makers, and negotiators in the societal process of sustainable resource use (Gata 1995, 36). This approach reflects the shift in the broader development debate and the move away from large-scale development projects to smaller, more manageable projects in collaboration with local people.

6 *Focus on gender*. This approach draws on the contributions of feminist environmentalism and feminist political ecology and focuses on social relations and the link between cultural and resource use practices, reflecting the importance of the

> macrocontext. Gender is seen as a factor among others (class, caste, ethnicity, age, and locality), in determining access to resources or interest in resource management (Joekes *et al.* 1996, 6).

This paper will look at the relationship between gender and natural resources from a perspective based on the following convictions: Women and men are active participants in societal processes, they are decision makers and negotiators in issues and activities concerned with resource management. Gender relations, as well as women's and men's relations with nature and the environment, are culturally and socially constructed, and they vary from place to place and from time to time. Women's perceptions of the environment are closely related to the gendered access to and control over resources and the sexual division of labor, and much of women's environmental knowledge is associated with their agricultural and forest work and the management and use of natural resources. While women are not a homogeneous group but are divided by age, class, ethnicity, and religion, and while they have different interests, objectives, and goals, there are features common to all women across social lines that define women's access to and perspective on resources. To be able to maintain the earth's biological wealth, both principles of sustainable development – principles of ecological sustainability as well as principles of equity – have to be taken into account.

The role of women in the management of biodiversity

Biodiversity – the totality of genetic resources, varieties and ecosystems – is the very foundation of all life on earth. The food security of local communities, and of the global community, is based on biodiversity in fields and forests. Biodiversity is of great economic value for plant breeding and new industrial uses. Breeding, maintenance of yields, and resistance to pests and diseases depend upon access to a wide range of genetic material. Beyond its monetary value, the richness of biodiversity ensures the present and future stability of the food supply as well as the adaptation of natural ecosystems to changing climatic conditions. The present economic world order, the destruction of natural habitats, and the widespread introduction of uniform height-yielding varieties are major causes of genetic erosion. In fact, ever since seed became a purchased farm input, the erosion of genetic resources has accompanied the modernization of agriculture.

Approaches to counteract genetic erosion include ex situ (off-site, normally in gene banks) and in situ (on-site) conservation. One of the main messages from the Earth Summit 1992 in Rio is that in situ conservation, through application in contemporary agriculture, is needed and should be promoted. Most biodiversity conservation efforts, however, derive from a "gendered vision of segmented sustainability," as Rocheleau (1995, 9) calls it, a vision that divides home (women's place) from workplace (men's domain) from protected habitats, devoid of humans. People are excluded from parks and wilderness reserves meant to maintain biodiversity. The spatial and conceptional separation of biodiversity and production, and the alienation of both from "home," does not correspond to people's life realities, and it undermined the biological basis of rural people's livelihoods. Shiva (1993, 20) also criticizes the dominant knowledge system, the "life-destroying paradigm," as opposed to the life-enhancing paradigm, which has the maintenance of conditions for renewability as its primary management objective, and which she finds in the ecological concepts of women in the Chipko movement in the Himalayan forests.

The international scientific and development community has tended to ignore local people's knowledge systems. Ethnobotanical research, however, has uncovered a rich store of local knowledge and practices concerning the use and management of food and medicinal plants, with gender-specific use and knowledge of plants (Appleton [illegible]

thus evolve into new landraces. Even today, the innovative capacity and activities of women and men farmers are hardly recognized. Farmers' experimentation results not only from actions related to the need to adapt to a situation or to solve problems but also from curiosity. The driving force for the latter is the farmer's own quest for additional knowledge as a result of some skills that she/he has acquired or encountered, "or an idea he/she just wants to try out" (Millar 1996, 43). Farmers do not hesitate to import foreign seed if they are not satisfied with the local material.

In many parts of the world, women play a significant role in agriculture and in managing the diversity of the ecosystem, owing to the social and sexual division of labor. In many rural communities, women are responsible for the production of daily subsistence, the reproduction of the workforce, and the maintenance of the complex ecosystems and particular species that support agriculture, livestock, and forest production. However, most women are not officially part of the workforce; a large part of their productive and reproductive work does not "count" in the calculation of GNP, and they are not paid for it. Women have many roles, and often they are simultaneously farmers, herders, forest gatherers, drawers of water, food processors, market vendors, soil conservationists, and keepers of the natural environment.

Women have developed multiple strategies for their farming systems, almost all of which are based on a sophisticated management of genetic diversity (Douma *et al.* 1994, 178). To spread the risk of crop failure, women practice intercropping and diversification of crops in the field and in their home gardens. "Agricultural biodiversity" actually includes not only food but fodder, fuel, medicines, clothing, and shelter, among other things. It is also the basis for survival and improvements in the standard of living. Almost all biodiversity within reach of rural societies is used, developed, and maintained by local women. What we commonly refer to as "wild" plants (plants gathered and used as foods, fodder, medicine, or building material in the proximity of the cultivated areas) could be more properly called "partner" plants, as they form part of people's livelihoods (Pat Mooney, personal communication). These resources, which are often found on community land, need little external input and little capital, and they are of vital importance to women and the poor (Scoones *et al.* 1992, 16).

It can be argued that because of women's responsibilities for securing food, fuel, and water, women tend to have a greater interest in preserving and conserving croplands, forests, and other natural resources for perpetual use (Domoto 1994, 220). Wild fruit, leaves, roots from trees and shrubs, which grow on common property or in between the main crops – "the hidden harvest" – are an important part of the daily food intake (Scoones *et al*. 1992, 15). In times of need, they are important storerooms and sources of food supply. To a large degree, the gathering of the hidden harvest is a women's task and responsibility. In Burkina Faso, for instance, the leaves and fruits of the Sahel trees, wild roots and tubers, grasses and herbs are important in the daily diet, and they are a welcome source of cash income (Coulibaly 1992, 27–31). Women also depend on tree and forest products for fuel, fodder, medicines, fibers, and other important products vital to the survival and well-being of their families.

Women have built up significant experience in the sustainable use of natural resources and are the unacknowledged experts on the sustainable use of the biotic wealth of forests and trees. In gathering and plucking wild fruit and leaves, they usually are careful not to overuse the natural resource base, and to care for and conserve a wide spectrum of wild plants and animals through sustainable use, thereby helping to maintain the ecosystem. The sustainable use and conservation of biodiversity are embedded in societal and cultural systems. A study showed that in Burkina Faso deeply ingrained norms and taboos protect against overexploitation. Only members of the family or the clan are allowed to use the trees. The trees are protected with a sign and a taboo is put on them. The few trees that are not protected are plundered before the fruits are ripe. The leaves and flowers of the tamarind, for instance, blossom at the same time, and in plucking the leaves one has to be very careful not to destroy the flowers and with them the fruit. The study also uncovered the rich knowledge of the women, which allows them to manage, use, and protect natural resources efficiently. This knowledge is passed on informally between family members, from the older to the younger generation. Because of natural resource shortages, it is now put into practice less often and gets lost, thereby intensifying the problem of desertification. Women migrating to towns unfortunately forget what they have learned about natural resources. Only those who sell forest products on the local markets preserve their skills in the new environment. Women migrating into other rural areas also retain their knowledge and expand it with new information in the new environment (Coulibaly 1992, 45–49).

In most societies in Africa, Asia, and Latin America, the seed has traditionally been in the care of women. For centuries, women and men have developed and continue to develop a wide spectrum of different crop varieties, which were adapted to specific needs within their farming system. In Peru, "slow-motion plant breeding" often depends on the observational powers of women who historically have been most associated with seed selection and thus notice "new varieties" that spontaneously appear in the field (Prain 1993, 106). In Zimbabwe, crops with multiple uses in form and function are considered women's crops. This illustrates the invaluable knowledge and experiences women have with the different uses of plant genetic material, which guaranteed options for responding to changing environmental conditions (Gata 1995, 15). As women and farmers know well, biological diversity cannot be conserved outside their ecosystems. To be conserved and protected, diversity has to be the basis of production and economic activity.

The vital role of women in selection and plant breeding in traditional systems gave them a position of influence, power, and respect (Mehta 1996, 199). The conservation, preservation, and germination of seeds involves highly intricate knowledge, which is transmitted from mother to daughter, from sister to sister, from mother-in-law to daughter-in-law. One has to be familiar with the delicate wisdom of seed propagation to know why some seeds should be dried under bright sun and others under shade. Seed has to be protected from insect attacks and degeneration, and its germination capability has to be tested before it is sown (Mazhar 1996, 261).

[illegible]

education, training, and empowerment of women in relation to men, without giving sufficient attention to the value of women's knowledge (Rojas 1995, 13). And most programs concerned with environmental issues and plant breeding were totally gender "neutral," which in practice usually translates into a male bias. While on a mission to collect germ plasm in southern Sudan, the Norwegian scientist Trygve Berg discovered local plant-breeding activities "by accident." As he relates it: "We came to a village where, after some discussion with the people, we thought we had been granted permission to take some heads of sorghum. But on picking the sorghum, a woman came shouting furiously after us" (Berg 1993, 75). Eventually they realized that it was the woman, the mother of the family, who was responsible for the seed. Before harvesting could start, she would select the best sorghum heads. Removing seeds before she had made her selection was strictly forbidden. After this eye-opener, the scientist became aware of the long and sophisticated selection process preceding the event, the careful observation of women, and the long discussions that took place within the family about the best sorghum.

The gender division of knowledge may be based on particular places, whether by land use type or by ecozone. Men's and women's knowledge and skills may be divided by plant and animal species, products, particular uses, or particular activities. Gender-specific knowledge of particular environments, plant species, their ecology, and their uses can be invaluable for identifying species or management practices for agricultural, forestry, and pharmaceutical uses. "We have no idea what is being lost in genetic resources due to 'gender blindness.' Plant collectors will miss a lot if they only talk to men," states Susan Poats, a consultant to international agricultural organizations (IGPRI 1991, 11). A well-known example of the expertise of women is the case study of the Kpelle rice farmers in Liberia, who grow more than 100 different local varieties. A plant specialist doing research tested local knowledge of these varieties by dividing farmers into two groups. Farmers in one group described the characteristics of a particular rice variety, while those in the second group were asked to name the variety being described. The first group was able to name and describe the characteristics of virtually all fifteen varieties used in the test, including details such as husk and seed color, length of hair at the tip of the rice, size of grains, suitability for different types of soil, cooking time, and so forth. Farmers in the second group provided very few correct answers.

The difference between the two groups was that the first, characterized by far greater knowledge, was composed entirely of women (IGPRI 1991, 11).

Diversity in nature often corresponds to, and results from, a diversity of cultures. Social and cultural diversity represents different solutions to the problems of surviving in particular environments, and helps society to adapt to changing conditions. The boundaries of gendered perception and knowledge systems are neither fixed nor independent but flexible and influenced by the gender division of rights and responsibilities in national, regional, and local contexts. All over the world, the gender division of knowledge, work, and responsibilities is changing rapidly. In societies and regions where men are preferentially drawn into cash crop production, local wage labor, and the urban workforce, women are increasingly responsible for the use and maintenance of the complex rural ecosystems. Where mostly men have migrated to towns, women may take care of subsistence and commercial production, in addition to performing the community and environmental maintenance work that they formerly shared with men.

An ethnobotanical survey in the Machako Region in Kenya showed the growing importance of women's local knowledge. The local population identified forty-five indigenous or naturalized wild plant species used for food and 118 for medicine. Priorities among men and women varied; they knew many of the same places but usually used different species, or, in some cases, different products of the same species. Some of the older men were very knowledgeable about specific classes of wild plants used for specialized purposes (charcoal, brick making, fuel, carving, and medicine), while younger men could name very few. Women retained a widely shared, high level of general knowledge about wild food and medicinal plants. The decline in indigenous knowledge was attributed to formal schooling, rejection of "primitive" traditions, male out-migration, and other reasons. Moreover, with new duties and responsibilities, women had to acquire an even broader range of new (formerly male) knowledge and skills (Rocheleau 1995, 13). Compared to men's local knowledge, women's local knowledge is gaining in importance, as more women than men not only retain traditional knowledge but add to it.

Modernization of agriculture and the growing emphasis on market-based transactions are contributing to the gradual erosion of local knowledge systems. On the one hand, as in the case study above, the relevance of women's local knowledge is growing, on account of formal schooling and out-migration of men. On the other hand, with the modernization of agriculture, drought, environmental degradation, and the destruction of biodiversity, the relevance of women's knowledge and their status, especially as the keepers of the seed, are eroding. An elderly woman in northern India, selecting seeds for storage, commented on the changes: "It takes a sharp eye, a sensitive hand and a lot of patience to tell the difference between these seeds. But these are not the things that are honoured any more" (Mehta 1996, 200; see also Mazhar 1996, 261). Modern biotechnologies will reinforce existing trends, and devaluate local knowledge, replace local plant breeding and seed keeping, and marginalize farmers even further, especially women (Zweifel 1995, 13).

With the erosion of biological resources and the marginalization of the representatives of knowledge about biological resources, an invaluable treasure, contained in the libraries of local knowledge, gets lost. When the elders who knew the diverse uses of plants and animals die, important elements of the science of survival are lost forever. Even if the resources survive, women, who cannot own land, who lose access to land and rely on resources outside their own land, will be unlikely to enjoy the same facility of access to common land in future, as resources become scarcer (Oosterhout 1996, 43). Another reason for the erosion of the local science of natural resource management is that traditional plant breeding and knowledge is not given the value it deserves, either by the local opinion leaders or by women themselves. As women have to spend more time on outside activities for sheer survival, as families migrate [illegible] male farmers often resort to a double strategy: traditional local and tasty species for home consumption, high-yielding varieties for sale. This way, a traditional, increasingly "female" system of plant breeding develops side by side with the modern "male" system of plant breeding.

Intellectual property rights

As previously mentioned, the Convention on Biodiversity recognizes "the vital role" of women in the conservation and sustainable use of biological diversity. The most relevant article of the convention for local communities and women, article 8, establishes the obligations of each "Contracting Party" to "respect, preserve, and maintain knowledge, innovations and practices of indigenous and local communities embodying traditional lifestyles relevant for conservation and sustainable use of biological diversity and promote their wider application with the approval and involvement of the holders of such knowledge, innovations, and practices and encourage the equitable sharing of the benefits arising from the utilization of such knowledge, innovations and practices" (UNEP 1992, 2).

Women thus have a key role to play in the implementation of article 8 of the convention. However, the typical project often fails to recognize the role of women in the sustainable use of resources and, as a result, has been biased against women in most countries. Moreover, the growing interest of researchers and policymakers in women's indigenous knowledge does not necessarily imply real appreciation of women's knowledge, skills, and capabilities. Studies of women's indigenous knowledge may well harm women. While indigenous knowledge of the use of certain plants, animals, and environments would benefit sustainable agriculture, "it could also be used against the local people, through the prevailing official – but questionable – development strategy and approaches" (Fernandez 1994, 12).

For thousands of years, information on plant genetic resources has been collected freely all over the world. With the emergence of modern biotechnology, living resourccs and ecological knowledge have gone from being the very basis of sustenance to being "raw material" for industry. For biotechnology companies, open access to and control over a wide range of genetic resources are of strategic importance. Biologists, agronomists, social anthropologists, and other scientists in the service of the industry scour the forests, bush, fields, and markets of the South in search of genetic material and the knowledge of local people (Mooney 1993, 170). Till now, private companies of the North obtained their source material freely from the fields and forests, as it was regarded as the "common heritage of mankind." The commodification of biodiversity has caused a shift in the ownership of genetic resources from communal to private. Biodiversity knowledge and resources are alienated from the original custodians and donors and become the monopoly of private industry. The patenting of live plants, animals, and microorganisms will strengthen the control of international companies over genetic resources. A patent gives a company monopoly rights of control over individual genes, plants, animals, and processes. When biotechnology companies invest in certain species and claim intellectual property rights on isolated genes, cells, and entire living beings, biological resources become private property (Hobbelink 1991, 106).

The developments of the last decades have already deteriorated local seed systems, and thereby the autonomy and the position of women. Patents on life will accelerate these tendencies and undermine the cultural fabric of the agricultural societies of the South. The appropriation of women's indigenous knowledge and the destruction of traditional seed exchange systems may take different forms. As mentioned above, scientists tend to overlook and ignore that women are plant breeders and experts in local biodiversity, or they do not perceive women's knowledge as real knowledge and call it "primitive," "intuitive knowledge," or "unconscious ecological wisdom." However, the qualifiers "scientific" for modern systems and "unscientific" for traditional knowledge systems have less to do with knowledge and more to do with power (Shiva 1994, 137). In the international system, only breeding in the scientific laboratories of the North is appreciated as a "creative act" that will be protected by "intellectual property rights." The work and time invested by women farmers and whole communities in creating and conserving the diversity in the first place are given no value.

The Convention on Biological Diversity now recognizes the innovative contributions of women and men farmers and indigenous communities, and states that there must be fair and equal sharing of benefits arising out of the commercialization of resources. It leaves many questions open, however, and it has not been put into practice so far. The Global Plan of Action for the Conservation and Sustainable Utilization of Plant Genetic Resources for Food and Agriculture (GPA), which was adopted at the Fourth International Technical Conference of the Food and Agriculture Organization (FAO) in Leipzig in June 1996, fails to recognize the contributions of farming communities and the issue of equitable sharing of benefits (Dasgupta 1996, 20–21). A few exceptional private companies and research organizations (Merck-InBio, Shaman Pharmaceuticals, Body Shop), recognizing the value of women's and men's indigenous knowledge and using local people as informants and collectors, offered private-sector arrangements with local communities or the state to compensate for the commercial exploitation. But these agreements raise many questions about just and equal compensation for indigenous knowledge (Zerner and Kennedy 1996, 103). The Merck-InBio deal, for instance, requires Costa Rica to provide Merck, one of the largest pharmaceutical companies, with roughly 10,000 plant, animal, or microbial samples, in return for $1.135 million. This does not compare to the high returns the company expects from plant-derived ingredients on the international market (RAFI 1994, 7).

The denial of the age-old right of farmers to save seeds from one growing season for the next, and to exchange and to experiment with them, will have a negative impact on local farmers. Breeders will no longer have free access to germ plasm for developing new varieties (Crucible Group 1994, 65). The Trade-Related Intellectual Property Rights (TRIPs) agreement of GATT, which accepts only the Northern, industrialized [illegible]

The recognition, reinforcement, and improvement of women's position, knowledge, and capabilities with respect to the sustainable management of biological diversity are key factors in the success of the conservation and use of natural resources, as well as in the empowerment of women. Programs and projects undertaken from a gender perspective that assign value to the perspectives, experiences, and voices of all concerned actors are likely to have far-reaching implications in respect to equity issues and the empowerment of women, as well as to the maintenance of biological diversity. Measures have to be taken at different levels: at the international level, such as improving the participation of women in the convention process and in other international fora, and at the national and local levels, such as putting into action conservation measures and sustainable development initiatives.

In conclusion, three key points must be mentioned regarding research on gender, biodiversity, and local knowledge carried out with a view to enhancing women's autonomy and access to and control over vital resources, and to supporting sustainable development.

1 A gender perspective needs to be considered in all measures aiming at the conservation of biodiversity and sustainable development. All over the world, women and men have developed partially different, partially common and interlinking sciences of survival in complex ecosystems. This knowledge of diversity, characteristics, selection, care, and conservation is not part of the knowledge system of men. The borderline between the knowledge of women and the knowledge of men is fluid, flexible, and dependent on the sociocultural and ecological context. The importance of women's local knowledge – in comparison with men's local knowledge – is expanding: because of changing structures, more women than men have not only retained their traditional knowledge and skills but even expanded them. As knowledgeable persons and practitioners of the science of survival, women play an important role in the conservation and preservation of the biological basis of future life.
2 "Local" and "modern"' knowledge are complementary: there are many different types of perception, as well as different knowledge systems, and the recognition of these differences allows for cooperation and the conservation of biological

diversity. Recognition of and respect for the local knowledge of women and men is an important starting point, but it has to be complemented by modern Western knowledge. As the sustainable use of natural resources and the conservation and preservation of diversity are linked with future conditions, they should be assessed from as many perspectives as possible: that is, besides the perspective of men, that of women; besides the perspective of local people, that of outsiders, researchers, development agents, and administrators.

3 Particular attention needs to be given to women's participation in research, decision making and implementation processes. True recognition of women's knowledge, however, would lead to the conclusion that women must play the key role of decision makers in designing the direction of research as well as research programs. Measures to improve women's control over resources, decisions, and actions are key factors in the success of any project or program designed to help solve environmental problems, promote sustainable management, and conserve biological diversity. The participation of women is needed from the very beginning, on all levels of research and implementation, in the definition of projects and programs and in the formulation of national biodiversity strategies. Participation is understood to involve responsibility, trust, and cooperation – not just consultation to help implement outside innovation more efficiently. This means "empowerment" for women to gain more autonomy and decision-making power over their own lives and the circumstances in which they live.

Works cited

Abramovitz, Janet N. 1994. "Biodiversity and Gender Issues: Recognizing Common Ground." In Harcourt 1994. 198–212.

Agarwal, Bina. 1992. "The Gender and Environment Debate: Lessons from India." *Feminist Studies* 18 (1): 119–58.

Appleton, Helen, Maria E. Fernandez, Catherine L.M. Hill, and Consuelo Quiroz. 1995. "Claiming and Using Indigenous Knowledge." In *Missing Links: Gender Equity in Science and Technology for Development*. Ed. Gender Working Group. Ottawa: IDRC. 55–82.

Baumann, Miges, Janet Bell, Forianne Koechlin, and Michel Pimbert, eds. 1996. *The Life Industry: Biodiversity, People and Profits*. London: Intermediate Technology.

Berg, Trygve. 1993. "The Science of Plant Breeding – Support or Alternative to Traditional Practices?" In Boef *et al*. 1993. 72–77.

Boef, Walter de, Kojo Amanor, and Kate Wellard, eds. 1993. *Cultivating Knowledge: Genetic Diversity, Farmer Experimentation and Crop Research*. London: Intermediate Technology.

Braidotti, Rosi, Ewa Charkiewicz, Sabine Häusler, and Siskia Wieringa. 1994. *Women, the Environment and Sustainable Development: Towards a Theoretical Synthesis*. London: Zed.

Bunning, Sally, and Catherine Hill. 1996. "Farmers' Rights in the Conservation and Use of Plant Genetic Reources: A Gender Perspective." Paper presented at the Second Extraordinary Session of the FAO Commission on Genetic Resources for Food and Agriculture, 22–27 April.

Coulibaly, Suzanne. 1992. "Femmes, Immigration et Gestion des Ressources Naturelles au Burkina Faso." Unpublished paper.

Cromwell, Elisabeth. 1996. *Governments, Farmers and Seeds in a Changing Africa*. Oxon: CAB International.

Crucible Group. 1994. *People, Plants and Patents: The Impact of Intellectual Property on Biodiversity, Conservation, Trade, and Rural Society*. Ottawa: IDRC.

Dankelmann, Irene and Joan Davidson. 1988. *Women and Environment in the Third World. Alliance for the Future*. London: Earthscan.

Dasgupta Sumita. 1996. "The Genepool War." *Down to Earth*, June, 20–21.

Agriculture: Food Systems and Natural Resource Management with Special Reference to Zimbabwe." Paper presented at a World Bank workshop on indigenous systems and peoples in Southern Africa, 20–22 April 1994, GDE (Group for Development and Environment). Sustainable use of natural resources. Berne: Development and Environment Reports No. 14. Institute of Geography, University of Berne.

Harcourt, Wendy. ed. 1994. *Feminist Perspectives on Sustainable Development*. London: Zed.

—— 1995. "Understanding Women, Environment and Development: Key Terms and Concepts." Paper presented at the SPPE Seminar on Women-Environment-Development, Berne, 31 October.

Hobbelink, Henk. 1991. *Biotechnology and the Future of World Agriculture: The Fourth Resource*. London: Zed.

International Board for Plant Genetic Resources (IGPRI). 1991. "Women and Plant Genetic Resources." *Geneflow*, 8–16.

Joekes, Susan, Cathy Green, and Melissa Leach. 1996. "Integrating Gender into Environmental Research and Policy." IDS Working Paper 27, Institute of Development Studies, University of Sussex, Brighton.

Leach, Melissa. 1992. "Gender and the Environment: Traps and Opportunities." *Development in Practice* 2.2: 12–22.

Mazhar, Farhad. 1996. "Naysakrishi Andolan: An Initiative of the Bangladesh Peasants for Better Living." in Sperling and Loevinsohn 1996. 255–67.

Mehta, Manjari. 1996. "Our Lives Are No Different from That of Our Buffaloes: Agricultural Change and Gendered Spaces in a Central Himalayan Valley." Ed. Dianne Rocheleau, Barbara Thomas-Slayter, and Esther Wangari. In *Feminist Political Ecology: Global Issues and Local Experiences*. New York: Routledge. 180–210.

Mies, Maria, and Vandana Shiva. 1993. *Ecofeminism*. London: Zed.

Millar, David. 1996. *Footprints in the Mud: Re-constructing the Diversities in Rural People's Learning Processes*. Wageningen: Thesis Wageningen.

Mooney, Pat Roy. 1993. "Exploiting Local Knowledge: International Policy Implications." In Boef *et al*. 1993. 172–78.

Oosterhout, Saskia van. 1996. "What Does in Situ Conservation Mean in the Life of a Small-Scale Farmer? Examples from Zimbabwe's Communal Areas." In Sperling and Loevinsohn 1996. 35–52.

Opole, Monica. 1993. "Revalidating Women's Knowledge on Indigenous Vegetables: Implications for Policy." In Boef *et al.* 1993. 157–64.

Prain, Gordon. 1993. "Mobilising Local Expertise in Plant Genetic Resources Research." In Boef *et al.* 1993. 102–10.

Rathgeber, Eva M. 1995. "Gender and Development in Action." *Feminism / Postmodernism / Development*. Ed. Marianne H. Marchant and Jane L. Parpart. London: Routledge. 204–20.

Rocheleau, Dianne E. 1991. "Gender, Ecology, and the Science of Survival: Stories and Lessons from Kenya." *Agriculture and Human Values* 8: 156–65.

—— 1995. "Gender and Biodiversity: A Feminist Political Ecology Perspective." *IDS Bulletin* 26.1: 9–16.

Rojas, Martha. 1995. "Women and Biodiversity in the Context of the Convention on Biological Diversity." Paper presented to the Workshop on Women and Biodiversity in North Africa, Marrakesh, Morocco, 25–27 April.

Rural Advancement Foundation International (RAFI). 1994. "Pirating Medicinal Plants." *Occasional Papers* 1.4.

Scoones, Ian, Mary Melnyk, and Jules N. Pretty, eds. 1992. *The Hidden Harvest: Wild Foods and Agricultural Systems*. London: International Institute for Environment and Development.

Shiva, Vandana. 1993. *Monocultures of the Mind: Biodiversity, Biotechnology, and the Third World*. Penang: Third World Network.

—— 1994. "The Seed and the Earth: Biotechnology and the Colonisation of Regeneration." In *Close to Home. Women Reconnect Ecology, Health and Development*. Ed. Vandana Shiva. London: Earthscan. 128–43.

—— 1996. "The Losers' Perspective." in Baumann *et al.* 1996. 119–36.

Sperling, Luise, and Michael Loevinsohn, eds. 1996. *Using Diversity: Enhancing and Maintaining Genetic Resources On-Farm*. New Delhi: IDRC.

United Nations Environment Programme (UNEP). 1992. Convention on Biological Diversity, 5 June. Na. 92–7807.

Zerner, Charles, and Kelly Kennedy. 1996. "Equity Issues in Bioprospecting." In Baumann *et al.* 1996. 96–109.

Zweifel, Helen. 1995. "Modern Biotechnologies in Agriculture: Impact on Women in the South." *Biotechnology and Development Monitor* 23: 10–13.

Chapter 23

Curtis L. Meinert

The U.S. National Institutes of Health (NIH) Revitalization Act of 1993 requires in the case of any clinical trial involving treatment of diseases common to both genders that the trial is:

> designed and carried out in a manner sufficient to provide for a valid analysis of whether the variables being studied in the trial affect women members or minority groups, as the case may be, differently than other subjects in the trial.[1] (p. 134)

The "valid analysis" mandate came about because of the perception that the clinical research enterprise in the United States is biased in favor of male participants. The perception has come to be an accepted fact by inductive reasoning from specifics to the general. Most arguments intended to establish the perception as true focus on a 1977 guideline from the US Food and Drug Administration that discouraged the participation of women of childbearing potential in phase 1 and 2 drug trials[2] and in a few large-scale heart trials, principally, the Physicians' Health Study[3] and the Multiple Risk Factor Intervention Trial.[4]

New guidelines

The NIH Revitalization Act has given rise to guidelines from NIH for implementing the valid analysis requirements of the legislation[5] and to a new bureaucracy for review of trials in relation to phase 3 trials (NIH has interpreted the Act to pertain exclusively to phase 3 trials; phase 1 and 2 trials have been exempted from the requirements of the Act). The Act has been challenged in a petition from the Society for Clinical Trials,[6] in a directive from the membership of the Society to the director of NIH,[7] and by various writers, including myself.[8]

For a treatment to be of value for general use, it must first be shown to be of value in some limited setting. There is no point in worrying about whether a treatment works the same or differently in men and women until it has been shown to work in someone.

Every trial involves a select, nonrepresentative study population. The requirement of consent alone is sufficient to ensure that fact. Hence, the strength of a trial lies in its internal validity. A comparison of treatment within a trial is valid as long as the demographic composition of the treatment groups is the same. There is no requirement for demographic coverage or representativeness for internal validity. Generalizations from the study population to the broader universe of patients are a matter of judgment and is always open to question, even when the trial involves a demographically heterogeneous population.

A preoccupation with subgrouping leads to a quagmire of confusion and to a mosaic with ever more parts. That the United States is headed in this direction seems apparent by the increasingly strident voices from constituent groups for their place in the mosaic. Each group argues that it is different from all others and, hence, must be represented in sufficient numbers to provide a valid analysis for them.

If we want to know more about the treatments we use in regard to demographics, we have to be prepared to pay the piper. We will not generate that information by simply subdividing a pie already too small for answering questions having to do with the main effects of treatments, let alone differences by gender or ethnic origin.

The attention given to clinical trials in the halls of the US Congress would be heartening if its mandate sprung from an inherent appreciation of the strength of trials as a basic evaluation tool. It does not. It springs, instead, from parochial interests in who is studied and in the politics of votes. Alas, the mandate itself is but one more example of an unfunded mandate from Congress.

Possible consequences

The tendency of funders to gravitate to quotas to fix perceived imbalances or as a means of fending off attack from the underrepresented is short-sighted and fraught with peril. Quotas carry political risks and raise serious ethical issues, especially in the case of treatment trials. Turning away some patients in need of treatment while continuing to enroll others simply to achieve specified demographic recruitment quotas is likely to be viewed as discriminatory and unfair by ethics committees and institutional review boards. It can be argued that they have a responsibility to challenge all demographically based selections or exclusions and to accept only those that can be justified on practical or scientific grounds.

Even in the absence of objection on ethical grounds, there are reasons to steer clear of quotas on practical grounds. Recruiting to quotas to achieve a stated total sample size is invariably more costly and time consuming than recruiting to that total with a floating economy of patients.

As envisioned by Congress and implemented by NIH, the reward for trying to mount a phase 3 trial is added expenditure of time and effort merely to satisfy review requirements. The investigator-initiated, large-scale, multicentered trial is already endangered.[9] The mandate and the resulting guidelines add to its endangerment and may well serve to move researchers involved in clinical trials away from phase 3 trials to other less politically risky undertakings. If so, the mandate will help no one.

Clearly, in an ideal world, treatments for diseases affecting men and women should be tested on men and women. But what if that is not practical, for example, as in the Veterans Administration Hospital system where the population is predominantly male? Should we forego doing a trial or should we live with a less-than-ideal study population? The answer is obvious. Information is information, and some, even if imperfect, is [illegible]

[illegible]

Better practice

The way to better, more robust trials is not by legislation and recruitment quotas, but rather by making them larger and more inclusive. Indeed, if treatments that work work more or less the same across demographic boundaries, then we should be designing trials for all people having the condition or disease of interest with as few enrollment restrictions as possible. To move in that direction we need to educate those who fund and do trials to devalue demographic selectivity in favor of demographic diversity.

The experimental scientist is taught to value selectivity as a vehicle for variance control and to hold fixed all variables other than the experimental variable. Hence, the laboratory scientist is taught to select animals of the same genetic strain and sex and to house and feed them in identical fashion.

Clinical researchers, dealing with free-living beings, seek to homogenize the populations they study by selection and exclusion. They are obliged to exclude those who are not suitable for treatment as well as those who cannot be assigned to receive one or more of the study treatments. They are not obliged to exclude on the basis of demographics, except where treatment is contraindicated in specified demographic subgroups. They may legitimately choose to exclude on the basis of demographic characteristics in order to enroll a population considered suitable for finding a treatment difference, as in the case of the Multiple Risk Factor Intervention Trial.[11] They may choose, as well, to select or exclude on the basis of specified demographic characteristics if there is reason to believe that the nature of the treatment effect observed will differ by gender, age, or ethnic origin. Demographically based inclusions or exclusions should not be imposed because others have done so in the past or as an act of conservatism in the absence of scientific rationale to justify the exclusions or inclusions.

There are advantages to being a minimalist when it comes to using demographic characteristics for selection into or exclusion from clinical trials. First, the fewer the restrictions, the easier it is to recruit. Second, the more unconstrained the flow of participants into a trial, the more likely it is that those enrolled will be reflective of the general population of people eligible for treatment. Third, the demographic heterogeneity allows for subgroup analyses otherwise precluded. Such analyses in regard to demographically based subgroups are informative, even if the resulting subgroups are not large enough to provide definitive answers to treatment questions within those subgroups. It is apparent in retrospect that everyone would have been better served by a Physicians' Health Study that had enrolled women physicians, even though their number was not adequate to provide a definitive answer as to the value of aspirin as a preventative for myocardial infarction in women. We would have been better off with some information on the question than none at all.

The goal should be to create a climate aimed at encouraging researchers to move toward demographic heterogeneity in the trials they perform. The fear is that the Congress's mandate, as written and implemented, will continue the tradition of demographic selectivity and exclusivity in the absence of scientific justification. We should be moving toward unconstrained heterogeneity not controlled representativeness through demographic selection and exclusion.

References

1 National Institutes of Health Revitalization Act of 1993. U.S. Statutes at Large **107** (1993): 122–219.

2 Food and Drug Administration, *General Considerations for the Clinical Evaluation of Drugs* (publication no. HEW (FDA) 77–3040, Government Printing Office, Washington, DC, 1977); R.B. Merkatz *et al.*, *N. Engl. J. Med.* **329**, 292 (1993).

3 Steering Committee of the Physicians' Health Study Research Group, *N. Engl. J. Med.* **321**, 129 (1989).

4 Multiple Risk Factor Intervention Trial Research Group, *J. Am. Med. Assoc.* **248**, 1465 (1982).

5 National Institutes of Health Department of Health and Human Services, *NIH Guidelines on the Inclusion of Women and Minorities as Subjects in Clinical Research*; Federal Register, vol. 59, no. 59, Washington, DC, 28 March 1994.

6 Society for Clinical Trials, *Controlled Clin. Trials* **14**, 558 (1993).

7 ibid., p. 559.

8 C.L. Meinert, ibid., in press.

9 ibid. **9**, 97 (1988).

10 *NIH Inventory of Clinical Trials: Fiscal Year 1979* (Division of Research Grants, Bethesda, MD, 1980); National Institutes of Health, Institute of Medicine. Committee on the Ethical and Legal Issues Relating to the Inclusion of Women in Clinical Studies, *Women and Health Research: Ethical and Legal Issues of Including Women in Clinical Studies*, Workshop and Commission Papers (National Academy Press, Washington, DC, 1994) (2 volumes); J.T. Holbrook, C.L. Meinert, A. Kaplan Gilpin, *Controlled Clin. Trials* **15**, 129S (1994); A. Kaplan Gilpin and C.L. Meinert, ibid., p. 64S; C. Levine, A. Kaplan Gilpin, C.L. Mienert, ibid., p. 65S.

11 Multiple Risk Factor Intervention Trial Research Group, *J. Chronic Dis.* **30**, 261 (1977).

SECTION FIVE

SCIENTIFIC RESEARCH IS OFTEN CONDUCTED to identify, quantify and reinforce differences between groups of people on the basis of gender, race, class, sexual preference, and age. "Difference" research seeks some essential, biologically pre-determined reason to accept certain attributes in some individuals, for example higher testosterone and aggression in men, and to expect the opposite condition in others, which, to complete this example, means passive women. A great deal of difference research has focused on the brain, from craniologists comparing brain sizes and "predicting" intelligence, to psychological tests that "reveal" differences in the ways that men's and women's brains function. Based on this kind of research, and the biological and genetic determinism it supports, people are placed in categories, the categories are naturalized and those who are not members of the socially dominant category are marginalized.

Gender expectations of women and men of course play a large role in how we interpret what are perceived to be sex differences and even the kinds of differences we choose to seek. Frequently, the interpretations are supported only by inferences that may or may not be supported by real evidence. Inferring that males are 'right brained' because spatial abilities are linked to the right hemisphere and that females are 'left brained' because language abilities are centered in the left hemisphere becomes an empty argument. Another difficulty with difference research, as pointed out by Lynda Birke, is that part of the problem with assessing differences between people comes with establishing what constitutes an absolute difference and in ignoring the large degree of variance that exists within populations. Focusing on the central tendency erases the large degree of overlap that occurs among people, probably for all characteristics.

We use the same rationale and social expectations to generate "differences" between racial groups, how the differences become naturalized, and how the categories are not as harmless as they appear. Kaplan and Rogers discuss the political, social and moral dangers associated with biological determinism and the devaluing of human life. Anne Fausto-Sterling writes about how the identity of black women was constructed by white, male scientists during the 1800s. Using comparative anatomy, usually with very few samples, natural scientists constructed a very clear identity of African women which served to align these women more closely to lower primates and distance them from (white) European women. Comparative anatomy (science) and the categorization of non-white humans to non-human categories could be used to justify the civilizing of indigenous peoples through colonial expansion.

Not only is science used to reinforce and hierarchically arrange perceived differences between groups of people, it is also used to examine sex determination or, typically, how the male sex is determined. Bonnie Spanier raises the issue of how "reinforcements at the 'scientific' level render the sociopolitical construction of gender totally invisible" (p. 368). She also uses a very specific example from the journal *Science* to show how publication of some research and suppression of other interpretations affirm which ideologies are upheld as normal in the scientific community.

Another example of what is perceived as normal and natural differences between males and females occurs in science classrooms where girls are expected to achieve less than boys. Liz Whitelegg discusses differences in the ways that boys and girls are educated in the science classrooms, the ways that gender-specific play and role-play work to shape students' choice of science-related activities in the classroom. The science education process serves to reinforce the misconception that girls choose not to do science and, at times, have not been given an opportunity to learn science, rather than considering the socio-cultural conditions that make it difficult for girls to succeed in science classes.

Chapter 24

Lynda Birke

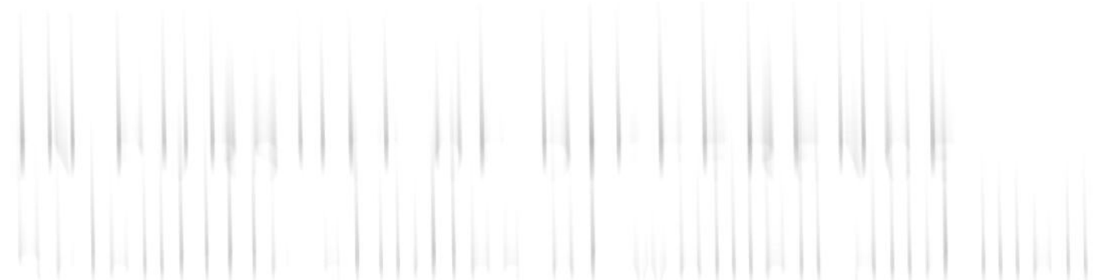

The fact that women and men are different has long fascinated people. Explanations for the origin of these differences have been plenty: evidence, on the other hand, has been in rather shorter supply. Aristotle suggested that a source of gender difference was that females were biologically defective. Their role in reproduction was merely, and passively, to give the foetus a home and some nourishment. The greater activity and importance of male seed (sperm) in reproduction were, in turn, related to the greater heat of males; women were imperfect because they lacked bodily heat (Tuana, 1989).

In the following centuries there have been many claims of difference between the bodies of women and men. For some, like Aristotle's idea of heat, there is no evidence. Yet there clearly are anatomical *differences between women and men*. My concern is not so much to list the various – and sometimes obvious – ways in which the two sexes differ, as to ask what we mean by the idea of difference in how bodies work. What is meant, for instance, when we read of sex differences in the way that human brains work? What does it mean to talk of sex differences in muscular strength? And why do we focus on sex as a source of difference rather than some other physical attribute?

This article will also address the question of how sex differences originate.[1] In part, this question can be answered in terms of human development: the chromosomes that we inherit from our parents largely determine what sex we become, for example. But human development does not cease at birth, and one theme running through this article is how we change throughout our life-spans – and, accordingly, what kinds of sex differences we see between people at different stages of their lives. In part, too, the question of where sex differences come from can be answered in terms of what causes the differences: why, for example, do men tend to have heavier arm muscles than women? There are many answers to these questions: but to begin to address them, we need to go back in our lives, to before a baby is even born.

Sex differences before birth

Immediately when a baby is born, we allocate it to one sex or the other, on the basis of what its genitals look like. We take this allocation very much for granted; so much so, that most people are horrified when mistakes are occasionally – if rarely – made, and a child is allocated to the 'wrong' sex. Culturally, we attach great importance to the existence of two, different, sexes: a child is brought up as either one or the other, and we expect that everyone we meet will be *either* male or female. But biology is not always as clear-cut as that simple dichotomy would imply.

The first step, then, in how sex differences develop is that we inherit particular sets of sex chromosomes. A person with two X chromosomes will be female: one with an X and a Y will be male. Occasionally, however, it is not so straightforward as that, and an individual is born who is neither XX nor XY.[2] Just how this happens does not concern us here. What is more important is that even the chromosomes are not as dichotomous as appears at first sight; even chromosomes cannot always indicate whether a person is 'male' or 'female'.

Indeed, women who are deemed to be too masculine in competitive sports may be subjected to 'sex tests' based on analysis of chromosomes in order to determine whether they are 'genuinely' female (tests are never done to see if men are genuinely male, however). The middle-distance Czech runner Jarmila Kratochvilova, for example, was alleged to be 'not really female' in the mid-1980s. An American doctor commented, 'This is not a normal physiological female body. I've treated Olympic female athletes in 34 countries but I've never seen a body like that' (quoted in Donahue and Johnson, 1986, 66). Despite medical misgivings, Kratochvilova passed the test. Chromosome tests were introduced in 1966 and Ewa Klobukowska, a Polish athlete, was the first to 'fail' the test; the doctors declared that she had 'one chromosome too many to be declared a woman for the purposes of athletic competition' (she had two Xs and one Y chromosome) (ibid., p. 77).

The next step in development depends upon the chromosomes. During the first few weeks of gestation it is not possible to tell the foetus's sex from its appearance. Even inside, the reproductive systems of male and female start out the same way. But, if a foetus has a Y chromosome, then these internal structures will begin to develop into testes and the tubes which carry sperm from the testes to the outside.[3] If the foetus has no Y chromosome (usually, this means it will be XX), then ovaries and uterus develop. Again, while this may hold true for most people, a few individuals are born whose internal reproductive systems are not straightforwardly 'male' or 'female' – a female born without ovaries, for example, or someone born with one ovary and one testis.

Ovaries and testes produce hormones, even at this early stage of foetal development (by this time, the foetus is still less than six weeks old). The third stage of sex development depends upon these hormones. Testes produce higher levels of certain hormones (androgens) than do ovaries; how the external genitals of the foetus develop next depends upon these levels. If the levels of androgens are high (as they would normally be if testes are present), then a penis and scrotum will develop; if they are low (for example, if the foetus has ovaries rather than a testis), then labia and a clitoris will develop.

Most people would think of the structure of the external genitals as one of the most basic differences between women and men; it is, after all, genital structure that allows us to assign newborn babies to one or other sex. Yet even here the differences are not absolute, and some individuals are born with ambiguous genitals (perhaps because they are producing higher or lower levels of particular hormones than might be expected). Babies that are chromosomally female, for example, may have a condition that makes them produce excess levels of androgens before they are born (the hormones are produced by the adrenal glands, adjacent to the kidneys). Because of the higher-than-usual levels of androgens, the baby's external genitals are relatively masculinized by the time she is born. Usually, this condition [illegible]

[illegible]

of chromosomes. (Chromosomes are usually arranged in pairs, although different species may have fewer or more pairs than we do.)

One of these pairs is called the sex chromosomes. When the body produces eggs or sperm (called gametes), each chromosome pair is split into two: thus a human gamete contains 23 single chromosomes. When sperm and egg fuse during the process of fertilization, chromosomes are once again paired up and the full 46 (or 23 pairs) are restored.

Sex chromosomes in mammals are called X and Y. Females usually have two Xs: so each egg they produce contains one X. Males usually have one X and one Y chromosome, so that each individual sperm can have either an X or a Y chromosome. This means that it is the sperm's sex chromosome (X or Y) that will determine what sex chromosomes the resulting child will have.

Because chromosomes are in pairs, the genes they contain are usually also paired. Often, the joint action of many pairs of genes influences the emergence of a particular characteristic – through interaction with the environment, of course. Skin colour, for example, is affected by the action of many genes.

Sometimes, however, a single pair of genes controls the manifestation of one particular trait. The ability to taste a particular chemical called PTC (which is bitter to those who can taste it) is one trait depending on a single pair of genes. But we inherit two copies of the gene – one from each parent: these can be the same as each other, or slightly different. So, we could either inherit two copies that are identical – two genes for tasting (call these TT) or two genes for non-tasting (call these tt) – or we could inherit one of each type of the gene (Tt). Having two identical genes means that we will be tasters (TT) or non-tasters (tt), but if we inherit one of each – Tt – then we will also be able to taste the chemical. The effect of the T gene is said to be *dominant* to the effect of the t gene, because, when the two occur together, only T affects the outcome. The t gene is said to be *recessive*. People who have both a dominant and a recessive gene for a particular trait are said to be *carriers* of that trait: that is they can pass on the recessive gene to their children but it does not have any effect in the parent who carries it.

Most genetic diseases, such as cystic fibrosis, are recessive. So, if both parents are carriers, there is a chance that a child will inherit the two recessive genes and so develop the disease. But any of their children who inherit only one recessive gene will not develop the disease. Genetic diseases based on dominant genes are rarer: Huntington's chorea is an example. If either or both parents have this gene, there is a much greater chance of the children developing the disease, since the gene for it is dominant.

The Y chromosome carries very few genes; these include a gene called the 'testis determining factor' that promotes the development of testes in the embryo. This usually means that the embryo will develop as a male; without that gene, the embryo will develop as a female. But because the Y chromosome carries so few genes, the genes on the X chromosome in a male are not usually paired; so in a boy a recessive gene on the X chromosome acts like a dominant gene. This is why only boys develop Duchenne's muscular dystrophy; the faulty recessive gene is on the X chromosome. A woman who inherits a faulty gene on the X chromosome is likely to have a normal gene on her second X chromosome; that is, she will be a carrier for the faulty gene which may then be passed on to some of her sons. Haemophilia and Lesch-Nyhan disease are two examples of genetic diseases passed on in this way.

Growing up

With the exception of the external genitals, there are rather few differences between girls and boys until they reach puberty. There are small differences in height, and there are differences in the rate at which children become mature: girls reach half their eventual adult weight at an earlier age than boys, and their adult teeth come through slightly earlier, but there is considerable overlap and similarity between girls and boys in their first decade of life.

Somewhat more pronounced differences emerge as puberty approaches, and the amounts of sex hormones produced by the child's ovaries or testes increase. The age at which different children enter puberty varies enormously; what varies much less is the sequence in which the different events occur.

Some of these differences reflect basic differences in the reproductive roles of males and females. Men, for example, develop larger testes as the testes begin to produce sperm; women begin to menstruate as their ovaries begin to produce mature eggs in preparation for pregnancy. Other differences are less directly concerned with pregnancy, but depend upon hormonal differences – the growth of breasts in women, for example. (These hormones are, of course, indirectly involved in reproduction.)

Even the hormonal differences are not absolute, however. There is no one hormone that is produced uniquely by either women or men. Men produce more of the hormones called androgens than women do, whereas women produce more of the hormones called oestrogens and progestins. These hormones are produced by both ovaries and testes; they are also produced by the adrenal glands, situated above the kidneys. It is thus not strictly accurate to refer to male and female hormones as though each belongs specifically to one sex. Strictly speaking, what is meant by 'male hormone' is that the hormone stimulates the development of male characteristics.

Unfortunately, however, the everyday use of terms such as 'male (or female) hormones' often implies that they belong specifically to one sex or the other.

Yet it is not only in reproductive anatomy and secondary sexual characteristics such as breasts or facial hair that women and men tend to differ physically. Accompanying the spurt of growth that takes place during puberty are changes in the child's skeleton, particularly the shoulders and hips. As boys grow into adolescence, the width of the shoulders increases particularly, whereas in girls it is the width of the hips [illegible] obvious that boys tend to become bigger and to have narrower hips than girls. But there are other differences that are less obvious. Women tend, for example, to have smaller hearts than men, and to have lower concentrations of haemoglobin in their blood. Haemoglobin is the chemical in our blood that carries oxygen around to wherever it is needed. Men's blood therefore tends to carry more oxygen: for every hundred millilitres of blood, the average amount of oxygen carried in a man's blood is 19.2 millilitres compared to 16.7 for a woman's.

Further differences emerge as we get older. Women's reproductive systems go through fairly dramatic changes at the menopause, as the ovaries cease to produce mature eggs. Men's reproductive system, by contrast, slows down less dramatically. One of the consequences of the menopause is that women's ovaries start to produce smaller quantities of oestrogen; some of the less pleasant problems of the menopause, such as hot flushes, are at least partly due to the decline in hormone levels.

As levels of these sex hormones decline in older people, the balance of hormones may shift. In women, for example, this can sometimes result in increased growth of bodily hair (a 'masculinizing' effect of the balance of hormones). Another consequence of declining hormone levels is a change in the way that bones are remodelled. Throughout our lives, bone is constantly being broken down and rebuilt. During early adulthood, the loss and rebuilding approximately balance each other; but, as we age, so the amount lost begins to exceed the amount built. As a result, bones can become thinner and more fragile as we approach old age (a condition called osteoporosis), and so more likely to fracture.

Women are more commonly associated with high risks of bone fracture due to osteoporosis than men, however. Partly, this is because women seem to lose bone at a faster rate after the menopause, owing to the more dramatic change in their hormone levels. Partly, too, they are collectively at higher risk because there are simply more older women than men in the population. So, towards the end of our lives, other differences emerge between women and men: women are more likely to suffer fractures because of osteoporosis, and they are likely to live longer.

What is a 'difference'?

Those, then, are some of the characteristics that someone might mention if asked what the physical differences are between men and women. But *what do we mean by difference?* I began the last section by outlining some aspects of human biology that show quite clear-cut differences (the possession of X or Y chromosomes, say, or having ovaries versus testes), and I have emphasized that even these are not absolute. But what is an absolute difference? *Are* there many ways in which women are absolutely different from men? To answer that, we have to distinguish between what characteristics *an individual has*, and those exhibited by the population. For example, there are differences between the mean heights for each sex, but there are more individuals in the middle range of height for that sex than very tall or very short individuals. But there is clearly overlap between the populations. So, to state that a difference is not absolute is to say that there is some degree of overlap between two populations, even if there is a marked difference in the mean (or average) values.

When we compare two populations, we can look at the mean (average) values of each population. If they are markedly different, then we can probably conclude that the two populations really are different. (We would say that the two populations are significantly different, statistically.) If they are very similar, then there may be little difference between the two populations. But we cannot be sure just from the mean values. Sometimes the distributions for two populations have the same mean values, but the spread of the two populations is clearly different. To assess statistically whether a difference is significant, we would need to know both the mean values for the two populations, and the amount of spread (which statisticians call *variance*).

For many of the sex differences mentioned in this article the degree of overlap between the two populations is considerable. So, although there are differences in the mean value for men and women (in the amount of fat on the body, for example), there are clearly many people who have very little – or a great deal – of body fat and are therefore far from the average. What we should remember is that not all differences between the sexes are necessarily statistically significant.

Yet these statistics tell us nothing about individuals. Individuals could fall anywhere on the curve. Thus, there are many very thin women, and many very fat men. It is important to remember that statements about 'sex differences' in some measurement are differences between populations. Yet it is all too easy to assume that the statement is saying something about 'typical' men and women; thus, the statement that 'the typical woman is less muscular than the typical man' could refer to hypothetical individuals who are 'typical' of their sex. That is, they have a roughly 'average' amount of muscle. But within the population as a whole, there are clearly individuals who deviate markedly from that average, women who are very muscular, for example, or unmuscular men.

A third problem with the notion of difference is that it seems to imply something rather fixed and unchanging, especially if the characteristic is a physical one (such as muscle width). Yet this may be true of neither populations nor individuals. Consider first a statistical description of sex differences in muscle mass (the weight of muscles); the data referred to above were obtained from a study of growth and development in British children. But this sex difference does not apply in all human societies. In some human communities, there is very little difference in the weight of men's and women's muscles: Oakley (1972) gives an example from Bali where men do not usually engage in heavy work so there is little difference between them and women. Some characteristics, moreover, may change with time: children's heights at any given age have increased over this century in the United Kingdom, while the age at which young girls experience their first menstrual period has decreased. As we have seen in the previous section, the extent and nature of sex differences vary throughout the life span. To talk about 'average sex differences' for the population usually means talking about people of very different ages.

has bigger muscles). That thigh muscles do not show the large differences we saw for arm muscles may be due to the fact that all children have to exercise their thigh muscles to about the same extent during childhood, as these muscles are particularly important in standing and walking – which all children do.

Exercise can also reduce the size of some of the sex differences in bodily function in adults. In studies which have compared highly trained athletes of each sex, differences in heart size or the capacity of the blood to carry oxygen are much less than they would be for equivalent men and women who were not athletic. So, for untrained people, the amount of oxygen that the blood can carry in women is smaller than that for men. But for trained athletes, the difference is very much less.

Another example of a way in which training can affect physiology comes from a study of the effects of carrying heavy loads. Until recently, scientists believed that doing hard work, such as carrying a load, causes a person's metabolic rate (the rate at which they burn up energy) to increase: the more work you do the faster you burn up the energy. This is true for most of us, and in one study applied to the young army recruits who were asked to carry very heavy loads in backpacks. But it did not apply to the women to whom the army men were compared. These were women from an African community who traditionally carried loads on their heads. The metabolic rate of the women in the study did not increase, even when they were asked to carry very heavy loads (Maloiy *et al.*, 1986).

One reason for this difference may be that these women were carrying heavy weights on their heads even when they were small girls; this 'training', the researchers suggest, could affect how the body uses energy. So, even something as obviously 'biological' as the rate at which we use energy can change with training.

Exercise also affects sex differences in older people. After about age 35, the rate at which bone material is lost begins to exceed the rate at which it is gained. So, during our forties and after, we are all losing bone, although in women, this seems to speed up after the menopause, leading to osteoporosis in many women. Yet osteoporosis (very brittle and fragile bones) is not inevitable. Bone loss undoubtedly exceeds gain in later life, but the amount lost depends upon how much was there in the first place. If a person has very dense bone in their early adulthood, then their bones will retain much of their strength into old age. The density of our bones, in turn, depends upon the stresses that are put upon them through exercise. Our muscles are attached to our bones. So, as a muscle contracts, it pulls upon the bone, causing it to move. Long bones such as the femur (the thigh bone) have large, powerful muscles attached to them, and the pull exerted on the bone is considerable. Frequent stresses on the bone make its cells respond by producing more hard bone. Thus, hard exercise in early adulthood helps to build up denser bone.

The sex difference, then, in the fragility of older people's bones may be partly due to the fact that women in our culture tend to take less strenuous exercise than men throughout their adult lives. (This is not true of all cultures: women in traditional African societies are no more prone to osteoporosis than men, for example.)[4] In Britain women's bones are, consequently, less dense than men's on average, even before they reach the menopause. As one researcher commented, "[Osteoporosis] has reached epidemic proportions as a consequence of increased longevity, compounded by lifestyles that have led to women's reaching their menopause with an inadequate bone mineral reserve" (Notelovitz, 1986, p. 224).

A fourth problem with focusing on sex *differences* lies in how to interpret them. For example, when researchers discovered that men tend to sweat more than women during exercise (whereas women tend to go red), they concluded that women regulate their body temperature inefficiently. Yet women seem to be no more likely to overheat than men during strenuous exercise, and their tendency to lose heat by 'glowing' may even lessen the risk of dehydration during prolonged exercise (Ferris, 1980). Another example is running speed. On the whole, men's speeds in athletic races are faster than women's, but, if the results are adjusted for body size – women are usually smaller than men – then women actually run faster than men on average (Dyer, 1982). Similarly, the fact that women tend to have more body fat has sometimes been seen as a disadvantage in relation to sport – more weight to carry, and smaller muscles, for instance. But this difference can also be interpreted another way: fat is an excellent source of stored energy and is a good insulator. So for long-distance running, such as marathons or ultra-long-distance (races of 24 hours or longer), women might have an advantage over men in having more ready access to long-term stores of energy (Dyer, 1982). The insulation provided by fat might also be an advantage in long-distance swimming. Sex differences, then, can be interpreted in different ways.

Before leaving the issue of physical differences, however, we should ask why it is that sex differences are deemed to be so important. Why, for instance, is sport organized around differences between men and women? The usual answer to this is that men have an intrinsic advantage – greater physical strength, say. But that may be an advantage in only some sports. In sports requiring stamina (such as long-distance swimming) or fine control of movements (such as fine-bore rifle shooting), gross physical strength may actually be a disadvantage. In some sports, height may be a more appropriate way to distinguish between people. In basketball and rowing, for example, there is considerable advantage to being tall; true, this will apply to more men, but there are also some very tall women.

On differences in the brain

Just as male dominance in sport is sometimes justified in terms of sex differences in physical strength, so male dominance in intellectual pursuits has been justified by explanations that men's and women's brains are different. In the late nineteenth century there were two forms of such explanations. Some scientists simply pointed to the greater weight of the average male brain: 'the skulls of a notable proportion of

has never been a female Mozart'). This led to beliefs that one writer summarized as: 'Girls' minds [were said to] excel at the common or pedestrian, whereas boys' ideas are wider ranging. Because girls are more like one another than boys [in this theory] they are, as a group, closer to the "ordinary"' (Shields, 1987, p. 191).

Evidence for both these theories is lacking. Critics have pointed, for example, to the fact that the weight of the brain depends upon the size of the whole body. If comparisons are made of brain weights adjusted for total body size, the sex difference disappears. Theories which simply assert that male brains are superior at all intellectual functions are much less evident today. They have been superseded by theories that focus on the different qualities and abilities of men's brains and women's brains.

Before going into the details of recent theories, I should emphasize that there are likely to be *some* – albeit slight – differences in how women's and men's brains work. One important reason for supposing this has to do with the fact that a tiny portion of the brain (called the hypothalamus) organizes how our hormones work – and there are some ways in which these are different in women and men. Obviously, women's sex hormones usually follow a monthly cycle associated with the pattern of menstruation. Men's sex hormones do not follow such a pattern. (This is not to say, however, that men's hormones are produced at a steady level. They, too, fluctuate – with time of day, for example, or because of stress. They also rise in anticipation of sexual activity.)

During the early development of a foetus, at about the time that the external genitals are developing into characteristically female or male form, the hormones responsible also enter the brain of the foetus. Here, they affect permanently how the hypothalamus works. As before, high levels of the hormones known as androgens will stop the hypothalamus from ever organizing hormone cycles. If there are low levels, then it will be cyclic. This difference will be present at birth (although obviously undetected until puberty). But clear evidence for other intrinsic differences in the way that women's and men's brains work is scarce.

There are various ways in which researchers could, in principle, find out if the sexes differ in the ways that their brains actually function. These include:

(a) studying the gross anatomy of the brains of people after death;
(b) investigating how particular parts or cells of the brain respond electrically or chemically, say;
(c) studies looking at people's skills in relation to what we know about how the two halves of the brain work.

Each approach has been used to provide evidence that male and female brains work differently. And each has its problems, which I will deal with in turn.

An example of (a) was a study of the nerve fibres connecting the two halves of the brain. Female brains, the researchers found, had relatively thicker fibres in this area (called the corpus callosum) than men's brains. An obvious problem, however, with focusing on gross anatomy in this way is that the person is dead: brain function during life cannot be directly assessed.[5] Gross anatomical differences, moreover, tell us nothing about the causes of those differences: we cannot tell whether they might be due to some biological factor, such as hormones, or to some difference in, say, lifestyle. So, even if we accept that men and women differ in the thickness of this part of the brain, we are far from knowing what it means.

Direct investigation of what nerve cells in the brain are doing (b) might be informative, but it is obviously something our society considers unethical in humans (although some limited assessment of this kind has been done during brain surgery in people). Scientists do, however, use non-human animals for such purposes. Studies of how brains work in animals may combine, for example, anatomical investigations (a) with electrical or chemical investigation of the animals' brains.

It is from these, and by making inferences from observations of humans who have suffered brain damage, that scientists found out that different parts of the brain specialize in particular ways. In humans, for instance, a large area of the left side of the brain specializes in speech; so, if someone's brain is damaged in this area when they are adult, their speech will be impaired in some way (in very young children, other parts of the brain may take over the job of the damaged area).

One important aspect of this specialization is that the two halves of the brain – the right and left hemispheres – have somewhat different functions. One example of such asymmetry is handedness; the right hand is controlled particularly by the left side of the brain.

If we cannot directly investigate human brain function, then we have to make inferences (c) based on observations of people's skills. Doctors faced with a person who loses the ability to speak after a road accident, for example, would have to infer that the person's brain was damaged, probably on the left side. But inference can be a problem if it is stretched too far. In relation to sex differences, the inference is made in the following way: if scientists believe that a particular skill is associated with the left side of the brain, say, then they might infer that someone who is very good at that skill, but less good at something associated with the right side, had a dominant right hemisphere.

The starting point for inferences about men's and women's brains is that there seem to be sex differences in certain cognitive (or thinking) skills. Because some of these skills are believed to be associated with one side or other of the brain, some researchers have argued that men and women differ in the degree of symmetry of their brains (that is, whether one side 'dominates' the other).

There have long been claims that women and men think differently – and perhaps they do. But the claims about brain symmetry are based largely on the results of a set of psychological tests. Some of these were designed by psychologists to test for verbal abilities (tests might include, for example, questions asking you to supply a missing word in a sequence). Females, psychology textbooks tell us, do better on these tests than males. Other tests are designed to assess spatial ability, such as the ability to imagine how a flat shape on a page would look if folded in three dimensions. Here the sex difference [illegible]

It is also easy to go beyond the available evidence. There may be enough weight of evidence to make inferences about brains in relation to handedness, say. But when it comes to sex differences, the scales are heavily loaded; the mass of inferences and assumptions far outweighs that of clear evidence.

One important strand of criticism concerns the psychological skills themselves, and how they are tested. Of all the tests designed to measure spatial ability, only a few show a difference between males and females. Tests may measure only a very limited range of appropriate skills; verbal skills, for example, include a wide range of abilities, such as reading, and may depend upon other abilities, such as reasoning.

If it is unclear just what is being measured, it is even less clear that there is evidence of a marked difference based on sex or gender. As we saw with physical characteristics, there is enormous overlap. Indeed, the overlap is such that spatial ability alone simply cannot explain why, for instance, there are still so few women engineers. Yet the difference is often portrayed as much greater. One 'popular' book claims, for instance, that – unequivocally 'men's brains are more specialized' and that 'A woman may be less able to separate emotion from reason because of the way the female brain is organized' (Moir and Jessel, 1989, pp. 43, 48). Overstating the case is not unique to popular accounts, however: Hugh Fairweather noted how little evidence there was of clear-cut sex differences, yet how often the textbooks reported it. He concluded that this was 'stuff indeed to make a myth' (Fairweather, 1976).

A second strand of criticism is that the alleged links between brain asymmetry and sex differences often contradict themselves. At one time women were said in some theories to have dominant right brains – a claim flying in the face of assertions that women were better at verbal (left side) and men at spatial (right side) skills. Rogers (1988) notes two reasons why this claim should be made: first, some researchers have claimed that emotions have to do more with the right side (again, a claim made largely without evidence: and if we can locate 'emotion' in the brain at all, it probably has more to do with the bits of the brain lying underneath the two hemispheres). And second, she points out, '. . . it is obviously not acceptable for females to have left hemispheric dominance as analytic ability is a property of the left hemisphere' (Rogers, 1988, p. 48; also see Birke, 1992).

The third strand of criticism is that we should not automatically assume that any difference between women and men in performance of psychological tests is due to biology. It is, moreover, a strange kind of biology – for these theories portray the differences as somehow etched into a fixed kind of brain. Yet surely the human brain is anything but fixed: on the contrary, it shows amazing capacities for learning and memory. If there *are* differences between populations of women and of men in performance on certain psychological tests, then this may have little or nothing to do with their biology at all.

It has much more to do with gender, and how that is perceived. Females tend to gain higher scores on some tests of verbal ability; but boys learn early in life to associate reading with femininity (Rogers, 1988). Parents, however, usually recognize the importance of acquiring verbal skills and try to ensure that sons *learn* them (McGuinness, 1976).

Such compensation is less evident, however, in relation to girls and learning mechanical/spatial skills. But neither parents nor schools have traditionally tried to give girls compensatory education specifically aimed at developing these skills.

Yet there is evidence that the sex difference in spatial abilities is not found in all human societies. It largely disappears, moreover, if girls and boys are taught science in ways that encourage initiative and appropriate cognitive skills. Jane Butler Kahle studied a group of American biology teachers whom she had selected as being particularly successful in encouraging children to study science – including the girls. These teachers made particular efforts to encourage all children to participate, and were more likely than most teachers to include plenty of opportunities for the children to do 'hands-on' work in the laboratory. The students of these teachers were given various psychological tests, including tests of spatial ability and tests designed to measure students' anxiety about doing science. Sex differences virtually disappeared (Kahle, 1985, p. 64).

Conclusions

There are undoubtedly differences between women and men, both physically and psychologically, and our society attaches a great deal of importance to them. So much so, indeed, that they are often exaggerated out of all proportion. Such differences as exist are easily portrayed as absolute instead of statistical (that is they imply that the difference is between all men and all women, rather than only some). The question of what is meant by 'difference' in these discussions is clearly of some concern to feminists: but so is the widespread tendency, which I have tried to outline here, to attribute difference to 'biological' causes. There are two major problems with this: the concept of 'biology' it invokes is one of fixity – 'biology' is not seen as something which might change. And, secondly, other factors that might contribute are excluded. Even such obviously biological parts of the body as your bones are subject to change. The psychologist, Helen Thompson Woolley, said in 1910 that,

> There is perhaps no field aspiring to be scientific where flagrant personal bias, logic martyred in the cause of supporting a prejudice, unfounded assertions, and even sentimental rot and drivel, have run riot to such an extent as here.
>
> (Quoted in Sayers, 1980, p. 58; also see Rosenberg, 1982)

She was referring to research into sex differences. Feminist critics might well wonder how much has changed in eighty years.

Notes

1 In this chapter, I have relied upon the distinction between sex and gender (although [illegible]

3 Scientists have identified a gene situated on the Y chromosome (in humans and other mammals) which promotes the development of testes. If that gene is absent, the internal structures will develop into ovaries, uterus and so on. In that sense, the gene on that chromosome could be called a 'male-determining' gene. Interestingly many scientific reports referred to it as did newspaper accounts as a sex determining gene, as though differentiating into two sexes is equal to becoming male (see Fausto-Sterling, 1985).

4 There are many reasons for women's lack of strenuous exercise, of course, that do not concern us here. Women may not wish to participate in organized sport, for example because of its image of trenchant masculinity, or because – unlike most men – they lack the leisure time. See the special issue of *Women's Studies International Forum* (edited by Ann Hall) on the 'The gendering of sport, leisure and physical education' (Vol. 10, No. 4, 1987). There is, however, rather more interest among women in taking exercise now than there was, say, twenty years ago – so the sex difference may be declining.

5 There were other problems specific to this study: the number of brains dissected was small, the significance of the thickness of this part of the brain not really understood. Later research failed to find the sex difference (see Bradshaw, 1989; and Rogers, 1988), yet the study was widely popularized.

6 For critical feminist analysis, and further details of these theories, see Rogers (1988), Bleier (1984) and Genova (1989). The theories agree that males and females differ in the degree of specialization of the two halves of the brain; they differ, however, in whether they see this as due to dominance of one half over the other (for example, male spatial ability seen as resulting from dominance of the right half of the brain), or due to one sex being less 'lateralized' (that is the two halves of the brain show more 'cross-talk' and less dominance of one by the other).

References

Birke, L. 1992. Transforming biology. In H. Crowley and S. Himmelweit, eds., *Knowing women: Feminism and knowledge*. Cambridge: Polity Press/The Open University.

Bleier, R. 1984. *Science and gender: A critique of biology and its theories on women*. New York and Oxford: Pergamon Press.

Bradshaw, J.L. 1989. *Hemispheric specialization and psychological function*. Chichester: John Wiley.

Donahue, T. and Johnson, N. 1986. *Foul play: Drug abuse in sports*. Oxford: Basil Blackwell.

Dyer, K. 1982. *Catching up the men: Women in sport*. London: Junction Books.

Fairweather, H. 1976. Sex differences in cognition. *Cognition* 4: 231–280.

Fausto-Sterling, A. 1985. *Myths of gender: Biological theories about women and men*. New York: Basic Books.

Ferris, E. 1980. Attitudes to women in sport. International Congress on Women and Sport, July, Rome.

Genova, J. 1989. Women and the mismeasure of thought. In N. Tuana, ed., *Feminism and Science*, pp. 211–227. Bloomington, IN: University of Indiana Press.

Kahle, J.B. 1985. Retention of girls in science: case studies of secondary teachers. In J.B. Kahle, ed., *Women in science: A report from the field*. Brighton: Falmer Press.

McGuinness, D. 1976. Sex differences in the organisation of perception and cognition. In B. Lloyd and J. Archer, eds., *Exploring sex differences*. London: Academic Press.

Maloiy, G.M.O., Heglund, N.C., Prager, L.M., Gavagna, G.A., and Taylor, C.R. 1986. Energetic costs of carrying loads: Have African women discovered an economic way? *Nature* 319: 668–669.

Moir, A. and Jessel, D. 1989. *Brain sex: The real difference between men and women*. London: Michael Joseph.

Notelovitz, M. 1986. Interrelations of exercise and diet on bone metabolism and osteoporosis. In M. Winick, ed., *Nutrition and exercise*. Chichester: Wiley-Interscience.

Oakley, A. 1972. *Sex, gender and society*. London: Temple Smith.

Rogers, L. 1988. Biology, the popular weapon: Sex differences in cognitive function. *Crossing boundaries: Feminisms and the critique of knowledges*. Sydney: Allen and Unwin.

Rosenberg, R. 1982. *Beyond separate spheres: Intellectual roots of modern feminism*. New Haven, CT: Yale University Press.

Russett, C.E. 1989. *Sexual science: The Victorian construction of womanhoods*. Cambridge, MA: Harvard University Press.

Sayers, J. 1980. Psychological sex differences. In Brighton Women and Science Group, eds., *Alice through the microscope: The power of science over women's lives*. London: Virago.

Shields, S.A. 1987. The variability hypothesis: The history of biological sex differences in intelligence. In *Sex and scientific inquiry*. Chicago: Chicago University Press.

Tuana, N. 1989. The weaker seed: The sexist bias of reproductive theory. In N. Tuana, ed., *Feminism and Science*, pp. 147–171. Bloomington, IN: University of Indiana Press.

Chapter 25

Gisela Kaplan and Lesley J. Rogers

Introduction

Over the past two decades we have seen the rise of the New Right. When the National Front supporters rally in the streets of London, the neofascists rampage in Leipzig and Berlin, and The Navigators, a fundamentalist religious sect, call for stoppage of Asian immigration to Australia, they invoke the supremacy of the white male, and they use arguments of genetic determinism to justify their position. To them race is not a social construct but, rather, a natural order ultimately determined by our genes. Equally, to the mounting band of patriarchs who have reacted in backlash to the gains made by the feminist movements in the 1970s and 1980s male privilege is not a social construct but a "natural," innate manifestation of biologically determined difference. The claim is that human behavior is the consequence of biochemical events in cells and that these are in turn determined by the action of the genes within those cells. Biological determinism is used as an arbiter of social issues. According to the biological determinist, all human behavior, and even society itself, is fixed and controlled by the genes.

This essay deals with the role that biological determinism plays, and has played, in influencing general opinion and public wisdom on issues of race and gender. Racism and sexism are two phenomena of persistent prejudice, and here we will discuss how theories of inheritance have helped to perpetuate them. By using science as a supposedly value free, or objective, method for understanding reality, new discoveries and measurements have helped old beliefs to be dressed up in a new garb. Seemingly objective evidence in the field of biology has consistently been used as justification for racism, imperialism, and sexism. Far from being *value free*, much biological research reflects the prejudices and ignorance of its time. To quote Steven Rose, "Biology is inexorably a historical science in a way that chemistry and physics have no need to be" (1988, 161). This is not to say that chemistry and physics have been, and are, without controversy and influence from social forces or religious attitudes (cf. the resistance to reexamining Newtonian physics) but, rather, that the biological sciences are in constant interface with the social attitudes of the time.

Recognition of phenotypes distinguishing broad categories of skin color and eye or nose shape (i.e., purely anatomical and physical features) may appear to be merely descriptive and harmless enough. Equally, the recognition that women are anatomically different from men in certain respects (reproductive organs) apparently does little harm and merely reflects facts. Yet neither research nor social norms have ever left "difference" at that. There are countless examples of the way in which these "harmless" categories and findings in biology were and are being used to explain complex behaviors of the human species. Giant theoretical somersaults have been performed in both the disciplines of biology and sociology in order to pander to prejudices in an apparently scholarly fashion. If the goal was to prove inferiority of "races," the female sex, or the working classes, a whole catalog of beliefs concerning abilities and generalized psychological characteristics was extrapolated from a few physical differences. As is frequently claimed today, complex human behavior is reduced to biological explanations at the level of a physical trait or the genes.

In a recent publication entitled *The Sociology of Race* Richardson and Lambert argue that "the sociologist can safely leave biology aside and concentrate on how race is socially constructed" (1986). This, however, is incorrect. Social constructions of reality cannot safely leave behind biology. Indeed, much of that construction is based on biological arguments. The processes of genetic determinist support for racist and sexist views are still active in our society today and in the last two decades have even gone through a period of reactivation. It therefore remains an urgent task in each new generation to point out the fallacies and, in view of the social implications, the enormity of these academic transgressions. Biological, or genetic, determinism is politically, socially, and morally dangerous. First, unitary theories are readily popularized and gain widespread publicity. Second, these theories lend legitimation to a range of undesirable prejudicial beliefs that are at odds with modern political thinking of social democracies, civil liberties, and citizenship. Third, they tend to slow down the frontiers of knowledge because the sludge that they create requires "cleanup" and diverts energies.

The dialectic relationship between the development of biological determinist thinking and the socioeconomic and political environment is no more readily demonstrated than in the second half of the nineteenth and early twentieth century. Industrialization, the development of nation-states, their ensuing imperialism and expansionary aims, and the formation of movements such as pan-Slavism and pan-Germanism coincided with the formation of new theories of races and gender. Based on Adam Smith's economic theories of laissez-faire and on Malthus population theory (let the poor die because they represent human surplus), industrialization then entered its most brutal entrepreneurial stage. In racial and gender research much of the new "scientific evidence" for the so-called inferiority of any *Homo sapiens* who was not male and white first appeared in the second half of the nineteenth century. In other words biological determinist arguments entered into these socioeconomic events at this point. They infused the interpretation of reality with new "scientific" ideas in such a way as to remove any accountability or responsibility from those in power.

Among the most respected proponents of racist imperialist ideas were Joseph Arthur, Comte de Gobineau (1816–82), and Houston Stewart Chamberlain (1855–1927). In 1855 Gobineau presented his fatefully popular work *Essai sur l'inegalité des races humaines*. His notorious oeuvre stands out in its simple doctrines and the far-reaching consequences of his views. He used a simple and dangerous weapon: he praised the superiority of the white race, which he claimed was superior to the "black" and "yellow" races, even stating that civilization had progressed only when Aryans had been involved. And he invoked fear. His apocalyptic vision of the decline and death of the white race as a result of being swamped by "inferior races" occupied Gobineau and one of his most prominent pupils, Comte Vacher de Lapouge (1854–1936). Allegedly, even strong

as Gobineau's, were internationally acclaimed.

Gobineau's theories, largely through his friendship with Richard Wagner and the Bayreuth circle, became very influential in Germany. In 1894 one of the members of the Bayreuth circle founded the Gobineau Society. This might seem surprising since in Germany Gobineau's message of the inferiority and degenerating effect of the so-called yellow and African inferior races never took hold as it did in France or Britain. This had to do with the timing of Germany's acquisition of overseas colonies. Germany took African colonial possessions only in 1884 and a Chinese holding in 1897. Nevertheless, Gobineau's Aryan message and the warning of the degenerative and "diluting" effect of other races were highly usable and could be adapted to the German situation. In one sense it fueled the pan-German movement by "reawakening the Aryan Germanic soul"; in another it became a powerful weapon in the hands of anti-Semites. In the absence of the "yellow and black perils," Germans used the Jew as the one "polluting" race (Mosse 1978, 56).

Craniology flourished in the second half of the nineteenth century, and after Gobineau there were many crude attempts to draw a close association between blacks, women, and apes (see Gould 1981). Arguments that were propagated to justify the domination of men over women and the domination or enslavement of one "racial" group by another often equated women and black people. Thus, sexism and racism were linked aspects of genetic determinist thinking (Richards 1983).

There were two beliefs to which theorists held firmly, one being that the white brain was better developed than the black and the other that the male brain was better developed than the female. Women were said to lack the center for intellect, and blacks too were seen to have inferior intellect. Putting it the other way around, Charles Darwin stated that "some at least of those mental traits in which women may excel are traits characteristic of the lower race" (Darwin 1871, 569). He also referred to the "close connection of the negro or Australian and the gorilla" (Darwin 1871, 201). To make the logical connection that he, perhaps deliberately, leaves to conjecture, women in his opinion must also be closer to gorillas.

Some of the most reputable scientists of the time concerned themselves with finding scientific evidence to support the belief in the inferiority of women and blacks, and they became obsessed with measurement of cranial size and brain weight. The assumption (shown later to be incorrect) underlying this approach was that smaller brain size and weight indicate lower intelligence. Negro and female brains were considered to be not only smaller and lighter in weight but also underdeveloped. Thus, the anthropologist E. Huschke wrote in 1854: "The Negro brain possesses a spinal cord of the type found in children and women and, beyond this, approaches the type of brain found in higher apes" (cited in Gould 1981, 103). Similarly, another anthropologist McGrigor wrote in 1869 that "the type of female skull approaches in many respects that of the infant, and still more that of the lower races" (cited in Lewontin *et al.* 1984). The French craniologist F. Pruner embodied the pulse of that time when he wrote: "The Negro resembles the female in his love for children, his family and his cabin. . . . The black man is to the white man what woman is to man in general, a loving being and a being of pleasure" (1866, 13–33). One notes here the equation of the "negro" *he* with the white *she*. The black woman was apparently considered too worthless to even feature in these debates, and so, for better or worse, she was relegated to oblivion.

The famous neuroanatomist Broca (1824–80), founder of the Anthropological Society of Paris, gathered much data demonstrating that the male brain is on average heavier than that of the female. The motivation for this work is clearly apparent in the following statement of a coworker of Broca, G. LeBon, written in 1879. LeBon was one of the founders of social psychology, crowd behavior in particular, and he influenced the thinking of Mussolini. He opposed higher education for women:

> In the most intelligent races, as among the Parisians, there are a large number of women where brains are closer in size to those of gorillas than to the most developed male brains. This inferiority is so obvious that no one can contest it for a moment; only its degree is worth discussion. All psychologists who have studied the intelligence of women, as well as poets and novelists, recognize today that they represent the most inferior forms of human evolution and that they are closer to children and savages than to an adult, civilized man. They excel in fickleness, inconstancy, absence of thought and logic, and an incapacity to reason. Without doubt there exist some distinguished women, very superior to the average man, but they are as exceptional as the birth of any monstrosity, as, for example, of a gorilla with two heads: consequently we may neglect them entirely.
>
> (LeBon 1879, quoted in Gould 1981, 104)

To compare the occurrence of an intelligent woman with that of a gorilla with two heads is no less astounding than is the claim that the Parisians are a race. Apparently, his views went entirely unchecked and uncriticized.

Nevertheless, quite early in the era of brain size measurement, scientists had run into a number of problems, which they had either to dismiss or argue around. For example, Broca's theory of brain size and intelligence was momentarily shaken when he found that "Eskimos, Lapps, Malays, Tartars and several other peoples of the Mongolian type" had larger cranial capacity than "the most civilized people of Europe?" (1873, 38). To circumvent the problem of, as he saw it, some "lowly" races having large brains he saw fit to claim that the relationship between brain size and intelligence may not hold at the upper end of the scale, because some inferior groups have large brains, but that it did hold at the lower end. That is, small brains belong exclusively to people of low intelligence. By this means he felt that he was able to hold on to "the value of a small brain size as a mark of inferiority" (Broca 1873). As Gould (1981) points out, Broca did not fudge his actual numbers, although some other scientists of the time did so; rather, he reinterpreted them in a way that allowed him to uphold his original, preconceived notions, even if this required the most incredible feats of logic.

It became fashionable to measure the brains of eminent men after their deaths. The brain weights of several of these men were above the European average and were taken as evidence of their superior intellect (e.g., Baron Georges Cuvier and Ivan [illegible] extremely unreliable was all of this early data on brain weight and volume.

Much was made of this claimed difference in brain weight between women and men until it was realized that no sex difference occurs when brain weight is expressed in relation to body weight. Then attention was shifted to structural differences in the skull or differences in subregions of the brain, such as the frontal lobes or the corpus callosum. The arguments of brain size and cranium shape held sway to support racial, sexual, and indeed class oppression until 1901 when Alice Leigh applied new statistical procedures to the analysis of the data and showed that there was no correlation between cranial capacity and intelligence or brain weight and intelligence. Nevertheless, it was in 1903 that the American anatomist E.A. Spitzka published a figure showing the brain size of a "Bushwoman" as intermediate between that of a gorilla and the mathematician C.F. Gauss and the number of convolutions of the surface of the brain of the Bushwoman as being closer to that of the gorilla (see Gould 1981, fig. 3.3). It is worth noting that the lower "white" classes were also slotted into having inferior, undeveloped brains (see Gould 1981), although this issue does not directly concern us here.

Other morphological measurements

Many other parts of the human body can be measured, as indeed they have been, in attempts to show the inferiority of blacks, women, and the lower classes. One such example was Broca's measurement of the ratio of the size of the radius bone in the lower arm to the humerus bone in the upper arm, the theory being that a higher ratio means a longer forearm, which, in turn, is more characteristic of the ape. While blacks were found to have a higher ratio than whites, Broca encountered an impasse for his ideology when he found that Eskimos and Australian Aborigines had a lower ratio than whites. He concluded that "it seems difficult for me to continue to say that elongation of the forearm is a character of degradation or inferiority" (1862, 11). In other words, the approach was to hold on to the belief that Europeans rank above races with darker skins and to count as irrelevant the particular nonfitting measurement that was going to be used in support of it. As with his data on brain size, he continued to adhere to a belief and preferred to ignore some of the contradictory data. Broca's decision to hold on to his social attitudes in the face of conflicting scientific evidence is a clear example of the influence of social attitudes on science.

Nose shape and size was another characteristic measured across human groups perceived as races. Indeed, this variable is of particular interest because it was taken up by some scientists who defended equality and were later called cultural relativists. They argued that nose size and shape was influenced by climatic conditions, temperature, and humidity in order to optimize breathing and minimize water loss (this idea was still maintained by J.S. Weiner, writing in 1954). The theory of environmental influence on the shape of the nose, however admirable at the time, was always discussed in terms of measurements that set the white, male nose as a standard. For example, the naturalist O. Beccari, who spent time in Borneo at the turn of the century, made frequent references which described the Malays as lacking a prominent nose and described the women as having even flatter noses than the men (Beccari 1904, 22, 24). The smaller, flatter nose was seen as more childlike and even more apelike. It was a feature considered to illustrate the inferiority of the "lower races." Interestingly, somewhere along the line in European culture a small nose became associated with beauty and femininity. Even today a small nose is considered by some to be more beautiful in women, presumably because it makes the face more childlike, and, therefore, it is seen as more female (rather than more apelike!).

Beccari paid credence to "the opinion that the races of Man are climatic productions" (216) and accepted that this is not inconsistent with the theory of evolution. He then discussed in some detail the possibility that "Man" may have evolved from the orangutan. After failing to find any remains of an anthropoid form in Borneo, he concluded that man must have evolved in Africa or "an ancient dependency of that continent." The chief basis of this premise was that Africans have black skins, and thus "it may be surmised that the first men were black" (220). By implication, despite their flat small noses, the Malays have whiter skin and, therefore, cannot be closely related to the earliest humans. Skin color, therefore, dominates over other characteristics. There is, of course, no fossil evidence of the skin color of early humanoid forms.

Most of the measurement nonsense was later abandoned, but the link between the brain as a measure of inferior status of women and blacks did anything but disappear. For example, the introduction of brain surgery, notably the introduction of prefrontal lobotomies by Ergas Moniz, for which he won the Nobel Prize in medicine in 1949, simply put the arguments in a different context. Walter Freeman, who introduced prefrontal lobotomies to the United States in 1936 and practiced these until his retirement in 1970, found that in these operations "women respond better than men, Negroes better than whites and syphilitics better than nonsyphilitics." He added that, of course to limit lobotomy to syphilitic Negro women would be the height of absurdity" (cited in Chorover 1979, 156). At about the same time an English physician in Kenya, J.C. Carothers, stated that the normal behavior of leucotomized or lobotomized European whites resembled the normal behavior of East African blacks. Such behaviors included talkativeness, poor judgment, and a "tendency to be content with inferior performance socially and intellectually" (Carothers 1950, 38; cf. Chorover 1979, 156).

The "justification" of racism

The alleged European superiority, seemingly so evident because of its technological advances, by a giant leap somehow incorporated morality and relegated other cultures to a status of contempt (Worsley 1972). Technological, including military, progress was seen to go hand in hand with moral progress. To the confident postindustrial Europeans and their descendants in "new world" and colonialized countries, the indices

[illegible]

moral superiority imposed grave responsibilities on the "developed" nation-states to instruct the "savages and natives" in the art and fruits of modern civilization. If actions were taken in the light of the latest scientific findings on racial matters, governments could be seen as acting in good faith and even with a degree of magnanimity. English Parliament had the interest "to fulfill the mission of the Anglo-Saxon race, in spreading intelligence, freedom, and Christian faith wherever Providence gives us the dominion of the soil" (cited in Banton 1977, 26).

Hand in hand with the idea of racial superiority came the idea of racial purity and the fear of "miscegenation," which Bloom called "quasi-magical" (Bloom 1972, 119). Gobineau, in his typically oblique ways, had already warned that "blood mixture" and "blood impurities" were the beginning of the downfall of even the best race, which was then condemned to become "human herds, no longer nations, weighed down by the mournful somnolence, [which] will henceforth be benumbed in their nullity, like buffalo ruminating in the stagnant meres of the Pontine marshes" (Gobineau 1855). Chamberlain, echoing a similar sentiment, suggested that, "where the struggle [for race purity] is not waged with cannon-balls, it goes on silently in the heart of society by marriages, by the annihilation of distances which further intercourse" (cited in Bloom 1972, 38).

Perhaps the most direct link between philosophy, biological determinism, the fear of racial pollution, and Nazi biopolicies is provided by Ernst Haeckel, whose most successful work, *The Riddles of the Universe* (1899), was translated into twenty-five languages and by 1933 had sold more than one million copies in Germany alone (Stein 1988). Here social Darwinism obtained a new twist by a new branch of eugenics. Independently of Gobineau and Chamberlain, Haeckel came to the same conclusion that lower races "such as the Vedahs or Australian Negroes – are psychologically nearer to the mammals – apes and dogs – than to the civilized European" and that "therefore [we must] assign a totally different value to their lives" (cited in Stein 1988, 55). The important idea that held together his work was that humans are not distinct from the biological world but rather are part of nature and, therefore, represent part of a natural continuum. Natural selection occurs, or should occur, among humans in the same manner as among animals or plants. Obviously, neither liberalism, democracy, nor the ideas of the Enlightenment fitted his scheme. And indeed, he regarded these political and humanistic proposals as quite false because they were based on an assumption of free will and individual autonomy. He dismissed both as an illusion and as the consequence of dogma of the French Enlightenment *philosophes*.

For Haeckel the *only* morality lay in the process of natural selection. According to him, this "morality" of natural selection in human society now required positive intervention in order to correct the errors humans had already brought upon themselves. He advocated the extermination of anybody with any failings – racial, physical, social, or otherwise – because such an artificial process of selection would make "the struggle for life among the better portion of mankind . . . easier." Those he believed should be exterminated included "hundreds of thousands of incurables – lunatics, lepers, people with cancer etc. – who are artificially kept alive . . . without the slightest profit to themselves or the general body." Moreover, he said they polluted the breeding pool and so did "incorrigible and degraded criminals" (cited in Stein 1988, 55). Anthropologists of the time and the Society for Racial Hygiene supported Haeckel and often pronounced very similar views. By the 1920s these various groups, all regarded as consisting of respectable scholars, were proposing concrete programs of euthanasia, sterilization, and other methods of artificial selection in order to "revitalize the genepool." In 1935 H.F.K. Gunther was awarded the prestigious Prize for Science for his less than scientific work *Racial Knowledge of the German People*.

The new era of brain measurement

Over the past two decades there has been renewed interest in measuring parts of the brain to see if there are sex differences. Once found, as with the early brain measuring studies of the nineteenth century, these differences are seen to provide evidence for the biological basis of a wide range of sex differences in behavior. The reappearance of brain measuring in a search for explanations for sex differences began in the 1960s and 1970s, and this interest has continued to gain impetus (see the later section on brain lateralization). The timing of its emergence coincided with the focus on "proving" sex and race differences in IQ. Although it is clearly part of the same resurgence of biological determinism, it has received much less debate and criticism in the public arena. Part of the reason for this may be that the new measurements of brain size and structure are looking mainly at sex differences, not black–white differences, and that the present-day public may be more prepared to confront racism than sexism. Another reason may be that most of the researchers in this area have generated their data by applying new technology to the study of animal brains (mainly rats) rather than human brains. The implications are there, reported in the scientific literature, but *so far* relatively little of it has leaked out or been taken up by the wider media to be used for social policymaking. Its use for political purpose to curtail the progress of women toward equal rights has, however, begun (see Moir and Jessel 1989).

It should also be noted that there has been a recent report of a study by J. Klekamp *et al.* (1991) in which the size and development rate of the hippocampus were measured in Australian Aborigines and Caucasians. Slower growth of this brain region was reported to occur in Aboriginal women, and the authors hypothesized this to be a result of either genetic differences, by implication sex-linked, or poor diet or both. Are we about to see a resurgence of racist science?

Sociobiology

During the 1970s genetic determinism led to the formation of a new discipline called "sociobiology," demarcated in particular by the publication of E.O. Wilson's book, *Sociobiology: A New Synthesis*, in 1975. The existence of genes for aggression, territoriality, and intelligence was claimed. As these behaviors are all characteristic [illegible] of Western capitalist society, sociobiology reinforces the [illegible] determined, and the gene[illegible] sole purpose of replicating and getting into the next generation (see Dawkins 1976). Gene replication is seen as the sole purpose of life, and genes are given personality characteristics, such as "selfishness." All the complexities of animal behavior, the richness of human achievement and endeavor, are mere trappings that spin off from the basic purpose of the replicator units. Thus, analysis of mating strategies and reproduction becomes the main area of study. This burgeoning area of research in sociobiology analyzes data using cost-benefit models. The cost of a certain mating and reproductive strategy is weighed against the benefit for the individual (not the group), and so the biological fitness ("rightness") of the particular mating strategy is determined. The terminology of capitalism is commonly used, and the ideology of individualism is clearly apparent. It offers capitalism feedback in the form of biological justification. To this end sociobiological theories have been readily taken up by the media and also incorporated into a range of other disciplines, including sociology and economics. They have also been taken up by the National Front in the United Kingdom and other neofascist organizations elsewhere.

There has been much disagreement over the existence of a gene for altruism (cf. de Lepervanche 1984). Most sociobiologists agree that no such gene could exist for long in a population as it would soon be lost because it would not compete successfully against the "selfish" genes. Yet according to Wilson (1975), the gene for homosexuality, which he hypothesizes to exist, must be linked to a gene for altruism, or it too would have been lost from the population. Wilson's idea is that the gene for homosexuality persists only because homosexual individuals also carry a gene for altruism, and this leads them to assist in the raising of their siblings and their siblings' offspring; that is, they assist the reproduction of individuals who carry a certain percentage of their own genetic material. Thus, "the gene" for homosexuality, so Wilson believes, is an aberration that persists only as a consequence of the coexistence of a protector gene, and the altruism, helping behavior, determined by this protector gene is confined to individuals with whom there is shared genetic material (see also Ridley and Dawkins 1981).

Sociobiologists take into account no aspect of sociology or developmental biology. Had Wilson turned to some sociological records, he might have been surprised to discover that a large percentage of homosexuals do reproduce. Perhaps a more important criticism of the sociobiological approach is its utter disregard for the biological processes of development. Organisms develop in constant interaction with their environment. Genes do indeed influence development, but through each step of the developmental process the expression of the genes interacts with environmental factors in an inseparable, intertwined manner so that, finally, the separate contributions of the genes and environment cannot be determined (Rose *et al*. 1973). Genes function in an environment, and they cannot be discussed without considering that environment (see Tobach 1972). That environment is not a unitary or easily defined thing. For example, there is the biochemical environment in the immediate vicinity of the gene; there is the environment surrounding the organism itself; and so on. No clear distinction can be made between the environment within and outside the organism (Hambley 1973). Furthermore, genes and environment are not discrete opposites (Tobach 1972); they are both entirely integrated aspects of the developmental process.

Genes cannot behave or be "selfish." By the same token behavior is not in the genome. Behavior is at an entirely different level of organization than the genes; many steps and functions separate the two. Genes are expressed as biochemical processes; behavior is expressed by the whole organism. This is not to say that genes play no part in behavior. Rather, it is not possible to ignore the processes of development, to ignore environmental influences on the expression of genes, and to extrapolate directly from genes to behavior as do the sociobiologists. Again, we see the selective use of information to use (pseudo)science to bolster sociopolitical causes.

Genes, hormones, homosexuality, and sex differences in behavior

Biological determinism can be applied to a wide range of social phenomena, and the model can shift and move to any subject in which the transgression between biological basis and social reality is seen as a possibility. We suggest that the "scientific" writing on homosexuality, rekindled by Alfred Kinsey's findings of 1948, took a very similar turn to the discussions on race and gender. Kinsey's findings showed to an astounded audience that a very high percentage of males and a much higher than expected percentage of females at one time or another had engaged in homosexual activity (Kinsey *et al*. 1948). This was morally and socially so unacceptable that studies were undertaken to show that homosexuality was not the behavior of "normal," well-adapted people but, rather, the consequence of a biological abnormality or a congenital defect (although the evidence should have invited some to regard it as far less of an aberration than it was seen to be). In psychiatry homosexuality was treated as a disease. In the 1950s and 1960s the assumed abnormality of homosexuality allowed for biopolicies in the medical field. Under Hitler homosexuals went to concentration camps and were killed; under Mussolini celibacy and being unmarried as an adult were punishable by a prison sentence (Kaplan 1992).

In the postwar Western world the punitive legal procedure was changed into an invasive, even mutilating "treatment" model. In Australia and the United States, as well as in other countries, psychosurgery has been used to "treat" and/or "cure" homosexuality. Frontal lobotomies, which involve surgical severing of connection between parts of the frontal lobes and deeper regions of the brain, became fashionable in the 1940s and 1950s. They were performed enthusiastically in the United States, and, even though the operation was approached with greater caution in the United

Kingdom, over ten thousand patients in the United Kingdom were lobotomized between 1942 and 1954 (Whitlock 1979).

Although the discoveries (by Western medicine) of psychoactive drugs in the 1950s led to a decline in the number of lobotomies performed, throughout the following two decades the operation was still performed on a large number of psychiatric patients and also political dissidents. During the 1970s other forms of psychosurgery, such as the cingulotracheotomy operation (lesioning of the cingulate gyrus, part of the limbic

[illegible]

of the brain have also been destroyed as a means of treating homosexuality; for example, lesions have been placed in the hypothalamus (a most risky area of the brain to lesion) to treat a symptom called "latent homosexuality" (Blakemore 1977).

Aversion therapy with electric shock and hot plate treatment were not uncommon forms of treatment for homosexuality in the 1950s to the 1970s. In addition, chemical castration by application of antiandrogen therapy or estrogen treatment has been known to be used in West Germany, South Africa, and Australia (Kaplan and Rogers 1987). In a publication entitled *Sex Variants* (Henry 1948), Dickinson, the writer of "The Gynecology of Homosexuality," concerned himself with lesbians and measured the "erectility" of breast and nipples, the labia majora and minora, pubic hair, clitoris erectility and size, uterus, etc. One needs to note that, as in the nineteenth century, measurement of physical features once again became the guiding procedure for establishing difference (i.e., inferiority or "abnormality"). Because of the sexual focus, however, the customary measurement of brain size had been dropped in favor of measuring the size of genitalia. From these measurements of a total of thirty-one women he claimed to have found significant differences in size and behavior of the sexual organs of lesbians in comparison to, as he calls it, his experience in "office practice." Of course, we do not see any data of his daily experiences, that is, his office practice. Variation of anatomical difference on an extremely small sample is read as abnormality for all lesbians and thus confirms the medical model of homosexuality as a disease. D.J. West's study, first published under the title *Homosexuality* in 1955, has gone through four editions and seven reprints in all, the latest in 1977, revised as *Homosexuality Re-Examined*. West worked as a psychiatrist and reader in clinical criminology at Cambridge, and his book was very influential. Even in the 1977 revised version he argues that "the possibility that homosexual behaviour in humans is caused by some glandular deficiency cannot be dismissed out of hand" (West 1977, 615). According to him, androgen levels influence the strength of sexual desire, and an excess of prepubertal androgen in girls "may masculinize certain aspects of their social attitude and temperament." He quotes lowered sperm count and "relative infertility" as another relationship between male homosexuality and biology (69).

In the psychomedical field there is a huge literature on the determination of sex differences in behavior by the sex hormones, these in turn determined by the genes

(X and Y chromosomes). This form of biological determinism was particularly popularized by the studies and writings, in both the scientific and popular press, of J. Money and his coworkers in the 1970s and 1980s (Money and Ehrhardt 1972: Money and Tucker 1975; Dörner 1976).

There are serious flaws in the theoretical basis to the hypotheses of Money and Dörner, and this is best demonstrated by looking more closely at some of their work. Money and Ehrhardt (1972) conducted a study that has had much influence on thought in this area. They scored a range of behaviors and attitudes considered to be gender related in a group of girls who had been exposed to either androgens (adrenogenital syndrome) or the drug progestin (which their mothers took to prevent miscarriage and which has androgenic action) during their fetal development. Compared to controls (the choice of which was rather dubious: see Rogers and Walsh 1982), the girls exposed to androgens during fetal development were said to be more like males in that they scored higher in "tomboyishness," chose boys' clothes and toys, chose career over marriage (note that they were all only teenagers), and, of special note, scored higher IQs. In addition, they were said to have confused gender identity and were late to reach the "romantic age of dating and boy friends." There were numerous faults with the design of these experiments, let alone the premise on which they were based, but we will not elaborate on them here, as they have been covered previously in some detail (see Rogers and Walsh 1982; Rogers 1981; Rosoff 1991). Suffice it to say that much of the data were collected retrospectively by telephone interviews with the mothers (a method most open to error of recall and distortion due to expectations), the format of the questions used in the interviews has never been revealed, the selection of controls was dubious (in one study there were girls suffering from Turner's Syndrome, genetically XO with reduced levels of sex hormones) and no other members of the subjects' families were investigated for possible similar behavior patterns. The assumption made was that the male sex hormones had acted on the developing brain to switch it into being more masculine.

Perhaps the main danger of this work is that it has been widely taken up in popular writings (e.g., Durden-Smith and de Simone 1983) and extrapolated to explain sex differences between women and men. Beyond that it has been used to explain the so-called biological determination of homosexuality, transvestism, and transsexualism. Money has placed the latter three categories on a continuum of increasing disturbance of androgen levels during development (Money 1974, 1976), the male transsexual, for example, being seen as having a "female brain trapped in a male body." There is no evidence that any of these groups has abnormal hormonal levels during development. Yet the thesis persists, and indeed it has been further propagated by Dörner, who asserts that homosexuality should be prevented by treating pregnant women with the sex steroid hormones (Dörner 1976, 1979). To Dörner male homosexuality is caused by insufficient levels of testosterone during fetal life and lesbianism by an oversupply of testosterone. He advocates that stress of the mother during pregnancy may lead to the fetus being exposed to lowered levels of testosterone, and that is why, according to him, more homosexuals were born in Germany during the war years. Thus, that which he sees as abnormal sexual behavior is to be explained as being biologically caused, even though here the ultimate influence is from the stressful environment, as it were, impeding the "proper" cause of nature (i.e., genetic expression). To take his hypothesis literally, he can only mean that more male homosexuals were born during this time, as by extrapolation stress during pregnancy should lower the chance of a lesbian being born.

Brain lateralization

Most of this recent research has focused on differences in lateralization between male [illegible] carry a long history of cultural associations, which are not irrelevant to us here. Left has been characterized as bad, dark, black, unclean, weak, female, and homosexual, whereas right has been characterized as good, light, clean, sacred, strong, white, male, and heterosexual (Star 1979). Left-handed people have been associated with evil, weakness, and all manner of detrimental characteristics throughout history. As we will see, these connotations are still with us today.

In humans, in most cases, language is processed in a site situated in the left hemisphere, and speech production is controlled from another site also in the left hemisphere. Women, however, appear to have an extra site for language in the right hemisphere (Bradshaw and Nettleton 1983; see also Obler and Novoa 1988). Sex differences in structure and function are increasingly being reported for nonhuman species, particularly rats (Denenberg 1981; Diamond 1984) and birds (Andrew and Brennan 1984; Rogers 1986). In rats there are, for example, left–right asymmetries in the thickness of various regions of the cortex and the direction and magnitude of these differ with age and sex (Diamond 1984). Additionally, there are sex differences in lateralization of brain neurochemistry (Denenberg and Rosen 1983).

In mammals the large neural tract, called the corpus callosum, which connects the left and right hemispheres, is considered to be important in generating and maintaining brain lateralization (Denenberg 1981; Gazzaniga and LeDoux 1978; Selnes 1974). Recently there have been reports that in rats the corpus callosum differs in size between females and males (Denenberg, Berrebi, and Fitch 1989). Although similar data for humans are still in dispute, one group of researchers have reported a sex difference in the size of the corpus callosum (Holloway and de Lacoste 1986; de Lacoste-Utamsing and Holloway 1982; de Lacoste, Holloway, and Woodward 1986). It is important to contest and debate the significance of the data reported for humans, particularly given the difficulty in having adequate controls in the studies of human brains and the low sample sizes. In the light of the data for animal species, however, it is perhaps even more important to ask how sex differences in the brain may be generated. Are they biologically determined by the action of the genes and sex hormones, or are they imposed on the brain by the differential cultural learning that occurs in women and men?

All too readily, many of the researchers opt for biological determinist explanations, even though they may not have attempted to test specifically for such an explanation.

For example, de Lacoste *et al.* (1986) are convinced that their reported sex difference in the size of the corpus callosum is biologically caused, as is most evident from the following statement: "We believe that our data provide further indirect evidence that the gonadal steroids and/or genetic sex play a role in the development of neural structures, linked with 'cognitive functions', in the human brain" (95). This is a rather remarkable (or foolhardy) statement given that their study did not investigate the role of hormones in the development of the corpus callosum or any other structure or function. This is yet another case of overstating the data and extrapolating to reinforce social norms.

Nevertheless, sex hormones can indeed influence the development of brain structures, including the cortex (Diamond 1984) and the corpus callosum (Berrebi *et al.* 1988; Fitch *et al.* 1991). But experience (environment) and age also influence these forms of lateralization. Lateralization in the developing chicken brain has also been demonstrated to depend on the interaction of sex hormones and environmental input in the form of light stimulation (Rogers 1986). The final form that lateralization takes in a given brain, be it human or nonhuman, has been shown clearly to depend on the interaction of the genes/hormones, environmental experience, and age. Just as it is impossible to separate the relative contributions of genes and environmental factors in determining IQ, so too is it impossible to separate the effects of genes, hormones, and environmental factors in determining brain lateralization.

There are two opposing views on possible differences in lateralization in women and men. One of the theories suggests that because females are more emotional than males they must be right hemisphere dominant (see Star 1979). This theory ignores the fact that women, for whatever reason, are superior in language ability compared to men and that language ability is a function of the left hemisphere. It is obviously not acceptable that women have left hemisphere dominance, as analytical ability is a property of the left hemisphere (Bleier 1984). Another theory argues that the brains of women are less lateralized than those of men (Levy 1977), the premise being that more lateralized brains (male) are better at visuospatial tasks. As left-handed men are said to be less lateralized than right-handed men, this theory suggests that women are more like left-handed men. Women and left-handed men are said to have more interhemispheric cross-talk and a greater degree of language processing in the right hemisphere. It is the latter that is said to interfere with spatial ability of the left hemisphere. While there is some evidence that women, compared to men in general, have an extra center for processing language in the right hemisphere, as far as we know this has not been investigated in left-handed men. Moreover, the claims of this theory are inconsistent with evidence that there is a higher than average representation of left-handed men among architects (Geschwind and Galaburda 1985).

A contrary theory suggests that the brains of women are more lateralized than those of men (Buffery 1981). Thus, the circular reasoning goes, women are inferior on visuospatial tasks because this ability requires use of both hemispheres and women cannot do this so well because their brains are more lateralized. Human females may be more or less lateralized than males, but this tells us only that lateralization in the brain reflects the different hormonal and environmental inputs to which female and male brains are exposed. It does not tell us something essential and unitary about the biological determination of sex differences in cognitive function, as de Lacoste *et al.* and others would want to believe.

N. Geschwind and A.M. Galaburda (1987) are influential researchers in the area of brain lateralization who have also opted for a unitary biological explanation for sex differences in lateralization. They have hypothesized that "normal" brain lateralization in males comes about as a result of testosterone influencing the development of the left hemisphere. Environmental and cultural influences are ignored. They claim that low levels of testosterone disturb development of the left hemisphere and that this is why left-handedness (the left hand being controlled by the right hemisphere) is more [illegible] J. Money and A.A. Ehrhardt (1972). Geschwind and Galaburda therefore appear to have resurrected a rather dubious hypothesis, with no further evidence to substantiate it, and they were prepared to extend their hypothesis to offer some biologically determined associations of homosexuality (Geschwind and Galaburda 1987). Here they displayed the often tortuous path of reasoning and tenuous assumptions so often used for biological explanations of difference. They were keen to explain some anecdotal, and definitely not proven, indication that homosexuals have a higher rate of "non-righthandedness" (175). First, they adopted a former study showing that stressing rats during pregnancy initially causes testosterone levels in the male fetus to rise and later, after birth, results in permanently lower levels of this hormone. Next they linked this finding to one of Dörner and his coworkers which reported higher levels of "homosexual" behavior in rats stressed in this manner. By extrapolation Geschwind and Galaburda concluded that stress in pregnancy in humans raises the level of testosterone in the male fetus and so disrupts the development of the left hemisphere and leads to more nonrighthandedness and it also causes homosexuality – hence, there are more left-handed homosexuals. Now they were prepared to go one step further. An elevated level of testosterone in the fetus also suppresses the development of the immune system. Thus, homosexuals may have impaired immune systems and this may be why they are more susceptible to AIDS. By adopting a unitary, biological cause for homosexuality, they were able, in one neat parcel, to suggest an explanation for the epidemiology of AIDS: thus, reductionist explanations subsume other sciences and social sciences.

This convoluted reasoning has taken us far from the original discussion of the new focus on sex differences in brain measurements. If this detour exemplifies anything, it is to show the nature of dead-end roads. They distract and mislead. Some of them have been hailed as new insights and as roads of knowledge for the future. Often this is doubly ironic. The very reason why some deterministic theories acquire publicity and are hailed as new, exciting knowledge is precisely because they do not offer anything new but at times confirm even the worst prejudices held in a society at the time – and they are produced by people who themselves commenced their research with a view of, implicitly or explicitly, confirming their own prejudices.

Conclusion

We have made it our particular concern to choose for discussion examples of reductionism, biological determinism, and biologisms by well-known and often well-respected scholars in the field. The impression should not be gained that the prejudices somehow belong to minor writers or outsiders. The problem is precisely that academic activity in this field has spawned so much that is socially highly approved, albeit scientifically most questionable. On the surface some of the research findings seem quite sophisticated, but in reality some of these tremendous constructs (e.g., modern sociobiology) rest on very shaky and simplistic premises.

The premise is that one biological fact – such as a gene, the size of a bone, weight of a skull, length of a forearm, or the absence or presence of one specific hormone – has explanatory power and can offer *singly* insight into social behaviors of individuals. Yet monocausal explanations in any field of scholarship rarely stand up under scrutiny. For the study and explanation of human behavior it is logically and scientifically impossible for one small facet to explain all when there are a multitude of variables which make up the human environment and human behavior. That is, of course, both the challenge and the difficulty in studying human behavior. In terms of experimentation human behavior is less accessible than is the equivalent in studies using animals, and when a theory comes along that makes the complexities disappear there may be a sense of relief by the general community that finally manageable answers to our searching questions are at hand.

The theories we have proposed here, which we have claimed represent examples of pseudoscience, have created and kept alive the modern monster of social Darwinism. Social Darwinism works back into the biological roots and therefore seeks to find the answers for differences in behavior via biological channels. In this way there hardly seems any difference between the explanations (and solutions) provided by Haeckel in pre-Nazi Germany and those of Wilson in 1975. If aggression and territoriality are biologically given traits, and genes are selfish, then Haeckel has a point that free will and individual autonomy do not exist other than as a fictitious account of the French *philosophes*. The only morality, as he concluded then, would be a morality of natural selection, of the survival of the fittest. Whatever is "given" by the genes presumably has a right to exist – a neat biological justification for wars, territoriality, and male aggression against women (see Hunter 1991).

We have shown that the ideas and the "proofs" in pseudoscience serve to state, confirm, and propagate a social or political belief rather than to advance science and knowledge. There are countless examples of poor experimental designs, omission of presenting data, and even falsified data to substantiate this point. We have given some examples of these in this chapter. Another method is to ignore a substantial body of data in order to arrive at the conclusion that the writer has wanted to reach in the first place rather than to work with the data (cf. the stories of Broca and Hutt).

One key element in the psychology of racism and sexism is the apparent need by some to identify a group of people as being inferior to themselves. Of course, the "pay-offs" may be very high, socially, economically, and politically (territorial gains, gains in powers, income, loss of guilt, etc.). Scientists are not free from racism and sexism, and biology has had more than a share in upholding or creating new myths of inequality. The psychology of those needing paradigms in which the world can be divided into inferior and superior can extend anywhere. If it were not racism or sexism, it might be homophobia or ageism: a whole range of items could usefully fill the "inferiority" niche. Racists and sexists may confine their biological determinist arguments to one category at a time, to single out and label a single group. Notwithstanding this, the designated inferior groups are to them, interchangeable. The construct of biological determinism is general and refers at one time to race, another to sex, and still another to class, sexual preference, or whatever identified inferior group is the [illegible]

of the past. Forms of control, structures, and curtailments of equality may change form and argument. Affirmative action programs may be here, but they may be undermined today and tomorrow. Indeed, there is evidence that it is already happening. Backlashes with outbreaks of virulent attacks on difference of any kind (gender, ethnicity, color, sexual preference, etc.) are making headline news in the early 1990s in the very countries that pride themselves on their own democratization and egalitarianism.

References

Andrew, R.J., and A. Brennan. 1984. "Sex Differences in Lateralization in the Domestic Chick: A Developmental Study." *Neuropsychologia* 22: 503–9.

Banton, M. 1977. *The Idea of Race*. London: Tavistock Publications.

Beccari, O. 1904. *Wanderings in the Great Forests of Borneo*. London: Archibald Constable.

Berrebi, A.S., R.H. Fitch, J.O. Denenberg, V.L. Friedrich, and V.H. Denenberg. 1988. "Corpus Callosum: Region-Specific Effects of Sex, Early Experience and Age." *Brain Research* 438: 216–24.

Blakemore, C. 1977. *Mechanics of the Mind*. London: Cambridge University Press.

Bleier, R. 1984. *Science and Gender*. New York: Pergamon.

Bloom, L. 1972. *The Social Psychology of Race Relations*. London: Allen and Unwin.

Bradshaw, J.L. 1989. *Hemispheric Specialization and Psychological Function*. New York: John Wiley and Sons.

Bradshaw, J.L., and N.C. Nettleton. 1983. *Human Cerebral Asymmetry*. New York: Prentice-Hall.

Broca, P. 1862. "Sur les proportions relatives du bras, de l'avant bras et de la clavicule chez les nègres et les européens." *Bulletin Société d'Anthropologie Paris 3*, no. 2: 1–13.

—— 1873. "Sur les crânes de la caverne de I'Homme-Mort (Lozère). *Revue d'Anthropologie* 2: 1–53.

Buffery, A.W.H. 1981. "Male and Female Brain Structure." In *Australian Women: Feminist Perspectives*, ed. N. Grieve and P. Grimshaw, 58–66. Melbourne: Oxford University Press.

Carothers, J.C. 1950. "Frontal Lobe Function in the African." *British Journal of Mental Science*.

Chorover, S.L. 1979. *From Genesis to Genocide: The Meaning of Human Nature and the Power of Behavior Control*. Cambridge, Mass.: MIT Press.

Corballis, M.C. 1983. *Human Laterality*. New York: Academic Press.

Darwin, C. 1871. *The Descent of Man*. London: John Murray.

Dawkins, R. 1976. *The Selfish Gene*. Oxford: Oxford University Press.

de Lacoste, M.-C., R.L. Holloway, and D.J. Woodward. 1986. "Sex Difference in the Fetal Human Corpus Callosum." *Human Neurobiology* 5: 93–96,

de Lacoste-Utamsing, C., and R.L. Holloway. 1982. "Sexual Dimorphism in the Human Corpus Callosum." *Science* 216: 1431–32.

de Lepervanche, M.M. 1984. "The 'Naturalness' of Inequality." In *Ethnicity, Class and Gender in Australia*, G. Bottomley and M.M. de Lepervanche, 49–71. Sydney: Allen and Unwin.

Denenberg, V.H. 1981. "Hemispheric Laterality in Animals and the Effects of Early Experience." *Behavioral Brain Sciences* 4: 1–49.

Denenberg, V.H., and G.D. Rosen. 1983. "Interhemispheric Coupling Coefficients: Sex Differences in Brain Neurochemistry." *American Physiological Society* R151–R153.

Denenberg, V.H., A.S. Berrebi, and R.H. Fitch. 1989. "A Factor Analysis of the Rat's Corpus Callosum." *Brain Research* 497: 271–79.

Diamond, M.C. 1984. "Age, Sex, and Environmental Influences." In *Cerebral Dominance: The Biological Foundations*, ed. N. Geschwind and A.M. Galaburda, 134–46. Cambridge, Mass.: Harvard University Press.

Dickinson, R.L. 1948. "The Gynecology of Homosexuality." In *Sex Variants: A Study of Homosexual Patterns*, ed. G.W. Henry, 1069–129. New York and London: Paul B. Hoeber.

Dörner, G. 1976. "Hormone-Dependent Brain Development and Behaviour." In *Hormones and Behaviour in Higher Vertebrates*, ed. J. Baltharzart, E. Prove, and R. Gilles. Berlin: Springer.

—— 1979. "Hormones and Sexual Differentiation of the Brain." *Sex, Hormones and Behaviour* (Ciba Foundation Symposium) 62: 81–112.

Durden-Smith, J., and D. de Simone 1983. *Sex and the Brain*. London: Pan Books.

Fitch, R.H., P.E. Cowell, L.M. Schrott, and V.H. Denenberg. 1991. "Corpus Callosum: Ovarian Hormones and Feminization." *Brain Research* 542: 313–17.

Gazzaniga, M.S., and J.E. LeDoux. 1978. *The Integrated Mind*. New York: Plenum Press.

Geschwind, N., and A.M. Galaburda. 1985. "Cerebral Lateralization: Biological Mechanisms, Associations, and Pathology," *Archives of Neurology* 42, 428–653.

—— 1987. *Cerebral Lateralization: Biological Mechanisms, Associations, and Pathology*. Cambridge, Mass.: MIT Press.

Gobineau, J.A. 1855. Essai sur l'inegalité des races humaines. Trans. and ed. A. Collins. 1915. *The Inequality of Human Races*. New York: Putnam.

Gould, S.J. 1981. *The Mismeasure of Man*. New York and London: W.W. Norton.

Hambley, J. 1973. "Diversity: A Developmental Perspective." In *Race, Culture and Intelligence*, ed. K. Richardson and D. Spears, 114–27. Harmondsworth: Penguin.

Henry, G.W. 1948. *Sex Variants: A Study of Homosexual Patterns*. New York and London: Paul B. Hoeber.

Holloway, R.L., and M.C. de Lacoste. 1986. "Sexual Dimorphism in the Human Corpus Callosum: An Extension and Replication Study." *Human Neurobiology* 5: 87–91.

Hunter, A.E., ed. 1991. *Genes and Gender VI: On Peace, War and Gender*. New York: Feminist Press.

Kaplan, G. 1992. *Contemporary Western European Feminism*. Sydney and London: Allen and Unwin. New York: New York University Press.

Kaplan, G., and L.J. Rogers. 1987. "Biology and the Oppression of Women." In *Feminist Knowledge as Critique*, ed. Women's Studies Collective, 175–95. Geelong and Victoria: Deakin University Press.

Kinsey, A.C., W.B. Pomeroy, and C.E. Martin. 1948. *Sexual Behavior in the Human Male*. Philadelphia and London: W.B. Saunders.

Money, J. 1974. "Prenatal Hormones and Post-Natal Socialisation in Gender Identity Differentiation." In *Nebraska Symposium on Motivation*, ed. J.K. Cole and R. Dienstbeir. Lincoln: University of Nebraska Press.

—— 1976. "Two Names, Two Wardrobes, Two Personalities." *Journal of Homosexuality* 1: 65–70.

Money, J., and A.A. Ehrhardt. 1972. *Man and Woman: Boy and Girl*. Baltimore: Johns Hopkins University Press.

Money, J., and P. Tucker. 1975. *Sexual Signatures*. Boston and Toronto: Little, Brown.

Mosse, C.L. 1978. *Towards the Final Solution: A History of European Racism*. New York: Howard Fertig.

Obler, L.K., and L.M. Novoa. 1988. "Gender Similarities and Differences in Brain Lateralization." In *Genes and Gender V. Women at Work*, ed. G.M. Vroman, D. Burnham, S.G. Gordon, 37–51. New York: Gordian Press.

Pruner, F. 1866. Article in *Transactions of the Ethnological Society* 4: 13–33. Quoted by E. Fee. 1979. "Nineteenth Century Craniology: The Study of the Female Skull." *Bulletin of the History of Medicine* 53: 415–33.

Radcliffe-Browne, A.R. 1952. *Structure and Function in Primitive Society*. London: Cohen and West.

Richards, E. 1983. "Darwin and the Descent of Woman." In *The Wider Domain of Evolutionary Thought*, ed. D. Olroyd and I. Langham. Boston and London: Reidl.

Richardson, I., and J. Lambert. 1986. *The Sociology of Race*. Ormskirk, Lancashire: Causeway Press.

Ridley, M., and R. Dawkins. 1981. "The Natural Selection of Altruism." In *Altruism and Helping Behavior: Social, Personality and Developmental Perspectives*, ed. J. Philippe Rushton, 19–39. New Jersey: Lawrence Erlbaum Associates.

Rogers, L.J. 1981. "Biology: Gender Differentiation and Sexual Variation." In *Australian Women: Feminist Perspectives*, ed. N. Grieve and P. Grimshaw, 44–57. Melbourne: Oxford University Press.

—— 1986. "Lateralization of Learning in Chicks." *Advances in the Study of Behavior* 16: 147–89.

Rogers, L.J., and J. Walsh. 1982. "Short-comings of the Psychomedical Research into Sex Differences in Behaviour: Social and Political Implications." *Sex Roles* 8: 269–81.

Rose, S. 1988. "Reflections on Reductionism." *Trends in Biological Sciences* 13 (May): 160–62.

Rosoff, B. 1991. "Genes, Hormones and War." In *On Peace, War and Gender*, ed. A.E. Hunter, 39–49. New York: Feminist Press.

Schwartz, J.H. 1987. *The Red Ape, Orangutans and Human Origins*. Boston: Houghton Mifflin.

Selnes, O.A. 1974. "The Corpus Callosum: Some Anatomical and Functional Considerations, with Special Reference to Language." *Brain and Language* 1: 111–39.

Star, S.L. 1979. "The Politics of Left and Right." In *Women Look at Biology Looking at Women*, ed. R. Hubbard, M.S. Henifin, and B. Fried, 61–74. Cambridge, Mass.: Schenkman.

Stein, G.J. 1988. "Biological Science and the Roots of Nazism." *American Scientist* (January–February): 50–57.

Tobach, E. 1972. "The Meaning of the Cryptanthroparion." In *Genetics, Environment and Behavior*, ed. L. Ehrman, G. Omenn, and E. Caspari, 219–39. New York: Academic Press.

Watson, L. 1979. "Homosexuals." In *Mental Disorder or Madness?* ed. E.M. Bates and P.R. Wilson, 134–61. Brisbane: Queensland University Press.

Weiner, J.S. 1954. "Nose Shape and Climate." Reprinted in *Race and Social Difference*, ed. R. Baxter and B. Sanson, 44–47, 1972. Harmondsworth: Penguin.

West, D.J. 1977. *Homosexuality Re-Examined*. London: Duckworth.

Whitlock, F.A. 1979. "Psychosurgery." In *Mental Disorder or Madness?* ed. E.M. Bates and P.R. Wilson, 181–201. Brisbane: Queensland University Press.

Wilson, E.O. 1975. *Sociobiology: A New Synthesis*. Cambridge, Mass.: Harvard University Press.

Worsley, P. 1972. "Colonialism and Categories." In *Race and Social Difference*, ed. P. Baxter and B. Sanson, 98–101. Harmondsworth: Penguin.

Chapter 26

Anne Fausto-Sterling

A note about language use: Writing about nineteenth-century studies of race presents the modern writer with a problem: how to be faithful to the language usage of earlier periods without offending contemporary sensibilities. In this chapter I have chosen to capitalize words designating a race or a people. At the same time, I will use the appellations of the period about which I write. Hence I will render the French word *Negre* as Negro. Some nineteenth-century words, especially "Hottentot," "primitive," and "savage," contain meanings that we know today as deeply racist. I will use these words without quotation marks when it seems obvious that they refer to nineteenth- rather than twentieth-century usage.

A note about illustrations: This chapter is unillustrated for a reason. The obvious illustrations might include drawings and political cartoons of Sarah Bartmann or illustrations of her genitalia. Including such visual material would continue to state the question as a matter of science and to focus us visually on Bartmann as a deviant. Who could avoid looking to see if she really was different? I would have had to counter such illustrations with an additional discussion of the social construction of visual imagery. But this essay is meant to focus on the scientists who used Bartmann. Thus an appropriate illustration might be the architectural layout of the French Museum, where Cuvier worked, or something of that order. Failing to have in hand a drawing that keeps us focused on the construction and constructors of scientific knowledge, I felt it would be better to have none at all. Readers who are dying to see an image of Bartmann may, of course, return to any of the original sources cited.

Introduction

In 1816 Saartje Bartman, a South African woman whose original name is unknown and whose Dutch name had been anglicized to Sarah Bartmann, died in Paris. Depending upon the account, her death was caused by smallpox, pleurisy, or alcohol poisoning (Cuvier 1817; Lindfors 1983; Gray 1979). Georges Cuvier (1769–1832), one of the "fathers" of modern biology, claimed her body in the interests of science, offering a detailed account of its examination to the members of the French Museum of Natural History. Although now removed, as recently as the early 1930s a cast of her body along with her actual skeleton could be found on display in case #33 in the Musée de l'Homme in Paris; her preserved brain and a wax mold of her genitalia are stored in one of the museum's back rooms (Lindfors 1983; Gould 1985; Kirby 1953).[1]

During the last several years Bartmann's story has been retold by a number of writers (Altick 1978; Edwards and Walvin 1983; Gilman 1985).[2] These new accounts are significant. Just as during the nineteenth century she became a vehicle for the redefinition of our concepts of race, gender, and sexuality, her present recasting occurs in an era in which the bonds of empire have broken apart, and the fabric of the cultural systems of the nations of the North Atlantic has come under critical scrutiny. In this article I once again tell the tale, focusing not on Bartmann but on the scientists who so relentlessly probed her body. During the period 1814–70 there were at least seven scientific descriptions of the bodies of women of color done in the tradition of classical comparative anatomy. What was the importance of these dissections to the scientists who did them and the society that supported them? What social, cultural, and personal work did these scientific forays accomplish, and how did they accomplish it? Why did the anatomical descriptions of women of color seem to be of such importance to biologists of the nineteenth century?

The colonial expansions of the eighteenth and nineteenth centuries shaped European science; Cuvier's dissection of Bartmann was a natural extension of that shaping. (By "natural" I mean that it seemed unexceptional to the scientists of that era; it appeared to be not merely *good* science; it was forward-looking.) But a close reading of the original scientific publications reveals the insecurity and angst about race and gender experienced by individual researchers and the European culture at large. These articles show how the French scientific elite of the early nineteenth century tried to lay their own fears to rest. That they did so at the expense of so many others is no small matter.

Constructing the Hottentot before 1800

Several of the African women who ended up on the comparative anatomists' dissecting tables were called Hottentots or, sometimes, Bushwomen. Yet the peoples whom the early Dutch explorers named Hottentot had been extinct as a coherent cultural group since the late 1600s (Elphick 1977). Initially I thought written and visual descriptions would help me figure out these women's "true" race; I quickly discovered, however, that even the depictions of something so seemingly objective as skin color varied so widely that I now believe that questions of racial origin are like will-o'-the-wisps. Human racial difference, while in some sense obvious and therefore "real," is in another sense pure fabrication, a story written about the social relations of a particular historical time and then mapped onto available bodies.

As early as the sixteenth century, European travelers circling the world reported on the peoples they encountered. The earliest European engravings of nonwhites presented idyllic scenes. A depiction by Theodor de Bry from 1590, for example, shows Adam and Eve in the garden, with Native Americans farming peacefully in the background. The de Bry family images of the New World, however, transformed with time into savage and monstrous ones containing scenes of cannibalism and other horrors (Bucher 1981). Similarly, a representation of the Hottentots from 1595 (Raven-Hart 1967) shows two classically Greek-looking men standing in the foreground, with animals and a pastoral scene behind. A representation from 1627, however, tells a

The Adamic visions of newly discovered lands brought with them a darker side. Amerigo Vespucci, whose feminized first name became that of the New World, wrote that the women went about "naked and libidinous; yet they have bodies which are tolerably beautiful" (Tiffany and Adams 1985: 64). Vespucci's innocents lived to be 150 years old, and giving birth caused them no inconvenience. Despite being so at one with nature, Vespucci found Native American women immoral. They had special knowledge of how to enlarge their lovers' sex organs, induce miscarriages, and control their own fertility (Tiffany and Adams 1985). The early explorers linked the metaphor of the innocent virgin (both the women and the virgin land) with that of the wildly libidinous female. As one recent commentator puts it:

> Colonial discourse oscillates between these two master tropes, alternately positing the colonized 'other' as blissfully ignorant, pure and welcoming as well as an uncontrollable, savage, wild native whose chaotic, hysterical presence requires the imposition of the law, i.e., suppression of resistance.
>
> (Shohat 1991: 55)

From the start of the scientific revolution, scientists viewed the earth or nature as female, a territory to be explored, exploited, and controlled (Merchant 1980). Newly discovered lands were personified as female, and it seems unsurprising that the women of these nations became the locus of scientific inquiry. Identifying foreign lands as female helped to naturalize their rape and exploitation, but the appearance on the scene of "wild women" raised troubling questions about the status of European women; hence, it also became important to differentiate the "savage" land/woman from the civilized female of Europe. The Hottentot in particular fascinated and preoccupied the nineteenth-century scientist/explorer – the comparative anatomist who explored the body as well as the earth. But just who were the Hottentots?

In 1652 the Dutch established a refreshment station at the Cape of Good Hope, which not long after became a colonial settlement. The people whom they first and most frequently encountered there were pastoral nomads, short of stature, with light brown skin, and speaking a language with unusual clicks. The Dutch called these people Hottentots, although in the indigenous language they were called Khoikhoi, which means "men of men." Within sixty years after the Dutch settlement, the Khoikhoi, as an organized, independent culture, were extinct, ravaged by smallpox and the encroachment of the Dutch. Individual descendants of the Khoikhoi continued to exist, and European references to Hottentots may have referred to such people. Nevertheless, nineteenth-century European scientists wrote about Hottentots, even though the racial/cultural group that late-twentieth-century anthropologists believe to merit that name had been extinct for at least three-quarters of a century. Furthermore, in the eighteenth and nineteenth centuries Europeans often used the word "Hottentot" interchangeably with the word "Bushman."[3] The Bushmen, or Khoisan, or hunter-gatherer Khoi, were (and are) a physically similar but culturally distinct people who lived contiguously with the Khoikhoi (Elphick 1977; Guenther 1980). They speak a linguistically related language and have been the object/subject of a long tradition of cultural readings by Euro-Americans (Haraway 1989; Lewin 1988; Lee 1992). In this chapter I look at studies with both the word "Bushman/ Bushwoman" and the word "Hottentot" in the titles. Cuvier, for example, argued vehemently that Sarah Bartmann was a Bushwoman and not a Hottentot. The importance of the distinction in his mind will become apparent as the story unfolds.

Constructing the Hottentot in the French Museum of Natural History

The encounters between women from southern Africa and the great men of European science began in the second decade of the nineteenth century when Henri de Blainville (1777–1850) and Georges Cuvier met Bartmann and described her for scientific circles, both when she was alive and after her death (Cuvier 1817; de Blainville 1816). We know a lot about these men who were so needful of exploring non-European bodies. Cuvier, a French Protestant, weathered the French Revolution in the countryside. He came to Paris in 1795 and quickly became the chair of anatomy of animals at the Museum of Natural History (Appel 1987; Flourens 1845). Cuvier's meteoric rise gave him considerable control over the future of French zoology. In short order he became secretary of the Académie des Sciences, an organization whose weekly meetings attracted the best scientists of the city, professor at the museum and the College de France and member of the Council of the University. Henri de Blainville started out under Cuvier's patronage. He completed medical school in 1808 and became an adjunct professor at the Faculté des Sciences, while also teaching some of Cuvier's courses at the museum. But by 1816, the year his publication on Sarah Bartmann appeared, he had broken with Cuvier. After obtaining a new patron he managed, in 1825, to enter the Académie and eventually succeeded Cuvier in 1832, as chair of comparative anatomy.

Cuvier and de Blainville worked at the Musée d'Histoire Naturelle, founded in 1793 by the Revolutionary Convention. It contained ever-growing collections and with its "magnificent facilities for research became the world center for the study of the life sciences" (Appel 1987: 11). Work done in France from 1783–1830 established the study of comparative anatomy, paleontology, morphology, and what many see as the structure of modern zoological taxonomy. Cuvier and de Blainville used the museum's extraordinary collections to write their key works. Here we see one of the direct links to the earlier periods of exploration. During prior centuries private collectors of great wealth amassed large cabinets filled with curiosities, cultural artifacts and strange animals and plants. It was the collections that enabled the eighteenth-century classifiers to begin their work.

Bruno Latour identifies this process of collection as a move that simultaneously established the power of Western science and domesticated the "savage by making the wilderness known in advance, predictable" (Latour 1987: 218). He connects scientific [illegible] (Latour 1987: 225). Cuvier literally lived, "for nearly forty years, surrounded by the objects which engrossed so great a portion of his thoughts" (James 1830: 9). His house in the museum grounds connected directly to the anatomy museum and contained a suite of rooms, each of which held material on a particular subject. As he worked, he moved (along with his stove) from one room to the next, gathering his comparative information, transported from around the world to the comfort of his own home (Coleman 1964).

As centers of science acquired collections, however, they faced the prospect of becoming overwhelmed by the sheer volume of things collected. In order to manage the flood of information, scientists had to distill or summarize it. Cuvier, de Blainville, and others approached the inundation by developing coherent systems of animal classification. Thus the project of classification comprised one aspect of domesticating distant lands. The project extended from the most primitive and strange of animals and plants to the most complex and familiar. The history of classification must be read in this fashion; the attention paid by famous scientists to human anatomy cannot be painted on a separate canvas as if it were an odd or aberrant happening within the otherwise pure and noble history of biology.

During the French Revolution the cabinets of the wealthy who fled the conflict, as well as those from territories that France invaded, became part of the museum's collections. The cabinet of the Stadholder of Holland, for example, provided material for several of Cuvier's early papers. Appel describes the wealth of collected material:

> . . . in 1822, the Cabinet contained 1800 mammals belonging to over 500 species, 1800 reptiles belonging to over 700 species, 5000 fishes from over 2000 species, 20,000 arthropods . . . and an unspecified number of molluscs. . . .
>
> (Appel 1987: 35–36)

Cuvier's own comparative anatomy cabinet contained still more. He championed the idea that, in order to classify the animals, one must move beyond their mere surface similarities. Instead, one must gather facts and measurements from all of the internal parts. Without such comparative information, he believed, accurate classification of the animals became impossible. By 1822, among the 11,486 preparations in Cuvier's possession were a large number of human skeletons and skulls of different ages and races.

The human material did not innocently fall his way. In fact he had complained unbelievingly "that there is not yet, in any work, a detailed comparison of the skeletons of a Negro and a white" (Stocking 1982: 29). Wishing to bring the science of anatomy out of the realm of travelers' descriptions, Cuvier offered explicit instructions on how to procure human skeletons. He believed skulls to be the most important evidence, and he urged travelers to nab bodies whenever they observed a battle involving "savages." They must then "boil the bones in a solution of soda or caustic potash and rid them of their flesh in a matter of several hours" (Stocking 1982: 30). He also suggested methods of preserving skulls with flesh still intact, so that one could examine their facial forms.

As we shall see, Egyptian mummies – both animal and human – supply another significant source that Cuvier used to develop and defend his theories of animal classification. These he obtained from the travels of his mentor-turned-colleague, and eventual archenemy, Étienne Geoffroy Saint-Hilaire. Geoffroy Saint-Hilaire spent several years in Egypt as part of the young general Napoleon Bonaparte's expedition. Cuvier declined the opportunity, writing that the real science could be done most efficiently by staying at home in the museum, where he had a worldwide collection of research objects at his fingertips (Outram 1984).[4] In 1798 Bonaparte took with him the Commission of Science and the Arts, which included many famous French intellectuals. During his years in Egypt, Geoffroy Saint-Hilaire collected large numbers of animals and, of particular importance to this story, several human and animal mummies. By 1800, British armies had defeated the French in Egypt; the capitulating agreement stipulated that the British were to receive all of the notes and collections obtained by the French savants while in Egypt. But in a heroic moment, Geoffroy Saint-Hilaire refused. In the end he kept everything but the Rosetta stone, which now resides in the British Museum (Appel 1987). Once again we see how the fortunes of modern European science intertwined with the vicissitudes of colonial expansion.

Cuvier and de Blainville used the technologies of dissection and comparative anatomy to create classifications. These reflected both their scientific and their religious accounts of the world, and it is from and through these that the views on race, gender, and nation emerge. In the eighteenth century the idea of biologically differing races remained undeveloped. When Linnaeus listed varieties of men in his *Systema Naturae* (1758), he emphasized that the differences between them appeared because of environment. There were, of course, crosscurrents. Proponents of the Great Chain of Being placed Hottentots and Negroes on a continuum linking orangutans and humans. Nevertheless, "eighteenth-century writers did not conceptualize human diversity in rigidly hereditarian or strictly physical terms. . . . " (Stocking 1982: 18).

Cuvier divided the animal world into four branches: the vertebrates, the articulates, the molluscs, and the radiates. He used the structure of the nervous system to assign animals to one of these four categories. As one of his successors and hagiographers wrote, "the nervous system is in effect the entire animal, and all the other systems are only there to serve and maintain it. It is the unity and the multiplicity of forms of the nervous system which defines the unity and multiplicity of the animal kingdom" (Flourens 1845: 98).[5] Cuvier expected to find similarities in structure within each branch of the animal world. He insisted, however, that the four branches themselves existed independently of one another. Despite similarities between animals within each of his branches, he believed that God had created each individual species (which he defined as animals that could have fertile matings). As tempting as the interrelatedness was to many of his contemporaries, Cuvier did not believe that one organism evolved into another. There were no missing links, only gaps put there purposely by the Creator. "What law is there," he asked, "which would force the Creator to form unnecessarily useless organisms simply in order to fill gaps in a scale?" (Appel 1987: 137).[6]

structures and developed those of other animals by comparison (Coleman 1964). In this sense, his entire zoological system was homocentric.

Cuvier's beliefs about human difference mirror the transition from an eighteenth-century emphasis on differences in levels of "civilization" to the nineteenth-century construction of race. His work on Sarah Bartmann embodies the contradictions such a transition inevitably brings. In 1790, for example, he scolded a friend for believing that Negroes and orangutans could have fertile matings and for thinking that Negroes' mental abilities could be explained by some alleged peculiarity in brain structure (Stocking 1982). By 1817, however, in his work on Sarah Bartmann, he brandished the skull of an Egyptian mummy, exclaiming that its structure proved that Egyptian civilization had been created by whites from whom present-day Europeans had descended (Cuvier 1817).[7]

Cuvier believed in a theory that all humans came from a single creation, a view we today call monogeny. He delineated three races: Caucasians, Ethiopians (Negroes), and Mongolians. Despite uniting the three races under the banner of humanity (because they could interbreed), he found them to contain distinct physical differences, especially in the overall structure and shape of the head. One could not miss the invisible capabilities he read from the facial structures:

> It is not for nothing that the Caucasian race had gained dominion over the world and made the most rapid progress in the sciences while the Negroes are still sunken in slavery and the pleasures of the senses and the Chinese [lost] in the [obscurities] of a monosyllabic and hieroglyphic language. The shape of their head relates them somewhat more than us to the animals.
>
> (Coleman 1964: 66)

Cuvier, it is worth noting, was opposed to slavery. His was "a beneficent but haughty paternalism . . . " (Coleman 1964: 167). In practice, however, his brother Fredéric, writing "under the authority of the administration of the Museum" (i.e., brother Georges), would include Georges Cuvier's description of Sarah Bartmann as the only example of the human species listed in his *Natural History of the Mammals* (Geoffroy

Saint-Hilaire and Cuvier 1824: title page). Accompanying the article were two dramatic illustrations similar in size, style, and presentation to those offered for each of the forty-one species of monkeys and numerous other animals described in detail. The Hottentots' inclusion as the only humans in a book otherwise devoted to mammalian diversity suggests quite clearly Cuvier's ambivalence about monogeny and the separate creation of each species. Clearly, his religious belief system conflicted with his role in supporting European domination of more distant lands. Perhaps this internal conflict generated some of the urgency he felt about performing human dissections.

Other scientists of this period also linked human females with apes. While they differentiated white males from higher primates, using characteristics such as language, reason, and high culture, scholars used various forms of sexual anatomy – breasts, the presence of a hymen, the structure of the vaginal canal, and the placement of the urethral opening – to distinguish females from animals. Naturalists wrote that the breasts of female apes were flabby and pendulous – like those in the travelers' accounts of Hottentots (Schiebinger 1993). Cuvier's description of Sarah Bartmann repeats such "observations." The Hottentot worked as a double trope. As a woman of color, she served as a primitive primate: she was both a female and a racial link to nature – two for the price of one.

Although Cuvier believed that the human races had probably developed separately for several thousand years, there were others, who we today call polygenists, who argued that the races were actually separate species (Stepan 1982). Presentations such as those in the *Natural History of the Mammals* provided fuel for the fire of polygeny. Cuvier's system of zoological classification, his focus on the nervous system, and his idea that species were created separately laid the foundations for the nineteenth-century concepts of race (Stocking 1982; Stepan 1982).

In search of Sarah Bartmann

In contrast to what we know about her examiners, little about Bartmann is certain. What we do know comes from reading beneath the surface of newspaper reports, court proceedings, and scientific articles. We have nothing directly from her own hand. A historical record that has preserved a wealth of traces of the history of European men of science has left us only glimpses of the subjects they described. Hence, from the very outset, our knowledge of Sarah Bartmann is a construction, an effort to read between the lines of historical markings written from the viewpoint of a dominant culture. Even the most elementary information seems difficult to obtain. Cuvier wrote that she was twenty-six when they met and twenty-eight when she died, yet the inscription in the museum case that holds her body says that she was thirty-eight (Kirby 1949). She is said to have had two children by an African man, but de Blainville (1816) says that she had one child. One source says that the single child was dead by the time Bartmann arrived in Europe. According to some accounts, she was the daughter of a drover who had been killed by Bushmen. According to others, she was herself a Bushwoman (Altick 1978; Cuvier 1817). One London newspaper referred to her as "a Hottentot of a mixed race," while a twentieth-century writer wrote that he was "inclined to the view that she was a Bushwoman who possessed a certain proportion of alien blood" (Kirby 1949: 61).

Some sources state that Bartmann was taken in as a servant girl by a Boer family named Cezar. In 1810 Peter Cezar arranged to bring her to London, where he put her on exhibition in the Egyptian Hall of Piccadilly Circus.[8] She appeared on a platform raised two feet off the ground. A "keeper" ordered her to walk, sit, and stand, and when she sometimes refused to obey him, he threatened her. The whole "performance" so horrified some that abolitionists brought Cezar to court, charging that he held her in involuntary servitude. During the court hearing on November 24, 1810, the following [illegible] did not issue a writ of habeas corpus because – according to secondhand accounts – Bartmann testified in Dutch that she was not sexually abused, that she came to London of her own free will in order to earn money, and that she liked London and even had two "black boys" to serve her, but that she would like some warmer clothes. Her exhibition continued and a year later, on December 7, 1811, she was baptized in Manchester, "Sarah Bartmann a female Hottentot of the Cape of Good Hope born on the Borders of Caffraria" (Kirby 1953: 61). At some point prior to 1814, she ended up in Paris, and in March of 1815 a panel of zoologists and physiologists examined her for three days in the Jardin du Roi. During this time an artist painted the nude that appears in Geoffroy Saint-Hilaire and Cuvier's tome (1824). In December of 1815 she died in Paris, apparently of smallpox, but helped along by a misdiagnosis of pleurisy and, according to Cuvier, by her own indulgence in strong drink.

Why was Bartmann's exhibition so popular? Prior to the nineteenth century there was a small population of people of color living in Great Britain. They included slaves, escaped slaves, and the children of freedmen sent to England for an education. Strikingly, the vast majority of the nonwhite population in England was male. Thus, even though people of color lived in England in 1800, a nonwhite female was an unusual sight (Walvin 1973). This, however, is an insufficient explanation. We must also place Bartmann's experiences in at least two other contexts: the London entertainment scene and the evolving belief systems about sex, gender, and sexuality.

The shows of London and those that traveled about the countryside were popular forms of amusement. They displayed talking pigs, animal monsters, and human oddities – the Fattest Man on Earth, the Living Skeleton, fire-eaters, midgets, and giants. Bartmann's exhibition exemplifies an early version of ethnographic displays that became more complex during the nineteenth century. After her show closed, "the Venus of South America" appeared next. Tono Maria, a Botocudo Indian from Brazil, publicly displayed the scars (104 to be exact) she bore as punishment for adulterous acts. In time, the shows became more and more elaborate. In 1822 an entire grouping of Laplanders shown in the Egyptian Hall drew 58,000 visitors over a period of a few months. Then followed Eskimos and, subsequently, a "family grouping" of Zulus, all supposedly providing live demonstrations of their "native" behaviors. Such displays[9] may be seen as a living, nineteenth-century version of the early-twentieth-century museum diorama, the sort that riveted my attention in the American Museum of Natural History when I was a child. The dioramas, while supposedly providing scientifically accurate presentations of peoples of the world, instead offer a Euro-American vision of gender arrangements and the primitive that serves to set the supposedly "civilized" viewer apart, while at the same time offering the reassurance that women have always cooked and served, and men have always hunted (Haraway 1989).

Sometimes the shows of exotic people of color involved complete fabrication. A Zulu warrior might really be a black citizen of London, hired to play the part. One of the best documented examples of such "creativity" was the performer "Zip the What-is-it," hired and shown by B.T. Barnum. In one handbill, Zip was described as having been "captured by a party of adventurers while they were in search of the Gorilla. While exploring the river Gambia . . . they fell in with a race of beings never before discovered . . . in a PERFECTLY NUDE STATE, roving among the trees . . . in a manner common to the Monkey and the Orang Outang" (Lindfors 1983: 96). As it turns out, Zip was really William Henry Johnson, an African American from Bridgeport, Connecticut. He made what he found to be good money, and in exchange kept mum about his identity. Interviewed in 1926, at the age of 64, while still employed at Coney Island, he is reported to have said, "Well, we fooled 'em a long time, didn't we?" (Lindfors 1983: 98).

The London (and in fact European) show scene during the nineteenth century became a vehicle for creating visions of the nonwhite world.[10] As the century progressed, these visions "grew less representative of the African peoples they . . . were meant to portray. . . . Black Africa was presented as an exotic realm beyond the looking glass, a fantasy world populated by grotesque monsters – fat-arsed females, bloodthirsty warriors, pre-verbal pinheads, midgets and geeks" (Lindfors 1983: 100). From this vision Britain's "civilizing colonial mission" drew great strength. And it is also from this vision, this reflection of the other, that Europe's self-image derived; the presentation of the exotic requires a definition of the normal. It is this borderline between normal and abnormal that Bartmann's presentation helped to define for the Euro-American woman.

Bartmann's display linked the notion of the wild or savage female with one of dangerous or uncontrollable sexuality. At the "performance's" opening, she appeared caged, rocking back and forth to emphasize her supposedly wild and potentially dangerous nature. *The London Times* reported, "She is dressed in a colour as nearly resembling her skin as possible. The dress is contrived to exhibit the entire frame of her body, and spectators are even invited to examine the peculiarities of her form" (Kirby 1949: 58). One eyewitness recounted with horror the poking and pushing Bartmann endured, as people tried to see for themselves whether her buttocks were the real thing. Prurient interest in Bartmann became explicit in the rude street ballads and equally prurient cartoons that focused on her steatopygous backside.[11]

According to the *Oxford English Dictionary*, the term *steatopygia* (from the roots for fat and buttocks) was used as early as 1822 in a traveler's account of South Africa, but the observer said the "condition" was not characteristic of all Hottentots nor was it, for that matter, characteristic of any particular people. Later in the century, what had been essentially a curiosity found its way into medical textbooks as an abnormality. According to Gilman, by the middle of the nineteenth century the buttocks had become a clear symbol of female sexuality; and the intense interest in the backside a displacement for fascination with the genitalia. Gilman concludes, "Female sexuality is linked to the image of the buttocks, and the quintessential buttocks are those of the Hottentot" (Gilman 1985: 210).[12] Female sexuality may not have been the only thing at stake in all of the focus on Bartmann's backside. In this same historical period, a new sexual discourse on sodomy also developed. Male prostitutes, often dressed as women, walked the streets of London (Trumbach 1991), and certainly at a later date the enlarged buttocks became associated with female prostitution (Gilman 1985). Until more historical work is done, possible relationships between cultural constructions of the [illegible] with him, but unable to attract his attention, disguises herself as the Hottentot Venus, with whom he falls in love, making the appropriate mating, even after the fraud is revealed. (The full story has many more twists and turns, but this is the "Cliff Notes plot" (Lindfors 1983: 100).)

Of all the retellings of Bartmann's story, only Gould's attempts to give some insight into Bartmann's own feelings. We can never see her except through the eyes of the white men who described her. From them we can glean the following: first, for all her "savageness," she spoke English, Dutch, and a little French. Cuvier found her to have a lively, intelligent mind, an excellent memory, and a good ear for music. The question of her own complicity in and resistance to her exploitation is a very modern one. The evidence is scant. During her "performances" "she frequently heaved deep sighs; seemed anxious and uneasy; grew sullen, when she was ordered to play on some rude instrument of music" (Altick 1978: 270). Writing in the third person, de Blainville, who examined her in the Jardin du Roi, reported the following:

> Sarah appears good, sweet and timid, very easy to manage when one pleases her, cantankerous and stubborn in the contrary case. She appears to have a sense of modesty or at least we had a very difficult time convincing her to allow herself to be seen nude, and she scarcely wished to remove for even a moment the handkerchief with which she hid her organs of generation. . . . [H]er moods were very changeable; when one believed her to be tranquil and well-occupied with something, suddenly a desire to do something else would be born in her. Without being angry, she would easily strike someone. . . . [S]he took a dislike to M. de Blainville, probably because he came too near to her, and pestered her in order to obtain material for his description; although she loved money, she refused what he offered her in an effort to make her more docile. . . . She appeared to love to sleep: she preferred meat, especially chicken and rabbit, loved (alcoholic) spirits even more and didn't smoke, but chewed tobacco.
>
> (de Blainville 1816: 189)

In this passage, de Blainville expressed the same conflicts evinced two centuries earlier by Vespucci. He found her to be modest, good, sweet, and timid (like any modern, "civilized" Frenchwoman), but he could not reconcile this observation with what seemed to him to be the remnants of some irrational wildness (including habits such as chewing tobacco), which were out of line for any female he would wish to call civilized.

It is also worth comparing de Blainville's language to that used by Geoffroy Saint-Hilaire and F. Cuvier in the *Natural History of the Mammals*. In the section describing *Cynocephalus* monkeys (which follows immediately on the heels of Sarah Bartmann's description), they write that "one can see them pass in an instant from affection to hostility, from anger to love, from indifference to rage, without any apparent cause for their sudden changes" (Geoffroy Saint-Hilaire and Cuvier 1824: 2). They write further that the monkeys are "very lascivious, always disposed to couple, and very different from other animals, the females receive the males even after conception" (Geoffroy Saint-Hilaire and Cuvier 1824: 3). Clearly, de Blainville's language echoes through this passage framing the scientists' concerns about human animality and sexuality.

Constructing the (nonwhite) female

Although a theater attraction and the object of a legal dispute about slavery in England, it was in Paris, before and after her death, that Bartmann entered into the scientific accounting of race and gender. This part of the story takes us from Sarah's meeting with scientists in the Jardin du Roi to her death, preservation, and dissection by Georges Cuvier – and to other scientific and medical dissections of nonwhites in the period from 1815 to, at least, the 1870s.[13]

The printed version of de Blainville's report to the Société Philomatique de Paris (given orally in December of 1815 and appearing in the Society's proceedings in 1816) offers two purposes for the publication. The first is "a detailed comparison of this woman [Sarah Bartmann] with the lowest race of humans, the Negro race, and with the highest race of monkeys, the orangutan," and the second was to provide "the most complete account possible of the anomaly of her reproductive organs" (de Blainville 1816: 183). De Blainville accomplished his first purpose more completely than his second. On more than four occasions in this short paper he differentiates Bartmann from "Negroes," and throughout the article suggests the similarity of various body structures to those of the orangutan.

De Blainville began with an overall description of Sarah Bartmann's body shape and head. He then systematically described her cranium (one paragraph), her ears (two long, detailed paragraphs), her eyes (one paragraph), and other aspects of her face (five paragraphs, including one each devoted to her nose, teeth, and lips). In terms of printed space, her facial structure was the most important aspect. The final segment of his paper includes brief accounts (one paragraph each) of her neck, trunk, and breasts. In addition, he briefly described her legs, arms, and joints, devoting a full paragraph, complete with measurements, to her steatopygous buttocks.

De Blainville's attempts to get a good look at her pudendum, especially at the "hottentot apron," which Cuvier finally succeeded in describing only after her death, were foiled by her modesty (see above). Despite this, de Blainville offers three full paragraphs of description. He verbally sketches the pubis, mentioning its sparse hair covering, and lamenting that, from a frontal view, one cannot see the vaginal labia majora, but that, when she leaned over or when one watched from behind as she walked, one could see hanging appendages that were probably the sought-after elongated labia minora.

De Blainville's ambivalences emerge clearly in the written text. He placed Bartmann among other females by reporting that she menstruated regularly, "like other women," but noted that she wasn't really like white women because her periodic flow "appear[ed] less abundant" (de Blainville 1816: 183). (Debates about menstruation [illegible] original" (de Blainville 1816: 183). Finally, de Blainville suggests "that the extraordinary organization which this woman offers" (de Blainville 1816: 189) is probably natural to her race, rather than being pathological. In support of his contention, he cites travelers who found the same peculiarities – of jaws, buttocks, and labia – among "natives" living in their home environments. Hence, he finishes with the assertion of natural racial difference.

In de Blainville's text different parts of the body carried specific meanings. To compare the Negro and the orangutan, he spent paragraphs on detailed descriptions of the head, face, jaws, and lips. He used these to link Hottentots to orangs, writing that the general form of the head and the details of its various parts, taken together, make clear that Hottentots more closely resemble orangs than they do Negroes. He repeatedly invoked Pieter Camper's facial angle (Gould 1981; Russett 1989), the shape and placement of the jaws, and – in somewhat excruciating detail – the arrangement and structure of the ears. These passages evoke the tradition of physiognomy elaborated by Lavater (1775–78), whose work, widely translated into French and other languages, offered a basis for Gall's phrenology and a method of using the face to read the internal workings of animals. Of humans Lavater wrote:

> The intellectual life . . . would reside in the head and have the eye for its center . . . the forehead, to the eyebrows, [will] be a mirror . . . of the understandings; the nose and cheeks the image of the moral and sensitive life; the mouth and chin the image of the animal life. . . .
>
> (Graham 1979: 48)

When de Blainville and then Cuvier offered detailed comparisons between Sarah Bartmann's cheeks and nose and those of Caucasians, they set forth more than a set of dry descriptions. Her "moral and sensitive life" lay evident upon the surface of her face.[14]

It is to the description of the genitalia that de Blainville turns to place Bartmann among women. Here he balances his belief in the civilizing effects of Europe against a scarcely hidden savage libido. The gender norms of white women appear as a backdrop for the consideration of "savage" sexuality. Although he gave detailed descriptions of most of her exterior, de Blainville did not succeed in fully examining Bartmann's genitalia. Where he failed on the living woman, Cuvier succeeded after her death. Clearly a full account of this "primitive woman's" genitalia was essential to putting her finally in her appropriate place. By exposing them to what passed for scientific scrutiny, Cuvier provided the means to control the previously uncontrollable. Triumphantly, he opened his presentation to the French Academy with the following: "There is nothing more celebrated in natural history than the Hottentot apron, and at the same time there is nothing which has been the object of such great argumentation" (Cuvier 1817: 259). Cuvier set the stage to settle the arguments once and for all.

Twentieth-century scientific reports open with an introduction that uses previously published journal articles to provide background and justification for the report to follow. In Cuvier's piece we see the transition to this modern format from an older, more anecdotal style. Rather than relying on official scientific publications, however, Cuvier relied on travelers' accounts of the apron and the steatopygia. In later works, although these anecdotal, eyewitness testimonials fade from sight, they remain the source for knowledge incorporated into a more "objective" scientific literature. (Sexologists William Masters and Virginia E. Johnson, for example, in their scientifically dispassionate work on the *Human Sexual Response*, include a claim that African women elongate their vaginal labia by physical manipulation; their cited source is a decidedly unscientific (by modern standards) compendium of female physical oddities that dates from the 1930s but draws on nineteenth-century literature of the sort discussed here (Masters and Johnson 1966: 58).)

To set the stage for his revelations about the Hottentot apron, Cuvier first needed to provide a racial identity for his cadaver (which he referred to throughout the article as "my Bushwoman"). Travelers' accounts indicated that Bushmen were a people who lived much deeper in "the interior of lands" than did Hottentots. The apron and enlarged buttocks were peculiarly theirs, disappearing when they interbred with true Hottentots. Cuvier believed that the confusion between Bushmen and Hottentots explained the inconsistent nature of travelers' reports, since some voyagers to the Cape of Good Hope claimed sightings of the Hottentot apron, while others did not. Nevertheless, he had to admit that many people did not believe in the existence of a Bushman nation. Cuvier threw his weight behind what he believed to be the accumulation of evidence: that there existed "beings almost entirely savage who infested certain parts of the Cape colony . . . who built a sort of nest in the tufts of the brush; they originated from a race from the interior of Africa and were equally distinct from the Kaffir and the Hottentot" (Cuvier 1817: 261). Cuvier believed that the Bushman social structure had degenerated, so that eventually "they knew neither government nor proprieties; they scarcely organized themselves into families and then only when passion excited them. . . . They subsisted only by robbery and hunting, lived only in caves and covered their bodies with the skins of animals they had killed" (Cuvier 1817: 261). By naming Bartmann as a Bushwoman, Cuvier created her as the most primitive of all humans – a female exemplar of a degenerate, barely human race. Despite his lack of belief in evolution, he constructed her as the missing link between humans and apes.

To the modern reader, several noteworthy aspects emerge from these introductory passages. First, Cuvier melds the vision of an interior or hidden Africa with the hidden or interior genitalia of the Hottentot Venus. This becomes even clearer in subsequent passages in which, like de Blainville, he complains that when he examined her as a living nude in the Jardin du Roi in 1815 she "carefully hid her apron either between her thighs or more deeply" (Cuvier 1817: 265). Second, he connected a hidden (and hypothetical) people from the deep African interior with an animal-like primitiveness. The passage about making nests from brush tufts evokes monkey and ape behaviors (chimps sleep each night in nests they weave from tree branches). Cuvier's goal in this paper was to render visible the hidden African nations and the hidden genitalia. By exposing them he hoped to disempower, to use observation to bring these unknown elements under

"capricious" movements resembled those of a monkey, while her lips protruded like those of an orangutan. Yet he noted that she spoke several languages, had a good ear for music, and possessed a good memory. Nevertheless, Cuvier's vision of the savage emerged: belts and necklaces of glass beads "and other savage attires" pleased her, but more than anything she had developed an insatiable taste for "l'eau-de-vie" (Cuvier 1817: 263).

For fully one-fifth of the paper we read of her exterior. Cuvier paints what he clearly found to be a picture gruesome in its contradictory aspects. Only four and a half feet tall, she had enormous hips and buttocks, but otherwise normal body parts. Her shoulders and back were graceful, the protrusion of her chest not excessive, her arms slender and well made, her hands charming, and her feet pretty. But her physiognomy – her face – repelled him. In the jutting of the jaw, the oblique angle of her incisors, and the shortness of her chin, she looked like a Negro. In the enormity of her cheeks, the flatness of the base of her nose, and her narrow eye slits, she resembled a Mongol. Her ears, he felt, resembled those of several different kinds of monkeys. When finally, in the spring of 1815, she agreed to pose nude for a painting, Cuvier reported the truth of the stories about the enormity of her protruding buttocks and breasts – enormous hanging masses[15] – and her barely pilous pubis.

When she died, on December 29, 1815, the police prefect gave Cuvier permission to take the body to the museum, where his first task became to find and describe her hidden vaginal appendages. For a page and a half the reader learns of the appearance, folded and unfolded, of the vaginal lips, of their angle of joining, the measurements of their length (more than four inches – although Blumenbach reportedly had drawings of others whose apron extended for up to eight inches) and thickness, and the manner in which they cover the vulval opening. These he compared to analogous parts in European women, pointing out the considerable variation and stating that in general the inner vaginal lips are more developed in women from warmer climates. The variation in vaginal development had, indeed, been recognized by French anatomists, but a mere ten years earlier, medical writers failed to connect differences in vaginal structures to either southern races or nonwhite women. In a straightforward account of "over-development" of vaginal lips, Dr. M. Baillie, a British physician and member of the Royal Society of Medicine of London (whose book was translated into French in 1807), wrote matter-of-factly of this variation, listing it among a number of genital anomalies, but not connected to non-European women (Baillie 1807). As Gilman (1985) points out, however, by the middle of the nineteenth century elongated labia had taken their place in medical textbooks alongside accounts of enlarged clitorises, both described as genital abnormalities, rather than as part of a wide range of "normal" human variation.

Cuvier acknowledged the great variation in length of the inner vaginal lips found even among European women. But nothing, he felt, compared to those of "negresses" and "abyssynians," whose lips grew so large that they became uncomfortable, obliging their destruction by an operation carried out on young girls at about the same age that Abyssinian boys were circumcised. As an aside that served to establish a norm for vaginal structure and a warning to those whose bodies did not conform, we learn that the Portuguese Jesuits tried in the sixteenth century to outlaw this practice, believing that it was a holdover from ancient Judaism. But the now Catholic girls could no longer find husbands because the men wouldn't put up with such "a disgusting deformity" (Cuvier 1817: 267), and finally, with the authorization of the Pope, a permission was made possible by a surgeon's verification that the elongated lips were natural rather than the result of manipulation, and the ancient custom resumed.

Cuvier contrasts the vaginal lips of Bushwomen with those of monkeys, the near invisibility of which provided no evidence to link them to these primitive humans. But the steatopygia was another matter. Bartmann's buttocks, Cuvier believed, bore a striking resemblance to the genital swellings of female mandrills and baboons, which grow to "monstrous proportions" at certain times in their lives. Cuvier wanted to know whether the pelvic bone had developed any peculiar structures as a result of carting around such a heavy load. To answer the question, he made use of his well-established method of comparative anatomy, placing side by side the pelvises of "his bushwoman," those of "negresses," and those of different white women. In considering Bartmann's small overall size, Cuvier found her pelvis to be proportionally smaller and less flared, the anterior ridge of one of the bones thicker and more curved in back, and the ischial symphysis thicker. "All these characters, in an almost unnoticeable fashion, resemble one another in Negro women, and female Bushwomen and monkeys" (Cuvier 1817: 269). Just as the differences themselves were practically imperceptible, amidst a welter of measurement and description, Cuvier imperceptibly separated the tamed and manageable European woman from the wild and previously unknown African.

But something worried Cuvier. In his collection he had also a skeleton of a woman from the Canary Islands. She came from a group called the Guanche (extinct since shortly after the Spanish settlement), a people who inhabited the islands before the Spanish and who, by all accounts, were Caucasians. An astonished Cuvier reported to his colleagues that he found the most marked of Bartmann's characters not in the skeleton of Negro women but in that of the Canary Islander. Since he had too few complete skeletons to assess the reliability of these similarities, he turned finally to more abundant material. In the last part of his account, he compares the head and skull (which "one has always used to classify nations" (Cuvier 1817: 270)) of "our Bushwoman" with those of others in his collection.

Bartmann's skull, he wrote, mixed together the features of the Negro and the Mongol, but, chiefly, Cuvier declared that he "had never seen a human head more similar to those of monkeys" (Cuvier 1817: 271). After offering more detailed comparisons of various bones in the skull, Cuvier returned in the last few pages of his paper to the problem that concerned him at the outset – did the Bushmen really exist as a legitimate people, and just how far into the interior of Africa did they extend? Here he relied once more on travelers' reports. Although modern voyagers did not report such people in northern Africa, Herodotus and others described a group that seemed in stature and skin color to resemble the Bushmen. According to some sources, these people invaded Abyssinia, although the evidence in Cuvier's view was too prescientific to rely on. But he could be sure of one thing: Neither the

[illegible]

do was compare the skulls of ancient Egyptians with those of the pretender races. One can picture him, as he spoke, dramatically producing from beneath his dissecting table the skulls of Egyptian mummies, those very same ones brought back by Geoffroy Saint-Hilaire from the Napoleonic incursion into Egypt.

Cuvier studied the skulls of more than fifty mummies. These, he pointed out, had the same skin color and large cranial capacity as modern Europeans. They provided further evidence for "that cruel law that seems to have condemned to eternal inferiority those races with depressed and compressed crania" (Cuvier 1817: 273). And finally, he presented to his museum colleagues the skull of the Canary Islander whose skeleton had so troublingly resembled Bartmann's. This too "announced a Caucasian origin" (Cuvier 1817: 2/4), which is the phrase that concludes his report. In this last section of his paper we watch him struggle with his data. First, he realized that he had a Caucasian skeleton that looked identical to Bartmann's. If he could not explain this away (what modern scientists call eliminating outliers – data points that don't neatly fit an expected graph line), his thesis that Bushmen represented a primitive form of humanity was in trouble. But that wasn't all that worried him: if his thesis was in trouble, so too was the claim of European superiority on which European and American colonization, enslavement, and disenfranchisement so depended. Thus, he went to considerable trouble to explain away the Guanche skeleton; ultimately he succeeded by using the scientific spoils of colonial expansion – the Egyptian mummies captured during Napoleon's Egyptian campaign.

Conclusion

This chapter places the scientific study of nonwhite women in several contexts. The investigations were, to be sure, part of the history of biology and, especially, a component of the movement to catalogue and classify all the living creatures of the earth. But this movement was in turn embedded in the process of European capitalist expansion. Not only did traders and conquerors, by collecting from around the world, create the need for a classification project, they also required the project to justify continued expansion, colonialism, and slavery. Further entangling the matter, the vast capital used to build the museums and house the collections came from the economic exploitation of non-European goods – both human and otherwise. This entire essay has been an argument against a narrowly constructed historiography of science; instead, I more broadly socialize the history of Euro-American biology in the first quarter of the nineteenth century by exposing its intersections with gender, race, and nation.

If one looks at the process less globally, one sees Cuvier and de Blainville as significant actors in a period of scientific change. From the perspective of the history of Euro-American biology, parochially extracted from its role in world expansion, one can say that the biologists of this period, and Cuvier in particular, made enormous scientific progress with the "discovery of the great information content of the internal anatomy of the invertebrates" (Mayr 1982: 183). According to this view, Cuvier "discovered" the importance of the nervous system as a way to organize animals. But "Cuvier's vision of the animal world was deeply coloured by that of the human society in which he was forced to make his way" (Outram 1984: 65). Far from reflecting some underlying natural system, Cuvier's use of the nervous system in his classification schemes had a homocentric starting point. The ideas formed a meshwork. Cuvier gave the focus on the nervous system and brain (obtained from his conviction that classification should proceed from the most complex – in this case human – structure to the simplest) the status of scientific fact by developing a reasonably coherent story about how the structure of the nervous system enabled him to classify all animals. Once scientists agreed on the validity of Cuvier's animal classification scheme, it fed back on the question of human classification. It seemed only "natural" to focus on the structure of the brain (as reflected in cranial and facial characteristics) to obtain evidence about the relative standing of the human races.

Sarah Bartmann's story is shocking to modern sensibilities. The racism of the period seems obvious – even laughable. But in the rush to create distance between nineteenth-century racist science and our modern, putatively less racist selves, even highly sophisticated scholars often lose sight of an important point. The loss becomes evident when I am asked (as I frequently am) what the *real* truth about Bartmann was. Just how big were those forbidden parts? The question reflects an ongoing belief in the possibility of an objective science. It suggests that, now that we have escaped all that silly racism of the nineteenth century, we ought to be able to get out our measuring tapes and find the real truth about other people's bodies. In this essay I argue that Bartmann's bodily differences were constructed using the social and scientific paradigms available at the time. The historical record tells us nothing about her agency, we can only know how Europeans framed and read her. Were she somehow magically alive today, contemporary biologists or anthropologists might frame and read her differently, but it would be a framing and reading, nevertheless. One contemporary difference might be that the varying worldwide liberation movements could offer her a context in which to contest the constructions of Euro-American science. In fact we see such contestations regularly in debates over such questions as brain size, race, and IQ (Maddock 1992; Schluter and Lynn 1992; Becker, Rushton, and Ankney 1992), brain shape and gender, and genetics and homosexuality (Fausto-Sterling 1992).

In *Playing in the Dark*, Toni Morrison (1992) makes her intellectual project "an effort to avert the critical gaze from the racial object to the racial subject; from the described and imagined to the describers and imaginers" (Morrison 1992: 90). By analogy I look at the fears and anxieties of the scientists, rather than worrying about the (in)accuracies of their descriptions of Sarah Bartmann and other people of color. To quote further from Morrison:

> The fabrication of an Africanist persona is reflexive; an extraordinary meditation on the self; a powerful exploration of the fears and desires that reside in the writerly conscious. It is an astonishing revelation of longing, of terror, of perplexity, of shame, of magnanimity. It requires hard work NOT to see this.

[illegible]

conquest	resistance
human	animal
surface	interior
tame	wild
sexually modest	libidinous
civilized	savage
compliant	angry
ruler	subject
powerlessness	hidden power
male	female
white	nonwhite
colonizer	colonized

The simultaneous anxiety about European women and the savage Other is especially clear in de Blainville's account. He identified Bartmann as a woman because she menstruated. But she also drank, smoked, and was alleged to be sexually aggressive – all masculine characteristics. And if Bartmann, a woman, could behave thus, why not French women? Furthermore, the soap opera dramas about Bartmann that played in contemporary Paris suggested that French men, despite their "civilization," actually desired such women; civilization kept the European woman under control, decreasing the danger of rebellion, by thwarting male desire. Minute scientific observation converted the desire into a form of voyeurism, while at the same time confining it to a socially acceptable location.

Cuvier most clearly concerned himself with establishing the priority of European nationhood; he wished to control the hidden secrets of Africa and the woman by exposing them to scientific daylight. The French Revolution had frightened him, and certainly the prospect of resistance from other peoples must have seemed terrifying (Outram 1984; Appel 1987). Hence, he delved beneath the surface, bringing the interior to light; he extracted the hidden genitalia and defined the hidden Hottentot. Lying on his dissection table, the wild Bartmann became tame, the savage civilized. By exposing the clandestine power, the ruler prevailed. But one need only look at the list of anxieties glossed from the scientific literature to know how uneasy lay the head that wore a crown.[16]

Notes

Acknowledgements: this paper was written with the financial support of the National Science Foundation, Fellowship #DIR-9112556 from the Program in History and Philosophy of Science. I would like to thank Evelynn Hammonds, Joan Richards, Gregg Mitman, and Londa Schiebinger, as well as the editors of this volume, for reading and commenting on recent drafts of this paper. Londa Schiebinger also kindly shared with me drafts of chapters of her book *Nature's Body: Gender in the Making of Modern Science* (Beacon 1993).

1 In 1992 the Musée de l'Homme had removed the remnants of the Bartmann exhibit. In its place was a modern one entitled "All relatives, all different," celebrating human genetic diversity. Discussion of Bartmann could still be found in a part of the exhibit devoted to the history of scientific racism.

2 There is also a book of poetry featuring the Venus Hottentot in the title poem: Elizabeth Alexander, *The Venus Hottentot* (Charlottesville: University Press of Virginia), 1990.

3 The Dutch word for Bushman is *bosjeman*, which translates as "little man of the forest." This is also the translated meaning of the Malay word *orangutan*.

4 This is in perfect accord with Latour's account of how scientific knowledge is constructed.

5 All translations from works cited in the original are mine.

6 In fact, de Blainville's break with Cuvier came over just this question. He devised a different classificatory system based on external, rather than internal characters, but he linked his divisions by creating intermediate groupings.

7 The question of the racial origins of European thought has been raised in our own era by the work of Martin Bernal (1987).

8 The detailed ins and outs of her sale and repurchase may be found in the references in note 11.

9 In contrast to the family groupings of Laps, Eskimos, and Zulus, the displays of Bartmann, Tono Maria, and Zip made no attempt to present a working culture.

10 Nonwhites were not the only "others" constructed. I plan to address the use of "freaks" in the construction of the Other in a book-length account of the construction of race and gender by biologists, anthropologists, and sociologists.

11 All the details cited here may be found in Altick (1978), Edwards and Walvin (1983), Gould (1985), Kirby (1949, 1953), and Lindfors (1983). Remarkably, prurient interest in the figure of the Hottentot continues to this day. Gould (1985) discusses a 1982 cover of the French magazine *Photo* that features a naked woman named "Carolina, La Venus hottentote de Saint Domingue." In the copy of the Geoffroy Saint-Hilaire and Cuvier held by the Brown Library, the frontal drawing of Bartmann (which exhibited her breasts in full form) has been razored out. The mutilation was first noticed by librarians in 1968. This is not the first time I have encountered such mutilation of material of this sort.

12 Although the bustle was not invented until 1869, various fashions in the eighteenth

and nineteenth centuries accentuated the backside of middle- and upper-class white women (Batterberry and Batterberry 1977). The relationship between these fashions and scientific accounts of the body has yet to be detailed.

13 There were at least seven articles, falling into three chronological groupings, published in scientific journals in England, France, and Germany. The first two, by Henri de Blainville and Georges Cuvier, exclusively on Sarah Bartmann, were published in 1816 and 1817, respectively. The second group, containing two by

Tiedemann's study represents a transition from a period in which scientists offered detailed examinations of the outside of the body, while focusing on a single individual and describing all body parts. Tiedemann awarded priority to one organ – the brain. A comparison of the brains of Europeans, Negroes, and orangutans convinced him that there was no difference among the humans. He used his results to condemn the practice of slavery. His method, though, is primitive compared to the approach of the scientists working in the 1860s (Marshall 1864; Flower and Murie 1867), whose work provides a useful contrast to the changing scientific and political times. In this paper I will consider the first two exemplars, reserving detailed examination of the other works for a future occasion.

14 Outram (1984) documents Cuvier's dispute with Franz Joseph Gall over the scientific nature of phrenology. But Cuvier clearly believed in the principle that the face could be read for deeper meaning.

15 In the seventeenth century, breasts – as natural and social objects – had undergone a transformation, as male social commentators launched a successful campaign to do away with wet-nursing and reestablish the breast as an object that connected women to nature through the act of nursing. For middle- and upper-class white women, doing the right thing with the right kind of breasts hooked them into a growing cult of domesticity, which exploded as the nineteenth-century ideal for gender relationships for the middle- and upper classes in Europe and America. This naturalization of motherhood worked hand in glove with the desexualization of white women (Schiebinger 1993; Perry 1991). Perry cites Thomas Laqueur (1986) as explaining "this cultural reconsideration of the nature of women's sexuality as part of a process committed to sweeping clean all *socially* determined differences among people" (Perry 1991: 212), instead relocalizing differences in the biological body. No part of the body escaped unscathed from this process.

16 In one of the lovely ironies of history, Cuvier himself was dissected when he died (in 1832), and his brain and head measurements were taken. In a ranking of 115 men of note Cuvier's brain weight came in third (Turgenev's was first). The French as a group ranked behind Americans and the British. The author of this 1908 paper concluded that "the brains of men devoted to the higher intellectual occupations, such as the mathematical sciences . . . [or] those of men who have devised original lines of research [Cuvier] and those of forceful characters, like Ben Butler and Daniel

Webster, are generally heavier still. The results are fully in accord with biological truths" (Spitzka 1908: 215). In a second, larger sample, Spitzka included four women – mathematician Sonya Kovaleskaya, physician Caroline Winslow, actress Marie Bittner, and educator and orator Madame Leblais – who ranked 134th–137th, in brain weight.

References

Altick, Richard D. 1978. *The Shows of London*. Cambridge: Belknap Press of Harvard University.

Appel, Toby A. 1987. *The Cuvier–Geoffroy Debate: French Biology in the Decades Before Darwin*. Oxford: Oxford University Press.

Baillie, Mathieu. 1807. *Anatomie pathologique des organes les plus importants du corps humain*. Paris: Crochard.

Batterberry, Michael, and Ariane Batterberry. 1977. *Mirror Mirror: A Social History of Fashion*. New York: Holt, Rinehart and Winston.

Becker, Brent A., J. Philippe Rushton, and C. Davison Ankney. 1992. "Differences in Brain Size," *Nature* 358: 532.

Bernal, Martin. 1987–91. *Black Athena: The Afroasiatic Roots of Classical Civilization*. New Brunswick, NJ: Rutgers University.

Bucher, Bernadette. 1981. *Icon and Conquest: A Structural Analysis of the Illustrations of de Bry*. Great Voyages. Trans. Basia Miller Gulati. Chicago: University of Chicago Press.

Coleman, William. 1964. *Georges Cuvier, Zoologist: A Study in the History of Evolution Theory*. Cambridge: Harvard University Press.

Cuvier, Georges. 1817. "Faites sur le cadavre d'une femme connue à Paris et à Londres sous le nom de Venus Hottentotte." *Mémoires du Musée nationale d'histoire naturelle* 3: 259–74.

de Blainville, Henri. 1816. "Sur une femme de la race hottentote." *Bulletin du Société philomatique de Paris*, pp. 183–90.

Edwards, Paul, and James Walvin. 1983. *Black Personalities in the Era of the Slave Trade*. Baton Rouge: Louisiana State University Press.

Elphick, Richard. 1977. *Kraal and Castle: Khoikhoi and the Founding of White South Africa*. New Haven: Yale University Press.

Fausto-Sterling, Anne. 1992. *Myths of Gender: Biological Theories about Women and Men*. 2nd ed. New York: Basic Books.

Figlio, Karl M. 1976. "The Metaphor of Organization: An Historiographical Perspective on the Bio-Medical Sciences of the Early Nineteenth Century." *History of Science* 14: 17–53.

Flourens, P. 1845. *Cuvier. Histoire de ses travaux*. 2nd ed. rev. and corr. Paris: Paulin.

Flower, W.H., and James Murie. 1867. "Account of the Dissection of a Bushwoman. *Journal of Anatomy and Physiology* 1: 189–208.

Geoffroy Saint-Hilaire, Etienne, and Fredéric Cuvier. 1824. *Histoire Naturelle des Mammiferes*, vols. 1 and 2. Paris: A. Belin.

Gilman, Sander L. 1985. "Black Bodies, White Bodies: Toward an Iconography of Female Sexuality in Late 19th-Century Art, Medicine and Literature." *Critical Inquiry* 12: 204–42.

Gould, Stephen Jay. 1981. *The Mismeasure of Man*. New York: Norton.

—— 1985. "The Hottentot Venus." In Stephen Jay Gould, *The Flamingo's Smile: Reflections in Natural History*, pp. 291–305. New York: Norton.

Graham, John. 1979. *Lavater's Essays on Physiognomy: A Study in the History of Ideas*. Berne: Peter Lang.

Gray, Stephen. 1979. *Southern African Literature: An Introduction*. New York: Barnes and Noble.

Guenther, Mathias Georg. 1980. "From 'Brutal Savage' to 'Harmless People': Notes

Latour, Bruno. 1987. *Science in Action: How to Follow Scientists and Engineers Through Society*. Milton Keynes: Open University Press.

Lavater, J.C. 1775–78. *Physiognomische Fragmente zur Beforderung der Menschenkenntnis und Menschenliebe*. Leipzig: Weidmanns Erben und Reiche, H. Steiner und Companie.

Lee, Richard R. 1992. "Art, Science, or Politics? The Crisis in Hunter-Gatherer Studies." *American Anthropologist* 94(1): 31–54.

Lewin, Roger. 1988. "New Views Emerge on Hunters and Gatherers." *Science* 240: 1146–48.

Lindfors, Bernth. 1983. "The Hottentot Venus and Other African Attractions in Nineteenth-Century England." *Australasian Drama Studies* 1: 83–104.

Linnaeus (Carl von Linne). 1758. *Caroli Linnaei Systema Naturae. Regnum Animale*. 10th ed. Stockholm.

Maddock, John. 1992. "How to Publish the Unpalatable?" *Nature* 358: 187.

Marshall, John. 1864. "On the Brain of a Bushwoman; and on the Brains of Two Idiots of European Descent." *Philosophical Transactions of the Royal Society of London*, pp. 501–58.

Masters, William H., and Virginia E. Johnson. 1966. *Human Sexual Response*. Boston: Little, Brown.

Mayr, Ernst. 1982. *The Growth of Biological Thought: Diversity, Evolution, and Inheritance*. Cambridge: Belknap Press of Harvard University.

Merchant, Carolyn. 1980. *The Death of Nature: Women, Ecology, and the Scientific Revolution*. San Francisco: Harper and Row.

Morrison, Toni. 1992. *Playing in the Dark: Whiteness and the Literary Imagination*. Cambridge: Harvard University Press.

Muller, Johannes. 1834. "Ueber die ausseren Geslechtstheile der Buschmanninnen." *Arch für Anatomie, Physiologie und Wissenschaftliche Medicin*, pp. 319–45.

Outram, Dorinda. 1984. *Georges Cuvier: Vocation, Science, and Authority in Post-revolutionary France*. Manchester: Manchester University Press.

Perry, Ruth. 1991. "Colonizing the Breast: Sexuality and Maternity in Eighteenth-Century England." *Journal of the History of Sexuality* 2: 204–34.

Raven-Hart, Rowland. 1967. *Before Van Riebeeck: Callers at South Africa from 1488 to 1652*. Cape Town: C. Struik.

Russett, Cynthia Eagle. 1989. *Sexual Science: The Victorian Construction of Womanhood*. Cambridge: Harvard University Press.

Schiebinger, Londa. 1993. *Nature's Body: Gender in the Making of Modern Science*. Boston: Beacon Press.

Schluter, Dolph, and Richard Lynn. 1992. "Brain Size Differences." *Nature* 359: 181.

Shohat, Ella. 1991. "Imaging Terra Incognita: The Disciplinary Gaze of the Empire." *Public Culture* 3(2): 41–70.

Spitzka, Edward Anthony. 1908. "A Study of the Brains of Six Eminent Scientists and Scholars Belonging to the American Anthropometric Society, together with Description of the Skull of Professor E.D. Cope." *American Philosophical Society Transactions* 21: 175–308.

Stepan, Nancy. 1982. *The Idea of Race in Science: Great Britain, 1800–1960*. Hamden, Conn.: Archon.

Stocking, George W., Jr. 1982. *Race, Culture, and Evolution: Essays in the History of Anthropology*. Chicago: University of Chicago.

—— 1987. *Victorian Anthropology*. New York: Free Press.

Tiedemann, Frederick. 1836. "On the Brain of a Negro, Compared with That of the European and the Orang-outang." *Philosophical Transactions of the Royal Society of London*, pp. 497–558.

Tiffany, Sharon W., and Kathleen J. Adams. 1985. *The Wild Woman: An Inquiry into the Anthropology of an Idea*. Cambridge, Mass.: Schenkman.

Trumbach, Randolf. 1991. "Sex, Gender and Sexual Identity in Modern Culture: Male Sodomy and Female Prostitution in Enlightenment London." *Journal of the History of Sexuality* 2: 187–203.

Walvin, James. 1973. *Black and White; The Negro and English Society, 1555–1945*. London: Allen Lane and Penguin.

Chapter 27

Bonnie Spanier

Not only does sex determination nearly always mean how *male* sex is determined, but many articles on sex determination in the past decade contain the following distortions:[1]

(1) The paradigm of sex/gender insists that subjects are either "manned" or "unmanned," polarizing male/female development into male and female beings, while categorizing physically intermediate beings as abnormal, ambiguous, or intersexed. An issue of *Science* devoted to sexual dimorphism in mammals left little room for ambiguity, though it exists both in strict biological and broader cultural terms.[2]

(2) The dominant theory guiding the relationship of sex dimorphism at the genetic and molecular level to human behavior holds that prenatal male sex hormones affect brain development and produce "sex-dimorphic" behaviors such as "energy expenditure," "social aggression," "parenting rehearsal," "peer contact," "gender role labeling," and "grooming behavior."[3] Authors make no reference to the historical and cultural overlay of bipolar sex onto hormones and minimal reference to the social construction of sex/gender.

(3) Scientists frequently make leaps between (nonhuman) animal research (for example, research on reproductive behavior such as lordosis (mounting) in rats) and implications for humans, to the advantage of the predominant theories. Or, with more subtlety, studies of rats, primates, and humans are cited *without* qualifying statements.

(4) Scientists often conflate the issue of sexual orientation with gender identity. The following illustrates the assumption that male hormones (androgens) produce a (normal male) sexual orientation to females:

> To test the validity of the prenatal hormone theory, we need to examine human subjects with endocrine disorders that involve prenatal sex-hormone abnormalities. The theory predicts that the effective *presence of androgens* in prenatal life *contributes to the development of a sexual orientation toward females* and that a deficiency of prenatal androgens or tissue sensitivity to androgens leads to a sexual orientation toward males, *regardless of the genetic sex of the individual*.[4]
>
> (Emphasis added.)

A more recent article by those authors explicitly uses the same paradigm to explain homosexuality.[5]

The conflation, based on heterosexism, reflects and reinforces what is normal and what is abnormal in sexual relations. Obviously, in this framework, gay men are deficient in maleness and thus are more female than "normal" males; conversely, lesbians are male.

(5) Little reference is made to the social construction of sex/gender or the conflation of biological sex with gender or gender identity. Compulsory heterosexuality or the historically specific social constraints against expressing or revealing homosexual interest, behavior, or lifestyle is not mentioned. Nor are feminist and gay liberationist perspectives on the whole set of issues. For example, an article concludes:

> In the light of these generalizations, we can consider our own species. The human, like the rhesus monkey, is a species in which masculinization, rather than defeminization, appears to be the predominant mode of sexual differentiation (60). It seems reasonable that the neural substrate for gonadal steroid responsiveness is represented in the human brain in much the same way that we know it to be represented in the brains of rhesus and bonnet monkeys. . . . Other articles in this issue (87) elaborate on the extent to which we are able to recognize, *in spite of the environmental influences of learning*, the components of human behavior which are influenced by hormones during development and in adulthood.[6]
>
> (Emphasis added.)

In a very reasonable tone, a leap is made between monkeys and humans, brains and behavior. Then, too, the general scientific methodology employed can see "the environmental influences of learning" *only* as *obscuring*,[7] rather than enlightening the mechanisms of sex development, since "mechanisms" are limited by definition to "biology." And "biology" excludes the dynamic interweaving of our physical beings with our experience within our environment. Further, the articles referenced within the quote above (note 87) are the two articles in the journal that address human sexual behavior, and they are the most guilty of the inaccuracies and questionable assumptions I have delineated. In this way, mutual reinforcements at the "scientific" level render the sociopolitical construction of gender totally invisible.

While the language in the *Science* articles is carefully tempered in the tradition of scientific discourse to sound objective, the content is rife with all the problems delineated by critics – such as inadequate controls, inadequate data collection, alternative explanations, and conflicting work on prenatal hormone exposure.[8] For example, the following summary statement implies that a hormonal role in sexual orientation or cognition has been demonstrated, but not conclusively, when it has not been demonstrated *at all*: "A role of the prenatal endocrine milieu in the development of erotic partner preference, as in hetero-, homo-, or bisexual orientation, or of cognitive sex difference has not been *conclusively demonstrated*" (emphasis added).[9] Such language obscures the conclusion based on the evidence cited in the article: that there is no valid data for humans to support a role of endocrine effects, prenatal or otherwise, [illegible] biosciences.

A striking example of this has been documented by neurophysiologist Ruth Bleier, whose research on brain structure demonstrated that claims about gender-specific differences in the size of the corpus callosum in humans are inaccurate. (Note that scientists connect claims about brain differences to sex hormones with the theory that prenatal hormones masculinize or feminize the brain.) In 1982, *Science* published an article that claimed to show that the corpus callosum (a sheet of nerve fibers linking the left and right halves of the brain) was larger in human females than in males.[10] Despite their flawed methodology and statistically inadequate sample size, DeLacoste-Utamsing and Holloway applied their conclusion about morphological differences to theories of human evolution to explain purported cognitive differences and brain (cerebral) lateralization in males and females. Bleier identified several significant scientific flaws in the article – "an unstated methodology in sample selection and an unacceptable sample size, unsupportable assumptions leading to overblown interpretations, a 'finding' without a minimum standard of statistical acceptability"[11] – and launched a scientifically valid study (thirty-nine subjects as compared to fourteen; magnetic resonance images) to compare male and female brains. Bleier's results – and three more studies by other researchers – failed to find sex-related differences in the size of the corpus callosum.[12]

The Bleier group's paper was rejected by *Science*. More telling is *Science*'s rejection of a review article by Bleier, delineating the errors in methodology, conceptualization, and interpretation in several areas of sex-difference research. Although one reviewer recommended publication, the second reviewer demurred:

> While many of Bleier's points are valid, she tends to err in the opposite direction from the researchers whose results and conclusions she criticizes. While Bleier states, toward the end of her paper, that she does not "deny the possibility of biologically based structural or functional differences in the brain between women and men," she argues very strongly for the predominant role of environmental influences.[13]

As Bleier comments, the reviewer rejects the validity of such arguments for environmental influences on observed gender differences in behavior and cognition, implying that Bleier, while "erring in the opposite direction," is less legitimate and less objective than those scientists whose work *has* been published in *Science*. Clearly, the prevailing paradigm of sex differences, not balanced presentation of differing perspectives, influences publication decisions.

Feminist perspectives are often charged with being biased, because they are overtly political and come from a set of defined interests. I suggest that Bleier's case illustrates this. What is ignored is that everyone has a set of interests, but they are not usually acknowledged, particularly in the sciences, where a cult of objectivity both denies and obscures social, cultural, and economic influences.

Disagreement among scientists is not uncommon and is understood as part of an ideal of open debate of all sides of an issue. The absence from the pages of *Science* of a comprehensive critique of biological determinist theories about gender differences – and the related topic of sexuality differences – strongly suggests that one position holds sway among the decision makers. Bleier spoke about this situation at the 1987 AAAS meeting on a panel about gender issues in the science. A newspaper reporter quoted Holloway (one of the authors of the original study) as saying he "felt horrible" about his small sample, but "it was so intriguing we decided to publish. I didn't think it was premature at all; I felt it was damned important to get it out right away . . . [and not] wait and wait like Darwin did – and almost lose [credit for] the whole thing."[14]

Scientists cannot always blame the media

What are the consequences of having the original, scientifically questionable claim about a sex difference in the corpus callosum published in *Science*, while the scientific proof of no such difference is published in more specialized and much less widely read journals? What are the consequences of *Science* publishing neither a visible retraction or correction to the claim nor a thorough critique of the field of sex differences in the brain? The January 20, 1993, issue of *Time* magazine shows how questionable scientific claims about biological determinism of sex differences in behavior and cognition reflect and reinforce prejudices about gender, with the special power of science. The magazine cover features a white boy making a muscle, while a white girl passively watches. The expression on her face conveys to me a mixture of perhaps admiration and perhaps annoyance. The public is asked "Why Are Men and Women Different?" The question itself is based on the prior assumption that men and women *are* different in important ways that do not have to be specified. Everyone *just knows* that the sexes are different. And the answer on the cover beams out from newsstands everywhere: "It isn't just upbringing. New studies show they are born that way."[15]

Under the heading, "differences that are all in the head," a picture of the brain illustrates the evidence mustered to support this assertion. Here we see the claim that the corpus callosum is "often wider in the brains of women than in those of men . . . possibly the basis for woman's intuition."[16] Six years after a spurious result is proven scientifically to be incorrect, it is presented as objective, accepted scientific fact supporting beliefs about inherent sex differences. Despite the effort to cast the sex difference as a positive attribute for women, the misleading belief in inherent biologically determined differences in behavior, cognitive skills, or approaches to problem-solving gives unjustifiable credence to biological determinism – as well as to the view that complex processes are products of singular biological entities, whether hormones, genes, or brain cells. While the article presents a range of views on the subject of biological determinism of sex differences, it does *not* treat the inadequacies of the scientific claims themselves, leaving assumptions about scientific objectivity untouched.

Another questionable claim about sex differences in the brain is made about the hypothalamus, stating that a group of nerve cells was larger in heterosexual men [illegible] of context. Close reading of LeVay's *Science* article reveals that, while he admits that his data do not distinguish *whether the bundle of cells cause or are the consequence* of sexual orientation – and that comparisons from rats to humans in sexual studies may not be valid – he nonetheless concludes without further justification that "it seems more likely that in humans, too, the size of INAH 3 is established early in life and later *influences sexual behavior than the reverse*" (emphasis added).[18] The abstract also states this conclusion: "This finding indicates that INAH [3] is dimorphic with sexual orientation, at least in men, and suggests that sexual orientation has a biological substrate."[19] LeVay does not (and *Science* editors did not require him to) discuss the discrepancies between his work and other research (buried in endnote 10) or the well-documented general disarray of the field of sex differences in brain studies.[20] The media cannot be blamed for taking the scientist at his or her word and trusting the peer review and editorial system to monitor scientific publication.

Notes

1 I cite primarily from an issue of *Science* devoted to "Sexual Dimorphism," ed. Frederick Naftolin and Eleanore Butz, *Science* 221 (March 20, 1981). While that issue was published a number of years ago, current articles reflect no significant change in assumptions and methodology; for example, articles published in *Science* 243 (January 6, 1989). *Science* is typical of scientific journals and other publications in using the dominant paradigm of sex determination. See a detailed critique in Fausto-Sterling, "Society Writes Biology."

2 See Kessler, for example, for physical ambiguities; and Julia Epstein and Kristina Straub, eds., *Body Guards: The Cultural Politics of Gender Ambiguity* (New York: Routledge, 1991), for cultural and historical examples.

3 Anke A. Ehrhardt and Heino Meyer-Bahlburg, "Effects of Prenatal Sex Hormones on Gender-Related Behavior," *Science* 211 (March 20, 1981): 1313. The original Money and Ehrhardt research on "masculinized" girls exposed prenatally to androgens and subsequent claims about that work have been comprehensively critiqued; for example, Anne Fausto-Sterling, *Myths of Gender: Biological Theories About Women and Men* (New York: Basic Books, 1985), chapter 5: "Hormones and Aggression: An

Explanation of Power," esp. 133–41; and Ruth Bleier, *Science and Gender* (New York: Pergamon Press, 1984), esp. 97–103.

4 Ehrhardt and Meyer-Bahlburg, "Effects of Prenatal," 1316. For an in-depth analysis, see Helen E. Longino, *Science as Social Knowledge: Values and Objectivity in Scientific Inquiry* (Princeton, NJ: Princeton University Press, 1990).

5 Anke A. Ehrhardt *et al.*, "Sexual Orientation after Prenatal Exposure to Exogenous Estrogen," *Archives of Sexual Behavior* 14 (1985): 57–77.

6 Bruce McEwen, "Neural Gonadal Steroid Actions," *Science* 211 (March 20, 1981): 1310.

7 The verb "obscure" is used this way in the introductory essay in this issue on sexual dimorphism (Naftolin, "Understanding the Bases," 1264).

8 See Fausto-Sterling, *Myths of Gender*; and Bleier, *Science and Gender*.

9 Ehrhardt and Meyer-Bahlburg, "Effects of Prenatal," 1312.

10 C. DeLacoste-Utamsing and R.L. Holloway, "Sexual Dimorphism in the Human Corpus Callosum," *Science* 216 (1982): 1431–32. This "misadventure" in science was published posthumously. See Ruth Bleier, "A Decade of Feminist Critiques in the Natural Sciences," *Signs* 14, no.1 (Autumn 1988): 186–95, esp. 191–93.

11 Bleier, " Decade of Feminist Critiques," 192.

12 R. Bleier, L. Houston, and W. Byne, "Can the Corpus Callosum Predict Gender, Age, Handedness, or Cognitive Differences?" *Trends in Neurosciences* 9 (1986): 391–94.

13 Quoted in Bleier, "A Decade of Feminist Critiques," 191. For her critiques, see Bleier, *Science and Gender*.

14 San Francisco *Examiner* (February 22, 1987), as quoted in Bleier, "A Decade of Feminist Critiques," 192–93.

15 *Time* (January 20, 1992).

16 Christien Gorman, "Sizing up the Sexes," *Time* (January 20, 1992): 42.

17 Simon LeVay, "A Difference in Hypothalamic Structure between Heterosexual and Homosexual Men," *Science* 253 (August 30, 1991): 1034; and Marcia Barinaga, "Is Homosexuality Biological?" *Science* 253 (August 30, 1991): 956.

18 LeVay, "A Difference," 1036.

19 Ibid., 1034.

20 Bleier, "A Decade of Feminist Critiques"; and *Science and Gender*; and Fausto-Sterling, *Myths of Gender*. For a more detailed analysis of LeVay's work, see Bonnie Spanier, "Biological Determinism and Homosexuality," *NWSA Journal* 7, no. 1 (Spring 1995): 54–71.

Chapter 28

Liz Whitelegg

If you want gain in one year plant rice, in 10 years plant fruit trees, in 100 years educate women!

An old Chinese proverb

Introduction

In this article I will examine why so few girls have been involved in and motivated by science at school and hence gone on to scientific careers. I will start with an historical perspective, and offer contemporarily relevant explanations for why girls generally have not achieved as well as their brothers in scientific endeavours. I will also consider the recent policy changes in science education and examine what hopes these have for the future of girls in science.

Most of the research into girls in science over the last decade or so has focused on secondary science. Although *all* research in this area has had and continues to have very little funding and most researchers and teachers interested in this area must work in their spare time and on shoestring budgets, the latest and most exciting work has more recently been undertaken on the primary phase of education and it is with this area that I will begin in order to give a better perspective of what happens to girls at secondary school.

I will also look briefly at science education in two nonindustrialized countries in order to broaden the debate and offer an alternative perspective. Although the situation and circumstances for science teaching are very different from those found in Britain and most other countries in Europe, there are some common problems and difficulties.

Historical perspective

Science education in primary schools is a relatively new phenomenon. Before the 1920s little or no science was taught to either girls or boys and only 30 per cent of girls attended school regularly anyway. Around this time science in the form of natural history was introduced. Most learning was by rote and many teachers using this method had no understanding of the underlying scientific principles themselves and indeed in some schools the teaching of science was specifically banned. It was not until the middle of the nineteenth century that some science training became compulsory in *teacher* education. Until then neither girls nor boys received a great deal of science education. Nevertheless, boys were still offered a broader education as the predominant view was that girls should be educated to be a social asset. (This view was not shared by the women of the time though. In the 1830s, they outnumbered men at the British Association for the Advancement of Science meetings!)

More recently science education has made significant advances and teachers are now encouraged to adopt an open-ended, enquiring, child-centred approach to science teaching. This method, however, makes considerable demands on teachers and requires them to be confident in their own science knowledge. It is still the case that infant and primary teachers are not well equipped to adopt this approach and a recent report showed that less than half of primary teachers had studied science beyond the age of 13 and less than 10 per cent of those teaching 10-year-olds had science as their main subject in teacher education (*Times Educational Supplement*, 1989). (Over the period 1990 to 1993, the Department of Education and Science (DES) has made funds available for primary teachers to attend in-service training courses to gain a grounding in science knowledge and content. The funding is barely adequate to train one teacher in half the primary schools in England and Wales.)

What happens in primary schools?

The way in which attitudes develop in the early years is vital. As Naima Browne writes:

> With the advent of the National Curriculum with its definition of science as one of the three core subjects and technology as one of the seven foundation subjects, preparation for the study of these subjects in the early years of schooling can be seen as vital, as crucial ideas about the relevance of science and technology to girls are formed in these early years and their motivation for engaging in these areas of the curriculum can be easily undermined.
>
> (Browne, 1991)

Until recently, before science became a compulsory element in primary schooling, it was thought that *offering* science to girls in secondary schools would solve the problem as they would engage with science in an equal way with the boys. However, as we now know, offering the same subjects to girls and boys at 11 or 13 does not alter the imbalance because of girls' exposure to the 'hidden curriculum' which has influenced their motivation and later decisions to do science. This 'hidden curriculum' in the primary school involves a complex web of taken-for-granted assumptions and procedures that can only be counteracted if there is a great deal of awareness and vigilance on the part of teachers and local authority advisers. Teachers need to recognize that they themselves are powerful agents of socialization, who also bring their own culturally acquired perspectives with them. It is recognized that attitude change does not necessarily follow presentation of information, no matter how compelling and relevant that information may be. For change to occur, teacher-educators and teachers must confront their own attitudes and perceptions and be given opportunities to [illegible]

> Toys can be, and are, used to reinforce gender conformity. The Lego play showed that boys appear more task-oriented, have developed superior construction skills and pre-plan models independently by 6 to 7 years of age. Girls, however, see Lego [as] mainly for boys, their models are more simple in design and are not incorporated into fantasy play. They appear to gain little satisfaction from such activities. Finally, as children move from 5 to 9 years of age the separation of girls and boys becomes more evident and members of the opposite sex are frequently ridiculed in peer group play if they do not conform to gender expectations . . . [In the study] children's choice of activity was not solely influenced by interest but also by confidence – girls who played with Lego were often unconfident but boys never were. Girls rarely chose a construction toy on first entering a classroom, but boys often did. Girls adopted various strategies to play with boys and 'boys' toys', compromising themselves by adopting submissive roles or playing by boys' rules. Sometimes girls did have enough confidence to join a boys' game and play on their own terms.
>
> (p. 146)

In another study (Skelton, 1989) the teachers gave the children a choice of activities based on the topic of 'house'. The teacher introduced the activity and left the children to proceed. The boys chose to construct an electric circuit for the doll's house whilst the girls chose to design a pattern for curtains. Some of the girls, however, would have liked to work on the electrical activity but said that the boys got there first. With some of the other activities that were offered to the same class, the girls were put off doing the construction activity (making a bird table) because it would have meant working with a group of boys. These are not isolated incidents; time and time again observations of girls' and boys' use of resources in classrooms notes similar issues.

An 'equal opportunities' approach to science teaching like those described does not ensure that girls and boys get the same experience of science learning. Simply ignoring gender in fact reinforces stereotyping because it does nothing to challenge the definition of certain aspects of the curriculum as masculine or feminine. Children (and teachers) bring the effects of socialization with them into the classroom and that affects how they interact with the teaching and resources offered in school.

Some schools have introduced a 'girls' hour' into the nursery class to try to counteract girls' lack of confidence in constructional play. In this hour, girls have unrestricted access to a range of resources without the presence of boys. This strategy enables girls to become more confident in using the resources and they use them in their own way: they don't build the same things as boys but their activities can be just as valuable in developing their spatial abilities. Development of spatial abilities is linked to increased mathematical ability and it is quite commonplace to find girls performing better at maths than boys in primary schools. Intervention strategies such as these can increase their interest and confidence in constructional play with no detrimental effect on the boys.

The learning method most favoured by teacher-educators currently is that of open-ended, child-centred learning. This method aims to treat every child as an individual and to teach each child from her or his current starting point and let the child determine where each particular topic leads. This method gives rise to the view that gender stereotyping is not an issue, as teaching is based on each individual child's needs. However, this method does not take account of the gender–power relationships that exist within the classroom or the amount of stereotyping that children experience outside the school. I do not wish to imply that this method has little to offer, as I do believe that 'starting from where a child is at' is an excellent beginning, but the current research and resulting teaching resources which are being produced with this perspective do not have a necessary (in my view) gender dimension.

Much attention has lately been paid to setting an appropriate context for children's learning and this has repercussions for the testing of children at ages 7, 11, 13 and 16 as part of the National Curriculum. Setting questions and activities that relate to children's own experience is a good way of encouraging them to engage with the question or activity; but if the context is more appropriate to a boy's world view than a girl's, it will have disastrous consequences for girls' achievement as measured by the National Curriculum levels of attainment. This, however, is a very complex area and as an Assessment of Performance Unit (APU) report says: 'Examples of gender-linked differences in performance can be found in most aspects of the assessment framework. These differences cannot be described in terms of [a single cause] . . . They are to be found in cognitive, affective and social functioning and very often any particular influence is inextricable from the others' (APU, 1988, p. 109).

The National Curriculum in general does not address the issue of equal opportunity in science although the Non-Statutory Guidelines produced by the National Curriculum Council have made some attempt to do so when they stated:

> . . . there are some groups of pupils who, according to their teachers and as shown by research, have not, in the past, realized their full potential in science. These groups include girls . . . The common, balanced curriculum which pupils will follow will help to eliminate problems of sex imbalance in the uptake of specific-science courses. Nevertheless, it is likely that the problems of low expectations of many girls, particularly in physical science, will remain.
>
> (NCC, 1989, p. A9)

Despite this rather defeatist attitude, the National Curriculum will, however, ensure that all children study science from 5 to 16 years, and so girls, who have previously opted to continue with biology and drop the other sciences at secondary school, may now feel more equipped to continue with all the sciences at secondary school. Previously many girls who continued with science beyond the age of 14 continued only with biology, having built up some knowledge and confidence by being exposed to 'nature study' at primary school.

[illegible]

positive outcome of the National Curriculum. However, examining this more closely, it may not have the beneficial effects for girls that could be hoped for. Firstly, there are two models for the science curriculum in key stage 4 (for students aged 14 to 16). The model that it is hoped the majority of students will follow (model A) demands that 20 per cent of the curriculum time is devoted to science. Model B allows only 12.5 per cent of time for science. It is feared that less able children and many girls will be directed towards model B. Model B will not equip students for science A-levels. The second concern over the National Curriculum is the straightjacket that it places on girls. If the science that is taught to them continues to be male science then girls who do not conform to this male view will still feel alienated and will not succeed or enjoy it.

However, having stated these reservations about the National Curriculum, it will ensure a broadening in the teaching of science and it does assimilate contemporary good practice in science teaching. Attainment target 1 (AT1) – the process of science – carries a 50 per cent weighting. Good practice in science teaching will integrate AT1 (learning science as a process, learning through doing science) with the remaining fact-based attainment targets and this is seen as a step forward. Active learning is a great confidence-builder. But, as Bentley and Watts comment on Kelly's (1987) work,

> . . . confidence-building was an approach which in the early days of research into girls and science was seen to be most reasonable. Girls opted away from science, it was said, because . . . there must be something wrong with their perceptions of science, the world or of themselves. The corollary of this was that intervention strategies were designed to boost girls' confidence and correct their misconceptions of science.
>
> (Bentley and Watts, 1989, p. 191)

Kelly no longer believes that girls' lack of science achievement is to do primarily with their lack of confidence and early socialization. She now puts more emphasis on the role of schools and teachers in dissuading girls from science, and less on girls' internal states and she now thinks that it is necessary to change science. Bentley and Watts, with Kelly, 'believe that treating girls as though they were the problem, and designing "girl-friendly" approaches to science, is not the most successful way to ensure that women have equal opportunities to impose their ideas on existing science frameworks' (Bentley and Watts, 1989, pp. 191–2):

> . . . to construe the problem as enticing girls into science may not be the most promising way of progressing. Rather, reconstructing science and in particular science education so that both are more in keeping with the experiences and explanations of the world that are familiar to women, might serve teachers better.
>
> (Kelly, 1987)

Alison Kelly has reached this view after setting up and working on the Girls into Science and Technology project (GIST) in Manchester from 1979 to 1984. GIST was the first major schools-based project addressing problems of sex-stereotyping at school, and was an example of action research; the project simultaneously took action to improve girls' achievement in science and technology and investigated their reasons for under-achievement. The final report of the project states:

> We found that boys acted [in the classroom] in a way which made science seem more masculine than it really was; the teachers also helped to create the impression that science is a very macho business. In the first lesson, teachers often pointed out the dangers of equipment and chemicals in the lab, delighting the boys, who in later sessions displayed a great deal of bravado, for instance using a magnet to have a tug-of-war, trying to give each other electric shocks with a 6V battery; for the girls the element of danger was more discouraging. Teachers and boys seemed to be unthinkingly collaborating to construct science as an area of masculine endeavour, excluding girls, who quickly took the hint.
>
> (Whyte *et al.*, 1985, pp. 81–2)

Alison Kelly views science as masculine in four distinct senses:

> The attitudes of teachers and pupils.
> The image presented by books and other resources.
> Practitioners of science are overwhelmingly male.
> Scientific thinking embodies an intrinsically masculine world view.

The fourth point is true if we cling to an irredeemably narrow conception of science and scientific thinking. The industrial and social impact of science on health, on people and on the environment, and a focus on the beauty and complexity of the natural world were all notable omissions from the school syllabus until their introduction in the National Curriculum. But the attainment target that is concerned with the nature/philosophy of science is only available for model A students, which, as I outlined earlier, may not include many girls. This is a great pity because this is an area that is likely to interest them. Girls are not uninterested in science; they are bored by the limited version of it they meet in school.

Reconstructing science

So, if changing the way girls interact with science does not solve the problem, how do we change science? Does feminism have anything to offer? As Helene Witcher (1985) suggests, a feminist who examines science teaching in schools does not simply note that girls are less likely to play with Lego than boys. She notes that:

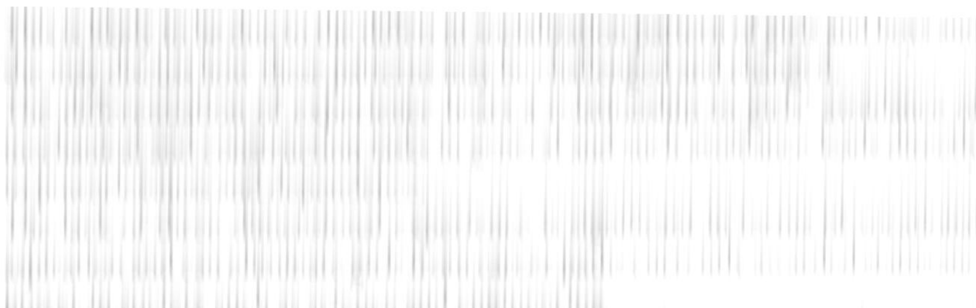

There are positive ways in which she can intervene to challenge this state of affairs, which a non-feminist researcher would not regard as a problem.

Few teachers of science would accept this feminist viewpoint. The idea that science education involves passing on a body of knowledge that is value-free has been the overwhelming and prevailing ideology of science educationalists. As Evelyn Fox Keller argues, modern science as we know it is a culturally specific activity, and what is considered 'good' science in any period is both historically and culturally determined.

> What all social studies of science see when they look closely at the process by which good science is named is a variety and range of practices, visions and articulations of science far in excess of any ideological prescriptions . . . In every period of scientific history, in every school of science, we can see a rich diversity of meanings and practices. In fact it would appear that where ideology makes its force felt most crucially is in its role in the process by which some theories, methodologies and explanations are selected as representative of good science and others are disregarded.
>
> (Fox Keller, 1986, p. 174)

Science education in underdeveloped countries

In underdeveloped countries science educators face a double dilemma. Two socio-cultural factors repel girls from entering science – the unfavourable conditions created by the general economic malaise (this is also a problem for boys, of course) and the common discriminators for girls in science education: different expectations of parents and teachers for girls; unequal treatment for girls and boys in the classroom; and packaging (illustrations in textbooks, etc.). Teachers who succeed in motivating girls into science are exemplary teachers who maintain well-equipped classrooms with posters on the walls, specimens and apparatus in the lab. Such learning environments are not common in poor countries. The situation in many African countries is particularly dire. In Sierra Leone, for example, there is little process-based teaching (only 10 per cent of teachers regularly use it) because of lack of time and resources (Amara, 1990). In the 1960s there was a major educational intervention programme with the objective of the dissemination of process-based learning in African countries but this is now largely defunct. Most teaching takes place via the old-fashioned 'chalk and talk' method. At the primary level, particularly, this is a further discouragement for girls. Julia Amara describes the classrooms in Sierra Leone as 'naked' – having nothing except chairs and desks in them. It is not possible for pupils to experience real science without access to equipment, especially at the primary level where experimentation is an integral part of process learning.

Pupils in underdeveloped countries often have to buy their own books – which most cannot afford to do – and there are very few libraries in primary schools. In general, all-girls' schools are disadvantaged more than boys' schools in terms of facilities. Of all the 16 girls' schools in Sierra Leone, only one is qualified to teach science in the sixth form, while there are many boys' schools which are able to teach sixth-form science. Much of the problem is to do with a shortage of educational materials.

In India the situation for urban girls and women is better. There has been some upturn in the numbers of women qualifying for and entering the professions. Science now has 31.4 per cent women, medicine has 30.4 per cent and engineering has seen a 4 per cent increase in women between 1976 and 1987. However, the unemployment rate among qualified women in science and technology is almost 50 per cent because work often involves interacting with male colleagues and clients as well as being on call for night duty. Small numbers of Indian women often succeed well at the postgraduate level and a higher proportion do so than at the undergraduate level. Once they have broken through the barriers of prejudice they are able to continue. Having said this, education is still a middle-class concern and huge numbers of rural Indian women remain uneducated (Raghuwanshi, 1990).

These two examples indicate the problems of developing good science education for women and girls in poor countries. The lack of resources and trained teachers may force a consideration of alternative models of science but even these cannot be taught well in a 'naked' classroom.

Where next?

My aim in this article has been to set out the multi-layered nature of the problem for girls in primary and secondary science schooling. In the United Kingdom new policy developments – the introduction of the National Curriculum and hence the broadening of science teaching away from the content-based, active learning approach – will go some way to addressing the problem. However, there are so many other factors to take into account that a one-dimensional solution does not exist.

Only nine months after the introduction of the National Curriculum into schools, it has already been modified as it was found that teaching 17 ATs was unmanageable. Under the new proposals recommended by the Secretary of State in May 1991, science has been reorganized into just 5 ATs. AT1, scientific investigation, has been retained but AT17, dealing with the social, cultural and historic ideas in science, has been lost. This does seem a backward step as far as interesting girls in science is concerned, as this AT did hold out some hope for introducing girls to scientific ideas through real-life contexts.

References

[illegible] Press.

Burn, E. 1989. Inside the Lego house. In C. Skelton, ed., *Whatever happens to little women*. Buckingham: Open University Press.

Fox Keller, E. 1986. How gender matters, or, why it's so hard for us to count past two. In J. Harding, ed., *Perspectives on gender and science*. Brighton: Falmer Press.

Kelly, A. 1987. *Science for girls?* Buckingham: Open University Press.

National Curriculum Council (NCC). 1989. *NCC Non-statutory Guidelines*. York: Department of Education and Science.

Raghuwanshi, C. 1990. Status of women in science and technology in India: current trends. Contribution to GASAT 1990 Conference, Jonkoping, Sweden.

Skelton, C. 1989. And so the wheel turns. In C. Skelton, ed., *Whatever happens to little women*. Buckingham: Open University Press.

Whyte, J., Deem, R., Kant, L. and Cruickshank, M. eds. 1985. *Girl-friendly schooling*. London: Methuen.

Witcher, H. 1985. Personal and professional: A feminist approach. In J. Whyte, R. Deem, L. Kant and M. Cruickshank (eds), *Girl-friendly schooling*. London: Methuen.

SECTION SIX

WHAT IS THE FUTURE OF FEMINIST science studies? These analyses can continue in multiple directions, shining new lights in still-hidden dark corners of science practice and its unspoken underlying theory. However, the analyses to date have illuminated enough about the androcentrism of science that it may be time to put these analyses into practice – to begin to change the way science is carried out and the way science is taught. Alteration in science teaching to include the results of feminist critiques is essential to prevent the perpetuation of sanctioned science *ad infinitum*.

One assumption is that if there are more women in science, the disciplines in which they work will be more receptive to change based in the feminist analyses. Kerr ("Toward a Feminist Natural Science: Linking Theory and Practice") interviewed women scientists concerning their familiarity with these analyses and whether the analyses had an influence on their own practice. Kerr is optimistic about the potential for change, noting practitioners' concerns to change science from within science, their desire for more diversity in practitioners, practices, and theories, and for more open exploration of uncertainty and social influences on scientific knowledge. But it is also possible to be pessimistic. One practitioner cited feminist theory as a potential threat to her and other women's ability to carry out scientific research, on the grounds that feminists may be perceived as thinking "differently," i.e., not well enough. While attempting to influence scientists both male and female, the feminist critiques must be advanced as one among many strategies to attain a richer understanding of the natural world, without stigmatizing particular groups or perpetuating already existing biases.

The results of Kerr's study show that these women scientists wish to change science from within, as do Weasel and Rose. Lederman ("Structuring Feminist Science") raises a challenge to the idea of changing science from within. Should this be the goal or is a more radical change required?

Shulman ("Implications of Feminist Critiques of Science for the Teaching of Mathematics and Science") contends that the perceived basis of all Western science, mathematics, long held as the tool that insures objectivity, is itself socially constructed. She cites the example of the Navajo's inter-connectedness with the natural world as influencing their children's ability to learn fractions, the Chinese lack of belief in God as the law-giver, and the non-universality of the notion that all things are susceptible to empirical testing. Can questioning the basis of Western science cause the entire structure to topple, in the hope of a new phoenix rising?

The authors of several essays make a plea for a science that values interconnection. Weasel ("The Cell in Relation: An Ecofeminist Revision of Cell and Molecular Biology") hopes for a reconceived cellular and molecular biology that incorporates metaphors focusing on "connection, communication, and interrelationship" (p. 431) within and between cells, as an alternative to overcoming the current destructive and hierarchical paradigms. Just because this discipline studies entities that are small is no a priori reason for reductionism, adopting the values of chemistry and physics that have to date not proven easily amenable to the feminist analyses. Shiva ("Democratizing Biology: Reinventing Biology from a Feminist, Ecological, and Third World Perspective") calls for re-inventing biology "to include respect for all species and all humans" (p. 461) and the value of diversity. This is a multi-faceted statement: respect for all species requires reconsideration of experimental biology and biotechnology; respect for humans requires reconsideration of the Human Genome Project and valuing the contributions to science of all non-white persons and women, especially considering women's role in preserving biodiversity.

Schiebinger ("Creating Sustainable Science") takes up this thread, requesting that we move away from epistemology and developing a successor science to focus instead on creating socially and environmentally responsible, sustainable science (pp. 473–477). She wishes that we stress what we know (reinforcing Harding's "strong objectivity") and why we know it (who gets to decide what we investigate) rather than *how* we know what we know. She believes that gender analyses of science, including dissection of language, institutions, and the effects of science on the environment, are the way to further women's participation in the sciences and their position in the world.

The feminist analyses offer many ways to approach androcentric science. A common theme of the essays in this section is avoidance of dominion over and destruction of nature, replacing it with Rose's love; "feminism brings love to knowledge and power. It is love, as caring respect for both people and nature, that offers an ethic to reshape knowledge, and with it society" (p. 489). Let us not argue about the best way to reshape knowledge; let us listen to our own rhetoric about valuing diversity. There are many individuals committed to the task; each will bring a unique perspective that is unlikely to be duplicated. Let us respect each other's contributions, realizing that as we improve the lives of women at all levels, we also improve the lives of all humans and all life on the planet, leading to the ultimate equality.

Suggested readings

We purposely do not suggest any readings, hoping to encourage our readers to develop new ways to analyze science and apply these analyses in any sphere that benefits all.

Chapter 29

E. Anne Kerr

TOWARD A FEMINIST NATURAL SCIENCE

Linking theory and practice

Synopsis

In this paper I tackle the gulf between feminist epistemologies of science and the practice of the natural sciences. I begin by considering the feminist epistemologies of science, focusing in particular on standpoint theories and objectivity in the work of Harding, Haraway, Longino, and Nelson, and identifying the problems in applying these theories in the natural sciences. I then move on to consider some of the views expressed by feminists with experience of practice in the natural sciences. I argue that this gives them a privileged standpoint from which to understand what a feminist natural science might mean, and use their views to elaborate my critique of the feminist epistemologies of science. I end by exploring practical strategies for moving toward a feminist natural science, emphasizing diversity amongst practitioners; unpacking established conceptual categories in science (especially gender); elaborating the role of subjectivity in guiding research questions and analysing data; and developing links between the different disciplines of science and with the local community.

Introduction

Feminist epistemologies of science are now an established part of feminist scholarship and have begun to penetrate mainstream teaching on social research methods, history, philosophy, and sociology (see Campbell, 1995). The standpoint theories of Sandra Harding (1986, 1991) are particularly well-received by feminists in the social sciences, most notably in sociology, geography, and psychology (see, for example, Harding and Hintikka, 1983).[1] But the feminist epistemologies of science have little apparent relevance to women in the natural sciences, particularly in the nonlife sciences (see Longino and Hammonds, 1990). Harding's feminist standpoint theory is particularly problematic in the natural sciences because of her emphasis on women's unique and privileged standpoint. This alienates many women natural scientists who rely heavily on demonstrating that their gender *does not* mark their contribution to knowledge (see Kerr and Faulkner, 1997). As Helen Longino argues, for many female scientists, theories that appeal to differences between men and women are invariably seen as "new clothing for the old idea that women can't do science" (Longino, 1989, p. 188).[2]

This is nevertheless not the only, or indeed the most important, difficulty that is

Yet, feminism has much work to do in challenging the hegemony of scientism, exemplified by scientists' appeals to their privileged "objective" representation of the natural world. The male domination of science in academe and industry also means that the natural sciences are urgently in need of feminist transformation.

In this article, I draw on research conducted as part of my Ph.D.[5] and begin to tackle the gulf between feminist epistemologies of science and the practice of the natural sciences. I begin by outlining some of the apparent divisions between feminist theorists and women in the natural sciences in the UK, USA, and Canada in more depth. A discussion of objectivity and subjectivity in standpoint and postmodernist theories and feminist empiricism follows.[6] I highlight the difficult epistemological and practical issues facing feminists working in the natural sciences. I argue that we not only need to explore practical and rigorous standards for inquiry to which feminists who are scientists could subscribe, we also need to explore the standpoint of scientists working toward a feminist natural science. I then move on to consider some of the views on these issues that feminists with experience of practice in the natural sciences have expressed in print and in interviews. These women share experiences in science and an interest in a variety of aspects of feminism: from promoting women in science to developing a feminist science. Despite the inevitable differences in some of their perspectives, I argue that these women do share a privileged standpoint from which to understand feminism, gender, and science, not only because they are women in a male-dominated environment, but because they are feminists involved in a pursuit commonly associated with masculinity. I end by synthesizing my preliminary analysis of the literature with the practical perspective of feminist scientists, with the aim of more fully understanding how to move toward a feminist natural science.

Negotiating the gap between theory and practice

The androcentrism and sexism in and of the natural sciences have been thoroughly criticized by many feminist scholars in the past 30 years (see, for example, Hubbard and Lowe, 1983).[7] Many feminists also argue that as we reach the end of the twentieth century, efforts to make science more "woman friendly" have failed. In the UK and

USA, scientists are predominantly male, particularly in the so-called, "hard" sciences of physics and chemistry. Despite recent "liberal feminist" (e.g., Hornig, 1984)[8] and government efforts (e.g., National Research Council, 1994)[9] to encourage more women into science, the association of science with masculinity prevails. The majority of women tend to feel ignorant, even frightened, of science (see Fausto-Sterling, 1992). Those that do try to become scientists often encounter sexism from teachers and peers, or find it difficult to cope with the culture of science, and leave. This leads to a progressive decline in the number of women scientists toward the top of the employment hierarchy (see Rose, 1994).

Instead of concentrating on how to get more women into science, many feminist critics of science have begun to question science itself. Their efforts have mainly been directed toward debunking some now notorious biological theories in support of sexist ideology – most recently sociobiology, which reifies the rape and suppression of women – and on unpacking the association between masculinity and science (see Birke, 1986, 1992; Janson Smith, 1980). This is also linked to more widespread criticism of science, particularly from the ecology movement, who criticize the destruction of the environment, which has resulted from recent advances in the industrial, military, and agricultural sciences. These critical approaches to science have led some feminist scholars to argue that the project of increasing women's representation in science is futile unless the association between masculinity and science is broken, that is, the practice of science is radically altered. Indeed, the most extreme ecofeminist position involves a total rejection of mainstream science on the grounds that it is intrinsically masculine (see Caldicott and Leland, 1983; Merchant, 1992; Shiva, 1988).

In contrast to ecofeminism, the emphasis in most of the "feminist science" literature tends to be more inclusive. However, it too exudes a prevailing unease with the natural sciences, or, more specifically, the physical sciences. With the exception of some work on the life sciences and geography (which spans the social and physical sciences), the main practical aspects of this literature concern the social sciences, with the fields of sociology and psychology apparently providing the most fertile ground for alternative practices. Indeed the physical sciences are portrayed as a definite "poor cousin" of the social sciences, and lambasted by some as the source of positivist ideology (Harding, 1986, 1991).

This apparent alienation and distaste for the natural sciences, which prevails in the community of feminist scholars in the social sciences and humanities, is reciprocated by similar feelings on the part of their female colleagues in the natural sciences. Women in the natural sciences, who have struggled for so long to survive and create a positive environment for their younger colleagues, do not have any time for those feminist critics who characterize their practice as akin to some kind of false consciousness. Even scholars who take a position more supportive of women in science are considered difficult to engage with, given their lack of interest and knowledge about studying the physical world (Fausto-Sterling, 1992).[10]

As a physics graduate and a feminist who is now working in the social sciences, I find myself caught between both of these groups. On the one hand, I understand women scientists' hostility to some feminists' criticisms of science. Women in science are accustomed to being told that they are out of place and the feminist analysis of masculinity and science can reinforce their sense of isolation. The tendency to concentrate on the social and life sciences is also frustrating for women in the physical sciences.

I am also deeply uncomfortable with the idea of adopting a feminist standpoint, because, as I shall go on to explain, I think that feminist-standpoint scholars over-emphasize women's shared experiences. In my view their appeals to the biological basis of women's standpoint are also flawed.[11] Equally problematic is feminist scholars' treatment of relativism, where science is treated as socially constructed. Despite the efforts of feminist scholars, such as Harding and Haraway, I shall argue that social constructivism [illegible] of the real world remain difficult to resolve when we [illegible] for my own approach to feminist [illegible] by privileging the insights of feminists with experience of practicing the natural sciences.

In order to understand what a feminist natural science would mean in practice, I must reconcile these tensions in my own views and negotiate the different perspectives of practitioners and critical theorists alike. Inspired by the earlier writings of feminist critics of science, who mostly combined an interest in feminist theory with the practice of biology, I aim to take a fresh approach to women, gender, feminism, and science. I suggest that much can be gained from a more detailed investigation of the perspective of science practitioners sympathetic to feminism. First though, it is necessary to review the feminist epistemologies of science.

Feminist epistemologies of science

There are three main types of feminist epistemologies of science that seek to bridge the gulf between traditional feminist theories and postmodernism: Sandra Harding's feminist standpoint theory (Harding, 1986, 1991), developed from the work of Nancy Hartsock (1983) and Hilary Rose (1983) amongst others; Donna Haraway's situated knowledge (Haraway, 1988); and Helen Longino's (1989) and Lynn Nelson's (1990) versions of feminist empiricism.

Sandra Harding integrates various feminist standpoint theories to argue for a feminist standpoint based on "strong objectivity." Her main argument is that science would be better if scientists developed the ability to *think from women's lives*. She combines the work of Hilary Rose, Nancy Hartsock, Gillian Ruddick (1989) (who developed "maternal thinking" theory), and Carol Gilligan (1982) (who developed theories on moral reasoning) amongst others. Harding argues that women have a privileged standpoint because their caring labor gives them a better understanding of the world. Rose and Hartsock both argue that this results from women's biological, as well as social, experiences. For example Rose argues that women's labor includes the labor of birthing, and she therefore advocates a "limited essentialism and constrained social realism" (Rose, 1994, p. 40). (See also Hartsock, 1983, p. 292.) In adopting the theories of Gilligan and Ruddick, Harding also accepts that women's psychological development, and by implication the feminist standpoint, is closely related to their biological experiences as mothers and daughters.

This emphasis on women's shared, biologically determined experiences implies that a feminist science based on a feminist standpoint would be woman only. Indeed, Rose and Harding both argue that feminist science is being practiced now, by women in the women's health and environmentalist movements, *in reaction* to mainstream science (Harding, 1991; Rose, 1994).

However, Harding does not make this position entirely explicit. Indeed, elsewhere she argues for more women in mainstream science and rejects biological determinism. She also argues that women must articulate the "gap they feel between their experience and the dominant conceptual schemes" of men (Harding, 1991, p. 70) and that this will enable scientists to *start their work from the perspective of women's lives*. In other words, scientists need to learn to see the world from the perspective of the marginalized and the oppressed, with the assistance of critical social theories generated by the emancipatory movements (Harding, 1991, p. 295). This would:

> . . . [increase] the objectivity of research by bringing scientific observations and the perception of the needs for explanation to bear on assumptions and practices that appear "natural" or unremarkable from the perspectives of the lives of men in the dominant group . . . [this] makes strange what appears familiar, which is the beginning of any scientific inquiry.
>
> (Harding, 1991, p. 150)

This type of critical reflection requires *strong* objectivity. Harding borrows here from the Edinburgh "strong programme" in the sociology of scientific knowledge, where David Bloor, for example, argues that sociologists must investigate the social construction of scientific claims that are considered by the scientific community to be true as well as those that are considered to be false (Bloor, 1976). She argues,

> . . . we must be able to identify the social causes of good beliefs, not just of the bad ones to which the conventional "sociology of errors" and objectivism restrict causal accounts. However, in contrast to the "strong programme," standpoint theory requires causal analyses not just of the micro processes in the laboratory but also of the macro tendencies in the social order which shape scientific practice . . . one can rationally distinguish social conditions giving rise to false beliefs from those giving rise to less false ones from the less false rather than more false beliefs.
>
> (Harding, 1991, pp. 149–167)

For Harding it is essential for feminists to remain able to judge between the validity of different knowledge claims by looking to the social conditions of the knowledge production.

Although sharing her desire to develop a more critical approach to scientific knowledge, Donna Haraway is critical of Harding's notion of a feminist standpoint, because she thinks that people have a multitude of different standpoints, based on differences in class, race, and sexuality, as well as gender. This means she has difficulty with Harding's notion of "seeing from below" as a means of judging the validity of knowledge claims when there are so many different standpoints that one could adopt. Instead she prefers to emphasize "situated knowledge" (Haraway, 1988; see also Haraway, 1979, 1986, 1987, 1989) and argues that people do not hold one perspective on the world, but many, some of which are contradictory. This also means that people can see from other people's perspectives, the result of which is a constantly shifting set of alliances – what she calls "coalition politics" (Haraway, 1988, p. 191). With [illegible] she says that scientists should allow their political commitments to guide their choice of particular models in science and not simply aim to uncover sexist bias. Nelson, instead, favors more empirical evaluation of knowledge and beliefs.

Although these theories have undoubtedly proved valuable in framing feminist discussions about methodology in the social sciences, their impact on practice cannot be assumed, given the isolation and minority status of many feminist researchers. This is particularly so in the case of the physical sciences. Harding, for example, only mentions the physical sciences in negative terms, calling them a "bad role model" for sciences because of their emphasis on distance from the objects of study and abstraction. Instead Harding promotes the social sciences, where she argues there is a greater emphasis on subjectivity and connection with the objects of study, usually other people (Harding, 1991), and proposes changes in the training of scientists and a model of science departments similar to the arts, where critics and practitioners are in equal numbers (Harding, 1993). In a related point, Haraway argues that the objects of study in the physical sciences – inanimate objects – should be given agency. This, she argues, would provoke a greater level of empathy and therefore self-awareness amongst researchers. Nelson and Longino also provide little detail about the physical sciences, with Longino arguing for theoretical pluralism across the sciences, and Nelson seeing more continuity in approach and theory across the social sciences, in contrast to the more abstract mathematical sciences.

Many questions remain about how to implement these theories concerning objectivity in the natural sciences. Despite her emphasis on women's diverse experiences and her rejection of biological determinism, Harding's feminist standpoint is particularly problematic because of its implied gender essentialism. By integrating the theories of Rose, Hartsock, Gilligan, and Ruddick she portrays women and men as having "some definable and discoverable nature whether given by biology or the environment" (Burr, 1995, p. 6). This means that she skirts dangerously close to the stereotypical and ultimately disempowering characterization of women that anti-feminists promote.

This brings into question the usefulness of adopting a feminist standpoint in the natural sciences. While the products of science would definitely improve if scientists were to think about their impact on women's caring labour, it is difficult to see how

Harding's feminist standpoint could be "achieved" by male or female scientists who have not experienced such activity, especially motherhood. The implication of this is that a feminist natural science will develop outwith the established scientific community (as Rose has already suggested). Although it is clearly important to promote unorthodox approaches to science (which I shall discuss later), we also need to transform the existing institutions of science. If feminists turn away to pursue a separate scientific project they, in effect, leave untouched the male domination of orthodox science.

Harding's acceptance of the influence of women's biology on the feminist standpoint, as opposed to a full account of the social construction of motherhood, and womanhood more broadly, also prevents us from gaining a deeper understanding of women's roles in society. Unless scientists are better able to appreciate women's many (biological and social) experiences, they will continue the current trend in much biological theorizing to adopt stereotypical imagery of women (and men).

Harding's feminist standpoint theory is not, however, the only aspect of feminist epistemologies of science that raises difficulties when we think about their role in the natural sciences. Aside from the problems that all of these proposals would raise for individuals trying to "know their own biases" (which would require a higher degree of self-awareness and honesty than most people operate with on a routine basis), group analysis of subjectivity could be equally difficult, given the inevitable subtext of political maneuvering amongst group members. The differences in perspectives amongst the emancipatory groups that Harding suggests would adjudicate between knowledge claims are likely to be difficult to resolve and Haraway's situated knowledge may be equally difficult to operationalize, given her emphasis on partiality and difference in perspective.

Thinking about implementing feminist epistemologies in the natural sciences raises further problems when we consider the "unpacking" of scientific knowledge, which they require. As sociologists and historians of science know, it is immensely difficult to untangle the social conditions that lead to particular forms of scientific knowledge, especially when this is without the benefit of hindsight or when the most obscure and reductionist theories of the physical sciences are concerned. In addition, having empathy with or giving agency to inanimate objects of study, as suggested by Haraway, might only exacerbate the problem of unpacking knowledge claims, by adding further layers of unreflective anthropomorphism. In short, how do we unpack empirical and social/political values from the "seamless web" of scientific knowledge?

These difficulties are compounded by a lack of thought or concern about the organization of the natural sciences in the feminist epistemologies. How would the different sciences be related in a feminist science based on the principles of feminist standpoint theory and strong objectivity or situated knowledge or feminist empiricism? The above theorists all seem to be suggesting a new paradigm of knowledge, rooted in the social sciences, with its emphasis on empathy and connectedness with the objects of study, but they disagree about the extent of similarity amongst the social and natural sciences. Large changes in the training and organization of scientists are radical steps, which are likely to be blocked by many different groups within the academic and political establishments. Would disciplinary divisions, to the extent that they exist, hinder change? Are the social sciences really the best model for change within the natural sciences?

To summarize, three main questions remain:

- How would scientists work together in a feminist natural science and how would they build an appreciation of the varied lives of women (and men) into their work?
- What practical standards for inquiry would a feminist natural science involve? How would these be established without losing sight of the social context of scientific knowledge?
- How would the different sciences relate to each other?

Feminist practitioners' perspectives

I now go on to explore in more depth the perspectives of feminist practitioners on these theories. I draw on the considerable body of literature by women scientists or ex-scientists who have an interest in feminism (see Hubbard, Henifin, and Fried, 1979, 1982).[12] Other work includes the numerous articles by Evelyn Fox Keller (see Keller, 1985)[13] and Longino's collaboration with two feminist scientists (Longino and Doell, 1983; Longino and Hammonds, 1990).[14]

In addition to considering this written material, I also draw on interviews with feminist practitioners and critics of science. Between 1993 and 1994 I interviewed 30 women from the UK, USA, and Canada, all with science backgrounds and who have either stayed in academia or retired, but are now variously involved in science as practitioners or, outside of science, as critics. These women's positions range from a liberal interest in promoting women and science through to a more radical criticism of science. The majority of active critical writers in this field are American (this can only really be noted here without more detailed consideration). The disciplines these women come from can be roughly categorized into physics, chemistry, and biology, with 13 each in physics and biology and a much smaller 4 in chemistry. Of the physicists, the vast majority, 11, were liberal women scientists and the majority of biologists were familiar with or active in feminist criticism of science. This mirrors the difficulty in conceptualizing and practicing a feminist physics. Interviews lasted for around an hour, and were tape recorded and transcribed (one was conducted over e-mail). I used a mixture of open-ended and more specific questions about background in research and interest in feminism; how science is sexist or gendered; how science might change for the better; and how feminist epistemologies of science relate to such a change. Interviewees were guaranteed anonymity. Where excerpts from interviews are used, interviewees are coded according to their principal activity (C = critic; P = practitioner; CP = both), the number of the interview, and their principal subject area (C = chemistry; B = biology; P = physics).

Feminist standpoint theory[15]

Feminist critics of science have looked in detail at sexist "bias" in the biological sciences. The Brighton Women in Science Group (1980) in the UK, and various women biologists in the US (e.g., Hubbard *et al.*, 1979, 1982)[16] and Canada, such as the late Margaret Benson (1982) (see also Franklin, Gay, and Miles, 1993), were especially active in debunking sexist assumptions in the biological and social sciences.[17] Lynda Birke, for example, highlights the numerous problems with research into sex difference (Birke, 1992). Taking into account the different sizes and shapes of people's genitalia, the existence of varying amounts of the sex hormones (androgens, progesterones, oestrogens) in both sexes, and the significant overlap in physical attributes between men and women, Birke argues that the dichotomy between male and female is ambiguous. She highlights the hidden inferences and assumptions that shape scientists' research; some of which are evident in the wider culture (e.g., the assumption that differences between men and women are biological); and others that may be more specific to this type of science (e.g., that animal brains can tell scientists about human brains). Birke also draws attention to the contradictory nature of much of the research and its role in legitimating the status quo.

Birke's emphasis on the immense variety in women and men's biological characteristics and the social construction of distinctive qualities compounds the difficulties with the notion of a feminist standpoint, which I identified earlier. It has already been emphasized that women's social experiences are very different, depending on their class, race, and sexuality amongst other criteria, and Birke shows us that their biological characteristics and, therefore, biological experiences are also different.[18] Moreover, Birke highlights the social construction of gender categories, noting the way in which women and men's shared biological experiences and differences between women's experiences are overlooked. In a similar vein to Birke, Evelyn Fox Keller (1985) also radically challenges feminist standpoint theory when she advocates a "gender-neutral" science that would involve "a transformation of the very categories of male and female, and correspondingly of mind and nature" (Keller, 1985, p. 178).

Birke and Keller seem to be making an argument for change from within science, which involves an appreciation of the social construction of biological categories and appreciation of diversity amongst the sexes. This challenges excessively stereotypical portrayals of women and men and the separatist agenda on which Harding's feminist standpoint seems to be based.

Feminist practitioners also made the case for appreciating diversity amongst practitioners when arguing for change from within science in interviews, for example:

> [Science] has to somehow become more decentralized – so that there is room for more diversity in the scientific endeavor. . . . What this probably means is smaller grants to more people to do lower tech things. . . . The way scientists work [also] has to be altered, and this is very reflective of the way I think all society has to change. I think it has to have a more open ended entry to the career, so that people who are older than 30 and who've had delays in their careers . . . should still be eligible to enter the field . . . and I think that once scientists start to work they have to be more flexible in terms of the way they work. . . . There should be a really generous approach in terms of people taking time out, or working part time. . . . I think these are very real impediments to women in science. (P13B)

This makes the feminist standpoint irrelevant to many feminist practitioners of science, for example:

> I don't care [about feminist theories in some ways], that's another issue. . . . I read articles . . . there's a whole issue about whether women think differently from men, whether they act differently, and whether there's a feminist way, and somehow I don't think I care. I want to be able to do science and I want other

> I think it's got its uses, I think that I wouldn't be a feminist if I didn't believe that women had some degree of commonality . . . otherwise . . . there is no physical grounds for feminism at all . . . but that's not to deny that there aren't important differences [amongst women] too. (C1B)

These feminist practitioners are arguing for diversity amongst women and scientists (without losing sight of their similarities). They also advocate exploring the social construction of and ultimately transforming traditional conceptual categories (particularly those concerned with gender) from within science. Haraway's emphasis on "situated knowledge" and "coalition politics" (Haraway, 1988) is a close fit with these suggestions. However, we need to explore objectivity in more depth before coming to a final conclusion about the usefulness of Haraway's and others' theories. The problems of uncovering scientists' subjectivity (at the group and individual level), identifying its influence on scientific knowledge, and developing a good relationship between the natural and social sciences remain.

Objectivity

Feminist critics of science have engaged in detailed criticism of the way the myth of objectivity encourages scientific elitism.

> The conventional view of objectivity is not simply a misconception that has occurred by chance. The rhetoric of objectivity serves to obscure the very real social and political biases of knowledge produced within universities. This knowledge is systematically more useful to the privileged than to the majority of people. It especially benefits businesses, the military and governments. However, if knowledge is seen as value-free then the question of who the knowledge serves can never arise. In fact the emphasis on objective knowledge acts to limit inquiry to topics which do not threaten the social order, since work that suggests changing the class structure or the gender or racial biases of our societies is seen as unsound.
>
> (Lowe, 1993, p. 8)

Lowe points to scientists' political maneuvering to suppress research that seeks to challenge existing power structures – one way of limiting the diversity in topics and practitioners that feminist practitioners called for above. However, this does not mean that feminists in science must entirely reject objectivity. Instead they have sought to identify different "levels" of objectivity. Anne Fausto-Sterling, for example, has argued for rigorous methodology, including proper controls and observational techniques that limit individual bias and thorough statistical analysis (Fausto-Sterling, 1985). Elizabeth Fee also argues that positive meanings of objectivity include the:

> . . . constant process of practical interaction with nature; willingness to consider all assumptions and methods as open to question . . . and the idea of individual creativity subjected to the constraints of community validation through a series of recognised procedures.
>
> (Fee, 1983, p. 16)

On the other hand, Fee rejects what she calls the "hierarchy of distances" in objectivity, which she argues is manifest in four ways: the portrayal of the process of production of knowledge as separate from its social use; the separation between scientific rationality and emotion in the language of science; the distance between the researcher and the object of study (which legitimates the domination of nature); and the view of science as separate and distinct from society. Interviewees also discussed objectivity in these terms, for example:

> Taking data and analysing I think are pretty objective – those are the tools we learn, how to measure the spectrum, how to plot up the results – but there are subjective parts at the . . . beginning and the end which is the choosing of the problem and the interpretation of the results . . . I think it's a shame that science is portrayed as reductionist and somehow dispassionate because it is absolutely subjective . . . at the beginning and the end points, and whatever you see up there in nature is going to be a product of what your eyes and brain are able to see and interpret. . . . I think that any scientist will say that it is, at a very personal level, very passionate. (P9P)

In the main feminist practitioners of science rejected the idea of separating knowledge from experience and politics. Instead these women argued for uncovering bias and subjectivities, in the sense of grounding knowledge back in experience. For example:

> I think there are different kinds of objectivity, and I think the objectivity that most of us were attacking is an objectivity that says I am nothing to do with this thing that I am studying and there is a great distance between this truth that's extracted from all human life and my ability to perceive what is going on, which is just sort of an empty screen . . . a more honest approach is certainly to admit that we're involved in the process of knowing the world, so there's a subjectivity you necessarily bring to any kind of science, that you bring to the kinds of questions that you want to raise . . . and for that matter . . . to the process of getting sensitive answers . . . now at the same time that doesn't mean there are no rules, no tests . . . I think the whole process of testing and confirming and debating and investigating and comparing results is going to go on. (PC4B)

This revamped version of objectivity is also associated with a more humble approach to the objects of study, characterized by less reductionist and more inductive (as opposed to deductive) methodologies, exemplified in the work of Barbara McClintock (Keller, 1985). For example:

> There's an analogy both in philosophy and in science . . . if you meditate on a point you meditate on something infinitely small in order to achieve something [illegible] think you can just narrow down . . . and somehow you are reductionist and missing the point . . . you have to do that in order to get the bigger picture. (P9P)

Meditation, or deep reflection, involves simultaneously holding a holistic and reductionist perspective.

Feminist practitioners' recognition of the way in which subjectivity shapes scientific practice, and therefore knowledge, challenges the way in which the rhetoric of objectivity is currently being used to stifle radical research. They accept that the production of knowledge is socially shaped; and want to bring the subject back into scientific writing; and to show respect for nature. This does not, however, entail a complete rejection of objectivity, because certain aspects of objectivity remain important, for example, tests that eliminate particular biases in the data and an acceptance of reductionism where it is most appropriate. A tolerance of diversity in methodology, explanations, and theories in science is another important aspect of feminist practitioners' arguments.

This approach has much in common with the emphasis on restrained relativism and realism in the feminist epistemologies – Haraway's "situated knowledge," Harding's "strong objectivity," and Longino's "contextual empiricism" – all modify the existing standards of inquiry, and recognize the subjective factors in science. However, from the perspective of feminist practitioners, when observing and theorizing scientists ought to be uncovering "biases" instead of deliberately using them to guide knowledge production. Their accounts also show that the methods of the social sciences cannot be simply imported into the natural sciences (despite their shared values, such as respect for the objects of study and bringing the subject into scientific writing). The predominance of qualitative methods in feminist research in the social sciences would clearly not be appropriate in the natural sciences. It is clear that each piece of research demands a different treatment of subjectivities in knowledge, depending on the research questions, albeit within the general rubric of critical reflection. However, they also accept that subjectivity cannot or should not always be eliminated (e.g., when choosing research questions).

Feminist practitioners stressed the need for financial support for alternative practices in science, and for a supportive network of colleagues, as well as diversity amongst scientists (which would generate critical reflection on a community-wide basis):

> Well I do [explore subjectivity] in the sense that I study the social context out of which the question has arisen and I know about its history, I know about how these ideas have come to be . . . [and where] my ideas are situated in regards to . . . the mainstream ideas, ones that are further out than mine, what I'm maneuvering through . . . but I'm a lonely person I don't have much . . . money . . . so it's a little bit different from . . . if I were negotiating through the NIH [National Institutes of Health, USA] or something like that. (C3B)

> I want to be able to work in a nurturing environment and I don't think there are many men who can fit in or provide that sort of environment. . . . I mean an environment where you can exchange ideas with people without fear of being judged, it's like working with friends. . . . I find women, if you want to talk about science with women, they're generally more supportive. (P4P)

> . . . ideas [about strong objectivity] are probably not practical. . . . I don't know that people are necessarily capable of being open about their biases, or to know what their assumptions about the world are all the time. Sometimes you know and you can lay them out, one, two, three . . . but often you don't really know until you're confronted by something that is different from you. (PC4B)

Diversity in topics is clearly related to diversity in scientists:

> Being more respectful of other human beings and widening the number of people, the kinds of people, from which scientists are drawn . . . would certainly change science. Now, that's certainly part of the feminist enterprise but it's not exclusive to the feminist enterprise . . . the sorts of notions about multiculturalism that other people would bring other kinds of questions . . . you [also have to be] more careful that you don't use the need for expertise automatically to exclude other kinds of knowledge, the kinds of traditional knowledge that are certainly useful ways of looking at nature and explaining nature. . . . I think all of that needs to be included in what science should be like. (C2B)

The call for more interdisciplinary research, for example between physics and biology in researching the effects of radiation on organic material, follows from this stress on diversity. Central to more collaboration is a less competitive environment:

> I think I'd start almost with social relations of science if I could design science. It would be slower, not so competitive, when you got negative results, or you had doubts about what you were doing, or something didn't quite turn out . . . you could report that and actually get it published, whereas now it's cut and dried. Meetings would be a lot more fun because people would be coming together to share ideas instead of to put one another down. (P8B)

Feminist natural scientists also emphasize changing society through research into questions of interest and importance to ordinary people. This would involve a different relationship between scientists and between scientists and the local community. Interviewees talked of involving the local community in research design and data collection, and not presenting scientific results as the objective truth but as a partial picture of nature, and therefore open to debate:

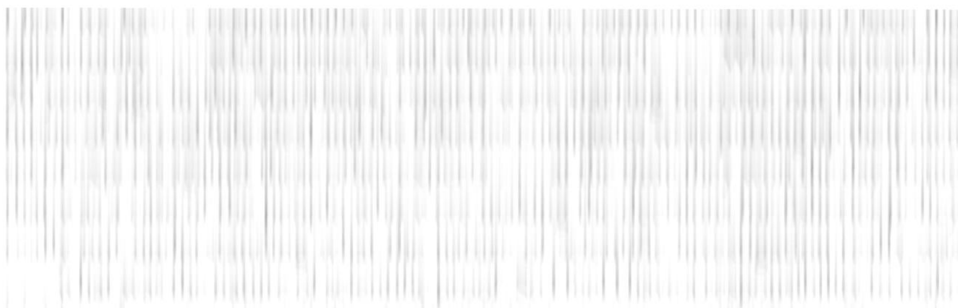

> it clear what science can say and what science cannot say. (P14C)

This community involvement would challenge boundaries between scientific disciplines, involving scientists in more collaboration and discussion. The moves that have been made by some feminist scientists toward increased community involvement bear this out. Despite the climate of cutbacks in research funding, some interviewees told of modest success in changing their scientific practice at a local level:

> We have here . . . a special set up . . . there are agreements between our university and three trade unions . . . there's also another arrangement between the university and women's groups and both of those types of agreements provide that if the groups ask for research or activities then the University system will provide those sorts of activities. . . . So, for example, the first time that I was asked for in this way was when a health centre asked for a course in women's bodies instead of giving four or five hours of regular teaching of undergraduates. . . . I've also been quite involved with women's groups, particularly in the trade unions, and particularly around issues of women and work. (P17B)

Concentrating on the links between organization and research practice offers pragmatic solutions to the problem of changing the natural sciences. The biological and social sciences are more open to feminist transformation because of their human subject matter, which means that the link between the local and scientific communities is stronger. The fact that there are already more women and, therefore, feminists in these disciplines also makes feminist transformation more likely. Changes in the physical sciences can, however, also be achieved by feminist promotion of diversity amongst its practitioners and community-based research initiatives.

Further discussion and conclusions

Feminist practitioners variously emphasize:

- The social construction of biological difference and gender categories
- Challenging conventional categorizations, that is, looking between groups for similarity and amongst groups for differences (particularly where gender is concerned)
- The value of many different perspectives and experiences amongst scientists
- Changing science from within science
- Tolerating diversity in practitioners, practices, and theories in science
- More open exploration of uncertainty and social influences on scientific knowledge
- The different levels and degrees of objectivity
- Switching between distance and connectedness with the objects of study and reductionist and holistic perspectives
- Flexible career paths
- Interdisciplinary research
- Collaboration between scientists and the local community
- Establishing funding structures for more innovative feminist-inspired research
- Developing support networks for women in science (as well as other minority groups).

These provide refreshing ideas about the epistemological and organizational changes involved in moving towards a feminist natural science.

Feminist practitioners argued that transforming the natural sciences involves opening up science to more diverse groups of people, and developing strong support networks amongst groups with common interests. They favored a nurturing environment where scientists could critically explore each other's work. This is required in the local laboratory and also at an interdisciplinary level. Instead of emphasizing gender differences, feminist practitioners favored a more critical perspective on gender. This means that where research concerns gender they are keen to dismantle the established preconceptions about gender, and to look carefully at the social construction of gender differences. This would also affect their relationships with each other – allowing for more collaboration between men and women, for example. The changes that they advocate are firmly placed within the existing institutions of science. This sits uneasily with feminist standpoint theory because of its implied essentialism and its resonance with a separatist agenda. However, the feminist standpoint theories' emphasis on standpoints that generate a more critical appreciation of knowledge claims, and on women's shared experiences and, therefore, solidarity are mirrored in these interviewees' accounts of feminism and science.

Feminist practitioners emphasized uncovering scientists' subjectivity through statistical tests that identify individual biases and critical reflection amongst a supportive yet diverse group of scientists. This differs from the feminist epistemologies in that the emphasis is on uncovering instead of extolling subjectivity when observing and analysing results. But it does involve a recognition and acceptance of subjectivity guiding research questions, as Harding, Haraway, Longino and Nelson all stress is important.

An appreciation of the social context of the questions being asked does not have to be at the expense of a commitment to better, more accurate knowledge. Importantly, these methods can be adopted in all the natural sciences, and emphasize the importance of the local context (avoiding generalizing to the physical sciences from the life sciences). In the more abstract areas of science, change can also be fostered at a philosophical level, with exploration of the mutuality of reductionism and holism, for example.

As well as fostering interdisciplinary research, involvement in the local community [illegible] suggests. Instead, Haraway's "partial perspectives" and "split and contradictory selves" is a more appropriate description of what interviewees favoured.

These organizational changes would also complement and reinforce new approaches to objectivity, as outlined in the feminist epistemologies. The current limitations in the traditional research environment (financial and cultural) mean that some feminist practitioners are looking to nontraditional sources of funding, for example, collaboration with workers' organizations, community groups, and social scientists. This does not just involve the life sciences, but could also involve the physical sciences (e.g., in developing more efficient and accessible transport systems or better energy provision).

Feminist practitioners' emphasis on diversity amongst scientists and on using the clash of perspectives that this engenders to generate deeper critical analysis and, therefore, better knowledge in science and their clear rejection of essentialism resolve the tensions with the notion of a feminist standpoint, which I identified at the start of this article. Their emphasis on different levels of objectivity and exploring subjectivity instead of being wholly guided by it also helps in the resolution of relativism and providing "better" accounts of the real world. The emphasis on collaboration between scientists in different disciplines and with people in the local community also reinforces my sense that the social sciences are not a simple model for change within the natural sciences. Instead, the overlap between the strategies of feminist practitioners in the social and natural sciences, such as their mutual emphasis on bridging the gap between the subject and object of study, ought to be put to good use in a relationship where social and natural scientists are equal partners. These strategies for moving toward a feminist natural science can be promoted in various ways. Feminist epistemologies perform a valuable role in making us think more deeply about what a feminist science might mean. And despite the constraints on moving toward a feminist science, feminist practitioners of science clearly have dynamic and imaginative approaches to knowledge creation in the sciences. Their accounts of their practice emphasize the local and incremental process of moving toward a feminist science, and the importance of "building bridges" between scientific and local communities. In order to bring more women into the project to transform the sciences feminists are best located within the sciences as well as outwith as critics and community activists.

Notes

1 See also Devault, 1996; Henwood and Pidgeon, 1995; Mattingly and Falconer-Alhindi, 1995.
2 See also Cowan, 1995; Keller, 1987a, 1987b, 1992; Longino and Hammonds, 1990.
3 See Haraway, 1988; Harding and Hintikka, 1983; Hartsock, 1983; Longino, 1988, 1989; Nelson, 1990; Rose 1983, 1994.
4 For a selection of "strong programme" work see Barnes, 1972, 1974, 1977; Barnes and Edge, 1982; Bloor, 1973, 1976.
5 Kerr, 1995.
6 Standpoint theory (drawn from Hegelian and Marxist philosophy) has been adopted by feminist theorists, such as Nancy Hartsock (1983) and Hilary Rose (1983), who argue that women understand the world more clearly because of their oppression. Postmodernist theories have influenced feminist scholars such as Jane Flax, who seeks to uncover political power within the academy, and resists generalizing about women's experience or the causes of their oppression (Flax, 1983, 1987, 1990; see also Nicholson, 1990). Deconstruction of modernist dichotomies – such as public and private, emotion and reason – is also favored by some postmodernist feminists because their dichotomies have played a role in women's oppression (Nicholson, 1990). On the other hand, postmodernism is viewed by some feminists as dangerously apolitical because of its relativism (Nicholson, 1990). Although empiricism is also dismissed by some feminist scholars because it implies that it is possible to generate "value free" knowledge, feminist empiricists argue that it can provide more empirically accurate accounts of the real world (see Longino, 1989; Nelson, 1990.
7 See also Bleier, 1984, 1986; Fausto-Sterling, 1985; Haraway, 1979; Kelly, 1981, 1987; Merchant, 1980; Rose, 1994, Rosser, 1990.
8 See Kahle, 1985; MacRae, Devine, and Lakey, 1991; Packer, 1993.
9 See also Office of Science and Technologies' Working Party on Women, Science and Engineering, 1993, 1994.
10 See also Harding, 1993; Fausto-Sterling, 1992; Rosser, 1990; Tuana, 1989.
11 See "Feminist Standpoint Theory" section for a full analysis. See also Cowan, 1995; Flax, 1987; Haraway, 1988; Holmwood, 1995 for various critiques of Harding's position.
12 See also Hubbard and Lowe, 1979, 1983; Bleier, 1984, 1986; Franklin *et al.* 1993; Brighton Women in Science Group, 1980; Birke, 1986, 1992; Fausto-Sterling, 1985, 1992.
13 See also Keller, 1978, 1982, 1983, 1985, 1987a, 1987b, 1992.
14 This work has developed in tandem with other critical perspectives on science, from both the Radical Science Movement and the sociology of scientific knowledge. Feminist critics have drawn on and extended the perspectives in the Radical Science Movement (see Rose and Rose, 1969, 1976a, 1976b) and the so-called "new sociology of science" (see Barnes, 1972, 1974, 1977; Barnes and Edge, 1982; Bloor, 1973, 1976; Collins, 1981; Gilbert and Mulkay, 1984; Knorr-Cetina, 1981; Knorr-Cetina and Mulkay, 1983; Kuhn, 1962; Latour, 1987; Latour and Woolgar, 1979), which rejected the notion that scientific knowledge is objective.
15 Feminist standpoint theory has, of course, been criticized from other perspectives (e.g., Cowan, 1995; Holmwood, 1995). The perspectives from feminist practice complement, rather than contradict these other critiques.

16 See also Hubbard and Lowe, 1979, 1983; Bleier, 1984, 1986.

17 See also Birke, 1986, 1992; Fausto-Sterling, 1985; Haraway, 1979, 1986, 1987, 1989; Tuana, 1989.

18 Biological characteristics shape but do not solely determine people's experiences. In distinguishing between "biological" and "social" experiences, I do not wish to imply that these are nonrelated, but it is important to emphasize that people experience their own bodies as well as the world around them. Biological experiences are, of [illegible]

Barnes, Barry. (1974). *Scientific knowledge and sociological theory*. London: Routledge and Kegan Paul.

Barnes, Barry. (1977). *Interests and the growth of knowledge*. London: Routledge and Kegan Paul.

Barnes, Barry, and Edge, David. (1982). (Eds.). *Science in context: Readings in the sociology of science*. Milton Keynes: Open University Press.

Benson, Margaret. (1982). Feminism and the critique of scientific method. In Angela R. Miles and Geraldine Finn (Eds.), *Feminism in Canada* (pp. 47–66). Montreal: Black Rose Books.

Birke, Lynda. (1986). *Women, feminism and biology*. New York: Methuen Books.

Birke, Lynda. (1992). In pursuit of difference: Scientific studies of women and men. In Gill Kircup and Laurie Smith Keller (Eds.), *Inventing women: Science, technology and gender* (pp. 81–102). Milton Keynes: Open University Press.

Bleier, Ruth. (1984). *Science and gender: A critique of biology and its theories on women*. Oxford: Pergamon Press.

Bleier, Ruth. (1986). (Ed.). *Feminist approaches to science*. New York: Pergamon Press.

Bloor, David. (1973). Wittgenstein and Manheim on the sociology of mathematics. *Studies in History and Philosophy of Science*, 4, 173–191.

Bloor, David. (1976). *Knowledge and social imagery*. London: Routledge and Kegan Paul.

Brighton Women in Science Group. (1980). (Eds.). *Alice through the microscope: The power of science over women's lives*. London: Virago.

Burr, V. (1995). *An introduction to social constructivism*. London: Routledge.

Caldicott, Leonie, and Leland, Stephanie. (1983). (Eds.). *Reclaim the earth: Women speak out for life on earth*. London: Women's Press.

Campbell, Rebecca. (1995). Weaving a new tapestry of research. A bibliography of Selected Readings on Feminist Methods. *Women's Studies International Forum*, 18, 215–222.

Collins, Harry. (1981). The place of the "core-set" in modern science: Social contingency with methodological propriety in science. *History of Science*, 19, 6–19.

Cowan, Ruth S. (1995). Women and science: Contested terrain. *Social Studies of Science*, 25, 363–370.

Devault, M.L. (1996). Talking back to sociology. Distinctive contributions of feminist methodology. *Annual Review of Sociology*, 22, 29–50.

Fausto-Sterling, Anne. (1985). *Myths of gender: Biological theories about women and men*. New York: Basic Books.

Fausto-Sterling, Anne. (1992). Building two-way streets: The case of feminism and science. *National Women's Studies Association Journal*, 4, 336–349.

Fee, Elizabeth. (1983). Women's nature and scientific objectivity. In Ruth Hubbard and Marion Lowe (Eds.), *Woman's nature: Rationalisation of women's inequality* (pp. 9–28). New York: Gordian Press.

Flax, Jane. (1983). Political philosophy and the patriarchal unconscious: A psychoanalytical perspective on epistemology and metaphysics. In Sandra Harding and Merrill Hintikka (Eds.), *Discovering reality: Feminist perspectives on epistemology, metaphysics, methodology and philosophy of science* (pp. 245–82). Dordrecht: Reidel Publishing.

Flax, Jane. (1987). Postmodernism and gender relations in feminist theory. *Signs: Journal of Women in Culture and Society*, 12, 621–643.

Flax, Jane. (1990). *Thinking fragments: Psychoanalysis, feminism and postmodernism in the contemporary west*. Berkeley, CA: University of California Press.

Franklin, Ursula, Gay, Hannah, and Miles, Angela. (1993). Women in science and technology: The legacy of Margaret Benson. *Canadian Woman Studies*, 13, 1–128.

Gilbert, Nigel, and Mulkay, Michael. (1984). *Opening Pandora's box: A sociological analysis of scientists' discourse*. Cambridge: Cambridge University Press.

Gilligan, Carol. (1982). *In a different voice: Psychological theory and women's development*. Cambridge, MA: Harvard University Press.

Haraway, Donna. (1979). The biological enterprise: Sex, mind and profit from human engineering to sociobiology. *Radical History Review*, 4, 21–36.

Haraway, Donna. (1986). Primatology is politics by other means. In Ruth Bleier (Ed.), *Feminist approaches to science* (pp. 77–118). New York: Pergamon Press.

Haraway, Donna. (1987). Animal sociology and a natural economy of the body politic, part 1: A political physiology of dominance. In Sandra Harding and Jean O'Barr (Eds.), *Sex and scientific inquiry* (pp. 217–232). Chicago, IL: University of Chicago Press.

Haraway, Donna. (1988). Situated knowledges: The science question in feminism and the privilege of partial perspective. *Feminist Studies*, 14, 575–599.

Haraway, Donna. (1989). *Primate visions*. New York: Routledge.

Harding, Sandra. (1986). *The science question in feminism*. New York: Cornell University Press.

Harding, Sandra. (1991). *Whose science? Whose knowledge? Thinking from women's lives*. Milton Keynes: Open University Press.

Harding, Sandra. (1993). Comments on Anne Fausto-Sterling's "Building Two Way Streets." *National Women's Studies Association Journal*, 5, 49–55.

Harding, Sandra, and Hintikka, Merrill. (1983). (Eds.). *Discovering reality: Feminist perspectives on epistemology, metaphysics, methodology and philosophy of science*. Dordrecht: Reidel Publishing.

Hartsock, Nancy. (1983). The feminist standpoint: Developing the ground for a specifically feminist historical materialism. In Sandra Harding and Merrill Himikka (Eds.), *Discovering reality: Feminist perspectives on epistemology, metaphysics, methodology and philosophy of science* (pp. 283–310). Dordrecht: Reidel Publishing.

Henwood, K., and Pidgeon, N. (1995). Remaking the link – Qualitative research and Feminist Standpoint Theory. *Feminism and Psychology*, 5, 730.

Holmwood, John. (1995). Feminism and epistemology: What kind of successor science? *Sociology*, 29, 411–428.

Hornig, L.S. (1984). Women in science and engineering: Why so few? *Technology Review*, 87, 31–41.

Hubbard, Ruth, and Lowe, Marion. (1979). *Genes and gender II: Pitfalls in research on sex and gender*. New York: Gordian Press.

Hubbard, Ruth, and Lowe, Marion. (1983). (Eds.). *Woman's nature: Rationalisation of women's inequality*. New York: Gordian Press.

Hubbard, Ruth, Henifin, Mary Sue, and Fried, Barbara. (1979). (Eds.). *Women looking at* [illegible]

Keller, Evelyn Fox. (1982). Feminism and science. *Signs*, 7, 589–602.

Keller, Evelyn Fox. (1983). *A feeling for the organism: The life and work of Barbara McClintock*. New York: W.H. Freeman.

Keller, Evelyn Fox. (1985). *Reflections on Gender and Science*. New Haven: Yale University Press.

Keller, Evelyn Fox. (1987a). The gender/science system: Or is sex to gender as nature is to science. *Hypatia*, 2, 37–49.

Keller, Evelyn Fox. (1987b). Learning about women. Gender, politics and power. *Daedalus*, 116, 77–91.

Keller, Evelyn Fox. (1992). How gender matters or why it's so difficult to count past two. In Gill Kircup and Laurie Smith Keller (Eds.), *Inventing women: Science, technology and gender* (pp. 42–56). Milton Keynes: Open University Press.

Kelly, Alison. (1981). *The missing half: Girls and science education*. Manchester: Manchester University Press.

Kelly, Alison. (1987). *Science for girls?* Milton Keynes: Open University Press.

Kerr, E. Anne. (1995). *Feminising science: Linking theory and practice*. Unpublished doctoral thesis, University of Edinburgh.

Kerr, E. Anne, and Faulkner, Wendy. (1997). On seeing broken spectres: Sex and gender in twentieth century science. In John Krige and Dominique Pestre (Eds.), *Science in the twentieth century* (pp. 43–60). London: Harwood Academic Press.

Knorr-Cetina, Karin. (1981). *The manufacture of knowledge: An essay on the constructivist and contextual nature of science*. Oxford: Pergamon Press.

Knorr-Cetina, Karin, and Mulkay, Michael. (1983). (Eds.). *Science observed: Perspectives on the social study of science*. London: Sage Publications.

Kuhn, Thomas. (1962). *The structure of scientific revolutions*. Chicago: University of Chicago Press.

Latour, Bruno. (1987). *Science in action*. Milton Keynes: Open University Press.

Latour, Bruno, and Woolgar, Steve. (1979). *Laboratory life: The social construction of scientific facts*. Beverly Hills, CA: Sage.

Longino, Helen. (1988). Science and feminist values. *Feminist Studies*, 14, 561–574.

Longino, Helen. (1989). *Science as social knowledge*. New York: Princeton University Press.

Longino, Helen, and Doell, Ruth. (1983). Body bias and behaviour. *Signs*, 9, 206–227.

Longino, Helen, and Hammonds, Evelyn. (1990). Conflicts and tension in the feminist study of gender and science. In Marion Hirsch and Evelyn Fox Keller (Eds.), *Conflicts in feminism* (pp. 164–183). London: Routledge.

Lowe, Marion. (1993). To understand the world in order to change it. In Ursula Franklin, Hannah Gay, and Angela Miles (Eds.), *Women in science and technology: The legacy of Margaret Benson. Canadian Woman Studies*, 13, 6–11.

MacRae, S., Devine, F., and Lakey, J. (1991). *Women in engineering and science: Employer's policies and practices*. London: Policy Studies Institute.

Mattingly, D.J., and Falconer-Alhindi, K. (1995). Should women count – A context for the debate. *Professional Geographer*, 47, 427–435.

Merchant, Carolyn. (1980). *The death of nature: Women, ecology, and the scientific revolution*. San Francisco: Harper & Row.

Merchant, Carolyn. (1992). *Radical ecology: The search for a liveable world*. New York: Routledge.

National Research Council. (1994). *Women scientists and engineers employed in industry, why so few?* Washington, DC: National Research Council.

Nelson, Lynn Hankinson. (1990). *Who knows; From Quine to a feminist empiricism*. Philadelphia: Temple University Press.

Nicholson, Lynda. (1990). (Ed.). *Feminism/postmodernism*. London and New York: Routledge.

Office of Science and Technologies' Working Party on Women, Science and Engineering. (1993). *Realising our potential: The 1993 White Paper on science, engineering and technology*. London: HMSO.

Office of Science and Technologies' Working Party on Women, Science and Engineering. (1994). *The rising tide: Women in science*. London: HMSO.

Packer, Kathryn. (1993). *Climbing the career ladder? The position of women and girls in UK science and technology*. Unpublished paper presented at Science Policy Support Group Policy Analysis Forum, A Gender Policy for British Science, 10th May 1993.

Rose, Hilary. (1983). Hand, brain and heart: A feminist epistemology for the natural sciences. *Signs*, 9, 73–90.

Rose, Hilary. (1994). *Love, power and knowledge: Towards a feminist transformation of the sciences*. Cambridge: Polity Press.

Rose, Hilary, and Rose, Steven. (1969). *Science and society*. Harmondsworth: Penguin.

Rose, Hilary, and Rose, Steven. (1976a). (Eds.). *The political economy of science*. London: Macmillan.

Rose, Hilary, and Rose, Steven. (1976b). (Eds.). *The radicalisation of science*. London: Macmillan.

Rosser, Sue. (1990). *Female friendly science: Applying women's studies methods and theories to attract students*. Oxford: Pergamon Press.

Ruddick, Sarah. (1989). *Maternal thinking: Towards a politics of peace*. Boston: Beacon Press.

Shiva, Vanda. (1988). *Staying alive: Women ecology and development*. London: Zed.

Tuana, Nancy. (1989). (Ed.). *Feminism and science*. Bloomington: University of Indiana Press.

Chapter 30

Bonnie Jean Shulman

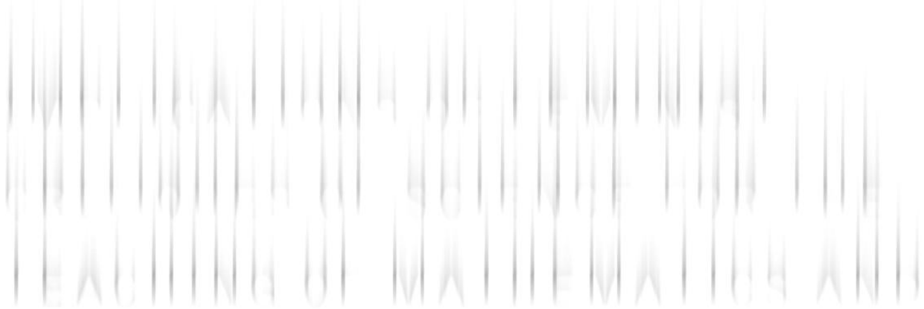

SCIENCE

Within the last half of the twentieth century, challenges to science as the bastion of true and certain knowledge have been mounted on many fronts. The specifically feminist contribution to this discussion is in framing the analysis in terms of gender ideology. This article includes a summary of some of these feminist critiques of science, which leads to an investigation of the role that language plays within science. In addition I explore the ramifications of gendered discourse to the teaching of science and mathematics, and examine some of the ways in which nature and culture interact in the production and dissemination of scientific knowledge.

Introduction

There is a core of assumptions about science that set it apart from other knowledge systems and confer upon it a special status. This status is based on the alleged superiority of the two fundamental attributes of scientific knowledge: its rationality and its objectivity. The position of science is further enhanced by the firmly held belief that the principled application of pure logical reasoning to unbiased observations is itself assured by strict adherence to the rules of scientific method. For over three centuries the veracity and reliability of other knowledge systems have been judged by how closely they follow the scientific model. However, within the last half of this century, challenges to science as the bastion of true and certain knowledge of the world have been mounted on many fronts. Historians, philosophers, sociologists, literary critics, and feminists alike have sought to dethrone the scientific method as the reigning method of inquiry of choice, with uniquely privileged access to "truth" and "reality." The specifically feminist contribution to this discussion is in framing the analysis in terms of gender ideology, our culturally constructed beliefs about what constitutes male and female nature.

By now an impressive body of literature[1] has accumulated that documents and critiques the interpenetrations and linkages between traditional notions of objectivity and traditional notions of masculinity. One of the most lucid and insightful writers investigating these issues is Evelyn Fox Keller (1985, 1992a), who has now extended her critique from reflections on gender and science to thinking about language, gender, and science. In considering what the consequences of a gendered discourse might be for science, she observes:

> It is easy enough to say, and to show, that the language of science is riddled with patriarchal imagery, but it is far more difficult to show – or even to think about – what effect a non-patriarchal discourse would have had or would now have (supposing that we could learn to ungender our discourse). In short, *what does language have to do with science?* This, I suggest, is the real task that faces not only feminist critiques of science, but all the history, philosophy and sociology of science.
>
> (Keller, 1992b, p. 48)

Sandra Harding is another highly original intellect in this field. Harding's work has evolved from considering the science question in feminism to asking questions about whose science and whose knowledge we are studying (Harding, 1986, 1991). She admonishes feminist critics of science to refrain from essentialist formulations that ignore differences in class, race, and sexuality among women. Just as a gender analysis of a particular discipline often exposes other implicit cultural assumptions, questioning the exclusion of women's voices from science leads inevitably to examining the consequences of the exclusion of other minority perspectives.

In this article I summarize some of the feminist critiques of science and try to indicate the wide range of philosophical, social, historical, and psychological issues that are encompassed under the rubric of "gender and science." In addition, I investigate the role that language plays in reflecting as well as perpetuating underlying cultural assumptions about and within science. In particular, I examine some of the reasons mathematics has evolved as the chosen language of science. (This is a natural subject for me to study, as I began my adult life as a poet and became a mathematician in my middle years.) Next, I weave Keller's concerns into one other abiding passion in my life besides mathematics and language, namely, teaching. I explore some of the ramifications of gendered discourse to the *teaching* of science and mathematics (with the emphasis on mathematics). Since, as René Thom has pointed out, "all mathematical pedagogy . . . rests on a philosophy of mathematics" (Thom, 1972), it makes sense to take these feminist critiques (which examine the underlying presuppositions and philosophy of science and mathematics) into account when considering pedagogical issues. Finally, I address the relevance of this entire discussion to women and minorities in science and engineering. Creating more inclusive environments in classrooms and laboratories will certainly help increase the participation of members of previously underrepresented groups in these fields. But as the composition of the community itself changes, so too will the disciplines evolve. It is precisely this blurring of boundaries between "the Changer and the Changed"[2] that embodies the very essence and promise of a feminist science.

Nature and culture

There are, in fact, not one but many feminist lenses through which the culture, content, and practice of science are refracted in what is sometimes referred to as the liberal feminist critique; the focus is on affirmative action and equal access for women and other minorities to education and employment. Many argue that these critiques do not go far enough, that there can be no true equality of opportunity in fields whose concerns

are constructed to make sense of the data and results, still does not address the question of what science *is*.

The most radical critique shakes the very foundations of science, questioning the assumptions of objectivity and rationalism that underlie the whole enterprise. These critics seek to reconceptualize objectivity as a *dialectical* process.[3] They distinguish the objective effort (an attempt to identify biases) from the objectivist illusion (ignoring the existence of self, and believing one's own perspective is objective and absolute). According to the modern Western tradition, scientific knowledge is achieved through rational, objective inquiry (attributes gendered as male), ensured by strict adherence to the rules of the scientific method. A postmodern relativist vision of reality denies the availability of a purely objective and direct experience of external events, and questions if indeed such an experience can be said to exist at all. "But," cries the working scientist, "science is not just a belief system! There is a Real World out there, and we can and do know something about it." How can one reconcile such differing perceptions of science, truth, and knowledge?

The problem is in insisting on a *single* view of reality. It is the privileging of the rational mode over, say, the empathetic mode of obtaining knowledge, and the power relations implied in the assumption of the superiority of reason (gendered as male) over feeling (gendered as female) that must be challenged. There is an underlying assumption in claiming that we can know the world through rational inquiry that is so "natural" that it goes unnoticed: that is, that the world we seek to know and understand is itself rational and orderly, and that human reason alone can discover principles and laws that govern the behavior of things. We forget that it takes a *leap of faith* to believe this. And we do not notice the role of language in perpetuating this belief, indeed masking the operation and very existence of an ideology at work.

> The particular conventions of language employed by a scientific community not only can permit a tacit incorporation of ideology into scientific theory but also can protect participants from recognition of such ideological influences and thus effectively secure the theoretical structure from substantive critical revision.
>
> (Keller, 1992a, p. 142)

It is worth pondering and making explicit the underlying assumptions of the world view implied when we say there are "laws" of nature that "govern" the behavior of inanimate objects in a gravitational field or animate biological organisms in an ecological system. Where did these laws come from?[4] Do the "rules" exist independently, apart from the reality they govern? Is this separation of nature into "the world" and "the laws" merely a cultural artifact (art + fact), a convenient artifice, artificial, one possible story about "the way things are" among many? Keller (1992a, p. 60) points out that most modern-day dichotomies were once seen as interlocking separations but grew into demarcations with rigid boundaries (God/Nature, Male/Female, Mind/Body, Nature/Culture, Animate/Inanimate, The World/The Laws). From a separatist perspective, the laws of nature appear as eternal truths upon which the universe is built, the bedrock of reality. Alternatively, if one perceives nature and culture as an interacting complementarity, there is no one unique set of laws toward which scientific knowledge converges. Laws and theories cannot be separated from the circumstances in which they are formulated. It is the highly contested claim of many of the most radical critics that culture can define what scientific knowledge *is* (as well as *whose* it is). They ask how nature (gendered as female) and culture (gendered as male) *interact* in the production of scientific knowledge. It is the implications of this critique that I wish to examine.

As a poet, I am keenly aware of the power of metaphor to shape our understanding of the world around us. Each age tends to use its most impressive technology as a metaphor for the cosmos or God. Thus the Greeks spoke of the music of the spheres (God the Geometer)[5] and the Age of Reason presented us with the clockwork universe (God the Watchmaker), while today's computer technology gives us the image of the universe as an information-processing system (God the Programmer). In order to understand better the influence a prevailing metaphor can have on the acquisition and interpretation of "facts," and to make more plausible the interaction between nature and culture in the production of scientific knowledge, I will examine more closely the animate/inanimate duality.

One aspect of Aristotle's cosmology that seems quite alien to us is that, in spite of all he says about *mechanisms* to explain the motions of celestial objects, he believes that the heavenly bodies are *animate*. To paraphrase his view, "[e]verything in Nature has a purpose and is animated by a soul fitted to its purpose . . . " (Toulmin and Goodfield, 1961). Apparently the ancient Maya had a somewhat similar image of the cosmos. They believed that

> . . . the everyday human world was intimately related to the natural world and that these two worlds functioned in harmony. The universe was a distinct whole, with all parts intricately laced together, each aspect influencing the others. Nature and culture were one. Their universe was animate – breathing, teeming, vibrant, and interactive.
>
> (Aveni, 1993)

Anthony Aveni, a professor of both astronomy and anthropology, elaborates the relationship between the Mayan world view and the kinds of knowledge they sought and glimpsed in the sky.

> The Maya were motivated not by a desire to express the workings of nature in terms of inert mathematical equations, but rather by the need to know how to mediate an alliance between the inherent power within the universe and their own direct physical well-being, between knowledge and human action. Today we might attribute a planet's change of color to an atmospheric effect, a shift in position to a dynamic effect, an alteration in brightness to a distance effect. The Maya would carefully watch the color, brightness, position, and movement of the planets
>
> (particularly for Mercury and Venus), dyadic and triadic bonds (sun, moon, and Venus).
>
> (Aveni, 1993)

This illustrates the important insights contributed by anthropologists (as well as sociologists, philosophers, historians, and feminists) in illuminating the connections between a particular culture (and the language in which it is embedded) and the presentations and understanding of the world.[6]

Mathematics as the language of science

Scientists like to explain things from "first principles," and some believe in the possibility of an "ultimate" level of explanation, perhaps even a "theory of everything."[7] They seek a logically coherent framework that can effectively predict a chain of causes and effects which account for and explain all observed phenomena. I can think of two ways that this project may fail. First, it may be that there are always certain starting assumptions (sometimes called "initial conditions") that must be built into any theory – God, logic, a set of laws – some foundation for existence from which all explanations can proceed. (Anyone who has ever been around (or simply remembers being) a two-year-old, knows the endless chain of whys – Why can't I stay up later? (Because you need your sleep.) Why do I need my sleep? (So your body can rest.) Why must my body rest? – which inevitably ends with some version of the fundamental statement, "Because I say so!") In mathematics, each subdiscipline has as its foundation a (small but necessary) list of undefined terms, concepts, or mathematical objects whose meaning and existence must be granted or "given" before the theory can be constructed. Perhaps any attempt at a comprehensive description of reality will confront the necessity of assuming some (arbitrary) starting conditions for the universe.

In any case, scientists must use language to represent what they learn about the world. And so there is a second, perhaps even more fundamental way in which the attempt to construct a theory of everything could fail: it may be that the very demands of the language in which science formulates its questions, a language of rationality and logic, impose restrictions on the sort of world we can know. Scientists value simplicity and analyzability. Thus legitimate questions are restricted to those capable of clear and unambiguous answers.

> The net effect is to exclude from the domain of theory those . . . phenomena that do not fit (or worse, threaten to undermine) the ideological commitments that are unspoken yet in language – built into science by the language we use in both constructing and applying our theories.
>
> (Keller, 1992a, p. 143)

But what is the language of science? Mathematics. Why is this so? Well, one would like to assume that something is either true or not true, and this would certainly seem to be the case when one is proving mathematical theorems. Thus, early on, physical scientists, with the goal of achieving the absolute certainty accorded to logic and geometry, tried as much as possible to model their enterprise upon mathematics, as exemplified by Euclid. In the words of Ptolemy,[8]

> The systematic study of *mathematical* theory alone can yield its practitioners solid conclusions, free of doubt, since its demonstrations – whether arithmetical or geometrical – are carried out in a manner that admits of no dispute.
>
> (Toulmin and Goodfield, 1961, p. 143)

And so the laws of nature were cast in mathematical form.[9]

The problem with the natural sciences is that they depend on observations, mediated by our senses or the instruments that extend them; and as any detective interviewing multiple witnesses to a single event soon realizes, the testimonies of our senses can be misleading. Furthermore, these observations must be classified and interpreted by human agents, and "[t]o identify the role of human agency in the making of an item of knowledge is to identify the possibility of it being otherwise" (Shapin and Schaffer, 1985, p. 23). Once we admit that we cannot trust our senses to provide absolute certainty about reality, we are inclined to agree with Ptolemy's claim that truth can be arrived at only through reasoned thinking. But we need some common grounds for belief. In mathematics we formalize reason, hoping to assure certainty by adhering to unassailable rules of logical deduction. Thus in the quest for the purest, most "disinterested" language in which to describe scientific discoveries, it would seem that the mathematics is the holy grail.

Even dyed-in-the-wool feminist scholars seem willing to exempt mathematics (and the "hardest" of the sciences, physics) from the basic tenet of feminist scholarship, that no knowledge is value free.

> Physics and mathematics may be possible exceptions to this statement. In these fields, the constraints on both the questions that can be asked and on the possible results are so great that they appear to unfold in a deterministic way, unaffected by social factors.
>
> (Lowe, 1993, p. 11)

Katherine Hayles, an interdisciplinary scholar in science and literature, has focused critical attention on these views. She notes that "[c]onvincing cases have been made for [cultural and gender encoding within] many of the biological sciences," but "[w]hen the theories are primarily mathematical rather than behavioral, the cases become more difficult to make. . . . For these reasons (among others), mathematical theories about nonliving physical systems remain largely an untouched preserve of masculinist science" (Hayles, 1992, p. 16).

If Keller's claim (1992a, p. 6) is true, that language mediates the course of science,

> and took various forms. . . .
>
> (Hayles, 1992, p. 22)

She makes strong arguments for "the power of the initial assumptions to influence the direction of subsequent theories," and challenges the state of "amnesia that made mathematical techniques seem natural solutions to obvious problems" (Hayles, 1992). On first reading, mathematicians often find Hayles's thesis challenging (at best), and even outrageous. Because Hayles herself is not trained as a mathematician, "insiders" find it easy to dismiss her critique as "uninformed." However, even when I may disagree on some of the technical details in her arguments, I take her challenges seriously and encourage others to examine them closely. Hayles is a pioneer and one of the few to attempt the difficult and necessary task of critiquing mathematics as a gendered discourse.

Clearly, much work remains to be done in uncovering the cultural assumptions encoded in and transmitted through mathematical language, and the ways in which this language mediates the course of science. One further point worth making is that feminists have also been arguing for at least two decades that "culture is classification" (Taylor, Kramarae, and Ebben, 1993). (And, as Marcia Ascher (1991, p. 8) points out, "how people categorize things is one of the major differences between one culture and another.") And mathematics is certainly, among other things, a system of classification. Thus choices are made in creating categories to include some things and exclude others (which then become "nonthings"), and I suggest that we seek out and study these choices to begin to uncover the imprint of culture within mathematics.

But here I want to address two related and perhaps somewhat easier questions. First I ask: what cultural values are encoded in the language of mathematics *education*? My second question arises from the observation made earlier that mathematics is perceived as totally depersonalized (i.e., objective, abstract, and rational). Paul Ernest, a mathematician in Great Britain, admits that "[t]he popular image of mathematics is that it is difficult, cold, abstract, ultra-rational, important and largely masculine" (Ernest, 1993, p. 53). Although most practicing mathematicians have a very different (insider's) view of their subject, it is this cold and heartless version that is promulgated by most textbooks and by our educational system in general. What is the relationship between this view of mathematics and the way it is taught? And most crucial for readers of this journal, I ask what impact might a shift from this view of mathematics as absolute and rigorous (as in rigor mortis?) have on pedagogy and accessibility to mathematics for women and minorities?

Mathematics and culture

It is commonly assumed that the language of mathematics is culture fair because it is culture free. However, recent articles and books (see Ascher, 1991, and references therein) support the view that "culture and language influence mathematics itself and that different societies have different versions of mathematics" (Schurle, 1993, p. 12). Indeed most mathematics, as it is taught, is not context free. Word problems are notorious for instances of sexist, racist, and other, more subtle cultural biases. As a blatant example, I quote the following problem from a teacher's handbook printed in Nazi Germany:

> Problem 200. According to statements of the Draeger Works in Luebeck in the gassing of a city only 50 per cent of the evaporated poison gas is effective. The atmosphere must be poisoned up to a height of 20 metres in a concentration of 45 mg/m^3. How much phosgene is needed to poison a city of 50,000 inhabitants who live in an area of four square kilometers?
>
> (Cohen, 1988, p. 244)

But there are value systems hidden in even the most innocuous problems. Quantification, comparison, and measurement are in themselves cultural activities, whose assumed values are not universally shared. Consider the following example from research conducted by Kathryn Crawford with Australian Aboriginal children:

> . . . students from Pitjantjatjara communities live in a culture that has evolved to meet the needs of subsistence in a harsh and relatively stable environment. Property rights are not clearly defined. Material possessions are not the key determinant of status in these communities. Aboriginal people view their physical environment as an extension of themselves rather than as something to be conquered. Traditional cultural activities typically revolve around small numbers of specifically named natural objects. Quantity is not usually considered and this low priority is reflected in a vernacular with few words to denote number. So they ask: "Why do you always own things?"
> "Why do you always compare?"
> "Why do you want to know how much?"
> "Why do you measure T?"
>
> (Crawford, 1989, p. 23)

Spatial conceptualization is culturally specific as well. Four faculty at the University of Alaska, with expertise in linguistics, mathematics, and education, studied language and its impact on mathematics learning among Native American and American Indian students in the interior of Alaska.

> Spatial conceptualization is an integral part of culture and world view and is expressed in the linguistic system. The manner in which a language encodes spatial relationships may affect the way a speaker acquires and understands concepts and principles of mathematics.
>
> (Bradley, Basham, Axelrod, and Jones, 1990, p. 8)

The authors observed that "the Western world developed the notion of fractions and [illegible]

Value conflicts occur even within our own culture. Martha Smith, a mathematician at the University of Texas at Austin, relates some anecdotes that helped her become aware of her "mathematically and scientifically related values and how they are often not shared by people outside these fields" (Smith, 1993, p. 1). For instance, one student "asked in his journal why we insist on proving things in mathematics. 'Why can't we just trust each other?' he asked. I had never realized until then that my value on proof might appear to conflict with a value on trust" (Smith, 1993, p. 1).

It has been argued by Chinese scholars that the Confucian virtues of loyalty, constancy, and gratitude precluded the development of the sort of questioning science that European and American culture has.[10] The differences in the development of science in the East and West have also been traced to theological differences in the two cultures. John Barrow claims that the Chinese lacked "the concept of a divine being who acted to legislate what went on in the natural world, whose decrees formed inviolate 'laws' of Nature, and who underwrote scientific enterprise" (Barrow, 1991, p. 35).

No doubt other factors are also responsible for the differential development of science in the two cultures, but the point needs to be made that the incompatibility of cultural values can also be a barrier in mathematics and science education. Comparing the Western "mathematico-technological" and the Islamic-Arab cultures, Murad Jurdak notes that the mathematical culture assumes that "values can be questioned and statements can be subjected to empirical test. In any religious culture, and certainly in the Islamo-Arabic culture, this assumption is not tenable because in such cultures there are some values which should not be questioned" (Jurdak, 1989, pp. 12–13).

A related issue that affects non-English-speaking and English-as-a-second-language (ESL) students is that since language is a cultural carrier, the language in which mathematics is taught affects the understanding and production of mathematical knowledge, as well as the ability to use it to cope with reality. There is even some evidence that formal deductive reasoning is language (and culture) specific (Jurdak, 1977, pp. 225–238). As teachers who value difference, we must give special attention to the conceptual understanding our students bring into the classroom, and build on what they know. We must not assume that (new) concepts are readily understood, simply because the words spoken by us are repeated back by the students. Further studies need to be done to compare the success in different types of problem solving among English-only speakers and ESL and non-English speakers, and the results of these investigations must be made available to teachers.

Mathematics and values

At this point it occurs to me to ask why one should learn mathematics, or, alternatively, why we should teach mathematics? Perusing the literature, I have found five goals proposed in answer to this question, and remarkable agreement about the goals among mathematicians and mathematics educators alike. First, we must prepare citizens to be users of mathematics (a societal goal). Second, it is important to provide examples of the contributions of mathematics to culture at large (a cultural goal). Third, the mental discipline that the study of mathematics provides should be available as an educative force in everyone's life (a personal goal). Fourth, we must train the next generation of mathematicians and scientists (a technical goal). And last, there is the beauty of mathematics for its own sake (an esthetic goal).

In light of the discussion above, I would add that we have a responsibility to acknowledge that we are also teaching values when we teach mathematics. For instance, in presenting mathematics as part of culture, it is necessary to specify whose culture and whose mathematics. When we invite our students to appreciate the elegance of a proof, we should keep in mind that such esthetic judgments also vary across cultures and genders. I am a mathematical physicist who has been well educated and fairly successful in the traditional school of "pure and unsullied" mathematics. It took some time and steady encouragement from patient colleagues in women's studies departments for me to accept that gender and culture are indeed encoded in even mathematics and physics. I offer here some specific suggestions as to *how* one might begin to realize what values one is transmitting and teach the next generation to assimilate this radical perspective as plain common sense.

It is essential that we encourage our students to look for hidden assumptions and make them explicit. Most of them will have absorbed the underlying biases of our culture about objectivity, truth, the scientific enterprise, and the nature of mathematics. We can start by helping them make their own ideas (however inchoate or ill formed) explicit and learn to question them. We must teach them to *expect* a standpoint in any scientific statement and include it as part of their observations, as well as to look for it in others. In mathematics, we should include more open-ended problems that require one to make assumptions in order to solve them. In standard word problems, we can append questions that ask students to list what assumptions have been made. Finally, we need to emphasize that there are many valid alternative approaches to the same problem, and even more important, there is often more than one single correct solution. In fact, why must problems always be *solved* and made to give up their secrets? What if we also gave open-ended problems that invite students to imagine more of the story, in order to understand the situation? Philip Davis makes the point very well:

> [M]athematics is a kind of language, and this language creates a milieu for thought that is hard to escape. . . . The subconscious modalities of mathematics and of its applications must be made clear, must be taught, watched, argued. Since we are all consumers of mathematics, and since we are both beneficiaries as well as

> victims, all mathematizations ought to be opened up in the public forums where ideas are debated. These debates ought to begin in the secondary school.[11]
>
> (Davis, 1988, p. 144)

It is also important that we do not present mathematics as a fixed body of knowledge – complete, certain, and absolute. In fact, scientists and mathematicians alike have a very different image of mathematics, and to some extent the public does too, thanks to

We owe it to our students to present this other image of mathematics, and to provide them with experiences of the personal, intuitive, creative (and culturally dependent) process of *doing* mathematics, rather than merely reading the codified and axiomatic presentation that appears in most textbooks. It is not enough that women and minorities be granted entry into the heretofore exclusive club of mathematicians (and scientists and engineers) if membership requires that one subscribe to the same rules and speak the same language. Radical feminist critics insist that forcing everyone to fit the same mold is a bad idea. Rather, they claim, the solution is to expand the definition of scientist to incorporate others, and that science will in fact profit by doing so. We must, as Leone Burton so aptly puts it, "broaden not only physical access to mathematics, but more crucially psychological access" (Burton, 1989, p. 17). A view of mathematics as based on incompleteness, conjecture, and relativity and a shift of emphasis from final product to process, will appeal to the minds and hearts of many previously "math-anxious" students, and invigorate our often stale classrooms with a gust of fresh air.

Finally, just as Barbara McClintock developed a "feeling for the organism" by taking the time to look and having the patience to "hear what the material has to say to you" (Keller, 1983, pp. 198–199), we need to look at and listen to our *students*. As we learn from standpoint theory, outsiders can often see alternatives to the beliefs and practices of a culture that remain invisible to insiders. And there are risks involved in posing awkward questions about "what everybody knows." Thus if one is already a member of the club and tries to lift the veil from some taken-for-granted assumptions, one may be labeled a troublemaker (at best), or, if one persists, even expelled. But our students can effectively critique the content and methodologies of science with innocence and impunity, if we permit them – before they have been inculcated with the dominant paradigm. It is like the parable of the Emperor's new clothes: they can often see the naked truth underneath the layers of assumptions that most of us have been persuaded are the objective facts. (Recall Martha Smith's student, who asked "Why can't we just trust each other?")

Here is an example that illustrates the kind of teaching I am advocating. Anneli Lax, a mathematician and educator, presented the following word problem from the standardized New York Regents Competency Test to a group of students in a high school remedial English class. They were asked to evaluate the problem, which many of them had missed on the exam, from a linguistic point of view, rewrite it however they liked, and only then try to solve it. The problem read:

> Shirts cost $7, pants cost $12, and jackets cost $25. Fred has $100 to buy 1 jacket, 2 pairs of pants, and some shirts. What is the greatest number of shirts he can buy?
> (Duncan, 1989, p. 235)

She reports that "[a]s the students were working out their revisions of the clothing problem, a girl in the back of the room raised her hand rather urgently. 'This doesn't have to do with math,' she said. 'But tell me what kind of a jacket can he buy for twenty-five dollars" (Duncan, 1989, p. 237). We smile, but the question is important from the student's point of view. The problem has taken on a kind of realism that was missing before she tried to deal with it on her own terms. Indeed, by involving herself in the story, this student has revealed a real weakness of the problem: it is not very convincing. This is a weakness shared by most word problems involving a silly story constructed around a preconceived solution. It is difficult to take such problems seriously, yet they are presented as real-world applications of mathematics. When students are invited to critique a problem and rewrite it, they may not only come to understand it in their own terms, but can be empowered as they become authors and pose their own questions, questions whose answers would be meaningful to them.

We must look at our students as well as listen to them, where, as Lax puts it, "[b]y 'look at' I mean finding out who our students are, how they learn, and why" (Lax, 1989, p. 264). Then we must ask ourselves what kinds of training and habits of thought do we want to foster and nourish in them? Taking a cue from the critiques outlined above, these should include habits of clear thinking, insistence on critical self-reflection (on process as well as product), and the relentless pursuit and questioning of hidden assumptions.

Conclusion

Many feminists who have turned their attention toward science teaching have concluded, along with Irene Lanzinger, that "the forming of a different kind of science classroom requires a reconceptualization of the nature of scientific thought as well as a redefining of gender roles" (Lanzinger, 1993, p. 98). I have tried to indicate the ways in which various feminist critiques of science can inform our efforts to reform and re-vision both the structure and content of mathematics and science education. Most important, we must replace the Eurocentric masculinist caricature of science and scientists as

> . . . the strict separation of subject and object, the priority of the objective over the subjective, the depersonalized and seemingly disembodied discourse, the elevation of the abstract over the concrete, the asocial self-identity of the scientist, the total commitment to the calling, the fundamental incompatibility between scientific career and family life, and, of course, the alienation from and dread of women. . . .
> (Noble, 1992, p. 281)

In its stead, we can offer a vision of science closer to that articulated by Stephen Jay Gould:

> Science . . . is a socially embedded activity. . . . Much of its change through time does not record a closer approach to absolute truth, but the alteration of cultural contexts that influence it so strongly. Facts are not pure and unsullied bits of information; culture also influences what we see and how we see it.[12] Theories,

> Otherwise, science will continue to produce skewed knowledge that . . . lessens the opportunities to reduce the distortion of scientific accounts that reflect the disproportionate influences of the dominant cultural group in science – white males.
>
> (Frankel, 1993, p. 9)

One of the questions most frequently asked by feminist critics of science is "Is there a feminist science, and if so, what does it look like?" As we continue to seek the answers, we should keep in mind that we have much to learn from our students and be sure to enlist them in this project. After all, the dissemination and re-creation of knowledge are largely effected through the educational system. And I believe it is in our roles as teachers and mentors that we can have the greatest impact on the perspectives of the next generation. As one woman scientist put it:

> I believe that part of my role as a good scientist is training good students, because, they are going to be telling my story long after I am gone. That's part of science. . . . That's not peripheral: learning from others how best to get students excited about science, to teach and to communicate, is at the heart of science.
>
> (Niewoehner, 1993, p. 14)

Notes

1 I will be citing some of this literature in this article, but I refer readers interested in the issues of feminism and science to the bibliography in Simons and Tuana (1988, pp. 145–155).

2 This is the title song of an album by Cris Williamson, a feminist singer/songwriter.

3 See, for instance, Harding (1991), who defines a "strong objectivity," and Haraway (1991), who discusses "socially situated knowledges."

4 In fact, the origin of the idea of a "law of nature" is intimately connected with the religion and politics of a particular era.

> Medieval Europe, subject on the one hand to the Christian doctrine of God's law manifested in nature, and on the other hand to a strongly enforced concept of civil law, provided a fertile milieu for the scientific idea of laws of nature to emerge.
>
> (Davies, 1992, p. 76)

See also John Barrow (1991) for a fascinating study of the religious and cultural origins of the concept of physical laws.

5 The discovery by Pythagoras (sixth century, BC) that numbers could describe music led to the belief that all phenomena could be described by relations between numbers. He and his followers associated geometric forms with certain numbers that they imbued with mystical significance. For example, a square was associated with the numbers 4, 9, and 16, and a triangle with the numbers 3, 6, and 10.

6 The outlook of our modern Western cosmology is inherited not from the Greeks, but rather influenced by later Christian ideas. We draw a sharp distinction between animate and inanimate objects, sharper than either the Greeks or Mayas found natural. "Yet as the philosopher Whitehead has recently argued, there may be just as much virtue in thinking of the universe as a single grand organism as there is in thinking of it as an enormously complicated machine" (Toulmin and Goodfield, 1961).

7 Note that not all scientists believe this is possible, nor is it only scientists who believe that science can explain everything.

8 Claudius Ptolemy lived from about 85 to 165 AD, and was a Greek astronomer in Alexandria.

9 That this should be so effective a praxis is, in fact, a great mystery. See, for example, Eugene Wigner (1960).

10 See "Isaac Newton Was Not Chinese," chap. 5 of Hsu (1992): and Joseph Needham (1969).

11 I would add, perhaps even earlier.

12 This reminds me of an aphorism from the Talmud: "We do not see things as they are – We see things as we are."

References

Ascher, M. (1991). *Ethnomathematics: A multicultural view of mathematical ideas*. Pacific Grove, CA: Brooks/Cole.

Aveni, A. (1993). Mediators in a universal discourse. *Archaeology*, 46(4), 10.

Barrow, J. (1991). *Theories of everything. The quest for ultimate explanation*. Oxford: Oxford University Press.

Bradley, C.B., Basham, C., Axelrod, M., and Jones, E. (1990). Language and mathematics learning. *UME Trends. News and Reports on Undergraduate Mathematics Education*, 2(5), 8.

Burton, L. (1989). Mathematics as a cultural experience: Whose experience? In C. Keitel (Ed.), *Mathematics, education, and society* (Science and Technology Education Document Series No. 35, pp. 16–19). Paris: UNESCO.

Cohen, E.A. (1988). *Human behaviour in the concentration camp*. London: Free Association Books.

Crawford, K. (1989). Knowing what versus knowing how: The need for a change in emphasis for minority group education in mathematics. In C. Keitel (Ed.), *Mathematics, education, and society* (Science and Technology Education Document Series No. 35, pp. 22–24). Paris: UNESCO.

Davies, P. (1992). *The mind of God. The scientific basis for a rational world.* New York: Simon & Schuster.

Davis, P.J. (1988). Applied mathematics as social contract. *Mathematics Magazine*, 61(3), 139–147.

Harding, S. (1986). *The science question in feminism*. Ithaca. NY: Cornell University Press.

Harding, S. (1991). *Whose science? Whose knowledge? Thinking from women's lives.* Ithaca, NY: Cornell University Press.

Hayles, K. (1992). Gender encoding in fluid mechanics: Masculine channels and feminine flows. *Dfferences*, 4(2), 16–44.

Hsu, K.J. (1992). *Challenger at sea. A ship that revolutionized earth science.* Princeton, NJ: Princeton University Press.

Jurdak, M.E. (1977). Structural and linguistics variables in selected inference patterns for bilinguals in grades six to ten. *Educational Studies in Mathematics*, 8, 225–238.

Jurdak, M.E. (1989). Religion and language as cultural carriers and barriers in mathematics education. In C. Keitel (Ed.), *Mathematics, education, and society* (Science and Technology Education Document Series No. 35, pp. 12–14). Paris: UNESCO.

Keller, E.F. (1983). *A feeling for the organism: The life and work of Barbara McClintock.* San Francisco: Freeman.

Keller, E.F. (1985). *Reflections on gender and science*. New Haven, CT: Yale University Press.

Keller, E.F. (1992a). *Secrets of life, secrets of death: Essays on language, gender and science.* New York: Routledge.

Keller, E.F. (1992b). How gender matters, or, why it's so hard for us to count past two. In G. Kirkup and L.S. Keller (Eds.), *Inventing women: Science, technology and gender* (pp. 42–56). Cambridge, MA: Polity Press.

Kline, M. (1972). *Mathematics and Western culture*. Oxford: Penguin.

Lanzinger, I. (1993). Toward feminist science teaching. *Canadian Woman Studies*, 13(2), 95–99.

Lax, A. (1989). They think, therefore we are. In P. Connolly and T. Vilardi (Eds.), *Writing to learn mathematics and science* (pp. 249–265). New York: Teachers College Press.

Lerman, S. (1989). A social view of mathematics – Implications for mathematics education. In C. Keitel (Ed.), *Mathematics, education, and society* (Science and Technology Education Document Series No. 35, pp. 42–44). Paris: UNESCO.

Lowe, M. (1993). To understand the world in order to change it. *Canadian Woman Studies*, 13(2), 6–11.

Needham, J. (1969). *The grand titration: Science and society in East and West*. London: Allen & Unwin.

Niewoehner, E.S. (1993). Mentoring works and here are the results! *AWIS Magazine*, 22(3), 14.

Noble, D.F. (1992). *A world without women: The Christian clerical culture of Western science*. New York: Knopf.

Schurle, A.W. (1993). Mathematics and culture (Review of Ethnomathematics). *Mathematical Connections*, 1(2), 12–18.

Shapin, S., and Schaffer, S. (1985). *Leviathan and the air-pump. Hobbes, Boyle, and the experimental life*. Princeton, NJ: Princeton University Press.

Simons, M.A., and Tuana, N. (Eds.). (1988). Feminism and science, Part 2 [Special issue]. *Hypatia*, 3(l).

Smith, M.K. (1993). Values and mathematics. *UME Trends. News and Reports on Undergraduate Mathematics Education*, 4(6), 1.

Taylor, H.J., Kramarae, C., and Ebben, M. (Eds.). (1993). *Women, information technology, and scholarship*. Urbana, IL: Center for Advanced Study.

Thom, R. (1972). Modern mathematics: Does it exist? In A.G. Howson (Ed.), *Developments in mathematical education* (pp. 194–209). Cambridge: Cambridge University Press.

Toulmin, S., and Goodfield. J. (1961). *The fabric of the heavens. The development of astronomy and dynamics*. New York: Harper & Row.

Wigner, E. (1960). The unreasonable effectiveness of mathematics in the natural sciences. *Communications in Pure and Applied Mathematics*, 13, 1–18.

Chapter 31

Synopsis

Ecofeminists must be aware of both the threats that the theories and practice of Western science hold for life on earth, as well as the goals that science shares with ecofeminism, namely to know and understand life. One way that feminists have addressed science is through their critiques, which provide a basis for understanding many of the inconsistencies between science and feminist principles. What is now called for is the revisioning of science along feminist lines. In this paper, I draw on a feminist theory of psychological development to describe a view of cell and molecular biology that is consistent with ecofeminist tenets. Such a revisioning of cell and molecular biology is important not only for broadened access and understanding of its theories amongst those groups of individuals traditionally underrepresented in science, including women, but also for providing new insights into health and disease at all levels of life.

Introduction

Ecofeminists considering the theories and practice of science are faced with both the sinister implications that the fruits of science hold for life on earth, as well as the potential resources that science offers for a healthy, sustainable connection to life. On the one hand, science and the technology that follows in its path have wreaked disaster upon much of nature as well as women. Science has provided the world with the knowledge to develop nuclear power and weapons as well as chemical warfare used not only as defense against human invaders, but in the form of pesticides and herbicides that grace our lawns and poison our soils, air and water.

In laboratories, hospitals and pharmacies, science has largely viewed women's bodies as though they were victims of raging hormones requiring control and domination by a predominantly male, medical elite. Ironically in light of this assertion, women have been excluded from much of the experimentation and safety testing performed by science for just this reason: their "unpredictable," wildly fluctuating bodies. Thus, the picture of "normal" human functions painted by science is one of the male of the species, further facilitating the domination and control of women's bodies and lives by science and technology.

On the other hand, there are some scientists and scientific theories that ecofeminism can draw upon for backing or inspiration. The Gaia hypothesis developed by James Lovelock (1979) and Lynn Margulis (Lovelock and Margulis, 1984) can be viewed as a scientific rendering of the connections that ecofeminism seeks to draw between all forms of life. The scientific theories of the "New Physics" (Capra, 1975, 1982), including relativity and chaos theories, can also be viewed as a scientific translation of ecofeminist tenets (Ruether, 1992). And the importance of science to humankind in general cannot be denied. Despite its limited perspective, it plays an important cultural role in organizing and structuring our knowledge of nature.

The polarization I have drawn here between the seeming goods and evils of science belies the complexity of the relationship that needs to exist between ecofeminism and science. While ecofeminists must, as Patsy Hallen (1989) states in her article of the same name, be "Careful of Science" they must also acknowledge that ecofeminism shares some of the same intentions, basically to know and understand the natural world and our selves in relation to it, that science also seeks.

Hallen (1989) explains that the ambiguity of her title implies that we must both be wary of science as well as cultivate it with care. Such ambiguity is a reflection of the equivocal character which science presents to ecofeminism. Because science and its one-sided perspective maintains such a powerful grip on most people's access to knowledge and understanding of the natural world, ecofeminism cannot afford to summarily dismiss science without a second look, but neither should it be tempted to embrace it unconditionally.

One way that feminists have addressed science is through their critiques of its theories and practice: looking at what is inconsistent between the way science investigates and portrays the natural world and the values and beliefs held by feminists. Examples of numerous feminist critiques of science (Bleier, 1984; Harding, 1986, 1992; Hubbard, 1990, 1995; Keller, 1983, 1985, 1992; Rosser, 1992) have appeared from all feminist orientations, including ecofeminism, and have provided an important starting point for an ecofeminist examination of science.

Yet criticism must be only one side of the story. Viable alternatives to the one-sided view of nature espoused by traditional, Western science must be sought and implemented by ecofeminists, whether inside or outside of the scientific establishment. For the value to the psyche that the role of science plays in offering an understanding of nature and self cannot be denied. Without it, humans would have no systematic manner of making the connections needed for physical, emotional and spiritual survival. Yet with it, it seems, the very connections that are drawn are often detrimental to life itself.

Rather than working for the abolishment of science altogether or celebrating science's benedictions where they occur while overlooking its harbingers of doom, advocates of ecofeminism must seek to reshape the way humans know and understand nature. What is being called for, as the relationship between humans and nonhuman nature continues to degrade and the conditions for life on earth move in the direction of extinction, is the development of an ecofeminist vision of science: a science that will seek to forge the connections now missing from science, and in doing so will open up such a vision of the natural world to a greater segment of individuals.

From my own perspective as a molecular biologist, I have had the opportunity to witness firsthand the aspects of my discipline which clash violently with philosophies of relation and mutual interdependence embodied by ecofeminisin (Davies, 1988). At [illegible] on earth, followed by suggestions for alternative viewpoints that might be instituted in their place.

An ecofeminist critique of cell and molecular biology

The field of cell and molecular biology (an appellation that often also includes areas of study such as genetics, microbiology and developmental biology) has perhaps been more immune to feminist intervention than have other biological disciplines (Hubbard, 1995; Rosser, 1992). This may be because its objects of study are one step removed from everyday life, unlike animals or individuals that we encounter on a regular basis and thus can readily identify with. It is much easier to spot outright sexism or even an androcentric bias in theories and experiments concerning women's reproductive anatomy, or in descriptions of mating behavior among nonhuman primates, than in theories concerning abstract concepts like genes, proteins and cells.

Another reason that cell and molecular biology has perhaps escaped thus far the degree of change that feminism has afforded other fields of biology may be its inherent abstruseness to the outsider, so that without substantial effort, only those with formal training are able to decipher the code of molecular notation and specialized jargon in which this field is mired, and within which much of the content deserving change is disguised. As a rule, the more abstract the science, the greater the challenge for both critique and revision.

Such a circumstance would seem to call for critique and change on the part of those already situated within the field. Unfortunately, very often those insiders who are most qualified to provide such a critique (namely women and members of other oppressed groups) hold the most fragile positions in the field with regard to power and privilege.

Thus, because of the threat to the very acceptance they have sacrificed so much to obtain, and their often tenuous position of authority, many cell and molecular biologists who do find fault with the system they are trying so hard to fit into are reluctant to speak (Aisenberg and Harrington, 1988; Keller, 1977). This is particularly true when such speaking might betray an individual's political, emotional or spiritual orientation or alignment. For to reveal such "biases," as science refers to these arenas of life, is one of the basic taboos of a scientific method which values detachment from the subject being studied over all else.

Much of the formal feminist criticism of cell and molecular biology also applies to science in general, spanning the subdisciplines of biology discussed here through to disparate scientific fields such as physics and chemistry. Although the basis of the critique may differ depending on the feminist orientation it arises from, many feminist critiques share a common denunciation of the following: (a) the historical and ideological exclusion of women from science as practitioners and shapers of its practice; (b) the impersonal, reductionist, and detached stance that science takes in its language and practice, which denies the existence of biases that nonetheless do exist and lead to (c) androcentric prejudice in many forms of scientific inquiry which is reflected in the unacknowledged androcentric bias of the resulting theories (Rosser, 1987, 1992).

Certainly, these factors maintain some relationship to one another; they are not merely individual flaws of science that coincidentally surface simultaneously. The division of labor in Western culture that relegates women to work in private – care-taking, domestic, embodied – arenas while awarding men the sole stewardship of the public – objective, external, authoritarian – world affects science no less, and if anything more, than it does other arenas of life activity.

The stark cultural division that leaves woman on one side of activities termed "work" (whether or not rewarded as so) and man on the other also meets a sharp divide through groups of individuals on the basis of traits or activities other than gender. Race plays a key role in establishing similar divisions, as does class, age, sexual orientation and expression. The imaginary geographic borders of nationalism cut through those within and without its bounds, as the third world remains divided from the first in ways larger than the mere physical distance between South and North.

Trailing closely behind this ranking of individuals follows a correlation between divided bodies and divided ideological concepts. Juxtapositions of terms like culture and nature, thinking and feeling, fall into place alongside human divisions of male/female, white/black and others. Science itself occupies a sacred niche in the company of all arenas claimed as male, culture and thinking being two important aspects for the discussion at hand.

Thus, just as science embodies and represents a certain manner of approaching knowledge, one rational, detached and historically privy to men, so too are those qualities confined to the realm of women and others who fall on the "wrong" (non-dominant) side of a dualistic divide considered inadequate and inappropriate for the serious undertaking science is constructed to be. Thus, intuition, feeling, and personal, lived experience are relegated to the sidelines of science, seen as threats and contaminants of scientific purity rather than the insightful, informative ways of knowing nature that they are. Likewise, those individuals espousing such ways of knowing are confined to the sidelines in scientific practice as well (for an example, see Keller, 1983).

Perhaps recognizing that those excluded from the heady privilege of knowing nature through the practice of science might attempt to claim their just place as knowers, science maintains a convoluted language which serves to obscure its practice and treatises from the uninitiated outsider, all the while contributing to its intended distancing from "real" life and personal experience. In this language, biases stemming from science's commitment to detachment and distance at the expense of other ways of knowing manage to miraculously disappear. Verbs become nouns; all reference to time and place is obliterated. Phrases like "it has been shown . . . " and "it has been determined . . . " declare the case closed to any intrepid individual who might even think of questioning science's singular authority.

That the historical tendency of all Western cultural institutions to employ a "divide and conquer" attitude by instituting dualisms and then rationing these out in hierarchical order surfaces in science is only to be expected. After all, science is imbedded in culture [illegible]

As one might expect, cell and molecular biology, as one of the most reductionist and fractionated forms of knowledge within biology, embraces hierarchy and dualism in its theories and investigations of the subjects it studies. If one is initially drawn to this field by a love of and awe for the beauty of nature as I once was, the first thing that becomes apparent is the inescapable paradox that in order to know something, one must kill it. With the sole exception of human beings, whose death often indirectly provides materials needed for scientific study, death and/or fragmentation of an organism's integrity must precede the procurement of the cells, DNA, RNA, or proteins needed to understand its existence. This most severe form of reductionism which breaks life down into its smallest form, namely death, is an example of one way in which the practice of cell and molecular biology clashes with the tenets of ecofeminism. Certainly the concept that life can only be understood and known once it has been extinguished seems at odds with an ecofeminist ethic of life-affirming ways of knowing.

On a greater scale, this example illustrates one of the approaches to study that feminists often criticize in science, which is pronounced in cell and molecular biology. The poking and prodding of nature as an inanimate subject that must be subdued and controlled underlies much of the methodology in this field[1] and is certainly inconsistent with a desire to portray women and all forms of life as active principles with intentionality and inherent wisdom and purpose, as has been expressed by ecofeminists (Davies, 1988; Diamond and Orenstein, 1990; Plant, 1989).

Just as cell and molecular biology breaks life down into smaller and smaller pieces so that the vision and existence of a living organism are often lost, so too do its theories reflect a shattering of connections, calling upon metaphors of domination and control to explain life. Feminist critiques of cell and molecular biology have focused upon the scientific conception of the cell within a context of domination and control (Birke, 1986; Bleier, 1984; Fausto-Sterling, 1985; Keller, 1983).

Scientific descriptions equating activity and control to sperm cells and passivity and subordination to egg cells, mirroring socially conceived gender roles, have been challenged by feminist thinkers (The Biology and Gender Study Group, 1988). Feminists have also critiqued the growing tendency to focus on genes at the expense of the rest of the cell, a view in which a cell is seen to operate under the exclusive control of its "master molecule," DNA (Hubbard, 1990; Keller, 1983). Marion

Namenwirth (1986) elucidates the implications of this metaphor: "In its extreme form, this model envisions the cell or organism as the passive, subordinate recipient of directions and orders from the master, the repository of the coded information without which nothing would get done" (p. 26). Here the passivity accorded to the cell is the same quality that has traditionally been afforded to women in Western society in general, and the domination/subordination dualism presented as necessary recalls not only the power of husband over wife, but the control of master over slave as well.

The ultimate aim of this scientific vision, which is depicted as a justification for the events that take place, is put forth in the name of "getting something done." The valuing of material accomplishment at the expense of the intricate and interconnected processes of life that ecofeminism recognizes is also a fundamental paradigm which leads to the acceptance of the scientific worldview, even when it seems skewed and socially constructed but is nonetheless difficult to challenge. Evelyn Fox Keller (1992) has eloquently described how science's ability to match its theories with perceived reality can make science appear to be impervious to alternative theories or constructions of reality. Viewed in this way, science can be seen not only as a means to an end, but as a means shaped by its end.

Thus, it should then come as no surprise to find metaphors of industrial society and its obsession with war (reflecting the values of the patriarchal, Western cultural milieu) turning up in popular depictions of cell biology. As Richard Lewontin, Steven Rose and Leon Kamin (1984) have described, "the imagery of the biochemistry of the cell [has] been that of the factory, where functions [are] specialized for the conversion of energy into particular products and which [has] its own part to play in the economy of the organism as a whole" (p. 58).

Even further, in the subdiscipline of molecular biology, the cell is envisioned as "an assembly line factory in which the DNA blueprints are interpreted and raw materials fabricated to produce the protein end products in response to a series of regulated requirements" (Lewontin *et al.*, 1984, p. 59). In many popular conceptions of molecular processes, viruses are depicted as "invaders" that the body must conquer by calling upon its department of defense, the immune system. In a relatively recent *Time* magazine article (Wallis, 1984), viruses are depicted as converting cellular "factories" to produce viral proteins, thereby disabling normal cellular functions.

In my own experience in science, I have found that metaphors of control and domination are not the only metaphors associated with the public, masculine side of life's equations to be found in cell biology. While metaphors of domination and control may be the most overtly recognizable metaphors of this type, and perhaps hold the deepest political implications, a more subtle bias in metaphorical description also exists in the undergirdings of cell biology.

Psychologically, the development of autonomy, distance, and individuality is traditionally associated with and observed to be a male-identified characteristic, while a valuing of connection, relationship and similarity is associated with women (Belenky, Clinchy, Goldberger and Tarule, 1986; Gilligan, 1982; Surrey, 1991). This gendering of the psyche is a further example of the dualistic division of individuals in Western culture. These social constructs are mapped onto biological bodies, so that once again theory appears to match reality not only as a means to an end, but as a means determined by its end.

Not surprisingly, the gendered division of these "ways of knowing" the self and others, whether that other is a person, place or thing, is also evident in the metaphors of cell biology. Take, for example, the commonly observed pictograph of a cell. Two concentric circles, one circumscribing the plasma membrane, the other the boundary of the all-powerful nucleus which contains the DNA, are its most salient features. Two continuous boundaries, separating inside from outside, nucleus from cytoplasm, master from controlled. The cell is shown as if autonomous, separate, disconnected from other

vation at hand may hold true, but so too do such actions obscure another picture of how cells actually exist: within the context of other cells, and in different states, continuous, relational, and interdependent.

The idea of cells as isolated individuals facilitated by the concept of a cell as a membraned boundary is carried further in the theoretical separation of different cellular "systems" from one another. Cells carrying out similar functions are grouped into organized systems, such as the immune system and the nervous system. Yet while such ordering is facilitated by the functions that these cells carry out, it often serves to mystify the all-important connections between the cells of different systems. It further implies a mutual exclusivity of cellular roles, so that a cell is seen as belonging to one system or another, even though it may act as a mediator between two or more functions, or perform multiple functions common to several systems.

Thus, metaphors of individuation, autonomy and separation underlie the picture of cell biology that is most commonly presented in textbooks, journal articles and presentations. Such depictions naturally have a strong influence on how scientists conceptualize, solve, and portray their version of how nature exists. They facilitate a vision of life, even at its most minute level, as one of separation, distance, and disconnection. From an ecofeminist perspective, the ramifications of such a conception of life, one that ignores and devalues connections and relationships, bodes doom for nature, women, and the fate of all life on earth.

An ecofeminist revisioning of cell and molecular biology

While scientists will often describe their observations as if no other alternative were possible, the reality of the situation is that just as a microscope can be adjusted to bring different views into focus, there exist a myriad of ways to describe a single observation. As much as physical reality may be said to exist, personal interpretation of that reality is very much a condition of one's life experiences and surroundings. While some basic elements can be agreed upon as common to many views, often just the way in which a scene is described can make it unrecognizable to another observer of that same scene.

By rendering views of the cell as an agent of connection with communication and cooperation invisible, which the scientific metaphors currently in widespread use certainly do, individuals who preferentially view life through a lens of relationship and empathic connection are discouraged and disadvantaged from this sort of knowledge. As referred to above, these ways of knowing and viewing life have been most cultivated, encouraged and associated with non-dominant (non-male) categories of knowers.

To envision the sight at the end of the microscope within the context of a different set of metaphors, namely those accorded to women and other groups currently underrepresented in science, could make a significant difference in the accessibility of cell and molecular biology to these populations. In doing so, it could also provide an important counterpoint for the view of life as disconnected, autonomous and individuated. Furthermore, I will venture to propose that such a standpoint could aid in bringing the focus of cell and molecular biology into a view more consistent with ecofeminist visions of the relationship between all forms of life on earth.

How can we envision the application of such metaphors to cell biology? Janet Surrey (1991), in her description of *The Self-in-Relation: A Theory of Women's Development*, eloquently foreshadows the application of such a conception of a relational self to science. Throughout the article, she discusses women's tendency to see themselves in the context of "an evolutionary process of development through relationship" (p. 59). Searching for an apt metaphor for the potentiality of such a concept of the self, she describes the recognition of a connected way of knowing in the sense that "perhaps this is like evolving from a language of three-dimensional space and Newtonian physics to four dimensional space and relativity theory" (p. 59).

I propose to go further with this association, drawing the sense of self-in-relation into the realm of cell and molecular biology. To know the cell as a unit of connection and communication, though different from traditional views of it as a unit of structure and function, provides a new dimensionality through which microscopic life can be experienced. And, counter to traditional, three-dimensional thought, difference in this case is not necessarily mutually exclusive. The cell can provide the fundamental unit of structure and function while at the same time carrying out functions of connection and communication.

An infusion of new metaphors into the scientific study of nature provides an effective way of opening up new avenues of thinking about and researching the processes of life, particularly at the cellular and molecular levels. Science at this level is mostly metaphorical, in that meaning is often transmitted through symbolic representation of observations (this characteristic of science is also what makes it "abstract"). What I am suggesting is not necessarily a substitution of metaphors of one kind for another, but a mutual acknowledgement that there may be many different kinds of metaphors for describing the processes of nature, just as there are multiple ways of knowing nature. By holding the possibility that such a multiplicity of metaphors may simultaneously exist, a new view of nature, as well as science, may be possible. Rather than seeking to find the singular way in which nature works through the discovery of a singular paradigm, a new way of knowing may emerge, one that, to echo Janet Surrey (1991), may be four-dimensional in its perspective, and may also be more attuned to ecofeminist perspectives.

Such a change in perspective necessarily implies a parallel change in the way that science is conceived and practiced. In its acknowledgment of personal, lived experience as a basis for knowledge claims, a science that draws on and incorporates multiple ways of knowing inherently replaces the goal of determining a singular objective truth with the aim of allowing for subjective exploration and description. Rather than seeking to deny personal bias, the presence of which most feminists as well as scientists have come to accept, a science aligned with ecofeminist tenets demands that we acknowledge the existence of our own biases, or subjectivities, and make use of them in our process of knowing nature.

[illegible]

Instead, I view the membranes of a cell as accomplishing both continuity with the cellular environment yet distinction and autonomy: basically, a cell "self" defined "in relation" to its environment.

Such metaphors of communication and interaction focus on the permeability of membraned boundaries, both delineating inside from out and serving as an interface between the two. Concentration gradients as well as osmotic pressure (the relative concentration of water inside and outside of the cell) can influence the movement of some substances through the membrane from inside to outside of a cell or vice versa. Thus, cell membranes are dynamic and versatile in adapting their specificity to cellular and environmental conditions.

Imbedded in membranes are many channels and proteins[2] forming a continuous interface between inside and outside of a cell. The fluid nature of the membrane allows for channels to constantly shift open and closed, depending on their surrounding conditions, and for membrane proteins to constantly shift position relative to one another. Many of these membrane proteins are receptors, the virtual sense organs of the cell. These receptors transmit cellular signals from outside to inside; changing cellular conditions, such as stage of growth or division (often a consequence of a cell's environment), can influence which receptors are displayed on the membrane and thus which signals can be communicated. Receptor expression at the membrane interface is often a consequence of intricate feedback loops, providing a further layer of communication and integration of the membrane within its cellular and environmental contexts.

Where in this view is the DNA – traditionally cordoned away in its nucleus, the master so central to currently prevailing views of the cell as the execution of its all-powerful genes? Focusing on cellular membranes as dynamic interfaces which facilitate relation and communication brings the nucleus itself into a different light. The membrane that encompasses the nucleus is directionally continuous with the cell membrane, through its connection with membranes of other "compartments" within the cell.[3] Thus, the nuclear environment of the DNA itself, which in turn influences the state of genes, is mediated by membranes. The "execution of genes" becomes just one of many interrelated, interdependent events in a cell's response to and interaction between inside and outside.

How might we envision the incorporation of new metaphors, focusing on connection and relationship, into the teaching and practice of cell and molecular biology? One source of new metaphors can be found in biological subdisciplines outside of cell and molecular biology, for example, in the fields of anatomy or ecology. Other metaphorical realignments of cell and molecular biology may come from shifting the focus of study from the knowledge "products" derived from such research to the process by which knowledge is made.

The following are examples of how such new metaphors might find their way into teaching and research in cell and molecular biology.

The cell as bodily organism

When we look for reflections between our own bodies and that of the cell, a rich world of metaphors opens up. The many receptors and ligands of the cell can be metaphorically viewed as sense organs, allowing the cell to "touch," "taste," "listen" and "smell." Membrane pores remind us of the connections between membranes and the pores of our own skin. Nobel laureate David Baltimore (1984) has likened the cell nucleus to a brain; while the context of his reference is questionable in ecofeminist terms, it nonetheless is an example of an organismal metaphor that can be applied to the cell. I would add the metaphor of nucleus as womb, the membranes its umbilical link to the environment. Metaphors of brain and womb need not be mutually exclusive; the simultaneous application of these two metaphors can aid in dismantling the parallel male/female, mind/body, and thinking/feeling splits found in Western culture.

The cell as ecosystem

Microbiologist Lynn Margulis (1981) has traced the different sources of DNA found in eukaryotic cells to show that some subcellular compartments evolved out of symbiotic relationships between different cell types, living together in cooperative harmony. This principle can provide a starting point for the introduction of ecological metaphors into cell and molecular biology. Within an ecological framework, the cell can be defined as a unit of life that exists in constant relation and exchange with its environment. The cyclical flow of membranes, as they travel between different cellular compartments as well as between the cell's interior and exterior, can be likened to the ecological process of succession. Emphasis can be placed upon the cycling and recycling of molecules within the cell, changing the focus of metabolic cycles such as the Krebs Cycle[4] from hierarchical orderings of enzymes and products into dynamic flows and exchanges of cellular resources. In a broader ecological perspective, organismal bodies can be viewed as cellular ecosystems, drawing on metaphorical comparisons such as that between the ecosystem of a river and that of the bloodstream.

Shifting metaphors of process in cell and molecular biology

Following a change in the metaphors of *what* is studied in cell and molecular biology needs to come a change in *how* those things are studied. Evelyn Fox Keller (1983), in her biography of geneticist Barbara McClintock, describes how this Nobel laureate approached her subject, seeking a "feeling for the organism" (p. 198). Plant physiologist

Winnie Devlin (1994) explains her approach to studying plant cells as "an energizing swim in their living fluid. A movement of interaction wherein my being merges with their biochemical flow" (p. 56). Molecular biologist Robert Pollack (1994) reinterprets the quest to understand DNA when he says that "to understand the linguistic properties, syntax, grammar, and semantics of a human genome, we have to look at how a gene speaks to a cell and at the meanings of what it says" (p. 68). Although Pollack disregards the other side of this conversation, in which the cell speaks to the genome, his metaphor

for structural support, such as in epithelial tissues as well as for the exchange of chemical components which support each other's growth and differentiation. A cell cannot exist isolated alone. It must have other cells and cell types if it is to grow and live. Healthy cells (those that have not been manipulated artificially outside of a living organism) have very accurate growth regulation mechanisms, which are a function of the cellular community to which they belong.

Many states of disease, in particular cancer, occur when such communities are deprived of their ability to interact with each other.[5] Some cancers result from cellular receptors which have lost their ability to receive signals from their environment but continue to transmit such signals to the inside of the cell anyway. Unable to sense its surrounding conditions, the cell proliferates, losing continuity with its environment. Most cancers result from cells becoming removed from the tissue or organ environment to which they belong. Lacking the signals needed to remain integrated into their community, such cells proliferate out of synchrony with their environment and become cancerous. Cancers can also be the result of the language of growth and development gone awry. Defects in biochemical pathways communicating developmental decisions can result in a cell misaligned with its surroundings, developing into a cancerous growth.

All of these conditions can be viewed as resulting from aberrant communication and maligned cellular relationships. Yet traditional views of cancer frame it as a crisis of control, in which mutated genes turn into malevolent dictators, overtaking the cell's growth and division cycles.[6] Conventional treatment options for cancer are likewise shaped by this framing. Radiation and chemotherapy seek to "kill off" the offending cells, while gene therapy "targets" the master molecule with little heed for its cellular or organismal environment.

Describing cancer as a failure in communication and relation rather than as a crisis of control leads to the possibility of different treatment options. Restoring the process of communication and relation by bringing the cellular community back into alignment may in some cases lead to more effective treatments than seeking to destroy the offender. In fact, cases of acute premyclocytic leukemia in which the condition did not respond to the conventional "seek and destroy" treatment tactics have been shown to be healed by a much more holistic approach (Shepherd, 1993). Cells were treated instead with compounds that enabled them to grow to maturity, completing their normal life cycle which had been interrupted and reversing the cancerous condition. Giving cells what they need to grow is an apt metaphor in itself for what women and nature often need in Western society (Brandenburger, personal communication (28 January, 1994)).

Viewing cancer in the context of relationality also enables us to link it to similar processes reflected at other levels of life, within an ecofeminist context. In this view of cancer, improper or disrupted communication between cells leads to anomalies in growth controls, and cellular communities become overpopulated, straining available resources just as overpopulated human communities might. And, just as overdrawing the resources of an environmental land base leads to a non-sustainable depletion of resources, so too does cellular overpopulation lead to an unsustainable depletion of organismal resources.

From this perspective then, the way back to health in both planetary and organismal senses is to reintroduce effective means of communication that will facilitate sustainable interactions with resources, whether these are environmental or organismal. The power of the mutually interchangeable metaphors of organism and environment can also be useful for stimulating new conceptions of the self. If we can learn to see ourselves as both organism and environment simultaneously, we may be able to breach rigid self–other boundaries in new ways.

Thus, the incorporation of new metaphors at the cellular and molecular level, really new ways of seeing life from a perspective of relationship and communication, has implications that spread throughout the many levels of awareness of self and nature that we as humans are able to grasp. My pursuit of such new metaphors has been stimulated by the dissonance that I have experienced between my own ways of knowing nature and the ways that are cultivated in traditional science.

I hope that I have begun to demonstrate here the powerful ways in which feminist critiques of science can move from expressions of dissatisfaction into stimuli for growth and change in ways consistent with ecofeminist views of nature and the self. I also hope that such an approach will be able to maneuver around the rigidity of dualistic and hierarchical characterization of the self and nature, and instead support a holistic, multifaceted view of life. Science holds a great deal of promise for ecofeminism, yet without an infusion of new life, it also poses dire threats to women, the environment and all life on earth. If we can learn to cultivate and encourage new ways of knowing inside of science, perhaps the outside will take care of itself.

Notes

1 For a historical analysis on parallels between the theoretical, scientific belief that both nature and women are subjects that must be subdued and conquered, see Merchant, 1980. The names of commonly used cell and molecular biology techniques speak for themselves: pulse chase, freeze fracture, radioactive probing, cell sonication.

2 Cell membranes are composed of 50% lipid material and 50% protein. Thus, these proteins are a significant component of the membrane (see Alberts, Bray, Lewis, Raff, Roberts and Watson, 1989).

3 The plasma membrane, golgi apparatus, endoplasmic reticulum, and nuclear envelope are all membranous structures that are either directly continuous (as in the case of the endoplasmic reticulum and the nuclear envelope) or they exchange membraned portions through processes such as exocytosis, endocytosis and "blebbing" (see Alberts *et al.*, 1989).

4 The Krebs cycle, also known as the citric acid cycle, is a fundamental biochemical pathway of digestion in which energy is extracted from sugar molecules through a

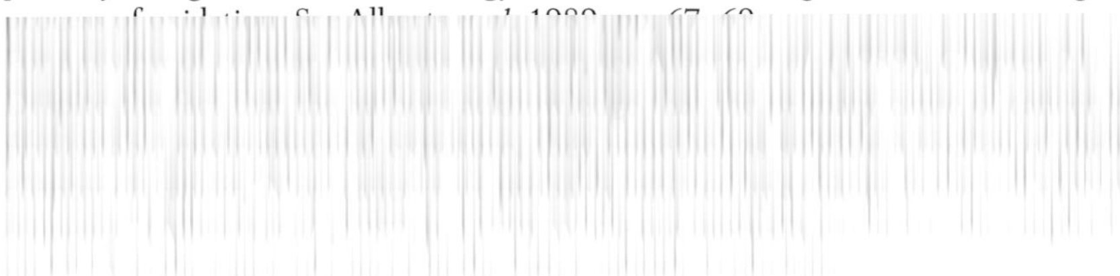

References

Aisenberg, Nadya and Harrington, Mona. (1988). *Women of academe: Outsiders in the sacred grove*. Amherst, MA: University of Massachusetts Press.

Alberts, Bruce, Bray, Dennis, Lewis, Julian, Raff, Martin, Roberts, Keith, and Watson, James D. (1989). *Molecular biology of the cell*. New York: Garland Publishing.

Baltimore, David. (1984). The brain of a cell. *Science, 84*, 149–151.

Belenky, Mary Field, Clinchy, Blythe McVicker, Goldberger, Nancy Rule, and Tarule, Jill Mattuck. (1986). *Women's ways of knowing: The development of self, voice and mind*. New York: Basic Books.

The Biology and Gender Study Group. (1988). The importance of feminist critique for contemporary cell biology. *Hypatia*, 3(l), 138–160.

Birke, Lynda. (1986). *Women, feminism and biology: The feminist challenge*. New York: Methuen.

Bleier, Ruth. (1984). *Science and gender: A critique of biology and its theories on women*. Elmsford, NY: Pergamon Press.

Capra, Frijof. (1975). *The tao of physics*. Berkeley: Shambhala.

Capra, Fritjof. (1982). *The turning point*. New York: Simon and Shuster.

Davies, Katherine. (1988). What is ecofeminism? *Women and Environments, 10*(3), 4–6.

Devlin, Winnie. (1994). Biochemical flowering. *Woman of Power, 23*, 56–58.

Diamond, Irene and Orenstein, Gloria Feman. (1990). *Reweaving the world: The emergence of ecofeminism*. San Francisco: Sierra Club Books.

Fausto-Sterling, Ann. (1985). *Myths of gender*. New York: Basic Books.

Gilligan, Carol. (1982). *In a different voice: Psychological theory and women's development*. Cambridge, MA: Harvard University Press.

Hallen, Patsy. (1989). Careful of science: A feminist critique of science. *The Trumpeter, 6*, 3–8.

Harding, Sandra. (1986). *The science question in feminism*. Ithaca: Cornell University Press.

Harding, Sandra. (1992). *Whose science? Whose knowledge? Thinking from women's lives*. Ithaca: Cornell University Press.

Hubbard, Ruth. (1990). *The politics of women's biology*. Cambridge, MA: Schenkman Publishing Co.

Hubbard, Ruth. (1995). *Profitable promises*. Monroe, ME: Common Courage Press.

Keeton, William T. (1980). *Biological science* (3rd ed.). New York: W.W. Norton & Co.
Keller, Evelyn Fox. (1977). The anomoly of a woman in physics. In Sara Ruddick and Pamela Daniels (Eds.), *Working it out* (pp. 77–91). New York: Pantheon Books
Keller, Evelyn Fox. (1983). *A feeling for the organism: The life and work of Barbara McClintock.* New York: W.A. Freeman & Co.
Keller, Evelyn Fox. (1985). *Reflections on gender and science.* New Haven, CT: Yale University Press.
Keller, Evelyn Fox. (1992). *Secrets of life, secrets of death.* New York: Routledge.
Lewontin, Richard, Rose, Steven, and Kamin, Leon. (1984). *Not in our genes: Biology, ideology and human nature.* New York: Pantheon.
Lovelock, James. (1979). *Gaia: A new look at life on earth.* Oxford: Oxford University Press.
Lovelock, James, and Margulis, Lynn. (1984). Gaia and geognosy. In M.B. Rambler (Ed.), *Global ecology: Toward a science of the biosphere.* London: Jones and Bartlett.
Margulis, Lynn. (1981). *Symbiosis in cell evolution.* San Francisco: W.H. Freeman.
Merchant, Carolyn. (1980). *The death of nature.* San Francisco: Harper & Row.
Namenwirth, Marion. (1986). Science seen through a feminist prism. In Ruth Bleier (Ed.), *Feminist approach to science* (pp. 18–41). Elmsford, NY: Pergamon Press.
Nanney, David L. (1957). The role of the cytoplasm in heredity. In W.D. McElroy and H.B. Glass (Eds.), *The chemical basis of heredity* (pp. 134–166). Baltimore: Johns Hopkins University Press.
Plant, Judith (Ed.). (1989). Healing the wounds: the promise of ecofeminism. Philadelphia, PA: New Society Publishers.
Pollack, Robert. (1994). *Signs of life: the language and meaning of DNA.* Boston: Houghton Mifflin.
Rosser, Sue V. (1987). Feminist scholarship in the science: Where are we now and when can we expect a theoretic breakthrough? *Hypatia*, 2, 3–14.
Rosser, Sue V. (1992). *Biology and feminism.* New York: Twayne Publishers.
Ruether, Rosemary Radford. (1992). *Gaia and god.* San Francisco: HarperCollins.
Shepherd, Linda Jean. (1993). *Lifting the veil: The feminine face of science.* Boston: Shambhala.
Surrey, Janet L. (1991). The self-in-relation: A theory of women's development. In Judith Jordan, Alexandra Kaplan, Jean Baker Miller, Irene Stiver and Janet Surrey (Eds.), *Women's growth in connection: Writings from the Stone Center* (pp. 51–66). New York: Guilford Press.
Thomas, Lewis. (1974). *The lives of a cell.* New York: Viking Press.
Wallis, Claudia. (1984). Knowing the face of the enemy. *Time, 123*, 66–67.

Chapter 32

Muriel Lederman

Synopsis

Many calls for a feminist science have ended with the disclaimer that there is no way to imagine such a science from within an androcentric society. Making the attempt requires dealing with two broad questions: "Is all or some of science socially constructed?" and "By what features is science recognized?" The strategy used here involves defining the components as we know them, asking if they are socially constructed, and, if they are, how they could be changed to be less androcentric. The conclusion is that all of science may be androcentric, and the approach to attaining feminist science may need to be radical, a total replacement of the scientific enterprise with one not based on the scientific method. Alternatively, we may accept a modification of current science, a "feminized" science (defined as doing the same science differently), as consistent with the political goal for feminist scientists.

Recently, there have been many calls for a feminist science. Most have ended with a statement reflecting the difficulty of envisioning a feminist science, saying that there is no way, from our current perspective, to imagine the form a feminist science might take. For example, Elizabeth Fee has stated that "For us to imagine a feminist science in a feminist society is rather like asking a medieval peasant to imagine the theory of genetics or the production of a space capsule" (Fee, 1982, p. 31). Sue Rosser has said "I do not think that we can further imagine how a feminist science might differ from traditional science until we have many feminists in top-level research and decision-making positions in science for a considerable period of time" (Rosser, 1988, p. 18). However, we should think about what may comprise such a science. If we fail even to try, we may be perceived as less than serious about our feminism and less than serious about the science that we conduct.

There is considerable agreement in feminist critiques of science that both the practice of science and the applications of that science reflect domination in subtle and overt fashions. Maria Mies has said:

> There is no abstract gain of knowledge which justifies the drastic destruction of vital links between self-sustaining living systems on earth, of the inherent worth of plants, animals, and humans in their living environment. *The marriage between knowledge and force must be dissolved*. It is imperative to alter this science. Another paradigm of science cannot start, however, with the famous male urge for limitless knowledge, omniscience and omnipotency.
>
> (Mies, 1990, p. 439)

However, this ideology of domination is deeply ingrained in the current practice of science, an ideology that entered, according to some, at the time of the Scientific Revolution.

> . . . The new epistemological principle upon which, since Bacon, the new scientific method is based is violence and power. Without violently disrupting the organic whole called Mother Nature, without separating the research objects by force from the symbiotic context and isolating them in the laboratory . . . the new scientists cannot gain knowledge. Violence and force are therefore intrinsic methodological principles of the modern concept of science and knowledge. They are not, as is often assumed, ethical questions which arise only on the *application of the results* of this science. They belong to the epistemological foundations of modern science.
>
> (Mies, 1990, p. 437)

As Susan Bordo says in her analysis of "The Cartesian Masculinization of Thought," "The otherness of nature is now what allows it to be known" (Bordo, 1986, p. 261).

One consequence of statements such as Mies' may be that current science will have to be replaced to attain feminist goals. However, these statements do not give much guidance about what might take its place. I explore another path to investigate the relationship of science as it is practiced now to a science that includes feminist viewpoints of many origins in the practices of biology. I realize that my analysis may be suspect to some, because I am a practicing scientist and therefore subject to the charge that I have been socialized during my training to accept androcentric science. I maintain that concerned, sensitized scientists may have the best perspective for a realistic assessment of science, because they might have two lenses with which to view science, the lens of feminism overlaid on the lens of their own research.

Science as we know it functions in an androcentric society. The first question to be asked is "By what features do we recognize science?" We need to be able to state clearly what is meant by "science" in order to define what counts as something to be changed. Then we need to ask "Is science socially constructed? – Is it defined by its practitioners and the society within which it thrives?" A positive answer to these last two questions, taken together with an androcentric society, means that if *all* facets of contemporary science are socially constructed, all of science is androcentric, and the call for a feminist science will necessitate the total replacement of the scientific enterprise. If only some aspects of science are socially constructed, then they alone have to be replaced or changed to develop or reveal a feminist science.

It is important to keep in mind that the search for a feminist model of inquiry is not separable from feminism as a political movement. Seeking to replace androcentric science with an alternative of any form is as much of a political act as entrenched androcentrism is a political reality. Implicit in the search for a feminist science is the assumption that once such a science can be characterized, it will be practiced. But can [illegible]

Is it possible, even with these constraints, to begin the process of inventing a feminist science? In the analysis to follow, I describe science as it is practiced today and attempt to identify which of its aspects are socially constructed and therefore androcentric. I attempt to show that it is necessary to be as rigorous in our critiques of the current versions of feminist science as we are of science within society. I hope to convince the reader in this exercise that at least some of the current analyses may not alter androcentric science in any fundamental fashion. I believe that what has emerged from the feminist critiques of science are versions of something that can be called "feminized" science (to be defined later). Any real change, to attain a truly feminist science, may require a much more radical approach.

Social construction of the practice of science

When analyzing the practice of science, we need to ask if science, in all or some of its components, is socially constructed and therefore androcentric. First, we must identify those components which exemplify science. If we can agree that these parameters are socially constructed, then the possibility emerges that they can be eliminated or replaced, thereby opening the way for a feminist science. I will take the scientific method as the current methodology of science. It is characterized by observation, description, the development of hypotheses, and the testing of these hypotheses by experimentation. To what extent is each of these components socially constructed? It is difficult, if not impossible, to discuss each of these categories separately, because the scientist comingles them in the process of carrying out an investigation. Observations are usually made within the context of experiments. Even if the science is not experimentally based, a hypothesis is still present and the interpretation of the data is a description which may confirm or refute the hypothesis.

Is the *process* of making an observation socially constructed? The process of observation has three components, the physiological act of observation, the instantaneous processing of information that produces an observation, and the description of that observation. I believe that the first component, the physiology of observation, is not socially constructed. If the difference between androcentric science and feminist science were grounded in differential perception, it would follow that men as opposed to women or individuals with diverse sexual orientation, or persons of different social classes or political persuasion would see, hear, or touch nature differently. Making the suggestion that individuals sense the physical world differently *depending on a social or biological grouping* would lead to the most dangerous, counterproductive kind of determinism. However, the second and third components, the "observation" and its description, may vary among members of different groups, based upon their different experiences in different social contexts. These alternatives could lead to a richness in interpretation that could benefit future experimentation, but more commonly the descriptions serve only to simultaneously reflect and reinforce prevailing social structures (Martin, 1991).

Within my own scientific field, molecular biology, the by now classic example of a description that is biased in a way which reflects the androcentrism of society is the naming of DNA as the "master molecule."The implication behind this naming is that DNA controls totally the metabolism of the cell, the overall metabolism of the organism, and the entire process of heredity. The implicit assumption of this term is that the DNA works in isolation, that it is preprogrammed for all these tasks. In this model, DNA functions solely to "read out" the program contained in its sequence of nucleotides, with no chance for any interaction with the cytoplasm or the environment (Biology and Gender Study Group, 1988). Is the process of generating hypotheses socially constructed? Very likely it is, because the already existing descriptors influence the way scientists pose new questions and the way they view the data they obtain.

Is experimentation socially constructed? By experimentation, I do not mean the nature of the questions asked in the experiment or the interpretation of the result, but rather the overall concept of experimental design. Experimentation itself can be subdivided into what I will call passive and active experimentation. One example of passive experimentation is the discovery of the periodicity in planetary movement. This involved observation, the generation of hypotheses, and the confirmation of hypotheses at a later time, again by observation. Passive experimentation can also be found in the field of ecology. Here, the investigator observes a natural situation, makes a hypothesis about the types of interactions occurring among the living entities in a region, and searches for confirmation of the hypothesis in *other naturally occurring situations*. A second situation may be, for example, a study of biological succession in an area which has suffered a forest fire. In neurobiology, hypotheses about the location in the human brain of areas which control different functions initially took advantage of individuals who had lost portions of their brains to accident or disease.

This is in contrast to what I call active experimentation, in which the investigator sets up a situation to test the hypothesis rather than patiently waiting for Nature to deliver the situation. A criticism of androcentric science which has been voiced persistently is that it is not "at one" with Nature. Active experimentation is the part of contemporary science which feminist critiques have singled out as exemplifying androcentric science, because this type of experimentation can be seen as an intrusion into Nature. For the examples given above of passive experimentation, the parallel active experiments might be burning an area to investigate ecological succession or surgically severing the corpus callosum in an animal, an early experiment in the development of the left brain–right brain distinction.

Let us instead entertain the idea that active science is female in origin by devising a hypothetical scenario. Imagine an individual in a pre-Scientific Revolution society posing herself the following questions: "Does the extract of the purple-leaved plant which grows on the hill a morning's walk toward the sun reduce the redness when applied to the wound caused by the bite of the spider? Does the liquid made by boiling this leaf stop the shivering of the fever which comes every year when the sun is low in the sky? If it stops the shivering, could the boiled leaves of the plant which grows by [illegible]

Sandra Harding has said:

> It is unclear how one would define this term (scientific method) in such a way that highly trained scientists and junior members of research teams in physics counted as scientists, but farmers in simple societies (or mothers!) did not.
>
> (Harding, 1987, p. 28)

Radical feminism as described by Rosser (1992) is "based on the women's experience . . . reject(ing) most scientific theories, data, and experiments because they not only exclude women but also because they are not women-centered" (p. 545). If there is any truth in the scenario I suggested for women's discovery of therapeutic botanicals, we are faced with a paradox. In the radical critique, active science would have to be valued because of its female origin. On the other hand, this woman-based effort might have given rise to one of the most androcentric parts of current science, after the co-optation and alteration of the contributions of women.

Reconstructing science

I have given examples which show that much of the practice of science is socially constructed and has been perceived to have an androcentric bias. How can we make the practice of science less androcentric? Let us begin with observation and description. There have been excellent examples of cases in science in which observations of the same systems resulted in alternative descriptions, one set of which was androcentric and the other set was gynocentric. Sue Rosser (1988, 1992) reports that the field of primatology altered drastically after the participation of women as researchers; the analyses of the organization of the animal families changed from an interpretation that was almost totally androcentric to one that recognized the contributions of the women.

Another instance is the description of DNA as the "master molecule." The concept of a nucleic acid (of whatever sort) as a reservoir of genetic information which is read out to determine genetic specificity has been challenged as a hierarchical construct which should be abolished. At some point, biologists must consider how an organism or a cell interacts with its environment. Strangely enough, one system which was very important in the early stages of attempts to understand the mechanism of gene expression was one in which expression was altered in response to changes in the environment which affected the growth of bacteria. The studies of Jacob and Monod (1961) on the *lac* operon of the bacterium *Escherichia coli* were among the first in which messenger RNA was demonstrated. The messenger RNA for the enzymes which allowed this bacterium to metabolize lactose appeared within the bacterial cell in response to the presence of lactose in the external growth medium. However, at the time, the environmental aspect was downplayed, and the utility of the system was the ability to detect and characterize the production of this newly made messenger RNA.

Indeed, 30 years after the experiments of Jacob and Monod, scientists are beginning formally to recognize the importance of a more interactive biology. The cover art on the Instructions to Authors for the first issue of a journal, *The Journal of Cell Regulation*, published by the American Society for Cell Biology (now called *Molecular Biology of the Cell*), showed a drawing of two adjacent cells. Superimposed on these cells was an arrow beginning in the cytoplasm of one cell, going to a box in the space between the cells. There is another arrow from the box to the cytoplasm of the second cell and a third arrow pointing from this cytoplasm to the nucleus. This diagram reflects both the sites of potential regulatory molecules and the directionality of the pathways thought to be operating in the regulation of gene expression. I wish to emphasize that there is an arrow from the cytoplasm to the nucleus; this implies that the cytoplasm has an influential role in affecting nuclear events. This in itself is a major shift from earlier paradigms, as there is no arrow from the nucleus to the cytoplasm; the major "controlling" role of the DNA in the nucleus is downplayed.

The term "master" has also been used to refer to genes, perhaps not surprisingly, to the putative genes for sex determination. The report of the human testis-determining factor by Page and co-workers (1987) explicitly uses the term "master." The view put forth by these workers (and five of the nine authors are women) is that the determination of "maleness" is the active process, with the expression of a gene(s) resulting in a phenotype. An alternative view (Eichner and Washburn, 1986) is that there are ovary-determining genes and testis-determining genes. The time at which these genes are expressed determines sex, with the "male" gene being expressed before the "female" gene. This perspective suggests that the default condition determines the phenotype. If the "maleness" gene is not expressed, the individual will be female. I leave it to the reader to decide for herself which hypothesis gives the most power to which sex. It must be noted that the hierarchical viewpoint is not absolutely correct: indirect effects come into play as well, both in mammals (Patek *et al.*, 1991) and in the worm *Caenorhabditis* (Hunter and Woods, 1992). Both points of view ignore other invertebrates (*Drosophila*) which have yet another mechanism of sex determination, and hermaphrodites. Unfortunately, the glib terminology of "master" was quickly picked up and disseminated to undergraduates. The genetics textbook, *The Science of Genetics* by George W. Burns and Paul J. Bottino (1989), refers to the testis-determining factor as the "master switch that . . . activates an entire series of genes whose function is sex differentiation" (p. 136).

Unfortunately, the term "master" is becoming ever more widely applied. The journal *Cell* recently had a review article titled "Translocations, Master Genes and

Differences between the Origins of Acute and Chronic Leukemias" (Rabbitts, 1991), that analyzed the genes on either side of sites where chromosomes break. These breaks correlate with recombination between individual chromosomes and with malignancy. Another review article covering essentially the same data was published in *Science*, without the sexist bias. It was "Chromosome Aberrations and Cancer" by Ellen Solomon, Julian Borrow, and Audrey D. Goddard (Solomon, Borrow, and Goddard, 1991). *Cell*, because of its reputation as perhaps the most prestigious cell and molecular [illegible] describe the device that alters the path of a railroad train from one track to another, has precisely the desired meaning.

As mentioned above, descriptions generally influence the generation of new hypotheses. The conception of DNA as the "master molecule" and the implication of unidirectionality inherent in it was a hypothesis, the Central Dogma; DNA makes RNA makes protein. Focusing on this hypothesis led to a series of experiments that were very productive. Scientists concentrated on those aspects of gene expression that *were* unidirectional. This led to the understanding of the mechanism of the synthesis of messenger RNA and the synthesis of protein based upon the nucleotide sequence of messenger RNA. It could be argued that this basic information was needed before studies on how gene expression is regulated in response to changing intracellular signals or altered environmental stimuli could be carried out. One potential problem with a conceptual framework that requires each component of a biological system to be accorded equal importance is that, under these circumstances, it is difficult to obtain information about the parts. It is not possible to know everything at once. Useful information is most often obtained by dividing biological systems into smaller packages; this information can then be reintegrated to give a complete picture.

One may wish to attribute equal standing to, for example, DNA, the magnesium ion, and water. However, one cannot study the role of these three components simultaneously. The relationship of water to DNA was crucial in discovering the structure of DNA, because X-ray diffraction studies were carried out on the molecules in different states of hydration. The role of magnesium in DNA replication was studied by enzymologists. When scientists came to study the role of DNA in gene expression, experiments had already been carried out and the results could be incorporated into the new studies. Although focusing on the role of DNA in gene expression could be seen as an example of hierarchical science, any one investigator picks out the things that are most interesting to her for her research program. She takes advantage of the research programs of other investigators, hoping someone else chooses a complementary area and that, in the long run, enough information is obtained so that a coherent view appears.

How do we deal with active and passive experimentation? At first glance, one solution might be to eliminate active experimentation from the practice of science.

There would be immense resistance to this proposal, as it would require the dismantling of almost all of the scientific establishment. Even passive experimentation may have to be discarded, at least in the extreme vision of feminist science that I suggest later.

If we cannot eliminate experimentation, how can we make it less androcentric? The liberal feminist critique believes that science is value-neutral and that androcentrism results from misapplication of the scientific method and is "bad science" (Rosser, 1992). Proper application of the scientific method could overcome this bias and result in "good science," with experiments properly controlled, for example, for effects of drugs on both sexes and with equal emphasis placed on diseases that affect both sexes, for example, prostate cancer and breast cancer. In my opinion, "good science" should be business as usual and not a goal to be attained in the future. That "good science" is just now beginning to be practiced points up how political the process of attaining even this first level of feminist science is. It is only through the agitation by the public and in the elected and executive branches of government that even modest progress has been made.

In all our analyses, we must remember that science eventually is constrained by the physical world. For there to be science at all, there must be something approaching a physical reality. Nucleic acid may be a "master molecule" in some sense. However, it is not the ultimate determinant. There are many genes which are subject to what is called "autogenous regulation," in which the amount of the protein produced from the genes regulates the production of messenger RNA for the protein which in turn redefines the amount of protein. As well, there are processes such as cortical contraction in ova that continue in the absence of a nucleus with its associated nucleic acid. We must be as aware as possible of the characteristics of many biological systems in our critiques of biology because many are not open to androcentric interpretations.

Evelyn Fox Keller (1988) has said " . . . a view of science as a pure social product, owing obedience to moral and political pressures from without . . . [leads to] extreme relativism, [in which] science dissolves into ideology" (p. 178). I would put a different slant on it. Without a physical reality, social construction of science could result in fraud. If absolutely everything were socially constructed, then anything goes. Any individual or social group could concoct a reality which could be explicated in a fashion totally consistent with the rules for carrying out science.

Constructing feminist science

The examples given in the previous section are representative of attempts to find alternative ways of doing science. How far have these changes, along with some institutional changes that have resulted in greater participation of women in science, gotten us? I think not very far. Although these changes are revisionist, they are still bound within the canons of androcentric science. I describe them as "feminized science," as "doing the same science differently."

Even if all the changes suggested in the section entitled "Reconstructing science" were made, the "feminist" science which would result would still be based on the scientific method. I suggest that the ultimate change leading to a feminist science might require the development of a science which is *not* based on the scientific method, especially if androcentrism is as deeply imbedded in science as some have suggested.

Indeed, the scientific method is so ingrained that it remains even in some of the feminist critiques. According to Rosser (1992), the liberal-feminist position explicitly accepts the scientific method. The Marxist-feminist viewpoint, along with believing in the social construction of science, rejects distancing the observer from the observed (Rosser, 1992). The examples given above of "passive" experimentation are consistent with this latter viewpoint but nevertheless share some features of the prevailing androcentric methodology, the generation of hypotheses and their testing. Even the hypothetical

[illegible]

precipice, we would be engaged in an extraordinarily exciting and strenuous intellectual activity that at least may bring back to current science new insights that will make it more accessible and relevant to all. Even if we can imagine this science, further difficulties may arise. How would we be sure this feminist science was a science when the only science we have now is by definition androcentric? We can get no guidance from philosophy of science in this matter. Philosophers relate different sciences, for example, transmission genetics and molecular biology, *both of which are based on the scientific method*. If there were two sciences, one based on the scientific method but not the other, they might truly be unrelatable by the current philosophical strategies. How would this science be distinctively feminist? What does feminist mean in this context? Would a science not based on the scientific method be a science accessible to all standpoint epistemologies? If it is not, we run the risk of both internal squabbles in the feminist community and further alienation of feminists from other oppressed peoples. Would a feminist science affect all sciences equally? Perhaps the most significant changes would be in areas such as ethology which can be interpreted in the mirror of human society. Would physics, chemistry, and molecular biology be as drastically affected?

There may be no real purpose in developing a truly feminist science. If we can make all the changes suggested above, resulting in a truly "feminized" science, would we, as feminists, still be unhappy with the scientific enterprise? Here we must return to the realization that feminism is a political movement. Is there a political advantage for women scientists, for the society at large and for science, in eliminating the scientific method? I believe this is the hard question we must ask. If we choose not to, we should direct our energies otherwise. We could continue our struggle to gain influence in the scientific establishment, attempt to alter both the practice of science at all levels and the technologies that result from the applications of the scientific method, in ways that are in line with our feminism.

References

Biology and Gender Study Group. (1988). The importance of feminist critique for contemporary cell biology. *Hypatia*, 3(1), 61–76.

Bordo, Susan. (1986). The cartesian masculinization of thought. In Sandra Harding and Jean F. O'Barr (Eds.), *Sex and scientific inquiry* (pp. 247–264). Chicago: University of Chicago Press.

Burns, George W., and Bottino, Paul J. (1989). *The science of genetics*. New York: Macmillan.

Eichner, Evelyn, and Washburn, Linda. (1986). Genetic control of primary sex determination in mice. *Annual Review of Genetics*, 20, 327–360.

Fee, Elizabeth. (1982). A feminist critique of scientific objectivity. *Science for the People*, 14(4), 8–35.

Ginzberg, Ruth. (1987). Uncovering gynocentric science. *Hypatia*, 2(3), 89–106.

Harding, Sandra. (1987). The method question. *Hypatia*, 2(1), 19–33.

Hunter, Craig R., and Woods, William B. (1992). Evidence from mosaic analysis of the masculinizing gene *her-1* for cell interactions in *C. elegans* sex determination. *Nature*, 355, 551–555.

Jacob, François, and Monod, Jacques. (1961). Genetic regulatory mechanisms in the synthesis of protein. *Journal of Molecular Biology*, 3, 318–356.

Keller, Evelyn Fox. (1988). *Reflections on gender and science*. New Haven: Yale University Press.

Martin, Emily. (1991). The egg and the sperm: How science has constructed a romance based on stereotypical male–female roles. *Signs: Journal of Women in Culture and Society*, 16(3), 485–501.

Mies, Maria. (1990). Women's Studies: Science, violence and responsibility. *Women's Studies International Forum*, 13(5), 433–441.

Page, David C., Mosher, Rebecca, Simpson, Elizabeth M., Fisher, Elizabeth M.C., Mardon, Graeme, Pollack, Jonathan, McGilvray, Barbara, de la Chapelle, Albert, and Brown, Laura G. (1987). The sex-determining region of the human Y chromosome encodes a finger protein. *Cell*, 51, 1091–1104.

Patek, C.E., Kerr, J.B., Gosden, K.W., Hardy, K. Muggleton-Harris, A.L., Handyside A.H., Whittingham, D.G., and Hooper, M.L. (1991). Sex chimaerism, fertility and sex determination in the mouse. *Development*, 113, 311–326.

Rabbitts, Terence H. (1991). Translocations, master genes and differences between the origins of acute and chronic leukemias. *Cell*, 67, 641–644.

Rosser, Sue V. (1988). Good science: Can it ever be gender free? *Women's Studies International Forum*, 11, 13–19.

Rosser, Sue V. (1992). Are there feminist methodologies appropriate for the natural sciences and do they make a difference? *Women's Studies International Forum*, 15(5,6), 535–550.

Solomon, Ellen, Borrow, Julian, and Goddard, Audrey D. (1991). Chromosome aberrations and cancer. *Science*, 254, 1153–1160.

Chapter 33

Vandana Shiva

Why biology needs to be democratized

The dominant paradigm of biology is in urgent need of reinvention and democratization because it is inherently undemocratic. There are three aspects to this. In the first place, it is socially undemocratic. The dominant paradigm casts patterns of human social behavior as biologically determined, thus ignoring the ways in which they are in reality outcomes of social prejudice and bias on the basis of race, class, and gender. Notions that human behavior is the product of biological determinism make such prejudice immune to democratic questioning and transformation, thus perpetuating social and economic inequalities.

Second, biology is the basis of all food production systems that are intimately linked to survival and to women's work and knowledge in the Third World. All of these are threatened by reductionist biology, particularly in the form of genetic engineering. The reinvention of biology is therefore also an economic imperative so that alternative production systems which are more socially just and ecologically sustainable have a chance to flourish.

Third, the dominant approach to studying biology is undemocratic with respect to nonhuman species. It is based on the metaphor of "man's empire over inferior creatures" rather than the metaphor of "the democracy of all life." It therefore contributes to a "war against species," manipulating them without limits if they are economically useful and pushing them to extinction if they are not. It also erodes biodiversity, leaving us materially impoverished. Last but not least, intellectual property rights in the area of life forms that are constructed on the basis of a reductionist biology deepen the exclusion of other knowledge systems.

The democratization of biology requires that culturally and socially determined behavior and characteristics are removed from the domain of biological determinism. This in turn makes it an imperative that excluded groups such as women and Third

World communities have a role in reinventing biology on democratic principles. Democratizing biology from the perspective of the democracy of all life requires that we reinvent biology to account better for the intrinsic worth and self-organizing capacities of all living organisms.

The democratization of biology involves the recovery of pluralism of knowledge traditions, both within the modern Western traditions and within ancient, time-tested, non-Western traditions of agriculture and health care. Democratizing biology requires that the latest application of biology, genetic engineering, be evaluated in the context of alternatives; it also needs to be evaluated in the context of empirical evidence that is undermining the basic tenets of genetic determinism and the assumption of immutable, unchanging genes. Democratizing biology, in addition, involves coherence and honesty both in the "owning" of benefits and the "owning" of risks of genetic engineering. There is therefore a need to have a coherent theory of "novelty" in the areas of intellectual property rights (which deal with ownership of benefits) and biosafety (which deals with the "owning" of risks and hazards).

These issues of the democratization of biology go to the very heart of democracy in the twenty-first century.

The undemocratic paradigm of biological determinism

The dominant paradigm of biology has been an imperialist one. Biological difference between human and nonhuman species, between white and colored peoples, and between men and women has been seen as reason and justification for the rule of the white man over nature, women, and all nonwhite races. Not only is the dominant biology based on these three exclusions; the exclusions themselves are interwoven and interlinked. And the exclusions are shaped by and in turn shape the mode of knowing and thinking about the world. It is these multiple and complex relationships between science, gender, and ecological survival that I want to explore.

Feminist critiques of dominant science emerged from analysis by feminist scientists, which showed how biology as a science was constructed on the basis of the gender biases of patriarchy, and these biased social constructions were then used to justify women's continued oppression.[1]

Central to the patriarchal construction of biology was the association of activity and creativity with the male and passivity with the female. Furthermore this construction was based on an artificial mind–body dichotomy, a dichotomy which was also seen as gendered. These distortions have led to the equation ot "biology" with lack of mind and intelligence, and intelligence as something outside biological organisms. The world was thus split into "thinking humans" and "vegetating other species." The relationship of domination of humans over other species and white men over other humans is based on and justified through the myth of the disembodied mind.

The Enlightenment was also a period in which human beings became seen as separate from other species. The ecological separation from the earth body went hand in hand with the epistemological separation from the human body. The human body was treated as "nature"; the disembodied mind alone was a truly human faculty. The mind–body split mirrored the culture–nature dichotomy in the Cartesian project of creating an "objective" science. As Susan Bordo has explained in "The Cartesian

Masculinization of Thought," Descartes split the world into two ontological orders based on the mutual exclusion of *res cogitans* and *res extensa*, and it made possible the conceptualization of complete intellectual transcendence of the body, which was viewed as a source of deceptive senses and distracting commotion. This also dislocated and excluded the natural world from the realm of the human. Nature for Descartes is pure *res extensa* totally devoid of mind and thought.[2]

This is in total contrast to other cultures of knowledge which do not split the mind [illegible]

[illegible]

What is there on the banks of the rivers, Doctor?
Take out your binoculars
And your spectacles
Look if you can.
Five hundred flowers
From five hundred different types of potato
Grow on the terraces
Above abysses
That your eyes don't reach
Those five hundred flowers
Are my brain
My flesh.

The Western patriarchal conceptualization of biology was based on robbing intelligence from organisms if they were female or nonhuman. Intelligence and "higher" faculties, for the production of "culture" and "science," were kept as a monopoly of men, particularly European men. By being robbed of their intelligence and minds, women, like Third World peoples, have been treated as not fully human. They have in fact been seen as closer to nature while godlike men have the exclusive capacity for creation of culture.

The treatment of other species mirrors the treatment meted out to the "others" of the human species. Furthermore, in artificially constructing "nature" out of these excluded others, the privileged knower is also artificially constructed as the creator of "culture and science," produced by a disembodied mind. Out of these multiple exclusions mutually exclusive dualities are carved:

Nature is opposed to culture
Human is opposed to nature
Human is opposed to animal
Man is opposed to woman
Mind is opposed to Body
Science is opposed to superstitions.

In most non-Western cultures, all species have been seen as part of an earth family. We have called it Vasudhaiva Kutumbkam in India. For native Americans, "kinship with all creatures of the earth, sky and water was a real and active principle."[3] As Carrie Dann stated at the Right Livelihood award ceremony, Earth has many children and humans are only one of them.[4] These non-Western perceptions have been viewed as a block in establishing "man's empire" over other species in the interactions of European men with other cultures in the process of colonization.

Robert Boyle, the famous scientist who was also governor of the New England Company, saw the rise of mechanical philosophy as an instrument of power, not just over nature but also over the original inhabitants of America. He explicitly declared his intention of ridding the New England Indians of their ridiculous notions about the workings of nature. He argued that "the veneration, wherewith men are imbued for what they call nature, has been a discouraging impediment to the empire of man over the inferior creatures of God."[5]

Modern Western science and technology have in fact been the continuation, not a break, with the Judeo-Christian myth of creation, according to which all species were made for man's use. The world view within which Western science is practiced is based on imperialism, not democracy. As Lyn White, Jr., has stated, "by gradual stages a loving and all-powerful God had created light and darkness, the heavenly bodies, the earth and all its plants, animals, birds, and fishes. Finally, God had created Adam and, as an after-thought, Eve to keep man from being lonely. Man named all the animals, thus establishing his dominance over them. God planned all of this explicitly for man's benefit and rule: no item in the physical creation had any purpose save to serve man's purposes."[6]

In Genesis, Eve (woman) created sin by forcing Adam (man) to eat the forbidden fruit. The story of "original sin" still underlies the dominant paradigm of biology. It is, for example, the metaphor in such popularizations of modern biology as Matt Ridley's *Red Queen*[7] and Richard Dawkins's *Selfish Gene*[8] and *The Blind Watchmaker*.[9]

The exclusion of all women and of men from non-Western cultures from the category "human" continues as biological determinism is articulated at newer and deeper levels. Non-Western men and all women are the "others" among the human species who have been excluded from the human family, just as the nonhuman species have been excluded from the earth family. "Western man's" relationship with nonhuman species mirrors his relationships with those who are cast as "others" of his own species.

Furthermore, the assumption of superiority of white men over other humans and other species has justified violence to and extinction of nonhuman species and non-Western cultures. Violence in human society has often been justified on the grounds that some humans are closer to "nature" and other species, and hence not fully human.

Biology and the Third World

The Western world view has sanctified European man as being made in the image and likeness of God. The Christian theology of man as the master of all species justified the domination over, and even the decimation of, all life that happened to be nonwhite and nonmale. St. Augustine said that "man but *not* woman was made in the image and likeness of God." And all non-Europeans were, of course, not in God's likeness because they were colored and in every way so different from the colonizers. Europeans had either to conceive of the naturalness of cultural diversity and invent cultural tolerance to go with it or to assume, given Christian dualism, that non-Europeans, being different, were not in God's image and therefore were "in league with Hell." Most Europeans made the latter choice. As Crosby observes, "Again and again, during the centuries of European imperialism, the Christian view that all men are brothers was to lead to persecution of non-Europeans – he who is my brother sins to the extent that he is

The decimation of original peoples everywhere was justified morally on the grounds that indigenous people were not really human. They were part of the fauna. As John Pilger has observed, the *Encyclopedia Britannica* appeared to be in no doubt about this in the context of Australia, stating that "man in Australia is an animal of prey. More ferocious than the lynx, the leopard, or the hyena, he devours his own people." In another Australian textbook, *Triumph in the Tropics*, Australian aborigines were equated with their half-wild dogs. Being animals, the original Australians and Americans, the Africans and Asians, possessed no rights as humans. They could therefore be ignored as people and exterminated. Their lands could be usurped as "Terra Nullius" – lands empty of people, "vacant," "waste," "unused."[12] European men were thus able to see their invasions as "discovery," piracy and theft as "trade," and extermination and enslavement as their "civilizing mission."

Since Columbus arrived in North America, the indigenous populations continue to be decimated, largely on the grounds of their not being treated as fully human. As Carrie Dann observes, "Since that time, the indigenous people of the Western Hemisphere have been described as savages, heathens, infidels and basically labelled as one of our relatives, the four legged, the wolf or coyote."[13]

The original inhabitants, who had populated the land for thousands of years were decimated after the arrival of Europeans in America. From a total population of seventy-two million in 1492, their population declined to about four million in a few centuries. Their land was conquered and colonized, their resources raped and destroyed. The world view of man's empire over lesser creatures rendered each act of invasion into other people's land as "discovery": in America in 1492, in Australia in 1788, in Africa and Asia through the past five hundred years of colonization.

In Australia, the aboriginal population numbered 750,000 in 1788. In the years following the European invasion, 600,000 of them had died. In Africa, an official of the Belgian Commission, reporting in 1919, reached the conclusion that the population of the Belgian Congo has been reduced by half since the beginning of the European occupation in the 1880s.

In Africa, depopulation was an obvious effect of the slave trade, which involved the deportation and death of several tens of millions of Africans over three or four centuries. The rate of mortality among slaves taken from Africa to the Americas was so high that whole "slave populations" had to be replaced every few years. The long-sustained destruction of African people is set forth in the German imperial records. "I know these African tribes," wrote Von Trotha, the general entrusted with the task of putting down the Herero and Nama in South Africa. "They are all the same. They respect nothing but force. To exercise this force with brute terror and even with ferocity was and is my policy. I wiped out rebellious tribes with streams of blood and streams of money. Only by sowing in this way can anything new be grown, anything that is stable."[14]

In 1904 it was estimated that there were 80,000 Herero and 20,000 Nama. In 1911, the estimates showed 15,130 Herero and 9,871 Nama remaining alive. Nearly 75,000 of them had paid the price for a "new" order based on the domination of the Europeans, who regarded themselves as naturally superior to the Africans and could use the most brutal forms of oppression and exploitation for their civilizing mission.

Western science continues to turn non-Western peoples into less than human objects of scientific enquiry. For example, US scientists have started a Human Genome Diversity Project to collect human DNA samples from indigenous communities around the world. The economic opportunity to collect and the push to preserve human genetic diversity has been fired by the development of new biotechnologies and the formation of the Human Genome Organization (abbreviated HUGO). Medical science has long been aware that there is not just one human genetic map. Each ethnic community may have a slightly different genetic composition. Some of the differences and mutations could someday prove to be invaluable to medicine.

Officials of the Human Genome Diversity Project estimate that an initial five-year sweep of relatively accessible populations will cost $35 million and will allow sampling from 10,000 to 15,000 human specimens. At an average total cost of $2,300 per sample, the project will spend more money gathering the blood of indigenous peoples than the per capita GNP of any of the world's poorest 110 countries.

White blood cells from each person will be preserved in vitro at the American Type Culture Collections in Rockville, Maryland. Human tissue (scraped from the cheek) and hair root sampling will be used in shorter-term studies. The project's leaders, concerned that human blood can survive only forty-eight hours outside of storage, are planning their collections carefully. "One person can bleed fifty people and get to the airport in one day," they calculate.

In the draft report of the Human Genome Diversity Project, preservation is the dominant theme, and there is an assumption that many or most of the human populations are inevitably going to disappear. The project's emphasis on preservation and its insensitivity to indigenous peoples is best exhibited by the term used to describe indigenous communities that have been targeted for human DNA sampling: "isolates of historic interest" (IHIs).

Sometimes the interest is more than historical. It is also directly economic as illustrated in the case of the patent claim WO 9208784 A1 lodged by the US secretary of commerce for the human T-lymphotropic virus type 2, drawn from the "immortalized" DNA of a twenty-six-year-old Guami Indian woman from Panama. The original blood sample is cryogenically preserved at the American Type Culture Collection in Rockville, Maryland. Under citizen pressure, the secretary of commerce was forced to withdraw the patent claim. However, no ethical or legal framework exists to prevent such patenting in the future. Meanwhile, similar patents have been claimed for indigenous communities from Papua New Guinea and the Solomon Islands.

The use of other peoples as raw material is one of the aspects of an imperialistic science of biology. Other aspects include the targeting of Third World women for population control and the treatment of Third World biodiversity and Third World biological knowledge as raw material for the economic empires of northern corporations in the age of biology. These issues, related to "intellectual property rights" and in the domain of biology, are dealt with later in further detail.

[illegible]

[illegible] room for diversity – only hierarchy. Woman, being different, is treated as unequal and inferior. Nature's diversity is not seen as intrinsically valuable in itself. It gets value only through economic exploitation for commercial gain. Within a commercial value framework, diversity thus is seen as a problem, a deficiency. Destruction of diversity and the creation of monocultures become an imperative for capitalist patriarchy.

The marginalization of women and the destruction of biodiversity go hand in hand. Diversity is the price paid in the patriarchal model of progress which pushes inexorably toward monocultures, uniformity, and homogeneity. In the perverted logic of progress, even conservation suffers. Agricultural "development" continues to work toward the erasure of diversity, while the same global interests that destroy biodiversity urge the Third World to conserve it. This separation of production and consumption, with "production" being based on uniformity and "conservation" desperately attempting to preserve diversity, guarantees that biodiversity will not be protected. It can only be protected by making diversity the basis, the foundation, the logic, of the technology and economics of production.

The logic of diversity is best derived from biodiversity and from women's links to it. It helps look at dominant structures from below, from the ground of diversity. From this ground, monocultures are not productive, they are unproductive, and the knowledge that produces monocultures is not sophisticated, it is primitive.

Diversity is, in many ways, the basis of women's politics and the politics of ecology. Gender politics is, to a large extent, a politics of difference. Ecopolitics too arises from the fact that nature is varied and different, while industrial commodities and processes are uniform and homogeneous.

The two politics of diversity converge in a significant way when women and biodiversity meet in fields and forests, in arid regions and wetlands. Diversity is the principle of women's work and knowledge. It is the reason that women's knowledge and work have been discounted in the patriarchal calculus. Yet it is also the matrix from which an alternative calculus of "productivity" and "skills" can be built, one that respects diversity instead of destroying it.

In Third World economies, many communities depend on biological resources for their sustenance and well-being. In these societies, biodiversity is simultaneously a means of production and an object of consumption. It is the survival base that has to be conserved. Sustainability of livelihoods is ultimately connected to the conservation and sustainable use of biological resources in all their diversity.

However, biodiversity-based technologies of tribal and peasant societies have been viewed as backward and primitive and have been displaced by technologies which use biological resources in such a way that they destroy diversity and people's livelihoods. There is a general misconception that diversity-based production systems are low-productivity systems. However, the high productivity of uniform and homogeneous systems is a contextual and theoretically constructed category, based on taking only one-dimensional yield and output into account. The low productivity of diverse, multiple-dimensional systems and the high productivity of uniform, one-dimensional systems of agriculture, forestry and livestock are therefore not based on a neutral, scientific measure, but are biased toward commercial interests for whom maximizing of one-dimensional output is an economic imperative.

This push toward uniformity, however, undermines the diversity of biological systems which form the production system. It also undermines the livelihoods of the people whose work is associated with diverse and multiple-use systems of forestry, agriculture, and animal husbandry.

As an example, in the state of Kerala, which derives its name from the coconut palm, coconut is cultivated in a multistoried, high-intensity cropping system along with betel and pepper vines, bananas, tapioca, drukstick, papaya, jackfruit, mango, and vegetables. Compared to an annual labor requirement of 157 person days per year in a monoculture of coconut palm, the mixed cropping system increases employment to 960 person days per year. In the dry-land farming systems of the Deccan, the shift from mixed cropping of millets with pulses and oilseeds to eucalyptus monocultures has led to a loss of employment of 250 person days per year.

When labor is scarce and costly, labor-displacing technologies are productive and efficient. When labor is abundant, labor displacement is unproductive because it leads to poverty, dispossession, and destruction of livelihoods. In Third World situations, sustainability has therefore to be achieved at two levels simultaneously – natural resources and livelihoods. Biodiversity conservation has to be linked to the conservation of livelihoods derived from biodiversity.

In India, agriculture employs 70 percent of the working population and about 84 percent of all economically active women.[15] For example, in the tribal economy of Orissa – shifting cultivation (*bogodo*) – women spend 105.4 days per year on agricultural operations compared to men's 59.1 days.[16] According to Vir Singh's assessment, in the Indian Himalaya a pair of bullocks work for l,064 hours, a man for 1,212 hours, and a woman for 3,418 hours a year on a one-hectare farm. Thus a woman works longer than men and farm animals combined![17]

K. Saradamoni's study of women agricultural laborers and cultivators in three rice growing states – Kerala, Tamilnadu, and West Bengal – shows that both groups of women make crucial contributions to production and processing.[18] Joan Mencher's studies in the Palghat region of Kerala reveal that apart from ploughing, which is exclusively men's work, women have a predominant role in all other processes. On the basis of this study, it is estimated that more than two-thirds of the labor input is female.[19] Bhati and Singh, in a study of the gender division of labor in hill agriculture in Himachal Pradesh, show that, overall, women contribute 61 percent of the total labor on farms.[20] A detailed study by Jain and Chand in three villages each in Rajasthan and West Bengal, covering 127 households over twelve months, highlights the fact that women in the age group nineteen to seventy spend longer hours than do men in a variety of activities.[21]

Women's work and livelihoods in subsistence agriculture are based on multiple use and management of biomass for fodder, fertilizer, food, and fuel. The collection of fodder from the forest is part of the process of transferring fertility for crop production and managing soil and water stability. The work of the women engaged in such activity [illegible]

economists as "work" or as "production" because it falls outside the so-called production boundary. These problems of data collection on agricultural work arise not because too few women work but because too many women have to do too much work. There is a conceptual inability of statisticians and researchers to define women's work inside and outside the house (and farming is usually part of both). This recognition of what is and is not labor is exacerbated by the great volume of work that women do. It is also related to the fact that although women work to sustain their families and communities, most of their work is not measured in wages.

Women's work is also invisible because women are concentrated outside market-related or remunerated work and are normally engaged in multiple tasks. Time allocation studies, which do not depend on an a priori definition of work, reflect more closely the multiplicity of tasks undertaken and the seasonal, even daily, movement in and out of the conventional labor force which characterizes the livelihood strategy for most rural women. Studies with a gender perspective which are now being published prove that women in India are major producers of food in terms of value, volume, and hours worked.

In the production and preparation of plant foods, women need skills and knowledge. To prepare seeds they need to know about germination requirements, seed preparation, and soil choice. Seed preparation requires visual discrimination, fine motor coordination, and sensitivity to humidity levels and weather conditions. To sow and strike seeds one needs to know about season, climate, plant requirements, weather conditions, microclimatic factors, soil enrichment; sowing seeds requires physical dexterity and strength. To care for plants properly, one needs information about the nature of plant diseases, pruning, staking, water supplies, companion planting, predators, sequences, growing seasons, and soil maintenance. Plant propagation also requires persistence and patience, physical strength, and attention to plant needs. Harvesting a crop requires judgments in relation to weather, labor, and grading and knowledge about preserving, immediate use, and propagation.

Women's knowledge has been the mainstay of the indigenous dairy industry. Dairying, as managed by women in rural India, embodies practices and logic rather different from those contained in the dairy science imparted at institutions of formal education in India, since the latter is essentially an import from Europe and North

America. Women have been experts in the breeding and feeding of farm animals, which include not just cows and buffaloes but also pigs, chickens, ducks, and goats.

In forestry too, women's knowledge is crucial to the use of biomass for feed and fertilizer. Knowledge of the feed value of different fodder species, of the value of firewood types, food products, and species, is essential to agriculture-related forestry in which women are predominantly active. In low-input agriculture, fertility is transferred from the forest and farm trees to the field by women's work, either directly or via animals.

It is in the "in between" spaces, the interstices of "sectors," the invisible biological flows between sectors, that women's work and knowledge in agriculture are uniquely found, and it is through these linkages that ecological stability and sustainability and productivity under resource-scarce conditions are maintained. The invisibility of women's work and knowledge arises from the gender bias which has a blind spot for realistic assessment of women's contributions. It is also rooted in the sectoral, fragmented, and reductionist approach to development, which treats forests, livestock, and crops as independent of each other.

The focus of the "green revolution" has been to increase grain yields of rice and wheat by techniques such as dwarfing, monocultures, and multicropping. For an Indian woman farmer, rice is not only food; it is also a source of fodder for cattle and straw for thatch. High-yield varieties (HYVs) can increase women's work. The destruction of biological diversity undermines women's diverse contributions to agriculture by eroding biological sources of food, fodder, fertilizer, fuel, and fiber. The shift from local varieties and local indigenous crop-improvement strategies can also take away women's control over seeds and genetic resources. Women have been the seed custodians since time immemorial, and it is their knowledge and skills which should be the basis of all crop-improvement strategies.

Women have been the custodians of biodiversity in most cultures. They have been selectors and preservers of seed. However, like all other aspects of women's work and knowledge, their role in development and conservation of biodiversity has been represented as nonwork and nonknowledge. Their labor and expertise have been defined into nature, even though it is based on sophisticated cultural and scientific practices. Women produce, reproduce, consume, and conserve biodiversity in agriculture. Women's role in the conservation of biodiversity, however, differs from the dominant patriarchal notions of biodiversity conservation in a number of ways.

The recent concern with biodiversity at the global level has grown as a result of the erosion of diversity due to the expansion of large-scale monoculture-based production in agriculture and the vulnerability associated with it. However, the fragmentation of farming systems which was linked to the spread of monocultures continues to be the guiding paradigm for biodiversity conservation. Each element of the farm ecosystem is viewed in isolation, and conservation of diversity is seen as an arithmetic exercise of collecting variety.

In contrast, biodiversity in the traditional Indian setting is a relational category in which each element gets its characteristics and value through its relationships with other elements. Biodiversity is ecologically and culturally embedded. Diversity is reproduced and conserved through the reproduction and conservation of culture, in festivals and rituals. Besides being a celebration of the renewal of life, these festivals are the platform for carrying out subtle tests for seed selection and propagation. These tests are not treated as scientific by the dominant world view because they are not embedded in the culture of the lab and the experimental plot; they are carried out not by men in lab coats but by village women. Yet they are reliable and systematic, and they help to preserve a rich biological diversity in agriculture.

Women have been the selectors and custodians of seed. When they conserve seed, they conserve diversity; and when they conserve diversity, they conserve a balance and harmony. *Navdanya*, or nine seeds, are the symbol of this renewal of diversity and [illegible]

worms through increasing their food supply, whether they feed directly on it or on the microorganisms it supports. Earthworms contribute to soil fertility by maintaining soil structure, aeration, and drainage and by breaking down organic matter and incorporating it into the soil. The work of earthworms in soil formation was Darwin's major concern in later years. When finishing his book on earthworms he wrote: "It may be doubted whether there are many other animals which played so important a part in the history of creatures."[24]

The little earthworm working invisibly in the soil is actually the tractor and fertilizer factory and dam combined. Worm-worked soils are more water stable than unworked soils, and worm-inhabited soils have considerably more organic carbon and nitrogen than parent soils. By their continuous movement through soils, earthworms make channels which help in soil aeration. It is estimated that they increase soil-air volume by up to 30 percent. Soils with earthworms drain four to ten times faster than soils without earthworms, and their water-holding capacity is higher by 20 percent. Earthworm casts, which can be 4.36 tons dry weight per acre per year, contain more nutritive materials containing carbon, nitrogen, calcium, magnesium, potassium, sodium, and phosphorus than the parent soil. Earthworms' work on the soil promotes microbial activity which is essential to the fertility of most soils. Yet the earthworm was never seen as a worker in "scientific" agriculture.[25] The woman peasant who works invisibly with the earthworm in building soil fertility has also not been seen as doing "productive" work or providing an "input" to the food economy. We need to look beyond the mentality that tells us that fertility is "bought" from fertilizer companies; we need to look beyond the fertilizer factory for maintaining soil fertility; and we need to recover the work of women and peasants who work with nature, not against it. In regions of India which have not yet been colonized by the green revolution, women peasants continue to work as soil builders rather than soil predators, and it is from these remaining pockets of natural farming that the ecological struggles to protect nature are emerging.

However, these sophisticated systems of agriculture which used biological diversity to provide internal inputs for pest control, fertility renewal, and soil and water conservation were displaced by the chemical-industrial model from the West, financed by aid and pushed by planning from international agencies like the World Bank under the label of the green revolution.

At the technological level, the instrumental and functionalist approach to non-human species tends to lead to the extinction of those species which capitalist patriarchy does not value. Distortion and mutilation in the name of "improvement" is likely to be the fate of those species that are found useful. In either case, entire communities of species become victims of imperialism. In this way, the so-called green revolution led to the displacement of thousands of varieties of crops and seeds. Wheat, maize, and rice were treated as the only crops of "value." To increase their commodity value, these crops were engineered to become dwarf varieties so that they could take up more chemical fertilizers. The engineered crops were vulnerable to pests and disease, so they needed more pesticides and fungicides.

The new plant biotechnologies will follow the path of the earlier HYVs of the green revolution in pushing farmers onto a technological treadmill. Biotechnology can be expected to increase the reliance of farmers on purchased inputs even as it accelerates the process of polarization. It will even increase the use of chemicals instead of decreasing it. The dominant focus of research in genetic engineering is not on fertilizer-free and pest-free crops but on pesticide- and herbicide-resistant varieties. For the seed and chemical multinational companies, this might make commercial sense, since it is cheaper to adapt the plant to the chemical than to adapt the chemical to the plant. The cost of developing a new crop variety rarely reaches $2 million, whereas the cost of a new herbicide exceeds $40 million.[26]

Like green revolution technologies, biotechnology in agriculture can become an instrument for dispossessing the farmer of seed as a means of production. The relocation of seed production from the farm to the corporate laboratory relocates power and value between the North and South and between corporations and farmers. It is estimated that the elimination of homegrown seed would dramatically increase the farmers' dependence on biotechnology industries by about $6 billion annually.[27]

It can also become an instrument of dispossession by selectively removing those plants or parts of plants that do not serve commercial interests but are essential for the survival of nature and people. "Improvement" of a selected characteristic in a plant also constitutes a selection against other characteristics which are useful to nature, or for local consumption. "Improvement" is not a class- or gender-neutral concept. Improvement of partitioning efficiency is based on the enhancement of the yield of the desired product at the expense of unwanted plant parts. The desired product is, however, not the same for rich people and poor people, or rich countries and poor countries; nor is efficiency. On the input side, richer people and richer countries are short of labor and poorer people and poorer countries are short of capital and land. Most agricultural development, however, increases capital input while displacing labor, thus destroying livelihoods. On the output side, which parts of a farming system or plant will be treated as "unwanted" depends on what class and gender one is. What is unwanted for the better off may be the wanted part for the poor. The plants or plant parts which serve the poor are usually the ones whose supply is squeezed by the normal priorities of improvement in response to commercial sources.

The destruction of people's livelihood and sustenance goes hand in hand with the erosion of biological resources and their capacity to fulfill diverse human needs while regenerating and renewing themselves. Attempts to increase commodity flows in one direction generate multiple levels of scarcities in related outputs. Increase of grain leads to decrease of fodder and fertilizer. Increase of cereals leads to decrease of pulses and oilseeds. The increase is measured. The decrease goes unnoticed, except by those who are deprived by virtue of the creation of new scarcity. Both people and nature are impoverished; their needs are no longer met by the one-dimensional production systems, which replace biologically rich and diverse ecosystems and put added burdens on remaining pockets of biodiversity that could satisfy these needs.

The extinction of people's livelihoods and sustenance is closely connected with the erosion of biodiversity. Protection of biodiversity can only be ensured by regenerating [illegible] biodiversity means to conserve the integrity of ecosystems and species, the rights to their resources and knowledge, and their production systems based on biodiversity. For commercial interests, such as pharmaceutical and agricultural biotechnology companies, biodiversity in itself has no value. It is merely "raw material" to provide "components" for the genetic engineering industry. This leads to a reductionist paradigm of biology and production based on biodiversity destruction, since local production systems based on diversity are displaced by production based on uniformity. The reductionist paradigm of biology leads to the paradigm of genetic engineering for production and reproduction. It is also closely associated with the treatment of living organisms as manufactured commodities, as "products of the mind," needing "intellectual property protection."

Intellectual property rights and intellectual imperialism

Even as feminists, environmentalists, and Third World scientists reshape our ideas of knowledge, the Cartesian and Baconian project of the disembodied mind as the model knower and control and domination as the goal of knowledge continues. Intellectual property rights (IPR) as related to biological organisms are the ultimate expressions of the Cartesian mind–body split and of knowledge as invasion to establish "man's empire over lesser creatures." In intellectual property rights, the legacies of Descartes, Locke, and Hobbes meet to create an antinature view of "creation." *Creation* here does not refer to the rich diversity of life but to the products of "godlike" acts of one group of humans. And through this distorted definition of creation, this group claims ownership of life in all its diversity.

The freedom that transnational corporations are claiming through intellectual property rights protection in the GATT agreement is the freedom that European colonizers have claimed since 1492, when Columbus set the precedent of treating the license to conquer non-European peoples as a natural right of European men. The land titles issued by the pope through European kings and queens were the first patents. Charters and patents issued to merchant adventurers were authorizations to "discover, find, search out and view such remote heathen and barbarous lands, countries and territories not actually possessed of any Christian prince or people."[28] The colonizers' freedom was built on the enslavement and subjugation of the people with original rights to the land. This violent takeover was rendered "natural" by defining the colonized people into nature, thus denying them their humanity and freedom.

Locke's treatise on property[29] effectively legitimized this same process of theft and robbery during the enclosure movement in Europe. Locke clearly articulates capitalism's freedom to build on the freedom to steal; he states that property is created by removing resources from nature through mixing them with labor. But this labor is not physical labor, but labor in its "spiritual" form as manifested in the control of capital. According to Locke, only capital can add value to appropriated nature, and hence only those who own capital have the natural right to own natural resources, a right that supersedes the common rights of others with prior claims. Capital is thus defined as a source of freedom, but this freedom is based on the denial of freedom to the land, forests, rivers, and biodiversity that capital claims as its own. Because property obtained through privatization of commons is equated with freedom, those commoners laying claim to it are perceived to be depriving the owner of the capital of freedom. Thus peasants and tribals who demand the return of their rights and access to resources are regarded as thieves.

Within the ambit of IPRs, the Lockean concept of property merges with the Cartesian concept of knowledge to give shape to a perverted world which appears "natural" in the eyes of capitalist patriarchy. During the scientific revolution, Descartes fashioned a new intellectual world order in which mind and body were deemed to be totally separate, and only the male European mind was considered capable of complete intellectual transcendence of the body. Intellectual and manual labor were thus pronounced to be "unrelated," even though all human labor, however simple, requires a degree of unity of "head and hand." But capitalist patriarchy denies the "head," the mind, to women and Third World peoples. The application of IPRs to agriculture is the ultimate denial of the intellectual creativity and contribution of Third World peasants, women and men who have saved and used seed over millennia.

The implication of a world view that assumes the possession of an intellect to be limited to only one class of human beings is that they are entitled to claim all products of intellectual labor as their private property, even when they have appropriated it from others – the Third World. Intellectual property rights and patents on life are the ultimate expression of capitalist patriarchy's impulse to control all that is living and free.

Corporations have patented naturally occurring microorganisms. Merck has a patent on soil samples from Mount Kilimanjaro in Kenya for production of an anti-hypertensive and a patent for soil from Mexico for production of testosterone. In Pimpri, India, Merck found a soil bacterium that led to patents for use in treatment of gastrointestinal and appetite disorders.[30] Corporations have patented the biopesticide and medicinal products from neem (*Azadirichta indica*), though Indian women in every village and every household have been processing and using neem products for crop and grain protection and as medicine for centuries.[31]

In cases where patent claims are not based on natural products or prior knowledge of non-Western cultures but on genetically modified organisms they are still false. In the case of plants that are not genetically engineered, patents given for medical and agricultural uses are often based on a theft of knowledge from non-Western cultures that use nonreductionist modes of knowing. Walter Bodmer, director of the Imperial

Cancer Research Fund and a major actor in the Human Genome Project, told the *Wall Street Journal* that "the issue [of ownership] is at the heart of everything we do." IPRs determine the issue of ownership.[32]

A shift to a postreductionist paradigm of biology that recognizes that biological organisms are complex and that ways of knowing their properties can be plural would undermine the epistemological basis of IPRs for life forms. In the area of IPRs and life forms, the issue is not merely *who* will own life but *whether* life can be owned. IPRs are [illegible]

organisms. This generates different ways of knowing and different claims to knowledge. Third World, feminist, and environmental approaches to science are converging in a reinvention of biology based on the recognition of creativity across cultures.

Third World, non-Western scientific traditions and feminist perspectives have sought to evolve noninvasive modes to know other organisms which are seen as live, not dead, matter. This tradition of seeing trees and plants as alive has been continued into modern times by eminent Indian scientists such as J.C. Bose, who did detailed experiments to show

> that the pretension of man and animals for undisputed superiority over their hitherto "vegetative brethren" does not bear the test of close inspection. These experiments bring the plant much nearer than we ever thought. We find that it is not a mere mass of vegetative growth, but that its every fibre is instinct with sensibility. We are able to record the throbbings of its pulsating life, and find these wax and wane according to the life conditions of the plant, and cease in the death of the organism. In these and many other ways the life reactions in plant and man are alike.[33]

Western scientific method to study biological organisms acts as if they were dead matter and confirms that assumption with its invasive and destructive methods of experimentation.

Mae Wan Ho has called this the "cataclysmic violence of homogenisation."[34] She, like Bose, is working toward a biology that allows organisms to inform. If organisms have intelligence, they can inform us: "This is the reason why sensitive, non-invasive techniques of investigation are essential for really getting to know the living system." The reinvention of biology is inspired by a convergence of non-Western scientific traditions and feminist approaches to science, exemplified so powerfully in Barbara McClintock's "feeling for the organism" and Rachel Carson's "listening to nature."[35]

The dominant paradigm of biology excludes knowledge in which organisms are treated as subjects, not mere objects of manipulation. In the genetic engineering revolution phase, species are being even further manipulated to serve the distorted and narrow ends of a small class of humans. Plants are being engineered to become poison factories, cows are being engineered to produce human protein in their milk, pigs are being engineered with human genes governing growth, carp, catfish, and trout have also been engineered with a number of genes from humans, cattle, and rats to increase their growth. Mammals are being genetically engineered to secrete valuable pharmaceuticals in their milk. As Robert Bermol of the University of Wisconsin has stated, "the mammary gland can be used as an impressive bioreactor."[36] Living organisms are being reduced to mechanical systems to be manipulated at will. A biotechnologist has said that "a cow is nothing but cells on the hoof."[37]

And while scientists play god with living organisms, they want no questions asked about the ethical and ecological implications of their "god tricks." Experts at fragmenting life take on the arrogant stance of being experts at everything. As James Watson has said, "Although some fringe groups thought this was a matter to be debated by all and sundry, it was never the intention of those who might be called the molecular biology establishment to take the issue to the general public to decide."[38] Besides excluding people from decisions of public concern, the new technologies have also worked out the exclusion of ethical concern which reinforces "man's empire over lesser creatures."

All life is precious. It is equally precious to the rich and the poor, to white and black, to men and women. Universalization of the protection of life is an ethical imperative. On the other hand, private property and private profits are culturally and socioeconomically legitimized constructs holding only for some groups. They do not hold for all societies and all cultures. Laws for the protection of private property rights, especially as related to life forms, cannot and should not be imposed globally. They need to be restrained.

Double standards also exist in the shift from private gain to social responsibility for environmental costs. When the patenting of life is at issue, arguments from "novelty" are used. Novelty requires that the subject matter of a patent be new, that it be the result of an inventive step, and not something existing in nature. On the other hand, when it comes to legislative safeguards, the argument shifts to "similarity," to establishing that biotechnology products and genetically engineered organisms differ little from parent organisms.

What counts as "nature" is constructed differently in patriarchal systems, depending on whether it is rights or responsibilities which have to be owned. When property rights to life forms are claimed, it is on the basis of them being new, novel, not occurring in nature. However, when environmentalists state that, being "not natural," genetically modified organisms will have special ecological impacts, which need to be known and assessed, and for which the "owners" need to take responsibility, the argument is that they are not new or unnatural. These organisms are "natural," and hence safe. The issue of biosafety is therefore treated as unnecessary.[39] Thus when biological organisms are to be owned, they are treated as not natural; when the responsibility for consequences of releasing genetically modified organisms is to be owned, they are treated as natural. These shifting constructions of "natural" show that the science that claims the highest levels of objectivity is actually very subjective and opportunistic in its approach to nature.

The inconsistency in the construction of the natural is well illustrated in the case of the manufacture of genetically engineered human proteins for infant formula. Gen Pharm, a biotechnology company, is the owner of the world's first transgenic dairy bull, called Herman. Herman was bioengineered by company scientists while an embryo to carry a human gene for producing milk with a human protein. This milk is now to be used for making infant formula.

The engineered gene and the organism of which it is a part are treated as nonnatural when it comes to ownership of Herman and his offspring. However, when the issue is safety of the infant formula containing this bioengineered ingredient extracted from the udders of Herman's offspring, the same company says, "We're making these proteins [illegible] lactoferrin might be of benefit to patients with cancer or AIDS. This change of direction has brought heavy criticism of both the company and the committee.[41]

However, this kind of opportunistic biology, in which species are manipulated arbitrarily for profits, is not inevitable. In its place we could have democratized biology in which diversity is recognized as the very basis of life and is treated as a reason for celebration rather than a reason for exploitation and in which ordinary citizens have a say in biotechnology policy.

Democratizing biology involves recognition of the intrinsic value of all life forms and their inherent ability and right to survival, independent of gender, race, and species differences. It also involves the recognition of the rights of all citizens in determining how we relate to diverse species. Through such democratization we could create sciences that respect all "others," and include all "others." In a democratized biology, knowledge of different cultures and groups has equal standing, and no arbitrary assumptions are made about the creative and self-organizational capacities of nonhuman species or about the expertise and ignorance of technocrats and citizens. The colonization of other species, other cultures, and all societies has threatened both biological and cultural diversity. The democratization of biology offers an opportunity to undo these colonizations and to create possibilities for the flourishing of diversity in nature and in our minds.

Notes

1 Linda Birke, *Women, Feminism and Biology* (Brighton: Wheatsheaf Books, 1986); Evelyn Fox Keller, *Reflections on Gender and Science* (New Haven, Conn.: Yale University Press, 1985); Sandra Harding and Jean F. O'Barr, *Sex and Scientific Injury* (Chicago: University of Chicago Press, 1987); Ruth Bleier, *Science and Gender* (New York: Pergamon Press, 1984); Ruth Hubbard, *The Politics of Women's Biology* (New Brunswick, NH: Rutgers University Press, 1990).

2 Susan Bordo, "The Cartesian Masculinisation of Thought," in Harding and O'Barr.

3 Chief Luther Standing Bear, quoted in *Touch the Earth* compiled by T.C. McLuhan (London: Abacus, 1982), p. 6.

4 Speech by Carrie Dann at the Right Livelihood award ceremony, Stockholm, December 9, 1993.

5 Quoted in Brian Easlea, *Science and Sexual Oppression: Patriarchy's Confrontation with Woman and Nature* (London: Weidenfeld and Nicolson, 1981), p. 64.

6 Lyn White, Jr., "The Historical Roots of Our Ecologic Crisis," in Ian Barbour, ed., *Western Man and Environmental Ethics* (Reading, Mass.: Addison Wesley, 1973), p. 25.

7 Matt Ridley, *The Red Queen* (Harmondsworth: Penguin Books, 1993).

8 Richard Dawkins, *The Selfish Gene* (Oxford: Oxford University Press, 1976).

9 Richard Dawkins, *The Blind Watchmaker* (Harmondsworth: Penguin Books, 1988).

10 Alfred Crosby, *The Columbian Exchange* (Westport, Conn.: Greenwood Press, 1972), p. 12.

11 Basil Davidson, *Africa in History* (New York: Collier Books, 1974).

12 John Pilger, *A Secret Country* (London: Vintage, 1989), p. 26.

13 Carrie Dann, acceptance speech, Right Livelihood award ceremony, Stockholm, December 9, 1993.

14 Davidson, *Africa in History*, pp. 178–179.

15 Vandana Shiva, "Most Farmers in India Are Women," FAO, Delhi, 1991, p. l.

16 Ibid., p. 2.

17 Vir Singh, "Hills of Hardship," *Hindustan Times Weekly*, Delhi, January 18, 1987.

18 K. Saradamoni, "Labour, Land and Rice Production: Women's Involvement in Three States," *Economic and Political Weekly*, vol. 22, no. 17, April 25, 1987.

19 Joan Mencher, "Women's Work and Poverty: Women's Contribution to Household Maintenance in Two Regions of South India," in *A Home Divided: Women and Income Control in the Third World*, ed. D.H. Dwyer and J. Bruce (Stanford University Press, 1987).

20 J.B. Bhati and D.V. Singh, "Women's Contribution to Agricultural Economy in Hill Regions of North West India," *Economic and Political Weekly*, vol. 22, no. 17, 1987.

21 Devaki Jain and Malini Chand Seth, "Domestic Work: Its Implications for Enumeration of Workers," in K. Saradamoni (ed.), *Women's Work and Society, Indian Statistical Institute*, Delhi, 1985.

22 Vandana Shiva, *Staying Alive: Women, Ecology and Development* (London: Zed Books, 1988).

23 Vandana Shiva, "Women's Knowledge and Work in Mountain Agriculture," paper presented at Conference on Women in Mountain Development, ICIMOD, Kathmandu, 1988.

24 Charles Darwin, *The Formation of Vegetable Mould through the Action of Worms with Observation on Their Habits* (London: Faber and Faber, 1927).

25 E. Satchel, *Earthworm Ecology* (London: Chapman and Hall, 1983).

26 C.E. Fowler *et al.*, "The Laws of Life," *Development Dialogue*, nos. 1–2 (1988) 1–350.

27 J. Kloppenburg, *First the Seed* (Cambridge: Cambridge University Press, 1988).

28 Djelal Kadir, *Columbus and the Ends of the Earth* (Berkeley: University of California Press, 1993), p. 90.

29 John Locke, *Two Treatises of Government*, Peter Caslett (ed.) (Cambridge: Cambridge University Press, 1967).

30 RAFI, "Conserving Indigenous Knowledge," UNDP, New York, 1994.

31 Vandana Shiva and Radha Holla Bhar, "Intellectual Piracy and the Neem Patents," Research Foundation for Science, Technology and Natural Resource Policy, Dehra Dun, 1993.

32 See R.C. Lewontin, *The Doctrine of DNA: Biology and Ideology* (London: Penguin, 1991), p. 75.

33 J.C. Bose, quoted in M.S. Randhawa, *A History of Agriculture in India* (New Delhi: Indian Council for Agricultural Research, 1980), p. 97.

34 Mae Wan Ho, "*The Physics of Biology*," manuscript, 1992.

35 See Evelyn Fox Keller, *A Feeling for the Organism: The Life and Work of Barbara McClintock* (New York: Freeman, 1983).

36 Quoted in Andrew Kimbrell,

Chapter 34

Londa Schiebinger

CREATING SUSTAINABLE SCIENCE

If we can identify the role of human agency in the making of knowledge, we – as women and as scientists – could know other things in new ways.

Joan Gero (1993)

My problematic is somewhat different from that set by the editors of this volume. My interest lies in the relationship between gender studies of science and scientists, centering on the following questions: What impact has gender studies of science had on the methods and practice of science? What kind of working relationships have been established between science studies scholars and scientists, and what fruitful relationships might be institutionalized? I take issue with Bruno Latour's suggestion that the purpose of science studies is to cultivate an appreciation of science, leaving undisturbed the object of study. Feminist science scholars not only study the "beauty of facts and discipline in science" but often seek to change them.[1]

The question is, how can this be done? The history and philosophy of science have themselves become exacting disciplines. We hold cozy conferences and put finishing touches on nuanced and complex theories. For the most part, however, our work does not reach the intended audiences in the sciences. The question of creating a vital working relationship between historians and philosophers of science and scientists is, for me, tied to the problem of increasing the numbers of women in science. I see the former as a necessary condition of the latter.

We have embarked on a new era in regard to the question of women in science. For the first time in history, institutions that for centuries have held women and minorities at arm's length are now courting them. There is genuine enthusiasm in this regard. As the former editor of *Science* put it, "It may cost some money, some effort, and some understanding, but the voyage to full equality can be even more exciting and worthwhile than the voyage into space."[2] And women have made unprecedented gains. Who, just five years ago, could have predicted that the chief scientist at the National

Aeronautics and Space Administration would be a woman (from 1994 to 1996 this post was held by the astrophysicist France Cordova)? Who would have expected that the Surgeon General of the United States would be a feisty woman (though only briefly), that the agency responsible for building US military weapons would be headed by an African-American woman, and that the Secretary of the Air Force would be a female professor of engineering from MIT? More dramatically, who would have predicted that the National Institutes of Health would devote nearly three-

[illegible]

the number of women in science, historians and philosophers of women and gender in science, and scientists. Because of the enormity of the task, those who design programs rarely discuss the restructuring of knowledge and institutions required to make them work. The National Research Council's Committee on Women in Science and Engineering, formed in 1990, for instance, narrowly limited itself to questions of education, recruitment, and advancement – that is, questions of how to make women more competitive as scientists. Missing from its bibliographies are the gender critiques of science offered by Sandra Harding, Evelyn Fox Keller, Sharon Traweek, and many others.[3] At the same time, feminist theorists and epistemologists rarely suggest concrete solutions or programs designed to overcome the problems they so ably uncover. Feminist science theorists often display the disdain for applied science characteristic of mainstream science theorists. Even more tragic is that scientists are by and large unfamiliar with the literature on gender in science.

These divides are reproduced in scholarship on women and gender in science, which includes diverse scholarly approaches that are often pursued in isolation from each other. First is the massive statistical literature, whose purpose is to demonstrate that women are underrepresented in science and to chart increases or decreases in their status. Second is the historical and sociological study of women in science, much of which reveals a clash of cultures between women and European and North American science. In 1959, C.P. Snow identified two cultures, scientific and literary, between which loomed a gulf of "mutual incomprehension . . . hostility and dislike, and most of all lack of understanding." Similarly, there exists a gulf between the cultures of science as we know them and women of diverse backgrounds, ethnic and national groups. The history and sociology of women in science have generally emphasized the consequences of the resulting conflicts for women: women have been banned from rarefied intellectual pursuits, their interests and concerns marginalized.[4] We have seen some institutional initiatives to solve some of these problems: spousal hiring programs, parental leave policies, policies for stopping the tenure clock – all of which leave basic academic structures in place.

What I want to focus on here is a third body of literature that analyzes the structure of knowledge crafted within institutions that have historically excluded women. The success of feminist critiques of science in the last ten years has been to reveal concrete examples of the gendering of science. But feminism is ultimately reactionary in the sense that it responds to and is structured by sexism. The critical task now is to turn critique into a resource for generating knowledge. It is not enough to understand how science has been made; we need to develop more practical, constructive ways to employ tools of gender analysis in creating what I will call "sustainable science." Only when gender analysis becomes an integral part of science research programs will the problem of women in science be solved.

Gendered science

Leaving aside for the moment the work of Christine de Pizan, Franqois Poullain de la Barre, Anna van Schurman, Dorothea Leporinin Erxleben, Antoinette Blackwell, Charlotte Perkins Gilman, Hedwig Dohm, and numerous other early critics of science, the modern feminist critique emerged in the 1970s. Much of this early critique sought to identify the distinctive masculine character of Western science. Objectivity and reason were identified not as neutral values but as notions intimately associated with Western masculinity and the public sphere.[5] Overarching critique provided the impetus and context for the fine-grained analyses of gender dynamics in particular scientific discoveries, theories, nomenclatures, instruments, techniques, and objects that began to emerge in the late 1980s and 1990s.

Feminists have enjoyed great success in revealing gender inequalities in the humanities, social sciences, and life sciences, where subject matters are sexed or easily imagined to have sex and gender. We can chant a litany of well-established examples of how the life sciences are gendered. We know, for example, how women's bodies have been read and misread by the medical sciences. We have seen how the long arm of gender has superimposed stereotypical attributes onto apes, plants' pistils and pollen, and cells and cell parts that do not necessarily have sex, let alone gender.[6]

A simple example of how gendered stereotypes have been written into cell biology can be found in textbook accounts of conception, where the active sperm and the passive egg long remained stock characters. After the mid 1980s, biologists no longer characterized the classical "passive" egg as drifting aimlessly along the fallopian tube until captured by the heroic, active sperm. Textbooks now more often portray the egg as an active agent, directing the growth of microvilli (small fingerlike projections on its surface) that tether the sperm and releasing digestive enzymes that allow a sperm to enter it. Critics have warned of problems ensuing from the regendered egg and sperm, which, in tune with more current gender stereotypes, are now often portrayed as "partners" – much like a dual-career couple – working together toward successful fertilization.[7]

The "exact" sciences, however, often claim for themselves a special epistemological status: freedom from social imprint. Confidence in this matter is so firm that critics of feminism often play "stump the speaker." The challenge goes something like this: Is there a concrete example of gender in the substance of physics or math? Can you point to gender distortion in Newton's laws or Einstein's theory of relativity? If not, then mathematics and the physical sciences are objective and value free, as we have claimed all along. This challenge is problematic, as Sandra Harding has pointed out and as I will discuss in what follows.[8] Considering it for a moment, however, as posed, can we identify gender in math and physics, whose subject matters have no recognizable sex, in the same way that we have done in the life sciences?

Take, first, mathematics, the "critical filter" for careers in science and engineering. Feminists have decoded sexism in student problem sets. Phyllis Rosser's extensive study of the mathematics portion of the Scholastic Aptitude Test (SAT) shows that the fifty-point spread between women's and men's scores results to a great extent from aspects of the test's format that work against women. Problems often exclude women actors [illegible]

first made this problem seem difficult and speculate that, had it not been for this tradition, the problem would have been solved fifty years earlier. The easiest solution requires that both be seated at once, giving preference to neither the women nor the men.[10] Bogart and Doyle do not comment on the rigidly Victorian character of the problem itself.

Other feminist critiques of mathematics have centered on its overwrought abstractness. There is in these critiques nothing peculiar to women or gender. Feminists join others who argue that a sense of certainty in mathematics has sometimes been bought at the price of oversimplification. N. Katherine Hayles has discussed, for example, how differential and integral calculus have difficulty modeling a world in motion and the problems this limitation raised for the development of fluid mechanics. According to Hayles, eighteenth-century calculus could see complex flow only as haphazard movement, as a deviation from its basic models rather than as a dynamic part of the environment. As in any tradition, what can be modeled is taken as the norm; what cannot becomes an aberration. Leonhard Euler's notion of a "fluid particle" (a body treated mathematically as a point having volume, mass, and density) was crucial to understanding hydraulics, since fluids conceived as points could never flow. As Hayles has pointed out, complex flow created difficulties for an analytic tradition that privileged constancy over change and discrete factors over dynamic interaction.[11]

The ultimate challenge to feminist science studies, however, is said to be physics. What is it about physics that so vehemently excludes women? It seems odd that in the biological sciences, where multiple negative images of females have been embroidered into foundational concepts and theories, 38 percent of the Ph.D.s are now awarded to women, while in physics, where far fewer examples of overt gendering have been brought forward, only about 11 percent of new Ph.D.s are women.[12] The low number of women in physics has no doubt helped to insulate it from gender analysis.

Another common explanation for the low numbers of women in the physical sciences is that those sciences are "hard." We are told repeatedly that the physical sciences are "hard" and that the life sciences, like the humanities and social sciences, are "soft." It is possible to distinguish at least four meanings of the supposed hardness of physics. First and foremost, the physical sciences are considered *epistemologically* hard. As disciplines, the physical sciences are held to be tough and analytical, yielding demonstrable answers grounded in fact, while the soft sciences and the humanities are characterized as having considerable breadth, permeable boundaries, and open-ended epistemological structure. Second, physics and the physical sciences are said to be *ontologically* hard. They study "hard," inanimate things – matter in motion – while the life sciences and humanities study "soft" animate organisms – plants, animals, humans, and their behaviors. Third, physics, chemistry, and the other physical sciences are thought to be *methodologically* "hard" because they are difficult, requiring a high degree of abstract thinking, strong analytical skills, hard work, and long hours. Finally, the physical sciences are said to be *emotionally* tough. In their ethos and telos, they are thought to be "dispassionate," distant, abstract, and quantitative, while the soft sciences are considered "compassionate" and qualitative, perhaps introspective, and closer to everyday concerns. The elaborate gendering of disciplines has led Robert Westman to suggest (presumably in all seriousness) that the history of science is "androgynous," combining, as it does, the "hardness" of science with the "softness" of history.[13]

The hardness of the science – in what it studies, how it studies it, the degree of difficulty attributed to it, and the emotional detachment involved – is also inversely proportional to the number of women in the field.

As with mathematics the epistemological hardness of physics may be illusionary – the result of carving out a narrow project. The cosmologist Martin Rees has suggested that the Big Bang is "a grand problem but perhaps a more straightforward problem . . . and far easier than anything in the biological world." While evolutionary geneticists are prone to suffer from "physics envy" (the desire to unveil incontrovertible laws governing the evolution of organisms with the same epistemic cash value as the laws of physics), it may turn out that biology is ultimately "harder" in the sense that the problems it undertakes encompass complexity not amenable to reduction to a few simple laws. The physicist Karen Barad has pointed out, further, that only Newtonian physics might be considered epistemologically "hard" in a strictly positivist sense. She argues that quantum physics, like history or literary criticism, depends on extensive theoretical and instrumental interpretation in identifying phenomena labeled "elementary particles."[14]

The epistemological "hardness" of the physical sciences has also been secured by the disciplinary separation of the practice of science from the critical examination of science. Questions of meaning, consequences, or social responsibility are rarely considered part of physics proper but to belong to other realms, such as philosophy, ethics, or sociology. This may help to explain the curious state of modern physics, which, at the highest theoretical end, couples unreflective materialism to highflying metaphysics. There are physicists who see "the face of God" (George Smoot), seek "the God particle" (Leon Lederman), and strive "to understand the mind of God" (Stephen Hawking), thus endowing their quest with religious verve. As Robert Wilson has remarked, "both cathedrals and accelerators are build at great expense as a matter of faith."[15] Yet the physicists' god is envisioned to be as apolitical as their science. Consequently, physicists can ascribe a higher meaning to their quest while ignoring the social realities of their undertaking,

Asking why there are fewer women in physics than in other fields of science may, however, emphasize the wrong axis of comparison. It might be more appropriate to realign physics with the military, for there are proportionally no more or fewer women in physics than there are in the United States Armed Forces. I do not mean to suggest that women are by nature peace loving, antimilitary, or antinuclear: Lise Meitner was

– fairly or unfairly – called "the mother of the bomb," some eighty women participated in the Manhattan Project, and women continue to number among weapons designers. My argument is that cultural conventions have long prohibited women from joining defense activities and that these attitudes may well spill over into some areas of physics, which since World War II has made strong contributions to national defense.[16]

Few women become physicists, then, for a number of reasons: its cultural image as a "hard" science, its overtly aggressive culture, its historic ties to the military, its [illegible] a more positive program. What is new and unprecedented is the growing agitation for change among scientists, especially women. The feminist ferment of the past decade has in many instances reshaped what is known and knowable: the simple process of taking feminists (men and women) seriously as makers of knowledge and a more respectful manner of including females as subjects of research have had a tremendous impact on methods, manners, and priorities in many of the sciences.[18]

The historical process by which gender analysis has come to influence aspects of science theory and practice has yet to be studied. In the absence of such research, it is astonishing how mainstream has become the idea that women (females of the human species) are changing science. While this view perhaps represents an improvement over the decades of assimilation fostered by liberal feminism, the brand of difference feminism (and its variant, standpoint theory) it embodies has begat its own distinctive set of problems.

In spring 1993 *Science* magazine jumped onto the difference feminist bandwagon (probably without realizing it) with its question: Is there a "female style" in science? Apparently not wanting to use the term *feminist*, the editors chose instead to focus on "female style"; unfortunately, in so doing they grounded gender in biology and placed the discussion in the essentialist camp. Nonetheless, the query was similar to that regarding feminist science posed in the late 1970s and early 1980s: When women enter science, do they bring with them different values and priorities? And *Science* encountered problems similar to those faced by many feminists – an all too-simple notion of a feminist or, in this instance, female science. From the articles in *Science* one can extrapolate the content of this prospective female style. It is warm; it is above all fuzzy. It is caring, relational, at times holistic and nurturing. Surprisingly, of the two hundred women and thirty men who responded to the magazine's follow-up survey, more than half said they believe that there is a female style in science, while only a quarter said that there is not. The respondents were, of course, highly self-selecting.[19]

This same issue of *Science* highlighted primatology as the prime example of a science remade by the influx of women, and in so doing it reinforced the myth that women *qua* women are the leavening agent producing change in the institutions and results of science (it is also significant that this article did not mention Donna Haraway's work).[20]

Is it women or feminists that have brought change to the sciences? It is true that gender ideology has been used historically to lock women (as a class of humans) out of the sciences, but this does not mean that bringing women into science automatically corrects gender biases. Having a significant number of women in a particular field, as Mildred Dresselhaus's theory of "critical mass" suggests, does seem a necessary condition for probing new research paradigms related to gender. (It would be highly paradoxical, if not impossible, to have a feminist science dominated by men.) But to say that women have changed science is overly simple. Many women primatologists, for example, have produced male-dominance theories indistinguishable from those of their male colleagues; by the same token, many men have been instrumental in opening new lines of feminist investigation.[21]

Increasing the numbers of women without increasing an awareness of gender issues will have little impact on science or its institutions. It is rarely mentioned that affirmative action can be abused by the political right. Women who consider themselves "old boys" become the darlings of conservatives; institutions gain respectability by showcasing a few high-profile women, but the fundamentals do not change. To make women the agents of change essentializes gender differences (even when those differences are said to be culturally produced) and unnecessarily excludes men as potential allies. It is not women per se, but women and men who have cultivated a critical awareness of gender, who are making a difference. More important, making women the agents of change depoliticizes the process, reducing to one dimension the multifactorial complex of economic, social, and attitudinal changes required to get women into science in the first place.

Take the example of the biomedical sciences, where the 1990 founding of the National Institutes of Health (NIH) Office of Research on Women's Health and the 1991 Women's Health Initiative represent at least a limited triumph for feminism. Taking women's health seriously did not require new technical breakthroughs or simply more women doctors (though that helped): it required new judgments about social worth and a new political will.

These new attitudes formed in the crucible of an active women's health movement. Since the 1960s and 1970s groups – including the Boston Women's Health Collective, the National Women's Health Network, the Black Women's Health Movement, and consumer lobbies for treatment and prevention of breast cancer – have drawn attention to how the US health care system has failed women. Women's health reform built on the work of women's movements that challenged fundamental assumptions about women's place in the professions and society more generally. These challenges required a host of legislative supports, such as the Civil Rights Act of 1964, the Equal Employment Opportunity Act of 1972, and the Equal Opportunity in Science and Engineering Act of 1980 (Title 42 of U.S. Code, sect. 1885–1885d), that specifically directed NIH and NSF to undertake programs to increase the participation of underrepresented groups in medicine, science, and engineering. The whole was shored up by affirmative action policies that insisted on equal opportunity for women and minorities within governmental agencies, universities, and industries doing business with the federal government.[22]

More specifically, national interest in women's health care required that there be a significant number of people dedicated to women's issues well placed within the medical profession. Florence Haseltine (director of the NIH Center for Population

Research), for example, founded the Society for the Advancement of Women's Health Research in 1990; William Harlan, then director of epidemiology and clinical applications at NIH, supported and coined the name for the Women's Health Initiative. Women's health reform also benefitted from the emergence of powerful people interested in gender issues, many of them women, in the Congress: in June 1990 the bipartisan Congressional Caucus on Women's Issues – including Democrats Patricia Schroeder and Barbara Mikulski and Republicans Constance Morella and Olympia [illegible] for women or are unique to women. The Women's Health Initiative, a fourteen-year, $625 million study (the largest ever undertaken by NIH), congealed in 1991 when Bernadine Healy, a Bush appointee, became NIH's first woman director. The initiative funds research into diseases that are more common or found only in women, such as osteoporosis, breast cancer, and cardiovascular disease – the leading causes of death and disability in older women.

The success of the women's health movement also required the opening of the academy to women and their concerns. It relied on gender analyses developed within women's studies and the history and philosophy of science and medicine. Finally, it benefitted from the emergence of a new class of professional women, ready to talk openly about and demand care for disorders long hidden behind the cloak of female modesty.

Change for women within the sciences, then, is a complex and broadly social process. It is not uniquely women, but women *and* men with a critical awareness of gender, who are the agents of that change. How this happens in concrete instances requires more study.

Sustainable science

I am suggesting that we move beyond the problems endemic to difference feminism and attempts to create a feminist science to something I call sustainable science. In a sense, a new label is not needed or perhaps even desirable; however, I offer the notion of sustainability as a useful heuristic. My notion of sustainable science resembles other new directions in feminist science theory, such as Donna Haraway's "situated knowledge," Sandra Harding's "strong objectivity," and Carolyn Merchant's "partnership ethic."[24] One element common to these various initiatives is emphasizing gender as one analytic among many required for creating socially and environmentally responsible science.

Much of what I mean by sustainable science is captured in the older notion of "socially responsible science." The movement for social responsibility in science arose after World War II, especially among physicists worried about the compromising of science goals by the militarization of science but also among physicians worried about the health effects of nuclear war and nuclear power. I am interested in broadening the notion to include responsibility toward nature as well as culture. The concept of sustainability comes from sustainable agriculture, which emerged in the 1970s as a challenge to conventional industrial agriculture with its emphasis on chemical fertilizers, monoagriculture, and hybrid seed. To my knowledge, the term *sustainable science* was first used by Helmut Hirsch and Helen Ghiradella in a Native American science journal; it incorporates the Native American notion of undertaking actions to meet the needs of the present in a way that can be sustained for many generations.[25]

What, then, is feminist about sustainable science? One might argue that feminism has to do only with women's equality and that once that is achieved the problem is solved. Most feminists, however, would disagree. Feminists are rarely advocates solely for women. What in the past has been advanced as "feminist science" offers strong elements of environmentalism and humanitarianism that have little to do with women's equality per se. Difference feminism ran amok in attempting to encompass a range of diverse political views – environmentalism, humanism, and pacifism – within feminism. In attempting to join feminism with environmentalism, for example, difference feminism (and much of ecofeminism) faltered on the shoals of essentialism by arguing that women have a special relationship with nature or that the oppression of women is connected with the domination of nature. Instead of being seen as characteristics attached culturally to women, feminist concerns for the environment might be seen as political goals held in common with a number of people whose first allegiance may or may not be to feminism.

Sustainable science shifts attention away from classical epistemology (how we know), which has exercised science and science theory since the seventeenth century, to focus on the goals and outcomes of science (what we know and don't know, and why). Key questions include: Science for whom? How is our knowledge influenced by who is included in science and who is excluded, which projects are pursued and which ignored, whose experiences are validated and whose are not, and who stands to gain in terms of wealth or well-being and who does not? And for how long? It is precisely in the choice of questions, in the priorities set for science, that much is determined. The questions we pose often determine the kinds of solutions we consider. Once a problem is set, there may be one best answer. When, for instance, the question of sexual equality is set into the realm of biological investigation, a particular set of debates and lines of investigation are opened and others closed off.

Donna Haraway's notion of situated knowledge (as a form of critique) is useful in this context. As postmodernists of various stripes have pointed out, feminists cannot, any more than anyone else, produce universal theories of science. In the early 1980s, when the notion of a feminist science arose, feminists were challenged to state precisely what it is or might become. This cannot be done in an abstract way; problems begin to arise when solutions are grounded in identity politics (the tendency to attach particular qualities to socially defined groups). While cultivating a cross-cultural understanding of the problem of gender in science, situated feminism calls for analyzing gender difference as one among many variables of power within concrete contexts.[26]

Sandra Harding's notion of strong objectivity is also useful in moving the focus from *how* we know to *what* we know and why we know it. Harding's notion of strong objectivity strengthens current notions of objectivity (which she calls "weak objectivity") by extending the concept to include the critical examination of all beliefs and interests forming a scientific project. Weak objectivity, she argues, prematurely cuts off the consideration of values, economics, and politics in the design of research projects. It is not enough to work on a piece of the puzzle; scientists (and other scholars) must also analyze the origins and long-term consequences of their work. Strong objectivity requires that the critique of science be joined to the generation of knowledge and not operate as jeremiad after the fact.[27]

Sustainable science requires tools for gender analysis. Tools for gender analysis are [illegible] the women's health research discussed earlier. Improving women's health care has not required new technical breakthroughs: it required new judgments about women's social worth and willingness to invest in women's health and well-being.

2. Gender analyses of populations chosen for study. The primatologist Linda Fedigan has discussed the 1950s "baboonization" of primatology, where savannah baboons, one of the most aggressive and male dominated of all primates, became the preferred model for ancestral human populations despite primatologists' knowledge of other, less aggressive primate populations.[28] In this instance, the choice of subject matter interjected a potent antifeminist element into understandings of human origins.

One of the basic tools of gender studies is, of course, the analysis of appropriate inclusion of females as subjects and objects of research. Since the 1980s, additional tools have been forged in this area to refine the analysis of gender in relation to class, race, ethnicity, and sexual preference. These tools have helped researchers become aware of the differences in disease among women and adjust resource allocation and treatments appropriately. Returning to the biomedical sciences, it has been learned that African-American women suffer fewer heart attacks than white women but more often die from them. Osteoporosis, one of the targets of the Women's Health Initiative, occurs most often in white women of non-Hispanic origin; this may mean that the initiative is not responding directly to the needs of minority women and that African-American and Hispanic women may not be screened and educated aggressively about the disease and consequently may be at risk.[29]

Yet other tools of analysis are used to encourage a global perspective when adjusting science and science policy to specific populations. Critics of US women's health reform, for example, point out that fine-grained inequalities in health research are not what haunts the majority of the world's population. Many women around the world suffer and die from diseases induced by poverty, malnutrition, and childbirth.

3. Analyses of how gender structures scientific institutions and the relationship between disciplines. Many modern disciplines have their origins in the German university system, from which women and their concerns were stringently excluded. The hierarchy of disciplines in US universities further correlates with the number of women, inequalities in intellectual authority, and often funding levels (as noted earlier). The archaeologist Joan Gero has shown, for instance, how disciplinary and subdisciplinary status hierarchies have placed women in both the discipline of archaeology and the study of prehistory.[30]

Disciplinary divisions have isolated gender studies of science from science studies (and vice versa) and the history and philosophy of science from science research and education (and vice versa). Solving the problem of women and gender in science will require not only reform of disciplines but deep and sweeping reform of disciplinary divisions.

4. Gender analyses of scientific language. Gender stereotypes are not innocent literary devices used to spice up texts and abbreviate thought. Analogies and metaphors, the theorist Susan Squier writes, function to construct as well as describe – they have both a hypothesis-creating and proof-making function in science. They can determine the direction of scientific practice, the questions asked, the results obtained, and the interpretations deduced.[31] We have already noted that gendering the egg as passive and the sperm as active places them within a predetermined and complex matrix of cultural meanings.

5. Gender analyses of criteria used in both determining what needs explanation and what counts as evidence. The archaeologists Margaret Conkey and Joan Gero discuss how male-identified stone tools figure among highly prized data for tracing the "progress of humankind." These potent symbols of "Early Man" obscure other important aspects of prehistoric life, such as nutting, leather working, grain harvesting, and woodworking – all of which were done with nonstandardized stone tools.[32] Gero argues that adopting a broader definition of tools will prove fundamental to a more comprehensive understanding of gender and tool use in prehistory.

6. Analyses of gender differentials in outcomes for the environment. Vandana Shiva has offered the example of forest management in India, where women developed a technique called lopping. Lopping, the selective thinning of trees, simultaneously provides feed for livestock and increases forest density and productivity. Shiva has suggested that "scientific forestry," with its emphasis on cash crops, has disproportionately displaced women (since traditional divisions in labor assigned this work to them) and undermined sustainable uses of the forest.[33]

7. Gender analyses of professions. What is the image of a successful professional in a particular field? Who is recruited? Who is rewarded – and for what reasons? Helen Longino has discussed how communities of researchers form "background assumptions" – the unquestioned givens that serve as the bases for mutual understanding and effective research. She also discusses how including representatives of alternative points of view in such communities can uncover social values and interests that become enshrined in research programs and unconsciously shape observation or reasoning.[34]

8. Analyses of gender dynamics in what is considered "science." Voltaire's 1764 proclamation that "all the arts have been invented by man, not by woman" was echoed recently in the assertion by two prominent sociologists of science that women have achieved less than men in science no matter how achievement is measured.[35] Women have generally been considered recipients, not generators, of knowledge. Exploring what is considered "science" – using ethnographic tools – can influence how women's contributions are evaluated.

Thus far I have offered examples primarily from Western-style science. Looking at alternative knowledge traditions may further expand Western definitions and practices of science. Within Western culture, as elsewhere, midwifery offers a key example of women's knowledge traditionally devalued by high science. This devaluing may have resulted more from the fact that midwifery has been practiced by women (not always of the highest classes) than from an evaluation of the knowledge involved or the value of the services.[36] Other practices explored to date have clustered around agriculture and forest management because women have traditionally been in charge of food and food preparation. A prime example is Andean potato breeding; for centuries Quechua women have bred and preserved potato seeds. (One might reflect on the [illegible] perishability, and the like. A single woman might manage up to fifty-six varieties of potatoes.

There is nothing sacred or mystical about the fact that particular knowledges have been developed by women. Women's work in birthing or seed preservation responds to sexual divisions of labor in particular cultures. The same kinds of knowledge could have been developed by men under different conditions – and may in that instance have been considered "science."

These tools of gender analysis, along with many others, aid in crafting sustainable sciences, sciences that have built into their research designs analyses of their long- and short-term effects and a consideration of their historical position within particular cultures and value systems. Sustainable science is the best way to realize the feminist goals of achieving equality for women in the sciences and creating sciences that address the concerns and needs of women around the world.

For some years now difference feminism has prescribed a quick and easy recipe for changing science and has in the process neglected the deep historical and philosophical analysis required to understand how science, culture, history, and environment shape one another. Much feminism has focused too narrowly (and reductionistically) on one variable – women – often leaving aside the complexities of the processes by which science is made. Neither changing women to fit science nor changing science to incorporate conventional feminine ideals will be sufficient: feminist goals based on either traditional divisions of labor or conventional gender representations are set in shifting sand. What is needed are collaborations between scientists, historians, and philosophers that will foster not only a diverse community of scholars but scientists critically attuned to their place in nature.

Notes

1 Bruno Latour, "Letter to the Editor," *The Sciences*, Mar./Apr. 1995, pp. 6–7.

2 Daniel Koshland, Jr., in *Science*, 25 Mar. 1988, 238: 1473. For bibliography on women in science, technology, and medicine see Alison Wylie, Kathleen Okruhlik, Sandra Morton, and Leslie Thielen-Wilson, "Philosophical Feminism: A Bibliographic Guide

to Critiques of Science," *Resources for Feminist Research / Documentation sur la Recherche Feministe*, 1990, 19(2): 2–36; Margarete Maurer, *Frauenforschung in Naturwissenschaften, Technik und Medizin* (Vienna: Wiener Frauenvertag, 1993); Elisabeth A. Bacus *et al.*, eds., *A Gendered Past: A Critical Bibliography of Gender in Archaeology* (Technical Reports, 25) (Ann Arbor: Univ. Michigan Museum of Anthropology, 1993); and Phyllis Holman Weisbard and Rima D. Apple, eds., *The History of Women and Science, Health, and Technology: A Bibliographic Guide to the Professions and the Disciplines*, 2nd ed. (Madison: Univ. Wisconsin System, Women's Studies Librarian, 1993).

3 National Research Council, Committee on Women in Science and Engineering, *Women in Science and Engineering: Increasing Their Numbers in the 1990s* (Washington, DC: National Academy Press, 1991); and National Research Council, Committee on Women in Science and Engineering, *Women Scientists and Engineers Employed in Industry: Why So Few?* (Washington, DC: National Academy Press, 1994). On the inequalities faced by women in science and engineering see National Science Foundation, *Women, Minorities, and Persons with Disabilities in Science and Engineering: 1994* (NSF94–333) (Arlington, Va.. 1994), p. xxxiii.

4 C.P. Snow, *The Two Cultures and the Scientific Revolution* (New York: Cambridge Univ. Press, 1962), p. 4. For the statistical literature, in addition to the National Science Foundation report on the status of women and minorities in science cited in note 3, above, see Betty Vetter, *Professional Women and Minorities* (Washington, DC: Commission on Professionals in Science and Technology, Jan. 1994). The literature on the history and sociology of women in science is voluminous. See, e.g., Margaret Rossiter, *Women Scientists in America: Struggles and Strategies to 1940* (Baltimore: Johns Hopkins Univ. Press, 1982); Rossiter, *Women Scientists in America: Before Affirmative Action, 1940–1972* (Baltimore: Johns Hopkins Univ. Press, 1995); Evelyn Fox Keller, *A Feeling for the Organism: The Life and Work of Barbara McClintock* (New York: Freeman, 1983); Margaret Alic, *Hypatia's Heritage* (London: Women's Press, 1986); Pnina G. Abir-Am and Dorinda Outram, eds., *Uneasy Careers and Intimate Lives: Women in Science, 1789–1979* (New Brunswick, NJ: Rutgers Univ. Press, 1987); Londa Schiebinger, *The Mind Has No Sex? Women in the Origins of Modern Science* (Cambridge, Mass.: Harvard Univ. Press, 1989); Harriet Zuckerman, Jonathan Cole, and John Bruer, eds., *The Outer Circle: Women in the Scientific Community* (New York: Norton, 1991); Evelynn Hammonds. "Science," in *Black Women in America: An Historical Encyclopedia*, ed. Darlene Hine (New York: Carlson, 1992), pp. 1015–1016; and Helena M. Pycior, Nancy G. Slack, and Pnina G. Abir-Am, eds., Creative Couples in the Sciences (New Brunswick, NJ: Rutgers Univ. Press, 1996).

5 Carolyn Merchant, *The Death of Nature: Women, Ecology, and the Scientific Revolution* (San Francisco: Harper & Row, 1980); Evelyn Fox Keller, *Reflections on Gender and Science* (New Haven, Conn.: Yale Univ. Press, 1985); and Sandra Harding, *The Science Question in Feminism* (Ithaca, NY: Cornell Univ. Press, 1986). For a history of pre-twentieth-century critique see Schiebinger, *Mind Has No Sex?* pp. 1–9, 160–188.

6 On the reading of women's bodies by the medical sciences see, e.g., Ruth Bleier, *Science and Gender: A Critique of Biology and Its Theories on Women* (New York: Pergamon, 1984); Anne Fausto-Sterling, *Myths of Gender: Biological Theories about Women and Men* (New York: Basic, 1985); Ludmilla Jordanova, *Sexual Visions: Images of Gender in Science and Medicine between the Eighteenth and Twentieth Centuries* (Madison: Univ. Wisconsin Press, 1989); Thomas Laqueur, *Making Sex: Body and Gender from the Greeks to Freud* (Cambridge, Mass.: Harvard Univ. Press, 1990); Cynthia Eagle Russett, *Sexual Science: The Victorian Construction of Womanhood* (Cambridge, Mass.: Harvard Univ.

Press, 1989); Ruth Hubbard, *The Politics of Women's Biology* (New Brunswick, NJ: Rutgers Univ. Press, 1990); Nancy Tuana, *The Less Noble Sex: Scientific, Religious, and Philosophical Conceptions of Woman's Nature* (Bloomington: Indiana Univ. Press, 1993); and Nelly Oudsboom, *Beyond the Natural Body: An Archaeology of Sex Hormones* (London: Routledge, 1994). On gender stereotyping in other fields see Donna Haraway, *Primate Visions: Gender, Race, and Nature in the World of Modern Science* (London: Routledge, 1989); Tuana, ed., *Feminism and Science* (Bloomington: Indiana Univ. Press, 1989); Marina Benjamin, [illegible]

[illegible]

Biology (Bloomington: Indiana Univ. Press, 1995), pp. 61–62. While many have hailed this new rendering of the drama as an example of prejudice vanquished, we might also see it as a narrative of masculinization. Not only is the egg energized; it is masculinized, that is, ascribed the valued "active" characteristics of the sperm. Like women themselves, female biology is here expected to assimilate the values of the dominant culture. Emily Martin warns that as the egg becomes active or masculinized, it is also seen as aggressive – a *femme fatale*, threatening to capture and victimize men. An active female can be valued differently than an active male. "New data," she writes, "did not lead scientists to eliminate gender stereotypes. . . . Instead, scientists simply began to describe egg and sperm in different, but no less damaging, terms" (Martin, "Egg and Sperm," pp. 498–499). The molecular biologist and professor of women's studies Bonnie Spanier interjects further that in this instance the notion of equality between the contributions of the egg and the sperm is misleading, hiding the fact that the egg (as females more generally) contributes more to biological reproduction than the sperm. Emphasizing equality in heredity, she argues, diminishes the actual role of the egg as the larger gamete that contributes nutrients, organelles such as mitochondria and ribosomes, the cell membrane, and proteins crucial to the development of the zygote.

8 To attempt to respond to this question on its own terms, of course, reinforces the privilege accorded physics. See Sandra Harding. "Why 'Physics' is a Bad Model for Physics," in *Whose Science? Whose Knowledge? Thinking from Women's Lives* (Ithaca, NY: Cornell Univ. Press, 1991), pp. 77–102.

9 Phyllis Rosser, *The SAT Gender Gap: Identifying the Causes* (Washington, DC: Center for Women Policy Studies, 1989); and Rosser, *The SAT Gender Gap: ETS Responds*, a Research Update (Washington, DC: Center for Women Policy Studies, 1992). The purpose of the SAT is to predict first-year college grades. Some universities, including the Massachusetts Institute of Technology, have begun admitting women with good academic records, even if they score lower on standardized tests than some of the men candidates, because they have found that these women perform just as well during their first academic year as men with higher scores. On the importance of mathematics see Lucy Sells, "High School Mathematics as the Critical Filter in the Job Market," in *Developing Opportunities for Minorities in Graduate Education*, ed. R.T. Thomas (Berkeley: Univ. California Press, 1973), pp. 37–39.

10 Kenneth Bogart and Peter Doyle, "Non-Sexist Solution of the Ménage Problem," *Mathematical Monthly*, 1986, 93: 514–518, on pp. 514–515.

11 N. Katherine Hayles, "Gender Encoding in Fluid Mechanics: Masculine Channels and Feminine Flows," *Differences*, 1992, 4: 16–44. On oversimplification in mathematics see Nancy Cartwright, *How the Laws of Physics Lie* (Oxford: Clarendon, 1983); and Philip Davis and Reuben Hersh, *Descartes' Dream: The World According to Mathematics* (Brighton, Sussex: Harvester, 1986).

12 For gender in physics see Keller, *Secrets of Life, Secrets of Death* (cit. n. 6), Pt. 2; Karen Barad, "A Feminist Approach to Teaching Quantum Physics," in *Teaching the Majority*, ed. Sue Rosser (New York: Teachers College Press, Columbia Univ., 1995); and Renée Heller, "The Tale of the Universe for Others" (unpublished manuscript, Physics and Women's Studies, Univ. Utrecht).

13 Julie Klein, "Blurring, Cracking, and Crossing: Permeation and the Fracturing of Disciplines," in *Knowledges: Historical and Critical Studies in Disciplinarity*, ed. Ellen Messer- Davidow, David Shumway and David Sylvan (Charlottesville: Univ. Press Virginia, 1993), p. 188; Zuckerman *et al.*, eds., *Outer Circle* (cit. n. 4), p. 31; and Robert Westman, "Two Cultures or One? A Second Look at Kuhn's *The Copernican Revolution*," *Isis*, 1994, 85: 79–115, on p. 92.

14 Martin Rees, "Contemplating the Cosmos," in *A Passion for Science*, ed. Lewis Wolpert and Alison Richards (Oxford: Oxford Univ. Press, 1988), pp. 34–35; and Barad, "Feminist Approach to Teaching Quantum Physics" (cit. n. 12). On the "illusion" that physics is epistemologically hard see Cartwright, *How the Laws of Physics Lie* (cit. n. 11), p. 45; on geneticists' "physics envy" see Virginia Morell, "Rise and Fall of the Y Chromosome," *Science*, 14 Jan. 1994, 263: 171–172, on p. 171.

15 Robert Wilson, cited in Margaret Wertheim, *Pythagoras' Trousers: God, Physics, and Gender Wars* (New York: Times Books, 1995). On the separation of the practice of science from its critical examination see Barad, "Feminist Approach to Teaching Quantum Physics"; and Robert Proctor, *Value-Free Science? Purity and Power in Modern Knowledge* (Cambridge, Mass.: Harvard Univ. Press, 1991).

16 Ruth Sime, *Lise Meitner: A Life in Physics* (Berkeley: Univ. California Press, 1996); Charlotte Kerner, *Lise, Atomphysikerin: Die Lebensgeschichte der Lise Meitner* (Weinheim: Beltz, 1986), pp. 102–111; and Caroline Herzenberg and Ruth Howes, "Women of the Manhattan Project," *Technology Review*, 1993, 96: 32–40. See also Teri Hopper, "'Radioactive Ladies and Gentlemen': Women and Men of the Radioactivity Community, 1919–1939," paper delivered at the annual meeting of the History of Science Society, Minneapolis, 28 Oct. 1995. On the contributions of physics to national defense since World War II see Peter Galison and Bruce Hevly, eds., *Big Science: The Growth of Large-Scale Research* (Stanford, Calif.: Stanford Univ. Press, 1992).

17 See Charlene Morrow and James Morrow, "Whose Math Is It, Anyway?" *Initiatives*, 1993, 55: 49–59, esp. p. 50; and Sharon Traweek, *Beamtimes and Lifetimes: The World of High Energy Physicists* (Cambridge, Mass.: Harvard Univ. Press, 1988).

18 Cheris Kramarae and Dale Spender, *The Knowledge Explosion: Generations of Feminist Scholarship* (New York: Teachers College Press, Columbia Univ., 1992).

19 Marcia Barinaga, "Is There a 'Female Style' in Science?" *Science*, 16 Apr. 1993, 260: 384–391; and *ibid.*, 23 July 1993, 261: 412.

20 Virginia Morell, "Primatology," *Science*, 16 Apr. 1993, 260: 420–429.

21 Mildred Dresselhaus, "Women Graduate Students." *Physics Today*, June 1986, 39: 74–75; Rosabeth Kanter, *Men and Women of the Corporation* (New York: Basic, 1977); and, on primatology, Haraway, *Primate Visions* (cit. n. 6), p. 252.

22 Evelyn White, *Black Women's Health Book* (Seattle: Seal, 1990); Sue Rosser, *Women's Health – Missing from U.S. Medicine* (Bloomington: Indiana Univ. Press, 1994); Eileen Nechas and Denise Foley, *Unequal Treatment: What You Don't Know about How Women Are Mistreated by the Medical Community* (New York: Simon and Schuster, 1994); Anna Mastroianni, Ruth Faden, and Daniel Federman, eds., *Women and Health Research* (Washington, DC: National Academy Press, 1994). Vol. 2; Vivian Pinn, Overview: Office of Research on Women's Health (Bethesda, Md.: National Institutes of Health, 1995); and Shirley Malcom, "Science and Diversity: A Compelling National Interest," [illegible]

26 Donna Haraway, "Situated Knowledges: The Science Question in Feminism and the Privilege of Partial Perspective," in *Simians, Cyborgs, and Women: The Reinvention of Nature* (New York: Routledge, 1991), pp. 183–203

27 Harding, *Whose Science? Whose Knowledge?* (cit. n. 8), Ch. 6. See also Helen Longino, "Can There Be a Feminist Science?" in *Feminism and Science*, ed. Tuana (cit. n. 6), pp. 45–57: and Regine Kollek, "Brauchen Wir eine neue wissenschaftliche Revolution?" in *Fortschritt Wohin?* ed. Hans-Jürgen Fischbeck and Kollek (Münster: Agenda, 1994), pp. 41–49.

28 Linda Fedigan, "The Changing Role of Women in Models of Human Evolution," *Annual Review of Anthropology*, 1986, 15: 25–66.

29 Vanessa Gamble and Bonnie Blustein, "Racial Differentials in Medical Care: Implications for Research on Women," in *Women and Health Research*, ed. Mastroianni *et al.* (cit. n. 22), Vol. 2, pp.174–191.

30 Joan M. Gero, "Genderlithics: Women's Roles in Stone Tool Production," in *Engendering Archaeology: Women and Prehistory*, ed. Gero and Margaret W. Conkey (Oxford: Blackwell, 1991), pp. 163–193.

31 Susan Squier, *Babies in Bottles: Twentieth-Century Visions of Reproductive Technology* (New Brunswick, NJ: Rutgers Univ. Press, 1994), Ch. 1.

32 Margaret W. Conkey, "Making the Connections: Feminist Theory and Archaeologies of Gender," in *Women in Archaeology: A Feminist Critique*, ed. Hilary du Cros and Laurajane Smith (Canberra: Australian National Univ. Occasional Papers, 1993), pp. 3–15; and Joan M. Gero, "The Social World of Prehistoric Facts: Gender and Power in Paleoindian Research," *ibid.*, pp. 31–40.

33 Vandana Shiva, *Staying Alive: Women, Ecology, and Development* (London: Zed, 1988), pp. 65–66. See also Shiva, ed., *Close to Home: Women Reconnect Ecology, Health, and Development Worldwide* (Philadelphia: New Society, 1994).

34 Helen Longino, "Subjects, Power, and Knowledge: Description and Prescription in Feminist Philosophies of Science," in *Feminism and Science*, ed. Evelyn Fox Keller and Longino (Oxford: Oxford Univ. Press, 1996), pp. 264–279.

35 François Marie Arouet Voltaire, *Dictionnaire philosophique* (1764; Amsterdam, 1789), Vol. 5, p. 255; and Stephen Cole and Robert Florentine, "Discrimination against Women in Science: The Confusion of Outcome with Process," in *Outer Circle*, ed. Zuckerman *et al.* (cit. n. 4), p. 205.

36 Jean Donnison, *Midwives and Medical Men: A History of Inter-Professional Rivals and Women's Rights* (London: Heinemann, 1977); Judity Leavitt, ed., *Women and Health in America* (Madison: Univ. Wisconsin Press, 1984); Ornella Moscucci, *The Science of Woman: Gynaecology and Gender in England, 1800–1929* (Cambridge: Cambridge Univ. Press, 1990); Schiebinger, *Mind Has No Sex?* (cit. n. 4), Ch. 4; Laurel Ulrich, *A Midwife's Tale* (New York: Vintage, 1990); Hilary Marland, ed., *The Art of Midwifery: Early Modern Midwives in Europe* (London: Routledge, 1993); and Adrian Wilson, *The Making of Man-Midwifery: Childbirth in England, 1660–1770* (Cambridge, Mass.: Harvard Univ. Press, 1995).

37 Mario Tapia and Ana de la Torre, *La mujer campesina y las semillas andinas* (Lima: FAO, 1993); Stephen Brush, "Potato Taxonomies in Andean Agriculture," in *Indigenous Knowledge Systems and Development*, ed. David Brokensha, D.M. Warren, and Oswald Werner (Washington, DC: Univ. Press America, 1980), pp. 37–47; and Arun Agrawal, "Indigenous and Scientific Knowledge: Some Critical Comments," *Indigenous Knowledge and Development Monitor*, Dec. 1995, 3: 3–6.

Chapter 35

Hilary Rose

In turning to this, the last chapter of my book, I have a double sense both of the achievements of feminist science criticism and feminist science theory and of the immense tasks that remain. I have wanted to celebrate that criticism and theorizing which has been created by feminists working within and without the sciences over the past twenty years. But in celebrating the achievements I do not want to gloss over the strains, not least between those feminists who do science and those who engage in the social studies of science. The work of the social studies of science feminists can easily be portrayed as weakening to women scientists; the insistence that the specific historical location of the producers of knowledge is important in critically understanding specific representations of nature can be cast as somehow gnawing at the truth-claims of all and every scientific fact. In Britain, powerful journals such as *Nature* pitch themselves on the side of a correspondence theory of truth, and because they do not take the feminist social studies of science seriously, they simply place it in the same witty but nihilist location where much (not all) of the mainstream social studies of science and technology lies.[1]

Against this I want to insist that the feminist studies of science and technology are different in that, while they include almost every conceivable methodological and disciplinary approach,[2] they are profoundly committed to the possibility of making better and more reliable representations of nature informed by new values. As part of a long haul to change knowledge, they have a place (or rather several places, for cultural struggles are never tidy and linear) within Peggy MacIntosh's five-phase model, which she describes modestly as 'curriculum integration' but which requires nothing less than entire transformation of knowledge.[3] Beginning with a pedagogic situation in which women and their concerns are totally absent from the mainstream curriculum, she sees the second phase as one where significant women are added to the curriculum. The third questions the absence of the realities of women's lives. The fourth moves beyond questioning to the generation of feminist knowledge; while the fifth, the last, seeks to produce a scholarship which is responsive to all of humanity. Of course, while it is entirely possible, indeed common, for every phase to happen simultaneously, MacIntosh's model gives a framework for reviewing the progress of feminist approaches to science and technology.

Feminist critics and science theorists unquestionably have very different and important things to say, and they do so with increasing confidence. They share a common wish to challenge the ethic of no ethic, the culture of no culture which lies at the universalizing core of modern science (that first phase which MacIntosh invites us to leave behind) and to rebuild the sciences as respectful and responsible. For historical and political reasons a great deal of feminist effort in the sciences has been directed towards reconstructing the life sciences, particularly as they relate to human and to collective reproduction, not least by making new conceptual relationships with the social, but feminist projects for the sciences and technologies by no means stop there.[4] As the Biology and Gender Study Group wrote in 1988: 'A theory about life affects life. We become what biology tells us is the truth about life. Therefore feminist critique of biology is not only good for biology but for our society as well. Biology needs it both for itself and for fulfilling its social responsibilities.'[5]

Part of our difficulty in working for change lies in recognizing how long and how subtle are the fingers of past cultural values. The century moves to its end in the context of an immense, confused and inconsistent struggle against the deadly weight of that Judaeo-Christian inheritance in which Man was made in the image of God and was therefore given dominion over the Beasts and the garden of Eden, and as Man dominion over Woman. Even the heretical Darwinian story of evolution draws strength from and sustains this inheritance, though its materialism appears to challenge religiosity. Darwin and his circle certainly worried about the threat to religious faith.[6] None the less, I want to suggest that at a more profound level Darwinism (and the more I read of Darwin the less convincing is the distinction between social Darwinism and Darwinism) shored up that inheritance of the domination of Nature and of Woman which has long shaped the accounts of men and their relationships to both. In this reading, Darwin's burial in Westminster Abbey was not some supreme expression of Victorian hypocrisy, but rather the recognition by church and state that at core the Darwinian theory of evolution sustained the Victorian rendering of the Judaeo-Christian belief in Western Man's right to treat nature, women and other others as his things. To recognize the genius of Darwin was to recognize the spirit of the age. Darwin's intense anxiety lest his science should disturb his social acceptability is, within a single biography, a metonym for the story of science as an institution both continuously seeking to represent nature and anxious about negotiating its place among the powers.[7]

Within this Judaeo-Christian and Western scientific tradition, nature, including women's nature, is there to be dominated, albeit these days there is a sort of defensive surface civility towards both, as the powerful movements of feminism and environmentalism insist on a greater respect. Within theology the notion of 'stewardship' has been proposed as a replacement for dominion, with God understood as both mother and father. Such images seek to foster new practices and new relationships. Yet the extent to which dominion is expressed every day in the laboratory is there in the language and practices which increasingly treat animals as if they were interchangeable with chemical reagents. As one example, the Harvard oncomouse was bred (though more and more the verbs typically and significantly used to describe the production of this and similar animals are 'constructed' or 'made') to facilitate cancer research, so that research can be speeded up. To talk and think in this way is to treat animals – living organisms – as if they were merely chemical reagents. (There are some minor satisfactions in that the oncomouse has so far failed to live up to its US patenters' hopes, and that Europe refused on ethical grounds to patent the oncomouse, as it is a living organism.)

For that matter it is quite complicated living with a biologist who uses (that is, kills) chicks in his research on learning and memory. Over the years I have moved [illegible] most part I do not.

Like many feminist science critics I want a science where all the actors take part in the construction of nature, so while I find somewhat intractable the problem of how a day-old chick might freely participate in constructing the facts of learning and memory, I recognize that moving practically towards a deep respect for nature offers at present only inconsistent and provisional way stations.[8] For me one of the more important aspects of the challenge from the animal rights movement has been the questioning set in train among experimental life scientists and their students.

As I tried to show in my discussion of feminist science theory, I think we can begin to see the possibility of new feminist philosophies of nature which do not abandon the task of making representations, of making scientific facts, but instead offer different approaches to the practice of science. Such critical work, although at times an uncomfortable ally, is not to be equated with anti-science feminism – a current which, while I may disagree with it, unquestionably exists within contemporary feminism. Instead, feminist critics of science are likely to be particularly respectful of the work of feminists within the sciences and their patient and technically demanding task of constructing new representations of nature sympathetic to feminist values. Despite the necessary differences between the feminist social studies of science theorists (necessary because we are not all looking at the sciences from the same place), my reading is that there is a commitment to creating facts about the natural world which build defensible, objective accounts of the real, accepting that the real is always understood through historically, geographically, politically located and embodied subjects. Thus who produces science is a powerful clue as to what science is produced.

Pragmatically, I also think that possible tensions between those of us who construct facts about nature and those of us who point to their social shaping are relatively easily overcome, not least because of issues of education, gender and generation. In our still highly inequitable academic labour market those women scientists and engineers who do manage to survive are likely to be extremely bright, and, as part of a generation still coming into its full creativity, are likely also to have been influenced by the feminist movement which has surrounded them for a great part of their lives. It is not surprising that there is common and increasingly unembarrassed talk among feminist scientists and engineers from different subjects and societies about how they feel they do science differently.[9] These are part of a generation with much greater self-confidence in being women; thinking dangerously and reflexively is wider spread. There were such exceptions in previous generations, but women – let alone feminists – were unlikely to secure more than the smallest toehold within the institutions of science.

What I see as a less discussed strain is that between the highly educated women of academic feminism (from whatever discipline) and primarily working-class women. There is an under-examined issue of class, in which 'race', because of the way it is entwined with class in women's lives, is also present. Thus, while I entirely support Anne Fausto-Sterling's criticisms of women's studies scholars and students who, while fluent in the higher reaches of feminist culture, literary and psychoanalytic theory, are content to claim that biology is 'too difficult', and I share her longing for a two-way street, what worries me even more is the gap of privilege, intensified by the recession and the world-wide lurch to the right. The intensification of poverty in women's lives both in the old industrial societies and in the third world is brutally evident.

Take two current examples, derived from third and first world, environment and health, both struggles within the politics of reproduction, whose intensity and scale have been immense. Thus third-world women move to the defence of the environment when its well being is the guarantor of everyday survival. We have learnt from Vandana Shiva's writing of the struggle of the Chipko women to save the trees, a practical struggle aided by the intellectual attempt to redefine the scientific problem from the perspective of those who are affected. More recently there has been the immense struggle waged by the Indian and international environmentalist movements to stop the building of the Sardar Sarovar dams which affect no less than three states, ultimately displacing 250,000 farming families. Environmentalist and feminist pressures eventually shamed the World Bank and the Japanese government into withdrawing funding, but the Indian government remained intransigent. A few months later, in the summer of 1993, India's best-known environmentalist, Medha Patkar, together with 500 of her fellow environmentalist activists, threatened mass suicide by drowning in the Narmada river, the site of the dam, to compel the government to come to its senses and stop the project. The government's response was to say that the dam would irrigate drought-ridden areas and provide electricity, and on the basis of this scientific claim it ordered the arrest and imprisonment of the protesters. However, it also climbed down, at least as far as ordering a review. In Kenya Wangari Maathai, founder and spokesman of the Green Belt Movement, has mobilized many thousands of women to plant literally millions of trees and build new lives, reversing human-made desertification.

Ironically, although many commentators, including myself, see these struggles as part of a profound ecofeminism and as a social movement which seeks to empower the dispossessed,[10] the women who play such leading roles within these struggles for the continued possibility of entire communities to reproduce themselves rarely claim themselves as feminist. Such a reflection troubles me: is it that feminism has been seen as too far away from the struggle for women's survival, too engaged, for example, in the possibility of a feminism without women, to be an evident ally of actual dispossessed women? Or is it, as Janet Biehl, a founding ecofeminist who now rejects the name, sees it, a problem of the growth of irrationality within the ecofeminist movement, where goddess worship, a biological essentialized account of women's caring, and a monolithic rejection of science and technology as male now dominate, throwing out the baby of feminist rationality along with the bathwater of masculine rationality?[11]

The women's health movement has been another bridge in the construction of new realities, and it is not by chance that feminists located in those countries where the Genome Programme is best funded and where the new genetics and reproductive technologies make their loudest claims spend so much energy criticizing them. In the summer of 1993 the political achievement of securing from the British government an [illegible] not least because it was a battle over whether the discourses of mind and body could be integrated, or whether the Cartesian split would be perpetuated.[12] What was also precious in this struggle was the refusal of key women's groups such as the Maternity Alliance to abandon the claims of low income women, pointing out that if the Royal College cared so deeply for the safety of babies it would campaign for better welfare provision, as poverty was the greatest threat to their well being.

In such struggles, Sandra Harding's question *Whose Science? Whose Knowledge?* becomes vivid. Where the stakes are survival itself, women's knowledge of what they need to survive comes into dramatic conflict with the constructions of a patriarchal science prejudicial to both the environment and the health of women and their families alike. Arguably, struggles on such a scale, requiring cooperation between many different groups, have something of the character of Peggy MacIntosh's fifth stage. Certainly, to reconstruct natural and social facts in this way, which is both 'true' and friendlier to the diversity and complexity of the lives of women, is to work with a significantly changed philosophy of nature and a significantly changed conception of who is to construct the new knowledge. Feminist representations of nature, as we saw in the work of the feminist primatologists or the environmentalists, seek to replace hostile – even deadly – representations without giving up on claims of objectivity. What is under siege from both feminists and deep green environmentalists is the power/knowledge couple, offered with zeal by Francis Bacon in the seventeenth century and critically exposed by Michel Foucault in the late twentieth. Integral to that power/knowledge couple is the cultural commitment of the West to the domination of nature, with technoscience serving as both culture and the technological means of domination. Against this a socialist ecofeminism can offer a respect for nature, a respect that is located in the embodied practices and values of caring – without slipping into celebrating those naturally nurturant women beloved by patriarchy and for that matter by mystical ecofeminism.

Love, power and knowledge in everyday life

The price of living in a scientific and technological culture is that most of the time we are enabled to do everyday extraordinary things without any understanding of how they work. I sit typing this text into a computer, believing that when I stop the cursor on the window for 'print' sheets of crisp white paper printed with beautiful black letters will, after sounds of ticking and clucking, fill the tray beside me. The manual typewriter, that artifact of marvellous transparent Victorian engineering, always seemed to me self-evident, the electric typewriter mysterious, and the electronic computer more or less magical. Virginia Woolf recognized this extraordinary development long ago in the height of the electrical revolution when she wrote about the mysterious lifts in Selfridges. The new revolutions in information handling, in mass transport, in biotechnology, are also magical to most users, so that the cultural relationship to technoscience increasingly becomes 'black-box' or 'press-button'.

In everyday life, people in a highly scientific and technological culture cope by what is called the press-button approach to the increasing proliferation of black goods – videos, cameras, televisions, camcorders and music centres – in our domestic lives. Few understand what goes on within the black boxes; the more modest ambition, differentially aged and gendered, is to know which buttons and in what order they should be pushed. We want to make our black boxes work; few of us care to know what goes on within.

But even at the button-pushing level, while there is a general recognition of the extraordinary skills of most 10-year-olds as against those of many adults in terms of picking up how to use the new video, research among adults shows that women's more frequent lack of skill than that of their male counterparts is often a matter of being smart socially rather than dumb technologically. Women, it seems, resist learning how to programme the video because they have a shrewd idea about who will be expected to do the family's programming if they learn. Such resistance is not without costs, but the point is that knowledge, ignorance and resistance to knowledge are all both socially structured and achieved through intentional action.

Something rather similar operates around the avalanche of new conceptualizations of the body produced by the life sciences. In the post-AIDS world, while few people understand the immune system many acknowledge its importance and genuflect to it in everyday speech. 'My immune system is down', 'These vitamins really give your immune system a boost', replace the older language of 'lowered resistance' to infection.

Despite this there is a tendency – which is why at intervals within *Love, Power and Knowledge* I become angered by the thesis of the two cultures – to suggest that the biggest cultural division is between the sciences and technologies on the one hand and the humanities and the arts on the other, unalloyed by the intersections of class, gender and race. There is a linked discourse called 'the public understanding of science' produced by elite science, in which society is portrayed as composed of two groups: the scientists and the public. The former arbitrate as to what is scientific knowledge and the latter are to be assessed in their competence within it. Such a division is only very superficially and at best momentarily true. It ignores the changing constructions of what counts as science and as non-science (think of Watson's arrogant assertion that there is only one science – physics – and that all else is 'social work', or the contempt of 'real' scientists for what is done in industrial labs), and it sets aside, for example, the very considerable technological expertise of many creative artists. But even more seriously, it ignores the problem of the huge proliferation of knowledges and their interconnections. The polymath, the Leonardo da Vinci, the Hypatia, who could operate at the cutting edge of all the knowledges, was historically possible; today we cope by focusing on what seems important to us, letting the rest blur into faith in the scientific and technological culture. This process of selection, black-boxing the rest, in order to [illegible]

[illegible]

scattered within *Love, Power and Knowledge* are what I see as harbingers of hope. They are not the outriders of some unidirectional cultural movement, a revolution which knows pretty much where it is going, as revolutionaries in the past have claimed; instead the harbingers are myriads of small and large, apparently disconnected struggles which are expressive of an immense and fragmented movement within and against the dominant construction of science. What all these fragments have in common, from the search for a holistic science amongst some physicists and biologists, through the ethnosciences with their respect for non-Western thought, to feminism's preoccupation with new ways of knowing, is the deeply subversive understanding that science is socially shaped. This understanding, fashioned over the last quarter-century, is out there, set loose in everyday life, making it possible for 'other others' to challenge the powers of technoscience. Few, except those convinced by anti-science, run a totalizing critique; rather within a knowledge-based society in which we black-box much of the techno-culture, some bits are inescapable. Specific sciences and technologies enter our everyday lives and dealing with them requires that we have greater knowledge of them and understand their meaning. Resisting specific parts of the technoculture, or seeking to renegotiate their relevance, requires that the lines between black-boxing and understanding are redrawn by the resisters. The examples within this and other chapters – and they can be multiplied many times – of third-world women's environmental struggles, and first-world women's campaigns over Genome and reproduction, show the capacity to go beyond black-boxing, to enter the terrain of science and to construct new definitions of reality, infused with a feminist understanding of caring. Within these examples we see feminism bringing love to knowledge and power. It is love, as caring respect for both people and nature, that offers an ethic to reshape knowledge, and with it society.

Notes

1 For a criticism of the erasing practices of mainstream science studies see H. Rose, 'Rhetoric, Feminism and Scientific Knowledge', in Richard H. Roberts and James M.M. Good (eds), *The Recovery of Rhetoric: Persuasive Discourse and Disciplinarity in the Human Sciences* (London: Bristol Classical Press, 1993).

2 Joan Rothschild, on the basis of her survey of feminist science, technology and society courses, argues that interdisciplinarity is a strength: *Teaching Technology from a Feminist Perspective* (Oxford: Pergamon, 1988).

3 MacIntosh, 'Interactive Phases of Curricular Revision', in Bonnie Spanier (ed.), *Toward a Balanced Curriculum: A Sourcebook for Initiative Gender Integration Projects* (Cambridge: Schenkman, 1984).

4 Innovators include Oakley, *Social Support and Motherhood*. Oakley fuses so-called 'soft' approaches – women's happiness and social support – with 'hard' quantitative approaches, crucially birth weight. In this she moves beyond that equation of feminist methodology with phenomenological approaches, a position which has dominated UK feminist social research in its resistance to the mathematization of reality. In a very different but again very male-dominated field, Sherry Turkle and Seymour Papert also argue for epistemological space. 'Epistemological Pluralism: Styles and Voices within the Computer Culture', *Signs*, 16 (1 1990).

5 Biology and Gender Study Group, 'The Importance of Feminist Critique for Contemporary Cell Biology', in Nancy Tuana (ed.), *Feminism and Science* (Bloomington: Indiana University Press, 1989).

6 Teaching or showing evolutionary theory is still problematic for many US school districts and science museums, because of the continued strength of Christian religious fundamentalism in the US.

7 Adrian Desmond and James Moore, *Darwin* (Harmondsworth: Penguin, 1991).

8 While the moral agony is clear the moral prescriptions are not. Thus while Josephine Donovan's brilliant survey endorses Peter Singer's opposition to animal experimentation, her own proposal for a feminist ethics of animal rights is more restricted. She opposes beauty and cleaning product tests, the notorious LD-50 test and the more vicious experiments such as those of Harlow's primate lab. My purpose is not to score points off Donovan, rather to underline the difficulty – which I share – of deciding what to support and what to oppose. 'Animal Rights and Feminist Theory', *Signs*, 15 (2 1990).

9 See the special supplement 'Women in Science: Gender and the Culture of Science', *Science*, 260, 1993.

10 Carolyn Merchant, *Radical Economy: The Search for a Livable World* (New York: Routledge, 1992).

11 Janet Biehl, *Rethinking Eco-Feminist Politics* (Boston: South End Press, 1991).

12 Bordo, 'The Cartesian Masculinization of Thought', *Signs*, 11 (3 1986).

Afterword

HOW DID WE ARRIVE AT a place where we were so committed to the feminist analyses of science that we were compelled to produce this anthology? We approached this project as women with quite different backgrounds, yet it is interesting (and evident) that we have come to a similar place in our journeys as feminist scientists. We both recognize the need for this volume as a teaching tool within science studies programs but also hope that its contents will affect science education and science practice. Without systemic change, individual efforts will be far less productive. We offer our individual stories, in the hope that our journeys may strike a chord and impact others' lives.

For me (M.L.), it's a fairly long journey that began when I was 7 or 8 years old. A young woman who lived in my apartment building in the Bronx was attending Barnard College (the women's undergraduate college of Columbia University), and I decided, out of the blue, that I would also. The time I was graduated from high school was the Sputnik era, and the State of New York offered Regents Scholarships to those who would major in the "hard" sciences. This scholarship made it financially possible for me to attend Barnard as a physics major. (This choice of major was no doubt influenced by competition with my cousin, who was going to MIT also to study physics!) Needless to say, after earning an "18" on my first physics exam, a major in physics was not to be. My sophomore year, I took biology and chemistry, and fell in love with biology. After graduation, not having a clue as to what "work" entailed, I entered a graduate program at Columbia. Three years of course work and a potentially very important but failed (for stupid technical reasons) research project led to my taking a leave of absence and actually working. Work was boring but the lack of intensity allowed time for political involvement, at the local level, and against the Vietnam War. I went back to school, completed a really good Ph.D. project, did a post-doc at Cal Tech, got married, followed my husband to a position, had two daughters, and was a post-doc, again, for way too long.

I now live in a place that is physically beautiful and am an associate professor at a university that is very conservative, intellectually and politically. The saving grace is that I early on found a group of historians and philosophers who were talking about science and technology studies, and two wonderful women, Doris Zallen and Ann LaBerge, also "trailing spouses." We formed a mutual mentoring group, encouraging each other to publish, with the goal of all of us obtaining tenure-track positions, which we did. Science fell a little by the way-side, with some papers in history of genetics and molecular biology. I joined a "women's discussion group" for graduate students in the Biology Department, organized by Robin Andrews; although I didn't know it at the time, this group was in response to perceived discrimination by faculty against these students. We met regularly, educated each other on women's issues in science and eventually developed a (subversive) university-wide reputation; people flocked to the meetings from all over campus, although some swore us to secrecy about their attendance. My contribution was my first efforts in feminist epistemology; it took at least five more years for the paper to be published. I became acquainted with the few feminist scholars on campus, a group of brilliant, dedicated women crying in the wilderness. There was no Women's Studies Program, no appreciation of the value of women-centered criticism, no hope for women working with this perspective to get tenured or promoted. It was with these women that I found an intellectual home.

Why here rather than in the discipline in which I had so many years of training and success? It was probably a combination of several factors. Even though I somehow missed the early women's movement and its consciousness-raising groups, my education at a women's college probably served as a substitute. The intellectual challenge I set for myself, developing a "successor science" that takes into account the problems with current science raised in the feminist critiques, was so much more interesting and difficult than doing traditional molecular biology. My scientific research was in a system that I don't think very many people cared about. While preparing the budget for a proposal to the National Institutes of Health, I realized that the cost of the two or three papers that the grant, if awarded, would produce, would be $500,000. What difference would three papers on bovine parvovirus molecular biology make? The cost/benefit ratio was laughable. As well, I am a little unhappy with the course of current molecular biology, with its emphasis on the genetic basis of everything. This may be a tautology; if I hadn't become involved with the feminist critique, I may never have known the term "biological determinism," which is the basis of my discontent!

I began to shift away from science and toward women's studies. By this time there was a fledgling Women's Studies program and I developed a course called "Gender and Science," being very careful to ground the syllabus in mainstream history and philosophy of science, so neither I nor the program would be accused of being too "radical." Teaching this course was terrifying. I had spent too long being the lecturer, dispensing information as the authority in front of seventy-five students, to feel secure in a situation that depended on my giving up control and rolling with the dialog that developed between myself and the student participants. Teaching the course was thrilling – virtually every class meeting someone would say something that took my breath away. Oddly (or not, perhaps), I have always received significantly better student evaluations in "Gender and Science" than in "Virology."

I have been a part-time administrator, a part-time scientist, a part-time science instructor, a part-time Women's Studies instructor and a part-time feminist researcher, who, ironically, shares manuscript drafts and ideas with above-mentioned cousin, also an ex-physicist, now a professor of English. Five professional lives, with two more as a wife and mother. What will be next? Very likely an effort to incorporate the feminist analyses into the teaching of science.

When I (I.B.) completed my Ph.D. in Plant Science (with two other degrees in [illegible]

One interesting and pivotal event that occurred during this period was that the Department of Biology, where I was employed as an adjunct, requested that I teach a course on "Women and Science." I categorize this as interesting because there was, and still is, no collaboration between departments of social and natural science on our campus. Furthermore, adjuncts are typically assigned to teach large sections of non-majors or introductory courses and this course drew a relatively small number of students who were taking it for elective credit. Although it was advertised as "Women in Science," with a flyer that challenged the students to name a famous woman scientist other than Marie Curie (of course, many are even unaware of her), developing and implementing that first class opened up a whole new series of readings for me, and provided me with an opportunity to see myself as a woman scientist and to begin to even consider women's issues. It also allowed me to understand that if I chose to pursue this "feminist" line, I would have to answer questions asked of me by faculty in the natural sciences such as "Why do we even need a class like 'Women and Science'?" and "You don't really believe that men and women are the same, do you?" Given that "Women and Science" is now a course recognized within the Florida State University System and that our institution has a faculty member who is doing everything possible to add feminist perspectives to natural science courses, the Department of Biology probably got more than it bargained for.

With this one experience in hand, I began to explore the possibility of teaching this course for the Department of Women's Studies. With my infant daughter in tow, the chair and I began a conversation that has, remarkably, resulted in a unique, tenure-earning position in the Department of Women's Studies. Unlike many women scientists who elect to combine feminist studies/science studies/natural science, this is not a shared position with a department within the natural sciences. The science research that I continue to do and to publish (always in collaboration) and the grants that I write are optional. The experience has allowed me to assume an unconventional position within my institution, which has been incredible in many ways. It has also allowed me to examine my own path in the sciences as I struggle to identify the positions of other women within, and with respect to, the culture of science. In retrospect, I realized that my choices of major and, later, of research and teaching were influenced by my discomfort with the abstract masculinity of science. I avoided reductionism, moving from an undergraduate degree with a research project that examined the narrow topic of respiration in a single plant species, to a master's degree that asked a much broader and more holistic question about the condition of whole communities and ecosystems. When I teach courses that focus on natural science, the focus is on concepts and discussion of broad connections rather than memorization of disconnected facts. Students who receive undergraduate degrees in the natural sciences are at a disadvantage as they enter post-graduate studies and/or the workforce. Armed with facts and little context, they are unprepared to apply their knowledge outside of the classroom.

I.B. says that her career has been influenced by an avoidance of reductionism. In contrast, M.L.'s attraction to cell physiology and later to molecular biology was because of its reductionism, the promise it offered of a mechanistic explanation of everything. It has taken a long time for her to realize that this promise is not possible, that the methodology required to define mechanism (*in vitro* experiments) is so far removed from anything that is alive that it is highly suspect. As Evelyn Fox Keller summarizes the writings of Nancy Cartwright and Mary Hesse, "the understanding of the remarkable convergences between theory and experiment that scientists have produced requires attention not so much to the adequacy of the laws that presumably are being tested, but rather to the particular and highly local manipulations of theory and experimental procedure that are required to produce those convergences." Rather than a science such as this, we hope for a new methodology that develops within the web of the feminist analyses and for a new pedagogy that insures its perpetuation.

Reference

Keller, Evelyn Fox (1992) *Secrets of Life, Secrets of Death*. New York and London, Routledge, p. 30.

Bibliography

Abir-Am, Pnina and Outram, Dorinda (eds) (1987) *Uneasy Careers and Intimate Lives: Women in Science 1789–1979*. New Brunswick, NJ: Rutgers University Press.

Alic, Margaret (1986) *Hypatia's Heritage: A History of Women in Science from Antiquity through the Nineteenth Century*. Boston: Beacon.

American Association for the Advancement of Science (1993) "Women in Science '93: Gender and the Culture of Science." *Science 260*: 383–430.

American Association for the Advancement of Science (1993) "Minorities '93: Trying to Change the Face of Science." *Science 262*: 1089–1134.

American Association for the Advancement of Science (1994) "Women in Science 1994." *Science 263*: 1467–1496.

Apple, R. (ed.) (1992) *Women, Health and Medicine in America*. New Brunswick, NJ: Rutgers University Press.

Barad, Karen (1998) "Agential Realism: Feminist Interventions in Understanding Scientific Practices." In Biagioli, Mario, *The Science Studies Reader*. New York: Routledge.

Barnes, Barry, Bloor, David, and Henry, John (1996) *Scientific Knowledge: A Sociological Analysis*. Chicago: University of Chicago Press.

Barr, Jean and Birke, Lynda (1998) *Common Science? Women, Science and Knowledge*. Bloomington and Indianapolis: Indiana University Press.

Barton, Angela Calabrese (1998) *Feminist Science Education*. New York and London: Teachers College Press.

Belenky, Mary Field, Clinchy, Blythe McVicker, Goldberger, Nancy Rule, and Tarule, Jill Mattuck (1986) *Women's Ways of Knowing: The Development of Self, Voice, and Mind*. New York: Basic Books.

Birke, Lynda (2000) *Feminism and the Biological Body*. New Brunswick: Rutgers University Press.

Birke, Lynda and Hubbard, Ruth (eds) (1995) *Reinventing Biology*. Bloomington and Indianapolis: Indiana University Press.

Bleier, Ruth (1984) *Science and Gender: A Critique of Biology and its Theories on Women*. Oxford: Pergamon Press.

Bleier, Ruth (ed.) (1991) *Feminist Approaches to Science*. New York and London: Teachers College Press.

Bordo, Susan (1986) "The Cartesian Masculinization of Thought." *Signs: Journal of Women in Culture and Society* 11: 439–456.

Bordo, Susan (ed.) (1999) *Feminist Interpretations of René Descartes*. University Park, PA: Pennsylvania State University Press.

Braidotti, Rosi, Charkiewics, Ewa, Hauster, Sabine, and Wieringa, Saskia (eds) (1994) *Women, the Environment and Sustainable Development: Towards a Theoretical Synthesis*. London: Zed Books.

Cartwright, Nancy (1983) *How the Laws of Physics Lie*. Oxford: Clarendon Press.

Cartwright, Nancy (1989) *Nature's Capacities and their Measurement*. Oxford: Clarendon Press.

Cole, Jonathan (1979) *Fair Science: Women in the Scientific Community*. New York: Columbia University Press.

Cudd, Ann E. (1998) "Multiculturalism as a Cognitive Virtue of Scientific Practice." *Hypatia* 3: 43–61.

Diamond, Irene and Orenstein, Gloria Feman (1990) *Reweaving the World: The Emergence of Ecofeminism*. San Francisco: Sierra Club Books.

Downey, Gary Lee and Dumit, Joseph (eds) (1997) *Cyborgs and Citadels*. Santa Fe: School of American Research Press.

Duran, Jane (1998) *Philosophies of Science/Feminist Theories*. Boulder and Oxford: Westview Press.

Eisenhart, Margaret A. and Finkel, Elizabeth (1998) *Women's Science: Learning and Succeeding From the Margins*. Chicago and London: University of Chicago Press.

Fausto-Sterling, Anne (1985) *Myths of Gender: Biological Theories About Women and Men*. New York: Basic Books.

Fuss, Diana (1989) *Essentially Speaking: Feminism, Nature and Difference*. New York: Routledge.

Gaard, Greta (ed.) (1993) *Ecofeminism: Women, Animals, and Nature*. Philadelphia: Temple University Press.

Garry, Ann and Pearsall, Marilyn (eds) (1989) *Women, Knowledge, and Reality*. New York and London: Routledge.

Gatens, Moira (1991) *Feminism and Philosophy: Perspectives on Difference and Equality*. Bloomington and Indianapolis: Indiana University Press.

Gates, Barbara T. and Shteir, Ann B. (1997) *Natural Eloquence: Women Reinscribe Science*. Madison: University of Wisconsin Press.

Gilligan, Carol (1982) *In a Different Voice*. Cambridge and London: Harvard University Press.

Goldberg, David Theo (ed.) (1990) *Anatomy of Racism*. Minneapolis and London: University of Minnesota Press.

Goldberger, Nancy, Tarule, Jill, Clinchy, Blythe, and Belenky, Mary (1996) *Knowledge, Difference, and Power: Essays Inspired by Women's Ways of Knowing*. New York: Basic Books.

Gould, Stephen J. (1981) *The Mismeasure of Man*. New York: W.W. Norton.

Gowaty, Patricia Adair (ed.) (1997) *Feminism and Evolutionary Biology*. New York: Chapman and Hall.

Hacking, Ian (1983) *Representing and Intervening*. Cambridge: Cambridge University [illegible]

[illegible] Cultural Studies." *Configurations* 1: 59–71.

Haraway, Donna (1997) *Modest-Witness@Second Millennium.FemaleMan-Meets Oncomouse: Feminism and Technoscience*. New York and London: Routledge.

Haraway, Donna and Goodeve, Thryza Nichols (1998) *How Like a Leaf: An Interview with Thryza Nichols Goodeve*. New York: Routledge.

Harding, Sandra (1986) *The Science Question in Feminism*. Milton Keynes: Open University Press.

Harding, Sandra (1991) *Whose Science? Whose Knowledge?* Ithaca: Cornell University Press.

Harding, Sandra (ed.) (1993) *The "Racial" Economy of Science*. Bloomington and Indianapolis: Indiana University Press.

Harding, Sandra (1998) *Is Science Multicultural? Postcolonialisms, Epistemologies*. Bloomington and Indianapolis: Indiana University Press.

Harding, Sandra and Hintikka, Merrill (eds) (1983) *Discovering Reality: Feminist Perspectives on Epistemology, Metaphysics, Methodology, and Philosophy of Science*. Dordrecht: Reidel.

Harding, Sandra and O'Barr, Jean F. (eds) (1987) *Sex and Scientific Inquiry*. Chicago and London: University of Chicago Press.

Harth, Erica (1992) *Cartesian Women: Versions and Subversions of Rational Discourse in the Old Regime*. Ithaca: Cornell University Press.

Heckman, Susan (1997) "Truth and Method: Feminist Standpoint Theory Revisited." *Signs: Journal of Women in Culture and Society* 22: 341–365.

Henrion, Claudia (1997) *Women in Mathematics: The Addition of Difference*. Bloomington and Indianapolis: Indiana University Press.

Hesse, Mary (1996) *Models and Analogies in Science*. Notre Dame, IN: Notre Dame Press.

Hirsch, Marianne and Keller, Evelyn Fox (eds) (1990) *Conflicts in Feminism*. London: Routledge.

Holloway, Margaret (1993) "A Lab of Her Own." *Scientific American*, November 1993, 94–103.

Hrdy, Sarah Blaffner (1999) *The Woman that Never Evolved.* Cambridge, MA, and London: Harvard University Press.

Hubbard, Ruth (1990) *The Politics of Women's Biology.* New Brunswick and London: Rutgers University Press.

Hubbard, Ruth and Wald, Elijah (1993) *Exploding the Gene Myth.* Boston: Beacon.

Hynes, H. Patricia (1989) *The Recurrent Silent Spring.* New York: Teachers College Press.

Hynes, H. Patricia (1991) *Reconstructing Babylon: Essays on Women and Technology.* Bloomington and Indianapolis: Indiana University Press.

Kass-Simon, Gabriele and Farnes, Patricia (eds) (1990) *Women of Science: Righting the Record.* Bloomington and Indianapolis: Indiana University Press.

Keller, Evelyn Fox (1983) *A Feeling for the Organism: The Life and Work of Barbara McClintock.* San Francisco: W.H. Freeman.

Keller, Evelyn Fox (1985) *Reflections on Gender and Science.* New Haven: Yale University Press.

Keller, Evelyn Fox (1992) *Secrets of Life, Secrets of Death.* New York and London: Routledge.

Keller, Evelyn Fox (1995) *Refiguring Life: Metaphors of Twentieth Century Biology.* New York: Columbia University Press.

Keller, Evelyn Fox and Longino, Helen (eds) (1996) *Feminism and Science.* Oxford: Oxford University Press.

Kelly, Alison (1985) "The Construction of Masculine Science." *British Journal of the Sociology of Education* 6: 133–154.

Kevles, Daniel and Hood, LeRoy (eds) (1992) *The Code of Codes: Scientific and Social Issues in the Human Genome Project.* Cambridge: Harvard University Press.

Kirkup, Gill and Keller, Laurie Smith (eds) (1992) *Inventing Women.* Milton Keynes: Open University Press.

Kohler, Robert E. (1994) *Lords of the Fly:* Drosophila *Genetics and the Experimental Life.* Chicago and London: University of Chicago Press.

Kohlstedt, Sally Gregory and Longino, Helen E. (eds) (1997) "Women, Gender and Science: New Directions." *Osiris* 12. Chicago: The History of Science Society, Inc./University of Chicago Press.

Kuhn, Thomas S. (1970) *The Structure of Scientific Revolutions. Second Edition Enlarged.* Chicago and London: University of Chicago Press.

Lasslett, Barbara, Kohlstedt, Sally Gregory, Longino, Helen, and Hammonds, Evelynn (1996) *Gender and Scientific Authority.* Chicago: University of Chicago Press.

Latour, Bruno (1987) *Science in Action.* Milton Keynes: Open University Press.

Latour, Bruno and Woolgar, Steve (1979) *Laboratory Life: The Social Construction of Scientific Facts.* Beverly Hills: Sage.

Laurence, Leslie and Weinhouse, Beth (1997) *Outrageous Practices: How Gender Bias Threatens Women's Health.* New Brunswick, NJ, and London: Rutgers University Press.

Lewontin, R.C., Rose, Steven, and Kamin, Leon J. (1984) *Not in Our Genes: Biology, Ideology and Human Nature.* New York: Pantheon.

Lloyd, Genevieve (1996) "Reason, Science and the Domination of Matter." In Evelyn Fox Keller and Helen Longino (eds) *Feminism and Science.* Oxford and New York: Oxford University Press.

Longino, Helen (1990) *Science as Social Knowledge: Values and Objectivity in Scientific Inquiry.* Princeton: Princeton University Press.

Lykke, Nina (ed.) (1996) *Between Monsters, Goddesses, Cyborgs: Feminist Confrontations with Science, Medicine and Cyberspace.* London: Zed Books.

[illegible] *Culture and Society* 16: 485–501.

Mayberry, Maralee and Rose, Ellen Cronan (1999) *Meeting the Challenge: Innovative Feminist Pedagogies in Action.* New York and London: Routledge.

Maynard, Mary (ed.) (1997) *Science and the Construction of Women.* London: UCL Press.

Mellor, Mary (1997) *Feminism and Ecology.* Washington Square, NY: New York University Press.

Merchant, Carolyn (1980) *The Death of Nature: Women, Biology and the Scientific Revolution.* San Francisco: Harper & Row.

Merchant, Carolyn (1996) *Earthcare: Women and the Environment.* London and New York: Routledge.

Mies, Maria and Vandana Shiva (1993) *Ecofeminism.* London: Zed Books.

Morse, Mary (1995) *Women Changing Science: Voices from a Field in Transition.* New York: Insight Books

National Science Foundation (1992) *Women and Minorities in Science and Engineering.* Washington, DC: National Science Foundation.

Needham, Joseph (1969) *The Grand Titration: Science and Society in East and West.* Toronto: University of Toronto Press.

Nelson, Lynn Hankinson and Nelson, Jack (1996) *Feminism, Science, and the Philosophy of Science.* Dordrecht/Boston/London: Kluwer Academic Publishers.

Noble, David (1992) *A World Without Women: The Christian Clerical Culture of Western Science.* New York: Knopf.

Pattatucci, Angela M. (1998) *Women in Science: Meeting Career Challenges.* London: Sage.

Pickering, Andrew (1992) *Science as Practice and Culture.* Chicago and London: University of Chicago Press.

Plumwood, Val (1993) *Feminism and the Mastery of Nature.* New York: Routledge.

Pycior, Helena M., Slack, Nancy, and Abir-Am, Pnina (eds) (1995) *Creative Couples in the Sciences.* New Brunswick, NJ: Rutgers University Press.

Rocheleau, Dianna, Thomas-Slater, Barbara, Wangari, Esther (eds) (1996) *Feminist Political Ecology: Global Issues and Local Experience*. New York: Routledge.

Rose, Hilary (1983) "Hand, Brain and Heart: Towards a Feminist Epistemology for the Natural Sciences." *Signs: Journal of Women in Culture and Society* 9: 73–96.

Rose, Hilary (1994) *Love, Power, and Knowledge: Towards a Feminist Transformation of the Sciences*. Bloomington and Indianapolis: Indiana University Press.

Rosser, Sue V. (1986) *Teaching Science and Health from a Feminist Perspective*. New York: Pergamon Press.

Rosser, Sue V. (ed.) (1988) *Feminism within the Science and Health Care Professions: Overcoming Resistance*. New York and London: Teachers College Press.

Rosser, Sue V. (1990) *Female-Friendly Science*. New York: Pergamon Press.

Rosser, Sue V. (1992) *Biology and Feminism*. New York: Twayne Publishers.

Rosser, Sue V. (1994) *Women's Health – Missing from U.S. Medicine*. Bloomington and Indianapolis: Indiana University Press.

Rosser, Sue V. (ed.) (1995) *Teaching the Majority: Breaking the Gender Barrier in Science, Mathematics, and Engineering*. New York and London: Teachers College Press.

Rosser, Sue V. (1997) *Re-Engineering Female Friendly Science*. New York and London: Teachers College Press.

Rosser, Sue V. (1998) "Applying Feminist Theories to Women in Science Programs." *Signs: Journal of Women in Culture and Society* 24: 171–200.

Rosser, Sue V. (2000) *Women, Science, and Society: The Crucial Union*. New York and London: Teachers College Press.

Rossiter, Margaret W. (1982) *Women Scientists in America: Struggles and Strategies to 1940*. Baltimore: Johns Hopkins University Press.

Rossiter, Margaret W. (1995) *Women Scientists in America: Before Affirmative Action 1940–1972*. Baltimore: Johns Hopkins University Press.

Sadker, Myra and Sadker, David (1994) *Failing at Fairness: How our Schools Cheat Girls*. New York: Touchstone.

Salleh, Ariel (1997) *Ecofeminism as Politics: Nature, Marx and the Postmodern*. New York: Zed Books.

Schiebinger, Londa (1987) "The History and Philosophy of Women in Science: A Review Essay." *Signs: Journal of Women in Culture and Society* 12: 305–332.

Schiebinger, Londa (1989) *The Mind Has No Sex: Women in the Origins of Modern Science*. Cambridge and London: Harvard University Press.

Schiebinger, Londa (1993) *Nature's Body: Gender in the Making of Modern Science*. Boston: Beacon.

Schiebinger, Londa (1999) *Has Feminism Changed Science?* Cambridge: Harvard University Press.

Seymour, Elaine and Hewitt, Nancy M. (1994) *Talking About Leaving*. Boulder, CO: University of Colorado Press.

Shapin, Stephen (1996) *The Scientific Revolution*. Chicago and London: University of Chicago Press.

Shepherd, Linda Jean (1993) *Lifting the Veil: The Feminine Face of Science*. Boston: Shambhala.

Shulman, Bonnie (1996) "What If We Change Our Axioms? A Feminist Inquiry into the Foundations of Mathematics." *Configurations* 3: 427–451.

Smaglik, Paul (1998) "Exodus of Women from Science is Jeopardizing Recent Gains." *The Scientist*, April 13, 1998.

Smith, Edward and Sapp, Walter (eds) (1997) *Plain Talk about the Human Genome Project*. Tuskeegee: Tuskeegee University.

Sonnert, Gerhard and Holton, Gerald (1995) *Who Succeeds in Science? The Gender* [illegible]

Toulmin, Stephen (1990) *Cosmopolis: The Hidden Agenda of Modernity*. New York: Free Press.

Traweek, Sharon (1988) *Beamtimes and Lifetimes: The World of High Energy Physics*. Cambridge and London: Harvard University Press.

Tuana, Nancy (ed.) (1989) *Feminism and Science*. Bloomington and Indianapolis: Indiana University Press.

Tuana, Nancy (1993) *The Less Noble Sex: Scientific, Religious, and Philosophical Conceptions of Women's Nature*. Bloomington and Indianapolis: Indiana University Press.

Tuomey, Christopher P. (1996) *Conjuring Science*. New Brunswick, NJ: Rutgers University Press.

van Wijngaard, Marianne (1997) *Reinventing the Sexes: The Biomedical Construction of Femininity and Masculinity*. Bloomington and Indianapolis: Indiana University Press.

Vetter, Betty M. (1992) "Women in Science: Ferment, Yes; Progress, Maybe; Change, Slow." *Mosaic* 23: 34–41.

Wajcman, Judy (1991) *Feminism Confronts Technology*. University Park, PA: Pennsylvania State University Press.

Warren, Karen (ed.) (1997) *Ecofeminism: Women, Culture, Nature*. Bloomington and Indianapolis: Indiana University Press.

Whitten, Barbara (1996) "What Physics is Fundamental Physics? Feminist Implications of Physicists' Debate over the Superconducting Supercollider." *National Women's Studies Association Journal* 8: 1–16.

Women and Scientific Literacy Project (1999) *Frequently Asked Questions About Feminist Science Studies*. Washington: Association of American Colleges and Universities.

Zuckerman, Harriet, Cole, Jonathan, and Bruer, John (eds) (1992) *The Outer Circle: Women in the Scientific Community*. New York: Norton.

Index

agriculture: and biodiversity 292, 454–456; modernization of 296
AIDS 337
American Association for the Advancement of Science (AAAS) 18
alchemy 64, 94
androcentrism 383, 386, 437
anthropomorphism 257, 260
Aristotle 63, 85, 180, 309

Bacon, Francis 65, 68–78, 95, 107
barriers: to success for women in science 31
bias 113, 232
biochemistry 272
biodiversity: agricultural 292; the role of women in 289
biological determinism 49, 180, 323, 338
biology: cell 272, 425; developmental 234; dominant paradigm of 50, 66; evolutionary 255; molecular 273–282, 425, 445, 462
biomedicine 42
biotechnology 40, 296, 458, 488

canon: biological 236
cancer 279, 423
capitalism 72
cell 429; biology 272, 425; egg 236, 312
chromosomes 310
cloning 238
cold war 239
colonialism 191–194, 253, 344, 352
Convention on Biodiversity 297
craniology 325
critique of science 20

Darwin, Charles 325
Darwinism 259, 329, 484
Descartes 65, 82–91, 107, 214, 229
decontextualizing 237
dialectics 258
difference 232, 236, 309–320, 330, 335
discrimination 42
DNA 237, 431, 440; recombinant technology 53, 272–280
dualism 90

ecofeminism 182, 291, 423, 486
education: reform 18; women 326
embryology 235
employment 14–17

engineering: enrollment in 24; genetic 234
Enlightenment 329
environment 291
epistemology 65, 87, 214, 232; feminist standpoint 145–152
essentialism 133–134
ethnography 254
eugenics 241, 329
Eurocentrism 191–194

feminism 262; African-American 131–132; essentialist 133; existentialist 134; lesbian separatism 138; liberal 55, 126–129, 409, 444; Marxist 129–130; psychoanalytic 134; radical 136, 441; Socialist 132
feminist: empiricism 215; epistemology 386, 392; standpoint theory 145–152, 216; theory 61
feminist critique: of science 50, 59
Freud 95

Gender and Development (GAD) 290
gender: gap 39; identity 367; ideology 55, 61; relations 292; studies 290
gene 244, 331
genetics 234, 272; engineering 448, 461; Mendelian 238
God 98, 105
Goodall, Jane 256, 259

Haraway, Donna 3, 221, 386, 474
Harding, Sandra 94, 264, 386, 474
Harvard Medical School 275
health: sciences 20; women's 464, 472
hierarchies: and biological classification 51; and dualism in science 272
homosexuality 331–332, 368
hooks, bell 132
hormones 283, 312, 333, 367
Human Genome Project 207, 275, 452, 487
hypothesis 111, 439

in vitro fertilization (IVF) 238
individualism 256
industry 39
Intellectual Property Rights (IPR) 459
interdisciplinary 400
intuition 257

Keller, Evelyn Fox 19–20, 94, 198, 221, 274, 394
knowledge: indigenous 297; intuitive 298; local 172, 289; masculine theory of 94–96; production of 64, 145; situated 173–175, 389, 395; systems 282, 295, 298, 347
Kuhn, Thomas 66

language: and science 105, 221, 412, 427, 476

marginalization 13
masculinized 283
mathematics 64, 411–418
McClintock, Barbara 135, 283
Mead, Margaret 258
mentoring 2, 40, 53
metaphors 243, 410
methodology: feminist 123; scientific 111–113, 124
minorities 38
molecular biology 52, 59
mythology 254

National Institutes of Health (NIH) 281, 303, 472
National Science Foundation (NSF) 15, 38
natural history 259, 354, 374
natural order 323
natural selection 329
nature 2, 51, 253; as animate 62, 410; as machine 93; dissection of 71; domination of 396, 484–486; gendered as female 100; laws of 59, 64; manipulation of 77; secrets of 69, 98–99
neuroscience 335
Newton 63, 101, 107
Nobel Prize 52, 283, 328, 489

objectivism 254
objectivity 2, 83, 89, 112, 114, 119, 154–163, 169, 226, 259, 356
oriental 191–195, 255, 281

physics 225, 469
positivism 228
pregnancy 312
[illegible]

race 324
racism 324–330, 355, 360
realism 59
reductionism 231, 276, 282, 338
reflexivity 164
relativism 219
religion 350
Renaissance 82
reproduction 313, 324
retention rates: of scientists 25
Royal Society 68

science: language of 105; social construction of 99, 130, 390; successor 172; sustainable 468; values in 111–118; wars 114, 117
science education 373–380, 407
scientific method 72, 218, 231, 407
scientific revolution 3, 63–65, 84–88, 98, 438
self confidence 31
sex determination 294
Shiva, Vandana 289
social constructivism 171, 180
social relations 236, 247
[illegible]

United Nations Conference on Environment and Development 1992 289
United Nations Women's Conference 1995 289

Watson, James 239, 276, 462
women: African 314, 344, 353; biology of 50; rural 293–295
Women in Development (WID) 290
women's health 467, 472
women's movement 49
women's studies 115
women's work 151
world view: mechanistic 63; reductionist 282; scientific 276
World War II 252

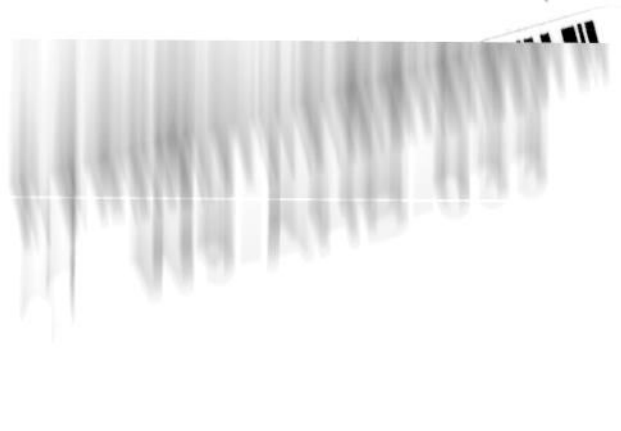

Readers are already raving about *Call Me Hope*, a powerful story about a young girl dealing with a verbally abusive mother:

"This beautiful, inspiring story should be read by mothers and daughters together. This captivating, healing novel brings extraordinary insight into the destructive emotional impact of verbal abuse on both mother and child. Together, with a promise and a pledge to one another, the gift of love is given."

—Ann S. Kelly, founder/executive director of Hands & Words Are Not For Hurting Project®

[illegible] difficult issues, which helps [illegible]

—Trudy Ludwig, children's advocate and bestselling author of *My Secret Bully, Just Kidding,* and *Sorry!*

"*Call Me Hope* introduces young readers to an amazing girl named Hope. Children who do not live in abusive homes may find her clever and creative. Those who DO live with the constant threat of abuse will surely find her inspirational."

—Pat Stanislaski, executive director of the New Jersey Task force on Child Abuse and Neglect, former executive director of the National Center for Assault Prevention

"A sensitive, heartrending book about parental verbal abuse and Hope's way of coping. Compassionately shared insight ending with promise for those involved. This book will be rewarding when shared with classroom discussion groups."

—Neva Huff, former educator

"Gretchen does a wonderful job of writing a hard story. I read this book aloud to twenty-five female inmates in jail, and they were captivated, as was I."

—Karen Rogers, Yamhill County Correctional Facility administrator

"A bittersweet *must-read* for every adolescent child and a powerful 'read-aloud' for those even younger. Gretchen has hit on a topic that is often very hidden from the world . . . verbal abuse. A remarkable story . . . As an educator for more than 30 years, I'm thrilled to see this issue faced head-on."

—Chris Morris, kindergarten teacher

a novel by Gretchen Olson

Also by Gretchen Olson:

Joyride

Little, Brown and Company

Hachette Book Group USA
1271 Avenue of Americas, New York, NY 10020
Visit our Web site at www.lb-kids.com

First Edition: April 2007

Library of Congress Cataloging-in-Publication Data

Olson, Gretchen.
Call me Hope / by Gretchen Olson — 1st ed.
p. cm.
Summary: In Oregon, eleven-year-old Hope begins coping with her mother's verbal abuse by devising survival strategies for herself based on a history unit about the Holocaust, and meanwhile she works toward buying a pair of purple hiking boots by helping at a second-hand shop.
ISBN-13: 978-0-316-01236-2
ISBN-10: 0-316-01236-X
[1. Child abuse — Fiction. 2. Mothers and daughters — Fiction. 3. Moneymaking projects — Fiction. 4. Schools — Fiction. 5. Stress (Physiology) — Fiction. 6. Oregon — Fiction.] I. Title.
PZ7.O5185Cal 2007
[Fic] — dc22
2006027896

10 9 8 7 6 5 4 3 2 1

Q-FF
Printed in the United States of America
The text was set in ITC Benguiat, and the display type is Day Dream.

For my Mother,

An *Angel Mom*

1923–1982

*Official pledge of the International Hands & Words Are Not For Hurting Project®.
Ann S. Kelly, Founder and Executive Director.

CHAPTER 1

Role Models

but I woke at exactly 6:06, which is lucky because it's perfectly balanced. Besides that, 6 is my favorite number. I kissed my fingers, touched the wall, and wished that 6th grade would be a great year.

Mr. Hudson looked over our class like he was figuring what kind of year he was going to have. Maybe he was looking for a good number, a lucky sign. He turned and wrote *role models* on the board, his bald spot bobbing along with his arm.

"What's the job of a role model?" he asked, turning back, wiping his hand on his pants.

My eyes shot down. I sucked in a deep breath. *Don't call on me. Please. Don't let sixth grade start with kids watching, waiting for an answer, remembering all the times I haven't paid attention.* I stared at my page of All-School Rules, the numbers and letters blurring. Rruulee ##1: BBeeSaafe.

"You have to be good for the little kids to see," answered Annette Stuckey.

Thank you, Annette.

"That's right." Mr. Hudson walked to the back of the room and took a sip of water from the fountain. "As sixth graders, you are now the oldest students at Eola Hills Grade School. You set examples for the rest of the school. Please take this responsibility seriously."

I slumped down in my chair. *You have to be good. You have to set examples. And—while you're at it—you have to be safe. Seriously. HA!* I crammed my pencil against the paper. *Snap!* The point flipped onto the desk, leaving flecks of black dust across Rule #2: Include Everyone.

Mr. Hudson cleared his throat. "I can't stress how important you are this year."

IMPORTANT. The pencil dust glowed and I brushed

(In case you're wondering why 6 is my favorite number, take a look at the circle part. It's like you're going round and round, which is okay if you're a clock, but if you're a person you'll get dizzy and sick and you gotta get out. That's what the curvy top is for — escape — and you fly away from all the bad stuff to something perfectly wonderful.)

"So what's the best thing about sixth grade?" Mr. Hudson was wandering between our desks.

"OUTDOOR SCHOOL!" we shouted.

"You got it!" He gave us two thumbs-up. "That means 'Boom Chicka Boom.'"

"And rappelling," said Brody Brinkman.

"Creek walks!" someone shouted.

"Tie-dyeing." "Campfires." "Ooga Booga."

"And," said Mr. Hudson, bending to eye level, getting all mysterious, "rattlesnakes," he hissed.

A few kids squealed and protested, but mostly we tried to act cool. "Tastes like chicken," said Peter Monroe.

"So," said Mr. Hudson, standing and crossing his arms, "this is the year that's finally come, after all those jogathons and candy bar and magazine sales. The year you've been waiting for. The week you've been waiting for. Nights sleeping beneath the moon and stars, listening to the crickets and coyotes, and coming home with unforgettable memories." He smiled like he had those memories himself. "This is also the year to be on your best behavior and try your hardest. Come next spring," he said, tapping the wall calendar, "if we decide a sixth grader hasn't been a good role model, he or she might not attend Outdoor School."

My ears rang: *role model, role model.* My heart pounded: *I'm going. I'm going.* I outlined Rule #4: **Have Fun.** I checked my watch — 8:44. YES. A double

CHAPTER 2

What's in a Name?

My official name is Hope Marie Elliot. My mother [illegible] Hope because it's a soap opera star's name and Marie for some singer, but Mom says I can't carry a tune to save my life. Sometimes Mom calls me Hopeless, which seems really weird. Does that mean I'm less than myself? Or not here at all?

My older brother, Tyler, calls me Hop, and if he wants my attention, it's HeyHop.

My father's name is Ryan Michael Elliot, but I don't know what he calls me. He never calls. Mom says he left us because I cried all the time when I was a baby.

I had colic: around-the-clock, 24-7 stomachache. Cry, cry, cry.

My mom's name is Darlene Delilah Elliot. Her big dream was to be an actress, but she had Tyler, then me (which she calls an accident), and then my dad left, so she couldn't go after her dream.

I'd rather be Hopeless than an accident, but that's still another problem to solve.

Even though Mom didn't become an actress, she still thinks she's going to be discovered, so she wears lots of makeup and crazy clothes. For example: high-heeled boots with jeans and a sweater that's too small. She keeps her hair long, partway down her back, and colors it blond, plus she wears these huge gold earrings, which you'd think would pull her ears off. She tells everyone to call her "D.D."

Mom probably could be a great actress because she's always rehearsing, especially at school things like the annual carnival. Last year she volunteered to call out bingo. "B 8," she breathed into the microphone. "B as in 'bathing beauty.'" She gazed across the lunch tables, flipped her hair back, and smiled into an invisible camera.

Everyone thinks she's amazing to work full time and do decorations for the '50s Sock Hop and plan the Spring Fling Talent Show and raise two kids all by her- [illegible] example: "Hope's been driving me nuts. She doesn't do anything I tell her. She's so *STUPID*."

By the time first grade arrived, Stupid Me was convinced I couldn't learn to read. But Mrs. Atkins was magical. She made sense out of all those alphabet letters and she made reading fun. Her book corner was piled with big pillows and stuffed animals and picture books with words I could figure out. And guess what? She read to her own kids every night. An Angel Mom.

I'll tell you my favorite name: Gabriela Feliciano. She's this amazing basketball player at Eola Hills High and her name's in the paper all the time. Doesn't it look pretty? All the high letters mixed with the low ones and the dots on all the *iii*'s looking like candles? It sounds pretty, too. Sometimes I say it out loud: *Gabriela Feliciano.* And, she's as beautiful as her name, with shiny, black, wavy hair pulled back from her face, plus thick, black eyebrows. The best part is she's always so happy. She has this big, glowy smile on her face. Even her dark eyes are happy. She probably doesn't have problems to solve. I bet no one calls her *STUPID*.

CHAPTER 3

Angels and Stars

and clanged as a bunch of Blue Eyes got up and glanced around at each other.

"This is just an experiment, but I want you to take it seriously and to focus on your reactions." Mr. Hudson took a piece of paper from his desk. "There are to be no comments as I read an announcement from the Yamhill County Commission on Youth Safety."

He cleared his throat. "From this day forward, no one with blue eyes may attend movies on the weekends, stay out past seven in the evening, shop at gas station convenience stores, or use skateboards on any public property."

Blue Eyes raised their brows, frowned, opened their mouths, and swallowed their words. Brody Brinkman rolled his very pale blue eyes and crossed his arms; Jessica Dobie bent to tie her shoe, muttering something about *insane.*

Mr. Hudson addressed the Seated Ones. "How do you feel about the Commission's announcement?"

"Why only kids with blue eyes?" asked Annette Stuckey. "That doesn't make sense."

"Yeah, like Brody is some gangster," said Justin Thayer. "You go, Bro."

Complaints flew: "Not fair." "Rip-off." "It stinks."

"This isn't for real, is it, Mr. H?" said Noelle Laslett.

My chest tightened and my skin tingled hot. But I should be okay. I had brown eyes.

"Blue Eyes, you may sit down." Mr. Hudson kept his serious voice.

Another round of restless chairs and grumbles.

"Okay. How do you feel, Blue Eyes?" Mr. Hudson went to the whiteboard.

"Are we allowed to talk now?" Peter Monroe shot back.

[illegible] Hudson, marker in hand.

[illegible]

Mr. Hudson wrote con[illegible]

"Yeah, a lot more than *confused*," said Peter, his voice rising, "but I can't say it in school except it starts with a *p* and rhymes with *missed*."

We choked back uneasy laughs as Mr. Hudson wrote *missed*. "More feelings," he said.

Annette raised her hand. "It's scary. Kids won't do it and there'll be fights and people getting hurt."

Scared went on the board. "Maybe there will be policemen watching," said Mr. Hudson, "guarding, checking IDs, arresting disobedient Blue Eyes."

"No way!" Justin practically jumped out of his seat.

"Come on, Mr. H, what's going on? This kind of thing doesn't happen here in Oregon, in the United States of America."

Mr. Hudson wrote *disbelief* and *trusting*. "I appreciate your heartfelt responses. To reassure those who didn't listen carefully, this is an *experiment* in this classroom — not in Yamhill County." He walked over to his desk and picked up a book. "This, however, was *not* a fictitious experiment." He turned a few pages, then began reading:

> After May 1940 good times rapidly fled: first the war, then the capitulation, followed by the arrival of the Germans, which is when the sufferings of us Jews really began. Anti-Jewish decrees followed each other in quick succession. Jews must wear a yellow star, Jews must hand in their bicycles, Jews are banned from trams and are forbidden to drive. Jews are only allowed to do their shopping between three and five o'clock and then only in shops which bear the placard 'Jewish shop.' Jews must be indoors by eight o'clock and cannot even sit in their own gardens after that hour. Jews are forbidden to visit theaters, cinemas, and other places of entertainment. Jews may not take part in public sports. Swimming baths,

> tennis courts, hockey fields, and other sports grounds are all prohibited to them. Jews may not visit Christians. Jews must go to Jewish schools. . . .

[illegible] book and looked out the win- [illegible]

[illegible] cover. A black-and [illegible] dark hair, deep-set eyes (were they blue?), and a [illegible] smile looking at our class. *Anne Frank: The Diary of a Young Girl.*

"This is the famous diary of a girl just about your age, who lived in hiding for two years, fearful of discovery by the German Nazis, who moved past rules and restrictions to removing Jews from their homes, placing them in ghettos, slave-labor camps, and death camps."

Mr. Hudson's voice had softened until he practically whispered *death camps.* "To begin our unit on European history, we are going to study the Holocaust, a very serious time in world history when human beings did horrific, inhumane things. No, there isn't a County Commission on Youth Safety, but maybe there's something less obvious lurking out there. More than anything, I want you to watch for prejudices in our lives today, compare them to events of the Holocaust, and observe how unspoken attitudes grow into a loud, collective voice."

He looked at us for a moment, letting the words sink in. "You are excused, now, to the library to get your own copy of Anne Frank's diary. Please study all the introductory photos and read to September 29, 1942, by Monday."

After checking out my book, I headed for Noelle and Jessica, but my steps slowed as I glanced at the cover, at Anne Frank's bright, unsuspecting eyes. *May not. Must. Only. Banned.* Mr. Hudson's words echoed in my ears. *Forbidden. Lived in hiding. Suffering.* My heart pounded faster, louder. Surely everyone could hear. I took a deep breath. It wasn't enough. Another breath and my legs and arms went limp. *I told you. You never listen.* A different voice now. *You're a pathetic loser.* My head spun in confusion. *Hopeless.* A woman's voice. *Helpless. Clueless.* My mother's voice! But why now? In the school library? And why did the sound of her voice make me sick? Could eleven-year-olds have heart at- [illegible] lowed my shaking body. I sat there, eyes closed, head spinning, the drumbeats in my ears slowly fading and my body sighing. Something nudged my arm and I cracked one eye open, expecting to see, of all people, my mother standing there, pointing her finger at me, telling me to *shape up or ship out.*

Instead, it was the half-free body of a mashed teddy bear. I rocked to one side, pulled him out, and allowed my arms to wrap around his fat chest, my head melting into his fuzzy, thick neck.

I'd made my way to the kiddie corner, empty and

quiet. Something hard jabbed my other side. Now what? I pulled out a picture book with pale blue stars and a big full moon, orange dancing flames in a black fireplace, and a cow jumping through the night sky. *Goodnight Moon,* sang the bright yellow letters. "In the great green room," I whispered to Bear, pulling him closer; turning the pages; floating on words about mittens and kittens, clocks and socks; stirring my first *Goodnight Moon* memory: Annette's sixth birthday and my first slumber party. I was so excited to be invited, to play games, eat cake, and sleep on the floor. But the best part was the bedtime story. Annette's mother sat on the sofa with Annette on her lap. A couple kids were cross-legged on the floor, one girl was on the sofa next to Annette's mom, and I was on the other side.

"Let's snuggle," said Mrs. Stuckey, hugging Annette. I inched closer and felt her mother's warm body next to mine. She began reading *Goodnight Moon* in a sparkly voice, stopping to show us the pictures and letting us find the mouse. She leaned forward and put her finger on her lips to whisper "hush." Then she slipped her arm around my shoulder, letting Annette turn the pages. An Angel Mom.

"Mr. Hudson's class — return to your room, please," came our librarian's voice. Kids jumped up, chairs [illegible] quietly." I gave Bear a tight [illegible]

[illegible]

That night I sat in bed, my lamp sending shadows around the room. I stared at the words I'd just read in Anne Frank's diary; honest, regretful words about her friends only having fun and joking, like they were stuck in one spot and could never get closer.

I thought of Noelle and Jessica and our conversations about school and teachers, music and movies. But what about deep, serious thoughts? I should have some by now. Shouldn't I? My only thoughts were getting through each day and staying out of trouble. *And* going to Outdoor School! That was enough. For now.

I crawled out of bed to the jumble of stuffed animals in the corner by my closet and chose my yellow and green turtle. She joined me back in bed, sitting on my lap, gazing at my bedroom walls — a dough map of Oregon with half of Mount Hood broken off, my Jefferson County mural from fourth grade, a poster of a sunflower, and my first-grade star chart. The shiny stars — for keeping my school desk clean, remembering my homework, walking in line to the cafeteria, and being a good listener at circle time — marched across the paper.

When Mrs. Atkins gave me my chart at the end of the year, she said, "Good job, Hope. Keep it up." I suppose she meant keep up the good work, but maybe she meant keep the chart up on my wall. I don't know for sure, but I do know it still makes me proud to see all those silver and gold and purple stars.

"Goodnight, stars," I said, smiling at the silliness. "Goodnight, map. Goodnight, Turtle, on my lap." Ha! Not bad. I closed my book and turned out my light. "Goodnight, Anne," I whispered, respecting the silence of her hiding.

CHAPTER 4

Stupid

[illegible]

birthday" at break[illegible]

with gold glitter and pink sequins.

"That's very sweet, Hope. Thank you, darling." She smiled, planted a kiss on my cheek, and put the card on the fridge with a heavy-duty magnet and a sigh.

"Happy over the hill," said Tyler, dropping bread into the toaster.

Mom eyed him. "Not funny." She sat down at the table with another, louder sigh.

I poured a bowl of cereal and whispered to Tyler, "What's *over the hill?*"

"You're anciently old," he whispered back. "It's all

downhill, one foot in the grave." His toast popped up. "It's a joke." Then he raised his voice. "But not everyone can take a joke."

Mom ignored him. She pulled something out of her bathrobe pocket and flicked a lighter. A cigarette! I'd never seen my mother smoke. Maybe it was a fortieth-birthday thing. *Over the hill* with a cigarette. I stood there staring as she sat there smoking and looking out the window.

So I ate my cereal, Tyler ate his toast, and we exchanged glances while Mom smoked *another* cigarette. I guess I couldn't blame her if she wasn't feeling so hot. I mean, 40 isn't exactly a great number. The 4 looks like it can't decide which way it wants to go and the 0 is that circle business again.

I put the Wheaties and the jug of milk away, made my bed, brushed my teeth, and was heading for the bus —

"Hope Marie Elliot! COME HERE RIGHT NOW!"

I froze. My heart sank. My brain raced for a defense, but what was there to defend? Mom always liked the beginning of a new school year. Back to a routine, she said every September. And I'd been role modeling like crazy, smiling and saying hi to the fifth graders, keeping my room picked up and my radio turned down. There'd even been good numbers: 6:42 when I went to the [illegible]

rhythm of my life. Good, then bad. High, then low. Cautious, then careless. As I returned to the kitchen, my entire body hit high alert, braced for the changing tide. The tidal wave.

Mom leaned against the sink, arms crossed, jaw clenched, eyes locked on mine, eyebrows raised, aimed, ready to fire.

"What do you see on the table?"

Warning. Trick question. Warning. Mind to mouth: Take your time. Get it right. Be sure. "Place mats . . . newspaper . . . jam . . . salt and pepper . . ."

"Don't be smart with me, young lady." Her finger stabbed the air in time with the sharp words. "You are so damn stupid. You know exactly what I'm talking about."

My mind whirled faster and faster like one of those carnival rides, spinning, twisting, turning upside down. I held my breath. Heat throbbed up my face and down my neck. If I knew exactly what she was talking about, why didn't I know the answer?

Maybe I should just give up, surrender. *Mind to eyes: sad, sorry, will never do it again.* I stared at the white puddle resting undisturbed in the bottom of my cereal bowl. What would it be like to float in a pool of silky, cool milk, gazing up at —

"You dumb shit! I am not the goddamned maid!" Mom snatched the bowl, milk slopping over the rim and down her bathrobe. "I have picked up after you for eleven lousy years. I'm sick and tired of it. You don't appreciate a single thing I do. You never listen. Get out! Get outta my sight! GET!"

Think Happy Thoughts. That's hard to do when you're sitting in the principal's office, but that's what the framed sign said, stitched in red and blue *X*s.

I wondered if principals had happy thoughts. At least Mrs. Piersma had a happy office: flowery wallpaper, a [illegible]

I took a deep breath and sat back in the soft chair. With the door closed, I could barely hear office voices — probably Mrs. Piersma telling the secretary my mom would be coming soon.

I shuddered. Of all days. I'd already made her mad. Forgetting my cereal bowl! How stupid was that? How could I have missed it? Probably laughing at one of Tyler's jokes. Now she had to come to the principal's office and do her acting thing. Thank goodness she had the day off and was going out to lunch with her old high school friend, Lydia Bishop. Or, maybe that wasn't such a good thing. I didn't know anymore.

Now the principal's door opened and Mrs. Piersma walked in. She closed the door and smiled. Her red lipstick matched her earrings. "It's good to see you, Hope. How are you doing?"

I shrugged and looked down at the carpet (no flowers).

"Am I kicked off the bus?"

Mrs. Piersma pulled a chair next to mine and sat down as if we were going to have a friendly little chat. She smiled again, like a grandmother smiles at her grandbaby.

"You know, Hope, about our zero-tolerance bus behavior?"

I nodded. But did she have to call Mom?

"I'm afraid you're not going to be able to ride for a week. Can your mother bring you to school?"

I cringed, knowing Mom's reaction: "Hope is such an inconvenience," like I was some 7-Eleven store that had closed at ten.

"So," said Mrs. Piersma, trying to sound all cheery, "how does it feel to be a sixth grader?"

"Okay," I muttered.

"And you have Outdoor School next spring. I bet [illegible] to that."

[illegible]

gripped the chair. [illegible] eyes nailed mine.

My head jerked back.

Mrs. Piersma stood up and offered her a seat, but Mom didn't move, her fists mashed into her hips. "Hope is so damn irresponsible. What did the little brat do *this* time?"

"Ms. Elliot," said Mrs. Piersma, lowering her voice, "I understand you're upset, but could you please refrain from swearing in the school?" Mrs. Piersma stood taller and straighter, like she was guarding Eola Hills Grade School.

I sat there, mouth open, eyeballs jumping back and forth, waiting for a fight.

Mom suddenly smiled sweetly, sat down, and folded her hands in her lap. "Excuse me, Mrs. Piersma," she said very businesslike. "It's my birthday today and I've got a lot on my mind. Could you please tell me again why Hope is in trouble?" She gave me a fake smile. "Can't Hope cope?"

Breakfast threatened my throat.

Mrs. Piersma spoke carefully. "I'm sure Hope didn't mean what she said on the bus. She has apologized to the girl and she'll be doing some cleanup work around the school. But she won't be able to ride the bus for a week."

"What in the world did you say, Hope?" I felt my mother's hot glare as I stared at *Think Happy Thoughts.* I tried thinking bad thoughts, about something happening to Mom, but it didn't make me feel better, just sad. I mean, there were some good times.

"Hope Marie." There. Just like that. A gentle voice, a soft hint of care. A happy flash. I longed to stay with my mother in that very moment, in Mrs. Piersma's office, forever.

I closed my eyes. "I called Danielle Moffat a 'dumb shit.'"

"Oh." It came out a relieved *oh.* My eyes opened.

[illegible]

"I'm sorry, Mrs. Elliot, but this is school policy."

Mom's face turned as hard as those presidents' faces carved in cliffs. She stood up. "Then Hope will just have to walk."

CHAPTER 5

Life Is Crazy

[illegible] stared at the [illegible] or at the windy showers of dried-up maple leaves. What a relief when Mr. Hudson pulled down the blinds and centered the TV/VCR in front of the room. Good, I could go to sleep.

Mr. Hudson held up the video cover. *Life Is Beautiful,* it said on it, with a man, lady, and little boy, all laughing and smiling. "This is the story of a Jewish father's daring imagination and quick thinking to protect his young son from racism and save him from the Nazi gas chambers."

He slipped the movie into the player. "How many of you have seen a foreign film?"

Silence.

"Okay. This is how it works. The actors will be speaking in Italian, but their words will appear in English at the bottom of the screen."

"Like you were deaf?" asked Katie Shelton.

Mr. Hudson nodded. "Yes, Katie, like closed-captioned TV."

"So we have to read?" Justin Thayer winced. "*While* we're watching the movie?"

"*And* write," said Mr. Hudson. "In the first part of the movie look for two signs of racism, and in the second part look for three survival strategies."

Darn. So much for my nap.

"Survival strategies?" Justin asked again.

"You know what a strategy is, don't you?" said Mr. Hudson.

"Like in basketball," said Brody. "We have offense and defense strategies."

"Right," said Mr. Hudson. "A plan. A means to reach your goal. And survival?"

"How you're going to live through something," said Brody.

"Right, again."

[illegible]

the craziness, the sadness, and the tragedy."

I had my paper on my desk and pencil in hand, ready to find the answers, but both were soon forgotten as I fell into a rhythm, listening to the Italian dialogue, reading the English subtitles, and trying to keep up with this guy named Guido who's always cracking jokes and doing wild things to make people smile or laugh.

One time he pokes fun at the Race Manifesto, which declares non-Jewish Italians are of a superior race. Before you know it, Guido is taking off his clothes, down to his underwear, and he pulls up his T-shirt, saying that Italians have great belly buttons.

Funny Guido marries sweet Dora and they have a little boy, Joshua. It seems the perfect life in this small Italian town, with sunny days and flowers and Guido always teasing and laughing with Dora and Joshua.

But I found my stomach tightening, sensing things were about to change. Just like for Anne Frank.

The little signs, like Mr. Hudson said, began showing up. Like the Nazi soldiers, marching down the streets. And a poster in the bakery: "No Jews or dogs allowed."

All of a sudden, Guido and Joshua are forced onto a Nazi army truck and hauled off to a train station. Guido tells his son they're going on a trip for Joshua's birthday, and they're so lucky because they got the last tickets for the train and they *get* to stand real close together because trains don't have seats.

But I knew different. I knew by now those trains led to a nightmare — the German concentration camps. I sat there in my safe classroom, so worried for Joshua, who had no idea that people hated him and wanted to kill him just because he was Jewish. *Get off the train!* I desperately wanted to warn them. *Run! Hide! Before it's too late!*

Then, out of nowhere, comes Dora, all dressed up [illegible] They finally let her climb into one of the packed box-cars. Joshua sees her through the metal grille of a nearby car and cries out, "They stopped the train to let Mama get on!"

When they reach the Nazi concentration camp, Guido tells Joshua they're playing a game and if they win, they get first prize. "What is it?" asks Joshua. Guido names Joshua's favorite toy, an army tank. "But I already have one," Joshua replies.

"A real one," Guido quickly responds, and explains the rules. They must accumulate one thousand points by not asking for a snack or wanting to see Mommy, or crying to go home. A plain piece of bread with no jam is worth sixty points.

"Is sixty points a lot?" asks Joshua. "It sure is," says his father. "And if you stay hidden all day it's a hundred and twenty points."

Every time I feared for Joshua's life, his father came up with a clever plan. Every time Joshua questioned the game or repeated horrible rumors, Guido zipped out a perfect answer or awarded more points.

Thank you, I thought, wishing Guido could hear me. *You are an amazing father.*

At the end of the movie, the United States Army is coming and the Germans are madly pushing Jewish prisoners into trucks, hoping to get rid of a few more loads. Guido is frantic. He quickly hides Joshua, urging him not to come out of the small cupboard, telling him they've earned a thousand points and they've won the grand prize, the tank. Then he's off again, disguised as a woman, racing to find Dora, madly searching, calling, then shouting at her to escape from the departing truck. As he's warning her, he is discovered and captured. A Nazi soldier marches him to a nearby alley. They disappear into darkness.

A gun fires.

[illegible]

comes around the corner and Joshua's eyes grow huge. "It's true!" he says. The tank stops right in front of him and out pops an army guy speaking English. "Want a ride?" he asks Joshua.

Everyone in the classroom started clapping. My throat tightened and my eyes blurred.

As the tank follows the road lined with departing prisoners, Joshua spots his mother in the crowd. "Mama!" he cries, and the soldier lowers him into his mother's arms. They sit alongside the road, hugging and kissing. "We won!" Joshua announces. "We came in first!" Then a man's voice tells us: "This is my story. This is the sacrifice my father made. This was his gift to me."

I shivered and realized Mr. Hudson had turned off the TV. The room was still dark but I could see him leaning against the TV cart, his head bent. My nose dripped but I didn't move to wipe it. Someone sniffled, sighed. A cough.

"I'm sorry." Mr. Hudson gently touched the silence. "I didn't plan this very well." He glanced at the clock. "The bell is about to ring and something this serious deserves more time. You'll probably feel a little strange going home with kids who have no clue what you just went through. Stay focused, if you can; try to remember what you saw; let it sink in; think about the questions; talk with your parents, as they allowed you to see this film."

The bell rang but no one moved.

Slowly, one by one, kids began shuffling their chairs and standing up.

Someone turned on the lights. I squinted and met Noelle's watery eyes. Justin walked to the door staring at the floor. I didn't want to go home; I wanted to rewind the film and stop at a happy spot, before all the hurting and pain.

ER 6

Next to New

[illegible]

trudged away from sc[illegible]

get wet in my backpack. Not that I had miles to g[illegible]

it was a good fifteen- to twenty-minute fast walk. I wasn't in any fast mood, though. Not after that movie. I kept thinking about Joshua and his mother and what I'd give for that kind of reunion. I could still hear his excited voice: "MAMA!" Maybe my mother would miss me if I was lost in the woods or held hostage in a bank robbery. "HOPE!" she'd shout as I raced into her arms.

I'd just passed Eola Hills Pizza and Coastal Bank, staying dry beneath their awnings, when I saw the boots.

They were purple. Well, mostly purple, with some brown and green designs. The bottoms were thick black rubber. There I stood, nose pressed to the window, my breath washing the cold glass, my heart craving those beautiful boots.

I barely noticed the yellow ski jacket and red backpack in the Next to New display. Actually, I'd barely noticed the store before. Mom said she'd never set foot in one of those musty-smelling consignment shops, let alone in someone else's shoes. But these boots looked brand-new and I could just see myself in them at Outdoor School.

A bell jangled as I opened the door. I braced myself for knockdown body odor and an instant skin rash, but nothing happened.

The woman behind the cash register smiled.

"Could I try on the purple hiking boots?" I pointed to the window display.

I sat on a bench and slipped off my tennis shoes.

The woman handed me the boots. Her name tag said "*Anita* — Owner/Manager." I quickly put them on, winding the leather laces around the top hooks and tying a thick bow. Oh, man, did they feel great. I stood and looked at Anita. She pushed her glasses into her orangish hair, examined my feet, and announced,

[illegible]

dresses, pants, [illegible] gowns. I stole glances into the full-length mirrors, [illegible] not to smile at cool me, taller me.

I bent over to check the price and wished I hadn't: $14. All I had was $5.45 sitting in a glass jar in my top dresser drawer.

I hiked over to Anita, now laughing and sorting through a pile of clothes with another name-tagged lady: "*Ruthie* — Asst. Manager."

"How do you pay for things here?" I asked. "I mean, can I put these on layaway?"

Ruthie inspected my feet. "You can pay for those

gorgeous boots by letting us sell your nice, outgrown clothes." She handed me a flyer: *Welcome. We're pleased you want to be part of our clothing family. Here's how it works.*

I was to wash and iron my clothes, place them on hangers, and bring them to the store. I'd receive forty percent of the selling price. My mind shot through my closet and drawers. Jeans, too small. T-shirt with teddy bears and valentines, too babyish. There was a lot of stuff crammed in the back of my drawers and under my bed.

"To hold the boots," said Anita, as if we were about to close a big business deal, "you'd need to give us twenty percent of the price. That would be two dollars and eighty cents."

"No problem. I've got that at home. I'll bring it right back. Please don't sell them while I'm gone."

As I tugged the boots off, she added, "The rest needs to be paid in two weeks."

Two weeks!

"Otherwise," she added, "you lose your down payment."

"How soon will my clothes sell?"

She shrugged. "You never know, but bring in winter clothes now and save your spring and summer things

[illegible]

ing against the streetlight, I felt my heart throbbing in my neck. It was a good throbbing, though, not a bad throbbing like in Mrs. Piersma's office that morning. But she'd been extra nice after Mom had left. "Are you okay?" she'd asked, handing me two pieces of candy.

"Yeah," I'd said, stuffing them in my pants pocket. *I could live here in your office, eat peppermint candies, and have happy thoughts. I'd never have to ride the bus again and I'd always be on time.*

"Come visit me again, Hope," said Mrs. Piersma, "just for fun."

Since when did you visit the principal *just for fun*? And why did she sound more sad than happy?

The sky had turned dark now with another rain cloud. Car headlights glowed in the road spray. I shivered and started jogging again. Better get home before Mom. Not that I was doing anything wrong, but there were always questions and she definitely wouldn't like the Next to New business. I'd have to hear all the reasons why I shouldn't even open their door.

My heart sank as I turned up our driveway and saw Mom's car in the garage. I fumbled in my pocket for a peppermint.

"Where have you been?" Mom stood in front of the open refrigerator, her back to me.

"I had to walk, *remember*?" I knew it was smarty to remind her, but I couldn't help it. My feet were freezing.

She jerked around, a plastic bottle of mustard in her hand, the nozzle pointed at me. I could imagine mustard splattering all over me and the kitchen and I couldn't help smiling.

"Wipe that nasty smirk off your face right this instant." She shook the bottle at me. "Your punishment was to stay in your room tomorrow. Now it's the *whole* [illegible]

"Don't argue."

"I'm not. Can't I come out at all?"

"You can go to the bathroom and eat in the kitchen. That's it."

"What about the laundry room? I gotta wash my clothes."

"So wash them."

"And dry."

"FINE."

"Iron?"

"SHUT your stupid mouth UP!" She slammed the mustard on the table. "God, girl, you really know how to push. Get out of here — right now."

My boots! I had to tell Anita I wasn't coming back. "Just one phone call."

"No calls."

I went to my room and fell onto my bed, my cold bare feet sticky against the comforter. *Shut up! Shut up! Shut up!* I said the words out loud, face crammed into my pillow, but my entire body ached to scream them as loud as my voice could carry them; right out my door, down the hall, into my mother's face. Why not? She said them to me.

CHAPTER 7

A Secret Place

[illegible]

black night. Rain splattered ag[illegible]

air slipped past the rattling wood frame. Maybe I should just open the window, slip out, and find a new life. It was an exciting thought, a huge relief, but one that should have a plan. Besides, I'd had enough wet feet for a while and I did have plans — not big ones like running away, but busy ones to keep my mind off Mom and the purple boots.

Plan A: Change into Dry Clothes. Sweats and slippers.

Plan B: Clothes for Next to New. I opened my dresser drawers one by one, took everything out, and laid them on my bed according to: 1) Save for me 2) Sell at Next to New 3) Give to Goodwill. Underwear, T-shirts, jeans, shorts, socks. Some of the stuff, like my rainbow pajamas, I hadn't worn in years.

I did the same thing with my closet clothes, getting rid of little-girl dresses, short skirts, blouses that untucked, wornout belts, and outgrown shoes. One final place: under my bed. Ugh. Scrunched clothes smothered in dust bunnies.

I like our laundry room. It's small and tidy — shelves for soap and bleach; baskets for ironing, mending, and rags; drawers with sewing supplies and wrapping paper. When I close the door and turn on the ceiling fan, I feel like I'm in charge: full load, one scoop soap, hot wash, cold rinse, extra spin. Check, check, check. All systems go.

I pushed *Start*. Water rushed against the metal tub. The laundry room echoed with a chorus of hum, drum, whirl.

Now I was in a cleaning mood. Without being told, I gathered rags, paper towels, Endust, and Windex, and headed back to my bedroom prison. Starting with my dresser, I went around the room spraying and wiping furniture, windows, and the mirrors on my closet sliding door. I even dusted my stuffed animals.

[illegible] out and cleaning [illegible] and normal.

With my next trip to the laundry room, I brought back extra blankets, a pillow and pillowcase. I stretched my bedside lamp into the closet and arranged the bedding in there. I lined all my stuffed animals along the back. Then I taped a newspaper picture of Gabriela Feliciano to the wall. Turtle sat on top of my pillow, and Anne Frank's diary lay on the blanket.

"Dinner's ready." Mom's voice approached. I jumped out of the closet and shut the door just in time. The bedroom door swung open and she examined the piles on my bed.

"I — I decided to wash everything," I said, avoiding her eyes.

"That'll keep you busy this weekend. You can do mine when you're done." She laughed like it was a joke. "Seriously, Hope, your room looks great."

My eyes shot to hers. Yes, they *were* smiling, along with her mouth. Wow. My face heated and I tried not to smile back, but I couldn't help it. Now maybe she'd visit every day and tell me — in a light, sunny voice — "Hope, your room looks great. You look great. You have great ears and a great nose and eyebrows and —"

"Wash your hands. They're filthy."

We sat across the table from each other, eating spaghetti. Flowers and a funny birthday card decorated Tyler's place. He'd given them to Mom, wished her happy birthday, then left for Egan McGowan's for the night. Smart guy.

Mom looked relaxed in her baggy Detroit Lions sweatshirt and flannel pj bottoms, no earrings, hair pulled back into a ponytail, makeup washed off.

She let out a huge sigh. "I can't tell you how stressed I am."

I concentrated on twirling noodles around my fork.

"I race off to work, put in a long day, stop by the gro- [illegible] you two to do homework, [illegible] ing to you."

I looked.

"Repeat my last sentence."

I hate the listening test. It always comes when you're not listening. "Look at me when I'm talking to you," I said, immediately regretting the wrong answer.

Mom's mouth tightened and I imagined a rattlesnake's tongue flicking out of her mouth, ready to strike. She dropped her fork into her spaghetti, crossed her arms on the table, and glared.

I felt the prick of tears but fought them back. As a little girl, I'd cried at my mother's angry face and stabbing words, but over the years I've tried to block them from my ears and from my gut, where they turned to inside tears. It doesn't always work, though. I just wished I understood how she could be so nice one minute and so angry the next — like she was two different people.

"My advice to you, young lady," Mom said, with her fork pointing at me, "don't get married and don't have kids."

With that bit of wisdom stuck in my brain and French bread stuck in my teeth, I returned to the laundry room. I plodded through another wash/dry cycle, folded clothes that were staying, sacked Goodwill stuff, and hung out clothes to iron. When I crawled into my closet that night, I was exhausted, but not so wiped out as to miss the sweet peacefulness drifting down . . . floating across my bed, my pillow, Turtle, and me. There, in my narrow, dark closet, with the sliding door barely opened, I felt strangely safe and happy. I hugged Turtle, settled into my pillow, and thought about my purple hiking boots. I could see the heavy, thick soles; I could smell the outdoors; and I crossed my fingers they'd still be there Monday.

CHAPTER 8

Number the Stars

[illegible] one of us having [illegible] straight up, into the uneven shadows of dresses, skirts, blouses, and pants. After all that sorting, washing, and cleaning business yesterday, these leftover clothes seemed like old friends.

Mom was still asleep and Tyler was still at Egan's. I like having breakfast by myself. I can fix whatever I want without anyone eyeing my every move, telling me I shouldn't cook the eggs so long or that I should toast the bread longer. That morning I made fluffy scrambled eggs, golden brown toast, and a pitcher of orange juice. When I was done eating, I cleared the table, put everything away, loaded my dishes in the dishwasher, and wiped sticky juice drops off the floor. Surely Mom would notice how clean I'd left things and then she'd drop the rest of my punishment.

I started another load of laundry and was folding clothes when Mom opened my bedroom door. "Don't ever take the last eggs. Someone else might want them, too, you know." I started to tell her about cleaning up, but she slammed the door. I opened it after her. "Can I iron in front of the TV?"

"No."

"Why not?"

She spun around. BIG SIGH. "Today is Saturday. I've worked hard all week and I need at least one day of peace and quiet. So don't bug me or I'll make it two weekends."

I closed the door, leaned against it, and inspected my room — the walls, the window, my swivel chair, desk, and star chart. Five hundred stars. That's what this punishment should be worth. I closed my eyes and imagined myself flying like a bird, free to go wherever I wanted, high above snowy mountains or skimming low across the ocean to a tropical island with palm trees and pineapples. Or into a sparkling night sky, dancing from star to star, making my own pattern: the Hope [illegible]

[illegible] he created the [illegible] the real army tank.

Problem Solve: I needed a distraction. And a prize. I deserved a prize for all the hours in this room. A prize for my mother's sighing and glaring, for "stupid," "brat," and "dumb shit."

That's when it hit — a great idea, a great distraction. I hurried to my desk and looked through the drawers, finding a little spiral notebook with a black Lab puppy on the front. On the first page I wrote "HOPE'S POINT SYSTEM." After lots of writing, crossing out, erasing, and rewriting, this is what came out:

FB = Feel Bad	20–150 Points
G = Grab	25 Points
SA = Sarcasm	35 Points
GL = Glare	40 Points
LO = Loser	50 Points
SH = Should	60 Points
HL = Hopeless	75 Points
LA = Laughed At	75 Points
B = Brat	85 Points
DS = Dumb Shit	100 Points
I = Interrupt	100 Points
SW = Swear Word	150 Points
S = Stupid	200 Points

Now I needed a prize, but not an army tank. I'd have to think about it.

Any thoughts about prizes disappeared the rest of the day as I read *Anne Frank: The Diary of a Young Girl.* I couldn't believe my eyes when I read the mean things people in hiding said to her. Check this out: "Am I really so bad-mannered, conceited, headstrong, pushing, stupid, lazy, etc., etc., as they all say? . . . Kitty, if only you knew how I sometimes boil under so many gibes and jeers. And I don't know how long I shall be able to stifle my rage. I shall just blow up one day."

It felt strange that someone so long ago could have had the same feelings I had. Anne needed a point sys- [illegible]

CHAPTER 9

Plans into Action

[illegible]

all the clothes I planned to keep. I'd discovered clothes I hadn't worn for a long time but still fit me, like a white blouse with glittery stars on the pocket and a pair of black jeans I didn't like before, but now I do. It was fun to think about wearing something different for a change.

I poked into the living room where Mom and Tyler were watching a football game. "Do you guys have any extra hangers?"

"In my closet," said Mom, her eyes glued to the TV.

"You can iron my stuff." Tyler tossed me his spongy football.

I threw it back, hitting his head, and stuck out my tongue. "Forget it."

"Careful, Missy," said Mom.

"Of what?" As soon as I'd said it, I knew I'd gone too far. WHY did I do that??? WHY did I push???

"Hope Marie." Firm but not a raised voice. Whew. Just a warning. But she GLARED. Yes! My first 40 points!

"I'm going." I practically skipped down the hall to her room, grinning like I'd just won a contest.

When I reached her bedroom door, I wasn't so excited. In fact, this was pretty stupid. Why would I want to win an arguing contest with my mom? It always made things worse. Yet, there was something itching inside me, scratching to get out, to stir her up, and I let it happen.

Problem Solve: Points for Not Talking Back. NTB: 50 Points. Just think, if I'd bitten my tongue on the bus, I wouldn't be a weekend prisoner.

Mom's closet door stood open like someone's mouth showing off a mishmash of partly chewed food. Mixed-up shoes spilled into the room; dresses hung lopsided; her bathrobe, nightgown, and last week's pants over-loaded the door hook; and a mountain of dirty clothes [illegible]

dresser. There she was, in that silver-framed photo, wearing the same blue-and-white-checkered sundress. Holding me. Brand New Me wrapped in a baby blanket. Just home from the hospital, she'd told me. She was smiling. Not a pretend actress smile. She looked like she was really happy to have me.

I dropped the empty hangers on the floor and slowly sat down on her unmade bed. Still hugging the check-ered dress, I snuggled under her sheet and blanket, nestling my head in her pillow, smelling her hair. I closed my eyes and tried to imagine my mother walking up to our house with me in her arms and Tyler running outside begging to see me, hold me. My throat tightened. Should I get points for not crying?

It was almost dinner and I was finally done. Everything was washed, ironed, hung up, or folded in dresser drawers.

I turned slowly in my swivel chair, surveying my room. The furniture glowed and the mirrors shined. But, now, without anything to do, I heard the silence. It moved slowly around my room, slipped along the walls, brushed across my arms, filled my ears, and gnawed my gut. Was this how it felt in prison? Was this how Anne Frank felt all those whispering, tiptoeing days in the "Secret Annexe"? It was a lonely silence shouting all the things you couldn't do, places you couldn't go.

Well, there's one thing you end up doing with a lot of silence — you think. You think about how life could be better and you make up little plans like getting a dog or cat to keep you company or having a best friend that tells you all her secrets. You put together big plans like running away, listing in your head the clothes you'll need, the kinds of food that won't smash or spoil, the backstreet route to the bus station; buying a ticket to [illegible]

[illegible] made me laugh with some funny story, imitating the teachers or lip-synching country-western singers. It's always been Tyler who's gotten me through the rough times with Mom. He's come to my rescue, teasing Mom out of her bad moods. Why she's nice to him, I don't know. Maybe she just likes boys better. Maybe he wasn't an accident.

Someone knocked on my door. "HeyHop! Let's go! Dinner!" Speaking of my brother.

I jumped up and whipped open my door.

"Out of my way!" I pushed him down the hall and stepped on his feet. He grabbed my arm and swung me into the kitchen.

"Enough, you two," said Mom, setting our plates on the table. Stew, tossed salad with apples and nuts, and corn bread. "Nice dinner, Mom." There. I meant it and you couldn't start an argument with that.

Mom smiled. "Thanks. I like weekends when I have time to cook." Good response.

Tyler was slurping down his stew.

"Where's the fire?" I asked.

He kicked my shin.

"Hey!"

"Okay," warned Mom.

I dipped my bread in the stew.

"Don't play with your food, Hope. Your manners are atrocious. You look like a baby eating with her fingers."

I glanced at Tyler.

"Why do you look at your brother when I'm talking to you?"

Oops. Forgot to be careful. My ears flashed hot.

Mom pointed her fork at Tyler and chuckled. "He's not going to help you out."

You're too late. He already has. Don't you remember Baby Me crying on the sofa and you yelling,

[illegible]

I set the dripping corn bread on my plate and stared at the microwave clock. 5:42. Maybe I should wait a minute for a better number. Until then, I'd calculate a few points: 20 for feeling bad, 75 for Mom laughing at me, and 50 for not talking back.

"Did you learn anything this weekend?" Mom asked.

I hesitated. "Yes."

"What?"

This was tricky. I could easily answer, *"I learned that you were once a Nazi prison guard."* Instead, for an additional 20 points, I spoke carefully. "I should keep my mouth shut most of the time . . . and . . . it takes half a box of Tide to wash everything in my room."

Her eyes pierced mine. I stopped breathing. *Funny, Mom, please think I'm funny.*

"Well," she said, all huffy, "just remember this weekend as you walk back and forth to school."

On an angry scale of one to ten, she was probably only a two, so I decided to try my luck. "Can I have my allowance? My room is perfectly clean."

"It means clean *all week*, Hope, not just one day. Plus, you need to do dishes *all* week, too, starting tonight."

"Tyler didn't have to do them last week, so why do I?"

"I —," started Tyler.

"He's in high school now, with lots of homework," Mom said, standing up, which meant the conversation was over.

"I have lots of homework, too."

"Don't whine, Hope," she said, walking out of the kitchen.

End of discussion. Turn your back and leave the room. Fifteen points.

Tyler silently cleared the table, stacking the plates and bowls in the sink. He even wiped off the table, then tossed the sponge in my face.

CHAPTER 10

#8726

[illegible]

store. I kept thinking about everything [illegible] up, and hid in my closet. I couldn't keep my mind on math; instead, I did my own figuring, adding what I'd make from my clothes and shoes, two belts, a stocking hat, and a pair of mittens.

"What were signs of hatred and intolerance toward the Jewish people?" Mr. Hudson's words made me feel guilty for counting my money, when Holocaust victims had everything taken from them. Once more I was inside *Life Is Beautiful* and the concentration camp, rooting for Joshua and his point system.

Brody remembered the sign in the bakery window and on Guido's bookstore door.

"Right," said Mr. Hudson, "but signs aren't always written. Like when daffodils bloom — they're a sign that spring is on the way."

"Like a clue," said Annette.

Mr. Hudson nodded. "What were some clues that the Jews were heading for trouble?"

"The Nazi soldiers marching into town?" said Peter.

"Yes," said Mr. Hudson. "And what about the two men taking Guido from his bookstore to see a city official?"

"Yeah," said Peter again, "and the one guy smashing his cigarette on Guido's window."

"Good observation, Peter. Now, if you could use only one word to say what this movie was about, what would it be?"

I heard "racism," "courage," "survival," "bravery," and "Holocaust." I thought of Guido's wife, Dora (*Principessa*, as he called her), who wasn't Jewish, who raced to the railway station and insisted on boarding the crowded boxcar. I thought of Guido, trying with all his might to save Joshua, to protect him from the horror and give him hope, and, in the end, sacrificing his [illegible] for his wife and son. My eyes watered as I saw [illegible] riding atop the army tank.

[illegible]

time [illegible]

"Love."

2:55. I dashed from the classroom, out the school doors, alongside buses, down the sidewalk, and past a zillion houses. Out of breath, I fumbled for the key in my backpack, jammed it into the lock, and flung open the door. Storming into my bedroom, I slammed on the brakes. I stood, frozen, staring.

My room. It looked awesome. For a moment, I sucked up all that tidiness, then announced: "100 points."

With my clothes on hangers slung over one arm and

a bag full of shoes and stuff on the other arm, I maneuvered back through the house, out the door, and down the sidewalk. Now my feet barely touched the ground. My body was light and airy. I watched cars pass and wondered if the drivers had any idea that I, Hope Elliot, was on a mission, that I was about to make a great business deal. I smiled.

Then panic hit. What if Mom came home early and saw me? Or someone told her I was hauling half the house away? I slowed my feet and my heart to a regular pace, my legs swish-swishing against the bag, but as soon as I spotted Next to New, my heart shot into double time. My eyes ached to see those purple hiking boots with the thick, black, sturdy soles. *Please, God, let them still be there.*

NO! They weren't in the window! Die. I was going to die.

Someone opened the PULL door for me, and I huffed and puffed my way back to the consignment counter.

Anita was sorting through a lady's resale clothes.

"Did you sell my purple hiking boots?" I blurted. "Sorry," I added as the lady looked at me with squinchy eyebrows. For a split second it seemed Anita didn't remember me or the boots or last Friday. *Remember.*

[illegible]

"Here, [illegible] clothes.

"I'm fine," I said, trying to look cool. The second Anita turned, I dropped my bag to the floor. *Oh, my arms!*

The lady left and Anita took my hanging bundle and arranged it on a tall clothes rack. "Now, let's set you up with an account." She clicked the computer mouse. "Name?"

"Hope Marie Elliot." I stood straight and tall, my feet tightly together, my hands at my sides, my eyes fixed on Anita's pumpkin earrings.

After entering my address and phone number, Anita asked, "If some of your clothes are stained or out of style or don't sell after a few months, would you like us to donate them to a local charity?"

I hadn't expected that question. I'd figured all my stuff would sell.

"The churches in town come by for —"

"Yeah," I cut her off, "it's okay."

While Anita typed, I glanced at my hanging clothes. I felt a strange mix of pride and sadness, saying good-bye to part of my life, a part that might live again on some little kid's head or feet. But how would I feel when I saw that bit of memory walking around town or on the playground? And just what kind of memory would it be?

Anita pulled a pen from her hair, now looking redder instead of oranger. She wrote on a small card. "Your membership number is 8726."

8726. A good number. Anita had even written my name in beautiful cursive lettering. It was official. I was a member. I even had a card to prove it. Did that mean

I could live at Next to New? Sleep in a changing room, curled up on the small bench, covered with —

"What about your down payment?"

I'd almost forgotten. I stuffed my hand in my jeans [illegible] pulled out two crumpled dollar bills plus [illegible] cans? Baby[illegible]

As if reading my mind, Anita said, "We have a Fifty-Fifty promotion going on right now." She held a bunch of narrow yellow papers. "Write your name on the back of these coupons and give them to all your friends and family. They'll get fifty percent off one item in the store and you'll receive fifty cents credit."

I nodded okay as I saw yellow coupons and shiny coins pouring from the sky, piling around me.

Anita set my purple boots on the counter. "I thought you'd like to see them — you know, visiting rights." She chuckled.

They looked beautiful. I picked them up and rubbed my hand across their tops and bottoms. I fingered the leather laces. I longed to put them on and wear them home. Setting them back on the counter, I smiled at Anita. It was time to earn money: $11.20.

CHAPTER 11

50-50 Club

[illegible] pop ca[illegible] when I discovered my key to the kitchen door still [illegible] in the lock and Mom not home yet.

I tried to hide my smile at dinner, working to look all sad about my life, but Tyler was telling funny stories about football practice and Mom was laughing.

My smile stopped when I returned to my bedroom and pulled out my Holocaust homework — a drawing of a concentration camp. I sharpened my colored pencils, not that there'd be much color in this. From Mr. Hudson's descriptions, I added sorting sheds where prisoners' belongings were divided into piles of clothes, shoes, jewelry, books, and toys. Using a ruler, I carefully drew the watchtowers and wooden fence, adding rolls of barbed wire to the top. I lined up prisoners for watery soup and the bathrooms. German soldiers marched with their stiff legs high in the air. Then I decided to put in something that probably wasn't there — a red rosebush — honoring all the Jewish prisoners who shed their blood. Maybe those poor Jews would have looked at that rosebush for hope. Maybe they would have given it a few spare drops of water, keeping it alive one more day. I think Anne Frank would have liked this; she was always looking for little things in her own hidden prison to be happy about, like a sliver of blue sky sneaking through a crack in the curtain or an extra ration of butter during the holidays.

The next morning I walked into the classroom wondering if my nervous heart was banging too loud. The Next to New yellow coupons were safe in a clear, zipped plastic bag, and I'd made a sign-up sheet with the title

"NEXT TO NEW SPECIAL COUPONS," using bright red and yellow markers. I'd even found a clipboard and tied a red pen to it with a piece of string.

But now what? Kids were still arriving, storing [illegible] checking the First Things First board. Jessica, [illegible] would suddenly appear, filling the empty spaces. I went all the way down the page, thirty lines. What was I thinking? What thirty people would want these coupons?

"What's that?" Annette stood next to my desk, pointing at the clipboard.

My chest grabbed, but I faked cool. "The Fifty-Fifty Club. Want to join?"

"How?"

I unzipped the plastic bag and took out one yellow coupon. "It's worth fifty percent off one thing at Next to New." I smoothed out my sign-up chart, knowing

Annette would love all the tidy lines and numbers. We used to play bank in kindergarten — she'd fill out the deposit slips and I'd run the cash register.

"If you want to join, sign your name on line number one."

"I don't know about Next to New," she said cautiously. "Isn't it just old, leftover clothes?" Her nose crinkled.

I pulled out the page of instructions. "It says they have to be in really good condition. I've seen the stuff — it's awesome. And fantastically low prices." I sounded like a car commercial.

Annette eyed the yellow coupon. "Well, I suppose it's okay. My mom loves half-off sales."

"Do you want to sign her up, too?"

She shrugged. "I guess." Annette picked up the red pen and carefully printed her name, and then her mother's on line two. I slipped one more coupon out of the bag, signed my name to the back of both, and handed them to Annette. Now she looked excited, probably because she had something to share with her mother. Before I could feel jealous or sad, Jessica and Lauren were standing there, rattling off questions, saying how they'd sold clothes at Next to New. Lines three and four, please.

"I love that store." It was Brody. My eyeballs practi- [illegible]

[illegible] made it a game when I was a little kid, searching for the best bargain. Now I go in sometimes just to find a sweet deal. I'll really make points when I tell her about this sale."

Before you could say "fifty percent off," Brody had a yellow coupon in one hand and a pen in the other. Line five, please.

CHAPTER 12

Surviving Should

mas. "What's all gone?"

"The coupons," I answered. A bunch of fourth grade girls at recess had gone crazy, dying to hold the clipboard and sign their names.

"Ah," she said, smiling. "What a saleswoman. Good job."

Good job. The words echoed in my ears as I looked around the store. Only a few customers at 3:16 on a Tuesday afternoon.

The bell above the door jangled and in walked Brody with his yellow coupon. That was fast. Maybe he really did love this place. He glanced around, then saw me and combed his fingers through his hair.

I leaned back against the counter.

He made his way to the rear of the store. "Hey," he said, dropping his backpack to the floor. "There was a Calvin Klein sweater here a few weeks ago, but" — he glanced toward Anita, who was busy tagging again — "it was too much money," he whispered.

I nodded.

"This helps." He held up the coupon. "I hope it's still here."

I nodded again. I felt like I should be directing him, but I had no idea where anything was, except for lay-away boots.

Brody picked up his backpack and gave a slight wave, then headed off toward the front corner.

"Do you have a few minutes to spare?" Anita handed me another stack of yellow discount coupons.

My mind clicked off the minutes: Tyler, football practice, home at 5:30. Mom, 5:45 if she stopped at the store. I checked the wall clock. 3:20. "Sure."

"I'm minus a gal today. How's your ironing?"

"Ironing? I thought everything came in ironed."

"We touch up special items — prom dresses, expensive shirts, whatever. The high school Homecoming dance is in a few weeks, so all the fancy clothes need [illegible]

The Next to New dresses were all shapes, lengths, sizes — a short, sparkly black dress with spaghetti straps; a red and green plaid crinkly skirt and matching blouse; a simple peach-colored long dress, almost like a nightgown; plus some silky pants and ruffly tops.

Now I wasn't so sure. I mean, I'd done piles of pants and shirts, but what if I put a huge iron hole through one of these gorgeous things? What if I had to pay for it? I sucked in a deep breath, blew it out, and spit on the iron. A low-heat iron should only produce a quiet sizzle, while high-heat spit makes snaps, crackles, and pops. Yup. Quiet sizzle. Good to go.

I arranged the black dress on the ironing board, wondering who had owned it and why they'd given it up. Like a ship, the iron glided across the flowing fabrics and I floated across a decorated gym. I saw myself in each dress as I pressed, smoothed, turned, hung, snapped, and zipped. Now all I needed were shoes, jewelry, and a date.

"Looks good." Anita poked her head in the doorway. She held up a yellow coupon and flipped it over, showing my name. "Calvin Klein sweater."

Five dollars for ironing and fifty cents from Brody's coupon. That left only $3.05 between my hiking boots and my feet.

I looked past Anita and scanned the store.

"He left a few minutes ago," she said.

Warm, warmer, warmest. (My ears.)

"He's nice." Anita flipped off the light in the storage room. "And he brings in good clothes."

Even though I'd done years of my own washing and ironing, I hadn't fixed things like rips or missing buttons. Neither had Mom or Tyler, so the pink plastic sewing basket bulged high and wide with bits of sad shirts [illegible] pants poking through narrow slots like [illegible]

of packed [illegible]

Mom, me, me, Tyler, Mom. It looked like most of my stuff had button problems. I found the button box and pawed through it, matching colors and sizes, then picked thread and a needle.

That night at dinner I decided to break the news. I hadn't said one thing yet about the Fifty-Fifty Club or the clothes I was taking to Next to New, but the purple boots were going to come home soon and they needed an explanation.

"I'm president of the Fifty-Fifty Club." The words nearly clogged my throat.

"What's that?" Mom asked, buttering her roll.

So far, so good.

"Next to New — the resale clothing store on Main Street," I said, my words racing to catch up with my pounding heart. "They have this deal where you can give out these discount coupons and whoever brings them in gets fifty percent off anything and you get fifty cents credit." I gulped for air.

"What possessed you to step foot in that disgusting store?" Mom set her knife down. "And how in the world did you get conned into a sales scheme? I'll bet those secondhand people spotted a real sucker when you walked in. How could you be so clueless, Hope?"

I shrugged. Now my heart banged in my ears like a band of miniature drums.

"How does the store know you get the credit?"

"I write my name on the back of the coupon before I give it to someone." I could barely hear myself over the drums.

"Isn't that just great? Your name is spread all over

Eola Hills." She waved her roll through the air. "I suppose you put our phone number and address on it, too, so we'll get crank calls and strangers at the door." Her jaw set tight. "When will you ever think before you act?"

[illegible] throat, but it didn't catch Mom's [illegible]

"No!"

Mom stared.

"I mean — please don't call." I paused, scrambling for words. "It's okay, really. I'm only giving them to kids at school. Really. They're not 'spread all over Eola Hills.'"

"Don't mimic me, Hope."

"I'm not, Mom. Honest." PLEASE LET THIS END. NOW.

I decided not to tell about my clothes, but I still had to mention the boots. "The credit is going for a pair of hiking boots."

"Hiking boots?"

I cringed.

"Sweet," said Tyler. "You'll need 'em for Outdoor School."

My eyes melted into Tyler's. He winked.

"Hope," Mom said firmly, "those boots have been worn by someone else. Probably several someones. You'll get athlete's foot or some strange disease and I don't have the time or the money to take you to the doctor. I don't want those boots in this house."

"Please, Mom, please, I really, really want them. I promise I'll keep them in the garage." Now I was begging for my life.

"You should save your money for a brand-new pair. Check the ads. They have sales all the time. You should get a better deal in the long run."

"But, Mom, these boots look like they've never been worn. I put them on layaway and I only have three dollars and five cents left to pay."

"You shouldn't put anything on layaway, Hope." Now

she was eating her roll. That slowed my heart. "If you don't pay it off on time, poof! There goes your hard-earned money. You should wait until you have the whole amount, then go in, buy it, and bring it home that same day."

[illegible]

my plan.

"I sure wouldn't spend my money that way." She shivered. "You wouldn't catch me dead in that store. Remember, Hope, you should start with new, not Next to New." She chuckled at her own cleverness.

Should, Should, Should. I hated *should.* It made me feel stupid. Really stupid. SHOULD needed points: 60. And, I still needed a Grand Prize.

As I watched Mom still making fun of me, my boots, and my coupons, it finally came to me:

CONGRATULATIONS!

* * *

YOU'VE REACHED THE 5,000 POINT GRAND TOTAL.

FROM THIS POINT FORWARD, YOUR MOTHER, D.D. ELLIOT, WILL NO LONGER SAY MEAN, HURTFUL THINGS, AND YOU WILL NO LONGER REQUIRE A POINT SYSTEM.

* * *

CHAPTER 13

Tangled Memories

[illegible]

my clothes going to Next to New, not that I was doing anything wrong. They were my clothes, after all. And I certainly couldn't wear them anymore. It's just that I got such a sick feeling whenever I thought I should tell Mom something. I knew exactly how it'd go: The minute I opened my mouth, I would've made all the wrong decisions, I'd be *should*ed to death, and I'd feel super stupid and guilty afterwards.

So, I kept pretty quiet, sewing in my closet, sneaking into the laundry room while Mom watched TV or talked on the phone. I didn't want to chance ironing; I planned to haul wrinkled clothes, in hopes of ironing them at Next to New.

The day our Holocaust project was due, I carefully rolled my concentration camp map, slipped rubber bands around each end, and placed it on a soft bed of outgrown dresses, skirts, and blouses, packed in Tyler's old Nike sports bag. With a few T-shirts and pants tucked along the sides, the map looked safe. My backpack hid the remaining clothes. I tried to convince myself I wasn't a thief, but my heart thought differently, shouting out confessions as I walked through the kitchen.

"Bye, Mom," I said, wishing the door closer.

"What's in the bag?" She started the dishwasher and wiped her hands on the towel.

I froze.

"Uh, it's my concentration camp map. Due today. I don't want it to get wet — since I have to walk." I guarded my voice. Not one hint of sarcasm. 50 points.

"And it's well-padded so it won't get squashed." I gave the side of the bag a gentle pat and moved again for the door. My ears prayed for silence.

"Good luck," said Mom.

Good luck! Better than silence! I couldn't believe it.

"Thanks."

Out the door and down the driveway. I reached the [illegible] knees turned to mush. I had to force [illegible]

home forever [illegible] ing, trying to disguise pants, vests, and stockings so the Nazis wouldn't suspect she was going into hiding.

When Mr. Hudson called for the maps, I slowly removed mine from its protective cocoon and carried it like long-lost treasure back to my desk. I slipped the rubber bands off and spread the map, smoothing it flat, my fingers moving gently across drab wooden barracks and dark smoky skies, guard towers and garbage dumps, yellow stars on striped shirts and red blooms on the lone rosebush.

When Mr. Hudson picked it up, I could tell he was

being careful, too. "Nice job, Hope," he said. I tried not to smile. Be cool. *Nice job.* That might even be better than *good job.* I wasn't sure. I'd have to think about it.

I had so many things on my mind that day, it wasn't until afternoon that I noticed Brody's sweater. My eyes moved up the brown and creamy white sleeve to his face. "Next to New," he mouthed from across the room, pulling at the elbow. He gave me a thumbs-up and my ears turned hot.

The bell jingled as I pushed open Next to New's heavy door. I waved to Jodi Huffman, the high-school girl who worked after school three days a week.

Anita was in SHOES.

"Hi," I said, sitting down on the bench.

She tossed a pair of pink fuzzy slippers into a reject pile. "Pink isn't selling these days."

I picked up the slippers and smoothed the helter-skelter hair. "They need mowing."

Anita chuckled. "You do lawns, too?"

"No, just ironing." I returned the slippers to the pile, stalling for time, mentally rehearsing my request. *Would it be okay, that is, could I please use the —*

"What's on your mind?" she asked, sitting down be- [illegible]

sundress [illegible]

I wore it as a top with pants.

"They're all washed and I checked for stains and fixed rips and sewed buttons, and I know they're supposed to be ironed." The words stumbled over my nervous tongue.

Anita stood up, handing me the dress and hat. "Be sure to fill the iron with bottled water, and use the smaller, children's hangers." She gathered her pile of reject shoes and slippers. "No rest for the wicked." She winked and I hoped she wasn't talking about me.

I passed through my childhood again — smoothing,

folding, and pressing memories: second-grade overalls so hard to undo that I peed in them more than once; a red flowery crop top too short during a time I wanted everything tucked in; a day at the beach in my blue shorts and sailboat T-shirt, when Mom built a sand castle with Tyler and me; a trip to the Eugene Zoo in Mickey Mouse sweats when Mom called me clumsy and clueless after I tripped down the stairs leading to the monkeys; Jessica Dobie's birthday party in my Winnie The Pooh dress and matching apron when Mom wished me a good time.

Why do happy memories come tangled with sad ones? Why can't you just pull out the good ones and leave the bad behind? Is it better to forget them all or remember them all? That was definitely a problem in need of a solution.

Anne took these things into hiding: her diary, hair curlers, handkerchiefs, schoolbooks, a comb, old letters. She wrote, "I put in the craziest things with the idea that we were going into hiding. But I'm not sorry, memories mean more to me than dresses."

CHAPTER 14

... Friends

Saturday afternoo... ball game and I was studying Am... test. Tyler said I was on his blacklist for staying ho... and that I'd better ace the test.

I took a break and wandered down to Tyler's room. Surely he had some outgrown clothes. I started with his chest of drawers, pulling out stuff I hadn't seen in years — sweatshirts, basketball T-shirts, football jerseys. The prize, though, was these jungle pajamas with lions and tigers, elephants, and parrots. Way too small. Besides, now he wore boxers and T-shirts to bed.

The phone rang. I dived across Tyler's rumpled bed and grabbed the receiver. "Hello."

"Hope?"

"Yes."

"There's a pair of purple hiking boots here with your name on them."

"Anita?"

"Yes, sweetie. I thought you'd like to know. A bunch of your coupons came in today. Your boots are paid off and you even have fifty cents' credit."

Purple hiking boots AND credit.

"I'll be there in a second."

I tore out of Tyler's room and snatched my tennis shoes off the back porch, hopping and tying my laces all at once.

In a flash, I was breathlessly leaning against Next to New's front door, allowing someone coming out to let me in. A fresh surge of anticipation swept me to the back counter, where I was sucked into a crowd of closet cleaners.

"Hope. Back here." Anita signaled from the storage room.

I weaved out of the crowd and slipped behind the [illegible]

[illegible] from behind her back, [illegible]

[illegible]

leather la[illegible] over and tried cramming my [illegible] on the floor and carefully pulled the laces tight, [illegible] at a time, then tied them in a double-knotted bow. Anita helped me up and we examined the finished look. "Perfect," she said.

Like Miss America taking her runway walk, I stood tall and gazed out across the audience of winter coats, men's suits, and maternity tops. Then I strolled past restrooms, dressing rooms, and the kiddie play corner. It's hard to be Miss America, though, when you're staring at your feet.

Back at the storage room, Anita and Ruthie were examining a white sweater, but they stopped as soon as they saw me.

"They're gorgeous," said Ruthie.

"As good as you remember?" asked Anita.

"Better." This must be heaven. Next to New and new-to-me boots.

Anita returned to the sweater. "What do you think, Hope? Is the stain noticeable?"

Ruthie handed me the sweater and I held it in different directions under the ceiling light. "Well," I hesitated, "it's not as bad in the shadows, but in bright light, I can see it. I probably wouldn't buy it." I raised my eyebrows, wondering if I'd answered okay, and gave the sweater back.

"I'd agree," Anita said. Ruthie nodded.

They must be good friends, I thought, glancing from Anita's XXL Halloween sweater to Ruthie's, then back to their ears. Tiny ghosts dangled from Anita's, witches on broomsticks swung from Ruthie's. And the hair color thing. Anita's now verged on red-red instead of orange-red. Ruthie seemed wrinkly enough for gray hair, but hers was as black as licorice.

"So, Hope," said Ruthie, flopping the white sweater [illegible] "I understand you're quite the sales- [illegible] with all these dis- [illegible]

[illegible]

"Congratu[illegible] jacket in the window is next on y[illegible]

I smiled. "Maybe," I said. Yellow and purple, a perfect combination. "I'd better get home — I have a test Monday."

Ruthie put her arm around my shoulder. "You take good care of those boots, now."

"I will."

"Check in with me next week, Hope," said Anita. "There might be some more ironing."

I rolled my eyes, pretending I was annoyed. Anita chuckled and something nudged my brain, like a baby chick poking at its shell, wanting out.

"See you later," I said, looking at them a moment longer.

"Bye," they said in unison, their earrings jangling.

I walked down the street, my tennis shoes in a paper bag, my purple boots strong against the pavement, and my thoughts on two crazy ladies who seemed to like me. I wondered if they lived together, and if I'd have to dye my hair in order to live with them.

I took a deep breath of cool fall air and picked out the hint of smoke from someone's leaves burning. One of my favorite smells. It was a good day. A Number 6 Day.

CHAPTER 15

Climbing Mountains

Later tha[illegible] room floor, a pile of his little bo[illegible] "I've got a business deal for you."

"What? You sell my clothes and you get the money?" He lay on his bed tossing a basketball in the air.

"No, smarty. I wash, iron, sew up rips, take everything on hangers to Next to New, and we split the money."

"Plus ten bucks for snooping through my stuff!"

"I wasn't snooping. I was just getting a head start."

He climbed off the bed, throwing the basketball in my lap. "Then let's get serious." He stood in front of his opened closet and began tossing Wrangler jeans and silver-buckled belts and long-sleeved Western shirts my way. "No more cowboy dress-up. I'm through playing the Lone Ranger." He even pulled out his really nice suede boots. Totally sweet. They should go for a great price.

"Tyler," I said hesitantly. He turned around. "I don't know what Mom would say, so I'm keeping this kinda quiet. Okay?"

"That'll be another ten bucks."

"No way!" I aimed his basketball at him.

"All right." He held his hands up. "But don't expect me to bail you out when you get caught."

"I won't get caught." I smiled and lowered the ball.

"How exactly do you plan to sneak this stuff out?" he asked, his head back in the closet.

"I have my ways."

With Tyler's clothes hiding in my closet, I tried studying again for my test. I shuddered, wondering if I could have endured Anne Frank's hidden prison and the constant fear of being found, aching for a breath of fresh air, craving to eat anything besides potatoes and beans. I skimmed the pages, feeling Anne's frustrations with [illegible]'s mean words, the longing for friends, the [illegible]

[illegible] the bus. [illegible] down on the plastic seat. Tyler [illegible] heading for the back with the other high schoolers. [illegible] eyed his bag. "Whatcha stealin'?" he whispered loudly.

"*Tyler.*" I scowled. "No half for you!"

"I'll tell."

"No, you won't!"

Noelle Laslett got on at the next stop, sat down beside me, and opened her jacket. "I got these overalls at Next to New."

"Good find," I said.

"Only five dollars with my coupon." She grinned.

And your coupon helped buy my boots, I thought,

moving them on the rubber mat: heel, toe, heel, toe, climbing Lava Butte.

❋

I held my breath as Mr. Hudson passed out the test, the paper turned over, silent questions daring me to remember.

"You have twenty minutes," he said.

I expected to see true-false, multiple choice, fill in the blank, but instead there was only one question: "How does the following story compare to the Holocaust? A frog jumped into a pan of very hot water and instantly jumped back out. Another frog jumped into a pan of cold water that slowly got hotter and hotter. The frog adapted to the increasing heat until the boiling water killed him."

I sat there for a moment feeling sick about the dead frog, then my mind wandered back to Guido, Dora, and Joshua and how they got used to the soldiers on every street corner, the stores closed to Jews and dogs. I thought back to Anne Frank's long list of forbidden freedoms, yet she wrote, ". . . things were still bearable." I remembered her words because I've said similar ones to myself — shut up in my bedroom, writing in [illegible] my closet bed — trying to [illegible]

thought about Anne [illegible] thoughts about the real thing; not just a twenty-minute test, but a twenty-four-hour-a-day test. A survival test. I felt bad for feeling tired.

After Mr. Hudson collected the papers, he began handing back our map projects. I scrunched my toes inside my boots and released them. Scrunched. Released. The wait was killing me. At last, standing beside my desk, Mr. Hudson paused and announced, "Please notice the great care that went into this project." He held up my concentration camp map for the entire class to see. Then, just to me he said quietly, "I like the rosebush." He lowered my map onto my desk like a royal crown.

A+.

What a beautiful letter. Those nice straight, even lines, meeting at the top, the mountaintop. And the prize "+" — the flag at the very tip of the mountain.

CHAPTER 16

Mountain Ranges

[illegible]

back down. That's [illegible] down. High and low. One mountain after another. It reminded me of those zigzag graphs coming out of heart-monitoring machines hooked up to hospital patients.

Mr. Hudson was definitely top-of-the-mountain. He was hard, but fair. And funny. For Halloween he painted a smiley pumpkin face on his bald spot and gave us orange glow sticks for Outdoor School. I'd never studied so much, but I wanted to be high on his Good Role Model List, plus I had to make up for that stupid bus referral. I didn't want a single question mark by my name.

I aced my Anne Frank test and left it on Tyler's bed;

it landed back in my room as an airplane with *Proud of You* written across the wings. Our half-book test was more difficult, but smarty Brody and I tied for the highest score.

Another mountaintop: Anita and Ruthie. They could make a sale day out of any occasion — Drizzly Days Deals, Two-for-One Tuesdays, Halloween Surprises — with signs, prizes, and decorations to match. They were the two best friends I'd ever seen. Of course, they'd had a long time to get there; they'd known each other since kindergarten. With both their husbands dead and their kids grown and gone, they'd moved in together and opened Next to New. I wondered if I'd have a lifetime friend, laughing over old memories, hugging and kissing cheeks, giving each other cards and flowers for no reason.

One more mountain high: purple hiking boots, now worn with thick woolly socks, which kept my feet warm even during recess.

In between the highs were the lows — not diving,

crashing, exploding lows, but rather nagging, poking, bugging lows. For instance: Garbage Day, every other Wednesday . . .

"Don't forget to put the . . ." Mom's voice bursts into [illegible] then fades. I'm clear at the end of the [illegible]

"It's garbag[illegible]

"Every other Wednesday. Can't you remember?"

I hear her voice, but it's like cafeteria rules. Pretty soon you don't hear the thousandth-time reminder words.

"Hope, you stupid shit! Answer me!" The words echo in my ears.

"Yeah, I know." I probably should yell louder, too, but I've lost all my yelling energy. It comes out a medium mumble. I turn the water back on and rinse my toothbrush.

"Hope Marie, get your dumb ass down here right now and take out the goddamn garbage!"

I sigh and inch my head out the door. Now she's standing halfway down the hall, her hands on her hips, her lips pressed tight.

"I'm just finishing my teeth." The words limp out, filling an excuse.

"I know you're going to forget." She's not yelling now, but the words are just as loud.

"I won't. I promise."

Garbage day. Every other Wednesday.

Another low: INTERRUPTING. Take Thanksgiving dinner, for instance. Mom's friend Lydia Bishop came over, which was good because she's nice. I passed the mashed potatoes and she asked how I was doing and what was new, but when I opened my mouth to answer, Mom's words came out. "She'll be lucky to make it through sixth grade."

Lydia smiled at me and tried again. "What are you doing in your spare time?" My lips parted and once more Mom's voice was there: "Hope is spending way too much time at that consignment store. Anyone for more turkey?" Conversation over. Onto pumpkin pie recipes and Christmas sales, and I quietly returned to my cranberry salad.

There was something new grinding at my life: head-

of nowhere. I'd be sitting in class, thinking about morning math, and *wham*. The pounding in my brain would start right while I was figuring miles from Seattle to San Francisco. The numbers blurred and nothing made sense. Or the pain would start behind my eyes, like someone had tied them into tight knots and was pulling them deep inside my head. Even my teeth hurt. Yeah, my teeth. Tops and bottoms, like I'd been chewing ten pieces of bubble gum for ten days straight.

If I complained about the pain, Mom gave me two aspirin and told me I shouldn't have headaches at my age. Sleeping used to help, but then I began waking up in the morning with a headache. How do you get a headache sleeping?

Highs and lows. Christmas was both. I'd climb up, take in all the beautiful lights and music, the school program, and TV specials. We'd decorate our classroom and have a party with red punch and ice cream, cookies, games, and secret pal gifts.

The low was my mom's belief in Christmas crafts. You know that song, "The Twelve Days of Christmas," with the turtledoves and lords a-leaping? Well, in our house, it was "The Twelve *Crafts* of Christmas," with at least twelve bulging bags from Fancy Fabrics crammed with pillow patterns, tassels, rickracks, sequins, and piles of red and green fabric covered with reindeer, snowmen, and Santas.

I used to get excited about Christmas crafts, but then I got tired of GRABBING — when someone decides you're doing something the wrong way and they're going to show you the *right way,* so they grab whatever you're doing out of your hands, saying, "You should do it this way." (Points Total: *Grabbing* + *Shoulding* + *Interrupting* + *Feeling Stupid* = 385.) I'd avoided the dining room workshop for years, but there was still crafty stuff scattered all over the house — half-finished [illegible] mas; we had a Crabby Christmas.

This year, however, Christmas wasn't too bad. We sat around the fake Christmas tree in bathrobes and slippers, drinking hot chocolate, opening presents. I got a basketball from Tyler; gloves, hiking socks, and a bead kit from Mom; twenty-five dollars from Grandma. I gave Tyler two shirts from Next to New. Mom got a warm red scarf that had never been worn. I'm not sure she liked it.

There is one more Christmas high: the day *after*

CHAPTER 17

Rain or Shine?

"Hmmm . . . let's see. Uh-huh." Dr. McKillip examined my teeth with his miniature mirror, then set the mirror on a tray hanging behind me and placed his hands on my jaw, moving it up and down, back and forth, pressing the sides of my face above my ears. "Does this hurt?"

"No."

He sat up straight on his stool and crossed his arms over his white jacket. "Well, young lady, I'd like to say you ate too many candy canes this Christmas. That's an easy fix. But it looks like you're grinding your teeth.

Your bicuspids and molars are getting the worst of it." He pointed to the back of his own mouth, then spoke to my mother leaning against the doorway. "That'll certainly cause her teeth to hurt and can bring on the headaches, too."

He turned back to me and looked right into my eyes. "Hope," he said quietly, like we were the only two people in the entire office, "how are you doing?"

A strange mix of panic and pride rushed over me while my ears tingled hot. He wanted to know how *I* was doing? A kid he only sees maybe once a year? My eyes turned misty and my throat was so tight I didn't think I could talk.

"Hope Marie," came my mother's words, "answer Dr. McKillip."

He gave her a sharp glance, then his eyes softened again as they studied mine. "Are you under any unusual stress at school?"

"Just regular stuff," I managed to say.

"There's no way she can be stressed," said Mom. "She's only in sixth grade. She's just too sensitive. If anyone should be grinding their teeth, it should be *me*. I've been stressed out for as long as I can remember."

Dr. McKillip frowned and looked out the window. "Mrs. Elliot," he said, studying the bare tree and hang- [illegible]

"Yeah."

He shifted around on his seat. "Uh, what about outside of school — anything bothering you?"

"She doesn't have a thing to be bothered about," said Mom, now standing in the middle of the doorway. "Like I said, she's only eleven years old."

Dr. McKillip patted my arm and stood up with a sigh. "I see many stressed-out eleven-year-olds, Mrs. Elliot. They may not have the same worries you or I do, but kids can be extremely concerned about a lot of things. You might want to look into this for Hope's sake."

Mom started to say something, then closed her mouth and looked down at the floor.

Dr. McKillip moved to the sink, turned on the water, and began mixing something in a small bowl. "I'm going to make impressions of Hope's teeth and have a special mouthpiece made for her to wear at night in order to protect her teeth and buffer her nerves. We'll be done here in a few minutes, Mrs. Elliot. You're welcome to relax in the waiting room with a cup of hot tea or coffee."

Mom was silent on the way home. Actually, she'd been pretty quiet the past few weeks. "After-Christmas blues," she called it. "Back to the same old routine. Same old, same old." I'd find her staring out the kitchen window while dinner fixings sat waiting on the counter, or she'd lose track of time, brushing her teeth for ten minutes.

"I'm sick and tired of these Oregon winters," she'd said one morning as rain dribbled down the window. "Rain, rain, rain." She snatched a piece of bread out of the toaster and mashed butter on it. "What I'd give for a spot of sun." That's when she'd bring up moving. Southern California, Arizona, New Mexico. Someplace, anyplace where the sky was blue and the sun shined hot.

[illegible]

and lay down. My entire body melted, my legs turning limp as noodles, my headache fading as my eyes wandered across the closet walls. Now they were covered with magazine pictures of sunflowers and waterfalls, seagulls flying above the ocean, a Christmas tree sparkling with white lights. There were the words to my favorite songs, my old star chart, my A+ Holocaust map, a newspaper picture of Gabriela Feliciano shooting a basket, and a quote from Anne Frank: ". . . I've found that there is always some beauty left — in nature, sunshine, freedom, in yourself; these can all help you."

Curled up in my closet bed, I felt like a bear, hibernating in my dark, safe cave. I closed my eyes and inspected my teeth with my tongue. There were still a few bits of dried guck from Dr. McKillip's impressions. He had me bite into this pile of gooey clay stuff, which was surely going to harden onto my teeth forever. But it was still nice being in his office. After Mom left for the waiting room, he got all chatty, talking about his plans to take his family to Disneyland for spring vacation. He asked if I'd ever been to Disneyland. I shook my head. He kept talking, like we were having this great conversation, with me grunting through gooey clay or nodding my head.

When he walked me to the waiting room, he put his hand on my shoulder and said, "Your mouthpiece will be ready in a week." He gave a quick squeeze. "Hang in there, Hope."

Now I blinked my eyes open and gazed up to the hems and cuffs, buttons and zippers of my hanging clothes. The view had changed. After Christmas, I'd gone through everything one more time, plus Tyler's, and hauled another load to Next to New. Our clothes were selling well, so along with coupon credits and ironing for Anita, I'd bought two pairs of jeans, a sweater, another pair of boots so I could save my purple ones for [illegible] a daisy necklace with matching [illegible] home from Next to [illegible] bought a bag of oyster crackers, cereal bars, canned cheese, red licorice, or green olives. I even found a small electric coffeepot at Goodwill so I could heat water and make hot chocolate or chicken noodle soup.

The bottom shelf was for my library. So far, *Anne Frank: The Diary of a Young Girl* was my only book. We'd finished our Holocaust unit months ago, but we hadn't finished the book. Mr. Hudson said we could borrow it if we wanted to read the second half. At first, I wanted to hurry up and get to the end, but now I was slowing down, figuring if I didn't finish, the Nazis wouldn't find the "Secret Annexe," arrest everyone, and haul them off to concentration camps. Anne Frank wouldn't die if I didn't finish her story.

I wrapped Turtle in my arms, nestled back into my pillow, and with the golden glow of lamplight falling softly on my eyes, I could see Dr. McKillip again, his hand on my shoulder. I could feel his gentle touch and hear his angel voice. I let the tears come. They pressed out the sides of my eyes, wandered into my hair and down to my ears, tickling as they turned cold. I wiped them away with Turtle's foot.

I wished I had a father like Dr. McKillip. If Mom moved to California, maybe I could move to Dr. McKillip's office. I'd have plenty of toothbrushes and little sample toothpastes, plus a bed on that big dental lounge chair.

CHAPTER 18

Name It and Tame It

classroom and

The puppet was freshly colored with crayon-yellow hair, black eyes, and a smiley red mouth. A big purple heart covered her brown chest.

"Remember first grade? Sitting in a circle on the floor, passing around Paper Bag Patty?" Mrs. Nelson's own black eyes moved from face to face, her pink mouth serious.

"Yeah," said Noelle. "We crumpled her every time we said something that hurt her feelings."

"Like what?" said Mrs. Nelson, bobbing Patty's head in time with her words.

"Moron," said Colin Davis.

Mrs. Nelson grabbed Patty's purple heart and squished it tight.

"Pimple face," said Annette.

Again, Mrs. Nelson twisted and wrinkled the puppet's body.

"Loser," "fatty," "dork," came the names, along with more crushes and creases.

"Stupid," I said, my own heart squeezing tight, sending a silent "sorry" to Patty.

By now you couldn't see any of the colors, just this brown wadded clump like a used lunch sack about to be tossed in the garbage.

"Then we tried to smooth out the lines," said Mrs. Nelson, "by saying nice things like 'smart,' 'awesome,' 'cool.'" Mrs. Nelson's fingers massaged Patty's heart, head, and body, unable to completely erase the wrinkles. "What was left behind?"

"Slime," said Brody.

"Right," said Mrs. Nelson, removing Patty, setting her

on Mr. Hudson's desk. "Hurting words are slugs that slime our hearts. What else?"

"Scars." I felt my mouth move and heard the word as if it had helped itself out.

[illegible] looked at me for a moment, then took [illegible]

to [illegible]

"Abuse. It's verbal abuse."

Now her right hand jabbed the air above our heads. "Verbal abuse is *as* damaging as physical abuse, or worse. It takes twenty-five to thirty positive comments to overcome the effects of one abusive comment. The scars from verbal abuse run just as deep, if not deeper, than physical scars."

With her strong words still hanging in the air, she assured us with softer words that it was important to properly name something. "When you name it, you tame it.

It's like putting a fence around a wild animal so you're safe to learn about it." Then she gave us words to help in abusive situations — *I feel* words, asking-for-a-change words.

An hour later, I stood in front of Next to New, staring at my reflection against green shamrocks. I couldn't think about St. Patrick's Day, though, with Mrs. Nelson's *abuse* word in my head. Why did she wait until sixth grade to tell us? Little kids should know that hurting words are not only slimy and scarring, but ***abusive***. I'd always liked Mrs. Nelson, but now I felt a knot of anger in my stomach. She should have told me sooner.

The knot tightened in my stomach as my mother's own words crashed through my head: *dumb shit, stupid as a stick, hopelessly lazy.* I couldn't believe she was doing something to me that had an official name, like chicken pox or the flu. I could just hear a doctor say, "You have a bad case of verbal abuse."

Now that it had a name it seemed more real, more serious, more important. Did that make me more important, too, in a weird sort of way? You know, like the kid who comes to school after a skiing accident, his leg in a cast, hobbling around with crutches. At first he's famous, everyone feeling sorry for him and a little jealous of all his attention, his cool crutches, someone carrying his books and lunch tray. But after a while, it's actually

[illegible]

tagged clothes." She hauled an armload of winter jackets and sweaters to the *50% Off* rack. "They've had their three months of glory," she said, hanging them back up.

"Think spring," said Ruthie as she dropped unsold sales clothes into a huge laundry basket set on wheels. A man and woman from some church came every Saturday for the leftovers, sending them off to places you see on the news after floods and hurricanes and wars. I kept looking for those pink fuzzy slippers to show up on someone's feet standing in desert sand. Sometimes I wondered if these people really wanted our clothes or if they just wore them for the TV cameras and *National Geographic* pictures.

"I'm selling chocolate candy bars." I held up plain milk chocolate and semisweet with almonds.

"Hope Elliot, you are a tease!" Anita shook her head.

Ruthie rolled her eyes. "Thanks a lot. You show up just when my stomach starts growling." She looked at Anita. "Are we going to be good?"

"What's it for?" asked Anita, like she needed an important cause in order to cheat on her diet.

"Outdoor School." I waved the white-and-gold-wrapped candy in the air. "Super delicious."

Anita shook her head. "Ruthie. We've lost eleven pounds between the two of us and Monday is weigh-in. I've got carrots and apple slices in the back room."

"Are they chocolate-covered?" Ruthie looked like she was in pain.

"How about I leave one for each of you?" I said. "And if you lose another pound by Monday night, you can pay me for them."

"What if we don't?" asked Ruthie.

"Pay me?"

"No — lose the weight?"

"I know," said Anita, "I'll buy the candy bars and *you* eat them, you skinny little thing." She eyed me up and down.

Dr. McKillip had bought two candy bars [illegible] picked up my mouth guard. "Hold it under warm water to soften it before you put it on. You don't want to break this expensive little number." He nodded toward the bathroom. "Try it before you leave."

I stood at the sink, hot water pouring over the clear plastic mold. Was this how people with dentures felt? Holding their fake teeth in their hands, scrubbing them clean, popping them back in place? Freaky.

I turned off the water, shook the horseshoe-shaped impression, then pushed it up, over my top teeth. It was smooth and thick, forcing my upper lip out, like a monkey.

I returned to the reception room. "I hhink iss okay."

The receptionist smiled while I drooled on the floor.

"You probably don't want to talk on the phone to your boyfriend with that in your mouth," Dr. McKillip said, smiling.

I quickly pulled the guard from my mouth and packed it back in its red container.

He handed me a piece of paper as I walked out the door. "Some headache tips," he said, and raised his hand, waving good-bye.

Now, watching Anita and Ruthie pulling, hanging, and rearranging clothes, I wished I was trying to lose weight rather than shake a headache. I wished I went to their weekly weigh-in meetings (they called it their *support group*). I wished I had someone to talk to, like Ruthie telling Anita she needed a chocolate fix. "Don't eat it," Anita would say. "Throw it away. Go for a walk, sweetie, or drink a glass of water." I wished there was a support group for verbal abuse. I'd go. Even by myself.

CHAPTER 19

Birthday Wishes

[illegible] big fuss with balloons and streamers and [illegible] chocolate-fudge cake and a special present like my clock radio. Other years she's given me ten dollars and told me to buy myself a present. When I turned nine, she didn't say a word. My birthday went right on by like a car driving straight through a red light. A few weeks later Tyler asked, "Don't you have a birthday sometime around now?"

Last year Annette and Noelle came over to watch movies and spend the night. I was carrying a huge bowl of popcorn and a plastic bottle of Coke into the living room when I tripped on the rug. Buttered popcorn and fizzing Coke splattered across the floor and furniture.

Annette and Noelle started laughing, but I just stared at the brown spotted ceiling, sick with dread. Before I could pick up the first piece of popcorn, Mom burst into the room. Annette and Noelle stopped laughing.

"You clumsy idiot," said Mom. "Get this cleaned up right now." She looked at Annette and Noelle. "You two call your parents. The party's over."

"But, Mom," I started, heat sweeping my body, burning my ears.

"SHUT UP! And do what you're told!"

With last year's birthday still a nightmare and just a week until my twelfth birthday, I tried to figure out Mom's mood.

"I'm really going to feel older when I'm twelve," I hinted.

"Uh-huh." Mom kept reading the morning paper.

"I'm eleven and I'll be twelve on the thirteenth."

"So?" She glanced up.

"So that's a good sign — three numbers in se- [illegible]

[illegible] remembered the [illegible]

Grand[illegible] months, with Mom [illegible] but always turning loud and angry [illegible] finally shouting, "Don't tell me how I should rai[illegible] kids!" and hanging up hard.

I couldn't give up, though, on the birthday business. "This is a really special year since it's my last at the elementary school, so I thought we could do something extra special, you know, maybe a day at the beach, or Night Lights at the Portland Zoo, or paintballing, or —"

"Hope, in case you've forgotten, and I tell you this every year, your birthday comes at our busiest time at work. I don't have the energy to plan a party."

"I'll plan it."

"Not after last year's disaster."

I stood there wondering if I was dismissed, but then she reached for her wallet and slapped twenty-five dollars on the table. "Spend this however you want. Take a friend to a movie and out for pizza. Or buy something. Or save it. Whatever."

Twenty-five dollars. At first I wasn't all that excited about the money. Somehow it felt more like a punishment than a present. Go figure.

But, then, a few days later, I found myself thinking what I could do with it. First I thought of the usual stuff. Then my twenty-five dollars stretched with my imagination: I saw the Humane Society animal ads and I felt a furry soft kitten sleeping next to me. I passed the Eola Hills Travel Agency and was jumping waves in Hawaii. I dreamed of going to a concert, flying in an airplane, a day at Disneyland.

I woke on my birthday still not sure what I was going to do. But I was excited it was Saturday and I still had my twenty-five dollars, even though I'd spent it a million times already in my head.

[illegible] birthday, Hope," said Mom, sitting at the [illegible] cigarette, ads spread across [illegible] I are going to [illegible]

[illegible] louder, [illegible] of stored conversation[illegible] *tell you . . . every year . . . our busie*[illegible] *don't have the energy to plan a party.*

"What about work?" I mumbled.

"Work's fine." Mom squashed her cigarette in a jar lid and began cutting coupons. "We're caught up for now."

I slogged through quicksand to the refrigerator. *It's okay,* my brain tried to reason with me. *It's your birthday and you're twelve. You can do anything you want today. Forget her. It's your birthday and you're okay. Give yourself one hundred points for DISAPPOINTED.*

After choking down a bowl of cereal, I took a shower,

checked out my bare reflection in the full-length mirror (nothing new or different), and put on a skirt, sweater, and my purple hiking boots. As soon as Mom was gone, I crammed my birthday money plus some Next to New earnings into my jacket pocket and walked out the door.

The air was cool and the pavement damp after a night rain, but there were splotches of blue between white and gray clouds. I sucked in the moist air, washing my insides. I wasn't sure where I was going, but my feet turned to town and started walking. The day was mine. All mine.

I stood in front of the Quail Run Bakery, studying row upon row of sprinkle doughnuts, maple bars, blueberry muffins, the fan above the door spreading frosting and coffee smells. In a flash I was walking down the street again, the first taste of a warm, magically sweet cinnamon roll in my mouth.

I passed outdoor coffee drinkers, paper readers, dog walkers, two little girls in ballet tights, a guy parking his motorcycle. The sun was shining warmer now as I studied French beaches, Alaskan cruises, and Mexican ru- [illegible] taped to the window at Eola Hills Travel Agency. I [illegible] three . . . someday. A little boy and his [illegible] of the Hallmark store, giv- [illegible] fur ball up to [illegible] stuffed kit[illegible] was mine.

By lunchtime, I'd wandered throu[illegible] clothes shops, Tyler's used-to-be-favorite Cowboy Cou[illegible]try, shoe stores, and an outdoor garden display with birdbaths and fountains and even a waterfall spilling down into a pond. I sat on a metal bench by the pond and watched huge goldfish wiggle-waggle around each other.

At the Second Street Deli, I ordered three turkey sandwiches and three chocolate-chip cookies. With a few dollars left in my pocket, I carried the white sack and my Hallmark bag down the street, over four blocks, and into Next to New.

The morning shoppers were gone and the closet cleaners hadn't arrived yet. I found Anita and Ruthie studying the Chinese restaurant menu. "But we can't eat the rice," said Anita.

"Just don't eat the fortune cookie," said Ruthie.

"How about turkey?" I said, holding up the sack.

"Hope!" they said together.

"Is a sandwich okay?" I began opening the bag. "You don't have to eat the chips, but you do have to eat the cookies, because they're for my birthday."

"Your birthday?" Ruthie practically shrieked. "But you shouldn't be here on a sunny spring Saturday — you should be out with your friends, shopping or —"

"Stuff it, Ruthie," Anita said, slamming her elbow into Ruthie's side. "Hope came to the right place. Let's celebrate."

Anita hustled us to the storage room and whipped out a card table and three folding chairs, flowery napkins, and the Easter globe off her desk. She cranked the globe key and shook the glitter while Ruthie and I handed out sandwiches, pickles, olives, chips, and chocolate-chip cookies. With "Here Comes Peter Cotton- [illegible]ming away, I told them about my twenty-five dol- [illegible] Eola Hills and passed around my [illegible] a pet," I said. "I think [illegible]

you[illegible] Diet Pepsi.

"Absolutely," said Ruthie, [illegible] coffee cup. "To Hope and to many [illegible] sandwiches."

"Thank you," I said, the cold turkey warming my stomach.

After "Happy Birthday" and the last bite of cookie, Anita announced, "Next to New will match your twenty-five dollars. Consider this your gift certificate." She handed me her napkin with *$25* scribbled across the flowers. "Not exactly fancy wrapped, but you didn't give us much notice."

"Enough notice for next year, though," said Ruthie.

And I knew they wouldn't forget.

CHAPTER 20

New Me

Anita needed su...

summer."

I'd already taken in my summery things and Ty...
warned me to stay out of his clothes. Mom had brought home two new dresses when she'd gone shopping with Lydia (on my birthday), which got me thinking, planning, and waiting for the right moment.

Monday morning, spring vacation, Tyler was still asleep and Mom had left for work. I tiptoed down the hall, past Tyler's bedroom, into Mom's room, and across the floor to her closet. I opened the door. It squeaked and I froze. *Forget it, Hope!* My eyes wandered to Mom's dresser and touched the photo of my baby self, curled in her arms, snuggled against her checkered dress, on that sunny day in March twelve years ago.

I could have stayed in that warm picture forever but reminded myself of the mission and quickly moved through the hanging clothes, stopping at the blue and white homecoming dress. My heart stopped as I grasped the hanger and pulled the dress from the closet.

At Next to New, I tested the iron while Anita fussed at her desk, coughed, glanced at Mom's dress, eyed me, opened and closed drawers, released a loud sigh, then sank down on her chair. "What *else* does your mother want to sell?"

I arranged the dress and began ironing. "Nothing."

"Hmm. That's odd. Most people bring in a pile of things they want to get rid of."

"She's too busy."

"Well, it's a lovely dress. Doesn't look like it's ever been worn."

"It was." I turned the fabric gently, my hands patting,

spreading, resting, longing to hug the blue-and-white-checkered dress one last time.

[illegible] her head and left the room.

[illegible] New turned into a party [illegible] prizes, and [illegible]

that tas[illegible] diet pop and apples a[illegible] olives.

I made chocolate-fudge brownies using [illegible] cholesterol-free directions, which meant I had to take out the egg yolks — a slimy mess. Instead of frosting, I just sprinkled powdered sugar all over, which looked pretty and *had* to be less calories.

Closet cleaners kept us pretty busy all week, with summer clothes coming in and sale stuff going out. One slower afternoon I was on hanger duty: gathering strays; sorting plastic, wood, wire; taking extras to the storage room. I was tidying the stack behind the consignment counter when a woman's voice drew my head around.

She was talking about the clothes she'd brought in like she knew exactly what we expected.

"Everything's washed and ironed. No stains or rips. It's all good."

There was a hint of something familiar in her voice, how she paused between sentences, the casual confidence. She smiled at Ruthie, her face shimmering under fluorescent lights, her forehead smooth, her reddish-blond hair curving softly under just below her ears. She wore a peach-colored sweater set and pearl earrings. She seemed so, I don't know, so — smart.

Just as I turned back to the tangle of hangers, I heard a *very* familiar voice. "Hey, Mom, there's some Liz Claiborne shirts on the New to Us rack."

Brody. Our eyes met while my arms were entwined in a hanger mobile.

"Hope! Hi. You working here?"

"Well, sort of, not really."

"She keeps the place going," said Ruthie, taking Mrs. Brinkman's clothes to a back rack.

"Mom," said Brody, "this is Hope."

“I’m happy to meet you, Hope,” said Mrs. Brinkman with a sparkly white smile.

“Thanks, me too.” I tried to return half a sparkly [illegible]

“Okay, [illegible] look at his mother.

“Mrs. Brinkman,” said Ruthie, now checking the computer screen, “you have twenty-seven dollars on your account.”

“Thank you,” said Brody’s mom. She smiled at me again. “Hope, could you join us? We’re going to play miniature golf.”

I didn’t know what to say. *Yes, I’d love to play golf with you, dress like you, sound smart like you, live with you.* Geezuz, Brody had an Angel Mom!

“Oh, thanks,” I mumbled, “but I’d better not.” I looked at Brody. “Maybe another time.”

Brody and his mom left with Brody giving me a wave at the front door.

"Ruthie," I said, combing my fingers through my hair, just as tangled as the hangers.

"Uh-huh."

"How do you think I'd look with shorter hair? Like below my ears? I mean, wouldn't it be better for summer?"

"Oh, darlin', you'd look spectacular — let's go for it."

I panicked. "*You're* going to cut it?"

"You think I'm just going to hack away at your lovely hair?" said Ruthie, leading me back to the storage room. "I'll have you know, I was a beautician in my former life."

Before I knew it, Ruthie had me sitting on a stool with a towel from LINENS around my shoulders. She began combing, brushing, untangling, and suggesting shampoos and conditioners.

I rolled my eyes. "Maybe I should just go bald."

"Hold still." She aimed the comb and scissors, poised for attack, then stopped. "What will your mother say?"

"She doesn't care." The words escaped before I could grab them. I panicked. I'd never said them out [illegible]yone.

[illegible] to her sides, her face shift- [illegible]

her a[illegible] against her chest.

"I care," echoed Anita, walking acros[illegible] an armload of sale signs, "but I certainly wouldn't let this lady near my hair with anything sharp."

"You be nice," said Ruthie, straightening up. "We're about to perform a little magic — just call me the Hairy Godmother."

"Bad, Ruthie, really stinks," said Anita.

"I asked her to," I said in Ruthie's defense.

"Oh, in that case, we're all in trouble." Anita sat at her desk to watch.

Ruthie pressed the cold scissors against my forehead and hair began to fall away. I closed my eyes until, at last, Anita handed me a small mirror. I saw my eyes first. They seemed bigger, browner — prettier. And I seemed older without those long, scraggly ends hitting my shoulders.

"I like it."

CHAPTER 21

The Prize

“Wh[illegible]

“It w-was my idea,” I stamm[illegible]

“WHO?”

“Uh, this lady at Next to New. She asked if you’d care and I said you wouldn’t.”

“I don’t,” she said, “but the boys will.”

“Huh?”

“Boys like girls with long hair.”

“Not all boys,” I said, wondering if Brody liked his mother’s hair short.

Mom threw her hands in the air. “Dye your hair green with purple stripes for all I care.”

Sarcasm: 35 points.

❋

The next morning I stood in front of Next to New, checking out my reflection. I touched the soft ends of my shampooed, conditioned, gelled, dried, and curled hair. Thank goodness I liked it after cramping my arm muscles with all that blowing and rolling.

Anita looked up from the cash register. "Ohmygosh. Ruthie! Come see who just walked in."

Ruthie appeared from ACCESSORIES, carrying an armful of belts and purses. "Oh, Hope."

I stiffened.

"It's beautiful," she said, dropping her load right on the floor and marching over to examine me.

I stood there, soaking up all their smiles and shiny eyes.

"Thanks," I said, and without thinking I gave them each a hug and a kiss on the cheek.

Thursday was slow. When we finished our two o'clock break, Anita brought out a cribbage board and deck of cards. "Winner gets a prize," she said.

"I love prizes," said Ruthie. "What is it?"

"You'll see," she said, shuffling the cards.

Cribbage — Anita and Ruthie's favorite game. I'd [illegible] of their nightly matches and a running winner- [illegible] the loser had to [illegible]

[illegible]

went, [illegible] wooden board.

When Ruthie moved her peg around the last corner, she announced, "Winner! Prize, please."

Anita smiled and took Ruthie's hand, leading her from the storage room to the men's bathroom.

"Excuse me, darlin', but I don't need to go," said Ruthie.

"Come on." Anita tugged.

"The MEN'S room?" Ruthie protested.

Anita didn't answer except for a "Shhh."

I walked behind them and heard a hushed "Ohhhhh."

"Come here, Hope," whispered Anita.

I walked cautiously between them, to a box, peeked over the edge, and smiled. I bent down and watched the gray and white kitten, curled on a bed of towels, stretch a tiny leg forward and arch its head with a slow-motion yawn, then snuggle back to sleep. Its tiny body moved ever so slightly with each quiet breath. I touched its silky fur and began stroking its back. A faint purr floated up from the box.

"Where did you get it?"

"A customer," said Anita, proud of her prize.

I picked up the little fluff ball and cuddled it next to my face.

After more ooohs and aaahs and petting and purring, we named him Resale after vetoing Ruthie's vote for Snickers.

"Looks like you've fallen in love with him already, Hope," said Ruthie. "Why don't you take him home? A companion for Peter."

I froze. "No, no, I couldn't do that." I handed Resale to Ruthie. Please don't ask me why and make me explain that my mother has never allowed pets, that they stink and pee and puke in the house.

"Then Resale will be a shop cat," said Anita, "with Hope in charge." She eyed me. "That means a clean lit- [illegible]

CHAPTER 22

Preparation & Permission

[illegible]

Mom, [illegible]

"What meeting?"

"*Outdoor School*. I've been reminding you for two weeks." I knew I was getting close to trouble, but I didn't care. This was too important. I held up the flyer I'd taped to the refrigerator. "All the sixth-grade teachers and ODS counselors will be there." My ears warmed a warning but I couldn't quit now. "There's a slide show and refreshments." How else could I convince her!?

"ODS," she said like she was imitating me.

"Outdoor School," I said, verging on angry impatience. "There are important forms to fill out."

"If they're that important, someone will send them to me." She clicked to another channel.

"Mr. Hudson is going to teach some fun campfire songs."

She looked at me. "I don't think so."

"*Please*, Mom. *Please* go. I'll get your jacket and car keys. You just *have* to go."

She sat up. "Hope Marie, stop your damn whining. I don't *have* to do anything." Her eyes narrowed. "And I *do not* take orders from a twelve-year-old."

My arms dropped and the flyer slipped to the floor. I turned and left the living room. The rest of the evening crept by as I stared at my math and out the window. I went to the bathroom and stared at myself in the mirror; I could see the twitching in my cheeks as I ground my teeth back and forth. Maybe Mom would change her mind, get off the couch, and drive to school. She'd be late but that'd be okay. She'd hear the songs and meet the counselors and —

"Hope," called Mom through the bathroom door. My heart jumped. She was going!

"Don't hog the bathroom."

I sighed and watched my eyes droop. "I'm coming." I flushed the empty toilet and ran the sink water.

When I opened the door, Mom smiled and kissed my [illegible] "Thanks, sweetie, you saved my life." There it [illegible] after be-

[illegible]

really was a chance — a big chance — [illegible] Outdoor School? No. It couldn't happen. But I felt like I was sinking into a deep hole, swallowed in cold darkness. *NO,* I wanted to scream, *I'm going!*

The next day, Mr. Hudson gave me a parents' packet. "It has everything in it except the slide show and counselors."

I pulled out the equipment list. Sleeping bag. Air mattress. Flashlight. Suntan lotion. Pajamas or sweats. Boots or sturdy shoes. My sturdy purple boots were ready. So was I. I was going.

❋

"I said a **boom** chicka boom." Mr. Hudson clapped his hands and slapped his legs.

"I said a **boom** chicka boom," we called back, clapping and slapping.

"I said a **boom** chicka rocka chicka rocka chicka boom."

Clap, slap, clap, slap. Mr. Hudson looked around the room.

We had pushed the desks against the walls and now sat cross-legged on the floor in a circle with Mr. Hudson sitting in front of the whiteboard.

"Oh, yeah," he said, nodding his head up and down.

"Oh, yeah," we answered, our voices rising, our hands burning.

"One more time."

"One more time."

Outdoor School was still three weeks away, but we were more than ready. We'd learned loud silly songs and quiet nighttime songs, ones with hand motions and some with full-body action, like the "Squirrelly" song where you turn around, bend over, and shake your rear, then hop on one foot in a circle.

We'd learned how *not* to put up a tent when Mr. H wound up in the middle of a green mess.

[illegible] out of empty [illegible]

Hudson filled with melted wax. [illegible] we stuck a piece of candlewick into the center.

"Buddy burners," announced Mr. Hudson, lighting his fire starter, then placing the open end of the coffee can upside down over the tuna can. He dropped a dab of butter on the flat top of the coffee can stove. The yellow glob sat there for a moment, then eased into a puddle and started bubbling. "There isn't a knob for *high* or *simmer*," he said, spreading the butter with a pancake turner.

We crowded closer as he cracked an egg on the

coffee can edge, then poured the insides onto the buttered griddle. Snapping and popping, the egg quickly changed from slime to a yellow and white eyeball. "You can try for easy-over," said Mr. Hudson, flipping the egg with the pancake turner. He winked at us. "It's in the wrist." With another flip, he had it on a paper plate and handed it to Peter Monroe.

We started to protest but shut up as Mr. Hudson spooned pancake batter on the stove and we all got a turn at flipping and eating.

The next afternoon we pulled all the blinds so the room was dark as a cave. Mr. Hudson turned on his laptop and projector and a bunch of students and parents appeared on the wall screen.

"This is the big ODS sendoff — good-bye for five whole days," he said. "If this is your first time away from home, your mother or father might get a bit teary-eyed. Go ahead and let them. They're just having trouble growing up. Or maybe it's seeing *you* grow up." Everyone except me chuckled politely, like they'd suddenly aged a couple years and were full of sympathy for their poor, sentimental parents.

"These are the showers," said Mr. Hudson, nodding at the small brick building on the screen. "You get one during the week."

[illegible] had snow some years. [illegible] campers around a snowman wearing an Eola Hills ODS T-shirt.

"And don't forget your counselor's camp name," warned Mr. Hudson as the picture changed. "If you're caught using his or her real name, it's a twenty-five cent fine." Counselors appeared on the screen, stacked in a three-layer pyramid. "Fungus, Cricket, and Gumdrop; Spice and Slug and Mole. They'll all be back this year, so memorize their names."

After the slide show, Mr. Hudson came by my desk. "Do you have your ODS packet, Hope?"

I sighed and inspected the floor. "I can't get Mom to fill out the forms."

"Do you want to go?"

My head jerked up so fast I thought it would snap off and spin across the room. "Are you kidding?"

"Attagirl." Mr. Hudson tapped on the desk with his knuckles. "I'll give your mom a call tonight in case she has any questions."

Each time the phone rang that evening, I inched down the hall toward the kitchen and held my breath. First it was Lydia, then someone for Tyler, then I heard Mom coo into the receiver, "Oh, Mr. Hudson, how very nice to hear from you. Yes, uh-huh. Well, I've just been so busy at work. Uh-huh. Oh, I'm sure it is. I just assumed Hope wouldn't be going since she's such a troublemaker. Oh, really? Outstanding? I haven't seen any pink slips. Uh-huh. Well, I'm sure it's a great experience. No, she's never been camping. I would have volunteered to go, but I just can't get away. Yes, her brother has a sleeping bag. Okay. No, I can't think of anything. Thank you so much for calling, Mr. Hudson. Bye, now." She put the phone down, flipped off the kitchen light, and walked back into the living room.

The next morning I hung around the kitchen, praying [illegible]

table. "Go on, catch the bus."

"Did you, are you, umm, could you —"

"For God's sake, Hope, spit it out."

"Outdoor School packet," I blurted.

She rolled her eyes. "I don't remember Tyler hauling so much garbage to and from school." She pushed her chair in. "I've never seen so many ridiculous permission forms."

"What about —?"

She eyed me, her hands on her hips. "You'll get your precious Outdoor Playschool forms."

"When?"

"When I get to it!"

I bit my tongue. 50 points.

CHAPTER 23

The Real Me

[illegible]

me worry, then she'd fill out the [illegible] ute, and I'd get my ODS T-shirt and pack my bag and climb onto the bus. But the possibility of not going to Outdoor School hung around like thick fog and I went through the next few days in a daze.

"Are you going to Next to New?" Brody asked.

"Huh?"

"Hope, wake up," he said, waving his hand in my face. "You just missed your bus. Are you working today at the store? You know — Next to New."

"No, I don't think so." I looked at him and then

around the school yard. The sun was warm, cutting through my fog, and I smelled the spring-come-summer tang of freshly cut grass. I didn't want to go to the store; I didn't want to go home. I just wanted to do — nothing.

Brody tossed his backpack on the grass. "Race you to the swings." He started running.

"No fair! You got a head start!" I dropped my back-pack and ran after him.

We fell into the black rubber seats gasping for air, hanging on to the cold metal chains.

Brody turned onto his stomach and pushed himself in little circles.

"You're going to get sick," I said, leaning back in my swing, looking at the wide blue sky.

"So are you." He reached over and pulled my chain.

"Hey! Stop it!" I laughed, then we both got quiet, our swings slowing to a stop.

"Do you get along with your parents?" I blurted with-out thinking.

"Yeah, I guess." He leaned down and picked up a handful of rubber pellets.

"Really? You never argue?"

He began tossing the pellets at me. "Not much. Just if I'm watching too much TV."

"I don't think my mom likes me." That whipped right out of my mouth like I had nothing to do with it. I felt [illegible] I was going [illegible] leaving. The hurting words. Angel Moms. [illegible] and my point-system notebook.

"Why so many points for *Stupid*?" he asked.

"I hate that word. I hate feeling stupid."

He nodded and was quiet for a moment. Then he asked, "How many points would it be if someone yells from another room, *'Come here!'*? You figure it's really important, or even an emergency, so you drop whatever you're doing and you holler back, *'Coming!'* You race to the next room or downstairs or upstairs, but then you discover they just want to show you something dumb, or have you hold something for a second, or they want to make sure you're not talking on the phone and that your homework's done."

My mind calculated as he rattled on. When he finished, I said, "Three hundred twenty-five points."

He stared.

I smiled.

Keeping my eyes on Brody, I pushed back my swing as far as it could go, my legs stretched up on tiptoe. Then I swung down and zinged past him, shouting, "See how high you can go!"

CHAPTER 24

Grounded

[illegible]

flat to the ground, our feet reaching high, [illegible] whipping straight down. The air swept against our faces. We laughed as we passed each other, one up, the other down. Once I laughed so hard, drool slipped out of my mouth and smeared my ear.

"Hope Marie." A woman's distant voice.

"Hope Marie Elliot!" Now a yelling voice.

My heart caught. My body stiffened as I strained to turn my head. The turning derailed my downswing and my legs swung the opposite direction as my head. I spotted my mother just as my legs flew back the other direction. My feet banged against the ground and jerked my body to a stop. Brody slowed and stopped. I choked and coughed, my insides threatening to throw up.

"Where have you been?" She stood cross-armed at the edge of the lawn.

I stood up, the swing resting against my rear. "Here," I said, confused and nervous, wondering why she wasn't at work, why she'd come looking for me.

"Is this what you do after school?" She glanced at Brody.

"Well, uh . . ." I stumbled for words, so embarrassed with Brody watching. "Not usually."

Was this a nightmare? Was my mother actually here? Pieces of the puzzle were missing, floating out there, somewhere.

"I have something to show you. Let's go." She snapped around and headed back to the parking lot.

"What happened?" Brody whispered.

"I don't know."

"Are you in trouble?"

"I guess so."

We grabbed our backpacks off the grass and Brody hurried to walk beside me. "Are you going to be okay?"

"Yeah, sure."

[illegible] a lot of points."

[illegible]

checkered [illegible]

"Recognize this?" Mom yanked it up and dropped it down.

"Yes," I said weakly.

"Get in."

I fell into the car and pulled the door shut. My face was so hot it stung. *Now what? How bad was this going to be?* The words whirled through my head, over and over.

Now we were passing Next to New. I had to look. There was a naked mannequin in the window.

"I leave the dentist's office and am driving home

when all of a sudden I see *my* dress on *that.*" Mom jabbed her finger at the faceless figure.

I closed my eyes, my heart sinking. "Can I go talk to Anita?" I opened my eyes, hoping to see Mom's nodding head.

She gripped the steering wheel. "We're done talking. We're going home."

We drove in silence. I watched the houses pass. Lawns, windows, trees in pink bloom, kids playing. Did they sleep in their closets? Did they have headaches? Or did they just play and have fun? I shivered and stared at the dashboard.

The car stopped. We were home. I felt myself open the door and follow my mother inside.

"Sit down." She dropped her dress on the kitchen table.

I sat.

"The lady with the dyed red hair said you brought this in. That *I* wanted to sell it. Who the hell do you think you are? Going into my bedroom, snooping through my closet, and *stealing* my clothes?"

I cringed at *stealing*, knowing she was right. I was a no-good, rotten thief.

"What else did you take?"

"Nothing," I said, relieved at the truth. "You never [illegible] it. I thought you didn't want it anymore."

[illegible]

I closed my eyes.

"And no Outdoor School — that's O — D — S."

My eyes shot open and head flew up. "*NO*, Mom, please, not that! I'll do eight weekends in my room. Ten. All summer. But not Outdoor School. *Please.*"

"You should have thought of that before taking my dress. Now think yourself into your bedroom."

My legs could barely stand with my gut in triple knots.

"And don't even try to change my mind."

My numb feet carried me down the hall, into my

room. I shut the door, saying good-bye to the whole wide world, and saw myself falling again into that dark hole, tumbling, spiraling out of control. My mouth turned watery and my knees wobbled. I stumbled to the wastebasket. My stomach clutched and released, lurched and heaved. Gross. Throwing up in my wastebasket. I waited for a minute, my head still leaning over the side; my body still jerked, but nothing more came up. I sat on the floor, wrapped my arms around myself, and began rocking back and forth, back and forth. *Why me? Why me?* I stared at the wastebasket, my eyes growing heavy, my body still rocking. Sometime later my legs began to ache and I crawled to my closet.

With Turtle tucked under my arm, I slid the door shut. I felt my way under the blankets and nestled my head in my pillow. But sleep wouldn't take me away. Instead, my body tensed from the memory of sharp words and shouting, of threats and punishments.

I clutched Turtle's body, squeezed it tight. Tighter. Then I threw her. She crashed against the closet wall and fell to the floor. Why did I take the dress? What was I thinking? Dumb! Stupid! Idiot!

My eyes stung and my throat swelled. It wasn't fair. Every time I thought things were better, they only turned worse. I'd get my hopes up and then — BAM — shot [illegible]

1:59. In limbo. Waiting for something to happen, for something to end, to begin, or to get better forever. HA. Like this was ever going to get better.

Exhaustion crept down my body, weighing heavy on my shoulders and legs, yet fighting sleep with sudden jerks and spasms until it finally gave up, gave in, gave out.

The closet door banged open. "You're late."

I squinted at my mother's outline. "I'm sick."

"Liar. You're a thief and a liar. Get going. You'll miss the bus and I'm not driving you to school. I mean it."

Somehow I made it. Tyler managed to prod me along, pouring me a bowl of stale cereal and a glass of sour orange juice. "Brush your teeth," he said, putting my empty bowl in the dishwasher. "Are you wearing yesterday's clothes?"

I shrugged.

"Wash your face — you've got something crusty on it."

I stared at him.

"And comb your hair."

We stood at the corner waiting for the bus, Tyler shifting his sports bag and backpack. "Boyfriend problems?"

I breathed in the cool morning air. A hint of the warming day rode the inhale and I shut my eyes. "No."

"Flunk a test?"

Frustration followed the exhale. "*NO.*"

"What then?"

"What do you think?" I eyed him.

"You and Mom."

"How'd you guess? I'm grounded and no Outdoor School."

"What?" He frowned. "Why?"

The bus stopped and the doors opened.

[illegible] back at him as I climbed the steps. "I took [illegible]

[illegible]

"You can't miss Outdoor School." Tyler leaned against the seat. "You have to go."

Brody met me at the classroom door and followed me to the coat hooks. "What'd your mom do?"

How many times could I say it? Only once more. "I'm grounded, I can't work at Next to New, I can't go to Outdoor School, and I don't want to talk about it." I walked past him to my seat, sat down, and stared at Mr. Hudson's bald spot as he wrote on the board.

The bell rang and someone led the flag salute,

someone read the lunch menu, and Mr. Hudson said something about counselors and wood cookies.

"I'm not sure I have everyone's attention," he said.

I'd been staring out the window. I looked at Mr. Hudson, who was watching me. My face warmed.

"Next week is Extra Credit Week," he said. "If you do a presentation to the class, you'll receive bonus points and something special. It can be on anything we've studied all year." *Points* gave me shivers. Why would I want more points? Besides, extra credit wouldn't earn me the only thing I wanted.

CHAPTER 25

The Pledge

[illegible] for my closet. My body [illegible] remembered waking to strange dreams and bad numbers: 1:13, 2:16, 3:08, 4:57. Each time I woke, I stared into the dark, trying to piece the dreams together.

It started out okay with me as the *Goodnight Moon* bunny, all cozy in my blue-and-white-striped pajamas, saying "goodnight" to the cow jumping over the moon and to the mittens and kittens. But then, the old lady whispering "hush" stood up and pointed her long, sharp knitting needles at me and yelled, "Shut up!" And she wasn't a lady bunny anymore, but a Nazi guard in a blue-and-white-checkered dress with all her fingers chopped off. She only had two thumbs. "Eat your mush," she shouted, "or I'll give it to the mouse and you'll lose your precious bowl forever!"

I madly gulped my mush, choking and coughing, nervously looking everywhere for the mouse, sure he was going to jump right in my bowl. As I swallowed the last spoonful, I threw up all over the green blanket. The old lady started for my bed. I scurried under the sheet and burrowed deep. Safe, I thought. But darkness closed in, my chest tightened, I gasped for air.

I thrashed for the closet light, whacked the lamp shade, then fumbled for the switch. Light, at last, precious light, filling my closet. My body shook in relief and I grabbed Turtle. With my knees to my chest, I rocked back and forth. *Dear God, please help me.*

"Are you okay, Hope?"

It wasn't God. It was Mr. Hudson. And I wasn't in my closet, but back in the classroom, rocking in my chair, my head still on my desk. I swallowed and followed the voice. He was kneeling down, his eyes meeting mine as I turned my head.

"Hope," he said again, quietly, "are you sick?"

"I don't know."

"Do you need to go to the sickroom?"

"I don't know." I stared at his eyebrows.

[illegible] Would you like to talk [illegible]

my feet. I thought my [illegible]

"What's up?" Brody came over. "You okay?"

"Yeah."

Mr. Hudson held my arm firmly, just above my elbow, as we walked to the door, and I knew he'd keep me from falling. "I'll be back in a moment, class."

We entered the hallway and I caught a deep breath of fresh air as the third graders headed outside to recess. My legs felt stronger and I stood up straight. Mr. Hudson dropped his hand and strolled alongside me like we were good friends taking a walk together. "Isn't this weather something else?" he said. "Did you hear the thunder last night? It woke my dog and she started howling."

I smiled. It felt good to smile even if I felt miles away.

We stopped in front of Mrs. Nelson's door. "Counselor," it said under her name, and I thought of Dr. McKillip.

Mr. Hudson tapped on the door, then pushed it open. The room was crammed with stacks of books and piles of stuffed animals and puppets. The walls were filled with yellow, orange, purple, and green posters with sayings like "Free to Be Me" and "Let Me Grow in Peace."

Mrs. Nelson looked up from her worktable and set her paintbrush in a glass jar filled with purple paint. Her shiny black hair swept across her shoulders as she stood up. She smiled, her mouth still morning fresh with pink lipstick. I wondered if she had kids and if they got to tell her how they felt.

"What can I do for you two?" she asked cheerfully.

Mr. Hudson put his hand on my shoulder. "Well, Hope isn't sure if she's sick or not, so I thought maybe you could talk to her and see if she needs to go home."

"No!" I practically shouted, then lowered my voice. "I don't need to go home."

Mrs. Nelson looked at Mr. Hudson, her thin black eyebrows raised like McDonald's arches.

"You came at just the right time," she said. "I could [illegible]

myself or others. The words floated easily through my mind. They should after six years. Six spring open houses when Mrs. Nelson urged parents and kids to take the pledge, then paint their hand purple, press it to the white paper, and sign their name alongside. Mom figured she'd done it once, so she didn't need to purple up her hand every year.

By the end of the open house, the hallways were filled with purple hands and names. The tiny kindergartner hands were so cute with their names spelled with backward letters and long, squiggly tails coming off *y* and *g*, looking like polliwogs.

Mr. Hudson had slipped out of the room and I wondered what I was really doing there.

"Why don't you start at one end of the sign, and I'll work at the other." Mrs. Nelson handed me another jar of purple paint and a brush. "We'll meet in the middle."

I nodded, dipped my brush in the paint, and followed the pencil-drawn *I.*

Mrs. Nelson smoothed the paper at the far end of the table and began writing backward. She didn't break the silence, leaving just the sound of our brushes dipping and tapping against glass, then swishing across dry paper. Quiet is nice. It lets your mind rest.

"So, Hope, how's school going for you?" I guess counselors can't go forever without asking questions.

"Okay, I guess." I kept my eyes on the purple *w*, trying for even curves.

"You guess?" She kept her eyes down, too. "Are you looking forward to Outdoor School?" She moved her paint jar closer to the middle.

"My mom says I can't go." The words sunk in and my stomach rolled. Not go to Outdoor School? Miss the experience of my life? Even snakes? I saw Mr. Hudson the first day of school, peering into our eyes and hissing the word

[illegible]

trated on finishing *will*. "I have headaches."

"So your mom is afraid to let you go because of your headaches?"

"She doesn't care about my headaches."

"She doesn't?"

"No."

"What does she care about?"

"How much things cost."

"She's a single parent, isn't she?" Mrs. Nelson painted away, her questions as smooth as her beautiful brushstrokes.

"Uh-huh."

"Do you remember your father?"

"He left us when I was a baby."

"I'm sorry."

"Me too."

Mrs. Nelson drew the *H* on *Hurting.* I was impressed she could lean her letters together while going the opposite way, like I was always amazed the way Mom could back our car down the driveway and turn into the street just by looking in the rearview mirror.

"How long have you had the headaches?"

I thought for a moment. "All this year, I guess."

"What do you do for them?"

"I wear a mouth guard thing at night so I don't grind my teeth."

"You're grinding your teeth?" Mrs. Nelson set her brush on top of her jar and turned to me. I looked up to see her troubled eyes and pressed pink lips.

"Is that Mr. Hudson giving you too much work?" She tilted her head to one side.

"Not really."

"Are you worried about junior high next year?"

"No."

She stared out the window, like the secret answer to my headaches was floating around the playground.

"What about your friends?" Mrs. Nelson's forehead [illegible] didn't even notice she'd made me wiggle the [illegible].

I stared at her hand.

"Do you know that a lot of students come and talk to me about their parents?"

"No." My eyes stayed on her hand.

"Some kids feel unsafe at home. Some parents yell or scream, hurt others in the family, or throw things, and students come in and share their concerns with me."

I set the brush on my jar and she cupped my empty hand in both of hers.

"Do you feel unsafe at home?"

My eyes went to the window and I studied the third graders swinging and climbing monkey bars and chasing after soccer balls. They seemed happy. Here, anyway. But what about after school, at home? Did they feel safe? Did I feel unsafe? I never thought Mom would hurt me, like burning me with a cigarette like some mothers do. I just felt sick to my stomach whenever I had to go home. Not even Turtle or my closet seemed to help much anymore.

I sighed and looked back at our hands, then at Mrs. Nelson's eyes. "My mother says I'm stupid. And – a dumb shit."

Mrs. Nelson's jaw clamped tight. She'd better be careful, I thought, or she'd need one of those plastic mouth guards. She squeezed my fingers so hard I thought they'd never move again. Dropping my hand, she moved to her desk and sat in her chair. She pulled an orange chair close and patted the seat. "The pledge signs can wait."

She looked out the window again. "Hope, you remember my visit to your classroom?"

"Uh-huh."

"And you know about *hurting words*?"

"Yes."

"That they're *abusive words*?"

"Yes." I didn't think this was a quiz, but I wondered

one can make you feel inferior without your consent.

Eleanor Roosevelt."

"Does anything else bother you at home?" I'd never seen Mrs. Nelson so serious, and I'd never had this much attention from her. I figured I should try to help her out. I read the quote on her pencil cup: "Albert Einstein's definition of insanity — doing the same thing over and over again and expecting different results." *Over and over again.* Was I going insane? Maybe so.

"I can't seem to do anything right. I try over and over

again but there's always something wrong. I don't do it fast enough or slow enough or good enough."

She glanced at the worktable. "See our sign?"

"Yeah."

"Well, I could have started at the beginning or at the end or in the middle and it would have come out basically the same. Then you came along at just the right time and we started at opposite ends and worked toward each other."

I wondered what this had to do with my mother.

She smiled — finally — then turned in her chair and leaned forward facing me, her arms resting on her legs. "There are many different ways to do the same thing, Hope, and usually they're all just as good. Always keep an open mind about that, would you?" Her strong eyes didn't budge from mine.

I nodded.

Her eyes softened and she spoke slower. "Hope, what do you wish for? How would you change your life if you could? What would make you really happy?"

My skin tingled, my stomach churned, and my heart

beat faster. I felt lighter with each question and wondered if I was about to take off flying, maybe to that tropical island. Any wish I wanted . . . to go to Outdoor School, of course . . . no more headaches . . . no more stomachaches . . . to live with Tyler, Anita, and [illegible] what I [illegible]

covered my face with my trembling [illegible] words fell in pieces from my lips, through my fingers, breaking apart in the air, "I — want — someone — to — love — me."

I felt arms around me, lifting me gently to my feet; and soft hair against my wet cheeks; a light, sweet whisper in my ear, "It's all right, it's okay"; and a gentle sway back and forth, back and forth.

Mrs. Nelson would probably have kept whispering and swaying all day, but I finally wiped my eyes and sat back in my chair. She patted my knee and waited.

"I'm okay," I said.

She nodded, then cleared her throat. "Hope, if there's any way you can talk to your mother about hurting words, about verbal abuse, it might help." She reached for a pink Sticky Note pad. "Remember, we've practiced *I Statements,*" she said as she wrote out an example: "I feel _____ when you _______, and I wish you would _______." She handed me the reminder note. "Look your mother in her eyes when you talk to her."

"I'll try."

"Good luck, Hope. I'll be thinking of you."

"Thanks."

We stood up and she put her arm over my shoulder while walking me to the door. "I feel *good,*" she said, "when you *come see me,* and I wish you would *do it more often.*"

CHAPTER 26

"I" Statements

gers clenched the pen, found the

letters, felt the relief: "I feel *sick* when you *are sarcastic* and I wish you would *say what you're really thinking*."

Then I set the table with our pretty yellow place mats and matching napkins. I put the silverware out just the right way, with the fork on the left and knife and spoon on the right. I made a pitcher of lemonade and put ice in the glasses and put the note on Mom's place mat.

The note was gone when I returned to the kitchen for

dinner. Tyler was washing his hands in the sink. Grass and mud stains covered his baseball uniform.

"You're not supposed to crawl to the bases," I said.

Tyler casually turned, then flicked his wet hands in my face.

"Ty-ler!" I wiped my face on his jersey and pretended to blow my nose.

He grabbed my wrists and yanked me toward the living room.

"No fighting," warned Mom, setting our plates on the table. "Time to eat."

I glanced around the kitchen, straining to discover even a hint of the flowery note. I tried to sneak looks at Mom's face. She was being way too cheerful, which made me way too nervous.

I suffered through leftover meat loaf and was about to clear the table when she cleared her throat. "Anyone know where *this* came from?" She pulled the missing note from under her place mat and tossed it onto the table.

Tyler read the message, then looked at me. I had no

idea what to do next. *Mrs. Nelson!* I clamped my cold hands together in my lap and tried to look Mom in the eyes, my whole self pleading for her understanding. The wall clock ticked loudly. I slipped one thumb inside my entwined fingers and squeezed it as tight as some-

[illegible]

once-confident words. "Sarcasm [illegible]

She snatched the note back, crumpled it, and tossed it on her dirty plate. "Now I feel *I want to clean this kitchen* and I wish *you would help me.*" She laughed and stood up.

Tyler mouthed to me, "Hang in there."

My body cautiously relaxed. I was relieved I didn't get lectured, but was I losing my mind? Was I really too sensitive? Maybe I did need to lighten up. Was she teasing or was she serious? All I knew for sure was my head ached. Again.

CHAPTER 27

Choices

ing in front of the class gave me the [illegible]
just maybe, the extra credit, plus Mr. Hudson's something special, would change my mother's mind about Outdoor School.

I finally decided after Mr. Hudson had talked about control. "Everyone wants to be in control — nations and neighbors, lovers and leaders, mothers and grandmothers, doctors and" — he gave us a little smile — "teachers."

He wrote *control* on the whiteboard.

"There's good control," he said, facing us, "when

people have choices and can pick the path of greatest advantage. There's also bad control, when people cross the path and become demanding, critical, and abusive of others. Somehow they seem to think they're more important than you.

"But," he said, pointing his finger at us, "you don't have to be an abuser; you can choose not to take that path. Nor do you have to be the victim. You always have choices, and the most important one is how you react. You can choose to be strong or choose to give up. You have to tell yourself, 'I am valuable. I am worth saving. I can be free.'

"Remember, you always have a choice over what's up here." He pointed to his head. "And what's in here." He touched his heart.

I felt Mr. Hudson's words all the way down to my feet. No one whispered or wiggled in their seats, so maybe they were feeling his words, too.

"The Hands and Words Are Not For Hurting Pledge is about good control," said Mr. Hudson, raising his right hand. Don't forget to take the pledge again at spring open house and encourage your family to take it, too."

I wish.

It wasn't until the end of the day, when we were put- [illegible] desks, that I approached Mr. Hud- [illegible]

that too soon."

I swallowed. "It's okay."

When Mom came home that evening, I met her at the back door and helped with the Bi-Mart bags.

"I'm doing an extra-credit report tomorrow."

Silence.

"That means I have to get up in front of the class and —"

"I know what it means." Mom pulled out dish soap and coffee filters from the paper bag.

I gripped the back of a chair. "Since I'm getting extra

credit, um, could I" — I paused, then whipped out the words — "could I go to Outdoor School?"

She stared at me, her arms filled with toilet paper and napkins. "Think about it, Hope. What did I tell you?"

I zoned after *think about it*. That told me all I needed to know, but it was too late.

"Answer me, Hope. What did I say?"

My mouth rescued my mind. "You said not to ask."

That evening I sat at my desk with paper, pencil, and pink Post-it notes. I stared at *Anne Frank: Diary of a Young Girl*. How had I gotten the nerve to do a class presentation? I'd even stopped by Next to New to borrow a few things. Anita and Ruthie were all over me, asking about my life, my mom, and saying they were so sorry about the dress business. They, too, hoped the extra credit would change her mind about the store and Outdoor School.

Deep breath. You can do it. *Control, Hope, control.*

I began flipping through Anne's diary, remembering

names and faces, strict schedules, skimpy meals, secret visits.

I reread sections, jotted notes on Post-its, and tagged pages. Then I drew a star, colored it yellow, and [illegible] it out.

[illegible]

pered, "Save the mouse," pointing to the [illegible] pointed back at the bunny. He shook his head and pointed sharply to the mouse that was leaning way over the edge of the top shelf. I slipped quietly behind the old lady's rocking chair while the kittens were busy wrestling yarn balls. With a quick snatch, the mouse was in my pocket, and I was out the door.

"Fifteen minutes, Hope, until your presentation," said Mr. Hudson.

In the girls' bathroom, I took off my jeans and pulled out a gray-and-white-striped dress from the Next to New bag. It was too big, going way past my knees, which was perfect. I found the rope-like belt and tied it around my waist. The shoes were mixed — one black and one brown.

I pushed up the left sleeve. With a blue marker, I wrote #8726 on my arm. I pinned on the yellow paper star and looked in the mirror. My heart clenched. I stared at the tired reflection, the drab striped dress, the yellow star. I wavered between past and present, between barbed-wire fences and playground swings, between Nazi guards shouting and Mr. Hudson singing, between brick chimneys and springtime daffodils. Was I coming or going? In Eola Hills or Auschwitz? Fear and relief swept through me at the same time. I shivered with an idea.

Pulling open the restroom door, I stuck my head into the hall. Noelle was coming back from the office with a stack of papers. "Noelle," I whispered loudly.

She paused. "What?"

"Could you bring me a pair of scissors?"

She wrinkled her forehead. "I guess."

When she returned, she stood in the half-opened doorway, staring at my dress. "Geezuz, Hope, what are [illegible]

With a gray [illegible] clothes in the bag, I walked back to the classroom. My throat was dry and my hands were wet as I opened the door. Anne Frank said she was petrified to go outside. I was petrified to go inside. Mr. Hudson looked up from his desk and the kids around him stared.

"Halloween's not till October," Peter snickered.

"Knock it off, Peter," said Brody.

But it was the whispers and giggles that almost sent me back to the restroom.

"That's enough." Mr. Hudson stood up. "It takes a lot of courage to talk in front of your peers, so let's give

Hope our respect and attention." The whispers stopped, everyone sat down, and I slowly walked to the front of the room gripping my book and notes.

"Hi," I said, my voice shaky. "My name is Anne Frank. I was born June 12, 1929. On Monday morning, July 6, 1942, I went into hiding with my mother, father, and sister. We left our home forever because the German Nazis were rounding up Jewish people like us and taking them to concentration camps and death camps where most of them died of hard work or disease or were killed in gas chambers. We lived for two years in a 'Secret Annexe,' which were some rooms hidden behind a bookshelf in my father's office building. Four other Jewish people lived with us."

I glanced at my notes and cleared my voice. "We had to do many hard things not to be discovered, like not talking and tiptoeing everywhere. Sometimes we couldn't even go to the bathroom."

My voice calmed and the words came easier. "I was scared most of the time. Scared we'd be discovered, scared of the bombs, scared for our friends taken away to work camps where their heads were shaved for lice and their arms tattooed with ID numbers." I pulled up my sleeve and showed my blue-numbered skin.

"It was hard for us to get along with each other, living day after day so close together. People argued over silly [illegible]

hiding from them stole my few remaining freedoms — to talk and laugh when I wanted, to look out a window and smell fresh air, to eat a decent meal. All I had left was what was in here." I pointed to my head. "I could think anything I wanted without anyone knowing. Without anyone stealing it. And I wrote a lot of it down." I held up Anne's diary, then turned to one of my Post-it note pages.

"I wrote this Thursday, November 19, 1942." My eyes swept the classroom and I was surprised how everyone was paying attention. "'I feel wicked sleeping in a warm bed, while my dearest friends have been knocked down or have fallen into a gutter somewhere out in the cold night. I get frightened when I think of close friends who have now been delivered into the hands of the cruelest brutes that walk the earth. And all because they are Jews!'

"Anne Frank hid for two years before getting caught and sent to a concentration camp. She died seven months later of a disease called typhus. That was over sixty years ago, but we remember her today because of what she said." I set the book and my notes on a table.

"Life is really unfair sometimes and it's hard to wait for good things to happen, but Anne Frank had courage. She played lots of little games to feel in control, like pretending that something was delicious when it was really disgusting. I wish she was alive today so she'd know how important she is."

I reached behind my head, untied my scarf, and slipped it off.

A gasp went through the classroom.

"I gave her the scissors," Noelle said loudly.

Everyone started talking.

"Quiet," said Mr. Hudson, stepping forward. "I don't think Hope is finished."

I waited until they'd settled back in their seats.

CHAPTER 28

The Last Link

from the thorny branches.

"It's believing in roses that makes them bloom," Mr. Hudson had said while handing out the extra-credit surprise. "A French proverb that speaks to having a dream, a goal, and working persistently and courageously to achieve it."

When I got my rosebush, he said, "I got the idea from your concentration camp map. I hope you'll take good care of it because that, too, will make it bloom." Brody got one for his report on the underground resistance — people who tried to secretly fight the Nazis.

There were extra-credit maps, science experiments, and special displays, but no other acting.

I leaned my extra-credit grade against the flowerpot. It was on a three-by-five card with these words: *"Remembering Anne Frank by Hope Elliot — A+."* It looked good. No, great. Mom would have to change her mind about Outdoor School once she saw the rosebush and my amazing grade. Then I remembered my hair and my heart sank. I fingered the stubby ends and wondered if Ruthie could salvage what was left.

"I'd never have the guts to do that," Jessica had said after my presentation. "Are you going to dye it, too?"

I almost told her "no," but quickly changed it to "maybe."

"My mom would never let me do that," she said.

"Mine said she didn't care if I dyed it green with purple stripes."

"Your mom is way cool."

My bedroom door opened and Mom leaned against the doorway. "What's with the farm girl look?"

I touched the red bandanna scarf tied around my hair. "Nothin'."

"Who's the rosebush from?" She seemed in a good [illegible]

you give it to the neighbors?"

"I'm supposed to take care of it myself."

Mom's eyebrows shot up like I had no business taking care of anything. Like I had no clue how to plant, water, fertilize. Maybe she was right. Maybe not.

She turned and walked out. From the hallway came: "Good job on your report." *Good job?* My heart skipped, but my brain interrupted: *Don't get so excited, heart. D.D. probably didn't mean it. Don't set yourself up for disappointment.*

❋

Saturday morning. The phone had rung five times by nine o'clock and someone had knocked at the front door. I hoped the calls weren't from Grandma. That would really put Mom in a crappy mood.

I lay on my closet bed and stared at my hanging clothes, then turned over and buried my head in my pillow. How could I have thought that extra credit and a rosebush would change Mom's mind? Maybe I *was* hopeless. But then I heard Mr. Hudson's voice: "You're not a victim. You have choices."

Right. I have choices. Just like the *Goodnight Moon* bunny, I can look at the ceiling or the walls or my comb and brush. Great choices. I can choose not to go to Outdoor School. My mind went blank and I nuzzled deeper into my flannel pillowcase. But, once again, Mr. Hudson's words intruded: "You can choose to be strong or choose to give up."

I wanted to be strong, but I didn't want to be like Anne Frank, working so hard, hoping things would get better, then losing everything in the end. The Jews should have known it was only going to get worse. They should have escaped at the first signs of trouble.

I sighed. I felt like the sad hum coming from my radio, the singer sending her heartache into my closet. Just [illegible] *those words?*

"Broken One, you are standing all alone. Broken One, is the pain deep inside or in your home?"

My *home*? My heart paused, waiting for an answer. *Yes,* I wanted to cry into the radio. *Yes, the pain is deep inside, in my home. Who are you, singing words wrapped in such hurt, yet sounding so sweet?* Now her angel voice turned strong and the words sparkled. "I believe there is hope. I believe there is peace. I believe there is love to feel the depth of your soul."

My heart began beating hard as the words rang in my

ears, swept past me, to the top of my clothes and out the closet, filling my room, urging me to get going.

"Take my hand, and I will walk this road with you. Take my hand, and I will carry you through." I sat up. Wide awake.

"I believe there is hope," came the chorus again. *Yes! There is Hope.* My insides shivered. I threw back my covers and sucked in a fresh start.

"Broken One, let your story make you strong as you begin to sing your song. Broken One, find joy once again, and your new life begins."

Maybe, just maybe, I wasn't too tired to do one last thing. I pushed myself up and rocked back on my heels. I found Tyler's sports bag in the back of my closet and opened it on my bed. I *wasn't* going to lose everything in the end. I *was* going to Outdoor School. AND I WASN'T COMING BACK. *There is Hope.*

My purple hiking boots went in the bag first. Then my two pairs of jeans and four T-shirts. Make that five. I tried to remember the list. Underwear and socks. Sweatshirt. That made sense. Toothbrush, toothpaste. I opened my door and crept down the hall, into the bathroom. Washcloth? Towel? I looked through the drawers and medicine cabinet. Band-Aids, sunscreen, mosquito repellent. Yes.

Back in my room, I checked my drawers and closet

[illegible]

"Yeah. I'm looking for something."

"I'm making blueberry pancakes."

"Okay," I shouted back. I grabbed the flashlight, zipped back to my room, tossed it in my bag, and hid the bag in my closet. My knees shook, but I entered the kitchen totally cool.

"What have you been up to?" Mom asked, sitting down across from me.

I tensed. "Uh, cleaning my room. Putting things away."

"I mean at school."

I buttered my pancakes and poured syrup over them. Where was she going with this? "Getting ready for Outdoor School," I answered carefully. "Learning songs, making these little stoves, stuff like that."

"Uh-huh." She lit a cigarette. "Have you made some new friends this year?"

Now she was making me nervous. I knew this wasn't a friendly little mom-daughter chat. It was heading somewhere I probably wouldn't like, but what could I do about it?

"What about some kid named Brody? Weren't the two of you swinging the other day?"

My fork clanked onto the plate and my face turned roasting hot. How did she know his name?

Mom grinned. "I think he likes you." She stood up and walked over to the counter, picked up a round tin, and opened the lid. "Brownies." She brought them to the table. "For me," she said, pushing the lid back on. "He came by this morning. Said he'd heard you were grounded and wondered if the brownies would change my mind about Outdoor School. Made them himself."

Brody had *that* much nerve? Wow.

"Pretty cute kid," Mom was saying. "Dressed like he was going to play golf or something. And his mother, waiting for him in a silver BMW." Mom tilted her head and eyed me. "You've got better taste than I thought."

smoke, then smashed the remains in an ashtray. "I goddamn don't know what the crap's going on, Hope, but I've had enough of this insane parade. First, your principal calls to tell me how important Outdoor School is and how much kids learn in just five days. Then she asks if I have any concerns about the trip." Mom rolled her eyes. "'No,' I tell her. Then Mr. Hudson calls saying I should be very proud of you and your efforts at school. I tell him I'm not exactly proud of your stealing. That shuts him up."

She crossed her arms on the table. "You'd better

stop this right now, young lady." She stared. "You can pass the word that I've made up my mind and not even a mountain can move it."

"I didn't do anything. Honest." I tried to sort it out, but my ears interrupted, beating to my dancing heart, ringing in glorious disbelief: Did all those people *really* stand up for me?

Back in my room, I tried to come up with a plan. I was going to Outdoor School, even if I had to walk. But where would I go after that? A crisis center? Teen runaway house? Abused women's shelter? I'd heard about some places in McMinnville. Yes, that's what I'd do.

Relief rushed through my body, followed by a burst of energy. Lots to do if I was moving out. I started with my closet, throwing away stale saltines, hard Red Vines, and a jar of moldy green olives. I sorted a pile of clothes, folding, hanging, and tossing dirties in my clothes hamper. I washed the dress and scarf from Anita and ironed my new sundress.

When I picked up my pillow to change the case, I saw my point system notebook, hiding there on my flannel sheet. I kneeled down and picked it up. I opened the cover. There was my code list and point values. I hadn't entered any numbers for a while. I don't know if I'd gotten tired of the system, or maybe it just seemed useless. I thumbed through the pages filled with dates

[illegible]

in seven months. Pride brought a smile to my lips, pride in all those moments I'd stood silent and had quietly beaten down those hateful words, the *dumb shits,* the *shoulds,* the stares and glares. I'd won. Guido and Joshua would have been proud of me.

My pride quickly faded, however, as I realized I had nothing to show for my hard work. No army tank. No blue ribbon. No gold star. No end to Mom's abusive words. I'd won the game but not the prize.

I walked over to the wastebasket and let my notebook slip from my hand.

I sat on my bed, held Turtle in my lap, and gazed at the wastebasket. Would I yell at my children? Call them *brat* and *stupid*? I'd heard that bad things like yelling and hitting can go down through families just like a bad heart, from mother to daughter, to grandson to great-grandson. Was I going to be a link in that chain? If only I wouldn't forget how the words hurt, how the sarcasm stung, and how the piercing eyes gagged my throat, burned my heart. I lay my head on Turtle's. Would I forget a year from now? Ten years from now?

Slowly I stood up and moved to the wastebasket. I reached down and picked up my notebook. Beneath it was the yellow star I'd worn for my Anne Frank presentation. I looked at both for a moment, then found a glue stick, smeared the back of the star, and pressed it carefully over the black Lab puppy on the front of my notebook. I ran my fingers over the star, feeling each line and point. I wouldn't forget. And I wouldn't be a link.

CHAPTER 29

Saving Hope

[illegible]

with Lydia. Tyler was at a baseball tournament. I looked through my packed bag ten times, adding more socks and ChapStick and a pair of sunglasses. I wandered around the house, stared out the front window, sat on the couch, went into the kitchen, opened the refrigerator, and studied the orange juice carton.

The telephone rang. I closed the refrigerator door and answered the phone. "Hello."

"Mrs. Elliot?"

"No, this is Hope."

"Oh, Hope, hi, this is Gabriela Feliciano. I'm at Eola High and I —"

Her words faded as I tried to convince myself that it really was Gabriela Feliciano, League MVP and All-State Team — calling *my* house. And not a wrong number. She asked for Mom. But why?

"It's my third year as a counselor, so I'm hoping that will convince your mother."

"What?"

"Convince your mother that she should let you go to Outdoor School," said Gabriela. "I'm going to be your counselor."

NO WAY! "But we don't find that out till the morning we leave."

"Counselors know ahead so we can make wood cookies."

I'd forgotten about our name tags, a competition among the counselors, who decorate the wooden circles with bright paint, tiny beads, and sparkly sequins in amazing designs, then string them on a leather cord.

Cool sixth graders return to school wearing them for the next week or two.

"I'll make you one, Hope, even if you don't get to go."

"I'm going."

[illegible]

"Well, then," said Gabriela, sounding relieved about Mom, "I'll get working on those wood cookies and I'll see you soon. Get lots of sleep — the coyotes keep us awake all night."

I could hear the smile in her voice. I couldn't wait. "Thanks for calling."

I was still glowing from Gabriela's call when Mom came home, glowing from too much champagne. She had two dresses draped over one arm and a Next to

New bag in her hand. My mother went into Next to New? Couldn't happen.

"Your lady friends showed up here just as I got home. Anita and Ruby."

"Ruthie," I said, completely confused.

She spread the dresses out on the couch — one silky purple and flowery yellow (cool iron) and the other a red, white, and blue (cotton/steam). "For the Fourth of July." Mom dumped the small sack and picked up American flag earrings.

I smiled, longing to be back at the store, then I braced for Mom's put-down.

"Their clothes aren't half bad." She dropped the earrings and picked up the purple and yellow dress, holding it to her shoulders, spinning around.

I swallowed in disbelief.

"They agreed with me — you shouldn't have taken in my dress without permission. They apologized over and over, saying they should have checked it out." Mom turned in another small circle, the silky dress flowing like flowers in a breeze. "They said I could have fifty percent off anything in the store the days you work there. And they practically wet their pants praising your work and begging to have you back."

The doorbell rang. "My God, stop!" Mom dropped the dress on the couch. "It'd better not be about you."

Please don't be about me. [illegible]

"I know who you are," Mom said stiffly, "and my answer is still no. Hope is not going to Outdoor School."

"That's fine," said Mrs. Nelson.

What? I wanted to shout. *You're the counselor. You're supposed to make things work out. Your job is to help kids. Don't give up now!*

Mom's shoulders relaxed and she opened the screen door.

"Happy Mother's Day." Mrs. Nelson handed Mom a small bouquet of flowers. "They're from my yard."

Mom held the flowers to her face as if soaking up all their beauty. "Thank you. They smell wonderful."

"I picked them," came a small voice, and a little girl walked right into the house. She grinned and held out a doll. "Samantha helped me."

"Maddie," said Mrs. Nelson, "please say *hello* to Mrs. Elliot and to Hope, her daughter."

"Hello, and Samantha says *hello.*" Maddie waved her doll's arm. "My real name is Madeline, but it's Maddie for short and I like horses. Someday I'm going to have a horse. Or maybe a kitten."

Mrs. Nelson shrugged and smiled at me.

We followed Mom into the living room. Mrs. Nelson's shiny black hair swayed across her pink blouse and Maddie hopped along, the bow on her dress bouncing behind her.

"I'm four," said Maddie, snuggling next to Mrs. Nelson on the couch.

"I'm ten times that old," said Mom, sitting down with a sigh.

"That's old," said Maddie, arranging Samantha on her lap.

Mrs. Nelson rolled her eyes. "Now, sweetheart, I'd like to visit with Mrs. Elliot."

I leaned against the wall hoping to blend in, wonder- [illegible]

[illegible] you can visit Hope's bedroom."

Maddie beamed. "I choose her bedroom." She hopped off the couch, hurried to my side, and grasped my hand.

"Well, we didn't exactly give Hope a choice, did we?" Mrs. Nelson laughed.

"That's okay," I said.

"Thank you," said Mrs. Nelson, her words as warm as Maddie's little hand.

As we left the living room, Mrs. Nelson cleared her throat. "Mrs. Elliot, I did stop by to talk about Outdoor School."

My heart clenched and I put my finger to my lips for Maddie to be quiet.

"I respect your decision," Mrs. Nelson went on before Mom or Maddie interrupted. "I'm sure it was difficult."

"No, it wasn't difficult," came my mother's abrupt words.

"Ow, you're squeezing too tight," Maddie whispered loudly, pulling her hand from mine.

"I'm sorry," I whispered back. "Would you like to meet my turtle?"

"Yes!"

I made several trips to the kitchen, getting drinks for Turtle and Samantha and cookies for Maddie, and for any other excuse to hear Mom and Mrs. Nelson.

"She screws up all the time," I heard Mom say. My knees went weak. "The dress was the last straw. She took something away from me; now I'm taking something away from her. Maybe it'll finally make an impression."

I inched to the end of the hall, my heart on hold.

"Why do you think she took it?" asked Mrs. Nelson.

"Money, what else?"

Pause.

"Did she take anything else?"

[illegible]

tal. There's a picture of us on my dresser."

I prayed Maddie would stay in my room.

"That must have been an amazing day," said Mrs. Nelson.

Right, I thought, *amazingly horrible.*

"Yes," Mom was saying, "a wonderful day."

I froze. *Wonderful?* Did I hear right?

"Does Hope know how you felt?" asked Mrs. Nelson.

"Do you have other children?" asked Mom.

"No, Madeline is our first," said Mrs. Nelson.

"It's a miracle to have a baby, an incredible miracle," said Mom slowly, "but there are a lot of things you never plan on, a lot of things you give up."

My shoulders slumped and my throat tightened.

"Did you have any help?" Now Mrs. Nelson's voice sounded concerned.

Mom laughed. "Are you kidding?"

"I'm sure it's hard being a single mom," said Mrs. Nelson. "But it looks like you've done a great job. Hope is a real joy to have at our school."

"She's got a mind of her own, that's for sure."

"She'll be a good leader," said Mrs. Nelson. "I can see her as an Outdoor School counselor."

I cringed.

"You think I should change my mind, don't you?" Mom asked.

"I think you're in a very uncomfortable situation and I'm sorry you had to make such a difficult decision." I could almost see Mrs. Nelson looking right into my mom's eyes. "But I also wonder if there might be another choice out there, one you'd both feel was more appropriate. Something we've found that works well at school is selecting a discipline closely related to the problem. Is there a consequence for Hope that somehow connects with taking your dress?"

"You mean like ironing my clothes?"

[illegible]

clothes."

"No, I won't." The words burst from the hallway into the living room.

"Hope." Mom stood up. So did Mrs. Nelson.

"I'm a good ironer." I walked straight into the living room. "I promise I am. I can iron silk and rayon and cotton. I know how to do pleats and ruffles. I can even steam. And I'm sorry about your dress, Mom. But I didn't think you wanted it anymore. You never wear it and I thought it reminded you of all my baby crying, and Dad — and, so" — I choked and felt a rush of tears to my eyes — "so I wanted to get it out of here."

Mrs. Nelson looked like she wanted to run right over and hug me. Mom's hands went to her hips. Panic stabbed my chest. My words had made things worse. Mom was angry at my outburst and now she'd add another punishment. A worse one.

But I had something to say. It was time to break my silence and release the agonizing, lonely hurt. I wasn't sure what to say, though. I wanted my words, each one, to tell exactly how I felt. This was my chance, maybe my only chance. *Please don't interrupt me.*

"Mom." I looked into her eyes and took a deep breath. "I feel sick to my stomach when you call me 'stupid.'"

"Well, I —" Mom started, but Mrs. Nelson put her hand on Mom's shoulder.

"And I feel really stupid when you tell me to 'think about it' and 'repeat what I've just said.'"

"But you stole my dress and tried to sell it." Same old stony voice. She didn't get it. *She didn't get it!* I covered my ears and closed my eyes. *Please, God, please take me away. Anywhere. Just take me away from here.*

Someone touched my shoulders but I didn't open my eyes. I took a shaky breath. "This . . . isn't . . . [illegible]"

[illegible]

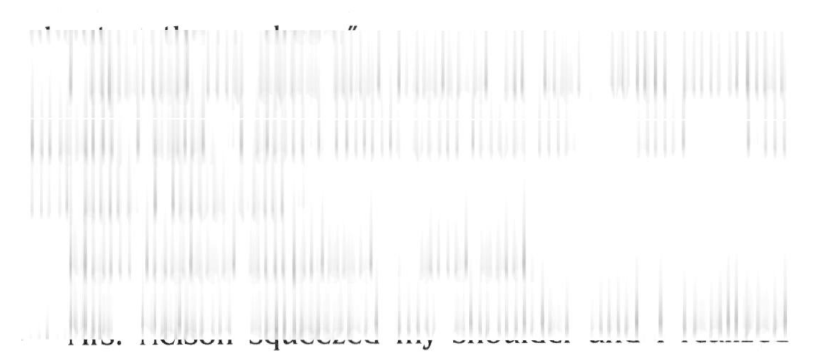

[illegible] she'd been standing by my side. Her eyes were also sad, but somehow hopeful.

A small hand patted my leg and I looked down to see Maddie holding up Turtle. "She'll make you feel better."

"Thank you," I said, taking Turtle to my chest for comfort and clutching Maddie's hand for strength.

I looked at everyone and suddenly felt confidence in my words. "I've tried to be good," I began again, wiping my eyes on the back of my hand, "but nothing I do ever works. I can't say the right things or do the right things.

I live in my bedroom trying to stay out of your way, Mom. I sneak around, trying not to disturb you. I don't ask for anything or to go anywhere. But maybe that's not enough. Maybe you want me out of here for good. Maybe I should go away."

"You can stay with me," said Maddie. "Mommy, can we go to Grandma's now and can Hope come, too, with her Turtle, and we'll get ice cream to feel better?"

Mrs. Nelson looked like she didn't know what to do next. At school she'd probably lead us in "There's Something We Can Do," but I didn't think she'd start singing in our living room.

"I need Hope to stay here with me." My mother blinked and a tear slipped out of her eye. She stepped closer and placed her hand on top of Maddie's and mine. "I need her here to help me, to iron my clothes."

Great, I thought, *more ironing for my poor arm.*

"And . . ." Mom paused. "Hope needs to pack for Outdoor School."

CHAPTER 30

Hug a Tree

one was snoring and Jessica's air mattress squeaked every time she rolled over. I inched quietly out of my sleeping bag, holding my breath so as not to wake Gabriela. I mean *Feliz.* That was her counselor name, meaning "happy" in Spanish, and she called us her *Campistas* (campers). Another counselor, Cricket, named her five kids *Ants,* and Fungus called his boys *Spores.*

I crawled to the tent door and slowly unzipped the canvas flap. Cold air washed my face and tingled my throat as I breathed in pine trees and campfire smoke.

I curled up next to the opening, forgetting the chill as I took in the perfectly still moonlit campground, tents scattered in a small meadow and along the river, the row of portable camp stoves lined up in front of the kitchen tent, and picnic tables ready for pancakes and pie-iron pizzas.

A million stars danced in the forever black sky and a brilliant yellow star shouted, "Look at me!" If I stared long enough, it turned white, or was it red, or purple? With all the surrounding darkness and stillness, and the giant sky, it seemed I was the only person on the entire earth taking in this magic. It was mine, all mine. But then I had this weird feeling that someone or something was out there, up there in the deep, throbbing heavens, staring back at me, hypnotizing me, urging my body to float up and join the dance.

I was so tired I should have slept like a rock. The past week had been crazy, trying to catch up and get ready. There was a rush of forms to fill out, schoolwork to finish, library books to find and return, and fund-raising money to collect. Tyler checked my packed bag and loaned me a sweatshirt and baseball cap plus his flannel sleeping bag. Mom bought a white T-shirt for tie-dyeing and surprised me with a disposable camera. She even got me a packet of three bandanna scarves — red, white, and blue — without a word, a single word, about

[illegible]

courage to break my long silence. I wished I could remember all I'd said, but I'll never forget the lightness that came with my final words, *"Maybe I should go away."* I smiled, thinking of Maddie's confidence and choices and carefree invitation to stay with them. And I clung to the watery shine in my mother's eyes.

"That's quite a brother you have," Mrs. Nelson had said Friday as she tagged my bags in the gym.

"Huh?" Tyler hadn't been home Sunday afternoon.

"Didn't you know?" She looked at me, her eyebrows raised in surprise.

"Know what?"

Mrs. Nelson lowered her clipboard. "Your brother was worried about you. He came to see me last week, concerned about your mother and her decision and how quiet you'd become."

"So you got everyone to call my mom?" I asked.

She shook her head, her ponytail bobbing. "No, Hope, Tyler was the spark. The fire spread by itself. People heard about your situation and wanted to do something. I don't even know who came to your aid."

Mr. Hudson had warned us to leave knives, hatchets, radios, and hair dryers at home. We were to bring everything Friday so the truck would be ready for our seven o'clock departure Monday morning. "Just bring a sack lunch," he said. "Tofu surprise and liver sandwiches are excellent." No comment.

After a long bus ride singing loud songs and waving at passing cars, we'd hiked into camp, unloaded the U-Haul and two pickups, pitched our tents, and were assigned camp duties. I helped clean the girls' bathroom — a small brick building with damp concrete floors and cold running water. There were funny mirrors above the sinks, some sort of smooth metal with faint, wavy reflections. I guess we wouldn't want to see our-

she finished her inspection, she glanced around, then wandered slowly between the tents and across the river.

The next morning before breakfast, Jessica leaned over and whispered in my ear, "Squid and Cougar are *too* cute." I followed her gaze to the high school counselors revving their campers to sing loudest for breakfast.

"Okay, gang," shouted Eagle Eye (Mr. Hudson), "let's

see who's going to line up first." He started singing, "There was a desperado —"

"From the wild and woolly west," we all chimed in, shouting our early morning best.

"Gumdrop's group goes first," Eagle Eye announced after voting with the other sixth-grade teachers, Miss Lindquist and Mr. Richmond. The rest of us protested, claiming horrid hunger pains.

Gabriela, uh, Feliz, corralled us in line. "Next time, we're first," she said, her arm draped around my shoulder.

"Yeah! All right!" we shouted.

"Who's number one?" she called out.

"*Campistas!*" we answered.

"*Rattlers!*" came a chorus from Snake's kids.

Settled at our table, we dived into sausage, scrambled eggs, and cinnamon rolls. I shook my milk carton, but it was frozen. "Do this," said Feliz, banging it on the wooden table. We all drummed away, then slurped out milky crystals.

After breakfast and camp cleanup, we split into study

sessions. Some headed to the fire pit to learn five kinds of fire making, then cooked Hunter's Stew in the coals. Others did water testing from the Deschutes River, or learned about the plants and animals of Central Ore-[illegible] My tent group was in Frog's survival-skills class. [illegible]

We sat around a picnic table with Frog standing at the end. "Ribbet," he said. "That means 'hi, how are you doin'?' in frog talk." We giggled and Shawna answered, "Ribbet." We giggled again.

He ran his hand through his black hair. "Okay," he announced, his thick eyebrows bobbing up and down. "Let's see what we've got here." He unzipped a backpack, then looked at us, getting all serious. "Anytime you head out on a hike, remind yourself that you could get lost and you could spend the night outdoors. Do you know the first rule if you get lost?"

No answer.

"Admit you're lost."

"Hi, tree, I'm lost," said Shawna.

I looked at the pines, their tops glowing warm in the morning sunlight.

"You can talk to the trees all you want," said Frog, "but be sure to hug one."

"And kiss it?" said Ellie Hoyt.

"Yuck," said Jenny.

"Hug a tree means to stay put," said Frog, pulling things out of his backpack. "Don't wander around trying to find your way out. Searchers will start looking where you were seen last."

Across the table Frog had lined up a pocketknife, a film canister housing waterproof matches, a plastic garbage bag, a whistle, a mirror, granola bars, and a water bottle. After explaining why we needed them in a survival kit, he gave us each our own whistle, then led us into the woods. We picked our tree to hug and Ellie really did kiss hers. Then we gathered leaves, grass, moss, pine needles, and dead fern fronds. Frog pulled the plastic garbage bag and pocketknife out of his backpack. "Let's say Hope is lost." I almost fell over at the sound of my name. I swallowed and my eyes zeroed in on Frog.

He motioned me to his side.

"Kiss a tree," said Ellie.

[illegible]

"Now, let's make sure Hope stays warm for her long night in the woods." He motioned for me to lie down on the ground and began filling my bag with our forest gatherings. "Hope needs a little insulation." I groaned. With great fun, everyone crammed pine needles and leaves and other dead things into my bag.

"The Abominable Snowman," Jenny announced.

"Snowwoman," said Shawna.

"I feel like a stuffed turtle," I moaned.

"Everyone — kneel down around Hope," instructed Frog, holding his camera.

Ellie whipped her fingers behind my head. "We're lost, come find us," called Jessica. But I didn't feel lost at all — I felt unbelievably found.

Shawna blew her whistle.

"Say 'we're hungry,'" answered Frog.

"We're hungry," came the chorus, and the camera clicked.

CHAPTER 31

What Is the Tie That Binds Us?

[illegible]

table lashing, knot tying, banana boats, and map and compass games.

We learned that Newberry Volcano covers five hundred square miles and the five-mile-wide crater contains two lakes and a lava flow of black glass called obsidian. Hiking up Lava Butte, we followed a twisting path cut into steep lava flows. (My purple boots were awesome.) At the top we could see the snow-covered Cascade Mountains stretching south toward California and north into Washington.

We learned to tell the difference between heatstroke and sunstroke; between ponderosa and lodgepole pines; and between skunk, coyote, and whitetail deer tracks. At Wizard Falls Fish Hatchery, a volunteer named Art showed us how nearly four million eggs hatch each year and become releasable fingerlings. We learned that feeding a tankful of fingerlings is way more exciting than sprinkling your goldfish bowl with those dried, pale-colored flakes. When you toss these specially made fish-guts nuggets into the concrete holding tanks, thousands of calm fish go crazy, thrashing in every direction, breaking the surface, churning the water like a giant blender. Afterward, we hit the restrooms, furiously scrubbing our stinky hands, before touching our lunch.

Other important things we learned: Peter was a sleepwalker and Noelle knew how to rappel because her uncle climbed mountains. Colin Davis recognized edible plants because his mother and grandmother had been Camp Fire girls. And Justin Thayer could really wiggle his tail. That's because he was always leaving his stuff around and had to sing the "Squirrelly" song to get it back. "Squirrelly, squirrelly, shake your bushy tail," we'd sing to him as he stood in front of the lunch line with other forgetful campers, turning and shaking their

[illegible]

sing. [illegible] and the song we were singing wasn't a shouting one, so I could hear his voice.

"In a cavern, in a canyon, excavating for a mine, dwelt a miner, 'forty-niner, and his daughter, Clementine."

It was nice hearing someone sing in tune, except I couldn't get the words out of my head the next day. And guess where we went? The Lava River Cave — down into this pitch-black cavern with small flashlights swinging around our necks, feeling like miners searching for gold. Counselors held big lantern flashlights and we started out in groups with lots of room between the cold, wet walls and drippy ceiling.

"Ohhh, wow, look at that," said Shawna, shining her light on a sparkling silver wall.

"It's bacteria from soil that's filtered down through the cave ceiling," said Feliz, moving her flashlight around the wall. "And a chemical reaction to your light causes the sparkle."

Gradually we found ourselves squishing closer together and lowering our heads, then going single file.

"We're near the end," came the warning. Mr. Hudson had explained how the cave gets so small at the very end that you have to crawl. If you want to touch the very, very end of the cave, you have to lie down on your back and push yourself feet first through this narrow opening, point your toes, and stretch your hardest. I already felt a little clammy and queasy, and I'd bumped my head twice on the hard ceiling, but my gut told me I had to do it.

When it was my turn, Mr. Hudson helped me get into position. "Okay, Hope, finish it."

With my arms kinda shaky, I managed to push forward. *Come on, come on, wall, hit my toes.* It seemed like forever, but then I felt the nudge on my left foot. One more push and my right foot touched. "Got it!" [illegible] hooted and hollered and something bright [illegible]

my mother[illegible]

Back at camp it was my day for a shower. Four days without one and I had to stink, but all I could smell was smoke and I liked that smell. I stood in the stream of hot water pouring off my head and down my back. This was our last night. I'd tried to put it out of my mind all day. One last campfire, one last round of skits. I hoped Mr. Hudson would do another one. He was hilarious in the makeup skit, where he was a woman wearing this wig and big shirt, and someone else, hidden behind him, slipped their arms into the shirtsleeves and tried putting makeup on him. Since the hidden person couldn't see, lipstick ended up on Mr. Hudson's nose and eye shadow on his chin and mascara on his forehead. When they were finished, Mr. Hudson looked in a little mirror. "Oh my," he said in this high squeaky voice, "how lovely!"

Walking back to my tent from the shower room, I felt incredibly clean, smelling of apple shampoo and peach conditioner. I passed the tie-dye trees — limbs covered with soaking-wet orange, green, and purple T-shirts, drying ahead of the nighttime frost. The parent volunteers were making our last dinner. Litter patrol was wandering between tents, and wood gatherers were hauling the last load of dead twigs and rotten sticks to the fire ring. I paused in front of my tent, removed my shoes on the little piece of muddy carpet, stepped past the sun-bleached gray flap, into the heavy odors of flannel sleeping bags and smoky clothes, sweaty socks, and damp towels. Jenny's aloe vera gel had oozed onto the tent floor and her banana-scented sunscreen gagged the air, but I already missed it.

At campfire that night, Brody's tent put on a skit called *J.C. Penney*. "Where'd you get your hat?" their counselor asked Peter. "J.C. Penney." "Where'd you get [illegible]

The parent volunteers sang a song they'd made up about all the counselors. Then Eagle Eye gave out camper awards for the most adventurous, the best fire builder, the fastest shower taker, the loudest singer. My name was called for best spelunker — that's a cave explorer. I got a ribbon and a hug.

"This is our twenty-third Outdoor School," said Mr. Hudson, when he'd finished the awards, "and I have to say one of the very best. You were great campers, eager to learn and willing to help. The weather cooperated, except for that one afternoon rainstorm." We laughed, remembering the surprise "shower" we gave Mr. Hudson as he climbed off the bus from the Metolius Headwaters trip.

"I expect you'll all return home tomorrow a little bit changed. How?" He shook his head. "I can't answer that, but for the better I'm quite sure." He looked up at the sky. "Before you go to bed tonight, I'd like you to make a wish for a camper next year — that he or she will have the same wonderful experience you had this week."

We formed our nightly friendship circle, crossing arms and holding hands, stretching wide around the campfire. "What is the tie that binds us," Eagle Eye began and we joined in, "friends of the long, long years? Just this — we have shared the weather, we have slumbered side by side, and friends who have camped together shall never again divide." We sang taps, gave each other's hands a sharp squeeze (the boys always gave torturous clamps, but we girls refused to utter a single peep), then walked to our tents for the last time. I searched the Central Oregon night sky, found the brightest yellow star, and made a wish for a future camper. I added a P.S., a wish for myself, that I'd come back again someday — as a counselor.

CHAPTER 32

A New Beginning

[illegible]

and broke them down and pa[illegible] ing the U-Haul and cleaning the bathrooms one last time, we posed for pictures: all-camp, tent groups, combinations of new camp friends, shots of the counselors in a giant, teetering pyramid, and the parent volunteers standing in front of the U-Haul. Jenny, Ellie, and I got Frog to hug a tree with us. Feliz took four pictures. We autographed each other's journals, T-shirts, and jeans. Then we piled into the buses, shouting out the windows to the parents and waving to anyone who'd wave back.

The buses crawled out the rutted campground road and crossed the Deschutes.

I leaned my head against the window frame. Good-bye river. Good-bye meadow and campfire, good-bye frozen milk and burned marshmallows. Good-bye. My chest ached and my shoulders suddenly felt very heavy. I closed my eyes.

The bus stopped. My neck was bent in half, my chin pressed against my chest. Slowly I untangled my body and looked around. Most everyone was asleep, leaning on their neighbor's shoulder, or with their head back, mouth opened. Hats were tilted, hair uncombed. Legs and arms slopped into the aisle. Wood cookies dangled every which way.

Almost home, I thought. My jaw tightened and my teeth ground together. I'd forgotten to wear my night guard at camp, but my headache had disappeared. Was it coming back? Please, no, not the headache. We'd problem-solved all week, but they were fun problems like starting a one-match fire or marking a trail. The thought of bad problems to solve sent pangs of panic through my body. I was wide awake now, staring at the outskirts of Eola Hills, wishing we could turn around, go back, begin the week over.

[illegible] as we stopped [illegible] my fingers, touched [illegible] good sign.

We turned the corner and drove two more blocks to the school, all the while my body tensing, my breath waiting, my eyes alert. Cars and pickups filled the parking lot. Parents chatted in small groups while younger brothers and sisters played on the swings and slides. I searched the parking lot with half of me hoping and half fearing. Then I spotted Mom's car and my heart jumped. I hadn't been forgotten.

When the bus stopped in front of the covered play

area, no one moved. "Come on, campers, we're home," said Miss Lindquist. Slowly we gathered our backpacks and extra blankets, hats and crumpled sack lunches. I fell in line, watching as parents greeted their sons and daughters with wide smiles and strong hugs. My throat tightened and my ears warmed. I stepped off the bus and someone moved out of the crowd.

"How are you, sweetie?" It was my mother's voice, but I barely heard. All I could do was stare at the blue-and-white-checkered dress.

With questions spinning like a roulette wheel, one finally settled on my lips. "Why are you wearing that dress?"

"Well," Mom said, "you came home for the very first time with me in this dress, and now you've come home again."

This had to be a dream.

We walked in silence to the soccer field where the U-Haul had parked. I didn't know what to say next, and I was afraid I'd break the spell.

We found all my stuff, and while Mom held Tyler's sleeping bag, I gave a final good-bye hug to Gabriela.

"I've been really busy while you were gone," said Mom as we headed for the car. "I went through all my clothes and took a bunch of things into Next to New.

[illegible] good money. Tyler's

[illegible]

fore I knew it I was rattling on about [illegible] ors and banana boats, river walks, compass hikes, and my award. I explained Mr. Hudson's makeup skit and we both started laughing.

"And when I'm in high school I'm going to be a counselor and I think my name will be —"

"What *are* you thinking, Hope?" Mom interrupted. "A counselor? Responsible for all those children?" Her voice pounced on the words. "You haven't even started babysitting. You won't possibly be able to —"

Wham! My mouth slammed shut, my words rear-ending each other. My head fell back against the seat and I closed my eyes. *Don't go there, Mom. Please, don't do it. Stop. STOP. I can't handle it. Not now, not after this week.* My heart beat so hard it hurt. *I know happiness and I won't trade it in. No, I won't. I choose to be strong and free. I believe in roses. I believe in hope.*

At the next streetlight I'm getting out and running back to the school. Gabriela will still be there for me and she'll take me home with her. Forever.

"Hope. Hope." The car had stopped. We were parked along the sidewalk. *I could jump out right now, grab my bag off the backseat, and—*

"Hope." Mom's hand was on my knee. With her other hand she was offering me a Kleenex. I took the Kleenex and slowly wiped the tears from my cheek.

Mom moved closer and put her arm around my shoulder. "I'm sorry, Hope. I didn't mean that. I — I'm —" She closed her eyes and I could feel her arm trembling through my T-shirt. "I'm taking Mrs. Nelson's parenting class." She laid her hand on top of mine. "I've already gone twice this week."

Her hand was warm and her bare arm felt soft on my neck. I didn't know what to say, and it seemed she was trying to come up with something else.

[illegible] out the window. We [illegible]

that went down [illegible]

"We're having a Southern Plantation party at work next Friday and we're supposed to dress accordingly."

I strained to see inside the store but couldn't get past the dreamy dress and backdrop.

"Any chance you can work here before Friday so I can get it half off?"

I stared at the dress and words spun in my head. *Parenting class. Twice a week. Work. Next to New. Dress. Parenting class.* My jaw relaxed and somehow the words came out. "I think so."

When we drove into the garage Mom turned off the car, but I couldn't move. My body that had hiked and climbed and crawled and sang and shouted had quit on me.

"Come on, let's get you inside before you fall asleep." Mom got out of the car and opened the kitchen door. I followed, banging my bag through the door, dropping it on the floor next to the table.

"I mixed a pitcher of lemonade," Mom said. She moved to the refrigerator and I about fainted. There, on the refrigerator door, was purple paper with Mom's outlined hand, her name signed and dated. She'd taken the pledge! I tried to imagine it: Mom standing in a classroom with other parents, raising her hand, and saying, "I will not use my hands or my words for hurting myself or others."

I fell into a chair, laid my head on my folded arms, and smiled. Maybe I'd sleep here tonight.

Ice clinked in the glass as Mom set it in front of me. She sat down across the table. "I watered your rosebush while you were gone."

"Thank you." *Please, God, let this be for real. Please.*

"We should plant it, don't you think? Maybe by the front door? Or do you like the back door better?"

Panic. If I planted my rosebush, then I'd have to dig [illegible]

could tell.

She took a sip of lemonade. "Hope, I need to tell you something."

Alert. Alert. People give those warning words just before saying something bad. I sat up straight. "What?"

Mom ran her fingers up and down the drippy sides of her glass. "I told you I'm taking this parenting class."

I stared but Mom was focused on her drink.

"I've never done anything like this before. I always thought parenting was supposed to come easy, like riding a bike. You have a baby and, bingo, you automatically know what to do. Well, being a parent's a lot harder than riding a bike, and I've fallen off a few times."

She looked at me with sorry eyes. "Hope, I really missed you while you were gone. I know I've said things that have hurt your feelings, but I didn't know how to stop. Sort of like people trying to quit smoking or drinking." She took a deep breath. "Anyway, what I'm trying to say is, I think this is going to be really hard for me. Mrs. Nelson's giving us lots of new stuff and I think it'll take me a long time. You know," she said, chuckling, "old dogs and new tricks." Now she looked at me, sort of worried. "I'll need your help."

My help. She'll need *my* help?

Then I had an idea. I pushed out my chair and stood up.

"Don't go." Now she really did look worried.

"Just a sec, I'll be right back." I zipped down the hall, opened my bedroom door, crawled across my bed and into my closet, reached under my pillow, and pulled out my point system notebook. I paused, then slowly, carefully, tore out my pages of numbers and symbols. I tucked them back under my pillow, pulled out the little bits of loose paper in the metal spiral, then hurried back to the kitchen.

Mom was still at the table and I set the notebook down in front of her.

[illegible] "Scratch paper?"

[illegible]

points for doing a good job. Take the [illegible] instance. You really don't want to call me that. So if you catch yourself, even if you say the *st* part, it's still not too late. Then you give yourself points, say two hundred, and maybe one hundred for not saying *brat.*"

I wrote down the date, the letters *S* and *BR,* and next to them 200 and 100.

Mom studied the page, flipped through the notebook, then closed it. "Good idea, Hope."

"Thank you." Was my heart going to break? "And you get one hundred points for telling me 'good idea.'"

"But what do I do with all the points?"

"You get to choose. Something special."

Mom's face relaxed, like she was already thinking of her prize. She ran her fingers over the cover, outlining the yellow star. "What's this for?"

As I gazed at the yellow star, I thought of Anne Frank and the starlit nights she watched from her secret hiding place. I thought of the Holocaust victims, branded with the yellow star because of their beliefs. I remembered the sparkling sky covering our campsite and last night's wishing star. I looked my mother in her eyes and said, "So you'll never forget."

Hope Notes

1. When you're too tired, confused, or frustrated to come up with a big plan, start with a small one.

2. When something's bothering you, talk to someone you trust, like a teacher, coach, or friend.

7. Keep trying. Don't give up.

8. Rain or shine? You decide.

9. Find a way to express your feelings, like writing in a journal or making up poetry or painting.

10. Make friends with people who listen without interrupting.

11. Learn more about verbal abuse on the Internet or at the library or local bookstore.

12. Stand up to verbal abuse. Help organizations that promote good relationships such as the Hands & Words Are Not For Hurting Project (*www.handsproject.org*).

13. Look for a verbal abuse support group, or help start one.

14. "I feel statements" don't usually work with verbal abusers. The abuser is often *glad* you feel *sad*. Ask your school counselor or another adult whose advice you trust to offer a different suggestion. One idea would be to take a stronger approach, saying something like: "I don't want to be with you when you hurt my feelings."

15. Call the Childhelp National Child Abuse Hotline: 1-800-4-A-Child (1-800-422-4453).

16. Give yourself gold stars, points, prizes, rewards, pats on the back. (We're never too old for star charts.)

17. Believe in yourself.

18. *Love yourself.*

ACKNOWLEDGMENTS

Call Me Hope

Thank you to my writing colleagues, Sharon Michaud and Kathy Beckwith, who painstakingly read countless revisions, offered wise suggestions, and passionately supported my dream for children to recognize verbal abuse and its devastating impact.

[illegible]

accuracy and offered the approval I needed to continue.

To the staff and students at Amity Elementary School, particularly fifth-grade teacher Jeff Geissler and counselor Marie Roth for graciously hosting numerous visits, answering endless questions, and reviewing the manuscript. Many thanks to others who took time to read and comment: Lauren Andreassen, Linda Ballard, Ginny Gardea, Melissa Hart, Susan Powell, and Bev Willius.

I am indebted to Carole Fewx, co-owner of Jackson's Books in Salem, Oregon, who introduced me to sales representatives at the Pacific Northwest Booksellers Association Tradeshow, and to Randy Hickernell for sending my proposal to Little, Brown and Company Books for Young Readers.

Enormous gratitude to editor Alvina Ling, who saw potential in that proposal and subsequent manuscript, then gave me the opportunity to revise. She pronounced it a "worthy project," presented it to the editorial staff, pitched it to the acquisitions committee, and offered me a contract. With a gentle touch, she guided me through the ensuing stages to this heartfelt creation.

Thanks to Alvina's assistants, Rebekah McKay and Connie Hsu; to copyeditor, Kerry Johnson; editorial director, Andrea Spooner; designer, Alison Impey; publisher, Megan Tingley; and to the entire editorial department for supporting Alvina and our project.

A published book can't go far if no one knows about it, so sincere thanks to the marketing department for spreading the word.

I am eternally grateful to Ann Kelly, founder and executive director of the Hands & Words Are Not For Hurting Project. Her incredible insight, compassion, and tireless work in the field of abuse and violence prevention will truly make this world a better place. Thank you for every piece of this program, but particularly for the pledge of hope and personal accountability that is changing and saving lives. Thank you for "The Power of One" and entrusting me with your message.

Thank you to the following research resources: Paul Kopperman, Oregon State University professor of history and chair of the OSU Holocaust Memorial Committee; Jerry Moe, national director of children's programs at the Betty Ford Center for "Name it and Tame it"; Josh Isgur, program coordinator at the Washington State Holocaust Education Resource Center; and volunteers in the Juliette's House Safe Kids Program.

I am especially grateful to a man of courage, sensitivity, and inspiration — Alter Wiener, Holocaust survivor.

Kockroach

KOCKROACH

TYLER KNOX

WILLIAM MORROW
An Imprint of HarperCollins*Publishers*

This book is a work of fiction. The characters, incidents, and dialogue are drawn from the author's imagination and are not to be construed as real. Any resemblance to actual events or persons, living or dead, is entirely coincidental.

HarperCollins books may be purchased for educational, business, or sales promotional use. For information please write: Special Markets Department, HarperCollins Publishers, 10 East 53rd Street, New York, NY 10022.

FIRST EDITION

Designed by Betty Lew
Illustrations by Will Staehle

Library of Congress Cataloging-in-Publication Data

Knox, Tyler.
Kockroach: a novel / Tyler Knox. — 1st ed.
p. cm.
ISBN-13: 978-0-06-114333-5
ISBN-10: 0-06-114333-2
1. Cockroaches—Fiction. I. Title.

PS3562.A75249K63 2007
813'.6—dc22

2006048138

07 08 09 10 11 WBC/RRD 10 9 8 7 6 5 4 3 2 1

For G.S.

And for Mr. G.
who introduced him to me

A story, for example, something that could never happen, an adventure. It would have to be beautiful and hard as steel and make people ashamed of their existence.

—JEAN-PAUL SARTRE
La Nausée

PART ONE

THE SWITCH

1

As Kockroach, an arthropod of the genus *Blatella* and of the species *germanica*, awakens one morning from a typically dreamless sleep, he finds himself transformed into some large, vile creature.

He is lying flip side up atop a sagging pad. Four awkwardly articulated legs sprawl on either side of his extended thorax. His abdomen, which once made up the bulk of his body, lies like a flaccid worm between his legs. In the thin light his new body looks ridiculously narrow and soft, its skin beneath a pelt of hair as pale and shriveled as a molting nymph's.

Maybe that is what has happened, maybe he has simply molted. He reflexively swallows air, expecting his abdomen to expand into its normal proud dimensions and the air to swell his body until the skin stretches taut so it can begin hardening to a comforting chocolate brown, but nothing happens. No matter how much air he swallows, his body remains this pale pathetic thing.

A flash of red rips through the crusts of Kockroach's eyes before disappearing, and suddenly, in the frenzied grip of positive thigmotaxis, he wriggles his legs wildly until he tumbles onto the floor. With his legs beneath him now, he scurries under the wooden frame supporting the pad, squirming back and

forth, ignoring the pain in his joints, until he has found a comforting pressure on his chest, his back, his side.

Better, much better. The red light snap-crackles on, hissing and glowing throughout the room, slinking beneath the wooden frame before disappearing just as suddenly. It snap-crackles on and disappears again, on-off, on-off. His fear of the light subsides as the pattern emerges, when something else draws his attention.

A rhythmic rush of air, in and out, an ebb and flow coming from somewhere nearby. He turns his head, trying to find the sound's source before he realizes that a peculiar undulation in his chest matches the rhythm of the rushing air.

Cockroaches don't breathe, per se. Instead, air flows passively into openings called spiracles and slides gently through tracheae that encircle their bodies. There is the occasional squeezing of air from the tracheae, yes, but nothing like this relentless pumping of air in and out, in and out. It is terrifying and deafening and unremitting. It is so loud it must be drawing predators. Kockroach spreads his antennae to check his surroundings and senses nothing. He reaches up a claw to clean the receptors and gasps upon finding no antennae there. The sound arising from his throat is shockingly loud, a great anguished squeal that frightens him into silence.

His shock wanes as quickly as it waxed. He doesn't wonder at how this grossly tragic transformation has happened to him. He doesn't fret about the blinking light or gasping breath, about his pale shriveled skin or missing antennae. Cockroaches don't dwell in the past. Firmly entrenched in the present tense, they are awesome coping machines. When his

their young, then they

Kockroach blinks his eyes at the growing brightness in the room. He is tired already. He is used to two bouts of feverish activity in the middle of the night and then a long sleep during the day. The dawn light signals him it is time to retire. Pressed against the edge of the wall, his aching limbs jerk beneath him, his back rises to touch the slats of the wooden frame, and he falls asleep.

When Kockroach awakens again it is dark except for the rhythmic pulse of the hissing red light. He is still wedged beneath the wooden frame. His four legs now ache considerably and a line of pain runs through his back.

From beneath the frame he can just make out the contours of the room, its walls and baseboards veined by inviting little cracks. There is a wooden object in the middle of the room, and beside it, floating above the floor, is a piece of meat, the top of which is obscured by the top of the frame.

Kockroach crawls quickly out from under the wooden frame, stops, crawls quickly again, dashes beneath the meat, heads for a lovely little crack he espied from afar. He dives into it and bangs his head on the wall.

He had forgotten for a moment what had happened to him.

Slowly he brings his face down to the crack that seems now so small. In the recess he sees two antennae floating gracefully back and forth. He reaches to the crack, tries to place his claw in the crevice to touch his fellow arthropod. His digits splay, the claw screams in pain. He articulates the digits, five of them, one by one before his face. What a grotesquely useless configuration. He reaches out one digit and guides it to the crack. Only the slightest bit of soft flesh slips in.

Suddenly, he is overwhelmed by a thousand different sensations that seem strangely more real than his bizarre altered presence in that room. The patter of hundreds of feet, the crush of bodies, the blissful stink of the colony. The feel of his antennae rubbing against the antennae of another, pheromones bringing everything to a fever pitch, being mounted from behind, his hooks grabbing hold. The taste of sugar, starch, the desperate run across a patch of open light. He is slipping back through his life. The shedding of old chitin, the taste of it afterward, the delicious feel of his mother's chest upon his back when he was still the smallest nymph. He slides his digit back and forth along the crack in the wall and falls into a pool of remembrance and emotion, both stunning and unexpected.

But sentimental nostalgia is not a cockroach trait, neither is regret, nor deep unsatisfied longing. He had never felt such sensations before and he fights against their unfathomable power with all his strength. Insectile resolve battles mammalian sentimentality for supremacy over this new body until, with a great shout, Kockroach triumphantly climbs out of the strange emotional swirl and falls back into himself.

He won't let this strange molt ruin him. He will stay true

He traces his digit up the wall, as if the tip itself is an arthropod making its way to the safety of the ceiling. Halfway to the top his claw alights on a dull white plate with a black switch. Cockroaches instinctively try every crevice, search every nook, climb every tilting pile of dishes. It is in their nature to explore. He flicks the switch.

Light floods the room. Panic. He would flee, but to where? He follows his second instinct to hide against a wall and freeze. He spins and presses himself into the corner and moves not a muscle.

He listens for the sound of a predator and hears nothing.

He presses his head so hard into the corner the vertex of his face throbs.

Still nothing.

With a start, he realizes he is standing and the ache he had been feeling in his legs, the pain in his back, are all slowly receding. This is a body that works best vertically. He will adapt, he is a cockroach.

Balancing precariously on two pale slabs of flesh at the bottom of his lower legs, he takes tiny steps as he turns around, his upper legs moving contrapuntally with his lower legs out of long-ingrained habit. And as he turns he examines the now-lit space in which he finds himself. It is in actuality

a small pathetic hotel room, green walls that can barely contain a bed and a bureau and a tiny desk, a single window through which the hissing red neon of the hotel's sign can be spied; it is a sad cramped piece of real estate but to Kockroach it is a palace. And in the center, hanging from the source of light, is the piece of meat.

Kockroach is frightened when he sees it there, shaped as it is like a predator, but it is just hanging, not moving, hanging. He determines it is not a threat and his fear subsides.

Still in the corner, he reaches out his upper appendage, an arm now that he is standing vertically, and with his claw flicks down the black switch on the white plate. Darkness.

He flicks it up. Light.

He flicks it down. Darkness.

So that is how they do it.

Up and down, up and down. After an hour of that he leaves the light on and practices walking.

He falls twice, thrice, six times, struggling to stand again after each fall. He is trying to retain the feel of his cockroach walk, when his legs moved forward three at a time while the other three maintained a steady tripod, allowing for sudden stops and quick switches of directions. This body is not so nimble or steady, the center of gravity is absurdly high, but finally, after much trial and error, he comes up with something that feels organic.

He leans back, his weight to the right as he steps forward with his left leg, his right arm rising reflexively with the step, with each step, stepping over and back, over and again, until it is mastered.

It isn't long before Kockroach wonders how he ever before crawled on his belly or why.

With his walk in place, Kockroach explores. The bed, the bureau, the small desk covered with bizarre fetishistic objects. He takes in the color, size, the shape of these things, without knowing their purposes or names. There is a door he can't open with all manner of metal running down its side, there is an open door leading to a cozy dark little room with cloths hanging from a rod, and there is another open door leading to another small room, slippery and cold, hard tile covering the floor.

In this room there is a large white seat that seems to fit his new proportions. In his many journeys he had seen seats like this before, in rooms much like this one, and from hiding places in baseboard cracks he had seen creatures sit on these white seats and let out horrible groans that had terrified him. It must be something dangerous, something awful, something truly bestial. Perfect reasons for a cockroach to try it.

He sits and groans, the sound rising, reverberating in the

tiny room, and he feels something, something not entirely unpleasant, causing him to groan ever more loudly. Cockroaches release desiccated pellets which grind as they are forced from the gut through the anus, but this, this is wet and slippery and strangely lovely. And the smell, the smell to a cockroach is ambrosial.

He groans again, louder, lets it out, tries for more, but it is over. There is nothing left. Maybe if he sits on that special seat long enough he can do it again. And again.

But what is that over there? A basin, with a strange panel atop it. He rises from the seat, steps to it. There is a single silver thing sticking out of the basin. He fiddles with it and cold water starts leaking out. He leans over and latches his mandibles around the thing to capture the water until it feels like his gut will burst apart. When he stands straight again what he sees in the panel above the basin sends him backing away with a shriek.

A predator face, staring at him, backing away as he backs away.

He approaches the panel again and stares at it. The face stares back. He tilts his head. The face tilts the same way. He reaches up a claw, points a digit to the face, and the other points a digit back. Kockroach moves his digit closer, closer, and so does the other, until just when their claws are about to touch they reach a barrier.

Twenty minutes later, after realizing that the other is himself and that the face staring back at him is now his own, he examines himself critically. The eyes are tiny and set low, there is a strange protuberance, like a beak, sticking out of the

palpi used to grind and test his food? This face he has now is both hideous and nearly useless.

As he stares in horror, the extent of the disaster that has befallen him slowly becomes manifest. He has become, of all things, a human.

Then he remembers where he saw before a face just like his new face: on the long piece of meat hanging from the ceiling.

He returns to the main room and circles the hanging thing with the exact same face as his own. It is a human, as is Kockroach now, naked, as is Kockroach now. A rope is fitted around the human's narrow prothorax and tied to a fixture overhead. Maybe all humans have the same face, he considers, unlike cockroaches with their infinite differences. The eyes of the human are closed, the hypopharynx is purple and hanging thickly from the mouth. He pushes the hanging human and jumps back, but there is no reaction other than a slow swaying.

Kockroach knows dead and this is it.

A sound erupts from his abdomen. Kockroach spins, scared. The sound comes again and with it he can feel a vibration and suddenly he is certain that it is time to eat.

How can he be so certain?

Because, for a cockroach, it is always time to eat.

Kockroach searches the apartment for food, pulls out drawers, inspects the room with the cloths, the room with the seat. There are the brown lumps in the bowl of the great white seat, but that is feces, he knows, and even cockroaches won't stoop so low as to eat their own feces, though the feces of other species are often a culinary treat.

In the desk he finds a thick black thing with shiny gold edges. He used to eat such things, used to delight in the tasty gobs of pale paste oozing from the back. He tries to gnash the thing in his teeth but his mandibles aren't strong enough. He splits it open and rips out a thin individual leaf with its black markings, stuffs it in his mouth. He chews and chews until it is soft enough to swallow. He leans down, throws it up on the floor, sucks it up and swallows it again. He still is hungry but he doesn't want to eat another leaf.

From the desk he takes a strange rectangular fetish and tries to bite it. Failing to turn it into food, he examines it instead. It is a picture, highly detailed in shades of gray, a picture of humans, a group of them, wearing cloths and shiny coverings on the tips of their legs. He is surprised to recognize variances among the humans. Their faces are not all the same, and somehow he can pick out the facial differences as if the ability is an integral part of this new body. Only one of the faces in the picture is identical to his own. Standing next

he had assumed was his wormlike abdomen has swelled and is now sticking straight out. He bats it down but it pops up again and the whole process, the batting down and the popping up, feels good, feels pretty damn terrific. He does it again and again. The abdomen grows even harder, longer, his head swarms as if inundated with pheromones.

He looks back at the picture, at the face with the light, curly hair. So that is a human female and the wormlike thing is not an abdomen. He is relieved that there are human females. And with the relief a new determination appears as if suddenly implanted in his brain.

He raises again the picture to his face. Yes, there are other females in the group, and a nymph, and all the faces are different except for the one that is just like his and just like the face on the hanging human. He turns around and looks at the dead thing. He does not like that they share the same face. Something tells him this is wrong, that he needs to be unique.

His stomach growls.

He slides over to the hanging piece of meat and chews off its face, regurgitates it onto the floor, scoops it up and swallows it.

He eats until he can eat no more. The thing hanging now is faceless, his head just a mass of red chewed meat. Good. Now there is only Kockroach.

He sits on the floor, opens his mouth, and begins to groom himself. He can't reach everywhere, but he cleans what he can with his tongue and teeth. What he can't reach with his mouth he rubs frantically with his legs and arms. It takes an hour.

Suddenly tired, he sees the sky outside his window begin to dawn. Someone must have flicked the switch. He crawls under the bed until he is again surrounded by pressure and falls back asleep.

In the middle of the day Kockroach is startled awake by a banging on the door he couldn't open.

"Hey, Smith, you in there?"

The voice is loud, deep. Kockroach slinks closer to the wall, stays silent and still.

"No one's seen your face since the girl left two, three days ago. You still in there?"

There is more banging, the door shakes but remains closed.

"Smith, hey. You okay? Is something the matter?"

More shaking. Kockroach crouches beneath the bed, ready to scurry away if the door opens.

"Look, Smithy, your week's up tomorrow and we want you out. There's been complaints about a smell. Can you flush the toilet or something, Jesus? People are living here, for Christ's sake. You're out tomorrow or we're gonna have to come in and

Kockroach knows he must leave. The predator that had been banging in the middle of the day will come back, they always come back he has learned, especially in kitchens in the middle of the night. Here, he knows, there is no good place to hide. But before he leaves he sits again on the white seat and groans loudly and feels the pleasure of the wet thing slipping out of him.

He stares a long time at the picture with the group of humans. The males in the picture are all covered in the same way and Kockroach, missing his chitinous armor, wants to be covered too. He remembers the cloths hanging in the small cozy room.

Using the picture as a guide, he attempts to place the cloths upon his body. He tries the long black tubes on his claws, on his ears, but finds they go best on the tips of his legs. He sticks his legs through the soft white thing with one big hole and three small holes. The center hole between his legs, he assumes, is to allow the wormlike thing between his legs to grow when he is mating. Based on the size of the hole it must grow very big indeed. The soft white thing with one stretchy hole and two smaller holes he puts on his head but finds he can't see and takes it off. Hanging from a hook is a narrow

loop with a knot which, from the picture, he can tell goes around his prothorax.

He has an easier time with the larger pieces because he can learn from the picture exactly how they go. The brown cloth to cover his legs, the white cloth to cover his thorax and arms. He spends a long time fiddling with the buttons but finally figures them out. The brown thorax covering goes over the white thorax covering and the narrow piece of cloth slides under the flaps around his prothorax. He discovers that the knot of the narrow piece of cloth slides. He slips it up until it is tight and he likes it, the tighter the better.

On the floor of the little room are two shiny brown things with some sort of pocked design. He caresses one, remembering the feel of his old chitin, before he slips them onto the tips of his legs. There are strings hanging off either side. He pulls hard at the strings and tucks them into the edges of the brown things.

All buttoned up, tightened and taut, feeling much more protected than before, he takes the photograph back to the panel over the basin and stares at his reflection.

Not everything is right.

There are little hairs on his face and none in the picture. He tries to pull them out one by one but it is impossible, they are too short to grip.

All the people in the picture are doing something strange with their mouths. He stares in the mirror and stretches his mouth to show the teeth atop his mandibles. It is a fearsome sight but it must serve some purpose in human culture, maybe a warning. He practices his warning grimace for many minutes.

to the basin and compares what he sees in the panel with what is in the picture. He turns the thing around. Better. He tilts it. Much better.

"Hey, Smith, you in there?" he says into the panel. His voice is high, almost twittering, but with a deep rumbling undertone that rises like a predator to swallow the high notes. He tries again. "Smith, hey. You okay? Is something the matter?" He keeps speaking, baring his teeth all the while, repeating the sequence of sounds he had heard through the door until his voice matches the voice of the human who had been banging.

He finds a storage pouch in the brown thorax covering for the picture. On the desk he finds something small and brown and shiny, a folder filled with little green papers with human faces on them. He puts this into a different pouch. He considers taking the thick black thing whose leaf he had eaten, but it is too big for the pouches and he hadn't found it very palatable and decides he can do without it.

It is time.

He searches for a way out of the room. He goes first to the window from where the blinking red light slithers. There is a

gap in the bottom. He sticks his claws in the gap and pushes the window up. The noise of the outside world attacks him, like a swarm of wasps. He sticks his head out. The red light is right next to him, painfully bright, hissing loudly at him every time it goes on. He wonders who is flicking the switch. He looks down and feels a burst of fear that tells him it is too high to jump. There are humans walking back and forth below him, little humans, a species no bigger than cockroaches. He will be a giant among them. But still he needs to find a way out.

He goes to the door that had been banged on that day. He tries to open it and fails. He fiddles with the hard shiny things along its side and tries again and still fails. He grips the knob on the side of the door and pulls as hard as he can and the door falls apart with a splintering crash.

Kockroach drops the knob, steps over the debris, and strides down the hall, his hat at a jaunty angle, the V's of his claws moving up and down with each step.

"Can you flush the toilet or something, Jesus?" he says as he makes his way down the hall and into the world. "People are living here, for Christ's sake."

2

They call me Mite. You got a problem with that?

Mite, as in Mighty Mite, on account of my size. They meant it as a joke, them bully Thomasson twins from the schoolyard, all gristle and snarl. They hoped the name it would sting, but I took it as a badge of honor and wear it proudly still. Mite. That's what you can call me.

You eating them shrimp?

Boss says I should stroll on over to the hotel, introduce myself, hand over the envelope what you're waiting for. It's all in there, everything I dug up on that son of a bitch Harrington what thought it was a brainy idea to run against the Boss. But I figured, whilst I'm at it, I'd also tell you a little something about the Boss hisself for that blab sheet you're writing for. Do you want to hear the real story, missy, the truth about the millionaire candidate for the U.S. Senate and his soon-to-be bride? The truth according to Mite?

Don't be so quick in saying yes, you might not like what you hear. It's my story and I don't like it one stinking bit.

Am I talking too fast for you? What was you, buried in the society pages afore they tapped you for this exposé? All parties and hemlines and Joes in bad toups trying not to stare

at them flush society tits? Hey, what's the difference between a Times Square whore and a society dame? Beats me.

But what I gots here for you is a story what could pull you out of the society racket and put you smack on the front page. A story of the rise and the fall and the resurrection. A story of a man searching for his place in an outsized world and finding nothing but a hole in his heart in which to fall. A story what will murder the Boss's chances for the Senate.

But the Boss's Senate run ain't all I'll be killing. Consider this my suicide note, because after this gets out I'm as good as gone too. But what the hell, I'm in the mood to bump my gums. And I gots my reasons for spilling. Alls I ask is that you write it straight.

So go ahead, missy, and fire up the reel-to-reel. I'm ready to begin.

They call me Mite, as in Mighty Mite, on account of my size.

I was born in Philly, same as the nation, Philadelphia, a city of alleyways and wild dogs. Nights, from the edges of Fairmount Park, you can hear them in the woods, the wild dogs, howling. Once, them Thomasson twins tied a string of wieners around my neck and dragged me into the dark depths of the park. A couple of cutups they was, them Thomasson twins, and when I peed my pants they held their sides and bent over as the laughter, it kicked the snot from their noses. I didn't fight back, didn't bust them boys, big as they was, in the snouts. Instead I ran away, pulling them wieners off my neck

guess he moved on up to the marathon because he took off long ago and best as I can tell he's still going. I often imagine what he would have been had he hung up them spikes. He might have grown fat, worn cardigans, affected a pipe, he might have called me sonny boy and tiger, had catches with me in the park, brought home toys in big white boxes. But all that hooey was my dream, not his. I was barely old enough to remember him afore he ran away from me. By then he could look at his son standing in the crib, his head still not reaching the top bar, and see him for what he was.

It's not like he was no giant hisself, the son of a bitch.

My mother was like a ghost in my life after my father left, always present and yet not really there. I can see her still, sitting at the kitchen table, thin elbows on the Formica, straggly blond hair falling limply across her face. Her tattered housecoat is belted around her waist. The veins in her ankles pulse slowly. Fluffs of cotton pill off them dirty blue slippers on her feets. She brushes the hair off her eyes and stares out at me from her prison of vast sadness.

"What am I going to do with you, Mickey? What am I going to do?"

"Nothing, Ma."

"Look at you. Let me get you some milk."

"Another glass of milk and I'm going to puke on the floor, Ma."

"Oh Mickey."

I grabs my books, heads to the back door, to the wooden stairwell that leads three flights down to the alley, and then I stop. Back inside I gives my mother a kiss.

A smile flits across her thin lips, it is forced, a gesture purely for my benefit, a feeble attempt to make me feel all is right, and strangely, against all odds, it does. Because in them days I still believed the world was good and that something would come along and save us. What a sap I was, I can't hardly tell. But still, I smiles back at my ma afore taking off for school, leaving her alone at the kitchen table.

My mother at the table, weighed down by her life, a husband long gone, an apartment infested with vermin, an affliction she can't control, a boy what refuses to grow no matter how much milk she pours down his throat.

But hey, life ain't fair, missy. You ever forget that, you're a goner. Life is like a heavyweight on the ropes; no matter how beat you think you got the sucker, it can still reach out with one well-timed hook and send you spinning.

I was nine first time it happened.

My dad now was long gone and I was nine and in school and my ma every day was staffing the register at Klein's Discount Clothes, where she fended off the advances of old man Klein and brought home my wardrobe from the clearance bins. Corduroy pants two sizes too big, stiff canvas shirts, shoes with rubber soles so thick they squeaked. I was like a one-man band when I walked down the school hallway, rub,

and a butter sandwich—when suddenly she turns around and I sees something in her eye, or more precisely something not in her eye. Whatever had been there before, the worry, the disappointment, the love, it all has vanished. She is less than a stranger, a wax dummy of my mother filled only with sawdust and the big empty. And she turns around again and again, spinning in ever-tighter circles. I wonders at first if she is playing, but then her body locks in on itself. I'm up in a snap and I grabs hold of her waist as the shaking starts. She hears not my pitiful cries of terror. She is rigid. I struggles to lay her gently on the rough wooden floor, and fails, and her head cracks onto the wood, and she doesn't feel it, she doesn't feel it, not a thing. I hugs her tight and wipes the foam from her mouth as she goes through it, her surface writhing and beneath the surface, scarier still, the big empty.

No comparisons here, missy, nothing to compare it to, had never seen nothing like it before and nothing has been the same since. You want the bright line in my life marking the before and the after, like a Charles Atlas ad at the back of them superhero comic books what I would lift from the drugstore? Well there it is, the bright line, when the big empty entered my life. It slipped inside my mother and latched on and never let go, and neither did I, even as the

brown smell of singed corn filled the kitchen, even as the shuddering ebbed and she calmed into a sleep.

She didn't remember what had happened when she awoke on the floor, told me she must have slipped and banged her head, that explained the headache, she said, and I let her tell me just that. But we both knew it was something worse, something simply too huge to talk about. She even later gave it a cute name, Hubert, telling me after I found her passed out on the floor that Hubert had come again to visit, like it was a gentleman caller paying his respects. And bit by bit, as Hubert returned once and then again, she hid herself from the world, left her job at Klein's lest the shame of it hit her there, and started her vigil in the apartment, alone with her sewing, waiting for Hubert to take over again, which he did and did and did and did, growing ever larger, growing ever more ravenous, until he swallowed her whole.

I knows what it is to lose the meaning of things. I knows what it is to watch the world spin around in a tight helpless circle and get eaten by a nothing bigger than everything there ever was.

Pass the sauce, hey, missy?

Them shrimp are tasty little critters. Tiny clots of muscle what slide around the ocean floor and feed on whatever garbage they can scavenge. Sounds familiar, don't it. For alls I know I could be eating a cousin.

What's the matter, you maybe got better things to do than

that stoolie Dean? I think this: Who gives a crap? He stays, he goes, it ain't going to change my life a stinking whit.

But this I knows: the Boss, he's been a big supporter from way back, from when the president he was still just an ex–vice president, a two-time loser eyeing the big chair from afar. The Boss has been a big supporter, and not just with a pat on the back. That money theys all talking about now, the hush money, well the Boss, he's been shoveling cash to the big guy from afore the first election. It was the Boss what convinced the president to hang in there all this time, and it was the president what convinced the Boss he ought to run hisself for that vacant Senate seat.

"The party needs people like you," he told the Boss in his deep skulking voice. How you like that apple?

In fact, you know that thing he does, the president I mean, his two arms raised, two fingers of each hand in the air, that thing? He got that thing from the Boss, from the queer way the Boss walks. "I like that," he says when he spied the Boss in the back of some hotel ballroom. "That's good." Next thing we knows the president, he's up on the stage, shoulders hunched, arms raised, doing his imitation of the Boss.

That's what you want, isn't it, the details, the dirt? Oh, I

know it ain't nothing personal, you digging the dirt, it's a trait of the profession. Lawyers sue, dentists drill, politicians drill aides named Sue. And reporters want the mud, the slime, want every last drop of excrement, raw and unfiltered. Well hold on tight, that's exactly what I'm giving here. But it's not just the envelope on Harrington you'll be getting, and not just my morsels about the Boss, neither. This ain't your story, this is my story, and I'll tell it like I choose or you won't get word one. You want the meat only, but you're getting the bone and gristle too.

So sit back, missy, and keep the reel-to-reel rolling 'cause it may take us a while.

We was talking about my life in Philly, afore ever I saw New York. Philadelphia, a city of lawyers and whores, of crooners and con men. Like Old Dudley, what found me in the Philadelphia Free Library, Logan Branch, and who was maybe a bit of each.

There I am, in my red jacket and corduroy pants, my thick-soled discount shoes, twelve but looking eight, reading through the fiction section, book after book, because it was safer hiding in the apple barrel with Jim Hawkins, or floating on that raft with Huck and Jim, than it was staying outside in the fresh air where them Thomasson twins could have their way with me. And there was Old Dudley, in his ragged black suit, gray hair pouring out both sides of his head like a torrent of the thoughts that kept his mind a-buzzing. He appeared as nothing so much as a lunatic, leaning over his battered old chess-

his breath, and said with that fake bluster of his, "Do you perchance, my boy, want to learn the game of chess?"

It wasn't no mystery what Old Dudley wanted from me, what with how he sat close beside me and squeezed my biceps beneath that red jacket as he taught me how them bishops moved on a slant. What wasn't so clear was what I wanted from him. Maybe I was seeking a substitute for the father who had sprinted off into the horizon, thin black track shoes pounding on the asphalt as he fled. Or maybe I imagined that this man could somehow teach me the mysterious ways of the world. Or maybe I was, even then, searching for a protector of my own, for by that early date I had already intuited the sad truth of my existence. I suppose at some level deep in my skull it was a combination of all of them maybes, and if so, then my instincts was spot on, because almost everything I could have hoped to get from Old Dudley came true. It all came true, with a price to be sure, steep as the crack in the Liberty Bell, but isn't that always the way of it?

And all them maybes, they burst into bloom a few evenings after that first squeeze of my biceps when I left out from the library and, on my way home, stepped into an alley to pee. I thought I was safe in the alley, behind a pair a garbage cans, facing the brick back of a row house, in the dim glow of

a bare yellow bulb, I thought I was safe. But in this world, when you're the size I am and you're alone, you are never safe. My knees are still bent slightly, my yard is still out, the stream is still hissing against the brick, when I hears a voice from behind me.

"Well look who it is, the Mighty Mite."

I jam my yard back in my pants, zip up, turn around. Them damn Thomassons.

"Hey, Mite, you hungry?" says the fat one.

"Who cares if he's hungry, let's just hit him," says the fatter one.

"Well if Mite's hungry, he might want a sandwich. Do you, Mite? Do you want a sandwich?"

"Why would we give him a sandwich?"

"A knuckle sandwich, dimwit. With mustard."

"Spicy brown?"

"Sure, that's it."

"Can I get one too?"

"Shut up and hit him."

The fatter one, he grabs the collar of my red jacket and cocks his fist and he is about to feed me my teeth when a figure appears out of the steam from some faulty pipe running through the ground, a silhouette what stands there, legs spread and arms on hips like a hero right out of them comic books. I catch just a glimpse of this heroic silhouette and my breath stops with hope, with hope that it is my daddy, returned from his run, home at last, ready to save my life as he should have from the start, my daddy.

And then the figure strides forward into the light.

that their heads resound like two blocks of wood and their noses mash one against the other and the blood first spurts and then streams down their cheeks as they stagger away.

"Well hello there, Master Mickey," says Old Dudley with a rheumy wink as he pulls me up off the concrete. "I doubt those young ruffians will bother you here on in. Children need to be instructed how to properly behave, even towheaded cretins like those two. But now, perchance, if 'tis not too much trouble, maybe you could do a small something for me."

3 **The world,** Kockroach discovers, is marvelously hospitable when your skin is pale and you walk on two legs.

Each morning now, just before dawn, his gut full to bursting, he scurries around corners, through marvelous dank alleyways strewn with aromatic scraps, to a pile of wooden cartons leaning against an old brick wall. He climbs over two cartons, tunnels under a third, arrives at a crate with one edge shattered. Through the shattered timbers lies a comfortably narrow space where he can sleep with pressure on three sides of his body. He carefully takes off his coverings, folds them neatly, grooms himself for an hour or more, and then slips into the narrow space.

At dusk he awakens, grooms himself again, cleans every inch of his coverings with his teeth, places them on his body in the precise order he learned from the picture, and slithers out of his carton, emerging into the night to feed.

Behind almost every building there are containers left out for the great monstrous collectors to devour in the morning, and from these containers Kockroach gorges himself nightly. Soggy breads, rotted fruit, the wilted leaves of great heads of

by a clutch of writhing maggots. He sucks off the maggots, shakes his head wildly as they slide down his throat, and then pulls off the red-blooded meat with his teeth.

From puddles, or from snaking green tubes, he washes down his nocturnal feasts with water.

There is far more in the containers than even he can eat, but this bounteous buffet is not without its risks. If he makes too much noise, rattling the containers as he searches, sometimes humans stick their heads out of windows and shout phrases at him which he dutifully shouts back. "Get the hell out of there." "Ain't you got no self-respect?" "Get a job, you bum."

Other times he is forced to share his food with creatures that fill him with a long-ingrained terror, slippery rats, narrow-muzzled dogs, raccoons, and, worst of all, cats, with their flat ugly faces and their quick paws. He remembers these brutal felines having lazy sport with the young cockroaches that scurried carelessly within the ambit of their gaze. They would flick out a paw, knock a cockroach on its back, lethargically pierce its abdomen with a claw. Even though he now stands five times taller than the largest cat, fear overwhelms him whenever he sees such a creature. But still he eats. Since when did fear ever long stop a cockroach from eating.

Once, when he regurgitated his food out of long habit, a

rat rushed between his legs and began to slurp. He has since learned there is no need to regurgitate in this body. His teeth are ugly yet marvelous things, and once he pulps the food in his mouth he can swallow it straightaway.

He should be hugely content in his new life, he is living a cockroach's dream, food and shelter, a nice brown suit and leather wingtips.

But something, something is missing.

Nightly now, after feasting, he makes tentative forays into the world of the humans. He has no longing for friendship, no pathetic need to blend within the jagged contours of human society, but still he feels an urge to insinuate himself among the specimens of this noisome species.

At first his fear and self-consciousness were debilitating. He shied away from anyone who came close, aware that he was being stared at, certain that every human was seeing him for what he truly was. Which of the humans, he wondered as his head swiveled back and forth in alarm, would lurch out and crush him. Which of the humans would dust him with their virulent powder. And no matter where he stood, no matter how far from the street, he threw himself against the nearest wall to avoid the vicious humped things that prowled like hungry yellow cats all hours of the night. But gradually his fears subsided, he felt more comfortable among this bizarre and repulsive species, and he began to explore.

Striding along the sidewalks, weight shifting, arms pumping, the V's of his claws rising and falling in opposition to his

keep his shoes from slipping. Another man lifts his hat as a female passes and Kockroach does the same. There is much he doesn't know, but he intends to learn.

The humans he follows seem to be headed toward some great glowing place in the distance, like a day in the middle of the night. He always turns away well before he reaches the glow, his fear of light is deeply ingrained, but each night he moves closer, closer to what he now is certain is the great center of human activity. And each night, as the great center nears, he finds himself surrounded by ever more humans. He even finds the jostling from large crowds pleasant; it reminds him of those times of plenty when his fellow cockroaches climbed each one over the other as they raced for the crumbs of sweet cookies or the stray swollen crust of bread.

As he walks among them, Kockroach listens to the way humans talk among themselves.

"Got a light?" "Looking for a date?" "Who ain't?" "It'll cost you five." "You got it, sweet pea." "Boy, bush, jam-a-lam." "And don't come back, you fresh bastard." "I'm from out of town." "Move along, pal." "Not so fast, big boy." "Girls,

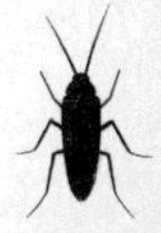

girls, girls." "I like it dark." "That'll cost you more than five, you filthy boy." "Enough with the blatta-blatta-blatta." "Gotta run." "Nothing personal, pal, just beeswax." "I'm hungry, Jerry. Jerry, you hungry?" "Jam-a-lam-a-lam." "Did you hear?" "No." "Yes." "Want to have some fun, honey? You look like you could use it."

Back in his shelter, naked and groomed, pressed against the sides of the crate, he manipulates his hypopharynx to form the sequences of sound he has heard. To get the sounds right, he repeats the phrases to himself, one after another, all the time remembering who said what when and what happened afterward. "Looking for a date?" "Who ain't?" "It'll cost you five."

Each night he learns something new and each day he becomes more ready to enter the great lighted place, the seeming center of all human activity.

Striding behind a human as they move together toward the light, the street growing dangerously bright, the human suddenly stops. Kockroach stops in turn.

There is a table set up on the sidewalk, a cloth over the table, and atop the cloth a myriad of strange objects. The human stands over the table to look and so does Kockroach. There are rows of shiny disks with straps on either side, the purpose of which remains a mystery to Kockroach. There are brown and black folders like the one Kockroach took from the room, though these don't have the green pieces of paper with the faces on them. There are little bottles with a colored fluid in-

ignores the disks, ignores the bottles and the folders. He reaches down, instead, for the fake black eyes. He has seen humans wearing such things, some clear, some dark like this, and so he knows how they are supposed to fit. Kockroach slips the black rods over his ears and suddenly the world has turned lovely. He looks around at the bleaked landscape, grim and shadowy, and as he does the constant buzz of fear at the back of his prothorax subsides. It is as if he is seeing the world now like he used to see it as a cockroach.

"You like? Ray-Ban. Special shipment. Fell right off truck. I give you nice price."

"I like it dark," says Kockroach.

"Five dollar."

"I'm from out of town," says Kockroach.

"You don't need tell me such ting, I'm not yet blind. Four dollar."

"Move along, pal."

"Hokay. Three-fifty, not penny less."

Kockroach, with the fake eyes still in place, turns and begins to walk toward the lights.

"Hey, you," the man behind the table shouts. "Four dollar you owe me."

Kockroach, still moving, shouts back, "Nothing personal, pal, just beeswax."

"Hey, you. Hey, tief. Stop tief," shouts the man behind the table, and Kockroach can hear the man yelling as he runs toward him.

Kockroach doesn't know why he is being chased, but he knows he must do something. On instinct Kockroach turns around and stands on the very tips of his legs. At the same time he reaches his arms high in the air, V's pointing right at the man. While fearsomely smiling, he jerks his body up and down and lets out a long loud hiss.

The human chasing him stops suddenly, his eyes widen.

Kockroach steps forward on his stilt-like legs.

The human backs away and raises his arms.

Kockroach has fought enough battles when still an arthropod to know that he has won. He turns around again and continues on his way, walking fast now, weaving through the humans.

"You pay later then, hokay," shouts the human. "Five dollar."

"You got it, sweet pea," shouts back Kockroach.

Kockroach keeps walking, fake eyes in place, his world turned comfortably gloomy, ready now to face the brightness and to solve the mystery at the center of human activity.

He is surrounded by lights, great piles of lights, frantically pulsing and glowing lights, shouting lights, shrieking lights, a miasma of lights. Even with his new fake eyes, the noise of

which will allow him to silence the lights. It will have to be larger than the one in the room, he knows, it will have to be monstrous, but he finds nothing and the lights keep calling, burning, shouting.

But as he spins around and takes in the entire scene, it is not the shocking volume of the lights that shakes him most deeply. Scattered high in the sky are pictures, like the one in his pouch, only far larger, representing a giant species of which he is not aware. And one picture grabs at his attention like the warning screech of a cat. A huge grimacing face, rising within the deafening expanse of lights, aiming a fierce stare directly at Kockroach, as if the huge creature recognizes Kockroach for exactly what he is. Gripped in the creature's giant claw is a large white fire stick, and pouring out of his fearsome grimace are great circular billows of smoke.

Kockroach has seen humans with the smoldering white sticks which they hold in their mouths or claws and use to spit out smoke, the sickening smell of burning floating about them. He had assumed the sticks were protection against some great predator, but now he knows they are also something else, a tribute to this totem of pure power with his brutal stare and grimace open in fierce warning. Kockroach suddenly has a great craving for a white fire stick of his own.

Cockroaches are not religious creatures. They take what they can as their due and live by a simple morality hardwired into their tiny brains. They never stop to contemplate their place in the great scheme of the universe for they have no doubts about their place in the great scheme of the universe. They are cockroaches. And whatever that sentence implies, they deal with it by surviving. Whenever a cockroach sits back and wonders what it's all about, he gets stepped on.

Cockroaches are not religious creatures, but still Kockroach can't help feeling a kind of awe while staring up at the wonderfully dreadful creature with the great smoking face. Awe is not an arthropod emotion, it is purely human, unfamiliar but not unpleasant, and so Kockroach doesn't fight it as he did the ugly emotional nostalgia that had almost defeated him before. He lets the awe sweep through him and he finds himself, somehow, in the strange, for him, act of prayer, directed toward the fierce creature staring down upon him.

There are no pat words, no liturgical screens placed upon the raw emotions, it is prayer at its purest and most vital, flowing straight from the gut, simple and heartfelt, representing the deepest yearnings of this mortal being. If you could somehow hear this prayer, the sounds would be simple and repetitive. A message of desire that transcends all posits of philosophy to reach a true measure of universality. A sweet, rhythmic song, like plates of chitin scraping one against the other, over and over, into the night. A song whispered reverently by all manner of species, by all manner of men. A song that is heard in every farm field, every suburban lawn, every urban tavern.

4

All right, I hears you. Enough with Mite's weepy childhood. Let's bring on the big guy, let's bring on the Boss.

I was in the city when first I spied him, this city, the Apple, handing out leaflets with a coupon for a buck off some second-floor peep show sporting a pack of girls what all needed a bath. And all the while I was keeping a wary eye out for Big Johnny Callas and his mauling fists, what personage I'd been told was looking for me hard and was frankly cheesed.

My moms by this time was dead, done in by the affliction what overtook her ever more frequently until her dying it was a gift. Hubert, which maybe started as something the size of an acorn, grew in her until at the end it was all that was left. I stayed with her to the last, and covered her with my tears, but in those final hours it wasn't my momma lying there no more, it was Hubert hisself, begging me to give him a new home.

"Mickey," he said to me in an empty voice no louder than a whisper. "Mickey, I'll take care of you. Don't let me die. Mickey."

And even after they wheeled her away, it was like that son of a bitch was still whispering in my ear.

I stuck it out a little while longer in Philly, but when the rent came due that was it for me. I dug into the cookie jar, her bert, a bus to New York and my future in the Square.

I'm talking now of Times Square, in the heart of the Fifties, my Times Square, shimmying in all its gaudy glory, where first I made my mark on this world. The Times Square of pinball palaces and shady dance clubs, of the grand old Sheraton-Astor and the fleabag junkie haunts what surrounded it, of the Broadway theaters where never I set foot and the Roxy Burlesque, with its second-rate strippers playing to a third-rate crowd, where certainly I did. I'm talking of knife fights over college girls at the White Rose, of hot dogs at Nedick's, of high-stakes pool at Ames Billiards, of the neon marketplace with its counterfeit suits and chest expanders, its little brown bottles of Spanish Fly. High heels and low brims, angry taunts and pearl-handled switchblades, jazz fiends looking for green, Benzedrine addicts looking for God, humped yellow taxis and Motogram headlines and politicians strutting and whores strumpeting and Satchmo trumpeting. Fleas pulling chariots, three-headed cows, rubberneckers and pickpockets, street-corner preachers, married suburban men looking for orgies and finding them, oh yes, with bad boys in tight tight jeans. Charlie Parker is blowing wild and incomprehensible at Birdland, Dizzy is blowing up them cheeks at the Onyx. The Criterion is showing *The Desperate Hours,* the

Lyric is showing *Killer's Kiss*. The Pepsi-Cola sign, the Canadian Club sign, the Admiral television sign, the Hit Parade cigarette sign with its slogan: "The Tobacco, the Tip, and the Taste!" Is that a blow job or what? Call for Philip Morris. The Warner is showing *Search for Paradise*, and missy, let me tell you, I emerged from that tunnel motherless and broke, with nothing to go back to but loss and nothing to go forward to but a forlorn hope, and I found my paradise, right there, in Times Square.

It was in the middle of that whole damn circus, beneath the Camel cigarette sign just off Forty-fourth Street, whilst I was handing out my leaflets with the sketch of a stripper looking oh so come-hither, that first I spots the Boss.

He wasn't the Boss then, just a Joe on the street, but there was something about him that caught my eye from the start. Maybe it was the way his brown suit twisted in strange ways around his torso, maybe it was the way he wore his dark glasses even in the thick of the night, maybe it was the clawlike fingernails or the smile plastered onto his bearded face, as if his lips was stapled into place. Or maybe it was the way he stared into the night sky as if scanning the very face of God.

I won't say I had the inkling even then of what he would be, my instincts are good, but not that good. First off I figure him for nothing more noble than a dope fiend looking to score. So even as I kept passing out them leaflets, I sidled up to the bizarre man in the brown suit, lifted the brim of my hat, looked away, and whispered my standard offer out the side of my mouth.

"Boy, bush, jam-a-lam-a-lam?"

He raises his head and points two fingers up to the Camel cigarette sign, you know, the one with the cat blowing smoke out his piehole.

"Smoke?" I says. "Smoke is it?"

"Smoke," he says. "Smoke is it. I'm hungry, Jerry. Jerry, you hungry?"

It wasn't just the words what confused me. His voice was strangely high, almost twittering, but with a deep rumbling undertone. To hear him speak was to hear two men who disliked each other talking at once, one munchkin, one gargantuan, two separate voices harmonizing badly. I looked at him as he continued to stare upward and realized, quite suddenly, that he was either a total nutjob or maybe the coolest, hippest cat on the Square, dropping on me a boatload of jazzman jive I hadn't yet cottoned to.

"Smoke it is," I tells him, hoping for the latter of the two possibilities. "You got the spinach?"

He stares down at me again, that blank stare, Hubert. I reach into my pocket and pulls out the thin wad I affected—a fiver wrapped around six ones, which was all I had just then to my name—and swish it back and forth. He aims his blank stare at the bills in my hand as if he had never seen a buck before.

Then he reaches into his jacket pocket, pulls out a wallet thick with cash, and swishes it in a perfect imitation of me.

"All right," I says, stuffing them leaflets into my pants. "Tag along and I'll take you to your dreams, palsy. What'd you say your name was? Jerry?"

"I'm hungry, Jerry. Jerry, you hungry?" he says.

I shakes my head in confusion.

"Enough with the blatta-blatta-blatta," he says.

"Blatta is it? Jerry Blatta?"

"Jerry Blatta?"

"Well, follow along then, Jerry Blatta, and I'll hitch up the reindeers for you."

"And don't come back, you fresh bastard."

I laugh, tap the brim of my hat over my eyes, and start off for Roscoe's place, where I knows he could cop whatever it was he was looking to cop and where I had business of my own. I glanced back once, maybe, to be sure he was following, but as I led him north, up through the Square along Broadway, I couldn't afford to be worrying about my new friend Jerry Blatta keeping up. Instead I had bigger concerns, like keeping my lamps peeled for Big Johnny Callas and those fists of his, thick enough it was like they had their own saps built in.

"Hey, Mite," says Sylvie, one of the girls what hooked for Big Johnny on the Square. "My man, he's looking for you."

I smiled, or maybe it was more like a wince, and hurried on.

"Mite, you scrawny half-pint," comes a voice, soft and mocking. It was a lean, leather-jacketed joint-swinger name of Tab. Tab was one of those Joes what strutted around like he was all [illegible] kidding? I wasn't running, but damn if I wasn't walking fast. See, just then I was in the middle of what you might call a situation.

Big Johnny Callas, with his big fists and blue-black pompadour, was the main man in the Square for that old geezer Abagados. The Abagados gang was a Greek crime outfit what covered the whole of midtown tight as a noose, and it was Big Johnny who did the squeezing on the Square. He was a sweet-dressing man-about-town, wearing flash suits, sawing steaks at Jack Dempsey's, paling around with Joe D. at Toots's place, pumping starlets in high-heeled pumps, and running a string what included Sylvie. He also booked numbers, booked bets, offered optional protection at a mandatory price, and lent out low amounts at a high vig, which was maybe where the trouble between him and me it began.

It had seemed like a good idea at the time, taking the two Bens off Big Johnny to give to Pepe to get in on a load of porno magazines what were coming up from Louisiana to be resold at obscene profits. As Pepe told me with that droopy smile of his, the hottest porno came from New Orleans, what with all the Frenchies there. In them days I was surviving night to night by handing out my leaflets, or selling reefer to hollow-eyed jazzmen looking to buy their inspiration, or

sending businessmen with that hunger in their eyes over to one of Big Johnny's sidewalk socialites for a short spurt of entertainment. My hustles was a step up from my first years in the Apple, when I racked balls for quarters and ran out on rainy nights to get some big dick a pack of cigs, but even so I was barely earning enough to keep me in feed and make the rent on my crappy flophouse bed with the toilet down the hall. I was heading nowheres, fast, and Hubert once again knew my name. He had tracked me to the Square, he was stalking me now like a panther stalks its prey. With my porno deal I thought I could rise to a level where he couldn't reach out and swipe me with his paw, but I should have known never to trust a mope like Pepe. Old Dudley had taught me better than that.

So I was hustling up Broadway, trying to avoid Big Johnny, when I caught a flash of pompadour coming the other way. I quickly ducks into a doorway and holds my breath until it passes on by. Strange thing is this guy, Jerry Blatta, he ducks in with me, faster than ever I could have imagined. I just looks at him, he looks back with them dark glasses.

"What are you doing?" I says.

"Looking for a date," he says back.

I give him a once-over. "Keep your mitts off, palsy."

Just then, down the street comes the pompadour, but not on Big Johnny Callas, instead on some silly snot-nosed stick from Jersey. I let out the breath I had been holding.

"Let's go," I says as I head back up Broadway.

"You got it, sweet pea."

Oh man he was hip, was he ever. I had then the first inkling whether he was the coolest cat on the Square, strutting like a jazz band throwing out a syncopated rhythm, or some physically disabled vet wounded terribly in the war. Except I had seen him duck into that alley after me quick and smooth as a snake.

Roscoe sold out of a crappy fifth-floor railroad flat on the West Side. We stepped over a junkie curled like a potato bug just inside the front door. The stairwell was dank and filthy, cockroaches scattered like councilmen at a cathouse raid as we climbed. At the right apartment, I knocks on the door. An eye appears in the peep, the door opens.

"Mite," says Roscoe in his soft, slurry voice. "This is a surprise."

Roscoe stands shirtless in the doorway, leaning carelessly on the right jamb, sweat glistening off the smooth flat plates of his chest. A lit cig dangles from his snarl. It was the era when every other Joe looked like they was ready to drop to theys knees and yell for Stella.

"I brought a customer," I says.

Roscoe's heavy-lidded eyes lift over my shoulder to take in the man in brown behind me. The edges of his mouth twitch. "What you having, friend?"

"Smoke," says Blatta.

Roscoe takes a deep drag from his cigarette. "You're in luck. Received myself a shipment of green just this week."

"But first, Roscoe," I says, "we needs to get square."

Roscoe stares down at me through the smoke from his cig. "Take a bite of air, Mite," he says finally. "The man and I are talking business."

"I must have sent thirty tea-heads up here in the last two months. You owe me my cuts. We had a deal."

"I've changed the arrangement. Go outside and play. We'll talk later."

"Roscoe, man. Man. I need it, the money. You know Big Johnny he's breathing down my neck. I gots to give him something. I figure you owe me like a hundred. That was our deal. Big Johnny, he'll crush me I don't pay."

"I've got two words for you, Mite: grey and hound."

"Roscoe, you're dicking me, man."

"Yes, well." He drags at his cig. "It happens, kid. It happens." With his left hand he quickly grabs my nose and gives it a twist.

Just then Roscoe's gaze, it falls to the floor. A fat cockroach was taking its main chance and sprinting across the threshold of his doorway. With his hand still grasping my nose, Roscoe reaches out the toe of his shoe and flicks the cockroach onto its back. The little bugger's legs spun wildly in the air, like it was trying to ride a bike, afore Roscoe, he brings his shoe down and squashes it with a loud snapping crunch that pops out the pale insides.

I hears a strange gasp from behind me.

"Get the picture?" says Roscoe.

shoot in some Joe's hand, so I am standing there, trembling, when it happens.

Blatta behind me suddenly grabs hold of Roscoe's wrist, the one connected to the hand still latched onto my nose. He grabs Roscoe's wrist and pulls it away from my face and then jerks the arm down with a terrible force. The sound of Roscoe's knees hitting the floor comes at the same time as the snap of the bones in his arm.

The howl Roscoe lets out as he sags back on his heels, cradling the flopping remnant of his arm, brings me out of my shock. I steps back and turns. He's standing there, smiling his maniac smile, Jerry Blatta, the Boss, though not yet the Boss, as calm as if what he had just done was as simple as flicking a switch.

"Who the hell are you?" I says.

"Blatta is it?" he says, "Jerry Blatta? Look, Smithy, your week's up tomorrow and we want you out."

I squints up at him, but not for long. Old Dudley had taught me that when things they slide in unexpected directions there is always advantages to be had. Things here had slid in an unexpected direction all right. I glance once more at Blatta and turns back to Roscoe, who is letting out a high-pitched wail and laying now in a puddle of his own drained dew.

"What about my money, you muscle-bound craphead?" I says.

Roscoe, still cradling his arm, keeps on howling even as he struggles to rise, his eyes steady on Blatta.

Blatta steps forward and smacks Roscoe's forehead with the palm of his hand. The son of a bitch sprawls backwards into the doorway.

I leans over, pats Roscoe's pants pockets, feel nothing but a slippery wetness, wipes my hand on his head, then steps over him into the bare apartment that smells now like some gypsy old-age home, all incense and urine. I toss a few cushions, empty a few drawers, scatter a shelfful of strange religious tracts as I remembers the vicious rumor going round that Roscoe was a Buddhist. The search, it doesn't take me long. For all Roscoe's talents, cleverness wasn't one of them.

The cigar box, it is slipped behind the tank of his toilet bowl, a box filled to the brim with sweet bills of many churches and all denominations. I consider carefully counting out the hundred I was owed, but then figure what the hell and takes it all. Six hundred and some dollars it turned out, enough to get me off the hook with Big Johnny Callas, for sure.

But already I wasn't so much worried anymore about Big Johnny Callas.

I stood inside the apartment, with the wad in my hand, and looked through the doorway, beyond the broken, prostrated body of Roscoe, to Jerry Blatta standing there in his dark glasses, smiling at me with that plastered-on smile. And right there I knew, in my heart, with the inbred instinct that has bee[illegible]

[illegible] on theys own, to embody the pioneering spirit what stretched America from one ocean to the next. Others, but not me. Because I am not enough. Let others fill their hearts with the lonely struggle to reach great heights, I need someone to carry me.

And I figured, if I played my cards just right, I had found my someone, a jive-talking, jazzy-walking, shady-eyed customer name of Jerry Blatta. Now all I needed was a plan.

I steps over Roscoe, whimpering as he was, still on the floor, and gives him a kick in the side for good measure. "Stiff me again, Siddhartha, why don't you?" Then I grabs at Blatta's sleeve and says, "Let's blow."

"But first, Roscoe, we needs to get square," says Blatta.

"What?" I says. "You want your cut now? Sure." I separate the bills into rough halves and offer Blatta the thicker share. When you're my size, muscle always gets the thicker share. "Here you go, palsy."

He takes the wad of bills I hand him and examines it, as if he were realizing the value of money for the first time, afore stuffing it in his pocket.

"All righty-rooty," I says. "Time to amscray the hell out of here."

"Not so fast, big boy," says Blatta.

I step backwards as Blatta leans over Roscoe. "Nothing personal, pal," he says. "Just beeswax."

Roscoe squirms backwards in fright, like a wounded spider trying to get away.

Blatta ignores him, staring instead at the still-lit cigarette lying on the floor, loosing a thin white string into the air. Blatta picks it up, looks at it queerly, sticks it in his teeth.

"Smoke," he says.

5 Kockroach doesn't question where the little man in the green cloths came from. One moment Kockroach was staring up in awe at the giant face breathing smoke into the night sky, and the next moment, as if upon decree from the great fearsome figure itself, the little man had appeared, spoken to him as if they already were familiar, and gestured for him to follow. Kockroach's immediate instinct had been to scurry into a hiding place, but something about this human, its size, its overt familiarity, the color of its cloths, made it seem a less threatening presence than the other humans he had observed. He decided instead to follow along and see what he could learn.

The little human had taken him to a fierce predator human with the smoking white stick, a human who had proceeded to grab onto the beak of the little human and then to kill one of Kockroach's former brothers. For some reason he couldn't fathom, Kockroach was now in the middle of a battle. It was a fight that Kockroach sensed wouldn't be won by a stilt-legged show of aggressiveness. So instead he had grabbed at the predator human and tried to pull his arm off, like the mouse had pulled off Kockroach's leg many molts ago. Kockroach had failed to detach the arm, but the attempt

was enough to injure the predator and just that fast the battle was won.

With a quick victory, and with the placing of the white fire stick in his mouth to pay tribute to the great smoking god, Kockroach's confidence swells. He still doesn't doubt that the humans would crush him had they half the chance, but now he knows it won't be so easy for them to do so. And with that realization comes a familiar and innate urge.

Rams butt heads over ewes, mustangs rear at one another for the right to mount mares. All animals fight over territory, battle over mating rights, struggle claw and breath for sheer superiority. It is the natural order of things for the strongest of a colony to impose his strength upon the others. Kockroach looks around himself, sees the little man, the injured predator human, remembers all those he has passed in the street. Maybe he is stronger than other humans. Delicious possibilities begin to open to him.

After the battle, the little human had given Kockroach more of those green pieces of paper with the faces on them. Those pieces of paper remain a great mystery to Kockroach. He has seen them passed back and forth among humans as a sort of token. He doesn't know what they mean or what they are used for, but he can tell they are important to the humans, so when the little man offered him a number of the papers, Kockroach understood immediately what was happening. The little human had given him a form of tribute, a token bespeaking clearly Kockroach's superior status. He likes the feeling. He

street back toward the seeming center of all human activity.

"So, Jerry Blatta," says the little human, "what can Mite get for you? Anything. I owes you, palsy. You did a job on Roscoe, you sure did."

"Smoke," says Kockroach. That word, which the little human had taught him, seems to have magical properties.

"Oh yeah, let's see."

The little human reaches his claw up to Kockroach's face and takes the white smoking stick from between Kockroach's teeth. It is now short and stubby, no longer glowing, no longer loosing its noxious burning smell.

"We need get you more, we do," says the little human, the human called Mite. "What's your brand?"

Blatta points up at the great visage in the sky with the smoke pouring out its fearsome open mouth.

"Camels it is. You got matches?"

"I like it dark," says Kockroach, pulling what seems to be appropriate from his stored inventory of human sounds.

The little human lets out a loud snort, pats Kockroach on the upper arm, disappears into one of the doorways off the street. Kockroach stares after him but doesn't dare follow. He

worries for a moment that the little human has left for good. It was a comfort having him close, someone who acknowledged an inferior status to Kockroach and yet was willing to usher him through the bizarre twists and turns of the human world. Kockroach's smile remains even as he searches with his gaze for the little human. Mite. Of all the humans, his is the only name Kockroach knows. Mite. He wants this Mite to stay near, to guide him through the thickets of this strange new territory.

After many minutes, the human returns. The relief Kockroach feels is both surprising and enjoyable. The little human gives him a small packet with silver at the top. Kockroach stares at it without understanding what it is. The little human takes the packet, rips off the top, taps the bottom so that three of the little white sticks appear. Kockroach takes them all. They are long but without the glowing tips. Still he puts them in his teeth. He tries to give the packet back to the little human, but the human refuses.

"My growth's stunted enough, don't you think? But I got you something else," says the little human. "A gift."

The little human shows him a small shiny thing, golden in color, a thin rectangle with a line running through it. Kockroach peers at it without comprehending its purpose. Then, shockingly, the little human opens the top and spins a little wheel.

Flame magically appears.

Kockroach backs away and squeals. The little man steps

himself that from now on, to remain as inconspicuous as possible, he will limit himself to one at a time.

Even as Kockroach is teaching himself moderation in his new smoking habit, the little human does something marvelous; he closes the top of the magic rectangle and places it in Kockroach's claw.

Kockroach rubs the magic rectangle with his digits. "Mite," he says in a soft, slurry voice. "This is a surprise."

"We're pals, ain't we, palsy?"

"You got it, sweet pea."

Kockroach opens the magic rectangle. He spins the wheel slowly. Sparks but nothing more. He tries again, harder, and suddenly a flame erupts. Fire: the bane of arthropods throughout all eras, scorcher of the bold, decimator of colonies. With a bright yelp, Kockroach drops the magic rectangle.

The little man picks the rectangle up, closes the top, and gives it back.

Kockroach opens it again, flicks the wheel: fire. He closes the top, opens it again, spins the wheel, repeats the act over and over, over and over. Fire. Fire. Fire.

Cockroaches have existed on earth for more than a quarter of a billion years. Fossil evidence shows hundreds of species of cockroaches living among the ferns and mosses that

covered Pangaea during the Paleozoic age, 150 million years before the coming of the dinosaur. From that distant age to this, cockroaches have evolved little. Any 350-million-year-old cockroach that magically appeared on the sparkling linoleum of a New York kitchen would be recognized for exactly what it was and squashed without a second's thought. They were cockroaches then, they remain so today, crawling along in the manner passed down for billions of generations with nary an advance. So it is safe to say that Kockroach's mastery of fire would qualify as the most stupendous leap forward ever in the bland, static, and yet oh-so-persistent history of his species.

"Hey, palsy," says the little human as Kockroach stares into the flame in utter fascination, "you hungry? You want some grub?"

For a cockroach, the question is rhetorical.

6

Each night after work, as she poured the cream into her coffee at the Times Square Automat, Celia Singer watched the ebbs and flows of lightness in her cup as if in the swirling shapes a private message about her future was being relayed, the meaning of which was just beyond her grasp. She was everywhere haunted by the vague terror that she was missing the meanings of things. It was an occupational hazard, she supposed, eight hours each night plugging lines, making connections, eight hours behind the huge grid, sockets connected by fraying cords over which endless words were streaming back and forth in a great communal conversation, words of which she caught the hum and rhythm and yet no meaning.

She added sugar and twirled her spoon in the cup. Her second cup. It was well after midnight and still the Automat was alive with comings and goings, with life. Maybe that was why she came here each night and sat by the window with her coffee and a slice of pie and let the night burn down around her, even as Gregory slept alone in their bed at the apartment. She preferred the tortured intimations of others' lives to the dead quiet of her own, and at the Automat there was a regular group of others on which to latch her attention.

Over there, at their usual table by the coffee spout, were the

politicians in their shabby suits, loudly arguing about the great issues of the day as they endlessly refilled their coffee cups. Celia admired their passion, it was obvious that their political beliefs were the most important things in their lives, certainly more important to them than their teeth.

And sitting as far from the cashier as they could sit were the college boys in their sweatshirts, slurping their makeshift tomato soups, concocted from ketchup, Worcestershire sauce, butter, and hot water. They split a sandwich bought with three precious nickels from one of the windows and talked with an uncontained excitement about the new jazz record bought by some hipster named Elmer, and the Céline novel being passed around, and the reform school kid on his way in from Denver, and their plans for getting out of the city and hitting the open open road. They were a jittery crew, slapping arms, jabbing fingers in the air, seeming to buzz with a pure current of energy that electrified the night for them but to which Celia was immune.

Far to the side, hunched over his pie, sat Tab, thin and good-looking, with his black leather jacket and ruined complexion, who trolled the shadows of the Square for men willing to buy what their wives could never give them. Tab made bravura come-ons to all the girls in the Automat, including Celia, just to be sure everyone knew that he was only doing what he did for the money, though no one believed him. Celia felt nothing but sympathy for the young boy, and the things he was forced to do to survive, but still, sometimes, in the mornings she would wake up beside Gregory with a start, realizing she had been dreaming of Tab stretching his lean

laughter, jealous of their direct connection to a brighter world, but jealous most of all of the pretty girls and their ability to dance. The very thought of it pressed tears to the back of her eyes, tears that should have dried and died years ago.

Not to forget Sylvie, on a break from the street, sitting alone, staring into her coffee as if it were to blame for what she had become. Celia supposed she should have felt sorry for Sylvie, in the way good girls feel sorry for girls like that, but Celia was no longer a good girl and what she felt instead of pity was a kind of bitter envy. Sylvie had the most magnificent body, long legs and wide hips, pillowy breasts, all of which she showed off with the sweaters and tight wool skirts and gorgeous high heels that Celia would never ever wear. When Sylvie walked through the dining room with her tray, each man in the restaurant watched the shifts of her body with some sad longing in his eyes. That it was as available as the lemon meringue pie behind the little glass doors if you had enough change didn't alter the way they looked at her.

"You're such a pretty girl," her mother had told Celia over and over. "You have the face of an angel. You'll have the family you deserve, a family to make you whole." This was not what she supposed her mother meant, this ragtag assortment of losers and late night hangers-on that surrounded her each

night at the Automat, but this was the closest thing she now had to a family. "The boys will come running, they won't let you slip by just because," had said her mother. Except they had, hadn't they, Mom? All but Gregory, who behaved as if he were doing her the greatest favor of her life, reaching down to help the disadvantaged, like they were two models in a March of Dimes poster.

Maybe Gregory actually was doing her the greatest favor and maybe she should be ever so grateful. He was basically decent and fairly upstanding and not bad-looking in a scholarly sort of way. But Gregory had no problem with indecipherable messages, he delighted in relaying to her the meaning of everything. Of course he was a graduate student in Russian history and so he knew just enough about everything to be unbearable. And of course he was a Communist, which meant his earnestness and self-importance were beyond endurance. But it was not like she had so many alternatives. And he seemed so certain of everything, which was comforting in its way because Celia was the most uncertain person she knew. Maybe his certainty was why she had stifled her doubts and let Gregory move into her little walk-up when his lease ran out.

So now she was living in sin. She laughed ruefully at that. Living in sin was what her mother called it when she spoke of the town strumpet or the widow in the next township. Oh, the image it brought to a young girl's mind. Other girls dreamed of marriage, of children, of the family Celia's mother so desperately wanted for her; Celia had dreamed of living in sin. Well, be careful what you wish for. Where was the canopied

times she stayed nights to feel a part of this. This was the juice in her life, not Gregory, not the job, not her pale hopes for the future, but her little table at the Automat, sitting with this strange dismal family, separated from the carnival of Times Square by a single pane of glass. It was sometimes hard to impress, even upon herself, exactly how pathetic her life had become.

Someone caught her attention in the throng outside the window. A man in brown, a handsome-faced man in sunglasses walking with a strange, jerky step. He had a ragged beard, his suit was on wrong, though how it was on wrong she was uncertain, his nails were long and unkempt, and he had a bizarre smile fixed around the cigarette in his teeth. Her immediate reaction to spotting him outside her window, just a few feet from her, was an irrational but very real fear. And her peculiar fear increased when he stopped right next to her, turned to the window, and stared inside.

She cowardly dropped her gaze to the tabletop before her. At all costs she wanted to avoid this strange man's gaze. "Please, please," she whispered to her coffee and still-uneaten pie, "don't come into the Automat." Celia loved being part of the midnight world, but only so long as she could maintain

sufficient distance from its inhabitants. That was her method of approaching all of her life, the rigid defenses of the maimed.

She stirred her coffee, lifted it to her lips, felt its tepid heat upon her teeth. When she put it down again she glanced up to the window. He was gone. Relief and disappointment both all at once and she wondered to herself at why that man had given her such unease.

It was his awkwardness, his hesitance. Celia could tell in some subliminal way that the mass of instinctual acts we take for a physical presence were not, in his case, being done instinctively. Nothing was easy, nothing was natural. That was it, his raw unnaturalness, and who felt more unnatural than Celia? In that way he was a mirror into her own uneasy place in the world and she mustn't have that. She had troubles enough, she didn't need some lunatic in a bad brown suit pointing out to her with utter clarity her own gnawing sense of alienation. So instead of reaching out, one alien to another, she hid in her coffee cup. How brave, Celia, how wondrously courageous. She felt sick, useless. Maybe that was why she didn't want to go home, so that even Gregory wouldn't find her out.

She glanced up and saw the man in the brown suit suddenly inside the restaurant, his right side brushing the wall as he scurried toward the food. It was a shock to see him and she had to fight a strange revulsion. But having castigated herself before, this time she bravely refused to look away.

He reached the glass serving doors and peered inside at all the offerings, the pies, the fruit, the sandwiches, tuna, egg salad, deviled ham, olive loaf, the crocks of baked beans, the

pulled harder. It still didn't open. He slid to another door, took hold of the handle. Then to another. He moved from one to the next, looking for a door that would open. He must be hungry and have no money. He shouldn't be in here if he didn't have any money. Why was he here, ruining it for everyone? Why did he insist on making everyone feel so uncomfortable?

She spun her gaze around the Automat. The politicians, the college boys, Sylvie, the comics, no one was noticing the strange man in brown. Even the cashier was more interested in her nails. It was only she whom he was making uncomfortable. Celia felt suddenly ashamed at everything she had been feeling, the revulsion, the anger, even the pity. Who the hell was she to feel any of those things for anyone else when she felt those exact same things for herself?

Almost as an act of penance she was about to stand and make her way toward him, to buy him a sandwich, when she realized he wasn't alone. There was a smaller man in a bright green suit bustling about him. She recognized the suit immediately.

Mite, the tiny young aspiring gangster who spent his evenings at the Automat huddled over a hot tea, eyes desperate and searching, ever vigilant for a mark to hustle. Mite introduced himself to everyone new at the Automat, sat down, told an

elaborate series of lies, and then asked to borrow thirty-nine cents. Always thirty-nine cents, as if the sheer specificity of the number made it hard to refuse the entreaty. He was short, thin, nervous, full of hope and despair all at once, and Celia, overwhelmed by the empathic sympathy only one loser can feel for another, had given up the thirty-nine cents more times than she could remember. Now they were close to friends.

She was shocked to see him there, in the Automat, that night. A few weeks ago he had told everyone about the big deal he was about to score. A little import-export, he had said. All he needed was some up-front cash, he had said. It was sad seeing the hunger that marked his face like a stain, a hunger that couldn't be satisfied in that Automat with all the nickels in the world. It was that hunger that had sent him to Big Johnny Callas, who often held court in that very Automat, to borrow the up-front cash at the Greek's brutal rates. And, as could only have been expected, Mite hadn't settled up when he was supposed to. She hadn't seen Mite for a couple of nights, she had heard he was on a bus to somewhere new, Moline, she had heard, or Fresno, away. She'd been glad he had escaped.

But now here he was, stunningly present, accompanying the strange man in brown. And now here he was leading the man by the elbow, bringing the man across the floor, past the politicians, past Tab and the comics, right smack to her table.

"Yo, Celia," said Mite. "This is my new friend, Jerry. You mind if we sits here with you?"

Celia kept her eyes off the strange man, always obedient to her mother's order not to stare whenever a strange or de-

"What are you still doing here, Mite?" she said. "I heard you were already on a bus out."

"You heard wrong, then, didn't you?"

"Big Johnny has been telling everyone about his plans for you. They're not very pretty."

"Let him talk." His nonchalance died quickly and he peered out at her warily. "What plans exactly?"

"Something to do with the spleen. You know where the spleen is, Mite?"

"Isn't that in New Jersey somewheres?"

"It's behind your liver. Big Johnny says he intends to remove it."

Mite sucked in a breath and then shrugged. "Well, the hell with him, excuse my Polish. He wants that spleen thing he can have it, I gots no need for it no more."

"Mite, you have to go. It's too dangerous for you here. Do you need money, bus fare?"

"Nah, I decided to maybe stick around a bit. It's a free country, ain't it? Believe it or not, things is looking up for me. Thanks to my friend Jerry, things is looking way up. So can my pal park hisself here while I grabs us some grub?"

"Sure, I suppose," she said. "Any friend of yours . . ."

Mite pulled a chair from the table. "Sit down, palsy. I'll take care your dinner. Keep an eye on him, Celia, won't you, whilst I load up? Anything you want?"

"No thank you, Mite. I'm fine."

Mite winked and then was off to the wall of food.

She watched him go before turning to the man in the brown suit, who was still standing.

"Sit, please, Mr. . . ."

He kept standing until she gestured at the seat Mite had pulled out for him and finally he sat.

The strange pull of revulsion she felt when she spied him outside the window, and then by the wall of food, strengthened in proximity. He had a peculiar smell, strong and furry, less the deep neglected tones of normal body odor, more the higher-pitched animal musk that arose with its own not-so-hidden message from the carnivora house at the zoo. His beard was dark, his hair, beneath his hat, long and greasy. There was something disconcertingly real about him, as if the rough edges of existence, normally smoothed by societal conventions or blurred by the plate of glass through which she viewed the world, were still jagged and sharp on him. He sat there in his dark glasses, unmoving, as if he were blind, but at the same time it seemed as if he were staring at her with a brutal intensity. She tried to stare back, to see beyond her own reflection in the dark lenses, but failed to connect with his eyes.

Suddenly he reached into his jacket pocket and pulled out something small and golden. He flicked open the top, spun

She felt strangely flattered, there was something almost gallant in the gesture. To be polite, she reached into her purse, took out a cigarette, leaned forward and lit it on the flame, all the while staring into the dark lenses.

"Thank you," she said. "Your name is Jerry?"

"Blatta is it? Jerry Blatta?"

"That's an interesting name."

He continued to stare.

Self-consciously she leaned back, crossed her arms over her breasts. "And you're a friend of Mite's?"

"Sure, I suppose. Any friend of yours . . ."

The register of his strange disjointed voice suddenly slipped higher, as if in imitation of her own, using even her own words. She began to laugh, she couldn't help herself, the charming gesture, the flattering imitation, the disconcerting stare.

He drew back as if under attack, and then through his fixed smile he laughed too, a laugh as high and girlish as her own.

Mite returned with a tray laden with plates and cups and glasses. Before his friend Jerry, Mite placed a ham and cheese sandwich, cut diagonally into two triangles, an apple, a tapered glass filled with tapioca pudding and topped with

whipped cream, a cup of coffee. Ever frugal, for himself Mite brought only a hard roll, two pats of butter, a glass of water, and a cup of tea. Mite sat himself next to Jerry, solicitously close, and edged the plate with the apple, red and shiny, toward his friend.

"Go ahead, Jerry," he said. "You know what they say, an apple a day keeps the coppers at bay."

Celia watched the strange maternalistic display with a curiosity that turned to amazement as this Jerry Blatta devoured the apple in four bites, swallowing skin, core, all, leaving only the tiny stem sticking out from his teeth.

"He's a hungry boy, your friend," says Celia.

"Ain't we all. Look at him close, Celia. He's my ticket."

"Your ticket?"

"Oh yeah."

"To where, Mite?"

"To the pineapple pie, sweetheart, where we all wants to go. Just like Pinnacio. You ever hear of Pinnacio, what worked out of the Square a few years ago?"

Celia shook her head.

"He's a legend now, sure, Pinnacio, but back then he was just an Alvin like me, a skinny hustler what styled hisself a show biz impresario with nothing but a single blue suit and a pretty face to get him through. He had two clients, a sad-sack comic who got the mokes laughing only 'cause he couldn't stop sweating on stage, and a contortionist what had a fatal fondness for chocolate and couldn't no longer touch her toes. Pinnacio used to hoard his nickels so he could sit over his coffee at the Automat and read

Blatta didn't answer but continued to stare at the cup filled with hot coffee. As Mite and Celia looked on, he stuck his finger into the cup, pulled it out, stared at it as it reddened from the heat.

Mite took hold of his own cup by the handle, pinkie sticking out absurdly, and lifted it to take a sip. Blatta, seeing this, did exactly the same. It is as if he is learning, thought Celia, as if he is a child learning his way in the world, latching onto the worst possible teacher in Mite.

"So one night, Pinnacio's at the Roxy and he sees a girl what looks no older than twelve doing a semistrip, and the geezers in the house theys just loving her show. She's got something, sweet little Suzy does, something a twelve-year-old shouldn't have, which makes sense 'cause this girl she's twenty-two and working a second shift on her back after the theater darks. But on stage she's playing the little-girl thing for all it's worth and the yards in the joint are springing to life like a crop of winter wheat, you get the picture? So Pinnacio, with this Suzy, he sees his ticket."

Jerry Blatta lifted half of the ham and cheese sandwich off the plate and squeezed the half in his fist until the cheese and mustard oozed out. He stuck the mess into his mouth, jamming

it all in until his lips could close one upon the other. Celia stared at him, dumbfounded. Blatta stared back with defiant humor, even as he reached for the other half.

"Well Pinnacio," continued Mite, "just the day before, in a *Variety* he hawked from a can, spied something about an opening for a juvenile in some second-rate C movie they was filming in Brooklyn. He strolls right up to little Suzy what wasn't so little and tells her he can get her an audition if she signs a management contract with him. She shrugs her shoulders and signs, figuring this skinny mope didn't have the pull to get the audition in the first place. But the thing was, this audition it was open, he didn't need no pull, and she didn't need no him, but there it was. And in that audition room she gives it the full twelve-year-old-with-a-glimmer-in-the-eye treatment and the director is a perv through and through and so hot to lay his mitts on a twelve-year-old he practically throws hisself at her feet. Now she's in Hollywood, a real star, and Pinnacio, he's riding around with a tan and a Cadillac, living flush in the pineapple pie. All because he found his ticket."

"Is that true, Mite, or just another one of your stories?"

"True, true, you could look it up. Her name is Susan Harrison or Susan Haywood or Susan something, they changed it for her, but it's true, I'll swear to it. And Celia, sweetheart. I have the damnedest feeling that Jerry here, he's my sweet little Suzy. Ain't you just that, palsy?"

Blatta ignored the question, maintaining his stare at Celia as he moved to the pudding. Reaching his hand into the tapered glass, he pulled out a glob of the yellow and white

thrilling. Watching him lick the gaps between his fingers with his tongue was like having a cat reposition itself over and over on her lap.

"What do you know about him?" said Celia softly.

"Nothing," said Mite.

"Where is he from? Where does he live?"

"No idea."

"So why do you think he can help you?"

"Oh he can, believe you me."

"And why do you think he will?"

"'Cause, Celia, I can help him too. See, he's something special, but he needs guidance, he needs management, he needs me. With him and me together, there's no telling where it will end."

"Just like Pinnacio."

"You got it."

"Did you know him personally, this Pinnacio?"

"Nah, not really, but I heard, I heard."

"So the whole story is apocryphal."

"A pocketful of what?"

"Posies, Mite. And what about Big Johnny?"

"What about him?"

"Mite, don't play the fool."

"Let me tell you a secret, Celia." He leaned forward, lowered his voice. "I gots the money."

"You have the money?"

"Like I said."

"How?"

"Sweet little Suzy here."

"You have enough?"

"More than enough. I could pay the dirty creep off and still have enough left over to take you and me to '21.' But it's no sure thing paying that creep off is the answer. See, Celia, I gots Jerry on my side now."

Just then Jerry Blatta reached into his jacket and pulled out a fistful of bills. He held his hand out and offered them to her. His face, his smile, had the same expression as when he flicked the lighter.

"Looking for a date?" he said. "Who ain't? It'll cost you five. You got it, sweet pea. Did you hear? No. Yes. Want to have some fun, honey? You look like you could use it."

Celia was taken immediately aback by the offer of money and the strange words. No hidden meanings here, despite the garbled sentences. He was offering to buy her, like one would buy Sylvie. It had never happened before, no one had ever confused her with a whore, and for a moment her emotions teetered.

Suddenly, involuntarily, she laughed.

She laughed and the strange man in brown laughed and Mite, whose jaw had dropped in disbelief and had stared at her with a worried gaze, he laughed too. And as they laughed

and the money in [illegible]

[illegible] political beliefs, but a commingling of desires too? That was the dream that had died in her, killed off by the virus that had lodged in her spine and the thick sole and brace she now wore on her left foot and the limp that scattered desire onto the floor like so many jacks with each pathetic step. Her mother had been wrong, the boys had not come, the dream had fallen into a deep hibernation, and with the dream went her courage to touch anything beyond the muffled voices of other lives seeping from a distant room. But now it stirred again, the dream, roused by the outstretched bills, the carnivora musk, the long pink tongue, the cat turning in her lap, the strange brutal reality of this man, all of it, and the muffled song of her own pale life seemed so ridiculously wan in its presence that she couldn't help but laugh.

The man in brown, this Jerry Blatta, he turned to Mite and let out a strange hissing sound, almost like a warning. There was a moment when he appeared to begin to rise from his seat.

She fought to regain control, let the laughter fade, tried to compose herself, not sure what was going on in Blatta's strange psyche, whether he took the laughter as an insult when that was not her intention, not her intention at all.

And then she imagined the expression on Gregory's face, the shock, when she would tell him that he absolutely had to move out, and she fell again into a hysterical fit that had them all looking, the politicians and the college boys, Sylvie, Tab, the comics and trombonists at the center table, all of them, and she didn't care, she didn't care, she did not care.

Kockroach feels a surge of excitement roll through him as the female makes her strange high-pitched bray, the same roll of excitement he had felt as a cockroach when the scent of a willing female's pheromones started his antennae to twitching. It must be part of the human mating ritual, that sound she makes, and so he echoes it as closely as he can, all the while holding out to her the green pieces of paper he means for a tribute. He is ready to mate, certain it is going to happen, when, to his shock, he hears the same mating bray from the little human beside him.

He turns to stare and lets out a warning hiss, but the little man continues to make the seductive sound. Normally this would be a time to fight, to rise up on stiff legs and battle for the attentions of the female, and he is about to do just that, to rise and attack with no mercy and destroy utterly the little man beside him, when something stops him.

The woman's braying subsides and she is looking at him, not at the little man named Mite. And Mite is offering up no tribute of his own, just his braying. And suddenly somehow Kockroach realizes that with this female Mite is not a threat, will never be a threat, as if he were of an entirely different spe-

cies. Kockroach turns back to the woman, makes the braying sound again, and the female joins in.

Kockroach is certain, absolutely, beyond any doubt, that now, finally, he is going to mate.

The female rises from the table and Kockroach rises with her. Will they do it here, right on the table, atop the scattered plates, like two cockroaches, or will they go instead to her lair? Humans, Kockroach has noticed, don't mate in the open, unless they mate in some strange way he has not heretofore recognized. Maybe that claw-to-claw thing he has seen so often in the street.

The female reaches out her claw to him. He reaches out his claw in the same way and she grabs hold. A jolt of power tingles through his arm and down into the worm between his legs.

"It was a pleasure to meet you, Mr. Blatta."

"Enough with the blatta-blatta-blatta."

She makes the braying sound again and lets go of his claw. Is that it, is that all there is to it for humans? If so, what a sad pathetic species.

"I'll see you around, Mite," says the female. "Be careful, please."

"It's them what oughts to be careful now," says Mite.

She turns her attention again to Kockroach. "Take care of my friend Mite, won't you?"

"You got it, sweet pea," says Kockroach, aware through his assimilation of the bizarre but handy human language that she

the female turns and walks away, walks away without him, her hip rising awkwardly with each step, walking away as if one leg had been twisted by some fearsome predator.

He stares at the female walking away, at the strange uneven gait, at the rods of metal attached to her leg, at the strange rocking motion of her tail. He feels the tingling in the worm again and begins to follow, until Mite grabs hold of Kockroach's arm.

"Is that what you want, palsy, you want a little barbecue?" says Mite.

"Girls, girls, girls."

"Well, why didn't you say so? Nothing could be easier. Half the girls in the Square this time of night have gone commercial, one way or another. Put the spinach back in your pocket and I'll get you one, no problem, anyone you want, just not her, all right? You got that, Jerry? Not her. She's a nice girl, Celia is. But I'll gets you someone else. Look over there. That's Sylvie, what with the tits like atom bombs. A bit mismatched too. We calls them Fat Man and Little Boy, we do, but variety, it's the spice of life, ain't it? What do you think of her? Hubba hubba hubba?"

"Hubba hubba hubba?" says Kockroach as he continues to watch the strange swaying of the first female's tail as she leaves through the spinning glass door.

Mite waves his claw in front of Kockroach's face. "Yo, Jerry, you listening? Anyone but her, all right? Not her. Celia ain't interested in that stuff. She's a cripple, for Christ's sake. No, the Norma Snockers what I was talking of, Sylvie, she's over there."

Kockroach slowly swivels his head in the direction of Mite's pointing digit until his gaze lights on a female sitting alone at a table. Her hair is yellow, her long legs are crossed, she has huge mounds deforming the chest of her thorax, mounds which Kockroach finds strangely appealing.

"Hubba hubba hubba?" says Kockroach.

"Attaboy. Wait here, I'll set it up."

Kockroach watches as Mite walks over to the female with the yellow hair. Kockroach turns for a moment to look at the door where he had last seen the first female, the one known as Celia, but she is gone. He turns back quickly enough to see Mite point at him. The second female, the one known as Sylvie, twists her face in a strange contortion and then shakes her head back and forth. Mite offers her a tribute, waving the green pieces of paper, and then clasps his claws together in a symbol of submission, and still she shakes her head back and forth.

Mite makes his way slowly back to Kockroach. With his eyes narrowed, he looks at Kockroach's face and then lets his gaze drop all along his body.

in slippery wisps and foul exhalations, it is colorless and hot and looks like smoke but it is wet to the touch and it now surrounds Kockroach on all sides with its heat and its pressure and the slime it leaves on his strange pale skin and his dark glasses.

At first, sitting next to Mite with only the glasses on and the single white cloth over his lap, Kockroach's nerves were shouting and he felt more defenseless than he had ever felt before, even more than when he was a white nymph and the mouse sprinted into their midst. There are other humans in the room with the hot wet smoke, sitting on the benches, water appearing on their soft round bodies as if by magic, and he was certain, naked before these other humans, he would be discovered, finally, for what he was and squashed. But the pale hot stuff, schvitz Mite called it, surrounded him and turned the walls dim and his never-ending urge to be protected on all sides eased and he now feels strangely comforted.

It is no wonder that he feels at home in the steam bath. Cockroaches developed in the steamy marshes of the tropical forests in the early millennia of earth's natural history, and while the heat tends to sap the energy of humans, Kockroach finds it positively invigorating.

"Schvitz," says Kockroach.

"It's a machiah, ain't it, bubelah," says an old human in the corner.

"Bubelah," says Kockroach,

"Hey, you Jewish?" says Mite.

"Right off back of truck," says Kockroach, with the accent of the man at the table where he found his dark glasses.

Mite laughs and shakes his head.

Through the smear of fog on his glasses, Kockroach examines the other humans in the schvitz. They all have glistening skin and big pink bellies and the same worm between their legs as does he, although his is bigger. What does that mean? he wonders. Is it good or bad? He is about to ask Mite when Mite speaks to him instead, speaking strangely, using only half his mouth to pronounce the words.

"Yo, Jerry. I might got an opportunity for you if you're interested. Something with huge possibilities what could put us both in the money."

"Opportunity?" says Kockroach.

"A little business."

"Beeswax?"

"Yeah, that's it, beeswax. Something rich. I thought up a plan, see. All you gots to do is follow my lead and let it happen. You interested?"

"Bubelah."

"Good. Great. This is gonna turn out, you'll see. All right, let's hit the shower. I suppose that's a word you ain't heard much lately, is it? Shower."

"Shower," says Kockroach.

"Attaboy."

[illegible] slurp it with their food, but they fear it when it comes from above, and at the first dangerous drops they scurry to a place of safety.

"What, too cold?" says Mite. He twists a knob. "Try this."

Kockroach sees Mite standing under one of the waterspouts, getting drenched, seeming to welcome the streaming fluid, lifting his face up to it as if it were a gift. Kockroach steps tentatively beneath the water and lets it pound on his belly, his shoulders, over his dark glasses, onto his head. He wonders why he had been afraid of it all those many molts.

Mite rubs a shiny white stone all over his body, creating a weird white froth. Other humans do the same thing. Kockroach takes the same white stone. It is slippery, easily bruised like no stone he has ever touched before. He licks it and spits out the bitter taste. He rubs it all over his own body as the other humans do, and the froth covers him head to toe until the water washes it off.

"The thing," says Mite, again using only half his mouth to speak, "is to let me do all the talking. I know these guys, what they're looking for. But there's going to be a time when you got to show your stuff. You'll know it when you see it, and then, baby, slam bam you do your little act."

"Your little act."

"Yeah, the thing what you did with Roscoe."

"Take care of my friend Mite, won't you?"

"Attaboy. We're a team, ain't we, Jerry? A team."

"You got it, sweet pea."

"Sweet pea. I love that sweet pea thing. You kill me, you know that, Jerry? You kill the hell out of me."

Mite brays and rubs the white stone over his hair and Kockroach does the same and as the water rinses off the froth he feels different than he ever felt before, looser, lighter, fresher.

One thing he has learned for sure. Never again will he lick himself clean.

"My friend Mite," says the tall thin human with the dark skin in a room filled with cats. "Always a pleasure. What can I do for you this morning?"

"I need a suit, Clive, with all the trimmings. Shirt, hat, skivvies, everything."

"Lovely. This suit, you're looking discount or executive?"

"Designer, baby."

"Designer? You're buying designer? Have you found God, little brother?"

"Something better. But I need a class look for it to go over."

"Do tell. But I'm sorry, darling. I don't think I have designer in your size."

"It ain't for me, Clive, I'm all set." Mite jerks his thumb at Kockroach. "It's for my pal Jerry here."

and dances around Kockroach as he stretches the cord along Kockroach's arms, his legs, around different parts of his thorax.

"Mr. Average, isn't he?" says the man, nodding with a smile. "Which is good, because that's what they grow in Des Moines. Forty-two jacket, best as I can tell. Seventeen-inch neck with thirty-five-inch sleeves. Waist thirty-four. I have some nice blues for you, or a lovely gray."

"What color you want, Jerry?" says Mite.

"Color?" says Kockroach.

"That's right, palsy. It's your choice."

Kockroach steps forward and reaches toward the tall thin man. His skin fascinates. It is the color of his old chitin. He misses his chitin, the strength and stiffness, the color. Running around with this white skin, he feels lost and frail, like the weakest of nymphs. He wishes his skin were like this man's, dark and rich and full of protection. He reaches up and touches the man's cheek. "Color," he says.

"Oooh," purrs the tall thin man. "Just so happens I have a forty-two in brown pinstripes, double-breasted. You want to see it?"

"Don't want to see it," says Mite. "I just want to buy it."

"No checks, Mite."

"No checks."

"My, you did find something better, didn't you?"

"How long to get it altered?"

"If you have time, I'll do it right now."

"Clive, my man, you are magic."

"Yes, yes I am."

Kockroach is lying back in the chair, a thick white cloth tight around his neck, surrounded by humans, all grooming him. One man in a red vest, having already smeared Kockroach's face with hot white foam, is now scraping his cheeks and chin with a brutal-looking edge of metal. One man is whipping a cloth back and forth across the shiny brown things on the ends of his legs. One female is cutting and scraping and rubbing the hard tips of his claws. Being so close to so many humans is frightening and yet comforting too. Kockroach feels as if the proper order of things has been established, as if these humans have indeed seen him for exactly what he is and, in lieu of squashing him, have exalted him to his rightful place.

But Kockroach knows it is not his inner self that has caused all this to happen. It is the little pieces of green paper Mite has been giving to all he meets: the human behind the counter at the schvitz, the human with the dark skin who gave him the new brown cloths and hat, the human with the brutal edge of metal who cut and greased his hair and now is scraping his cheeks. He is beginning to understand the power of the little green pieces of paper. He can use them to maintain the proper

"It's a great game," says Mite. "The game of kings, which is what you and me, we're going to be. An old geezer learned me the game in Philly. It teaches you how to use your noggin."

"Your noggin," says Kockroach as the man in the vest takes a towel and starts wiping what's left of the white goop off his face.

"That's it, baby. That's how to get ahead in this world. When this is all over, I'm going to teach you how to play. We'll have usselves a game, you and me."

"You and me."

"What do you think here, Mite?" says the man in the vest when all the goop is wiped off Kockroach's face.

"Nice, Charlie," says Mite. "Very nice. He cleans up good, don't he?"

"Yes he does."

"It's like looking at someone new without the beard. You want a look there, palsy?" says Mite. "Spin him around, Charlie."

The man with the vest dusts Kockroach with a sharp white powder, brushes the back of his neck, pulls away the towel, spins around the chair until Kockroach is staring at a man in a chair staring back at him. He moves his shoulders and so

does the other man in the chair. It is the thing he saw before, in the small white room, the thing that shows him himself. He hasn't seen his face since the early days of his strange new molt, and never before without the little hairs on his cheek. He examines himself carefully. He reaches into a pocket of his new jacket and pulls out the picture of the humans he took from the room at the time of his molt. He compares what he sees now with the face that is his in the picture.

Yes, this is the way he is meant to look.

"What you got there, palsy?" says Mite. He steps toward the chair, looks down at the picture. "There you are. I didn't know you was married. Boy, she's a looker, ain't she?"

"Hubba hubba hubba," says Kockroach as he stares at the female in the picture. She has light hair, like the female known as Sylvie, but she reminds him of the female known as Celia.

"Where she at now?" asks Mite.

Kockroach shrugs his shoulders.

"She die on you or what?"

"Or what."

"Oh man, women will get you every time, won't they? That's why I stay away from them. I gots a weak heart, the doctors they told my momma that when I was a tyke. But that's what's so good about them girls in the Square. They're always there for you. Even when theys with someone else, grab a cup of joe, a cig, and next thing you know it'll be your turn at the wheel. You ready for some trucking?"

"Ready for some trucking."

"Good. Let's go find Sylvie."

hear the sound beneath the roar in his head. He sniffs the air, her sweet floral scent, shakes his head, the roar grows louder. This is more like it, absolutely. He slows his step to watch the twitch of her tail but the woman pulls him forward. He lurches into her and the roar turns into a tempest.

She stops at a door. He lurches into her once again. He rubs against her as she fits a key into the lock and turns it. She spins around until she is facing him, her arms behind her, her mounds against his own flat chest. She grimaces at him and brays. He places his claws on either side of his forehead and reaches out two digits like two antennae. She tilts her head and brays again.

"You're a crazy one, you are," she says.

"Sweet pea," he says, wagging his digits.

"You're certifiable, you are."

"Sweet pea, sweet pea, sweet pea."

She stares for a moment at his wagging digits and then places her claws at the same positions on her own head, raises two of her digits into antennae. He reaches down to rub his antennae against hers. She rubs back, her braying turning to squeals.

"Sweet pea, sweet pea, sweet pea, sweet pea."

He leans down to bite her. She pushes him away, turns, opens the door, falls into the room.

He lunges in after her.

The mating ritual of the cockroach differs slightly from species to species within the order, but is generally initiated by the female, who raises her wings and secretes powerful pheromones from a special membrane on her back. Sensors in the male antennae pick up the sweet pheromonal scent from as far away as thirty feet and direct the male to the ready female. This release of pheromone can be accompanied by stridulatory singing or hissing by one or both sexes to help bring the partners together. Some cockroach songs comprise as many as six complex pulse trains, a melody more musically advanced, actually, than many Ramones songs.

When a sexually receptive female and male cockroach do finally meet face to face, they begin whipping and lashing each other over and over with their antennae. Antennae fencing serves to excite the varied sensory receptors up and down the antennae, which begin to tingle as the two cockroaches are near overwhelmed by tactile and chemical stimuli. This electrically charged S&M foreplay can last as long as two minutes among certain European species, though it has been observed to be remarkably abbreviated or ignored altogether by the male American cockroach, which often simply charges and thrusts its genitals at the female. Scientists have wondered if this behavior explains the infestations of female American cockroaches in the holds of transatlantic flights landing in Paris.

wings to a sixty-degree angle, revealing a lobe on his seventh abdominal tergite. This lobe, called an excitator, releases the male's sex pheromone, called seducin. The male's excitator is small and bristly and yet irresistible to the female, like a cone of rocky road or a medical degree.

Overwhelmed by the seducin and fooled by the male's submissive posture, the female steps forward, climbs upon the male's back, wraps her legs around his torso, and begins to nuzzle and lick the excitator.

Suddenly the male pushes backwards, arches his abdomen, and extends his genitals toward those of the female. The longest of the male's genital hooks reaches up and clamps itself onto the abdominal tip of the female. Once this connection is made, two other smaller hooks reach into the slim genital orifice of the female and grab hold, forming an unbreakable bond between male and female.

The female, as if in reaction to the male's sudden brutal move, tries to escape from the male and break off contact. She is able at first to move only sideways, stepping off his back and around and around until, still hooked up, she is facing directly away from him.

In this position, tip to tip, the male's genitals reaching deep inside the female's, the struggle stops and male and female this

way remain, for an hour at least, sometimes far longer, one inside the other, together, motionless except for the slow internal humming of their bodies. They stay connected long enough for the male to slowly transfer to the female an oval-shaped packet called a spermatophore, filled to the brim with sperm.

After copulation, it is cockroach tradition for the female to relax with a dose of urates, a supplemental source of nitrogen donated by the male. In some species, the urates are contained in the shell of the spermatophore itself. After the sperm cells are drained, the spermatophore is pushed out of the abdomen and devoured by the female. In other species, after copulation, the male will raise its wings, direct the tip of his abdomen toward his mate, and from special glands secrete a whitish urate-rich ooze, which is swallowed by the female in a feast that can last many minutes. This part of the process can often be seen, late at night, on the tiny televisions in arthropod motels. With no females to swallow this whitish ooze, an excess of urates can accumulate in the male's body, bit by bit in a toxic swell, until the male's own urates eventually poison him, or so young male cockroaches often claim.

The mating ritual completed, the male cockroach parts, quickly, washes his claws of the entire enterprise, and hurries off. Male cockroaches are positively Washingtonian in their determination to avoid foreign entanglements and hold no interest in the newborn nymphs that emerge from the female's egg capsule many days later, except as a quick snack if hunger strikes. Once safely away, the male cockroach feeds and defecates, scratches his belly, lays a few bets on the silverfish, and awaits the next intoxicating whiff of female pheromone.

[illegible], he squeezes his tie tight and places his hat on his head at the jaunty angle. It is time, he knows in his bones, to leave.

Something scurries across the sink. He lifts a glass, turns it over, traps the small brown thing. He leans forward to examine his prize. It is a cockroach. Slowly he lifts the glass. The cockroach remains motionless.

Kockroach reaches down a single digit and gently pets the back of the arthropod. The cockroach seems to lift higher on its legs, responding to the touch.

On the pad where they mated, he sees the female with the yellow hair, Sylvie. She is lying naked, twisted in the white cloths. Her eyes are open and they follow him as he walks about the room. Her grimace is soft and dreamy. As she looks at him, she opens her arms, revealing the mounds on her thorax, two large whitish things, one slightly bigger than the other, both with dark brown tips. Kockroach feels roaring through him the strange desire to fall upon his bent legs and place the dark brown tips in his mouth. But even stronger is the craving to flee. It grows within him like a sickness.

"Gotta run, sweet pea," he says.

"So soon, handsome?"

"Blatta, blatta, blatta."

"You know where I'll be."

"Lucky me," he says.

Before he leaves he takes from his wallet a few green papers, as a tribute. He places them on the small table next to the pad, beside the glass which he filled in the bathroom, its amber fluid reaching almost to the rim, its uric acid rich in nitrogen.

Kockroach finds Mite outside the building, leaning against the wall by the door, tossing a silver disk into the air.

"Took your time, didn't you?" says Mite.

"I'm from out of town."

"Aw hell, it's the same everywhere, ain't it? Except maybe in New Orleans, what with all the Frenchies there."

"Want to have some fun, honey? You look like you could use it."

"I got no time for such distractions," says Mite. "There's business to attend. You ready?"

"Ready."

"Remember what I told you? How to play it?"

"Nothing personal, pal, just beeswax."

"Absolutely."

Kockroach takes out his wallet and from the wallet takes out the green pieces of paper. "This," he says.

"Oh yeah, don't you know it. We're going to be drowning in it, you and me. That's what it's all about."

"What it's all about."

"The pineapple pie."

"All right, partner, it's off to see the wizard."

8

Was a geezer what hung around the Square name of Tony the Tune, on account of he was always humming to hisself. Missing half his teeth, bent back, wild white hair, voice like a frog, hum hum hum, crazy old Tony the Tune. Had enough money from somewheres that each night at the Automat he would buy hisself from the steam table a Salisbury steak, with masheds and broccoli, two rolls with butter, pick up a cup of joe from the big metal urn, a wedge of lemon meringue from the wall. Many was the night I nursed my single cup of tea and stared longingly as the old mope sat alone and hummed some cheery song to hisself whilst he sopped up the gravy with a thickly buttered roll.

"Hey, Tony. I got something coming down this week, but I'm a little short right now. You got thirty-nine cents you could lend me just till Tuesday?"

"Get away from me, you little scalawag," he'd spit at me. "I got no time to waste on the likes of you."

Tony the Tune.

So one night, Tony started coming into the Automat with some beefy-looking pretty-boy blond with dark eyes and arms like legs. Old Tony would shuffle in and the blond would

together and Tony would spend the whole meal patting the boy's hand, whispering in his ear, opening his milk cartons, humming some Sousa march, fetching straws and napkins, buying more food if the pile on the tray wasn't enough to fill the boy's gob.

I figured Tony for a queen in love, simple as that, but it was Sylvie what set me straight. Tony styled hisself a boxing aficionado, spent his days picking up towels at the Gramercy Gym on Fourteenth Street, looking to get his mitts on a palooka with a chance. Now any fighter with any kind of promise could find hisself a sharper manager than old Tony the Tune, so Tony was left to scrape the canvas for the sad saps with slow hands and glass jaws what were dead meat afore ever they stepped into a ring. A no-chancer, such was Tony's boy, a colorful pug only so long as the colors they was black and blue.

A few weeks after it started, the boy followed Tony in one night but he wasn't so pretty no more. His left eye was closed on him, his maw was a swollen mess, his nose busted but good. That night it was soup and milk and pudding mixed with cream, all sucked down by the palooka through a straw. It wasn't long afore Tony started again to come in alone, humming his tunes

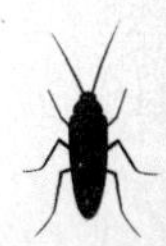

and ordering his Salisbury steak and masheds and broccoli and two rolls with butter. We never again spied the pretty-boy blond who wasn't so pretty no more.

If you asked me then, I would have told you Tony the Tune was the worst kind of fool, starving hisself so some no-chancer could prove exactly what he was. The worst kind of fool, a fool in love with hope. Because Hubert, that sack of nothing what sacked my ma, he seeks out hope, like he seeks out fear, waits for the instant when hope wanes to rise up and seize your soul. My momma, she showed me that. Tony the Tune was Hubert bait without even knowing it. But suddenly, with the coming of Jerry Blatta into my life, I had a whole new understanding of the grumpy old mope. See, even though I knew the dire consequences of relying on hope alone, I couldn't bring myself to reject its blandishments neither. So just like Tony, I brought my hope into the Automat, loaded his tray with food, groomed him for a shot at the title.

I had my doubts about Jerry Blatta to be sure. Like when I put him to bed the night we met, sacking out myself on the floor so he could have the mattress. I woke the next morning to find Blatta buck naked and curled into a ball beneath the bedsprings. What that was all about I never figured. Or when I noticed he put his legs through the armholes of his undershirt and pulled it up as high as he could. I had to near bite my lip through to stop my laughing at that. He was a queer one, and I had my doubts, but I had no doubt at all about what he had done to Roscoe. And so, when the choice was to save what I needed to pay off Big Johnny or to spring the bills I needed to clean up my Suzy like he needed to be cleaned, I

White Way. Can't you see us? Me in the front like a herald of sorts, and Jerry Blatta behind, drawing attention what with his fancy new double-breasted suit and dark glasses, his sharp cheekbones, his syncopated jazzy jazz walk, the lit cig bobbing in his lips, the cocky air of the newly laid. He was a sight, he was, as Times Square as Georgie M. hisself, who was so Times Square they gave him a statue. Jerry Blatta, bucking for a statue of his own, following behind as I led him north through the Square. And then a few blocks west, past all them restaurants, one next to the other, French and Irish and Spanish and Italian, a whole marketplace of cheap European cuisine, until we reached a Greek joint called the Acropolis, where in the back room the *Nonos,* what ran all the rackets in Times Square, held court.

Whoa, that perked you up in a hurry, hey, missy? A little organized crime never hurt a story, did it?

Abagados. The *Nonos.* Which in Greek means Godfather, or maybe murderous bastard, either one, didn't much matter the way things played out. Was a time the very whisper of his name sent a shiver through the Square. Prostitution, drugs, extortion, loan-sharking, pocket-picking, tit-shaking, cheap booze, cheap cigs, the more than occasional heist, the more than occasional murder. Abagados ruled his midtown empire

from a room behind the kitchen of the Acropolis, hiring soldiers like Big Johnny Callas to patrol his streets, and he took a cut out of every crime and caper what went down, from the garment district, through the theater district, into the restaurant district, and beyond. He was a shadowy figure, no pictures in the press, no gossip in the columns, I couldn't have ID'd him if he strolled up and bit my nose, but every step I took as I struggled to slip a score out from under his shadow, I felt the terrible weight of his power.

And word was out on the street that Abagados, no longer content to feast on midtown, was getting ready to expand south and north and east, into territory controlled by the coloreds, the Italians, the Jews, oh my, getting ready to expand and looking to build an army.

"What fug you doing here, Mite? Get hell out afore Yonni, he take off your head."

"Yo, Stavros, it's sweet seeing you too," I says. "Is Nemo around?"

Stavros, tall and thin with a black fedora and an absurd black mustache, jumped off his stool at the bar of the Acropolis and lifted both his long palms at me like a copper stopping traffic.

"I'm no kidding, Mite. Word is Yonni gonna make example you. He tells whole world he reach in you throat and pull out you *arhidis*."

"Yeah, well, whatever the hell that means, let him try."

"But the *Nonos*, he don't want no trouble in restaurant."

"Well then I picked the safest spot in New York, didn't I, Stavros, old pal? I need to see Nemo."

band, three men in puffy shirts and red vests, played maudlin Greek melodies with tears rolling down their cheeks.

Stavros takes a step toward me, like he's about to bounce me out of the joint, when he spies the man behind me.

"Who laughing boy?"

"His name's Blatta." I close an eye and thinks for a moment. "Jerzy Blatta."

"He Greek?"

"How the hell should I know? I didn't check his papers. Look, Blatta and me, we needs to see Nemo."

"He no here for you."

"It's important, Stavros. And believe me, it'll be worth his while."

"He no here. Now spam you."

"The word is scram. Spam is what you feeds the touristas here and call it souvlaki. And the answer is no. I came to see Nemo. I'll just check for myself to see if he's around."

As I push by him, Stavros grabs hold of me. Two other boneheads with fedoras at the bar jump off theys stools and reach into theys jackets as if about to recite the Pledge of Allegiance.

"Boys, boys, boys," I says. "Good to see you all. You're looking swell. But you might want to step aside or I'll start to

screaming bloody murder, I swears I will. Won't the *Nonos* like that, me screaming like a siren here in his quiet little restaurant? If you think that gut scraper on the violin can screech, wait till you gets a load of me. Ready?"

I takes a deep breath, screws up my face, open my mouth wide, like I'm about to make like some fat lady with horns, when Stavros, he lets loose my arm.

"Wait here," says Stavros to me. "I go see if Nemo, he wants talk to a *malakas* like you."

A few minutes later Stavros returned, followed by a huge round man who squeezed through the doorway from the kitchen and made his way to the bar. The man had no neck, lips like Capone, a cigarette was held daintily in his thick fingers. Fat Nemo.

Nemo was some sort of high underboss—the hierarchy of the Abagados organization was always Dutch to me—and yet seemed a decent sort for a gangster. As he made his tours through the Square, oozing his bulk down the crowded streets with Big Johnny Callas and Stavros behind him, he was all smiles and glad hands, tossing cigarettes and bills to the beggars, caressing the heads of the hookers with his fat fingers, buying rounds at the taverns he stepped into so as to renegotiate the payment schedules. And whenever he passed my way he always had a warm word of greeting. *How is it with you, Mite? Dressing mighty sharp this evening, Mite. Someday, Mite, you and me, we're going to do some business.*

"Mite," says Nemo, leaning now on the bar of the Acropolis, fiddling carelessly with his cigarette, his grin a little less

"Aaah, a fellow countryman perhaps? Then please, use one of our imported bottles, none of that swill we mix up in the bathtub."

The bartender, a lean dark man with hair plastered back, replaced the unmarked bottle in his hand with another, foggy on the outside, sweetly pink on the inside, and filled two of them water glasses like they had at the Automat. I took a sip, sharp like turpentine. I nodded at Blatta and he downed his in one swallow. His eyebrows, they danced just above his dark glasses.

"Now, Mite, I need to get back to the party, so please be brief."

"Word on the Square, Nemo, is you boys is soldiering up."

Nemo carefully raised his cigarette to his lips. "The word?"

"That's right."

Nemo stared down at me as he inhaled. "On the Square."

"The word."

"And you think you, you are the very soldier we may be looking for?"

"Absolutely."

Nemo blew the smoke out in a stream above my head.

"Let me be frank, my friend. I have craps bigger than you."

"That just mean you're eating well, Nemo, and I'm glad to hear it. But it's not only me I'm talking about."

Nemo tilted his head.

"My palsy Jerzy."

"Is that so?" Nemo turned his attention to Blatta. "I haven't seen you around before, Jerzy."

"He's new in the Square," I says.

"I'm from out of town," says Blatta.

"You got much experience there, Jerzy? You a fighting man? You single-handedly destroyed a regiment of Japs in the war?"

Blatta didn't say nothing, he just smiled his smile and Nemo's eyes they narrowed.

"Thank you for thinking of me, Mite, but I've no need now of your help. And I particularly have no need for strangers from out of town who as far as I know couldn't slap their way out of a pita."

"But Nemo," I says, "you don't understand."

"I do, Mite," he says, leaning forward now, his great bulk towering uneasily over me. "Believe me, I do. We don't want nobody nobody sent. The cops are pouring all kinds of finger men into the street to snitch for them, all kinds of lowlifes. And you, Mite, are about the lowest life I know. So now you might want to leave before Johnny steps through that door."

His gaze passes over my shoulder and a dark grin appears.

"Too late," he says.

I didn't need to turn around to know what Nemo was grinning at, the hairs what pricked up on the back of my neck

... deep chest bobbing up and down as he pointed first to his left, then to his right, acknowledging associates here, clients there, bobbing and pointing as he made his way to the center of the bar where stood yours truly, facing away from him. And it didn't matter that I was facing away from him, he'd know who I was right off. There wasn't too many guys my size who worked the Square, and none in a suit as green as mine.

"I been looking for you, you little parasite," he says.

"Johnny, I'm sorry. I'm trying—" I says. But before I turns around fully, I slams his fist with my face and flip sprawling onto to my back.

"You little parasite," he says, leaning over me now. He sucks his teeth and slaps me on the face. "I give you the two bills for your deal of a lifetime and what do I get in return? Nothing. And then you score on Roscoe and clean him out and what do you do with that cash? You buy a fancy suit, a good sweat, a fancy shave, you splurge at the Automat and buy a ride from Sylvie. You get all that and what do I get? Nothing. You little parasite. I'm going to take you apart. But before I do, I want my five C's."

"I only owes you two-fifty."

"There's a late fee of fifty and I get a cut out of the Roscoe deal. I get a cut out of everything goes down in my territory, just like I got to give a cut myself, you understand?"

"I don't got the money no more, Johnny."

"You know, Mite, I was hoping you would say that. I haven't kicked the crap out of nobody in almost two whole days and I miss it."

"Not in the restaurant, Johnny. You can't do it in the restaurant."

"The hell I can't," says Big Johnny.

"What about the *Nonos*? The *Nonos*."

"Well he ain't here now to tell me no, is he?" says Big Johnny. "Stavros, get the band to playing a little louder, and the rest of you boys gather round. No one need see what I do to this loser."

There it was, missy, my defining moment. Not just here, in the bar of the Acropolis, but through all the stages of my pathetic life. Whatever strides I made, whatever precautions I took, it all still ended right there, with me on my back and some bully boy about to turn my face into mincemeat. Look closely and you can see the scars, under my eye, across the bridge of my nose, the white line what runs through my lower lip. My face is a road map of violent despair.

Big Johnny grabbed my lapel, jerked me off the floor, cocked his fat fist and gave it a twirl. It was like poetry, the rightness of it, the beating of my life what was coming as surely as I deserved it. That I thought I could ever put one past the bully boys, manage a situation so over my head, stiff a stiff like Big Johnny and get away with it, all of it was proof that I had goodly earned every last stitch they was going to need to sew up my head. Off to the side Hubert was laughing at my foolish hopes. And I gave him a look of surrender, I

[illegible] your worst,
[illegible] lick of it. All right, Hubert, hope is dead, come and fill me with your sweet wisdom.

I felt a jerk forward and then a lurch and then I fell back hard on the floor. And the blow must have been worse than anything I had been dished before because I didn't feel it, didn't feel it, it must have numbed every nerve in my face because I didn't feel it.

I slowly opened my eyes and I saw why I didn't feel it.

Big Johnny Callas was high in the air, his legs kicking, his arms twirling, held high in the air by my own palsy Jerry Blatta. He held him there, did Blatta, in the air, held him there as if it were an actual comic book hero doing the holding. And then Big Johnny wasn't held aloft no more, he was flying in the air, over the ducking barkeep, against the three rows of bottles up against the wall, smashing the bottles even as his own head smashed against the mural of the la-di-daing maidens, afore his carcass fell with a thud to the floor, alcohol gushing down upon him.

The music stopped. The deep murmur of the restaurant died.

"My God," says Nemo.

"Take care of my friend Mite," says Blatta.

The two mokes who had come in with Big Johnny made their move and in a flash Jerry Blatta had each by his necktie. As

the shouts started flying, Blatta lurched forward and lifted both men in the air. Theys hung there, arms and legs swinging wildly, clutching at theys throats and fighting to find theys breaths.

Stavros pulls his big black gun and points it at Blatta's chest.

I jumps to my feet and stands between the gun and Blatta, the two mokes in the air kicking me as they struggle. "Nemo," I says. "Don't let him. Don't."

But afore Nemo could answer, the door to the kitchen, it opens and a skinny old man, bent like a question mark, leaning on a cane, hobbles hisself forward. Smoldering in his teeth is a short cigar, thick as a thumb. The crowd silences and parts for the man as if it were the Red Sea and the old man was Moses.

"What happen here?" the old man croaks in a thick Greek accent. "Who stop music?"

He looks at Blatta without an ounce of shock, or even admiration, in his eyes, as if it was an everyday sight to see a man hang two of his gunsels in the air by their ties.

"And who the hell you?" he says to Blatta.

"There's been complaints about a smell," says Jerry Blatta. "Can you flush the toilet or something, Jesus?"

The old man looks at the two men held in the air and then at the mess on the far side of the bar. He casually leans over the rail to see a dazed and doused Johnny Callas struggle to pull hisself to his feet. The old man stares down his long nose at Big Johnny.

"Yonni, you *skata*. I should a known you was in middle this. He's right. I should a flush you long ago."

drops the two gorillas, who fall into gasping heaps on either side of him.

"You come back with me," says the old man, eyes still focused on Blatta. "We need talk."

"He's with me, Mr. Abagados," I says quickly. "We're partners. My name's Pimelia. Mickey Pimelia. But they call me Mite, as in Mighty Mite, on account of my size. You might have heard of me? I certainly heard of you, yes I have. I'm very pleased to meet you sir. It's an honor. Really. If there's anything I can do to help you, sir, just let me—"

"Nemo," says Abagados.

Nemo raises an eyebrow. "Shut up, Mite."

Abagados shakes his head wearily. "Both then. And Nemo, my music."

Nemo looks at Stavros, who holsters his gun and yells, "Play, you fools."

The music started up again, gayer than before, and after a moment, the crowd it began again its loud murmur. The old man leaned on his cane, shrugged his shoulders like he had seen everything and was surprised by nothing, turned, and hobbled his way into the kitchen.

And with Big Johnny Callas and Hubert now both routed, Jerry Blatta and me, side by side, we followed the old man, the *Nonos*, followed the old man into our futures.

PART TWO

THE NONOS

9

Celia Singer stared down at the thick slab of beef bleeding on her plate.

There were times, when first she came to New York City, still living in the women's residence hotel, watching her meager savings thin, that the mere thought of a steak so thick could have sent her swooning. In those days, and even in the later days when she lived with Gregory and earned barely enough for her nightly dinners at the Automat, the desperately hoped-for New York success consisted, for her, of a myriad of nights at the popular spots, treated to steaks by one after the other of her imagined beaus—not Gregory, who saw meat as the purest manifestation of capitalists as carnivores, devouring their cows before they devoured their proletariat—but others, the faceless others, linking their arms with hers to drink champagne and laugh at the witty conversation that swirled about them like the smoke of their fashionable cigarettes. She hadn't wanted much, she thought, just everything.

And now, against all odds, here she was, in the barroom of the "21" Club, with a steak the size of a small dog on her plate and almost everything she had ever hoped for having come true . . . well, almost everything. Like the steak, for instance.

The steak she had always imagined would be discreetly well grilled, fully cooked without a hint of blood. But strangely, now, she found the cut of meat on the plate before her, raw enough to still twitch, more to her liking.

"So what happened to him?" she said.

"He was taken care of is all," said Mite. "I was just trying to tell you the way some people are, how they'll try anything to make a fool of you. I mean, the one thing you can be sure is that anyone what claims to be CIA ain't CIA."

"Did Blatta do something to him?"

Mite tried to shush her quiet.

"The things I've heard." Her eyes widened, she smiled slyly. "Did Blatta bite off his ear? Did Blatta break his leg?"

"Look, don't use his name, especially in a joint like this. He don't like that, all right?"

"The things I've heard."

"No one's supposed to use his name, even me. Dig in, why don't you?"

"Don't you trust me, Mite?" There was a flirtatious whine in her own voice that she found disturbing, it was the voice of one of those women who talked to their husbands like they talked to their dogs. *Don't you twust me, my sweet wittle wovey-dovey.*

"I trust you, course I does, Celia. It's just not important to the point of the thing. The point was about how careful you gots to be, how everyone's out for his own self and you can't trust a one of them. What, is something wrong with your steak? You want I tell the chef to stick it back in the frypan a few minutes?"

…pped his fingers.

She shrugged her shoulders, looked away and scanned the crowd. Gray suits and black wingtips, women in pearls, mink stoles, highballs and high-handed greetings, a swirl of meat eaters and greeters three deep at the long wooden bar or floating table to table, as if at a big party celebrating their own glorious selves. Actors and writers, internists to the stars, theater producers and publicity agents and columnists with phones at their tables, moguls and their second wives, politicians and their girlfriends and their aides playing the beard. Not to mention the gangsters and their molls, smiling fiercely, which she supposed included the two of them, though Mite was an unlikely gangster with his small stature and his loud green suits and Celia an even more unlikely moll. Still, they came once a week, Mite and Celia, sitting side by side at the same fine table beneath the shelves of athletic trophies, facing out at the room so that Mite could sit with his back to the wall. "Gots to keep an eye out for trouble," he explained to her.

From their red leather banquette they spied the famous and the faux famous. Was that Richard Rodgers there, in the corner, sitting next to Ed Sullivan, or just two dour lawyers talking shop? Was that Jackie Gleason with a cigar and a girl singer that looked like she was seventeen, or just some fat man from Toledo and the hooker he picked up off the street? Was that, my God, Ernest Hemingway, throwing

his head back in great gales of masculine laughter, his big hand gripped around his Papa *Doble*, or just some Madison Avenue stiff with a beard and a loud voice trying very hard to look like Ernest Hemingway, or maybe, strangest possibility of all, Ernest Hemingway trying very hard to look like Ernest Hemingway?

The glamorous crowd in the barroom of "21" was not at all like the ragtag assortment at the Automat, where never there was a complaint of a Salisbury steak being underdone. Occasionally, at the end of a night out, Celia would stop back in at the Automat and have a look around, the scene remarkably unchanged: the never-ending argument at the politicians' table; the college boys discussing Céline; the prostitutes with their weary expressions; the showbiz types with their forced gaiety. Even Tab, the boy hustler, was still around, though no longer looking so young or so innocent. She liked to visit the old place, see the old crowd that had once been like a family to her, she liked to take it all in and feel the bitter gratitude at having escaped its clutches. No longer did she hoard her nickels to have enough for a piece of pie, no longer would she sit dreamily by the window and watch the world stream by beyond the plate glass.

"Is there a problem, Mr. Pimelia?"

"Yeah, Peter, look at this thing." Mite stuck his fork in Celia's steak and lifted it off the plate, blood dripping down. "It's like you herded the cow through the kitchen and the chef sliced it right onto the plate."

"I'm terribly sorry, Mr. Pimelia. I'll have a new sirloin cooked to order. Medium well, madam?"

"Yes, thank you."

," said Celia, "finally promoted to management."

"What's that?"

"Nothing, Mite."

"Anything else you need, let me know."

He winked at her, winked as if this kid who had made good could do any sort of magic with a simple gesture, a snap of his fingers, a twitch of his lid. And maybe he could. He had started as a raggedly dressed waif with thrift-shop clothes, but like a hero out of Horatio Alger he had risen. Now his shoes were from Regal, his suits from Bonds, his shirts from Arrow, his watch from State Jewelers, his ties from King of Slims. He was a man of the Square, absolutely, linked so closely and inextricably to the mysterious Jerry Blatta that full-grown men shivered when he came close.

It was strange the way things had shifted and her own reaction to it. Celia liked being seen now with a big man on the Square, no matter his size, liked being given the best tables, the complimentary bottles of wine. She caught herself showing inflated exhibitions of interest in Mite's conversations, tilting her head and lowering her eyes at opportune moments, letting the light catch her teeth as she laughed at his jokes. When she got right to it, Mite was the most important person she knew, and because of that some Darwinian instinct had clutched at her good sense. He is important, it told her, he has power; these acts of flirtation were geneti-

cally compelled and, in the presence of his power, she was powerless to halt them.

She placed her elbows on the table, leaned her shoulder toward his, tilted her head just so. "Is that Jimmy Durante?"

"Where?"

"Over there, at the table by the bar."

"Sure it is. You want he should come over, say hello?"

"You can't do that."

"Sures I can. I'll ask Peter next time he comes around."

"How do you know Jimmy Durante?"

Mite shrugged. "He lives at the Astor. We did him a favor once. I'll ask. By the way, how's the day shift working out for you?"

"Fine, thank you. It's nice to wake up with the rest of the world for a change."

"Yeah good. That Barney guy is all right. He was more than willing to do a favor once I tuned him in. He's treating you all right?"

"Like a queen," she said gaily.

The promotion to the day shift had come well ahead of those with far more seniority at the phone company. She had mentioned it once, an offhand comment that she was tired of sleeping all day and working all night, and suddenly her boss, Mr. Rifkin, had put his arm on her shoulder and squeezed and told her she had been doing such a wonderful job that she was being promoted. He did this in front of everyone and the other girls eyed her suspiciously, which secretly thrilled her, better suspicion in their eyes than pity. She wondered at what Mite had done to convince Barney Rifkin to do him the favor,

windows and light streaming through their shades.

She lifted her empty wineglass and a waiter quickly filled it. Another waiter deftly placed a new steak before her, its surface dark and sizzling.

"So tell me, Mite," she said, "how do you break someone's legs?"

"What?"

"I mean, do you just crack them like twigs—" she snapped a piece of celery with her fingers—"or do you use tools? I know they call your friend Jerry a leg-breaker, so I was wondering."

"It's just an expression," said Mite. "It don't mean nothing. You know what I been thinking? I been thinking I oughts to go see an opera."

"Why on earth would you want to do that?"

"You know, culture. You think I'd like opera?"

"No, I don't. So he's never broken anyone's leg?"

"I don't know, maybe. A couple arms I know for sure. He just twists them behind the mope's back like a chicken wing and that's it."

"What's it like to watch him do it? Do you hear the crack?"

"You don't want to know," he said, but he was wrong, she did, every detail, every scent and sound. She was fascinated by his work, even the dark parts, especially the dark parts, the

Jerry Blatta parts. That the strange man in brown, seeming to be totally lost in the world when first she spied him, could end up being the source of all power in the Square amazed her. She hadn't seen him since that night in the Automat, but she constantly sensed his presence through Mite, and, somehow, it felt as if he were coming ever closer. The thought of ending up face to face with Jerry Blatta again secretly thrilled her.

This thing with Mite, this peculiar relationship, was now the richest part of her life. She first went out with him as a favor, reluctantly agreeing because he seemed so anxious to impress her, but now she looked forward to their dinners with a breathless anticipation. Mite was her lone connection to a more dangerous, more awe-inspiring world, and she wouldn't give this connection up, or the gifts Mite tossed to her as if they were nothing more than trifles. The dark blue dress she was wearing tonight, and the pearls, were from him. But she figured it was a square deal. In exchange for the weekly dinners and the gifts, Mite bought a companion, someone he could sit and talk to without the pressure of having to pretend to be other than he was, a kid who had latched onto something and was riding it high, someone to laugh with as Times Square opened up to him like an oyster. And it wasn't like she didn't pay a price for all he lavished on her: thrilling and dangerous this new world might be, but also distressingly barren. Everyone assumed there was something between her and Mite and no one anymore ever wanted to be on the wrong side of Mite. So she was like a vestal virgin without the virgin part, lavished with gifts and yet remaining untouched, as if being prepared for some great destiny.

[illegible] his wine at dinner. At another point, she had decided that she wouldn't, that Mite would have to take only what she was willing to offer, her time, her friendship, her smile, and be satisfied or go on his way. But then she realized that Mite wouldn't ever make that pass. She would have been insulted except she could sense it simply wasn't in him, boiling away like it was in the other men she had known.

"Why wouldn't I like opera?" he asked. "The swells all seem to lap it up."

"If you're having trouble sleeping, Mite, buy a pillow."

"What about that guy with the name what writes them plays. I hear he's pretty good."

"With the name?"

"Like a state."

"Tennessee Williams? Yes, he's wonderful. He has something opening up in the Morosco soon, something about a cat stuck up in a tree or something."

"A show about cats? It'll never go over."

"Maybe, but I'd still love to go."

"Okay, I'll get us ducats, then. Front row good?"

"He's a fruit, you know."

"Is he? Well maybe we'll see something else. There's plenty else, isn't there?"

"So why is he not called an arm-breaker, if that's what he does. I just want to get the lingo down."

"Why are you so interested in the Boss all of a sudden?"

"I'm just curious, Mite. Just curious."

"It's an expression, is all. Look, it's just beeswax. We make deals, we expect them kept. We don't go looking for trouble, but when someone starts talking about the CIA being the reason he can't pay what he owes, we can't go to no police, we gots to take care of it ourselves, that's all."

"Do you hear the crack?"

"All you hear are the pleading and the shake in the voice and then the scream, that's all you hear. A lot of screaming."

"It's the same in opera, too." She leaned toward him. "How does it make you feel, all the screaming?"

"Like my suit's too tight."

She pulled back quickly. It was not what she was expecting. She had expected to hear of the blood pounding, the fingers tingling, she had expected to learn something of the thrill in the raw exercise of power. What she felt now was like going down a fast elevator, a deflating sense of disappointment. Disappointment, she realized with a touch of shame, in Mite.

"Did you ever think, Mite?" she said enthusiastically, trying to mend a rent maybe only she felt. "When I first saw you, you looked like a drowned rat. It was raining, ferociously, and you ran into the Automat, your jacket pulled over your head. And then you hit on each table, one after the other, looking for a piece of change."

"I remembers."

"And after a while you finally came over to my table, water still dripping off your hair onto your face, and asked me for your usual thirty-nine cents."

met me in the public library of all places."

"What were you doing in a public library?"

"I was reading, what do you think? I used to be quite the reader, and not just comic books, thick books. *The Count of Monte Cristo*. You ever read that?"

"It's a boys' book."

"Yeah, especially for a boy what's been getting his butt kicked all over the schoolyard. Anyhoo, this old guy he taught me when you're asking from dough always be specific, a set amount it gives comfort to the mopes paying out. He taught me a lot. Everything I done in the Square, it's like I'm following his blueprint."

"He did you a favor."

"I suppose."

"Suppose? Why look at you. Look at all the money you have now, eating in the finest restaurants. Look at the way they treat you, like royalty. You're Pinnacio."

"Pinnacio?"

"The guy you told me about, the manager now in Hollywood. You told me about Pinnacio like he was a talisman, a symbol that everything was possible. I bet the up-and-comers don't talk about Pinnacio anymore. I bet they talk about you."

"Go off."

"You found it, Mite. What did you call it?"

"The pineapple pie?"

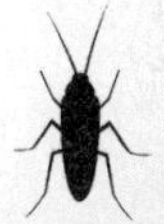

"That's it. It always sounded so tasty."

"But still, sometimes I feel the suit is too tight."

"Buy another," she snapped.

"See the thing is, Celia, the thing is," said Mite, who was clearly trying to tell her something, who was obviously struggling to make himself understood, "my mother was trapped. I don't know I ever told you about my mother."

"No," said Celia, not sure she wanted to hear about his mother, there, in the "21" Club, drinking red wine and eating red meat and watching Jimmy Durante tell stories at his table.

"She was . . . she had . . . I never told no one before, but she had these episodes, she called them. Episodes. They was more like the whole world crashing down. She would spin around and her eyes would roll up the back of her head and she'd be shaking and quivering and she'd fall down bang to the floor and there'd be nothing there, nothing there. The first was this big surprise and the second was not such a surprise and after that she just didn't want to go nowhere in case it happened right there, on the street, with everyone watching. So it was like she was trapped by this thing, this affliction of emptiness which I never told no one about but which scared me small. It still does."

"Do you want more wine?"

"Yeah, sure. And now I see those mokes in their suits, wage slaves Old Dudley called them—Old Dudley was the guy what set me on my way—the suckers riding the train in and working on someone else's money and then riding the train back. Better they hang themselves with them ties, he used to say. Except what are they going back to, Celia? The wife, the

“That’s not you, Mite.”

“Why not? Why the hell not? I could wear gray, not green. I could fold my paper on the train, fold once, fold twice, a little bend and there it is, the baseball scores ready for my perusal. Hey, Don, how’d them Gints do yesterday? I could like opera, maybe, or that queen from Tennessee.”

“Mississippi, actually.”

“Well, nows I understand. But see there’s a whole ’nother layer in the Square that I know nothing about. All them theaters, all them parties at Sardi’s, all them books I don’t read no more. Look around, these mokes are all part of it, why can’t I be too? Sometimes I feel as trapped as my mother she ever was, like I got the same affliction and the emptiness it’s pouring down on me like rain.”

“Mite, stop. Please.”

She didn’t want to hear this, his anxieties and doubts, the weepy telling of his childhood traumas. It was selfish, she knew, he was trying so hard, she could tell, but still his confession was more than she could bear. She needed him to be a cartoon, an amiably winning surface of strut and language whose number had hit and who now was taking her along for the ride. And that other stuff, that darker stuff, the Blatta stuff that tightened his collar, for her that was more than just part of his color, his charm. For her that was, somehow, the root of everything. So she didn’t want to see the undersized

boy tending to his epileptic mother after his father had run away. She didn't want to see the gangster straining against the violence of his trade and yearning for the bland homilies of suburban life. She didn't want to see the man, naked and alone, bewildered by his existential anxieties. For God's sake, did he think he was the only one with the specter of emptiness threatening to swallow him? Didn't he realize that the surface he wanted to discard, that edge of darkness that sickened him, was the only thing protecting her from the same damn specter? So no, she didn't want to hear any of it, not because of what it said about him, but for what it said about her taste for pearls and wine, her new job on the day shift, her growing hunger for animal flesh cooked rare.

"I'm sorry, Celia. I don't want to ruin your dinner. I just thought you'd understand what it meant, and all, feeling trapped."

Like she was slapped. "I don't feel trapped."

"You know what I meant. We all of us are in—"

"Mr. Pimelia, sir?"

The man who appeared at their table was portly and sweating as he stood, literally, hat in hand. She had seen others just like him on other nights, all clothed with either greater or lesser aplomb but all with the same terror in their eyes. This one had a golden ring on one of his fat fingers and the neatly trimmed beard of a man who wasn't used to standing, literally, hat in hand. She was so relieved to see him it was like he was a reprieve from the sentence Mite was about to impose upon them both.

"Aw hell, Cooney," said Mite, who didn't rise to greet

"I'm sorry to disturb your dinner, Mr. Pimelia."

"Yeah? So come back when we're done."

"Can we talk?" The man glanced at Celia. "In private?"

"What's to talk about?" said Mite, sticking a piece of meat in his mouth, chewing, continuing to talk all the while. "You're late again. Two weeks this time."

"The closing, Mr. Pimelia, they keep putting it off. Now it's a problem with the deed. The buyer is ready and willing, but they keep putting off the closing."

"And that's supposed to be our problem? You knew the terms. More wine there, Celia?"

"Yes please," she said brightly. Mite poured the last of the bottle into her glass, raised his hand, snapped his fingers.

"Yes, Mr. Pimelia," said Peter, who had appeared quickly and silently, and was now standing just behind the man with the beard. "Is there a problem? This man said he was a friend of yours."

Mite glanced up at the man in the beard and then said, "No, no problem. We're out of wine here, is all. And get Jimmy over by the bar another bottle of whatever it is he's drinking and tell him I gives my regards."

Peter leaned over, snatched the empty bottle from off the table. "Very good, Mr. Pimelia."

The man with the beard watched until the maître d' had left and then began again with his pleading. "I can't make the

two-fifty, per, Mr. Pimelia. I just can't. You'll get it all when we close, I swear, with some extra. But just now, I tried to get the five I owe you."

"And this week's too."

"Of course, yes, I tried. And I can't."

"You got a house, don't you?"

"And three kids, Mr. Pimelia, and a wife and a mother-in-law living in a first-floor bedroom."

"Aw, Cooney, we don't want to hear about your mother-in-law, please, we're eating here. Look, you got something to say, you want to make a deal, make it with the big guy."

The man's eyes swam like two fish, left, right, bulging forward. "No please, God, no. That's why I came to you, Mr. Pimelia, to avoid going to him."

"But Cooney, there's nothing I can do. If you can't make the payments or a deal with the big guy, there is nothing I can do."

Mite sawed at his steak and then looked up at Celia. Celia glanced at the man and though she believed she should have felt pity, compassion, horror over what was being done to him and his family, what she felt instead was a familiar tremor of thrill at being part of some force powerful enough to shake a man like that to his core. The affection she felt that instant for Mite grabbed at her heart, and if he had asked her just then for anything, anything, she would have given it gladly and without hesitation.

"What about that ring you're sporting there, Cooney?" said Mite, while still staring at Celia. "The big gold one. How much it worth?"

"How big?"

"Half carat each maybe."

Mite raised his eyebrows and smiled, still looking only at Celia. "All right, you're lucky you got me on a night when my mood is sweet and I might just be in the market for a ring. I'll need to resize it, and that will cost me, still I figure it's good for seven-fifty."

"But, but—"

"Take it off."

The man hesitated and then, quickly, he began scrabbling at his finger, trying to yank off the ring. It wouldn't budge past the knuckle. He gave it a twist, tried again, his face strained with the effort.

"I'll tell him you're clear up to this week. But next time don't come back to me like this. Either bring the money or go see him. And Cooney, believe me when I tell you this, it's better you find him than he finds you."

"I understand," said the man, his voice slow and constipated as he struggled with the ring.

"All right, all right, let's have it."

"I'm trying, Mr. Pimelia," the man said, his face twisting grotesquely from the effort. "All the nervousness, my hands are swollen, but I'm trying."

Celia edged a small crock of butter his way.

She was still feeling a quivering thrill at what she had done when she looked up. Her heart leaped when she saw him. He was coming toward them, energetically darting through the crowd, arms outstretched. His bent back, his famous nose, a great gleam in his eye.

"Mickey, you son of a gun," came the celebrated rasp, full of merriment and rhythm, "how you ended up with the swellest dame in the room I'll never know. It's a mystery, it is. Guess my good news. Guess. All right I'll tell you. I made a killing today in the market. Yes indeed. I shot my broker. Mickey, my friend, you look like a million. So how the hell are you?"

10

Kockroach does not dream. The inner mechanisms of his brain won't admit to gorgeous flights of fantasy and it need not trouble itself with working through the unsolved dilemmas of the day because Kockroach's day has no unsolved dilemmas. He does what he needs to get what he wants and moves on. In fact, Kockroach's life has little day in it. He falls peacefully to sleep at the earliest announcement of the early dawn, the dreamless sleep of the innocent, if innocence is remaining true to inner character, and arises only as the promise of night begins whispering in his ear. What song he hears from the onset of night is the song that has serenaded his species awake for a hundred thousand millennia:

"Darkness comes, sweet darkness, so arise, ye scions of the night, and devour."

At the first rap on his door Kockroach scurries from beneath his bed. He has slept his peaceful slumber in the lovely narrow gap between the bedsprings and the floor, but still the covers and sheets of the bed are tossed and twisted with some fierce abandon. For a cockroach, a night without sex is like . . . well, how would one even know? He pushes himself

to standing, protects his eyes with the dark glasses, strolls, naked and unabashed, arms rising languidly in his contrapuntal step, to the door, which he opens.

The man in the red jacket studiously keeps his gaze averted as he rolls in the cart with its twin domes, like two great silver breasts. He parks the cart, bows stiffly, and silently backs out of the suite, leaving Kockroach alone.

Kockroach lifts one dome to find a huge bowl of ice topped with thick pink shrimp, cooked but still in their shells, their little legs clutching at the ice. He dips his hand into the red spicy sauce, licks his fingers clean with his long tongue, and then one by one jams the shrimp into his mouth. He masticates with abandon, letting out a strange series of chortles with each snap of the jaw. He has taken a great liking to shrimp, their briny sweetness, like the briny marshes in which his great and noble forebears first evolved. The lovely crunch of their thin shells reminds him of the crunch of chitin eaten after a molt.

Beneath the second dome lies a great rack of lamb, the bones arranged in a crown, pink paper hats on the tip of each rib. Kockroach lifts the rack, each hand grabbing a number of ribs, lifts it above his head, and then, in a savage jerk, rips it apart. He snaps at the tender chunks of meat rolling off each rib, first from one hand, then the other, and back again, ripping the meat with his teeth, mashing it to pulp with his molars, swallowing the sweet roasted muscle before snapping at more. His lips, his cheeks, his body is smeared with the grease of the rack. When the meat is gnawed off he starts on the bones, crushing them in his teeth, sucking out the marrow.

[...] a great evolutionary step forward, a natural progression from the discovery of fire. This is how cockroaches would eat had they the wherewithal to hunt larger prey, to cook their victims over savage fires, to smear the grease of their roasted conquests across their abdomen, their legs, their genital hooks.

He struts around, his back arched, his legs stepping high, holding the final remnants of the ribs in the air as the light reflects off the smears of fat on his body, struts and laughs and revels.

He is in the shower when the man in the red coat arrives to roll out the cart. The shrimp are gone, muscle and shell. All that's left of the rack of lamb are the tiny paper hats, tossed carelessly across the floor.

Kockroach sits back in the stiff, high chair, the white robe cinched around his body, his glasses on, his grimace fixed, the lower part of his face covered with hot white foam. A man scrapes at the foam with a straight razor. A female rubs his nails with a yellow stick. A man is in the corner shining his shoes. Mite sprawls on the couch, his feet on a coffee table, talking.

"The girls are all out, Jerry, all but Sylvie what says it's so

painful she can barely walk. Don't know what it is with her lately, but she ain't bringing in what she was, no surprise the way the skin it hangs off of her like a baggy sack of nylons. She's on the sleeve, I think, but everyone knows not to sell to our girls so I don't know where she's getting it. Having her around, it's bad for business, gets the other girls upset and, truth be told, she ain't so appetizing to the buyers. We need do something about her soon."

Kockroach says little when Mite speaks, but it is not out of a paucity of words. He has learned much of the language, picked it up on the run from conversations overheard, from statements barked by his associates, from the movies Mite sometimes takes him to on hot, slow nights. He now knows the names of the parts of his new body, the names of the human things that surround him. He has collected strung-together bits of noise that he sounds out during the gaps in his sleep until they are polished and ready for the world. The sentences he has learned are short, to the point, active, orders aped from the most powerful humans he has come across. And along with the sentences he has learned a trick about speaking with humans: the fewer sounds you make, the more they respect and fear you; the fewer sounds you make, the more you maintain control.

"The protection's been coming in like clockwork, no worry there, not after what you did to Paddy's place and then to Paddy's wife. Once word got out, the others what was holding back all fell in line like tenpins. Oh she's walking again, by the way, case you was worried, Paddy's wife, though she ain't walking so well."

[illegible] somewheres underneath a mattress so it pays to let him get behind. Rickland paid, Somerset paid, Bert is out of town but his girl's still around so he'll come through. And you'll love this. Seven twelve came up, which is Toddy's number, son of a bitch. He owed us six plus, but as soon as I heard the number I got to his runner afore he did, so he's up to date."

"Show me," says Kockroach.

"Sure, Jerry, sure. You know I'm always square with you."

Mite reaches into his jacket, pulls out a thick envelope, drops it onto the coffee table with a solid thwack. The female working on Kockroach's nails slips and digs a knife into the cuticle. Kockroach's hand suffers not a twitch as blood wells on his fingertip. The female cleans it off nervously with a white towel.

"I'm sorry, sir," she says. "I'm sorry."

"Who isn't?" says Kockroach.

"I marked out with a paper clip the *Nonos*'s cut, for you to give him the way you like," says Mite.

Kockroach nods.

"The *Nonos* wants to meet everyone at midnight. Nemo made sure for me to tell you not to be late."

Kockroach shrugs.

"That's it, I guess." Mite drops his feet from the table, slaps

his thighs and stands. "I'll see you at midnight then. Have yourself a good night, Jerry."

"What about Cooney?" says Kockroach.

Mite freezes for an instant, and from behind his glasses, Kockroach notices.

"I told you he made up three payments a couple weeks ago," says Mite.

"I didn't see the cash."

"He made it up in trade. He gave us this." Mite screws a thick gold ring off his finger. "I had it sized for me and took the spinach out of my cut, but if you want it, Jerry, be my guest."

Mite flips the heavy ring to Kockroach, who examines it carefully, notices how small it is, notices the shiny metal, the square diamonds, the ruby, and then bites into it as he has seen others bite into gold.

"Swell," Kockroach says, tossing it back to Mite. "Keep it for yourself. But what about this week?"

"He's due, yeah," says Mite, examining the ring with evident disappointment, a bite mark ripping now through its face, "but I think we should give him time. He's been jabbering something about the city holding up his deal. I checked out what he's saying and it's on the up. Once the deal closes and he flips the building he'll have plenty to pay what he owes and a premium to boot. He's got a wife and three kids, he needs a break."

"I think so too, sweet pea," says Kockroach, his grimace, half hidden by the foam, growing wider.

Mite nods, turns to leave.

"Hey, Mite," says Kockroach, "how about a game?"

wooden pieces. Together they are performing a human ritual that Mite has taught to Kockroach, a ritual called chess.

"What are you up to, Mite?" says Kockroach as he stares at the board.

"You know me, Boss. I'm never up to nothing."

"Sweet pea."

Kockroach has learned to enjoy the give-and-take over the board. Mite's was the first name he learned in the human world and he relies on Mite for much as he runs the business of running Times Square, but Kockroach is not certain he can trust Mite anymore. If you know what a human wants, you have control. But Kockroach is no longer sure of what Mite wants. At first he assumed that Mite wanted exactly what he himself wanted: money, power, sex, shrimp, sex. But Mite was never about sex, and money, power, and shrimp seem no longer enough for him, and that is the cause of Kockroach's concern. This mistrust has leaked into all their business dealings. The hesitancy Kockroach noticed this very night is merely another example. But Mite, who is suitably deferential to Kockroach in business, is anything but deferential in the ritual. He schemes, he traps, he attacks without mercy. The only time now Kockroach feels Mite is being completely honest with him is during the ritual of the game.

It took Kockroach a long time to gain an understanding of the ritual. Not the pieces and the moves, that was easy. The slopey pieces move entirely on an angle. The piece shaped like the head of a wasp jumps up and over. The moves and rules of this chess were easy, it was the purpose of the ritual that confused him. It seemed to him at the start a type of battling. When Mite first slipped his large female piece into Kockroach's side of the board like a knife and knocked over Kockroach's boss piece with the cross on top, Kockroach felt a spurt of fear. Now what? he wondered. He tensed his whole body, ready for a confrontation, sad at what he'd have to do to the little man. But Mite merely reached out his hand. "Good game, Jerry," he said. "Keep at it and you'll get the hang," and that was it. Everything after the ritual was the same as before. It seemed to have no meaning. Kockroach didn't understand. Time after time Mite toppled Kockroach's boss piece and nothing changed.

Until something did change, and it slammed into Kockroach like a revelation.

In his first games, Kockroach examined the board and made what appeared to be the strongest move. If a square could be occupied he occupied it, if a piece could be killed he killed it. Cockroaches live eternally in the present tense and he performed the ritual like a cockroach, but each game ended with Mite knocking Kockroach's pieces off the board one after the other before swooping in and killing his all-important boss piece.

"Where did you learn this chess?" said Kockroach early in their practice of the ritual.

"From Old Dudley, what taught me the ways of the world,"

... little piece, Mite could kill a stronger piece. If Kockroach moved here, Mite would move there. If Mite moved there and Kockroach moved there, then Mite would move there. Kockroach saw deeper into the game, the rituals lengthened, Kockroach came closer and closer to killing Mite's boss piece.

But that wasn't the fantastic change. As Kockroach stared at the board, sequences of moves played out in his head in glorious ribbons of possibility that grew and lengthened and weaved from the now to the then until, like some sort of strong magic, he was no longer playing only in the present, he was playing in the future, too.

"You're getting tougher, Boss," says Mite as their current ritual heads toward its conclusion. "You been taking lessons?"

"From you, Mite. Only you."

"You got me pinned here. You got me pinned there. Looks like I'm in serious trouble."

"Looks like."

"Except watch this." Mite moves his wasp. "Check."

Kockroach stares at the board. The ribbons of possibility that had been reeling through his head suddenly shrivel. His boss piece is under attack. He has one possible move. He makes it.

Mite moves the female piece that had been protecting his boss piece, leaving his boss piece vulnerable. Kockroach is

ready to rush in and kill Mite's boss when Mite says, "Checkmate."

Kockroach stares at the board for a moment longer before he topples over his own boss piece.

"Nice game," says Mite, reaching out his hand as he stands. "It won't be long afore you own me."

Kockroach, still staring at the board, ignores Mite's outstretched hand as he says, "I own you already."

"Maybe next time, Boss," says Mite. He pulls back his hand, hitches up his pants, heads to the door. "Maybe, but I doubt it."

Kockroach keeps staring at the board, willing the ribbons of possibility to reappear and flutter in his brain. The purpose of the ritual, he has learned, is not the game itself, not who kills whose boss. The purpose of the game is these ribbons rippling into the future. Through the practice of the ritual, he has leaped out of the arthropod's slavish devotion to the present tense.

And suddenly, a whole new territory has opened up for Kockroach to plunder.

Pressed and pleated, shaved and shined and buffed, tie tightened, belt cinched, shoes double-knotted, jacket double-buttoned to his throat, glasses on, hat on, grin on, cigarette burning like a warning in his teeth, Kockroach saunters out of the elevator and greets the world.

"Good evening, Mr. Blatta."

"Step away, please, and let Mr. Blatta through."

A path is cleared as if for a tycoon and doors are opened as if for a starlet. Kockroach walks through the crowded lobby, leaving gapes and green tributes in his wake.

Istvan is waiting for him outside, leaning on the hood of the big humped Lincoln, chocolate brown and encrusted with chrome. Istvan is Kockroach's driver, promoted by Kockroach from the pack of lowly gangsters who police the Square. Istvan's huge arms are crossed, his peaked cap is tipped up on his wide blond head, his narrow blue eyes light up with devotion when he sees Kockroach exit the hotel. Istvan jumps away from the hood and reaches for the door.

"Good evening, Mr. Blatta."

Kockroach ducks into the car without breaking stride.

"What's on the agenda tonight, Mr. Blatta?" says Istvan, his accent thicker than his arms.

"Beeswax."

The Murdock Hotel is a desiccated pile of cracked brick wedged between a dusty supply warehouse to the east and a failing shirtwaist factory to the west. The desk clerk, perched

on a stool, hunched over something pornographic, glances up to see Kockroach standing before him and jerks back so hard he slams into the boxes behind him, sending mail and keys clattering to the floor.

"Room two-two-four," says Kockroach.

"Right away," says the clerk as he drops to his knees and searches the floor for the key.

Kockroach climbs the steps slowly, sensing their rotting boards, their foul stench. He slams his fist on the damp wall and a slab of plaster dislodges to crash upon and tumble down the steps. He opens the door to Room 224 without a knock and finds Sylvie shivering beneath a blanket on her bed. She startles when she sees him, sits up, teeth chattering. The blanket slips down, baring her sagging, mismatched breasts and the ribs beneath them.

"Get dressed," he says. "We're going out."

"I can't, Jerry. God, I can't. Don't you see how sick I am?"

Kockroach steps forward and sits on the bed. He gently caresses the side of her face. She leans into his touch.

"I don't want to see you like this," he says.

"I miss you too, Jerry. We're never together anymore. Remember when you used to take me out, when I taught you to dance at the Latin Club? Those were times, weren't they? I know I haven't been working enough, but I'm still sick. Even with the medicine you been giving me, I can't do it anymore. I have to get away. I got a sister in Pittsburgh. I was thinking of visiting her, just for a while, to get back my strength."

"You'll be swell. You need to get up, step out. We'll go for a ride."

[illegible]," says Sylvie, "the sickness or the cure."

"Get dressed," he says, standing. "I'll be waiting for you outside."

Sylvie stares at the bundle with the red thread for a long moment, as if deciding on something, and then snatches it to her chest.

"And Sylvie," he says, his smile brightening, "put on something sharp."

Istvan drives the Lincoln slowly through Times Square, the phantasm of light and color reflecting off the brown, the chrome, the glass like a scrambled message from a neon god. Kockroach sits jammed into the corner of the backseat, a cigarette in his teeth, one hand clamped on Sylvie's knee. She is in a black dress with sequins, high heels, a fluffy boa wrapped around her neck. Her face is pale, pale as death, but her lips are painted red.

Istvan slows the car and then stops. Kockroach's door opens, a red-haired woman in a tight sweater and bangle earrings leans into the car. "Sylvie," she says, "dragged your skinny ass out of bed, did you?"

Sylvie snuggles up to Kockroach and licks his ear. Without

turning her head, she slips a stare at the woman. "Get back to work, Denise. There might be a sailor still who hasn't filled your mouth."

"Leastways I'm working, baby."

"Since you're in the dough, let me give some advice. Do something about them snaggleteeth."

The red-haired woman smiles.

"Please," says Sylvie, "before you start frightening small children."

"How's beeswax?" says Kockroach.

"Started slow, must be a Bible convention in town, but it's picking up."

"Let me see."

The woman pulls a wad of bills from inside her sweater. Kockroach takes them, sniffs them, jams them into his jacket. "Any trouble?" he asks.

"A tall hat from Texas thought he was so good he should get it for free. Janine whispered your name and he near pissed himself trying to take the wallet out of his pants."

"I'll be back before dawn. Tell Janine I want her to wait for me."

The red-haired woman nods her head at Sylvie. "Why she get to ride tonight?"

Sylvie leans over Kockroach. "'Cause Jerry is tired of your fat ass and wanted a dose of class."

"Dose of clap is more like it."

Kockroach pushes the red-haired woman out the door and slams it shut. Istvan pulls away, down Broadway, as Sylvie leans over and sticks her tongue out at the window.

“Where are we going?” asks Sylvie.

“I have something to show you.”

Sylvie cuddles up. “Some out of the way club? Some exotic gangster hangout?”

“Something like that.”

“Anyplace is fine,” she says, drowsily leaning her head on his strong left arm. “Surprise me.”

“That’s the intention,” he says. “Feeling better?”

“Much.” She yawns.

“Are you too tired to dance?”

“Don’t be silly,” she says, rubbing his stomach with her left hand. “I’m never too tired to dance with you.”

The streets narrow, twist and turn. The car purrs along, turns right, squeezes through an alleyway. It comes out on a wide stretch of asphalt, lined with blocky brick buildings fronted by wooden frames, the frames empty now of the carcasses hanging daily in the mornings. The thick smell of meat, rotting, luscious, hovers over the puddles and the cracked sidewalks, the dim streetlights, the overturned trash bins being scavenged by rats.

A huge dog in an alley, gnawing on the raw haunch of something, bends in respect as the brown car passes.

“Where are we?” says Sylvie, suddenly sitting up.

“Go to the end, Istvan,” says Kockroach.

"Is that the club?" says Sylvia.

"The far end."

The car pulls to the end of the street, turns right, then left again, where they reach a wide, uneven strip of cobbles leading to a row of desultory wooden piers, ill lit, swirling with fog, seeming to be in the very process of slowly, agonizingly, collapsing into the Hudson River. Sylvie shrinks from Kockroach when she sees the piers.

On one, a shadow leans on a post, its very posture a signal of defeat. On another, toward the street, are two shadows, one walking fast, head swiveling, the other, well behind, dragging itself toward the light. A car rumbles along the cobblestones, stops at still another pier, a shadow slips in, the car moves off.

"Why'd you bring me here?" says Sylvie, unable to hide the desperation in her voice. "What business do you have here?"

"Do you see the pier straight ahead?"

"What about it, Jerry?"

"It's yours now, sweet pea."

"Go to hell. I'm no pier monkey. It's only dope fiends and toothless scags that need work the piers."

Kockroach loops a finger around her lower lip and pulls it down. There is a large gap between her front teeth and her back molar. "I'd say you're a bit of both."

"It was you that gave me the medicine. It was you that did this to me."

"You were sick, you needed to be working. Like now."

[illegible] than [illegible] queen of the Square. I was prime once, don't you remember? We had something, didn't we? We had nights. I taught you to dance at the Latin. Don't do this, please, please, I'm begging you, please."

Kockroach leans over and opens Sylvie's door. "Nothing personal, pal, just beeswax."

"Don't, no, God, don't make me, please, please, not the piers. I'll do anything, anything."

He lets her cry on as a wisp of fog floats in the door. He doesn't have to shove her out, he sits there and waits until she cries herself into silence and then climbs out all on her own.

"You did this to me, you stinking cockroach," she yells as she slams the door shut, losing her balance in the effort.

Kockroach watches silently as she staggers over the wide, uneven expanse of cobbles, reaches the pier, collapses against a wooden pole. He remembers that this is the first human with which he ever mated and wonders if that matters. He decides that it doesn't. Kockroach does not read, but if he did he would agree with Shakespeare that "what's past is prologue." And if Kockroach did, in fact, ever have a book in his hand, he would certainly skip past the prologue and get right to the meat of it, which is the desiccated woman gripping desperately the wooden pole, now, turning from a drain on his

finances to a productive member of his organization, now. Something needed to be done.

"You'll check on her later, Istvan, make sure she stays all night."

"No problem, Mr. Blatta. Where to?"

"The Acropolis." Kockroach lights a cigarette. "Word is the *Nonos* wants to talk."

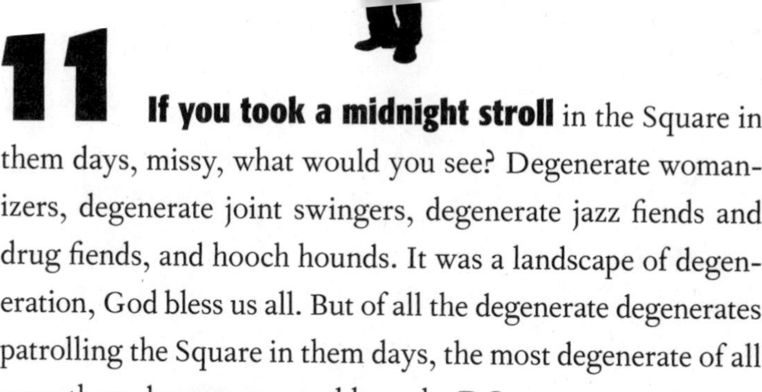

11

If you took a midnight stroll in the Square in them days, missy, what would you see? Degenerate womanizers, degenerate joint swingers, degenerate jazz fiends and drug fiends, and hooch hounds. It was a landscape of degeneration, God bless us all. But of all the degenerate degenerates patrolling the Square in them days, the most degenerate of all were them degenerate gamblers, the DGs.

Was a DG what made his life on the Square when first I arrived name of Jimmy Slaps. He had scuffed shoes and a long face and he wore his greasy old raincoat rain or shine, its filthy beige tail trailing after him like an ugly rumor as he cruised the Square looking for a bet, any bet, at any odds. If was a craps game going off in an alleyway south of Forty-fourth, Jimmy Slaps was there. If was a poker game being dealt in some fleabag flophouse, Jimmy Slaps was scratching behind his ear and raising hard on his two pair. His bible was the racing form, his drug of choice was long-shot odds, he jacked off to queens full.

See, the thing about a DG is he believes he's found the answer to Hubert, the very purpose of life, and that the Main Street fools living without the thrill of seeing if the up card matches the two jacks down are the ones what are missing

out on the true sweetness of the world. That's why a sure thing don't never interest guys like Jimmy Slaps. You want a sure thing, sell shoes for a living; Jimmy Slaps, he wanted to gamble.

And here's the killer. If to be good at the thing you love to do is to be blessed in this world, then Jimmy Slaps was a limp-dick Mongol in a Chinese whorehouse.

So there was a poker game going down in the Chelsea Hotel off Forty-first, a big-money game organized by two pros from Chicago, and all the DGs on the Square was hot to take part. I'm talking about legends now. There was Shifty Mahoose, there was Kings Dagboy, there was Ices Neat, there was Tony Marrone. Big game, hot game, and naturally Jimmy Slaps wanted—no needed—to buy in. But the buy-in was a grand and Jimmy Slaps just then didn't have enough to fade a game of nickel craps.

Old Jimmy was left out in the cold until Kings Dagboy, never a generous soul to begin with, agreed to cover Jimmy Slaps's buy-in in exchange for nothing more substantial than a signature. It was a puzzling turn of events, more puzzling still when you knew that the Slap in Jimmy Slaps came from the way Jimmy's eyes lit and he tapped the table with his fingertips whenever the card he was looking for came through.

With a tell like that, it wasn't long afore Jimmy Slaps slapped hisself right out of that game, a thousand off the nut to Kings Dagboy. And Kings started immediately putting the squeeze on Jimmy, literally, throwing him in the crapper of that room at the Chelsea, taking Jimmy's head in his meaty hands and squeezing that long face until Jimmy's eyes near popped.

[illegible] setup from the start, see, all a way for Kings to entertain the two pros from Chicago and make a profit on the thou in the process. And with his back against a toilet and Kings Dagboy's fist aiming once again for his face, Jimmy Slaps had no choice but to agree.

When word got out, every DG on the Square wanted in on the action. Kings was making book and within five hours of the deal there was twenty thou on the line one side or the other, with Kings bound to make a couple G's on the vig alone no matter how it all turned out. They set it up in the basement of an old garment factory on Thirty-ninth and the crowd poured in, a festive high-spirited crowd as interested in the show as in the welfare of their bets. Kings's runners was working the crowd, taking bets to the last minute. Entrepreneurial souls was edging through the room with a bottle and a glass selling whiskey pure for a buck a swallow. Long-lost pals was shouting greetings back and forth like at a county fair.

It were a party until Jimmy Slaps hisself appears like magic beside a crate at the back end of the basement. Hoots and cheers and a few more bets taken and then the crowd quiets. Jimmy Slaps, shivering now, steps up on the crate, sweat pouring down his bloodied face, his filthy raincoat swirling about him, a revolver in his shaking right hand.

"This is my last bet, boys," he tells the crowd in a quavering

voice. "Life is all snake eyes without faith in something purer than a string of numbers hit. No more will I put my faith in a king-high straight, now I pledge myself to the King of Kings, the only shooter worth a bet. I have promised God I am finished with the life, and I want you all to keep me to it. If I make it through, no matter how I whine or beg, I'm asking you not to take my bets. Will you do that for me, will you, boys?"

The crowd lets out a roar, but not a roar of assent. It is a roar of disdain, a full-throated bellow of heckles and crude remarks, telling old Jimmy Slaps to quit the Bible-punching and get right to it. A crowd of DGs don't want to hear about no change, no redemption, no promises to the great good Lord. All they wants is the bet laid and the race run so they can head to the window and lay another.

Jimmy Slaps smiles right into that roar, smiles as if, by God, he means every word of it, that he is finished with it all, that face to face with death itself, he has found an answer to Hubert and is ready to change. And in the middle of the crowd, selling my whiskey for a buck a shot, I believe him, that he really has found an answer. And I cheers for the son of a bitch, I does, I cheers as loud as my larynx allows.

Until right then, in the middle of the crowd's disapproving roar and my cheers of hope, Jimmy Slaps puts that gun smack to his head and pulls the trigger.

We was royalty, the Boss and me. We ruled the Square, under the kingly benediction of the *Nonos*. We was funny kind of partners; I did what the Boss told me and he, well, he told

ambitions myself, but as long as he let me tell him what I needed to do, and then I followed his directions like a lapdog, we got along like gangbusters and we was both of us making out. I had climbed as far as ever I could hope to climb, I was the key man under the key man in Times Square and life was ever so grand.

Or was it?

Jimmy Slaps, what did he want in this world? He wanted to gamble, to bet, to feel the probabilities work their smooth impartial magic on his life. But when it became too real, when the hammer was cocked and the barrel faced his temple at a smooth six-to-one, suddenly he didn't want the magic of them odds no more. You see, sometimes everything you're hustling for it comes true and then you wonder if all that time you been hustling for the wrong damn thing.

In the spare moments between collecting the protection moneys and collecting the sharking moneys and collecting from our whores and collecting our cuts from the beer and drugs and smuggled cigs what was sold on our turf, in the spare moments I began to wonder if maybe I'd be in a whole different line if Old Dudley hadn't sidled up to me in that library and started whispering about chess in my ear and that maybe the whole other line might have been the right line for me.

I see you trying to hide your sniggers. What the hell could

Mite ever hope to be except a hustler, a chiseler, a thief? What other could Mite ever expect for hisself except the bowl of crap he fell into in hitching a ride on the back of the Boss. But see, maybe our fates ain't as fixed as you would have it. Maybe it ain't so set in stone, the way our lives they turn out. What better proof of that than old Jimmy Slaps, swearing afore the whole of his peers that his life would change and never would he take another bet.

I thought about going the Jimmy Slaps route, hitting my knees and asking God to save me, I even strolled every now and then up to old St. Pat's and slipped into the cool calming darkness and watched the light twist blue and red through them windows. But in the end, when it came time for the actual praying, I couldn't go through with it.

I mean let's say He is everything them street-corner preachers say He is, let's just say it. Then He is everything, ain't He? The sun, the moon, the scrap piece of trash floating like a beam of light on the shiv of the wind. And if He's everything, then He's nothing too. Which meant when Hubert came a-visiting my mom, filling her with nothing, maybe he was really filling her with God, and hell with that. I couldn't help the feeling that if ever I dropped to my knees and said the words and tried to open my heart, it would never be what I hoped would come rushing in, some guy with a long white beard and a cardigan and a pipe calling me sonny boy and tiger. No, it would be Hubert hisself jumping in my head and making hisself at home and sending me spinning in the air afore I fell on the floor with foam coming out my mouth.

So no, it wasn't never going to be prayer that saved me, no

coffee. Flawlessly beautiful, the line of her jaw, the bump of her nose, the pale white skin, eyes the blue of a sky you don't never see in the city, the blue of a sky over an Iowa cornfield, and missy, I had never been to Iowa and still I knew. And when I saw her, all at once my little hustler dreams they faded like a fog beneath the sun and I understood, with the vicious cruelty of a bully boy, exactly what I was and all them things that would never be mine.

And then she stood and walked her crippled walk over to refill her coffee cup and my heart, my twisted black heart, it cracked open with hope. For I knew then that we was two of a kind, this woman and me, two bodies marked with misfortune, two lonely souls looking for comfort in a world what starts out cruel on the schoolyard and goes downhill from there. You could see the goodness in her, how could there not be with her leg in a brace, and her face it glowed with her goodness, just like my mother's face, even in the throes of her episodes, maybe especially then. And the goodness there, along with her affliction, it gave me the courage to hitch up my pants and slide over to her table and sit down uninvited and tell her a story and ask for my thirty-nine cents. And there it began between Celia and me.

By the time of now I'm speaking, we was painting the town once a week, rubbing shoulders with the hoit-toit at "21,"

chugging wine, chewing steaks so thick you had to cuts each piece twice, longways and then sideways, just to get it in your mouth. Good times we had then, and I could confide in her everything about my life except the one thing what mattered most, the desire what kept me up at night, the desire to take care of her, to protect her, to matter to her, just like it was with me and my ma. And we wanted the exact same things, Celia and me, I could tell, security, peace, a place of our own, a family, with the kids reaching up theys little arms to us.

Silly, ain't it, a guy like me dreaming that hackneyed picket-fence dream, but when you're my size normalcy suddenly ain't so normal.

Yeah there it is, what would save me from Hubert's grasp, the only thing worth the game. Love, dammit, love would save me. I loved Celia Singer, not like the cricket's love some moke with a highball and a hard-on feels for the dancer what's grinding away on his lap, no, missy. My love was purer than that, higher than the meat and kidneys what rule the day on this soiled heap of dust. It was like a hard cold star in the night sky, like the flight of a white pigeon skimming the rooftops as it makes its way home, like the explosion in my heart when my momma let the emptiness flow through her one last time.

Can you feel it, missy? I still can. From the first moment I laid eyes on her, it never stopped glowing.

I could never tell Blatta about what I was hoping for with Celia because Blatta wasn't the type in who to confide your soft intimate yearnings. And I couldn't tell our girls what were working the Square, and I couldn't tell the barkeeps what fiding to was the one Joe what could make it all come true.

Fat Nemo drummed the tabletop with his fat fingers. He was dressed to the nines, double-breasted pinstripes, tie tight. When Nemo, with that neck of his, so thick it was like he had no neck, had his tie tight it meant business. I'm setting the scene, all right, just sos you understand how what happened happened. It ain't so easy to see sometimes. Sometimes it's like the smallest breath of air changes everything. Fat Nemo, I knew by then, was the number two in the organization. Sitting beside Nemo was Mr. Abagados, the *Nonos*. The old man appeared to be sleeping, his hands on his cane, his chin falling down to his throat.

"He knows to come?" said Nemo to yours truly.

"I tolds him so myself," I said.

"Then where the hell might he be, Mite?"

"He's having problems."

"Is that so?"

"With a whore."

"Well, that is a surprise, isn't it, problems with a whore."

The back room behind the kitchen of the Acropolis was set for a banquet, a banquet without no food, the long tables

arranged in a O, with the *Nonos* and Nemo at the head table and the bottom U filled with men in slouch hats and bulky jackets, all the headmen of the Abagados mob, sitting back, yawning, rubbing their noses.

"What about we order up some grub," said one of the men.

"And a liter of retsina," said another.

"Any moussaka left in the pan?"

"Maybe some bread and feta."

"And the retsina."

"This isn't a party, Cos," said Nemo. "This is business."

"Is that what it is, sweet pea?" said the Boss, barging through the door. "Business?"

"Thank you for joining us, Jerzy."

"I had a thing to deal with."

"We hope it came off all right," said Nemo.

The Boss, he kept smiling as he strided to the head table. When he reached Mr. Abagados, he stuck a hand into his jacket. He pulled out a bundle of cash and dropped it in front of the *Nonos*. With his chin still on his chest, the old man reached out his three-fingered claw and took hold of the stack.

The Boss then he moved along the head table to the other side of Nemo, where he pulled out a chair and sat down as if that were his very spot, right there beside Nemo, number three, which it was. He had risen fast, had the Boss. With my brains and his cold brutality, he had become an essential member of the Abagados outfit, especially as the outfit geared for war. Big Johnny Callas had been letting things slip as he tried to slip hisself into the glitter of Square society, but the Boss and me, we didn't care about no ball stars or starlets. We

duffel. That was the final bit, the little power play what put Blatta at the head table.

"We are being squeezed, gentlemen," said Nemo, "like a ripe tomato. We have every organization in the city looking with envious eyes at all we have done to develop our territory. When we took over the Square it was a place of honest revelry and burlesque, with only a few pitiful operations that barely wet a whistle. Now who doesn't want to own it? The raiding operation run by that greaseball Stanzi was just the most recent attempt at our territory, and not all have turned out so well. At the same time you know it is not enough that we stay still because, in the world in which we live, you stay still you might as well paint red circles on your back. But to where can we expand? To the east is Tartelli. To the south is that madman Zwillman. And to the north we have the most troublesome of all, that *nothos mauvros*, J. Jackie Moonstone and his colored all-stars.

"Everyone wants to expand, everyone is eyeing their neighbors like they eye their neighbors' wives. The fuse is lit. That's why we've spent the last months enlarging our ranks, building our arsenal, sucking up all the surplus war materials we could graft our hands onto and placing it into a secure location known only to the *Nonos* and myself. We are ready, but for what? If we let it get out of control, we are going to end up

ripping each other to shreds like wild dogs. And then, with blood on the streets, the last one standing will inherit nothing but indictments.

"So we've come up with a better plan. The *Nonos* has brokered a series of agreements that serves to divide much of the disputed territory. Zwillman gets the South Bronx, Spanish Harlem, and Washington Heights. Tartelli gets the main part of Harlem from river to river. We get south Harlem and the area north of our current territory."

"But that is all Moonstone's turf," said one of the men. "What does he say about it?"

"He is delighted to help out," said Nemo. "He has invited us all to the party."

"Really?"

"No, not really," said Nemo. "We have no choice but to wipe that *nothos mauvros* off the map. Moonstone has bigger numbers than all of us individually, which is why he's the biggest threat, but together we can destroy him. So long as we work together."

"When do we start?"

"When we give the word, not before. Moonstone is a barbarian, anyone tips him off it will be ten times as bad for all of us. But the purpose of this meeting is not to start a war with Moonstone, it is to let you all know that we now have new friends. Do you trust *koproskilo* like Tartelli and Zwillman? Neither do I, but for now they are our friends. It's like Roosevelt making kissy-face with Stalin during the war. We're going to be allies until it is over, save Berlin for later. No actions against them, no incursions, no fights. We're going to make nice until Moonstone is taken care of. And we all have to take care of that *nothos mauvros* when the time is ripe. Are there any questions? Do you all understand how crucial it is we all follow direction? Do you all understand what is at stake?"

As the meeting was breaking, Nemo, he gave me the signal, a surreptitious flick, so I didn't storm out the joint with most the rest of them, the Boss included, back to the street to take care of business. Instead I stayed at the Acropolis, buying drinks for Stavros and the boys, cracking jokes and rolling dice for quarters to pass the time, as if I had nothing but time to pass. After my third beer I hopped off the bar, hitched up my pants.

"Remember, boys, you never buys the beer, you only rents it."

So what if the joke was as stale as the brew they served in that joint, a cloud of laughter followed me as I headed to the bathroom. I could still hear it as I rounded the corner, slipped through the kitchen, and nodded at the gunsel guarding the back room.

He let me pass.

We was alone, the two of us. Nemo made hisself scarce,

quite the feat for someone the size of Nemo, and so it was just me and Mr. Abagados at the table, sitting across the one from the other. He was still pitched forward, leaning on his cane, still in his posture that seemed to be one of sleep. But now his eyes instead of being closed were open and focused like twin gunsights on me.

"Tell me, Mickey, how goes things with that girl?"

"Good, *Nonos*, things with Celia are going good. You know."

"Does she yet understand how you feel?"

"I don't know, maybe. She gots to suspect, what with all the cash I'm laying out on her. You don't give pearls to your palsies, now do you?"

"But you didn't yet say."

"No, not yet. The time it ain't just ripe. I don't got nothing set up, no place to take her that she'll want to be, and I don't want to be scaring her off untils I does."

"With women is always better to scare than to bore." Abagados, he reached into the outside pocket of his jacket. "Let me show you this."

From out his jacket pocket he pulled his loppy three-fingered hand, closed over something big and round, as big and round as a grenade. Slowly, he turned over his palm and flipped his hand so as to roll the object across the table at me.

I snatched it off the table afore it fell into my lap. "It's a lemon."

"Tell me, of what does it smell?"

I took myself a sniff. "It smells like a lemon."

California. I bought my own grove in California. Place to retire when my time here is over."

"That's a good racket, I'd bet, letting the sun do all the work and then picking fruit off them trees like they was dollar bills."

"You'd think yes. The foreman he knows *lemoni,* and he is Greek, but he is also thief. I need someone watch him, someone I trust. Someone sharp enough to turn sun into money."

I took the lemon in my hand, rolled it back and forth, lifted it to my nose, let its fragrance, sweet and rich, rise through me like a Louis Armstrong song, like a movie kiss.

"What does it smell like, Mickey?"

"Like a lemon."

"See, that's why I enjoy you. You know how to hold back. You are a man who will go far."

"How far?"

"Think three thousand miles to the west."

Without saying nothing, I took another sniff.

"And not alone, you understand," said the *Nonos*. "Never again alone. This is dangerous time. The wolves are circling. They smell something too. What do they smell?"

"Lemons?"

"Betrayal. And this I found in my life. Two sweetest scents

in all the world, *lemoni* fresh from tree and betrayal. The wolves are circling and I need something from you, my friend. Something of the utmost importance."

When I left the Acropolis that night, I had a lemon in my hand and a knot of fear in my gut, but more than that, dead in my sights I had my main chance. It ain't no easy thing to change the world; how much harder is it to change yourself? Some, they say it can't be done, that early on the bones is thrown and everything after is simply a matter of the odds. An Alvin like me what makes good is still just an Alvin what hit his point. It's easy enough to believe it, to shrug your shoulders and say there is nothing to be done and go on going on. It's easy enough, except I had an example to guide me. Jimmy Slaps, what stood on that crate and proclaimed his change to all the world afore he placed the gun to his head.

And it didn't much matter to me if the change claimed by old Jimmy Slaps, it didn't take, if soon as the chamber it clicked empty he slipped back into his old ways, flashing his newly gapped grin as he threw the dice or peeked at his hole cards. His face it grew longer, his raincoat it grew grimier, the gaps in his smile grew wider, the odds against him grew filthy long.

Last I saw of Jimmy Slaps was in an alleyway off Forty-fourth where he spun the cylinder like you spin the dice and put another gun to his head. Before him in a box lay assorted bills, a fiver, two tenners, a pile of ones, the paltry payoff for which Jimmy Slaps was letting once again the odds work their smooth magic on his life. It hadn't been enough no more to watch the odds work on the cards or the dice or the ponies.

hand and a knot of fear in my gut. I tossed the lemon in the air and hoped to hell it worked out better for me than it did for good old, dead old, Jimmy Slaps.

12

Kockroach waits patiently in the car. He has an inhuman patience, the patience of a fly on the wall, a spider in its web. Istvan taps the steering wheel with his fingers as they wait, but Kockroach moves not a muscle. The car is parked half a block before the restaurant, behind a wide truck that bars much of the car's view of the street, but from the rear seat Kockroach can see the entrance of the Acropolis. He waits, patiently.

"Maybe he went out back," says Istvan.

"No," is all Kockroach says.

"You want I check he's still there?"

"No."

Istvan taps his fingers. Kockroach waits. The door opens and a small man in a green suit and a green fedora steps into the night. There is something in his hand, something small and yellow. The man tosses it into the air.

"What is he holding?" says Kockroach.

"*Lemoni*, Mr. Blatta."

Kockroach watches as Mite turns down the street and walks away, toward the Square, still tossing the lemon up and down. In the past, Kockroach would only have seen a man with a lemon, but that was before he learned the ritual of

"No need." It is like the ritual of chess, being played out by the two of them on the streets of the city. And Mite, as usual, is planning a trap. But Kockroach has taken to heart the lessons of the ritual, he has plans of his own now, his own ribbons of possibility reaching out like clawed legs to strike at the future, to battle it and subdue it and turn it to his will.

"To Yonkers then?" says Istvan.

"Yes, to Yonkers."

The Lincoln pulls away from the curb, turns left on Eighth, and begins heading north, toward a place called Yonkers. Kockroach has never stepped foot there, Yonkers, has only heard the name a few times, Yonkers, but already he likes it. Yonkers. Yonkers. It feels in his mouth like the sound of lamb bones crunching between his teeth.

The house is large and white and sits on a leafy street on the crest of a hill a few miles north of Yonkers Raceway. A shallow white picket fence surrounds the front of the property. Outside there are lights blazing, streetlights, security lights, a light on the post that announces the address. Outside is bright, inside is as dark as terror.

"Wait here," says Kockroach before slipping quietly out of the car. He makes a quick circle around the house, spies the

weakness with an unerring instinct, crawls through the gap in the basement window, dusts off his suit, straightens his glasses, his tie, his hat, begins his ascent up the stairway.

Since his earliest days in this strange body, Kockroach has learned much about the humans. They are a species, he has discovered, governed by emotion. Some of these emotions he understands, emotions such as greed. Greed is the second strongest of all cockroach emotions. His incessant hunger is merely a manifestation of his boundless greed, for a cockroach always hungers, always, even with its belly full and its uric acid spent. To see something is to want it, a speck of starch, a drop of water, a shed plate of chitin, a cozy hiding place, a female rising on her hind legs, to see something is to want it, need it, got to have it. But a cockroach's greed has boundaries, a cockroach's view is necessarily limited by its height and size, the narrowness of its territory. How much more can a human desire with its better viewpoint, its stronger eyes, its ability to traverse great breadths of territory.

Yes, Kockroach understands greed, and its cousin envy. For why should one human have something when Kockroach himself could have it just as well, be it food, be it a woman, be it money, be it turf, be it power, be it favor in the eyes of the great god of smoke rising high over the Square. Kockroach knows not Abel but understands Cain.

Other emotions Kockroach has yet to fathom. Love is a word he hears in every song and in every one of the movies to which Mite drags him, it is a word he overhears in many human conversations, yet of it he still has no understanding. It has something to do with sex, yes, and sex he understands, sex

knows for sure is that every human wants it, and so, therefore, does he: greed and envy work their magic beyond the realm of understanding.

Just as he has no understanding of love, he has no understanding of hate. Yes, he can be violent, brutal and swift, but it is all for him a matter of business, a matter of greed. He does what he must to get as much as he can. It is never personal because for Kockroach nothing is personal. Even to see Mite slink out of the Acropolis long after he should, even to assume he is plotting something with the powers inside, even that is not a personal affront. Mite has greed too, of course he does, is he not also a creature of this world? To see him toss that lemon up and down causes no hate to flash across Kockroach's calm. Kockroach doesn't hate, he handles.

Similarly Kockroach fails to understand the way some humans are angry at other humans simply because of the sound of their last names, the shape of their eyes, the color of their skins. To him they are all of the lower orders, all humans, and to differentiate among them because of color or accent or the vowels in their last names is to differentiate among different orders of feces, all tasty, sure, but still.

And pride, embarrassment, vanity, all things that seem to cripple humans have no meaning for a cockroach. Such traits denote a struggle to change, to grow, to fulfill a dream of

becoming something different. But cockroaches don't dream of being crickets and singing sweetly into the night, don't dream of being spotted hawks and soaring to great heights, don't dream of being humans and expressing all the world's joy and sorrow in discrete lines of poetry. *I too am not a bit tamed, I too am untranslatable, I sound my barbaric yawp over the roofs of the world.* What human would not have wished to write such a line, what cockroach would even consider it, though for a cockroach it be more apt? Cockroaches embrace their cockroachedness. If they have a charm that is it. They are content with what they are and so are beyond vanity, beyond the possibilities of pride and embarrassment, beyond poetry.

But with all Kockroach still cannot understand of the human matrix of emotion, there is one emotion other than greed that he understands completely. If you could examine the twin strands of a cockroach's emotion, rising like the twining strands of its DNA, you would find fear and greed, greed and fear, fear and greed, always the two, one with the other, yes and no, stop and go. It is greed that drives a cockroach forward, toward the wet slop of goop upon which it desires to feast—a near-uncontrollable desire to obtain, to mount, to devour—but it is fear that stops him cold, that spreads his antennae, that sends him sniffing for predators before he heads once more toward the goop. Fear. It is why cockroaches sleep in the tightest spaces, why cockroaches are silent, why they scurry, why they scurry in darkness.

Kockroach understands fear, and in dealing with the human he has learned that, of all the emotions, it is fear that drives it,

…, devouring your food with great noisy chomps while the light bathes his front, ripping meat off bones, swallowing raw eggs whole, and, though still not sated, wiping the residue off his mouth with the back of his hand before passing the door of your mother-in-law's room and rising ever farther up your stairs, skulking past your three sleeping children, entering your very own bedroom, sitting on the side of your very own bed, where you and your wife sleep the sound sleep of the unsuspecting.

Shaking you awake in the darkness.

Startling you awake with a shake in the darkness.

"What? What?" you ask, as if the darkness itself will hold some answers. And it is the darkness itself that responds, darkness in the shape of a shadow, a shadow with broad shoulders and a fedora cocked on its head, a shadow whose voice is both twittering and deep, the deranged voice of fear itself.

"Cooney," it says. "Cooney. You're late."

Kockroach sits in the back of the car as it speeds through the Bronx toward Manhattan. He examines a spot on the cuff of his shirt, a dark splatter. He rubs at it with his thumb but the splatter has soaked into the fabric.

"Back to the Square?" asks Istvan.

"Yes," says Kockroach, still rubbing futilely at the spot, "but first stop at Kirschner's."

In Manhattan, the brown car double-parks in front of a small storefront, Kirschner's Delicatessen. In New York, all creatures have a favorite deli, even cockroaches, especially cockroaches. The neon beneath the name reads: OPEN ALL NIGHT.

"The usual?" says Istvan.

"Two."

"Hungry tonight, Mr. Blatta?"

Kockroach doesn't respond. It is a foolish question; he is hungry every night. After a few moments, Istvan steps out of the delicatessen with a brown paper bag, nearly translucent with grease on the bottom.

With the car again on its way south, Kockroach opens the bag, takes a deep whiff. The rich oily scent, starchy and sweet, reminds him of his childhood.

Sitting now beside Kockroach in the back of the car is a woman with dark hair piled high. Her heels are spiky, her earrings dangle, her white blouse is tucked into her tight gray skirt: a secretary tarted up for a late night assignation with the boss. The look is catnip for conventioneers. Her thin mouth shifts and wriggles like a nervous worm on a hook. The brown car jerks east between two cabs on Forty-second Street.

"He was going to stiff me, the bastard," she says.

Okay. Sure. She's been tough to take lately anyway, still thinking she was some kind of queen bee even with her junkie shakes. She's better off on them piers, how skinny she got. I'm tired and hungry and my dogs are barking. What's in the bag?"

"It's not for you."

"C'mon, Jerry. I'm hungry. Just a bite. It smells good."

"I need something from you, sweet pea."

"Of course you do."

She slips off the seat onto her knees, begins to unhook his belt buckle. He pushes her away.

"There is a man in a bar."

"There's always a man in a bar," she says.

"He's tall, thin, his suits are expensive and too tight. You can tell him by the way his hair grows down to his eyebrow. You'll go in. He'll make a move. You'll promise him a freebie and take him to the alley behind the bar."

"Then what?"

"That's it. I'll take over from there."

"Never knew you liked the other side, Jerry."

"I like everything, sweet pea. And you mention my name again, you'll be strolling the piers with Sylvie."

"You wouldn't."

"Here we are. Hair down to his eyebrow. Put on a smile and make nice."

Kockroach waits in the alley behind the bar. He stands stock-still, in the darkest crevice of shadow, well out of the single shaft of light that pierces the darkness. He waits with his inhuman patience.

He doesn't imagine what is happening inside the bar, the music, the smoke, the laughter and slapped backs, doesn't imagine the woman sitting on her stool, turning her head, smiling at the tall man in the tight suit, taking a cigarette from her purse, placing it in her fingers, waiting for the man to leave his friends, step over and light it. Kockroach doesn't imagine the repartee, the sexual innuendo, the flitting erotic imaginings that slip through the man's brain as the woman places the lit cigarette in her mobile lips. He has already worked out the moves in advance and so now he simply stands there. The brick of the alley is weeping. A cat scampers around a puddle and jumps atop a metal trash can. The intermittent sound of cars passing by the narrow alley rises and falls in an endless series, the closest Kockroach has ever gotten to the sound of ocean waves. If you ever wondered what a cockroach was thinking when standing motionless on your kitchen floor, don't. It doesn't move, it doesn't think, it merely waits for the proper stimulus.

A world opens, the sound of trumpets and piano, of talking, of clinking glasses and celebration, then the sound dies

"Someplace private."

"This is private enough, what I got in mind."

"Just over here."

They step into the narrow shaft of light. The man's suit is tight, his glossy black hair pulled back from low on his brow. There is a bland cruelty in his eyes.

"You're a hot one, ain't you, baby?" he says.

He roughly opens the woman's white blouse, popping a button as he reaches for a breast. He grabs hold of her rear and squeezes.

"One hot baby."

He leans his mouth into her long pale neck. The woman unbuckles his belt, pulls down his suit pants. His knees are bony, bristly. He takes his hand from her rear, yanks down his own boxers, reaches now under her skirt, growls and laughs at the same time.

With a quick press of her arms, she pushes herself away, leaving him alone in the light, his pants and boxers pooled around his ankles.

"No more teasing, baby. Let's just get to it."

"I can't," she says.

"You can't? Don't act shy now, you tease. Come on, baby, Papa needs to sing."

"Got to go, *baby*."

"Oh no, no you don't. Not till I say you go, understand? Get on your knees, bitch, or I'm going to rip apart your—"

"Hello, Rocco," says Kockroach, taking a step from the shadows.

Rocco Stanzi's head swivels as if slapped. "Blatta?"

"Wait for me in the car."

The woman nods and scampers out of the alley, tucking her blouse in all the while.

"Hey, Blatta, what are you doing? I was just about to get a little action here. Can't you wait until—" Stanzi stops speaking, looks at the girl rushing off. "One of yours?"

Kockroach takes another step forward.

"What, you didn't hear the news? They didn't tell you?" Stanzi grapples for his pants, pulls them up, fiddles unsuccessfully with the belt. "There's a citywide truce. Zwillman's guys and your guys and our guys, all of us, we're on the same side now. Didn't you hear?"

"I heard," says Kockroach.

"Good, yeah. Isn't that something? One day we want to rip each other's guts out and stamp them into the dirt, the next we're bosom buddies. You want a drink or something, to celebrate? No hard feelings about that thing we had, right? That's all past us now. It was only business. But now we gots bigger fish to fry. Moonstone's a bear, he's going to be tough. But together, man, we're going to fry his black ass. And let me tell you, no one's gladder than me to have you on my side. You want a drink? Let me get you a drink. To celebrate our

Kockroach steps forward, takes Rocco's hand in his own. "Partners," he says. They shake on it, once, twice—and then Kockroach squeezes.

The bones in Rocco Stanzi's hand press against each other, press into each other, grind into each other, grind and twist and split.

As Rocco Stanzi begins to scream Kockroach's free hand dives at Stanzi's throat and clamps hold. The scream is choked off like a stalled engine. Still gripping hand and throat, Kockroach lifts Stanzi in the air.

Stanzi, face now bursting red, swings his arm and feet wildly. He kicks Kockroach in the chest, in the legs, grabs at his eyes. Kockroach pulls Stanzi close, holds him face to face so the flailing limbs lose their leverage. Kockroach's breath washes across Stanzi's purple face. Stanzi's pants drop, binding his ankles together. His flailing grows wilder. Kockroach's smile deepens. The grip on Stanzi's neck tightens. Stanzi's struggle eases. Stanzi's breathing falters, fails.

After, Kockroach slaps the dust off his pant legs. He takes a bag out of his jacket pocket, the brown paper bag with the greasy bottom. From the bag he pulls out a small brick of pastry. He takes a bite. Potato. Kirschner's has the best knishes in the Square, they have them delivered daily from Yonah

Schimmel's on the Lower East Side. He takes another bite and then leans over Rocco Stanzi's body, opens Rocco Stanzi's slack jaw, jams the rest of the knish in Rocco Stanzi's mouth so that it sticks out like a thick beige tongue.

"Nothing personal, pal, just beeswax."

Kockroach puts the bag back in his pocket, wipes his hands on the dead man's shirt, heads back to the car.

Kockroach has a hobby.

It is a very human trait to have a hobby, a pastime with which to while away the hours, and so one might be surprised to learn this of Kockroach. It is hard to imagine him dabbling in watercolors, working with wood, collecting stamps from foreign countries. But Kockroach's hobby is not philately.

Greed and fear, fear and greed. For a cockroach, a perfect hobby would combine the two, obsessively collecting something that also provides protection. Guns would seem then perfect, but Kockroach does not carry a gun and has never fully understood their allure. Oh, the mechanics he understands. Pull a lever and a shard of metal flies out and puts a hole in an enemy at a distance. Marvelously efficient, yes, but the fascination, the glorification is beyond him. Cockroaches don't fight at a distance, they fight up close, claw to claw, mandible to mandible, the desperate hot breath of your adversary pawing across your face. That is how it has always been done from time immemorial. To kill from a distance seems to Kockroach unnatural and, in a way, obscenely human. No, a cockroach wouldn't turn to guns for protection,

wrists named Albert Gladden who, before he met Kockroach, managed a few desolate properties scattered along the West Side. Albert owed Big Johnny Callas a debt that was on the books still when Johnny mysteriously disappeared. When Kockroach paid the awkward, mournful Albert Gladden a visit in the dusty office in one of his buildings, the realtor raised his palms and sadly pleaded poverty before proposing a deal: a deserted tenement on Ninety-fourth Street in exchange for the debt.

Kockroach toured his new building, sniffed the ruined plaster, bent his head beneath the leaking roof. In the dining area, his foot stepped through a rotted floorboard. The house smelled of old trash, of dead rats, of animal droppings, of desolation: it smelled wonderful.

Immediately Kockroach wanted more.

Now Albert Gladden works out of an office on a high floor in the Empire State Building, managing the properties of a generically named holding company whose primary shareholder he never reveals and whose empire continues to grow under Gladden's watchful eye. He has a staff of four, including a title man, and each morning finds him carefully perusing the list of property foreclosures. He is still mournful and awkward, Albert Gladden, but now he lives on the East Side, drinks aged Scotch, smokes hand-rolled cigars, is married to a former Rockette with

sturdy legs and breasts like huge smothering marshmallows.

As Kockroach drives through the city, he enjoys passing by the properties he owns, run-down brownstones in Harlem, shabby apartment buildings, shabby storefronts, sad sagging hotels like the Murdock, including the Murdock, old industrial buildings, ragged office buildings with long empty halls, a deserted warehouse teetering two blocks off the Square, which Gladden rents to Abagados without ever divulging the name of the true owner. And now, in his inside jacket pocket, Kockroach holds the deed to a large white house in Yonkers that he has just obtained from Cooney. He has a plan for this house, but if this plan of his fails, then he will leave it to his realtor to decide whether to keep it and rent it out or to sell it and use the proceeds to buy something in the city. He leaves everything to Gladden, allows him to buy, rent, sell as he sees fit so long as Kockroach is kept completely informed. Gladden makes his reports in person, at clandestine midnight meetings in deserted alleys so that Kockroach's hobby is kept secret. The only building Albert Gladden is forbidden to sell is the original property on Ninety-fourth Street, sagging, leaking, stripped of all pipe and wire, its front boarded up with plywood, a disaster of a ruin before which the brown Lincoln is now parked.

Istvan taps his fingers on the steering wheel, the woman is asleep alone in the backseat.

Kockroach roams through the dark ruin, stepping around holes in the floorboards, ripping cobwebs from his path,

cay, molder, rot. Home, it smells of home. In this place, of all the places he has been since his molt, he can best remember what he was.

He stops in a stray beam of light floating through the cracked window of the rear door, standing now before a beaten and blackened stove, so worthless with misuse and age it has survived the multiple strippings of the property. Atop the stove sits the photograph Kockroach took from the room where he first awoke with this body. He keeps it in this house for safekeeping. He picks it up, stares at the face that is identical to his and the woman's face beside it. For Kockroach the photograph has become a talisman of both his past and his future. He puts the photograph back upon the stove and stoops down on the filthy wooden floor. He reaches out a hand. From a crevice beneath the stove he sees two strands of brown, waving softly.

He waits.

The strands wave softly, wave, softly wave. And then, slowly, jerkily, with scurries and stops, a lone cockroach emerges and makes its way toward the outstretched hand, stopping just before it, letting its antennae brush the hand's flesh. The cockroach stays there, motionless for a second, for two, before rising slightly on its hind legs. With the tip of his forefinger, Kockroach gently strokes the arthropod's chest. The cockroach sways affectionately into the touch.

Kockroach takes the greasy paper bag from his pocket, reaches inside, pulls out the second Kirschner knish. He twists off a piece, rolls it into a ball, lays it on the floor.

The cockroach approaches carefully, rubs it with its antennae and then mounts the tiny ball, working the greasy piece of starch with its legs, devouring it with its ironlike mandibles and chitinous teeth.

Kockroach twists off another piece, and two more, and ten more, laying them side by side by side.

In the crevice beneath the stove he sees two more softly waving strands, and then two more and then twelve more. One by one the cockroaches emerge, one by one, one by one by one, from under the stove, from a crevice in the corner, through the holes in the wooden floorboards of the dining room, dropping like a battalion of airborne from the ceiling, they stream forward in a great army, scurrying madly now to the feast. The floor itself is alive with their frantic race.

"There is plenty, my brothers," he whispers.

Kockroach twists off more pieces, leaves them in his palm, lets the army swarm over his hand as they battle for the food, swarm so thickly not a speck of flesh is left uncovered. He places the remainder of the pastry on his shoulder and the army drives forward until his hand, his arm, his shoulder and neck, his entire right side is covered with a boiling mass of brown. The feel of them dancing on his flesh, piling one on the other, scurrying around his neck, across his face, nibbling his fingernails, his eyelashes, is lovely, warm, scratchy, familiar, rich,

jerking his body or shaking off any of the swarm, he turns his head and smiles at the man in the now-open doorway even as a cockroach dashes from his mouth to his ear.

"My good Lord. Blatta, you are one aberrant son of a bitch, yes you are. Don't be denying it."

"Want to feed my friends?" says Blatta.

"No no no. I spent enough nights with those critters biting at my toes. My bedroom was like a gymnasium when I was growing up. They'd come in, work the light bag, do a few rounds just to keep in shape, then hang in the corner and smoke reefer, snickering at my skinny ass, at the hand-me-downs I was forced to wear. I fed them enough to last me."

The man in the doorway wears a powder blue suit, a powder blue hat. He has a long nose, a small pursed mouth. In one hand he holds a gold-tipped walking stick, the other sports a diamond as big as an eye. His skin is as black as the coal from which the diamond was formed. His name is Moonstone.

"No surprises?" says J. Jackie Moonstone.

"No," says Kockroach.

"They're carving me up like a turkey, Blatta, like it's Thanksgiving already and I'm the only thing in the forest that gobbles. Well, they'll find critters in the forest other than turkeys, won't they? What about Stanzi?"

"Stuffed."

"And they're going to blame Zwillman, like you said?"

"Like I said."

"So everything is smooth, no problems?"

"Nothing I can't handle."

"Like what, for example?"

"Like nothing I can't handle."

"You're holding out on me, Blatta, not a good way to start. Is your boy Pimelia on board?"

"He will be."

"You're sure."

"One way or the other."

"My Lord, you are marvelous, Blatta, yes you are. A couple weeks from now it's just going to be you and me, just you and me on top of the heap."

"And then it's between us."

"No sir, no more fighting. There's more than enough to keep us jazzed and balled the rest of our lives. Whatever split of the other's turf you think is fair is fine with me, just leave me with what I got now and I won't fight it. I know enough not to mess with someone who keeps roaches for pets. We're going to get along like brothers. Here, what you asked for."

Moonstone drops onto the floor a handful of small wax-paper bundles, each tied with a bright red string. A mass of cockroaches sprints from the rest and swarms over the bundles until all that can be seen is a writhing mass of brown.

"Just like you asked for," says Moonstone. "Waxy Red, finest scat in New York City. Pretty soon you're going to have

Over the rooftops to the east, the first tentacles of dawn reach through the sky like a warning. Istvan is pulling the Lincoln up to the hotel. The woman in the car, awake now, leans her head on Kockroach's shoulder.

"You want me?" she says.

"Not tonight."

"Please, Jerry, let me come up. We haven't been together in ages. I miss you."

"Take her home, Istvan. I won't need the car until the usual time this evening."

"Yes, Mr. Blatta."

"Before then, find Mite and take him wherever he wants to go."

"Yes, Mr. Blatta."

"And then tell me where that is."

"Of course, Mr. Blatta."

Kockroach pats the woman's knee and slips out of the Lincoln. On the way to the entrance, he feels something squirm up his sleeve. A small cockroach climbs out and halts on the cuff, its antennae waving gently. Kockroach lets it climb onto his finger, pets its back, drops it through a grate in the street leading to the sewer, the promised land.

"Good morning, Mr. Blatta," says the doorman in his tall brown hat.

"Busy night, Mr. Blatta?" says the porter standing by the door.

Kockroach slaps green tributes into their hands as he walks through the door into the lobby.

"Your guest is waiting for you, Mr. Blatta," says the desk clerk.

"Very good," says Kockroach.

With a ding of the bell the elevator arrives, white gloves slip out and hold the door as Kockroach steps in.

"Going up, Mr. Blatta?" says the operator.

"To the top," says Kockroach.

13

Was one more player you needs to know about, missy, one more piece what moved across the Square like a deranged knight.

I can see him still, swaggering into some Times Square titty shake. His hat is shiny with grease. His cheap suit is rumpled, like he slept in it two nights running, which maybe he did. His tie is loose, his loose jaw unshaven, his socks smell like old socks.

"Shoot the sherbet to me, Herbert," he says to the barkeep in a voice with more hoarse in it than what's running at Aqueduct. He leans an elbow on the bar and checks out the merchandise. "Gin, straight up. On the house."

"On the house?" says the bartender, whose name is not Herbert and who is new on the Square so he ain't tuned in.

"And put an olive in it."

"Who the hell are you to be getting a drink on the house?"

This Joe he flips up his fedora with his pinkie and stares at the sap for a moment. Then he grabs the barkeep by his bow tie and jerks his fist down till the bartender's forehead it slams smack into the bar. He drags the bleeding face an inch from his own. His breath smells of cheap cigars, of raw onions on street-corner dogs, of wanton unwashed women.

"The name's Fallon, you piece of dick," he says. "Lieutenant Nick Fallon. Vice."

He rose from the mean streets of Hell's Kitchen, and he fell back into them streets afore it was over, but whilst he patrolled the Square, collecting his envelopes and pulling in rubes by the truckload, Fallon was a power. He kept his thumb up everyone's ass, just to be sure of the temperature, and everyone smiled whilst he did it, because he could make things easy for you on the Square, or make them very very hard. And missy, easy was better than hard when it came to Fallon. Manys the poor sap what ended up in the precinct house cage with Lieutenant Nick Fallon's fists asking the questions and the answers already written down afore ever they let slip a word. But he wasn't all hardworking cop, he had a sweet tooth of his own. What else could you expect from a man with vice in his very name?

"You ever have yourself a threesome, Mite?" said Lieutenant Nick Fallon, Vice.

"No, Lieutenant."

"I had one going on last night. Two girls. One of them had legs up to here, the other had Himalayas out to there, and they both still had all their teeth. Fancy that."

"Why you telling me, Lieutenant?"

"I'm telling everyone."

Fallon had yanked me by my collar out to the beach, the thin triangular strip of cement and grate just south of Forty-sixth, and now he was lighting one of his Cuban candles as cars and trucks wheezed by on either side. With the hubbub, the traffic, the backfires and horns, the pall of smoke and noise ris-

looks like me, setting up a with two broads look like that and still got all their teeth."

"I'm guessing raw."

"All their teeth."

"I'm happy for you, Lieutenant."

"Yeah, well don't be. Just as it was getting interesting, a call comes in from my captain. The only bite mark I got on my ass was from his chewing me out, Mite. So I am angry, I am blue, and I want to know what the dick is going on."

"Just the usual, Lieutenant."

"You think it usual for one of Tartelli's boys to end up dead in an alley? You think it usual for the Abagados clan to have a powwow just a few hours before the killing? You think it usual for my captain to suddenly take an interest in what goes on in my territory. You think that's good for any of us? Get smart, Mite. Something's up and I need to know about it. You owe me."

"Hell if I owes you anything."

"Hell you do. Take a gander," he said, spinning around to view the whole of Times Square. "Everyone your eye can spy owes me. I keep it safe, I keep it running, I keep everyone in business. You want they replace me with another Johnny Broderick, the cop who handled the Square before I did?

Johnny Broderick, tapping you on the shoulder with a newspaper wrapped around a lead pipe. He stuffed Legs Diamond headfirst into a garbage can one block down from here, stuffed him into that can and good as finished him off right there. You want another Broderick running the Square?"

When he talked of that Johnny Broderick, something fierce and hard glazed Fallon's bloodshot eyes, and looking at him then, and his thick lips wrapped around that cigar, I saw a touch of froth flit around the corner of his mouth. Just a touch, but it was enough to roil my stomach.

It was going to end up bad, the whole thing, I could see it in his eyes, in the froth at his mouth, the way his hand rolled into a fist for emphasis. It was like a curtain was dropped and I could suddenly see he was made of the same cement and asphalt what we was standing on, what ran from our feets east and west, north and south, off the beach, through the streets, in a great stinking sea of stuff what died at both rivers, made of the same grist as was all the raw matter of the city. He was a cop, but that was a lie, because it made him sound like he was something different from the rest of it when he was the same as everything else of it, all of it, even me, all of it. And his lips they was foaming and his eyes they was glazed and he spun around to make a point and it wasn't no more a cop before me or even a man but a piece of the world what was animated only by Hubert.

I held my stomach and looked down Broadway and tried to blink the sickness away and I did, this time I did, and when I turned back it wasn't this nameless piece of matter facing off

“What do you know, Mite?” he said.

“I don’t know nothing.”

“A midnight meeting at the Acropolis. Every big dick from Abagados down. I even heard Blatta was there.”

“Who?”

“Don’t be coy with me, you son of a dick. Start motivating your mouth. What did you boys talk about?”

“Moussaka.”

“Is that a fact? So tell me,” elbow in the ribs, ready for the coded clue, “what was decided?”

“The key is salting the eggplant. Kosher salt works best.”

“Kosher salt, huh? Is that why Zwillman he dicked Stanzi? Not enough *kosher* salt?”

“Zwillman? Is that what happened? I heard Stanzi, he choked on a knish. That Stanzi, he always liked a good knish.”

Fallon looked at me, licked the froth off his lips, filled his mouth with smoke, blew it in my face. “We got a good thing going here, Mite. Don’t let them ruin it for us.”

“Them? Who them?”

“That’s the question, isn’t it? The coroner says you can’t swallow dick if your throat’s crushed, as you could find out firsthand. I won’t let a war break out on my turf unless it’s my war, understand? I find out who is starting up I’ll get an army in here to finish it, understand? I'll be back, and when I do, don't dick with me, Mite. I want answers."

Didn't we all, just then, didn't we all.

What that iceberg it was to the Titanic, the knish sticking out of Rocco Stanzi's mouth, the most famous potato knish in the history of gang warfare, was to our peace. The whole delicate arrangement forged between Abagados and Zwillman and Tartelli, the whole beautiful alliance against J. Jackie Moonstone, was shot to hell. Tartelli, he immediately blamed Zwillman for the Stanzi hit, using as his proof the Yonah Schimmel knish, what was baked in the Lower East Side, Zwillman's territory. And with that accusation Zwillman, slipping into his normal state of apoplectic paranoia, pointed his thick finger at Abagados, what had had his troubles with Stanzi in the past. And Abagados, an old man who had fought too many battles, who had actually lost his fingers as a young Greek soldier in the century afore this one, Abagados struggled with all his powers, political, physical, and persuasive, to bring back the peace. But his efforts were stymied by a series of hit-and-run massacres on the border territories that kept the general uproar uproarious. And nobody knew nothing, nobody, including me, especially me, nobody except those what did, who weren't saying.

"Same as it always was, *Nonos,*" I said, alone with Abagados in the back room of the Acropolis. "Everything's the same with him. I been looking like you asked and I ain't found nothing."

"Look harder," said Abagados.

"I don't know what it is I'm looking for."

[illegible] in the eyes.

"He's always been loyal to you, *Nonos*."

"You know why he wears dark glasses? So I can't see into his soul. But when I shake his hand I feel it. It is my talent, I could always feel it. His is cold, hard, ruthless, it is like something dark and small, like something that crawls across your skin in the night. It is why I liked him at the start, a valuable friend he can be. Also a deadly enemy. But so am I, Mickey, so am I."

"I'll keep looking."

"You will find, you will bring me proof of his deceit. And this proof, it bind together once again all the families. And together we will destroy him and dance the dance of wolves on his carcass."

"Add some dip and a swing band and it sounds like a party, Mr. Abagados. But what about me? Blatta and me, we came in together."

"Mickey, my friend, Mickey." He lifted his big mangled hand and slapped the side of my face gently afore clasping his claw onto my cheek. "Find. Bring. They tell me there is no winter in California, just sun. Do you know how to swim?"

"No, *Nonos*."

"You will learn."

"Or die trying?"

He didn't smile, he didn't nothing. Whatever reassurance I was hoping to see in his bitter old eyes, all I saw was a vacancy as dark as Blatta's dark glasses.

So nows you know, missy. Me sitting here, spilling out the whole story for your snitch-sheet exposé, this ain't the first time I betrayed the Boss. Mr. Abagados, what he had wanted that long-ago night at the Acropolis when he rolled me the lemon was for me to spy on Blatta. And I had agreed. Playing Judas, I suppose, is simply my natural role in the Boss's little passion play.

But this I knew with a searing certainty. That thing what happened with Fallon on the beach, that lowering of the curtain and seeing all the city and the fools within it as nothing but the grist of the world? It was happening. Again and again. It was filling me like a fever. It was only a matter of time afore I started spinning and foaming myself. I needed to make something happen, fast. I needed to get on the train west with Celia, fast. I needed to take hold of her love and clutch it like a sword and swing with all my might and separate old Hubert from his head, and I had to do it fast. Because I was losing it, losing it, I was losing it.

"Anything that is different," had said the *Nonos*, "anything that is wrong." I crisscrossed the Square looking for something what didn't make no sense to me, I asked whoever would stand still for the asking, and then the something, it hit me like a punch in the face.

[illegible] into a taxi afore [illegible] in the middle of a wide deserted street smelling of blood.

A fog was rolling off the Hudson, a sickly mist. And I walked right into it, turning right then left, crossing a wide cobbled street.

It took me a while to find her, them piers they was one just like the next, hard to tell apart, and telling apart the girls what inhabited them was even harder, each a scabrous spider, clinging precariously to her collapsing web. In the cloaking mist I wrongly approached two strange creatures what grabbed at me like I was a last pitiful hope until I broke away.

But eventually I found the right pier. I stood under the single light and observed a peculiar shadow at the river's edge. An irregular shadow, moving about in slow motion with a steady skritch heard just over the lapping of the water, an inhuman skritch skritch, evidence of some readjustment of finances and fluids.

"Come to check on me, Mite?" she said after half the shadow had scuffled off and she had slipped back into the dim cone of light. "Come to make sure I'm not taking too many coffee breaks?"

"How you doing there, Sylvie?" I said, but I didn't need no answer from her.

She seemed as if she was in the middle of some great fever, bone skinny, shivering and sweating both, her swollen hands shaking at her sides. Her skirt was ragged and filthy, her blouse torn, a long scab darted across her neck. Dirt was streaked on her leg, her forehead, so that she blended into them shadows like a ghost.

"Spend a night here," she said, "in this fog that soaks through to the bone, and see how you hold up. Got a cigarette?"

"Sorry. Gum?"

"Thanks for nothing. What, did Jerry send you to tell me something? Does he even still know I'm alive? Does he care?"

"Sure he does."

"Tell the creep if he wants to send a message he knows where to find me. All right, let me have a stick."

I reached into my pocket, pulled out a Doublemint, watched her unwrap the foil. The boards creaked beneath our feets, some ship offshore, hidden in the fog, belched its horn.

"And this, after all I did for him," she said. "I was the one who spread the word about him to the other girls. I taught him to dance."

"Is that true, Syl?"

"Sure. One night at the Latin Club, after he took over for Johnny. My feet were aching for days after, the way he stepped all over them. I was his first girlfriend in New York, did you know that?"

"That I knew. Don't you remember? I was the one what paid."

"Don't be a silly goose, Mite. I did it for free. It wasn't ever [illegible] back to Pittsburgh and get healthy. I got a sister there, a married sister. I told him, let me go back and I'll return, better than ever."

I reached into my pocket, pulled out my roll, peeled off more than enough. "Here."

"What's this?"

"It's your ticket to Pittsburgh. The Boss, he wants you to go, to get well. But you gots to go now, tonight, run up to the terminal and leave right away while still you can and not say nothing to no one."

"Is that what Jerry wants? He wants me to get well?"

"Sure he does. You always been his favorite, Syl."

"Still?"

"Sure. Go to your sister, she'll take care of you."

She looked at the money for a moment afore grabbing at it and stuffing it under her dress, into the top of her stocking.

"It will be grand back in Pittsburgh," she said. "I was a queen there. You know, my sister, she was always jealous of me. I was the one that had the way with the boys. She didn't invite me to her wedding, afraid I'd steal the groom. Won't it be something when I go back, won't it be a stir. She better hold tight to her man, my sister, that jealous witch, yes she better."

"So tell me something, Sylvie. After what Blatta he done to that Turkish bastard what was supplying Christine, remember her, after that everyone knowed not to supply any flea powder to our girls."

"Course they knew. No one crosses Jerry."

"Not thems that's smart, anyway. So, Sylvie, the question I gots, the question what's suddenly been racking my noggin, is this: Who is it who's been selling to you?"

"What are you talking about? I don't have the least idea what you are talking about."

"Come down off it, Syl. The world can tell you're smacked back just by looking at you."

"Did Jerry say something? Jerry told you, didn't he? And you acting like you don't know, like you don't know when you know everything about everything. What are you playing at, Mite? What's the game?"

I stared at her for a moment, at her reddened nose, her twitching mouth, her eyes narrowing suspiciously at me, and then I knowed, and then I knowed, just like I knowed that she was never going back to Pennsylvania.

"Let me see what the Boss gave you," I said, and she did.

I found him at the Paddock, hard by the Winter Garden, sitting in a back booth in the back room, his hat on and his jaw hanging, a cigar in one hand, a gin in the other, a near-naked broad shimmying in his lap. Lieutenant Nick Fallon, Vice.

"Got a minute, Lieutenant?"

[illegible] so damn joyful, that I suppose for him they wasn't vices at all. He didn't feel embarrassed or degraded by them, they was simply worldly pleasures what made life something other than a wait for death. But there was one thing, one need that did embarrass him with its dark power, one secret desire which just then, clever little me, I was beginning to suspect.

Fallon slapped the bare thigh of the girl what was kneeling astride him and she squealed and pinched his cheek and hiked a leg over his lap so as to slide off the seat and leave us alone in the booth. He watched her go with a sweet regret on his ugly mug and then turned that mug on me.

"What's the agenda, Brenda?"

"I've been asking around. I ain't got nothing firm yet."

"And I haven't cracked a little pissant's head yet. You understand what I'm saying?"

"Not yet."

He leaned over and rapped his knuckle into my noggin, loosing a sharp spot of pain. "You are a cute one. You could make some real scratch cruising the Square in a pair a tight jeans and a T-shirt, playing at being a juvenile."

"That ain't my game."

"Mite, you don't know your game."

"I got a question for you, Lieutenant."

"I don't need questions, I got questions up and down my dick. What I need is answers."

Without responding, I reached into my jacket and pulled out the little wax-paper bundle with red thread I got from Sylvie and tossed it onto the middle of the table. It sat there, small and delicate, like a little ornament designed to hang from a Christmas tree.

"I could run you for possession right now," he said slowly.

"I found this on one of our girls. I needs to know who it came from."

"One of your girls? Which one?"

"That don't matter."

"The one you been with at '21,' the one with the bum leg?"

"Shut up, she ain't nothing to do with this, nothing to do with nothing. Leave her out of it."

"She isn't one of your girls?"

"That's what I said. She's pure civilian."

"Not so pure as you might think."

"Don't even start, you scum bastard."

He grabbed my tie, pulled it toward him until I was out of my seat, bent over the table, my face inches from the smoldering tip of his cigar.

"It's Lieutenant Scum Bastard to you, Mite. Don't be forgetting your place."

He let go. I slid back across the table and pooled down to the seat as if my backbone had just been neatly extracted with a filet knife.

"I'll take this," he said, swiping the ornament from the

[illegible] you. He got word the sucker was eating dinner in the Automat. Broderick strolled in, took a sugar bowl, whacked the pimp in the head, and then, over his collapsed carcass, he said, 'Case closed.' Johnny Broderick. In his off hours he was Dempsey's bodyguard. They made a movie about him. Edward G. Robinson. Johnny Broderick."

It happened right on cue, Fallon started talking about Johnny Broderick and suddenly the curtain it dropped and everything went nameless and strange on me again. What was this thing sitting across from me? Best I could tell it seemed to be made of cement, with granite lips and asphalt eyes, some great yet jolly creature built with the bones of the earth. And it was talking to me, this thing what had no name and no meaning, talking to me in a voice as deep as the Grand Canyon.

"You keep playing your game, holding out," came the canyon voice out of them gray stone lips, "and I'm going to close the case on you. Time to come clean."

I sat there, trying to blink it away like I done before, but it wouldn't disappear, this thing in front of me. I closed my eyes for a longer time and opened them again, but it was still there, the cement creature with the granite lips and Hubert's voice.

"Suddenly you don't look so good, Mite. You look like you're about to lay a puddle right here on the table. Just keep it the hell away from my suit, it's not even shiny yet."

The cement creature leaned forward, waved a burning tree trunk in the air.

"Go outside and what do you see?" it said. "Sucker bait over every last surface. Signs selling liquor, magazines, movies and televisions, selling sex even, if you can read between the neon. God bless Artcraft. It's the new age, Mite, everything is marketing now. Pretty soon we'll be billboards ourselves, with signs on our hats and shoes."

I closed my eyes to the cement man, just listened to his words, and slowly, gradually, like a lifting fog, the voice lightened and the meanings came clear.

"They call it Waxy Red on the street, or Wacky Red, depending. The thread is the key, the thread is the sign they ask for. Prime quality, expensive as far as horse goes. For junkies who know enough to demand the very best. You can always count on J. Jackie Moonstone to have the fiercest stuff in the city and to know the power of a label."

I opened them suddenly, my eyes, and he was back, Lieutenant Nick Fallon, Vice, no longer cement and stone and asphalt, but a man, a cop with a name and a purpose in life which unbeknownst to him was about to reach a glorious fulfillment.

"Now agitate the gravel," he said, "and don't come back till you have something to tell me about what's going on."

I did as he said, I hustled out of there fast as I could hustle. Time, it was running out on me, it was running out, it was almost gone, and I was almost lost. But I had my answer now. Wasn't I the little detective? I had my answer and I knew

14

Within the hard brown exterior of the Lincoln, wedged in a corner of the backseat, Kockroach feels safer than anywhere else in his new world. As the Lincoln cruises the streets of the city, dodging lane to lane, moving shoulder to shoulder with other cars and trucks, twisting down side streets, turning, stopping, starting, stopping again, as the car transports him through the city in a familiar rhythm, he comes closest to recovering the old sensations: comfort in his skin, purpose, community, the great fear of something coming from above to squash him flat. That is why he sits always in the rear seat's corner, jammed as tight against the door as he can manage, one eye looking out, one eye looking up.

The Lincoln now is double-parked across Broadway from a small, narrow bar called the Paddock. Cars are honking angrily as they stream past but Istvan, in the front seat, doesn't so much as twitch at the hostile sounds. The Paddock is one of Fallon's places, Fallon, whom Kockroach knows to be an enemy.

Kockroach does not have a subtle system of classification. He wants, he fears, those are his twin guiding lights, and when he applies that simple matrix to the humans who sur-

who supply him with the material things he craves but also nurture the dread that gnaws at his liver with the constant hunger of an arthropod. These others, these in the middle, might give a human some pause, but not Kockroach. They too are enemies, fear is that strongly embedded in the cockroach emotional DNA, enemies to be used as long as possible and then destroyed. Abagados is such an enemy, as is J. Jackie Moonstone, as is Fallon.

Yes, Fallon keeps the Square calm and for a small price allows Kockroach's collections to go unimpeded, but there is something in Fallon that Kockroach doesn't trust, some streak of angry honor that Kockroach believes Fallon will one day turn against him, and so Fallon feeds the fear. And now, from a bartender at the Paddock who is paid to keep tabs on the scum with whom Fallon meets each night, Kockroach has learned that the scum with whom Fallon is meeting this night is Mite.

Mite steps out of the Paddock, hikes up his pants, tilts down his fedora to cover his eyes, looks left and right, slips into the pharmacy next door.

"Pick him up," says Kockroach.

Istvan pulls the Lincoln in front of a green Oldsmobile,

speeds across two lanes, cutting off a Checker cab, makes a fast U-turn, and stops with a squeal and a jerk in front of the drugstore. When Mite exits with a pack of chewing gum, Istvan is outside, holding open the car door. Mite is unwrapping the foil on one of the sticks when he looks up and sees Istvan, the car, the open door. His jaw drops.

Mite takes a hesitant step forward, peers into the car. "What's the word, Boss?"

"The word," says Kockroach from inside, "is Fallon."

"I had a question for Fallon, is all," says Mite, sitting now in the backseat as the brown car cruises north, headed out of the city. "Where are we going?"

Kockroach doesn't answer.

"It was something what was happening with Sylvie. After what you done to the Turk what was doping up Christine, I didn't expect no one would be such a stupid tit-face as to be selling to our girls. But someone was, see, it was obvious with her. So I figured it was good business to find out who. Whoever it was we needed to do something about it, don't you think?"

Kockroach doesn't answer. He is jammed into the corner of the car, staring. He smells something coming from Mite, it smells like cat urine, like the breath of a mouse, it smells like fear. Kockroach lets the silence between them grow until Mite can't help himself from filling it.

"So I went and talked to Sylvie and then to Fallon and this is what I found out. The stuff she's getting, it's coming from up north, from Harlem, from Moonstone. How about them

"So you gots to tell me what to do about it. Somehow, Moonstone's slipping it through some tit-face into our territory and taking money out of our pockets. You want I tell what's happening to the *Nonos*?"

Kockroach doesn't answer.

"Where we going, Jerry? I got someplace in the city I got to be. Where you taking me?"

"Did you find out who the tit-face is?" says Kockroach.

"Sure I did," says Mite. "The tit-face is you."

Kockroach doesn't react with surprise, his smile stays broad, his head still, his hands calmly one in the other on his lap.

"Did you tell Fallon?" says Kockroach.

"Nah."

"Did you tell Abagados?"

"Don't needs to, he knows already you're in league with Moonstone without me saying a word. He wants me to prove it is all."

"Can you?"

"Sures I can."

"Will you?"

Mite looks again outside the window, at the unfamiliar landscape passing by. "I suppose you're going to knish me like you done Stanzi."

"That reminds me," says Kockroach. "On the way back, Istvan, we need to stop at Kirschner's."

"Why wasn't it enough what we had?" says Mite. "That's what I don't understand about you getting messed up with Moonstone. We started with nothing, we ended up as kings. Take your cuts, protect your territory, work with Nemo and the *Nonos*, roll in the clover. Why wasn't it enough?"

Kockroach considers Mite's question. One thing Kockroach has learned in his time among the humans is that all humans lie. They lie to get what they want, they lie because they are afraid, they lie to express the very essence of their humanity. Cats prowl, mice devour, cockroaches scurry, humans lie. Kockroach, therefore, had fully expected Mite to lie, he had planned for it, seen the ribbons of possibility float into the future with each expected falsehood. But Mite has turned the tables by telling him the truth. It is why Mite still beats him at the ritual of chess, his maneuvers are always full of surprises. Kockroach considers how to respond, and decides to battle claw with claw. For the first time since the change he will tell Mite the absolute truth about himself and his plans, and he begins with the biggest truth of all.

"I'm hungry," says Kockroach.

"Well, there's the problem right there. You know what you need? You need let me take you out to dinner at Mama Leone's. Seven courses that will split your belly. If the mama don't kill your hunger, nothing will."

"Nothing can. I'm hungry all the time."

"That's not what I want."

"Then what is it you want, big fellow? Tell me. What?"

"Everything."

"Well, that ain't happening. Sometimes you just gots to accept the way things are. I'm small, I'm never going to be big, I accept it. I'm never going to be a swell, I accept it. I'm never going to write one of them thick books, fine. I'm always going to have a boss, I accept it, so it don't matter who it is so long as I get my cuts. You gots to learn to accept things."

"I accept my hunger."

"You should show a little more gratitude to the *Nonos*. He took us in when we had nothing, gave us responsibility, allowed us to rise. He was the one what okayed the move on Big Johnny. He don't deserve what you're doing to him."

"Why should he be the *Nonos*?"

"Because that's the way it is, that's what he is. He's the *Nonos*. Who else but him?"

"Me."

"You? You're not even remotely Greek. That Jerzy thing I made up on the spot. You don't even know what it means to be the *Nonos*."

"Everyone feeds him. I want to be fed."

"Don't we all. But why you? Why not Nemo, what's been around longer than both of us, or Stavros, or even me. Everyone's got to wait their turn to move up. Why the hell do you think you got the right to take over out of turn?"

"The player that knocks over the boss piece wins the ritual."

"And that's going to be you?"

"Sweet pea."

"But we have it cushy as it is. Why you want to risk it all to be top dog?"

"Because I can."

"I suppose that's why you're going to kill me too, because you can. How are you going to do it? You going to crush my throat like you done Stanzi? Or are you going to let Istvan lead me out to one of these deserted woods and put a bullet in my brain. Oh, no answer to that? Well look, I got one request, all right? Two maybe. Two. Don't let it hurt, please. Just don't let it hurt. That's the one I just thought of, but the other, the more important, do me a favor and take care of Celia for me, will you? Will you, Jerry?"

"Sure I will."

"Thanks. You're a pal."

"Palsy."

"Yeah, you son of a bitch."

"Don't you ever think about what the other guy's feeling, Jerry? Don't you ever wonder, when you got the moke's

asking something different. He tries to remember the most recent moments when he triggered the greatest amount of fear in the humans, Sylvie at the piers, Cooney in his house, Stanzi in the grip of death. In those triumphant moments, did he feel anything that they were feeling, even the least intimation of their emotions?

"No," he says finally.

"Then you're lucky. I does. I can't help it. I looks into their eyes and I feels what they feel."

"I don't understand," says Kockroach.

"Well, yeah, maybe neither does I. This frigging world don't make no sense."

"But it does. Perfectly."

"Go to hell."

"You see what you want and you take it. Others try to take it for themselves. Whoever is stronger wins. What does not make sense?"

"It ain't that easy."

"Sure it is, Mite. It is only you that makes it hard. The world is all beeswax, everything."

"There's more to life than business, Boss."

"Only that something above is ready to squash you flat if you step into the light."

"That's the only part I believe, you ask me. But when you're going after them the way you do, Jesus, I can't help but suffer for them. And when there's the screaming, forget about it. It turns out I don't got the stomach for it. Who would have guessed? It's 'cause I been there, I guess, on the wrong side of the big boy's fist. And when finally I'm on the right side, it's still there, them feelings."

Kockroach wonders if that is a great weakness or a great strength. It could stay an opponent's hand at the crucial moment, but it might also be why Mite still beats him at chess.

"I couldn't take it no more," says Mite. "I had to get out. Them feelings was why I done what I done, if you gotta know. It was never nothing personal. I just saw a way."

"The lemon," says Kockroach.

"Son of a bitch, what don't you know? Where are we going? I got a right to know. Where?"

"Someplace special for you."

"You don't got to be so damn cheery about it. So what do you feel, Jerry? When you got some moke up against the wall and you're there twisting his arm behind his back and he's screaming and the arm is snapping, what do you feel then? What?"

"Hunger."

"Christ, you got it bad, don't you? You got a tapeworm the size of a snake inside your gut. I almost feel sorry for you, you starving son of a bitch. Why don't you just frigging eat me instead of killing me."

"I want to eat the entire city. I want to devour the world."

"You know what, Jerry, all this time I never realized how crazy you are."

Mite's head swivels quickly to look outside. "What is it? Where are we?"

"Get out, Mite," says Kockroach.

"Sure, Jerry. Sure. But can you do me a favor and not let Istvan do it to me? It ought to come from you. Can you do that for me, that little thing?"

"Istvan, stay in the car."

"Sure, Boss."

"Thanks, Jerry, really. You know, when it comes it ought to have the personal touch, don't you think. Most of my life it's been cold, noways reason my death it should be the same."

"Get out, Mite."

Mite nods, opens his car door, steps out. Kockroach steps out the other side. Mite is crouched, as if readying himself to be leaped upon, but when his gaze spins crazily around and he sees where he is he stands straight. They are on a street, a suburban street with thick trees hanging over the curbs and houses on either side. There are lights, streetlights, security lights, cars parked in driveways.

"This ain't no deserted field."

"No," says Kockroach.

"I thought you was sending me straight to hell. Where are we?"

"Yonkers."

"Same difference, then. What are we doing here?"

"Look over there," says Kockroach, pointing. Mite's head twists as he follows the direction until his gaze alights on a large white house on the crest of a hill. A light on the post announces the address and a shallow white picket fence surrounds the front of the property.

"This Cooney's place?"

"It was. Now it's your place. Cooney signed the deed over to me and I'm signing it over to you."

"Me? Why?"

"It's what you want, isn't it? A place out of the city. A plot of grass. A fence."

"Stop that, all right? Just stop it. You know too damn much."

"I don't understand about the fence, it's like putting yourself in a cage."

"I was getting ready to sell you down the river. Why would you do this for me?"

"When I was young, I was left to scuttle for myself. I survived but it was always on my own. I never knew it could be otherwise. And then, after the change, I was a blank in this world."

"What change?"

"You found me and took me to Abagados and taught me chess. Whatever I have become, it is because of you."

"You means you weren't a gangster before this? Is that the change?"

Or if I took you to a fire station, you would be saving lives now instead of taking them?"

"I was a blank."

"You was a piece of clay and I was your Old Dudley. Oh God, I really stepped in it, didn't I? I really am damned, ain't I?"

"We are brothers now, Mite. Our possibilities are intertwined. For me it is so foreign a concept, I wouldn't even know it existed if there wasn't a word: *we*. You want a house with a fence, we want the house, and here it is."

"What do you want in return?"

"Loyalty. The loyalty of a brother."

"I never had no brother."

"I've had hundreds, thousands."

"I won't even ask. I won't even frigging ask, you freak. But since you've had so many you needs to clue me in. What does that loyalty-of-a-brother crap mean?"

"It means, Mite, I won't eat you unless I have to."

Istvan stops the big brown car at Kirschner's Delicatessen, double-parking in front of the entrance. "The usual?" says Istvan.

"I'll take care of it," says Kockroach. "Wait here, both of you."

"Get me a pastrami," says Mite. "Funny how thinking you're getting whacked and then not getting whacked it builds an appetite."

Mite and Istvan stay in the car as Kockroach steps out, looks around, heads into the store.

"Look who it is," says the short man behind the counter, his round gray head barely peeking above the white porcelain surface. "Always a treat it is to be seeink you. You want maybe potato or spinach?"

"No knish tonight. They've been hard to swallow lately. Give me two pastramis."

"Don't tell me. On rye, no mustard, no Russian, nothink but meat."

"You got it, sweet pea," says Kockroach before heading to the rear of the store, through a small kitchen, out the swinging back door into an alley. Hunched amidst the Dumpster and cans is a tall man in a beige raincoat, his bony wrists sticking out of the raincoat sleeves.

"I've been waiting," says Albert Gladden, Kockroach's real estate man.

"That's your job," says Kockroach.

"I made the changes you asked for in the deed to the property in Yonkers. As soon as I file the deed, the house becomes his for as long as he lives. Shall I go ahead?"

"Yes. Anything else?"

"An opportunity has arisen. There is a foreclosure on three contiguous brownstones on the East Side. Run-down

[illegible] they have the only copies.”

Kockroach tosses the keys in his hand, feeling their heft, seeing the dark ribbons of possibility that flow from them. “Is there insurance on the building?” he says.

“Some, but the building itself is not worth as much as the land so the insurance only covers the cost of demolition in case of a fire.”

“Get more.”

“It doesn’t make—”

“Get more,” says Kockroach. He grips the keys tight in his palm. “If things go bad, I might need to disappear for a while. I want you to continue as you have so far. But I will be back and I will expect an accounting.”

“Of course, Mr. Blatta.”

“Do not disappoint me.”

“Never, Mr. Blatta.”

“How’s the wife?”

“She’s a whore.”

“Lucky you,” says Kockroach.

In the alleyway at the side of an old, crumbling warehouse, Kockroach waits as Mite fiddles with the keys. The alley leads around to a loading dock in the back. The warehouse is dark,

only a thin strip of light illuminates the side door, where Mite works the keys into the three locks. He has all three keys inserted, but it is hard to tell whether an individual lock is opened or closed. No matter what combination of turns he applies, the door stays tightly locked. Kockroach stands patiently as Mite works.

"What the hell is this place?" says Mite.

"Open the door."

"I'm trying. You got a flashlight?"

"I don't need a flashlight," says Kockroach.

Finally a combination works, the door opens with a shriek to Mite's push. Kockroach steps through the open door and Mite follows. It is cool, clammy, oily and dark. It smells of must, of sulfur. The windows are painted over, the thin light from the alley dies at the doorstep. Kockroach climbs a set of impossibly dark stairs with nary a hesitation, the stairway echoes with Mite's fumbles as he follows.

"Hey, Jerry, what's up?" says Mite. "Turn on a light or something."

Kockroach reaches the top of the stairs and stops. Mite bumps into his back and bounces off.

"Is that you, Jerr?"

"Welcome," says Kockroach.

"Where are we? I can't see a thing. What is this place?"

"Our future."

There is a hiss of light, a flickering flame from a safety match. The diffuse light seems to flow outward slowly, like a fluid, as if Einstein's theory had died at the doorway. With [illegible]y, huge and endless, filled with bullets and grenades. Giant guns on tripods, standing like insects ready to march to war. Squat mortars and mortar shells piled haphazardly like bowling pins. Stacks of giant Chinese firecrackers which are not Chinese and not firecrackers.

Kockroach moves the match to his teeth, where a cigarette waits. He lights the cigarette and carelessly tosses away the still-lit match.

"Jesus, Jerry," says Mite as the match lands on the floor, sputters, and dies harmlessly. Darkness returns as slowly as it was erased. "Who owns all this? The frigging army?"

"The *Nonos*."

"The stuff he's collecting?"

"The stuff, yes."

"And you have the key?"

"We have the key."

"It's enough to wipe out the frigging city."

"That's what I'm planning on."

"You're going to blow it up, you're going to level everything?"

"The *Nonos* has set up his pieces. I'm advancing mine. Let's kill all the pawns and see who survives."

"I felt it first time I ever looked in them eyes. You're Hubert, you son of a bitch, ain't you?"

"I am what you have made me," says Kockroach.

Because cockroaches are not religious creatures, they have no theology, none of the glorious jewels of thought that inevitably follow from a simple belief in God. The very concepts of faith, purpose, redemption, grace, life after life, concepts that have warmed and informed the hearts of humans for millennia, have no meaning for a cockroach. But there is one theological concept of which each cockroach does have some understanding, a concept burned into its genetic history and hardwired into its DNA by the crises of the past.

At the end of the Devonian age, 360 million years ago, a great cataclysm occurred. It is unclear whether this cataclysm arose from the sulfurous fire of volcanic eruptions, from the deep freeze of an extended ice age, or from some terrible extraterrestrial impact, but what is clear is that this disaster destroyed a great majority of the newly evolved species on the earth. It was from the shadow of this mass extinction that the first cockroach emerged. Another mass extinction, 248 million years ago, killed up to 95 percent of all marine species, and still another mass extinction, 64 million years ago, caused the destruction of 85 percent of all animal species, including the mighty dinosaur. The cockroach has experienced hellfire from below, ravages from above, the very shifting of the earth, and survived when others, bigger, stronger, smarter, had been blown

It is simply a fact of existence, something of which it is aware, just as it is aware of water and air, of the sound of footsteps, the smell of feces. For the order it has no name and so no word enters Kockroach's mind as he stands among the massive piles of armaments and explosives, but Kockroach knows of it in the blood and the bone and the marrow, knows of it as clearly as if his ancestors had tapped him on the shoulder and explained it all, and in so knowing he understands exactly where now he stands.

And the seventh angel poured out his vial into the air; and there came a great voice out of the temple of heaven, from the throne, saying, It is done. And there were voices, and thunders, and lightnings; and there was a great earthquake, such as was not since men were upon the earth, so mighty an earthquake, and so great.

Armageddon.

15

The train, it shivered as it pulled out of Penn Station, heading west, and I shivered with it. I wasn't alone in that train, they was two of us, and we leaned on each other and had our arms around each another and we whispered pledges of undying fidelity one to the other as the train took us both out from the city and into the great empty West. But stills I shivered.

It wasn't only the late night cold or the effect of the row of martinis I'd swilled. And it wasn't only the new adventure we was embarked upon, just as I had planned, though not as I had planned. I was facing the future, as blank as a white sheet of paper with just one black fact upon it which I could try the rest of my life to erase without succeeding, and that was terrifying, sure it was, but it was interesting too to see the black fact clear for the first time, so it wasn't only that which caused my shivers. It was something else, something I had spied outs the corner of my eye, just a glimpse of a thing, a silhouette against a backdrop of hell, something what would haunt my dreams through the long bland years to come.

After the Boss he showed me that pretty white house in Yonkers with my name on the deed, Celia and me we had ourselves some options. But there wasn't no time to waste. I had at the warehouse, to load a convoy of trucks and take the whole damn arsenal up to Harlem, leaving clues what blamed Tartelli for the theft. It was all coming to a head, the explosion was only hours away.

So I set up the meeting what would decide it all, the fate of my life and Times Square to boot, set it up at our usual place, Jack and Charlie's place with them wooden jockeys standing guard. I bought a new shirt and a new tie and a new pair of roach-stompers with points at the toes, and I ordered the best champagne in the joint because that's what I thought it took. And it was flowing, missy, but then shouldn't it flow on the night what sets you on the direction you'll follow for the rest of your cursed life?

"What's the big surprise, Mite?" asked Celia, sitting next to me at our table, her blue eyes shining in the candlelight, brighter than ever I saw them before, her face more alive, more beautiful, her whole being more vibrant, like she was a different girl altogether, a different girl playing at a different pitch. And tell me if I was a fool to think she had an inkling—the hints I had been giving had not been so subtle, not so subtle at all—and it was the inkling that had brought the flush of life to her cheek.

"You ever been out west?" I said.

"Where, like Montana? Wyoming? The Wild West?"

"I'm talking California."

"California?" Her eyes lit even brighter. "Hollywood?"

"I don't know, anyplace. Just California."

"No, I've never been. Girls from small towns in Ohio get one move. I came to New York."

"You want to go?"

"California? Sure, Mite. Who wouldn't? See some stars, see the Pacific."

"Not for a visit."

"Mite?"

"Call me Mickey, can you do that? Just for the night."

"Sure. Mickey. I didn't know you minded."

"I don't, it's just that some things are changing and maybe others ought change too. I got an opportunity out there. California. I thought I might go for it."

"In Hollywood? In the movies?"

"No, not the movies. I ain't the Bogart type, am I? What would I say, 'Here's looking up at you, sweetheart'? No, not the movies. Agriculture."

Her laughter was lighter than ever I remembered it.

"Mite? Excuse me. Mickey. Mickey? What do you know about agriculture?"

"Things grow, you hire Mexicans to pick the things what grow, trucks take them away and you gets money in return. Seems like an easy racket to me. Hey, don't laugh, I'm serious here. I could do it, why not?"

"Because you're a street kid. You'd be lost on a farm."

"Not a farm. I'm talking trees here. And maybe I don't want to be a street kid no more."

question the worth of everything. Let's just have fun tonight, let's just be gay. You're on top, in the greatest city of the world. Why would you want to go anyplace else? You should find someone for yourself, spend a night or two dancing at the Stork Club, live it up."

"How about Yonkers, then? I got a line on a place in Yonkers. Nice white house, grass, picket fence, the whole schmear, and just a train ride into the city. A great place for kids."

"Kids?"

"What do you say?"

"What do I say about what?"

"Look." I glanced side to side, lowered my voice. "It's gonna explode, the whole thing down here. It's gonna be ugly and I don't want to have nothing to do with it. I can't take it no more. My suit's so tight it's choking me. I'm getting out."

"You need a vacation."

"It's more than that. I got plans. I got dreams other than this dream. So if I gets what you're telling me, you're thinking Yonkers over California. It's a suit and a tie and a commute to the city instead of long sunny days in the orchard. Fine. What about advertising? Maybe I could snag a job selling toothpaste. Who knows? I got skills I can use in a different way than I'm using them now. And truth be told, I got a feeling he's going to end up on top somehows anyway."

"Mite?"

"Mickey, right?"

"I don't understand what you're talking about."

"California or Yonkers? Take your pick."

"Jesus, Mite—Mickey, I don't know."

"But if you had to choose."

"I suppose anything's better than Yonkers."

"So that's it then."

"What?"

"Look, I got something I need to ask you."

"Sure, Mite. What? Anything."

It was time, I was ready. I had practiced for hours in my room. I had bought the ring from State Jewelers, next to the Loews State, the ring a gaudy diamond on a thin gold band. I stepped out from around the table, took the box out from my jacket pocket. I ignored the look on her face, a puzzled worried look, and slipped to one knee. The box, it opened with a muffled snap. The diamond it truly sparkled in the dark room, sparkled as if lit by a strange inner fire, as if it were the brightest thing in the entire room, in the entire city, as if it had fallen into that box right out from the midnight sky.

And then and there I let slip the words I knew she was hoping for, the words what I was sure would give her everything I supposed she ever could have dreamed.

Late the next day, I climbed to the roof of a building on the West Side, pigeons fluttering about within a wire cage, the birds cooing their sad unrequited songs.

I laid flat on the tar, peeked my head over the shallow lip of the roof, and waited for it all to happen. It was like the whole of the city was a white-suited jazz band and I was the leader with my baton, like Benny Goodman or the Duke. Introducing Mickey Pimelia and his Mighty Mites.

Who the hell said I couldn't be no swell?

The sun set, the light faded, the night turned cold, the sky above grew dark and empty, the stars elbowed out of the heavens by the lights of Times Square just a few blocks off. It was time for the rhythm section to open with a wild dangerous beat, soft yet insistent, thump thump, thump. I raised my baton with a flick of my wrist and the drums started in and it began.

I never saw Blatta show. I thought I'd spy the brown Lincoln but I spied nothing, he must have slid in with Istvan through the alley entrance without so much as giving the street a sniff. But he was there, I could sense it, the way you can sense a bloodsucker landing on your neck even afore the needle nose pricks the skin. And when the trucks started arriving like a bass line plucked note by note, one after the other in a rhythm as steady as the drummer's beat, I knew it for sure. The line of trucks passed the front of the warehouse and then slipped into the alleyway that led to the loading dock at the back. Blatta was there, and now so was J. Jackie

Moonstone and the bulk of his boys, ready to pick Abagados's arsenal clean.

But tonight it wouldn't be so easy, tonight there'd be crashers at the party. Mite had seen to that. Good old Mite, loyal Mite, brother Mite.

It wasn't no surprise to me when, soon as the trucks they slipped down the alley and enough time had passed for the occupants to slip inside, the street it came alive like a sweet serenade of saxophones, blowing one against the other, with a licorice stick dancing riffs around them all. Slowly, quietly, as if in response to my very direction, an army rose from the gutters, as insidiously as if an army of insects, and then another and then a third, lining up on the various sides of the building. Three armies, armed and dangerous, led by three bosses standing now side by side by side right out in front.

Tartelli. Zwillman. Abagados.

Abagados lifted a hand, and like a solo blast from the big trombone, a pane in a warehouse window, it was blasted into shards of light.

"Blatta, you *poutana*," Abagados yelled in a voice shocking strong. "Show you stinking face."

There was silence. Then another window shattered, this time broken from inside the warehouse, and Blatta's voice poured into the street in a starkly inhuman yet hearty yelp. "Hello, *Nonos*."

"Everything in there it is mine," said Abagados.

"Come and get it."

"And how be your new black friend?"

"I'm always easy to find, *Nonos*. Look to the money, that's where I am."

"I never trust you."

"Trust?" Blatta yelled back. "You humans and your words. Are you ready to fight, *Nonos*?"

"No," said Abagados in a weary voice. "Not fight. In my life I had enough fight." He paused, let his shoulders slump for a moment, and then raised his jaw. "But I ready to kill."

Just then an explosion from inside the warehouse blew out the entire first floor of windows, scattering shards of glass across the street and high in the air, so that small slivers landed atop the far rooftops, even landed atop of me, pricking my exposed skin like sharpened teeth.

Abagados wasn't no doomed Confederate general, there wasn't going to be no valiant charge into the teeth of the enemy's firepower. The boys ringing the warehouse was only there to keep them what was inside from getting out. Earlier that day Nemo had taken a squad into the warehouse, a squad what included me, and set it up just the way he wanted. We took the ammunition out of them boxes, so them big guns they couldn't hurt you unless they was throwed at you. And we wired up the explosives so that a series of fuses lit from outside could start the thing inside to going kaboom. And missy, now them fuses they was lit.

It wasn't going to be a battle, it was going to be murder, pure and simple.

Them fuses they was lit, just like I expected, but they was lit too soon. I looked left, looked right. It was time for the coronets, as if led by Louis Armstrong hisself, with his fanfare entrance and his sweet tone of righteousness. But where was them coronets? I was wondering just that when a second explosion blew another set of glass choppers chewing through the sky.

Where was them coronets?

And then they opened up, as if I had brought them in myself with a swift wave of my baton. Lieutenant Nick Fallon, Vice, and his army of coppers came a-charging. They came a-charging, but not with no chorus of paddy wagons, no ma'am. This wasn't going to be just another raid with all them gunsels down in the street ending with a short pull in the poky afore the mouthpieces showed with piles of cash to spring them like springs. There wasn't no paddy wagons because there wasn't going to be no survivors. Lieutenant Nick Fallon, Vice, sent his army down both sides of the street, two battalions with guns blazing, like a loud blast of brass, shooting away at them boys outside the warehouse, forcing them back, back, back toward the very building they had set to blow.

The entire underworld was going to go up in one great torrent of fire and brimstone to slake the hunger what was burning inside my own damned soul.

Do you desire me like a man desires a woman, and don't you think I deserve that? Don't you think me worthy of that? Mite? How dare you, Mite.

I had never felt so small in all my life, smaller even than when them Thomasson twins took their turns with me. I knew what her laughter it was saying, what it was shrieking. And it was while I was still on my knees, and feeling the acid truth of her laughter wash through me, that I decided to follow her and see where she was getting what she couldn't get from me.

And I found out, without a doubt, and threw that moldy old lemon at his door, damn me to hell.

So I told the *Nonos* what I told the *Nonos*. And when I learned what he had in store, to turn that warehouse into a crematorium, I had an even cleverer idea, and so I told Fallon what I told Fallon. He talked about keeping the rackets going, did Lieutenant Nick Fallon, Vice, keeping the status quo so all could take their pleasures and their cuts, but he had hisself his own tidy dream, didn't he? He spilled it to me every time we met, and Hubert showed up laughing every time he spilled it, and it was in Fallon's dream that I spied the means to the ultimate obliteration. For Fallon wanted to be Johnny Broderick but better than Johnny Broderick. Johnny Broderick cleaned up the Square, Fallon was going to clean up the whole stinking town, scrub it fresh in one purifying burn, and in the process earn his own damn movie.

And the world I knew burst into flame. And the smoke billowed. And the heat grew hotter than even I could stand. And the black tar melted against my pants, my suit jacket, my tie. And just at the height of it all, I spotted something across the street, I spotted something, and in a blind fear I tore myself from off the roof, leaped the gap, sprinted back to the open door, raced down the stairs and out, back to the Square.

It was only a few short blocks to Penn Station and the love what was waiting for me on the train, but I had one thing more to do as I made my way out from the Square for the last time, one thing more to do. So I stopped at the Paddock for a drink and then at Benedict's for a drink and then at Kennedy's for a drink, and so Mite is suitably out of his skin and ready, yes he is, for that one thing more to do.

"Hey, Mite," says Tab, what Mite passes on the street, Tab the hustler what was always kidding hisself about who he was. "What happened to your threads, man?"

"Go to hell, you faggot," says Mite.

"I got something just for you, sweetheart."

"Shut up," says Mite. "Shut the hell up, you tit-face queer."

"Hey, baby, I might just be your last chance at heaven."

"You think so, dick-breath?" says Mite. "You really think so?"

"Sure I do."

"Then prove it."

"What? You mean—"

most of all from something else, from the thing I had spied afore I had sprinted off that roof.

But leastways I wasn't alone, I couldn't have stood my own damn self if I was alone. We was together now, now and forever. We leaned on each other and held to one another and we whispered pledges of undying fidelity one to the other, Hubert and me, lovers at last.

And Hubert, he was a great teacher, better even than Old Dudley. Old Dudley taught me the way to advance in the world: Behave yourself and eat your spinach and take them mopes for all they was worth. But Hubert, he knew better and showed it to me clear. There is no way, there is no advancement, there is no worth. Everything it is false, everything it is empty. And them things what behave as if it is any different, them things ain't only lies, theys worse than lies. And it isn't good enough to just see them for what they are and let them be, whether the *Nonos* or the Boss or the whole stinking life, no that isn't good enough at all. He lit a hunger in my soul, did Hubert, and there was only one thing what would satisfy it, one delicious thing.

Up on that roof, with the tar melting onto my clothes, I was tasting it. There was a third explosion, and then a fourth, like the sharp final exclamations of my great opus, and it was this fourth explosion what seemed to catch onto something else and blossom wild until the whole building collapsed into the center of a huge flower of fire. And out from the fire billowed a pillar of smoke, gray and thick, and I swear, I swear, it towered so high it fell back down on itself and from the light of the fire I could see the shape of a thick gray mushroom in the sky.

It was biblical, missy, and it devoured everything what was in its orbit, everything and everyone, everything and everyone but one.

A shadow what I swear I saw climb out from the center of the fire and appear to me for just an instant against the surging orange backdrop of flame. A shadow what intruded into my grand finale like the long bass note of an angry tuba. It stood there for an instant, the shadow, staring up as if right at me for just long enough to show me it survived, afore it somehow disappeared. A shadow with broad shoulders and a fedora still in place and a posture so distinctive and jaunty it could only be the shadow of one Joe, one Joe, the same Joe what I followed Celia to after she had laughed me down and set me on my path, the one Joe what was sticking it to her after she done stuck it to me.

Blatta.

And it was that shadow what scared me senseless and sent me running and set me to shivering on the train, with Hubert clutching and smothering me in his long gray arms.

But this I can tell you, missy, this, the strangest thing of all. It was in the outline of that shadow, that jaunty inhuman

16

Singed and smoldering, driven relentlessly by fear, Kockroach slithers through the encircling line of police thugs with Thompson machine guns at their hips. He moves stealthily, from shadow to shadow, scuttling as quickly as his leg, burning from some interior fire, allows. When one of Fallon's cops turns in his direction, he slips into darkness and holds deathly still. He is working from deepest instinct, trusting what he had been to lead what he has become to safety.

He is crouching now against the scorching skin of a building across from the blazing warehouse. His hand reaches down to his thigh and feels a warm wetness. He brings his fingers to his mouth and licks them clean with his tongue. Briny, like his evening shrimp. Shrimp. The delicious crackle in his teeth, the sweetness. That, he knows, is now over. All of it is over.

Across the street, his plan to wrest power from the *Nonos* is burning with an intensity that pains the exposed sections of his fragile human flesh. There was a moment when his pieces were in perfect position and the human dream of great power was within his grasp. But now the entire chess board is being devoured by fire. He was betrayed from within, betrayed by Mite.

Mite was up there, on the roof, looking down upon the

to the wall and wood. And yet, even after seeing the scattered pulp, he continued with his plan. He thought he had enough power to topple the *Nonos* despite Mite's betrayal, but he should have known better. No matter how skillfully he arrays his pieces, Mite always beats him at chess. Maybe there was something in Kockroach that rejected the human dream even as he reached to grab it in his fist.

Kockroach stares at the great conflagration and the burgeoning gray acrid smoke and he feels not bitterness nor anger nor a deep thirst for revenge. It is over. The world he knew and its possibilities are destroyed. He lets the fact of it wash over him and through him until it is part of him.

Deal with it, that is the cockroach way.

He has survived, he will move on, maybe even to molt once more back to his original form. He is through with the gangs, through with the whores, the protection rackets, through with twisting legs and snapping arms, through with humans altogether. The money he has out on the street will stay there and that is the only thing he regrets, along with no more shrimp.

The fear that pushed him out of the burning building and past the police rises up in his throat. It swivels his head, left and right, he searches for a way to escape, left and right. Then he spies something. A hole, in the street, the heavy cover tossed to the side by one of the invading armies. He scans the scene quickly to be sure no one is watching, glances nervously up at the sky, and then dives down into the darkness.

He slops into the slop. The smell is sweet, the darkness a balm, something squeals as it races across his shoe. Kockroach has found the sewers, and like the prodigal son of whom he knows nothing, he has come home.

Chased by fear, Kockroach hobbles through the tunnels, dragging his injured leg behind him. He veers left, hops right, travels straight for a long distance, and then bounds again to the left. He is rushing away from danger and to safety and judges each choice by some instinctive measure which he understands not at all and trusts completely.

When he reaches an obstruction he can't pass he stops, searches for a new route, and finds a long metal ladder climbing to a tiny shaft of light. He clambers up the ladder, places his hands on a metal disk with a single hole letting in the light. A roar reaches through the metal and vibrates into his bones. He stiffens his uninjured leg and pushes upward.

The traffic on Eighth Avenue buzzes ferociously. Taxis and long black cars. A huge gray truck thunders by.

He ignores the traffic, throws the metal lid to the side, lifts his head out of the hole.

A taxi swerves to avoid him, a delivery van sideswipes the taxi. Brakes squeal, a truck blows its horn as it roars right over him. A big black car avoids him by darting to the left before slamming into a parked car.

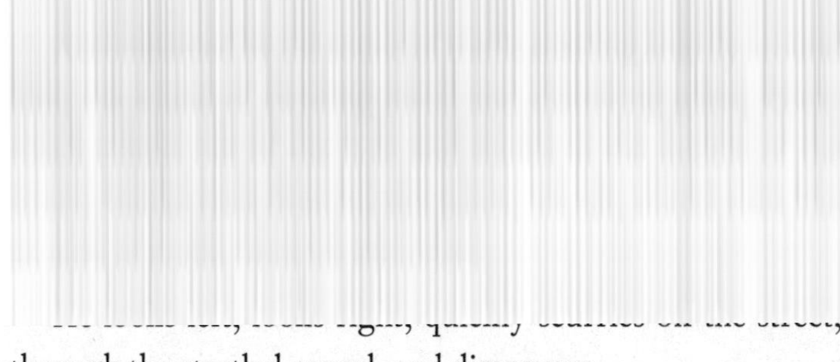

through the startled crowd, and disappears.

Kockroach knows now to where he is headed. In the underground sewers, his instincts were leading him to an indeterminate place of safety, but now, as he slides quietly uptown through dark alleys, as he hides in shadows as humans pass, he knows to where he is headed. Something inside of him rises as he comes closer, as he recognizes the neighborhood, the street, as he recognizes the very sheets of plywood sealing up the windows.

He pulls opens the rear door and slides inside his house on Ninety-fourth Street, the one property his real estate man, Albert Gladden, is never permitted to sell.

Once inside, he staggers through the kitchen and falls. The pain and weariness have finally taken him down like a fierce predator leaping onto his back, a panther maybe, black and heavy, or, in his earlier incarnation, a mouse. He drags himself to a corner of the living room, strips off his human clothes, curls up so that three sides of his body are protected.

His leg burns where it is bleeding, his ears ring still from the explosions, his skin throbs red from the heat, his mouth and tongue are raw from smoke, his vision is spotted from the

great balls of fire that blossomed about him. He is in a dangerous state, he knows, his new body is failing him and he has no idea of what the future will hold. Yet his senses are as overstimulated as if he had been antennae fencing with a fleshy palmetto bug drunk on Sterno. Even as his body burns, and even as fear shrieks in his ear, he finds himself in the mood to mate. This is no surprise, really. Kockroach is always in the mood to mate.

And to a cockroach the crackle of destruction is as seductive as a Barry White sigh.

He awakes with a start at the tiny skritch he feels on his finger. One of his brothers has come to visit.

With his thumb, Kockroach gently rubs the arthropod's wings. It straightens its legs and lifts its back in response, antennae swaying all the while. A moment later another comes to be stroked, and then another, and still another until they swarm over his hand, his arm, his entire body. They are nibbling his nails, gnashing his lashes, crawling in and out of his ears in search of tasty morsels of wax. They dive beneath his limbs and massage his skin with their tiny tarsi. Once again a feeling of connection rises within him, a feeling lovely, warm, scratchy, familiar, rich, sensuous, luxurious, loving, and it continues to rise, beyond what he felt before, to almost overwhelm him.

They are after food, he knows. They are searching for the delicious balls of knish he has hand-fed them before and he feels their disappointment, as if it were he himself who was

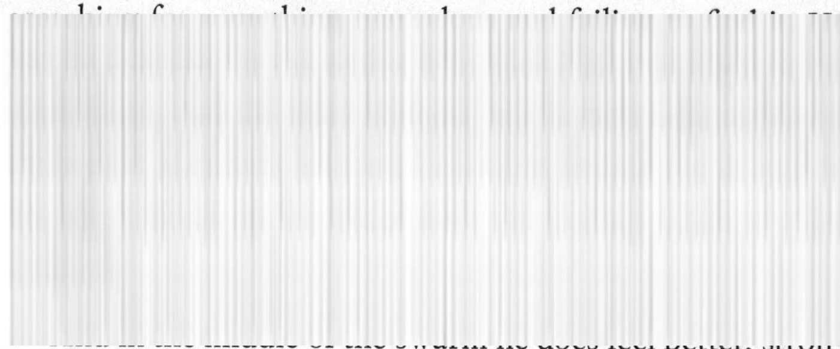

ger, he does feel revitalized. The world in which he had found himself, the world Mite had led him to, the world of power and death, the world of the *Nonos,* dissolves for him as if he had awakened from a strange dream.

He feels himself revert to a simpler and superior thing.

Kockroach is back on the street, clothed again, haunting the back alleys, the Dumpsters, darting with his limp through the darkness as he searches for food to feed the colony he now supports. The city is no longer a mystery to him, he knows now where to find quickly and safely what he needs. Each night he scours his favorite spots for bits of rotted vegetables, of maggoty meat, of glops of congealed noodles dumped behind chop suey houses. He eats all he can stuff into his throat and brings all he can carry back to his colony.

No more do they move hesitantly in his presence. They rush him as soon as he appears, a great swarm, far more than ever before survived in that house. From the neighboring houses they have come, from the street, from the sewers they have come. They arrive in great heaving armies, racing each madly as they make their dash to the provider. He leaves his

special treats and watches as they climb one over the other over the next to devour them. Small white nymphs scurry among the legs of the adults, snapping up the morsels too small for the older ones to bother with. The sight of it fills him with a strange feeling, warm and rich, a feeling that, most strangely of all, has a name.

Satisfaction.

He is living the same way he had lived before ever he met Mite and was led into the dream world from which he escaped. But he is also not living the same way.

He tried to groom himself and his clothes, but that proved unsatisfying. He found the taste and hairs in his teeth to be unpleasant, and he was never as clean as he remembered from the showers. He also missed the fresh feel of the razor scraping his cheeks and jaw. So he has found a bathhouse nearby that is open all night, and a place to buy new clothes after dark, and a barber that cuts his hair and shaves his beard even after midnight. He spends what money that remained in his pockets after the destruction to keep himself clean and his new clothes pressed.

And he understands that this whole provider business is not the way it ever was before, when he was still an arthropod. Cockroaches are not selfless drones, working themselves to death for the common weal. One for one and all for one, is the cockroach motto, so long as you are the one. And yet, Kockroach somehow derives great satisfaction from being the provider.

That word again.

Therein lies the most momentous difference between what

he was before ever he met

covers that words themselves have intruded upon his new life.

He had considered them to be handy things, words, little arrays of strange garbled sound that helped him assuage his fear and feed his greed. He had considered them to simply be tools, which only indicates the depth of the intrusion, because Kockroach had no conception of what was a tool before he learned the word.

Immediately after his escape from the warehouse, lying in the corner of his home, still bleeding, he had been frightened of what the future would hold when, before he was taught the ritual of chess and learned the word future, all his concern was rooted firmly and solely in the present. And then there was that peculiar satisfaction word, a troubling word indeed, because it carries with it a concept so foreign as to be shattering. For when is a cockroach's hunger ever sated, his thirst slaked, his fear eased? For when, simply, is a cockroach ever satisfied?

And it wasn't just that words brought with them strange concepts that had insinuated themselves like a colony of earwigs in his brain. The concepts fed one upon the other, and led to still other concepts in a vertiginous climb of words and ideas that could only be classified as thought.

Thought.

But cockroaches don't think: they do or don't do. When they are still, their sides pushed tightly against the base of a kitchen cabinet, cockroaches are devoid of thought. They are simply waiting for the stimuli to align themselves in such a way that their instincts tell them it is safe again to move forward, to seek out something to mount and devour. Look into the mind of a motionless cockroach and you'll find nothing, a lovely, quiet nothing. Practitioners of the Eastern religions spend their lives training their minds to reach the pure empty state that is first nature to a cockroach. But in fairness to the devout, a cockroach has a natural advantage: no words.

In the human world, even before the destruction, the perverse practice of thought had crept into his mind on hushed little feet. But in the bustle of that world it had all seemed, well, almost natural. Now, among his original species, the flaw is glaring. In the moments between his daytime sleeps and nighttime forays for food and cleanliness, when Kockroach lies naked and awake in his corner, he experiences not that lovely quiet nothing but, instead, the bilious hubbub of words and concepts clashing and climbing in an incessant blabber. In short, he thinks.

He thinks of the future, he thinks of finding satisfactions in the future, he thinks of the tools he'll need to find satisfactions in the future.

He thinks of eating shrimp. He thinks of mating. He thinks of eating shrimp while mating. Of dipping his hands in

which he holds, the hot breath when he brings the victim's face close to his own, the gurgling sound when the throat collapses from the pressure.

He thinks of Celia Singer, her naked body stretched beneath him, above him, away from him even as their genital bond remains ever solid. Her shivering excitement, her blatant need, the way she would place her face wet with tears upon his chest.

He thinks of Mite, but not of his betrayal. He thinks of sitting in the schvitz with Mite, of playing chess with Mite. And he thinks of the conversation they had in the big brown Lincoln as they drove together to see the house in Yonkers, using words like gratitude, feeling, hunger. They had just been words, passed back and forth, tools, but even in the car, Kockroach had known they were more. And he would like now to talk again to Mite about those words and others, words like loyalty and satisfaction. Words like violence and opportunity and power.

This desire to talk, to communicate, is completely foreign to a cockroach and yet it grows ever stronger within him. He knows it is alien, this desire, he knows it is a corruption, and yet it is too strong to deny. Just as words infected him with concepts and concepts infected him with thought, thought infects him with the strange need to talk, to talk in words, to start it all again.

He brings back a great ball of starchy gluck to feed his colony and they swarm over the food and swarm over him, burying him in their writhing brown mass, and it feels still as good as ever it felt, and his genital flap swells and throbs in the middle of it, yes, but it is no longer enough.

He needs to mate, but his molt has made the allure of the female cockroach a vague remembrance and nothing more. He hungers for shrimp, to devour again their crackly briny sweetness. He opens his mouth and a cockroach crawls in and he chews it and swallows and repeats with two more, four more, and it is good, yes, musty and crunchy with a soft gooey interior, yes, but it is not shrimp. And he wants to talk, but his family, his swarm, they have no words, no concepts, no thoughts, and so the talk is painfully one-sided.

He hoped it would be enough, to live as once he had lived and to provide for his flock, he hoped it would be enough, but it is not enough, not anymore, not after being infected with words.

Kockroach needs again to enter the human world.

Kockroach moves now through the streets of the city in the bright light of day.

The sun is painful and frightening, even as he keeps his dark glasses on and his hat low, yet he has no choice but to walk among the humans in the daytime. He is no longer afraid of giant predators, and he is no longer afraid that a human will recognize him for what he is and crush him, but that does not mean he is not afraid. Fear and greed, greed and fear, they are always with him, his boon companions. He was in the middle of the explosion. He saw humans flying through the air, humans riddled with bullets, humans torn apart like cockroaches at the many many hands of a millipede. The biggest danger he faces in the human world is to meet up with those who will recognize him and want to finish what he started. So he stays away from the world of his former life, away from Times Square, away from the places in which he had once been known. And, most painfully, he stays away from the night.

Kockroach moves now through the streets of the city in the bright light of day and he is looking for something. He is not sure exactly for what it is he is looking, but he is looking for something and the something has a name, a word Mite had taught him.

Opportunity.

He has thought it through. In his house, in his corner, in the darkness, he has thought it through. What went wrong. Why he continued to the warehouse even after he was certain of Mite's betrayal. From wherein came the destruction. He has thought it through, he could not help but think it through—that is the way of thought he has discovered, it is self-perpetuating and it never shuts up—and the answer he came up with was that violence had guaranteed his failure. Not the violence perpetrated against Kockroach, but the violence Kockroach perpetrated himself.

Two cockroaches chasing after the same female, the same morsel of goop, two cockroaches battle, the stronger wins, the winner mates, the winner eats, it is so simple. And among the humans he discovered that he is the strongest and so it was natural for him to think that anything he saw, any female, any territory, was his to take. But he was wrong.

Human violence is very different from the cleanliness of cockroach violence. There is a battle and one human wins and that should be the end of it, but one battle is never enough. Human violence spirals. And each battle ever after grows in size and intensity as the combatants reach each for their tools. The beaten human comes back with a knife. The stabbed human comes back with a gun. The shot human comes back with a bomb. The bombed human comes back with an army. It continues, back and forth, until one side is utterly vanquished or both sides are utterly destroyed.

That is why Kockroach went to the warehouse even after he was certain that Mite had betrayed him. The fight would spiral into something cataclysmic, it was so destined, it

destruction. It is the human way with violence. Cataclysm is cleansing, yes, but surviving the cleansing fire of the warehouse had been mostly a matter of luck. He was lucky once, he couldn't be sure he'd be lucky twice.

And so Kockroach has decided he will have to find a different way to rise again in the human world. And so he is looking for opportunity. He remembers when Mite first gave him the word. "A little business," had said Mite. "Beeswax. Something rich."

Yes, that is what he wants, something rich, a little beeswax, opportunity, that is what he is seeking as he stalks the city's streets.

"You're looking for opportunity, young man?" says the woman behind the desk. She has high gray hair, clear glasses on a chain around her neck, and she looks like she just bit into a mouse.

"You got it, sweet pea."

"Well, we don't wear sunglasses at the bank, or our hats inside, and we don't use words like 'sweet pea.' We maintain a certain decorum. Are you sure this is where you want to work?"

Kockroach looks around. The ceiling is high, men and women behind glass partitions are sorting through money. He wants to be rich again, he wants the green bills to be thick in his wallet and ready to buy food, women, grooming, shrimp. Why would he want to work anyplace else but a bank? "I'm sure."

"Then fill this out." She hands him a sheet of paper. "And don't leave out the references. Three. We do nothing without references."

Kockroach looks at the sheet of paper in his hand, covered with human writing and long blank lines. He looks up at the woman, who is staring at him through those clear glasses.

"I don't read," he says.

"I'm very sorry to hear that," says the woman, without sounding very sorry at all. "But if you don't read, what makes you think you can work at a bank?"

He leans over, tickles her chin. "Because I can count."

Kockroach places the gray tub on the table and starts tossing in the dishes, the silverware, glasses and food. Shards break off as the plates and glasses hit one another from the tossing, but he continues. He is wearing still his suit, his hat, his tie, his dark glasses, but he has now an apron tied around his waist.

"You want opportunity?" had said the man at the register of the restaurant, a short man with a pointed beard. "Why not? This land of opportunity, right?"

"So they say, sweet pea."

"You ever bus?"

"I had a Lincoln."

clash of the dishes is lovely, and the smell too. He likes the work, he would do this for free.

A half a sandwich, soggy with spilled coffee, gray with ash, lies on a plate in the tub. He likes his starch soggy. He grabs the sandwich, stuffs it in his mouth.

"What you do?" says the man with the pointed beard, standing now in front of him.

Kockroach looks up at him, bits of sandwich sticking to his grinning lips.

"Get hell out of here. What, you some sort of animal?"

Kockroach drops the tub on the floor, pulls off the apron, wipes his mouth with it, tosses it in the tub.

"As a matter of fact," he says before leaving.

It is harder than he anticipated, this opportunity beeswax.

It seems opportunity is available only to those who can fill out the form that is held in a desk drawer in every building and the form can only be filled out by someone who can read. He needs to learn, he realizes, but who can teach him? He thinks of Mite. If Mite were here, Mite would take care of him, Mite would fill out the form, Mite would teach him how

to read. It was Mite after all who had taken him to Abagados where he could find a job without the form. He hadn't realized how difficult it is to navigate the human world without a Mite by his side.

Every attempt to find opportunity fails. The market with all that luscious food, the clothing store, the barbershop, every place is closed to him. He crosses avenues, he hops along streets, he skulks the back alleys, he is looking for something, anything, he is looking for a sign.

And a sign is exactly what he finds.

Through an alley, on a short cobbled street surrounded by the butt ends of huge factory buildings, atop a small building with a ground-floor office, he sees a sign. There are words that Kockroach can't yet read but it is what is above the words that pulls him in. Huge, brown, oval, with six little legs sticking out, two beady eyes, two stubby antennae. It is a giant arthropod, a giant cockroach to be exact, not an accurate rendering, as Kockroach surely knows, but close enough to leave no doubt of what it is.

Kockroach rubs a finger across his teeth, twists his ears.

"Irv," yells the woman at the front counter in a voice that resembles the screeching of a cat with a truck parked on its tail and which Kockroach finds positively lovely. "Is someone here looking for a job."

Her blond hair is piled atop her head like a hornet's nest. She rubs a stick across one of her fingernails. The mounds on her chest are astounding.

"Mr. Brownside is busy," says the woman.

Kockroach leans over the front counter and takes the woman's hand in his own. She tries to tug it away but he holds it fast and brings it to his lips. He licks the middle finger lightly with the dry tip of his tongue.

"What did you go and do that for?"

"I couldn't help myself, sweet pea."

"Well, don't do it again."

He does it again, sees her eyelids flutter. Still holding her hand, he says, "What is your name?"

"Cassandra, with a *C*."

"That's a pretty name. What do you do here, Cassandra, with a *C*.?"

"I'm the receptionist."

"I mean you and Mr. Brownside."

"None a your frigging business. What are you, some sort of gumshoe for his . . . Oh, you don't mean . . . Well, jeez, didn't you see the sign? We're the Brownside Extermination Company. We get rid of bugs."

"Get rid of bugs? How?"

"How do you think? We exterminate them."

"What does that mean?"

"It means you don't want to be no bug around Irv."

"Do you like wine, sweet pea?"

"What does that got to do with exterminating?"

"Let me in to talk to Mr. Brownside and you'll find out."

"What if I don't want no wine?"

"Then we'll drink champagne."

"What if the bubbles set me sneezing?"

"I'll get you a tissue and pour another glass."

"What if I ain't interested?"

He lowers his head, lets his tongue roll out its full ungodly length before gently brushing once again her finger with its tip.

"Irv," she screeches. "Youse got a visitor."

"It ain't so easy as it looks," says Irv Brownside, rumpled and unshaven, big-bellied, big-jawed, wearing a filthy brown coverall. His desk is piled with papers, journals, files, invoices, cans of poison, a thick pastrami sandwich. His work boots sit atop his desk, alongside his feet in their dirty woolen socks. He leans forward, picks up his sandwich, leans back, takes a bite. "You don't just go in and spray. Oh it looks good, you in your uniform with the tank on your back, but when those little buggers they're back that night it's hell to pay. You want to kill 'em, you got to think like 'em. Not just any crack will do. They like it warm, they like it tight, they like it moist."

"Don't we all," says Kockroach.

“What? Oh yeah, right. Good one. You got any

guy, huh? Is that why the smile?”

“I always smile.”

“I don’t like funny guys. Funny guys like to talk instead of work.”

“I like to work.”

“You don’t seem the type.”

“I’m a fool for work.”

“Look, if you got no experience, I can’t use you. I don’t got time to train. Fill out a form, and if things change, I’ll maybe give you a call.”

“No forms.”

“Everyone’s got to fill out a form. We need your numbers. The government and all.”

“No forms.”

“No forms?”

“No numbers.”

“What are you, on the lam?”

“Rack of lamb.”

“Heh? Oh yeah, again with the funny. So you’re talking something off the books. No taxes, no withholding, none of that Social Security bullcrap. Cash.”

"Perfect."

"And with everything in cash—" he rubs an eyebrow—"you'd be expecting less than minimum, I suppose. Ain't that so?"

"So."

"And you think you can think like them little buggers?"

"I'm sure of it."

Brownside takes a bite of his sandwich, swings his feet from the desk, pushes out of the chair, ambles off into a closet. He brings back a black chest the size of a small suitcase. He opens the chest on the desk. Inside rests an empty cage with a steel frame, wire-mesh sides, a small latched door.

"How many roaches in this city?" he says. "A hundred million or so? Bring me back just fifty and you got the job. Just a measly fifty. It should be the easiest thing in the world, but you got to know where to look. We open at seven. Show me at seven that you know where to look and I'll give you the job."

"No problem."

"Don't be so sure of yourself. Sixteen years in this business I been sending rooks out with that case and not a single one came back with more than twelve. Even pros can't find twenty, nine times out of ten. It's funny how when you don't want them it's all you can find, and when you're looking you can't find a one. Still think you can handle it?"

"Piece of cake," says Kockroach.

Kockroach waits outside the Brownside Extermination offices with the black chest gripped in his hand. He has been waiting since before dawn [illegible]

about how the thoughts now don't ever stop and leave him be. It doesn't make him better, this curse of thought, of that he is certain, but it does make him different. And why, he wonders, should that difference make a difference?

He thinks about the members of his colony, their hungers, their fears. Cockroaches do whatever they need do to survive. They would eat him if they had the wherewithal to bring him down and teeth sharp enough to chew the meat off his bones. That he is ready to do the same to them is only proof of the continuing purity of his cockroach nature.

But why must he even try to justify his actions to himself when greed and fear were justification enough before? If only the woman in the bank had given him an opportunity, he wouldn't be here, now, beneath this sign, with the case in his hand. That too is something new, along with thought comes what? Regret? He has no doubt about what he is going to do, and yet still he thinks of the reasons why, as if the reasons mattered. This thinking, he thinks, is like a sickness, only you can't squeeze it out with your morning crap.

A boxy brown van drives to the front of the office and shudders to a stop. On the side of the van is an identical sign to that atop the small building, with an identical drawing of

an arthropod. Irv Brownside steps out of the van holding a steaming mug and a bag, wipes his mouth, checks his watch.

"You are an eager beaver, ain't you?"

Brownside doesn't wait for a reply. He unlocks the door, steps around the counter and into his office. Kockroach follows.

"Cassie don't come in till eight-thirty," he says when he is seated behind the pile on his desk. He clears a spot in front of him and papers flutter to the floor. He puts down the mug, reaches into the bag, pulls out six donuts, one after the other, lays them on a stack of invoices, licks his finger. "What'd you say your name was again?"

"Blatta. Jerry Blatta."

"What is that? Italian?"

"Greek."

"Son of a bitch. All right. Show me what you got."

Kockroach lays the chest on the floor, unsnaps the latch.

"It ain't so easy, I told you," says Brownside. "Didn't I tell you?"

"You told me," says Kockroach even as he lifts up the small steel cage and unlatches the door.

They fall in a torrent, a waterfall of brown, scurrying madly once they hit the pile, diving beneath the papers, climbing around the canisters of poison, swarming in thick piles over the donuts, hundreds and hundreds, dropping with audible snaps to the floor and dashing to the far walls and crevices.

Brownside jumps back for a second and then raises his gaze from the undulating desktop to Kockroach's face.

"Piece of cake," says Kockroach.

Brownside's unshaven face cracks into a

"Welcome aboard," says Brownside. "Let's get you a uniform."

Kockroach stands beside the brown van, outside a tall tenement with cracked windows and weeds sprouting through the brick.

He is wearing a brown coverall zipped to his throat with the crude drawing of a cockroach on the breast, brown gloves, brown boots, a brown baseball cap. His eyes are covered by goggles tinted yellow. Strapped onto his back is a heavy metal tank and in his gloved hands is a metal nozzle shaped like a gun with an extralong barrel. His smile is broad and white and pearly. He looks up at the building rising before him as if he were looking at his hope.

Irv Brownside stands beside him in an identical outfit, though not so well pressed.

"You ready to clean up Tombstone, Jerry?" asks Brownside.

"I'm ready, Irv," says Kockroach. "I've been ready all my life."

EMPIRE STATE

Eight years after, after it all went to hell, eight years after I came back to face the ghosts.

It was Champ what was driving the old '55 Packard over the Georgie W. and he wasn't none too happy about it, no ma'am. Far as he was concerned, he wanted nothing ever more to do with this burg. I knowed that because it's what he tells me while we're stalled in traffic smack in the middle of the bridge.

"I want nothing ever more to do with this burg," he says in his soft voice scarred forever from one too many jolts to the throat. "Look at it there, all towers and lights, leaning forward like a hungry southpaw, just waiting again to knock me on my keister."

"It wasn't the city," I says. "It was Izzy Berg and Fighting Paddy Conaghan what did the knocking."

"They were just the front men, Mick. It was the promoters, the cops, the managers, the cut men, the whole damn city. Slipping that shiv so clean across my brow I didn't feel a thing, ruining me just because I had the local Irish boy in the deep."

"You sure it wasn't a chop to the eye what started you to bleeding?"

"Whatever else I was, Mick, I wasn't a bleeder."

"Excepts for that night. Keep your eyes on the road."

"I hate this city. We've got no call to come to this city. What about we head to the coast?"

"Let me see what I need see, and if it ain't worth our while, then we'll blow."

"We could head out to Santa Cruz, buy a boat. Catch fish for a living."

"What do you know about catching fish?"

"They don't punch back, I know that. And it don't cost nothing to snatch them out of the ocean. It's like gold just floating around, waiting to be hooked and pulled in."

"With all we knows about fishing, we might as well throws a hook into a bathtub."

"I always wanted to own a boat. And what I heard about Santa Cruz, cheap rooms, cheap eats. Man can fish all day, fill his belly at night, and sleep sound in Santa Cruz."

"Things work out like I expect, Champ, we won't need to be watching our dimes no more."

"I miss old Chicago. Best damn hot dogs in the world in old Chicago."

"Well we can't go back to Chicago, now can we?"

"No we can't."

"You took care of that, didn't you?"

"Yes I did."

"Nedick's."

"What say?"

"Nedick's got good dogs. Or I'll take you up to Nathan's on Coney Island. Take my word, there's good dogs in New York."

“Better than Chicago?”

city always climbing the ropes for more. After the big blowup I had meant to take the train from New York all the way across to the far ocean, but when it stopped in Chicago, the thought of all them rolling prairies, them palm trees swaying and beaches filled with stuffed bikinis, all of it turned my stomach. I stepped out of the train into the grit of the big city, breathed in the industrial stench, and you know what it smelled like, missy? It smelled like mother’s milk, that pure. It smelled like home.

What would I do on a beach, all that sand getting in my Regal shoes, in my fedora, shining up my green suit? What would a guy like me do on a beach, I ask you that?

So I dusted off my suit and stayed, in Chicago. I found a small room with a bed and a sink on the North Side, close enough to the ballyard I could hear the yobs cheering through my window whenever Big Ernie, he parked one on Waveland Avenue, and that’s where I stayed to figure it all out between me and Hubert, which is where that lawyer he came in.

“Th-th-thank you for coming to see me, Mr. P-P-Pimelia,” he says, sitting at one end of the long conference table, desirous to keep his distance from something so distasteful as the likes of me sitting at the other. “I’m afraid we have some unpleasant b-b-business to which to attend.”

His name was McGreevy. He was tall and pale, with a sharp pointy nose. When he spoke his eyelids fell so low you couldn't see the green of his eyes. He wasn't much older than me, but still, with his pale skin, his black vested suit, with his long banker's jacket, he reminded me of the old-money Philadelphia I heard tale of when I was a boy but what I never got a whiff of firsthand, ancient, secret, wealthy, powerful, incestuous, grasping.

"It is your uncle, your dear Uncle R-R-Rufus, third cousin twice removed of your dear departed mother. I am grieved to inf-f-form you your Uncle Rufus has passed away. A tragedy yes. But as in many such tragedies, there is a b-b-benefit to the survivors. Uncle Rufus left a will."

McGreevy, the lawyer, he come along at a low point, that's for sure. It had been four years since I arrived in Chicago and things with Hubert and me hadn't gone so swell, no ma'am. First of all I had run out of money, and the little hustles I had undertaken, the tired scams, the small-time dealing, all of it had proven less than profitable and sent me to the slammer more than once. I was struggling, yes I was, struggling to even make the pitiful rent on my pitiful room. It got so bad I took a job, that's right, a job, bagging groceries, a job. How low had I sunk don't even ask 'cause that will tell you everything. And I was drinking too, and that's not a good thing because I'm not a drinker, never was, could never hold nothing, but I was drinking nightly at the corner tavern to fill the hole.

You see, Hubert, he scoops something out of you and leaves a hole, and you needs to fill it somehow, and I tried, first

enough, then Hubert again starts whispering in your ear and you get faster ideas, and a knife it ain't no longer just a knife and a gun it ain't no longer just a gun and a bottle of pills it's more than a bottle of pills, or maybe less is what I mean, less than anything, an invitation to nothing. And that's where I was when the letter came from McGreevy asking me to meet hisself in the Loop, in the legal offices of some bluenosed firm called Hotchkiss and Tate.

"The will is still in pr-pr-probate, Mr. Pimelia, and pr-pr-probate could last years, decades even. But we are prepared to advance you a sum to tide you over."

"How much of a sum?" I asks.

"A handsome sum, and there will be other payments in the future, so long as you don't in any way c-c-contest the distributions I make to you."

"I should just sit back and takes what you gives and ask no questions."

"Yes, that is exactly what you should do. And you'll need to sign a full agreement to that ef-f-fect, of course."

"And what if I does contest," I says. "And what if I hires my own three-piece suit to make sure I gets all that's coming my way. How do I know I'm not being played for the patsy

here? My dear dead Uncle Rufus, I loved the man like a father, I did, and the rest of the family was just ingrates. Maybe I'll decide to muck it up for everyone untils I get maybe even more than my fair share, like old Uncle Rufus would have wanted. What then?"

"Then our b-b-business," he says, "is at an end."

"I noticed your name, McGreevy, it ain't on the door."

"Hotchkiss and Tate is our local counsel."

"So where's your digs?"

"Think c-c-carefully before you decide."

"Tell me this, then. Where did dear old Uncle Rufus kick it for good? Philly? Where should I tell my lawyer to start digging?"

"If you d-d-decide to sign, I can be very helpful in the future. If you need anything, you can simply get in touch with Mr. Tate. If you d-d-decide not to sign, then I won't disturb you further."

"This is screwy. Something it ain't right."

"They say there is a p-p-pot of gold at the end of every rainbow, Mr. Pimelia, but the trick, as in everything in the world, is f-f-finding it."

I signed, course I did. And the payouts they came steady, just as McGreevy promised. And whenever I got the square idea of jumping out for more, it wasn't the paper I signed what stopped me, it was the memory of that bloodless bastard with the stammer telling me about rainbows and pots of gold like he hisself was the leprechaun what could make it all disappear and would, believe you me, of that I had no doubt.

But strangely, McGreevy, that pale bastard, he started me

care of us, that someone had cared, that did the trick. Funny how much Hubert he hates that.

I had questions, sures I did, but I buried them and went about my life. And with old Uncle Rufus's benediction I began to feel things I hadn't felt in a long time. Connected, is what I mean. I saw a kid in trouble and I was that kid in trouble and I helped him out with a dime or a dollar when I could. I'd look at a Joe struggling with something and I'd feel the strain and lend a hand so I could struggle with him. I wasn't no saint, believe you me, but I was feeling things again.

And then I found Champ. And he filled a hole even Hubert hadn't dug. And Chi-town, when it all slipped into place, became for me a different world where different dreams was dreamed in colors I never knew existed.

But Chicago was dead to us now, both of us, and we couldn't never go back, and so there we was, crossing the Hudson, heading into the Apple, another place that had died to me.

Rate I was going, Santa Cruz would be all I had left.

But first I was coming back to the big town, chasing my ghosts, coming home. Funny, ain't it? I grows up in Philly, spends eight years in the distant wilderness of the Midwest, yet it's New York what I still thought of as home. What did that Joe say, the Joe what wrote all those long sentences that fly around

like twittering birds and end up nowheres, didn't he say you can't never go home again? Well, maybe he was right, but there we was, the two of us, driving over the Georgie W., trying to make a liar out of him as I reached out for some shadow barely glimpsed in the midst of an apocalypse. You see, them questions I had buried had risen from the dead and it was time to finds some answers.

"Head south off the bridge," I says. "We'll check out first the Square."

The Square, Times Square, my square, ever the same and yet. And yet.

The signs, sure, still there, brighter than before, but different faces, different products being hustled to the mokes, different names on the movie marquees, half of them with sex in the title or tagline. "Raw Naked Violence." "Sex Without Shame." The whole scene filthier, seedier, sad. The Astor Hotel, the grand old dame of the Square—shuttered up for the wrecking ball. The Latin Quarter—all shot to hell. The Roxy, the frigging Roxy—gone. The life of the place had been chewed off by Sister Time.

I stepped in the Automat, the land of promise for me as a boy, but it too was changed completely. Once an elegant refuge full of promise, a direct link to the grand parade flowing outside its windows, now it was dirty, muted, inhabited by a bunch of low-life bums sitting miserably alone at the tables, no punch or laughter or thrilling sense of possibility.

"What are we doing here?" says Champ.

“I don’t know,” I

“Get away from me, you little scalawag. I got no time to waste on the likes of you.”

It was the loveliest thing I heard since we crossed the Hudson.

On the street, I met a hustler with his T-shirt and tight jeans and I asked about Tab, but alls I got was a drugged-out pout and a halfhearted come-on, more pathetic than enticing. The hookers was all strangers too. Not a one of our girls was still on the street. There had always been turnover, sure, that was the nature of the game, but I hadn’t noticed how relentless it was whilst I was in the middle of it. But in eight years it must have turned over a couple times or more. Still I took aside what girls I found and asked them some names. Blatta? What’s that? Abagados? Who? Fallon? Nothing. Who’s in charge now? I asked. A name I never heard of, a name I didn’t want to remember.

“You ever hear of Pinnacio?” I says, but not a one a them did.

The legends was all dead.

In the Paddock was a barkeep I never seen before, a broad bus with a bully boy’s face who eyed Champ a good long moment afore wising up and giving him a beer.

"Does a copper name of Fallon still come in here?" I asks.

"Who's asking?" he says.

"Just someone what used to work the Square is all."

"Who were you with?"

"Blatta."

"Never heard of him."

"Abagados."

"Never heard of him."

"The extent of what you ain't heard of would float the Hindenburg."

"I got nothing for nobody I never heard of. Get lost."

"Answer his question, Pops," says Champ with that soft ruined voice of his, "and we will."

The barkeep glances again at Champ, takes in his dark face, scarred and mashed, his ears engorged from rabbit punches, his neck thick from all that training, his huge hands laying still and heavy on the bar.

"There's an old wino comes in sometimes, begging for drinks," says the barkeep, talking to me but his eyes all the time on Champ, which was the way of it. "Goes on and on about how he used to be somebody before he starts the shouting and we need to toss him. He says he was a cop and once I heard his name, something like Fallon."

"Where can I find him?" I says.

The barkeep snorts. "Where do you think you find winos like that?"

It didn't take long. I had picked up a new line of work in Chicago. It was all part of that strange feeling I had that I

an office, set up a phone, hired a dame with attitude to answer it, and just like that I had my new line.

Mickey Pimelia, P.I., licensed and all.

Fallon wasn't hard to find for a licensed gumshoe. He was holed up in a sad sagging flophouse on the Bowery, a fleabag called the Sunshine. I bought him a sandwich, what kind didn't matter, he probably couldn't taste the difference no more, and a jug of rotgut wine, anything harder he wouldn't be able to stomach, and Champ and me, we walked past the suspicious eyes of the night clerk and climbed the hotel's stairs to pay our respects.

The stench was enough to stagger you, piss and puke and crap like it was rubbed along the walls, the rot of ages. Cockroaches climbed the banisters and clung to the ceiling.

"Go away," was the response to our banging from the other side of the door.

"I'm looking for Fallon," I said, "Lieutenant Nick Fallon, Vice."

Pause. "He's dead."

"I'm an old friend."

"He doesn't have any."

"I got some food and some wine for him."

"Keep it," says the voice, but then we hears the sag of bedsprings and the shuffle of feet and the door it opens.

"Mite," says Nick Fallon when he gets a good look at me out of his rheumy eyes. "You look like dick."

"But you, Lieutenant, you're the goddamn queen of England."

He glances at Champ, back at me, raises his eyebrows, takes the wine out of my hand.

"You don't wants the sandwich?" I says.

"What do you take me for?" he says.

Think of a balloon, all pumped up and proud, its belly sticking out with the authority of the inflated, that was Lieutenant Nick Fallon, Vice, when I knew him when. He was inflated by his position, by his arrogance, by his secret ambition to out-Broderick Johnny Broderick and become a legend hisself. But then the air leaks out as it always leaks out until the balloon is only a ghost of what it was. That was Fallon now, in his ragged suit pants, his filthy undershirt, the sockers with his toes sticking out. He had aged a quarter of a century in the eight years I was away, disheveled hair white beneath the grease, bristly gray beard, skin a haggard sack of wrinkly white rubber hanging off his bones. A deflating balloon with only the final desperate hope that if it drinks enough it will shrink all the way to nothing.

"Oh, Mite, it was something it was, when that warehouse blew into the sky." We weren't so much in a room as in a closet, with only a bed, a locker, and one bare bulb hanging through a chicken-wire ceiling. Fallon was lying on his side

"The greatest piece of crime fighting ever to hit this town. Wiping out four crime organizations at once. Front page of every tabloid. 'Fallon's War,' they called it. But it wasn't just mine, was it, Mite? Have a drink with me."

"No thanks."

"Old times."

"Get that out of my face."

"Afraid of my little germs?"

"Your germs they the size of small dogs. I can hear them barking."

He smiles, takes another long pull of the wine.

"You find all the bodies?" I ask.

"Most."

"You find Blatta's?"

"I said most."

"But not Blatta's?"

Fallon shrugs. "Gone. Disappeared. Poof. Maybe incinerated, maybe not, who knows? Who could know? Except it wasn't just his body that disappeared."

"Talk to me."

"Where'd you go off to anyways?"

"Fiji."

"Fiji, huh? That where you found Queequeg over there?"

"Watch your mouth."

"Don't be sore, Mite. I just see you found your game after all."

"Talk to me about Blatta."

"Sure, Mite. Don't be so touchy. Was a time you'd eat any crap I'd serve."

"It's a new day, palsy."

"You don't need to tell me. When the Square was still my territory, I kept a file on every hood whose name I even heard whispered. Had a file on you inches thick and a file on your boy Blatta too. There wasn't much there, no one talked about him, it was mostly rumor and a stray piece from a snitch here or a whore there. He was more like a ghost than anything else, with the way you were protecting him. Some in the department even thought he was someone you made up on your own to project some authority. But I had seen him coming out of that hotel of his, heading to his car, I knew he wasn't a ghost. And then, after my victory, he disappeared like the rest of them. No body, but no Blatta either. Case closed, right? File sent to storage and life moves on.

"So one day I'm out of the territory, me and a dame are celebrating, a real special dame, a high-priced hooker doing a pal a favor, which was why I was where I was. This is three or four years after, understand. I'm on the Upper East Side, strange place the Upper East Side, and I was heading down to the El Morocco, and I see this big brown limo slip up the street. The driver has an eye patch and he looks familiar and that's what draws my attention first. And then I notice the

room, the morgue, to pull his file and word comes back there isn't a file. How can that be? I made it myself. I send a request to the morgue for yours, since you two were so tight, and yours isn't there either. So I pull the whole Abagados file, the whole thing. My desk is covered with paper, and I go through it page by page, the first time anyone's looked at it since it all went down, but it wasn't the first time anyone's looked at it since it all went down. See, someone else had combed through it with a razor blade and every mention of Blatta or you had been sliced out so neat you wouldn't have known it had ever been there unless you were the guy that put it there in the first place, understand? Far as the department knew, you and Blatta, the two of you never existed."

"Who could do something like that?"

"Someone with the pull of an elephant. It takes pull to get hold of a file from the morgue and take it to a place where you got time to razor it clean. The same kind of pull it takes to haul my ass before the Police Corruption Commission, to get six witnesses to testify to everything I ever done which was hunky and not dory, and then to strip me of my rank, my job, my pension, my life. That kind of pull. Which is how I ended up here, in this lovely abode. Sure you don't want a drink?"

"Revenge for what you did at the warehouse."

"No," said Fallon. "You're not getting it, are you? I didn't end up on Bowery Row because of what I did at the warehouse. I ended up here because I happened to glimpse a face in a window."

"Jesus."

"And if he could do that to me, Mite, for just glimpsing his face, imagine what fun he's going to have with you."

Yonkers in the twilight.

Sounds like a swing-band ballad, don't it? *Yonkers in the twilight, dancing cheek to cheek.* What's the matter, missy, you don't like my chops? As if Louis Armstrong's got a voice of velvet.

We was parked on a hill, Central Avenue down to our left, the Bronx River down to our right, and we was waiting. In front of us sat a lovely white house with a picket fence. Cooney's old house. My old house, except it wasn't really my old house, first because it wasn't really never my house since I never lived there, and second it wasn't my old house, like in something that had passed away long ago, because my name, imagine that, was still on the deed. A life estate, the clerk said, which meant it was mine until I died. But I hadn't paid no taxes on it, had I? And yet the taxes they was paid. And I hadn't been up on the ladder painting that siding, had I? Yet the house it was still all nice and white.

"So who paid them taxes?" I asks the property clerk, a tenner slipped along with the question to grease the wheels of information.

"The reversionary party," he says.

"What the hell does that mean?" I asks.

"The party to whom the property reverts after the death of this Mickey Pimelia listed on the deed."

"And who might that be?" I asks.

[illegible]

Can you smell him, missy? Can you? I could, [illegible] bloodhound. I was on his trail, I was getting closer, and the blood scent it was coursing through me like a drug. It was only a matter of time afore the Boss and me we was finally, after all these years, once again face to face.

"What are we doing here, Mick?" asked Champ.

"Just want to see who's been living in my house."

"I mean in this city, this state. Didn't you hear what that wino said? He wasn't jiving us, Mick. This Blatta of yours, he ruined that cop just for catching his face. Can't imagine what he's going to do with you once you track him down."

"He's going to give me a hug and wrap a mink round my shoulders."

"Don't you start getting all biblical on me, Mick. Had enough preaching when I was a boy to know life doesn't work out like the stories. Lazarus isn't rising, and those we betray, they don't give us minks."

"You singing the blues, Champ?"

"Who has the right if I don't, Mick, tell me that. Who the hell more than me has the right?"

I first met Champ in an uptown Chicago joint when I was looking for some muscle in the new line I was trying. I asked him to tag along to some West Side motel one night and he came in mighty handy when the mark didn't like me taking that flash picture of him and his secretary tied all in knots. The mark, he lunged, but afore he could get his mitts on the camera, Champ grabbed him by the neck so tight the mark's yard near popped. Then I knew, Champ, he was just what I needed. See, most gumshoes carried a gun, but I never thought guns made much sense. You bring out a cannon and someone's liable to start shooting. I had firsthand experience where that ended, with me on a roof watching the world go mushroom. Hell with that. Champ, he kept things clamped down cool. One look at Champ and even the most pissed-off Joes, they settled into reason.

After that first night, Champ he was by my side whenever I stepped into the night to do any detecting and I was in his corner in the dusty prairie arenas where his title dreams falled and rised and falled again. In Champ I suppose I had found more of the muscle on which I relied account of my size. My fate was ever my fate, by my lonesome I was not near enough, and it was the same in the Midwest as it was in the East, excepting with Champ it was different. First off, with Champ I was in charge, it was my name painted on the door. My name, my license, my line. I was the one making the decisions for once and I liked that, I liked that fine.

And second off, well, yeah it was different all right. It

wasn't like the hard pure thing I felt for Celia. And it wasn't like the desperate empty thing I felt with Hubert, which I got [illegible] hell of a relief. What with my Uncle Rufus's

their place, don't you think, but better late than never.

So things was jake, with Uncle Rufus's money and with Champ by my side, things was oh so jake. I had no reason to want to leave Chicago, no reason to heed the faint calls I was hearing from the past. Until, in the middle of a case, I found a kid with a strange welt on his arm and I looked at it closer and it was a burn, perfectly round like the tip of a cheap ten-cent cigar. Champ took care of the cigar smoker, worked him like the heavy bag hanging from the ceiling of the gym, whilst I stood back and watched it all with a satisfaction that was more personal than ever it should have been. But the cigar smoker turned out to be a cop, and the other cops they didn't want to hear about no burns on some skinny waif's arm. So that was it, goodbye Chicago.

"Ever feel, Champ," I said as twilight in Yonkers descended into evening in Yonkers, "like someone's watching over you?"

"Over my shoulder, sure. The cops, waiting for one wrong move to bust me proper."

"Well, someone's been watching over me. You know that money I keep getting from my dead Uncle Rufus?"

"Good old Uncle Rufus."

"I gots the suspicion, Champ, that he ain't dead and he ain't my uncle and his name it ain't Rufus."

"Whoa, Mick, looky there. Is that who we're waiting on?"

I leans forward in the Packard. There are two figures heading down the sidewalk, hand in hand. I can't see their faces, just their silhouettes, heading down the sidewalk and then turning up the little stone path that led to Cooney's house. One is a child, a boy, stocky and thick, his arm raised up to hold the hand of the other. And the other, well the other there was no doubtsky aboutsky. It was that walk, who could ever mistake that walk.

"That's the one," I says.

"You sure you want to be doing this, Mick? No telling what kind of damage you could end up causing."

"The only thing I ever been sure of, Champ, wheresever I go, disaster it follows sure as blood from a wound."

We walked side by side together up the sidewalk, Champ and me, and then we turned into the stone path. This was something I knew I had to do, but even so my step slowed as I approached the house. My house. I had once felt the person inside to be the most important person in my life, someone I believed to be the fulcrum around which my life swayed and tottered. It's not so easy running away from that and not so easy coming back to it again.

"We can turn around now," says Champ. "Let's say we turn around now, fill up the tank, hightail it out of this burg. What about Nogales?"

"You never been to Nogales."

“Be on your best behavior,” I says as I punch the button. “And smile. We don’t wants to scare the kid.”

We waits a while, a while longer. I rings again and then the footsteps, the footsteps, and the door opens, and despite my best intentions my heart it takes a leap. It takes a leap, yes it does. It don’t matter what we are, the heart it’s a strange thing, inexplicable as life itself. It takes a leap and then it settles and I wait as comes first the gasp and then the face in front of me composes itself into a mask of stunned surprise.

“Mite?”

“Hello there, Celia,” I says. “It turned out to be Yonkers for you after all, now didn’t it?”

19

The night of Mite's reappearance after eight long years, Celia dreamed of the Empire State Building.

In the dream, she hovered over the art deco tower, jaunty and impossibly high, as it danced to the music of some riotous jazz band, twisting its upper-floor windows into a smile, whistling out its piercing crown, snapping to the music with cartoon fingers at the end of stick arms. The shimmying skyscraper, swelling and bopping to the rhythm of the trumpet's Dixieland beat, filled her with joy and fierce longing, emotions so powerful they blistered her heart. And then the skin of granite and glass began to peel away from the top of the tower in one elastic piece, like a sheath being pulled back, and what she saw being revealed was monstrous and dark and she woke with a start.

Well now, thought Celia, catching her breath as she lay next to her husband, Gregory, who snored gently. Not so hard to figure that one out, is it? No need to call in Freud to make sense of that.

"How'd you end up here, in Yonkers?" asked Mite after she invited him and the huge Negro with the scarred face, named Champ, into her house, and spent an awkward time in small talk. Gregory was in a faculty meeting at the college,

from seeing Mite after all these years. But she needed one, she decided, definitely, and she half filled a second glass. "Gregory found the house and brought me here and instantly I loved it. There's some financial arrangement Gregory worked out. Through the college, I think. I don't know how he does it, but he's a genius like that."

"I'll bet he is," said Mite.

"And a small inheritance I received helps," she said as she walked the drink over to Champ, who was sitting next to Mite on the coach.

"That was sure a lucky break," said Mite.

"It was. I love it here," she said, taking a sweet burning sip. "Norman is in third grade now. I walk him to school, just down the road. And there's a small park just the other way, and the neighbors."

"You ever hear from Blatta?"

"Jerry? No, of course not. Didn't you know? You had to know. He died. In the thing. I thought for sure you knew. I was just so happy to hear from that grubby little policeman that you were okay. Mite, tell me what happened. How did you escape?"

"I wasn't in that warehouse when it went down. I was tipped before, you see."

"And Jerry?"

"He wasn't."

"Wasn't what?"

"Tipped."

"Mite? You didn't tell him? Mite? You let him go in there, all the time knowing?" She felt something rise in her, a pain still so fresh it was as if it was only yesterday when the world exploded and a part of her was buried away forever. "Mite?"

"Call me Mickey," he said.

She looked at him, took a swallow from the drink, tried to fight back the emotion, succeeded, because that was what she had become so accomplished at over the last eight years, drinking and fighting back her emotions.

"That was a long time ago," she said finally.

"No it wasn't," said Mite. "I can still smell the smoke."

"Are you sure you don't want anything? Champ, are you hungry? I have cheese and crackers and some grapes. How does that sound?"

"That sounds jimmy, ma'am."

"Good, just give me a minute."

She was headed into the kitchen when Mite said, "He didn't die, Celia."

She stopped without turning. "Who?"

"You knows who. He didn't die."

She spun. "Of course he did."

"It's my house, this house. It's my name on the deed, you can check it for yourself. You didn't get it through no college. He pays the taxes and he made sure you got it for nothing. You had to suspect, ending up in this house, in Yonkers. This

glass and steel. But the monstrosity in her dream wasn't inside the building, she knew, no matter what Freud would have said about it. The dark thing she glimpsed beneath the skin of the building was herself, as she might have been had not everything in her old life gone to a fiery hell.

And yet, like a phoenix, from the ashes she had been reborn into what now she was. Everything her mother had always wanted for her, a husband who supported her, a child whom she adored, a beautiful house with a picket fence, all of it had come into her life. Respectable. That was what she had become, against all odds, and she owed it all to Gregory.

She had gone to him after all of it was over, had gone to him as if just to talk, but all the time hoping that he would save her, and he did, exactly that. Gregory. Without any questions or lectures. The arrogance had somehow been burned out of him in the years after she had sent him packing from the apartment. Gregory. Still the idealist, but more practical than ever she could have imagined. He knew what to do right away. The quick civil ceremony, the new place with room for a nursery, the introductions to the junior faculty at the college. And he did it all without making her feel that he was doing her the greatest favor of her life, even if he actually was. He did it all as if he were doing it out of love, imagine that. It would have been easier if he had turned out like so many of the other professors he worked with, if he drank too much and stomped around like the second coming of Hegel and slept with his young and pretty research assistants, it would have been a relief. Then they would have been even. But he didn't. He was the perfect husband, the perfect father, a more attentive lover th

and she didn't, truly, know why she was there. Just to be sure one way or the other, she told herself. Her son deserved that, at least, she told herself. She would only go as far as she needed to find out if it was true, she told herself.

"What if he's not so happy to see us, Mick?" said Champ, who stood like a scarred ebony pillar on the other side of Mite.

"Oh, he'll be happy," said Mite. "He'll be bursting his buttons, he will. It's why he took care of us all these years. He was waiting for us to return."

"You think?" said Celia.

"No doubtsky aboutsky," said Mite.

The very scent of the lower offices of Brownside Enterprises, on the eighty-ninth floor of the Empire State Building, raised the thin black hairs on the back of her neck. The elevator had taken off so fast it was as if a part of her had been left behind in the rise and maybe that was the main cause of her vertigo. But there was also the faint scent of raw animal power that worked on her emotions like a memory. It floated here among the pretty girls with their perfect legs, busily typing at desks arrayed in neatly ordered rows and columns in the middle of

the floor. It floated among the executives in their suits, bustling in and out of glass-walled offices ringing the floor. And it seemed to flow down the broad staircase that reached grandly from this floor to the next, from this level of worker bees to something high up in the reaches of power.

The buttons of the elevator had gone straight from 89 to 91.

Before the stairs sat a woman in a dark suit, cold and perfect, as if carved from alabaster. There was no typewriter on her desk, just a single flower in a fluted vase and a single phone. Behind her stood a guard with a gun on his hip. The woman at the desk smiled stonily at the three of them as they stepped off the elevator.

"Can I help you?" said the woman at the desk.

"What's upstairs?" said Mite.

"Executive offices."

"That's where we're going."

"Do you have an appointment?"

"No appointment," said Mite.

"Then I'm sorry," she said with a firm smile, "but no one is allowed up without an appointment."

"How abouts you gets us an appointment?" said Mite.

"That is not possible. I am not authorized to make appointments."

"Then why don't you call up on that phone of yours and gets the authorization?" said Mite. "Tell them we're here to see Blatta."

The woman looked at the three of them for a moment and then opened her desk drawer, took out a small book, paged through it. "There is no Mr. Blatta listed, Mr. . . ."

“Pimelia, but he’ll know me as Mite.”

his hand slipped onto the grip of his gun.

Quick as a clap, Champ grabbed the guard’s arm with one hand and the holstered gun with the other and lifted the guard slightly into the air so it was impossible for the gun to be drawn.

The guard flailed about for a moment.

“Easy now, Pops,” said Champ in his low growl.

Mite stepped toward the desk, sat on its edge, raised the handset of the phone. “About that appointment,” he said.

Celia’s skin began to itch at the way the woman blanched.

A man came down to get them, a stocky man in a chauffeur’s uniform and chauffeur’s peaked cap. He walked with a limp, wore a black eye patch over his left eye.

“Well, well, well,” said Mite. “Look who it is. I see Uncle Rufus found you too, hey, Istvan?”

It was only then that Celia recognized the man with the eye patch as Jerry’s former driver, who eight years before had come with the message from his boss that had started everything.

“Good morning, Mr. Pimelia,” said Istvan. “You too, Miss Singer.”

“Hello, Istvan,” she said softly. “It’s Mrs. now.”

"Very good."

"Looks like you survived the worst of it, huh, palsy?" said Mite.

"This way, please," said Istvan in a dry voice, before turning toward the stairs and starting up again.

Champ eased the guard down, gently let go of his arm, brushed away the palm mark on his sleeve. Then Mite and Champ, with Celia behind, followed Istvan up the stairs.

The smell grew stronger as they rose, furry, more animal than human, of some great power waiting to be unleashed. The scent flushed through her as if injected straight into her veins. The itch in her skin increased, her heart started kicking beneath her breast.

He was here, she could sense it in every nerve. The presence of Istvan proved it even further. There was no reason to go on, she should turn away, now. And yet she didn't.

They were in a dark imposing space, all wood paneling, with maroon leather chairs like in some fussy old men's club. Istvan led them to a reception desk next to a set of large double doors. The woman behind the desk was pretty, with high blond hair and huge breasts. The nameplate on her desk read: C. Peppers. Behind her was a portrait of a greasy-looking man with an unshaved face and a bemused smile. The bronze plaque under the portrait read: IRVING BROWNSIDE—FOUNDER.

"And how can we help you today?" said C. Peppers, her screech of a voice wildly out of place in the powerful hush of the office.

"We's here to see Blatta," said Mite.

"Whom can I tell them is here and what can I tell them is

the purpose of the visit?” She

The woman stopped writing on her pad to eye Celia carefully, her gaze riding down from Celia’s face to her waist to the brace on her leg. She seemed relieved to see it and then looked back up with a breath of pity on her face.

So, thought Celia, that’s how he has been entertaining himself.

“We just came to wish him Happy New Year is all,” said Mite.

“It’s May,” said the woman with the high hair.

“So maybe we’s a little late, but like my momma always said, it’s the sentiment what matters.”

“My mother wasn’t much on sentiment,” said the woman. “She preferred diamonds. All right, wait here and I’ll see what I can do.”

Celia watched as the woman ripped a sheet off her pad, stood, smoothed out her skirt. The blond woman had high heels, and she walked so that she led with her breasts, like a battleship with two great prows. It had been years since Celia felt what she felt as she watched the woman walk to the double doors: envy, bitterness, the strange competitive desire to rip the woman’s face off and stuff it down her cleavage.

Whoa, where did that come from?

It was the scent, the dream, the sight of Istvan, the way Champ and Mite abused the woman and her guard on the floor below, it was in the very possibilities that had been raised by Mite's visit. Whatever civilizing had happened to her in the last eight years as a faculty wife and mother in the suburbs had been stripped from her as quick as a snap of the finger. Whose finger? His, of course.

It was time to leave, this was too much for her. Go, she told herself, run away. You have a son, a husband, a family, a life. Run while you can, she told herself, but it was as if the paralysis rose from her leg to overtake the whole of her body as she watched the woman step softly to the large double doors, knock lightly, and push one of them open.

In the moment the door swung wide, Celia caught a glimpse of the room inside. It was large, huge, with a great granite table in the middle and a huddle of men around the table, a strange huddle, like a swarm of insects crowding around something, a huddle of drones dancing and circling and serving the master. And then one of the drones in the huddle lifted his face and stared at the woman in heels and then stared through the doorway at the three of them, stared at her. And in the instant before the door was closed she recognized the face.

Pale skin, pointy nose, lidded green eyes. McGreevy. The lawyer. Her dead uncle's lawyer.

She almost fainted at the sight. The scent, the height of the building, the emotions, everything weakened her. She put a hand on the desk to steady herself and then backed up to one of the chairs and collapsed into it. It was too much, everything was too much. She should never have come, never.

"Mr. Mite," said the woman in her screetch. "Mr. Champ. I can bring you in now."

"What about me?" said Celia in someone else's voice, a little girl's voice, some strange orphan girl afraid of being left behind.

"Not now," said the woman, "but we may be in touch," as if Celia had just failed her job interview and was being told that, no, they would never be in touch.

Mite gave her a chuck on the arm. "I'll put in the good word for you, Celia," he said, "don't you worry," and then he and Champ and Istvan followed the woman into the room. The door closed solidly behind them all, leaving Celia alone.

20

Kockroach can feel it in his bones. Mite is close, closer, Mite will soon be within his grasp.

He sits at the granite table as his employees move in a flurry about him. Before him on the table are papers, files, photographs. He listens to what they tell him, he signs his name where they tell him to sign, he sits quietly while they plot and plan around him. It isn't lost on him that what used to be done by Mite alone now takes dozens. Of course the operation is far bigger, the possibilities of growth in business are endless and Brownside has been growing like a weed from the moment Kockroach sprayed his first building and murdered his first colony. But still he remembers how it was, just him and Mite running the Square together. There were no papers then, no teams of lawyers and bankers and agents. Just money.

Until Mite betrayed him and blew it all into the sky.

But now Kockroach is in the world of business, and business, Kockroach has learned, is all about information. His lines of informants spread throughout the country like great antennae, keeping data flowing from the farthest reaches into his headquarters. And his informants have kept him apprised of Mite's progress.

The lawyer Tate, in Chicago, informed McGreevy of the

Gladden of the visit to Fallon's room by the little man in green and his huge friend. The title clerk in Yonkers earned his envelope by informing Gladden the moment anyone asked about the small white house which is owned by one Mickey Pimelia in a life estate.

And now Mite is getting closer, so close Kockroach's ears begin to twitch.

He hears something, just a rustle of a disturbance, but it grabs his attention. As his men continue their work all about him, he leans forward. Footsteps rising up the stairs, stopping at Cassandra's desk, a conversation. The words are muffled but the cadence of one of the voices is shockingly familiar. He is startled at the excitement he feels, like the buzz before mating. Or before squeezing the life out of a human throat.

The door opens, Cassandra enters, closes the door behind her, walks quietly to the table, leans over to whisper in his ear.

"There is a man called Mr. Mite here to see you," she says. "Istvan says you know him."

"Yes," says Kockroach.

"And someone called Mr. Champ."

"Send them in," says Kockroach.

"And a woman called Celia."

Kockroach lets out a gasp that quiets the room.

He had been expecting Mite and his associate, but he had not been expecting Celia. Leave it to Mite to always arrive with a surprise. His head turns left, right, as if he is trapped in a maze and searching for a way out. He spies the wall of windows staring out over the rooftops of the city and imagines himself spreading his wings and flying to safety.

The men surrounding him all stare. McGreevy steps forward.

"Is everything all right, Mr. Blatta?"

"Celia is outside."

"Yes, I saw her. She is with Mr. P-P-Pimelia."

"I don't want her here."

"That's fine, Mr. Blatta," says McGreevy. "Cassandra, send the woman home, please. Tell her that m-m-maybe we'll be in touch in the future."

Cassandra nods and then makes her way out of the room. As she opens the door, Kockroach strains his neck to see outside. Framed in the doorway is a black dress, a heavy shoe. Fear spurts in the back of his throat and he can't help but duck before the door closes.

And then the door opens again.

Mite enters the room with his familiar lively stride, but Kockroach notices immediately that he is not the same Mite. He is older now, there are cracks around the edges of his face now. And he doesn't shift back and forth with an uncontained energy as he did before.

Alongside Mite is a human who is huge and dark and scarred

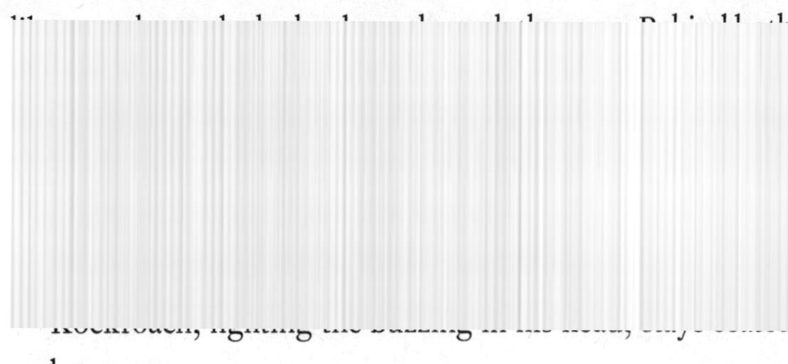

and stares.

"Long time no see," says Mite. "Looks like you done all right for yourself. What line you in, anyway?"

"Exterminations," says Kockroach.

"So you found your place in the world at last."

"Who's your palsy, Mite?" says Kockroach.

"Oh, I'm sorry. That was rude of me. Boss, this is Champ. He's with me now. Champ, meet my Uncle Rufus."

"It's a pleasure, Pops," says Champ.

"Do you think he can protect you?" says Kockroach.

"Do I need protection, Boss?"

"Everyone leave," says Kockroach. "Everyone but Mite."

The men surrounding Kockroach quickly gather their folders and papers before streaming out a door behind them. McGreevy stands still for a moment, raising his chin and staring down his long pointy nose at Mite before following the crowd and closing the door. On the far side of the room, Istvan opens the door to the reception area, but the big dark man doesn't move.

"It's okay, Champ," says Mite, patting one of the giant man's arms with his hand. "Go on out. Me and the Boss, we got things to talk about."

"Maybe I'll stay," says Champ. "Keep them waters calm."

"I bets they got some premium java in this joint," says Mite. "Go on out with Istvan. Have yourself a jolt. Don't worry yourself about me. The Boss and me are old friends. We just got some unfinished business, is all. Ain't that right, Boss?"

Kockroach, still seated, says nothing.

Istvan holds the door open for Champ, who bobs his head a couple of times as he takes a long look at Kockroach before turning and stepping through the door. Istvan closes the door behind them, leaving Kockroach and Mite alone in the huge conference room.

"What's on your mind, Boss?" says Mite.

Kockroach places his hands on the great granite table, presses himself to standing.

"Can't say you don't got the right to be sore," says Mite.

Slowly Kockroach walks around the table. His hands are still, his head is tilted.

"Here we are again, ain't we, Boss?" says Mite. "Just like on that trip up to Yonkers."

Kockroach closes in on Mite until he is looming over him, staring down through his dark glasses, his smile viciously in place. He can smell the fear, like the urine of a cat.

"How about a game?" says Kockroach.

Kockroach and Mite sit on either side of the granite table. The board is set between them, the pieces are arrayed in their lines of battle.

"You been playing much, Boss?"

a pawn. He plays the same as he ever played, with traps and feints, relying on his little pieces to control the board. Mite has a natural affinity for the pawn. His pawn positions used to bedevil Kockroach, but not anymore. With each combination of moves, Mite's lines of defense are swiftly being mauled.

"You've gotten better, Boss."

"I learned the trick."

"What trick?"

"The trick to everything. When you first taught me the ritual of chess, I thought it was all about the pieces on the board. Then I learned the pieces didn't matter."

"What does matter?"

"The human who's moving them. Find what he wants and give it to him, on your terms. That's beeswax. Check."

Mite stares at the board and then pulls his king out of trouble.

"How'd an exterminator end up in the penthouse, Boss, you don't mind me asking?"

"There were just two of us at the start," says Kockroach, "me and Irv, the human who gave me my opportunity in the world of beeswax. A company called us in about a bug problem in their factory. The company made shoes, wingtips. I always liked wingtips. The owners were squeamish about bugs. Imagine that. We murdered their cockroaches, but somehow a nest of rats found their way into the basement."

"Convenient."

"Things happen, Mite. And no matter how hard we tried, we couldn't kill them off. After a few weeks of rats running across their desks, the owners couldn't wait to sell, they even gave us the money to buy the factory. Suddenly we had two companies."

"Clever."

"It's all about information. You'd be surprised how much you can learn in the middle of the night, searching through the nooks of an office building, spraying poison wherever you go. Once I learned to read, the world of information opened up to me."

"You learned to read, Boss? Good for you. Who taught you?"

"Cassandra."

"The one with the melons, what sits outside?"

"She's smarter than she looks."

"God, I hope so."

"Wherever we sprayed, we learned just enough to know what they wanted and then we gave it to them."

"That the other guy's portrait hanging there in the reception room?"

"Irv."

"What happened to him?"

"His wife shot him."

"They tend to do that."

make more money in a week than we ever saw in a year in the Square. But one company never gets sold."

"What's that?"

"Brownside Extermination. Every now and then I still put on the goggles and the tank. You can never have too much information."

Kockroach moves a bishop.

"I think I'm in trouble here, Boss."

"More than you know," says Kockroach. "The ritual has made me stronger. I can see farther into the future now. And I learned the trick."

"So what is it that I wants?"

"To come home."

"What's the chance of that?"

"Check."

Mite rubs his chin and stares at the board. He blocks Kockroach's attack with his knight.

Kockroach pushes ahead his other bishop.

Mite squirms in his seat as his rook retreats.

Kockroach kills a pawn.

Mite pulls his king farther back.

Kockroach sweeps his queen across the board. "Checkmate."

Mite examines the board for a moment, topples over his king, then sits back and stares at Kockroach.

"You going to kill me now, Boss?"

"No, Mite, I'm going to hire you."

"I need information," says Kockroach.

In the conference room, the chessboard has been removed and replaced with a huge urn of ice and shrimp. The table is littered with shells, Mite's shells. Kockroach still eats his shrimp whole. Kockroach and Mite are leaning back in their chairs, smoking cigars. Kockroach sucks the smoke into his lungs in deep drafts. Mite coughs. The smoke billows about them like the steam in the schvitz.

"Information's good," says Mite.

"It is better than money."

"I don't knows about that."

"Information isn't something you put into a bank, it is what allows you to buy the bank."

"Do you own a bank, Boss?"

"Just a small one," says Kockroach, holding his cigar out in front of him, staring at the glowing tip. "I once looked for opportunity there. A woman sent me home because I couldn't fill out the form."

"What happened to the woman when you bought the place?"

"I promoted her."

"That's funny, Boss. You know, I got myself a new line."

"I heard."

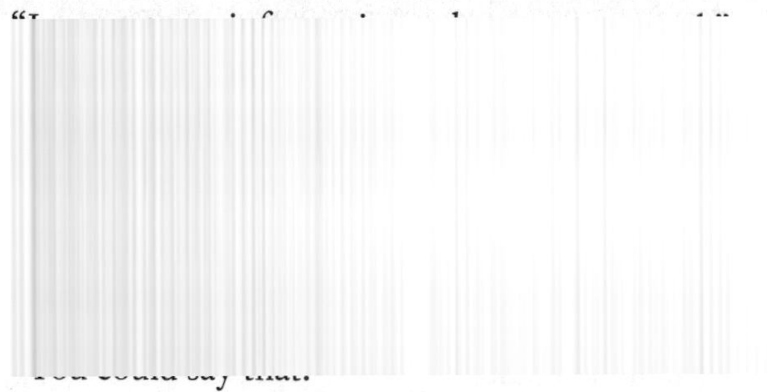

"The two of you can live in the house."

"What house?"

"My house. Istvan lives there. Cassandra. Now you and Champ."

"For a time, I suppose."

"So it is settled."

"What about Celia?"

"No," Kockroach says quickly. The same spurt of fear as before. "Not her."

"She's a good girl," says Mite. "She wants to see you. And she's got a kid now."

"I know."

"It wasn't she what betrayed you, Boss. It was all my doing."

"I know that, Mite."

"She just wants to see you."

"I don't work like that."

"Think about it, Boss. All this time she thought you was dead. When she heard you was still breathing she looked like she swallowed a goat."

"No."

"It's your call. But it don't seem fair to me."

"When was I ever fair?"

Mite frowns at his cigar. "Why ain't you wringing my neck right now for what I done?"

"I never expected anything different from you."

"And still you want me on?"

"Brother Mite."

"I'll be square from here in, Boss. I promise."

"Don't bother," says Kockroach. "We are what we are."

Kockroach, alone in the conference room after sending Mite to the house, stares out the wall of windows and thinks. He can't stop himself from thinking. It is the curse of this body.

He stands now high over the city, far higher than even the great smoking face in Times Square. From this vantage the city stretches like a chessboard before him. He can pick out the blocks he owns. That one, and that one, and that one with the tall building there. And the rest he wants to own. The world of business, he has learned, is a marvelous machine for feeding his greed. There are still those who feed his fear. The regulators who paw through his deals. The prosecutors who ask their questions. Fallon, a ruined drunk now but with continuing dreams of rising again to destroy him. It is not a place without fear, the world of business, but those who feed his fear are still without the power to bring him down. The world of business is as close to a perfect spot as a cockroach could ever hope to find.

And yet, it all does not feel the same to him as it once did. Working with Mite, cruising the Square in his brown

It is why he took care of Mite all these years, waiting like a patient spider for Mite to come home. And now he has. It is good to have Mite back, like old times, but something is still missing. Mite is back and his colony is growing and the world outside falls building by building under his dominion, but still something is missing. And the something that is missing has a name.

Celia.

He was willing to support her, but he wants nothing else to do with her, ever. The very thought of her fills him with an uneasy dread. She has a child now, a boy, and everything in Kockroach's being screams at him to stay away from a female and her nymph. It is why he reacted with such alarm when he learned Mite had brought Celia here, that she was outside this very room. And what about the boy? Was he here too?

The fear overwhelms him and he lets out a yelp.

The door opens, Istvan steps inside. "Is everything okay, Mr. Blatta?"

"Fine, Istvan," he says without turning from the window. Istvan quietly closes the door again.

Celia.

Kockroach had thought the world of business would give

him less opportunity for sex than the world of prostitutes and violence, but he was wrong. Money, he has learned, draws women like flies to feces. There is a parade of women into his bed, Cassandra of course, and the wives of his business opponents, and the girls Istvan finds for him in the Square, and the writers and the realtors and the ambitious young things. He is gorging on sex as he once gorged on gloop from the Dumpsters in the back alleys. What more could a cockroach want? But something gnaws at him.

Male cockroaches know only sex, they care nothing of the result, have no interest in the act of breeding. Clever as they are, male cockroaches still wonder where all these annoying white nymphs have come from as they go about their business of screwing every female in sight. But Kockroach has begun to imagine Celia's long pale body, and as he imagines it, in the ribbons of possibility that flow from the present to the future, he sees her eyes turn dark and her stomach swell.

And in those moments he can't help but think of the boy.

This is all wrong, this is a corruption of his character. He thinks of all the corruptions he has tolerated so far. The taste for roasted meat, the use of impersonal mass violence, the use of words, the curse of thought and its bastard cousin, regret. He has allowed himself to change so much, is this another change he must abide?

No, this is too much, a connection like this would alter him too fundamentally. This would be worse than thinking, he thinks. He must never allow Celia and her nymph back into his life.

And yet, as he stands before the window to look out at the

The door opens.

"Mr. Blatta?"

"Send in Cassandra," says Kockroach.

21

Celia moved through the days after her visit to the Empire State Building as if the dancing edifice had been the reality and it was her life that was the dream.

Yonkers felt as if it were deep underwater, slow, cold, colorless, distant. She stopped taking her afternoon walks, she resisted her husband's entreaties to perform the rudimentary duties of the faculty wife, no cocktails at the chairman's house, no dinner parties for the young bucks of the department. Gregory sat her down and told her he was worried that she had become depressed, but she didn't feel depressed, instead she felt detached. Nothing made an impression, the sidewalk beneath her feet, the laugh track on the television, the touch of her husband's hand on her arm. Only the golden flecks in the brown of her son's eyes seemed to burn with life. And it was her son, her lovely Norman, with the chubby limbs and mop of brown hair, that revealed to her the truth.

"Who are we hiding from, Mommy?" he said one afternoon.

"We're not hiding," she said.

"Then why don't we go out anymore?"

"We don't?"

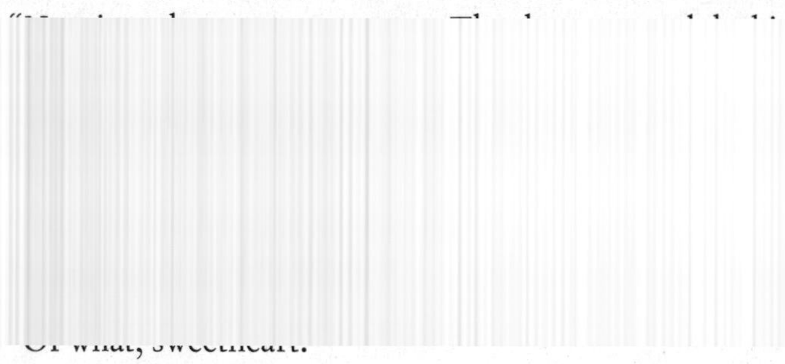

"Who were they, Mommy?"

"Old friends. Just that."

"I think it's good to hide. Sometimes at night I slip under my bed. I like it there for some reason. I feel safe."

"Norman?"

"But who are we hiding from, Mommy?"

Who indeed? Because Norman was right, she was hiding, and she realized now she had been hiding for the last eight years. And it wasn't from that grubby policeman who had given her the business after it all went to hell, and it wasn't from Mite or the other gangsters, and it wasn't from Jerry. She reached out and patted her son's hair and saw again the bright golden flecks in her son's eyes. It was a familiar color, that gold. When she closed her eyes she saw it, a streak of that same golden color, like a flaw running through her soul. It was this that she was hiding from, this part of her, this flaw. It had seemed to shrink in her years in Yonkers, it had blended in. She could almost imagine that it had disappeared, but no more. Now that golden flaw vibrated with color, it glowed as if on fire.

And what was it really? The thrill she felt from her proximity to the raw exercise of power? A sensuality that left her weak and clenched at the same time? A taste for shrimp? A desire for more than that of which she was capable of dreaming? How ridiculously shallow it all was, and yet. Take away the flaw and what was she? A mother, a wife, a daughter, a member of the PTA. Wasn't that just as shallow, to be nothing on her own, someone only defined by the others in her life. The one thing that was truly her own, the one thing that was truly her, was the flaw. And so maybe it wasn't a flaw after all, maybe it was the truest expression of her deepest yearnings.

Maybe what she had been running from all this time was her one true self.

The phone call came four weeks later in the middle of dinner. She had made a meat loaf with ketchup on top, mashed potatoes. She could barely muster enough energy to open the can of green beans. Gregory was talking about the most recent faculty meeting when the phone rang and she knew, immediately, what it was.

She stood, answered it, listened to the message. Then, pausing only long enough to depress the button and get a dial tone, she spun the dial of her phone, called the cab company, gave her address.

"I have to go," she said to her husband.

"Who was it?"

"I have to go," she said simply.

"Where are you going?" said Gregory. "Why? Who was it?" But by then he was talking to her back as she slowly climbed the stairs to the bedroom.

She wasn't up there debating, weighing her options, she wasn't trying to figure out what to do. Instead she pinned up her hair, applied the base to her cheeks, the blush, the

Gregory was demanding an answer, but he would never understand it if it came. It lay in that glimpse through the open doorway, in the huddle of the drones dancing and writhing around a source of great power. Dancing and writhing around him. That was where she belonged, there.

When the horn blared from outside, Gregory stood in the doorway, blocking her path. "I won't let you go," he said. "You're my wife."

"I'm going home," she said.

"This is your home."

"Why didn't you tell me how we got this house?"

"I did tell you. It's from the college."

"He came to you, the lawyer. He made you an offer."

"Celia."

"Tell me the truth for once, Gregory."

"The truth is I love you. And then the lawyer, he showed up at the college and gave us a beautiful house, rent-free. The only condition was that you shouldn't know. What was I supposed to do?"

"You were supposed to tell me. What else did he give you?"

"Nothing, I swear."

"Well, don't fret, dear. I expect you'll be getting something soon."

"It's happening again, isn't it?" he said. "After all I've done, you're doing it to me again."

"I am what I am."

"And what's that, Celia? What kind of woman runs away from her husband and child?"

She looked into his eyes, saw the pain, the fear. The sight filled her with both pity and triumph and the combination gave her a familiar thrill.

"Norman has school tomorrow," she said. "You'll have to take him and pick him up in the afternoon."

"Celia."

"I don't know when I'll be back."

On the way out, she leaned over to kiss her son goodbye. She thought she'd feel a tinge of guilt here, at this moment, but there was none. Was she imagining that the look in his eyes was full of understanding, as if he sensed what was happening, what was driving her, where she was heading, and what it would mean for both of them? Was she imagining that he wished he could go with her?

The address given her over the phone was on the Upper East Side. A large brownstone. It was Istvan, in his chauffeur's uniform, who opened the door. He smiled when he saw her. And behind Istvan stood Champ, wearing a tailored black suit, shiny black shoes.

"Lovely to see you again, Miss Celia," said Champ. "Welcome. I'm sorry that Mickey is out on business, he would love to have been here for you. Are you ready?"

peared from outside, three houses had been combined to create a single, glorious mansion, elegant and rich and shiny. The carpet beneath her feet was thick and red, the scent of the place was of polished wood and cigars. At the top of the steps, a long hallway led to the right, with a dark door at the end. She stepped slowly, almost reverently, toward the door, knocked lightly, closed her eyes.

It glowed white hot, her flaw. She could see it now in the darkness beneath her lids, watch it flow like a river of lava, widen, she could feel its heat. And slowly all the steady darkness around it burned away until it was no longer a flaw, until it was all there was in her soul. This, her.

She opened her eyes again and the door was now open and he was now before her. In a brown smoking jacket and ascot, in brown velvet pants and patent leather slippers. His dark glasses were on, his smile was bright. One hand held a cigar, the other was holding something large and pink and doused with thick red sauce. He raised it toward her.

"Shrimp?" he said.

She bowed her head, snapped a bite of crustacean in her teeth, passed him as she made her way into his bedroom.

22 Kockroach is ill at ease.

Possibly it is the outfit he is wearing, a cacophonous clash of stripes and diamonds, a riot of color that makes his skin crawl. Kockroach is only comfortable in brown, he has closets full of suits, racks and racks of them, all in brown. Brown wingtips, brown socks, brown hats, brown ties. Only the shirts are white. But today there is no brown on him, except for the shoes. He must admit he likes the shoes, the way they dig into the carpet, the way they crunch on cement. Yes, the shoes he very much likes, he should wear them all the time, but the rest of the outfit leaves him slightly nauseous.

It was Mite who bought these clothes for him, it was Mite who told him to put them on. "It's what the fat cats will be wearing out there, I'm telling you, Boss," he had said. And Kockroach had gone along. This wasn't pleasure, this was business. So he had put on the colorful socks, the short green pants that buckle below the knee, the yellow shirt, the vest, the hat, not his usual fedora but a slouchy herringbone cap. So maybe it is the clothes that have him ill at ease, but he doesn't think so.

He has felt this before, this unease, and is feeling it now, more and more often. Something has gone astray. For a while,

meeting. When something is not right in Kockroach's life, he knows what to do. He is a cockroach, he devours.

And today he will devour a company.

"Drive around the side," says Mite, leaning forward from the backseat to get a view.

They are somewhere in the country, everything is green and tidy. The building before them is overly grand, with a tall flagpole in the front. The Stars and Stripes. It is tasty, that flag, like a great cake ready to be eaten. The sight of it stirs his hunger.

Mite isn't wearing the funny colors, the stripes and diamonds, just his normal green suit. And Istvan, driving, is dressed in his normal uniform, and Champ, sitting beside Istvan in the front seat, is dressed in his normal black. Only Kockroach is wearing the ridiculous outfit. He knows in some animal species the strongest male is clad in the gaudiest finery. Maybe that is why Mite had him wear these clothes. So be it, if that is what it takes.

They are meeting today with a man named Gorman. Gorman is the boss of the company Kockroach wants to devour. This is supposed to be just a friendly face-to-face, Mite had

told him. Kockroach isn't sure what is friendly about a face-to-face. Business is business, the only question is whose face is going to get chewed off. Gorman started his company from a single dry cleaning store. Now he owns newspapers, magazines, a motorcycle factory. Gorman's cash flow, Mite has said, is like a great green river.

Cash flow. Kockroach has always loved those two words. The sound, the taste. Cash flow. It fizzles on the tongue like champagne.

"Keep going," says Mite.

"The drive ends here," says Istvan. "You want I should drive on the grass?"

"Why not? Let's announce our presence to the swells."

The car lurches as it drives over a curb and then rocks softly across the lawn, coming to a stop beside a closely mowed area with little flags all across its curvy surface. A number of men are bowing down with sticks in their hands, as if praying to the white round fetishes at their feet.

As Kockroach steps out of the car, all the men straighten and stare, their jaws dropping. Kockroach takes a cigar out of his pocket. Mite pulls out a lighter, flicks it alive.

"What do they do here?" says Kockroach, waving at the huge expanse of long green meadows and tall trees.

"It's a golf course," says Mite as he lights the cigar. "It's where Gorman plays golf."

Kockroach rolls his cigar over the flame, sucks in a mouthful

shaking Kockroach's hand with great enthusiasm. Gorman is one of those humans with a deep chest and a ruddy complexion who squeeze hard when they shake hands. Kockroach has learned not to squeeze back. "I've heard nothing but grand things about Brownside. Our people say your books are shipshape."

"We do our best," says Kockroach.

They are on a flat area overlooking one of the long green meadows. In the distance is a round circle of green with a flag planted in the middle. Gorman is there with his son and two men with green vests who are carrying long bags with metal and wooden implements sticking out of the top. Champ, in his black suit, is carrying the same sort of bag, holding similar implements.

"So what's your number?" says Gorman. "I'm a six. Herman here"—he thumbed at a tall handsome young man with dark wavy hair—"my son, is a scratch."

"Number?" says Kockroach.

"Your handicap."

"Handicap?"

"You don't have a handicap? Where do you play?"

"Play?"

"Golf. Where do you play golf?"

"I don't."

"I was told you played golf," says Gorman, looking now at Mite. "Was I mistaken?"

"He'll do fine, Mr. Gorman," says Mite. "Don't you worry. What say we make a little wager?"

"But he doesn't play," says Gorman.

"That's the beauty of it. He never played before, but I figure he'll pick it up quick. Let's just say he's a natural. No bad habits, right? What about a hundred a hole, against each of you," says Mite. "Even up?"

"Even up, when he's never played before?" says Gorman. "That would be like stealing thirty-six hundred dollars."

"What?" says Mite. "It ain't enough?"

Gorman's son steps up. "Let's not be pikers then," he says, his easy grin showing his even white teeth. "A thousand a hole. Ties carry over."

Kockroach grins back at him. "Sweet pea," he says.

"Herman, stop this," says Gorman. "Mr. Blatta is our guest. This isn't right."

"But of course it is," says Gorman's son. "We're all sporting men here, aren't we?"

"Sure we are, sport," says Kockroach.

"See?"

"You gots a game," says Mite. "Step on up and whack it, why don't you."

As Gorman the younger steps between two large blue balls pressed into the flat ground, Mite sidles up to Kockroach. "Champ used to caddy in New Orleans growing up," says

of wood in the grass, steps up to the ball, and swings the stick. The little ball sails into the sky and lands far off in the meadow, about two thirds of the way to the green circle in the distance. The young man turns and grins. Gorman sends his ball also into the sky, landing it short of where his son's ball lies.

"Want me to show you how to grip it, Blatta?" says Gorman.

"I can figure it out," says Kockroach.

Champ takes a stick out of the bag, hands it to Kockroach. It is metal, long, with a big blob of wood on the far end. Champ takes a ball, sets it on a small peg in the ground. "Hit it down the middle, Boss," says Champ.

"How far?" says Kockroach.

"See that flag?" says Champ. "That's the target. Right where that flag is, there's a little hole. You want to hit the ball into that hole."

Kockroach steps up, places the wooden blob behind the ball as he saw the two other players do. Swaaaaack. The ball flies as if being chased, rises high, sails long, and then falls far far far beyond the other two balls, before rolling onto the circular green area, stopping just short of the flag in the distance.

"I missed," says Kockroach.

"Well, now you knows to hit it harder for next time," says Mite.

"What do I do now?" says Kockroach.

"You go on up and knock it into the hole," says Champ.

Kockroach looks at Gorman and his son, who are staring at Kockroach with their jaws dropped and something lovely in their eyes.

"You mean I get another chance?" says Kockroach.

"Yes you do, Boss," says Champ, shouldering the bag.

"How sweet is that?" says Kockroach as he tosses the club to Champ and strides off toward his ball, the Gormans staring after him.

Kockroach doesn't understand this thing about humans and their games. The ritual of chess he understands, an exercise in controlling the future, but these other games make no sense to him.

The humans take it so personally, like it is combat, when it is exactly the opposite. Combat between arthropods is a life-and-death affair where everything is on the line, that morsel of food, that attractive female with enlarged glands, leadership of the colony. The beauty of combat is that the stakes are so high. But after the human game is over, everything is the same. And yet humans take it all so seriously. Like this golf. There is a bet, but it is air. A few thousand dollars. The number means nothing to Kockroach, it means even less to the Gormans, who are wealthier. And yet, to watch the Gormans play their game with

"I've never seen anything like it," says Gorman after Kockroach sends his ball skittering across the green until it drops into the cup. "You've never played before? Really?"

"Really," says Kockroach. "But how hard can it be? It's just a game."

"He hustled us," says Gorman's son as he steps toward Kockroach, the small flat-faced stick still in his hand. The boy's features are twisted in anger, his throat is close enough for Kockroach to grab hold and crush if he so desired. "You're a goddamned sandbagger."

"Herman," says Gorman, "stop it."

"I'm definitely a bastard," says Kockroach, grinning into the boy's face. "And if being a sandbagger's a profitable thing, then I'm that too."

Gorman's son raises his stick into the air like a sword.

Kockroach doesn't flinch.

Champ steps forward, but before he can reach the raised stick, Gorman's son brings the stick down with tremendous force so that its face buries in the soft green ground.

"Herman, enough."

"He cheated us, Dad. Don't you see? You better triple-check his books. He's a swindler."

"You're being rude to our guest."

"Soon enough he'll be an employee," says Gorman's son as he pulls his stick out of the ground and stalks away.

"Pleasant guy, ain't he?" says Mite. "And a good loser, to boot."

"Does this mean the game is over?" says Kockroach.

"I'm afraid so," says Gorman, watching the boy's exit with a pained expression on his face. "And I must apologize for my son's behavior. He's always been quite competitive."

"Aren't we all," says Kockroach, handing his stick to Champ. "So, enough pleasantries. Let's talk business. How much?"

Gorman's gaze snaps back to Kockroach, his face turns impassive. "We haven't gone over all the figures yet, but our accountants have put a preliminary price on the whole of Brownside Enterprises, one I think you'll be pleased with."

"Sweet pea," says Kockroach, "there's been a mistake."

"Excuse me?" says Gorman.

"A mistake. You've made a mistake. You're not buying me," says Kockroach. "I'm buying you."

"I like the shoes," says Kockroach.

He is in the backseat of the car. They are driving away from the golf place, driving toward the big house in the city. "I want to wear them all the time."

"They'll be hell on the wooden floors," says Mite, sitting beside him. "You'll have to get that by Celia."

"But they're my floors."

"So they are," says Mite. "Still, you be the one to tell her

you had in mind."

"He'll come around," says Kockroach.

"Don't think so, Boss," says Mite. "Not the way he was acting out there. I think he wants to keep the business for that son of his to take over."

"The sport."

"Yeah. He wants to keep it in the family. They get like that, fathers do. At least some of them. And the son of his has a son of his own to get the company in turn. So it don't look to me like Gorman will be willing to sell, no matter how much we offer."

"He'll sell," says Kockroach. "Get the goods, Mite. Get the goods and we'll convince him."

"How, Boss? I already looked into the guy. There ain't nothing there."

"There's always something."

"I tell you, Boss, I asked around, did the sniffing on my own. Gorman's clean."

"You're looking in the wrong place."

"Where should I be looking?"

"Not at the old man," says Kockroach. "At the sport."

There is a moment of quiet. Kockroach watches as Mite and

Champ glance at each other, and in that moment Kockroach senses that Mite had found something and is holding back. He can feel it in the air, what he felt before, the misty scent that always swirls around Mite like a sour pheromone. Betrayal.

Is that where it comes from, this unease that has once again come over him, is it from Mite? No, nothing there is out of sorts. With Mite there is always a whiff of betrayal in the air. It is part of him, he can't help himself. No, the unease comes from someplace else. For the time he was with Gorman he had lost it, business always puts his mind at ease. But the business now is concluded. After playing the game with the Gormans, he knows it is only a matter of time. They will sell, he saw the weakness in their knocking knees as they tried to roll the ball into the hole. They will sell, willingly, and be ever grateful. And so it is as good as over and Kockroach once again is ill at ease.

He wonders why. It is a puzzle. Something is troubling him. Outside the car window, great fields pass by. The car is deep in the country, the fields are green and stretch on forever and their very greatness is what troubles him.

Business has made him rich, powerful in the world of men. It has allowed him to rise, to support his colony, it has brought Mite back, and Istvan, and Celia, and Norman. But business, he now sees, has its limitations. The more he buys, the more there is to buy. In the ribbons of possibility floating into the future he sees the positions of his pieces on the chessboard advance and then retreat. There are too many other players who all want to be on the same blocks, there is too much money that will never be his. His fear has been greatly eased in the world of business, McGreevy has seen to that, but with the lessening of his fear, his greed has concomitantly grown to

mered through the soles beneath his feet, he wants to spill his seed along the furrows, he wants to make his claim, he wants to mark, control, dominate the entire breadth of the world.

"I like the shoes," he says.

23

I suppose I gots a problem with saying goodbye.

Maybe it's something in my genes. My daddy he wasn't no good at saying so long neither, but at least he would just take a powder. I leans toward the powder keg. Why I can't just get on with it, like other Joes, what shake a hand and are on their ways, is a mystery. Champ, for instance, didn't make no big thing of leaving. It was just, "Goodbye, Mick," two words, a nod, and quick as that he's off in the old Packard for points west.

I ever tell you how I said goodbye to Old Dudley, what first taught me chess and the ways of the world? This was after my mother got swallowed whole by Hubert and I checked out her rainy-day cookie jar and found not a dollar, not a cent, just an IOU signed by, wouldn't you know it, Old Dudley hisself. So we were pulling one of our inside jobs, scouring some house shiny of its jewels and silver and cash, all placed in that white sack of his. And then, just as he's shimmying legs-first back out the window, I slams the frame on his back, locking him in. "Mickey, my boy," he says, that puzzled look on his puss. But the puzzlement it disappears when I takes the sack and starts to bashing his face with it. It was his blood and my

You want to blame it on something, that soft goodbye? Then blame it on them envelopes, just like the one with Harrington's name you gots your eye on. You been looking at it all this time like it was the holy grail, like it was something powerful and golden, when let me tell you, missy, it is a steaming pile of crap. And how does I knows? Because I'm the rodent what scours them sewers until I finds the tastiest morsels. The lowest rat in the lowest stream of sewage in this whole damn town ain't got nothing on Mite. This is what the Boss has made of me.

"I need information," the Boss told me, all the time knowing I was the one to get it for him. With the new line I had picked up in Chi-town, I could get the goods, I could fill them envelopes. And believe me when I tells you, in the land of money where the Boss now was plying his trade, there was plenty of filling to find.

I thought the Times Square of my young manhood was a place of vice and degeneration, a place where all the lowliest desires could find a few moments of release, but let me tell you this, missy, Times Square never had nothing on the dark and desolate landscape of money. I found thievery and perversion, falsehoods and incest, violence, boorishness, bad breath, and murder. And, worst of all, fools what thought that

money it could cleanse the darkest secrets of the soul. And maybe it could have, if I wasn't there with my envelopes. Like I was for a muck-a-muck what faced off against the Boss, name of Nicholas Van Ater.

Van Ater was a society type, loaded to the gills and liked showing it. Short, squat, thick fingers, thick cigars, his black hair slicked back like a cartoon. To see Van Ater was to see a soul swelled fat on money pure. And his wife was so thin, if she turned sideways you could see the bone in her throat. Van Ater had a lien on a property the Boss, he wanted to buy, and Van Ater was leaning a bit too hard. So the Boss, he put me on the case. When it came time for the sit-down with Van Ater, Boss had more than enough information to slap that fat face into submission.

"How'd it go, Boss?" I said when he left out of Van Ater's building with the envelope still in his hand.

"Not so good, Mite."

"You tell him you knows the girl she's only fourteen?"

"He said he likes to reach out to the nation's youth."

"What about the girl afore her, what he beat near to senseless?"

"A lovers' spat."

"And about his wife, the powder up her upturned nose and the tennis instructor what is instructing her plenty with his forehand?"

"He was pleased he was getting value for his money."

"Son of a bitch," I said. "The bastard's shameless."

"I admire that," said the Boss.

"So does I. Want me to spill it all to the press?"

that money in the first place. It had to be something different, something what would make that society hound he had married and the boys at the club take notice. And I found it, sures I did. Because the Boss is right, damn it to hell, it's always there.

"What does that bastard Blatta want now?" says Van Ater. He talks in an affected gangsterese, like he had suckled at the droopy breast of Edward G. Robinson hisself.

I leans back, props my feet on the rim of his huge mahogany desk. "He wants you to mark the lien settled."

"Tell your boss to find some young bear cub he can steamroll," says Van Ater.

"Oh, I thinks you'll do as we wants," I says.

"You know, you're just the size, I'd have fun working you over myself."

"You wouldn't be the first to try, believe me," I says, "I've got a face like a hardball, all stitches and horsehide already."

And then I pulls the envelope out my jacket. I drops my feet, puts the envelope on the desk, pushes it oh so slowly toward his grinning mug.

I watch as he snatches it up, watch as he opens it, takes out the note, unfolds it, watch as the smile is wiped off his fat face just like the Boss, he wanted. Within the week the lien was

settled and the property was slipped into the Boss's side pocket. Now Van Ater's one of the Boss's big supporters in the run for the Senate. Funny how it works, isn't it, all from a single name on a folded-up slip of paper?

See, that's how the Boss did business in them days, how he does it still. Because the Boss, he don't strong-arm no more. Now it's all what you know and who you're willing to tell. That's what this envelope is too, a little treat for that son of a bitch Harrington who thinks the open Senate seat is his for the taking, so long as he gets the most votes. Stupid son of a bitch, he don't have the foggiest damn notion of what he got hisself into.

And neither did Champ.

It wasn't like there wasn't no happy times riding along with the Boss. We was a family then, or the closest thing I ever had to one, other than that tight threesome in my boyhood: me, my momma, and Hubert. In the Boss's triple townhouse there lived the Boss and Celia, and Norman, Celia's boy. And there was Istvan, and Cassandra too. And then there was me, the envelope man, and Champ hisself, who from the first day was treated like one of the family. That was the thing about the Boss, he didn't have no hang-ups about color or twisted dispositions. And we couldn't forget the money boys what was always skulking about, McGreevy, looking after all the details, and Albert Gladden, the real estate man, his sad-sack face putting a damper on everything. Not to mention the passel of servants what served us all.

There was one more member I don't want to slight, Glenda,

Glenda was already under the protection of the Boss, and so no matter how many dishes was throwed, Glenda stayed and Celia just had to learn to live with it.

But then, what's a family without a little family strife.

Look at us there, the family that we was. It's all in the snapshots. Champ and me smoking stogies in Miami. Celia and Norman and the two of us in Hollywood, with our hands on the cement in front of that Chinese Theatre. Norman on the beach, fat and white, standing over a buried Mite, me with my hat still on. Norman in horse pants, getting taller, wider, his smile getting a little too familiar. The whole gang, including McGreevy and Cassandra, Istvan and Glenda and the Boss, on the Strip in Vegas, dressed in our finery, all of us all smiles, excepting of course the way Celia she looks at Glenda as the Boss wraps his arm around Glenda's whippet waist.

It was anything any of us ever could have hoped for, but it wasn't enough for Champ. Not after that last envelope.

It was just another get, nothing big. A fat cat named Gorman had something the Boss wanted to buy, a conglomeration of companies bigger than anything the Boss had bought before. McGreevy worked out a whole new financing arrangement to provide the cash. My job was to get Gorman to sell.

Except the Boss told us right off the key it wasn't Gorman hisself, but the son. And even afore I started looking I knew what I would find. Champ and me, first time we laid eyes on the boy we both of us knew.

And finding proof, what did that take?

Follow the car to the joint west by the Hudson, not far, actually, from the very pier what Sylvie used to work. Wait until the son, he slips out that bar and back to his car with a new pal. Take a few pictures and then slip inside yourself.

Smoke and fancy lights and music what was like a throbbing in your head. A place what was on the other side of the rainbow from where Champ and me we lived our lives. And the ways they dressed, with their feathers and finery, made my green outfit seem pale. Champ and me, we sat at the bar, ordered our drinks, rubbernecked like we was tourists.

"What do you think, Mick?"

"I don't likes it," I said. "It's a damn costume party. When I first came to the Square there wasn't no filly-fallying like this here. When I first came to the Square—"

"I heard it all already," said Champ. "What, are you going to tell me again about Jimmy Slaps?"

"He was an interesting guy, is all. And that's my point. There was a way of doing things then. There was a world to aspire to. But this, this is like giving up. I don't likes it."

"I don't think they care, Mick."

"Shows you what they know. Let's get to work. I'll talk up the barkeep, you start to asking around."

"I don't think so."

I stopped at that, stared at Champ, acted like I didn't know

"But this one is, Mick, can't you see?"

"It ain't no different than Van Ater."

"No, it's not. But I didn't learn about that one till later. You purposely kept that one from me."

"Don't act like some holy shaman. You've been filling them envelopes too."

"But what those fools did is different than what they are."

"Van Ater done plenty."

"But that's not what you put in the envelope."

"I put his name is all."

"His old name."

"That he was passing hisself off as something he never was, acting like there was something to be ashamed of in being the same race as you, that didn't piss you off?"

"Just made me sad for him, Mick. Just that. You don't know what it is."

"Don't tell me I don't know what it is. It's all I ever knowed."

"And now with this boy, it's the same."

"He's a creep."

"He might be that, but that's not what you'll be putting in the envelope, is it? You give what he is to the Boss, you be betraying nothing but yourself."

"Can't say I don't deserve it."

"Maybe not, but you be betraying me too, and I won't be staying around to see that."

"I promised I'd be square with him here on in," I said. "I left him once, I can't leave him again. I don't got no choice."

"Sure you do, Mick."

But did I? Did I ever in the presence of the Boss? Not really. My fate in this world is to latch on to the strong, and no one was ever stronger than the Boss. So, yeah, I handed the envelope with the facts and the photos over to the Boss and he handed it to the Joe what owned the company and, yeah, to keep it quiet from the country club world that his married boy preferred to tango with other boys, Gorman caved. And Champ, well, he was as good as his word.

"Goodbye, Mick."

And goodbye to you, you son of a bitch.

And out of my life went something I never had before and I won't near see again. It's been a year already and still it slays me. Every day. But it was me who said goodbye first, wasn't it? And now I'm saying goodbye again, but not so quietly as Champ.

So here's the envelope what should make the race a one-horse exhibition. Look inside and you'll find everything what Harrington done to make the fortune he's using to buy his seat. All the thieving, all the swindling, an insider stock deal what already has the SEC boys hard just thinking about it. Not to mention the name of his lady friend, with the Spanish eyes and the tits like urns of soft butter, what he keeps in a pad on Park Avenue.

But when betrayal it's in your blood and bones, [illegible]

missy. Pulitzer will be calling, and the Republican Party will soon enough be looking for a new boy to carry its hat into the race. With Champ safe and away in Mexico, I figure it's time to call in my chips.

You don't spend a chunk of your life in a place like Times Square without learning a thing or two. And what I learned was this: People, theys all liars, and the ones they lying to most of all is theyselves. Like Tab, what hustled the men's rooms and back alleys, selling hisself to men, but who insisted all along he wasn't no queer. And Tony the Tune, what was just one fighter away from the big time. And Jimmy Slaps, what was devoting his life to Jesus. And Sylvie, what was going to visit her sister and get herself well. And Old Dudley hisself, what always claimed him bloodying my lip and diddling my yard was done for my own damn good. My own damn good. And even my mother, telling me time and again everything was going to be all right. All of them, every one of them, was just lying to theyselves so they could stand the company for the next couple months or days or hours.

But I'm done with the lying, I'm here to face it all head-on. It wasn't just the last envelope what sent Champ scampering away, it was all them envelopes, taken together. He had seen enough of what I had become in the land of money, the twisted creature you see before you now, without hope or reason, hating everything about his own self, without nothing to hold on to but nothing. Like I was when I set old Times Square on fire. Infected again.

I thought I had finally beaten him away in Chicago, I thought I was free of him for good. But this is what I didn't yet know; in the land of money, Hubert prowls like a god. And in the service of the Boss, once again I was easy prey. But I've stopped fooling myself. There's only one true prescription for the son of a bitch. And I just filled it.

See, the Boss won't be letting me get away with it this time. This time he's going to finish it once and for all. With the end of the story, it's the end of me, too. But no weeping here, it's also my last chance to save myself. I'm looking forward to the fireworks. They'll burn away, finally, the leech on my soul.

So stop the tape and start to typing. Whatever's coming to smite my soul when the story runs is a gift. I'll open my arms to it like it's a lover, tall and black with big teeth and raw scarred flesh and hands like soft leather mitts to wrap you up and keep you safe.

Goodbye, missy. So long.

Kaboom.

As Celia Singer sewed the beads on the wedding dress, the delicate teardrops of crystal caught the morning light and sprinkled upon her a rainbow of promise.

Celia was arranging the beads in a pattern across the midriff, above the bunches of pleated silk at the top of the skirt and below the delicate sheet of lace designed to expose the swell of the breasts. It was an intricate and difficult job and Celia wore reading glasses low on her nose to be sure each stitch was exact. She could have had the seamstress do this part—these days she could have someone do everything for her and often did—but she was enjoying the task.

The wedding seemed to be happening around her as if conjured by a spell. It was being planned by planners, catered by caterers, the guest list was being compiled by high-priced political consultants. The ceremony and reception were being covered by the press as if it were the marriage of a prince instead of a politician, which was all part of a political strategy to turn candidate into celebrity. Jerry had hired hired-guns from the publicity departments of Hollywood studios, he had bought space in gossip columns coast to coast. The wedding was simply another leg of the marketing campaign. But it was more than that to Celia, this wedding, and that was why she insisted on sewing the beads herself, stitch by careful stitch.

She couldn't help but remember her mother in the same pose, glasses perched on her nose as she sewed in the parlor. In those days, Celia was always with a book, one Brontë or the other, Balzac, Flaubert, anything that made the librarian sniff. Sometimes, in the evenings, she would look up from the tumescent prose and see her mother sitting quietly, working slowly within the ambit of the lamp, and believe quite earnestly that her mother must be the most boring woman alive. For the whole of her life, she had felt as if she were fleeing the banal priorities her mother had tried to impose upon her. Yet now here she was, having made all her choices, in the same pose as her mother, peering through her reading glasses at the needle, the fabric, the thread.

Her feelings about her mother had changed markedly. Partly it was the conversion that happens to every daughter upon the death of her mother, the bleeding out of anger that accompanies the lowering of the coffin. But it was also a realization that came to her slowly in the past few years. Those long-ago nights in the parlor, her mother wasn't simply sewing on sleeves, embroidering towels, darning socks, knitting scarves, her mother wasn't simply manufacturing objects. She was knitting together the fabric of her family. And that's what Celia felt she was doing now, as she fastened each bead in its proper place. Celia had shed the trappings of religion long ago, and no longer even pretended to the false piety that made life easier among polite folk, but still, this wedding had acquired for her a transcendent significance.

The familiar shuffle across the early morning hush, the

ing room and an unbidden smile brightened her countenance. The same jaunty stride, the same loud suit, the wiseacre's half grin. He was unchanged since the first time she saw him in the Automat, except for the eyes. The desperate hope of the rain-soaked teenage hustler had been replaced by the weary sadness of a short, middle-aged man who had gotten more than he ever could have dreamed in this life and found it wasn't enough. Poor Mite, she thought. It was part of all that desperate wanting, never to be satisfied.

"He's not up yet," said Celia.

"I figured as much," said Mite as he picked an apple out of the bowl, tossed it, snatched it from the air, rubbed it on his sleeve. "But I thought it'd be better to get here early. Don't want him waiting on me, not today."

"I didn't know you two had an appointment."

"Not officially," he said, falling into a chair and biting the apple all in one graceful movement, "but he'll be wanting to see me, I knows that."

"How'd it go yesterday? We were expecting you back."

"It went a little long," said Mite.

She lowered her chin, peered over her glasses. "Everything go as planned?"

"What could go wrong? A piece of birthday cake, it was. Except for the missy, who to tell you the truth wasn't so bright. I had to spell out some things. What, was the Boss asking after me?"

She noticed the worry in his face. Mite never could hide his emotions. It was the one thing she found most annoying in him.

"No," said Celia. "He was busy meeting with the former governor."

"That stuck-up sumbitch?"

"He's been very helpful."

"You gots to watch out for a guy you can't buy, Celia. You can't never trust them. The boy up yet?"

"Already scrubbed and fed and off to school."

Mite glanced at his apple. "Surprised there's still a piece of fruit left. Glenda take care of him?"

"Hardly. She's still in bed."

"With all she's putting away each night, that's no surprise. But that dress is looking jimmy."

"Thank you." She pushed herself out of the chair, held the dress high so that the hem of the skirt barely brushed the floor. "Almost ready."

"Smashing," he said. "The hit of the evening, you ask me. I'd love to see it sashaying down the aisle, I would."

"You will."

"Maybe not, Celia. I might be busy that day."

"Don't be silly. Of course you'll be there. The governor's going to be the best man."

"Rockefeller?"

"Isn't that thrilling?"

"Papers arrive?" he said.

"Not yet. Cassandra went out to get them. Can't wait to see the headlines."

"Oh, they'll be something, they will."

"I never much cared for Harrington," said Celia, leaning back in her chair, turning her attention back to the beads. "He doesn't know how to smile. That should be a fundamental requirement for being considered human, don't you think?"

"The Boss gots no problem there."

"I guess our friend Mr. Harrington will be smiling even less after this morning."

"He won't be the only one with an itch."

She let out an exaggerated sigh of resignation as she continued to work. "What did you do, Mickey?"

"Only what I should have done afore all this started."

"And what is that?"

"I told the missy everything."

"About what?"

"About the Boss. From the beginning. From when I found him, to the times on Times Square, to the money he was shoveling to the president."

She tried to hide her dismay. Still staring at the dress, she said as calmly as she could manage, "Mickey, you shouldn't have."

"Sures I should. Isn't that what I've become? Isn't that what he's made of me? A teller of tales? And who's got a richer tale to tell, let me ask you, than the Boss?"

She leaned close to the fabric, positioned a bead exactly atop the mark on the pattern. She felt the fear rise in her, unsteadying her hand. There's always something upsetting the balance, turning everything on its head. Just when you make your peace with all you've given up and think all is settled, it starts breaking apart. One more thing to take care of. She took a deep breath before plunging the needle.

"Maybe you shouldn't be here when he finds out," she said.

"Where else would I be?"

"While you're away, I could talk to him. Calm him down."

"I don't wants him calm. If you're gonna sing, you gots to face the music."

She looked up, smiled at him. "You always do, don't you? I'll give you that. This is just like before."

"Before what?"

"Big Johnny Callas. Remember how you stayed around even after you stiffed him his two hundred dollars?"

"That Greek meatball? Yeah, I remembers."

"And then when you came back to Jerry after the explosion. It's the same thing over again."

Mite turned his head away. "Maybe so."

"You know what it was that brought you back? You couldn't leave him. None of us can. But you beat yourself up about it when you should embrace it. You love him. Y

"But not no more, Celia. Not after what I done to his run for the Senate. I thought it was a crap idea from the start. There was no percentage in it, no profit. What was we going to do in a place like Washington, nobbing with the hobs?"

"It will be fabulous," said Celia. "The balls, the intrigue."

"It ain't for me. And now it's done."

"Oh, Mickey, how long have you been with him? And you still don't understand?"

"He won't take it lying down."

"Maybe not," she said. She glanced up at him to be sure he was listening. "Why don't you take a small vacation? Maybe even leave the country. I'll have Cassandra make the arrangements. You can fly to San Diego, catch a bus to Ensenada."

"Ensenada? Why would I go to Ensenada? With the water they got, I'll be crapping out my brains."

She smiled. "And that's a problem how?"

"There ain't nothing for me in Mexico."

"Now who's not facing the music? You can't keep blaming Jerry for what happened, Mickey."

"I'll blame who the hell I want to blame."

"Don't you think it's time you pay him a call?"

"Nope."

"He owns a fishing boat. He takes the tourists out to catch tuna and sea bass."

"I don't care."

"McGreevy set it up for him without him knowing it was set up."

Mite looked up. "You think he doesn't know?"

"I don't know, Mickey. Maybe he does."

"It don't make no difference even so. I ain't going down to Mexico and what's in Mexico ain't got nothing to do with what I done."

"You know what it's called? The boat?"

Before she could tell him, Cassandra entered the living room, striding forward in her heels, clutching a stack of newspapers. "Shocked is what I am," she said in her Bronx screech. "Shocked."

Celia couldn't help but admire the woman who stood before her. Her hair had thinned over the years, but it was still high, her legs were still sturdy. She was older than Celia, and it showed on her face, but she had kept her figure with all its luxuriant curves, and her waist hadn't yet thickened with age as had Celia's.

"Something in the papers?" said Celia calmly.

Mite shrank back into his chair, readying himself for the inevitable.

"Who would have thought," said Cassandra, a sly smile breaking out on her face, "that our nice Mr. Harrington was such a rotten tomato?"

Mite sat up. “Let me see them things,” he said, reaching

WITH PARK AVENUE LOVE NEST

SENATE SWINDLE,
HARRINGTON’S SORDID ROAD TO RICHES

HARRINGTON UNDER INVESTIGATION BY SEC

HARRINGTON DENIES BEATING WIFE

Mite picked through the papers, staring dumbly at the headlines, before grabbing one and opening it. He paged quickly through, looking for something specific. Finally, he looked up at Celia with an expression of disbelief on his face.

“There ain’t nothing in the missy’s rag about the Boss,” said Mite.

“Of course not,” she said.

“I don’t understand.”

“What did you think, M-M-Mite?” said the pale-faced McGreevy from the doorway. He was in his black-vested suit, he was leaning against the doorframe. “That we’d let you ruin everything?”

"The missy," said Mite with a bite of anger in his voice. "I knowed there was something I didn't like about her."

"Bought and p-p-paid for, before ever we let you get close to her."

"I should have seen it right off," said Mite. "What with all the shrimp. What kind of reporter's got shrimp in her suite?"

"Ours," said McGreevy.

"You bastards set me up."

"They were protecting you," said Celia, her attention back on the dress. She tightened a thread, another bead slipped into place.

"They were protecting the Boss," said Mite.

"Oh, sweetheart," said Celia, "you still don't understand. He doesn't need our protection."

"I'll just tells someone else," said Mite, standing.

"No you won't," said Jerry, now passing McGreevy as he strode into the room.

Behind him, the dour-faced Albert Gladden slunk beside McGreevy, forming a sort of wall of business, barring the door.

Jerry wore his sunglasses, a white silk ascot, a brown silk robe belted tight around his waist. He reached out and patted Cassandra's neck. She bent her head toward his hand like a cat. He leaned over the chair where Celia sat with the wedding dress on her lap and kissed her on the lips. Celia's hands gripped tightly the silk as she felt the rasp of his tongue in her mouth. Like someone was reaching inside and gently squeezing the breath out of her. It was always like that, even after all these years.

"I betrayed you," said Mite. "I told her everything."

"I'm through."

"No you're not," said Jerry, rising up again and turning toward Mite. "The two of us, we'll never be through."

Celia stared at her men as they went back and forth, Mite and Jerry, and still suffused as she was with the emotions of the kiss, she saw something she had never seen before. But it was now so clear, she didn't understand how she could have missed it. It was in the connection, the rebellion, the unbreakable bond. Their relationship wasn't just boss to employee, or like brother to brother, it was stronger. Jerry had become to Mite like a father. And that explained Mite's twin needs to both please and destroy. And Jerry seemed to understand it too. It was why he always allowed Mite to stray, and why he always took him back. And it was part of what Jerry felt for Istvan too, and McGreevy, and Cassandra, and Norman, and even for herself, in a way that both appalled and thrilled her. He had become as a father to them all.

There was a moment when they stood face to face, Jerry and Mite, father and son, and their future together seemed to tremble.

"Sweet pea," said Jerry as he reached out a hand.

Mite didn't step forward, Mite didn't grasp the hand or hug

the man before him or turn around and bolt. Instead, he looked at the outstretched hand, and then Jerry's face, and then he slipped down again into the chair, as if something had collapsed inside him.

"So it is settled," said Jerry.

"You're a son of a bitch," said Mite.

"I never knew my mother," said Jerry, "so you're probably right. Now, boys. What's the word?"

"Harrington is scrambling to stay alive," said McGreevy. "But our inside sources tell us he got a call this morning from the m-m-mayor. He's being pressed to drop out."

"He'll be gone by the end of the week," said Gladden. "They'll draft Paglia."

"Is that trouble?"

"Paglia is popular in the outer boroughs," said Gladden.

"I'll need you again, Mite," said Jerry.

But Mite didn't respond. Still slumped in the chair, his chin resting on his chest, Mite was lost. The men continued their discussion, walking to the wet bar at the end of the room to plan and plot. Cassandra went into the hallway to answer the ringing phone. Celia held the wedding dress on her lap and waited for Mite. When he looked up, finally, his lips were quivering and it was as if his eyes were focused on some distant shore.

"You never got around to telling me," he said softly.

"The boat's called *Mick's First Mate*," she said.

"Damn," said Mite.

"Should I tell Cassandra to get the tickets?"

"Three words and he's routed again," said Mite, softly, to himself. "It shouldn't be so easy."

"I'll have her get the tickets," said Celia Singer, the soft

because he was part of it, surely. And now even Champ would return and join them again. He wouldn't stay on that old boat of his when Mite beckoned him back. This wedding, she knew, was going to be the greatest day of her life. And then, at the edge of her vision, she spotted something swaying in the doorway, all in white.

It was Glenda, in a gauzy white dressing gown, her feet bare, an empty glass in her hand, swaying, as if the slightest of reeds swaying in the wind. Her skin was pale, her blue eyes watery, her lips swollen red. Her beautiful heart-shaped face seemed to float above her narrow shoulders, which in turn seemed disconnected from her thin waist, her slim hips, her long slender legs which showed through the gossamer gown. She looked about the room as if comprehending nothing.

"I don't . . ." she said. "I can't . . ."

"Jerry dear," said Celia, "it's Glenda."

Jerry turned to her, lifted his arms wide. Glenda rose on her toes, staggered slightly to the left.

"Look, Jerry," said Celia, standing now, with the dress in her hands. "Look how exquisite she'll be."

She stepped over to Glenda and lifted the wedding dress so that its shoulders were at Glenda's shoulders, its arms at

Glenda's arms. The pattern of beads traced along Glenda's waist and the hem of the skirt just barely brushed the floor at Glenda's feet. Glenda staggered again, as if under the weight of the garment.

"Lovely," said Jerry. "Just lovely."

Celia was filled with an exultant joy. She leaned forward and kissed Glenda on the forehead. "You'll make the most beautiful, beautiful bride," she said. And she meant every word of it.

Kockroach stands at the center of his world. He can feel them all around him, on every side of him, rubbing him and patting him, grabbing him and hugging him. Since his strange molt, it is the closest he has come to feeling, among the humans, the purity of the colony as it huddles and writhes together. There are shouts, shrieks of jubilation, there is a shiver of exultation running through them all. He can smell all of them, each one of them, as they clamber about him. Celia and Glenda, Norman, Cassandra, Champ back from Mexico, Istvan and Gladden, McGreevy and Mite. His colony.

In the distance, the chanting of a name as if it were the name of a god.

Blatta. Blatta. Blatta. Blatta.

The excitement sparks all about him like the burning of a fuse rushing toward some great pile of explosives. The enthusiasm puzzles him, the prize seems so small. To be a senator is to be a barnacle on the rear end of a whale, a parasite along for a pointless ride. Senators are cheaper to buy than buildings. Better to sit on a toilet seat than in the Senate. But every rise needs a first step. In the world of crime, he first was an enforcer. In the world of business, he first was an exterminator. In the world of politics, he first will be a senator.

As he stands in that room behind the stage, surrounded by his colony, he closes his eyes and watches the ribbons of possibility float like writhing snakes into the future. He sees a chessboard of white and brown squares that stretches beyond the city, beyond the country, that spans continents and bridges oceans. His pieces move forward in brutal ranks along columns and diagonals, thwarting attacks, smashing defenses, always advancing. And slowly, magnificently, the chessboard itself begins to change. The white squares shift and darken until the whole board is one huge surface of brown. The brown of his chitin in his earlier life. It will cover the world, he can make it happen.

"It's t-t-time," says McGreevy.

Kockroach knows what to do, as if he were reborn for this moment. The colony parts. He grabs Glenda's hand, steadies her, and then pulls her from behind the curtain and onto the stage. There is more chanting, there are bright lights, there is music. A writhing mass of people stand before him, clapping and jumping and shouting. At the lectern, with his human name emblazoned in red white and blue, Kockroach raises his hands, fingers splayed into twin V's, and quiets the crowd.

"Tonight," he says in a voice that resounds through the ballroom and races across the night sky to the televisions of an entire nation, "tonight is the dawning of a new and glorious era for America."

For their brilliant assistance with, and support for, this novel, I wish to thank the following:
David Roth-Ey;
Carolyn Marino;
Amy Robbins;
Will Staehle;
Lisa Gallagher;
Michael Morrison;
Wendy Sherman;
Larry Gringlas;
Nate Allen;
My wife; and
My dog.
For any failures of substance, craft, or taste, blame the dog.

My primary entomological reference was an apartment in the East Village, where I was able to study at close hand the fauna of New York City. Among a host of other sources used were *The Compleat Cockroach*, by David George Gordon, a series of Insect Morphology Posters produced by B. K. Mitchell and J. S. Scott at the University of Alberta, and a quite peculiar paper on the effect of parasitoid wasp venom on cockroach grooming behavior, written by Aviva Weisel-Eichler, Gal Haspel and Frederic Libersat at Ben-Gurion University of the Negev in Israel. Less well known than the cockroach is the common cockroach mite, found within the genus *Pimeliaphilus*, notable for its small size and deficient grammar.

T. Knox